WATER RESOURCE MANAGEMENT

A Casebook in Law and Public Policy

SIXTH EDITION

by

A. DAN TARLOCK
Distinguished Professor of Law
IIT Chicago–Kent College of Law

JAMES N. CORBRIDGE, JR.
Professor Emeritus
University of Colorado School of Law

DAVID H. GETCHES
Dean and Raphael J. Moses Professor of Natural Resources Law
University of Colorado School of Law

REED D. BENSON
Professor of Law
University of New Mexico School of Law

FOUNDATION PRESS
2009

THOMSON REUTERS

© 1971, 1980, 1988, 1993, 2002 FOUNDATION PRESS

© 2009 By THOMSON REUTERS/FOUNDATION PRESS

 195 Broadway, 9th Floor

 New York, NY 10007

 Phone Toll Free 1–877–888–1330

 Fax (212) 367–6799

 foundation–press.com

Printed in the United States of America

ISBN 978–1–59941–438–6

 TEXT IS PRINTED ON 10% POST CONSUMER RECYCLED PAPER

Dedicated to

Vivien, Robert, Katherine and Marc

ADT

Pauline

JNC

My grandchildren Harrison, Benjamin, and Owen

DHG

Melinda

RDB

*

Eventually, all things merge into one,
and a river runs through it.

NORMAN MACLEAN

*

PREFACE

This book was originally conceived by the late Dean Charles J. Meyers of Stanford University, an extraordinary law professor and lawyer. His impact on the field of water law in the 1960s and 70s was enormous and his work continues to be widely consulted and cited. His many contributions include his role as clerk to the Special Master in the landmark *Arizona v. California* litigation, his work for the National Water Commission in the 1970s, his powerful scholarship urging market approaches and state primacy, and his role as Special Master in the Pecos River litigation, *Texas v. New Mexico*. See A. Dan Tarlock, *Tribute*, 29 Natural Resources J. 328 (1989) and G. Emlen Hall, High and Dry: The Texas–New Mexico Struggle for the Pecos River, Chapter 7 (2002). Charlie was the guiding spirit for the book until he entered private practice in 1981. His untimely death came in 1988, but the question, "is this text up to Charlie's high standard?", is never far from our minds.

Professor Tarlock was Dean Meyers' coauthor for the 1971 First Edition, and was primarily responsible for the Second Edition. Since the Third Edition in 1988, Professors James Corbridge and David Getches have been coauthors with Professor Tarlock. For this edition, the three of us are extremely pleased to welcome Professor Reed Benson, University of New Mexico, as coauthor to continue the tradition began by Charlie Meyers.

The evolution of this book through six editions reflects the changes in the field of the past four decades. In that time, the big dam era has ended, notions of demand management have emerged, and the work of lawyers has expanded from compliance with state allocations laws to include complicated environmental protection issues under federal law. Today, policy focuses on reallocation from long-established agricultural uses to urban demands created by burgeoning populations, and attempts to respond to the relatively new demands for instream flows to satisfy recreation and ecosystem needs. The single-minded concern with fulfilling utilitarian purposes that has always prevailed in water policy now is challenged by the new ethic of sustainability. Water is increasingly understood as an integrating resource that links development and preservation demands. Water decision-making is the crucible for achieving equity as well as economic and ecological health in resource use.

The fifth edition reflected a new pedagogical approach to water law. The sixth edition retains and updates this framework. Chapter One's introductory materials set the book's overall theme of scarcity, using recent readings and data on hydrology, demographics, climate change, demands for water, and economics. Instead of trying to maintain unrealistically sharp divisions between riparian and prior appropriation law, we present the historical development of water law as it occurred–in response to society's varied demands for particular uses. The rules were invented to serve those purposes, and in a short Chapter Two, we collect the basic rules of water law as they were generated, use by use. No single doctrine lasted long in its rigid form. Courts created exceptions to respond to evolving needs of society with only passing allegiance to doctrine. This is the subject of Chapter Three which covers the principles for acquisition, enjoyment, transfer, and loss of water rights. It is divided into two sections emphasizing eastern and western law. An individual professor may choose to design the course so that selections of materials will emphasize geographic and subject matter preferences.

Today, nearly all states, eastern and western, have administrative permit systems that look remarkably similar. Thus, after introducing the basic concepts as articulated by courts, Chapter Four discusses comprehensive permit systems and then treats the major statutory embellishments that deal with instream flows, the public interest, out-of-priority use, transbasin diversions, and efficient use.

Chapter Five provides a unified treatment of public rights, ranging from navigation, the public trust doctrine, surface use and Fifth Amendment takings. The succeeding chapters cover Groundwater, Environmental Regulation, Development and Distribution Programs and Organizations, and Federal and Indian Reserved Rights. A final chapter covers transboundary water issues, both interstate and international.

An important theme emerges in chapters Eight, Nine and Ten. The twentieth century tradition of the Bureau of Reclamation and the United States Army Corps of Engineers in planning, developing and managing large river systems has proved unworkable as the power of these agencies has diminished. Water use conflicts, however, have intensified. To protect endangered species and to stabilize degrading aquatic ecosystems in the face of competing demands, we have often turned to ad hoc government-stakeholder processes to reach consensus-based solutions. We also began to modify the missions of the water resource agencies. These chapters have discussions of this transition and illustrate it though case studies of current water conflicts and processes such as the California Bay–Delta, the Columbia River, the Great Lakes, the Klamath River, the Jordan River, and the Platte River. Related emerging policy concerns are introduced, such as the use of negotiation and collaboration to solve problems; the linkage between water policy and urban growth management; increased use of market mechanisms; transboundary water issues; and the place of global climate change in water decision making.

As in the past, we have tried to refer readers, teachers, and students alike, to selected supplemental materials to facilitate additional reading and research. Appropriate references are found in the text. Appendix B includes our favorite books on water law and policy.

One may question why we focus on a preponderance of western cases, and the inclusion of so many Colorado cases. The answer is easy. The West is dry, and this has heightened anxiety and conflict over water. As one court observed: "Water litigation is a weed that flowers in the arid West." United States v. Orr Water Ditch Co., 256 F.3d 935, 940 (9th Cir. 2001). And in Colorado, issues that are usually resolved elsewhere by administrative agencies are brought to the courts, often resulting in appeals with reported decisions. In searching for the best vehicles for teaching issues likely to arise anywhere, then, it has been more than the zip codes of two coauthors that has guided our selection of cases.

In preparing this and previous editions, several colleagues favored us with written and oral comments or contributed materials that helped to guide our revision. We have tried to incorporate the thoughts of all, and especially their corrections. Continuing thanks to each of them.

Our deepest gratitude goes to our research assistants who did yeomen's service in researching recent developments, finding obscure materials, and tirelessly editing copy. We thank Nathan Maxon, University of Wyoming College of Law, Class of 2009, Susan Tehlirian, University of Colorado Law School Class of 2009, Matthew Hoppe, University of Colorado Law School Class of 2009, William Wombacher University of Colorado Law School Class of 20q0, and Douglas Enzor, Assistant Dean, University of Colorado Law School. We are grateful to Chicago–Kent College of Law faculty assistant Kevin Jones, Wheaton College Class of 2008, for his careful preparation of the manuscript for publication. A word on our use of excerpted material: In reprinting excerpts of cases and other materials we have indicated our omissions with asterisks (* * *), while preserving the author's omissions from original quoted material with ellipses (. . .). We have, however, omitted citations to cases and other authority and footnotes from excerpted work without notation. Where we have included footnotes we retained the original numbering. Footnotes added by us are signaled with an asterisk and the notation "Eds."

We hope that teachers and students who do us the honor of using this book will share our excitement for this subject.

R.D.B.

J.N.C.

D.H.G.

A.D.T.

Boulder, Colorado

January, 2009

*

ACKNOWLEDGMENTS

We have reproduced portions of the following publications and wish to express our appreciation to the copyright holders and others for permission to reprint them. Except as noted, permission was granted by the copyright holder.

Robert H. Abrams, Replacing Riparianism in the Twenty–First Century, 36 Wayne L. Rev. 93 (1989). Copyright © 1989 by the Wayne State University Law School.

Terry L. Anderson & Pamela Snyder, Water Markets: Priming the Invisible Pump 7–12 (1997). Copyright © 1997 by the Cato Institute.

Joe S. Bain, Richard Caves & Julius Margolis, Northern California's Water Industry 77–79 (1966). Copyright © 1966 by Resources for the Future. Published for Resources for the Future by The Johns Hopkins University Press.

Sarah F. Bates, David H. Getches, Lawrence J. MacDonnell & Charles F. Wilkinson, Searching Out the Headwaters: Change and Rediscovery in Western Water Policy 4–8 (1993). Copyright © 1993 by Island Press.

Robert E. Beck, Use Preferences for Water, 76 N.D. L. Rev. 73, 767–68 (2000). Copyright © 2000 by the North Dakota Law Review. Reprinted with permission.

William Blomquist, Dividing the Waters 146–150 (1992). Copyright © 1992 by ICS Press.

Conservation Foundation, America's Water: Current Trends and Emerging Issues 34–35, 42–43, 47, 48 (1984). Copyright © 1984 by the Conservation Foundation.

James H. Davenport, Softening the Divides: The Seven Colorado River basin States' Recommendation to the Secretary of the Interior Regarding Lower Basin Shortage Guidelines and Operation of Lakes Mead and Powell in Low Reservoir Conditions, 10 University of Denver Law review 287, 289–290, 296–306, 311 (2007). Copyright © by University of Denver College of Law.

Peter N. Davis, Australian and American Water Allocation Systems Compared, 9 B.C. Indus. and Comm. L. Rev. 647, 680–82 (1968). Copyright © Boston College Industrial and Commercial Law Review.

Deborah A. de Lambert, Comment, District Management for California Groundwater, 11 Ecology L.Q. 373, 391–93 (1984). Copyright © 1984 by Ecology Law Quarterly.

Joseph W. Dellapenna, Waters and Water Rights § 6.01(c) (Robert E. Beck, ed., 1991). Copyright © 1991 by The Michie Company.

Joseph W. Dellapenna, Issues Arising Under Riparian Rights: Replacing Common–Law Riparian Rights with Regulated Riparianism, in Water Rights of the Eastern United States 35–48 (Kenneth R. Wright, ed. 1995). Copyright © 1998 by the American Water Works Association. Reprinted by permission.

Timothy De Young, Special Water Districts: Their Role in Western Water Use, in Western Water: Expanding Uses/Finite Supplies, Seventh Annual Summer Program, Natural Resources Law Center, University of Colorado School of Law (1986). Copyright © 1986 by Natural Resources Law Center.

Harrison C. Dunning, The "Physical Solution" in Western Water Law, 57 U. Colo. L. Rev. 445, 448, 458–61, 472–74, 477–78 (1986). Copyright © 1986 by the University of Colorado Law Review, Inc. Reprinted with permission of the University of Colorado Law Review and Harrison Dunning.

Peter A. Fahmy, The Public Trust Doctrine as Source of State Reserved Water Rights, 63 Denv. U.L. Rev. 585, 600–01 (1986). Copyright © 1986 by Denver University Law Review. Reprinted by permission of Denver University Law Review.

Kenneth D. Frederick, ed., Scarce Water and Institutional Change 7–11 (1986). Copyright © 1986 by Resources for the Future.

Kenneth D. Frederick & Peter H. Gleick, Water and Global Climate Change: Potential Impacts on U.S. Water Resources iii-vi, 4–9, 18–20 (1999). Copyright © 1999 by The Pew Center on Global Climate Change.

David H. Getches, Competing Demands for the Colorado River, 56 U. Colo. L. Rev. 413, 415–29 (1985). Copyright © 1985 by the University of Colorado Law Review, Inc.

David H. Getches, The Metamorphosis of Western Water Policy: Have Federal Laws and Local Decisions Eclipsed the States' Role, 20 Stan. Envtl. L.J. 3, 42–48 (2000). Copyright © 2000 by Stanford Environmental Law Journal.

David H. Getches, Water Allocation During Drought in Arizona and Southern California: Legal and Institutional Responses 1–3 (Natural Resources Law Center Research Report Series, Jan 1991). Copyright © 1991 by the Natural Resources Law Center, University of Colorado.

David H. Getches, Water Planning: Untapped Opportunity for the Western States, 9 J. Energy L. & Pol'y 1 (1998). Copyright © 1998 by the Journal of Energy Law and Policy.

David Getches, Water Wrongs: Why Can't We Get it Right the First time, 34 Envt'l Law, 1–19 (2004). Copyright © by the Lewis and Clark Law School. Reprinted also with permission of David Getches.

A. Dan Tarlock, The Endangered Species Act and Western Water Rights, 20 Land & Water L. Rev. 1, 13, 17, 26–30 (1985). Copyright © 1985 by the University of Wyoming. Reprinted with permission of the Land & Water Law Review.

A. Dan Tarlock, The Law of Equitable Apportionment Revisited, Updated, and Restated, 56 U. Colo. L. Rev. 381, 385–400 (1985). Copyright © 1985 by the University of Colorado Law Review, Inc.

A. Dan Tarlock, Law of Water Rights and Resources § 3:69 (2000). Copyright © 2000 by the West Group.

William R. Travis, New Geographies of the American West, 31–32, 46–48, 51–55, 59, 63, 67 (2007). Copyright © 2007 William R. Travis and the Orton FamilyFoundation. Reproduced by permission of Island Press, Washington, D.C.

George Vranesh, Vranesh's Colorado Water Law 336–350 (James N. Corbridge, Jr. & Teresa A. Rice, eds., Rev. ed. 1999). Copyright © 1999 by University Press of Colorado.

Richard W. Wahl, Markets for Federal Water: Subsidies, Property Rights, and the Bureau of Reclamation 27–46 (1989). Copyright © 1989 by Resources for the Future.

Jonathan M. Wenig, Water and Peace: The Past, the Present, and the Future of the Jordan River Watercourse: An International Law Analysis, 27 N.Y.U. J. Int'l L. & Pol. 331, 363–64 (1995). Copyright © 1995 by the New York University Journal of International Law and Politics.

Samuel C. Wiel, Fifty Years of Water Law, 50 Harv. L. Rev. 252, 256–59 (1936). Copyright © 1936 by the Harvard Law Review.

James D. Williams & Ronald M. Nowak, Vanishing Species in Our Own Backyard: Extinct Fish and Wildlife of the United States and Canada, in The Last Extinction 107, 127–128 (Les Kaufman & Kenneth Mallory, eds., 1986). Copyright © 1986 by The MIT Press.

The World Commission on Dams, The Report of the World Commission on Dams, Dams and Development: A New Framework for Decision Making xxxi-xxxv (2000). Copyright © 2000 by World Commission on Dams. Reprinted with permission of the World Commission on Dams Secretariat. Published by Earthscan Publications Ltd.

*

SUMMARY OF CONTENTS

PREFACE iii
ACKNOWLEDGMENTS xi
TABLE OF CASES xxxi

Chapter One. Water Law: A Response to Scarcity 1

A. A Special Kind of Scarcity 1
B. Water Supply: The Hydrologic Cycle 4
C. Demands for Water 7
D. Geographic Differences 19
E. Climate Variability 26
F. Economic Forces 33
G. Water Scarcity: The Role of Law and Policy 47

Chapter Two. Inventing Rules to Allocate a Scarce Resource 58

A. Milling 60
B. Mining 67
C. Agriculture 71
D. Electrical Power 84
E. Cities 94
F. Recreation 97
G. Fish, As Proxies for Protection of Aquatic Environments 99
H. Indian Reservations 102

Chapter Three. Principles of Acquisition, Enjoyment, Transfer, and Loss of Water Rights 112

A. Riparian Principles 112
B. Prior Appropriation Principles 154

Chapter Four. Modern Statutory Administration of Water 266

A. The Structure of Permit Systems 268
B. Issues Under Water Allocation Statutes 308

Chapter Five. Shared Public and Private Use of Waters 399

A. The Public Trust in Navigable Waters 400
B. Rights to Surface Use Among Riparians 449
C. Expanding Public Rights to Surface Use 460
D. The Navigation Servitude 479

E. Shoreline Access --- 487
F. Water Rights and Constitutional Takings ------------------------- 496

Chapter Six.   Groundwater Management ---------------------- 545

A. Introduction to the Geology and Dynamics of Groundwater --------- 550
B. Individual Rights in Groundwater ------------------------------- 559
C. Groundwater Allocation and Public Policy ----------------------- 598

Chapter Seven.   Environmental Protection and Water Law ----- 655

A. The Water Quality—Water Law Interface ------------------------- 657
B. Federal Regulation of Water Quality --------------------------- 673
C. "Waters of the United States": Wetlands and Small Streams ------- 701
D. Federal Power Act Licensing ----------------------------------- 714
E. State Certification and Federal Actions ------------------------ 728
F. Endangered Species Conservation ------------------------------- 737
G. Accommodating Federal Regulation and State Water Law ---------- 747
H. Environmental Quality and the Future of Dams------------------- 760

Chapter Eight.   Developing and Distributing Water Supplies -- 768

A. Water Supply Organizations ------------------------------------ 768
B. Federal Planning and Development of Water Resources ------------ 796

Chapter Nine.   Reserved Rights for Indian and Federal Lands 859

Chapter Ten.   Transboundary Waters: Interstate and International Allocation --- 938

A. Interstate Allocation--- 938
B. Federal Limits on State Export Restrictions ------------------- 1029
C. International Water Allocation Law---------------------------- 1049

Appendix A.   Table of Water Equivalents --------------------- 1069

Appendix B.   Sources of Water Law and Resources Literature 1070

INDEX --- 1081

TABLE OF CONTENTS

PREFACE iii

ACKNOWLEDGMENTS xi

TABLE OF CASES xxxi

Chapter One. Water Law: A Response to Scarcity 1

A. A Special Kind of Scarcity 1
B. Water Supply: The Hydrologic Cycle 4
    Note: Water Measurement 6
C. Demands for Water 7
    U.S. Geological Survey, Estimated Water Use in the United States in 2000 7
    David M. Gillilan & Thomas C. Brown, Instream Flow Protection ... 11
    William R. Travis, New Geographies of the American West: Land Use and the Changing Patterns of Place 15
D. Geographic Differences 19
    Western Water Policy Review Advisory Commission, Water in the West: Challenge for the Next Century 19
    Joseph W. Dellapenna, Issues Arising Under Riparian Rights: Replacing Common–Law Riparian Rights With Regulated Riparianism *in* Water Rights of the Eastern United States (Kenneth R. Wright ed.) 25
E. Climate Variability 26
    Committee on Environment and Natural Resources, National Science and Technology Council, Scientific Assessment of Global Change on the United States 26
    Notes 32
F. Economic Forces 33
    Terry L. Anderson & Pamela Snyder, Water Markets: Priming the Invisible Pump 33
    Charles W. Howe, Protecting Values in a Water Market Setting: Improving Water Markets to Increase Economic Efficiency and Equity 36
    Sandra Postel, Last Oasis: Facing Water Scarcity 41
G. Water Scarcity: The Role of Law and Policy 47
    The Conservation Foundation, America's Water: Current Trends and Emerging Issues 47
    Scarce Water and Institutional Change 48
    David Getches, Water Wrongs: Why Can't We Get It Right The First Time? 49
    Sarah F. Bates, David H. Getches, Lawrence J. MacDonnell & Charles F. Wilkinson, Searching Out the Headwaters: Change and Rediscovery in Western Water Policy 56
    Questions 56

Chapter Two.   Inventing Rules to Allocate a Scarce Resource   58

A. Milling -- 60
    Tyler v. Wilkinson --- 60
    Note -- 63
    Note: History of Riparian Doctrine -------------------------------- 63
B. Mining -- 67
    Irwin v. Phillips --- 67
    Notes --- 69
C. Agriculture --- 71
    Coffin v. Left Hand Ditch Co. ----------------------------------- 71
    Notes --- 75
    Note: History of the Appropriation Doctrine --------------------- 76
    Wells A. Hutchins, Water Rights Laws in the Nineteen Western
        States -- 77
D. Electrical Power -- 84
    Herminghaus v. Southern California Edison Co. -------------- 84
    Note: History of the "California Doctrine" ------------------------ 89
E. Cities -- 94
    City and County of Denver v. Sheriff ---------------------------- 94
F. Recreation --- 97
    Empire Water & Power Co. v. Cascade Town Co. ------------- 97
    Note -- 99
G. Fish, As Proxies for Protection of Aquatic Environments ----------- 99
    *Colorado River Water Conservation District v. Rocky Mountain
        Power Company* --- 99
    Note -- 102
H. Indian Reservations -- 102
    Winters v. United States -- 102
    Notes --- 105
    Note: The Federal Interest in Western Water -------------------- 106

**Chapter Three.   Principles of Acquisition, Enjoyment, Trans-
        fer, and Loss of Water Rights** ----------------------------------- 112

A. Riparian Principles -- 112
    1. Acquisition -- 112
    2. Enjoyment --- 115
        Kundel Farms v. Vir–Jo Farms, Inc. --------------------- 115
        Note: Preference for "Natural" Uses --------------------------- 117
        Mason v. Hoyle -- 118
        Notes --- 122
        Note: Custom and Riparian Rights in Hawai'i --------------- 125
        Harris v. Brooks -- 126
        Notes --- 130
        Note: The Restatement and Rights Among Riparians --------- 132
        Pyle v. Gilbert -- 137
        Notes --- 140
    3. Transfer --- 142
        Note: Use of Water on Non–Riparian Land or Outside the
            Watershed --- 145
        Note: Accretion and Avulsion ------------------------------------ 147
    4. Loss --- 150
        Pabst v. Finmand --- 150
        Notes --- 153

B. Prior Appropriation Principles ------------------------------------ 154
    Justice Greg Hobbs, Colorado Supreme Court, How Like a River:
      The Evolution of Western Water Law -------------------------- 155
    1. Acquisition -- 158
        State ex rel. Reynolds v. Miranda ---------------------------- 159
        Notes --- 160
        *In the Matter of the Adjudication of the Existing Rights to the
          Use of all the Water, Both Surface and Underground, Within
          the Missouri River Drainage Area* ---------------------------- 161
        Notes --- 167
        Sand Point Water & Light Co. v. Panhandle Development Co. ---- 168
        Notes --- 170
        *City and County of Denver v. Northern Colorado Water Conser-
          vancy District* -- 171
        Notes --- 177
        Note: Water Storage Rights -------------------------------- 180
    2. Enjoyment --- 182
        State ex rel. Cary v. Cochran ------------------------------- 184
        Notes --- 188
        State ex rel. Crowley v. District Court --------------------- 190
        Notes --- 193
        State Department of Ecology v. Grimes ----------------------- 195
        Notes --- 201
        A–B Cattle Company v. United States ------------------------- 203
        Note -- 207
        Lawrence J. MacDonnell, From Reclamation to Sustainability:
          Water, Agriculture, and the Environment in the American
          West -- 208
        Estate of Steed v. New Escalante Irrigation Co. ------------- 213
        Notes --- 218
        City and County of Denver v. Fulton Irrigating Ditch Co. ---- 220
        Notes --- 222
        *Southeastern Colorado Water Conservancy Dist. v. Shelton
          Farms, Inc.* --- 223
        Notes --- 229
    3. Transfer -- 230
        Lawrence J. MacDonnell, Transferring Water Uses in the West -- 230
        Economics of Water Transfers ------------------------------- 233
        Clifford T. Lee, The Transfer of Water Rights in California --- 233
        Note: Transaction Costs ------------------------------------ 235
        Green v. Chaffee Ditch Co. ---------------------------------- 238
        Notes --- 241
        Orr v. Arapahoe Water and Sanitation District -------------- 244
        Notes --- 249
        *Metropolitan Denver Sewage Disposal Dist. No. 1 v. Farmers
          Reservoir & Irrigation Co.* ---------------------------------- 251
        Notes --- 253
        City of Boulder v. Boulder & Left Hand Ditch Co. ----------- 254
        Notes --- 256
        National Research Council, National Academy of Science, Wa-
          ter Transfers in the West: Efficiency, Equity, and the Envi-
          ronment --- 257

4. Loss -- 259
    Jenkins v. State, Department of Water Resources ------------------ 259
    Notes -- 262
    Note: Prescription -- 265

Chapter Four.   Modern Statutory Administration of Water ----- 266

A. The Structure of Permit Systems ------------------------------------ 268
  George William Sherk, Meetings of Waters: The Conceptual Con-
    fluence of Water Law in the Eastern and Western States ---------- 268
  1. The Rise of Statutory Systems ------------------------------------ 275
    Frank E. Maloney, Sheldon J. Plager & Fletcher N. Baldwin,
      Water Law and Administration: The Florida Experience ------ 275
    Note -- 276
  2. The East Modifies Riparianism ---------------------------------- 277
    Robert H. Abrams, Replacing Riparianism in the Twenty–First
      Century -- 277
  3. Regulated Ripariansim --- 281
    a. What Is It? --- 281
    b. The Scope of Regulated Riparian Permit Systems ------------- 281
    c. The Florida Model for Stressed Humid States ----------------- 282
      Richard Hamann, Law and Policy in Managing Florida's
        Water Resources, *in* Water Resources Atlas of Florida 282
      Notes --- 288
  4. Western States -- 294
    a. Overview --- 294
      Wyoming Hereford Ranch v. Hammond Packing Co. ---------- 295
      Note --- 297
    b. Other State Variations -------------------------------------- 299
    c. General Stream Adjudications ------------------------------- 305
B. Issues Under Water Allocation Statutes --------------------------- 308
  1. Threshold Issues --- 308
    a. Availability of Water --------------------------------------- 308
    b. Rights for Future Uses ------------------------------------- 311
    c. Preferences --- 318
  2. Promoting the Public Interest ----------------------------------- 319
    a. New Uses --- 322
      Little Blue Natural Resources Dist. v. Lower Platte North
        Natural Resources Dist. ------------------------------------ 322
      Notes -- 325
      Shokal v. Dunn -- 326
      Notes -- 330
      David H. Getches, Water Planning: Untapped Opportunity
        for the Western States ------------------------------------- 333
      Note: Impact Assessment ------------------------------------ 337
    b. Changes in Existing Rights --------------------------------- 339
      Bonham v. Morgan -- 340
      Notes -- 342
    c. Limitations on the Exercise of Rights ---------------------- 343
      Alamosa–La Jara Water Users Protection Ass'n v. Gould ----- 343
      Notes -- 349

3. Statutory Protection for Instream Flows ----------------------- 350
   State, Department of Parks v. Idaho Department of Water
      Administration -- 351
   Notes --- 356
   City of Thornton v. City of Fort Collins -------------------- 360
   Notes --- 363
   Note: Water Trusts -- 364
4. Transfers and Changed Uses in Statutory Systems --------------- 367
   a. Improving Efficiency Through Transfers and Exchanges ----- 368
      National Research Council, National Academy of Science,
         Water Transfers in the West: Efficiency, Equity, and the
         Environment -- 368
      National Research Council, National Academy of Science,
         Water Transfers in the West: Efficiency, Equity, and the
         Environment -- 372
      Note: Bureau of Reclamation Transfers ------------------- 375
   b. Out of Priority Use -------------------------------------- 377
      Board of Directors of Wilder Irrigation Dist. v. Jorgensen ---- 377
      Notes -- 379
      Harrison C. Dunning, The "Physical Solution" in Western
         Water Law -- 381
      Cache LaPoudre Water Users Ass'n v. Glacier View Mead-
         ows --- 384
      Notes -- 387
   c. Area of Origin Protection from Transfers ----------------- 389
      National Research Council, National Academy of Sciences,
         Water Transfers in the West: Efficiency, Equity, and the
         Environment -- 390
      Colorado River Water Conservation Dist. v. Municipal Sub-
         district, Northern Colorado Water Conservancy Dist. ------- 391
      Notes -- 394
      Note: Area of Origin Protection ------------------------- 395

Chapter Five. Shared Public and Private Use of Waters -------- 399

A. The Public Trust in Navigable Waters ------------------------- 400
   1. Public Ownership of Beds ---------------------------------- 400
      a. Ancient Origins of Public Ownership ------------------- 401
      b. Navigability for Title -------------------------------- 403
      c. Federal–State Conflicts Over Ownership ---------------- 405
         Hughes v. Washington --------------------------------- 408
         Notes -- 411
   2. The Public Trust Doctrine as a Limit on Private Use ------- 415
      Illinois Central Railroad Co. v. Illinois --------------- 416
      Notes -- 420
      National Audubon Society v. Superior Court of Alpine County --- 426
      Notes -- 432
      In re Water Use Permit Applications, Petitions for Interim
         Instream Flow Standard Amendments, and Petitions for
         Water Reservations for the Waiahole Ditch -------------- 434
      Notes -- 439

3. Allowable Private Use of Submerged Lands 440
    Wilbour v. Gallagher 441
    Notes 446
B. Rights to Surface Use Among Riparians 449
    Beacham v. Lake Zurich Property Owners Ass'n 450
    Notes 452
    Thompson v. Enz 455
    Notes 459
C. Expanding Public Rights to Surface Use 460
    State v. McIlroy 461
    Notes 466
    People v. Emmert 470
    Notes 477
D. The Navigation Servitude 479
    United States v. Rands 479
    Notes 483
E. Shoreline Access 487
    Gion v. City of Santa Cruz 491
    Notes 496
F. Water Rights and Constitutional Takings 496
   1. Changing to Statutory Systems 496
    In re Waters of Long Valley Creek Stream System 497
    Notes 503
    Note: Objections to Statutes Converting a State System from Riparian to Prior Appropriation 503
    Franco–American Charolaise, Ltd. v. Oklahoma Water Resources Board 505
    Note 511
   2. Controls and Limits on Use of Existing Rights 514
    Enterprise Irrigation District v. Willis 514
    Note 517
    Note: U.S. Supreme Court Cases Regarding Constitutional Takings 517
    Joseph L. Sax, The Constitution, Property Rights and the Future of Water Law 521
    Note 526
   3. Environmental Restrictions on Water Use as Physical Takings 527
    Notes 528
    Casitas Mun. Water Dist. v. United States 533
    Notes 540
    Questions 544

Chapter Six. Groundwater Management 545

A. Introduction to the Geology and Dynamics of Groundwater 550
    E.C. Pielou, Fresh Water 550
    Note 556
B. Individual Rights in Groundwater 559
    Jack Hirshleifer, James C. De Haven and Jerome W. Milliman, Water Supply: Economics, Technology, and Policy 559
   1. Rights of Landowners 561
    Higday v. Nickolaus 562

Notes -- 566
Note: Land Subsidence and Groundwater Pumping --------------- 568
2. Prior Users' Rights --- 570
Wayman v. Murray City Corp. ------------------------------------ 571
Notes -- 574
Michigan Citizens for Water Conservation v. Nestlé Waters
    North America, Inc. -- 577
Notes -- 583
Musser v. Higginson -- 583
Notes -- 587
Note: Integration of Surface Water and Groundwater Adminis-
    tration --- 595
C. Groundwater Allocation and Public Policy ------------------------- 598
U.S. National Water Commission, Water Policies for the Future ---- 600
U.S. Geological Survey, National Water Summary, 1983: Hydro-
    logic Events and Issues -- 601
1. Administrative Regulation ------------------------------------- 602
Baker v. Ore–Ida Foods, Inc. ----------------------------------- 602
Notes -- 604
Mathers v. Texaco, Inc. --- 606
Notes -- 609
2. Permit Systems --- 610
3. Special Groundwater Management Districts ------------------ 613
Fundingsland v. Colorado Ground Water Commission ----------- 613
Note -- 616
Note: Statutory Control of Groundwater in Colorado ------------ 616
Note: State Variations in Local District Control of Groundwa-
    ter -- 621
4. Arizona: Legislative Redefinition of Rights and Strong State
    Control -- 624
Town of Chino Valley v. City of Prescott ---------------------- 626
Notes -- 632
5. California: Basinwide Adjudication ------------------------------ 633
Pasadena v. Alhambra -- 634
Notes -- 640
Los Angeles v. San Fernando ----------------------------------- 642
William Blomquist, Dividing the Waters ----------------------- 649
Note -- 650
Deborah A. de Lambert, Comment, District Management for
    California Groundwater --- 652
Note -- 653
6. Prevention and Clean–Up of Contamination -------------------- 653

Chapter Seven.   Environmental Protection and Water Law ----- 655

A. The Water Quality—Water Law Interface ------------------------- 657
1. Traditional State Approaches --------------------------------- 657
David H. Getches, Lawrence J. MacDonnell & Teresa A. Rice,
    Controlling Water Use: The Unfinished Business of Water
    Quality Protection --- 657
Note -- 664

2. Tort Remedies -- 665

Borough of Westville v. Whitney Home Builders ------------------- 666

Notes-- 669

Arizona Copper Co. v. Gillespie------------------------------------- 671

Notes-- 672

B. Federal Regulation of Water Quality-------------------------------- 673

1. Surface Water—The Clean Water Act------------------------ 673

a. Basic Structure-- 673

b. NPDES Permit Program: Technology Versus Receiving Water Quality and Quantity ------------------------------- 675

c. Water Quality Standards and TMDLS -------------------- 677

d. Point Versus Non–Point Pollution: The Case of Inter–Watershed Transfers ------------------------------------- 678

Catskill Mountains Chapter, Trout Unlimited v. City of New York--- 679

Notes --- 685

Note: Federal Pollution Control and the Common Law ------- 686

2. Federal Control and Clean–Up of Groundwater Contamination 688

Attorney General v. Thomas Solvent Co.--------------------- 692

Notes--- 695

C. "Waters of the United States": Wetlands and Small Streams ------- 701

Rapanos v. United States --- 705

Notes -- 712

D. Federal Power Act Licensing ------------------------------------- 714

Notes -- 716

Note: Dam Removal -- 717

City of Tacoma v. FERC--- 718

Notes -- 727

E. State Certification and Federal Actions ---------------------------- 728

PUD No. 1 of Jefferson County v. Washington Department of Ecology--- 728

Notes -- 736

F. Endangered Species Conservation --------------------------------- 737

Riverside Irrigation District v. Andrews ---------------------------- 737

Notes -- 741

A. Dan Tarlock, The Endangered Species Act and Western Water Rights --- 745

Note: National Environmental Policy Act --------------------------- 746

G. Accommodating Federal Regulation and State Water Law ----------- 747

1. Federal Regulation of Water -------------------------------- 747

David H. Getches, The Metamorphosis of Western Water Policy: Have Federal Laws and Local Decisions Eclipsed the States' Role?-- 748

Notes--- 751

The Bay–Delta: A Case Study in Reasoning Together ------------ 753

Notes--- 756

H. Environmental Quality and the Future of Dams---------------------- 760

The Report of the World Commission on Dams, Dams and Development: A New Framework for Decision–Making -------------------- 761

Chapter Eight. Developing and Distributing Water Supplies -- 768

A. Water Supply Organizations ----- 768
    Note on Adequate Water Supply Laws ----- 773
    1. Public Utilities ----- 774
    2. Municipal Service ----- 774
    3. Mutual Irrigation Companies ----- 778
    4. Special Districts ----- 782
        John D. Leshy, Special Water Districts—The Historical Background, in Special Water Districts: Challenge for the Future 11–27 (James N. Corbridge, Jr., ed., 1983) ----- 782
B. Federal Planning and Development of Water Resources ----- 796
    John R. Mather, Water Resources: Distribution, Use, and Management ----- 796
    1. The Reach of Congressional Power ----- 801
        United States v. Appalachian Elec. Power Co. ----- 802
        Notes ----- 809
        First Iowa Hydro–Electric Cooperative v. Federal Power Commission ----- 811
        Notes ----- 817
        California v. United States ----- 818
        Notes ----- 825
    2. The Reclamation Act and Reclamation Policy ----- 828
        Note: Restrictions on the Delivery of Reclamation Project Water ----- 829
        O'Neill v. United States ----- 833
        Notes ----- 839
        Note: Reclamation Project Subsidies and Water Transfers ----- 840
        Richard W. Wahl, Markets for Federal Water: Subsidies, Property Rights, and the Bureau of Reclamation ----- 841
        Department of the Interior, Principles Governing Voluntary Water Transactions That Involve or Affect Facilities Owned or Operated by the Department of the Interior ----- 844
        Note ----- 846
        Note: Corps of Engineers Water Project Operations ----- 846
        Southeastern Federal Power Customers v. Geren ----- 847
        Notes ----- 855

Chapter Nine. Reserved Rights for Indian and Federal Lands 859

    1. Nature and Extent of Reserved Rights ----- 862
        Winters v. United States ----- 863
        Notes ----- 863
        Arizona v. California ----- 864
        Notes ----- 867
    2. Jurisdiction to Determine Reserved Rights ----- 873
        United States v. District Court in and for Eagle County ----- 873
        Notes ----- 875
    3. Intent to Reserve ----- 878
        United States v. New Mexico ----- 878
        Notes ----- 885
        High Country Citizens' Alliance v. Norton ----- 890

Notes -- 896
United States v. Adair --- 899
Notes -- 905
Note: Federal Powers, Reserved and Nonreserved Federal Water Rights --- 907
4. Quantification -- 910
In re General Adjudication of All Rights to Use Water in the Big Horn River System ------------------------------------- 911
Notes -- 920
Note: Quantification of Indian Reserved Water Rights Without Litigation --- 923
5. Tribal Water Management --- 929
Steven J. Shupe, Water in Indian Country: From Paper Rights to a Managed Resource ----------------------------------- 930
Notes -- 934

Chapter Ten. Transboundary Waters: Interstate and International Allocation -- 938

A. Interstate Allocation -- 938
1. Adjudication -- 939
   a. Litigation Between Water Users ------------------------------- 940
      Bean v. Morris -- 940
      Note -- 942
   b. Litigation Between States ----------------------------------- 943
      Kansas v. Colorado --- 943
      Notes --- 946
      New Jersey v. New York ------------------------------------- 948
      Notes --- 951
      A. Dan Tarlock, The Law of Equitable Apportionment Revisited, Updated, and Restated ------------------------- 951
      Note -- 955
      Colorado v. New Mexico ------------------------------------- 956
      Note -- 960
      Colorado v. New Mexico ------------------------------------- 961
      Note -- 964
      Arkansas v. Oklahoma --------------------------------------- 966
      Note -- 973
      Note: Interstate Pollution Remedies ------------------------- 973
      Note: On the Future of Equitable Apportionment ------------- 976
2. Allocation by Interstate Compact --------------------------------- 977
   State ex rel. Dyer v. Sims ------------------------------------ 979
   Notes -- 982
   Intake Water Company v. Yellowstone River Compact Commission --- 985
   Notes -- 986
   David H. Getches, Competing Demands for the Colorado River ---- 987
   The Colorado River Compact -------------------------------------- 989
   Notes -- 992
3. Congressional Apportionment: The Special Case of the Colorado River -- 995
   The Boulder Canyon Project Act ---------------------------------- 996

Notes--- 999
Charles J. Meyers, The Colorado River -------------------------------- 999
Arizona v. California --- 1001
Note --- 1010
4. Interstate Problem Solving in the Colorado River Basin ---------- 1011
David H. Getches, Water Allocation During Drought in Arizona
and Southern California: Legal and Institutional Responses 1011
Notes-- 1013
Note: A Frustrating Quest for Solutions --------------------------- 1013
James H. Davenport, Softening The Divides: The Seven Colo-
rado River Basin States' Recommendation to the Secretary
of the Interior Regarding Lower Basin Shortage Guidelines
and the Operation of Lakes Mead and Powell in Low Reser-
voir Conditions --- 1021
Notes-- 1026
Note: Congressional Approval of Multi–Party, Multi–Issue In-
terstate Dispute Resolution--------------------------------------- 1026
B. Federal Limits on State Export Restrictions ------------------------- 1029
Sporhase v. Nebraska ex rel. Douglas --------------------------------- 1030
Notes --- 1037
Note: The Great Lakes—A Case Study in Diversion Policy Making 1043
Note: Export Restrictions and International Trade Law -------------- 1046
C. International Water Allocation Law---------------------------------- 1049
Daniel F. Luecke et al., A Delta Once More: Restoring Riparian
and Wetland Habitat in the Colorado River Delta ------------------ 1049
Notes --- 1054
Convention on the Law of the Non–Navigational Uses of Interna-
tional Watercourses-- 1056
Notes --- 1060
*Case Concerning The Gabcikovo–Nagymaros Project (Hung. v.
Slovakia)* -- 1062
Note: Water Allocation in the Middle East--------------------------- 1066

Appendix A.   Table of Water Equivalents ----------------------- 1069

Appendix B.   Sources of Water Law and Resources Literature 1070

1. Introduction-- 1070
2. The Law-- 1070
3. History--- 1072
4. Official Documents--- 1077
5. Economics --- 1078
6. Political Science--- 1079
7. Law Reviews --- 1079
8. Popular Literature--- 1079
9. Miscellaneous --- 1080

INDEX --- 1081

*

TABLE OF CASES

Principal cases are in bold type. Non-principal cases are in roman type. References are to Pages.

A–B Cattle Co. v. United States, 196 Colo. 539, 589 P.2d 57 (Colo.1978), **203**

Ace Equipment Sales v. Buccino, 273 Conn. 217, 869 A.2d 626 (Conn.2005), 453, 455

Acton v. Blundell, 152 Eng. Rep. 1223 (Ex.Ct. 1843), 562

Adair, United States v., 723 F.2d 1394 (9th Cir.1983), 863, **899**

Adams v. Lang, 553 So.2d 89 (Ala.1989), 569

Adams v. Star Enterprise, 51 F.3d 417 (4th Cir.1995), 688

Adirondack League Club, Inc. v. Sierra Club, 92 N.Y.2d 591, 684 N.Y.S.2d 168, 706 N.E.2d 1192 (N.Y.1998), 470

Adjudication of the Existing Rights to the Use of All the Water, In re, 311 Mont. 327, 55 P.3d 396 (Mont.2002), **161**

Adjudication of the Water Rights of Upper Guadalupe Segment of Guadalupe River Basin, In re, 642 S.W.2d 438 (Tex.1982), 505

Adjudication of Water Rights in the Llano River Watershed of Colorado River Basin, In re, 642 S.W.2d 446 (Tex.1982), 505

Adkins v. Thomas Solvent Co., 440 Mich. 293, 487 N.W.2d 715 (Mich.1992), 654

Alabama v. United States Army Corps of Engineers, 424 F.3d 1117 (11th Cir.2005), 854, 942

Alameda Gateway Ltd., United States v., 213 F.3d 1161 (9th Cir.2000), 440

Alameda Water & Sanitation Dist. v. Reilly, 930 F.Supp. 486 (D.Colo.1996), 714

Alamosa–La Jara Water Users Protection Ass'n v. Gould, 674 P.2d 914 (Colo. 1983), 310, **343,** 544, 597

Alaska, United States v., 521 U.S. 1, 117 S.Ct. 1888, 138 L.Ed.2d 231 (1997), 412

Alaska, United States v., 423 F.2d 764 (9th Cir.1970), 411

Albuquerque, City of v. FAA, 97 F.3d 415 (10th Cir.1996), 936

Alburger v. Philadelphia Elec. Co., 112 Pa. Cmwlth. 441, 535 A.2d 729 (Pa.Cmwlth. 1988), 146

Allegretti & Co. v. County of Imperial, 42 Cal.Rptr.3d 122 (Cal.App. 4 Dist.2006), 532, 541

Alpine Land & Reservoir Co., United States v., 697 F.2d 851 (9th Cir.1983), 202

Alsea Valley Alliance v. Department of Commerce, 358 F.3d 1181 (9th Cir.2004), 759

Alsea Valley Alliance v. Evans, 161 F.Supp.2d 1154 (D.Or.2001), 759

American Falls Reservoir Dist. v. Idaho Dept. of Water Resources, 143 Idaho 862, 154 P.3d 433 (Idaho 2007), 181, 189, 594

American Rivers, Inc. v. FERC, 129 F.3d 99 (2nd Cir.1997), 736

American Wildlands v. Browner, 260 F.3d 1192 (10th Cir.2001), 678

Anaheim Union Water Co. v. Fuller, 150 Cal. 327, 88 P. 978 (Cal.1907), 115, 145

A & N Cleaners & Launderers, Inc. v. United States v., 788 F.Supp. 1317 (S.D.N.Y. 1992), 696

Anderson v. Bell, 433 So.2d 1202 (Fla.1983), 453

Anderson v. Cumpston, 258 Neb. 891, 606 N.W.2d 817 (Neb.2000), 147

Anderson, United States v., 736 F.2d 1358 (9th Cir.1984), 907

Anita Ditch Co. v. Turner, 389 P.2d 1018 (Wyo.1964), 299

Apfelbacher, State v., 167 Wis. 233, 167 N.W. 244 (Wis.1918), 142

Appalachian Elec. Power Co., United States v., 311 U.S. 377, 61 S.Ct. 291, 85 L.Ed. 243 (1940), **802**

Application A–16642, In re, 236 Neb. 671, 463 N.W.2d 591 (Neb.1990), 331

Application for Water Rights of Certain Shareholders in Las Animas Consol. Canal Co., In re, 688 P.2d 1102 (Colo.1984), 781

Application for Water Rights of Hines Highlands Ltd. Partnership, 929 P.2d 718 (Colo.1996), 314

Application for Water Rights of United States, In re, 101 P.3d 1072 (Colo.2004), 897

Application of (see name of party)

Applications A–16027, In re, 242 Neb. 315, 495 N.W.2d 23 (Neb.1993), 326

Arizona v. California, 531 U.S. 1, 121 S.Ct. 292, 148 L.Ed.2d 1 (2000), 869

Arizona v. California, 530 U.S. 392, 120 S.Ct. 2304, 147 L.Ed.2d 374 (2000), 868

Arizona v. California, 460 U.S. 605, 103 S.Ct. 1382, 75 L.Ed.2d 318 (1983), 868, 871

Arizona v. California, 439 U.S. 419, 99 S.Ct. 995, 58 L.Ed.2d 627 (1979), 868, 872

Arizona v. California, 376 U.S. 340, 84 S.Ct. 755, 11 L.Ed.2d 757 (1964), 868

Arizona v. California, 373 U.S. 546, 83 S.Ct. 1468, 10 L.Ed.2d 542 (1963), 106, 862, **864,** 907, 956, 996, **1001**

Arizona v. California, 298 U.S. 558, 56 S.Ct. 848, 80 L.Ed. 1331 (1936), 956

Arizona v. California, 292 U.S. 341, 54 S.Ct. 735, 78 L.Ed. 1298 (1934), 3

Arizona v. California, 283 U.S. 423, 51 S.Ct. 522, 75 L.Ed. 1154 (1931), 810

Arizona v. San Carlos Apache Tribe, 463 U.S. 545, 103 S.Ct. 3201, 77 L.Ed.2d 837 (1983), 877

Arizona Copper Co. v. Gillespie, 12 Ariz. 190, 100 P. 465 (Ariz.Terr.1909), **671**

Arkansas v. Oklahoma, 503 U.S. 91, 112 S.Ct. 1046, 117 L.Ed.2d 239 (1992), 687, 940, **966**

Ashford, Application of, 50 Haw. 314, 50 Haw. 452, 440 P.2d 76 (Hawai'i 1968), 489

Ashmore, State v., 236 Ga. 401, 224 S.E.2d 334 (Ga.1976), 490

Ashwander v. Tennessee Valley Authority, 297 U.S. 288, 56 S.Ct. 466, 80 L.Ed. 688 (1936), 811

Aspen, City of v. Colorado River Water Conservation Dist., 696 P.2d 758 (Colo.1985), 170

Aspen Wilderness Workshop, Inc. v. Colorado Water Conservation Bd., 901 P.2d 1251 (Colo.1995), 360

Associated Enterprises, Inc. v. Toltec Watershed Imp. Dist., 578 P.2d 1359 (Wyo. 1978), 311

Associated Home Builders etc., Inc. v. City of Livermore, 135 Cal.Rptr. 41, 557 P.2d 473 (Cal.1976), 777

Attorney General v. Thomas Solvent Co., 146 Mich.App. 55, 380 N.W.2d 53 (Mich.App.1985), **692**

Attorney General ex rel. Natural Resources Com'n v. Balkema, 191 Mich.App. 201, 477 N.W.2d 100 (Mich.App.1991), 460

Aurora, City of v. Commerce Group Corp., 694 P.2d 382 (Colo.App.1984), 776

Aurora ex rel. Utility Enterprise, City of v. Colorado State Engineer, 105 P.3d 595 (Colo.2005), 229

Avoyelles Sportsmen's League, Inc. v. Marsh, 715 F.2d 897 (5th Cir.1983), 705

Babbitt v. Sweet Home Chapter of Communities for a Great Oregon, 515 U.S. 687, 115 S.Ct. 2407, 132 L.Ed.2d 597 (1995), 742

Bach v. Sarich, 74 Wash.2d 575, 445 P.2d 648 (Wash.1968), 449

Badger v. Brooklyn Canal Co., 922 P.2d 745 (Utah 1996), 780

Badgley v. New York, 606 F.2d 358 (2nd Cir.1979), 942, 983

Baeth v. Hoisveen, 157 N.W.2d 728 (N.D. 1968), 504

Bailey v. State, 95 Nev. 378, 594 P.2d 734 (Nev.1979), 311

Baker v. Ore–Ida Foods, Inc., 95 Idaho 575, 513 P.2d 627 (Idaho 1973), **602**

Baker Ditch Co. v. District Court of Eighteenth Judicial Dist., 251 Mont. 251, 824 P.2d 260 (Mont.1992), 267

Ball v. James, 451 U.S. 355, 101 S.Ct. 1811, 68 L.Ed.2d 150 (1981), 788, 789

Barney v. Keokuk, 94 U.S. 324, 4 Otto 324, 24 L.Ed. 224 (1876), 403

Barrett v. Atlantic Richfield Co., 95 F.3d 375 (5th Cir.1996), 654

Bar 70 Enterprises, Inc. v. Tosco Corp., 703 P.2d 1297 (Colo.1985), 170

Barshop v. Medina County Underground Water Conservation Dist., 925 S.W.2d 618 (Tex.1996), 624

Barstow, City of v. Mojave Water Agency, 99 Cal.Rptr.2d 294, 5 P.3d 853 (Cal.2000), 183, 640

Basin Elec. Power Co-op. v. State Bd. of Control, 578 P.2d 557 (Wyo.1978), 243

Battle Creek, City of v. Goguac Resort Ass'n, 181 Mich. 241, 148 N.W. 441 (Mich.1914), 670

Baumgartner v. Stremel, 178 Colo. 209, 496 P.2d 705 (Colo.1972), 257

Bausch v. Myers, 273 Or. 376, 541 P.2d 817 (Or.1975), 264

Bausch & Lomb Inc. v. Utica Mut. Ins. Co., 330 Md. 758, 625 A.2d 1021 (Md.1993), 281

Bay–Delta Programmatic Environmental Impact Report Coordinated Proceedings, In re, 77 Cal.Rptr.3d 578, 184 P.3d 709 (Cal. 2008), 757

Bayou Land Co. v. Talley, 924 P.2d 136 (Colo. 1996), 620

Bayview Land, Ltd. v. State ex rel. Clark, 950 So.2d 966 (Miss.2006), 149

Beacham v. Lake Zurich Property Owners Ass'n, 123 Ill.2d 227, 122 Ill.Dec. 14, 526 N.E.2d 154 (Ill.1988), **450**

Bealey v. Shaw, 102 Eng. Rep. 1266 (K.B. 1805), 131

Bean v. Morris, 221 U.S. 485, 31 S.Ct. 703, 55 L.Ed. 821 (1911), 939, **940**

Beckendorff v. Harris–Galveston Coastal Subsidence Dist., 558 S.W.2d 75 (Tex.Civ. App.-Hous (14 Dist.) 1977), 570

Bell v. Town of Wells, 557 A.2d 168 (Me. 1989), 490

Bell, United States v., 724 P.2d 631 (Colo. 1986), 876

Belle Fourche Irr. Dist. v. Smiley, 84 S.D. 701, 176 N.W.2d 239 (S.D.1970), 504

Bell Petroleum Services, Inc., In re, 3 F.3d 889 (5th Cir.1993), 691, 696

Beneficial Water Use Permit, Matter of Application for, 278 Mont. 50, 923 P.2d 1073 (Mont.1996), 878

Bergh v. Hines, 44 Mass.App.Ct. 590, 692 N.E.2d 980 (Mass.App.Ct.1998), 150

Berkeley, City of v. Superior Court, 162 Cal. Rptr. 327, 606 P.2d 362 (Cal.1980), 422

Bersani v. Robichaud, 850 F.2d 36 (2nd Cir. 1988), 714

B.F. Goodrich Co. v. Murtha, 958 F.2d 1192 (2nd Cir.1992), 696

Biddix v. Henredon Furniture Industries, Inc., 76 N.C.App. 30, 331 S.E.2d 717 (N.C.App.1985), 686

Big Cottonwood Tanner Ditch Co. v. Shurt-liff, 56 Utah 196, 189 P. 587 (Utah 1919), 194

Bighorn–Desert View Water Agency v. Verjil, 46 Cal.Rptr.3d 73, 138 P.3d 220 (Cal. 2006), 641

Big Horn Power Co. v. State, 23 Wyo. 271, 148 P. 1110 (Wyo.1915), 298

Biodiversity Legal Foundation v. Babbitt, 943 F.Supp. 23 (D.D.C.1996), 752

Birchwood Lakes Colony Club, Inc. v. Borough of Medford Lakes, 90 N.J. 582, 449 A.2d 472 (N.J.1982), 687

Black Hawk, City of v. City of Central, 97 P.3d 951 (Colo.2004), 314

Blue Springs, City of v. Central Development Ass'n, 831 S.W.2d 655 (Mo.App. W.D. 1992), 566

Board of County Comm'rs v. Crystal Creek Homeowners Ass'n, 891 P.2d 952 (Colo. 1995), 229, 310, 314, 333

Board of County Com'rs of Arapahoe County v. Denver Bd. of Water Com'rs, 718 P.2d 235 (Colo.1986), 777

Board of County Com'rs of County of Park v. Park County Sportsmen's Ranch, LLP, 45 P.3d 693 (Colo.2002), 577

Board of Directors of Wilder Irr. Dist. v. Jorgensen, 64 Idaho 538, 136 P.2d 461 (Idaho 1943), **377**

Board of Trustees of Internal Imp. Trust Fund v. Levy, 656 So.2d 1359 (Fla.App. 1 Dist.1995), 440

Board of Trustees of Internal Imp. Trust Fund v. Medeira Beach Nominee, 272 So.2d 209 (Fla.App. 2 Dist.1973), 150, 440

Boehmer v. Big Rock Creek Irr. Dist., 117 Cal. 19, 48 P. 908 (Cal.1897), 114

Boggs v. Merced Mining Co., 14 Cal. 279 (Cal.1859), 70

Bohn v. Albertson, 107 Cal.App.2d 738, 238 P.2d 128 (Cal.App. 1 Dist.1951), 448

Boise–Kuna Irr. Dist. v. Gross, 118 Idaho 940, 801 P.2d 1291 (Idaho App.1990), 265

Bollinger v. Henry, 375 S.W.2d 161 (Mo. 1964), 455

Bonelli Cattle Co. v. Arizona, 414 U.S. 313, 94 S.Ct. 517, 38 L.Ed.2d 526 (1973), 412

Bonham v. Morgan, 788 P.2d 497 (Utah 1989), **340**

Borax Consolidated v. Los Angeles, 296 U.S. 10, 56 S.Ct. 23, 80 L.Ed. 9 (1935), 113

Borough of (see name of borough)

Bott v. Commission of Natural Resources of State of Mich. Dept. of Natural Resources, 415 Mich. 45, 327 N.W.2d 838 (Mich. 1982), 466

Botton v. State, 69 Wash.2d 751, 420 P.2d 352 (Wash.1966), 459

Boulder, City of v. Boulder & Left Hand Ditch Co., 192 Colo. 219, 557 P.2d 1182 (Colo.1976), **254**

Boyer, Application of, 73 Idaho 152, 248 P.2d 540 (Idaho 1952), 264

Branch v. Western Petroleum, Inc., 657 P.2d 267 (Utah 1982), 688

Brannon v. Boldt, 958 So.2d 367 (Fla.App. 2 Dist.2007), 144

Braren, United States v., 338 F.3d 971 (9th Cir.2003), 906

Briggs v. Golden Valley Land & Cattle Co., 97 Idaho 427, 546 P.2d 382 (Idaho 1976), 604

Bristor v. Cheatham, 75 Ariz. 227, 255 P.2d 173 (Ariz.1953), 625

Bristor v. Cheatham, 73 Ariz. 228, 240 P.2d 185 (Ariz.1952), 625

Brookens v. City of Yakima, 15 Wash.App. 464, 550 P.2d 30 (Wash.App. Div. 3 1976), 777

Brose v. Board of Directors of Nampa & Meridian Irr. Dist., 24 Idaho 116, 132 P. 799 (Idaho 1913), 781

Brown v. Chase, 125 Wash. 542, 217 P. 23 (Wash.1923), 505

Bryant v. Yellen, 447 U.S. 352, 100 S.Ct. 2232, 65 L.Ed.2d 184 (1980), 830

Buffalo River Conservation & Recreation Council v. National Park Service, 558 F.2d 1342 (8th Cir.1977), 468

Burger v. City of Beatrice, 181 Neb. 213, 147 N.W.2d 784 (Neb.1967), 776

Burkart v. City of Fort Lauderdale, 168 So.2d 65 (Fla.1964), 113

Burket v. Krimlofski, 167 Neb. 45, 91 N.W.2d 57 (Neb.1958), 148

Burlington Northern & Santa Fe Ry. Co., United States v., 520 F.3d 918 (9th Cir. 2008), 691

Burr v. Maclay Rancho Water Co., 154 Cal. 428, 98 P. 260 (Cal.1908), 634

Byrd, United States v., 609 F.2d 1204 (7th Cir.1979), 704

Cache LaPoudre Water Users Ass'n v. Glacier View Meadows, 191 Colo. 53, 550 P.2d 288 (Colo.1976), **384**

California v. FERC, 495 U.S. 490, 110 S.Ct. 2024, 109 L.Ed.2d 474 (1990), 714, 826

California v. United States, 438 U.S. 645, 98 S.Ct. 2985, 57 L.Ed.2d 1018 (1978), **818**

California ex rel. Air Resources Bd. v. EPA, 774 F.2d 1437 (9th Cir.1985), 558

California ex rel. State Lands Com., State of v. Superior Court, 44 Cal.Rptr.2d 399, 900 P.2d 648 (Cal.1995), 150

California Oregon Power Co. v. Beaver Portland Cement Co., 295 U.S. 142, 55 S.Ct. 725, 79 L.Ed. 1356 (1935), 107, 860, 908

California Trout, Inc. v. State Water Resources Control Bd., 207 Cal.App.3d 585, 255 Cal.Rptr. 184 (Cal.App. 3 Dist.1989), 432

California, United States v., 509 F.Supp. 867 (E.D.Cal.1981), 825

California, United States v., 694 F.2d 1171 (9th Cir.1982), 825

Cambridge Water Co. v. Eastern Counties Leather Plc, 2 A.C. 264 (H.L. 1993), 688

Campbell v. Wyoming Development Co., 55 Wyo. 347, 100 P.2d 124 (Wyo.1940), 265

Cappaert v. United States, 426 U.S. 128, 96 S.Ct. 2062, 48 L.Ed.2d 523 (1976), 885

Capune v. Robbins, 273 N.C. 581, 160 S.E.2d 881 (N.C.1968), 441

Carnahan v. Moriah Property Owners Ass'n, Inc., 716 N.E.2d 437 (Ind.1999), 452

Carson–Truckee Water Conservancy Dist. v. Clark, 741 F.2d 257 (9th Cir.1984), 741, 936

Carter v. Territory, 24 Haw. 47 (Hawai'i Terr.1917), 125

Cartwright v. Public Service Co. of N.M., 66 N.M. 64, 343 P.2d 654 (N.M.1958), 769

Cary, State ex rel. v. Cochran, 138 Neb. 163, 292 N.W. 239 (Neb.1940), **184**

Case Concerning The Gabcikovo–Nagymaros Project (Hung. v. Slovakia), 1997 I.C.J. 7 (I.C.J.1997), **1062**

Case of the Royal Fishery of Banne, 80 Eng. Rep. 540 (K.B. 1611), 401

Casitas Mun. Water Dist. v. United States, 543 F.3d 1276 (Fed.Cir.2008), **533,** 840

Casitas Mun. Water Dist. v. United States, 76 Fed.Cl. 100 (Fed.Cl.2007), 532

Catskill Mountains Chapter of Trout Unlimited v. City of New York, 451 F.3d 77 (2nd Cir.2006), **679**

Cave v. Tyler, 133 Cal. 566, 65 P. 1089 (Cal. 1901), 69

Central Florida Investments, Inc. v. Orange County Code Enforcement Bd., 790 So.2d 593 (Fla.App. 5 Dist.2001), 670

Central Green Co. v. United States, 531 U.S. 425, 121 S.Ct. 1005, 148 L.Ed.2d 919 (2001), 811

Central Neb. Public Power Co. & Irrigation Dist. v. Abrahamson, 226 Neb. 594, 413 N.W.2d 290 (Neb.1987), 596

Central Platte Natural Resources Dist. v. Wyoming, 245 Neb. 439, 513 N.W.2d 847 (Neb.1994), 359

CF & I Steel Corp. v. Rooks, 178 Colo. 110, 495 P.2d 1134 (Colo.1972), 242

CF & I Steel Corp. Purgatoire River Water Conservancy Dist., 183 Colo. 135, 515 P.2d 456 (Colo.1973), 263

Chadd v. Lower Platte South Natural Resources Dist., 261 Neb. 90, 621 N.W.2d 299 (Neb.2001), 1037

Chance v. BP Chemicals, Inc., 77 Ohio St.3d 17, 670 N.E.2d 985 (Ohio 1996), 688

Change of Appropriation Water Rights, In re Application for , United States v., No. CDV 99–28 (Mont. 1st Jud. Dist. 1999), 219

Chatfield East Well Co. v. Chatfield East Property Owners Ass'n, 956 P.2d 1260 (Colo.1998), 620

Chemical Waste Management, Inc. v. EPA, 976 F.2d 2 (D.C.Cir.1992), 691

Cherokee Nation of Oklahoma, United States v., 480 U.S. 700, 107 S.Ct. 1487, 94 L.Ed.2d 704 (1987), 486

Cherry v. Steiner, 543 F.Supp. 1270 (D.Ariz. 1982), 632

Chevron v. NRDC, 467 U.S. 837, 104 S.Ct. 2778, 81 L.Ed.2d 694 (1984), 703, 936

Chicago Park Dist., People ex rel. Scott v., 66 Ill.2d 65, 4 Ill.Dec. 660, 360 N.E.2d 773 (Ill.1976), 420

Chino Valley, Town of v. City of Prescott, 131 Ariz. 78, 638 P.2d 1324 (Ariz. 1981), **626**

Choctaw Nation v. Oklahoma, 397 U.S. 620, 90 S.Ct. 1328, 25 L.Ed.2d 615 (1970), 414

Choudhry v. Free, 17 Cal.3d 660, 131 Cal. Rptr. 654, 552 P.2d 438 (1976), 790

Christian Activities Council v. Town Council of Glastonbury, 249 Conn. 566, 735 A.2d 231 (Conn.1999), 600

Cinque Bambini Partnership v. State, 491 So.2d 508 (Miss.1986), 421

City and County of (see name of city)
City of (see name of city)

Clark v. Nash, 198 U.S. 361, 25 S.Ct. 676, 49 L.Ed. 1085 (1905), 487

Clark Fork River Drainage Area, In re, 274 Mont. 340, 908 P.2d 1353 (Mont.1995), 263

Cleaver v. Judd, 238 Or. 266, 393 P.2d 193 (Or.1964), 218

Cline v. American Aggregates Corp., 15 Ohio St.3d 384, 474 N.E.2d 324 (Ohio 1984), 568

Cochran, State ex rel. Cary v., 138 Neb. 163, 292 N.W. 239 (Neb.1940), **184**

Coffin v. Left Hand Ditch Co., 6 Colo. 443 (Colo.1882), **71**

Colberg, Inc. v. State ex rel. Dept. of Public Works, 67 Cal.2d 408, 62 Cal.Rptr. 401, 432 P.2d 3 (Cal.1967), 487

Coleman v. Schaeffer, 163 Ohio St. 202, 126 N.E.2d 444 (Ohio 1955), 461

College Sav. Bank v. Florida Prepaid Postsecondary Educ. Expense Bd., 527 U.S. 666, 119 S.Ct. 2219, 144 L.Ed.2d 605 (1999), 1040

Collens v. New Canaan Water Co., 155 Conn. 477, 234 A.2d 825 (Conn.1967), 123

Collier v. Arizona Dept. of Water Resources, 150 Ariz. 195, 722 P.2d 363 (Ariz.App. Div. 1 1986), 595

Colorado v. ASARCO, Inc., 608 F.Supp. 1484 (D.Colo.1985), 696

Colorado v. Kansas, 320 U.S. 383, 64 S.Ct. 176, 88 L.Ed. 116 (1943), 946

Colorado v. New Mexico, 467 U.S. 310, 104 S.Ct. 2433, 81 L.Ed.2d 247 (1984), 940, **961**

Colorado v. New Mexico, 459 U.S. 176, 103 S.Ct. 539, 74 L.Ed.2d 348 (1982), **956**

Colorado Dept. of Natural Resources v. Southwestern Colorado Water Conservation Dist., 671 P.2d 1294 (Colo.1983), 620

Colorado River Water Conservation Dist. v. City and County of Denver, 640 P.2d 1139 (Colo.1982), 178

Colorado River Water Conservation Dist. v. Municipal Subdistrict, Northern Colorado Water Conservancy Dist., 198 Colo. 352, 610 P.2d 81 (Colo. 1979), **391**

Colorado River Water Conservation Dist. v. Rocky Mountain Power Co., 158 Colo. 331, 406 P.2d 798 (Colo.1965), **99,** 351

Colorado River Water Conservation Dist. v. Twin Lakes Reservoir and Canal Co., 181 Colo. 53, 506 P.2d 1226 (Colo.1973), 178

Colorado River Water Conservation Dist. v. United States, 424 U.S. 800, 96 S.Ct. 1236, 47 L.Ed.2d 483 (1976), 877

Colorado River Water Conservation Dist. v. Vidler Tunnel Water Co., 197 Colo. 413, 594 P.2d 566 (Colo.1979), 179, 313

Colorado Springs v. Bender, 148 Colo. 458, 366 P.2d 552 (Colo.1961), 574

Colorado Water Conservation Bd. v. Upper Gunnison River Water Conservancy Dist., 109 P.3d 585 (Colo.2005), 364

Colville Confederated Tribes v. Walton, 752 F.2d 397 (9th Cir.1985), 907

Colville Confederated Tribes v. Walton, 647 F.2d 42 (9th Cir.1981), 907

Commonwealth, Dept. of Highways v. Thomas, 427 S.W.2d 213 (Ky.1967), 487

Committee To Save Mokelumne River v. East Bay Mun. Utility Dist., 13 F.3d 305 (9th Cir.1993), 679

Commonwealth of (see name of Commonwealth)

Conatser v. Johnson, 194 P.3d 897 (Utah 2008), 470

Concerned Area Residents for Environment v. Southview Farm, 34 F.3d 114 (2nd Cir. 1994), 685

Concerned Citizens of Putnam County for Responsive Government, Inc. v. St. Johns River Water Management Dist., 622 So.2d 520 (Fla.App. 5 Dist.1993), 288, 360

Concerning Application for Plan for Augmentation of City and County of Denver ex rel. Bd. of Water Com'rs, In re, 44 P.3d 1019 (Colo.2002), 664

Concerning the Application for Water Rights of the City of Golden, No. 98CW448, Dist. Ct. Water Div., No. 1 (Colo. Jan. 13, 2001), 363

Confederated Salish & Kootenai Tribes v. Clinch, 336 Mont. 302, 158 P.3d 377 (Mont.2007), 878

Confederated Salish & Kootenai Tribes v. Clinch, 297 Mont. 448, 992 P.2d 244 (Mont.1999), 878

Conrad/Dommel, LLC v. West Development Co., 149 Md.App. 239, 815 A.2d 828 (Md. App.2003), 144

Consejo de Desarrollo Economico de Mexicali v. United States, 482 F.3d 1157 (9th Cir. 2007), 1019

Consolidated Edison Co. of New York, Inc. v. UGI Utilities, Inc., 423 F.3d 90 (2nd Cir. 2005), 691

Cook v. Evans, 45 S.D. 31, 185 N.W. 262 (S.D.1921), 504

Cool v. Mountainview Landowners Co-op. Ass'n, Inc., 139 Idaho 770, 86 P.3d 484 (Idaho 2004), 144

Cooper Industries, Inc. v. Aviall, 543 U.S. 157, 125 S.Ct. 577, 160 L.Ed.2d 548 (2004), 691

Corpus Christi, City of v. City of Pleasanton, 154 Tex. 289, 276 S.W.2d 798 (Tex.1955), 195

Coryell v. Robinson, 118 Colo. 225, 194 P.2d 342 (Colo.1948), 265

County of (see name of county)

Cowden v. Kennewick Irrigation Dist., 76 Wash.App. 844, 888 P.2d 1225 (1995), 788

Crandall v. Woods, 8 Cal. 136 (Cal.1857), 70

Creedmoor Maha Water Supply Corp. v. Barton Springs–Edwards Aquifer Conservation Dist., 784 S.W.2d 79 (Tex.App.-Austin 1989), 653

Crookston Cattle Co. v. Minnesota Dept. of Natural Resources, 300 N.W.2d 769 (Minn.1980), 610

Crowley, State ex rel. v. District Court, 108 Mont. 89, 88 P.2d 23 (Mont.1939), **190**

Cundy v. Weber, 68 S.D. 214, 300 N.W. 17 (S.D.1941), 262, 380

Current Creek Irr. Co. v. Andrews, 9 Utah 2d 324, 344 P.2d 528 (Utah 1959), 574

Curry v. Hill, 460 P.2d 933 (Okla.1969), 461

Custis Fishing & Hunting Club, Inc. v. Johnson, 214 Va. 388, 200 S.E.2d 542 (Va. 1973), 453

Danielson v. Castle Meadows, Inc., 791 P.2d 1106 (Colo.1990), 621

Danielson, People ex rel. v. City of Thornton, 775 P.2d 11 (Colo.1989), 263

Dardar v. Lafourche Realty Co., Inc., 55 F.3d 1082 (5th Cir.1995), 486

Dateline Builders, Inc. v. City of Santa Rosa, 146 Cal.App.3d 520, 194 Cal.Rptr. 258 (Cal.App. 1 Dist.1983), 776

Daubert v. Merrell Dow Pharmaceuticals, Inc., 509 U.S. 579, 113 S.Ct. 2786, 125 L.Ed.2d 469 (1993), 688

Day v. Armstrong, 362 P.2d 137 (Wyo.1961), 470

Deadman Creek Drainage Basin in Spokane County, In re, 103 Wash.2d 686, 694 P.2d 1071 (Wash.1985), 505

Delaware River Basin Com'n v. Bucks County Water Authority, 545 F.Supp. 138 (E.D.Pa.1982), 983

Delaware River Joint Toll Bridge Commission v. Miller, 147 F.Supp. 270 (E.D.Pa. 1956), 982

Del Norte, County of v. City of Crescent City, 84 Cal.Rptr.2d 179 (Cal.App. 1 Dist.1999), 776

Denver By and Through Bd. of Water Com'rs, City and County of v. Snake River Water Dist., 788 P.2d 772 (Colo.1990), 263

Denver, City and County of v. Board of Com'rs of Arapahoe County, 113 Colo. 150, 156 P.2d 101 (Colo.1945), 775

Denver, City and County of v. Fulton Irrigating Ditch Co., 179 Colo. 47, 506 P.2d 144 (Colo.1972), **220**

Denver, City and County of v. Middle Park Water Conservancy Dist., 925 P.2d 283 (Colo.1996), 262

Denver, City and County of v. Northern Colo. Water Conservancy Dist., 130 Colo. 375, 276 P.2d 992 (Colo.1954), **171**

Denver, City and County of v. Sheriff, 105 Colo. 193, 96 P.2d 836 (Colo.1939), **94**

Denver, United States v., 656 P.2d 1 (Colo. 1982), 888, 907

Department of Fish & Game v. Anderson–Cottonwood Irrigation Dist., 11 Cal. Rptr.2d 222 (Cal.App. 3 Dist.1992), 742

Department of Highways v. Sebastian, 345 S.W.2d 46 (Ky.1961), 556

Diana Shooting Club v. Husting, 156 Wis. 261, 145 N.W. 816 (Wis.1914), 461

Dillard v. Bishop Eddie Long Ministries, Inc., 258 Ga.App. 507, 574 S.E.2d 544 (Ga.App. 2002), 454

Dimmock v. City of New London, 157 Conn. 9, 245 A.2d 569 (Conn.1968), 124

District Court In and For Eagle County, Colo., United States v., 401 U.S. 520, 91 S.Ct. 998, 28 L.Ed.2d 278 (1971), **873**

District Court of Sixth Judicial Dist. in and for Gallatin County, State ex rel. Crowley v., 108 Mont. 89, 88 P.2d 23 (Mont.1939), **190**

District 10 Water Users Ass'n v. Barnett, 198 Colo. 291, 599 P.2d 894 (Colo.1979), 617

Diversion Lake Club v. Heath, 126 Tex. 129, 86 S.W.2d 441 (Tex.1935), 448

Dobie v. Morrison, 227 Mich.App. 536, 575 N.W.2d 817 (Mich.App.1998), 143

Dodge v. Ellensburg Water Co., 46 Wash.App. 77, 729 P.2d 631 (Wash.App. Div. 3 1986), 223

Doherty v. Pratt, 34 Nev. 343, 124 P. 574 (Nev.1912), 194

Dolan v. City of Tigard, 512 U.S. 374, 114 S.Ct. 2309, 129 L.Ed.2d 304 (1994), 519

Drinkwine v. State, 131 Vt. 127, 300 A.2d 616 (Vt.1973), 562

Dublin Water Co. v. Delaware River Basin Commission, 443 F.Supp. 310 (E.D.Pa. 1977), 983

Duckworth v. Watsonville Water and Light Co., 158 Cal. 206, 110 P. 927 (Cal.1910), 142

Dugan v. Rank, 372 U.S. 609, 83 S.Ct. 999, 10 L.Ed.2d 15 (1963), 875

Dyball v. Lennox, 260 Mich.App. 698, 680 N.W.2d 522 (Mich.App.2004), 144

Dycus v. Sillers, 557 So.2d 486 (Miss.1990), 453

Dyer, State ex rel. v. Sims, 341 U.S. 22, 71 S.Ct. 557, 95 L.Ed. 713 (1951), **979**

East Jordan Irr. Co. v. Morgan, 860 P.2d 310 (Utah 1993), 780

East Twin Lakes Ditches and Water Works, Inc. v. Board of County Com'rs of Lake County, 76 P.3d 918 (Colo.2003), 263

Edgemont Imp. Co. v. N.S. Tubbs Sheep Co., 22 S.D. 142, 115 N.W. 1130 (S.D.1908), 262

Edmondson v. Edwards, 111 S.W.3d 906 (Mo. App. S.D.2003), 137

E.I. du Pont de Nemours & Co. v. Train, 430 U.S. 112, 97 S.Ct. 965, 51 L.Ed.2d 204 (1977), 675

E.I. DuPont De Nemours & Co. v. United States, 460 F.3d 515 (3rd Cir.2006), 691

Elder v. Delcour, 364 Mo. 835, 269 S.W.2d 17 (Mo.1954), 461, 470

El Dorado Irr. Dist. v. State Water Resources Control Bd., 48 Cal.Rptr.3d 468 (Cal.App. 3 Dist.2006), 397, 759

Elk–Rifle Water Co. v. Templeton, 173 Colo. 438, 484 P.2d 1211 (Colo.1971), 171

Ellingsworth v. Swiggum, 195 Wis.2d 142, 536 N.W.2d 112 (Wis.App.1995), 144

El Paso v. Reynolds (Reynolds II), 597 F.Supp. 694 (D.N.M.1984), 1039

El Paso v. Reynolds, 563 F.Supp. 379 (D.N.M. 1983), 1039

El Paso County Water Imp. Dist. No. 1 v. City of El Paso, 133 F.Supp. 894 (W.D.Tex.1955), 376

Emmert, People v., 198 Colo. 137, 597 P.2d 1025 (Colo.1979), **470**

Empire Lodge Homeowners' Ass'n v. Moyer, 39 P.3d 1139 (Colo.2001), 389

Empire Water & Power Co. v. Cascade Town Co., 205 F. 123 (8th Cir.1913), **97, 350**

Englewood, City of v. City & County of Denver, 123 Colo. 290, 229 P.2d 667 (Colo. 1951), 777

Ensenada Land and Water Association v. Sleeper, 107 N.M. 494, 760 P.2d 787 (N.M.App.1988), 343

Ensenada Land and Water Association v. Sleeper, No. RA–84–53(C) (District Court, Rio Arriba County, New Mexico, June 2, 1985), 343

Enterprise Irr. Dist. v. Willis, 135 Neb. 827, 284 N.W. 326 (Neb.1939), **514**

Environmental Defense Fund, Inc. v. East Bay Mun. Utility Dist., 142 Cal.Rptr. 904, 572 P.2d 1128 (Cal.1977), 203

Erickson v. Queen Valley Ranch Co., 22 Cal. App.3d 578, 99 Cal.Rptr. 446 (Cal.App. 3 Dist.1971), 194

Erie R. v. Tompkins, 304 U.S. 64, 58 S.Ct. 817, 82 L.Ed. 1188 (1938), 973

Esmeralda, County of v. United States Dept. of Energy, 925 F.2d 1216 (9th Cir.1991), 700

Estate of (see name of party)

ETSI v. Missouri, 484 U.S. 495, 108 S.Ct. 805, 98 L.Ed.2d 898 (1988), 847, 856, 1042

Eureka, Town of v. Office of State Engineer, 108 Nev. 163, 826 P.2d 948 (Nev.1992), 264

Evans v. Merriweather, 4 Ill. 492 (Ill.1842), 117

Exxon Corp. v. Train, 554 F.2d 1310 (5th Cir.1977), 689

Fairfield Irr. Co. v. White, 18 Utah 2d 93, 416 P.2d 641 (Utah 1966), 183

Fairhurst v. Hagener, 422 F.3d 1146 (9th Cir.2005), 685

Fallbrook Irrigation District v. Bradley, 164 U.S. 112 (1896), 787

Farmers High Line Canal and Reservoir Co. v. City of Golden, 975 P.2d 189 (Colo. 1999), 250

Farmers Highline Canal & Reservoir Co. v. City of Golden, 129 Colo. 575, 272 P.2d 629 (Colo.1954), 249

Farmers Inv. Co. v. Bettwy, 113 Ariz. 520, 558 P.2d 14 (Ariz.1976), 625

Farm Inv. Co. v. Carpenter, 9 Wyo. 110, 61 P. 258 (Wyo.1900), 298

Farmers Reservoir & Irr. Co. v. City of Golden, 44 P.3d 241 (Colo.2002), 251

F. Arthur Stone & Sons v. Gibson, 230 Kan. 224, 630 P.2d 1164 (Kan.1981), 504

Federal Power Commission v. Oregon, 349 U.S. 435, 75 S.Ct. 832, 99 L.Ed. 1215 (1955), 868

Fellhauer v. People, 167 Colo. 320, 447 P.2d 986 (Colo.1968), 575

Finley v. Teeter Stone, Inc., 251 Md. 428, 248 A.2d 106 (Md.1968), 569

First Iowa Hydro–Elec. Co-op. v. Federal Power Commission, 328 U.S. 152, 66 S.Ct. 906, 90 L.Ed. 1143 (1946), **811**

First Peoples Bank of New Jersey v. Township of Medford, 126 N.J. 413, 599 A.2d 1248 (N.J.1991), 776

Flint v. United States, 906 F.2d 471 (9th Cir.1990), 653

Florida Wildlife Federation v. State Dept. of Environmental Regulation, 390 So.2d 64 (Fla.1980), 666

Forni, People ex rel. State Water Resources Control Bd. v., 54 Cal.App.3d 743, 126 Cal.Rptr. 851 (Cal.App. 1 Dist.1976), 183

Fort Lyon Canal Co. v. Catlin Canal Co., 642 P.2d 501 (Colo.1982), 779

Fort Mojave Indian Tribe v. United States, 32 Fed.Cl. 29 (Fed.Cl.1994), 868

Fort Morgan Reservoir & Irrigation Co. v. McCune, 71 Colo. 256, 206 P. 393 (Colo. 1922), 218

Foster v. Sunnyside Valley Irrigation Dist., 102 Wash.2d 395, 687 P.2d 841 (1984), 790

Four Counties Water Users Ass'n v. Colorado River Water Conservation Dist., 159 Colo. 499, 414 P.2d 469 (Colo.1966), 312

Fox River Paper Co. v. Railroad Com'n of Wisconsin, 274 U.S. 651, 47 S.Ct. 669, 71 L.Ed. 1279 (1927), 503

Fox, State ex rel. Haman v., 100 Idaho 140, 594 P.2d 1093 (Idaho 1979), 488

Franco–American Charolaise, Ltd. v. Oklahoma Water Resources Bd., 855 P.2d 568 (Okla.1990), **505,** 567

Freeman v. Blue Ridge Paper Products, Inc., 229 S.W.3d 694 (Tenn.Ct.App.2007), 666

Fresno, City of v. California, 372 U.S. 627, 83 S.Ct. 996, 10 L.Ed.2d 28 (1963), 825

Friends of Pinto Creek v. EPA, 504 F.3d 1007 (9th Cir.2007), 973

Friends of Wild Swan, Inc. v. United States Fish & Wildlife Service, 945 F.Supp. 1388 (D.Or.1996), 752

Friendswood Development Co. v. Smith–Southwest Industries, Inc., 576 S.W.2d 21 (Tex.1978), 570, 623

Fundingsland v. Colorado Ground Water Commission, 171 Colo. 487, 468 P.2d 835 (Colo.1970), **613**

Fuss v. Franks, 610 P.2d 17 (Wyo.1980), 218

FWS Land & Cattle Co. v. State Div. of Wildlife, 795 P.2d 837 (Colo.1990), 314

Gagnon v. French Lick Springs Hotel Co., 163 Ind. 687, 72 N.E. 849 (Ind.1904), 562

Galt v. State, 225 Mont. 142, 731 P.2d 912 (Mont.1987), 467

Game & Fresh Water Fish Commission v. Lake Islands, Ltd., 407 So.2d 189 (Fla. 1981), 670

Gamer v. Town of Milton, 346 Mass. 617, 195 N.E.2d 65 (Mass.1964), 569

Garrarapata Water Co., In re, State Water Resources Control Decision No. 1639 (June 17, 1999), 651

General Adjudication of All Rights to Use Water in Big Horn River System, In re, 48 P.3d 1040 (Wyo.2002), 922

General Adjudication of All Rights to Use Water in Big Horn River System, In re, 835 P.2d 273 (Wyo.1992), 871, 922

General Adjudication of All Rights to Use Water in Big Horn River System, In re, 803 P.2d 61 (Wyo.1990), 922

General Adjudication of All Rights to Use Water in the Big Horn River System, In re, 753 P.2d 76 (Wyo.1988), **911**

General Adjudication of All Rights to Use Water in Gila River (Gila IV), In re, 201 Ariz. 307, 35 P.3d 68 (Ariz.2001), 871, 923

General Adjudication of All Rights to Use Water in Gila River System and Source, In re, 198 Ariz. 330, 9 P.3d 1069 (Ariz. 2000), 596

General Adjudication of All Rights to Use Water in Gila River System and Source, In re, 195 Ariz. 411, 989 P.2d 739 (Ariz. 1999), 922

General Adjudication of All Rights to Use Water in Gila River (Gila III), In re, 175 Ariz. 382, 857 P.2d 1236 (Ariz.1993), 596

Georgia v. South Carolina, 497 U.S. 376, 110 S.Ct. 2903, 111 L.Ed.2d 309 (1990), 149

Gerlach Live Stock Co., United States v., 339 U.S. 725, 70 S.Ct. 955, 94 L.Ed. 1231 (1950), 811

Gibbs, Matter of v. Wolf Land Co., 856 P.2d 798 (Colo.1993), 314

Gila Valley Irr. Dist., United States v., 31 F.3d 1428 (9th Cir.1994), 194

Gilbert v. Smith, 97 Idaho 735, 552 P.2d 1220 (Idaho 1976), 262

Gion v. City of Santa Cruz, 84 Cal.Rptr. 162, 465 P.2d 50 (Cal.1970), **491**

Glacier View Meadows for Water Rights in Larimer County, In re Application of, Nos. W–7438 and W–7629 (Colo. Dist. Ct., Water Div. No. 1, Oct. 6, 1976), 388

Glass v. Goeckel, 473 Mich. 667, 703 N.W.2d 58 (Mich.2005), 490

Glenn–Colusa Irr. Dist., United States v., 788 F.Supp. 1126 (E.D.Cal.1992), 742

Glenn Dale Ranches, Inc. v. Shaub, 94 Idaho 585, 494 P.2d 1029 (Idaho 1972), 195

Goat Hill Development Co. v. Lake Lotawana Ass'n, 134 S.W.3d 807 (Mo.App. W.D. 2004), 144

Golden Feather Community Assn. v. Thermalito Irrigation Dist., 209 Cal.App.3d 1276, 257 Cal.Rptr. 836 (Cal.App. 3 Dist. 1989), 439

Grand River Dam Authority, United States v., 363 U.S. 229, 80 S.Ct. 1134, 4 L.Ed.2d 1186 (1960), 484

Greater Providence Chamber of Commerce v. State, 657 A.2d 1038 (R.I.1995), 421

Great Western Sugar Co. v. Jackson Lake Reservoir and Irrigation Co., 681 P.2d 484 (Colo.1984), 781

Green v. Chaffee Ditch Co., 150 Colo. 91, 371 P.2d 775 (Colo.1962), **238**

Green v. City of Williamstown, 848 F.Supp. 102 (E.D.Ky.1994), 454

Gros Ventre and Assiniboine Tribes of Fort Belknap Indian Community of the Fort Belknap Indian Reservation v. Hodel, No. CV–85–213–GF (D. Mont. August 22, 1985), 864

Gunby v. Olde Severna Park, 174 Md.App. 189, 921 A.2d 292 (Md.App.2007), 144

Gurley Refining Co., United States v., 788 F.Supp. 1473 (E.D.Ark.1992), 696

Gwathmey v. State Through Dept. of Environment, Health, and Natural Resources Through Cobey, 342 N.C. 287, 464 S.E.2d 674 (N.C.1995), 420

Haaser v. Englebrecht, 45 S.D. 143, 186 N.W. 572 (S.D.1922), 504

Hagan v. Upper Republican Natural Resources Dist., 261 Neb. 312, 622 N.W.2d 627 (Neb.2001), 942

Half Moon Bay Land Co. v. Cowell, 173 Cal. 543, 160 P. 675 (Cal.1916), 124

Hall v. Kuiper, 181 Colo. 130, 510 P.2d 329 (Colo.1973), 617

Hall v. Mayor & Council of Calhoun, 140 Ga. 611, 79 S.E. 533 (Ga.1913), 775

Hallenbeck v. Granby Ditch & Reservoir Co., 160 Colo. 555, 420 P.2d 419 (Colo.1966), 262

Haman, State ex rel. v. Fox, 100 Idaho 140, 594 P.2d 1093 (Idaho 1979), 488

Hammond v. Johnson, 94 Utah 20, 66 P.2d 894 (Utah 1937), 265

Hanapi, State v., 970 P.2d 485 (Hawai'i 1998), 489

Hardin v. Jordan, 140 U.S. 371, 11 S.Ct. 808, 35 L.Ed. 428 (1891), 407

Hardy v. Higginson, 123 Idaho 485, 849 P.2d 946 (Idaho 1993), 331

Harloff v. City of Sarasota, 575 So.2d 1324 (Fla.App. 2 Dist.1991), 612

Harris v. Brooks, 225 Ark. 436, 283 S.W.2d 129 (Ark.1955), **126**

Harris v. Hylebos Industries, Inc., 81 Wash.2d 770, 505 P.2d 457 (Wash.1973), 447

Harrison County v. Guice, 244 Miss. 95, 140 So.2d 838 (Miss.1962), 149

Hartman v. Tresise, 36 Colo. 146, 84 P. 685 (Colo.1905), 475, 496

Hawaii, County of v. Sotomura, 55 Haw. 176, 517 P.2d 57 (Hawai'i 1973), 489

Hays, State ex rel. Meek v., 246 Kan. 99, 785 P.2d 1356 (Kan.1990), 477

Hay, State ex rel. Thornton v., 254 Or. 584, 462 P.2d 671 (Or.1969), 488

Hayes v. Adams, 109 Or. 51, 218 P. 933 (Or.1923), 556

Head, State v., 330 S.C. 79, 498 S.E.2d 389 (S.C.App.1997), 448

Headwaters, Inc. v. Talent Irrigation Dist., 243 F.3d 526 (9th Cir.2001), 685

Heldermon v. Wright, 152 P.3d 855 (Okla. 2006), 512

Heller, State v., 123 Conn. 492, 196 A. 337 (Conn.1937), 670

Herminghaus v. Southern California Edison Co., 200 Cal. 81, 252 P. 607 (Cal. 1926), **84, 154**

Hess v. Port Authority Trans–Hudson Corp., 513 U.S. 30, 115 S.Ct. 394, 130 L.Ed.2d 245 (1994), 983

Higday v. Nickolaus, 469 S.W.2d 859 (Mo. App.1971), **562**

High Country Citizens' Alliance v. Norton, 448 F.Supp.2d 1235 (D.Colo.2006), **890**

High Plains A & M, LLC v. Southeastern Colorado Water Conservancy Dist., 120 P.3d 710 (Colo.2005), 243, 313

Hinderlider v. La Plata River and Cherry Creek Ditch Co., 304 U.S. 92, 58 S.Ct. 803, 82 L.Ed. 1202 (1938), 974, 983

Hinderlider, People ex rel. Park Reservoir Co. v., 98 Colo. 505, 57 P.2d 894 (Colo. 1936), 303

Hines v. Davidowitz, 312 U.S. 52, 61 S.Ct. 399, 85 L.Ed. 581 (1941), 909

Hitchcock and Red Willow Irr. Dist., In re Application of, 226 Neb. 146, 410 N.W.2d 101 (Neb.1987), 326

Holly v. Confederated Tribes and Bands of Yakima Indian Nation, 655 F.Supp. 557 (E.D.Wash.1985), 935

Holt State Bank, United States v., 270 U.S. 49, 46 S.Ct. 197, 70 L.Ed. 465 (1926), 413

Homestake Min. Co. v. United States Environmental Protection Agency, 477 F.Supp. 1279 (D.S.D.1979), 678

Hoover v. Crane, 362 Mich. 36, 106 N.W.2d 563 (Mich.1960), 131

Huber v. Merkel, 117 Wis. 355, 94 N.W. 354 (Wis.1903), 562

Hudson River Fishermen's Ass'n v. City of New York, 751 F.Supp. 1088 (S.D.N.Y. 1990), 942

Hufford v. Dye, 162 Cal. 147, 121 P. 400 (Cal.1912), 380

Hughes v. State, 67 Wash.2d 799, 410 P.2d 20 (Wash.1966), 491

Hughes v. Washington, 389 U.S. 290, 88 S.Ct. 438, 19 L.Ed.2d 530 (1967), **408**

Ickes v. Fox, 300 U.S. 82, 57 S.Ct. 412, 81 L.Ed. 525 (1937), 376, 789

Idaho v. Coeur d'Alene Tribe, 521 U.S. 261, 117 S.Ct. 2028, 138 L.Ed.2d 438 (1997), 415, 423

Idaho v. United States, 533 U.S. 262, 121 S.Ct. 2135, 150 L.Ed.2d 326 (2001), 415

Idaho Conservation League v. State, 128 Idaho 155, 911 P.2d 748 (Idaho 1995), 433

Idaho Dept. of Fish & Game v. National Marine Fisheries Service, 850 F.Supp. 886 (D.Or.1994), 744

Idaho Power Co. v. State, Dept. of Water Resources, 104 Idaho 575, 661 P.2d 741 (Idaho 1983), 181

Illinois v. Milwaukee, 731 F.2d 403 (7th Cir. 1984), 975

Illinois v. Milwaukee, 406 U.S. 91, 92 S.Ct. 1385, 31 L.Ed.2d 712 (1972), 974, 1044

Illinois Cent. R. Co. v. Illinois, 146 U.S. 387, 13 S.Ct. 110, 36 L.Ed. 1018 (1892), **416**

Imperial Irrigation Dist. v. State Wat. Resources Control Bd., 225 Cal.App.3d 548, 275 Cal.Rptr. 250 (Cal.App. 4 Dist.1990), 219, 1017

In re (see name of party)

Intake Water Co. v. Yellowstone River Compact Com'n, 769 F.2d 568 (9th Cir. 1985), **985**

International Paper Co. v. Ouellette, 479 U.S. 481, 107 S.Ct. 805, 93 L.Ed.2d 883 (1987), 687, 940, 975

Intracoastal North Condominium Ass'n v. Palm Beach County, 698 So.2d 384 (Fla. App. 4 Dist.1997), 440

Inyo County of v. Los Angeles, C004068 (3d Dist. 1997), 339

Irwin v. Phillips, 5 Cal. 140 (Cal.1855), **67**

Ivanhoe Irr. Dist. v. McCracken, 357 U.S. 275, 78 S.Ct. 1174, 2 L.Ed.2d 1313 (1958), 832

Jacobs Ranch, L.L.C. v. Smith, 148 P.3d 842 (Okla.2006), 567

Jacobucci v. District Court In and For County of Jefferson, 189 Colo. 380, 541 P.2d 667 (Colo.1975), 782

James City County v. E.P.A., 12 F.3d 1330 (4th Cir.1993), 714

Jarvis v. State Land Dept., 113 Ariz. 230, 550 P.2d 227 (Ariz.1976), 625

Jarvis v. State Land Dept., 106 Ariz. 506, 479 P.2d 169 (Ariz.1970), 625

Jarvis v. State Land Dept., 104 Ariz. 527, 456 P.2d 385 (Ariz.1969), 625

Jenkins v. State, Dept. of Water Resources, 103 Idaho 384, 647 P.2d 1256 (Idaho 1982), **259**

Jennison v. Kirk, 98 U.S. 453, 8 Otto 453, 25 L.Ed. 240 (1878), 860

Johnson v. Bryant, 350 So.2d 433 (Ala.1977), 440

Johnston v. Little Horse Creek Irr. Co., 13 Wyo. 208, 79 P. 22 (Wyo.1904), 380

Joint Bd. of Control of Flathead, Mission and Jocko Irr. Districts v. United States, 832 F.2d 1127 (9th Cir.1987), 906

Jordan v. City of Santa Barbara, 54 Cal. Rptr.2d 340 (Cal.App. 2 Dist.1996), 687

Joslin v. Marin Municipal Water Dist., 67 Cal.2d 132, 60 Cal.Rptr. 377, 429 P.2d 889 (Cal.1967), 137

Joyce Livestock v. United States, 144 Idaho 1, 156 P.3d 502 (Idaho 2007), 84

Kaiser Aetna v. United States, 444 U.S. 164, 100 S.Ct. 383, 62 L.Ed.2d 332 (1979), 448, 485, 809

Kandra v. United States, 145 F.Supp.2d 1192 (D.Or.2001), 743

Kansas v. Colorado, 543 U.S. 86, 125 S.Ct. 526, 160 L.Ed.2d 418 (2004), 947, 948

Kansas v. Colorado, 533 U.S. 1, 121 S.Ct. 2023, 150 L.Ed.2d 72 (2001), 947

Kansas v. Colorado, 514 U.S. 673, 115 S.Ct. 1733, 131 L.Ed.2d 759 (1995), 942, 952

Kansas v. Colorado, 206 U.S. 46, 27 S.Ct. 655, 51 L.Ed. 956 (1907), 810, 862, **943**

Kansas v. Colorado, 185 U.S. 125, 22 S.Ct. 552, 46 L.Ed. 838 (1902), 946

Kansas City Life Ins. Co., United States v., 339 U.S. 799, 70 S.Ct. 885, 94 L.Ed. 1277 (1950), 484

Ka Pa'akai O Ka'Aina v. Land Use Com'n, 7 P.3d 1068 (Hawai'i 2000), 489

Katz v. Walkinshaw, 141 Cal. 116, 70 P. 663 (Cal.1902), 634

Kearney Lake, Land & Reservoir Co. v. Lake DeSmet Reservoir Co., 487 P.2d 324 (Wyo. 1971), 265

Kelly Ranch v. Southeastern Colorado Water Conservancy Dist., 191 Colo. 65, 550 P.2d 297 (Colo.1976), 389

Kennecott Utah Copper Corp. v. Department of Interior, 88 F.3d 1191 (D.C.Cir.1996), 696

Kerr–McGee Corp., State ex rel. Martinez v., 120 N.M. 118, 898 P.2d 1256 (N.M.App. 1995), 872

Kiwanis Club Foundation, Inc. v. Yost, 179 Neb. 598, 139 N.W.2d 359 (Neb.1966), 454

Klamath Irrigation Dist. v. United States, 75 Fed.Cl. 677 (Fed.Cl.2007), 532

Klamath Irrigation Dist. v. United States, 67 Fed.Cl. 504 (Fed.Cl.2005), 532

Klamath Water Users Protective Ass'n v. Patterson, 204 F.3d 1206 (9th Cir.1999), 743

Kline v. Oklahoma Water Resources Bd., 759 P.2d 210 (Okla.1988), 567

Knight v. Grimes, 80 S.D. 517, 127 N.W.2d 708 (S.D.1964), 504

Knight v. United Land Ass'n, 142 U.S. 161, 12 S.Ct. 258, 35 L.Ed. 974 (1891), 406

Knudson v. Kearney, 171 Cal. 250, 152 P. 541 (Cal.1915), 422

Kootenai Environmental Alliance, Inc. v. Panhandle Yacht Club, Inc., 105 Idaho 622, 671 P.2d 1085 (Idaho 1983), 433

Kraemer, People v., 7 Misc.2d 373, 164 N.Y.S.2d 423 (N.Y.Police Ct.1957), 453

Kuiper v. Well Owners Conservation Ass'n, 176 Colo. 119, 490 P.2d 268 (Colo.1971), 597

Kukui (Molokai), Inc., In re, 174 P.3d 320 (Hawai'i 2007), 439

Kundel Farms v. Vir–Jo Farms, Inc., 467 N.W.2d 291 (Iowa App.1991), **115**

Lac Lanoux Arbitration, (Spain v. France), 12 U.N.R.I.A.A. 281 (1957), 1061

Lake Michigan Federation v. United States Army Corps of Engineers, 742 F.Supp. 441 (N.D.Ill.1990), 420

Lambert Gravel Co. v. J.A. Jones Const. Co., 835 F.2d 1105 (5th Cir.1988), 529

Lamprey v. Metcalf, 52 Minn. 181, 53 N.W. 1139 (Minn.1893), 461

Landers v. East Tex. Salt Water Disposal Co., 151 Tex. 251, 248 S.W.2d 731 (Tex.1952), 696

Laramie Rivers Co. v. Watson, 69 Wyo. 333, 241 P.2d 1080 (Wyo.1952), 781

League of Wilderness Defenders/Blue Mountains Biodiversity Project v. Forsgren, 309 F.3d 1181 (9th Cir.2002), 685

League to Save Lake Tahoe v. Tahoe Regional Planning Agency, 507 F.2d 517 (9th Cir.1974), 982

Leavitt v. Lassen Irr. Co., 157 Cal. 82, 106 P. 404 (Cal.1909), 257

Lechuza Villas West v. California Coastal Com'n, 70 Cal.Rptr.2d 399 (Cal.App. 2 Dist.1997), 490

Lee County v. South Florida Water Management Dist., 805 So.2d 893 (Fla.App. 2 Dist.2001), 664

Left Hand Ditch Co. v. Hill, 933 P.2d 1 (Colo.1997), 780

Lehigh Falls Fishing Club v. Andrejewski, 735 A.2d 718 (Pa.Super.1999), 400

Lewis v. General Elec. Co., 37 F.Supp.2d 55 (D.Mass.1999), 688

Leydon v. Town of Greenwich, 57 Conn.App. 712, 750 A.2d 1122 (Conn.App.2000), 490

Lindsley v. Natural Carbonic Gas Co., 220 U.S. 61, 31 S.Ct. 337, 55 L.Ed. 369 (1911), 599

Lingle v. Chevron U.S.A. Inc., 544 U.S. 528, 125 S.Ct. 2074, 161 L.Ed.2d 876 (2005), 519

Lionelle v. Southeastern Colorado Water Conservancy Dist., 676 P.2d 1162 (Colo. 1984), 314

Little v. Kin, 249 Mich.App. 502, 644 N.W.2d 375 (Mich.App.2002), 143

Little Blue Natural Resources Dist. v. Lower Platte North Natural Resources Dist., 210 Neb. 862, 317 N.W.2d 726 (Neb.1982), 326

Little Blue Natural Resources Dist. v. Lower Platte North Natural Resources Dist., 206 Neb. 535, 294 N.W.2d 598 (Neb.1980), **322**

Lockary v. Kayfetz, 917 F.2d 1150 (9th Cir. 1990), 778

Long Beach, City of v. Marshall, 11 Cal.2d 609, 82 P.2d 362 (Cal.1938), 421

Long Beach, City of, People v., 51 Cal.2d 875, 338 P.2d 177 (Cal.1959), 421

Long Island Pine Barrens Soc., Inc. v. Planning Bd. of Brookhaven, 178 A.D.2d 18, 581 N.Y.S.2d 803 (N.Y.A.D. 2 Dept.1992), 600

Lopez, United States v., 514 U.S. 549, 115 S.Ct. 1624, 131 L.Ed.2d 626 (1995), 705

Los Angeles v. San Fernando, 123 Cal. Rptr. 1, 537 P.2d 1250 (Cal.1975), **642,** 873

Los Angeles, City of v. Aitken, 10 Cal.App.2d 460, 52 P.2d 585 (Cal.App. 3 Dist.1935), 132

Los Angeles, City of v. County of Inyo, Case No. 12908 (Super. Ct. Inyo County, Cal. 1997), 339

Los Angeles, City of v. Venice Peninsula Properties, 182 Cal.Rptr. 599, 644 P.2d 792 (Cal.1982), 423

Los Osos Valley Associates v. City of San Luis Obispo, 36 Cal.Rptr.2d 758 (Cal.App. 2 Dist.1994), 570

Lower Colorado River Authority v. Texas Dept. of Water Resources, 689 S.W.2d 873 (Tex.1984), 310

Lucas v. South Carolina Coastal Council, 505 U.S. 1003, 112 S.Ct. 2886, 120 L.Ed.2d 798 (1992), 520

Lucas v. South Carolina Coastal Council, 304 S.C. 376, 404 S.E.2d 895 (S.C.1991), 150

Lukrawka v. Spring Val. Water Co., 169 Cal. 318, 146 P. 640 (Cal.1915), 776

Lundberg v. University of Notre Dame, 231 Wis. 187, 282 N.W. 70 (Wis.1938), 470

Lux v. Haggin, 69 Cal. 255, 10 P. 674 (Cal. 1886), 90, 91, 787

Machipongo Land &d Coal Co. v. Commonwealth, 569 Pa. 3, 799 A.2d 751 (Pa.2002), 665

Mack v. Eldorado Water Dist., 56 Wash.2d 584, 354 P.2d 917 (Wash.1960), 322

Maddocks v. Giles, 728 A.2d 150 (Me.1999), 568

Madera Irr. Dist. v. Hancock, 985 F.2d 1397 (9th Cir.1993), 832, 839

Madison v. Graham, 126 F.Supp.2d 1320 (D.Mont.2001), 467

Maerz v. United States Steel Corp., 116 Mich. App. 710, 323 N.W.2d 524 (Mich.App. 1982), 568

Maine v. Taylor, 477 U.S. 131, 106 S.Ct. 2440, 91 L.Ed.2d 110 (1986), 1038

Mally v. Weidensteiner, 88 Wash. 398, 153 P. 342 (Wash.1915), 154

Marbled Murrelet v. Babbitt, 83 F.3d 1060 (9th Cir.1996), 742

Maricopa County Municipal Water Conservation Dist. No. 1 v. Southwest Cotton Co., 39 Ariz. 65, 4 P.2d 369 (Ariz.1931), 595

Marks v. Whitney, 98 Cal.Rptr. 790, 491 P.2d 374 (Cal.1971), 421

Martin v. Waddell's Lessee, 41 U.S. 367, 16 Pet. 367, 10 L.Ed. 997 (1842), 402

Martinez, State ex rel. v. Kerr–McGee Corp., 120 N.M. 118, 898 P.2d 1256 (N.M.App. 1995), 872

Mason v. Hoyle, 56 Conn. 255, 14 A. 786 (Conn.1888), **118**

Mathers v. Texaco, Inc., 77 N.M. 239, 421 P.2d 771 (N.M.1966), **606**

Mattaponi Indian Tribe v. Virginia, 261 Va. 366, 541 S.E.2d 920 (Va.2001), 360

Matter of (see name of party)

Matthews v. Bay Head Imp. Ass'n, 95 N.J. 306, 471 A.2d 355 (N.J.1984), 490

Mayer v. Grueber, 29 Wis.2d 168, 138 N.W.2d 197 (Wis.1965), 453

McBryde Sugar Co. v. Robinson, 55 Haw. 260, 517 P.2d 26 (Hawai'i 1973), 126

McDonald v. Bear River and Auburn Water & Min. Co., 13 Cal. 220 (Cal.1859), 237

McDonald v. State, 220 Mont. 519, 722 P.2d 598 (Mont.1986), 301

McIlroy, State v., 268 Ark. 227, 595 S.W.2d 659 (Ark.1980), **461**

McNamara v. Rittman, 107 Ohio St.3d 243, 838 N.E.2d 640 (Ohio 2005), 568

Mead Corp., United States v., 533 U.S. 218, 121 S.Ct. 2164, 150 L.Ed.2d 292 (2001), 712

Meek, State ex rel. v. Hays, 246 Kan. 99, 785 P.2d 1356 (Kan.1990), 477

Meng v. Coffey, 67 Neb. 500, 93 N.W. 713 (Neb.1903), 117

Metalclad Corporation v. United Mexican States, Award, Case No. ARB (AF)/97/1 (August 30, 2000), 1048

Metropolitan Denver Sewage Disposal Dist. No. 1 v. Farmers Reservoir & Irr. Co., 179 Colo. 36, 499 P.2d 1190 (Colo.1972), **251**

Metropolitan Suburban Water Users Ass'n v. Colorado River Water Conservation Dist., 148 Colo. 173, 365 P.2d 273 (Colo.1961), 177, 312

Metropolitan Utilities Dist. of Omaha v. Merritt Beach Co., 179 Neb. 783, 140 N.W.2d 626 (Neb.1966), 546

Metropolitan Water Dist. v. Imperial Irr. Dist., 96 Cal.Rptr.2d 314 (Cal.App. 2 Dist. 2000), 1018

Michels Pipeline Const., Inc., State v., 63 Wis.2d 278, 217 N.W.2d 339 (Wis.1974), 567

Michigan Citizens for Water Conservation v. Nestlé Waters North America Inc., 479 Mich. 280, 737 N.W.2d 447 (Mich.2007), 460

Michigan Citizens for Water Conservation v. Nestlé Waters North America Inc., 269 Mich.App. 25, 709 N.W.2d 174 (Mich.App.2005), 102, 568, **577**

Middlesex County Sewerage Authority v. National Sea Clammers Ass'n, 453 U.S. 1, 101 S.Ct. 2615, 69 L.Ed.2d 435 (1981), 686

Miller v. Cudahy Co., 567 F.Supp. 892 (D.Kan.1983), 654

Mills, State ex rel. Sprynczynatyk v., 523 N.W.2d 537 (N.D.1994), 422

Milwaukee v. Illinois (Milwaukee II), 451 U.S. 304, 101 S.Ct. 1784, 68 L.Ed.2d 114 (1981), 686, 940, 973, 1044

Milwaukee, City of v. State, 193 Wis. 423, 214 N.W. 820 (Wis.1927), 420

Miranda, State ex rel. Reynolds v., 83 N.M. 443, 493 P.2d 409 (N.M.1972), **159**

Mississippi Commission on Natural Resources v. Costle, 625 F.2d 1269 (5th Cir. 1980), 678

Mississippi State Highway Com'n v. Gilich, 609 So.2d 367 (Miss.1992), 149

Montana v. United States, 450 U.S. 544, 101 S.Ct. 1245, 67 L.Ed.2d 493 (1981), 413

Montana v. Wyoming, ___ U.S. ___, 128 S.Ct. 1332, 170 L.Ed.2d 56 (2008), 987

Montana Coalition for Stream Access, Inc. v. Curran, 210 Mont. 38, 682 P.2d 163 (Mont.1984), 466

Montana Coalition for Stream Access, Inc. v. Hildreth, 211 Mont. 29, 684 P.2d 1088 (Mont.1984), 466, 467

Montana v. EPA, 137 F.3d 1135 (9th Cir. 1998), 936

Montana Trout Unlimited v. Montana Dept. of Natural Resources and Conservation, 331 Mont. 483, 133 P.3d 224 (Mont.2006), 359

Montgomery v. Lomos Altos, Inc., 141 N.M. 21, 150 P.3d 971 (N.M.2006), 609

Monument Farms, Inc. v. Daggett, 2 Neb. App. 988, 520 N.W.2d 556 (Neb.App. 1994), 150

Morrison, United States v., 529 U.S. 598, 120 S.Ct. 1740, 146 L.Ed.2d 658 (2000), 705

Moses, United States v., 496 F.3d 984 (9th Cir.2007), 712

Motl v. Boyd, 116 Tex. 82, 286 S.W. 458 (Tex.1926), 505

Mount Emmons Min. Co. v. Town of Crested Butte, 40 P.3d 1255 (Colo.2002), 315

Moviematic Industries Corp. v. Board of County Com'rs, 349 So.2d 667 (Fla.App. 3 Dist.1977), 611

Muckleshoot Indian Tribe v. Trans–Canada Enterprises, Ltd., 713 F.2d 455 (9th Cir. 1983), 907

Muench v. Public Service Commission, 261 Wis. 492, 53 N.W.2d 514 (Wis.1952), 449

Municipal Subdistrict, Northern Colorado Water Conservancy Dist. v. Chevron Shale Oil Co., 986 P.2d 918 (Colo.1999), 178

Municipal Subdistrict, Northern Colorado Water Conservancy Dist. v. OXY USA, Inc., 990 P.2d 701 (Colo.1999), 315

Musselshell River Drainage Area, In re, 255 Mont. 43, 840 P.2d 577 (Mont.1992), 263

Musser v. Higginson, 125 Idaho 392, 871 P.2d 809 (Idaho 1994), **583**

Mutual Life Ins. Co. of New York v. Mobil Corp., 1998 WL 160820 (N.D.N.Y.1998), 689

National Ass'n of Home Builders v. Defenders of Wildlife, 551 U.S. 644, 127 S.Ct. 2518, 168 L.Ed.2d 467 (2007), 745

National Ass'n of Home Builders v. New Jersey Dept. of Environmental Protection, 64 F.Supp.2d 354 (D.N.J.1999), 489

National Audubon Society v. Superior Court of Alpine County, 189 Cal.Rptr. 346, 658 P.2d 709 (Cal.1983), **426**

National Wildlife Federation v. Babbitt, 128 F.Supp.2d 1274 (E.D.Cal.2000), 752

National Wildlife Federation v. FERC, 801 F.2d 1505 (9th Cir.1986), 715, 747

National Wildlife Federation v. Gorsuch, 693 F.2d 156 (D.C.Cir.1982), 679

National Wildlife Federation v. National Marine Fisheries Service, 481 F.3d 1224 (9th Cir.2007), 744

Natural Soda Products Co. v. City of Los Angeles, 23 Cal.2d 193, 143 P.2d 12 (Cal. 1943), 454

Nebraska v. Iowa, 143 U.S. 359, 12 S.Ct. 396, 36 L.Ed. 186 (1892), 147, 148

Nebraska v. Wyoming, 515 U.S. 1, 115 S.Ct. 1933, 132 L.Ed.2d 1 (1995), 953, 1028

Nebraska v. Wyoming, 507 U.S. 584, 113 S.Ct. 1689, 123 L.Ed.2d 317 (1993), 952

Nekoosa–Edwards Paper Co. v. Public Service Commission, 8 Wis.2d 582, 99 N.W.2d 821 (Wis.1959), 289, 291

Nekoosa Edwards Paper Co. v. Railroad Commission, 201 Wis. 40, 228 N.W. 144 (Wis. 1929), 320

Nevada v. United States, 463 U.S. 110, 103 S.Ct. 2906, 77 L.Ed.2d 509 (1983), 871, 889

New England Power Co. v. New Hampshire, 455 U.S. 331, 102 S.Ct. 1096, 71 L.Ed.2d 188 (1982), 1045

New Jersey v. Delaware, ___ U.S. ___, 128 S.Ct. 1929, 170 L.Ed.2d 743 (2008), 965

New Jersey v. Delaware, 291 U.S. 361, 54 S.Ct. 407, 78 L.Ed. 847 (1934), 965

New Jersey v. New York, 523 U.S. 767, 118 S.Ct. 1726, 140 L.Ed.2d 993 (1998), 149

New Jersey v. New York, 347 U.S. 995, 74 S.Ct. 842, 98 L.Ed. 1127 (1954), 951

New Jersey v. New York, 283 U.S. 336, 51 S.Ct. 478, 75 L.Ed. 1104 (1931), 940, **948,** 983

New Mexico v. Aamodt, 537 F.2d 1102 (10th Cir.1976), 872

New Mexico v. General Elec. Co., 335 F.Supp.2d 1266 (D.N.M.2004), 697

New Mexico v. General Elec. Co., 335 F.Supp.2d 1185 (D.N.M.2004), 281, 666, 697

New Mexico ex rel. Reynolds v. Aamodt, 618 F.Supp. 993 (D.N.M.1985), 872

Martinez, State ex rel. v. City of Las Vegas, 135 N.M. 375, 89 P.3d 47 (N.M.2004), 769, 873

New Mexico, United States v., 438 U.S. 696, 98 S.Ct. 3012, 57 L.Ed.2d 1052 (1978), 871, **878**

Newton v. City of Groesbeck, 299 S.W. 518 (Tex.Civ.App.-Waco 1927), 670

New York v. Shore Realty Corp., 759 F.2d 1032 (2nd Cir.1985), 691

Nilsson v. Latimer, 281 Ark. 325, 664 S.W.2d 447 (Ark.1984), 113

Nollan v. California Coastal Com'n, 483 U.S. 825, 107 S.Ct. 3141, 97 L.Ed.2d 677 (1987), 491, 519

Northeastern Pharmaceutical & Chemical Co., United States v., 579 F.Supp. 823 (W.D.Mo.1984), 691

North Gualala Water Co. v. State Water Resources Control Bd., 43 Cal.Rptr.3d 821 (Cal.App. 1 Dist.2006), 651

North Kern Water Storage Dist. v. Kern Delta Water Dist., 54 Cal.Rptr.3d 578 (Cal. App. 5 Dist.2007), 265

North Sebago Shores, LLC v. Mazzaglia, 926 A.2d 728 (Me.2007), 144

Norton v. Southern Utah Wilderness Alliance, 542 U.S. 55, 124 S.Ct. 2373, 159 L.Ed.2d 137 (2004), 889

No Spray Coalition, Inc. v. City of New York, 351 F.3d 602 (2nd Cir.2003), 685

Nuclear Energy Institute, Inc. v. EPA, 373 F.3d 1251 (D.C.Cir.2004), 700

NRDC v. Interior Dept., 2007 WL 14283 (E.D.Cal.2007), 759

NRDC v. Patterson, 791 F.Supp. 1425 (E.D.Cal.1992), 826

NRDC v. Patterson, 333 F.Supp.2d 906 (E.D.Cal.2004), 826

NRDC v. United States Dept. of the Interior, 113 F.3d 1121 (9th Cir.1997), 752

NRDC, Inc. v. Costle, 568 F.2d 1369 (D.C.Cir. 1977), 679

Nueces County Water Control and Improvement Dist. No. 3 v. Texas Water Rights Comm'n, 481 S.W.2d 930 (Tex.Civ.App. 1972), 788

Nueces County Water Control & Improvement Dist. No. 3 v. Texas Water Rights Comm'n, 481 S.W.2d 924 (Tex.Civ.App. 1972), 788

Office of State Engineer v. Morris, 107 Nev. 699, 819 P.2d 203 (Nev.1991), 605

Ohio v. Department of the Interior, 880 F.2d 432 (D.C.Cir.1989), 696

Ohio v. Wyandotte Chemicals Corp., 401 U.S. 493, 91 S.Ct. 1005, 28 L.Ed.2d 256 (1971), 974

Ohio, State of v. EPA, 784 F.2d 224 (6th Cir.1986), 558

Okanogan, County of v. National Marine Fisheries Service, 347 F.3d 1081 (9th Cir. 2003), 910

Okanogan Wilderness League v. Town of Twisp, 133 Wash.2d 769, 947 P.2d 732 (Wash.1997), 263

Okaw Drainage Dist. v. National Distillers and Chemical Corp., 96 F.3d 1049 (7th Cir.1996), 147

Okaw Drainage Dist. v. National Distillers and Chemical Corp., 882 F.2d 1241 (7th Cir.1989), 146

Oklahoma v. New Mexico, 501 U.S. 221, 111 S.Ct. 2281, 115 L.Ed.2d 207 (1991), 994

Oklahoma ex rel. Phillips v. Guy F. Atkinson Co., 313 U.S. 508, 61 S.Ct. 1050, 85 L.Ed. 1487 (1941), 811, 847

Omernick v. Department of Natural Resources, 71 Wis.2d 370, 238 N.W.2d 114 (Wis.1976), 289

Omernik v. State, 64 Wis.2d 6, 218 N.W.2d 734 (Wis.1974), 289

O'Neill v. United States, 50 F.3d 677 (9th Cir.1995), **833**

Opal Lake Ass'n v. Michaywe' Ltd., 47 Mich. App. 354, 209 N.W.2d 478 (Mich.App. 1973), 460

Operation of Missouri River System Litigation, In re, 421 F.3d 618 (8th Cir.2005), 858

Opinion of the Justices, 365 Mass. 681, 313 N.E.2d 561 (Mass.1974), 490

Opinion of the Justices (Public Use of Coastal Beaches), 139 N.H. 82, 649 A.2d 604 (N.H.1994), 490

Orchard City Irr. Dist. v. Whitten, 146 Colo. 127, 361 P.2d 130 (Colo.1961), 181

Orchard Mesa Irr. Dist. v. City and County of Denver, 182 Colo. 59, 511 P.2d 25 (Colo. 1973), 178

Oregon ex rel. State Land Bd. v. Corvallis Sand & Gravel Co., 429 U.S. 363, 97 S.Ct. 582, 50 L.Ed.2d 550 (1977), 412

Oregon Natural Desert Ass'n v. Dombeck, 172 F.3d 1092 (9th Cir.1998), 736

Oregon Natural Resources Council v. Daley, 6 F.Supp.2d 1139 (D.Or.1998), 752

Oregon Waste Systems v. Department of Environmental Quality, 511 U.S. 93, 114 S.Ct. 1345, 128 L.Ed.2d 13 (1994), 1038

Oregon, United States v., 44 F.3d 758 (9th Cir.1994), 876, 877

Orr v. Arapahoe Water and Sanitation Dist., 753 P.2d 1217 (Colo.1988), **244**

Orr v. Mortvedt, 735 N.W.2d 610 (Iowa 2007), 453

Orr Ditch Co., United States v., Equity Docket No. A3 (D. Nev. 1944), 1027

Osterman v. Central Nebraska Public Power and Irrigation District, 131 Neb. 356, 268 N.W. 334 (Neb.1936), 326

O.W.L. Foundation v. City of Rohnert Park, 86 Cal.Rptr.3d 1 (Cal.App. 1 Dist.2008), 773

Pabst v. Finmand, 190 Cal. 124, 211 P. 11 (Cal.1922), **150**

Pacific Coast Federation of Fishermen's Associations v. United States Bureau of Reclamation, 426 F.3d 1082 (9th Cir.2005), 743

Pacific Coast Federation of Fishermen's Associations v. Bureau of Reclamation, 138 F.Supp.2d 1228 (N.D.Cal.2001), 742

Pagosa Area Water and Sanitation Dist. v. Trout Unlimited, 170 P.3d 307 (Colo. 2007), 180, 313

Pajaro Valley Water Mgmt. Agency v. Amrhein, 59 Cal.Rptr.3d 484 (Cal.App. 6 Dist. 2007), 641

Palazzolo v. Rhode Island, 533 U.S. 606, 121 S.Ct. 2448, 150 L.Ed.2d 592 (2001), 521

Palila v. Hawaii Dept. of Land & Natural Resources, 649 F.Supp. 1070 (D.Hawai'i 1986), 742

Palm Beach Isles Associates v. United States, 42 Fed.Cl. 340 (Fed.Cl.1998), 529

Panetta v. Equity One, Inc., 190 N.J. 307, 920 A.2d 638 (N.J.2007), 144

Park Center Water Dist. v. United States, 781 P.2d 90 (Colo.1989), 876

Park Reservoir Co., People ex rel. v. Hinderlider, 98 Colo. 505, 57 P.2d 894 (Colo.1936), 303

Pasadena v. Alhambra, 33 Cal.2d 908, 207 P.2d 17 (Cal.1949), **634**

Peabody v. City of Vallejo, 2 Cal.2d 351, 40 P.2d 486 (Cal.1935), 94

People v. _____(see opposing party)

People ex rel. v. _____ (see opposing party and relator)

Pernell v. Henderson, 220 N.C. 79, 16 S.E.2d 449 (N.C.1941), 118

Peterson v. United States Dept. of Interior, 899 F.2d 799 (9th Cir.1990), 831, 832

Phelps v. State Water Resources Control Bd., 68 Cal.Rptr.3d 350 (Cal.App. 3 Dist.2007), 398, 759

Phelps Dodge Corp. v. Arizona Dept. of Water Resources, 211 Ariz. 146, 118 P.3d 1110 (Ariz.App. Div. 1 2005), 168

Platt v. Rapid City, 67 S.D. 245, 291 N.W. 600 (S.D.1940), 504

Pleasant Valley Canal Co. v. Borror, 72 Cal. Rptr.2d 1 (Cal.App. 5 Dist.1998), 153

Pollard v. Hagan, 44 U.S. 212, 3 How. 212, 11 L.Ed. 565 (1845), 405

Ponderosa Ridge LLC v. Banner County, 250 Neb. 944, 554 N.W.2d 151 (Neb.1996), 1038

Portage Cty. Bd. of Commrs. v. Akron, 156 Ohio App.3d 657, 808 N.E.2d 444 (Ohio App. 11 Dist.2004), 143

Port Authority Bondholders Protective Committee v. Port of New York Authority, 270 F.Supp. 947 (S.D.N.Y.1967), 982

Port of Seattle v. Oregon & Wash. R. R., 255 U.S. 56, 41 S.Ct. 237, 65 L.Ed. 500 (1921), 447

Postema v. Pollution Control Hearings Bd., 142 Wash.2d 68, 11 P.3d 726 (Wash.2000), 557

Potlatch Corp. v. United States, 134 Idaho 916, 12 P.3d 1260 (Idaho 2000), 897, 898

Potlatch Corp. v. United States, 134 Idaho 912, 12 P.3d 1256 (Idaho 2000), 897

Pronsolino v. Nastri, 291 F.3d 1123 (9th Cir. 2002), 678

Propeller Genesee Chief v. Fitzhugh, 53 U.S. 443, 12 How. 443, 13 L.Ed. 1058 (1851), 403

Providence & Worcester R.R. Co. v. Pine, 729 A.2d 202 (R.I.1999), 421

Prudential Ins. Co. v. Benjamin, 328 U.S. 408, 66 S.Ct. 1142, 90 L.Ed. 1342 (1946), 986

Public Access Shoreline Hawaii v. Hawai'i County Planning Com'n, 903 P.2d 1246 (Hawai'i 1995), 489

Public Service Co. of Colorado v. Board of Water Works of Pueblo, 831 P.2d 470 (Colo.1992), 313

Public Service Co. of Colorado v. Willows Water Dist., 856 P.2d 829 (Colo.1993), 223

Public Utility Dist. No. 1 v. City of Seattle, 382 F.2d 666 (9th Cir.1967), 486

Publix Super Markets, Inc. v. Pearson, 315 So.2d 98 (Fla.App. 2 Dist.1975), 453

PUD No. 1 of Jefferson County v. Washington Dept. of Ecology, 511 U.S. 700, 114 S.Ct. 1900, 128 L.Ed.2d 716 (1994), **728**

Purdie v. Attorney General, 143 N.H. 661, 732 A.2d 442 (N.H.1999), 490

Pyle v. Gilbert, 245 Ga. 403, 265 S.E.2d 584 (Ga.1980), **137**

Pyramid Lake Paiute Tribe of Indians v. Morton, 354 F.Supp. 252 (D.D.C.1972), 889

Pyramid Lake Paiute Tribe of Indians v. Washoe County, 112 Nev. 743, 918 P.2d 697 (Nev.1996), 331

Query v. Burgess, 371 S.C. 407, 639 S.E.2d 455 (S.C.App.2006), 420

Quivira Min. Co. v. United StatesE.P.A., 765 F.2d 126 (10th Cir.1985), 675

Raleigh Avenue Beach Ass'n v. Atlantis Beach Club, Inc., 185 N.J. 40, 879 A.2d 112 (N.J.2005), 490

Ramada Inns, Inc. v. Salt River Valley Water Users' Ass'n, 111 Ariz. 65, 523 P.2d 496 (Ariz.1974), 455

Rancho Santa Margarita v. Vail, 11 Cal.2d 501, 81 P.2d 533 (Cal.1938), 146

Rands, United States v., 389 U.S. 121, 88 S.Ct. 265, 19 L.Ed.2d 329 (1967), **479**

Rapanos v. United States, 547 U.S. 715, 126 S.Ct. 2208, 165 L.Ed.2d 159 (2006), **705, 802**

Ravndal v. Northfork Placers, 60 Idaho 305, 91 P.2d 368 (Idaho 1939), 673

R.D. Merrill Co. v. State, Pollution Control Hearings Bd., 137 Wash.2d 118, 969 P.2d 458 (Wash.1999), 243

Ready Mixed Concrete Co. in Adams County v. Farmers Reservoir and Irrigation Co., 115 P.3d 638 (Colo.2005), 230

Red River Roller Mills v. Wright, 30 Minn. 249, 15 N.W. 167 (Minn.1883), 123

Reeves, Inc. v. Stake, 447 U.S. 429, 100 S.Ct. 2271, 65 L.Ed.2d 244 (1980), 1040

Reitsma v. Pascoag Reservoir & Dam, LLC, 774 A.2d 826 (R.I.2001), 469

Rencken v. Young, 300 Or. 352, 711 P.2d 954 (Or.1985), 263

Republic Steel Corp., United States v., 362 U.S. 482, 80 S.Ct. 884, 4 L.Ed.2d 903 (1960), 674

Rettkowski v. Department of Ecology, 122 Wash.2d 219, 858 P.2d 232 (Wash.1993), 433

Reynolds v. City of Roswell, 99 N.M. 84, 654 P.2d 537 (N.M.1982), 223

Reynolds, State ex rel. v. Miranda, 83 N.M. 443, 493 P.2d 409 (N.M.1972), **159**

Rice v. Harken Exploration Co., 250 F.3d 264 (5th Cir.2001), 705

Richmond v. Shasta Community Services Dist., 9 Cal.Rptr.3d 121, 83 P.3d 518 (Cal. 2004), 641

Rio Grande Dam & Irrigation Co., United States v., 174 U.S. 690, 19 S.Ct. 770, 43 L.Ed. 1136 (1899), 860, 1044

Rio Grande Silvery Minnow v. Keys, 333 F.3d 1109 (10th Cir.2003), 745

Ripka v. Wansing, 589 S.W.2d 333 (Mo.App. S.D.1979), 124

Ritter v. Standal, 98 Idaho 446, 566 P.2d 769 (Idaho 1977), 433, 479

Riverside Bayview Homes, United States v., 474 U.S. 121, 106 S.Ct. 455, 88 L.Ed.2d 419 (1985), 703

Riverside Irr. Dist. v. Andrews, 758 F.2d 508 (10th Cir.1985), **737**

Riverside Superior Court, California v., 93 Cal.Rptr.2d 276 (Cal.App. 4 Dist.2000), 399

Rivoli Trucking Corp. v. American Export Lines, 167 F.Supp. 937 (E.D.N.Y.1958), 982

R.J.A., Inc. v. Water Users Ass'n of Dist. No. 6, 690 P.2d 823 (Colo.1984), 350

Robertson v. Seattle Audubon Soc., 503 U.S. 429, 112 S.Ct. 1407, 118 L.Ed.2d 73 (1992), 1019

Robinson v. Ariyoshi, 753 F.2d 1468 (9th Cir.1985), 514

Robinson v. Booth–Orchard Grove Ditch Co., 94 Colo. 515, 31 P.2d 487 (Colo.1934), 781

Robinson v. City of Boulder, 190 Colo. 357, 547 P.2d 228 (Colo.1976), 776

Robinson, United States v., 570 F.Supp. 1157 (M.D.Fla.1983), 704

Rocky Ford Irr. Co. v. Kents Lake Reservoir Co., 104 Utah 216, 140 P.2d 638 (Utah 1943), 264

Rogers, People ex rel. v. Letford, 102 Colo. 284, 79 P.2d 274 (1938), 790

Romey v. Landers, 392 N.W.2d 415 (S.D. 1986), 123

Rose v. State, 24 N.Y.2d 80, 298 N.Y.S.2d 968, 246 N.E.2d 735 (N.Y.1969), 137

Roswell, City of v. Reynolds, 86 N.M. 249, 522 P.2d 796 (N.M.1974), 257, 609

R.T. Nahas Co. v. Hulet, 106 Idaho 37, 674 P.2d 1036 (Idaho App.1983), 167, 203

Rudd v. Electrolux Corp., 982 F.Supp. 355 (M.D.N.C.1997), 688

Rushton ex rel. Hoffmaster v. Taggart, 306 Mich. 432, 11 N.W.2d 193 (Mich.1943), 470

Rylands v. Fletcher, L.R. 3 H.L. 330 (1868), 455

Safranek v. Limon, 123 Colo. 330, 228 P.2d 975 (Colo.1951), 557, 616

Sagewillow, Inc. v. Idaho Dept. of Water Resources, 138 Idaho 831, 70 P.3d 669 (Idaho 2003), 264

Salt River Val. Water Users' Ass'n v. Kovacovich, 3 Ariz.App. 28, 411 P.2d 201 (Ariz. App.1966), 219

San Bernardino, City of v. City of Riverside, 186 Cal. 7, 198 P. 784 (Cal.1921), 634

San Carlos Apache Tribe v. Superior Court, 193 Ariz. 195, 972 P.2d 179 (Ariz.1999), 434

Sanderson v. Salmon River Canal Co., 34 Idaho 303, 200 P. 341 (Idaho 1921), 781

San Luis Rey Water Conservation Dist. v. Carlsbad Mun. Water Dist. (San Diego County Superior Court No. 184855, Aug. 3, 1959), 641

Sand Point Water & Light Co. v. Panhandle Development Co., 11 Idaho 405, 83 P. 347 (Idaho 1905), **168**

Sandusky Marina Ltd. v. Ohio Dept. of Natural Resources, 126 Ohio App.3d 256, 710 N.E.2d 302 (Ohio App. 6 Dist.1998), 421

San Mateo County Coastal Landowners' Assn. v. County of San Mateo, 45 Cal. Rptr.2d 117 (Cal.App. 1 Dist.1995), 776

Santa Fe Trail Ranches Property Owners Ass'n v. Simpson, 990 P.2d 46 (Colo. 1999), 251

Sause, State v., 217 Or. 52, 342 P.2d 803 (Or.1959), 150

Save Our Beaches, Inc. v. Florida Dept. of Environmental Protection, 2006 WL 1112700 (Fla.App. 1 Dist.2006), 150

Scheer v. Virginia, 2001 WL 803840 (Va.App. 2001), 360

Schero v. Texas Dept. of Water Resources, 630 S.W.2d 516 (Tex.App.-Waco 1982), 505

Scheufler v. General Host Corp., 126 F.3d 1261 (10th Cir.1997), 673

Schodde v. Twin Falls Land & Water Co., 224 U.S. 107, 32 S.Ct. 470, 56 L.Ed. 686 (1912), 189, 193

Schodde v. Twin Falls Land & Water Co., 161 F. 43 (9th Cir.1908), 194

Scott v. McTiernan, 974 P.2d 966 (Wyo. 1999), 263

Scott, People ex rel. v. Chicago Park Dist., 66 Ill.2d 65, 4 Ill.Dec. 660, 360 N.E.2d 773 (Ill.1976), 420

Scribner v. Summers, 84 F.3d 554 (2nd Cir. 1996), 688

S.D. Warren v. Maine Bd. of Environmental Protection, 547 U.S. 370, 126 S.Ct. 1843, 164 L.Ed.2d 625 (2006), 736

Sheep Mountain Cattle Co. v. State, Dept. of Ecology, 45 Wash.App. 427, 726 P.2d 55 (Wash.App. Div. 3 1986), 264

Shell Oil Co., United States v., 605 F.Supp. 1064 (D.Colo.1985), 691

Shellow v. Hagen, 9 Wis.2d 506, 101 N.W.2d 694 (Wis.1960), 469

Shelton Logging Co. v. Gosser, 26 Wash. 126, 66 P. 151 (Wash.1901), 491

Shirokow, People v., 162 Cal.Rptr. 30, 605 P.2d 859 (Cal.1980), 265, 302

Shively v. Bowlby, 152 U.S. 1, 14 S.Ct. 548, 38 L.Ed. 331 (1894), 406, 413, 440, 491

Shokal v. Dunn, 109 Idaho 330, 707 P.2d 441 (Idaho 1985), **326**

Shore Village Property Owners' Ass'n v. State, 824 So.2d 208 (Fla.App. 4 Dist. 2002), 144

Sierra Club v. Andrus, 487 F.Supp. 443 (D.D.C.1980), 425, 888

Sierra Club v. Block, 622 F.Supp. 842 (D.Colo.1985), 889

Sierra Club v. Lujan, 1993 WL 151353, 36 ERC 1533 (W.D.Tex.1993), 623

Sierra Club v. Lyng, 694 F.Supp. 1260 (E.D.Tex.1988), 742

Sierra Club v. Watt, 659 F.2d 203 (D.C.Cir. 1981), 889

Sierra Club v. Yeutter, 911 F.2d 1405 (10th Cir.1990), 889

Silkwood v. Kerr–McGee Corp., 464 U.S. 238, 104 S.Ct. 615, 78 L.Ed.2d 443 (1984), 827

Silver Blue Lake Apartments, Inc. v. Silver Blue Lake Home Owners Ass'n, 245 So.2d 609 (Fla.1971), 447

Simpson v. Cotton Creek Circles, LLC, 181 P.3d 252 (Colo.2008), 350

Sims, State ex rel. Dyer v., 341 U.S. 22, 71 S.Ct. 557, 95 L.Ed. 713 (1951), **979**

Sipriano v. Great Spring Waters of America, Inc., 1 S.W.3d 75 (Tex.1999), 623

Smith v. Carbide and Chemicals Corp., 298 F.Supp.2d 561 (W.D.Ky.2004), 665

Snyder Ranches, Inc. v. Oil Conservation Com'n, 110 N.M. 637, 798 P.2d 587 (N.M. 1990), 688

Solid Waste Agency of Northern Cook County v. United States Army Corps of Engineers, 531 U.S. 159, 121 S.Ct. 675, 148 L.Ed.2d 576 (2001), 705, 802

Solomon v. Sioux City, 243 Iowa 634, 51 N.W.2d 472 (Iowa 1952), 148

Sorensen v. Lower Niobrara Natural Resources Dist., 221 Neb. 180, 376 N.W.2d 539 (Neb.1985), 632

Sotomura v. Hawaii County, 460 F.Supp. 473 (D.Hawai'i 1978), 489

Southeastern Colorado Water Conservancy Dist. v. City of Florence, 688 P.2d 715 (Colo.1984), 314

Southeastern Colorado Water Conservancy Dist. v. Rich, 625 P.2d 977 (Colo.1981), 310

Southeastern Colorado Water Conservancy Dist. v. Shelton Farms, Inc.,

187 Colo. 181, 529 P.2d 1321 (Colo.1974), **223**

Southeastern Federal Power Customers v. Geren, 514 F.3d 1316 (D.C.Cir.2008), **847,** 976

Southern Idaho Fish and Game Ass'n v. Picabo Livestock, Inc., 96 Idaho 360, 528 P.2d 1295 (Idaho 1974), 479

South Florida Water Management Dist. v. Miccosukee Tribe, 541 U.S. 95, 124 S.Ct. 1537, 158 L.Ed.2d 264 (2004), 736

South Plains Lamesa Railroad, Ltd. v. High Plains Underground Water Conservation Dist. No. 1, 52 S.W.3d 770 (Tex.App.-Amarillo 2001), 624

Spear T Ranch, Inc. v. Knaub, 269 Neb. 177, 691 N.W.2d 116 (Neb.2005), 546, 568

Sporhase v. Nebraska, ex rel. Douglas, 458 U.S. 941, 102 S.Ct. 3456, 73 L.Ed.2d 1254 (1982), 612, **1030**

Sprynczynatyk, State ex rel. v. Mills, 523 N.W.2d 537 (N.D.1994), 422

SRBA, Case No. 39576, In re, 1999 WL 778325 (Idaho 1999), 898

Staats v. Newman, 164 Or.App. 18, 988 P.2d 439 (Or.App.1999), 161

State v. _____ (see opposing party)

State, United States v., 135 Idaho 655, 23 P.3d 117 (Idaho 2001), 898

State by Burnquist v. Fischer, 245 Minn. 1, 71 N.W.2d 161 (Minn.1955), 496

State Dept. of Ecology v. Grimes, 121 Wash.2d 459, 852 P.2d 1044 (Wash.1993), **195**

State, Dept. of Ecology v. Theodoratus, 135 Wash.2d 582, 957 P.2d 1241 (Wash.1998), 315

State, Dept. of Environmental Protection v. Ventron Corp., 94 N.J. 254, 463 A.2d 893 (N.J.1983), 688

State, Dept. of Parks v. Idaho Dept. of Water Administration, 96 Idaho 440, 530 P.2d 924 (Idaho 1974), **351**

State Engineer of Nevada v. South Fork Band of Te–Moak Tribe, 114 F.Supp.2d 1046 (D.Nev.2000), 877

State ex rel. v. _____ (see opposing party and relator)

State of (see name of state)

State Water Resources Control Bd. Cases, 39 Cal.Rptr.3d 189 (Cal.App. 3 Dist.2006), 398, 758

State Water Resources Control Bd., People ex rel. v. Forni, 54 Cal.App.3d 743, 126 Cal. Rptr. 851 (Cal.App. 1 Dist.1976), 183

Statler v. Catalano, 293 Ill.App.3d 483, 229 Ill.Dec. 274, 691 N.E.2d 384 (Ill.App. 5 Dist.1997), 453

Steed, Estate of v. New Escalante Irr. Co., 846 P.2d 1223 (Utah 1992), **213**

Stefanoni v. Duncan, 282 Conn. 686, 923 A.2d 737 (Conn.2007), 113, 144

Stelzel v. South Indian River Water Control Dist., 486 So.2d 65 (Fla.Dist.Ct.App. 1986), 790

Stempel v. Department of Water Resources, 82 Wash.2d 109, 508 P.2d 166 (Wash. 1973), 331

Stevens v. City of Cannon Beach, 317 Or. 131, 854 P.2d 449 (Or.1993), 488

St. Germain Irrigating Co. v. Hawthorn Ditch Co., 32 S.D. 260, 143 N.W. 124 (S.D.1913), 504

Stockton East Water Dist. v. United States, 76 Fed.Cl. 497 (Fed.Cl.2007), 532

Stockton East Water Dist. v. United States, 75 Fed.Cl. 321 (Fed.Cl.2007), 532

Stokes v. Morgan, 101 N.M. 195, 680 P.2d 335 (N.M.1984), 342

Stratton v. Mt. Hermon Boys' School, 216 Mass. 83, 103 N.E. 87 (Mass.1913), 145, 153

Stupak–Thrall v. Glickman, 988 F.Supp. 1055 (W.D.Mich.1997), 450

Stupak–Thrall v. United States, 89 F.3d 1269 (6th Cir.1996), 450

Sturgeon v. Brooks, 73 Wyo. 436, 281 P.2d 675 (Wyo.1955), 264

Summa Corp. v. California ex rel. State Lands Com'n, 466 U.S. 198, 104 S.Ct. 1751, 80 L.Ed.2d 237 (1984), 423

Superior Court of Lake County (Lyon), State v., 172 Cal.Rptr. 696, 625 P.2d 239 (Cal. 1981), 422

Superior Court of Placer County, State v., 172 Cal.Rptr. 713, 625 P.2d 256 (Cal. 1981), 422

Swaim v. Stephens Production Co., 359 Ark. 190, 196 S.W.3d 5 (Ark.2004), 149

Swanson Min. Corp. v. FERC, 790 F.2d 96 (D.C.Cir.1986), 716

Swasey v. Rocky Point Ditch Co., 617 P.2d 375 (Utah 1980), 779

Swift v. State, Dept. of Natural Resources & Conservation, 226 Mont. 439, 736 P.2d 117 (Mont.1987), 300

Tacoma, City of v. FERC, 460 F.3d 53 (D.C.Cir.2006), **718**

Tacoma, City of v. Taxpayers of Tacoma, 357 U.S. 320, 78 S.Ct. 1209, 2 L.Ed.2d 1345 (1958), 817

Tahoe–Sierra Preservation Council, Inc. v. Tahoe Regional Planning Agency, 535 U.S. 302, 122 S.Ct. 1465, 152 L.Ed.2d 517 (2002), 530, 567

Tanner v. Bacon, 103 Utah 494, 136 P.2d 957 (Utah 1943), 321

Tapoco, Inc. v. Peterson, 213 Tenn. 335, 373 S.W.2d 605 (Tenn.1963), 453

Taylor v. Tampa Coal Co., 46 So.2d 392 (Fla. 1950), 131

Tehachapi–Cummings County Water Dist. v. Armstrong, 49 Cal.App.3d 992, 122 Cal. Rptr. 918 (Cal.App. 5 Dist.1975), 634

Ten Eyck v. Warwick, 59 N.Y.St.Rep. 636, 27 N.Y.S. 536 (N.Y.Sup.Gen.Term 1894), 453

Tennessee v. Lane, 541 U.S. 509, 124 S.Ct. 1978, 158 L.Ed.2d 820 (2004), 414

Tequesta, Village of v. Jupiter Inlet Corp., 371 So.2d 663 (Fla.1979), 610

Territory of Montana v. Drennan, 1 Mont. 41 (Mont.Terr.1868), 3

Texaco, Inc. v. Short, 454 U.S. 516, 102 S.Ct. 781, 70 L.Ed.2d 738 (1982), 505

Texarkana, City of v. Wiggins, 151 Tex. 100, 246 S.W.2d 622 (Tex.1952), 777

Texas v. New Mexico, 467 U.S. 1238, 104 S.Ct. 3505, 82 L.Ed.2d 816 (1984), 994

Texas v. New Mexico., 446 U.S. 540, 100 S.Ct. 2911, 64 L.Ed.2d 485 (1980), 993

Texas County Irr. and Water Resources Ass'n v. Oklahoma Water Resources Bd., 803 P.2d 1119 (Okla.1990), 567

Thayer v. California Development Co., 164 Cal. 117, 128 P. 21 (Cal.1912), 774

Thayer v. City of Rawlins, 594 P.2d 951 (Wyo.1979), 223

The Confederated Salish and Kootenai Tribes of the Flathead Reservation v. Stults, 312 Mont. 420, 59 P.3d 1093 (Mont.2002), 922

The Daniel Ball, 77 U.S. 557, 19 L.Ed. 999 (1870), 403, 701

The Steamboaters v. FERC, 759 F.2d 1382 (9th Cir.1985), 715

Thies v. Howland, 424 Mich. 282, 380 N.W.2d 463 (Mich.1985), 143

TH Investments, Inc. v. Kirby Inland Marine, L.P., 218 S.W.3d 173 (Tex.App.-Hous. (14 Dist.) 2007), 453

Thompson v. Colorado Ground Water Commission, 194 Colo. 489, 575 P.2d 372 (Colo.1978), 616

Thompson v. Enz, 379 Mich. 667, 154 N.W.2d 473 (Mich.1967), 143, **455**

Thompson v. Salt Lake City Corp., 724 P.2d 958 (Utah 1986), 778

Thornton, City of v. Bijou Irr. Co., 926 P.2d 1 (Colo.1996), 171, 313, 343, 664, 780

Thornton, City of v. City of Fort Collins, 830 P.2d 915 (Colo.1992), 171, **360**

Thornton, City of v. Farmers Reservoir and Irr. Co., 194 Colo. 526, 575 P.2d 382 (Colo.1978), 775

Thornton, City of, People ex rel. Danielson v., 775 P.2d 11 (Colo.1989), 263

Thornton, State ex rel. v. Hay, 254 Or. 584, 462 P.2d 671 (Or.1969), 488

Tiegs v. Watts, 135 Wash.2d 1, 954 P.2d 877 (Wash.1998), 686, 687

Town of (see name of town)

Trail Smelter Arbitration (United States v. Canada 1941), 3 U.N.R.I.A.A. 1938 (1949), 1054

Trepanier v. County of Volusia, 965 So.2d 276 (Fla.App. 5 Dist.2007), 496

Trout Unlimited v. Lohn, 2007 WL 1730090 (W.D.Wash.2007), 760

Tulare Irr. Dist. v. Lindsay–Strathmore Irr. Dist., 3 Cal.2d 489, 45 P.2d 972 (Cal. 1935), 183, 184

Tulare Lake Basin Water Storage Dist. v. United States, Verdict, Agreement and

Settlement, 2004 WL 3728318 (Dec. 21, 2004), 529

Tulare Lake Basin Water Storage Dist. v. United States, 59 Fed.Cl. 246 (Fed.Cl. 2003), 529

Tulare Lake Basin Water Storage Dist. v. United States, 49 Fed.Cl. 313 (Fed.Cl. 2001), 527

Tulkisarmute Native Community Council v. Heinze, 898 P.2d 935 (Alaska 1995), 311

Turner v. James Canal Co., 155 Cal. 82, 99 P. 520 (Cal.1909), 113

Twin Lakes Reservoir & Canal Co. v. City of Aspen, 193 Colo. 478, 568 P.2d 45 (Colo. 1977), 257

Tyler v. Wilkinson, 24 F.Cas. 472 (C.C.D.R.I.1827), **60**

Udall v. Federal Power Commission, 387 U.S. 428, 87 S.Ct. 1712, 18 L.Ed.2d 869 (1967), 714

Uintah Basin, In re, 133 P.3d 410 (Utah 2006), 376, 789

Umatilla Waterquality Protective Ass'n v. Smith Frozen Foods, Inc., 962 F.Supp. 1312 (D.Or.1997), 689

United Plainsmen Ass'n v. North Dakota State Water Conservation Commission, 247 N.W.2d 457 (N.D.1976), 433

United Proteins, Inc. v. Farmland Industries, Inc., 259 Kan. 725, 915 P.2d 80 (Kan. 1996), 688

United States v. _____(see opposing party)

United States, State v., 134 Idaho 940, 12 P.3d 1284 (Idaho 2000), 898

Upper Black Squirrel Creek Ground Water Management Dist. v. Goss, 993 P.2d 1177 (Colo.2000), 618

Upper Snake River Chapter v. Hodel, 921 F.2d 232 (9th Cir.1990), 747

Urie v. Franconia Paper Corp., 107 N.H. 131, 218 A.2d 360 (N.H.1966), 687

Utah v. Kennecott Corp., 801 F.Supp. 553 (D.Utah 1992), 698

Utah v. United States, 403 U.S. 9, 91 S.Ct. 1775, 29 L.Ed.2d 279 (1971), 405

Utah Div. of State Lands v. United States, 482 U.S. 193, 107 S.Ct. 2318, 96 L.Ed.2d 162 (1987), 411

Valparaiso, City of v. Defler, 694 N.E.2d 1177 (Ind.App.1998), 569

Van Sickle v. Haines, 7 Nev. 249 (Nev.1872), 70

Varjabedian v. City of Madera, 142 Cal.Rptr. 429, 572 P.2d 43 (Cal.1977), 687

Vaughn v. Vermilion Corp., 444 U.S. 206, 100 S.Ct. 399, 62 L.Ed.2d 365 (1979), 448, 486

Village of (see name of village)

Vineyard Area Citizens for Responsible Growth v. Rancho Cordova, 53 Cal. Rptr.3d 821, 150 P.3d 709 (Cal.2007), 773

Virginia v. Maryland, 540 U.S. 1101, 124 S.Ct. 1127, 157 L.Ed.2d 884 (2004), 964

Virginia v. Tennessee, 148 U.S. 503, 13 S.Ct. 728, 37 L.Ed. 537 (1893), 983

Vought, In re, 76 P.3d 906 (Colo.2003), 171

Wadsworth Ditch Co. v. Brown, 39 Colo. 57, 88 P. 1060 (Colo.1907), 782

Waiola O Moloka'i, In re, 83 P.3d 664 (Hawai'i 2004), 439

Warner Val. Stock Co. v. Lynch, 215 Or. 523, 336 P.2d 884 (Or.1959), 183

Washington v. Washington State Commercial Passenger Fishing Vessel Ass'n, 443 U.S. 658, 99 S.Ct. 3055, 61 L.Ed.2d 823 (1979), 727

Washington Dep't of Ecology, United States v., 375 F.Supp.2d 1050 (W.D.Wash.2005), 922

Washington, United States v., 157 F.3d 630 (9th Cir.1998), 414

Wasserburger v. Coffee, 180 Neb. 149, 141 N.W.2d 738 (Neb.1966), 503

Waterbury, City of v. Town of Washington, 260 Conn. 506, 800 A.2d 1102 (Conn. 2002), 289

Water Rights of Fort Lyon Canal Co., In re, 762 P.2d 1375 (Colo.1988), 780

Water Rights of Park County Sportsmen's Ranch LLP v. Bargas, 986 P.2d 262 (Colo. 1999), 389

Waters of Long Valley Creek Stream System, In re, 158 Cal.Rptr. 350, 599 P.2d 656 (Cal.1979), **497,** 640

Water Use Permit Applications, In re, 9 P.3d 409 (Hawai'i 2000), 399, **434,** 489, 621

Wayman v. Murray City Corp., 23 Utah 2d 97, 458 P.2d 861 (Utah 1969), **571**

Wehby v. Turpin, 710 So.2d 1243 (Ala.1998), 453

Weibert v. Rothe Bros., Inc., 200 Colo. 310, 618 P.2d 1367 (Colo.1980), 249, 389

Wernberg v. State, 516 P.2d 1191 (Alaska 1973), 487

West Dauphin Ltd. v. Callon Offshore Production, Inc., 725 So.2d 944 (Ala.1998), 150, 421

West Elk Ranch, L.L.C. v. United States, 65 P.3d 479 (Colo.2002), 315

Western Nebraska Resources Council v. EPA, 943 F.2d 867 (8th Cir.1991), 690

Westminster, City of v. Church, 167 Colo. 1, 445 P.2d 52 (Colo.1968), 242

West Palm Beach, City of v. Board of Trustees of the Internal Improvement Trust, 746 So.2d 1085 (Fla.1999), 421

Westville, Borough of v. Whitney Home Builders, 40 N.J.Super. 62, 122 A.2d 233 (N.J.Super.A.D.1956), **666**

Weyerhaeuser Co. v. Costle, 590 F.2d 1011 (D.C.Cir.1978), 676

White v. Massachusetts Council of Const. Employers, Inc., 460 U.S. 204, 103 S.Ct. 1042, 75 L.Ed.2d 1 (1983), 1040

White's Mill Colony Inc. v. Williams, 363 S.C. 117, 609 S.E.2d 811 (S.C.App.2005), 461

Whitten v. Coit, 153 Colo. 157, 385 P.2d 131 (Colo.1963), 617

Wiggins v. Brazil Coal & Clay Corp., 452 N.E.2d 958 (Ind.1983), 568

Wilbour v. Gallagher, 77 Wash.2d 306, 462 P.2d 232 (Wash.1969), **441**

Williams v. City of Wichita, 190 Kan. 317, 374 P.2d 578 (Kan.1962), 504

Williams v. Skyline Development Corp., 265 Md. 130, 288 A.2d 333 (Md.1972), 144

Williams Pipe Line Co. v. Bayer Corp., 964 F.Supp. 1300 (S.D.Iowa 1997), 686

Winans, United States v., 198 U.S. 371, 25 S.Ct. 662, 49 L.Ed. 1089 (1905), 105, 863

Winters v. United States, 207 U.S. 564, 28 S.Ct. 207, 52 L.Ed. 340 (1908), **102,** 861, 863, 898

Wisconsin v. Illinois, 388 U.S. 426, 87 S.Ct. 1774, 18 L.Ed.2d 1290 (1967), 1044

Wisconsin v. Illinois, 281 U.S. 179, 50 S.Ct. 266, 74 L.Ed. 799 (1930), 955

Wisconsin v. Illinois, 278 U.S. 367, 49 S.Ct. 163, 73 L.Ed. 426 (1929), 1044

Wood v. Picillo, 443 A.2d 1244 (R.I.1982), 688

Woods v. Johnson, 241 Cal.App.2d 278, 50 Cal.Rptr. 515 (Cal.App. 1 Dist.1966), 440

Woodsum v. Pemberton, 172 N.J.Super. 489, 412 A.2d 1064 (N.J.Super.L.1980), 566

Wright v. Goleta Water Dist., 174 Cal.App.3d 74, 219 Cal.Rptr. 740 (Cal.App. 2 Dist. 1985), 640

Wyoming Hereford Ranch v. Hammond Packing Co., 33 Wyo. 14, 236 P. 764 (Wyo.1925), **295**

Yellowstone River, In re, 253 Mont. 167, 832 P.2d 1210 (Mont.1992), 301

Yeo v. Tweedy, 34 N.M. 611, 286 P. 970 (N.M.1929), 609

Young & Norton v. Hinderlider, 15 N.M. 666, 110 P. 1045 (N.M.Terr.1910), 320

Zabel v. Tabb, 430 F.2d 199 (5th Cir.1970), 702

Zepp v. Mayor & Council of Athens, 180 Ga.App. 72, 348 S.E.2d 673 (Ga.App. 1986), 777

*

WATER RESOURCE MANAGEMENT

*

CHAPTER ONE

WATER LAW: A RESPONSE TO SCARCITY

This evening, as I write, the sun is going down, and the shadows are settling in the canyon. The vermilion gleams and roseate hues, blending with the green and gray tints, are slowly changing to somber brown above, and black shadows are creeping over them below; and now it is a dark portal to a region of gloom—the gateway through which we are to enter on our voyage of exploration tomorrow. What shall we find?

John Wesley Powell, The Exploration of the Colorado River 15 (U. of Chicago Press, 1957) (1875).

A. A SPECIAL KIND OF SCARCITY

The challenge of water law is to ensure the best use for society of a scarce resource. The central issue is not the allocation of a declining supply, as it is with oil and gas. Water scarcity results from a geographic and temporal mismatch of supply and demand exacerbated by competition among users and changing societal values of alternative uses. Areas of high municipal, agricultural, and industrial water demand often coincide with areas of low precipitation, particularly in the western and southwestern United States. Increasingly serious water supply problems are also being felt in the humid eastern states where political inattention to water needs and decentralized allocation systems have allowed growth in demand to overtake available supplies.

Although overall water consumption is not increasing significantly in the United States, the demand for water in certain sectors is rapidly growing. Urbanization makes municipal water use the most palpable source of new demand for water, and for water lawyers. The nation's burgeoning population is settling primarily in metropolitan areas, with the fastest growing cities located in the arid Southwest.

For most of the nation's history expanding demand could be satisfied by developing new supplies. Water development projects dammed, stored, and delivered water. In many areas, especially in the East, wells were drilled more deeply into aquifers and equipped with more powerful pumps. Now, the opportunities for new water development are limited because most supply sources have been fully exploited for existing uses.

New urban demands, therefore, either have to be met by reallocating water from other uses—more often than not from agriculture—or methods have to be found to reduce demand. Agricultural demand is not increasing and technology offers methods to make irrigation more efficient. Transfers of water present a variety of challenges for lawyers, however, because of the social and economic factors involved in removing water from one use and putting it to another use, often in another place. In addition, the water laws of some states can inhibit transfers.

Even as municipal uses grow, the public is demanding more water for instream uses to maintain sustainable aquatic ecosystems or to restore degraded ones. Agricultural, municipal, and industrial uses remove water from streams and therefore are in direct competition with public uses of water for recreation, fishing, habitat for fish and wildlife, and aesthetics. Other uses are also "instream," like hydroelectric power generation and navigation; however, the dams and locks they require to be built in rivers can also be at odds with the public's instream uses.

At another level, sovereigns contest with one another for the prerogative to control and allocate water. States compete with one another for the use of interstate rivers and with Indian tribes over waterways that they share with Indian reservations. The United States as trustee for Indian tribes pursues many tribal claims to the waters needed to make reservations viable homelands. It also asserts claims to water needed for federal lands ranging from parks to military bases.

Historically, the federal government has dominated much of the water development activity in the West and required the subordination of some state laws and policies to federal objectives in return for large subsidies. Today, federal activity related to water is focused primarily on environmental protection rather than development. Federal environmental laws restrict water pollution, regulate the use of rivers for hydroelectric power generation, protect endangered species, and prohibit filling in wetlands. These laws are now the most influential factor in whether or not new water development can proceed. On the other hand, solving the environmental problems created by large dams built by the federal government in the past is one of the most challenging tasks for water law and policy today.

Climate variability presents new challenges for the law and for water managers. Seasonal variations in precipitation have long plagued water planners. Water law is essentially a risk allocation system. Most water users, however, are extremely risk averse and seek to use the law to protect investments that depend on water use. A deep-seated fear of drought has compelled water users to secure supplies sufficient for dry years and caused public officials to expend funds for large storage facilities as insurance against shortages. The reality of long-term global changes in precipitation is now widely accepted by climatologists, although they differ on projections of the timing, extent, and location of the impacts. This has created a wild card frustrating efforts of water planners. Although nature's weather patterns have always created uncertainty for water users and placed cyclical limits on "rights" to receive water, the prospect of permanent changes casts fresh doubt on the reliability of water supplies.

Coping with disparities between supply and demand and competition among water users has always been a contentious matter. Scarcity, especially of a resource so important to the economic viability of land and entire communities, has moved people to conflict and violence. Water scarcity is not an issue of human survival in the United States, as human consumption is minimal; we could find no record of a person dying of thirst. Nonetheless, water conflicts can be life-and-death matters. For instance, at one time Arizona mobilized its National Guard to prevent the construction of Parker Dam on the Colorado River. See Arizona v. California, 292 U.S. 341, 54 S.Ct. 735, 78 L.Ed. 1298 (1934). Likewise, the first reported water dispute in the Montana courts was a criminal case. A miner sought to assert as a defense to his prosecution for shooting another man the fact that the victim had cut off water running through a gulch that he had been using to work a mining claim. Territory of Montana v. Drennan, 1 Mont. 41 (1868).

It is the job of the law to prevent violence and to mediate and resolve conflict. Water law therefore presents a particularly colorful study in society's attempts to allocate a scarce and universally desired resource. The battles are played out in courtrooms, in legislatures, in agency proceedings, in Congress, and, more than ever before, in multi-party negotiations. Conflicts range from minor disputes among neighbors, to interstate and international disagreements over the entitlements of sovereigns to use the rivers they share. In between are the claims of competing users: farmers, cities, power generators, fishers, boaters, and industries.

Public uses for water—nominally a public resource—are increasingly drawn into competition with entrenched private uses. Water uses may be conveniently divided into instream (or "in situ") and offstream uses. Instream uses include transportation, hydroelectric power generation, recreation, fish and wildlife, dilution of water pollution, and aesthetics. These uses are typically considered "public uses." Offstream uses include agricultural irrigation and municipal and industrial water supply. Although these uses are often based on private rights, even they can be imbued with the "public interest." Domestic water uses—drinking, cooking, and washing— are necessities of life.

In the chapters that follow, we first explore the various responses of the law to society's demands for water for different economic uses. Legal principles emerged from these experiments and were institutionalized into systems of riparian law, mainly in the eastern states, and prior appropriation law, mainly in the West. The fact that a majority of the judicial decisions in this book are drawn from western states reflects the reality that most disputes over water and most legal activity in water law have arisen in the West. Although the legal responses to water scarcity differed at first in the East and the West, the systems they created were continually adapted to meet changing needs. Today they closely resemble one another,

and are most are embodied in similar permitting laws enacted and administered by the states.

This book examines early legal responses to the water scarcity problem, the resulting principles for acquisition, enjoyment, transfer, and loss of
water rights under the riparian and prior appropriation doctrines, the
permit systems that evolved under both doctrines, and the relation of the
public's interest in water to the creation of private rights. The book then
explores laws pertaining to groundwater, federal environmental protection
laws, special water districts, federal and Indian reserved rights, and interstate and international issues. We begin, however, with selected readings
that elucidate the nature of the scarcity problem.

B.   Water Supply: The Hydrologic Cycle

Water is present in many different forms everywhere on earth. Most of
the globe's surface, in fact, is covered with water. This water is not all
available for human use, however, as most of it is tied up in non-potable
forms as oceans (97% of the total water resource), glaciers and ice caps
(2%), and in soil or rocks. With 77% of the inland water in glaciers, the
remaining forms of water—in lakes, rivers, vegetation, and the atmosphere—contain less than 0.5% of the total. About 0.6% is in groundwater.

Rain and snow are the source of virtually all freshwater. Because
precipitation varies regionally as well as seasonally, water is distributed
unequally. In the aggregate, however, the world's total supply of water does
not change. The problem is that water is not a static resource. In economic
terms, it is a "flowing," not a stock resource (some aquifers excepted).
Therefore, any description of its distribution must include its constant
movement in the hydrologic cycle:

> The atmosphere receives water through evaporation and loses it as
> precipitation, mostly in the form of rain or snow. The average resi-
> dence time for water in the atmosphere is 10 days. A drop of rain can
> have a multitude of fates, depending on where and when it falls. Some
> rainfall never reaches land surface; instead, it evaporates as it falls (a
> phenomenon known as virga) and returns to the atmospheric reservoir.
> A falling raindrop could land on a leaf of a tree, from where it might
> fall to the ground, evaporate, or perhaps be imbibed by the plant.
> Another drop might land directly on the ground. That water could
> puddle in a depression, travel over the surface to a lower elevation
> (runoff), or enter the sub-surface (infiltrate). Water in a puddle will
> likely evaporate or infiltrate. Water that runs off may infiltrate at a
> more favorable location or travel to a stream and ultimately be
> transported to an ocean; at any point on this journey, that water can
> evaporate. The average residence time for water in free-flowing rivers
> ranges between 16 and 26 days. Streams that run through reservoirs
> can have substantially longer residence times. Not all surface water
> flows to oceans. Some lakes and wetlands have no surface drainage.

They lose water to evaporation and to ground water. Humans withdraw water from streams and reservoirs, thus interrupting its migration to the ocean.

Water moves much more slowly in the subsurface than in the atmosphere or on land surface. Water that infiltrates the subsurface can remain in the unsaturated zone where it will most likely be returned to the atmosphere by evaporation or plant transpiration; it can discharge to the surface in a channel or depression, thus becoming surface flow; or it can traverse the unsaturated zone to recharge an underlying aquifer. Most water that infiltrates the subsurface is returned to the atmosphere by evaporation from bare soil or by plant transpiration. That returned water typically resides in the subsurface for less than a year. Discharge to land surface of unsaturated-zone water, sometimes referred to as interflow, may occur days to months after that water has infiltrated, depending on the distance between the points of infiltration and discharge. Infiltrated water that travels downward past the depth of the root zone may eventually reach the saturated zone, thus becoming aquifer recharge. Travel times of water through the entire thickness of the unsaturated zone span a very large range: from hours, for thin unsaturated zones in humid regions, to millennia, for thick unsaturated zones in arid regions. Water that reaches the saturated zone may reside there for days to thousands of years. Under natural conditions, ground water discharges to surface-water bodies such as streams, wetlands, lakes, or oceans, or it is extracted by plants and returned to the atmosphere by transpiration. Humans also extract ground water for agricultural, domestic, and industrial uses; such water is ultimately reapplied to land surface, returned to the subsurface, or discharged to surface-water bodies.

Precipitation in the form of snow can follow several courses. In many environments, snow accumulated on land surface melts in a few days or less. In other areas, a seasonal snowpack exists throughout winter and melts in the spring. Still other areas, such as Greenland and Antarctica, have snow and ice fields that are thousands of years old. In any of these cases, the melting water flows to a surface-water body, infiltrates into the subsurface, or is evaporated back into the atmosphere.

Healy, R.W., Winter, T.C., LaBaugh, J.W., and Franke, O.L., 2007, Water budgets: Foundations for effective water-resources and environmental management: U.S. Geological Survey Circular 1308 3–5 (2008).

Figure 1. Hydrologic Cycle

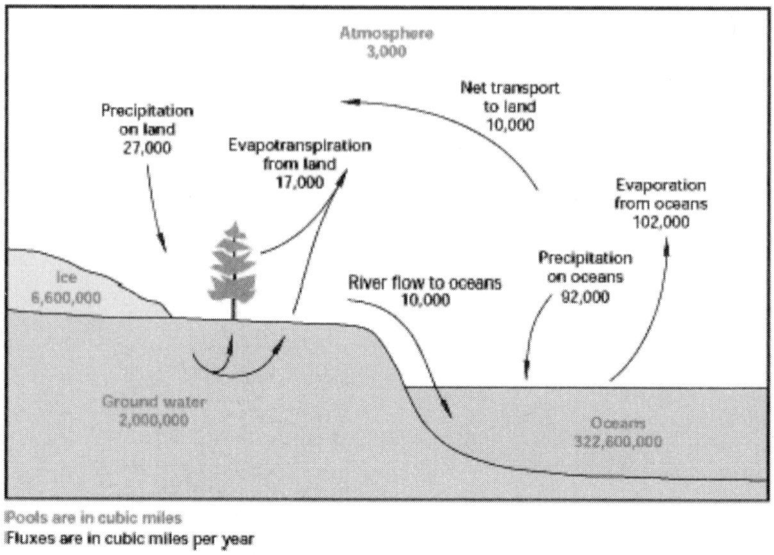

Pools are in cubic miles
Fluxes are in cubic miles per year

Source: U.S.G.S. Ground Water and Surface Water as a Single Resource: U.S. Geological Survey Circular 1139 (1998).

There is an emerging awareness that the quality of water is linked to the quantity available for use. For example, contamination forecloses most uses of ground and surface water. The popular desire for clean water has led to a complex administrative structure to control waste disposal, pollution from municipal, agricultural, and industrial users, groundwater contamination, and the increasingly serious problem of unsafe hazardous waste storage and disposal.

NOTE: WATER MEASUREMENT

Water is measured by different units, depending on the purpose: storage capacity, consumption, streamflow rates, or rainfall determination. For example, the basic unit of storage capacity measurement or consumption is the "acre-foot." One acre-foot is enough water to cover one acre of land to a depth of one foot, and is equivalent to 325,851 gallons. This is about enough water to supply the domestic needs of five people for one year at a rate of 180 gallons per person per day. Water flowing in a stream is measured by "cubic feet per second" (cfs); one cubic foot per second equals 7.48 gallons of water per second. A flow of one cfs will produce 1.98 acre-feet per day. Rainfall is measured by inches of precipitation, and often is expressed as inches per year. One inch of rain over an acre of land delivers 27,200 gallons of water. Large-scale descriptions of water supply frequently use the terms "million gallons per day" (mgd) or "billion gallons per day" (bgd). Finally, there is an older measurement of water flow encountered infrequently, the "miner's inch" or "statutory inch." Used by California miners in the 1800s, the miner's inch is measured by allowing water to flow at a specified pressure through an orifice of a specified size. The amount of water represented by a miner's inch varies among states from 0.02 cfs to 0.028 cfs. A table showing common water measurement equivalents and metric conversion factors is found in Appendix A, *infra* p. 1069.

C. DEMANDS FOR WATER

The most authoritative sources of water use data in the United States are the U.S. Geological Survey's five year reports. Given the amount of data that must be collected, standardized and synthesized, estimates are almost always a decade behind. However, the basic trends have been holding relatively constant, even as the United States continues to add population. As you read the excerpts from the 2000 survey, keep in mind the fundamental distinction between gross and net withdrawals. Some withdrawals, especially for hydroelectric production, are non-consumptive uses because most of the water is returned to the river or lake; in contrast, agricultural uses consume a much higher percentage of the withdrawn water and are thus classified as consumptive rather than non-consumptive uses.

U.S. Geological Survey, Estimated Water Use in the United States in 2000

4, 10, 39–42 (2004).

Total water use in the United States for 2000 was determined from estimates of water withdrawals for the eight categories of public supply, domestic, irrigation, livestock, aquaculture, industrial, mining, and thermoelectric power. Total freshwater and saline-water withdrawals for 2000 were estimated to be 408,000 Mgal/d, or 457,000 thousand acre-feet per year. Freshwater withdrawals were 85 percent of the total, and the remaining 15 percent was saline water. Estimates of withdrawals by source indicate that for 2000, total surface-water withdrawals were 323,000 Mgal/d, or 79 percent of the total withdrawals for all categories of use. About 81 percent of surface water withdrawn was freshwater. Total ground-water withdrawals were 84,500 Mgal/d, of which 99 percent was freshwater. Nearly all (98 percent) saline-water withdrawals were from surface water.

* * *

For 2000, most of the fresh ground-water withdrawals, 68 percent, were for irrigation. About 52 percent of the fresh ground-water use nationwide was in California, Texas, Nebraska, Arkansas, and Florida. About three-fourths of ground-water withdrawals in California and Texas were for irrigation; in Nebraska and Arkansas, 94 percent of the ground-water withdrawals were for irrigation. Ground-water withdrawals for public supply and irrigation in Florida were nearly identical. Nationwide, ground-water withdrawals for irrigation were about 3.5 times larger than the withdrawals for public supply. * * *

[T]he largest category of water withdrawals was thermoelectric power (48 percent of total withdrawals). Irrigation accounted for 34 percent of the total withdrawals; public supply, 11 percent of the total; self-supplied industrial, 5 percent of the total; and self-supplied domestic, livestock, aquaculture, and mining combined accounted for around 2 percent of the total withdrawals.

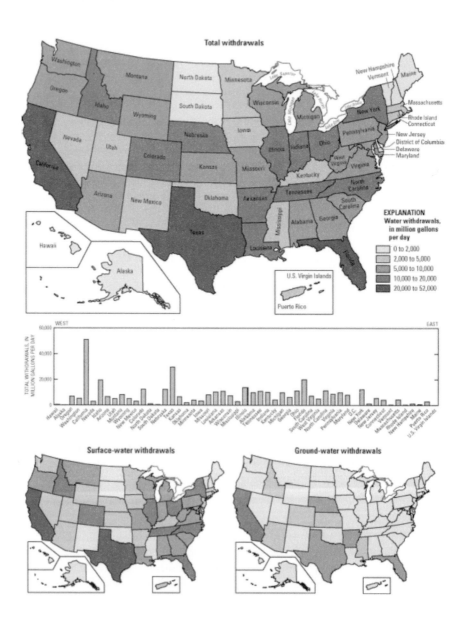

Figure 2. Total, surface-water, and ground-water withdrawals, 2000

The geographic distribution of total, total surface-water, and total ground-water withdrawals is shown in Figure 2. California, Texas, and Florida accounted for 25 percent of total withdrawals. California and Texas accounted for 17 percent of total surface-water withdrawals, and California accounted for 18 percent of total ground-water withdrawals. With respect to fresh and saline water withdrawals, California and Texas accounted for 18 percent of the total freshwater withdrawals, and California and Florida accounted for 40 percent of the total saline-water withdrawals.

* * *

Trends in Water Use, 1950–2000

The USGS first conducted the water-use compilations for 1950 and has published them every 5 years since. Groupings of categories and data elements have changed through the years. Water-use categories were combined in some compilations and were published as separate categories in others. Summaries of withdrawal estimates from 1950 to 2000 are shown graphically in Figures 13 and 14. * * *.

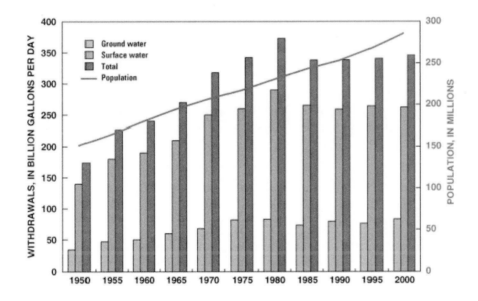

Figure 13. Trends in population and freshwater
withdrawals by source, 1950–2000

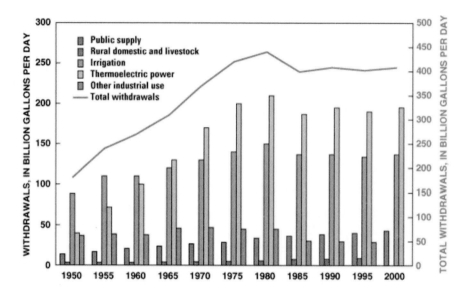

Figure 14. Trends in total water withdrawals
by water-use category, 1950–2000

* * *

Estimates in Figure 13 show total withdrawals increased steadily from 1950 to 1980, declined more than 9 percent from 1980 to 1985, and have varied less than 3 percent between the 5–year intervals since 1985. Total withdrawals peaked during 1980, although total U.S. population has increased steadily since 1950. Estimates of water use peaked during 1980 because of large industrial, irrigation, and thermoelectric-power withdrawals. Total withdrawals for 2000 were similar to the 1990 total withdrawals, although population had increased 13 percent since 1990.

Total withdrawals have remained about 80 percent surface water and 20 percent ground water during the 50–year period. * * *

Estimated withdrawals for public supply increased continually since 1950 (Figure 14) along with population served by public suppliers. Public-supply withdrawals more than tripled during this 50–year period and increased about 8 percent from 1995 to 2000. * * *

Since 1950, irrigation has represented about 65 percent of total withdrawals, excluding those for thermoelectric power. Withdrawals for irrigation increased by more than 68 percent from 1950 to 1980 (from 89 to 150 Bgal/d). Withdrawals have decreased since 1980 and have stabilized at between 134 and 137 Bgal/d between 1985 and 2000. Depending on the geographic area of the United States, this overall decrease can be attributed to climate, crop type, advances in irrigation efficiency, and higher energy costs.

* * *

The total number of acres irrigated in the United States steadily increased from 25,000 thousand acres for 1950 to 58,000 thousand acres for 1980. The estimated number of acres irrigated remained relatively constant from 1980 to 1995, and then increased to 61,900 thousand acres during 2000. * * *

David M. Gillilan & Thomas C. Brown, Instream Flow Protection

95–96, 297–298, 302–305 (1997).

* * * Ideally, in a world without scarcity, all water uses would receive, at the appropriate times, sufficient water to maximize benefits. But there is not enough water to supply all instream and offstream uses at levels that would produce maximum benefits from each, so some balancing of needs must occur. * * *

Some people believe that because water is scarce, its primary uses should be human consumption and commodity production, that only the amount of water not needed for these purposes—if any—should be left in streams. A competing view is that because water is scarce, we should restrict offstream consumption to only the bare minimum needed to support human populations and thereby preserve the West's comparatively rare aquatic and riparian environments. Most people, to the degree that they think about the issue at all, probably fall somewhere between, recognizing a need to divert water for a variety of purposes but also a need to leave water instream.

Two broad principles often used to guide society in the quest to properly allocate water among competing needs are efficiency and equity. The efficiency principle proposes that water be allocated among competing uses so as to produce the maximum possible benefit to society. "Maximum benefit" does not refer solely to financial returns; financial returns are important, but benefits not typically assigned a dollar value must also be considered. This means that the whole array of use and nonuse values must be considered, including the value of water in producing commodities, providing recreational opportunities, supporting domestic and municipal uses, and maintaining stream channels and water quality, together with the existence and bequest values of preserving fish, wildlife, and a healthy environment.

Considerations of equity have played a highly visible role in the debate over instream flow protection. Some of the more common notions of fairness expressed in these debates include the desire to ensure that all members of society benefit from resource use, that particular individuals are not placed in a position from which to either reap all the benefits or suffer all the costs of water allocation decisions, and that property owners should not be deprived of their property in the absence of just and adequate compensation. * * *

Water used offstream has caused the desert to bloom and cities and towns to prosper—but these developments have not been without cost. Only in some of the uppermost river stretches and smaller tributaries, and in a few of the West's most isolated areas, does streamflow remain unaltered by diversion or storage projects. Streamflow volumes throughout the rest of the West have been diminished. With the loss of instream flows has come a significant loss in aquatic and riparian habitat, recreational opportunities, and water quality.

Society values instream flows more highly now than at the turn of the century. The primary concern of the great majority of westerners at the dawn of the 20th century was to secure the basic elements of life, such as food, shelter, and safety. If these could be obtained by using water offstream, then the water was quickly diverted. As urban areas have grown to dominate the population and economy of the West, and average real incomes have risen substantially, residents have become more concerned about the quality of the surrounding environment and about the existence of recreational opportunities and other amenities. The beauty and proximity of the western landscape, including the West's rivers and streams, have much to do with the desirability of the West as a place to live and work. Today, people are moving West not to be farmers, ranchers, lumberjacks, or miners but to find work in the cities, to retire, and to seek a better quality of life, including access to the West's scenic beauty and outstanding recreational opportunities. Although it may dismay those westerners who still make their living directly off the West's land and water, the character of the West has changed dramatically. With that change has come an increase in the demand for the integrity of the natural environment, including the existence of instream flows.

* * *

It is easy to understand why attempts to retroactively protect instream flows—i.e., to put water that has already been allocated to offstream use back into streams—raise serious objections. Some people argue that water uses that have lowered instream flows below the minimum levels necessary to, say, maintain healthy fish populations, should never have been allowed in the first place, so that retroactive reallocation is merely correcting a past wrong. But the fact is that these uses were allowed, and even encouraged, to occur at a time when values and conditions were different. Retroactive protection without compensation essentially asks just a portion of the population, current water users, to bear the entire cost of the larger public's benefit. This issue cannot be resolved solely by technical measurements of benefits and costs, for it is essentially an issue of fairness. The issue of who will pay for instream flow improvements in streams that have previously been allocated to offstream use will ultimately have to be settled in the legislatures, and perhaps in the courts.

It is less obvious why attempts to protect flows currently in streams from future appropriation should raise objections, particularly when such attempts do not go beyond protecting the most valuable instream flows. Part of the explanation lies in the general lack of information about instream flow protection among water users, water agency officials, and the general public. It is easy to fear, reject, or ignore that which is not known, particularly when long-established property rights are at issue. Many, probably even most, water users have little understanding of the effects that instream flow protection measures would have on their own current and future water uses. But objections based on lack of knowledge should gradually subside as information about instream flow protection becomes more widespread and people gain familiarity with instream flow protection measures that have already been implemented.

Some people object to instream flow protection on the grounds that it limits future diversions and therefore constrains future economic activities, such as agricultural expansion or urban development, for which diversions are necessary. It is true that instream flow protection measures constrain future diversions; that is, in fact, the purpose of the measures. But objections based on this fact should be tempered by at least four major considerations.

First, if there is not enough water to meet all possible needs—the usual situation virtually everywhere—then water should be allocated in such manner as to produce the greatest value. If a certain portion of the streamflow on a given reach of stream can produce more value to society if left instream than if diverted for offstream use, then it is entirely appropriate for that streamflow to be left instream.

Second, objectors often overlook the fact that more efficient use of diverted water can provide for new and expanded offstream uses of water without the need to increase diversions. Water conservation is often complicated by issues concerning ownership of water that has not previously been used efficiently, but conservation has nevertheless been growing in importance and effectiveness in many locations throughout the West.

Third, objectors frequently fail to realize that choosing to leave water instream does not categorically exclude offstream uses of water. Leaving some water instream, for some period of time, over some length of the stream, does not make water totally unavailable for offstream use. It is a rare situation indeed in which 100 percent of the natural flow of a watercourse is allocated to instream use. Instream flow protection generally involves the allocation of only a part of a stream's flow to instream purposes. And because instream uses are essentially nonconsumptive, the water is still available for offstream use after it has flowed through the protected reach. The decision to fight over every drop of water as if it were the only drop can be an effective political and legal tactic—often used by both sides of the instream flow controversy—but in most situations it does not square with reality.

Fourth, objectors either don't realize or fail to mention that instream flow protection is not irreversible. Relative to existing allocations and values, instream flows currently have too little protection. But values and conditions can change. If at some point society determines that water being used instream would have greater value if used offstream, a new allocation can be made.

Fortunately, instream flow protection measures often do not have any adverse impact on other water uses. The fact that instream water uses are nonconsumptive greatly reduces the potential for conflict with other water uses. Rather than prohibiting the consumptive use of water, instream flow protection measures merely constrain the location at which diversions can occur. The impact of an instream flow requirement on other water uses decreases, all else being equal, as the location of the protected reach moves upstream. Though certainly not all river and stream reaches with valuable instream uses needing flow protection are located in headwater areas, the availability of sites where there is little potential for conflict—such as many sites in national forests and parks—provides instream flow protection advocates with opportunities to demonstrate to other water users that protection measures do not necessarily have to disrupt existing patterns of water use.

We do not mean to imply, however, that instream flow protection does not ever require hard choices and substantial costs. There are still many unprotected instream flows, particularly at lower elevations, that would provide greater benefits if left instream than if diverted for offstream use. In fact, the relative ease with which higher-elevation streams can be protected has caused much of the existing protection activity to take place there, leaving stream segments at lower elevations with very little protection. Many of the most substantial instream flow protection controversies are taking place, and will continue to take place, over river segments flowing through lower elevations. It is in these areas that the most care will have to be taken to ensure, first, that the water truly would be more valuable if used for instream purposes than if diverted for offstream use, and second, that the concerns of existing offstream water users are adequately addressed.

Because the protection of instream flows will require that at least some water currently allocated to offstream use be reallocated to instream use, we should not close without briefly discussing the sensitive topic of where that additional flow is to come from. Clearly, the answer in any given case will depend on the physical, legal, and economic circumstances of the particular river or stream at issue. And all current offstream uses are potential sources of increments in instream flow. Cities, because of their rapid growth, are generally viewed as a source of expanding need for offstream water use. However, the extensive water infrastructure built by municipalities—dams, reservoirs, canals, pipelines, and treatment facilities—provides many opportunities for enhanced instream flows through more efficient, better coordinated water flow management. And, as the Mono Lake decision made clear [see *infra* pp. 426–434], even relatively high-valued urban water uses are not immune to the sacrifices necessary to accommodate the new water allocations demanded by changing societal values.

The agricultural industry, however, is likely to provide most of the water that will eventually be reallocated to instream use, primarily because it is by far the largest offstream user of water. Irrigated agriculture accounts for 77 percent of all freshwater withdrawn from rivers, streams, and lakes and 90 percent of all water consumption in the West. Furthermore, most irrigation water in the West is used to grow feed grains and forage for livestock, or to grow cotton, rather than to directly feed the urban masses. The value added by water consumption in irrigated agriculture tends to be lower—especially when the water is used to grow feed grains, forage, and other low-value crops—than in other consumptive water uses.

It is important to keep in mind that the possibility of transferring water from agricultural use to instream use is likely to be fiercely resisted by many—though definitely not all—agricultural water users. Much of this resistance is due to fears that water will be taken from farmers involuntarily. Much is also due to the fact that instream flow protection is often perceived as a threat to a rural way of life that is increasingly challenged for other reasons as well. Instream flow advocates are not the only ones looking at the huge proportion of the West's water being used for agriculture. Municipalities, in particular, have been actively seeking to obtain a greater share of that water, and the adverse impacts of agricultural practices on water quality have drawn increased scrutiny now that so much headway has been made in controlling point sources of pollution. Other threats to the rural way of life such as expanding residential development, economic difficulties, and changing values and uses of our public lands have also contributed to a defensive mind-set on the part of many longtime rural residents.

William R. Travis, New Geographies of the American West: Land Use and the Changing Patterns of Place
31–32, 46–48, 51–53, 54–55, 63, 67 (2007).

* * *

The West's dry climate would seem to place an absolute limit on population growth, and its big spaces, its geographic barriers such as mountain ranges and canyons, and its widely separated cities should, in theory, retard development. The "friction of distance" should make commerce of any type slow and costly.

But instead of limiting growth, the West's large swaths of public land and its dramatic mountain, canyon, and desert terrain now *attract* and encourage development, from desert golf communities in Arizona and California to ranchettes in Montana and Wyoming. Newcomers, including CEOs who bring entire companies with them, cite the West's landscape and outdoor lifestyle as reasons for locating there. Even the region's aridity, long assumed to be the preeminent limit on western development, seems to have lost its power to retard growth. Enormous dams, tunnels, and canals that collect and move water across mountain ranges and through deserts, built originally for agriculture, now enable the spread of residential and commercial land uses throughout the region. If anything, there is too much water in the West, so much irrigation water (some 80–90 percent of water use in the region is still agriculture) looking for industrial and municipal buyers in a poor agricultural market that we have annihilated the West's aridity, or at least the role it might have played in limiting development. Rather than water attracting growth—or lack of water limiting it—growth itself attracts water. Even the worst-case drought can be managed by the region's adaptable, interconnected water systems.

Finally, our changing attitude toward wilderness (once dreaded, now loved; once only a place to visit or exploit, now a place in which to live or, at least, to live near) encourages western development. Instead of a foreboding, coarse landscape that resists settlement, we have made the West into a frictionless geography that welcomes settlement and development, even, perhaps especially, in its more remote, natural reaches.

* * *

Most explanations of regional growth start with population growth, but the real driving forces come one step before population growth. They include preferences that affect where people live, the economic and political forces driving immigration, and the demographic forces that govern in situ population growth. The New West School focuses on people's preferences as a force behind population growth. They are impressed with evidence that many—maybe most—Americans prefer small-town and rural life if they can get it. The West—even the West's cities—seems to offer this lifestyle. Geographers William Beyers and Peter Nelson argue that people are increasingly able to act on this preference because the West's economy, even in rural areas and small towns, has diversified. Increasing the value attached to outdoor amenities also drives both urban and nonurban growth in the west. The in-migration process reinforces itself, they contend, because amenity-seeking new arrivals create further economic opportunities for others in preferred locations.

* * *

Population Growth

Both components of immigration to the West—domestic and international migration—are strongly positive (meaning that more people arrive than leave). During most of the 1990s, for example, the Rocky Mountain states attracted more immigrants from all other census regions than they sent back. Even California showed a net out-migration to the Interior West for much of the 1990s. But California still grew because of net international immigration. * * *.

International immigration is a large, and controversial, driving force in western development. Although data on immigration are poor, we do know that most of the roughly 1 million documented immigrants to the United States each year settle in the West. * * *. Another 700,000 or so (perhaps significantly more) undocumented immigrants also enter the country each year, mostly in the West, and many stay permanently. * * *.

It is also worth noting that immigrants tend to be relatively young and exhibit relatively high fertility, thus ensuring future natural population increase in the region. Immigrants also build wealth, becoming consumers and homeowners. * * *.

The West also exhibits relatively high rates of "natural" population growth, meaning births over deaths. Its fertility rates are well above the national norm: the eleven western states average 71 births per 1,000 women of childbearing age, with Utah topping the chart at 92 births per 1,000 (compared to the national average of 66). This keeps the West relatively young, as evidenced by the broad-based current and projected population pyramids for most western states. But the region also attracts older domestic migrants. The coming American retirement boom will affect more than the traditional retirement spots in the desert Southwest. When author David Savageau updated *Retirement Places Rated* in the mid–1990s, he found his surveys pointing to nontraditional retirement magnets such as Sandpoint, Idaho, Kalispell, Montana, and Fort Collins, Colorado (which showed up as the highest-rated retirement spot in the country). * * *. With the United States on the verge of its biggest retirement surge in history (the U.S. population over 65 will grow from 31 million in 1990 to 53 million in 2020), retirees will continue to add their numbers and wealth to a region already booming with immigrants spanning the economic spectrum.

* * *

Thus the West presents a rare regional demographic profile: strong growth of all age cohorts and strong net positive immigration, both domestic and international. Indeed, many westerners sensed that their region was growing fast in the 1990s, and the 2000 census substantiated that feeling. The eleven western states grew by 10.2 million people in the 1990s, or by 20 percent (the national average rate was 13.2 percent). This growth continues a historical trend that has put the West ahead of the national growth rates for four consecutive decades. The Interior West topped the national charts of population growth, with Nevada, Arizona, Utah, Colorado, and Idaho making up the five fastest-growing states in the United States. These five states grew from 10.8 million to 14.9 million residents (4.1 million additional people, or a 37 percent increase: almost three times the national rate) during 1990–2000. The region's strength in all the components of population change is why most demographers expect it to lead the nation in growth for decades, and the Census Bureau's release in 2005 of population projections out to the year 2030 offered no real surprises for westerners. Current trends will continue, and the West will grow faster than the country as a whole, over the next three decades. Arizona and Nevada will more than double in population, and several Rocky Mountain States, such as Colorado, Utah, and Idaho, will add another one-third to one-half to their 2000 population. Even California, building on a huge base

(33.9 million), will grow by more than one-third. In all, some 28 million more people will live in the West by 2030 than in 2000.

Economic Growth

* * *. The traditional economic model puts jobs first: jobs created by industries located in a place because of some geographic attraction, such as an ore deposit, hydroelectric dam, or transportation node. In this "base economy" model, people then move to the jobs, earn incomes exporting raw materials or manufactured products, and create an economic ecology of additional jobs and a tax base that round out the community. Most economic analysts and development directors accept this model and put most of their efforts into luring employers. The director of Colorado's Office of State Planning and Budget, alluding to (and dismissing) the notion that Colorado is attractive to immigrants even when job growth is slow, stated what almost all development officers fundamentally believe: "The only reason people will be coming is if there are jobs."

A year later, Colorado's state demographer, noting a falloff in jobs, told the *Rocky Mountain News*: "What's sort of remarkable is the fact that we have lost a heck of a lot of jobs, and we still have people coming in." Still later, the *Denver Post* quoted the state's new demographer: "That we could lose 100,000 jobs from 2001 to 2003 and still see people moving here totally surprised us . . . It's completely contrary to the idea that people will follow jobs."

* * *

[T]he New West School believes that communities should pay more attention to the role that quality of life and individual preferences about where to live (preferences that might not maximize income) play in regional growth. They argue that indiscriminate job-grubbing, especially if it includes, as it often has in communities across the West, trying to keep a lumber mill or a mine open, or even to reopen closed mills and mines, may harm the very amenities that can secure the new economy. Towns that thrive after the chief old-economy employer closes down provide evidence for their argument. * * *

* * *. Urban economic development directors everywhere, from Phoenix to Seattle, argue that recreational attractions such as open space, trail systems, ski areas, and mountain and desert scenery are important selling points in their box of lures for relocating corporations (which, of course, also includes urban amenities such as professional sports teams, well-connected airports, and tax breaks).

But employees' locational preferences might also drive corporate strategy, to some extent, via both push and pull factors. * * * Level 3's CEO reported that he chose the Colorado Front Range location because a national survey of 500 college seniors and current high-tech employees revealed where and how his potential workforce wanted to live. He told the *Denver Post* that the area beat out high-tech enclaves near Boston, San Francisco, and the other usual suspects. Such corporate decisions can have multiplier effects. A local newspaper, profiling newcomers to the state, told the story of one family lured from Maryland by a Level 3 job (becoming four of the 44,614 immigrants to Colorado from other states in 1999). Besides the job, they cited quality of life as a draw, but we also learn in the profile that their move was presaged by a sister's move to Colorado from Texas and a brother's move from Pennsylvania. Then, after the family settled in, the husband's retired parents arrived from Florida. Our own preferences, and our ties to family and friends, help drive growth.

* * *

* * * Higher energy prices should be a brake on sprawl, but in the West, where the nation's largest energy reserves lie, higher energy prices mean more economic development and population growth.

* * *

Still, the physical environment seems to matter less and less. Development now attracts water, rather than vice versa: some towns with lots of water grow slowly, while others, including some of the driest, grow spectacularly. Build it and water will come, grow it and more water will come, in the New West.

D.   GEOGRAPHIC DIFFERENCES

Western Water Policy Review Advisory Commission, Water in the West: Challenge for the Next Century

2–1—2–9 (1998).

Water Defines the West

Topography and Climate

Water defines "the West." In this sense, the West is the 17 coterminous states located on and westward of the 100th meridian (North Dakota, South Dakota, Nebraska, Kansas, Oklahoma, Texas, Montana, Wyoming, Colorado, New Mexico, Idaho, Utah, Arizona, Washington, Oregon, Nevada, and California). The 100th meridian is a useful dividing point in the context of water use and management.... [P]recipitation rates east of the Great Plains average 40 inches or more but, beginning around the 100th meridian, much of the West sees less than 20 inches each year. John Wesley Powell, in his classic report on settlement possibilities in the region, pointed out that areas receiving less than 20 inches of rainfall annually would require supplemental irrigation to support agriculture.

Not all of the land contained within the western states meets the definition of "arid," however. Western Washington and Oregon and parts of the northern Rockies experience annual precipitation well above the 20–inch mark. The greatest amount of precipitation in the western United

States occurs on the Olympic Peninsula in western Washington, where more than 100 inches of rain falls each year. Streamflow to the Pacific Ocean, mostly from the Pacific Northwest region, is estimated to be over 335 million acre-feet per year, or nearly 70 percent of all runoff for the entire 17 western states.

Western precipitation is determined by the interaction of topography and marine influences. Air masses carrying atmospheric moisture over the region move generally from west to east, releasing moisture as they are forced to climb over the Sierra Nevada and Cascade mountain ranges of the Pacific coast and the Rocky Mountains. The lands to the east of these ranges experience a "rain shadow" effect, as the descending air masses are relatively dry. Precipitation also may vary dramatically from one year to the next as a result of a phenomenon called "El Nino/Southern Oscillation," in which changes in atmospheric pressures over the South Pacific affect sea surface temperatures in the Pacific Ocean and, consequently, influence precipitation through the western region.

In the years to come, the West's water supplies may also be influenced by human-induced climate change. The report prepared for the Western Water Policy Review Advisory Commission by Dr. Kathleen Miller describes a growing body of research indicating that many parts of the region may experience reduced water availability, particularly during the high-demand summer months. At the same time, the risk of winter or early spring floods may increase, especially in the West Coast states where warmer winter temperatures could be coupled with precipitation increases and an increased frequency of rain or snow in some areas. After reviewing the literature, Miller concluded that

> ... *the potential impacts of climate change on western water resources are serious enough to warrant attention in discussions of long-term policy directions and in the design of programs and institutions that are expected to have enduring impacts on the control and allocation of water resources (Miller, 1997).*

In particular, she suggested that water policies should include sufficient flexibility to respond to a wide range of possible hydrologic changes.

Streamflows and the River Environment

Once it leaves the atmosphere, water moves through the terrain in a variety of forms that determine the availability of water for human use and influence how aquatic systems function. Many areas of the West get the majority of their streamflows from melting snow, while parts of the Southwest depend on summer thunderstorms. Streamflow is made up of three components, all related to precipitation:

(1) Surface runoff, which depends on evaporation, plant transpiration, and the rate of soil infiltration.

(2) Subsurface runoff, composed of precipitation that infiltrates the soil and moves laterally toward water bodies.

(3) Base flow, or precipitation that percolates through the soil into groundwater and then enters the stream channel after a time lag.

Western streamflows are noted for their great variability because they are dependent on unstable and unpredictable atmospheric processes that operate well beyond the region. Each year, approximately 1.5 billion acre-feet of water is added to the western United States as precipitation, the majority of which is consumed by evapotranspiration; roughly 500 million acre-feet (maf) constitute the measured flow in western streams, and 50 maf are added annually to groundwater.

The Colorado River illustrates the great variability in western river-flows. During the period immediately preceding negotiation of the Colorado River Compact in 1922 (from 1906–21), the estimated natural annual flow of the river averaged 18.1 maf. Negotiators assumed they had a surplus of water by basing their discussions on an estimated flow of 16.5 maf, but subsequent experience and tree-ring studies revealed that the river's annual natural flow from 1906–94 averaged 15.1 maf. Moreover, yearly fluctuations have been dramatic, ranging from 4.4 maf to more than 22 maf.

Native plant and animal communities have adapted to the dramatic variations in western water supplies. For example, the Southwest once contained many marshlands (ciénegas) adjacent to rivers, which moderated fluctuations, retained and recycled nutrients, and served as refuges, nurseries, and rich feeding grounds for aquatic animals. Many riparian plant species have evolved to depend on periodic flooding for successful propagation. Native fish, too, adapted their reproduction patterns around natural fluctuations. Some species require the slow, warm backwaters created by seasonal drops in river levels for successful egg and young fish survival; others depend on fast runoff flows to flush young fish out to sea.

River ecosystems extend beyond their flowing waters. The riparian zone includes virtually all of a river's flood plain, where river water supplements water available from other sources. The abundant vegetation growing in a riparian zone serves many purposes: reducing soil erosion rates; slowing floodwaters; enhancing groundwater recharge and maintaining an elevated water table; improving water quality by filtering sediment, nutrients, and pollutants from surface runoff; maintaining biodiversity by providing critical habitat to species using adjacent uplands; supplying shade and overhanging banks for fishes and other aquatic organisms; and offering diverse and increasingly popular recreational opportunities for human populations. Until recently, many of these important functions were not recognized, and riparian zones were under-appreciated as important components of functioning rivers.

Western Water: A Working Resource

Harnessing Water for Human Uses

Given the variable precipitation (seasonally and year-to-year), storage of water during high-flow periods has been necessary to ensure reliable deliveries during times of high demand. In the United States as a whole, there are 2,654 reservoirs and controlled natural lakes with capacities of 5,000 acre-feet or more; together they hold about 480 million acre-feet of water. Over two-thirds of this total capacity (324.6 million acre-feet) is provided by reservoirs in the western water regions. Reservoir capacity as a proportion of land area is greatest in the Upper Colorado region (defined as the Colorado River drainage above Lee's Ferry), where 366 acre-feet of water is stored per square mile; in the Great Basin region, by contrast, only 24 acre-feet of storage exists per square mile.

Dams on the Colorado River can store 4 years of the river's typical annual flow. * * *

Groundwater aquifers serve as both primary and secondary sources of water supply. In 1985, approximately 92.7 maf of the United States' freshwater supply came from groundwater—nearly a quarter of the total supply for the nation. Of the pumped groundwater, 62.5 maf (67 percent) went to irrigation. In 1990, water uses in the 17 western states pumped about 58 maf of groundwater, of which nearly 46 maf (79 percent) went to irrigation. About two-thirds of all the groundwater pumping in the nation was concentrated in eight states: California (23 maf), Texas (8.9 maf), Nebraska (8 maf), Idaho (7 maf), Kansas (6.3 maf), Arizona (4.7 maf), Arkansas (4.5 maf), and Florida (4.2 maf).

A large proportion of the West's groundwater comes from the High Plains regional aquifer, which underlies about 174,000 square miles in six states (Nebraska, Colorado, Kansas, New Mexico, Texas, and Oklahoma) and includes the 134,000 square-mile Ogallala aquifer. The High Plains aquifer sustains 20 percent of the irrigated acreage and provides 30 percent of all irrigation water pumped within the United States. About 16,000 square miles of the regional aquifer experienced water level declines of more than 50 feet as of 1980, and 50,000 square miles declined more than 10 feet, attributed to accelerated pumping for irrigation. A maximum decline of almost 200 feet occurred in Floyd County, Texas. In some locations in Nebraska, aquifer levels have risen as a result of recharge from canal irrigation using water directly from the Platte River. Overall, however, the U.S. Geological Survey (USGS) has projected severe depletions in the High Plains region by the year 2020, with Texas suffering more than the other states that share this water source. Throughout the region, groundwater overdraft continues to be a problem.

Water is being increasingly reclaimed through wastewater treatment and reuse. In 1990, approximately 553,000 acre-feet of reclaimed wastewater was used in the 19 western states, an increase of about 25 percent from 1985. The USGS has identified a trend in tapping reclaimed water as a source for industrial uses, with four states dominating the statistics: Arizona, California, Nevada, and Texas. Since 1960, use of reclaimed water in the industrial sector has increased from 784 acre-feet to 30,800 acre-feet in 1990, but its role as an alternative source of supply remains limited because of cost and public concerns. Several studies have shown that the public is wary about accepting reclaimed wastewater for domestic uses, although people tend to view it as appropriate for such applications as fighting fires, watering golf courses and parks, and cleaning streets. Water recycling is particularly advantageous in Pacific or Gulf Coast States where wastewater is otherwise discharged to the ocean, or in states where wastewater is irretrievably lost to saline sinks.

Water supplies are being augmented by new technologies to supplement the West's traditional reliance on storage. Most experts agree that the era of large federal dam building, as experienced in the first 70 years of this century, is over. However, municipal and industrial water suppliers expect to construct smaller facilities, many of which will provide offstream water storage. Several such projects are under construction in California, among them the Eastside Reservoir in Riverside County and Los Vaqueros Reservoir in Contra Costa County. In addition, existing dams are being altered to enlarge reservoir capacities. In Arizona, for example, the Theodore Roosevelt Dam was renovated to add 300,000 acre-feet to its reservoir, and the New Waddell Dam enlarged the existing Lake Pleasant Reservoir by nearly 700,000 acre-feet.

Other strategies to stretch water supplies include: groundwater recharge and conjunctive use of surface and groundwater (managing surface and groundwater supplies as a single source); reoperation or management modification of existing storage facilities; encouraging water efficiency improvements; providing incentives for land fallowing, either permanently or only on a "dry-year option"; desalination and treatment of seawater or other brackish waters; using "gray water" for irrigation; weather modification (cloud seeding); delaying snowmelt through vegetative manipulation in upper watersheds; and importing water from areas of available water supply to areas of growing demand.

* * *

Benefits of Federal Water Storage and Delivery Systems

In physical terms alone, the accomplishments of water developers in the West are impressive, and the key role of the federal government is obvious. Working together, federal and state governments and local interests have provided the water infrastructure to support a high level of agricultural and urban growth.

The U.S. Bureau of Reclamation (Reclamation) is responsible for the largest portion of water storage in federal reservoirs in the West. Reclamation has sole responsibility for the operation of reservoirs with a total capacity of more than 119 maf and shares responsibility for the operation of reservoirs with an additional 16 maf of storage. A recent report by the General Accounting Office estimated that the federal government, through Reclamation, has spent $21.8 billion to construct 133 water projects in the western United States. Water provided by Reclamation in 1991 produced agricultural crops valued at nearly $9 billion; 48 billion kilowatt hours of electricity sold for $727 million; and more than 50 million recreational visitor days.

The U.S. Army Corps of Engineers (Corps) is solely or partially responsible for the operation of reservoirs in the West with a total capacity of more than 103 maf. The U.S. Department of Agriculture (USDA), primarily through the Forest Service, operates and maintains reservoirs totaling more than 25.7 maf. The Bureau of Indian Affairs operates and maintains reservoirs with a total storage capacity of more than 2.3 maf, and the U.S. Fish and Wildlife Service (Service) operates reservoirs with a total capacity of slightly more than 704,000 acre-feet. The Department of Energy, through the Federal Energy Regulatory Commission, shares responsibility for the operation of more than 2.1 maf of storage throughout the West.

As it has in irrigation water supply, the federal government has played an important role in hydroelectric power generation constructing and operating more than half of the total hydroelectric generating capacity in the West. The total installed hydropower capacity in the United States, according to Federal Energy Regulatory Commission, is 73,494 megawatts, or roughly 10 percent of total national electric generation capacity. (By comparison, coal is used in 40 percent of the nation's capacity). However, in the West, especially in the Pacific Northwest, hydropower plays a larger role.

* * *

Figure 3. Average Annual Precipitation

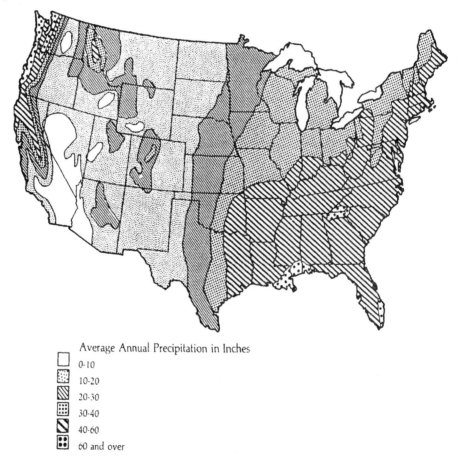

Average Annual Precipitation in Inches
☐ 0-10
▦ 10-20
▨ 20-30
▦ 30-40
◪ 40-60
⦂ 60 and over

Source: Mohamed T. El–Ashry & Diana C. Gibbons, Troubled Waters: New Policies for Managing Water in the American West 8 (1986).

[T]here are 51,468 megawatts of installed hydropower capacity on western river basins. This is roughly 70 percent of national hydropower capacity. It amounts to about one-third of all installed electric generation capacity in the region, a substantially higher percentage than its share nationally. The higher percentage of hydropower in the West is largely a result of hydropower's dominant position in the Pacific Northwest, where hydropower comprises about 68 percent of all generation capacity.

Joseph W. Dellapenna, Issues Arising Under Riparian Rights: Replacing Common–Law Riparian Rights With Regulated Riparianism *in* Water Rights of the Eastern United States (Kenneth R. Wright ed.)

35–48 (1998).

* * *

To the east of Kansas City, people have always considered water to be readily available at little or no cost. Although there might be serious problems with water quality arising from human activities, shortages historically were rare and short-lived. * * * To the West of Kansas City, people considered water to be scarce, or at least misplaced. * * *

* * *

In the eastern states, demand for water continues to increase and precipitation patterns seem to have become more erratic, with recurring water shortages becoming more frequent. For example, the Delaware River Basin Commission has declared no less than four water emergencies since 1980. There no longer is enough water to satisfy all needs in eastern states. For the first time, users of water in eastern states frequently find that their need for water is in conflict with the needs of other, formerly compatible users. The predictable result is a considerable increase in the number of disputes over the allocation of water (quantity disputes), although disputes over the pollution of water (quality disputes) remain common and generally are better publicized. Pollution itself is one source of the growing inadequacy of water relative to demand in eastern states.

E. CLIMATE VARIABILITY

Perhaps the greatest challenge facing water managers is adaptation to global climate change. There is a widespread consensus in the scientific community that global temperatures are rising, due in part to the continued emission of greenhouse gases. Society faces three choices: do nothing, mitigate, oradapt. If we do nothing, which is the current approach; greenhouse emissions will continue to increase. Addressing the problem means mitigating the change by reducing emissions or adapting to the changed conditions or a combination of mitigation and adaptation. Water managers must consider adaptation since the benefits of mitigation will not be felt, if ever, until decades after the initial reductions take place. That is, they must assume that there will be a drier, warmer atmosphere with major impacts on the hydrological assumptions for the operation of water projects and upon which water rights systems and pollution control regimes are based.

Most scientific forecasts are that climate is becoming more variable. Both floods and droughts may become more frequent. Lower net run-offs on major river and lake systems will disrupt hydropower production and navigation. Warmer lakes will see prolonged oxygen depletion in the lower levels and significant changes in their ecosystems. Groundwater recharge may decrease in some areas such as the Ogallala Aquifer of the Great Plains and increase in others.

The following excerpt from a U.S. government report draws heavily on the findings of the Intergovernmental Panel on Climate Change (IPCC), an international scientific body that analyzes the science of climate change and provides information to government decision makers.

Committee on Environment and Natural Resources, National Science and Technology Council, Scientific Assessment of Global Change on the United States

145–149, 154–155 (2008).

* * *

Overall, the IPCC made the following conclusions:

- The negative impacts of climate change on freshwater systems outweigh the benefits (*high confidence*).

- All IPCC regions show an overall net negative impact of climate change on water resources and freshwater ecosystems (*high confidence*).

- Areas in which runoff is projected to decline are *likely* to face a reduction in the value of the services provided by water resources (*very high confidence*).

- The beneficial impacts of increased annual runoff in other areas will be tempered by the negative effects of increased precipitation variability and seasonal runoff shifts on water supply, water quality, and flood risks (*high confidence*).

- The impacts of climate change on freshwater systems and their management are mainly due to the observed and projected increases in temperature, sea level, and precipitation variability (*very high confidence*).

- More than one-sixth of the world's population lives in glacier- or snow-melt-fed river basins and will be affected by the seasonal shift in streamflow, an increase in the ratio of winter to annual flows, and possibly the reduction in low flows caused by decreased glacier extent or snow water storage (*high confidence*).

Surface water and precipitation

The primary driver of the land surface hydrologic system is precipitation. Current vulnerabilities of the system are strongly tied to precipitation variability. Observed trends in both are reviewed here. The IPCC Fourth Assessment Report found that climate induced changes in river flows and lake and wetland levels depend on changes in the volume, timing, and intensity of precipitation and snowmelt, as well as the amount of precipitation falling as snow or rain. Precipitation is expected to increase globally with important regional variations. Current observations show increased precipitation over land north of 30° N from 1901 to 2005 and decreases over land between 10° S and 30° N after the 1970s. Snow cover and glaciers are decreasing in most regions, particularly in spring. Permafrost is thawing between 0.02 m per year (Alaska) and 0.4 m per year (Tibetan Plateau). In many cases, precipitation may be more variable, with increases in one season followed by decreases in another. Intensified droughts have been observed in some drier regions since the 1970s. Changes in evapotranspiration driven by temperature, radiation, atmospheric humidity, increased atmospheric CO_2 concentration, and wind speed can offset small increases in precipitation and intensify the effects of decreased precipitation on surface waters.

Effects vary across catchments depending on specific physical, hydrological, and geological characteristics. Current observations have identified highly variable streamflows globally, with increases in some basins and declines in others. Warming temperatures have resulted in earlier spring peak flows and increased winter base flows in North America and Eurasia. Catchments that are already stressed due to non-climatic drivers are highly vulnerable to additional impacts. In addition, vulnerability to precipitation variability is highest in semi-arid and arid low-income countries, where precipitation and streamflow are concentrated over a few months, and where year-to-year variations are high. Without adequate storage infrastructure, these regions are highly vulnerable to current climate variability and expected increases in variability with future climate change.

Human water use has resulted in reduced water levels in many lakes worldwide. In some cases, declining precipitation was also a significant cause (e.g., in the case of Lake Chad, where both decreased precipitation and increased human water use account for the observed decrease in lake area since the 1960s). For the many lakes, rivers, and wetlands that have shrunk mainly due to human water use and drainage, climate change is expected to exacerbate the situation if it results in reduced net water availability (precipitation minus evapotranspiration). Observations have also identified warming lake temperatures and reduction in ice cover on lakes worldwide.

Surface water availability and precipitation differ greatly across the United States. Generally, conditions become increasingly dry from east to west. However, conditions in the upslope areas of the Cascade and coastal mountain ranges, especially in the Pacific Northwest, are much more humid. The driest climates occur in the Intermountain West and the Southwest. Precipitation variability follows similar trends with less variability in the humid areas (eastern United States and Pacific Northwest) and the greatest variability in the arid and semiarid West. The IPCC concluded with *high confidence* that semi-arid and arid areas are particularly exposed to the impacts of climate change on freshwater.

Specific to the United States, the IPCC identified the following trends in surface water supply, precipitation patterns, and snowpack (Field et al., 2007):

- Streamflow in the eastern United States has increased 25% in the last 60 years, but over the last century has decreased by about 2% per decade in the central Rocky Mountain region.

- Since 1950, stream discharge in both the Colorado and Columbia River Basins has decreased, while over the same time period annual evapotranspiration from the conterminous United States increased by 55 mm.

- In regions with winter snow, warming has shifted the magnitude and timing of hydrologic events. The fraction of annual precipitation falling as rain (rather than snow) increased at 74% of the weather stations studied in the western mountains of the United States from 1949 to 2004.

- In Canada, warming from 1900 to 2003 led to a decrease in total precipitation as snowfall in the West and on the Prairies.

- Spring and summer snow cover has decreased in the U.S. West. April snow water equivalent has declined 15 to 30% since 1950 in the western mountains of North America, particularly at lower elevations and primarily due to warming rather than changes in precipitation.

- Streamflow peaks in the snowmelt-dominated western mountains of the United States occurred one to four weeks earlier in 2002 than in 1948.

- Breakup of river and lake ice across North America has advanced by 0.2 to 12.9 days over the last 100 years.

Data from 167 stream gauge stations over the period 1939 to 1998 found increasing streamflows over time in the eastern United States with a more or less reverse pattern in the western United States, with an onset of dry conditions beginning in the 1980s. Similar to global observations, U.S. effects will vary from region to region.

As for the Arctic, research reviewed in the Arctic Climate Impact Assessment concluded that precipitation has increased by about 1% per decade over the past century although the results are highly variable spatially. Much of the increase has fallen as rain, with the largest increases occurring in autumn and winter. The ice season has been reduced by one to three weeks in some areas from a combination of later freeze-up and earlier breakup of river and lake ice. Glaciers throughout North America are melting. Alaskan glaciers are melting particularly fast and represent about half of the estimated loss of glacial mass worldwide. Permafrost plays an important role in providing an impermeable surface and forming lakes and ponds. The spatial pattern of lake disappearance strongly suggests that permafrost thawing is driving the changes. In the Arctic, river discharge to the ocean has increased during the past few decades, and peak flows in the spring are occurring earlier. These changes are projected to accelerate with future climate change. Snow cover extent in Alaska is projected to decrease by 10 to 20% by the 2070s, with greatest declines in spring.

Projected impacts

The following conclusions were drawn * * *:

- There is a trend toward reduced mountain snowpack and earlier spring snowmelt runoff peaks across much of the western United States. Evidence suggests this trend is very likely attributable, at least in part, to long-term warming, although some part may have been played by decadal-scale variability, including a shift in the Pacific Decadal Oscillation (PDO) in the late 1970s. Where shifts to earlier snowmelt peaks and reduced summer and fall low flows have already been detected, continuing shifts in this direction are expected and may have substantial impacts on the performance of reservoir systems.

- The most recent (IPCC Fourth Assessment Report) climate model simulations project increased runoff over the eastern United States, gradually transitioning to little change in the Missouri and lower Mississippi, to substantial decreases in annual runoff in the interior of the West (Colorado and Great Basin). The projected drying in the interior of the West is quite consistent among models. These changes are, very roughly, consistent with observed trends in the second half of the 20th century, which show increased streamflow over most of the United States, but sporadic decreases in the West.

- Snowpacks in the mountainous headwaters regions of the western United States generally declined over the second half of the 20th century, especially at lower elevations and in locations where average winter temperatures are close to or above 0°C. These trends toward reduced winter snow accumulation and earlier spring melt are also reflected in a tendency toward earlier runoff peaks in the spring, a shift that has not occurred in rainfall-dominated watersheds in the same region.

- Climate model projections of increased temperatures and slight precipitation increases indicate that modest streamflow increases are expected in the East, but that larger (in absolute value) declines are expected in the West, where the balance between precipitation and evaporative demand changes will be dominated by increased evaporative demand. However, because of the uncertainty in climate model projections of precipitation change, future projections of streamflow are highly uncertain across most of the United States. One exception is watersheds that are dominated by spring and summer snowmelt, most of which are in the western United States. In these cases, where shifts to earlier snowmelt peaks and reduced summer and fall low flows have already begun to be detected, continuing shifts in this direction are generally expected and may have substantial impacts on the performance of reservoir systems.

Groundwater

Relatively few studies have assessed the sensitivity of groundwater systems to a changing climate.

The available research suggests that groundwater systems generally respond more slowly to climate change than surface water systems. In general, groundwater levels correlate most strongly with precipitation, but temperature becomes more important for shallow aquifers, especially during warm periods. With climate change, availability of groundwater is expected to be influenced by changes in withdrawals (reflecting development, human and agricultural demand, and availability of other sources) and recharge (determined by temperature, timing, and amount of precipitation, and surface water interactions) (*medium confidence*). In general, simulated aquifer levels respond to changes in temperature, precipitation, and the level of withdrawal.

According to the IPCC, base flows were found to decrease in scenarios that are drier or have higher pumping rates, and increase in wetter scenarios on average across world regions. The IPCC projects that efforts to offset declining surface water availability due to increasing precipitation variability will be hampered by the fact that groundwater recharge will decrease considerably in some already water-stressed regions (*high confidence*) where vulnerability is often exacerbated by the rapid increase in population and water demand (*very high confidence*). This is expected to be particularly acute in some waterstressed regions, such as the southwestern United States. Projections for the Ogallala aquifer region show that natural groundwater recharge decreases more than 20% in all simulations with different climate models and future warming scenarios of 2.5°C or greater. Groundwater resources can also be adversely impacted in coastal areas by saltwater intrusion from sea level rise. In addition, they conclude that sea level rise will extend areas of salinization of groundwater and estuaries, resulting in a decrease in freshwater availability for humans and ecosystems in coastal areas (*very high confidence*).

* * *

Implications for water users

On global water use, the IPCC drew the following conclusions:

- Climate change affects the function and operation of existing water infrastructure as well as water management practices (*very high confidence*).

- Adverse effects of climate on freshwater systems aggravate the impacts of other stresses, such as population growth, changing economic activity, land use change, and urbanization (*very high confidence*).

- Globally, water demand will grow in the coming decades, primarily due to population growth and increased affluence. Regionally, large changes in irrigation water demand as a result of climate change are *likely* (*high confidence*).

- Current water management practices are *very likely* to be inadequate to reduce the negative impacts of climate change on water supply reliability, flood risk, health, energy, and aquatic ecosystems (*very high confidence*). Improved incorporation of current climate variability into water-related management would make adaptation to future climate change easier (*very high confidence*).

In the United States, many competing water uses will be adversely affected by climate change impacts on water supply and quality. The IPCC reviewed a number of studies describing the impacts of climate change on water uses in the United States that showed the following:

- Decreased water supply and lower water levels are likely to exacerbate challenges relating to navigation in the United States. Some studies have found that low flow conditions may restrict ship loading in shallow ports and harbors. However, navigational benefits from climate change exist as well. For example, the navigation season for the Northern Sea Route is projected to increase from the current 20 to 30 days per year to 90 to 100 days by 2080.

- Climate change impacts on water supply and quality will affect agricultural practices, including the increase in irrigation demand in dry regions and the aggravation of nonpoint source water pollution (e.g., pollution from urban areas, roads, or agricultural fields) problems in areas susceptible to intense rainfall events and flooding.

- The U.S. energy sector, which relies heavily on water for generation (hydropower) and cooling capacity, will be adversely impacted by changes in water supply and quality in reservoirs and other water bodies.

Less reliable supplies of water are expected to create challenges for managing urban water systems as well as for industries that depend on large volumes of water. U.S. water managers currently anticipate local, regional, or statewide water shortages over the next 10 years. Threats to reliable supply are complicated by high population growth rates in western states where many resources are at or approaching full utilization. The IPCC reviewed several regional-level studies of climate change impacts on U.S. water management that showed the following:

- In the Great Lakes–St. Lawrence Basin, many, but not all, assessments project lower net basin supplies and lake water levels. Lower water levels are *likely* to influence many sectors, with multiple, interacting impacts. These impacts are projected with *high confidence*, in which atmosphere—lake interactions contribute to the uncertainty in assessment.

- Urban water supply systems in North America often draw water from considerable distances, so climate impacts need not be local to affect cities. By the 2020s, 41% of the water supply to southern California is *likely* to be vulnerable due to snowpack loss in the Sierra Nevada mountains and the Colorado River Basin.

- The New York area will *likely* experience greater water supply variability. New York City's system can *likely* adapt to future changes, but the region's smaller systems may be vulnerable, leading to a need for enhanced regional water distribution plans.

Drawing on these studies, the IPCC concluded that climate change will constrain North America's over-allocated water resources, increasing competition among agricultural, municipal, industrial, and ecological uses (*very high confidence*). Rising temperatures will diminish snowpack and increase evaporation, affecting seasonal availability of water. Higher demand from economic development, agriculture, and population growth will further limit surface and groundwater availability. In the Great Lakes and major river systems across the United States, lower water levels are *likely* to exacerbate challenges relating to water quality, navigation, recreation, hydropower generation, water transfers, and bi-national relationships.

NOTES

1. You are the manager of an irrigation district in the western United States near an expanding urban area. Should you try to resist the conversion of land from agriculture to housing because climate impact assessments predict decreased crop yields in Mediterranean areas in Europe, Australia, and South America that face increased aridity? Or should you encourage the conversion? The IPCC Report summarizes studies that predict a decline in irrigated acreage and withdrawals of water for irrigation in the United States due to higher temperatures and greater yields by rain-fed crops as precipitation increases in non-arid areas. In addition to reducing the demand for irrigation, some experts recommend that imports of food be increased to create virtual water. However, the IPCC Report also counsels that "[t]hese studies do not take into account the increasing variability of daily precipitation, and, as such, rain-fed yields are probably overestimated." Intergovernmental Panel on Climate Change, Climate Change and Water: IPCC Technical Paper VI at 62 (2008).

2. Although there is consensus on the reality of climate change, is there enough information for water resource planners to take action? The IPCC Report says that uncertainty pervades all stages of assessment "from the range of climate model projections for a given scenario, the downscaling of climate effects to local/regional scales, impacts assessments, and feedback from adaptation and mitigation activities." *Id.* at 135. It also says that "[e]xamples of concrete actions in the water sector to adapt specifically and solely to a changing climate are very rare. This is partly because change may only be one of the many drivers affecting strategies and investment plans (and it may not be the most important one over the short-term planning horizon), and partly due to uncertainty in projections of future hydrological changes." *Id.* at. 49.

3. As you learn more about water law, ask yourself how well existing legal regimes lend themselves to adaptation. One strategy is the construction of new dams and reservoirs, and water law has long promoted the capture and storage of water. Likewise, the increased use of groundwater will be allowed under many groundwater laws. Water transfers have long been a part of water law at the urging of economists but they remain controversial. Water conservation from the farm to the city was a policy objective before global climate change but now it becomes increasingly more important. Does current law provide the kind of flexibility for water managers and users to adapt to climate change impacts? What further legal changes could provide such flexibility?

F. Economic Forces

Terry L. Anderson & Pamela Snyder, Water Markets: Priming the Invisible Pump

7–12 (1997).

What Causes a Crisis?

It is true that "the energy crisis and the water shortage are inextricably linked," but the connection is probably more subtle than most people understand. Rising energy prices have made supplying water more costly, but the general link between energy and water is more directly related to the extent to which prices are allowed to influence demand and supply. In economic terms, a crisis exists when the quantity demanded is greater than the quantity available and when there is little time to adjust either of them. This is exactly what the energy crisis was and what any water crisis is likely to be. The question is, why does quantity demanded not equal quantity supplied?

The 1970s taught us an important lesson: When government regulations keep fuel prices below market-clearing levels, shortages inevitably follow. Further, once shortages occur and as price controls block normal market mechanisms, government is forced into the business of allocating scarce supplies. Federal price controls for gasoline and the blundering attempts to allocate gasoline in 1974 and 1979 had social costs that far exceeded the limited relief provided to gasoline purchasers. Experience around the world has demonstrated over and over again that the only successful way to avoid fuel shortages is to rely on free-market pricing and allocation.

The same circumstances are causing problems with water. Water prices have been kept artificially low, and the inevitable shortages have followed. Governments have responded by attempting to restrain demand, ration water, and increase the available supply. For example, in the face of the California drought in the late 1980s through early 1990s municipalities implemented rationing, began constructing desalinization plants, paid thousands of dollars for cloud seeding, and in 1991, the state cut off supplies to farmers. Nevertheless, except in isolated cases where shortages have been caused by drought and where a cooperative community spirit has developed, efforts to ration water have not been successful. Increased water supplies have only been made possible through the construction of massive water projects, which have dammed many of our free-flowing rivers. These projects have been extremely costly, and it is doubtful that Congress will continue to fund them. If not, water crises will continue to arise apart from a price mechanism operating on water supply and demand.

Could Markets Do Better?

In arguing that the price mechanism has not been allowed to work for allocating water, there is the implicit assumption that price rationing could help resolve water crises. At higher prices people tend to consume less of a commodity and search for alternative means of achieving their desired ends. Water is no exception. * * *

The actual responsiveness of water consumption to price changes will vary among regions with the variations depending on such variables as income and precipitation. In their study of six subregions of the United States, Bruce Beattie and Henry Foster (1980) found that a 10 percent increase in the price of water would produce between a 3.75 and 12.63 percent decrease in urban residential water consumption. The Northern California and Pacific Northwest region, with its abundant rainfall, was the most responsive, and the arid Southwest region was the least responsive. While these estimates may suggest that higher water prices could reduce consumption, it must be noted that in 57 percent of the 23 cities studied real water prices declined between 1960 and 1976. Only three cities had real water rate increases of more than $1 per 1,000 cubic feet per year. Beattie and Foster concluded that

> the water utility industry has done a good job for consumers. Unfortunately, because of this good job water users have adjusted their way of life so that needs for water are great.... Thus, how much water consumers need depends not only on willingness and ability to pay, but most importantly on the real price charged. If it is a lot, only a modest amount of water is needed. If the charge is a little, a lot is needed. The choice is largely up to the water utility industry.

Similar data suggest that the agricultural sector demand for water is also price-responsive. Demand responsiveness varies by crops, of course, but some aggregate estimates for California show that a 10 percent increase in price would bring about a 6.5 percent decrease in water consumption. The same price increase would cause an overall average consumption decrease of 3.7 percent for the 17 Western states. Estimates for homogeneous production areas in California show that at a price of $17, a 10 percent increase in price would yield a 20 percent decrease in water use. These relatively large responses in quantity demanded to changes in price, known as elasticity of demand, indicate that farmers in homogeneous production areas

> would not be using all the water DWR (the California Department of Water Resources) was planning to send them—at the price DWR was planning to charge.... [T]he marginal cost of water to the farmer would have to be reduced between $4 and $6 per acre-foot (from a contractual price of $14.70 per acre-foot in one HPA [homogeneous production area] and $16.36 in the other) before DWR's projected 1 million acres would be brought into production.

The implications are significant. If water prices are kept low, more demands will be placed on water resources. The additional water use will be subject to diminishing returns—the last units consumed will generate much less value than the first. What is seen as waste or inefficient water use in rural and urban areas is simply the users' rational response to low water prices. When water for lawns is left to run into storm gutters or when irrigation water erodes the field without reaching the roots of the plant, it is easy to say that users are being wasteful. But users can afford to be wasteful only when water is cheap. In agriculture, if water carried a higher price, it is likely that less water would be applied to any given crop, that different irrigation technology or water application practices would be used, and that different cropping patterns might appear.

Research conducted at the University of California suggests that reduced water application would decrease most crop yields but that at higher water prices such reduction would be economical. Flood irrigation techniques conserve labor but use large amounts of water. With high water prices, it makes sense to substitute labor and capital for water and to use drip irrigation or similar techniques. * * *

In motivating agricultural consumers to reduce consumption through improved irrigation techniques and modified cropping patterns, higher water prices would free up irrigation water for municipal and other uses. It is estimated that if 5 percent of agricultural water were transferred to municipal use, the needs of urban areas in the western United States would be met for the next 25 years. Higher water prices would also reduce the need to build costly supply projects and delivery systems that dam and divert free-flowing streams. Higher prices would encourage private, profit-making firms to enter the water supply industry, taking the burden off the public treasury. If the price mechanism were allowed to operate, demand could be reduced, supply could be increased, water would be reallocated, and water crises could become obsolete.

Five years of drought moved Californians toward various pricing mechanisms to reduce demand for water and reallocate the scarce supplies. In

1991, when water supplies from the State Water Project and the federal Central Valley Project were cut, some cities, such as Santa Barbara, began using an escalating price scale for water to encourage conservation. Rather than regulating water consumption, or using the state's regulatory power to shift water from one use to another, California Governor Pete Wilson opted to facilitate water marketing by creating the California Drought Emergency Water Bank. Under the Bank system, the Department of Water Resources bought water from farmers for $125 per acre-foot (most farmers pay less than $50 per acre-foot), and made the water available for other uses according to extreme critical needs. In so doing, the Department "guarantee[d] sellers that the transactions [would not] be regarded . . . as evidence of available surplus water or of wasteful or inefficient use on the part of the seller." Apart from this guarantee, sellers would risk losing their water rights under the "use-it-or-lose-it" rule of California water law. Water users jumped at the opportunity afforded by the Bank, which quickly exceeded its goal of purchasing 500,000 acre-feet of water.

While the Water Bank was a step in the right direction, Governor Wilson stopped short of creating a true market, because only the Bank was authorized to buy water under the plan. In addition, limitations on the sale of federal water from the Bureau of Reclamation's Central Valley Project effectively prevented those water users from selling their water to the state.

Passage of the Central Valley Project Improvement Act changed that by allowing water from the Central Valley Project to be traded outside the project area at fair market prices. The act, part of an omnibus water bill signed by President Bush on October 30, 1992, also established a tiered pricing system for project water, a major change from the long-held policy of providing federal reclamation water to farmers at subsidized prices. Both the water trading and the tiered pricing system for project water provide market incentives to farmers for improved efficiency and conservation.

In addition to providing market incentives to conserve water, however, the Central Valley Project Improvement Act also set aside 800,000 acre-feet, or about 10 percent of project water, for environmental purposes, such as restoration and protection of fisheries, wetlands, and water quality. Exactly where this water will come from and how it will be used remains to be seen.

Charles W. Howe, Protecting Values in a Water Market Setting: Improving Water Markets to Increase Economic Efficiency and Equity

3 Denv. U. Water L. Rev. 357, 361–66 (2000).

* * *

Public values are values that are unlikely to be taken into account by private transactors in the market process. In the water resources area, these values include the unique importance of social and cultural values generated by water, the important instream values that are not protected by property rights, external costs imposed directly on other parties due to jurisdictional boundaries that relieve water users of liability for damage, and the "secondary economic impacts" imposed on areas-of-origin, especially agricultural communities when agricultural water use is substantially reduced. The importance of these values, in the case of water transfers, implies that market-based transactions in water are likely to generate inefficiencies and inequities to a greater extent than market-based transactions in other sectors of the economy. Ignoring or under-weighting these values can occur for various reasons as discussed in detail below.

Due largely to these highly visible, negative impacts on public values, there has been increasing resistance to water marketing and, in particular, to out-of-basin transfers of water. Recent newspaper citizen letters have expressed concerns. In Colorado, legislation has been introduced in several recent legislative sessions to prohibit or constrain out-of-basin transfers. It is worthwhile, therefore, to identify these public values, to determine the extent to which they warrant protection, and to explore ways in which this protection might be provided without foregoing the advantages of water markets.

A.   SOCIAL AND CULTURAL VALUES GENERATED BY WATER

Many community values cannot be captured in monetary terms but warrant consideration in decisions about water transfers. A recent study points out that water is one of the most attractive visual elements of the landscape and that in arid landscapes, especially, there is a wide range of cultural, spiritual, and religious values related to water. Current policies for water management address only a few of the relevant human values. This is particularly true in traditional, low-income communities in which water often plays an important symbolic, cultural role. In the Southwestern United States, the acequia system not only supports local agricultural needs, but also maintains social cohesion because maintenance of the canals and distribution of the water are community efforts. Costilla County, Colorado, provides a good demonstration of the acequia community's cohesion: the village of San Luis, Colorado has banded together to fight the degradation of its waters caused by logging on the adjacent Taylor Ranch.

In these old systems, the water rights typically belong to the community, so that community-wide decisions have to be made if water is to be sold and transferred outside the community. While this appears to require a consensus on water sales, the low-income levels and the seemingly high prices offered for water make such decisions difficult, requiring a tradeoff not only between the level of agricultural activities and alternatives made possible by the proceeds from water sales but between lifestyles and cultures. In a well-known New Mexico water rights case, the judge is said to have stated: "[I]t is simply assumed by the applicants that greater economic benefits are more desirable than the preservation of cultural identity. This is clearly not so ... I am persuaded that to transfer water rights, devoted for more than a century to agricultural purposes, in order to construct a playground for those who can pay is a poor trade indeed." Although this decision was reversed on appeal, it stands as a classic statement of the importance of historic patterns of water use. In another New Mexico case, the state engineer negotiated a compromise between the acequia and industry that sought to purchase and transfer 45.35 acre-feet of surface rights from one of the acequia landowners on the historic Anton Chico Land Grant. The judge stated that "the thirty to forty-five acres of land that would have gone fallow might not seem significant to the outside observer, but within the acequia system, custom and tradition require that all water users participate in the upkeep and maintenance of the entire system."

Cultural values associated with water are not confined to particular ethnic groups. Farm families place a high value on the farm or ranch lifestyle. Kenneth Weber interviewed farmers engaged in agriculture in the Arkansas Valley of Colorado, farmers who "stick it out" on marginally profitable farms because they value the farm lifestyle. Even after selling the water from their lands, many farmers retain their farm homes. Weber found that of thirty-six Crowley County, Colorado farmers who had sold their water, thirty-four remained in the county. This is not to argue that traditional societies should forever remain unchanged, but it is to argue that the economic "playing field" is uneven between low-income traditional societies and the more advanced sectors, and that maintenance of these cultures is of concern to society at large.

B.   ENVIRONMENTAL, RECREATIONAL, AND ECOSYSTEM VALUES GENERATED BY WATER SYSTEMS: THE PROBLEM OF "PUBLIC GOODS"

Some of the undervalued services provided by water systems, like the environment and recreation, share two unique characteristics: (1) the benefits can be enjoyed by many people without diminishing the quality of the benefit for others; and (2) it is impractical to require people to pay for the benefit. An example would be an improvement in water quality that can be enjoyed by many downstream parties including recreationists, urban utilities, agricultural irrigators, and all parties who value healthy riparian ecosystems. Such a benefit or good is called a "public good" in economic jargon, not that it is necessarily publicly provided, but that it provides widespread, non-rival benefits. Public goods are significant because private parties tend not to provide for or be concerned about them. For these reasons, public good values associated with instream flows are likely to be slighted by private water rights owners and even by public agencies that cannot gain revenues from their provision.

It is clear that water transfers can affect water quality, instream values, and riparian habitat. It is axiomatic that out-of-basin transfers will have a negative effect on the basin-of-origin and a positive one on the basin-of-destination. Diminished flows in the basin-of-origin eventually affect the streambed and riparian vegetation, which in turn affect wildlife dependent on certain bank and vegetation conditions. This is only an example of the negative effects.

A highly visible negative effect occurs when irrigated land is dried up. If revegetation is not undertaken, noxious weeds and blowing dust are likely to result. Revegetation of long-irrigated land has proven to be very difficult due to the changes in the composition of the soil. In the case of the Rocky Ford minority transfer, the water court required that part of the water not be removed from the land until revegetation had been successfully carried out.

C. PUBLIC AND PRIVATE VALUES LOST THROUGH "JURISDICTIONAL EXTERNALITIES"

In all water administration systems, there remain unrecognized "opportunity costs" of water abstraction. These are downstream benefits that are lost by virtue of upstream abstraction. At the intrastate level, one can again cite the Vaux and Howitt study of transfer opportunities in California as evidence of institutional barriers to water transfers; barriers that obfuscate the true opportunity costs of the water being used in different parts of the state. A current case in Colorado exhibiting the same shortcoming is the Eastern Slope's rapidly-growing Arapahoe County's application for the import of 60,000 acre-feet per year from the headwaters of the Gunnison River on the western slope. While there is "unappropriated water" in the Gunnison system, large downstream values are generated by every acre-foot of water left in the stream. As noted earlier, Howe and Ahrens have estimated that these values for the Gunnison are at least $140 per acre-foot.[36]

A prime example of losses occasioned at the interstate level due to failure to recognize downstream costs is the increase in salinity caused by the Grand Valley Irrigation Project in Western Colorado. Prior to the Bureau of Reclamation's salinity control program for the Project, [it was] estimated that the Grand Valley Project was contributing ten (short) tons of salt to the Colorado River per irrigated acre per year. This addition of salt occurs just before the River flows out of the State of Colorado and hence through Utah to the Lower Basin. Since 10,000 tons of salt added to the Upper Basin results in an increase in a Lower Basin Imperial Dam total-dissolved-solids concentration of approximately 1 mg/l, it has been estimated that each ton of salt in Upper Basin return flows results in Lower Basin damages in the range of $16 to $48 per ton. Thus, one acre of irrigated land in the Grand Valley has historically contributed damages between $160 and $480 to Lower Basin.

These patterns continue not from illegal activity or ill intent but from the institutional framework for water administration. The Colorado River framework is divided into Upper Basin and Lower Basin state-by-state areas, with each assigned allowable uses under existing compacts and state

---

36 *See* Charles W. Howe & W. Ashley Ahrens, Water Resources of the Upper Colorado River Basin: Problems and Policy alter- natives, in Water and Arid Lands of the Western United States 169 (Mohamed T. El–Ashry & Diana C. Gibbons eds., 1988).

laws. These jurisdictions were established to solve various political and equity problems in water administration, such as a fair, reliable sharing of water. However, the lack of coincidence between political boundaries and river basins has allowed decision-makers to ignore downstream opportunity costs. The resultant downstream externalities can be called "jurisdictional externalities." As a consequence, while the resulting patterns of water use may be considered fair in an historical context, they have become increasingly inefficient from an economic point of view. The implication is that the geographical extent of the markets is not great enough to allow the markets to reflect total system opportunity costs.

D.   THE PROBLEM OF "SECONDARY ECONOMIC IMPACTS" OF WATER TRANSFERS

The phrase "secondary economic impacts" of water transfers refers to changes in the levels of economic activity experienced by those who supply inputs to or process the outputs of the seller or the buyer in a water transfer. Since the majority of transfers in the Western United States are from agricultural to urban uses, the negative secondary impacts associated with the sale of irrigation water would consist of the reduced sales of agricultural inputs like seed, fertilizer, chemicals, and equipment, and reduced levels of further processing of agricultural products. In economic terminology, these activities are said to be either "backward linked" (suppliers) or "forward linked" (processors) to the water selling and buying activities. The positive side of the transfer provides the benefits generated by new-urban supplies.

The usual economic view of secondary impacts is that they are simply the way the market works to withdraw or supplement resources at the two ends of a resource transfer. In the private sector, businesses are not held liable for losses imposed on forward or backward linked firms, so why pay attention to these effects when evaluating resource transfers that are under public sector jurisdiction? Furthermore, the secondary economic gains at the buying end presumably more than offset the secondary losses at the sale end. Thus, the usual practice in cost-benefit analysis is to omit consideration of secondary impacts.

This attitude ignores the uniqueness of water as a social and environmental value, especially in rural areas. It also ignores the following: (1) that the secondary losses are felt in one location, while the secondary gains are generally felt elsewhere; (2) that the transfers of human and other resources away from the point of sale often take many months at the cost of job search, moving expenses, and social disturbance; and (3) that the timing of the gains and losses differ since the losses occur either prior to or during the water transfer while offsetting gains are typically in the future since cities and industry typically buy water in anticipation of future needs.

Sale of water is most frequently from marginal, depressed agricultural areas, often resulting in long-term unemployment of human and nonspecialized resources. From the point of view of economic efficiency, the idleness of resources that would otherwise have been employed constitutes a real economic cost. Especially in the case of large water transfers, the negative secondary impacts in the area-of-origin are highly visible and attract public opposition to transfers. The absence of compensation and assistance to the area of origin exacerbates the malaise.

Sandra Postel, Last Oasis: Facing Water Scarcity
165–182 (1997).

* * *

Moving toward more efficient, ecologically sound, sustainable patterns of water use requires major changes in the way water is valued, allocated, and managed. Appropriate pricing, the creation of markets for buying and selling water, and other economic inducements for wise water use hardly exist in most places. They have a central role to play in the transition to an era of scarcity. In addition, protecting the many functions water performs that a marketplace does not adequately value—such as habitat protection, species preservation, recreational uses, and aesthetic benefits—requires limiting the amount of water that cities, industries, and agriculture collectively claim. And finally, with the stability of the water cycle so dependent on the land over which water flows, regulations on how we use critical parcels of the earth are also necessary to achieve water security.

Many of the water shortages cropping up around the world stem from the widespread failure to value water at anything close to its true worth. Grossly underpricing water perpetuates the illusion that it is plentiful, and that nothing is sacrificed by wasteful practices. Benjamin Franklin once said, "When the well's dry, we know the worth of water." A key challenge is to begin valuing it appropriately and using it more wisely so as to avoid learning Franklin's lesson the hard way.

Setting prices closer to the real cost of supplying water is a key component of both urban and industrial conservation. [T]his would encourage both city-dwellers and manufacturers to conserve, recycle, and reuse their supplies, thereby fostering greater efficiency among those accounting for a third of the world's total water use.

Pricing water properly is most important in agriculture, however, because wasteful irrigation constitutes the single largest reservoir within the "last oasis." Water subsidies are larger, and more pervasive in agriculture than in any other realm of water use. Governments often build, maintain, and operate irrigation systems with public funds, and then charge farmers next to nothing for these expensive services. Irrigators in Mexico, for instance, pay on average just 11 percent of their water's full cost, and those in Indonesia and Pakistan, about 13 percent. In Egypt, a land of extreme scarcity, farmers are not charged directly for their irrigation water at all.

In India, the world's third largest food producer, government spending to operate and maintain medium and large canal projects exceeds the total revenue collected from farmers by 23.5 billion rupees ($816 million).

Adding in capital cost subsidies would lift this figure even higher. Irrigation officials set water charges according to the size of farmers' plots and the crops they are growing, so payments bear no relation to the amount actually used on the fields. Moreover, charges are so low—typically amounting to 2–5 percent of the harvest's value—that they have no influence on farmers' management decisions. Water prices have not been raised in most Indian states since the mid-eighties and in a few, including the Punjab and water-short Tamil Nadu, since the mid-seventies.

Such extreme undercharging not only fosters waste and the planting of water-intensive crops, it also deprives government agencies of the funds needed to maintain canals and other irrigation works adequately. As a result, agriculture usurps far more water than is necessary for the harvest it yields, farmers grow thirsty crops like sugarcane even in water-tight areas, and irrigation works fall into disrepair, which reduces efficiency even further.

The situation is little better in the United States. The federal Bureau of Reclamation supplies water to a quarter of the West's irrigated land— more than 4 million hectares—under long-term (typically 40–year) contracts at greatly subsidized prices. This practice dates back to the 1902 Reclamation Act, which aimed to settle the western frontier by helping family farmers obtain irrigation water and power. Over time, the degree of federal assistance deepened with the Bureau's decision not to charge interest on water project construction costs, to lengthen the repayment period, and to limit repayment to farmers' "ability to pay."

As a result, subsidies ballooned over time, with farmers large and small drinking heavily at the public trough for decades. As of the mid-eighties, irrigators benefiting from California's huge Central Valley Project had repaid only 4 percent of its capital costs: $38 million out of $950 million. U.S. taxpayers have footed the bill for the remainder.

As in poorer countries, this free ride has discouraged farmers from investing in efficiency improvements and has led them to choose crops ill-suited to a semidesert and to devote scarce water to low-value uses. A third of the water delivered by the Bureau of Reclamation is used to irrigate hay, pasture, and other forage crops destined for livestock. Meanwhile, western cities and industries scramble for more water, and drum up plans to dam yet another canyon or divert even more from a distant river.

Correcting these perverse situations is easier said than done. It requires bucking deeply entrenched and politically influential special interests, instilling irrigation bureaucracies with a broader sense of mission, and decentralizing water management so that local water suppliers and users have more responsibility and accountability for the performance of their operations. In some cases, it even means challenging religious and cultural beliefs. Islamic norms, for instance, hold that water must be free, which has generally precluded governments in Muslim countries from charging anything more than the cost of delivery.

Requiring farmers in developing countries to at least pay for the operation and maintenance of their irrigation systems is often frustrated by the notion that they cannot afford higher prices. Yet those benefiting from irrigation typically earn far more than those cultivating rainfed lands do. Lessening irrigation subsidies would free up funds to invest in the productivity of rainfed farming, which accounts for the bulk of the world's cropland and provides the livelihood of most of the rural poor. Moreover, Third World irrigators have shown time and again that they are willing and able to pay more for water that is reliable and over which they can exercise control. With an assured and timely supply, they can invest in fertilizers, high-yielding seeds, and better management practices, often boosting their crop production and income enough to offset any rise in water prices.

Reducing irrigation subsidies would thus tend to promote both efficiency and equity while stemming problems of waterlogging, soil salinization, and other forms of environmental degradation. * * *

In the United States, meaningful reform of the Bureau of Reclamation's irrigation policies has repeatedly fallen victim to the powerful western agricultural lobby and the politicians beholden to them. With hundreds of federal irrigation contracts coming up for renewal this decade, a timely opportunity exists to establish new rules for what has become a very different water game. A first step is to reduce the subsidies that give farmers water for a small fraction of the price cities and industries pay. Prices could be raised gradually, say over five years, to avoid sudden disruptions. Once farmers know that water prices will be much higher in the next round of contracts, the government could induce them to renegotiate sooner by offering to help pay for conservation investments undertaken immediately.

* * *

In the western United States, competition for scarce supplies has spawned an active market that is fostering transfers of water from farms to cities. Where farmers have clear property rights to water, as they do in much of the West, they have the option of selling those rights to a willing buyer. If an irrigator can earn more by selling water to a nearby city than by spreading it on alfalfa, cotton, or wheat, transferring that water from farm to city use is economically beneficial. If it prevents the city from damming another river to increase its supplies, the transfer can also benefit the environment. In this way, marketing can be an effective means of reallocating a finite pool of water.

* * *

Exactly how far U.S. water trading ultimately will go in reallocating supplies remains unclear. According to some estimates, redirecting 7 percent of western agriculture's water to cities would be sufficient to meet the growth in urban demand projected for the end of the decade. After that, larger shifts would be needed. Unless cities stabilize their water use through conservation, reuse, and, where necessary, limits on the size of their populations and economies, agriculture ultimately could lose more water—and land—than socially desirable, given the challenge that lies ahead of feeding a much larger world population.

To the extent that agricultural supplies are freed up by increasing irrigation efficiency or by switching crops, land need not come out of production. For instance, the Metropolitan Water District (MWD) of Southern California—water wholesaler for roughly half the state's 30 million residents—is financing the lining of canals and other conservation projects in the neighboring Imperial Irrigation District in exchange for the 100,000 acre-feet of water per year the investments will save. * * *

In some cases, buyers pay cash for the water, but often they pay in kind, either by lending their labor, sharing a portion of their harvest with the seller, or some combination of these two approaches. Where electricity is priced according to a flat fee geared to the horsepower of the pump, as is common in many areas, a farmer has an extra incentive to sell water, since there is no real cost to the extra pumping. Although this makes relatively inexpensive water available to poorer farmers, it also creates a strong inducement to overpump the resource, especially because tubewell owners often have de facto ownership rights to as much groundwater as they can extract. To serve the goals of efficiency, equity, and sustainable resource use simultaneously, water marketing would need to be accompanied by limits on groundwater pumping, the reduction of energy subsidies, and assurances that markets do not further concentrate water rights in the hands of the rich.

Indeed, wherever pricing and marketing fail to take into account the full social, environmental, and intergenerational costs of water use, some additional correction is needed. In areas with declining groundwater levels, for instance, governments can limit the total amount pumped to the average rate of aquifer recharge. In the United States, Arizona pioneered this approach in 1980 with passage of a law requiring that groundwater basins undergoing depletion achieve a balance between pumping and recharge by the year 2025. Unfortunately, many cities affected by this legislation have not met their conservation targets, and, as noted earlier, have sought to buy land and water rights from farms.

Another option is to tax groundwater pumping that exceeds natural replenishment. A 1991 Arizona law moves toward this approach in the Phoenix area, requiring those who have overdrawn their groundwater accounts to pay a "replenishment tax" or to purchase credits from someone who has pumped less than the allowable level. The tax rate reflects the cost of supplying enough water to balance the whole district's account, and is thus high enough to induce conservation.

In the case of fossil aquifers, such as the Ogallala in the U.S. High Plains or the deep desert aquifers in Saudi Arabia and Libya, this approach could take the form of a "depletion tax" on all groundwater extractions. In this way, those profiting from the draining of one-time reserves would at least partially compensate society for the loss of these supplies, which will be valued far more highly by future generations faced with feeding a much larger world population. A groundwater depletion tax would help promote equity among generations—a basic tenet of a sustainable society—while also helping slow the depletion rate by encouraging conservation.

Public action is also needed to ensure that ecological systems get the water they need to remain healthy. Open markets that allow water to be purchased and dedicated to this purpose can help. For instance, 11 of the 127 water transactions in the western United States in 1991 were aimed at securing more water for rivers, wetlands, and nature preserves.

But the task at hand is far larger than private conservation initiatives alone can handle through the marketplace. According to Defenders of Wildlife, a U.S. conservation group, in 1989 (a drought year) wildlife refuges in California's Central Valley got less than 8 percent of the water needed in order for migrating waterfowl to winter there successfully. Private action simply cannot secure the large volumes of water needed to serve the public's interest. Collecting money from the millions of people who are willing to pay for protection of these ecological values is far too difficult and costly. Economists call this a problem of excessively high "transaction costs," and it is an important reason the market fails to protect the environment adequately.

In such instances, regulations are needed to preserve and restore ecological health. The water laws and practices of most countries are heavily biased toward the individual's right to withdraw water for private gain and against the public's common interest in leaving water "instream" to maintain fisheries, recreational values, and the integrity of ecosystems. Where water is plentiful, the consequences of this bias may be negligible; but where it is scarce, severe ecological damage results, as is now so evident in many parts of the world.

One way of protecting water's life-support functions is simply to limit the total amount that can be diverted from a river, lake, or stream. Until fairly recently, this was difficult in the western United States, since water rights had to be put to "beneficial use," which was interpreted as removing water from its natural channel for some productive purpose. Most states, however, now recognize water left "instream" to protect ecological functions as a legitimate beneficial use to which water rights can be attached. Only a few allow individuals and private entities to hold instream rights; in most cases, a state agency must acquire them. Montana, for instance, passed a law in 1973 that allows the state and federal governments to reserve water for instream uses. As a result, about 70 percent of the average annual flow in the upper basin of the Yellowstone River and half to two thirds of the lower basin flow have been reserved to protect aquatic life, water quality, and other ecological services.

Where excessive diversions have already caused ecological damage, as with central Asia's Aral Sea or Florida's Everglades, new laws and regulations will be needed to restore ecosystems to health. One such instrument is a legal principle called the "public trust doctrine," which asserts that governments hold certain rights in trust for the public and can take action to protect those rights from private interests. Widespread application of this doctrine could have sweeping effects, since even existing water rights could be revoked in order to prevent violation of the public trust.

In a landmark decision handed down in February 1983,* the California Supreme Court declared that the water rights of Los Angeles, which permit diversions from the Mono Lake basin, are subject to the public trust doctrine. Mono Lake—a hauntingly beautiful water body on the eastern side of the Sierra Nevada whose algae and brine shrimp support hundreds of migratory bird species—has had its volume halved and its salinity doubled because of excessive diversions from its major tributaries. Since 1989, the courts have prevented the Los Angeles Department of Water and Power from siphoning off any Mono basin water, which previously had constituted some 1.5 percent of the urban utility's supply. With a final determination of the city's rights to Mono water not expected until 1993, Judge Terrence Finney called Mono Lake "a national environmental, ecological and scenic treasure [that] should not be experimented with even for a few brief years."

Protecting water systems also depends on regulating the use of those critical areas of land that help moderate water's cycling through the environment. Degradation of the watershed—the sloping land that collects, directs, and controls the flow of rainwater in a river basin—is a pervasive problem in rich and poor countries alike. Besides contributing to flash floods and loss of groundwater recharge, which can exacerbate the effects of drought, it leads to soil erosion that prematurely fills downstream reservoirs with silt, shortening the useful life of these expensive water projects.

* * *

Land use planning in and around cities and suburbs can be equally important for the protection of local water supplies. Unplanned development can end up paving over rainwater's main point of entry into a key drinking-water source. Especially in areas dependent on local groundwater, protecting these critical aquifer recharge areas is essential to ensure that water sources get replenished. Suffolk County, Long Island, recently spent $118 million to acquire 3,440 hectares of open space in order to preclude development in recharge zones vital to the region's underground water supply, its sole source of drinking water. Voters approved a one-quarter cent increase in the county sales tax to fund the land purchases, which remains in effect until the end of the decade.

Local ordinances can also set landscaping requirements with an eye toward protecting water supplies. Across the United States, cultivated lawns cover 10–12 million hectares, an area about the size of Kentucky. Not only do lawns fail to promote recharge effectively in many cases, the fertilizers and pesticides used to maintain them are troubling sources of pollution. The town of Southampton, Long Island, requires that at least 80 percent of each home lot situated in a critical aquifer zone be kept in its

---

* National Audubon Society v. Superior Court, *infra* p. 426 [Eds.].

natural (typically wooded) state and that no more than 15 percent be put in lawns or vegetation that require fertilizer.

A number of states—including Connecticut, Georgia, New York, and North Carolina—have adopted laws and regulations specifically designed to control land use in watersheds. North Carolina passed a law in 1989, for instance, requiring the development of minimum statewide standards for watershed protection, which were due out by July 1992. Cities and towns are required to develop land use plans and ordinances that are at least as strict as the state's standards, which include, for example, limits on impervious surface areas and certain agricultural practices.

Here and there, pricing, marketing, and regulatory actions are being used effectively to tap the "last oasis" of conservation and efficiency and to promote sustainable water use. But nowhere have all the elements been brought together into a strategy ensuring that human use of water remains within ecological bounds and that the integrity of water systems overall is protected. We can muddle through by fine-tuning antiquated policies, but only for so long. And the longer we wait to make the needed adjustments the costlier they are likely to be—with a greater loss of ecological assets in the interim.

G. WATER SCARCITY: THE ROLE OF LAW AND POLICY

The Conservation Foundation, America's Water: Current Trends and Emerging Issues
34–35, 42–43, 47, 48 (1984).

Many experts agree that most water problems do not result primarily from physical limitations or technical inadequacies. Water shortages, while growing in number and seriousness, are still fairly unusual. And, certainly, technical means are available for dealing with most contamination problems—at least of surface water. But, as in the case of energy, water problems could be compounded as a result of imprudent and misguided human choices. Such choices typically are shaped by market imperfections and by unwise government policies, including narrow-purpose programs, long-established subsidies, and inappropriate legal constraints. Because many of today's water crises stem largely from government policies and human desires and habits rather than physical or technological limitations, crises over water often are susceptible to, and prevented by, changes in the ways legal, political, economic, and social institutions deal with water. The real question is whether the institutional adjustments necessary to respond to conditions of increased scarcity can be made before it is too late.

Such changes, necessary as they may be, generate bitter conflict. Farmers, urbanites, industrialists, professional and sport fishers, environmentalists, and officials of different states all find themselves competing for water, the purity and availability of which suddenly carry a high price.

Water administrators and legislators accustomed to distributing largess to appreciative constituencies now find that the limited availability of both water and money forces decisions that outrage various parties. In short, water allocation and treatment programs developed under conditions of surplus and subsidy must adapt to conditions of mounting shortages and heated competition.

Water problems, obviously, are most likely to be noticed when they become tangible—be they manifested as groundwater pollution in New Jersey, flooding along the Colorado River, groundwater depletion in Illinois, or the drying up of the Everglades Swamp in Florida. These situations may worsen, and others, less pressing now, are likely to erupt. But underlying all these specific problems are some generic issues relating to water use and management in the United States. Three of the most fundamental issues are: For what purposes are supplies of water to be used? Who should decide how to allocate water? Who should pay for water investments?

Scarce Water and Institutional Change

7–11 (Kenneth D. Frederick ed. 1986).

Water Law

Water is not treated like any other resource. The states reserve the power and prerogative to establish the institutions for allocating all the waters within their boundaries not encumbered by federal law or interstate compact. The states grant water use rights based on either a common law doctrine that calls for all users to cut back in time of shortage or a system in which the earliest users have the most senior rights. In almost all cases, water is treated as a free commodity; charges are not made for extracting water from surface or groundwater sources, but only for the costs of moving the water. The rights to the water, however, are often constrained in ways that limit or at least raise doubts about the legality of transfers to other uses and users.

The earliest state laws controlling surface waters were based on the common law doctrine of riparian rights, which grants the owner of land adjacent to a water body the right to use the water. Riparian rights are inseparable from the land and are constrained to uses that are "reasonable" and do not unduly inconvenience other riparian owners. There is no priority of use, so all riparian owners must share in curtailing use in time of shortage. Riparian doctrine still underlies the water codes of almost all the relatively water-abundant eastern states.

In regions where streams are less numerous and their flows smaller and less reliable, extensive development required diverting water beyond riparian lands with greater assurance of availability. Consequently, the seventeen western states adopted the doctrine of prior appropriation as the basis of their water laws. Under this doctrine, water is allocated according to the principle of "first in time, first in right." Thus, the holders of senior water rights have priority over all subsequently acquired rights, and the full burden of any water shortage is borne by the holders of the most junior rights.

Appropriative rights eliminate a major obstacle to water transfers and markets by breaking the link between water and land. However, a variety of legal provisions in states using the appropriation doctrine inhibit the creation of well-defined, transferable property rights in water. Appropriative rights are acquired by diverting water from a stream and putting it to some beneficial use; the right originates only at the point of diversion and is contingent upon continued beneficial use. The acquired right can be sold or transferred, but the right is limited to use (not ownership) of the water, and there may be restrictions as to how and where it can be used. Twelve western states specify a ranked preference of use that allows preferred uses (municipal and domestic first, often followed by agriculture) to supersede water rights destined for less-preferred uses in time of scarcity. And the right to transfer water to other uses and locations is complicated by the fact that return flows are public property, freed for appropriation by downstream users.

State laws and institutions guiding the allocation and use of water have evolved over time in response to new conditions. However, * * * changes enabling institutions to deal efficiently with water scarcity have lagged well behind need. Most of the laws and institutions remain more appropriate for an era when water was in actuality as well as in law a free resource. These provisions served their regions reasonably well when new demands could be met by developing new supplies. But their shortcomings are apparent when there is need to apportion existing supplies among alternative uses or respond to short-term shortages.

David Getches, Water Wrongs: Why Can't We Get It Right The First Time?

34 Envt'l Law 1–19 (2004).

Water policy has faltered throughout the ages. Our water decisions have often created more problems than they have resolved, leaving severe environmental and social disasters in their wake. In most cases, it is not that we did not know better. On the contrary, we have been making the same errors for thousands of years by replicating policies that failed societies both ancient and modern. But this destructive trend need not continue and can be reversed by integrating and accepting old knowledge and responding to new knowledge about the uncertainty and limits of water supply. It requires modesty about our ability to control nature.

The stories begin in Iraq, long predating the multiple sins of Saddam Hussein. What we know as Iraq today was once Mesopotamia, the Fertile Crescent region where civilization began. For thousands of years societies flourished in the sprawling lands where Iraq, Syria, and Turkey converge. Here originated the first written language, sophisticated commercial systems, metal tools, and art, thousands of years before Christ.

These scientific and cultural advances were achievable because ample food could be produced on fertile lands, allowing time for people to put their intellects to work. Today, the area is a sparse, unpopulated desert. The ancient Sumerians who lived there around 3500 BC are credited with creating irrigation systems that supported major production of wheat and barley. By 2500 BC wheat production was largely phased out, a trend that resulted from salt accumulation in the soil. Although more salt-tolerant barley continued to be produced, overall agricultural production declined. Conquests and the fall of Sumerian civilization followed. People emigrated and those who remained were impoverished. Today, most scholars posit that it was environmental degradation from intensive irrigation that led to the demise of the region's flourishing economy, culture, and political structure.

The decline came slowly and, as there were then no textbooks on the subject, it may be understandable and excusable that the Sumerians did not identify and reverse the process. Those who left the area as the Sumerian civilization dissolved moved north, transporting the same irrigation practices. More salinity crises occurred in the new regions. Apparently, the emigrants did not learn the lessons of Sumeria: Repeated soil irrigation without adequate drainage in an arid climate leads to salt buildup.

What about those who developed irrigation systems on the Colorado River in the American Southwest? The Colorado forms in the Rocky Mountains, runs through the Grand Canyon, and ends in the Sea of Cortez in Mexico. It is the only major river serving most of the states of the Southwest and the Mountain West. This hot and dry climate is characterized by poor and naturally saline land. Without irrigation, farming stood no chance of success in much of the region. In the early part of the twentieth century, boosters pleaded with the U.S. government to put up capital when private investors refused.

The U.S. Bureau of Reclamation eagerly went to work on building dams and canals to serve farmers and later to expand cities with water from the Colorado. Dam building continued throughout the first half of the twentieth century. The massive developments began with the Hoover Dam in the 1930s, one of the human-made wonders of the modern world. Hoover was a success in many ways. It came in under budget and ahead of schedule, and provides a year-round source of water to the seven Colorado River Basin states. In addition, it was emulated not only in the U.S. system but all over the world, and kicked off the era of big dams, a frenzy of dam building during the first sixty years of the twentieth century.

Glen Canyon Dam was the capstone of the Colorado River projects, approximately the same capacity and height as the Hoover Dam. No sooner was Glen Canyon finished, and the government was filling it with water, than the salinity in the river spiked to such a level that irrigation water diverted in Mexico destroyed crops. This touched off an international dispute with Mexico. Domestically, the crisis also affected farmers who were beginning to experience declining crop yields from the increased salinity. Cities also realized the negative and costly effects of using water with increased salinity.

An agreement was reached with Mexico to curtail the salinity in the water and was embodied in a document interpreting the Treaty recognizing the right of Mexico to use a share of Colorado River water. This—coupled with U.S. concerns with the salinity problem—necessitated an elaborate and expensive federal salinity control program. Hundreds of millions of dollars were spent on major engineering projects to prevent salt accumulation and to clean up polluted water. The most expensive single investment was for the construction of a huge desalination plant designed to take salt-laden agricultural return flows, treat them to a pristine level, and then dump the clean water back into the polluted river to dilute the flowing water to the salt levels promised to Mexico.

The desalination plant has lain virtually unused since it was completed. Thanks to high river flows that diluted the salt, coupled with physical measures, the salinity problem in the Colorado River has been held at bay. The enormously expensive solutions have been trial and error and, at best, will attenuate the worst of the effects of heavy development of the Colorado. But was all this necessary when the adverse impacts of irrigation could have been foreseen and avoided? Perhaps we can make excuses for the ancient Sumerians, but how forgiving should we be of those who repeated their mistakes in the twentieth century?

Although dam builders have made engineering mistakes—resulting in disaster and deaths from the collapse of dams—more typically the engineers achieved what they set out to do: They built bigger, stronger dams that harnessed great rivers and promoted economic activity. Some of these projects have produced great benefits for society, but even they caused environmental and social problems—and sometimes disasters. The negative consequences were typically unintended, but no less negative. Although we have improved our engineering techniques, the methods used to irrigate most farmlands in the world, including in the American West, are not much different from the methods used by the ancients. Sandra Postel writes, "[i]rrigation's historical record spans six millennia.... The overriding lesson from history is that most irrigation-based civilizations fail ... the question is: Will ours be any different."

* * * As with the dams on the Colorado, spectacular canyons and falls were necessarily flooded and the flow regime was permanently changed. The once roaring Columbia is now a series of slack water pools. This has had a devastating effect on the salmon, as the hydropower system affects every stage of salmon life.

In some cases the government built fish ladders for returning fish, but neglected to provide a means to protect the young fish trying to pass from tributary streams down to the ocean. These crude efforts were not universal and allowed only the hardiest to survive. It is estimated that annual salmon runs have diminished from as high as 16 million to around 1 million. "Currently, approximately 60% of the salmon stocks in the Columbia River basin are listed as depressed, threatened, or endangered." Additionally, over 100 of the native stocks have already gone extinct.

* * *

In pursuing the impressive benefits of large dams, politicians and boosters across the West, and experts within government agencies, have ignored the consequences—consequences that were inevitable and should have been obvious. As international experts pointed out in a recent paper: "The authors are unaware of even a single large dam whose benefits and costs have been properly and systematically documented after 10–20 years of operation." Moreover, when cost-benefit analyses were made, the calculations were often distorted to justify constructing dams.

Recent technical reports have demonstrated some damning facts: 1) Dams are the predominant factor in the decline of aquatic life; 2) water development is the largest single factor in species extinction; and 3) the great masses created by large dams concentrated in parts of the world have altered the earth's rotational pattern.

In addition to environmental harm, dam building has displaced indigenous people around the world and locked them in poverty. The Garrison Dam on the Missouri River caused the flooding of the Fort Berthold Reservation, dividing families and destroying an economy. * * *

* * *

John McPhee has chronicled some of the most heroic efforts to control nature in the United States. Since 1950, the U.S. Army Corps of Engineers (the Corps) has been locked in a war with the mighty Mississippi River, attempting to protect New Orleans and Baton Rouge and countless millions of dollars in industrial investment from flooding. The scheme depends on structures designed to contain the growing tendency of the Mississippi to shift its flow to the Atchafalaya River where floods imperil development that now lies behind fragile dikes. The Corps sought to reverse millennia of channel shifting as sediments built up and gravity forced the river to find a more direct and less resistant course to the Gulf of Mexico. Congress declared that the then-normal flow of about a third of the Mississippi to the Atchafalaya must be maintained. It charged the Corps with diverting the rest of the river away from the course beckoned by nature. Professor Oliver Houck regarded as arrogant the assumption that engineers could train the Mississippi River to go where they wanted it to go instead of where it was wont to go. Indeed, in the major floods since it was built, parts of the system have been lost and rebuilt. McPhee convinces us that it is just a matter of time before it all fails. [Editor's note: Hurricane Katrina occurred August, 2005, inundating 80% of New Orleans as the levees and flood control system failed.]

In the West, Americans have tried to defy nature since the first settlers arrived. The very settlement and development of the semi-arid West was conceived under the mindless belief that the "endless" lands could accommodate as many people as chose to settle there. However, John Wesley

Powell knew better and espoused a vision of the West being settled in a nature-conscious pattern, with small, cooperative communities, widely dispersed over large expanses of the arid West, under counties divided by watershed boundaries. His wise counsel was disregarded.

Powell's revolutionary ideas simply did not fit the nation's goals of populating untamed western lands, justifying railroad investments, and fulfilling the romantic ideal of Jeffersonian yeoman farmers. So one homestead program after another offered more land for less money, and promised that water would be available according to the simple gold miner's rule that whoever discovered the water could keep using it. But we know from subsequent history that there was not enough water to sustain this pattern in many parts of the west—just as Powell predicted. Large numbers of homesteaders quickly failed. Many of those who stayed on the Great Plains were finally driven out by the Dust Bowl.

Common sense was not only disregarded, but science was invented to overcome it. The westward movement and particularly homesteading on the Great Plains was accelerated by the boosters' myth that "rain follows the plow." This nonsense amounted to wishful thinking that more cultivation would reward farmers with more rainfall. "God speed the plow.... By this wonderful provision, which is only man's mastery over nature, the clouds are dispensing copious rains ... [the plow] is the instrument which separates civilization from savagery; and converts a desert into a farm or garden.... To be more concise, Rain follows the plow."

During the 1870s and early 1880s, unusually heavy rainfall made these claims sound plausible, and within ten years nearly two million people had sunk roots into the prairie soil. But when the wet years finally came to an end, the high plains again became a place where only the luckiest or most determined could survive.

There are multiple examples of water institutions being founded on ignorance of science or poor science. The frailties of the prior appropriation doctrine itself were frankly identified by a lawyer-engineer, Elwood Mead, who would became one of the great leaders in creating state water institutions. Mead, Wyoming's first State Engineer and later Director of the U.S. Bureau of Reclamation, warned in 1903 that irrigation practices sanctioned by a doctrine based on the rule of capture without a complete water code or adequate record-keeping practices lead to waste and inefficiency.

* * *

Climate change exacerbates nature's uncertainties. Various scientific models provide scenarios with different regional impacts and ranges of severity. But scientists now agree that we are clearly heading into an era of greater and more frequent fluctuations in the naturally available water supply.

Meanwhile, the West's population grows, and with it grows demand. If we assume that demand is a steadily rising curve, or even an inflexible constant, our encounters with nature's limits are bound to be more frequent. So what should we do?

In the face of uncertainty, it becomes more important that decisions be based on sound scientific data. This does not argue that decisions should await perfect information, rather it counsels a quest for and acceptance of the best available information. Most water resource decisions have ignored climate change, either because decision makers have just not included its consideration in the past or because they are discouraged by the presence of many uncertainties in the data. * * *

If we cannot avoid uncertainty, it would be rational to try to reduce our vulnerability to uncertainty in water supply. To accomplish this we have to integrate and accept old knowledge about the uncertainty and limits of water supply, and respond to new knowledge concerning the limits of our ability to control nature. Also, demand can be effectively controlled. Unlike the natural phenomena that dominate water supply, demand is something that humans create. Thus, humans ought to be able to manipulate demand more readily than we can manipulate nature.

* * *

* * * Markets and pricing tempt water away from low-valued uses; regulations prevent harmful or wasteful uses. * * * The great virtue of creating property rights in water—the right to use water is itself property—is that it can be bought and sold. Therefore, the enduring and realistic social goal of adaptability reflected in prior appropriation is achieved by transferability.

When drought focuses attention on water policy, lawmakers have an opportunity to take advantage of the present system to achieve optimum use through market mechanism and to enact laws to control demand. This has rarely been their response. * * *

So, what does it mean to "get it right" in addressing water problems? Doing it right requires no technological breakthroughs. It primarily requires attention to the natural world and sufficient will to exercise restraint. This may be a tall order given our past performance. However, there are four concepts that will help us avoid and correct the errors of the past. These ideas are not revolutionary, not even new. They simply are not practiced.

First, we must look at water problems primarily as demand problems, not supply problems. * * *

Second, we must incorporate all of the values of water into the water decision-making process. * * *

[R]ecently, integrated water management has taken on the mantle of sustainable development. It stands for a broader consideration, not just of the multiple potential benefits of water development, but of the multiple potential consequences. It recognizes the links between human-made and natural capital, and integrates social, cultural, political, economic, and environmental issues.

* * *

A third approach that will help us get water decisions right is institutionalization of the precautionary principle. This is a rather revolutionary concept in the realm of water decisions. The precautionary principle is an emerging concept that has found its way into domestic laws, mostly outside of the United States. The principle counsels that decision makers should act to prevent environmental harm before it occurs by erring on the side of caution.

The precautionary approach—minimizing irreversible impacts or irretrievable commitments of resources—is accepted widely in environmental decision making in Europe and as an international norm. "[I]t dictates that indication of harm, rather than proof of harm, should be the trigger for action—especially if the delay may cause irreparable damage."

Some international treaties and declarations that have incorporated this theory into their documents are the 1995 Agreement on Fish Stocks, the Convention on Biological Diversity, and the Framework Convention on Climate Change. * * *

The precautionary principle is reflected in environmental statutes of several countries and explicitly in the treaty forming the European Union (EU). Courts have begun to apply it in some countries and it is emerging as a norm of international law.

* * *

We can address demand, pursue integrated water management, and institutionalize the precautionary principle to deal with future water problems and decisions. But the reality is that most water is already in use. Much of the damage, especially in a developed country like the United States, is already done or occurring.

This requires a fourth approach: restoration. Restoration efforts are afoot throughout the United States and are enormously popular. * * *

Communities are rebuilding streams that were despoiled or destroyed by development activities. * * *

For the past twenty years, saving the salmon runs has been a huge priority in the Northwest. * * *

* * *

At this point, a major overhaul in planning and management of the Columbia River Basin is needed to recover endangered fish species. Removal of some dams appears to be the most controversial but effective way to restore the system. * * * Although dam breaching will be costly, "failure to breach the dams would cause greater, irreparable damage." Some have suggested that dam breaching is probably the only solution to save the fish. Even the Army Corps of Engineers called the "natural flow alternative" the "biological option if salmon and ecosystem restoration is the primary goal."

How can we avoid repeating history? How can we get it right next time? The tools are there and relatively simple: 1) Shift the focus to controlling water demand; 2) consider all the values by using integrated water management to achieve the goal of sustainability and using cost-benefit analysis responsibly, as an analytical tool and not to justify a preconception; 3) adopt the precautionary principle in water decisions; and 4) invest in restoration.

* * *

Sarah F. Bates, David H. Getches, Lawrence J. MacDonnell & Charles F. Wilkinson, Searching Out the Headwaters: Change and Rediscovery in Western Water Policy
4–8 (1993).

The root difficulty with preserving the status quo is that western water is governed by one of the most outmoded collections of rules found anywhere in American public policy. The society that created the current system well over a century ago saw the rivers of the American West through a particular lens: Water was a commodity that needed to be removed from the river channel and "put to use." Water left wild and flowing in the channel was "wasted." Extravagant government expenditures to impound and transport water were justified in the name of "conservation."

This single-minded focus on the extraction of water at any cost was overwhelmingly successful in achieving the objectives of official nineteenth-century policy: to encourage American citizens to settle the broad, dry, and inhospitable western lands. The federal and state governments made western water development—dams, reservoirs, transmountain tunnels, pipelines, and canals—a first-line priority and laid out a sprawling program of subsidies that led to engineering triumph after engineering triumph. The human effort and ingenuity were extraordinary, and the benefits were many, whether measured by solid farming and ranching communities, construction jobs, or the museums and symphonies of the region's urban centers.

* * *

There are other new perceptions. Westerners now view water as more than a commodity. They see western rivers and lakes, like the mountains, forests, and wide-open spaces, as public assets of inestimable value. By and large, today's populace came west, not to wrestle an existence out of a harsh land, but to capture the privilege of living, working, and raising their families in a blessed place. To do that requires some water development, but it does not require the radical posture that water policy adopted and has held since the middle nineteenth century.

QUESTIONS

1. You are asked to suggest a water policy for a country with a federal system and which has the following characteristics:

- a mix of humid and arid areas and a variable rainfall pattern, with a history of extended periods of severe drought in both humid and arid areas; rapidly growing urban areas, an indigenous population dependent on farming, energy shortages; considerable subsidized irrigated agriculture devoted both to export crops and livestock feed crops;

- rivers, some of which are degraded by human use, and some of which flow freely through spectacular canyons and have minimal natural or human-introduced pollution.

The Ministry of Water wants to know the best way to allocate water. Should it be declared a state resource and allocated entirely through government licenses? If so, should licenses be issued solely by the national government or should this function be entirely delegated to state governments? What criteria should govern the issuance of licenses:

- priority of application?

- need for the water?

- the comparative economic value of alternative uses of water?

- the public interest?

2. Should water instead be declared a commodity, private rights assigned to users and the market used to allocate it? If so, could environmental values be adequately protected?

CHAPTER TWO

INVENTING RULES TO ALLOCATE A SCARCE RESOURCE

The rules for allocating water have deep, richly historical origins that reflect continual adaptations to different water needs. Although the field of water law is dominated by statutes, it began as common or customary law. Rules were invented to facilitate meeting society's practical needs. Those needs have varied over time and from place to place. Almost invariably, rules started out simple and became more complicated and riddled with exceptions; starkly simple rules are often rigid.

In making rules for allocating a limited supply of water, consider the options. If a group of people all want some of it and there is not enough for all, how should it be parceled out? Should it matter who began using it first? Who is nearest to the source? Who will produce the greatest economic value? Whose use is more urgent or socially beneficial? And who will decide, the state or the market? Why not share the supply that is available equally? Should the risk of changed conditions be factored in to water rights?

Rules were first made case-by-case, typically after a dispute broke out and the parties sought the aid of the law in resolving it. Coherent theories of water rights did not emerge until the 19th century in England and the United States. See Joshua Getzler, A History of Water Rights at Common Law (2004). Reliance on judicial allocation resulted in the development of two distinct bodies of state law, one based on riparian rights and the other based on prior appropriation. Riparian law attributed to landowners rights to make use of waters abutting their property. Prior appropriation allowed anyone with a beneficial use to begin using water and thereby to secure rights to continue using the water that were superior to the rights of anyone who began using water later. A third group of states developed hybrid systems that recognized to some extent legal rights of both riparians and appropriators.

The systems chosen by courts in particular states were products of time and place and, most of all, the nature of the dispute that first gave judicial attention to the matter. The rules adopted in early cases were then applied in other disputes, and modified to fit new situations. Legislatures later got involved and built on common law doctrines. Often, they modified water law systems to the point that their riparian or appropriation roots were difficult to discern.

Water law has had to reconcile two objectives that are often at odds with each other. As the use of water became more valuable, water rights became a species of property rights. The law tried to make them as secure and exclusive as possible. At the same time, water users face higher risks of curtailment or loss of use compared to other property users. Water rights are by nature correlative so the right to use must be defined in relation to other existing and potential future uses. But, there is a higher public interest in the allocation of water compared to other natural resources because water is essential for human survival and no substitute exists. Finally, water rights are vulnerable to year to year climatic variations. A right is useless if the water is not available. This has always been the case in arid areas, but global climate change increases the risk for arid, semi-arid and humid areas. In 2008, researchers at the Scripps Institution of Oceanography shocked water users by predicting that the two reservoirs that backstop the Colorado River water rights of Arizona, California and Nevada could go dry by 2021. Pierce and Barnett, When Will Lake Mead Go Dry? Journal of Water Resources Research (2008). The study was immediately contested, but it illustrates the increasing risks faced by water users. The allocation of the Colorado and stresses the system faces are discussed at pages 987–1026, *infra*.

The objective of this chapter is to introduce the basic concepts of water law in the milieu in which the rules—and some of their exceptions—were created. We illustrate the utilitarian basis of most water laws by organizing this introductory material by types of uses. One of the earliest uses of water in the United States that called for a set of rules was milling. Mills were located along streams to exploit the power of moving water. In the West, miners needed water to help them extract and refine minerals, but mines were often located far from streams. They had to have an allocation system that allowed them to use water away from a stream. Farmers in the West confronted a similar problem. Later, their uses conflicted with cities that typically wanted to secure future rights to water to support future growth. Electric power generation conflicted with both uses, requiring that rivers be controlled by dams and water released according to power demands. Recreational uses, mostly dependent on keeping water in a stream or lake, eventually emerged as important, but confronted systems where most of the available water was already committed to uses off the stream. Similarly, allocation of water for fish was an afterthought and a misfit for established water law. Indian tribes, located mostly in the West, also demanded and received a share of water, or at least rights on paper, based on major exceptions to the system.

As you study the response of the law to different types of demands, consider what values are being promoted by each rule that is created. Ask what motivated the court to reach its decision? What other options were available to the court? What problems are inherent in the rule that was adopted?

A. MILLING

Tyler v. Wilkinson

Circuit Court, District of Rhode Island, 1827.
24 F.Cas. 472.

Bill in equity [by Ebenezer Tyler and others against Abraham Wilkinson and others] to establish the right of the plaintiffs to a priority of use of the waters of Pawtucket river.

* * *

■ STORY, CIRCUIT JUSTICE. * * *

The river Pawtucket forms a boundary line between the states of Massachusetts and Rhode Island, in that part of its course where it separates the town of North Providence from the town of Seekonk. It is a fresh water river, above the lower falls between these towns, and is there unaffected by the ebb or flow of the tide. At these falls there is an ancient dam, called the lower dam, extending quite across the river, and several mills are built near it, as well on the eastern as on the western side of the river. The plaintiffs, together with some of the defendants, are the proprietors in fee of the mills and adjacent land on the eastern bank, and either by themselves or their lessees are occupants of the same. The mills and land adjacent, on the western bank, are owned by some of the defendants. The lower dam was built as early as the year 1718, by the proprietors on both sides of the river, and is indispensable for the use of their mills respectively. There was previously an old dam on the western side, extending about three quarters of the way across the river, and a separate dam for a saw-mill on the east side. The lower dam was a substitute for both. About the year 1714 a canal was dug, or an old channel widened and cleared on the western side of the river, beginning at the river a few rods above the lower dam, and running round the west end thereof, until it emptied into the river about ten rods below the same dam. It has been long known by the name of "Sergeant's Trench," and was originally cut for the passage of fish up and down the river; but having wholly failed for this purpose, about the year 1730 an anchor-mill and dam were built across it by the then proprietors of the land; and between that period and the year 1790, several other dams and mills were built over the same; and since that period more expensive mills have been built there, which are all owned by some of the defendants. About thirty years before the filing of the bill, to wit, in 1792, another dam was built across the river at a place above the head of the trench, and about 20 rods above the lower dam; and the mills on the upper dam, as well as those on Sergeant's trench, are now supplied with water by proper flumes, & c. from the pond formed by the upper dam. The proprietors of this last dam are also made defendants.

* * *

The principal points, which have been discussed at the bar, are, first, what is the nature and extent of the right of the owners of Sergeant's trench; and, secondly, whether that right has been exceeded by them to the injury of the plaintiffs.

* * *

Prima facie every proprietor upon each bank of a river is entitled to the land, covered with water, in front of his bank, to the middle thread of the stream, or, as it is commonly expressed, usque ad filum aquae. In virtue of this ownership he has a right to the use of the water flowing over it in its natural current, without diminution or obstruction. But, strictly speaking, he has no property in the water itself; but a simple use of it, while it passes along. The consequence of this principle is, that no proprietor has a right to use the water to the prejudice of another. It is wholly immaterial, whether the party be a proprietor above or below, in the course of the river; the right being common to all the proprietors on the river, no one has a right to diminish the quantity which will, according to the natural current, flow to a proprietor below, or to throw it back upon a proprietor above. This is the necessary result of the perfect equality of right among all the proprietors of that, which is common to all. The natural stream, existing by the bounty of Providence for the benefit of the land through which it flows, is an incident annexed, by operation of law, to the land itself. When I speak of this common right, I do not mean to be understood, as holding the doctrine, that there can be no diminution whatsoever, and no obstruction or impediment whatsoever, by a riparian proprietor, in the use of the water as it flows; for that would be to deny any valuable use of it. There may be, and there must be allowed of that, which is common to all, a reasonable use. The true test of the principle and extent of the use is, whether it is to the injury of the other proprietors or not. There may be a diminution in quantity, or a retardation or acceleration of the natural current indispensable for the general and valuable use of the water, perfectly consistent with the existence of the common right. The diminution, retardation, or acceleration, not positively and sensibly injurious by diminishing the value of the common right, is an implied element in the right of using the stream at all. The law here, as in many other cases, acts with a reasonable reference to public convenience and general good, and it is not betrayed into a narrow strictness, subversive of common sense, nor into an extravagant looseness, which would destroy private rights. The maxim is applied, "Sic utere tuo, ut non alienum laedas."

But of a thing, common by nature, there may be an appropriation by general consent or grant. Mere priority of appropriation of running water, without such consent or grant, confers no exclusive right. It is not like the case of mere occupancy, where the first occupant takes by force of his priority of occupancy. That supposes no ownership already existing, and no right to the use already acquired. But our law annexes to the riparian proprietors the right to the use in common, as an incident to the land; and whoever seeks to found an exclusive use, must establish a rightful appropriation in some manner known and admitted by the law. Now, this may be, either by a grant from all the proprietors, whose interest is affected by the particular appropriation, or by a long exclusive enjoyment, without interruption, which affords a just presumption of right. By our law, upon principles of public convenience, the term of twenty years of exclusive uninterrupted enjoyment has been held a conclusive presumption of a grant or right.

* * *

With these principles in view, the general rights of the plaintiffs cannot admit of much controversy. They are riparian proprietors, and, as such, are entitled to the natural flow of the river without diminution to their injury. As owners of the lower dam, and the mills connected therewith, they have no rights beyond those of any other person, who might have appropriated that portion of the stream to the use of their mills. That is, their rights are to be measured by the extent of their actual appropriation and use of the water for a period, which the law deems a conclusive presumption in favor of rights of this nature. In their character as mill-owners, they have no title to the flow of the stream beyond the water actually and legally appropriated to the mills; but in their character as riparian proprietors, they have annexed to their lands the general flow of the river, so far as it has not been already acquired by some prior and legally operative appropriation. No doubt, then, can exist as to the right of the plaintiffs to the surplus of the natural flow of the stream not yet appropriated. Their rights, as riparian proprietors, are general; and it is incumbent on the parties, who seek to narrow these rights, to establish by competent proofs their own title to divert and use the stream.

* * *

In this view of the matter, the proprietors of Sergeant's trench are entitled to the use of so much of the water of the river as has been accustomed to flow through that trench to and from their mills (whether actually used or necessary for the same mills or not), during the twenty years last before the institution of this suit, subject only to such qualifications and limitations, as have been acknowledged or rightfully exercised by the plaintiffs as riparian proprietors, or as owners of the lower mill-dam, during that period. But here their right stops; they have no right farther to appropriate any surplus water not already used by the riparian proprietors, upon the notion, that such water is open to the first occupiers. That surplus is the inheritance of the riparian proprietors, and not open to occupancy.

* * *

* * * [If] there be a deficiency, it must be borne by all parties, as a common loss, wherever it may fall, according to existing rights; that the trench proprietors have no right to appropriate more water than belonged to them in 1796, and ought to be restrained from any further appropriation; and that the plaintiffs to this extent are entitled to have their general right established, and an injunction granted.

It is impracticable for the court to do more, in this posture of the case, than to refer it to a master to ascertain, as near as may be, and in conformity with the suggestions in the opinion of the court, the quantity to which the trench owners are entitled, and to report a suitable mode and arrangement permanently to regulate and adjust the flow of the water, so as to preserve the rights of all parties.

In respect to the question of damages for any excess of the use of the water by the trench owners, beyond their right, within six years next before the filing of the bill, I have not thought it my duty to go into a consideration of the evidence. It is a fit subject, either for a reference to a master, or for an issue of quantum damnificatus, if either party shall desire it.

The decree of the court is to be drawn up accordingly; and all further directions are reserved to the further hearing upon the master's report, & c. Decree accordingly.

NOTE

What are the "rules" of riparian water law as articulated in *Tyler*? What would the result have been if the rules were strictly applied?

NOTE: HISTORY OF RIPARIAN DOCTRINE

Tyler v. Wilkinson is the foundational American riparian case. According to Samuel C. Wiel, the great early twentieth century treatise writer and water law scholar, it was "the first expression * * * of the familiar notation of 'riparian' in reference to rights in watercourses." Samuel C. Wiel, *Waters: American Law and French Authority,* 33 Harv. L. Rev. 133, 136 (1919). *Tyler* and an English case decided a few years later, Mason v. Hill, 110 Eng. Rep. 692 (1833), provoked a lively twentieth century academic dispute about the historical roots of riparian rights. Wiel posited that modern riparian doctrine was grounded in civil, more particularly French, law. He argued that French ideas were more welcome in the United States during the post-Revolutionary War era than those of England. He believed that Justice Story and Chancellor Kent had borrowed their "riparian doctrine" from the Code Napoleon, which states that property rights accrue to those with property adjacent to a watercourse and that water must be returned to its ordinary course after being used.

Two scholars, Arthur Maas and Hiller B. Zobel, argued that English common law was the true source of riparianism as we know it. They theorized that English common law had developed riparianism over centuries and that Justice Story and Chancellor Kent built upon both English and American precedent to create riparian law. Arthur Maas & Hiller B. Zobel, *Anglo–American Water Law: Who Appropriated the Riparian Doctrine?,* 10 Pub. Policy 109 (1960). This is difficult to document in reported English decisions. More recently, Professor Carol M. Rose of Yale Law School has traced a different developmental path based on her research. Theoretically, as the scarcity of a natural resource increases, property rights will become more individualized and articulated. History reveals, however, that in Britain as water resources became scarcer, the status quo favoring ancient, established uses prevailed until the late eighteenth century. Carol M. Rose, *Energy and Efficiency in the Realignment of Common-Law Water Rights,* 19 J. Legal Stud. 261 (1990).

> An evolutionary view of property rights would suggest that this no-change approach occurs only in a zone between a perceived plenty and an increased demand that threatens to make a given resource scarce. Accordingly, no-change doctrines may crumple when the resource comes under more serious pressure. But the seventeenth- and eighteenth-century watercourse law tells us that the no-change approach may also be fairly stable, at least under certain conditions.

> These conditions are, first, that rivalries are relatively infrequent; second, that they involve one-on-one conflicts so that, in the normal case, it is fairly easy to negotiate reallocations from the baseline of no-change property allocation; third, that it is relatively easy to go elsewhere if negotiation fails; and finally, that the actual use of the resource is fairly stable over time so that one can reasonably presume that an established use is the most valuable one. All these conditions combined to maintain a certain stability in the doctrinally rigid water law of preindustrial Britain. It was stable precisely because the legal arrangements did not matter very much and were marginal to most ordinary behavior.

Id. at 273.

As Britain became more industrialized, new uses were deemed the most valuable ones and the conditions identified by Professor Rose no longer prevailed. Rose's research shows that England moved to an occupancy system, favoring the first person to alter a stream from its natural condition. By the early nineteenth century, the law in England and in the eastern United States had adopted a form not unlike the prior appropriation approach that, as we will see, developed in the western United States a few years later. Such a system worked well because the typical water dispute involved few parties in areas with abundant water supplies.

> The Massachusetts courts, then, were well on the way to an occupancy regime similar to that which would emerge in the American West. The first person to install works for utilizing the power of the fall would be entitled to keep that power, either against a prior unimproving user—however ancient his use—or against a subsequent improver along the same watercourse.

* * *

* * * [A] major difference between ancient use and occupancy doctrines lay in their implicit assessment of the relative value of water uses: ancient use assumed that the use in place for many years was superior, whereas occupancy assumed that the first capital expenditure marked the more valuable use.

But what was not different was that the occupancy cases, like the older ancient-use cases, took place in a microcontext of one-on-one conflicts between owners of neighboring sites. Until the middle of the nineteenth century, the leading Massachusetts occupancy cases were back-flow cases, and these almost certainly involved few parties: usually a downstream neighbor with a new dam and an upstream neighbor whose earlier waterwheel was swamped by the new dam. In these two-party site-use conflicts, whether governed by ancient use or by occupancy, it should have been relatively easy for most parties to organize a bargain, particularly before a new mill was constructed. Indeed, the cases themselves show that, in both Britain and America, fall-line riparian owners entered quite complex contractual arrangements for the distribution of given sites' waterpower.

Id. at 280–281.

Both ancient use and occupancy functioned well at first, but as flow interruptions and pollution problems dramatically increased transaction costs, the law quickly adapted. A new system of correlative rights appeared in New York at the turn of the nineteenth century. This system was labeled riparianism twenty years later in *Tyler v. Wilkinson,* and gave riparians equal rights to use a watercourse. Riparianism was well suited to areas where water power, not consumption, was the major use. According to Rose, Britain and Massachusetts soon followed in New York's footsteps as their industrialization demanded water allocation with minimal transaction costs. Thus, they all moved from a more individualized property system to a common property system. While the movement toward common property discounts Rose's theoretical construct, she concludes that the subject matter of disputes and low consumptive uses account for the variation. Yet, as *Tyler* illustrates, the "rules" of riparianism were almost immediately subject to exceptions that accommodated the economic realities of the situation.

The significance of economic pressures on changes in water law during America's first century was developed in the foundational work of Morton J. Horwitz in The Transformation of American Law, 1780–1860 (1977). Horwitz argues that the judiciary's willingness to adapt established common law rules to promote economic growth and social change led to a general transformation of the conception of law in the nineteenth century. For water law, this meant a departure from the theoretical riparian idea of natural flow to the "prior occupancy" and "reasonable use" values evidenced by the result reached in *Tyler v. Wilkinson.*

The natural flow ideal expressed by some courts inhibited the use of water as a productive asset. Diversions were allowed for water needed for domestic uses. Other uses had to be made without diminishing the quantity or quality of the stream. As a result, water law was effectively anti-development, as a literal application of the law would deny entrepreneurs the ability to divert or appropriate water for economic uses:

Two basic assumptions determined the approach of the common law to conflicts over water rights. First, since the flow of water in its natural channel was part of nature's plan, any interference with this flow was an "artificial," and therefore impermissible attempt to change the natural order of things. Second, since the right to the flow of a stream was derived from the ownership of adjacent land, any use of water that conflicted with the interests of any other proprietor on the stream was an unlawful invasion of his property.

Id. at 35.

Horwitz argues that the "reasonable use" doctrine did not prevail until the second quarter of the nineteenth century. He says that the 1805 New York case of *Palmer v. Mulligan* was the first to hold that an upper riparian could impede the flow of the water for a mill. "[Judge] Livingston understood that a rule making all injuries from obstruction of water compensable would, in effect, confer an exclusive right of development on the downstream property. The result, he concluded, would be that 'the public, whose advantage is always to be regarded, would be deprived of the benefit which always attends competition and rivalry.' " Id. at 37.

By the time of the Civil War, courts commonly recognized "reasonable use." Thus, the idea of property and water had undergone a transformation—from a "static agrarian conception entitling an owner to undisturbed enjoyment, to a dynamic, instrumental, and more abstract view of property that emphasized the newly paramount virtues of productive use and enjoyment." Id. at 31. Although that transformation was still subject to change, Horwitz theorized that prior appropriation lost in the East because the economic situation changed. Once the initial developers had taken the risks, prior appropriation promoted monopolies for those first users, while reasonable use allowed competition to thrive.

A later book challenged the idea that there ever was a "transformation" of judicial attitudes in the nineteenth century. Peter Karsten, Heart Versus Head: Judge–Made Law in Nineteenth–Century America (1997). Karsten argues that the evolution of the natural flow rule was present long before Horwitz acknowledges, and that American courts did not change many of the common law rules in the nineteenth century. He also argues that those rules that were changed were for the benefit of poor plaintiffs, rather than to promote economic efficiency.

For example, Karsten argues that *Merritt v. Parker*, a 1795 New Jersey case, demonstrates the early adoption of common law variations. The judge offered the "natural use" rule as the basic rule in giving jury instructions. But he also read the jury the rules of prior occupancy and reasonable use, rules that Horwitz argues "evolved" in the nineteenth century. According to Karsten: "Yes, all riparians had a right to the 'natural use' of the water. But prior milldam owners had claims affecting more recent ones, who had the right to use water so long as they did not diminish significantly the flow to the prior millowner. All of Horwitz's 'stages' of legal development were already there in this charge to the New Jersey jury: natural use, prior occupancy, and reasonable use." Id. at 42. In the end, the judge and jury decided that the plaintiff had not been justified in cutting a trench and draining water power from the defendant's previously established millpond.

Thus, Karsten argues that the case, like others cited by Horwitz, established that "one cannot unreasonably cause damage to an existing mill." Id.

Karsten cites the work of another scholar, William Nelson, who looked at county and supreme court decisions in Massachusetts from 1760 to 1830. "He tells us that the rule in the 1760s was that one who was first on a stream with a milldam acquired the continued right to water necessary to operate his mill and the power to 'bring suit against anyone who interfered with that use.' " Id. at 45. Karsten adds that many other states followed the same pattern. Karsten's disagreement with Horwitz is not only about the timing of judicial departures from crabbed rules of natural flow. He surmises that courts worked their way to "just" resolutions and introduced innovation into doctrine that often favored poor litigants over corporate interests.

Whatever historical and theoretical bases there may be for riparian rights, it is striking that in *Tyler* the basic principles are no sooner announced than exceptions are found to avoid applying them.

B. MINING

Irwin v. Phillips

Supreme Court of California, 1855.
5 Cal. 140.

■ HEYDENFELDT, J., delivered the opinion of the Court. MURRAY, C. J., concurred.

The several assignments of error will not be separately considered, because the whole merit of the case depends really on a single question, and upon that question the case must be decided. The proposition to be settled is whether the owner of a canal in the mineral region of this State, constructed for the purpose of supplying water to miners, has the right to divert the water of a stream from its natural channel, as against the claims of those who subsequent to the diversion take up lands along the banks of the stream, for the purpose of mining. It must be premised that it is admitted on all sides that the mining claims in controversy, and the lands through which the stream runs, and through which the canal passes, are a part of the public domain, to which there is no claim of private proprietorship, and that the miners have the right to dig for gold on the public lands was settled by this Court in the case of Hicks *et al.* *v.* Bell *et al.*, 3 Cal., 219.

It is insisted by the appellants that in this case the common law doctrine must be invoked, which prescribes that a water course must be allowed to flow in its natural channel. But upon an examination of the authorities which support that doctrine, it will be found to rest upon the fact of the individual rights of landed proprietors upon the stream, the principle being both at the civil and common law that the owner of lands on the banks of a water course, owns to the middle of the stream, and has the right in virtue of his proprietorship to the use of the water in its pure and natural condition. In this case the lands are the property either of the State or of the United States, and it is not necessary to decide to which they belong for the purposes of this case. It is certain that at the common law the diversion of water courses could only be complained of by riparian owners, who were deprived of the use, or those claiming directly under them. Can the appellants assert their present claim as tenants at will? To solve this question it must be kept in mind that their tenancy is of their own creation, their tenements of their own selection, and subsequent, in point of time to the diversion of the stream. They had the right to mine where they pleased throughout an extensive region, and they selected the bank of a stream from which the water had been already turned, for the purpose of supplying the mines at another point.

Courts are bound to take notice of the political and social condition of the country, which they judicially rule. In this State the larger part of the territory consists of mineral lands, nearly the whole of which are the property of the public. No right or intent of disposition of these lands has been shown either by the United States or the State governments, and with the exception of certain State regulations, very limited in their character, a system has been permitted to grow up by the voluntary action and assent of the population, whose free and unrestrained occupation of the mineral region has been tacitly assented to by the one government, and heartily encouraged by the expressed legislative policy of the other. If there are, as must be admitted, many things connected with this system, which are crude and undigested, and subject to fluctuation and dispute, there are still some which a universal sense of necessity and propriety have so firmly fixed as that they have come to be looked upon as having the force and effect of *res judicata*. Among these the most important are the rights of miners to be protected in the possession of their selected localities, and the rights of those who, by prior appropriation, have taken the waters from their natural beds, and by costly artificial works have conducted them for miles over mountains and ravines, to supply the necessities of gold diggers, and without which the most important interests of the mineral region would remain without development. So fully recognized have become these rights, that without any specific legislation conferring, or confirming them, they are alluded to and spoken of in various acts of the Legislature in the same manner as if they were rights which had been vested by the most distinct expression of the will of the law makers; as for instance, in the Revenue Act "canals and water races" are declared to be property subject to taxation, and this when there was none other in the State than such as were devoted to the use of mining. Section 2 of Article IX of the same Act, providing for the assessment of the property of companies and associations, among others mentions "dam or dams, canal or canals, or other works for mining purposes." This simply goes to prove what is the purpose of the argument, that however much the policy of the State, as indicated by her legislation, has conferred the privilege to work the mines, it has equally conferred the right to divert the streams from their natural channels, and as these two rights stand upon an equal footing, when they conflict, they must be decided by the fact of priority upon the maxim of equity, *qui prior est in tempore potior est in jure.* The miner, who selects a piece of ground to work, must take it as he finds it, subject to prior rights, which have an equal equity, on account of an equal recognition from the sovereign power. If it is upon a stream the waters of which have not been taken from their bed, they cannot be taken to his prejudice; but if they have been already diverted, and for as high, and legitimate a purpose as the one he seeks to accomplish, he has no right to complain, no right to interfere with the prior occupation of his neighbor, and must abide the disadvantages of his own selection.

It follows from this opinion that the judgment of the Court below was substantially correct, upon the merits of the case presented by the evidence, and it is therefore affirmed.

NOTES

1. In 1850 California adopted a statute that provided: "The common law of England, so far as it is not repugnant to or inconsistent with the constitution of the United States or the constitution or laws of this State, is the rule of decision in all the courts of this state." 1850 Cal. Stat. 219. Answering the argument that the case should have been decided by the common law of riparian rights, the court in *Irwin* reasoned that riparian rights were not involved because there was only public, not private land, along the stream. In his great treatise, Samuel Wiel wrote of the miners:

> They took possession of the public lands, mines, water and timber wherever they located, following out as between themselves the customs and rules of prior appropriation of all of these things prevailing in California, and not hearing from Congress one way or the other. Private rights to real estate all rested upon this rule of priority of occupation upon public land. "For a long period the general government stood silently by and allowed its citizens to occupy a great part of its public domain in California, and to locate and hold mining claims, water-rights, etc., according to such rules as could be made applicable to the peculiar situation; and when there were contests between hostile claimants, the courts were compelled to decide them without reference to the ownership of the government, as it was not urged or presented. In this way—from 1849 to 1866—a system had grown up under which the rights of locators on the public domain, as between themselves, were determined, which left out of view the paramount title of the government."

Samuel C. Wiel, Water Rights in the United States 88 (3d ed. 1911), quoting Cave v. Tyler, 133 Cal. 566, 65 P. 1089, 1090 (1901).

2. Presumably, if riparian rights existed in the public lands, they would belong to the government. Should a federal patent conveying title to public land carry with it riparian rights? In 1857 the California Supreme Court recognized the existence of riparian rights as between two claimants who located on and applied for patents to public lands. It acknowledged, however, the superior title of the federal government. "One who locates upon public lands with a view of appropriating them to his own use, becomes the absolute owner thereof as against every one but the government, and is entitled to all the privileges and incidents which appertain to the soil, subject to the single exception of rights antecedently acquired." Crandall v. Woods, 8 Cal. 136, 143 (1857). Is *Crandall* consistent with *Irwin*? *Hicks v. Bell*, cited in the principal case, had provided two answers to any possible federal claims to natural resources on public lands. First, California, not the federal government, succeeded to the sovereign's common law right to valuable minerals; second, the federal government was only a private proprietor of the public domain.

3.   Justice Stephen J. Field of the California Supreme Court affirmed the federal government's superior title in a major and controversial opinion that upheld the mining claim of a lessee of John C. Frémont against a miner who simply entered the land and began mining. Frémont, who was the leader of major western expeditions in the 1840s and the first Republican candidate for President, traced his claim as a riparian owner to a Mexican land grant. See Allan Nevins, Frémont: Pathmarker of the West (2d ed. 1955). Frémont's lessee, of course, characterized the entrant as a trespasser on the public domain, and the entrant argued that he was a licensee. Justice Field rejected the license theory but laid the foundation for the ultimate recognition of title in those who entered and grabbed according to custom. "There is no license in the legal meaning of the term. * * * The most which can be said is, that the government has forborne to exercise its rights." Biddle Boggs v. Merced Mining Co., 14 Cal. 279, 374 (1859), aff'd 70 U.S. 304, 18 L.Ed. 245 (1865).

The logic of *Biddle Boggs* was followed by the Nevada Supreme Court, which held in 1872 that a subsequent federal patentee obtained riparian rights superior to a downstream prior appropriator who entered and diverted the stream while that land was part of the public domain. Vansickle v. Haines, 7 Nev. 249 (1872). A concurring justice observed that the rule that a federal patent carried with it riparian rights would disappoint expectations that had been long considered by the public to be well founded. These decisions are important today because they illustrate that western water institutions were developed prior to the federal government's consistent assertion of any interest; thus the western states based their laws on the assumption that the United States permanently gave up whatever interests it might have had. The Supreme Court later found evidence that the federal government's silence was broken in a series of mining and public land laws passed between 1866–1872, as discussed *infra* at p. 107.

4.   While prior appropriation became the law of all the Great Basin states, it apparently was not the early law of the first white irrigators in the West, the Mormons. Originally a theocracy, the early church and government were one. In 1850 Congress refused to admit the state of Deseret and created the territory of Utah. An 1852 Utah Territorial statute provided that "county courts shall * * * have control of all * * * water privileges * * * and exercise such powers as in their judgment shall * * * subserve the interests of settlement in the distribution of water for irrigation." Moses Lasky, *From Prior Appropriation to Economic Distribution of Water By the State—Via Irrigation Administration*, 1 Rocky Mtn. L. Rev. 161, 167 (1929). Mormon collectivism survived only until 1880, perhaps because of the increased secularization of state government and the general tendency toward individualism in the late nineteenth century. It may be, however, that the mutual water companies, discussed *infra* at pp. 778–782, that abound in Utah are an offspring of the earlier community control of water.

Utah was not the only place where settlers tried collective water distribution. A commonly-held assumption that the western states quickly and uniformly adopted prior appropriation is not accurate. Western history shows that the earliest irrigation developed around various quasi-utopian colony schemes, and these colonies were receptive to a variety of water allocation practices. Irrigation colonies in southern California and Colorado following the Mormon model were founded in the 1870s and early 1880s. In Colorado Nathan C. Meeker, the agricultural editor of Horace Greeley's enormously influential New York Tribune, founded a utopian irrigation colony in 1870 along the Cache la Poudre River. The settlement was named Greeley. The story of the Union Colony and other attempts to construct irrigation colonies before the triumph of prior appropriation in the late 1880s is well told in Robert G. Dunbar, Forging New Rights in Western Waters 9–85 (1983).

C. Agriculture

Coffin v. Left Hand Ditch Co.

Supreme Court of Colorado, 1882.
6 Colo. 443.

■ Helm, J. Appellee, who was plaintiff below, claimed to be the owner of certain water by virtue of an appropriation thereof from the south fork of the St. Vrain creek. It appears that such water, after its diversion, is carried by means of a ditch to the James creek, and thence along the bed of the same to Left Hand creek, where it is again diverted by lateral ditches and used to irrigate lands adjacent to the last named stream. Appellants are the owners of lands lying on the margin and in the neighborhood of the St. Vrain below the mouth of said south fork thereof, and naturally irrigated therefrom.

In 1879 there was not a sufficient quantity of water in the St. Vrain to supply the ditch of appellee and also irrigate the said lands of appellant. A portion of appellee's dam was torn out, and its diversion of water thereby seriously interfered with by appellants. The action is brought for damages arising from the trespass, and for injunctive relief to prevent repetitions thereof in the future.

* * *

It is contended by counsel for appellants that the common law principles of riparian proprietorship prevailed in Colorado until 1876, and that the doctrine of priority of right to water by priority of appropriation thereof was first recognized and adopted in the constitution. But we think the latter doctrine has existed from the date of the earliest appropriations of water within the boundaries of the state. The climate is dry, and the soil, when moistened only by the usual rainfall, is arid and unproductive; except in a few favored sections, artificial irrigation for agriculture is an absolute necessity. Water in the various streams thus acquires a value unknown in moister climates. Instead of being a mere incident to the soil, it rises, when appropriated, to the dignity of a distinct usufructuary estate, or right of property. It has always been the policy of the national, as well as the territorial and state governments, to encourage the diversion and use of water in this country for agriculture; and vast expenditures of time and money have been made in reclaiming and fertilizing by irrigation portions of our unproductive territory. Houses have been built, and permanent improvements made; the soil has been cultivated, and thousands of acres have been rendered immensely valuable, with the understanding that appropriations of water would be protected. Deny the doctrine of priority or superiority of right by priority of appropriation, and a great part of the value of all this property is at once destroyed.

The right to water in this country, by priority of appropriation thereof, we think it is, and has always been, the duty of the national and state governments to protect. The right itself, and the obligation to protect it, existed prior to legislation on the subject of irrigation. It is entitled to protection as well after patent to a third party of the land over which the natural stream flows, as when such land is a part of the public domain; and it is immaterial whether or not it be mentioned in the patent and expressly excluded from the grant.

The act of congress protecting in patents such right in water appropriated, when recognized by local customs and laws, "was rather a voluntary recognition of a pre-existing right of possession, constituting a valid claim to its continued use, than the establishment of a new one." *Broder v. Natoma W. & M. Co.* 11 Otto 274.

We conclude, then, that the common law doctrine giving the riparian owner a right to the flow of water in its natural channel upon and over his lands, even though he makes no beneficial use thereof, is inapplicable to Colorado. Imperative necessity, unknown to the countries which gave it birth, compels the recognition of another doctrine in conflict therewith. And we hold that, in the absence of express statutes to the contrary, the first appropriator of water from a natural stream for a beneficial purpose has, with the qualifications contained in the constitution, a prior right thereto, to the extent of such appropriation. See *Schilling v. Rominger*, 4 Col. 103.

The territorial legislature in 1864 expressly recognizes the doctrine. It says: "Nor shall the water of any stream be diverted from its original channel to the detriment of any miner, millmen or others along the line of said stream, *who may have a priority of right,* and there shall be at all times left sufficient water in said stream for the use of miners and agriculturists along said stream." Session Laws of 1864, p. 68, § 32.

The priority of right mentioned in this section is acquired by priority of appropriation, and the provision declares that appropriations of water shall be subordinate to the use thereof by prior appropriators. This provision remained in force until the adoption of the constitution; it was repealed in 1868, but the repealing act re-enacted it *verbatim.*

But the rights of appellee were acquired, in the first instance, under the acts of 1861 and 1862, and counsel for appellants urge, with no little skill and plausibility, that these statutes are in conflict with our conclusion that priority of right is acquired by priority of appropriation. The only provision, however, which can be construed as referring to this subject is § 4 on page 68, Session Laws of 1861. This section provides for the appointment of commissioners, in times of scarcity, to apportion the stream "in a just and equitable proportion," to the best interests of all parties, *"with a due regard to the legal rights of all."* What is meant by the concluding phrases of the foregoing statute? What are the legal rights for which the commissioners are enjoined to have a "due regard?" Why this additional limitation upon the powers of such commissioners?

It seems to us a reasonable inference that these phrases had reference to the rights acquired by priority of appropriation. This view is sustained by the universal respect shown at the time said statute was adopted, and subsequently by each person, for the prior appropriations of others, and the corresponding customs existing among settlers with reference thereto. This construction does not, in our judgment, detract from the force or effect of the statute. It was the duty of the commissioners under it to guard against extravagance and waste, and to so divide and distribute the water as most economically to supply all of the earlier appropriators thereof according to their respective appropriations and necessities, to the extent of the amount remaining in the stream.

It appears from the record that the patent under which appellant George W. Coffin holds title was issued prior to the act of congress of 1866, hereinbefore mentioned. That it contained no reservation or exception of vested water rights, and conveyed to Coffin through his grantor the absolute title in fee simple to his land, together with all incidents and appurtenances thereunto belonging; and it is claimed that therefore the doctrine of priority of right by appropriation cannot, at least, apply to him. We have already declared that water appropriated and diverted for a beneficial purpose is, in this country, not necessarily an appurtenance to the soil through which the stream supplying the same naturally flows. If appropriated by one prior to the patenting of such soil by another, it is a vested right entitled to protection, though not mentioned in the patent. But we are relieved from any extended consideration of this subject by the decision in *Broder v. Natoma W. & M. Co., supra.*

It is urged, however, that even if the doctrine of priority or superiority of right by priority of appropriation be conceded, appellee in this case is not benefited thereby. Appellants claim that they have a better right to the water because their lands lie along the margin and in the neighborhood of the St. Vrain. They assert that, as against them, appellee's diversion of said water to irrigate lands adjacent to Left Hand creek, though prior in time, is unlawful.

In the absence of legislation to the contrary, we think that the right to water acquired by priority of appropriation thereof is not in any way dependent upon the *locus* of its application to the beneficial use designed. And the disastrous consequences of our adoption of the rule contended for, forbid our giving such a construction to the statutes as will concede the same, if they will properly bear a more reasonable and equitable one.

The doctrine of priority of right by priority of appropriation for agriculture is evoked, as we have seen, by the imperative necessity for artificial irrigation of the soil. And it would be an ungenerous and inequitable rule that would deprive one of its benefit simply because he has, by large expenditure of time and money, carried the water from one stream over an intervening watershed and cultivated land in the valley of another. It might be utterly impossible, owing to the topography of the country, to get water upon his farm from the adjacent stream; or if possible, it might be impracticable on account of the distance from the point where the diversion must take place and the attendant expense; or the quantity of water in such stream might be entirely insufficient to supply his wants. It sometimes happens that the most fertile soil is found along the margin or in the neighborhood of the small rivulet, and sandy and barren land beside the larger stream. To apply the rule contended for would prevent the useful and profitable cultivation of the productive soil, and sanction the waste of water upon the more sterile lands. It would have enabled a party to locate upon a stream in 1875, and destroy the value of thousands of acres, and the improvements thereon, in adjoining valleys, possessed and cultivated for the preceding decade. Under the principle contended for, a party owning land ten miles from the stream, but in the valley thereof, might deprive a prior appropriator of the water diverted therefrom whose lands are within a thousand yards, but just beyond an intervening divide.

We cannot believe that any legislative body within the territory or state of Colorado ever *intended* these consequences to flow from a statute enacted. Yet two sections are relied upon by counsel as practically producing them. These sections are as follows:

"All persons who claim, own or hold a possessory right or title to any land or parcel of land within the boundary of Colorado territory, * * * when those claims are on the bank, margin or neighborhood of any stream of water, creek or river, shall be entitled to the use of the water of said stream, creek or river for the purposes of irrigation, and making said claims available to the full extent of the soil, for agricultural purposes." Session Laws 1861, p. 67, § 1.

"Nor shall the water of any stream be diverted from its original channel to the detriment of any miner, millmen or others along the line of said stream, and there shall be at all times left sufficient water in said stream for the use of miners and farmers along said stream." Latter part of § 13, p. 48, Session Laws 1862.

The two statutory provisions above quoted must, for the purpose of this discussion, be construed together. The phrase "along said stream," in the latter, is equally comprehensive, as to the extent of territory, with the expression "on the bank, margin or neighborhood," used in the former, and both include all lands in the immediate valley of the stream. The latter provision sanctions the diversion of water from one stream to irrigate lands adjacent to another, provided such diversion is not to the "detriment" of parties along the line of the stream from which the water is taken. If there is any conflict between the statutes in this respect, the latter, of course, must prevail. We think that the "use" and "detriment" spoken of are a use existing at the time of the diversion, and a detriment immediately resulting therefrom. We do not believe that the legislature intended to prohibit the diversion of water to the "detriment" of parties who might at some future period conclude to settle upon the stream; nor do we think that they were legislating with a view to preserving in such stream sufficient water for the "use" of settlers who might never come, and consequently never have use therefor.

But "detriment" at the time of diversion could only exist where the water diverted had been previously appropriated or used; if there had been no previous appropriation or use thereof, there could be no present injury or "*detriment.*"

Our conclusion above as to the intent of the legislature is supported by the fact that the succeeding assembly, in 1864, hastened to insert into the latter statute, without other change or amendment, the clause, "*who have a priority of right,*" in connection with the idea of "*detriment*" to adjacent owners. This amendment of the statute was simply the acknowledgment by the legislature of a doctrine already existing, under which rights had accrued that were entitled to protection. In the language of Mr. Justice Miller, above quoted, upon a different branch of the same subject, it "was rather a voluntary recognition of a pre-existing right constituting a valid claim, than the creation of a new one."

* * *

The judgment of the court below will be affirmed.

Affirmed.

NOTES

1. Colorado became a state in 1876. Its constitution embraced prior appropriation by including a provision stating that: "[t]he right to divert

the unappropriated waters of any natural steam shall never be denied."
COLO. CONST. ART. XVI, § 6. The 1861 and 1862 territorial statutes, however,
were relevant in *Coffin* because any water rights of the parties were
established before statehood. What regime did the statutes establish in the
Territory of Colorado? Did the court correctly construe the statutes?

2. Do you agree with the court that climate and the sparse distribution of
water sources in the West dictated adoption of the prior appropriation
doctrine? Suppose the court had applied Colorado's riparian statute in
Coffin. Is it likely that this would have resulted in "disastrous consequences" and "prevent[ed] the useful and profitable cultivation of the
productive soil, and sanction[ed] the waste of water upon the more sterile
lands"? How might the parties have avoided such consequences if riparian
law had been applied?

NOTE: HISTORY OF THE APPROPRIATION DOCTRINE

The arid climate and geography of the West are usually cited as the
forces shaping western water institutions by necessitating a rejection of
riparianism and inexorably moving to a prior appropriation system. Today,
however, many leading scholars argue persuasively that economic expansion and social conditions of the nineteenth century were the most profound influences. See Terry L. Anderson & P. J. Hill, *The Evolution of
Property Rights: A Study of the American West* 18 J.L. & Econ. 163 (1975);
Donald J. Pisani, *Enterprise and Equity: A Critique of Western Water Law
in the Nineteenth Century*, in 18 Western Hist. Q. 15 (1987).

The origins of western water law lie in the conquest of the region by
the early miners and pioneers. This conquest, which is responsible for so
much of our national identity, has taken on the aura of a sacred myth that
has important and continuing consequences for modern water lawyers. The
history of western water law is first a history of mining and then of
irrigation. It is a history of costly trial and error. Some of the failures were
based on fantastic, scientifically unsound theories about aridity.

Josiah Gregg's 1844 book, Commerce of the Prairies, the standard
work on the Santa Fe trade, first expressed the naive idea that was to
dominate the settlement of the West until the 1890s. "The extreme
cultivation of the earth," he observed, "might contribute to the multiplica-
tion of showers, as it certainly does to fountains." Scientists, visionaries
and land promoters reduced this observation to the dictum: "rain follows
the plow." It took scientific studies, such as John Wesley Powell's Report
on the Lands of the Arid Region of the United States, With a More Detailed
Account of the Lands of Utah (1879) (essential reading for any serious
student of water law), and the droughts of the 1880s to convince westerners that this dictum was false and that European and eastern agricultural
practices must be modified in the West to adapt to the limiting condition of
aridity.

Walter Prescott Webb's The Great Plains (1931) is the classic study of
human effort to adapt to the limitations of the western climate and
landscape. He shows that it was not until the battle for open range was lost

by the cattle industry that irrigation emerged as a national agricultural strategy. After flirting with the occult and semi-occult of rainmaking, see W. Eugene Hollon, The Great American Desert: Then and Now 141–80 (1966), western farmers eventually turned to dry farming (the retention of seasonable moisture by techniques such as deep plowing and vegetation cover) and eventually to irrigation to cope with the imbalance between land and water in the West. These early farmers ultimately adopted techniques that had been used for centuries by Indians of the Southwest.

Capping a life's study of western water law, the leading scholar, Wells A. Hutchins, summed up the conventional understanding in his treatise.

Wells A. Hutchins, Water Rights Laws in the Nineteen Western States

159–67 (1971).

The prevailing Western doctrine of prior appropriation, as it is now recognized and applied throughout the 17 contiguous Western States and Alaska, is traceable chiefly to local customs and regulations developed spontaneously on public lands. The basic principles resulted from experience under varying conditions which, however, had an outstanding feature in common—inadequacy of water to supply completely the rapidly growing demands of industry and agriculture with use of the water control facilities then available. With considerable uniformity, these simple but effective principles became formalized into legal doctrine by decisions of courts and enactments of legislatures. Upon this foundation have been built the current complicated and voluminous water codes and case laws of the West.

As of the middle of the 19th century, the seeds of the appropriation doctrine are discernible in the status of three general movements of great historical and economic importance, which for the most part were probably unrelated—(1) Spanish settlements in parts of the Southwest, (2) the Mormon colonization of Utah, and (3) the California Gold Rush. Irrigation, although on the whole in its infancy, was being practiced in parts of the Southwest, chiefly under the Spanish–American community acequias and to a moderate extent by individuals in other scattered western areas. The Mormon irrigation agriculture development in Utah was getting under way. In California, the Gold Rush had started and mining ditches were being dug.

The early Utah and California water law situations have been the subject of much legal and historical literature, which facilitates appraisals of prevailing doctrine. In the southwestern areas, however, the situation with respect to appropriation of water is less clear and opinions concerning it differ.

Spanish Settlements in Parts of the Southwest

Irrigation in Arizona and New Mexico in aid of crop production is of prehistoric origin.

* * *

Opinions differ as to just how the appropriation doctrine came to the southwestern areas that had been occupied by the Spaniards and Mexicans. According to one school of thought, the Spanish settlers brought this doctrine from Europe with their civil law, which had been derived from the civil law of Rome. Thus, with respect to the Spanish, French, and Mexican penetration of what is now the American Southwest, it is said that:

> The extent to which this early western development has spread over and influenced the customs and laws of the subsequently created states may be debatable. But that such an influence existed, having as its background the old Roman water law, cannot be denied. How remarkably alike, in many vital respects, are the Roman laws concerning water and water rights and the doctrine of appropriation as interpreted and applied, for example, in Colorado. * * *

Another view is that exclusive rights in the Spanish and Mexican settlements arose only by way of grants from the sovereign, or as the result of local custom * * * which would be prescription.

Apparently, exclusive rights to the use of water on nonriparian lands in the New World of Spain were obtainable and, in various instances, they doubtless were obtained from the sovereign. Perhaps some form of "appropriation" of water can be found in some of the local customs. But in view of the paucity of historical examples, establishment of the well-known principle of *priority of appropriation* under the Spanish–Mexican regime, in the form in which it is so widely applied in the West today, is lacking in satisfactory proof and therefore, to say the least, is questionable.

Mormon Colonization of Utah

The colonization of Utah began in 1847 when the Mormons, under the personal leadership of Brigham Young, entered the Great Salt Lake Valley.

* * *

In the year following the arrival of the first pioneers, this region was ceded to the United States by the Treaty of Guadalupe Hidalgo, which was proclaimed July 4, 1848. Without direction or interference from the United States Government, the Mormons improvised a temporary system of land titles, pending the acquisition of definitive Federal grants, and the roots of a permanent system of water titles.

* * *

* * * During the earliest years, in the absence of political law, the Mormon Church approved the custom of diverting water by group effort and applying it to beneficial use, and supervised these operations. Early legislation made grants of water privileges, authorized the making of grants, and vested in the county courts control over appropriations of water. A statute passed in 1880 recognized accrued rights to water acquired by appropriation or adverse use, but did not contain a specific authorization to appropriate water. The principle of priority in time appears to have been recognized by custom before there was any general law on the subject.

California Gold Rush

Gold was discovered in the foothills of the Sierra Nevada, California, in January 1848. This development and the resulting mining industry had a profound influence upon the political and economic growth of California and on the development of water law throughout the West. As water was required in much of the gold mining processes, rights to the use of water were of fundamental importance. This mineral area was Mexican territory when gold was discovered but was ceded to the United States less than 6 months later by the Treaty of Guadalupe Hidalgo. There was no organized government there in the early years, nor much law except that made by the miners who helped themselves to the land, gold, and water under rules and regulations of their own making as they went along. In the words of the United States Supreme Court, speaking through Justice Field who had been Chief Justice of California, the miners "were emphatically the law-makers, as respects mining, upon the public lands in the State."

The rules and regulations of the miners were made by and for the individual camps and hence varied from one locality to another, but essentially the principles that they embodied were of marked uniformity. These principles related to the acquisition, holding, and forfeiture of individual mining claims, based upon priority of discovery and diligence in working them. And to the acquisition and exercise of rights to the needed water were applied comparable principles—posting and recording notice of intention to divert a specific quantity of water, actual diversion and application of water to beneficial use with reasonable diligence, continued exercise of the right, priority in time of initiating the appropriation, and forfeiture of priority for noncompliance with the rules—in other words, the doctrine of prior appropriation of water for beneficial use. These property rights in land and water were thus had, held, and enjoyed under local rules and were enforced by community action.

The California legislature took note of the miners' practices, but did not authorize appropriation of water until 1872. This was done in a short statute which essentially codified principles and practices that had been developed in the mining camps of the Sierra. In the meantime, these customs had been copied in mining areas of other States and Territories. Many water cases decided in the early years in several Western States involved relative rights to the use of water for mining purposes or for milling connected with mining. The miner's inch unit for measuring water in the mining camps is still used in some Western States, although its quantitative value varies from one area to another. The spreading influence of these mining customs is attested to by the considerable number of western jurisdictions in which early statutes authorizing appropriation of water contained the requirements of posting notice of appropriation, filing it for record, and diverting the water and putting it to beneficial use which were featured in the California statute of 1872. The present long, detailed "water codes," with their centralized administrative procedures, developed inevitably from these early brief declarations of a few basic principles.

There is no doubt that the major contribution to the arid region doctrine of appropriation as it is now recognized and applied throughout the West was made by these gold miners. But as to whether the mining water rights doctrine was actually made up out of whole cloth in the Gold Rush days, substantial doubt has been expressed. A writer who studied the scene on the ground a few decades after its height,[29] and another whose research was published in 1935,[30] concluded that the rules and regulations then established were strikingly characteristic of much earlier mining enterprises in the Old World. The earlier writer compared the principle of "mining freedom" of the Germanic and Cornwall miners with that of the modern mining camps in California and other western jurisdictions. A half-century later, Professor Colby's well-documented article discussed the right of free mining and free use of flowing water for mining purposes as a part of the customs of Germanic miners in the Middle Ages, and the similarity of conditions under which the California and Germanic miners developed their rules, usages, and customs related to mining practices and uses of water for mining purposes. This principle of "free mining," with free use of water therefor, spread from the Germanic lands to various European countries and their colonies. In fact, Professor Colby's main thesis, with numerous examples, is the widespread existence of the doctrine of prior appropriation of water in the important mining regions of the world. Certain it is that the "Forty-niners" came to California from many countries. They may well have brought with them some knowledge of the old Germanic customs and applied this knowledge in their new environment.

Development of the Appropriation Doctrine

State and Local Laws and Customs

Possessory rights on the public domain. The appropriation doctrine developed chiefly on the public domain. For years the owner of these lands—the Federal Government—made no move either to assert or to grant away its water rights. The miners were trespassers, and so their claims to the use of water were not good as against the Government. However, in the absence of specific State or Federal legislation authorizing the appropriation of water, the customs established in the mining camps of recognizing rights to the use of water by appropriation—"first in time, first in right"—eventually became valid local law. This came about because of the policy of the courts to recognize miners' claims as possessory rights that were good among themselves and as against any other claimant but the Government.

An enlightening account of the events leading up to the establishment of the appropriative doctrine in California is contained in an opinion of the United States Supreme Court written in 1879 by Justice Field, who had been Chief Justice of the California Supreme Court during a part of this

---

29. Shinn, C. H., "Mining Camps, A Study in American Frontier Government," pp. 11–35 (1948, originally published in 1885).

30. Colby, William E., "The Freedom of the Miner and Its Influence on Water Law," published in "Legal Essays, in Tribute to Orrin Kipp McMurray," pp. 67–84 (1935).

dynamic period.[31] Justice Field said that the discovery of gold was followed by an immense immigration into the State; that the gold-bearing lands, which belonged to the United States, were unsurveyed and not open to settlement; that the immigrants in vast numbers entered the Sierra Nevada with a love of order, system, and fair dealing. He continued:

> In every district which they occupied they framed certain rules for their government, by which the extent of ground they could severally hold for mining was designated, their possessory right to such ground secured and enforced, and contests between them either avoided or determined. These rules bore a marked similarity, varying in the several districts only according to the extent and character of the mines; distinct provisions being made for different kinds of mining, such as placer mining, quartz mining, and mining in drifts or tunnels. They all recognized discovery, followed by appropriation, as the foundation of the possessor's title, and development by working as the condition of its retention. And they were so framed as to secure to all comers, within practicable limits, absolute equality of right and privilege in working the mines. Nothing but such equality would have been tolerated by the miners, who were emphatically the law-makers, as respects mining, upon the public lands in the State. The first appropriator was everywhere held to have, within certain well-defined limits, a better right than others to the claims taken up; and in all controversies, except as against the government, he was regarded as the original owner, from whom title was to be traced. But the mines could not be worked without water. Without water the gold would remain forever buried in the earth or rock. To carry water to mining localities, when they were not on the banks of a stream or lake, became, therefore, an important and necessary business in carrying on mining. Here, also, the first appropriator of water to be conveyed to such localities for mining or other beneficial purposes, was recognized as having, to the extent of actual use, the better right. The doctrines of the common law respecting the rights of riparian owners were not considered as applicable, or only in a very limited degree, to the condition of miners in the mountains. The waters of rivers and lakes were consequently carried great distances in ditches and flumes, constructed with vast labor and enormous expenditures of money, along the sides of mountains and through canons and ravines, to supply communities engaged in mining, as well as for agriculturists and ordinary consumption. Numerous regulations were adopted, or assumed to exist, from their obvious justness, for the security of these ditches and flumes, and the protection of rights to water, not only between different appropriators, but between them and the holders of mining claims. These regulations and customs were appealed to in controversies in the State courts, and received their sanction; and properties to the values of many millions rested upon them. * * * Until 1866 [when Congress passed the first

---

31. Jennison v. Kirk, 98 U.S. 453, 457–458 (1878).

public lands mining law], no legislation was had looking to a sale of the mineral lands. * * *

———

Donald Worster brings a different perspective to the history of the appropriation doctrine. He argues in Rivers of Empire: Water, Aridity, and the Growth of the American West (1985) that the economic situation of the West was interlinked with a new, instrumental view of nature, and prior appropriation "offered a greater freedom to exploit nature." Id. at 89.

> By that thinking, nature was assumed to exist for no other purpose than to be turned into private profit, and the first man on the scene was the one who could claim that profit. Older notions of property, along with any restraints on its exploitation, were no longer taken as sacrosanct.

> But western miners were only late, rough, derivative exponents of the new instrumentalism being articulated throughout the rising world of enterprise. In its broadest terms, the doctrine of prior appropriation was the product of a new capitalist economic culture and its attitudes toward nature. Appearing first in England, that culture was organized around the institutions of the free, competitive marketplace and of private property. It promised to overcome the supposed scarcity of nature with the abundance provided by new technology.

Id. at 90.

Because the drive for economic efficiency had changed the natural flow doctrine in the East as explained by Morton Horwitz, *supra* p. 65, Worster argues that by the middle of the nineteenth century the riparian doctrine was only alive in the sense that water users still had to own land on the banks of the river to get water rights. Therefore, the West simply eliminated the last requirement remaining from the old common law rule. However, while the East adopted "reasonable use" as the rule that would most encourage economic efficiency and discourage monopoly, westerners held on to their prior appropriation rights as vested rights.

Another western legal historian, Donald Pisani, also built on Horwitz's work to show that an instrumental approach to water law allowed the rise of prior appropriation in the West. Pisani calls the West's arid climate "at best, half an answer." Donald J. Pisani, Water, Land, and Law in the West: The Limits of Public Policy, 1850–1920, at 10 (1996). He argues that the water systems of the Mexicans and Spanish who inhabited the Southwest, as well as the Mormon system in Utah, demonstrate that prior appropriation was not inevitable in an arid climate. None of these cultures followed prior appropriation, instead adapting some form of community-based sharing, or correlative rights, to their situations. Their systems were far more linked to public rights than to the private rights that were later considered "necessary" in the West, in order to gain the capital needed to mine. Thus,

Pisani argues that economic demands most dictated the creation of prior appropriation:

> When easterners moved west, they carried with them several interlocking assumptions: first, that in the absence of a formal legal structure, or when that structure broke down, "popular sovereignty"—in this case "squatter sovereignty"—should prevail; second, that "liberty" meant freedom from government interference in the individual search for wealth; third, that the right to pursue wealth was not a gift of the state; but rather, derived from an individual's inalienable right to the product of his labor; fourth, that no person should be able to secure more land or water than he or she could make use of; and fifth, that the initiative and energy needed to develop a natural resource did more to create property than a formal title. Miners looked at the law in terms of self-interest, not protection of the "general interest."

Donald J. Pisani, To Reclaim a Divided West: Water, Law, and Public Policy, 1848–1902, at 22 (1992).

Mining was the dominant economic activity in the early settling of the West. Since the miners were digging on federal land, they could not secure riparian rights based on ownership. Pisani describes miners as "disseisors" of the United States, meaning that they held the right of a landholder to evict a trespasser when title belonged to a third party. Water, Land, and Law in the West, at 11. Thus, the solution for the disseisors of the United States to protect the rights they had in the water was to give priority to the first possessor.

Even so, neither miners nor every mining camp universally embraced prior appropriation. See To Reclaim a Divided West, at 12. "Miners disagreed over which water rights were stronger: those senior in time, those used on land closest to the water, or those whose holders had invested the greatest amounts of money developing their claims." Id. at 20. In areas where gold deposits were not extensive enough for large investments, prior appropriation was not seen as inevitable. However, "by 1852, money began to pour into the construction of diversion ditches, and argonauts began to recognize that water was more valuable than gold." Id.

Early western court decisions were conflicting as they obeyed the local customs, but several used economic justification to choose the prior appropriator over a riparian owner. For example, in 1854, the Ninth Judicial District Court in California "responded to immediate economic interests rather than the dictates of doctrinal purity or consistency," in rewarding water to the appropriator. Id. at 34. The judge justified his decision by describing how the construction of canals will "yield good wages to miners for years to come, and furnish thousands with constant employment, who otherwise would be compelled to lay idle, except during the rainy season." Id.

Finally, prior appropriation continued to be popular among the large irrigators who replaced the miners as the dominant water users, despite contemporary critics who foresaw monopolies and other inequities. In essence, Pisani argues "[t]he pursuit of wealth took precedence. Enterprise triumphed over equity." Id. at 23.

The view that *Coffin* is just another 19th century example of the creation of private property rights to promote the efficient allocation of resources, e.g. Stuart Banner, *Transitions Between Property Regimes*, 31 J. Legal Studies 359 (2002), has been challenged by Professor David B. Schorr, *Appropriation as Agrarianism: Distributive Justice in the Creation of Property Rights*, 32 Ecology L.Q. 3, 66 (2005):

> Early Colorado law attempted to spread the ownership of this scarce and valuable resource as widely as possible through a variety of rules, including limiting appropriations to the amount that could be beneficially used, abolishing the common-law disqualification of non-riparian lands from water use, and subjecting riparian lands to easements in favor of other water users. Temporal priority was a secondary principle, meant to ensure that these egalitarian-minded rules did not lead to a situation where rights were so small as to be worthless. Even the culminating moment of *Coffin*, in which the Colorado doctrine of prior appropriation was most clearly annunciated, mostly involved the law's opening the opportunity to appropriate water to all comers, not just a narrow class of landowners near the stream.

The Idaho Supreme Court, Joyce Livestock Co. v. United States, 144 Idaho 1, 156 P.3d 502, 512 (Idaho 2007), recently stated that "[t]he doctrine of prior appropriation grew out of the sense of justice of the miners who came to the west in search of gold and other precious metals." Does the opinion refer to distributive or corrective justice?

D. ELECTRICAL POWER

Herminghaus v. Southern California Edison Co.

Supreme Court of California, 1926.
200 Cal. 81, 252 P. 607.

■ RICHARDS, J. This appeal is from a judgment in the plaintiffs' favor in an action brought by them to obtain an injunction preventing the defendants from an alleged actual and proposed diversion of the waters of the upper San Joaquin river and its tributaries to the irreparable injury of the plaintiffs, through the interference thereby with riparian rights of the latter in and to the flow and use of the waters of said river upon, along, and across their lower lying lands contiguous to the banks and course of said river. The plaintiffs in their original complaint herein allege that they are the owners and tenants in possession of a certain large tract of land containing about 18,000 acres in the counties of Fresno and Madera, state of California, and extending along the bank of the main channel of the San Joaquin river for a distance of about 20 miles; the said land being as to the whole thereof riparian to said river, and the said plaintiffs having, for many past years, in the exercise of their riparian rights therein, made appropriate use of the waters of said river for the irrigation, overflow, and enrichment of their said lands and of the whole thereof. The plaintiffs proceed to allege that the defendants, being the occupants of lands lying along the reaches of the San Joaquin river and its tributaries above to the location of the plaintiffs' lands, claim some right in and to the waters of said river and to the use thereof adversely to the rights of the plaintiffs therein, and by virtue of such claims are threatening by dams, reservoirs, and other works to stop the flow of said river and to impound the waters thereof in and thereby to divert the waters of said river impounded and to convey the same away from said river at points above the plaintiffs' said lands so as to prevent the waters of said river from flowing through the courses and channels thereof down to and along, across, and over the said lands of plaintiffs, and to thus deprive the latter of the use and enjoyment thereof to their great and irreparable injury. * * *

[The trial court found in favor of plaintiffs.] * * * We are satisfied, from a careful review of the evidence in this case, that it sufficiently sustains the findings of the trial court * * * and, this being so, it becomes necessary for us at this point to review the history and development of the law of riparian rights in this state. We are saved the necessity of an extended elaboration of the earlier stages of that development by the decision of this court in the leading case of Lux v. Haggin, 69 Cal. 255, 4 P. 919, 10 P. 674, wherein, in the longest opinion in the judicial history of this court, the growth and development of the doctrine of riparian rights under the common law, in other jurisdictions, and finally in California, since its adoption of the common law in the year 1850, through a course of judicial decision down to the date of the determination of that cause upon appeal, is exhaustively reviewed. While it is true that the decision in the case of Lux v. Haggin was that of a divided court, we think it is also true, as stated by Mr. Chief Justice Shaw in his most able review of the "Development of the Law of Waters in the West," to be found in the appendix to 189 Cal. at page 779 et seq., that:

"It declared that the rights of the riparian owners to the use of the waters of the abutting stream were paramount to the rights of any other persons thereto; that such rights were parcel of the land and that any diminution of the stream against the will of the riparian owner by other persons was an actionable injury. The question was settled by that case and the riparian right has never since been disputed."

* * *

The doctrine of riparian rights thus abstractly stated has been clarified, though not materially changed, by this court in its application to the particular cases which have come before it since the decision of the case of Lux v. Haggin, *supra*. * * *

* * *

* * * The plaintiffs herein are riparian owners along the course or courses of the San Joaquin river, and their tract of land is practically all

riparian to said river, either directly along and beside the main channel thereof or through the contiguity of the upper portions thereof to the numerous sloughs putting off from said river and interpenetrating these higher areas of their said tract of land. As such riparian owners said plaintiffs are abstractly entitled to the reasonable use of the said waters of said river at all seasons of the year. Their right thereto is to the usufruct of said flowing stream in the usual and ordinary course of its flow, and this right is a vested right inherent in the soil of their said lands and not a mere incident or appurtenant thereto. It is a right which is neither gained nor lost by use or disuse abstractly and in the absence of adverse rights gained by others by prescription or of their loss by laches creating an estoppel under certain conditions hereinafter to be noted. It is a right which they partake of in common with other riparian proprietors along said stream entitled to a similar usufruct in its waters. It is a right which appropriators of water from said stream do not, as we shall see, share with the riparian owners thereon, in the absence of rights to the use of said waters gained by such appropriators by grant or by prescription.

* * *

We are * * * entirely satisfied that the foregoing utilization by the said plaintiffs of the waters of said river and the flow and underflow and overflow thereof constitutes a reasonable use thereof within the intent and meaning of the foregoing definitions of the riparian right of land owners along such or similar streams. * * * To admit the right to such interference to the extent of taking away from the individual his initiative in deciding to which of several adaptable uses he shall devote his property would be to divest him to that extent of his most precious right of ownership therein. * * *

We have now reached the point in this discussion where the rights and claims of right of the appellant in and to the use of the waters of the San Joaquin river and its tributaries come into view. The appellant is a riparian owner of considerable lands along the upper reaches of said river and its tributaries. * * * Generally speaking, it has the same usufruct in the waters of said river as all other riparian owners along the course thereof possess. It is entitled to the reasonable use of said waters and of the ordinary and usual flow thereof for such customary and domestic uses as inhere in riparian owners along similar streams, and for irrigation of their said riparian lands. Being an upper riparian owner along said stream and the tributaries thereof, it is entitled to the benefit of whatever reasonable waste or diminution in the volume of said waters occurs during and in the course of the reasonable exercise of its riparian rights therein. In addition to the foregoing usual and customary uses of said waters, the appellant is entitled to make appropriate use of the same for the development of power and electric energy. * * *

* * * [D]efendants [claim] that, in the course and exercise of their conceded right to a reasonable use of the waters of said stream for the development of power and electric energy, they have the right to build reservoirs at various points along the upper reaches of said river and the tributaries thereof for the storage of the waters of said river to the extent set forth with much of detail in their said answer. * * * The trial court found that * * * the system of reservoirs shown to be partially in course of construction and wholly within the contemplation and plans of the defendants, would * * * have the effect of causing a diversion of the waters which constitute the usual and ordinary flow of said river for periods, and to an extent which would practically effectuate a withdrawal of said waters from a large portion of the lands of said plaintiffs during the period in each season when they are benefited by its flow and overflow * * *. * * * [T]he defendants frankly admit that their proposed plans for the storage of the waters of said river in its vast system of reservoirs hold in contemplation the retirement of said waters for long and indefinite periods of time, in fact, admit that as to certain of said reservoirs, the sequestration of the portion of the said waters stored therein will be cyclic, and as to said waters as a whole and to the extent of their retention in said reservoirs, their ultimate return to the river would depend, not at all upon the claims and asserted rights of lower riparian owners to the usual, natural, and ordinary flow of said waters, but altogether upon the will and convenience of the defendants in their proposed utilization of said waters for power production.

* * * The asserted right of the defendants herein as riparian owners along said river and incidentally the asserted rights and claims of all those who have appeared herein as amici curiae claiming similar rights in similar rivers in this state, would, if permitted, put an end to the whole doctrine of riparian rights, not only as to these plaintiffs and all other lower riparian owners similarly situated, but also as to the defendants themselves, since any person or aggregation of persons having the financial ability and acquiring a riparian ownership in lands above those of the defendants along the yet higher reaches of said river would thus become entitled to exercise all the rights which the defendants are here claiming, even against them, with the resultant drying up of the defendants' own reservoirs. Two answers might well be suggested to the claims of the defendants and of their supporting amici curiae of a present right to thus break down and destroy the long-established doctrine of riparian rights upon the ground of public policy. One of these is to be found in the apt expression of our Chief Justice Shaw in his admirable review of the "Development of the Law of Waters in the West" above referred to, wherein he says:

"The obvious answer on the question of policy is that the objection comes too late, that it should have been made to the Legislature in 1850, prior to the enactment of the statute adopting the common law. When that was done, the riparian rights became vested, and thereupon the much more important public policy of protecting the right of private property, became paramount and controlling. This policy is declared in our constitutions, has been adhered to throughout our national history, and it is through it that the remarkable progress and development of the country has been made possible."

And the other equally apt answer is to be found in the opinion of Mr. Justice Sloss in the case of Miller & Lux v. Madera Canal, etc., Co., *supra*, wherein that learned jurist said: "The riparian owners have a right to have the stream flow past their land in its usual course, and this right, so far as it is of regular occurrence and beneficial to their land is, as we have frequently said, a right of property, 'a parcel of the land itself.' Neither a court nor the Legislature has the right to say that because such water may be more beneficially used by others it may be freely taken by them. Public policy is at best a vague and uncertain guide, and no consideration of policy can justify the taking of private property without compensation. If the higher interests of the public should be thought to require that the water usually flowing in streams of this state should be subject to appropriation in ways that will deprive the riparian proprietor of its benefit, the change sought must be accomplished by the use of the power of eminent domain. The argument that these waters are of great value for the purposes of storage by appropriators and of small value to the lower riparian owners defeats itself. If the right sought to be taken be of small worth, the burden of paying for it will not be great. If, on the other hand, great benefits are conferred upon the riparian lands by the flow, there is all the more reason why these advantages should not without compensation, be taken from the owners of these lands and transferred to others."

* * *

■ SHENK, J. I dissent. The decision in this case is important because of its effect generally upon the conservation of the waters of the state. The main opinion, it seems to me, will result in checking the progress of the state of California in conserving this most important natural resource. It unnecessarily pulls the teeth of the Water Commission Act. In order to have the beneficial use of less than 1 per cent. of the maximum flow of the San Joaquin river on their riparian lands, the plaintiffs are contending for the right to use the balance in such a way that, so far as they are concerned, over 99 per cent. of that flow is wasted. This is a highly unreasonable use or method of the use of water. * * *

The rule that limits the right to the use of water to that which is reasonably necessary for beneficial purposes is now general throughout the Western states, and prevails in this state except as between a riparian owner and an appropriator. * * *

In 1850 the Legislature provided that the common law of England should be the rule of decision in all of the courts of this state in so far as it was not inconsistent with or repugnant to the state and federal constitutions and laws of this state. This provision was codified in 1872. One of the characteristics of the common law is that it contains within itself its own repealer; that is to say, it changes as conditions change and adapts itself to new conditions, ex proprio vigore. It should be applied to our conditions when our conditions are similar to those out of which the common law arose, but, when the common law is not applicable, because of different conditions, it should not be applied. 1 Kinney on Irrigation, §§ 509, 510; Motl v. Boyd (Tex. Sup.) 286 S. W. 458. In Lux v. Haggin, 69 Cal. 255, 4 P. 919, 10 P. 674, the common-law doctrine of riparian rights was applied to water rights in this state. But the conditions prevailing over 40 years ago when that case was decided were far different from the conditions existing at the present time when the growth and prosperity of the state are so dependent upon the proper conservation of the excess waters of its rivers by storage for irrigation and power uses. * * *

Citation of authority would seem to be unnecessary to support the proposition that no one may acquire a vested right to waste water in any form. That precise statement was made in the case of Eden Irrigation Co. v. District Court, 61 Utah, 103, 211 P. 957, in the following language:

"Let it be remembered that no one can acquire a vested right to waste water in any form. In this arid country water is life and may not be wasted. In this connection it is of the utmost importance to remember that no one can acquire an absolute title to water as he can to other property. A person having absolute title to property generally may ordinarily waste it, destroy it, or permit it to go to decay and become utterly useless at his pleasure. This he may not do with water."

Abundant authority to the same effect could be cited. The asserted right of a riparian owner in this state to have the waters of a river flow over or past his land, regardless of the reasonableness of the use or the benefit that such use may be to him, should therefore not be confirmed, especially when such use results in a needless waste and the deprivation of the rights of the state and of those who would use such waters for beneficial purposes under the authority of the state. * * *

As to the particular facts in this case: The appellant is both a riparian owner and an appropriator on the upper reaches of the San Joaquin river. The plaintiffs are the owners of some 18,000 acres of land bordering on the river below. This tract is an uncultivated area of grazing land, not devoted to cultivated crops. In the spring and early summer it is inundated by the waters of the river to such an extent that as such waters flow down the valley they resemble a moving lake. During that season of the year the flow amounts to from 10,000 to 20,000 cubic feet of water per second. The court found that a constant flow of 180 cubic feet per second from April 1 to October 1 of each year would irrigate the lands of the plaintiffs if the same were prepared for intensive cultivation.

* * *

The plaintiffs do not pretend to use or to be able to use the great volume of water that flows by their land on to San Francisco bay in the sense that the term "use of water" is ordinarily employed, namely, for the purpose of sinking into or moistening the soil of their lands. The use they demand is to employ this tremendous flow as a booster or a means of conveyance or of transportation to lift the very small percentage of the flow so useful to them to and over their pasture lands. A more extravagant or wasteful use of water could not be well imagined. * * *

NOTE: HISTORY OF THE "CALIFORNIA DOCTRINE"

The court in *Herminghaus* reached its result by invoking the riparian doctrine, thereby allowing farmers the full flow of the San Joaquin River.

California and some other states had distinguished themselves doctrinally from Colorado and most of the West. After the bold stroke seen in *Irwin v. Phillips, supra* p. 67, incorporating prior appropriation as the system of allocating water rights among miners on the public land, California recognized the common law of riparian rights as between landowners in a factually similar precursor to *Herminghaus,* Lux v. Haggin, 69 Cal. 255, 10 P. 674 (1886). The case is a colorful slice of California history and it is the spiritual foundation of the mixed, or hybrid, system of water law that prevails or once prevailed in the two tiers of states that bracket the arid, mountainous, "pure" prior appropriation states. The hybrid system states once included the West Coast states—California, Oregon and Washington—and those along the one-hundredth meridian, an arid-humid line that bisects the country—North Dakota, South Dakota, Nebraska, Kansas, Oklahoma, and Texas.

Samuel C. Wiel, writing in 1936, described *Lux* and its impact as follows:

> In 1886 the Supreme Court of California was concerned with flooding for wild hay in one of its most noted cases, *Lux v. Haggin.* The principal plaintiff was the West's greatest "Cattle King", the late Henry Miller. The locality was the portion of the central valley of California comprising the south end of San Joaquin Valley. * * *
>
> * * *
>
> "This land was in what might be called the overflow basin of Kern River. Through it the river flowed in various channels or sloughs, the principal one being known as Buena Vista Slough, but in flood time the lands were entirely inundated, because the sloughs were inadequate to carry the water, which flowed over the land and finally drained into Tulare Lake."
>
> * * *
>
> "As fast as land was acquired along the San Joaquin River, dams were thrown in the slough, levees were thrown up, and the water spread over large tracts for the production of grasses. The economy and effectiveness of this method of wild irrigation were remarkable. * * * [Henry Miller] became the wizard of the west in making green grass grow. * * * In order to control the water he acquired land on both sides of the river for a distance of over a hundred and twenty miles. * * * "9

The Haggin interests, also very wealthy, were promoting an irrigation and land development to divert the water above Miller. Emphasizing the disproportionately little benefit that Miller's wild haying was getting as compared to the vast volume of water, they urged that Miller was not making the beneficial use required by a test based upon prior appropriation.

---

9. The foregoing facts are quoted from Treadwell, The Cattle King (1931) 80, 62–63.

This was a test that, given up in England, appeared anew among the Forty Niners of California in their mining on the public domain. * * *

* * * The trial court favored priority of appropriation and was reversed by the supreme court. The reversal sustained Miller, his land being private, in the common-law riparian right for flow of the water against the defendants, unlimited by use. The defendants persuaded the supreme court to grant a rehearing. Much public attention followed, and had its reflection in the length of the rehearing opinion, two hundred pages, bringing up in a heap most of what the books contained upon the subject of waters at that time. [The court] sustained Miller again. The first opinion of 1884, because it is shorter, is the better reading. It had been a concise embodiment that "Property rights are essentially the same and quite as secure here as elsewhere." An earlier period, also against much pressure, had ruled similarly in the analogous litigation over the once-famous Mariposa Grant of General Fremont. On that occasion Mr. Justice Field (subsequently of the United States Supreme Court) established as Chief Justice of California that free location of mines is confined to minerals on the vacant public domain and is barred from land that became private before the mining location is attempted. Numerous California cases had made like rulings about appropriating water, and *Lux v. Haggin* in 1886 was giving recognition to this legal history. It held, therefore, that questions of use were immaterial in the case.

Samuel C. Wiel, *Fifty Years of Water Law*, 50 Harv. L. Rev. 252, 256–59 (1936).

In limiting the appropriation doctrine to public lands still in federal ownership, the court in *Lux* held that:

> *A grant of public land of the United States carries with it the common-law rights to an innavigable stream thereon, unless the waters are expressly or impliedly reserved by the terms of the patent, or of the statute granting the land, or unless they are reserved by the congressional legislation authorizing the patent* * * *.

Lux v. Haggin, 69 Cal. 255, 10 P. 674, 720 (1886).

The court reconciled its earlier decisions and stressed the significance of federal legislation concerning mining on the public lands that recognized the rights of water appropriators (discussed and quoted *infra* p. 107):

> It has never been held by the supreme court of the United States, or by the supreme court of this state, that an appropriation of water on the public lands of the United States (made after the act of congress of July 26, 1866, or the amendatory act of 1870) gave to the appropriator the right to the water appropriated as against a grantee of riparian lands, under a grant made or issued prior to the act of 1866, except in a case where the water so subsequently appropriated was reserved by the terms of such grant.

* * *

* * * In the case at bar the grant of the lands to the state (containing no reservation of the waters of flowing streams, express or to be implied from its terms) was made nearly 30 years before the first appropriation of water by the defendant, which was *after* the act of congress of July, 1866, and the amendatory act of 1870.

In *Osgood v. Water Co.*, 56 Cal. 571 [(1880)], it was held that where a person acquired a right, by appropriation, to water upon the public lands of the United States, *before* the issuance of a patent to another for lands through which the stream ran, the patentee's rights were, "by express statutory enactment, subject to the rights of the appropriator." The court cited the [1870] amendatory act of congress * * *.

* * * [O]ne who acquired a title to riparian lands from the United States prior to the act of July 26, 1866, could not (in the absence of reservation in his grant) be deprived of his common-law rights to the flow of the stream by one who appropriated its waters after the passage of that act. * * *

* * * The statutes passed long afterwards cannot affect rights acquired by the state by virtue of a [Swamp Land Act] grant made in 1850, [and later conveyed to Miller and Lux], nor can the subsequent policy of the United States (which is supposed to be indicated by a failure, by express laws, to prohibit the occupation of portions of its lands for mining, etc., and by the omission of the executive officers to attempt to remove miners and other occupants by force) be held to affect the rights acquired by the state through the grant of 1850. * * *

10 P. at 724–30.

After *Lux*, when can a holder of a prior appropriative right prevail over a subsequent riparian? The *Lux* court distinguished *Coffin v. Left Hand Ditch Co.*, *supra* p. 71, based on the unequivocal incorporation of the prior appropriation doctrine by the Colorado Constitution of 1876. Article XVI, § 5 provides:

The water of every natural stream, not heretofore appropriated, within the State of Colorado, is hereby declared to be property of the people of the State, subject to appropriation as hereinafter provided.

Coffin, however, involved rights that arose before the state constitution was adopted, and the Colorado court therefore never mentioned the provision.

Western states developed both appropriation and riparian systems on the assumption that both were sanctioned by the federal government. The western states also began to assume that the United States would assert no interest in allocating waters arising on the public domain. This assumption arose during what is called the "disposition era" of public land policy. Congress passed a variety of statutes to transfer land from public to private ownership. However, the disposition era came to an end before the federal government had disposed of all the public domain. In 1891, federal policy began to shift toward a policy of selective retention of public lands with the passage of legislation authorizing the presidential creation of forest reserves. In addition, the President made large-scale withdrawals of western

lands from entry and the establishment of private rights. But the consequences of this shift for western water law were largely ignored. In his
third edition in 1911, Samuel Wiel observed that "[t]he future of Western
law of waters will depend much on the course of the policy of conservation;
at present that policy is in the ascendant, and demands a great change of
the existing law." Samuel C. Wiel, Water rights in the United States 166
(3d ed. 1911).

Wiel's account of Lux v. Haggin does not do full justice to the epic
nature of the case and the consequences it had for the future development
of California. The case pitted two monopolizers of land with different ideas
about the best system of water law to promote the large-scale reclamation
of an area of rich soil but with hydrological extremes. See Mary Catherine
Miller, Flooding the Courtrooms: Law and Water in the Far West (1993).
Miller and Lux were two German butchers who came to the state during
the Gold Rush and eventually amassed 80,350 acres of swamp land by
entries, some fraudulent, in the Tulare Basin under the Swamp Land Act of
1850. This Act had its genesis in efforts to stimulate further reclamation in
Louisiana but was extended to other states with these "worthless" lands.
Other acquisitions gave them an empire of over 300,000 acres in the
southern San Joaquin Valley. See David Igler, Industrial Cowboys: Miller &
Lux and the Transformation of the Far West, 1850–1920 (2001). The
dubious classification of much of the Tulare Basin, a series of ancient lakes
which rose and fell drastically depending on the seasonal rainfall surrounded by an alkali desert, as swamp land was already under investigation by
the California legislature as their entrymen fanned out over the area. Paul
W. Gates, History of Public Land Law Development 327 (1968). James
Haggin amassed his land through entries under the Desert Land Act of
1877, for which his company, The Kern County Land Company, successfully lobbied. Miller & Lux's lawyer argued that prior appropriation would
fundamentally alter nature whereas riparian rights would preserve it.
David Igler, When Is a River Not a River? Or, Reclaiming Nature's
Disorder in Lux v. Haggin, 2 Environmental History 52 (1996). In reality,
after the decision, the two giants agreed to share the costs of building a
reservoir so the River's supply could be used by both of them, and the
process of transforming the Valley into one of the world's most productive
agro-business areas that came to fruition in the 20th century began.
California's dual system both confirmed that power of large land riparian
land owners, and creatd powerful pressures incentives to limit this "monopoly." Valley farmers quickly turned to groundwater pumping, which
then and now remains largely unregulated. In 1887, the state passed the
Irrigation District Act which "gave less wealthy landowners a means to
compete against the Henry Millers and James Ben Ali Haggins." The Great
Central Valley: California's Heartland 45 (Stephen Johnson ed. 1993).
Finally, after decades of sustained criticism, voters finally enshrined reasonable use in the state's constitution.

In 1928, two years after *Herminghaus*, California responded to the
impracticality and waste permitted by the court's rather pure version of

riparianism by amending its constitution. The amendment to what was then article XIV (now art. X, § 2) states:

> It is hereby declared that because of the conditions prevailing in this State the general welfare requires that the water resources of the State be put to beneficial use to the fullest extent of which they are capable, and that the waste or unreasonable use or unreasonable method of use of water be prevented, and that the conservation of such waters is to be exercised with a view to the reasonable and beneficial use thereof in the interest of the people and for the public welfare. The right to water or to the use or flow of water in or from any natural stream or watercourse in this State is and shall be limited to such water as shall be reasonably required for the beneficial use to be serviced, and such right does not and shall not extend to the waste or unreasonable use or unreasonable method of use or unreasonable method of diversion of water. Riparian rights in a stream or water course attach to, but to no more than so much of the flow thereof as may be required or used consistently with this section, for the purposes for which such lands are, or may be made adaptable, in view of such reasonable and beneficial uses; provided, however, that nothing herein contained shall be construed as depriving any riparian owner of the reasonable use of water of the stream to which his land is riparian under reasonable methods of diversion and use, or of depriving any appropriator of water to which he is lawfully entitled. This section shall be self-executing, and the Legislature may also enact laws in the furtherance of the policy in this section contained.

The amendment was designed to adjust the relationship between riparian and appropriative rights. See Peabody v. City of Vallejo, 2 Cal.2d 351, 40 P.2d 486 (1935). This tempered the riparians' commanding advantage that had been reinforced in *Herminghaus*.

E.   CITIES

City and County of Denver v. Sheriff

Supreme Court of Colorado, 1939.
105 Colo. 193, 96 P.2d 836.

■ OTTO BOCK, JUSTICE.

* * *

* * * In 1918, when Denver acquired its water system, the population was between 150,000 and 200,000. The population served by the system at this time is approximately 350,000. The city has not been unmindful of its obligation to seek further water sources for its growing needs. As early as 1914 its Public Utilities Commission made investigation through employed engineers. After the city acquired the Denver Union Water Company, and in 1921, it caused a location survey to be made for projects of Western

Slope water, and particularly the Fraser river and Williams Fork diversion projects, these latter being involved in the instant case, and which the trial court decreed as of July 4, 1921, as the appropriation date. The filing of the map for these projects with the state engineer occurred January 28, 1922. The claims as filed seek water for irrigation as well as for domestic and other purposes. To bring water over the divide so that it may be applied to a beneficial use by the city, engineering and financial problems always have been a serious concern. Several futile attempts were made until the successful culmination in the organization of the Moffat Tunnel District in 1922, which provides two tunnels, one for rail transportation and a similar one for irrigation purposes. The tunnel commission continued work on the water tunnel until January 2, 1929, when it was turned over to the city by lease, under the terms of which provision was made that it be finished by the lessee and placed in operation to bring water to Denver. The expense of the construction of the water tunnel is estimated at $5,000,000. At the time of the trial it had a usable capacity of 600 second feet * * *. When completed and lined its capacity will be 1280 cubic feet per second. In addition to the completion of the water tunnel by the city to a capacity of 600 second feet, it constructed various gathering ditches, conduits, diversion works, tunnels and pipe-lines necessary to bring the water to Denver at an expense of approximately $12,000,000. It is hoped that by this development about 74,000 acre-feet of water will be made available at a cost of approximately $160 per acre-foot, which it is asserted is a considerably higher sum than farmers could afford to expend for water for the irrigation of agricultural land.

* * * As related to the Fraser river diversion project, the court found and decreed "that the maximum rate of diversion of water through said project accomplished prior to the date of this decree is 335 cubic feet per second." The balance of the appropriations are decreed conditionally upon actual diversion and storage within a reasonable time from the date of the decree to the maximum of 1280 cubic feet per second, this being the completed carrying capacity of the Moffat water tunnel. * * * The assignments of error raise but two questions, namely:

First, that the trial court, in giving the city its priorities from the Western Slope streams, made such priorities subject to unlawful and burdensome restrictive conditions; and,

[Discussion on the second question is omitted.]

In each of the three divisions of the decree we find the paragraph of which the city complains, as follows: "Any waters decreed herein, whether decreed therefor, to be for direct flow or for storage, and whether the said decree be absolute or conditional, be diverted, taken and used as supplemental to the decreed water rights now belonging to claimant, which said decrees are from the waters of the natural streams of the State of Colorado and that the said claimant be required to satisfy its needs for waters from said existing decrees owned by it before it shall be held to require or need waters herein decreed or shall be entitled to take the same. That the waters herein decreed shall be held by the said claimant as a water supply supplemental to its present supply of water available under water decrees which the said claimant now holds and to be used only to the extent necessary to fill the needs and requirements of the claimant for municipal purposes, after it has made full and economical use of the waters available to it under water decrees now owned by it."

* * *

It will be noted that the restrictions relate to "water decrees now owned by it," being the Eastern Slope water rights, and "any waters decreed herein" being the Western Slope water rights.

We shall first discuss these restrictive conditions to the decrees of the city as they relate to its Eastern Slope water rights. These appropriations are all based upon unconditional and absolute decrees. That they take on the attribute of property rights cannot be questioned. Counsel for defendants in error do not question this. This carries with it the right, under certain circumstances, to lease, sell and convey title.

* * *

The trial court's purpose in these restrictive conditions is disclosed in the record, wherein it is stated: "In making this right a supplemental right to the rights already owned by Denver, we are guarding against the City of Denver going into the business of selling water or disposing of a part or all of her present water rights and substituting the water acquired or to be acquired in this proceeding for her present water supply."

In part, the express purpose is to prevent any sale, lease or alienation of the Eastern Slope water. This would operate to prevent the city from leasing Eastern Slope water to farmers, which, under certain circumstances, we have said it had a right to do. Denver v. Brown, 56 Colo. 216, 233, 138 P. 44. If the city, for some legitimate reason, desired to abandon or sell any of its Eastern Slope water, it would, by so doing, and under these restrictions, jeopardize its water rights on the Western Slope. The furnishing of an adequate supply of water to 350,000 people requires managerial judgment and involves an ever-changing problem. To so freeze and straight-jacket the city's Eastern Slope water rights, by the restrictions involved here, would be an arbitrary invasion of vested property rights of the city.

* * *

* * * [I]t is not speculation but the highest prudence on the part of the city to obtain appropriations of water that will satisfy the needs resulting from a normal increase in population within a reasonable period of time. * * *

Neither a private nor a governmental agency may obtain a right to use a portion of the public's water resource unless it establishes intent to make a non-speculative appropriation.

For a private entity to meet its intent burden, it must have contractual commitments for any appropriations that are not planned for its own use, or the application will fail as unduly speculative. On the other hand, a governmental water supply agency has a unique need for planning flexibility because it must plan for the reasonably anticipated water needs of its populace, taking into account a normal increase in population. *City & County of Denver v. N. Colo. Water Conservancy Dist.*, 130 Colo. 375, 384, 276 P.2d 992, 997 (1954); *City & County of Denver v. Sheriff*, 105 Colo. 193, 202, 96 P.2d 836, 841 (1939).

The governmental agency does not have carte blanche to appropriate water for speculative purposes; in effect, the statute provides for a limited exception from certain requirements otherwise applicable to private appropriators. Public agencies must still substantiate a non-speculative intent to appropriate unappropriated water, and they must "have a specific plan and intent to divert, store, or otherwise capture, possess, and control a specific quantity of water for specific beneficial uses."§ 37–92–103(3)(a)(II). Accordingly, the governmental agency has the burden to demonstrate that its conditional appropriation is not speculative.

* * *

Sherrif is an example of the growing cities doctrine. The Court's willingness to exempt Denver from the duty to put its water to beneficial use in a relatively short time became the legal foundation of Western urban growth. In the past decade, the idea that cities must continue to grow endlessly in water-short areas has been challenged. Pagosa Area Water and Sanitation Dist. v. Trout Unlimited, 170 P.3d 307 (Colo. 2007), ch. 3, *infra* p. 313. GENERATED DIVIDER LINE OF TYPE 29

F. RECREATION

Empire Water & Power Co. v. Cascade Town Co.

United States Court of Appeals, Eighth Circuit, 1913.
205 Fed. 123.

[Cascade Town Company was the owner of a tourist resort located along Cascade Creek near the City of Colorado Springs, Colorado. The creek descended into the resort rapidly from the mountains through a deep, beautiful canyon whose "floor and sides are covered with an exceptionally luxuriant growth of trees, shrubbery, and flowers. This exceptional vegetation is produced by the flow of Cascade creek through the canon and the mist and spray from its falls." A hydroelectric power company proposed to make a diversion from Cascade Creek upstream from the defendant's property to generate electric power. Cascade sued for an injunction, which was granted by the trial court, and the power company appealed.]

■ HOOK, CIRCUIT JUDGE.

* * *

* * * In this branch of the case the controversy was over the character of complainant's use, its relation to that proposed by defendants, and the extent of complainant's appropriation and application of the water. It is urged that a use for a summer resort is not a beneficial use for either domestic or agricultural purposes. Counsel say that the views and standards of the early settlers were reflected in the state Constitution, and that it should be construed accordingly; that they did not plan for rest and recreation, and that to them "domestic" had to do with sustenance for man and beast, and cleanliness; and that "agricultural" related to the raising of crops. We think such a view is too narrow. If the commerce clause of the federal Constitution had been construed in that way, much of the growth of this country would have been arrested. In framing Constitutions wisdom frequently requires the use of general terms, which should be held as progressively adaptable to natural development and as open to embrace new instances as they arise and come clearly within the spirit of the provisions. * * * Places such as that described here, favored by climatic conditions, improved by the work of man, and designed to promote health by affording rest and relaxation are assuredly beneficial. They are relatively as important as sanitariums or hospitals, and should not be dismissed by calling them mere resorts for idleness. They are a recognized feature of the times, are important in their influence upon health, and multitudes of people avail themselves of them from necessity. Cascade is well described as a place of this kind. With its railroad station, hotels, cottages, waterworks, park, roads, and trails and its 12,000 or 15,000 annual visitors, it is a summer city. That it is not an incorporated municipality, but is largely a private venture, is, we think, unimportant. Nor need the purpose to which the waters of the stream are devoted be a single one of those named in the classification in the Constitution. It need not be exclusively domestic nor exclusively agricultural. It may be and is both, like that of the ordinary city with its homes, business places, parks, and public grounds.

It is clear that complainant intended to appropriate the waters of the stream to its purpose. The intent was openly manifested by the extensive improvement of its property by buildings, roads, etc., in reliance, not only on the use of the water in the ditches that were constructed, but also on the continued natural falls and flow of the stream. At this point, however, we experience the most difficulty with complainant's case. The laws of Colorado are designed to prevent waste of a most valuable but limited natural resource, and to confine the use to needs. By rejecting the common-law rule they deny the right of the landowner to have the stream run in its natural way without diminution. He cannot hold to all the water for the scant vegetation which lines the banks but must make the most efficient use by applying it to his land. See Schodde v. Water Co., 224 U.S. 107, a case from Idaho, where a landowner claimed the whole current of a stream to raise part of the water to his land. The case before us is exceptional, but we think complainant is not entitled to a continuance of the falls solely for their scenic beauty. The state laws proceed upon more material lines. Complainant also relies upon the distribution by the falls of moisture for the trees and other vegetable growth on its lands, which it has extensively improved. As we have said, its intent to appropriate the waters has been shown by its expenditures and improvements beyond what is served by its ditches. Has there been that actual application which the law requires? Undoubtedly a landowner may rely upon an efficient application by nature, and need do no more than affirmatively to avail himself of it (Thomas v. Guiraud, 6 Colo. 530; Larimer, etc., Co. v. People, 8 Colo. 614, 9 Pac. 794); but the use in that way should not be unnecessarily or wastefully excessive. If all the water flowing over the falls, directly applied to the lands in the usual way of irrigation, would be required to produce the effect of the distributed mist and spray as now utilized, we think defendants would have no right to divert it for a manufacturing purpose. If nature accomplishes a result which is recognized and utilized, a change of process by man would seem unnecessary. But the trial court based its decision of this branch of the case largely upon the artistic value of the falls, and made no inquiry into the effectiveness of the use of the water in the way adopted as compared with the customary methods of irrigation. In all other respects the conclusions of the court were in accord with the views we have expressed. It may be that if the attention of the lawmakers had been directed to such natural objects of great beauty they would have sought to preserve them, but we think the dominant idea was utility, liberally and not narrowly regarded, and we are constrained to follow it.

* * *

The decree of the trial court is reversed and remanded for further proceedings in conformity with this opinion.

NOTE

The court seemed to recognize the benefits of recreational and aesthetic uses of water but rejected the idea that prior appropriation law could protect a use of water to maintain the falls "solely for their scenic beauty." It leaves any expansion of the concept of beneficial use to the legislature. In the western states, a consciousness of the economic benefits and public enjoyment of recreation has continued to expand. Along with raised environmental consciousness, this has brought pressure for legal recognition of rights to maintain streamflows. As the next case illustrates, the concept of beneficial use was not the only barrier to change in water law doctrine.

G. Fish, As Proxies for Protection of Aquatic Environments

Colorado River Water Conservation District v. Rocky Mountain Power Company

Supreme Court of Colorado, 1965.
158 Colo. 331, 406 P.2d 798.

■ Moore, Justice.

Plaintiff in error, to whom we will refer as the district, claimed certain water rights in a statutory supplemental adjudication of water rights which was conducted in the trial court. The defendant in error, hereinafter referred to as the power company, protested allowance of the claims made by the district by filing a motion to dismiss them. The trial court granted the motion, denied the motion of the district for a new trial, and entered an appropriate judgment to review which the district is here on writ of error.

* * *

The language contained in each of the [three] claims, which is pertinent to the question to be decided, relates to the nature of the beneficial use to which the water in dispute has allegedly been applied. The allegation is that:

> "For the purposes herein claimed, water is not to be diverted from the natural stream, but is to be preserved and kept in the stream to the extent necessary for the preservation of fish life and the propagation of fish."

In each of the claims the areas along the streams where the water rights were allegedly initiated were described, together with the volume of water claimed, measured in cubic feet per second of time. The date claimed for the initiation of all the appropriations is set forth as June 7, 1937. The claims all contain the assertion that the streams involved, ". . . have been a habitat for fish and the propagation and preservation thereof for over 40 years, and have been used by the public to fish and for the recreational activities connected therewith during all of said period of time."

The district appeared in the adjudication proceedings and filed the disputed claims under the powers allegedly conferred by C.R.S. 1963, 150–7–5(10) which, among other powers placed in the district, includes the following:

> "To file upon and hold for the use of the public sufficient water of any natural stream to maintain a constant stream flow in the amount necessary to preserve fish, and to use such water in connection with retaining ponds for the propagation of fish for the benefit of the public."

As grounds for reversal of the judgment counsel for the district assert that:

* * *

"In pursuing this power the District is entitled to adopt and show in proof of its claims the acts of the public, if any, evidencing the intention of that public to appropriate the necessary portion of such waters for recreational purposes. A portion of these acts, all open, notorious and well known and publicized, indicating such intention are as follows:

"1. The construction of camp grounds and access roads and trails.

"2. The construction of fish hatcheries and the stocking, at public expense, of the rivers and streams affected by the claims.

"3. The utilization, by the general public, of such streams for fishing purposes.

"4. The studies of the Colorado Game and Fish Department, the Forest Service, the Bureau of Sport Fisheries and Wildlife, and others, conducted on the streams, determining what flows are necessary to sustain fish life, and provide for natural propagation."

* * *

The argument of the attorneys for the district consists of two basic propositions. One is that the use of flowing water in a stream is an appropriation of water; and the second is that such a use of water is a "beneficial use." Numerous opinions of this court have defined the essential requirements of an "appropriation" of water. We direct attention to Denver v. Northern Colorado Water Conservancy District, 276 P.2d 992, in which we find the following pertinent language:

"Further, the rule is elementary that the first essential of an appropriation is the *actual diversion of the water* with intent to apply to a beneficial use. * * * Water can be actually diverted only by taking it from the stream. * * * "(Emphasis supplied.)

* * *

There is no support in the law of this state for the proposition that a minimum flow of water may be "appropriated" in a natural stream for piscatorial purposes without diversion of any portion of the water "appropriated" from the natural course of the stream. By the enactment of C.R.S. 1963, 150–7–5(10) the legislature did not intend to bring about such an extreme departure from well established doctrine, and we hold that no such departure was brought about by said statute.

Cases relied on by the district, in which it is held that the diversion of water into retaining ponds for fish culture is a diversion for a beneficial use, are clearly distinguishable from the case under consideration. The case of Schodde v. Twin Falls Land and Water Co., 224 U.S. 107, contains language applicable to the instant controversy. * * *

The contention of the plaintiff that he was entitled to have the flow of the stream maintained * * * as to power the waterwheels by which he raised the water [to irrigate his land], was rejected by the supreme Court of the United States. It was pointed out in that opinion that the right to the maintenance of the "flow" of the stream is a riparian right and is completely inconsistent with the doctrine of prior appropriation. We quote from the opinion the following:

"We say this because it may not be doubted that the application here sought to be made of the doctrine of riparian rights would be absolutely destructive of the fundamental conceptions upon which the theory of appropriation for beneficial use proceeds, since it would allow the owner of a riparian right to appropriate the entire volume of the water of the river, without regard to the extent of his beneficial use.''

* * *

The judgment is affirmed.

NOTE

The Colorado law was later changed by creating a program for protection of instream flows which eliminated the requirement of a diversion. This and other state schemes for protecting instream flows are discussed *infra*.

The modern environmental movement was just being formed at the time of the case. We now value relatively undisturbed or restored aquatic environments much more than we once did. Efforts to incorporate these values into water law permeate the book. However, water law largely retains its 19th century utilitarian focus. One exception is the intermediate courts of appeals opinion in Michigan Citizens for Water Conservation v. Nestle Waters North America Inc., 269 Mich.App. 25, 709 N.W.2d 174 (2005), Chapter 4, pages 577–583.

H. Indian Reservations

Winters v. United States

Supreme Court of the United States, 1908.
207 U.S. 564, 28 S.Ct. 207, 52 L.Ed. 340.

This suit was brought by the United States to restrain appellants and others from constructing or maintaining dams or reservoirs on the Milk River in the State of Montana, or in any manner preventing the water of the river or its tributaries from flowing to the Fort Belknap Indian Reservation.

* * *

The allegations of the bill, so far as necessary to state them, are as follows: On the first day of May, 1888, a tract of land, the property of the United States, was reserved and set apart "as an Indian reservation as and for a permanent home and abiding place of the Gros Ventre and Assiniboine bands or tribes of Indians in the State (then Territory) of Montana, designated and known as the Fort Belknap Indian Reservation." The tract has ever since been used as an Indian Reservation and as the home and abiding place of the Indians. * * *

Milk River, designated as the northern boundary of the reservation, is a non-navigable stream. Large portions of the lands embraced within the reservation are well fitted and adapted for pasturage and the feeding and grazing of stock, and since the establishment of the reservation the United States and the Indians have had and have large herds of cattle and large numbers of horses grazing upon the land within the reservation, "being and situate along and bordering upon said Milk River." Other portions of the reservation are "adapted for and susceptible of farming and cultivation and the pursuit of agriculture, and productive in the raising thereon of grass, grain and vegetables," but such portions are of dry and arid character, and in order to make them productive require large quantities of water for the purpose of irrigating them. * * * It is alleged with detail that all of the waters of the river are necessary for all those purposes and the purposes for which the reservation was created, and that in furthering and advancing the civilization and improvement of the Indians, and to encourage habits of industry and thrift among them, it is essential and necessary that all of the waters of the river flow down the channel uninterruptedly and undiminished in quantity and undeteriorated in quality.

It is alleged that "notwithstanding the riparian and other rights" of the United States and the Indians to the uninterrupted flow of the waters of the river the defendants, in the year 1900, wrongfully entered upon the river and its tributaries above the points of the diversion of the waters of the river by the United States and the Indians, built large and substantial dams and reservoirs, and by means of canals and ditches and waterways have diverted the waters of the river from its channel, and have deprived the United States and the Indians of the use thereof. And this diversion of the water, it is alleged, has continued until the present time, to the irreparable injury of the United States, for which there is no adequate remedy at law.

The allegations of the answer, so far as material to the present controversy, are as follows: * * *

That the individual defendants and the stockholders of the Matheson Ditch Company and Cook's Irrigation Company were qualified to become settlers upon the public land and to acquire title thereto under the homestead and desert land laws of the United States. And that said corporations were recognized and exist under the laws of Montana for the purpose of supplying to their said stockholders the water of Milk River and its tributaries, to be used by them in the irrigation of their lands.

* * *

That for the purpose of reclaiming the lands, and acting under the laws of the United States and the laws of Montana, the defendants, respectively, posted upon the river and its tributaries, at the points of intended diversion, notices of appropriation, stating the means of diversion and place of use, and thereafter filed in the office of the clerk and recorder of the county wherein the lands were situated a copy of the notices, duly verified, and within forty days thereafter commenced the construction of ditches and other instrumentalities, and completed them with diligence and diverted, appropriated, and applied to a beneficial use more than 5,000 miners' inches of the waters of the river and its tributaries, or 120 cubic feet per second, irrigating their lands and producing hay, grain and other crops thereon. * * *

■ MR. JUSTICE MCKENNA, after making the foregoing statement, delivered the opinion of the court.

* * *

The case, as we view it, turns on the agreement of May, 1888, resulting in the creation of Fort Belknap Reservation. In the construction of this agreement there are certain elements to be considered that are prominent and significant. The reservation was a part of a very much larger tract which the Indians had the right to occupy and use, and which was adequate for the habits and wants of a nomadic and uncivilized people. It was the policy of the Government, it was the desire of the Indians, to change those habits and to become a pastoral and civilized people. If they should become such the original tract was too extensive, but a smaller tract would be inadequate without a change of conditions. The lands were arid and, without irrigation, were practically valueless. And yet, it is contended, the means of irrigation were deliberately given up by the Indians and deliberately accepted by the Government. The lands ceded were, it is true, also arid; and some argument may be urged, and is urged, that with their cession there was the cession of the waters, without which they would be valueless, and "civilized communities could not be established thereon." And this, it is further contended, the Indians knew, and yet made no reservation of the waters. We realize that there is a conflict of implications, but that which makes for the retention of the waters is of greater force than that which makes for their cession. The Indians had command of the lands and the waters—command of all their beneficial use, whether kept for hunting, "and grazing roving herds of stock," or turned to agriculture and the arts of civilization. Did they give up all this? Did they reduce the area of their occupation and give up the waters which made it valuable or adequate? And, even regarding the allegation of the answer as true, that there are springs and streams on the reservation flowing about 2,900 inches of water, the inquiries are pertinent. If it were possible to believe affirmative answers, we might also believe that the Indians were awed by the power of the Government or deceived by its negotiators. Neither view is possible. The Government is asserting the right of the Indians. But extremes need not be taken into account. By a rule of interpretation of agreements and treaties with the Indians, ambiguities occurring will be resolved from the standpoint of the Indians. And the rule should certainly be applied to determine between two inferences, one of which would support the purpose of the agreement and the other impair or defeat it. On account of their relations to the Government, it cannot be supposed that the Indians were alert to exclude by formal words every inference which might militate against or defeat the declared purpose of themselves and the Government, even if it could be supposed that they had the intelligence to foresee the "double sense" which might some time be urged against them.

Another contention of appellants is that if it be conceded that there was a reservation of the waters of Milk River by the agreement of 1888, yet the reservation was repealed by the admission of Montana into the Union, February 22, 1889, c. 180, 25 Stat. 676, "upon an equal footing with the original States." The language of counsel is that "any reservation in the agreement with the Indians, expressed or implied, whereby the waters of Milk River were not to be subject of appropriation by the citizens and inhabitants of said State, was repealed by the act of admission." But to establish the repeal counsel rely substantially upon the same argument that they advance against the intention of the agreement to reserve the waters. The power of the Government to reserve the waters and exempt them from appropriation under the state laws is not denied, and could not be. The *United States v. The Rio Grande Ditch & Irrigation Co.*, 174 U.S. 690, 702 (1899); *United States v. Winans*, 198 U.S. 371 [1905]. That the Government did reserve them we have decided, and for a use which would be necessarily continued through years. This was done May 1, 1888, and it would be extreme to believe that within a year Congress destroyed the reservation and took from the Indians the consideration of their grant, leaving them a barren waste—took from them the means of continuing their old habits, yet did not leave them the power to change to new ones.

Appellants' argument upon the incidental repeal of the agreement by the admission of Montana into the Union and the power over the waters of Milk River which the State thereby acquired to dispose of them under its laws, is elaborate and able, but our construction of the agreement and its effect make it unnecessary to answer the argument in detail. For the same reason we have not discussed the doctrine of riparian rights urged by the Government.

Decree affirmed.

NOTES

1. The United States based its case on behalf of the Indians primarily on riparian rights. The Court did not deal with that argument but embraced a rationale for "reserved" water rights that had been articulated by the lower court. This was entirely new to water law but was based on Indian law principles. In Indian treaties it is well-established that tribes reserve to themselves all rights not explicitly granted to the United States. See David H. Getches, Charles F. Wilkinson & Robert F. Williams, Cases and Materials on Federal Indian Law 136–39 (4th ed. 1998). Five years before *Winters* Justice McKenna who wrote the *Winters* opinion, decided United States v. Winans, 198 U.S. 371, 25 S.Ct. 662, 49 L.Ed. 1089 (1905) dealing with fishing rights. He held that a provision reserving treaty fishing rights on lands ceded by the tribes to the United States carried with it an implied easement for the Indians to cross private property the government had granted to non-Indians. He said: "the treaty was not a grant of rights to the Indians, but a grant of rights from them—a reservation of those not granted." 198 U.S. at 381.

2. In the dry season immediately after the Supreme Court decision, the lower court determined that the water rights reserved for the Fort Belknap

Reservation by the 1888 agreement that were needed to fulfill the agricultural purposes of the agreement entitled the United States to virtually the full flow of the Milk River and enjoined the upstream non-Indian irrigators from diverting water. Although the government relented and settled for half the water, the impact of the decision was enormous.

NOTE: THE FEDERAL INTEREST IN WESTERN WATER

One hundred years after it was decided, *Winters* remains the foundation of Tribal efforts to secure water or money to sustain reservations. Its impact also extends beyond reservations. In Arizona v. California, 373 U.S. 546, 83 S.Ct. 1468, 10 L.Ed.2d 542 (1963), *infra* page 1001, the reserved rights doctrine was applied to all public land withdrawals for a water-related purpose. See Chapter 9 for the evolution of Indian and non-Indian reserved rights law. *Winters* and *Arizona v. California* shocked the western states, which had convinced themselves that no federal water rights existed, because the raised the specter of ''super-riparian'' rights with priority dates superior to many state appropriative rights. Resistance followed. The notes after Coffin v. Left Hand Ditch Co., *supra* page 71, explained why the states believed they could develop water rights systems free from any federal rights during the settlement of the West.

In the early settlement of the West, Congress's silence about water rights on the public lands had been at once confusing and convenient. The states did as they pleased. As we have seen, California developed a hybrid system that was built in part on the state court's recognition of the paramount title of the United States to water on the public lands. Prior appropriation worked as a rule to be applied as between those who used the public lands and their successors, but the United States owned and could convey riparian rights that attached to its lands. Indeed, this conceptual concern with federal rights was partly responsible for the dual or hybrid nature of California law.

Most other western states opted for the simplicity of prior appropriation as applied to waters on all lands before and after federal conveyance to private homesteaders, miners, and the like. They did not assume, as California had, that the federal government would ever assert water rights for its lands.

Water law was being built differently by individual states as embodied in state judicial rulings and local customs. This situation of inconsistent laws could have been upset if the federal government had abruptly asserted its previously undefined rights. Instead, Congress only obliquely mentioned water in a few late-nineteenth century laws.

The *Winters* decision was based on neither riparian nor prior appropriation doctrine. But it inserted federal rights to a substantial quantity of water with an early priority date into Montana's system under which the Milk River had been fully allocated. Had the states incorrectly assumed that the federal government intended to allow private rights to be created in water on the public lands? Where public lands were patented to private parties as part of the government's scheme to lure settlers to the West, could their water rights under state law be upset by future federal claims to water for the remaining public or Indian lands?

Many years after *Winters* the Supreme Court said that, simply by passing three post-Civil War statutes that scarcely mentioned water, Congress had deferred to the states to fashion their own water law systems. The same decision reconciled this state prerogative with the retention of broad federal powers to protect water for the public lands and for navigation. In the seminal case of California Oregon Power Co. v. Beaver Portland Cement Co., 295 U.S. 142, 55 S.Ct. 725, 79 L.Ed. 1356 (1935), a power company that owned land as a successor to a homesteader, who had gotten it under a federal patent, asserted riparian rights to try to stop a mining company from interfering with the natural flow of the Rogue River. The mining company had appropriative rights under a 1909 state law to use water in the process of mining gravel. Oregon court decisions had recognized water rights under both riparian and prior appropriation law, and so the Supreme Court was called upon to clarify the intentions of the federal government concerning rights to water originating on the public lands and the prerogatives of the states to allocate such water.

The question with which we are here primarily concerned is whether—in the light of pertinent history, of the conditions which existed in the arid and semi-arid land states, of the practice and attitude of the federal government, and of the congressional legislation prior to 1885—the homestead patent in question carried with it as part of the granted estate the common-law rights which attach to riparian proprietorship. * * *

For many years prior to the passage of the Act of July 26, 1866, the right to the use of waters for mining and other beneficial purposes in California and the arid region generally was fixed and regulated by local rules and customs. The first appropriator of water for a beneficial use was uniformly recognized as having the better right to the extent of his actual use. The common law with respect to riparian rights was not considered applicable, or, if so, only to a limited degree. Water was carried by means of ditches and flumes great distances for consumption by those engaged in mining and agriculture. The rule generally recognized throughout the states and territories of the arid region was that the acquisition of water by prior appropriation for a beneficial use was entitled to protection; and the rule applied whether the water was diverted for manufacturing, irrigation, or mining purposes. The rule was evidenced not only by legislation and judicial decision, but by local and customary law and usage as well.

This general policy was approved by the silent acquiescence of the federal government, until it received formal confirmation at the hands of Congress by the Act of 1866. Section 9 of that act provides:

"That whenever, by priority of possession, rights to the use of water for mining, agricultural, manufacturing, or other purposes, have vested and accrued, and the same are recognized and acknowledged by the local customs, laws, and the decisions of courts, the possessors and owners of such vested rights shall be maintained and protected in the same; and the right of way for the construction of ditches and canals for the purposes aforesaid is hereby acknowledged and confirmed: * * *." * * * And in order to make it clear that the grantees of the United States would take their lands charged with the existing servitude, the Act of July 9, 1870, amending the Act of 1866, provided that—

" * * * all patents granted, or preemption or homesteads allowed, shall be subject to any vested and accrued water rights, or rights to ditches and reservoirs used in connection with such water rights, as may have been acquired under or recognized by the ninth section of the act of which this act is amendatory."

The effect of these acts is not limited to rights acquired before 1866. They reach into the future as well, and approve and confirm the policy of appropriation for a beneficial use, as recognized by local rules and customs, and the legislation and judicial decisions of the arid-land states, as the test and measure of private rights in and to the non-navigable waters on the public domain.

If the acts of 1866 and 1870 did not constitute an entire abandonment of the common-law rule of running waters in so far as the public lands and subsequent grantees thereof were concerned, they foreshadowed the more positive declarations of the Desert Land Act of 1877, which it is contended did bring about that result. That act allows the entry and reclamation of desert lands within the states of California, Oregon, and Nevada (to which Colorado was later added), and the then territories of Washington, Idaho, Montana, Utah, Wyoming, Arizona, New Mexico, and Dakota, with a proviso to the effect that the right to the use of waters by the claimant shall depend upon *bona fide* prior appropriation, not to exceed the amount of waters actually appropriated and necessarily used for the purpose of irrigation and reclamation. Then follows the clause of the proviso with which we are here concerned:

" * * * all surplus water over and above such actual appropriation and use, together with the water of all lakes, rivers and other sources of water supply upon the public lands and not navigable, shall remain and be held free for the appropriation and use of the public for irrigation, mining and manufacturing purposes subject to existing rights."

For the light which it will reflect upon the meaning and scope of that provision and its bearing upon the present question, it is well to pause at this point to consider the then-existing situation with respect to land and water rights in the states and territories named. * * * [T]he lands capable of redemption, in the main, constituted a desert, impossible of agricultural use without artificial irrigation.

In the beginning, the task of reclaiming this area was left to the unaided efforts of the people who found their way by painful effort to its inhospitable solitudes. * * *

* * * [I]t had become evident to Congress, as it had to the inhabitants, that the future growth and well-being of the entire region depended upon a complete adherence to the rule of appropriation for a beneficial use as the exclusive criterion of the right to the use of water. The streams and other sources of supply from which this water must come were separated from one another by wide stretches of parched and barren land which never could be made to produce agricultural crops except by the transmission of water for long distances and its entire consumption in the processes of irrigation. Necessarily, that involved the complete subordination of the common-law doctrine of riparian rights to that of appropriation. And this substitution of the rule of appropriation for that of the common law was to have momentous consequences. It became the determining factor in the long struggle to expunge from our vocabulary the legend "Great American Desert," which was spread in large letters across the face of the old maps of the far west.*

In the light of the foregoing considerations, the Desert Land Act was passed, and in their light it must now be construed. By its terms, not only all surplus water over and above such as might be appropriated and used by the desert-land entrymen, but "the water of all lakes, rivers and other sources of water supply upon the public lands and not navigable" were to remain "free for the appropriation and use of the public for irrigation, mining and manufacturing purposes." If this language is to be given its natural meaning, and we see no reason why it should not, it effected a severance of all waters upon the public domain, not theretofore appropriated, from the land itself. From that premise, it follows that a patent issued thereafter for lands in a desert-land state or territory, under any of the land laws of the United States, carried with it, of its own force, no common law right to the water flowing through or bordering upon the lands conveyed. * * *

As the owner of the public domain, the government possessed the power to dispose of land and water thereon together, or to dispose of them separately. The fair construction of the provision now under review is that Congress intended to establish the rule that for the future the land should be patented separately; and that all non-navigable waters thereon should be reserved for the use of the public under the laws of the states and territories named. * * * The terms of the statute, thus construed, must be read into every patent thereafter issued, with the same force as though expressly incorporated therein,

* Mr. Justice Sutherland immigrated with his parents to the Utah Territory in 1863 when he was 18 months old, his father having been converted to the Church of Jesus Christ of Latter–Day Saints. Sutherland practiced law in Utah from 1883 to 1905, when he was elected U.S. Senator. His account of the development of the West rests, therefore, on more than a cold record. [Eds.]

with the result that the grantee will take the legal title to the land conveyed, and such title, and only such title, to the flowing waters thereon as shall be fixed or acknowledged by the customs, laws, and judicial decisions of the state of their location. If it be conceded that in the absence of federal legislation the state would be powerless to affect the riparian rights of the United States or its grantees, still, the authority of Congress to vest such power in the state, and that it has done so by the legislation to which we have referred, cannot be doubted.

* * *

* * * Nothing we have said is meant to suggest that the act, as we construe it, has the effect of curtailing the power of the states affected to legislate in respect of waters and water rights as they deem wise in the public interest. What we hold is that following the act of 1877, if not before, all non-navigable waters then a part of the public domain became *publici juris*, subject to the plenary control of the designated states, including those since created out of the territories named, with the right in each to determine for itself to what extent the rule of appropriation or the common-law rule in respect of riparian rights should obtain. For since "Congress cannot enforce either rule upon any state," *Kansas v. Colorado*, 206 U.S. 46, 94, the full power of choice must remain with the state. The Desert Land Act does not bind or purport to bind the states to any policy. It simply recognizes and gives sanction, in so far as the United States and its future grantees are concerned, to the state and local doctrine of appropriation, and seeks to remove what otherwise might be an impediment to its full and successful operation.

295 U.S. at 153–164.

California Oregon Power deftly upheld the power of each state to adopt any type of water law that it deemed appropriate and, in the process, to defeat (or uphold) the riparian claims of the federal government or its successors in interest. But the Court stressed a major exception to the government's deference to state water law systems and authority to allocate water from the public lands when those prerogatives come into conflict with federal objectives. Citing an important 1899 case the Court said:

In *United States v. Rio Grande Irrigation Co.*, 174 U.S. 690, the government sought to enjoin the irrigation company from constructing a dam across the Rio Grande in the Territory of New Mexico, and from appropriating the waters of that stream. The object of the company was to impound the waters and distribute the same for a variety of purposes. The company defended on the ground that the site of the dam was within the arid region, and that it had fully complied with the water laws of the Territory of New Mexico in which the dam was located and the waters were to be used. The supreme court of the territory affirmed a decree dismissing the bill. This court reversed and remanded the case, with instructions to inquire whether the construction of the dam and appropriation of water would substantially diminish the navigability of the stream, and, if so, to enter a decree restraining the acts of the appellees to the extent of the threatened diminution. The opinion, dealing with the question of riparian rights, said that it was within the power of any state to change the common-law rule and permit the appropriation of the flowing waters for any purposes it deemed wise. Whether a territory had the same power the court did not then decide. Two limitations of state power were suggested: first, in the absence of any specific authority from Congress, that a state could not by its legislation destroy the right of the United States as the owner of lands bordering on a stream to the continued flow—so far, at least, as might be necessary for the beneficial use of the government property; and second, that its power was limited by that of the general government to secure the uninterrupted navigability of all navigable streams within the limits of the United States. With these exceptions, the court, however, thought that by the acts of 1866 and 1877 "Congress recognized and assented to the appropriation of water in contravention of the common law rule as to continuous flow," and that "the obvious purpose of Congress was to give its assent, so far as the public lands were concerned, to any system, although in contravention to the common law rule, which permitted the appropriation of those waters for legitimate industries." * * *

295 U.S. at 158–159.

Winters was decided just nine years after the *Rio Grande* case discussed in *California Oregon Power*. It illustrated the power of the exceptions to congressional deference to state water law.

The materials in the next chapter show how the riparian and appropriation "doctrines" continued to adapt to changing needs. As social and economic conditions compelled change, courts and especially legislatures were quite willing to leave some of the basic principles of doctrine behind.

Nonetheless, *California Oregon Power* continues to float through western water law. In *Joyce Livestock Co., supra*, 156 P.3d 502 at 520–521, the Bureau of Land Management claimed stock raising water rights under state law, but argued that the Supremacy Clause of the federal constitution freed it from the beneficial use requirement. The court brushed the argument aside as inconsistent with *California Oregon Power's* recognition of the severance of the right to use water, as opposed to ownership, from public lands.

CHAPTER THREE

PRINCIPLES OF ACQUISITION, ENJOYMENT, TRANSFER, AND LOSS OF WATER RIGHTS

A. RIPARIAN PRINCIPLES

Since the earliest cases, riparian doctrine has been announced in the form of absolute rules so stringent that they were impractical to enforce. Chapter Two shows that decided cases may faithfully recite the rules but then adjust and accommodate the rights of competing users by tempering the rules. Although riparianism is a form of property law that recognizes water rights as an attribute of ownership of land bordering a waterway, the rules have emerged in tort cases. The resulting "doctrine" is essentially the same rule of reason that dominates decisions in negligence and nuisance law, where subjectivity, balancing, and equitable considerations determine outcomes.

In this chapter we build on the glimpse of the system provided in Chapter Two, and examine how the common law evolved to make riparian doctrine work in a complex and changing society. The rules that governed the acquisition, enjoyment, transfer, and loss of riparian rights inspired many of the statutory rules that govern the use of water today in most states that have adopted the administrative systems that are studied in Chapter Four. These systems have been adopted in riparian and prior appropriation states alike. Yet, the common law of riparian rights that is the subject of this chapter remains relevant not only for historical purposes, but because, even in states with comprehensive statutory systems, tort suits still arise among water users. Moreover, in the eastern, so-called riparian states, modern statutes continue to be interpreted and applied in the shadow of the riparian tradition.

1. ACQUISITION

Land Abutting a Watercourse

In the riparian system, only the owners of lands abutting a watercourse are entitled to use the water. Several complications lurk behind this apparently straightforward statement. The first is the meaning of "abutting." Most courts hold that one claiming riparian rights must own land that reaches the high water mark of the waterbody; occasionally ownership to the low water mark is required. Riparian rights might be seasonal depending on the water level of the watercourse at peak versus low flow periods. Turner v. James Canal Co., 155 Cal. 82, 99 P. 520 (1909).

Determining the exact location of these boundaries may prove troublesome, especially where tidal waters are involved. These complexities are discussed in Borax Consol. v. Los Angeles, 296 U.S. 10, 56 S.Ct. 23, 80 L.Ed. 9 (1935) and Frank E. Maloney and Richard C. Ausness, *The Use and Legal Significance of the Mean High Water Line in Coastal Boundary Mapping*, 53 N.C. L. Rev. 185 (1974). A riparian normally need not own submerged lands to claim rights, but for some purposes—the right to fill, for instance—ownership of the bottom of the waterbody may be required. Typically, these situations are limited to non-navigable waters because private ownership of navigable bottoms below the high or low water mark is subject to public uses, *infra* p. 399.

Where bottom ownership is required, the calls of the deed must be examined, to ascertain the intent of the grantor. The landowner is assisted by the common law presumption that "absent an express reservation by the grantor, a conveyance of riparian property conveys title to the thread of the stream unless a contrary intention appears or is clearly inferrable from the terms of the deed." Nilsson v. Latimer, 281 Ark. 325, 664 S.W.2d 447, 449 (1984). The rule also applies to lakes, where the landowners' correlative rights are technically classified as "littoral" rights. Bottom ownership is ordinarily determined by extending property lines from the points at which they touch the high water mark to the center of the lake. Determining the boundaries of bottom ownership of irregular lakes can be a challenge to the surveyor's art. See Curtis M. Brown et al., Evidence and Procedures for Boundary Location 219–215, 329–354 (3d ed. 1994).

Nature of Interest in Riparian Land

Must the person claiming riparian rights show fee title, or may a lessee be a riparian? What if the fee owner of riparian land conveys rights to an easement, the exercise of which necessarily involves the assertion of riparian privileges? Is the easement holder the "owner" of the riparian rights? See Burkart v. City of Fort Lauderdale, 168 So.2d 65 (Fla.1964) and Stefanoni v. Duncan, 282 Conn. 686, 923 A.2d 737 (2007). The question frequently arises in lake subdivisions in conflicts between littoral owners and back lot owners. See pp. 143–144, *infra*.

"Source of Title" and "Unity of Title" Rules

A major limitation on water use under the riparian system may relate to the derivation of title to the land. Even though land appears to be riparian, it may be considered nonriparian under the "source of title" rule. This rule, and the more inclusive "unity of title" rule are discussed in Peter N. Davis, *Australian and American Water Allocation Systems Compared*, 9 B.C. Indus. and Comm. L. Rev. 647, 680–82 (1968):

> Two major doctrines have emerged defining just which land that abuts a stream is to be considered riparian land. The "source of title" test states that water may be used only on land which has been held as

a single tract throughout its chain of title. This means that any nonabutting portions of the original tract which have been severed forever lose their riparian character unless a contrary intention is manifested. Reuniting such severed tracts with the abutting tract will not reestablish their riparian status.* The total amount of riparian land under this rule cannot be enlarged by the purchase of contiguous back tracts.

Another rule followed in some states, the "unity of title" rule, provides that any tracts contiguous to the abutting tract are riparian if all of them are held under single ownership regardless of the times when the various tracts were acquired. This means that a riparian proprietor may enlarge the amount of his riparian land by purchasing contiguous back tracts within the watershed. The general rule that water may not be diverted to lands outside the watershed of the originating stream follows from the rule that water diverted for any extraordinary purpose must be returned to the stream above the next lower riparian's land.

The difference in the amount of land available for riparian water use under these two rules can be considerable. A recent study in northwestern Wisconsin indicates that the "unity of title" test would encompass 64 percent more land than the "source of title" test. This substantial increase results from the fact that most farms today have different boundaries than the original farms and that many back tracts have changed hands.

Although riparianism generally restricts use of water to riparian land, there is considerable authority for the proposition that in many instances water may be used by riparians on nonriparian land. These cases, admittedly the minority rule, state that water may be diverted to and used on nonriparian land provided that lower riparians are not damaged. Two states in this group allow use on nonriparian land, even though riparians are damaged, if the use is reasonable. To the contrary

---

* The author here cites, *inter alia*, Boehmer v. Big Rock Creek Irrigation Dist., 117 Cal. 19, 48 P. 908 (1897). In justifying the application of the source of title rule, the court said:

> [I]t has been the policy of the general government to subdivide the public domain into small tracts, and to dispose of them as such, and for the purpose of carrying out such policy restricted the right of entry under the homestead and pre-emption laws to 160 acres. Even in its grants to railroads, by granting alternate sections, it prevented the acquisition from the government of large bodies of contiguous lands, and a similar policy is pursued by the state in disposing of state lands.

Id. at 910.

In the case at bar the stipulation is that these fourteen quarter sections were granted each by a separate patent, each patent being based upon a separate entry, and these fourteen quarter sections therefore constitute fourteen distinct tracts of land, and mere contiguity cannot extend a riparian right which is appurtenant to one quarter section to another, though both are now owned by the same person.

An additional explanation for the adoption of the rule in California was the policy of that state to enlarge the amount of water available for appropriation and prescription. [Eds.]

is the majority rule that riparian rights may not be exercised on nonriparian land. Many eastern states have not decided which rule to follow.

Place-of-use restrictions have not yet raised any obvious problems in the East, where development of industry has been concentrated at streamside. The problem of locational restrictions probably will be more relevant for the East if irrigation becomes prevalent, or if severe water shortages should occur.

California, where expansion of riparian rights is disfavored because new water rights may be obtained under the appropriation system, applies the "source of title" rule. As stated in Anaheim Union Water Co. v. Fuller, 150 Cal. 327, 88 P. 978, 980 (1907), discussed *infra* p. 145: "If the owner of a tract abutting on a stream conveys to another a part of the land not contiguous to the stream, he thereby cuts off the part so conveyed from all participation in the use of the stream and from riparian rights therein, unless the conveyance declares the contrary." This suggests a means of ameliorating the sweeping, sometimes harsh effect of the source of title rule.

After reviewing the theories of riparian ownership from an eastern perspective, Professor Farnham argued that the humid states should not adopt the source of title rule because "the policy in aid of which these practices were inaugurated—the policy against concentration of land ownership in too few hands—should not now be pursued in the East in view of the economic and scientific factors currently affecting agriculture," and recommends legislation that would require only that the land be both within the watershed of the stream and a reasonable distance from the stream. William F. Farnham, *The Permissible Extent of Riparian Land,* 7 Land & Water L. Rev. 31, 54 (1972).

2. Enjoyment

Kundel Farms v. Vir–Jo Farms, Inc.

Court of Appeal of Iowa, 1991.
467 N.W.2d 291.

Kundel Farms (Kundel) and Vir–Jo Farms (Vir–Jo) are adjoining landowners. Kundel owns land to the east, north, and west of Vir–Jo. * * *

* * * Vir–Jo filed an equity action against Kundel in the district court. Vir–Jo claimed Kundel was obstructing the natural waterflow over its land.

* * * The master filed his report finding: * * * Vir–Jo failed to show Kundel's alterations of the embankment substantially harmed Vir–Jo's land.

* * *

* * * [W]hen Kundel bought the property in 1978 * * * a thirty-six-inch steel culvert at creek bed level allowed the creek to flow through the

dam. The dam itself is actually a causeway traversing a low-lying swampy portion of Kundel's land. This low-lying area extends down into Vir–Jo's property.

* * *

The dam as presently constructed has two fifteen or eighteen inch steel culverts. The first is about two feet above the creek bed level. The second is about nine inches or so above the first. There is no question the positioning and decreased diameter of the present culverts substantially affect the flow of water onto Vir–Jo's servient property.

* * *

Now, each riparian owner has a right to use the water of a surface stream for ordinary or natural uses, and, under certain circumstances, for artificial uses, such as for irrigation and the like; and the better law seems to be that he may use the water for his natural and ordinary wants, regardless of the effect upon other proprietors on the stream; that is, as we understand the rule, one riparian proprietor may, for his natural wants, if necessary, use all of the water in a surface stream, to the exclusion of every other such proprietor, certainly so as against the other proprietor using the water for artificial purposes. In case, however, such a proprietor puts the water to an extraordinary or artificial use, he must do so in such a manner as not to interfere with its lawful use by others above or below him upon the same stream. As to extraordinary or artificial uses, the rights of all proprietors on the stream are equal; and the artificial use is held to be always subordinate to the natural use. If there is not water enough to more than supply the natural wants of the several riparian owners, none can use the water from the stream for artificial purposes. Ordinary or natural uses have been held to include the use for domestic purposes, including household purposes, such as cleansing, washing, and supplying an ordinary number of horses or stock with water, and it is said that natural uses are limited to the purposes above stated. Now, what is a reasonable use of the water of a surface stream for artificial purposes? Clearly, such a use as permits the return of the water used to the stream in its natural channel, without corruption or sensible diminution in quantity. By this is not meant that all the water must be returned to the stream, because in the use some will necessarily be lost or wasted. What is or constitutes such reasonable use must be determined in view of the size and capacity of the stream, the wants of all other proprietors, the fall of the water, the character of the soil, the number of proprietors to be supplied, and all other circumstances.
* * *

Willis v. City of Perry, 92 Iowa 297, 302–04, 60 N.W. 727, 729 (1894).

Vir–Jo desires to use the water in Crane Creek for watering stock and other agricultural purposes. Kundel uses the water to make a wetland so four hunters may rent the land for $1,000 a year. While we find neither use unreasonable, creating a wetland for hunting certainly is an artificial use.

As such, Vir–Jo's natural use of the stream to water his livestock takes precedence.

The two foot minimum depth of Kundel's pond will substantially diminish the flow of water onto Vir–Jo's property, especially in drier years. Also, the smaller size of the two pipes and their relative height will further diminish the flow.

We determine Kundel's alteration of the previously agreed upon thirty-six-inch culvert to be impermissible in light of the diminished flow of water to servient properties. Kundel is ordered to return the dam to the former dimensions, with a thirty-six-inch culvert set at creek bed level.

We reverse the trial court on this issue.

NOTE: PREFERENCE FOR "NATURAL" USES

Under riparian law, domestic or "natural" uses have always enjoyed a preference over other uses which the courts refer to as "artificial." In distinguishing between the two, the court in an Illinois case, Evans v. Merriweather, 4 Ill. (3 Scam.) 492, 495 (1842) noted:

[I]t is proper to consider the wants of man in regard to the element of water. These wants are either natural or artificial. Natural are such as are absolutely necessary to be supplied, in order to his existence. Artificial, such only as, by supplying them, his comfort and prosperity are increased. To quench thirst, and for household purposes, water is absolutely indispensable. In civilized life, water for cattle is also necessary. These wants must be supplied, or both man and beast will perish.

Compare the analysis offered by Roscoe Pound, one of the seminal figures in American jurisprudence, when he was a young commissioner in his native Nebraska:

This subject has been confused needlessly by the unfortunate use of the words "natural" and "ordinary" in this connection to distinguish those uses which the common law does not attempt to limit, and "artificial" or "extraordinary" to designate those which are required to be exercised within reasonable bounds. It is no doubt true that irrigation is a very natural and a very ordinary want and that use of a stream for such purpose is natural and ordinary in semiarid regions. But such is not the question. The law does not regard the needs and desires of the person taking the water solely to the exclusion of all other riparian proprietors, but looks rather to the natural effect of his use of water upon the stream and the equal rights of others therein. The true distinction appears to lie between those modes of use which ordinarily involve the taking of small quantities, and but little interference with the stream, such as drinking and other household purposes, and those which necessarily involve the taking or diversion of large quantities and a considerable interference with its ordinary course and flow, such as manufacturing purposes.

Meng v. Coffey, 67 Neb. 500, 93 N.W. 713, 717–18 (1903).

The domestic preference has generally not been extended to municipalities or other large institutional suppliers. See Pernell v. Henderson, 220 N.C. 79, 16 S.E.2d 449 (1941). The question of municipal supply is further considered in Chapter Eight.

Mason v. Hoyle

Supreme Court of Errors of Connecticut, 1888.
56 Conn. 255, 14 A. 786.

* * * The plaintiff Mason, during all that time, has owned and operated a saw-mill, grist-mill, and wagon-shop, with machinery driven wholly by water-power, under a head and fall of about eight feet, supplied from a small pond owned by him, covering not over an acre and a half, and raised by a dam across the bed of the stream. About eighteen inches only upon the top of this pond, when full, is available for power. When the flow of water into the pond is scant, but adequate for the purpose, the ordinary practice at this mill has been to run the machinery until the pond is drawn down some six or eight inches from the top, and then cease running till it fills again, when the use is resumed as before. This privilege is an ancient one. * * * [The water uses of other plaintiffs were described.] The machinery and business at each is and has been such that the ordinary flow of the stream, during the dry seasons of the year, as they ordinarily occur, would (except for the acts of the defendant mentioned hereafter) have been ample to continue the business, and meet its ordinary demands. The defendant Hoyle, since the year 1875, has been owner and possessor of land, mills, and mill privileges in the town of Willington, on the same stream, next above the mill of the plaintiff Mason, and about four hundred and fifty rods therefrom, which are and long have been used for the manufacture of woolen goods. The privilege consists of a head and fall of twenty feet, the water being drawn onto the wheel directly from a small pond near the mills, which is supplied by means of a canal or ditch connecting with a larger pond or reservoir, owned by him, about a quarter of a mile above, on the same stream, where there is an additional fall, when the reservoir is full, of about eleven feet; and some five acres are covered with the water. The dam at the reservoir was repaired and enlarged by the defendant about the year 1881. In addition to water-power, the defendant has at his mills a steam-boiler and engine, capable of driving his machinery independently of the water-wheel, but it is so arranged that it may be used with facility, and without detriment to the business, in connection with the water-power. As a usual thing, for eight or nine months of each year, extending from September or October to May or June following, there has been flowing in the river an ample supply of water for all the privileges and mills thereon, and during such periods there has been no complaint, or ground of complaint, against the defendant, or any other mill-owner, as to the mode of using the water; but during the remaining three or four months, between May and October, (subject to a few exceptions in extraordinary seasons,) the supply of water has been comparatively small. And during such dry seasons the amount of machinery to be driven at the defendant's

mill has been and is greatly disproportionate to the diminished capacity of the stream, and it has been impossible for the defendant, at such times, to run all his machinery by water-power alone, except for a small part of the time. The mill and privilege now owned by the defendant was owned and occupied by other parties, for the same purposes, many years before the defendant obtained the same. These prior owners and occupants, during the season of deficient supply of water, as a general rule, used steam and water power in connection; and in this way the water naturally flowing in the stream was allowed to pass regularly to the several privileges of the plaintiffs, furnishing a supply sufficient to meet the ordinary demands of their business; so that no complaint was made by them, or either of them. But about the year 1881 the defendant adopted a practice in this respect different from that of his predecessors, and during the season of the year when the water supply has been inadequate for his use he has been in the habit of shutting his gates, wholly or partially, so that the water would accumulate in his reservoir, meanwhile running his machinery wholly by steam-power from two to five days, until there was an accumulation of water in his reservoir sufficient to run by water-power alone continuously for five or six hours; and, after so running, he would return again to the exclusive use of steam, and continue, as before, the alternative use of steam and water power. By these means the defendant has detained, for periods varying from two to five days in the week, and for many weeks, during the dry season of each year, substantially all the natural flow of the stream, except so much as he required daily for washing wool and cloth, and for his boiler, (which usually has been much less than the natural flow of the stream;) and then, by the use of water-power alone, for periods of five or six hours a day, once or twice during the week, and sometimes oftener, the water has flowed from his wheel in quantities far in excess of the natural flow of the stream during such seasons, which has resulted in quickly filling the small ponds of the plaintiffs, and then running to waste over their several dams. * * *

■ Loomis, J. The rule that now obtains in all jurisdictions, as recognized by all the authorities, is that the use made by mill-owners of a stream must, in its relation to other mill-owners on the same stream, be a reasonable use. The rule is obviously one that applies solely to the relation of the several occupants of the stream among themselves. Where one mill-owner is the sole occupant, there is in law no limitation upon his use. The rule being that of reasonable use, the application of the rule becomes a matter for each particular case. The question, while in some sense a mixed question of law and fact, is yet essentially a question of fact. Whether the use be reasonable must depend less upon any general rule than upon the particular circumstances. But there are certain conditions essential to a reasonable use so long recognized by common consent, or so obviously just, that we may safely generalize with regard to them. In the first place, the use must be as near as possible an equal use, or, rather, an equal opportunity to use. "Equity delighteth in equality." Every owner improving a mill privilege has a right to consider the law as protecting him against any unfair use by any other owner who may establish a mill above him. The term "unfair use" is the equivalent of "unreasonable use." When the owner above him has established his mill, he is bound, not merely by this obvious rule of the stream, but by another more general rule of universal application, that no one may so use his own as to injure the property of another. This golden rule of the law is not, of course, to be taken literally; for where there is a concurrent use of water, and at the same time a deficiency, the use of one will, to some extent, injure another. In the next place, a reasonable use is one adapted to the character and capacity of the stream. Indeed, there is no other factor of so much importance that comes into the question as that of the capacity of the stream; and, in determining this capacity, its condition throughout the year is to be considered. * * * In the next place, a reasonable use must permit the water to flow in its accustomed way, so far as this can be done, and a beneficial use, though a limited one, be made of the reduced stream, each riparian mill-owner having his fair proportion. It is the right of every mill-owner, large or small, on the stream, that the water be allowed to run in its usual way, except where detained by another to secure his fair proportion of beneficial use. A policy of the state may come in to affect the question. It is for the public interest that all our streams be improved as far as they can be. This rule has sometimes been applied to favor the larger mill-owner, but it should have regard also to small mill-owners, who are the great majority of those in such business, or who incline to go into it. These men of moderate capital, investing their means in mills upon our lesser streams, should be protected against such a use of the streams by mills disproportioned to their capacities as would practically deprive them of water and ruin their privileges. And, where the water is sufficient only for a few hours' use in a day, it is a reasonable demand of these lesser mills that they should be allowed water enough to run a part of every day, rather than it should be detained by any larger mill in such a way as to compel them to crowd into a single day or night all the work of a week. There would be no way in which the lesser mills could hold their own against the disproportionately large ones, with reservoirs of great capacity, but to enlarge their own reservoirs and ponds to an equal capacity; thus compelling all to enlarge their works in a manner not demanded by the capacity of the stream, and involving an unnecessary and perhaps ruinous expenditure. If a large mill-owner has made a reservoir which it requires several days to fill in the dry season, he has no more right, on that account, to detain the water for a week, to fill it, than he would have to detain it a month. His rights are not measured at all by the capacity of his reservoir, for he may be able to double or fourfold its capacity, and the law will not allow him to establish for himself the rule that shall decide his rights between himself and another. The question is not as to the capacity of the reservoir, but what is a fair use of the water between him and his neighbor below? Where the reservoir, as in the case at bar, is simply to store the water, and not to furnish the head and fall, he can as well use the water when it is a half or a quarter filled as the lower owner can use it when his smaller pond is wholly filled. A reservoir used to store surplus water, when the supply is abundant, for use at a time when it is deficient, is a great benefit to all the lower proprietors; but, if used to detain the water in the dry season, it may occasion great injury, as in this case.

* * *

But the general principle stated by us at the outset of the discussion, to the effect that, to justify a detention of the water by the upper proprietor long enough to make an advantageous use of it, his machinery, or so much of it as he operates, must be adapted to the fixed character of the stream (if it has any) as to deficiency of water during the dry seasons, apparently conflicts with the rule laid down in many cases, that the adaptation referred to must be to the usual quantity of water in the stream, or other equivalent expressions, by which we have no doubt was meant, as applicable to those cases, the medium average flow between a high and low stage of water. But in none of the cases where the rule has been applied, so far as we have examined them, did the seasons of great scarcity of water occur with such regularity, year after year, as in the case at bar. * * * "And during such dry seasons the amount of machinery to be driven at the defendant's mill has been and is greatly disproportionate to the diminished capacity of the stream; and it has been impossible for the defendant at such times to run all his machinery by water-power alone, except for a small fraction of the time." And the other fact found, that five days' detention of the water has enabled the defendant to run only five hours, shows still more forcibly the enormous disproportion of his machinery to the capacity of the stream during the dry season. * * * The reasoning of the court, however, in *Drake v. Woolen Co.*, 99 Mass. 574, suggests the point that the rule to be adopted should be one to promote the largest possible utilization of water-power, which can only be accomplished by conceding to the mill-owner the right to erect machinery requiring the full average flow of the stream, with the incidental right to detain the water as may be necessary during the dry season, as otherwise the workmen must remain idle till the wet season returns and the scarcity is over. We find no fault with this rule applied to cases where the season of scarcity cannot be anticipated, but the reason of the rule makes it inapplicable to the case at bar, where it is manifest from the finding that, if water-power alone was used, the workmen could be employed only a small fraction of the time during the summer months. So if we concede to the defendant the right to detain the water, as claimed, for the propulsion of his entire machinery, the certain result would be that there could be no beneficial employment for men and machinery at the defendant's own mill, nor at the several mills of the plaintiffs. There can be no public policy in a rule thus applied.

Now, the defendant insists that any reasoning which is to determine his water-rights must leave out of the account the fact that he has steam-power which he can use with facility and without detriment, and this position we accept as substantially correct. At the same time the fact that steam-power must be used or the mill must stop, and that it always has been used, is a significant admission that his machinery has overburdened the water-power. It is found that his predecessors in the ownership of the mill, and who were carrying on the same business, so used the water in connection with their steam-power as not to injure the plaintiffs in the use of their mills. While the defendant has, of course, lost no rights to the water by the possession of steam-power, yet the fact that he is using such power, and can, by using the water in connection with it, get a reasonably advantageous use of the latter, without injury to the owners below, making his present mode of using it unnecessary, is a matter proper to be considered in determining whether he should be restrained from such injurious use.

If the principle we have been contending for is not sufficiently established to be accepted as controlling this case, still the fact of a regularly recurring deficiency of water is at least one important element in determining the question of reasonable use. The defendant knew the fact when he bought the property, and afterwards when, in 1881, he repaired and enlarged his reservoir, and when, with presumptive knowledge of the result to the plaintiffs, he changed the long-established mode of running the mill. And this suggests another element with which to test the reasonableness of the defendant's use of the water. The immemorial local custom upon the stream, down to the time of the defendant's interposition, to let the water flow to the plaintiffs' mills without any long or injurious detention, according to the authorities in this and other jurisdictions, has an important bearing upon the question. Again, there is still another element of great significance as it exists in this case, namely, the extent of benefit to the defendant by his detention as compared with the injury to the plaintiffs. * * * If we take the period of greatest detention, which has often occurred, we find that the three mills belonging severally to the three plaintiffs must each be idle five days to enable the defendant to enjoy the slight benefit of a five hours' use.

NOTES

1. Suppose the defendant's mill and large pond had been on the stream *before* plaintiffs located their mills on the stream. Same result?

2. Is it clear that efficiency is promoted by this decision? Recall the Horowitz promotion of industrial development thesis on pages 65–67, *supra*, as well as the Rose thesis. Joshua Getzler, A History of Water Rights at Common Law 332–343 (2004) criticizes these efforts to reduce the evolution of the doctrine of riparian rights to general efficiency explanations for failing to appreciate that "[t]he inheritance of concepts from Roman law and medieval early-modern formulary law was the major determinant in shaping...." it. Id. at 342. Still, borrowing from the work of the political scientist Elinor Ostrom[1] and others who have argued that the tragedy of the commons sometimes can be avoided by community collective action, he argues that "the history of English riparian law is a story of the evolution of institutions and agencies able effectively to enforce

1. Elinor Ostrum, Governing The Commons: The Evolution of Institutions for Collective Action (1990), eds.

the norms of commons management," and this purpose "remained constant notwithstanding the instability of the riparian doctrine." Id. at 350. Does this thesis explain Mason v. Hoyle? How does the commons management hypothesis differ from the Horwitz and Rose theses?

3. In Romey v. Landers, 392 N.W.2d 415, 417 (S.D.1986), an upstream riparian constructed a series of earthen dams that cut off the flow of a prior downstream cattle rancher. Because of inadequate flow for irrigation and livestock watering, the rancher claimed that he suffered crop losses and was forced to sell some of his cattle. He also had to haul water to cattle that "could smell the impounded water, causing Romey to reinforce his fences." The injured rancher petitioned the state Water Management Board which issued an order requiring removal of all but two of the dams because they represented an unreasonable and wasteful use of water. On appeal, the court rejected the argument of the upper riparian that a South Dakota statute prohibiting waste was void for vagueness.

> Although "waste" and "reasonable use" are not statutorily defined, the Legislature's general intent is capable of understanding and this general intent, coupled with the case law hereinbefore cited, sufficiently apprises riparian owners of forbidden water use and provides the Board with guidelines for enforcing these statutes.

392 N.W.2d at 420.

4. *Tyler v. Wilkinson, supra* p. 60 is generally cited for the introduction of riparian rights into American law. Was it a natural flow or reasonable use case? Courts after *Tyler* did sometimes hold that any diversion by an upper riparian was a violation of the lower's rights, but the natural flow theory was frequently challenged because it impeded industrial development. By the late nineteenth century the natural flow theory had been widely rejected and replaced by the reasonable use doctrine which required a showing of actual damages as a prerequisite to judicial protection of a riparian right and made protection of a use dependent on the reasonableness of the competing uses. *E.g.,* Red River Roller Mills v. Wright, 30 Minn. 249, 15 N.W. 167 (1883).

5. Pure natural flow decisions are historically rare and virtually absent from modern cases. One still encounters natural flow language in the occasional case. This characteristically occurs where an upstream riparian takes so much of the flow that it would interfere with most reasonable uses of downstream users. In Collens v. New Canaan Water Co., 155 Conn. 477, 234 A.2d 825, 831 (1967), for instance, downstream riparians sued to enjoin defendant from diverting water from the Noroton River, thereby substantially diminishing the flow of the stream. The court granted the injunction and punitive damages because "[t]he plaintiffs, as riparian owners along the Noroton River, are entitled to the natural flow of the water of the running stream through or along their land, in its accustomed channel, undiminished in quantity or unimpaired in quality." As the court pointed out, defendant had alternative supplies available and had failed to prove that the injunction would prevent it from meeting the demands of its customers. The court also indicated that defendant could condemn the rights if it needed them. See Dimmock v. City of New London, 157 Conn. 9, 245 A.2d 569 (1968).

6.   Under the reasonable use theory of riparian rights, of which *Mason v. Hoyle* is an oft-cited example, each riparian owner's right is correlative. It is protected from harm by other, unreasonable uses of water, but the use of the stream must be shared among all reasonable users. Eastern riparian cases seldom require a court to apportion the use of a stream among similar users. Often the court is not convinced that a shortage exists. *E.g.*, Ripka v. Wansing, 589 S.W.2d 333 (Mo.App.1979). As one would expect, what there is of the law of riparian apportionment comes from dual system states in the arid West. In California, the courts developed a device for quantifying the water rights of competing riparians. In Half Moon Bay Land Co. v. Cowell, 173 Cal. 543, 160 P. 675, 678 (1916), Justice Shaw, the judicial architect of many important California water law doctrines, commented on an apportionment decree as follows:

> In apportioning the waters of a stream among the riparian owners, where there is not sufficient for the needs of all, many different facts are to be considered. In Harris v. Harrison, 93 Cal. 681, 29 Pac. 326, the court, in considering this question, said:

> "The length of the stream, the volume of water in it, the extent of each ownership along the banks, the character of the soil owned by each contestant, the area sought to be irrigated by each—all these, and many other considerations, must enter into the solution of the problem."

> See, also, Southern etc. Co. v. Wilshire, 144 Cal. 71, 77 Pac. 767. So far as we are aware, no court has ever undertaken to lay down a comprehensive rule on the subject. We are satisfied that the court may also consider the practicability of irrigation of the lands of the respective parties, the expense thereof, the comparative profit of the different uses which could be made of the water on the land, and that when the water is insufficient for all the land or for all of the uses to which it might be applied thereon, and there is enough only for that use which is most valuable and profitable, the shares may properly be limited to and measured by the quantity sufficient for that use, and the proportions fixed accordingly. The party taking, under such a decree, could, of course, put his share so fixed to another beneficial use if he so desired. The decree here does not, and it should not, prohibit him from doing so. The apportionment made appears to have awarded to each his reasonable share of the limited quantity of water flowing in the stream during the dry season of the excessively dry year taken as the basis upon which the apportionment was made. The fact that it was made with regard to the area of land capable of profitable irrigation does not of necessity make the apportionment inequitable. It was a reasonable division for a year of that character. No reason appears why it should not be equally fair and reasonable to divide the water in the same proportions in other years when there is more water.

7. Would an allocation of a specific amount of water to each riparian be superior to a percentage allocation? What is the effect of the failure to join a riparian owner as a party in litigation to apportion the water of a stream? Do apportionment decrees quantify the parties' water rights in perpetuity, or are such decrees subject to being reopened?

NOTE: CUSTOM AND RIPARIAN RIGHTS IN HAWAI'I

Recent scholarship recognizes that custom is the source of many property rights, although the "modern" positivist push for uniformity has obscured those origins. Hawaiian water law is a striking example of the interplay between custom and riparian rights. Prior to Hawai'i's annexation by the United States, land was divided into *ahupua'as* and *ilis*.

An *ahupua'a* was a parcel of land, roughly wedge-shaped, extending from the highland to the ocean. Typically, the side boundaries ran down ridges, and the *ahupua'a* encompassed an entire watershed. Each *ahupua'a* was under the direction of a *konohiki*, or chief. Commoners lived on the *ahupua'a*s and cultivated them, giving a portion of the crops to the *konohiki* and later to the King after the islands were unified under one sovereign. An *ili* is a smaller tract of land granted to a chief.

All Hawaiian land and water was held in common for the benefit of the people. After unification, land and water were under the ultimate control of the King. There were no individual land titles so westerners seeking land in the nineteenth century brought pressure to make land transferable. In 1848 the Great *Mahele* (division) took place. The King quitclaimed his interest in certain lands to the *konohiki*s, and they in turn quitclaimed other lands to the King. This is the source of Hawaiian allodial land titles.

Water rights were based on the Hawaiian land tenure system. Traditionally there were two types of water rights: the appurtenant right and the *konohiki* right. The appurtenant right was based on the water requirements of taro farming. Taro is a root crop used to make a staple of the Hawaiian diet, *poi*. An owner of an *ahupua'a* had the right to use as much water from the watercourse of that *ahupua'a* as was needed for the cultivation of taro. Taro farming requires large diversions because the crop must be inundated with flowing water at regular intervals. However, it is not a highly consumptive use and much of the water returns to the watercourse. The *konohiki* right provided that rights in water not required to fulfill appurtenant rights (surplus waters) were controlled by the *konohiki*.

In Carter v. Territory, 24 Haw. 47 (1917), the territorial court superimposed the riparian doctrine over traditional Hawaiian allocation systems. At issue was the right to storm waters in a stream that flowed through two adjacent *ahupua'a*s. The court held that the owner of the upstream *ahupua'a* had the right to use of storm water but not to diminish its quantity or quality. The court's language sounded like the "natural flow" approach to riparianism but in fact it dealt only with storm waters. It also said that water rights could be acquired by prescription. Early cases had held that appurtenant rights could be obtained by prescription.

The development of large water-consumptive sugar cane plantations led some Hawaiians to view water as a salable commodity. A line of cases appeared to hold that appurtenant and prescriptive rights were "owned" by the landowner and could be severed and put to use in other watersheds. Large sugar plantations were made possible by investments of millions of dollars in irrigation systems which transported water from one *ahupua'a* (and thus watershed) to another.

The practices on which many enterprises were built were thrown into question in McBryde Sugar Co. v. Robinson, 55 Haw. 260, 517 P.2d 26 (1973). For all surplus waters, the court adopted a version of the natural flow theory of riparian rights. Relying on ancient Hawaiian customary law, the court held that ancient appurtenant rights, which passed with the land at the Great *Mahele,* were merely usufructuary, not possessory rights. A series of unsuccessful constitutional challenges followed, see *infra* p. 512, and in 1987 the state adopted a transferable permit system applicable to certain designated areas. HAW. REV. STAT. § 174C–59 (1993); In the Matter of Water Use Permit Applications, *infra* p. 434.

Harris v. Brooks

Supreme Court of Arkansas, 1955.
225 Ark. 436, 283 S.W.2d 129.

■ WARD, JUSTICE.

* * *

Appellant, Theo Mashburn, lessee of riparian landowners conducts a commercial boating and fishing enterprise. In this business he rents cabins, sells fishing bait and equipment, and rents boats to members of the general public who desire to use the lake for fishing and other recreational purposes. He and his lessors filed a complaint in chancery court on July 10, 1954 to enjoin appellees from pumping water from the lake to irrigate a rice crop, alleging that, as of that date, appellees had reduced the water level of the lake to such an extent as to make the lake unsuitable "for fishing, recreation, or other lawful purposes." After a lengthy hearing, the chancellor denied injunctive relief, and this appeal is prosecuted to reverse the chancellor's decision.

Factual Background. Horseshoe Lake, located about 3 miles south of Augusta, is approximately 3 miles long and 300 feet wide, and, as the name implies, resembles a horseshoe in shape. Appellees, John Brooks and John Brooks, Jr., are lessees of Ector Johnson who owns a large tract of land adjacent to the lake, including three-fourths of the lake bed.

For a number of years appellees have intermittently raised rice on Johnson's land and have each year, including 1954, irrigated the rice with water pumped from the lake. They pumped no more water in 1954 than they did in 1951 and 1952, no rice being raised in 1953. Approximately 190 acres were cultivated in rice in 1954.

The rest of the lake bed and the adjoining land is divided into four parts, each part owned by a different person or group of persons. One such part is owned by Ed Harris, Jesse Harris, Alice Lynch and Dora Balkin who are also appellants. In March 1954 Mashburn leased from the above named appellants a relatively small camp site on the bank of the lake and installed the business above mentioned at a cost of approximately $8,000, including boats, cabins, and fishing equipment. Mashburn began operating his business about the first of April, 1954, and fishing and boat rentals were satisfactory from that time until about July 1st or 4th when, he says, the fish quit biting and his income from that source and boat rentals was reduced to practically nothing.

Appellees began pumping water with an 8 inch intake on May 25, 1954 and continued pumping until this suit was filed on July 10, and then until about August 20th. They quit pumping at this time because it was discovered fish life was being endangered. The trial was had September 28, 1954, and the decree was rendered December 29, 1954.

The Testimony. Because of the disposition we hereafter make of this case, it would serve no useful purpose to set out the voluminous testimony in detail or attempt to evaluate all the conflicting portions thereof. The burden of appellants' testimony, given by residents who had observed the lake over a period of years and by those familiar with fish life and sea level calculations, was directed at establishing the *normal* or *medium* water level of the lake. The years 1952, 1953 and 1954 were unusually dry and the water levels in similar lakes in the same general area were unusually low in August and September of 1954. During August 1954 Horseshoe Lake was below "normal", but it is not entirely clear from the testimony that this was true on July 10 when the suit was filed. It also appears that during the stated period the water had receded from the bank where Mashburn's boats were usually docked, making it impossible for him to rent them to the public. There is strong testimony, disputed by appellees, that the *normal* level of the lake is 189.67 feet above sea level and that the water was below this level on July 10. Unquestionably the water was below normal when this suit was tried the latter part of September, 1954.

* * *

Issues Clarified. In refusing to issue the injunction the chancellor made no finding of facts, and did not state the ground upon which his decision rested. Appellants strongly insist that the chancellor was forced by the testimony to conclude first that the normal level of the lake was 189.67 feet above sea level and second that the water in the lake was at or below this level when the suit was filed on July 10th. This being true, appellants say, it was error for the chancellor to refuse to enjoin appellees from pumping water out of the lake. If it be conceded that the testimony does show and the chancellor should have found that the water in Horseshoe Lake was at or below the normal level when this suit was filed on July

10th, then appellants would have been entitled to an injunction provided this case was decided strictly under the uniform flow theory mentioned hereafter. However as explained later we are not bound by this theory in this state. * * *

Two Basic Theories. Generally speaking two separate and distinct theories or doctrines regarding the right to use water are recognized. One is commonly called the "Appropriation Doctrine" and the other is the "Riparian Doctrine".

Appropriation Doctrine. Since it is unnecessary to do so we make no attempt to discuss the varied implications of this doctrine. Generally speaking, under this doctrine, some governmental agency, acting under constitutional or legislative authority, apportions water to contesting claimants. It has never been adopted in this state, but has been in about 17 western states. This doctrine is inconsistent with the common law relative to water rights in force in this and many other states. One principal distinction between this doctrine and the riparian doctrine is that under the former the use is not limited to riparian landowners.

Riparian Doctrine. This doctrine, long in force in this and many other states, is based on the old common law which gave to the owners of land bordering on streams the right to use the water therefrom for certain purposes, and this right was considered an incident to the ownership of land. Originally it apparently accorded the landowner the right to have the water maintained at its normal level, subject to use for strictly domestic purposes. Later it became evident that this strict limitation placed on the use of water was unreasonable and unutilitarian. Consequently it was not long before the demand for a greater use of water caused a relaxation of the strict limitations placed on its use and this doctrine came to be divided into (a) the natural flow theory and (b) the reasonable use theory.

(a) *Natural Flow Theory.* Generally speaking again, under the natural flow theory, a riparian owner can take water for domestic purposes only, such as water for the family, live stock, and gardening, and he is entitled to have the water in the stream or lake upon which he borders kept at the normal level. There are some expressions in the opinions of this court indicating that we have recognized this theory, at least to a certain extent.

Reasonable Use Theory. This theory appears to be based on the necessity and desirability of deriving greater benefits from the use of our abundant supply of water. It recognizes that there is no sound reason for maintaining our lakes and streams at a normal level when the water can be beneficially used without causing unreasonable damage to other riparian owners. The progress of civilization, particularly in regard to manufacturing, irrigation, and recreation, has forced the realization that a strict adherence to the uninterrupted flow doctrine placed an unwarranted limitation on the use of water, and consequently the court developed what we now call the reasonable use theory. This theory is of course subject to different interpretations and limitations. In 56 Am.Jur., page 728, it is stated that "The rights of riparian proprietors on both navigable and unnavigable streams are to a great extent mutual, common, or correlative.

The use of the stream or water by each proprietor is therefore limited to what is reasonable, having due regard for the rights of others above, below, or on the opposite shore. In general, the special rights of a riparian owner are such as are necessary for the use and enjoyment of his abutting property and the business lawfully conducted thereon, qualified only by the correlative rights of other riparian owners, and by certain rights of the public, and they are to be so exercised as not to injure others in the enjoyment of their rights." It has been stated that each riparian owner has an equal right to make a reasonable use of waters subject to the equal rights of other owners to make the reasonable use. * * *

* * * We do not understand that the two theories will necessarily clash in every case, but where there is an inconsistency, and where vested rights may not prevent, it is our conclusion that the reasonable use theory should control.

In embracing the reasonable use theory we caution, however, that we are not necessarily adopting all the interpretations given it by the decisions of other states, and that our own interpretation will be developed in the future as occasions arise. Nor is it intended hereby that we will not in the future, under certain circumstances, possibly adhere to some phases of the uniform flow system. It is recognized that in some instances vested rights may have accrued to riparian landowners and we could not of course constitutionally negate those rights.

* * *

The result of our examination of the decisions of this court and other authorities relative to the use by riparian proprietors of water in non-navigable lakes and streams justifies the enunciation of the following general rules and principles:

(a) The right to use water for strictly domestic purposes—such as for household use—is superior to many other uses of water—such as for fishing, recreation and irrigation.

(b) Other than the use mentioned above, all other lawful uses of water are equal. Some of the lawful uses of water recognized by this state are: fishing, swimming, recreation, and irrigation.

(c) When one lawful use of water is destroyed by another lawful use the latter must yield, or it may be enjoined.

(d) When one lawful use of water interferes with or detracts from another lawful use, then a question arises as to whether, under all the facts and circumstances of that particular case, the interfering use shall be declared unreasonable and as such enjoined, or whether a reasonable and equitable adjustment should be made, having due regard to the reasonable rights of each.

* * *

We do not minimize the difficulties attendant upon an application of the reasonable use rule to any given set of facts and circumstances and particularly those present in this instance. It is obvious that there are no definite guide posts provided and that necessarily much must be left to judgment and discretion. The breadth and boundaries of this area of discretion are well stated in Restatement of the Law, Torts, § 852c in these words: "The determination in a particular case of the unreasonableness of a particular use is not and should not be an unreasoned, intuitive conclusion on the part of the court or jury. It is rather an evaluating of the conflicting interests of each of the contestants before the court in accordance with the standards of society, and a weighing of those, one against the other. The law accords equal protection to the interests of all the riparian proprietors in the use of water, and seeks to promote the greatest beneficial use of the water, and seeks to promote the greatest beneficial use by each with a minimum of harm to others. But when one riparian proprietor's use of the water harmfully invades another's interest in its use, there is an incompatibility of interest between the two parties to a greater or lesser extent depending on the extent of the invasion, and there is immediately a question whether such a use is legally permissible. It is axiomatic in the law that individuals in society must put up with a reasonable amount of annoyance and inconvenience resulting from the otherwise lawful activities of their neighbors in the use of their land. Hence it is only when one riparian proprietor's use of the water is unreasonable that another who is harmed by it can complain, even though the harm is intentional. Substantial intentional harm to another cannot be justified as reasonable unless the legal merit or utility of the activity which produces it outweighs the legal seriousness or gravity of the harm."

* * *

Our Conclusion. After careful consideration, an application of the rules above announced to the complicated fact situation set forth in this record leads us to conclude that the Chancellor should have issued an order enjoining appellees from pumping water out of Horseshoe Lake when the water level reaches 189.67 feet above sea level for as long as the material facts and circumstances are substantially the same as they appear in this record. * * * Our conclusion is based on the fact that we think the evidence shows this level happens to be the level below which appellants would be unreasonably interfered with. * * *

Reversed with direction to the trial court to enter a decree in conformity with this opinion.

■ McFADDIN, J., concurs.

NOTES

1. In *Harris,* Mashburn's fishing business apparently began in the spring of 1954, whereas Brooks had been growing rice for a "number of years" before that. Does the court attach any significance to Brooks' status as a prior user? Should it, and if so, how much significance? Priority of water use has traditionally carried weight with riparian courts, even those that purported to accept the "natural flow" theory. See, *e.g.*, Bealey v. Shaw, 102 Eng. Rep. 1266 (K.B. 1805) (using a "prior use" test to prevent newer mills from using water in a way that interfered with earlier mills).

2. What standard does the court in *Harris* employ in comparing the reasonableness of the two competing uses? Did Brooks' rice growing become less reasonable when the Mashburn fishing business started up? What would happen if another rice grower now began withdrawing water from the lake? What is the relationship between the "normal" level of Horseshoe Lake and the "reasonable" level? Will they always be the same?

3. How do the results in *Harris* measure up to the criteria for sound resource allocation based on economics as discussed in Chapter One, *supra* p. 33?

4. Are nonconsumptive uses presumptively more "reasonable" than consumptive uses? In *Harris*, a consumptive use—the irrigation of rice—and a nonconsumptive use—commercial fishing and boating—are in conflict. Does the distinction between the two types of uses have an impact on the outcome? The court says that the irrigators "had merely been exercising their lawful rights as riparian owners." What are those rights, and why does their exercise not "disturb" the rights of other riparians on the lake?

In Hoover v. Crane, 362 Mich. 36, 106 N.W.2d 563, 566 (1960), the court approved a decree which allowed an irrigator to take "the total metered equivalent in pumpage of ¼ inch of the content of Hutchins Lake to be used in any dry period in between the cessation of flow from the outlet and the date when such flow recommences." The littoral owners were unable to prove that the irrigator caused the decline in the water level., The court noted:

> Both resort use and agricultural use of the lake are entirely legitimate purposes. Neither serves to remove water from the watershed. There is, however, no doubt that agricultural use does occasion some water loss due to increased evaporation and absorption. Indeed, extensive irrigation might constitute a threat to the very existence of the lake in which all riparian owners have a stake; and at some point the use of the water which causes loss must yield to the common good.

> The question on this appeal is, of course, whether the chancellor's determination of this point was unreasonable as to plaintiffs. On this record, we cannot overrule the circuit judge's view that most of the plaintiffs' 1958 plight was due to natural causes. Nor can we say, if this be the only irrigation use intended and the only water diversion sought, that use of the amount provided in the decree during the dry season is unreasonable in respect to other riparian owners.

In Taylor v. Tampa Coal Co., 46 So.2d 392, 394 (Fla.1950), littoral recreational users succeeded in enjoining withdrawals from a twenty-six acre lake for citrus irrigation. The court quoted from Henry Phillip Farnham, Waters and Water Rights § 477a (1904), that "[t]he owner of land on the margin of a natural lake or pond has a right to have the natural level of the water maintained, so as to permit him to enjoy the advantages attendant upon riparian ownership, and to protect him from the disadvantage of having a strip of uncovered lake bottom left in front of his property," and concluded "it is plain that when the water of the lake here involved is at normal level the lake is too small in area and content to allow water to be pumped therefrom for irrigating purposes without consequent damage to other riparian owners."

Should courts consider possible future nonconsumptive uses of riparians in determining reasonableness of a consumptive use? The respective rights of riparians to use the surface of a waterbody are considered *infra* p. 439.

5. Is there a riparian right to have a water level maintained even if the surface is not to be "used" in the ordinary sense?

The City of Los Angeles condemned rights in two streams that contributed 90 per cent of the inflow to Mono Lake, a closed mountain lake so permeated with alkaline compounds as to be unfit for domestic or irrigation use. Diversion of the streamflow into the city water system would cause the lake to dry up, leaving exposed salt flats. Condemnees were owners of resort properties around (and on an island in) the lake. The jury awarded damages which took into consideration the water-related values of the littoral land. Los Angeles appealed on the ground that the condemnees were making no beneficial use of the water of the lake and that under article XIV, § 3 of the California Constitution, only nominal damages for littoral rights were due. The Court of Appeals affirmed.

> For the reason that the existence of Mono Lake in its natural condition, with all of its attractive surroundings, is the vital thing that furnishes to the respondents' marginal land almost its entire value, and that the draining of the lake will nearly destroy the value of their properties and the incident littoral rights thereto, it seems clear that the lake is not being used by the respondents for an unreasonable or nonbeneficial purpose, but, upon the contrary, that their use of the lake in its natural condition is reasonably beneficial to their land, and the littoral rights thereof may therefore not be appropriated, even for a higher or more beneficial use for public welfare, without just compensation therefor.

City of Los Angeles v. Aitken, 10 Cal.App.2d 460, 52 P.2d 585, 592 (1935). In recent years, litigation over diversions of water away from Mono Lake has raged. See *infra* p. 426.

NOTE: THE RESTATEMENT AND RIGHTS AMONG RIPARIANS

Rules have been developed that modify property concepts to account for conduct that seems "reasonable" in an era of economic growth. They are reflected in the Restatement (Second) of Torts, though it has not yet been embraced as perfectly containing any state's water law.

For historical reasons, water allocation rules have been assigned to the Restatement of Torts. Riparian water cases are usually after-the-fact claims for redress for a specific activity alleged to have caused harm rather than proceedings to allocate the risk of future shortages. Riparian cases are often resolved by the use of principles similar to the law of nuisance, and thus they have been seen as tort rather than property cases. The Restatement (Second) of Torts § 850 (1979) states:

> A riparian proprietor is subject to liability for making an unreasonable use of the water of a watercourse or lake that causes harm to another riparian proprietor's reasonable use of water or his land.

Restatement (Second) of Torts § 850A (1979) describes the principles applicable in determining reasonableness:

> The determination of the reasonableness of a use of water depends upon a consideration of the interests of the riparian proprietor making the use, of any riparian proprietor harmed by it and of society as a whole. Factors that affect the determination include the following:
>
> (a) The purpose of the use,
>
> (b) the suitability of the use to the watercourse or lake,
>
> (c) the economic value of the use,
>
> (d) the social value of the use,
>
> (e) the extent and amount of the harm it causes,
>
> (f) the practicality of avoiding the harm by adjusting the use or method of use of one proprietor or the other,
>
> (g) the practicality of adjusting the quantity of water used by each proprietor,
>
> (h) the protection for existing values of water uses, land, investments and enterprises, and
>
> (i) the justice of requiring the user causing harm to bear the loss.
>
> Comment:
>
> *a. Determination of reasonable or unreasonable use.* The reasonableness or unreasonableness of a use of water by a riparian proprietor must be determined by a court or jury from a number of points of view and upon the consideration of a number of factors. A conflict arising out of a claim of harm to one riparian proprietor caused by the water use of another proprietor involves an examination of the use or interest alleged to be harmed, the use causing the harm, the effect that the latter has upon the former and the effects upon society, the economy and the environment of making the uses and of resolving the conflict.
>
> In a suit between two riparian users of water the reasonableness of both uses is in issue. The plaintiff, in order to show he has a right that has been violated, must establish that his use of the water is reasonable. (See § 850, Comment *c.*) This will normally call for the application of the first four factors stated in this Section. Clause (a) requires that the use be made for a beneficial purpose; Clause (b) that

it be suited to the water source in question. Clauses (c) and (d) require the use to have both economic and social value. If the use serves no beneficial purpose and requires an inordinate amount of water, factors (a) and (b) are not met. If the product of the use has only slight or trifling economic value and the use has destructive or harmful side effects on other persons or the public, factors (b) and (c) are not met.

Illustration:

> 1. A, a riparian proprietor, uses almost all the water of a small stream to flood his pasture for the purpose of drowning gophers. Other cheap and easy methods of eliminating gophers are available. B, an upstream riparian, uses a substantial portion of the stream to irrigate valuable crops and does not leave enough water for A's use. A's use is not reasonable, and B is not subject to liability to A.

The defendant's use must in the first instance meet the same tests. If the plaintiff proves that his use is reasonable and has been harmed and that the defendant's use does not serve a beneficial purpose, is not suited to the source or has little or no economic or social value, he has established a prima facie case that the defendant's use is unreasonable. Most cases, however, are not so simple, since few uses of water are of such a sterile character. The typical case involves two riparians who are each making a beneficial use by suitable means and are each producing desirable values. The controversy arises because the two uses are inconsistent and both cannot be enjoyed, since one interferes with the other by reducing the availability of water in the source or the opportunities for its enjoyment.

In this case the courts must test the reasonableness of each use by considering the additional factors listed in this section. A major policy underlying the law of riparian rights is that of accommodating as many reasonable riparian uses of a stream or lake as possible. Clause (e) requires the court to find that the harm inflicted is substantial. If one water use causes no serious harm to another it cannot be said to be unreasonable, and accommodation can be reached by requiring the complaining proprietor to bear a minor inconvenience. Clause (f) directs an inquiry into the relative efficiency of the means of accomplishing the uses. If harm can be avoided by changing the practices, methods or facilities of one user or the other, the reasonableness of the uses may depend upon the determination of which party should make the change or bear the cost of making the change. Clause (g) directs attention to the possibility of finding a solution by adjusting the quantity of water used by each party. If one user takes more water than is necessary, reasonableness may be achieved by the elimination of waste. When a concurring cause of the harm is a drought or temporary water shortage, it is usually reasonable to require the water and the harm to be shared.

There will remain cases in which the defendant's use causes serious harm that cannot be avoided by these adjustments. These cases will arise when the demand for water exceeds the supply and there is not enough for both uses. The defendant's new use takes the plaintiff's water supply or makes the plaintiff's use and enjoyment of the water impossible in some other way. When this is the case, the controversy cannot be solved by a simple balancing of the interests of the parties or by determining the relative values of the uses and awarding the water to the user with the paramount interest or the better use. Often the two uses are essentially the same or are of equal utility. Even if one is more valuable than the other a transfer of a wealth-producing resource has taken place and the court must decide whether the act or conduct of the defendant in taking the water from the plaintiff is tortious.

Restatement (Second) of Torts § 850A cmt. a (1979).

Clause (h) of Section 850A suggests a preference for uses in place over new uses to provide a reasonable assurance of continuity to existing investments. The late Professor Jacob Beuscher of the University of Wisconsin, a pioneering water law scholar, observed over forty years ago that "[t]here is actually much more protection given to the prior user of water as against a subsequent water claimant than one would have any reason to expect from a mere recitation of black-letter riparianisms." J. H. Beuscher, *Appropriation Water Law Elements in Riparian Doctrine States,* 10 Buf. L. Rev. 448, 451–52 (1961). The late Dean Frank J. Trelease was the Associate Reporter for the Water Law Revisions. He proposed to restate protection of existing uses as the law of riparian rights, but intense opposition ensued and § 850A(h) was the resulting compromise. Despite the incorporation of prior appropriation principles into the Restatement, there are significant differences between the protections given to prior users under the riparian doctrine and those afforded senior users under the appropriation doctrine. For example, riparian doctrine contemplates sharing in times of shortage while the appropriation system does not. And, riparian rights cannot be quantified in advance of litigation.

Clause (i) deals with whether the person causing the harm should bear the burden of the resulting loss. The Restatement (Second) of Torts comments:

The court must inquire whether imposing liability upon the innovator will discourage or deter desirable progress. Ordinarily it will not. If a shift from one water use to another can be characterized as progress, it should result in an overall increase of welfare. In economic terms, a desirable new use is one that produces benefits that exceed its costs, including as a cost the loss of the benefits of the old use. Quite generally, an increase in welfare is not regarded as desirable if it is achieved by the method of impoverishing one person to enrich another. A new use may have much social and economic value, but if it will cause substantial harm by taking the water supply from an existing use, even one with less value, it may nevertheless be characterized as unreasonable unless compensation is paid. The new user who produces greater wealth can ordinarily afford to compensate the person whose less productive use he displaces.

Restatement (Second) of Torts § 850A cmt. on clause i (1979).

There is some debate about the impact of the Restatement of Torts (Second) on the solution of riparian conflicts, especially inasmuch as few cases have explicitly relied on it. In his treatise on water rights, one of the editors of this casebook, Professor Tarlock, endorses the Restatement position:

> The Restatement of Torts (Second) is an important recodification of the doctrine of riparian rights. The Restatement (Second) attempts to promote the more efficient use of water by making riparian rights a more complete property system. In many cases, doctrines that discourage efficient use are modified and replaced by advocates doctrines that encourage efficient use. Because the Restatement (Second) both attempts to restate the law of riparian rights in terms of what courts in fact do and is forward rather than backward looking, it has already had a substantial influence on modern decisions and is likely to have an even greater influence in the future.
>
> Riparian law is not a complete system of property rights allocation, as is the law of prior appropriation. Most of the cases impose after the fact liability on one use for interfering with another. The courts try to do equity between the parties before the court and do not try to formulate general rules to guide future behavior. In short, the law of riparian rights follows a tort compared to property approach. Thus, it is not surprising that the American Law Institute assigned the law of riparian rights to the Restatement of Torts not to the Restatement of Property.
>
> The water rights sections of the Restatement were extensively revised in the 1970s and a new approach to reasonableness was developed. The distinguished water law expert, Frank J. Trelease of the University of Wyoming, was made Associate Editor of the water rights chapter. He tried to substitute a prior appropriation rule for the common law balancing test, arguing that was, in fact, what courts did in the vast majority of riparian rights cases. His argument was unfortunately rejected by those who wanted to preserve judicial flexibility to trim or terminate inefficient or otherwise socially undesirable uses, but the core idea of protecting prior uses was retained in the new Restatement.

A. Dan Tarlock, Law of Water Rights and Resources § 3:69 (2008).

The modern debate centers on the merits of the Restatement's incorporation of priority versus the merits of regulated riparianism. The successors to the original protagonists, Deans Maloney and Trelease, square off in Joseph W. Dellapenna, The Law of Water Allocation in the Southeastern States At the Opening of the Twenty–First Century, 25 U. Arkansas Little Rock L. Rev. 8 (2002) and George A. Gould, A Westerner Looks at Eastern Water Law: Reconsideration of Prior Appropriation in the East, 25 U. Arkansas Little Rock L. Rev. 89 (2002). In brief, Professor Dellapenna portrays prior appropriation as a primitive, inflexible vigilante law which fosters premature development, results in an inefficient all or nothing result as opposed to a more efficient risk pooling of regulated riparianism, and thus is unsuited to "an economically mature, humid eastern state." Criticisms of The Restatement (Second) are academic because it has had almost no influence in surface, as opposed to groundwater, cases, in part because most of the conflicts involve non-consumptive uses. This said, the protection of long-established uses continues to be a relevant factor in the cases. Without citing Section 850, Edmondson v. Edwards, 111 S.W.3d 906 (Mo.App. 2003), protected a downstream cattle rancher from an upstream recreational dam that dried up the stream. The dam was not a reasonable use because it diverted water "to the exclusion of its long-standing use" downstream. As Chapter 4 illustrates, eastern states are finding that they cannot avoid incorporating a measure of priority into their evolving permit systems to protect the expectations of established users.

In Joslin v. Marin Mun. Water Dist., 67 Cal.2d 132, 60 Cal.Rptr. 377, 429 P.2d 889 (1967), a riparian in the rock and gravel business brought an inverse condemnation action after the defendant water district constructed an upstream dam that decreased the deposit of sand and gravel onto plaintiff's land. The value of the plaintiff's land was diminished by $250,000 when it became useless as a sand and gravel operation. The trial court's order granting defendant's motion for summary judgment was affirmed by the California Supreme Court because use of water to carry gravel was unreasonable "as a matter of law." It therefore found that there was not a compensable property interest "in the amassing of mere sand and gravel which for aught that appears subserves *no* public policy." Id. at 895 (emphasis in original). Can *Joslin* be reconciled with the principles of Clause (i) of the Restatement? With the Fifth and Fourteenth Amendments? Does the California Supreme Court's decision promote the efficient allocation of resources? Is it distributively fair? Does a sand and gravel operation satisfy no social purpose? Suppose that the defendant upstream riparian had been another sand and gravel operator. Do you think the outcome would be different? Compensation was required in Rose v. State, 24 N.Y.2d 80, 298 N.Y.S.2d 968, 246 N.E.2d 735 (1969), a case similar to *Joslin*. A 1928 California constitutional amendment was intended to curtail the expansion of riparian rights in preference to greater use of appropriative rights. See *supra* p. 93. Professor Brian Gray argues that *Joslin* "is the cornerstone of modern California water law" because it holds that article X, section 2 "requires all water rights to be exercised in accordance with contemporary economic conditions and social values." Brian E. Gray, *"In Search of Bigfoot": The Common Law Origins of Article X, Section 2 of the California Constitution*, 17 Hastings Const. L.Q. 225, 228, 230 (1989).

Pyle v. Gilbert

Supreme Court of Georgia, 1980.
245 Ga. 403, 265 S.E.2d 584.

■ HILL, JUSTICE.

This is a water rights case involving a non-navigable watercourse. It presents a confrontation between the past and the present. Plaintiffs are the owners of a 140–year–old water-powered gristmill. They emphasize the natural flow theory. Defendants are upper riparians using water to irrigate their farms. They emphasize the reasonable use theory of water rights.

The plaintiffs, Willie and Arlene Gilbert, own property commonly known as Howard's Mill located on Kirkland's Creek, a non-navigable stream in Early County which goes into the Chattahoochee River. * * * Until August 31, 1978, the Gilberts owned and operated a water-powered gristmill on their property. They also rented boats for profit and permitted fishing and swimming in the 40–acre pond. (On August 31, 1978, the mill was destroyed by fire.)

On July 7, 1978, the Gilberts filed a complaint against Sanford Hill, who is an owner of property that is upper riparian in relation to the Gilbert's property, alleging that since 1975 he has been diverting and using water from Kirkland's Creek for irrigation * * *. * * * The Gilberts characterized Hill's diversion of waters from Kirkland's Creek for irrigation as both a nuisance and a trespass and sought injunctive relief as well as actual and punitive damages and attorney fees.

The testimony at a hearing on July 18, 1978, revealed to plaintiffs that other upper riparian owners also had irrigated with water from the creek. The plaintiffs subsequently added four defendants: George Edgar Pyle, Jimmy Doster, Philip Buckhalter and Vinson Evans.[2] Following discovery, the trial court made an extensive examination of our water law and granted the plaintiffs' motions for summary judgment as to liability against all defendants, holding that the defendants' use of the water for irrigation constituted a diversion, a trespass, a nuisance and an unreasonable use as a matter of law, and enjoining any future use. The issue of damages was reserved for trial. The defendants appeal.

1.   Over 100 years ago, when this court first considered riparian rights in *Hendrick v. Cook*, 4 Ga. 241 (1848), several bedrock principles were established. First, the court firmly rejected the doctrine of appropriation and instead applied riparian principles to the dispute. And in stating the principles of riparian rights, the court also adopted the doctrine of reasonable use. * * * The court also held that an injury to one's riparian rights gave rise to an action for damages for trespass even in the absence of proof of actual damage.

Subsequently, two statutes were enacted and codified in the Code of 1863. Section 2206 of the Code of 1863 appears today almost verbatim at Code § 85–1301: "Running water, while on land, belongs to the owner of the land, but he has *no right to divert it* from the usual channel, nor may he so use or adulterate it as to interfere with the enjoyment of it by the next owner." (Emphasis supplied.) (See also Code § 85–1305.) Section 2960

---

2. Vinson Evans owns non-riparian property which he admits having irrigated with the alleged permission of a riparian owner. The evidence does not show that he owns any riparian property. * * *

of the Code of 1863 now appears at Code § 105–1407: "The owner of land through which nonnavigable watercourses may flow is entitled to have the water in such streams come to his land in its natural and usual flow, subject only to such detention or diminution as may be caused by a *reasonable use* of it by other riparian proprietors; and the *diverting of the stream, wholly or in part,* from the same, or the obstructing thereof so as to impede its course or cause it to overflow or injure his land, or any right appurtenant thereto, or the pollution thereof so as to lessen its value to him, shall be a trespass upon his property." (Emphasis supplied.)

* * *

Thus it is clear that under both court decisions and statutes, Georgia's law of riparian rights is a natural flow theory modified by a reasonable use provision.

* * *

In this case, the trial court found that irrigation with modern equipment was a "diversion" which is entirely prohibited by Georgia law, Code §§ 85–1301, 105–1407, *supra*; i.e., the trial court found that irrigation with modern equipment constituted a trespass as a matter of law. We disagree. The use of water for agricultural purposes was recognized as a reasonable use along with domestic use in the first reported Georgia case on riparian rights. * * *

* * * When our riparian rights statutes were enacted, irrigation apparently was practiced only moderately here and in other "humid" states. Thus the General Assembly would not have contemplated prohibiting the use of water for irrigation in enacting these laws. * * *

* * * Rather we think the General Assembly intended to prohibit the diversion of water from a watercourse for other purposes, such as to drain one's own property or to create a new watercourse on the diverter's property. That this latter use would have been of some concern to the General Assembly is evidenced by the adoption of the natural flow theory, which recognizes that the mere presence of a watercourse on one's property generally enhances it.

* * *

In sum, we find that the right of the lower riparian to receive the natural flow of the water without diversion or diminution is subject to the right of the upper riparian to its reasonable use for agricultural purposes, including irrigation.

* * *

3. In its detailed analysis of Georgia water law, the trial court had to apply *Hendrix v. Roberts Marble Co.*, 175 Ga. 389, 394, 165 S.E. 223, 226 (1932), to the effect that "... riparian rights are appurtenant only to lands which actually touch on the watercourse, or through which it flows, and that a riparian owner or proprietor can not himself lawfully use or convey to another the right to use water flowing along or through his proper-

ty. . . ." Thus *Hendrix* held water could only be used on riparian lands.[9] Yet four years later, in reversing the denial of an injunction against the use of water on non-riparian land, the court did not rely heavily on *Hendrix, supra.* Instead the court (Russell, C.J., writing the opinion in both cases) based its decision more on general riparian water law principles than on the non-riparian use. *Robertson v. Arnold,* 182 Ga. 664, 671, 186 S.E. 806 (1936). To the extent that *Robertson v. Arnold* might reflect ambivalence as to the rule announced in *Hendrix,* that concern is well-founded.

A major study of Georgia water law concluded that "Another disadvantage of this doctrine is that it permits the use of stream water only in connection with riparian land." Institute of Law and Government, University of Georgia Law School, *A Study of the Riparian and Prior Appropriation Doctrines of Water Law* (1955), p. 104. Likewise, the American Law Institute now recommends allowing use of water by riparian owners on non-riparian land, Rest. Torts 2d § 855, as well as allowing non-riparian owners to acquire a right to use water from riparian owners. Id., § 856(2), (see also 7 Clark, Waters and Water Rights 71–72, § 614.1 (1976)). The Restatement relies on two principles: that riparian rights are property rights and as such could normally be transferred, and that water law should be utilitarian and allow the best use of the water. Id., Comment b. Also, the Institute considers the acquisition of water rights by condemnation a "grant of riparian right." Id., comment c.

Georgia recognizes the power to condemn riparian rights. * * * We agree with the American Law Institute that the right to use water on non-riparian land should be permitted and if that right can be acquired by condemnation, it can also be acquired by grant. Thus we find that the right to the reasonable use of water in a non-navigable watercourse on non-riparian land can be acquired by grant from a riparian owner. The contrary conclusion in *Hendrix v. Roberts Marble Co., supra,* will not be followed.

* * *

Judgment reversed.

NOTES

1. The first Restatement of Torts dealt with nonriparian uses in § 855: "In determining what the law regards as the utility of a use of water (§ 853) or the gravity of the harm from an interference with a use of water (§ 854), the classification of the use as riparian or non-riparian is important." Restatement of Torts § 855 (1938). The drafters of the Restatement (Second) of Torts took an approach more typical of the prior appropriation doctrine by de-emphasizing the locus of the use. In Restatement (Second) of

---

9. It should be noted that the use of water in steam locomotives was a non-riparian use of that water unless the railroad right of way was considered riparian land wherever it went. See, for example, *Goodrich v. Ga. R. & Bkg. Co., supra,* where such use apparently was approved.

Torts Tentative Draft No. 17 § 855 (1971), the following "Note to Council" appears:

> The Restatement of Torts, § 855, says that the classification of the use as riparian or non-riparian is "important" in determining reasonableness. It then states that "there is no reason in strict logic why an arbitrary distinction should be made." However, it goes on to note that "in a number of jurisdictions, it is definitely a policy of the law, where uses of the stream or lake are conflicting, to recognize riparian uses as preferred over non-riparian uses even though the latter are of considerable importance to those who benefit by them." It expounds the latter theory in three comments and five illustrations.
>
> The Restatement 2d should take a positive stand on the split of authority on this question. The approach of the drafters of the Restatement 1st was ambivalent. They obviously seemed to prefer the rule stated in the recommendation made here, but they gave considerable aid and comfort to the more restrictive rule. The Restatement 2d should clearly prefer the rule most conducive to good use of water resources. The policy reasons for the suggested rule are given in the Comments.

The drafters proposed replacing the earlier language with a new § 855: "The reasonableness of a use of water by a riparian proprietor is not affected by the classification of the use as riparian or non-riparian." This was apparently too strong for the Institute. In § 855 as finally adopted, "affected" is replaced by "controlled." Restatement (Second) of Torts § 855 (1979).

Uses by nonriparians, as contrasted with nonriparian uses by riparian owners, remain disfavored in the Restatement (Second) of Torts. Section 856, Harm by Riparian Proprietor to Nonriparian–Effect of Grants, Permits and Public Rights states:

> (1) Except as stated in Subsections (2), (3) and (4), a riparian proprietor is not subject to liability for making a use of the water of a watercourse or lake that causes harm to a use of water by a nonriparian.
>
> (2) A riparian proprietor is subject to liability for making an unreasonable use of the water of a watercourse or a lake that causes harm to a reasonable use of water by a nonriparian who holds a grant from another riparian proprietor of the grantor's right to use the water.
>
> (3) A riparian proprietor is subject to liability for making a use of the water of a watercourse or lake that causes harm to a nonriparian exercising a right created by governmental authority, permit or license to use public or private water.
>
> (4) A riparian proprietor is subject to liability for making a use of public waters that interferes with the exercise of a public right to use the waters.

Restatement (Second) of Torts § 856 (1979).

In sharp contrast is the liability of nonriparians under § 857: "Except as stated in Subsections (2), (3), and (4), a non-riparian is subject to liability for a use of the water of a watercourse or lake that interferes with the right of a riparian proprietor to use the water." Restatement (Second) of Torts § 857 (1979). As in § 856, the reference in § 857 to Subsection (2) refers to a nonriparian who holds a grant from a riparian, Subsection (3) to a nonriparian "exercising a right created by governmental authority, permit, or license to use public or private water," and Subsection (4) to a nonriparian exercising a public right. Public rights will be treated in Chapter Five.

2.   Under the approach of the Restatement (Second) of Torts, what would be the treatment of defendant Evans in *Pyle v. Gilbert?*

3.   TRANSFER

When land with which riparian rights are associated is transferred, the riparian rights are presumed transferred as well, absent a reservation or severance in the granting instrument. Attempts to transfer riparian rights apart from the land, however, have generated controversy. The general rule is that riparian rights may be severed from the land, either by grant or reservation, and conveyed separately.

It is not clear whether a contract between a riparian owner-seller and a nonriparian owner-buyer is a covenant by the riparian not to sue for infringement of riparian rights or is a transfer of the riparian right itself, such right having been severed from the riparian land. The riparian owner who purports to transfer the full right to make use of the supply to a nonriparian thereafter has no right to complain of the nonriparian's use and, further, has no right to make use of the water supply over the objection of the transferee. Moreover, this set of legal relationships is binding on successors in interest to the transferor and it benefits successors in interest to the transferee. See Duckworth v. Watsonville Water and Light Co., 158 Cal. 206, 110 P. 927 (1910). Thus, if a seller owned the land on both sides of a stream from source to mouth, a sale of the right to use all the water of the stream to a purchaser in another watershed would extinguish any private claims of successors in interest to maintenance of the flow of the stream.

Other riparians not party to the transfer contract, however, remain unaffected by the transfer. Thus in State v. Apfelbacher, 167 Wis. 233, 167 N.W. 244 (1918), an upper riparian mill owner contracted to sell water to the state to maintain a fish hatchery. Under the contract the upper riparian agreed to maintain the level of the lake behind his dam at twelve inches above the average high water mark. In periods of low flow the state enforced this right by shutting off releases at the dam. A lower riparian mill operator suffered substantial injury from this detention of the flow and recovered judgment against the state on the theory that the state took only the rights of the vendor-riparian. "The condition of reasonable use attached to it [the water] before he conveyed it, and remained with it after such conveyance." Id. at 246. Accord: Portage County Board of Commissioners v. City of Akron, 156 Ohio App.3d 657, 808 N.E.2d 444, aff'd on transfer issue, 109 Ohio St.3d 106, 846 N.E.2d 478 (2006).

The possible operation of a bargaining system is illustrated by *Mason v. Hoyle, supra* p. 118. If it had been worthwhile to do so, defendant could have bought from plaintiffs the right to alter the timing of the flow of the stream. This exchange would take place only if the value of the detention by the defendant exceeded the sum of the values to plaintiffs of a normal flow. The granting of an injunction in that case could raise problems of monopoly power in the plaintiffs, although defendant did have alternative sources of energy.

Interbasin and interstate transfers of water in riparian jurisdictions raise both legal and political questions. For a discussion of these issues, see Robert Haskell Abrams, *Interbasin Transfer in a Riparian Jurisdiction*, 24 Wm. & Mary L. Rev. 591 (1983).

Interesting questions have arisen as subdividers have attempted to convey riparian surface use rights to lot owners in the subdivision. Feuding neighbors on Michigan's Gun Lake have litigated a variety of issues. See Thompson v. Enz, 379 Mich. 667, 154 N.W.2d 473 (1967), *infra* p. 455, involving asserted riparian surface use rights on Gun Lake by owners of subdivided lots. In another case, a developer in 1907 platted a twelve-foot wide "walk" along the shore for the benefit of all lot owners in the subdivision. An owner of a first-tier lot (separated from the lake only by the walk) got into a fight with owners of second-tier lots over the docking and anchorage of pleasure boats. The first-tier lot owners were held to be riparians but all other lot owners had only an easement to use the walk. Thies v. Howland, 424 Mich. 282, 380 N.W.2d 463 (1985). The second-tier lot owners "are not riparian owners because they only possess an easement interest in the walk * * * [and] the construction of docks and permanent anchorage of boats is not within the scope of the plattors' dedication of the walk." Id. at 469. Where the developer platted a park for the benefit of the back owners who had no lake frontage, the court held that they received only an easement and not fee ownership. The front lot owner retained ownership in fee and therefore the riparian rights to the park. The court based its ruling on the language of the conveyance, which dedicated the park to "the use of the owners of lots in this plat which have no lake frontage." Dobie v. Morrison, 227 Mich.App. 536, 575 N.W.2d 817, 819 (1998). The court did find that the easement included traditional and historical riparian rights, however, including swimming, fishing, picnicking, sunbathing, constructing one dock within specified limits, and temporary mooring of boats. An intermediate Michigan appellate court suggested in dictum that back lot owners' easements entitled them to erect piers, but the state supreme court held only that the issue is the scope of the easement and whether it burdens the servient estate. Little v. Kin, 249 Mich.App. 502, 644 N.W.2d 375 (2002), aff'd, 468 Mich. 699, 664 N.W.2d 749 (2003). Courts have split on whether access easements include the right to erect a pier. Compare Stefanoni v. Duncan, 282 Conn. 686, 923 A.2d 737 (2007); Dyball v. Lennox, 260 Mich.App. 698, 680 N.W.2d 522 (2004); and Ellingsworth v. Swiggum, 195 Wis.2d 142, 536 N.W.2d 112 (Wis.App. 1995) (no) with Shore Village Property Owners' Assoc. v. State, 824 So.2d 208 (Fla.App. 2002) (yes). The scope cases vary on the right to make other riparian uses. Many construe the easements narrowly. Eg., Brannon v. Boldt, 958 So.2d 367, 374 (Fla.App. 2 Dist. 2007) (back lot access eaement to water does not include lingering on beach "for extended period of time to view the water, fireworks, or the sunset."); Cool v. Mountainview Landowners Co-op. Ass'n, Inc., 139 Idaho 770, 86 P.3d 484 (2004) ("swimming" easement allows sunbathing but not picnicking or hanging out on the association's beach); and North Sebago Shores, LLC v. Mazzaglia, 926 A.2d 728 (Me. 2007) (easement to sunbathe and swim on beach does not encompass right to land boat). Others are more generous. Eg., Goat Hill Development Co. v. Lake Lotawana Ass'n, 134 S.W.3d 807 (Mo.App. 2004) (easement permitting sailboat slip includes docking power boats).

Allowing riparian rights to be severed and retained by the grantor (or transferred to a third party) can have dramatic and frustrating consequences for those who purchase waterfront residential property. In Williams v. Skyline Dev. Corp., 265 Md. 130, 288 A.2d 333 (1972), the expectations of purchasers of bayfront lots with unobstructed bay views at the time of purchase were disappointed when they discovered that their grantors had retained the riparian rights to wharf out and fill so that their lots became lagoonfront rather than bayfront and faced similar condominiums rather than the bay. As one would expect, courts require a strong showing of intent to sever riparian rights because a subsequent exercise by their owner could deprive the riparian tract of considerable value and encourage fragmentation of interests in property. *Williams* was followed in Conrad/Dommel, LLC v. West Development Co., 149 Md.App. 239, 815 A.2d 828 (2003), but no general severance of riparian rights was found in a deed which permitted lot owners to use streets in a subdivision bordering a river. Gundy v. Olde Severna Park, 174 Md.App. 189, 921 A.2d 292 (2007). The severance of riparian rights in New Jersey is complicated because of the practice of riparian grants; these are tideland grants which must be offered first to riparian owners when the state decides to sever the land from the public trust. N.J.S.A. 12:3–10 (2008). Panetta v. Equity One, Inc., 190 N.J. 307, 920 A.2d 638 (2007), holds that the presumption that riparian rights pass with the transfer of riparian lands applies to the transfer of riparian rights but not to riparian grants. The difference is that when a riparian right is transferred, it can be appurtenant, although the deed does not mention it, "but a riparian grant cannot." 920 A.2d at 647. In *Panetta*, the owners of upland and a riparian grant mortgaged the property and failed to expressly include the riparian grant, so the mortgage only attached to the upland portion of the property

Is transferability of riparian rights subject to a reasonableness standard, or is the standard only applicable to uses once the transfer has taken place?

NOTE: USE OF WATER ON NON–RIPARIAN LAND OR OUTSIDE THE WATERSHED

The transfer issue often arises in riparian jurisdictions because of the apparent restriction against use of riparian rights on non-riparian land. If one could use or allow others to use water on non-riparian land, many transfers would not be necessary. The rigid common law rule was that any use of water on nonriparian land may be enjoined. In Stratton v. Mt. Hermon Boys' School, 216 Mass. 83, 103 N.E. 87 (1913), plaintiff owned a mill on a small stream, and defendant, an upstream riparian owner, diverted water from the stream and clearly used it on nonriparian land. Nevertheless, the court opined that there would be no restriction on nonriparian uses by the riparian owner absent proof of actual injury to other riparians. There the plaintiff showed injury and recovered damages. What are the consequences of denying an injunction (or nominal damages where there is no harm)? Does the court's approach amount to granting a private right of condemnation to riparians as against one another? Is the result, and the analysis used to reach it, any different from that which would be used if all the uses were on riparian lands? In determining the reasonableness of a use of water on nonriparian lands, does it matter how much land the user owns that is riparian to a stream? If a landowner with a tiny parcel of riparian land, only large enough to accommodate diversion works, can take water for an enormous tract of nonriparian land, why should it matter that the user is technically a riparian? Does it make any practical difference to other riparians whether it is a riparian or a nonriparian who uses water on nonriparian land? The cases suggest that the early prohibition of non-riparian use of water has been relaxed in many jurisdictions.

The plaintiff in *Stratton* had an independent ground for objecting to the defendant's use beyond the fact that it was on nonriparian land. The water was being applied in another watershed. Why should it matter that water is used in a watershed apart from the stream of origin? Is there a modern rationale for the watershed limitation beyond protection of downstream return flows for the benefit of present and future consumptive uses? See Lynda L. Butler, *Allocating Consumptive Water Rights in a Riparian Jurisdiction: Defining the Relationship Between Public and Private Interests,* 47 U. Pitt. L. Rev. 95, 111–17 (1985). Today, transfers to other watersheds are generally allowed, subject to review.

Some lands actually abut more than one stream. If so, might water then be withdrawn from stream A and applied to a portion of the tract that lies within the watershed of stream B? Does it matter if both streams join together to form a large stream and therefore that the land is all in the watershed of the larger stream? In Anaheim Union Water Co. v. Fuller, 150 Cal. 327, 88 P. 978 (1907), the Santa Ana River ran from east to west, consisting in its eastern reaches of two forks that joined to form the mainstream. Defendant's parcel of land lay athwart both forks, and plaintiff's land was downstream from defendant's, on the north fork and upstream from the confluence of the two forks. Defendant diverted water from the north fork over a ridge into the watershed of the south fork, where the water was used for irrigation. The court held that plaintiff may enjoin the diversion, explaining the purpose of the watershed rule:

> The principal reasons for the rule confining riparian rights to that part of lands bordering on the stream which are within the watershed are, that where the water is used on such land it will, after such use, return to the stream so far as it is not consumed, and that as the rainfall on such land feeds the stream, the land is, in consequence, entitled, so to speak, to the use of its waters. Where two streams unite, we think the correct rule to be applied, in regard to the riparian rights therein, is that each is to be considered as a separate stream, with regard to lands abutting thereon above the junction, and that land lying within the watershed of one stream above that point is not to be considered as riparian to the other stream.

Id. at 980.

Compare Rancho Santa Margarita v. Vail, 11 Cal.2d 501, 81 P.2d 533 (1938), where plaintiff was a riparian located below the junction of the two branches on which the defendant owned land. It was held that the plaintiff could not complain of the defendant's use of water outside of one of the two tributary watersheds because the plaintiff failed to show injury. There was no actual injury to the plaintiff in *Anaheim* either; the non-watershed use was sufficient ground for an injunction. The difference between the two cases seems to be that in 1928 California adopted a constitutional amendment imposing a reasonable use rule. Making any non-watershed use actionable would be inconsistent with the amendment which states that "because of the conditions prevailing in this State the general welfare requires that the water resources of the state be put to beneficial use to the fullest extent." Cal. Const. art. X, § 2 (quoted in full *supra* at pp. 93–94).

Apparently there was another ground for the result in *Anaheim*. The court also applied the "source of title" rule to hold that the land in the south fork watershed had once been severed by conveyances from the land in the north watershed and, though later it came back into common ownership, it was technically "nonriparian."

Can a riparian use a natural stream as a conduit to transport water to a point where it would be extracted and used? In Alburger v. Philadelphia Elec. Co., 112 Pa.Commw. 441, 535 A.2d 729 (1988), a public utility sought to discharge water diverted from the Delaware River into a small, non-navigable creek, where it would be transported to a nuclear power plant and there used for cooling and water supply for surrounding towns. The court enjoined the transport of foreign water as exceeding the flowage easement that the company had, as an upstream riparian, over the lands of downstream riparians.

In Okaw Drainage Dist. v. National Distillers and Chemical Corp., 882 F.2d 1241 (7th Cir.1989), National Distillers pumped groundwater and transported it down the Kaskaskia River in central Illinois for use at its alcohol plant and for resale to nearby towns. The water flowed through a stretch of the river maintained by the district, which opposed the use of the stream as a conduit because it interfered with farmland drainage by eroding the banks and raising the level of the river. The district argued that National's continued use of the ditch was a nuisance. Judge Posner said injunction should be denied because the plaintiff failed to present any evidence to offset the balance of equities which favored the downstream municipal purchasers of the flow. On the fourth appeal, the court recognized the district's right to damages. The damages, however, were based on National's failure to dredge the ditch and clear brush, as called for in the original contract between the parties. Okaw Drainage Dist. v. National Distillers and Chemical Corp., 96 F.3d 1049 (7th Cir.1996).

Can theories that limit the amount of land owned by a riparian that can be served with water be justified today because they tend to make more water available for instream uses such as recreation and fish and wildlife preservation? As a means of making more water available for downstream uses? Some states, such as California, have dual systems of water rights; riparian rights are available to those who own land along a stream, and appropriative rights are available for others. Is there a greater justification for a restrictive definition of riparian land in dual system states?

NOTE: ACCRETION AND AVULSION

In their natural state, the shorelines of rivers and lakes are rarely fixed or permanent. Through the action of erosion, rock is dissolved and soil washed away. During the process of *accretion,* alluvion (composed of soil, sand, and other sediment) is deposited on the shore, gradually extending the banks into the bed of the waterway. *Reliction* occurs when water slowly recedes to expose land which was formerly submerged. A change in the course of a waterway, however, may be rapid, in which case the process of changing stream configuration is called *avulsion.* A storm or heavy flood may cause a sudden shift in the location of the banks of a waterway, as soil is carried off and deposited downstream. Each of these natural events alters the shape and location of the shoreline, and can have important and different consequences for the enjoyment of riparian rights.

Title to new land added by the process of accretion vests in the landowner whose property abuts the water.

> The question is well settled at common law, that the person whose land is bounded by a stream of water which changes its course gradually by alluvial formations, shall still hold by the same boundary, including the accumulated soil. * * * Every proprietor whose land is thus bounded is subject to loss by the same means which may add to his territory; and, as he is without remedy for his loss in this way, he cannot be held accountable for his gain.

Nebraska v. Iowa, 143 U.S. 359, 360–61, 12 S.Ct. 396, 36 L.Ed. 186 (1892). The same rule has been applied to human-caused changes. See Anderson v. Cumpston, 258 Neb. 891, 606 N.W.2d 817 (2000) (sudden changes in Platte River caused by bridges and dams treated as avulsion).

The Court in *Nebraska v. Iowa* noted that one justification for the rule can be found in the principle of reciprocal compensation: those who may lose their land through erosion should keep any gains attributable to accretion. A further rationale is the important protection provided riparian rights by the common law rule. Vesting title to the new shoreland in the abutting owner assures that the necessary contact between riparian land and water will not be lost.

Although accretion and reliction are distinct physical processes, the law generally does not distinguish between them. A landowner whose property abuts relicted land is typically awarded title to the exposed soil. However, some jurisdictions recognize an exception for land created as a result of state-authorized drainage operations. Where riverbottom has been reclaimed as part of a governmental program to improve the waterway, title to the reclaimed land may vest in the state, as owner of the riverbed, as discussed below.

The law deals differently with title to land suddenly altered by avulsion. Because such events are considered "acts of God," affected landowners are expected to bear their own losses and others are not benefitted by the windfall. Boundaries do not shift with the river, but remain as described in their original location.

When states were established, waterways often formed the basis for political boundaries. Gradual changes in shorelines have not provoked major disputes. Rapid, avulsive changes, however, have created substantial disagreements over boundary locations. For example, the Missouri River, an extremely active waterway, formed the political boundary between Iowa and Nebraska. Every spring, heavy flooding altered the shorelines and changed the course of the river. In Nebraska v. Iowa, 143 U.S. 359, 12 S.Ct. 396, 36 L.Ed. 186 (1892), the Supreme Court declined to treat these sudden changes in the Missouri as accretion, despite being urged to do so by both states. Because these changes were considered to be avulsive, the two states were continually forced to relocate their boundaries. Today, many states, including Nebraska and Iowa, have fixed their boundaries by compacts. As a result, river changes, rapid or slow, have no effect on boundaries.

In most jurisdictions, changes are presumed to be by accretion. The resulting burden of proof may be difficult for those asserting avulsion to carry. The issue is how slowly a change must occur to be considered accretive. In Solomon v. Sioux City, 243 Iowa 634, 51 N.W.2d 472 (1952), the court quieted title in the upland owner on the basis of accretion despite the city's claim that major alterations over a period of only three years should be characterized as avulsive. Contrast this result with the outcome in *Nebraska v. Iowa*, where the changes were annual.

When accretion adds land to the property of two adjacent landowners along a watercourse, how should ownership of the new land be divided? Some courts give each owner a share of the accreted land proportionate to the original ownership of the shoreline. Others base the allocation of title on the location of the beginning point of accretion. For example, in Burket v. Krimlofski, 167 Neb. 45, 91 N.W.2d 57 (1958), the court examined a series of photographs which documented a gradual transformation from island to peninsula. Because the alluvion had adhered to the island, rather than the mainland, the island's owner received title to all of the new land, while the mainland owner suffered the loss of his riparian status.

What of mineral interests under the accreted land? Should it make any difference that the mineral interest is severed from the surface estate? See Swaim v. Stephens Production Co., 359 Ark. 190, 196 S.W.3d 5 (2004).

When accretion occurs as a result of artificial improvements to the waterway (such as the construction of dams or dikes), the rules governing vesting of title may be altered. An upland owner who benefits from the accretion, but had no part in its creation, will generally be allowed to claim title. But a riparian cannot extend owned property by filling or purposely causing accretion. This is the general rule, but in an original action to locate the boundary between South Carolina and Georgia at the mouth of the Savannah River, the Supreme Court awarded Georgia one mile of riverfront land connected to South Carolina as a result of the deposit of dredged soil by the U.S. Army Corps of Engineers. "The rapidity of some aspects of the dredging and other process led the Special Master to conclude that the changes in the Savannah River were primarily avulsive. Although the question is close, on balance, we think this particular record * * * supports the recommendation * * *." Georgia v. South Carolina, 497 U.S. 376, 404, 110 S.Ct. 2903, 111 L.Ed.2d 309 (1990). The United States Supreme Court also applied the avulsion rule to a dispute between New Jersey and New York over Ellis Island where the federal government, as owner of the island, had added fill to enlarge the island. Ellis Island is on the New Jersey side of the Hudson River but New Jersey ceded sovereignty over the island and the surrounding submerged lands to New York in an 1834 interstate compact setting the boundary between the two states. The Supreme Court held that New Jersey nevertheless had sovereignty over the 24.5 acres of filled lands added to the original three-acre island. It held that the common law of property should govern where the boundary agreement between the two sovereigns was silent on the issue. New Jersey v. New York, 523 U.S. 767, 118 S.Ct. 1726, 140 L.Ed.2d 993 (1998). Mississippi first held that artificial accretions belonged to the upland owner to avoid opening a beach to African–Americans, Harrison County v. Guice, 244 Miss. 95, 140 So.2d 838 (1962), and then reversed itself, Mississippi State Highway Comm. v. Gilich, 609 So.2d 367 (Miss. 1992), but then qualified the reversal. Bayview Land, Ltd. v. State ex rel. Clark, 950 So.2d 966 (Miss. 2006) (artificial accretions by third party strangers to title vest in upland owner).

Governmental programs to stabilize soil and improve navigation are common. When such projects result in accretion, title disputes may arise between the state, as owner of navigable riverbottoms, and the upland owners. Until recently, many courts vested title in the riparian. In addition to the usual preservation of access justification, courts have stressed that a contrary rule would jeopardize the marketability of riparian titles and would not adequately compensate riparians for erosion control programs "gone awry." Board of Trustees of the Internal Improvement Trust Fund v. Medeira Beach Nominee, Inc., 272 So.2d 209 (Fla.Dist.Ct.App.1973). Questions of eminent domain and just compensation may be involved. See Save Our Beaches, Inc. v. Florida Dept. of Environmental Protection, 2006 WL 1112700 (Fla.App. 1 Dist.). However, on the ground that the state should not lose land as a result of projects undertaken to promote the public interest, courts today tend to award ownership to the state. A major California opinion rejected the common law rule because it would result in the transfer of state tidelands to private owners. State *ex rel.* State Lands Comm'n v. Superior Court, 11 Cal.4th 50, 44 Cal.Rptr.2d 399, 900 P.2d 648 (1995). Other states refuse to follow the common law rule if the riparian causes the accretion. Lucas v. South Carolina Coastal Council, 304 S.C. 376, 404 S.E.2d 895 (1991), rev'd on other grounds 505 U.S. 1003, 112 S.Ct. 2886, 120 L.Ed.2d 798 (1992). See also Bergh v. Hines, 44 Mass.App.Ct. 590, 692 N.E.2d 980, 982 (1998), review denied 427 Mass. 1106, 699 N.E.2d 850 (1998), which held that the holder of a beach access easement could follow the easement to the new, artificial littoral boundary because "accretion by steam shovel is not a recognized method of changing littoral boundaries." A state may be forced to justify its need against an upland owner's beneficial use of the land, as in State v. Sause, 217 Or. 52, 342 P.2d 803 (1959), where the state's attempt to force the upland owner who constructed a log dump on a river bank to purchase the resulting accreted land failed because it could not demonstrate a beneficial use of its own. However, many courts continue to apply the common law rule. *E.g.*, West Dauphin Ltd. v. Callon Offshore Prod., Inc., 725 So.2d 944 (Ala.1998), review denied (1998) and Monument Farms, Inc. v. Daggett, 2 Neb.App. 988, 520 N.W.2d 556 (1994) (island in North Platte formed by decreased flows from upstream Wyoming dams).

4. Loss

Pabst v. Finmand

Supreme Court of California, 1922.
190 Cal. 124, 211 P. 11.

■ LENNON, J. This action was instituted by the plaintiffs, Charlie Lee Pabst and the Priors, against H.H. Finmand and N.H. Finmand and the Cambrons, to quiet title to the waters of Eagle creek, in the county of Modoc, state of California. Eagle creek, rising in the Warner Mountains, west of the lands of both plaintiffs and defendants, flows in a single channel until just before it reaches the land of the plaintiffs, Priors, and the defendant, N.H. Finmand. There it forks and the north branch flows across the northwest corner of N.H. Finmand's lands and across the Prior lands. The south branch flows across the south portion of N.H. Finmand's lands and thence onto and across the lands of plaintiff Pabst.

The lands of the other defendant, H.H. Finmand, are not riparian to the creek. They lie to the west of the lands of the plaintiffs Priors and to the northwest of the lands of the plaintiff Pabst and the defendant N.H. Finmand, and are irrigated by means of two ditches, the "Gee" and the "Grider" ditches, which run from the main channel of Eagle creek before it forks, northerly to the lands of H.H. Finmand.

* * *

The N.H. Finmand lands being riparian, whereas the H.H. Finmand lands are nonriparian, the rights arising from the use of water on these different tracts are necessarily based upon different principles, and for this reason these different tracts of lands will be considered separately.

As to the rights of the N.H. Finmand lands, it is conceded by counsel for defendants that the right to the amount of water awarded to the defendants by the judgment of the trial court must rest upon a prescriptive right alone. This is so for the reason that, as admitted by defendants, the right by appropriation is not supported by the evidence, and, while the trial court found that N.H. Finmand was a riparian owner, no judgment was given such defendant based upon his right as a riparian owner, and no attempt was made to apportion the waters among the plaintiffs and defendants as riparian owners.

The judgment for a prescriptive right was given in favor of the N.H. Finmand lands against both the Prior lands and the Pabst lands. The N.H. Finmand lands claimed this right, and it was adjudged to those lands upon the theory that said lands had gained it by adverse use of the water which was taken from the south fork of the creek. As to the Prior lands no right could be gained by prescription. This is so because the water used on the N.H. Finmand lands was taken from the south fork of the stream, which runs below and does not border the Prior lands, where as the water diverted for use on the Prior lands is taken from the north fork of the creek, which runs by a small portion of the northwest corner of the N.H. Finmand lands and on to the Prior lands. The Prior lands, therefore, are riparian only to the north fork of the stream. A right can be gained by prescription only by acts which operate as an invasion of the rights of the person against whom the right is sought and which afford a ground of action by such party against such claimant, and it is a rule of law so well settled by decisions in this and other states as to scarcely need any citation to support it that a lower use, since it interferes in no way with the flow above, constitutes no invasion of the upper riparian owner's right, and cannot, therefore, afford any basis for a prescriptive right.

As to the Pabst lands, the N.H. Finmand lands are the upper riparian lands, and the Pabst lands are lower riparian lands. It is the contention of defendants that the continuous use of a certain amount of water each year for the statutory period of time gave to them a prescriptive right to that certain quantity of water so used by them, and this in spite of the fact that the use of the water by the lower riparian owner was never in any manner interrupted or interfered with by such use, and in the absence of any indication or bringing of knowledge home to the lower riparian owner that the upper riparian owner was claiming such right, not as a riparian owner, but adversely to him. This contention cannot be maintained. In the absence of a showing that the upper owner is using the water under a claim of prescriptive right, the lower owner has the right to presume that such owner is only taking that to which he is entitled as a riparian owner by virtue of his riparian right. Such use was not hostile unless there was an actual clash between the rights of the respective owners. While there was sufficient water flowing down the stream to supply the wants of all parties, its use by one was not an invasion of the rights of the other.

A riparian owner is entitled to a reasonable amount of water for use on his riparian lands. What is a reasonable amount varies with the circumstances of each particular case and also varies from year to year, for the amount which might be reasonable in a season of plenty might be manifestly unreasonable in a season of drought. Nor is the question of reasonableness to be tested solely by the needs of the upper riparian proprietor. The rights of riparian proprietors are correlative, and the "reasonable" amount to which any one riparian owner is entitled is to be measured by comparison with the needs of the other riparian proprietors. The fact that there was always sufficient water coming down the creek for the Pabst lands with the exception of the two years prior to the trial is undisputed by any evidence offered by the defendants. And, so long as defendants left sufficient water in the stream for the use of the lower riparian proprietors, it cannot be said that they were using an unreasonable amount, and, so long as they were not using an "unreasonable" amount, the plaintiffs had no cause to complain, nor was any right of theirs invaded.

The adverse use must be such as to raise a presumption of a grant of an easement as the only hypothesis on which to account for the other party's failure to complain thereof. Lakeside Ditch Co. v. Crane, 80 Cal. 181, 22 Pac. 76. In the absence of any facts showing an actual knowledge by plaintiffs of the adverse nature of defendants' claim or of any facts sufficient to create a presumption of a knowledge of that claim, it cannot be said that a failure of plaintiffs to assert their rights by bringing an action against the defendants was such a submission as could be accounted for only on the hypothesis of a grant. Indeed, defendants have not shown such an unreasonable use of the water on their lands as to put plaintiffs on notice of their claim. We do not mean to hold that a right may not be gained by an upper riparian proprietor by prescription, but to do so it must be clearly shown either that actual notice of the adverse claim of such owner has been brought home to the other party, or that the circumstances are such, as, for instance, the use of all of the water of the creek, that such party must be presumed to have known of the adverse claim. In the instant case there was nothing to indicate to the lower riparian owners that the owners of the N.H. Finmand lands were exercising, or attempting to exercise, any more than their riparian rights, and, in the absence of such indication to plaintiffs that the owners of the N.H. Finmand lands were asserting a right hostile to the rights of the plaintiffs, no prescriptive title was acquired. Even if the upper riparian owner is using all the water of the stream, still, if the lower riparian owner is not then using any and has no desire to do so, such use by the upper riparian owner would not be adverse, and, if continued five years, would not gain him a prescriptive right.

* * *

It is the contention of plaintiffs that there was no invasion of plaintiffs' riparian rights by the nonriparian owners of the H.H. Finmand lands by the diversion by such nonriparian owners of water which the riparian owners did not need, and therefore no prescriptive right to the use of the water could be acquired in the absence of a showing of actual damage to the lands of the riparian owners caused by a deprivation of the water. As to a nonriparian owner the riparian owner is under no duty to share the waters of the creek, and the slightest use by such nonriparian owner diminishes to some extent the flow of the stream. Obviously, there is no question of reasonable use in the sense in which that term is applied to the rights of respective riparian owners, since a riparian owner, as against a nonriparian owner, is entitled to the full flow of the stream without the slightest diminution. The initial step in the diversion of the water by the nonriparian owner is therefore an invasion of the right of the lower riparian owner, and every subsequent diversion is a further invasion of that right. Against a person who seeks to divert water to nonriparian lands, the riparian owner is entitled to restrain any diversion, and he is not required to show any damage to his use. Although no damage to the present use of the riparian owner results from the diversion, yet damage to the future use may result, and an injunction will be granted to prevent the diversion from growing into a right by the lapse of the statutory period. In the instant case the adverse use of the water on nonriparian lands was continued "openly and notoriously" for a period longer than five years, and, the slightest use by the owners of these lands being notice to all the lower riparian owners that a hostile right was being asserted, a prescriptive right was acquired by such adverse use by those lands.

* * *

Judgment reversed.

NOTES

1. Did N.H. Finmand have a prescriptive right as against Prior? Why? As against Pabst? Why? Under what circumstances might he have obtained prescriptive rights from Pabst? Did H.H. Finmand have prescriptive rights? Why? Can this case be reconciled with Stratton v. Mt. Hermon Boys' School, 216 Mass. 83, 103 N.E. 87 (1913), *supra* p. 145. What is the rationale for allowing prescription in a riparian jurisdiction when the plaintiff demonstrates no present harm?

2. A prescriptive right cannot be perfected without a showing of adversity. Ordinarily, a downstream riparian cannot adversely affect an upper riparian's use. It is therefore said that "prescription does not flow upstream." The key element is that the prescriptor's use actually deprives the downstream user of water to which he or she is entitled. Pleasant Valley Canal

Co. v. Borror, 61 Cal.App.4th 742, 72 Cal.Rptr.2d 1, 29–30 (1998). In order to perfect a prescriptive right, a claimant must show adverse use over a specified period of time. The prescriptive period starts as soon as injury occurs to other users. If injury is presumed, the prescriptive period begins as soon as the claimant initiates an impermissible use, regardless of the injury to the downstream riparian. How would a riparian demonstrate the necessary adversity in a reasonable use jurisdiction? The modern American rule entitles each riparian to as much water as can be reasonably used, subject to being enjoined if the use unreasonably interferes with the rights of others. A prescriptor must show that use of the water caused actual injury to other riparians. This rule ensures that injured riparians will have notice of a prescriptor's hostile use before the statutory period begins to run.

3. *Prescription in a Dual System.* In California, where the appropriation and riparian systems exist side-by-side, prescriptive rights have played a significant role. At the time of *Pabst,* it was unclear whether California followed the reasonable use rule. As *Pabst* illustrates, prior to the 1928 amendment to the state constitution, *supra* p. 93, any diversion for use outside the watershed in California created a prescriptive right against downstream riparians after five years of uninterrupted use. This rule operated without regard to the dates of the respective patents, and without the necessity of showing harm. The amendment applied the rule of reasonableness to the exercise of all water rights, making the acquisition of riparian rights by prescription much more difficult because only harm to reasonable use was actionable. Before that, "any diminution of the stream against the will of the riparian owner by other persons was an actionable injury." See Herminghaus v. Southern California Edison Co., 200 Cal. 81, 252 P. 607, 613 (1926), *supra* p. 83.

4. Once prescriptive rights have been recognized, courts must determine the quantity of water to which the claimant is entitled. Some jurisdictions treat a prescriptor like any other riparian, awarding only a proportionate share of the total flow of the waterbody. In times of shortage, each user's share is reduced in direct proportion to the decreased amount of water available in the stream. Other courts quantify the amount of water used during the prescriptive period, and award the claimant the right to use that quantity regardless of the amount of water available in the stream. This could put holders of prescriptive rights in a better position than other riparians in times of drought. A more practical approach is shown by Mally v. Weidensteiner, 88 Wash. 398, 153 P. 342 (1915). A nonriparian obtained a prescriptive right to 1.5 cfs. The court, however, limited the right to one-third of the water actually available at any time.

B.   PRIOR APPROPRIATION PRINCIPLES

The courts have continually ushered changes into prior appropriation law, modifying its characteristic features as necessary to respond to society's evolving demands and values. Chapter Two illustrated that the creation of water law doctrine, whether riparian, prior appropriation, or hybrid versions of the two, was a response to social and economic needs of eras and regions. And if doctrine did not fit the situation, it was altered or exceptions were announced. Today, riparian law and prior appropriation law have grown together into similar, if not identical, types of administrative systems that are examined in Chapter Four. To understand why those statutory measures were embraced, and to understand how courts interpret and fill gaps in those statutory systems, it is important to study how the courts developed the principles of acquisition, enjoyment, transfer, and loss of water rights under the prior appropriation system. The courts typically have identified how to escape inflexibilities in doctrine. Legislatures often have adopted programs that institutionalized these common law modifications and exceptions. The judicial role continues to be significant in applying the statutes, and it draws on the traditions of the common law doctrine.

Justice Greg Hobbs, Colorado Supreme Court, How Like a River: The Evolution of Western Water Law

Speech to the Colorado Water Workshop, July 26, 2000.

Geography and Experience

It's the natural order of geography for a river to keep on moving—and for those who would understand rivers—to walk in their path, sometimes pushing against the current, sometimes going with the flow. Western water law has always been changing—and remaining the same. From the earliest days of the states and territories, it's been so.

There's no contradiction in this. Law courts exist to decide actual cases, based on constitutions and statutes—state and federal—in light of the facts of each case and prior precedent, with a peek at the future, always hoping the decisions made at the time are as good as they can be. Oliver Wendell Holmes said: "The law embodies the story of a nation's development through many centuries, and it cannot be dealt with as if it contained only the axioms and corollaries of a book of mathematics."

* * *

Major Currents

For all his knowledge of the western landscape, his audacious physical and political explorations, his commitment to progressive planning and management, his fascination with irrigated agriculture as the enduring heritage of the western movement, pioneer river runner John Wesley Powell could not have foreseen the multi-dimensional role of water in future economies of the settled West. He predicted in his 1879 Arid Lands Report, for example, that, "All of the waters of all the arid lands will eventually be taken from their natural channels, and they can be utilized only to the extent to which they are thus removed, and water rights must of necessity be severed from the natural channels."

The western states have discovered that they lack the means, the right, and the will to dry up all the streams. Downstream states, Native Americans, federal reservations, the utility and joy of a flowing stream for fishing and boating and walking along through urban drainage ways and rural meanderings—in sum, the changing values and customs of the people at work and at play, have intruded.

Major active currents of western water law are: (1) Congress severed water from the title to public lands and provided for the territories and states to establish water rights under their own laws; (2) the western states chose prior appropriation as their basic water allocation and administration law for waters of the natural stream; (3) under prior appropriation law, water remains a public resource, the states continue to create property rights to the use of this resource, and beneficial use is the basis, measure, and limit of these water rights; (4) in times of short supply, state water officials have a duty to curtail junior water rights in favor of senior water rights; (5) the reserved water rights of the United States and of Native American tribes are entitled to recognition and administration along with all other rights in order of their adjudicated priority; (6) interstate water compacts and equitable apportionment decrees allocate water between the states, with congressional approval, and are enforceable; (7) new water demand is created predominantly by the public sector, namely municipalities and special districts that serve the west's municipal and commercial growth; (8) federal environmental laws significantly constrain new development of surface water resources, shifting water supply planning towards increased reliance on groundwater, changes of water rights from their prior uses, and conservation measures; (9) the changing values and customs of the people of the West and of the United States include clean and flowing water for recreation, instream flow, and restoration of disturbed riverine habitat; (10) optimum use, efficient water management, and priority administration are fundamental adaptive principles of western water law increasingly important to meeting water needs in the twenty-first century.

Adaptive Law of Beneficial Use

State constitutions and statutes do not generally confine the content of the term "beneficial use." Instead, beneficial use tracks the economic and community values of the people. The western states are the most rapidly urbanizing region of the United States. Citizen demand for water-related amenities in all forms drives the direction of water law and policy. The list of recognized beneficial uses now includes irrigation, stock watering, domestic, municipal, commercial, industrial, power generation, fire protection, flood control, residential environment, recreation, fish and wildlife culture, release from storage for boating and fishing flows, snowmaking, dust suppression, mined land reclamation, boat chutes, fish ladders, nature centers, augmentation of depletions for out-of-priority diversions, and minimum stream flows for preservation of the environment to a reasonable degree. The list is growing as new and changed uses are proposed for state permits and judicial decrees.

Instream flow use has been the most dramatic innovation. Thirteen western states now recognize instream water rights in some form. * * *

Thus, prior appropriation law can evolve to protect environmental values through enforceable water rights that are subject to the exercise of senior rights. * * *

Federal Constraints and Water Supply Alternatives

Through such laws as the Clean Water Act, the Endangered Species Act, and the Federal Land Policy and Management Act, United States policy favoring western water development has shifted to environmental protection and preservation.

* * *

Existing reservoirs have become even more critical to meeting western water needs—as new reservoirs face a long, difficult, and uncertain permitting course. Since water rights are perfected under prior appropriation law only by application of water to beneficial use, the obligation to obtain required federal approvals and permits directly affects whether water users are in a position to obtain absolute decrees. Until the structures are built to turn water to beneficial use a water right cannot be perfected.

Flowing into the Future

Beneficial use and preservation are the two chambers of our western heart, the two lobes of our brain. State and federal public land, land use, water, and environmental laws mirror this duality of feeling and response. Land use decisions will be instrumental in determining the look and feel of the western states.

We coexist in the land of little rain with other living creatures we must respect and help to survive. Westerners will proceed into the twenty-first century with values that will be reflected in water decisions at every level. From town to city to rural reaches, trashways are being turned back into waterways for walking and biking and boating. Local citizens will react to proposed diversions that threaten their economic livelihood and love for their home place. They will appear in administrative, legislative, and judicial proceedings to protect these interests. It is not possible to build a new water project without extensive public consultation and study of alternatives, including not building the project.

As the western states enter closely upon living within their interstate apportioned water shares, management will become even more necessary. Efficient means of diversion and storage, beneficial use without waste, recognition of all purposes that westerners value, these have always been fundamental precepts of western water law. The era of their fuller implementation is upon us.

Water supply decisions will involve examination of all options: among them, conservation, exchange, ground water recharge, joint use projects, conjunctive use of ground water and surface water, out-of-priority diversion and use through decreed augmentation plans, and the sale of water rights for change of use.

* * *

Inevitably, as each generation must learn, the land and the waters will instruct us in the ways of community.

1.   ACQUISITION

A prerequisite to obtaining a water right in a prior appropriation state is the availability of unappropriated water in a natural stream or lake. Once it is determined that water is in a natural watercourse, an official or court must also determine how much impact or inconvenience of senior users will be allowed.

The sources of water from which appropriations may be made include natural watercourses; diffused water (runoff) is usually left to the control of landowners. The definition of watercourses establishes the extent of public control of waters. Some western states assert greater control by adopting a more inclusive definition of the natural stream. The tendency to consider water to be within natural watercourses, and thus under state regulation, is motivated in part by considerations of efficiency that can be enforced under the prior appropriation system.

Prior appropriation assumes that water users will follow a series of steps leading to a perfected water right with priority over subsequently acquired rights. The requirements for establishing a water right were first defined by nineteenth century courts and incorporated in some state constitutions before states set up their statutory systems. They were commonly described as: (1) the demonstration of an *intent to appropriate* water, (2) the *diversion* of water from a watercourse, and (3) the application of the water to a *beneficial use.*

States have implemented these requirements by statute, and have added a host of regulatory provisions applicable to the acquisition, use, transfer, and loss of water rights. Regulations are designed to allow for fuller, more efficient uses of water, for better record keeping, and for more secure investments in water-using enterprises. All the appropriation states but Colorado have permit systems; Colorado uses a water court system to accomplish the same purposes. Some of the statutory enactments are mentioned in this chapter, but a fuller treatment of statutory systems is found in Chapter Four.

Intent and Diversion

Can water be appropriated without a physical diversion? Cases involving stockwatering directly in a stream, irrigation by natural flooding, storage in on-stream reservoirs, and the like all ultimately involve traditional consumptive uses of water that are identifiable and quantifiable. But they fundamentally lack one of the three requisites of an appropriative right: diversion. The problem is exacerbated today with the growing desire to maintain flows of water in streams for fish, wildlife, recreation, and aesthetic purposes. These efforts have been met with objections that keeping water in a stream is not a beneficial use (see *Empire Water & Power v. Cascade Town Co.*, *supra* p. 97) and that rights to instream flows cannot be secured because there is no diversion (see *Colorado River Water Conservation Dist. v. Rocky Mountain Power Co.*, *supra* p. 99). Programs securing statutory legal protection for the maintenance of instream flows are discussed *infra* p. 350.

State *ex rel.* Reynolds v. Miranda

Supreme Court of New Mexico, 1972.
83 N.M. 443, 493 P.2d 409.

■ MONTOYA, JUSTICE.

* * *

Across the defendant's property from east to west runs a water course called the Abo Wash, which has its source in the mountains approximately 18 miles from the Rio Grande River into which it empties. Following certain rains, water would flow intermittently through the wash, across defendant's property, and into the Rio Grande River. In earlier times, farmers would turn their stock into the wash to graze upon the tall, thick grass which grew in the wash and, in the fall season, the farmers would cut and store the grass for winter use. Sometime after World War I, a natural arroyo was formed and water flowing into the wash was naturally diverted from the wash into the arroyo. As a consequence, irrigation of the grassland began to decline. From that time until the present, the wash has diminished as a source of pasture for stock.

In 1969, defendant filed a declaration of ownership of water rights, claiming perfection thereof prior to 1907, and filed two applications to change the point of diversion, seeking to drill two water wells to be used for irrigating lands belonging to defendant.

Defendant's claims evidently are based upon the fact that his predecessors had made beneficial use of the grasses grown in and near the wash and that this would be a sufficient appropriation to entitle him to water rights in the Rio Grande Underground Basin. This contention is bolstered by testimony of two witnesses who can recall defendant's predecessors using the grass from the wash prior to 1907. However, neither witness could recall any man-made diversion of the waters from the wash, nor could defendant offer evidence of man-made diversion.

* * *

In support of his contention that man-made diversion is not necessary to appropriate water rights, defendant relies upon Town of Genoa v. Westfall, 141 Colo. 533, 349 P.2d 370 (1960). There an injunction was sought to prohibit the town from diverting waters forming the source of certain springs located on plaintiff's property. The court found that the water being diverted into town wells was a tributary to the springs on plaintiff's land, and that plaintiff, by watering of cattle and domestic use, had appropriated the water for a beneficial use. Defendant in the instant case cites the following language from Town of Genoa v. Westfall, *supra*:

> "It is not necessary in every case for an appropriator of water to construct ditches or artificial ways through which the water might be taken from the stream in order that a valid appropriation be made. The only indispensable requirements are that the appropriator intends to use the waters for a beneficial purpose and actually applies them to that use."

We believe that defendant's reliance on the Westfall case is misplaced. The Colorado court has established the dual requirements that the appropriator intend to use the water, and that he actually apply it to a beneficial use in order for man-made diversion to be unnecessary to an appropriation of water. Even if man-made diversion were unnecessary, defendant would be required to show that his predecessors in interest intended to appropriate water for beneficial use. The mere cutting of the grasses would not be sufficient to manifest an intention to appropriate the water for beneficial use, nor can it be said that defendant's predecessors applied the waters to beneficial use by grazing cattle upon the grasses in the wash. These acts only manifested an intention to reap nature's bounty gratuitously provided by water flowing through the Abo Wash, not to appropriate the water itself. The lack of intention to appropriate the water in the wash is also buttressed by evidence in the record which shows that defendant and his predecessors in interest made no attempt to divert water from the arroyo into the wash when the waters flowing into the wash became diverted into the arroyo. The grazing on and harvesting of grasses does not constitute appropriation of the water in the Abo Wash.

* * *

We hold that man-made diversion, together with intent to apply water to beneficial use and actual application of the water to beneficial use, is necessary to claim water rights by appropriation in New Mexico for agricultural purposes.

The decision of the trial court is affirmed.

It is so ordered.

NOTES

1. If Miranda had immediately redirected waters back into the wash after the arroyo formed, would that have made a significant difference? Suppose Miranda and his predecessors tossed rocks in the wash on his property to cause the runoff to spread out across the fields where he harvested grasses. Would that have satisfied the diversion requirement?

2. Water can be used to irrigate crops without passing over the surface. Many crops are watered by "subirrigation," or the natural seepage of water underground. It has been held that only "artificial" application of water deviated from a stream is sufficient to sustain an appropriation. See Staats v. Newman, 164 Or.App. 18, 988 P.2d 439 (1999).

In the Matter of the Adjudication of the Existing Rights to the Use of all the Water, Both Surface and Underground, Within the Missouri River Drainage Area

Supreme Court of Montana, 2002.
311 Mont. 327, 55 P.3d 396.

■ LEAPHART, JUSTICE.

The Montana Department of Fish Wildlife and Parks (DFWP) appeals a ruling by the Chief Water Judge on five pre–1973 water rights claims in the Missouri River basin. The five claims are based on diversions of water for purposes of fish, wildlife or recreation. The Water Court ruling refers to *In the Matter of Dearborn Drainage Area* (1988), 234 Mont. 331, 766 P.2d 228 (Bean Lake) in remarking on the potential invalidity of the claims.

* * *

To provide guidance to the Water Court, we must resolve the Bean Lake confusion and address not only the question of whether fish, wildlife and recreation uses are recognized as beneficial uses for appropriation purposes, but also whether a diversion is required for appropriation purposes.

* * *

Was *Bean Lake* correct in its holding that "under Montana law before 1973, no appropriation right was recognized for recreation, fish and wildlife, except through a Murphy right statute?"

Water Law in the American West: The Doctrine of Prior Appropriation

Miners in California developed a water use system as an alternative to the riparian water system prevalent in England and the eastern United States. While riparians allowed owners of land abutting the water source to control it, the more arid climes of the American West required a different approach. Prior appropriation, adapting flexibly to the needs of a developing society, allowed diversion to a distant location and simply required use of the water for a beneficial purpose. Western states adopted the miners' customs through both court decisions and codification, and the doctrine of prior appropriation became the law of the western states. A. Stone, *Selected Aspects of Montana Water Law* 7 (1978); Christine A. Klein, *The Constitutional Mythology of Western Water Law*, 14 Va. Envtl. L.J. 343, 347–48 (1995).

The common law elements of a valid appropriation are intent, notice, diversion and application to beneficial use. However, in Montana, as in many western states, the flexibility of the prior appropriation doctrine has allowed acquisition of the right to use a specific amount of water through application of the water to a beneficial use. A. Stone, Montana Water Law (1994). Judicial opinions and scholarly commentators have repeatedly stated the rule that application to a beneficial use is the touchstone of the appropriation doctrine. See, e.g., A. Stone, *Selected Aspects of Montana Water Law* 30 (1978); *Thomas* v. *Guiraud* (1883), 6 Colo. 530, 533 ("[t]he true test of appropriation of water is the successful application thereof to the beneficial use designed, and the method of diverting or carrying the same, or making such application, is immaterial").

Bean Lake

Bean Lake involved a claim for inlake water rights for fish, wildlife and recreation purposes in a natural pothole lake. In *Bean Lake* this Court stated, "[i]t is clear therefore that under Montana law before 1973, no appropriation right was recognized for recreation, fish and wildlife, except through a Murphy right statute."[1] *Bean Lake,* 234 Mont. At 343, 766 P.2d at 236.

The *Bean Lake* decision appears to be inconsistent with earlier case law in which the Court recognized appropriations for fish, wildlife and recreation. See, e.g., *Osnes Livestock Co. v. Warren* (1936), 103 Mont. 284, 62 P.2d 206, and *Paradise Rainbows v. Fish and Game Commission* (1966), 148 Mont. 412, 421 P.2d 717. In holding that no appropriation right was recognized for fish, wildlife and recreation, the *Bean Lake* Court ignored *Osnes* and misread *Paradise Rainbows*. The *Osnes* Court ruled that an earlier diversion of water, even if used only to maintain a swimming pool or fish pond, had priority over a later appropriation and stated, "it is not clear that such a use [swimming pool or fish pond] would not be a beneficial use and hence the basis of a valid appropriation." *Osnes*, 103 Mont. at 302, 62 P.2d at 214. The *Bean Lake* Court neglected to discuss or acknowledge the *Osnes* precedent.

In *Paradise Rainbows*, the Court again recognized the diversion of water for fish ponds as a valid appropriation of water. The *Paradise Rainbows* holding explicitly validated a diversionary appropriation for fish. In Bean Lake, however, the Court concentrated solely on the *Paradise Rainbows* Court's unwillingness, under the peculiar facts of that case, to protect an instream fish and recreation right and, consequently, overlooked the fact that in *Paradise Rainbows* the Court upheld a diversionary appropriation of water for fish.

* * *

A.   Did the *Bean Lake* Court correctly hold that prior to 1973 Montana did not recognize water rights for recreation, fish and wildlife purposes under the appropriation doctrine?

In *Bean Lake*, the Court cited and discussed *Paradise Rainbows*, in which this Court specifically recognized as a valid appropriation a diversion

---

1. The 1969 Montana Legislature created a procedure by which the Fish and Game Commission could appropriate instream flows for fish, wildlife and recreation purposes on certain designated streams. Section 89–801, RCM (1947).

of water for fish propagation. There is no hint in the *Bean Lake* decision of an intent to overrule *Paradise Rainbows*. *Bean Lake* is no model of clarity, ignores *Osnes* altogether, fails to appreciate the ultimate holding in *Paradise Rainbows* precedent and incorrectly states Montana law. Prior to 1973, Montana explicitly recognized water rights for fish, wildlife and recreation uses. Montana was not alone in recognizing as beneficial the use of water for fish, wildlife and recreation purposes. See, e.g., *Faden v. Hubbell* (1933), 93 Colo. 358, 28 P.2d 247, 250–51 ("[i]t is self-evident that water diverted and employed for the propagation of fish is devoted to a useful purpose, and all of the parties completed their appropriations of water by its application to the beneficial use designed"); *State ex rel. State Game Commission v. Red River Valley Co.* (1945), 51 N.M. 207, 182 P.2d 421, 428 ("we are unable to find authority, or justification in reason, to support the claim that the 'beneficial use' to which public waters, as defined in this and other jurisdictions, may be put, does not include uses for recreation and fishing").

To the extent *Bean Lake* suggests that fish, wildlife and recreation are not beneficial uses, it simply misstates Montana precedent and is hereby overruled. We next address whether *Bean Lake* correctly held that non-diversionary water rights for fish, wildlife *335 and recreation purposes were not recognized in Montana under the doctrine of prior appropriation.

B. Does *Bean Lake* correctly hold that claims for the non-diversionary use of water for fish, wildlife and recreation are not recognized in Montana law under the prior appropriation doctrine?

* * *

After the *Bean Lake* Court concluded that prior to 1973, Montana did not allow appropriation of water for fish, wildlife and recreation purposes, the Court essentially skipped the traditional appropriation analysis. Rather than evaluating whether DFWP had intended to appropriate water and whether DFWP provided notice of its intent, the Court simply stated that because Montana did not recognize water rights for fish, wildlife and recreation purposes, DFWP could not have intended to appropriate water for those purposes, and thus adverse water users could not have had notice of any such intent. It is unclear from the opinion itself, whether the Court denied the appropriation for *Bean Lake* because there was no diversion or because it found there was no notice of intent to appropriate. To resolve the confusion engendered by *Bean Lake*, we now determine whether a valid appropriation of water may be established without a diversion where no diversion is physically necessary for the intended use.

While most traditional uses necessitated a diversion of water for application to beneficial use, the appropriation doctrine's history of flexibility and practicality support a holding that a diversion is not required where the application to beneficial use does not physically require a diversion. Common sense rebels against a rigid diversion requirement that would refuse to recognize an acknowledged beneficial use simply because application to the use does not require removal from and depletion of the water source. In accordance with the doctrine's flexibility, we find that a diversion is not a requisite element of an appropriation when it is not a physical necessity for application to a beneficial use.

More than one commentator has warned against the strict adherence to traditional elements, such as diversion, when the element no longer serves its original purpose. These scholars also note that beneficial use is the only essential element of a valid appropriation. See, e.g., Tarlock, *Appropriation For Instream Flow Maintenance: A Progress Report on "New" Public Western Water Rights*,1978 Utah L.Rev. 211, 221 ("Most western water experts agree that the actual diversion requirement serves no function that cannot be served by other water law doctrines and statutory procedures. Thus the real issue is whether these uses are beneficial"); Christine A. Klein, *The Constitutional Mythology of Western Water Law*, 14 Va. Envtl. L.J. 343, 351 (1995) ("Rigid adherence to the diversion requirement has increasingly restricted the traditional flexibility of the ideas of beneficial use and waste. Although appropriation to beneficial use is the true measure of a water right, diversion has frequently been substituted as the constitutional requirement").

Under prior appropriation, a diversion traditionally served dual purposes providing notice of a user's intent to appropriate water, and defining the extent of the use. In *Wheat v. Cameron* (1922), 64 Mont. 494, 210 P. 761, this Court explained that intent to appropriate is to be determined from the specific facts and circumstances pertaining.

* * *

Justice Rice in his dissent states that, in recognizing instream uses prior to 1973, we are rewriting Montana history. Justice Rice's protestations to the contrary, Montana has a legendary history of cattle and sheep ranching. No doubt Montana's stockgrowers would be surprised to learn, as the dissent suggests, that Montana law would not have recognized a right to water stock directly from a stream, lake, pond or slough without a man-made diversion. Justice Rice's assertion that Montana law is "monolithic" and absolute in requiring a diversion as a prerequisite element for all pre–1973 water appropriation claims is belied by the fact the Montana Legislature recognized that pre–1973 claims for stock use and individual use *based upon instream flow* were valid. Such non-diversionary, instream claims were exempted from the mandatory filing requirement of Title 85, Chapter 2. ("Every person ... asserting a claim to an existing right to the use of water arising prior to July 1, 1973, is ordered to file a statement of claim to that right with the department no later than June 30, 1983. Claims for stock and individual as opposed to municipal domestic uses *based upon instream flow* or ground water sources are exempt from this requirement; however, claims for such uses may be voluntarily filed." Section 85–2–212, MCA (emphasis added)).

* * *

Ample case law depicting the evolution of the prior appropriation doctrine, and emerging from throughout the west, supports a conclusion that the doctrine should not rigidly demand a diversion where unnecessary to achieve the intended beneficial use. See, e.g., *Empire Water & Power Co. v. Cascade Town Co.* (8th Cir.1913), 205 F. 123, 129 ("[i]f nature accomplishes a result which is recognized and utilized, a change of process by man would seem unnecessary"); *In re Water Rights in Silvies River* (1925), 115 Or. 27, 237 P. 322, 336 ("[w]hen no 'ditch, canal, or other structure' is necessary to divert the water from its natural channel, the law does not vainly require such works, prior to an appropriation"); *Town of Genoa v. Westfall* (1960), 141 Colo. 533, 349 P.2d 370, 378 ("It is not necessary in every case for an appropriator of water to construct ditches or artificial ways through which the water might be taken from the stream in order that a valid appropriation be made. The only indispensable requirements are that the appropriator intends to use the waters for a beneficial purpose and actually applies them to that use"); *State, Dept. of Parks v. Idaho Dept. of Water Admin.* (1974), 96 Idaho 440, 530 P.2d 924, 933 (Bakes, J., concurring) ("[w]here an appropriative water right does not require a diversion to make it effective and beneficial, in the absence of a statute requiring a diversion there appears to be no practical reason why a diversion should be required").

* * *

Any perception that Montana law required a diversion as a *sine qua non* to an appropriation arises from the fact that most traditional uses, such as agriculture and mining, had a practical need for a physical diversion. That necessity combined with the practice of using diversions as evidence of a user's intent to appropriate has undeniably led to confusion in our precedent, which likewise recognizes instream uses of water where no diversion is necessary for the beneficial use. See, e.g., *Axtell v. M.S. Consulting,* 1998 MT 64, 288 Mont. 150, 955 P.2d 1362; *Donich v. Johnson* (1926), 77 Mont. 229, 250 P. 963; *Montana Coalition,* 210 Mont. at 44, 682 P.2d at 166; and *Greely,* 219 Mont. at 91, 712 P.2d at 763. Given Montana's long history of beneficially using water for purposes of agriculture, mining, cattle and sheep ranching, logging, railroading, fishing and recreation, we resolve the confusion in favor of the *Axtell, Donich, Montana Coalition and Greely* line of authority and hold that the doctrine of prior appropriation does not require a physical diversion of water where no diversion is necessary to put the water to a beneficial use. Thus, instream/inlake appropriations of water for beneficial uses may be valid when the purpose (e.g., stock-watering, fish, wildlife and recreation) does not require a diversion.

Because beneficial use rather than diversion is the touchstone of the prior appropriation doctrine; because Montana has long recognized as beneficial the use of water for fish, wildlife and recreation; and because Montana has validated non-diversionary appropriations, we now hold that Montana law prior to 1973 did not absolutely require a diversion for a valid appropriation of water.

* * *

■ RICE, JUSTICE, concurring in part and dissenting in part.

I concur with the Court's holding herein that recreational use is a beneficial use of water, and that the language in *Bean Lake* which purports to invalidate all pre–1973 recreational claims is erroneous. To the extent that it is necessary to clarify that pre–1973 recreational claims which meet all of the elements of the appropriation doctrine, including diversion, are valid, I concur with the Court's decision herein. However, I must dissent from the remaining, substantial portion of the Court's opinion. *Bean Lake* properly held that pre–1973 claims involving "non-captive," i.e., instream or inlake, recreational uses have never been recognized, as also acknowledged by this Court in *Paradise Rainbows*.

The Court offers a lengthy discussion in an effort to market its conclusions that the doctrine of prior appropriation is a "historically flexible" concept, and that the strict necessity of establishing diversion is mere "perception." The Court further holds that the doctrine recognizes appropriations of water without a diversion whenever a diversion is not necessary for the use. Finally, the Court holds that pre–1973 instream appropriations have already been recognized and approved in our law. These conclusions, which blatantly ignore controlling statutes and case law, are all erroneous. A proper review of the applicable law establishes that diversion, or a form thereof, such as impoundment or capture, is a long-standing, foundational and requisite element for all pre–1973 water appropriation claims, including recreational uses. That the law clearly required it is an inescapable conclusion.

* * *

Clearly, the Court is remaking the law, but more than that, it is rewriting history. Its holding does not simply pronounce a rule of law for future application. Rather, the holding declares the state of the law prior to 1973—that instream, non-diversion rights were then recognized. If that assessment of the law is correct, the Court should be able to cite to a Montana case which approved of such a pre–1973 right, but, of course, it is unable to do so. The only two cases which recognized pre–1973 recreational claims, *Osnes Livestock Co. v. Warren* (1936), 103 Mont. 284, 62 P.2d 206, and *Paradise Rainbows v. Fish and Game Comm'n* (1966), 148 Mont. 412, 421 P.2d 717, were based upon diversion. There are no other cases in our history to which the Court can cite in support of recreational claims—and certainly none which established a recreational right without diversion. In fact, every Montana case cited in the opinion stands precisely for the opposite conclusion than the one reached by the Court here.

The Court attempts to divert attention from the obvious lack of support in our precedent for its analysis by denouncing this dissent as a "simplified rendition of Montana's water usage history." If the Court deems this discussion of our law simplified, the objection lies not with the dissent, but with the law. Indeed, this Court has previously acknowledged the truth of the dissent's central premise: "Such a public right has never been declared in the case law of this state." *Paradise Rainbows*, 148 Mont. at 419, 421 P.2d at 721. While the Court claims to disdain fiction within legal analysis, its inability to point to a single Montana case supporting its position belies its asserted literary preference.

The Court also responds to this criticism by stating that stockgrowers, loggers, and railroaders would be surprised to learn that the diversion requirement would have affected their water use, and that the Court "would have" approved of such uses, had it been given the opportunity. While I have not suggested, as the opinion states, that Montana law would not have recognized the withdrawal of water by stock as a water right, I respectfully suggest that it is our duty to apply the law as it exists, not the law that "might have been," in seeking to explain the correct status of the law prior to 1973.

* * *

The Court has now re-created pre–1973 water law in Montana. Its opinion is a smoothly written, seamless essay which attracts an unsuspecting reader to the conclusion that the holding is completely correct and justified under the law. Indeed, I cannot disagree with the proposition that "[c]ommon sense rebels against a rigid diversion requirement which would refuse to recognize an acknowledged beneficial use simply because application to the use does not require removal from the water source." If this issue had been presented to the Court as a prospective revision to the common law properly arising out of litigation, I would most seriously consider it. However, the issue of instream rights is not even before the Court; only diversion-based claims are before us. The Court chooses to go outside the issues actually raised here, outside the arguments presented, outside the relief requested, and outside 100 plus years of precedent to retroactively redefine pre–1973 law. I submit that the Court is also going outside its judicial obligation to apply the law that is, electing instead to remake pre–1973 law in accordance with what it wished the law had been.

NOTES

1. If, as the dissent suggests, stating, or even "re-creating," pre–1973 Montana water law was unnecessary to decide the issues in the principal case, why did the majority engage in this exercise?

2. Do the principal case and State ex rel. Reynolds v.Miranda, *supra*, arrive at fundamentally different principles, or merely different outcomes based on the fact situations of each case?

3. *Town of Genoa v. Westfall*, discussed in the principal case and in *Miranda*, involved stockwatering. Because no artificial means of diversion are usually involved, stockwatering has been one focus of the debate regarding the need for a diversion. Most states allow it to be the basis of an appropriation. In R.T. Nahas Co. v. Hulet, 106 Idaho 37, 674 P.2d 1036, 1043 (App.1983), the court concluded that "we cannot justify imposing an economic burden, by requiring a diversion, which will not advance the interests of the public by promoting more efficient use of water, or reducing waste."

4. In a recent case, Phelps Dodge Corp. v. Arizona Dep't of Water Resources, 211 Ariz. 146, 118 P.3d 1110 (Ariz.App.Div. 1 2005), the Arizona Court of Appeals declined to follow *State ex rel. Reynolds v. Miranda* and also rejected the notion that stock watering was a diversion. In upholding the granting of an instream flow permit to the U.S. Forest Service, the court held that neither the common law in Arizona nor the water statute required a diversion for a valid appropriation.

5. What policies are served by requiring appropriators to divert water? In light of the judicial and legislative recognition of a variety of acts short of diversion of water from the stream in order to demonstrate due diligence, does the diversion requirement have a purpose? One of the editors has suggested that the original function of the requirement—to give notice to subsequent appropriators—is better performed by modern permitting and recordation systems than by an actual diversion requirement. A. Dan Tarlock, *Appropriation for Instream Flow Maintenance: A Progress Report on "New" Public Western Water Rights*, 1978 Utah L. Rev. 211.

Sand Point Water & Light Co. v. Panhandle Development Co.

Supreme Court of Idaho, 1905.
11 Idaho 405, 83 P. 347.

■ AILSHIE, J.

* * *

This action was commenced by the respondent corporation to restrain the appellant corporation from diverting and appropriating the waters of Sand creek and Switzer creek in Kootenai county, and to restrain and enjoin the defendants from interfering with or diverting the waters of those streams in any way or manner that would interfere with the rights and appropriation of the plaintiff. The case went to trial upon complaint and answer, and resulted in a judgment for the plaintiff, from which judgment and an order denying a motion for a new trial, the defendant has appealed.

* * *

On December 16, 1902, appellant's grantors located a water right on West Sand or Mill creek in Kootenai county, and the location notice thereof was posted and duly filed and recorded in the office of the county recorder of Kootenai county, and thereafter, in due time, was filed in the office of the State Engineer at Boise city. Within a few days thereafter the same parties duly and regularly made two additional locations on these streams. On the 14th day of January, 1903, and about 29 days after making the first location, work was commenced, which consisted in cutting out a trail up the canyon, and making a survey for flumes and ditches. Work was continuously prosecuted from that time until the date of the trial of this cause, with at least one man on the ground all the time engaged in building a road, and a flume and ditch through which to carry the waters of these streams, and the general work incident to the construction of the diverting work for carrying out the purposes for which the appropriation was being made.

* * *

* * * The fact stands upon the record practically undisputed, that on the 29th day of September, 1903, the date on which respondent's grantor obtained his permit from the State Engineer to divert and appropriate the waters of these streams, the appellant was actively engaged in the construction of its diverting works, and had at that time expended from $700 to $800 in the prosecution of the work.

It should be observed that appellant's location and the prosecution of its work was made under the act of February 25, 1899, while the respondent's right was initiated under act approved March 11, 1903. By the latter act a permit is obtained from the State Engineer to divert and appropriate the waters of any of the public streams of the state, while under the act of 1899, notice was required to be posted and a copy thereof filed and recorded with the county recorder, and a duplicate thereof filed with the State Engineer. By section 6 of the act of 1899, under which appellant initiated its right, it is provided: "Within sixty days after the notice is posted, the claimant must commence the excavation or construction of the works by which he intends to divert the water, and must prosecute the work diligently and uninterruptedly to completion, unless temporarily interrupted by snow, rain, or cold weather." Respondent claims that the appellant failed to show that it had prosecuted the construction of its diverting works with the diligence required by section 6, and for that reason, if for none other, the judgment was properly entered against appellant. It seems to us, however, when we consider that this work was being prosecuted in a mountainous section of the state where there is a heavy snow fall and a long winter season with much rough and stormy weather which would interrupt and delay the character of work that was being carried on, that the amount and kind of work which is shown to have been done evidences good faith, reasonable diligence, and a purpose to complete the work and apply the waters to the beneficial use designated. Saying nothing of the record notice which the respondent had, the work upon the ground and its continued prosecution was ample actual notice to respondent, or any other subsequent claimant to these waters, as to the nature of the claim asserted by appellant.

It seems to us that the real difficulty in this case has arisen from a wrong construction and misapplication of the word appropriate as used in our statutes. Section 8 of the act of February 25, 1899, provides that where an appropriator has complied with the preceding sections in the posting and recording of notices and the commencement and prosecution of work, "the claimant's right to the use of water relates back to the time the notice was posted." Section 7 of the act provides that by a completion of the work "is meant conducting the waters to the place of intended use." A person desiring to appropriate the waters of a stream may do so either by actually diverting the water and applying it to a beneficial use, or he may pursue the statutory method by posting and recording his notice and commencing and prosecuting his work within the statutory time.

* * *

* * * In other words, by pursuing the successive steps prescribed in the statute, and completing his diverting works, and applying the water to a beneficial purpose, the appropriation is completed.

* * *

It appears that the lower court proceeded on the theory that the appropriation, regardless of the posting of notice, dates from the actual diversion of the water, and its application to the use intended, and the court accordingly finds that "the plaintiff did on or before the 14th day of August, 1904, complete its water system and did actually appropriate the waters flowing in the said stream described in the complaint, and has ever since said date actually appropriated and used all the waters in said stream described in the complaint in supplying the inhabitants of the village of Sand Point with water for domestic uses and fire purposes." This theory is incorrect as applied to appellant, so long as appellant continued to prosecute its work with reasonable diligence. So long as it did so, it was entitled to have its appropriation relate back to the posting of its notice; and, in that event, appellant would be entitled to protection as a prior appropriator as against the respondent.

NOTES

1. What economic objective does the relation back doctrine serve? Does the decision in the principal case further this objective?

2. In *Sand Point*, intent was manifested by posting a location notice according to statute, and subsequently recording it. In the absence of such a statutory requirement, intent may be demonstrated in many ways, including having a surveyor mark out the proper location for ditches. In the case of a corporate appropriator, action by the board of directors approving a water development plan may suffice, provided it is accompanied by a physical manifestation such as some excavation or even placement of survey stakes. City of Aspen v. Colorado River Water Conservation Dist., 696 P.2d 758 (Colo.1985), holds that such manifestations need not be on the land, but must be an overt act sufficient to satisfy the purpose of affording adequate notice to all interested third parties. But compare Bar 70 Enterprises, Inc. v. Tosco Corp., 703 P.2d 1297 (Colo.1985). The court held that a reconnaissance walk in the White River basin to look for reservoir and diversion points for a planned (now dormant) oil shale project did not constitute the necessary concurrence of intent to appropriate water for a beneficial use and the performance of an overt act in furtherance of that intent. The 1976 junket did not manifest the requisite intent to appropriate because "Tosco did not conduct a survey of the reservoir or diversion sites, failed to set stakes or to locate monuments, and did not post signs or publish notices." Id. at 1307–1308. Nor did the "field trip" demonstrate the taking of a substantial step toward application of the water to a beneficial use. "Tosco's field crew did not conduct a field survey at all, but simply hiked along most of the route of the proposed pipeline * * *." Id. at 1308. Finally, the court held that the field crew's modest activities were not sufficient to put third parties on notice of the contemplated diversion. Similarly, a city's surveys that involved limited contact with individuals and no public notice other than hastily posted signs did not constitute adequate notice. City of Thornton v. Bijou Irrigation Co., 926 P.2d 1 (Colo.1996).

In the permit states, application for a permit to make an appropriation demonstrates the necessary intent. In Colorado, filing for a conditional decree will demonstrate intent and serve to manifest that intent. Further activity by the applicant may well be necessary to take the required "substantial step" toward putting the water to a beneficial use. See In re Vought, 76 P.3d 906 (Colo. 2003).

3.   Should the priority date relate back to the date of the overt act or the date at which a decision was made to proceed with the project, thus manifesting the requisite intent? In Elk–Rifle Water Co. v. Templeton, 173 Colo. 438, 484 P.2d 1211, 1215 (1971), the Colorado Supreme Court chose the latter of the two dates: "[w]hat is required is that at some point in time the two requirements—the open physical demonstration and the requisite intent to appropriate—co-exist, with the priority date to be set not earlier than the date on which both elements are present." For a discussion of the "first step" test, including consideration of what factors and actions qualify as manifestations of intent, see City of Thornton v. City of Fort Collins, 830 P.2d 915 (Colo.1992), *infra*.

4.   Originally, relation back of a priority was necessary to allow time for digging a ditch. In an era of multistage projects that require long lead times for planning, financing, and construction, relation back raises more difficult questions. Consequently, states have passed laws giving discretion to an official to prescribe a time within which certain work must be done and water applied to a beneficial use. See *infra* p. 182. Colorado continues to rely on demonstrations of due diligence to maintain a conditional water right.

City and County of Denver v. Northern Colorado Water Conservancy District

Supreme Court of Colorado, 1954.
130 Colo. 375, 276 P.2d 992.

[Denver appealed a decision of the District Court for Summit County awarding it a conditional decree in connection with the city's Blue River Project, which involved a proposed transmountain diversion from the Western Slope of the Rocky Mountains. Denver claimed 1600 c.f.s. with a priority date of March 21, 1914; the District Court awarded 788 c.f.s. as of June 24, 1946. On appeal, the Colorado Supreme Court addressed several issues, including Denver's need for the water, its intent to make an appropriation, and the doctrine of relation back. It then turned to Denver's demonstration of due diligence in the prosecution of the conditional decree.]

■ STONE, CHIEF JUSTICE.

* * *

The Colorado River Water Conservation District and others protested the awarding of any decree whatever to Denver's Blue River project and here assign error to the decree awarded it on the ground that Denver now has an adequate water supply, and that a conditional decree should not be given for a larger quantity of water than it can reasonably expect to put to beneficial use. The uncontradicted evidence in the record discloses that Denver had adequate water supply at the time of the hearing without the Blue River water here sought. As to its further growth and consequent future need, there were divergent estimates, all necessarily without actual knowledge. We cannot hold that a city more than others is entitled to decree for water beyond its own needs. However, an appropriator has a reasonable time in which to effect his originally intended use as well as to complete his originally intended means of diversion, and when appropriations are sought by a growing city, regard should be given to its reasonably anticipated requirements. Van Tassel Real Estate & Live Stock Co. v. City of Cheyenne, 49 Wyo. 333, 54 P.2d 906; City and County of Denver v. Sheriff, 105 Colo. 193, 96 P.2d 836. Particularly is this true in considering claims for conditional decrees. * * * While the witnesses as to Denver's future water requirements were not in agreement, there was substantial evidence to support a finding of future need for water from the Blue River within a reasonable time. This is amply confirmed by the City's rapid subsequent growth.

* * *

In each of the plats filed by Denver as its Exhibits A, B and D, it is recited that work was commenced by survey on the 21st day of March, 1914. In its statement of claim, Denver asserts the same commencement date. However, from the evidence submitted, it appears without dispute that the 1914 date was based entirely on reconnaissance surveys made in that year by the Public Utilities Commission not followed by any construction, and in its briefs Denver now abandons that date and claims right to conditional decree to the Blue River project for 1200 second feet as of July 4, 1921, and 400 cubic feet as of October 19, 1927, the former being the date when it is contended that survey was begun on a project planned to divert 1200 second feet, but some two years before filing any plat thereof, and the latter date being the date of the filing of its plat Exhibit B, showing plan to divert 1600 second feet.

There is no evidence that any work, even of survey, on the Blue River project was begun on July 4, 1921, or at any time prior to the summer of 1922. The claim for the 1921 date is based solely on the fact that survey was started on that date on Denver's Williams Fork and Fraser River projects and the contention that those two projects and the Blue River project constitute in fact a single irrigation project, and consequently that in the determination of the date when the first step was taken, and also in the determination of reasonable diligence since such date, the three projects should be considered as a single project.

In determining the date "when the first step was taken," a survey made on the Fraser River or on the Williams Fork would of itself be no evidence of intent to appropriate water from the Blue River. Certainly such a survey in a far distant basin supplying water to another stream would constitute no notice to another appropriator of such intent. The filing of a plat of method of diversion from the Fraser or Williams Fork would be no evidence of intent to appropriate water from the Blue or notice of such intent. Therefore, there is nothing to support the contention that the priority should be dated as of July 4, 1921. At most, the priority for the Blue River project could date back only to the time when the first step was taken in construction of a project on the Blue River.

In determining reasonable diligence, also, we find no ground for holding, as urged by Denver, that the Blue River project, the Williams Fork project and Fraser River project are each units of a single project so that the construction work on those projects and the expenses incurred thereon can be considered as part of the construction of the Blue River project. Denver's claim for its Blue River project was made by survey, plat and filing entirely separate from those of its Fraser and Williams Fork projects. It seeks priority to water from an entirely separate stream, not even confluent with the Fraser River or Williams Fork except to the extent that each is ultimately a tributary of the Colorado River. It seeks water to be diverted from an entirely separate drainage basin. It was surveyed and planned after those projects. It directly affects other claimants who are protestants here but not directly affected by those projects. It is to be carried through an entirely separate conduit—the Fraser River being diverted through the Moffat Tunnel and the Williams Fork through the Jones Pass Tunnel, and the Blue, as now planned, to be carried in the Montezuma tunnel to be bored through the Continental Divide many miles to the south of the others. Its water rights are here sought to be adjudicated as entirely separate from the rights of those projects. It has even less relation to the Fraser River and Williams Fork projects than to Denver's South Platte water system with which it will share the same river channel and reservoirs. In fact, the only relation between the Blue River project and these other projects is that their several waters may ultimately rest in common filtration and concentration plants, and that by means of exchange they may be used cooperatively for supplying prior rights or filling storage reservoirs such as would be probable in the case of any other independent water right. The priority of appropriation which gives the better right under our Constitution is priority on a stream rather than on a project, and any diligence in construction to permit dating back of priority on the Blue River must be diligence relating to and promoting the Blue River appropriation. No such relation here appears. Therefore, diligence in the prosecution of the Fraser and Williams Fork projects cannot be imputed to the Blue River project. However, the fact that the City of Denver was engaged in the construction of these or other enterprises may properly be considered together with all other evidence as to existing facilities and ability of the city in determination of the issue of reasonable diligence.

* * *

* * * During the entire period from 1927 to 1946, substantially all the work done and all the money spent by Denver in connection with its Blue River project was for investigation and exploratory work or work in connection with Eastern Slope reservoirs which were not dependent on any one plan for diversion or even on Blue River water. This and similar evidence before the trial court presented substantial support to the contention of protestants that Denver had no fixed and definite plan and no definite point of diversion prior to the report and recommendation of said board in 1946, and supported the decree of the trial court consistent therewith.

As to the second question, that of diligence:

In summary, the evidence showed that the Exhibit A plan of 1923 has been abandoned without any construction whatever; that following the filing of the Exhibit B plan in 1927, no evidence of actual excavation work in connection with its proposed tunnel appeared until 1942, some fifteen years later, when a cut was made and a small exploratory tunnel was driven about 400 feet at a place then intended to be the west portal to ascertain the condition of the ground. The proposed location of the portal has since been changed and a part of the excavation has caved in. No other work was performed on the ground until July 1946 when work at the east portal of the tunnel was started. Denver's Chief Engineer testified that "That was the first actual construction work." It had been driven 2850 feet out of a total distance of approximately twenty-four miles in the period from 1946 to the date of hearing. In addition to the tunnel, Denver's plan of diversion as last approved at the time of the trial included the large Dillon Reservoir on the Blue River at the intake, plat of which was filed in 1942 but no construction begun before 1946.

As satisfying the requirement of reasonable diligence, Denver showed that after the filing of the plat in 1927, the tunnel line was staked in 1931-2, and triangulation survey monuments installed for geological studies. These surveys brought about an unfavorable report on the straight tunnel as platted and a recommendation that a dog-leg tunnel be constructed by way of Montezuma. But the new line was not staked and geologized until sometime in 1943, 1944 and 1945. Over a period from 1928 to 1948, Denver's witnesses testified that survey was made and rights of way acquired for the Two Forks Reservoir, but that reservoir is to be located on the South Platte River and, as shown in the application for right of way, was planned for regulation of that river, storage of its flood waters and power development. It has no essential connection with direct use diversion from the Blue River; even its construction would not indicate any plan for Blue River diversion or give another appropriator any notice of such plan. Between 1928 and 1932 surveys were made for power lines to carry the electrical energy proposed to be generated by the project. In 1932, right of way was granted for the twenty-three mile tunnel, but for a period of ten years no step was taken toward its construction. It appears that throughout the period from 1936 to 1941 efforts were made by the City to induce the United States Bureau of Reclamation to build the project, but without success. There was no evidence of any effort by Denver to finance the project itself prior to the year 1946, but only of efforts to induce the United States to do so.

To support its contention that this work was sufficient to satisfy the requirements of reasonable diligence, Denver cites Taussig v. Moffat Tunnel Co., 106 Colo. 384, 106 P.2d 363, wherein it was held that surveys, preparation of maps, acquiring of rights of way and options and obtaining a contract for the carriage of water through the Moffat Tunnel, drilling of test holes, clearing of timber along proposed ditch lines and other similar work was sufficient to satisfy the requirement of reasonable diligence in construction of a ditch leading to the Moffat Tunnel. However, there the party seeking diversion of the water was a private company of apparently limited resources. The dating back was apparently for a period of less than five years, and the decision of this court affirmed the finding of the trial court, holding that there was due diligence; while here, we are asked to hold that such expenditures on the part of a great city, without shown limitation upon its financial capacity, spread out over a period of nearly twenty years would require us to reverse the decision of the trial court and say that such expenditures were evidence of reasonable diligence as a matter of law.

Kinney, in his great work on irrigation, says: "Probably the best definition of the word diligence was given by Lewis, C. J., in rendering the opinion in an early Nevada case, Ophir Silver Min. Co. v. Carpenter, 4 Nev. 534. It is there defined as 'the steady application to business of any kind, constant effort to accomplish any undertaking.' 'It is the doing of an act or series of acts with all possible expedition, with no delay except such as may be incident to the work itself.' " Kinney on Irrigation and Water Rights, Vol. 2, § 735.

Our statute authorizing conditional decrees requires that each claimant shall offer proof in support of his claim and "if it shall appear that any claimant * * * has prosecuted his claims of appropriation and the financing and construction of his enterprise with reasonable diligence", 35 C.S.A. c. 90, § 195, the court shall enter decree determining the priority of right.

It is undisputed that during a period of about twenty years, Denver had not even begun the actual construction of its project and had made no effort whatever as appears from the record towards financing it, but only a laudable but fruitless attempt after nine years of inaction to induce the United States Reclamation Service to finance it for the joint use of Denver and the South Platte Water Users Association. Meanwhile others have worked diligently and long to put a part of this water to actual use. The record before us does not show such conclusive evidence of "steady application" to the business of constructing the project or of such "constant effort to accomplish" it as to require us to hold that the trial court erred in refusal to date back Denver's appropriation, to the loss of such prior users. On the contrary, in order to sustain Denver's claim, we should have to establish as a law of Colorado that a great city or a great corporation, by the filing of a plat of a water diversion plan and the fitful continuance of surveys and exploratory operations, could paralyze all development in a river basin for a period of nineteen years without excavating a single shovel full of dirt in actual construction and without taking any step towards bond issue or other financing plan of its own for carrying out its purpose; that for nineteen years no farmer could build a ditch to develop his farm and no other city or industry could construct a project for use of water in that area without facing loss of their water when and if the city or corporation which filed the plat should actually construct its project. This we cannot do.

* * *

Accordingly, the decree of the trial court herein is affirmed. * * *

■ MOORE, JUSTICE (dissenting).

I agree generally with the views expressed by Mr. Chief Justice STONE in the opinion written by him, except for the disposition which he makes concerning the claim of the City and County of Denver. * * *

* * *

* * * In fact, as we pointed out in the Taussig case, a conditional decree may be necessary to furnish that "reasonable assurance" essential to financing a private project. We see no reason why public funds are not entitled to equal assurance.

The question under discussion cannot be answered in terms applicable to all controversies. The facts must govern each individual case. The basis for examining the facts, under the law of Colorado as announced by our Court over the years, may well include the following:

(a) The appropriator's acts should evidence a fixed and definite intention to take a fixed amount of water for application to a beneficial use.

(b) A change in plan, which indicates a lack of fixed purpose or which shows only a general desire without a fixed determination to fulfill the desire, would not support an appropriation.

(c) Changes undertaken with the apparent intent to improve or make more efficient or less costly the whole work to be undertaken, should be regarded as the natural diligence of a prudent man rather than the want of constancy in the prosecution of the undertaking.

Within these three pertinent principles I think it is abundantly clear that, at least from and after the 19th day of October, 1927, the City and County of Denver made no change in its plan to develop the water right claimed, which would amount to a relinquishment of the plan and purpose then fixed upon to appropriate 1600 second feet of water.

* * *

It appears * * * that the test of the extent to which work on one part of a water system may properly relate to another for the purpose of determining due diligence, is whether the parts of the work relate to a single integrated purpose intimately enough that progress on one part has a direct bearing upon another part. What we are really considering is whether or not the work done is within the limits of what is reasonably to be considered as customary to an enterprise unified under single management * * *.

* * *

* * * [T]he majority opinion brushed off most pertinent and undisputed evidence, as well as facts concerning which our Court has judicial knowledge, concerning the desperate need, in the early years of the 1930 decade, for speedy increases in the water supply of the city, and the heavy demands upon the city for completion of developments of other related works for the diversion of water from streams tributary to the Colorado river. * * * Unmentioned is the fact, which every citizen then living well knows, that in 1929 the whole nation trembled and lay prostrate in depression; that the public treasuries were empty; that for years thereafter any attempt to finance such a large undertaking upon the local level would have been sheer folly; and that the only hope for resources sufficient to warrant a start at construction was to seek the financial backing of the United States. In those years all business, both public and private, looked only to Washington for rescue from total collapse.

At about the time when another approach to the financial problem might reasonably have been expected to succeed, World War II broke out and thereafter for several years the productive energies of all the people were concentrated on the war effort. Men and materials were not to be had for any development of this kind, which could possibly wait. Just as soon as the conflict ended and war demands relaxed, construction of the tunnel began, and, despite inadequate financing and disappointments, the city has gone forward with the work. * * *

From an examination of the whole record it appears that Denver, with respect to its Blue River project has done what might reasonably have been expected of any city similarly situated.

NOTES

1. Are the policies supporting the relation back doctrine furthered by the decision in the principal case? What is the practical effect of limiting Denver's right to the tunnel's capacity? Are future water projects likely to be more or less costly? Efficient?

2. Since the principal case, the concept of due diligence in connection with conditional decrees in Colorado has undergone a substantial evolution, commensurate, at least at first, with Justice Moore's dissent. In Metropolitan Suburban Water Users Ass'n v. Colorado River Water Conservation Dist., 148 Colo. 173, 365 P.2d 273 (1961), the court treated Metro's

Homestake Project and its Eagle–Arkansas River Project as one "overall integral plan" and granted a conditional right for the whole project relating back to the date the original surveys were begun, even though the evidence indicated that not all parts of the project had been worked on with equal diligence. In Colorado River Water Conservation Dist. v. Twin Lakes Reservoir and Canal Co., 181 Colo. 53, 506 P.2d 1226 (1973), the court again held that the priority belongs to the total project (citing *Metropolitan Suburban*) and added that occasional changes that do not drastically alter or constitute abandonment of the overall plan are permissible. The same year, however, in Orchard Mesa Irrigation Dist. v. City and County of Denver, 182 Colo. 59, 511 P.2d 25 (1973), the court indicated that stricter standards might be applied in future diligence cases. In cancelling a conditional decree where no steps had been taken for fifty years to apply the decreed water to a beneficial use, the court stated that a record showing only a hope to use the water, but no concrete action to finalize the intended appropriation, was insufficient to show diligence.

Orchard Mesa was cited with approval in Colorado River Water Conservation Dist. v. City and County of Denver, 640 P.2d 1139 (Colo.1982), where conditional rights were cancelled when no on-site work or activity specifically related to individual parts of a general water development scheme were performed during the diligence period. Litigation and political activities designed to promote the overall project were held insufficient to constitute due diligence, in the absence of efforts to develop each conditionally decreed right individually.

Cancellation of conditional rights for failure to demonstrate diligence is now the exception, however. Indeed, the Colorado Supreme Court seems to have retreated from its insistence on actual, on-site work, so long as the activity pertains to a specific site. The court now stresses that it will make essentially a case-by-case examination of factors such as economic feasibility, status of permit applications, expenditures, conduct of engineering and environmental studies, design and construction of facilities, and land holdings or contracts showing demand for water that the rights will serve. This has allowed the water courts considerable discretion to rely entirely on planning, litigation, and research supported by little or no on-the-ground work whatsoever. See Municipal Subdistrict, Northern Colorado Water Conservancy District v. Chevron Shale Oil Co., 986 P.2d 918 (Colo.1999), where the court allowed $1.5 million in expenditures over six years for such activities to constitute reasonable diligence in light of the fact that the oil shale development for which the water was intended was economically infeasible when the rights were first sought 45 years before and might not be feasible for another 50–85 years. Is this the kind of economic exigency that Justice Moore thought should be considered in the principal case? Does *Chevron* indicate that the less feasible water development plans are, the more relaxed the standard of due diligence should be? What justifies a lax approach that allows the perpetuation of conditional decrees? The Colorado Supreme Court, citing *Metropolitan Suburban*, has noted that conditional decrees serve as an incentive for water development.

3. One purpose served by legislation in states that place statutory time limits on the commencement of a diversion for those who seek the benefit of the relation-back rule is to prevent speculation. In Colorado, where there is no definite time limit, some developers have sought to use conditional decrees to reserve a priority date while the would-be appropriator shops for a specific beneficial use.

In Colorado River Water Conservation Dist. v. Vidler Tunnel Water Co., 197 Colo. 413, 594 P.2d 566 (1979), the trial court had awarded Vidler a conditional storage decree for 156,238 acre-feet of water for its proposed Sheephorn Reservoir on the mainstem of the Colorado River. Vidler planned to bring water, except for a portion it intended to use on its own lands, to the Eastern Slope of the Continental Divide for sale to various municipalities. The Colorado Supreme Court disallowed the conditional decree, because Vidler had not demonstrated an intent to put the water to a beneficial use. Noting that there was "no firm contractual commitment from any municipality to use any of the water," the court added:

> While Vidler's efforts possibly went beyond mere speculation, there was no sufficient evidence that it represented anyone committed to actual beneficial use of the water not intended for use on its own land. Indeed, there is not even evidence of firm sale arrangements. In essence, water rights are sought here on the assumption that growing population will produce a general need for more water in the future. But Vidler has no contract or agency relationship justifying its claim to represent those whose future needs are asserted.

Id. at 569. The conditional decree for the small amount of water intended to be used on land owned by Vidler was approved, however. After *Vidler,* the legislature modified the judicial anti-speculation rule announced in the case to require a showing that water "can be and will be diverted" and "will be beneficially used" within a reasonable time. COLO. REV. STAT. § 37–92–305(9)(b). The statute and the courts' interpretation of it are discussed more in depth at pp. 314–315.

Vidler involved an appropriation by a private entity. As noted earlier, *supra* p. 94, cities are often given some relief from anti-speculation rules that apply to other appropriators. This is suggested by language in the principal case and in *Denver v. Sheriff, supra* p. 94. The Colorado Supreme Court has now stated explicitly that the *Vidler* anti-speculation doctrine does not apply with equal force to municipalities. *City of Thornton v. Bijou Irrigation Co.* stated that when the legislature enacted the *Vidler* rule in Colo. Rev. Stat. § 37–92–103(3)(a) (2000), it excepted government entities. The court went on to say that:

> [T]he General Assembly endorsed the *Vidler* holding with respect to private parties but also recognized the need for governmental agencies, which include municipalities and other agencies responsible for supplying water to individual users, to exercise some flexibility with respect to future water needs. This exception, however, does not completely immunize municipal applicants from speculation challenges. * * * [A] municipality may be decreed conditional water rights based solely on

its projected future needs, and without firm contractual commitments or agency relationships, but a municipality's entitlement to such a decree is subject to the water court's determination that the amount conditionally appropriated is consistent with the municipality's reasonably anticipated requirements based on substantiated projections of future growth.

926 P.2d at 38–39.

What is wrong with speculation? Professor (now Senior Judge) Stephen F. Williams has argued that by forcing water to be put to beneficial use prematurely, the prior appropriation doctrine can result in waste. *The Requirement of Beneficial Use as a Cause of Waste in Water Resource Development*, 23 Nat. Resources J. 7 (1983). He suggests instead a system of auctioning "anticipatory water rights" to be held for future uses. Is Judge Williams's proposal superior to the present system?

NOTE: WATER STORAGE RIGHTS

In the arid West, storage of water is treated as an appropriation of water from a stream. While storage alone is not a beneficial use, storage for future use in irrigation or other beneficial purposes is considered a beneficial use.

Direct flow rights attach to water that is put to immediate beneficial use, and often are expressed in terms of the rate of flow, such as cubic feet per second, though they may also be defined by maximum volume in acre-feet. Storage rights, on the other hand, apply to water that is retained for later beneficial use, and are expressed in terms of storage volume, such as acre-feet. Storage rights may also be limited by the rate of flow into a reservoir and times when water may be stored. See generally Funk, Storage 101, 9 U. Denver Water L. Rev. 519 (2006).

Storage rights attach to on-channel and off-channel facilities. On-channel storage involves retaining streamflow behind a dam in a streambed. Off-channel storage involves a diversion through a canal or pipeline to a storage facility away from the stream. An offstream reservoir by definition involves diverting water from the stream. Utilizing structures to store water in onstream reservoirs is also considered a diversion, even though the water is merely detained, rather than actually diverted. Pagosa Area Water and Sanitation Dist. v. Trout Unlimited, 170 P.3d 307 (Colo. 2007) held that an appropriation for the storage of water for recreation, wildlife and aesthetic purposes showed requisite intent to appropriate and that the actual application to beneficial use could and would be evaluated in subsequent due diligence proceedings.

Under the one-fill rule, a reservoir may only be filled once a year. In other words, the reservoir appropriation to impound water is limited to the capacity of the reservoir, though the reservoir may be alternately filling and draining down throughout the year. The sum of all additions to the reservoir count against the single filling allowed under the rule.

Where the rule is applied strictly, as in Colorado, inefficiency may result. Larger reservoirs may be built because reservoirs may not be successively refilled during the year. Further, the one-filling restriction may limit creative means of obtaining water. For example, in Orchard City Irrigation Dist. v. Whitten, 146 Colo. 127, 361 P.2d 130 (1961), a reservoir owner had decrees on two streams in the watershed, so that water from the second stream could make up for deficiencies in the first stream during dry years. The state engineer had approved rights equal to twice the storage capacity of the reservoir. This was disallowed by the court, however, as a "double filling." The court summarized Colorado precedent: "a reservoir is limited to one annual filling from whatever source the water may be derived * * *." Id.

The inefficiency of the one-fill rule is compounded if carryover storage (water remaining in the reservoir from one year to another) is debited against the single filling. If it is not so debited, a reservoir can have a long term storage pool to protect against drought and an "active pool" that will be allowed to be filled and drawn down several times, with fillings cumulatively not to exceed the capacity of the reservoir.

Should the same rules apply to storage for hydroelectric power as for irrigation? A is a hydroelectric power generator located low on a stream and holding storage rights. For most of the year, A does not retain water in the reservoir for more than a few days, allowing it to flow through the turbines as necessary to generate power. Is A nevertheless considered to have "stored" the cumulative total of any waters held behind the dam in excess of natural flow, no matter how briefly, for purposes of the one-fill rule? There is surprisingly little law on this subject, probably because the operations of hydroelectric facilities are heavily regulated. See *infra* p. 714; *e.g.*, Idaho Power Co. v. State, Dept. of Water Resources, 104 Idaho 575, 661 P.2d 741 (1983).

The prior appropriation doctrine has long been back-stopped by carryover storage. Are there any limits on the appropriator's ability to retain stored water until the really big drought? In upholding Idaho's conjunctive surface and groundwater use rules [discussed *infra* at pages 587–595], which give the Director of the Department of Water Resources the discretion to require a surface right holder to draw on storage rights, the Idaho Supreme Court observed that "[t]o permit excessive carry-over of stored water without the need for it would be in itself unconstitutional." American Falls Reservoir Dist. v. Idaho Dept. of Water Resources, 143 Idaho 862, 154 P.3d 433, 449–451 (2007). The rules, however, do guarantee storage right holders a reasonable amount of carry-over storage.

Almost all the large reservoirs throughout the country are operated by either the Bureau of Reclamation or the US Army Corps of Engineers. The law controlling the operation of these reservoirs is a mix of federal Reclamation law, Congressional authorizing legislation, state water law, interstate compacts and, more recently, federal environmental law. See Chapters 7 and 10. Symposium on New Mexico's Rio Grande Reservoirs, 43

Nat. Res. J. No. 3 (2007) is a good case study how all these laws impact the use of water on this interstate and international river.

2.   ENJOYMENT

"Beneficial use" is said to be the basis, measure, and limit of an appropriative right. State constitutions, statutes, and judicial decisions throughout the western states recognize the concept. Is beneficial use the same as the reasonable use requirement applied in riparian states?

In the settlement of the West, the concept of beneficial use had both an allocative and a distributive function. The initially important societal uses that led to the doctrine were mining and agriculture. Of course, domestic uses have always been the most important to society but because they demanded so little water no legal doctrines were needed to protect them. State constitutions and statutes enshrined a utilitarian list of beneficial uses, indicating purposes to which water rights were properly allocated. But because the list was not complete or detailed, new and nontraditional uses of water sometimes required a legislative or judicial determination of whether they were "beneficial." In the mid-twentieth century, for example, recreation was added to the list (usually by statute), and this ultimately led to efforts by the western states to protect instream flows, a concept that challenged basic aspects of traditional appropriation doctrine. To the nine-teenth century mind that created the doctrine, leaving water in place was simply not a use. Societal values changed, however, and with them changed the interpretation of "beneficial use."

The distributive function of the beneficial use requirement was to promote widespread access to scarce supplies. Under the pure appropriation system as it was originally applied, the beneficial nature of a use was not dependent on the amount of water in the stream, nor were comparisons made with the uses of other appropriators. But a common theme running through the cases is that wasteful uses were not beneficial. This judgment can only be made in the context of surrounding use patterns. Theoretically, every water user operates under a threat that a water use can be chal-lenged as wasteful and thereby held to be in excess of a decreed appropria-tive right. A successful challenge would result in more water being left in the stream for the benefit of junior appropriators. Such challenges have been rare, and successes even rarer. A more seriously perceived threat is from non-use. Appropriators have operated under the specter of "use it or lose it," not "use it efficiently or lose it." Thus, far greater quantities of water than are needed to fulfill particular purposes have been diverted in the false hope of protecting rights to use quantities of water awarded in permits or decrees. In fact, however, recent cases indicate that water rights are not "protected" by wasteful overapplication.

Beneficial Use and Efficiency

Critics of the beneficial use doctrine have long observed that it does not effectively force users to adopt conservation practices. *E.g.*, Janet C. Neuman, *Beneficial Use, Waste, and Forfeiture: The Inefficient Search for*

Efficiency in Western Water Use, 28 Envtl. L. 919 (1998). Extensive techniques for using water efficiently are available, such as drip irrigation to replace flood irrigation in agriculture and low flush toilets to reduce municipal use. A major premise of modern environmental law is that polluters should be forced to adopt control technologies. An issue in beneficial use today is whether the concept can serve an analogous technology-forcing function.

There is an increasing tendency of courts and administrative agencies to insist that water be used in a manner that is "reasonable" or "efficient" relative to other uses. The right to use water simply does not extend to wasteful uses. Yet, historically courts have rarely restricted a nominally beneficial use—agriculture, mining, domestic—for the sake of another use that was more efficient or productive.

Recall that California's "solution" to the wastefulness built into the natural flow doctrine of riparianism was a constitutional amendment requiring that all uses of water be "reasonable." See *supra* p. 93. Other states embraced reasonable use as a matter of common law. See *supra* p. 118. Is beneficial use the same as the reasonable use requirement applied in riparian states? See City of Barstow v. Mojave Water Agency, 23 Cal.4th 1224, 99 Cal.Rptr.2d 294, 5 P.3d 853, 863 (2000) (discussing California's principle of reasonable beneficial use and citing casebook).

The opinion in *Empire Water & Power Co.*, *supra* p. 97, observed that the trial court "made no inquiry into the effectiveness of the use of the water in the way adopted as compared with the customary methods of irrigation." The law of prior appropriation has consistently required diverters to make reasonably efficient diversions. The standard of reasonableness has changed over the years, but generally requires a method of diversion consistent with prevailing community practices. For example, overflow or natural flood irrigation has been held inefficient, inasmuch as it ties up the whole stream, to supply an appropriator's right to a lesser amount of water. Warner Valley Stock Co. v. Lynch, 215 Or. 523, 336 P.2d 884 (1959). Other extreme agricultural practices have been curtailed in the name of beneficial use. In People *ex rel.* State Water Resources Control Bd. v. Forni, 54 Cal.App.3d 743, 126 Cal.Rptr. 851 (1976), the court found that pumping water directly from a river for frost protection of vineyards might not be a reasonable and beneficial use of water as required by the California Constitution. See also Fairfield Irrigation Co. v. White, 18 Utah 2d 93, 416 P.2d 641 (1966) (irrigation of fields during non-growing season); Tulare Irrigation Dist. v. Lindsay–Strathmore Irrigation Dist., 3 Cal.2d 489, 45 P.2d 972 (1935) (winter flooding of fields to control gophers).

Efficiency has an economic as well as a technical meaning. Economic efficiency was also potentially implicated in *Empire Water & Power Co.* Should the court have been concerned if the profits to Cascade from tourism attributable to the falls exceeded Empire's profits from power generation. Indeed, would not use of the water for power generation at the expense of the resort be economically wasteful under such circumstances? Suppose a court finds Cascade's use the more profitable use and therefore "beneficial." Can Cascade and Empire nevertheless allocate the water among themselves?

Can yesterday's beneficial use be deemed wasteful tomorrow? A California court applying that state's constitutional prohibition of waste said that reasonableness depends on conditions at any given time:

> What is a beneficial use, of course, depends upon the facts and circumstances of each case. What may be a reasonable beneficial use, where water is present in excess of all needs, would not be a reasonable beneficial use in an area of great scarcity and great need. What is a beneficial use at one time may, because of changed conditions, become a waste of water at a later time.

Tulare Irrigation Dist. v. Lindsay–Strathmore Irrigation Dist., 3 Cal.2d 489, 45 P.2d 972, 1007 (1935). As streams become more fully appropriated and new, economically productive uses come into conflict with established uses that may be wasteful, junior users and states (confronted with demands that may force them to develop expensive new sources) are beginning to challenge whether particular uses or manners of using water are truly "beneficial." One of the most lively issues in contemporary water law is whether courts, administrative agencies, and legislatures should impose stringent conservation duties on historic use patterns in order to make water available for new uses or for wider distribution among similarly situated users. Should the resolution of such a conflict depend on today's standards of efficiency or those that prevailed at the time the challenged appropriation was initiated?

State *ex rel.* Cary v. Cochran

Supreme Court of Nebraska, 1940.
138 Neb. 163, 292 N.W. 239.

■ CARTER, JUSTICE.

* * *

The North Platte river is a nonnavigable stream which has its source in the mountains of Colorado and flows across a part of Wyoming and Nebraska to a point approximately 200 miles from the Wyoming–Nebraska line, where it joins the South Platte river to form the Platte river. The present case involves the administration of irrigation and power rights on the North Platte and Platte rivers from the Wyoming–Nebraska line to the headgate of the Kearney canal located 13 miles west of Kearney, Nebraska.
* * *

The flow of the river even in the summer months is affected by the amount of snow falling in the mountains of Colorado within its drainage basin. The river passes through parts of Colorado and Wyoming, both of which states require irrigation water in excess of the available supply. Storage and control dams under the control of the federal government also exist along the river west of the point where the river enters Nebraska.

Water rights, both senior and junior to existing rights and priorities in Nebraska, coupled with the uncertainty of their accurate administration, add to the indefiniteness of the amount of water that passes at any given time across the state line and under the control of the administrative officers of this state.

Losses from evaporation and transpiration are heavy, due to the wide and shallow character of the river. Changes of temperature and varying types of wind add to the uncertainty of the losses resulting from these changing conditions. Losses from percolation vary along the various sectors of the river. The evidence shows that the river valley from the Wyoming–Nebraska line to North Platte or thereabouts is underlaid with impervious formations which do not permit losses of subterranean waters into other watersheds. At some unknown point between North Platte and Gothenburg, the river cuts through the impervious formations and runs into the sheets of sand and gravel with which the territory is underlaid. Losses begin to occur at this point due to the percolation of river water through this sand and gravel formation, in a southeasterly direction into the basin of the Republican river. * * * Experts with experience on the river estimate that the loss in delivering water from North Platte to the headgate of the Kearney canal with a wet river bed amounts to three times the amount of delivery, and with a dry river bed that it is almost impossible to get water through without a flood or a large sustained flow. In other words, it requires approximately 700 second-feet of water at North Platte to deliver 162 second-feet at the headgate of the Kearney canal when the river bed is wet. The underlying sand and gravel beds thicken as the river moves east. With the bed of the river on the surface of these sand and gravel deposits, it requires a huge amount of water to recharge the river channel and surrounding water table after the river bed once becomes dry. Until the water table is built up to the surface of the river bed, the river channel will not support a continuous flow. It is also shown that the water table has been affected materially by pump irrigation. It was estimated that there are 500 irrigation pumps in Dawson county alone, which pump as much as 40,000 acre-feet of water in a single season. The evidence bears out the statement that the Platte river east of Gothenburg is a very inefficient carrier of water. In addition to the subterranean losses noted, the river spreads out, causing a broad surface of water and channel bed to be subjected to large evaporation losses. It is further established by early settlers along the river that it was not unusual for the river to go dry in July and August before irrigation was generally practiced along the river. That the river is generally considered a gaining stream, and can be so established by an examination of the statistical records of the mean flow for the calendar year, is borne out by the record. But it is just as clearly shown that the river is ordinarily a losing stream during the months of July and August, when the mean flow for that period is considered. These conditions and activities establish the cause of the huge losses of water between Gothenburg and the Kearney canal. They are important only as factors that must be considered by the officers of the state in distributing an insufficient supply of water to appropriators in the proper order of priority.

Appropriations of water are made throughout the length of the river. The priority dates of these appropriations have no relation whatever to their location on the stream. Hence, very early appropriations may be found at the upper and lower ends of the stream, while very late appropriations are likewise found at both ends. In times of water shortage, the later appropriators are the first to be deprived of water. The closing of canals in accordance with the inverse order of their priority dates necessarily requires certain canals to close their headgates all along the stream at the same time. Water moves down the stream at approximately 25 miles per day with the result that it requires approximately ten days to deliver water from the state line to the Kearney headgate under normal conditions. The resulting lag therefore becomes an important factor to be considered. During the lag period, conditions over which the administrator of the river has no control may change or disrupt all calculations. Excessive heat, continued drought, and unusual winds may greatly reduce estimated quantities of river-flow, or, on the other hand, low temperatures, rains and floods in the lower river basin may relieve immediate demands. These elements of uncertainty must be considered in protecting the rights of all on the stream. The position of relators at the lower end of the stream is in itself a recognized condition, and while they have the second oldest priority on the river, it is inescapable that their location subjects them to unfavorable conditions which are practically impossible to eliminate.

* * *

The use of water for irrigation in this state is a natural want. The inadequacy of supply to meet the demands of the public requires strict administration to prevent waste. It is therefore the policy of the law that junior appropriators may use available water within the limits of their own appropriations so long as the rights of senior appropriators are not injured or damaged. And so, in the instant case, junior appropriators may lawfully apply water to their lands within the limits of their adjudicated appropriations until the Kearney canal fails to receive its full appropriation of 162 second-feet. Until the senior appropriator is injured, there is the ever-present possibility of changed weather conditions, precipitation, or other sources of water supply which might alleviate the situation and supply the needs of the Kearney canal. To pursue any other rule would greatly add to the loss by waste of the public waters of this state. We conclude therefore that the use of water by a junior appropriator does not become adverse to or injure a senior appropriator until it results in a deprivation of his allotted amount, or some part thereof. This rule is supported, we think, by our decisions as well as the decisions of other states.

The real question to be decided, however, is the determination of the duty imposed upon the officers of the state in administering the waters of the stream when the available supply of water at the headgate of the Kearney canal is reduced to an amount less than the 162 second-feet to which the relators are entitled. The rights of relators to the use of this water as against all appropriators subsequent to September 10, 1882, cannot be questioned. It is the duty of the administrative officers of the state to recognize this right and to give force to relators' priority. This requires that junior appropriators be restrained from taking water from the stream so long as such water can be delivered in usable quantities at the headgate of the Kearney canal. If it appear that all the available water in the stream would be lost before its arrival at the headgate of the Kearney canal, it would, of course, be an unjustified waste of water to attempt delivery. Whether a definite quantity of water passing a given point on the stream would, if not diverted or interrupted in its course, reach the headgate of the Kearney canal in a usable quantity creates a very complicated question of fact. It therefore is the duty of the administrative officers of the state to determine from all available means, including the factors hereinbefore discussed, whether or not a usable quantity of water can be delivered at the headgate of the Kearney canal. * * *

After determination that a given quantity of water passing a certain point on the river would not, even if uninterrupted, reach the headgate of the Kearney canal in usable quantities, the administrative officers of the state may lawfully permit junior appropriators to divert it for irrigation purposes. This results ofttimes in having junior appropriators receiving a head of water at a time when an appropriator farther downstream is getting none, though he is prior in time. Such situations are not therefore conclusive evidence of unlawful diversions.

Amici curiae urge that the doctrine of reasonable use is in force in this state and that it should be applied to the case at bar. We recognize the principle that the public has an interest in the public waters of the state and it is the use thereof only that may be appropriated. Even though an adjudicated appropriation may be vested, it may be subjected to regulation and control by the state by virtue of its police power. It may likewise be circumscribed to the extent that a limited diversion for a specified purpose will not permit of an undue interference with the rights of other appropriators on the stream. But we cannot agree that the doctrine of reasonable use can be applied in a case where delivery of a usable quantity of water can be made, although the losses suffered in so doing are great. To permit the officers of the state the right to say whether prospective losses would or would not justify the delivery of usable quantities of water would clothe such officers with a discretion incompatible with the vested interests of the relators, and destroy the very purpose of the doctrine of appropriation existent in this state. When upstream appropriators applied for and received adjudicated priorities, they did so with the knowledge that there was an earlier appropriator at the lower end of the stream whose rights had to be recognized. When the relators applied for and received their adjudications, they are likewise presumed to have known that other appropriators would obtain inferior rights above them that would have to be recognized. Each is required to respect the vested rights of the others, even though some hardships may be thereby imposed. We therefore hold that the doctrine of reasonable use does not extend so far as to authorize the administrator of the waters of the stream to refrain from delivering a usable quantity of water to a senior appropriator because it might appear to him that excessive losses would result. The duty of the administrator, in administering the waters of the stream by virtue of the police power of the state, is to enforce existing priorities, not to determine, change or amend them. But in regulating the distribution of water it may become incidentally necessary for him to ascertain for that purpose only whether a prior appropriator is injured by a diversion above him. This finding of fact must be made, not to change existing priorities, but in order to determine whether or not a distribution of water may be made to a junior appropriator in accordance with existing priorities.

NOTES

1. The prohibition against the waste of water and the limitation of reasonable use on the exercise of an appropriative right would seem to be correlative doctrines; that is, water cannot be wasted because there is no right to use water in a non-beneficial manner. Observe, however, that the loss between a flow of 700 cfs (second-feet) at North Platte and a flow of 162 cfs at the Kearney Canal is nearly 77%. Even if the senior appropriators on the Kearney Canal make an efficient application of their 162 cfs of water after it is received, can it be said that they have made a beneficial use of the 538 cfs lost in transit? If the cost of building a pipeline from North Platte to the Kearney Canal is less than the value of 538 cfs of water saved, can it be said that the 538 cfs are being wasted? If the upstream junior appropriators installed a pipeline that would deliver 162 cfs at Kearney, could they use the remaining 538 cfs themselves to fulfill their water rights? Assuming the answer is "yes," why did they not adopt such a scheme? Would it not have been economically feasible? Assuming the value of 700 cfs of water at and around North Platte is greater than 162 cfs at the Kearney Canal, has the 538 cfs been wasted? What happened to the "lost" water? Might the answer to this question mitigate criticism of the decision?

A careful analysis of the *Cary* case was made by a lawyer-economist (who was U.S. Secretary of Agriculture from 1989–92), Clayton K. Yeutter, *A Legal–Economic Critique of Nebraska Watercourse Law*, 44 Neb. L. Rev. 11, 39–43 (1965).

2. Seniors faced with a shortage of water needed to satisfy their full water rights generally may "call" upstream juniors, requiring them to forgo diverting water until the seniors are fully satisfied. But if, as in *Cary*, there are conditions that will prevent water from reaching the seniors in a manner or at times that will enable it to be put to use, the juniors may continue to divert out of priority. In Colorado, this is known as the "futile call doctrine." COLO. REV. STAT. § 37–92–502(2)(a) (2006) states:

> Each division engineer shall order the total or partial discontinuance of any diversion in his division to the extent the water being diverted is required by persons entitled to use water under water rights having senior priorities, but no such discontinuance shall be ordered unless the diversion is causing or will cause material injury to such water rights having senior priorities * * *. * * * In the event a

discontinuance has been ordered pursuant to the provisions of this paragraph (a), and nevertheless such discontinuance does not cause water to become available to such senior priorities at the time and place of their need, then such discontinuance order shall be rescinded.

3. *Cary* is one of the most famous priority enforcement cases in western water law. However, strict priority enforcement is often—but not always—avoided for equity or efficiency reasons. See A. Dan Tarlock, *Prior Appropriation: Rule, Principle, or Rhetoric?*, 76 N.D. L. Rev. 881 (2000). *Cary* and the futile call doctrine relate to natural conditions causing carriage losses. Should the analysis be different when losses occur in conveyances or systems that are constructed or controlled by appropriators?

4. Beneficial use, priority and the futile call doctrine came together in the coordination of older surface appropriations with newer groundwater rights in Idaho's Snake River Plain. Starting in 1993, senior appropriators have made calls on junior pumpers. The initial calls have been averted but the possibility of future calls is real. For example, in2005 two trout farms in south-central Idaho's Magic Valley made a call and rejected an initial offer of 45,000 acre feet of replacement water. The Department of Water Resources eventually threatened to shut down pumps for 33,000 acres and several towns and industries in the Valley. To try and avoid this drastic remedy, the state adopted Rules for the Conjunctive Management of Surface and Ground Water Resources. IDAPA 37.03.22.002. In brief, the rules allow the Director of the Idaho Department of Water Resources to apply a combination of the traditional futile call doctrine and the doctrine, developed in the Snake River Plain, that a senior's use must be reasonable before a call will be honored. See Schodde v. Twin Falls Land & Water Co., 224 U.S. 107, 32 S.Ct. 470, 56 L.Ed. 686 (1912), *infra*, p. 193. A district court held that the Rules violated the constitutional right to divert because they do not permit the timely administration of water rights and failed to include a presumption that any junior withdrawal in times of shortage is a per se interference with senior surface rights. The Idaho Supreme Court reversed. American Falls Reservoir Dist. v. Idaho Dept. of Water Resources, 143 Idaho 862, 154 P.3d 433 (2007). The court first observed that "[w]hile the Constitution, statutes and case law in Idaho set forth principles of the prior appropriation doctrine, these principles are more easily stated than applied. These principles become especially more difficult, and harsh, in their application in times of drought." The need for a presumption of interference was rejected because the Director of the Department of Natural Resources, the state engineer of old, needed the discretion to decide when to honor a call and thus the Rules contained sufficient standards and did not constitute a readjudication of decreed water rights. It also held that a contrary ruling would ignore "the constitutional requirement that priority over water be extended only to those using water." 154 P.3d at 437.

Is it more important to have an administrative agency charged with allocating this public resource make a scientifically-informed decision about the extent of injury to a senior, rather than make a speedy delivery of water based on a reflexive enforcement of priorities?

State *ex rel.* Crowley v. District Court

Supreme Court of Montana, 1939.
108 Mont. 89, 88 P.2d 23.

■ JOHNSON, CHIEF JUSTICE.

* * *

* * * The suit in question is for damages for alleged interference with plaintiff's use of irrigation water from the Madison River in 1935, 1936 and 1937.

* * *

* * * [The plaintiff alleges] that the defendants impounded by their dams the entire natural flow of the river so that the water level at plaintiff's point of diversion was so low that he could not divert water into his ditches by his diversion dam, although the latter was suitable and efficient for the purpose and was a reasonably adequate means of diversion, and reasonably constructed and maintained to divert water from the river to plaintiff's land in spite of the fluctuations in flow incidental to the reasonable and lawful use of water by all persons lawfully entitled to use the same.

* * *

* * * Defendants' contentions are that plaintiff has no cause of action merely because their acts so reduced the flow that he could not divert his appropriated water by his reasonably efficient diversion system; that he should have alleged that not enough was left to permit his diversion without leaving any water in the stream. In other words, they contend that plaintiff has no cause of action if there are 200 inches of water at his point of diversion, even though he cannot get the water into his ditches without a pump; that an appropriator's vested interest is only in the use of the quantum of water appropriated by him without reference to his means or manner of diversion, however reasonably efficient; that not reasonable efficiency but absolute efficiency is required. To this theory we cannot assent without doing violence to the entire principle of water rights by appropriation. If it is to be followed, there are few, if any, irrigation water rights in the state of Montana, however long established, which could not in effect be destroyed entirely by subsequent appropriations. One hundred per cent efficiency can be furnished by no system of diversion, and certainly by none financially available to the average water user. The law does not defeat its own end by requiring the impossible. The marginal character of many farming enterprises, and especially of the smaller ones, is well known, and if defendants' argument is followed, vested interests will be seriously affected and rights limited by the necessity of installing diversion systems by which the last drop may be taken from the stream.

There is no question that waste of our water resources must be minimized in the general interest, but it is equally manifest that there is a vanishing point at which the possible waste of water would be more than

overcome by the waste incidental to the abandonment of reasonably efficient diversion systems and the establishment of diversion systems whose
expense is neither warranted nor permitted by the benefit to be derived
from the water.

It is well established that subsequent appropriators take with notice of
the conditions existing at the time of their appropriations. In making their
appropriation of storage or other water and their expenditures in connection therewith, defendants and their predecessors were chargeable with
knowledge of the existing conditions, with reference not only to the amount
of prior appropriations, but also to the existing diversion systems of prior
appropriators. They cannot now argue that they are limited by the amount
but not the means of prior appropriations, however reasonably efficient
under the circumstances, or that so long as they leave the exact amount of
plaintiff's appropriation in the river at his point of diversion, they have no
further duty and that it is his worry and not theirs how or whether he can
divert it upon his land. His right is to divert and use the water, not merely
to have it left in the streambed; that is the essential difference between
riparian and appropriation rights.

In Salt Lake City v. Gardner, 39 Utah 30, 114 P. 147, 152, appellants
had appropriated water from Utah Lake by means of natural gravity flow,
aided by a storage dam and pumping plant. The question was whether the
respondents should be allowed to appropriate and divert water by means of
a pumping plant, thus reducing or stopping the gravity flow and placing
upon appellants an additional burden for installation and operation of
pumps. The court said: "Counsel for respondents, however, insist that the
prior appropriator acquires no right in his means of diversion, but obtains a
prior right only to use the quantity of water appropriated and applied to a
beneficial use by him. We cannot yield assent to this view. We think the
original taker or appropriator from a stream or body of water also acquires
the right to continue to use his method or means of diverting which he has
installed. If this be not so, then prior appropriators, who have appropriated
only in small quantities, and whose means of diversion from the stream are
simple but sufficient for their purpose, could have their means made
entirely ineffective by a subsequent appropriator of a large volume of water
the diverting of which would so lower the stream that the water would no
longer reach the point of diversion of the small appropriator. In this way it
may well be that the cost to the small appropriator to make the water
appropriated by him available for his purpose might under changed conditions be prohibitive if not ruinous. Upon the other hand, the cost of making
the change might not be so great as to prevent the larger appropriator from
supplying and paying for some means whereby the prior rights to the use of
the water appropriated by the small user might be preserved, and the
wants of the large appropriator could nevertheless be met and supplied. In
this way, perhaps, very large quantities of water theretofore wasted, or
used only to aid the original appropriator to obtain his meager supply,
would be put to a useful and beneficial purpose without destroying the
rights of any one. If it be held, therefore, that a subsequent appropriator of
water need have no regard for the diverting means or methods of the prior

appropriator, but may in fact or effect make prior appropriations of water unavailable with impunity, then there is in fact no such a right as a prior right, but all rights may, at any time, be invaded or destroyed by a subsequent appropriator by simply making the diverting means used by the prior appropriator useless. To permit such an invasion of a prior right would, in effect, amount to an indirect taking of a prior appropriator's water. This neither the legislative nor the judicial power can allow without permitting confiscation of property rights. * * * If all rights can be protected and preserved, a mere change in prior established means or methods of diversion, if possible, ought not to prevent the use of water which could otherwise not be beneficially applied. But, in our judgment, the risk of interfering with prior rights and the cost of any change in the prior appropriator's means or methods of diversion should be assumed and borne by the subsequent appropriator, and a court should in no case permit a subsequent appropriation unless all prior rights can by some feasible means be protected and maintained."

Defendants contend that the case of Schodde v. Twin Falls Land & Water Co., 224 U.S. 107 sustains their contention that a prior appropriator has no vested interest in his means of diversion. It cannot be so construed. * * * Obviously, of course, under the circumstances of that case, it was unreasonable to prevent the irrigation of 300,000 acres by an unusual and inefficient method of diverting water for 429 acres. The complaint there was not that the defendant had taken water out of the stream so as to interfere with the waterwheels; as a matter of fact, the defendant had confined more water there. What it had deprived plaintiff of was not the water, but the force of the water, which was no part of his appropriation. This can be made clear by an analogy. If, instead of building water wheels to utilize the force of the stream, he had constructed windmills to employ the force of the wind, it would have been entirely clear that his complaint was not of water right interference, but of something entirely different. If the conditions were such that he could have recovered for an obstruction to the flow of the wind to his windmills, it would still have been something entirely apart from and not appurtenant to his water right.

* * *

The rule in this connection is well stated as follows in Long on Irrigation, 2nd ed., 202, 203, sec. 116: "The irrigator may employ any means best suited to the existing physical conditions, and all the circumstances of the case, though undoubtedly he will be required to employ reasonably economical means, so as to prevent unnecessary waste. * * * As already stated, the means of diversion employed must not be unnecessarily wasteful, but when ditches and flumes are the usual and ordinary means of diverting water, parties who have made their appropriations by such means cannot be compelled to substitute iron pipes, though they will be required to prevent unnecessary waste by keeping their ditches and flumes in good repair."

* * *

Plaintiff alleges that he has diverted the water by means of a wing dam of brush, rocks and dirt, and proceeds to allege that the means of diversion was at the time in question "suitable and efficient for the diversion of water," and "a reasonably adequate means of diversion and reasonably constructed and maintained" for the purpose, notwithstanding the fluctuations incidental to the reasonable and lawful use of water by all those entitled, including defendants. * * * It follows that the demurrers should have been overruled.

NOTES

1. The court discusses the United States Supreme Court's decision in Schodde v. Twin Falls Land & Water Co., 224 U.S. 107, 32 S.Ct. 470, 56 L.Ed. 686 (1912). The following excerpt from *Schodde* presents the factual setting and the essence of the decision:

"Plaintiff is the owner of three tracts of land on the banks of Snake river, containing in the aggregate 429.96 acres. Two of these tracts, containing 263.96 acres, are on the south bank, and one tract of 160 acres is on the north bank. One of the tracts on the south bank is agricultural land, and the other is partly agricultural land and partly mining ground. The tract of land on the north bank is agricultural. In the year 1889 plaintiff's predecessors in interest, and in 1895 the plaintiff himself, appropriated certain quantities of water of the flow of Snake river for use on said lands. * * * The aggregate of water appropriated as alleged in the three counts is referred to in the briefs as 1,250 miner's inches. Soon after this water was appropriated the parties in interest erected water wheels in the river to lift the water to a sufficient height for distribution over the land. Nine of these wheels were erected opposite or near the tracts on the south side of the river, and two near the tract on the north side of the river. These wheels vary in height from 24 to 34 feet. The parties also constructed wing dams in the river adjoining or in front of the lands owned by them, for the purpose of confining the flow of the water of the river and raising it at such points above the natural flow of the river, so that the current would drive the water wheels and cause them to revolve and carry the water in buckets attached to the wheels to a height where it would be emptied into flumes and distributed over the lands by ditches and used thereon to irrigate and cultivate the agricultural land and work the mining ground. * * * In the year 1903, while plaintiff was using the appropriated water of the river upon the described premises, the defendant commenced the construction of a dam across Snake river at a point about nine miles westerly from and below the lands of the plaintiff. The work was prosecuted on said dam until its completion in March, 1905. This dam is so constructed as to impound all the water of Snake river flowing at said point, and to raise the water about forty feet in height. * * * It is alleged that by reason of this dam the waters of Snake river have been backed up from said dam and to and beyond plaintiff's premises and have destroyed the current in the river by means of which plaintiff's water wheels were driven and made to revolve and raise the water to the elevation required for distribution over plaintiff's lands. * * * ''

* * *

'' * * * It is unquestioned that what he has actually diverted and used upon his land, he has appropriated, but can it be said that all the water he uses or needs to operate his wheels is an appropriation? As before suggested, there is neither statutory nor judicial authority that such a use is an appropriation. Such use also lacks one of the essential attributes of an appropriation; it is not reasonable.''

* * *

''The only way in which his wheels can be used for the purpose he intended them, is to preserve the river in the condition it was when he erected them. And with what result, it may be asked. * * * ''

''Suppose from a stream of 1000 inches a party diverts and uses 100, and in some way uses the other 900 to divert his 100, could it be said that he had made such a reasonable use of the 900 as to constitute an appropriation of it? Or, suppose that when the entire 1000 inches are running, they so fill the channel that by a ditch he can draw off to his land his 100 inches, can he then object to those above him appropriating and using the other 900 inches, because it will so lower the stream that his ditch becomes useless? This would be such an unreasonable use of the 900 inches as will not be tolerated under the law of appropriation. In effect this is substantially the principle that plaintiff is asking to have established.''

224 U.S. at 114–119 (quoting Schodde v. Twin Falls Land & Water Co., 161 F. 43 (9th Cir.1908)).

Did the court in *Crowley* satisfactorily distinguish *Schodde*?

2. What practical difference would it make in *Crowley* if the ''reasonable efficiency'' of an appropriator's means of diversion were determined based on present conditions instead of conditions at the time the diversion was made? Unlined ditches were found to be ''reasonably efficient'' because they were found to be ''the usual and ordinary means of diverting water.'' United States v. Gila Valley Irrigation Dist., 31 F.3d 1428, 1434 (9th Cir.1994).

3. Particularly egregious transportation losses through unlined, leaky ditches, have been categorized as inefficient means of diversion. Examples are Big Cottonwood Tanner Ditch Co. v. Shurtliff, 56 Utah 196, 189 P. 587 (1919) (diversion of 323,000 gallons of water per day through an open ditch 807 feet long over porous and gravelly soil to supply a continuous flow of 20,000 gallons per day of pure and potable water for domestic and culinary purposes for a small family and a few head of stock); and Doherty v. Pratt, 34 Nev. 343, 124 P. 574 (1912) (loss of 2/3 of water conveyed by 3–mile open ditch through 300–acre swamp). But see Erickson v. Queen Valley Ranch Co., 22 Cal.App.3d 578, 99 Cal.Rptr. 446 (1971) (loss of 5/6ths due to evapotranspiration and seepage in 2½–mile open ditch); City of Corpus Christi v. City of Pleasanton, 154 Tex. 289, 276 S.W.2d 798 (1955) (63–74% loss through evaporation, transpiration and seepage of water flowing from artesian wells down a natural streambed and through lakes for a distance of 118 miles), where the courts held the losses did not result in waste. The Idaho Supreme Court has said in dictum that an appropriator is not entitled to divert approximately double the amount needed to irrigate his crops in order to compensate for carriage losses which occur as the water is conducted from the stream or canal to the place of use. Reviewing a long line of previous cases the court stated, " * * * the public policy against wasting water prohibits additional diversion to compensate for unreasonable loss. * * * Accordingly, waters appropriated will be measured for their sufficiency from the point of diversion, not at the place of use." Glenn Dale Ranches, Inc. v. Shaub, 94 Idaho 585, 494 P.2d 1029, 1032 (1972).

State Department of Ecology v. Grimes

Supreme Court of Washington, 1993.
121 Wash.2d 459, 852 P.2d 1044.

■ SMITH, JUSTICE.

* * *

In September 1981, the Department of Ecology filed a petition in the Pend Oreille County Superior Court for clarification of existing rights to divert, withdraw, or otherwise make beneficial use of the surface and ground waters of the Marshall Lake and Marshall Creek drainage basin (Marshall Lake basin). Ecology investigated the Marshall Lake basin and the locality served by it and found that the interests of the public and users of the surface and ground waters would be served by an adjudication and determination of the relative rights of all claimants to the use of these waters.

* * *

The Grimeses submitted five claims for water rights, only the first of which is at issue in this appeal. This claim was for the use of waters for domestic supply, irrigation and recreational purposes. The Grimeses requested an instantaneous flow rate of 3 cubic feet per second (c.f.s.) for irrigation purposes, and a storage right of 1,520 acre feet of water in the Marshall Lake reservoir. The referee recommended that this claim be confirmed, but limited it to an instantaneous flow of 1.5 c.f.s. during irrigation season, and a storage right of 183 acre feet plus 737 acre feet for evaporative loss, for a total storage right of 920 acre feet.

* * *

On January 5, 1990, after hearing testimony on the Grimeses' exceptions, the Superior Court entered its "Decree Adjudicating Water Rights Pursuant to RCW 90.03.200." The decree approved the "Report of Referee", as amended by the "Report of Referee Pursuant to Order on Exceptions of May 19, 1988." * * *

* * * The surface water rights of the Grimeses in this case are pre–1917 rights, established 11 years before adoption of the Water Code of 1917 and 65 years before adoption of the Water Resources Act of 1971. Subsequent amendments to the 1917 Water Code have clearly stated that nothing in the act "shall affect or operate to impair any existing water rights." To confirm existing rights, the referee must determine two primary elements of a water right: (1) the amount of water that has been put to beneficial use and (2) the priority of water rights relative to each other.

Appellants contend that they or their predecessors in interest have owned and continuously used all waters of Marshall Lake since 1906, and that the State has no authority to limit, control, or regulate their impoundment rights or the quantity of their use of those waters. * * *

The Doctrine of Prior Appropriation

The law of prior appropriation was established in this state by the Territorial Legislature in 1873 and recognized by this court in 1897. * * *

> The key to determining the extent of plaintiffs' vested water rights is the concept of "beneficial use." ... An appropriated water right is established and maintained by the purposeful application of a given quantity of water to a beneficial use upon the land.[33]

* * *

"Beneficial use" is a term of art in water law, and encompasses two principal elements of a water right.

First, it refers to the purposes, or type of activities, for which water may be used. Use of water for the purposes of irrigated agriculture is a beneficial use. The Grimeses' use of water to irrigate alfalfa fields is not at issue in this case.

Second, beneficial use determines the measure of a water right. The owner of a water right is entitled to the amount of water necessary for the purpose to which it has been put, provided that purpose constitutes a beneficial use. To determine the amount of water necessary for a beneficial use, courts have developed the principle of "reasonable use". Reasonable use of water is determined by analysis of the factors of water duty and waste.

In his findings establishing the measure of the Grimeses' water right, the referee stated that:

> [A] valid right for irrigation purposes only exists for the benefit of these claimants and such right is derived from the original 1906 Linsley notice. It is, therefore, recommended that a right be confirmed to these defendants, with a July 13, 1906 priority for the irrigation of 73 acres from Marshall Lake. Quantification of the amount of water to

---

33. (Citations omitted.) *Neubert,* 117 Wash.2d at 237, 814 P.2d 199.

which this right is entitled creates somewhat of a problem in that there has been no direct testimony regarding the amount of water placed to beneficial use other than a reference in the state's investigatory report that 56 sprinklers are utilized in the system. . . . Therefore, the Referee will allow the standard duty of water which would be 1.2 cubic feet per second plus an additional 25 percent for transportation loss, thus making an aggregate amount of 1.5 cubic feet per second identified with this right. . . .

A second element concerning this right is the amount of storage of water to which these claimants are entitled. . . . [T]hese waters also have recreational benefits, not only to the riparian owners around the lake but also to the general public through the use of resort facilities located on the lake. . . . Therefore, the Referee recommends that a related but separate right be confirmed to these defendants for the storage of 920 acre-feet in Marshall Lake for irrigation and recreation purposes. The priority shall be fixed as of July 13, 1906. The period during which waters may be stored shall be identified as those periods of the year which do not include the April 1 to October 31 irrigation season.

The Grimeses challenge the referee's "consideration of the evidence" and his application of the law in making these findings. We first consider the evidence used by the referee in establishing the factors of water duty and waste. We then consider the test of "reasonable efficiency" employed by the referee, and adopted by the Superior Court, to evaluate these factors.

Water Duty

"[Water duty] that measure of water, which, by careful management and use, without wastage, is reasonably required to be applied to any given tract of land for such period of time as may be adequate to produce therefrom a maximum amount of such crops as ordinarily are grown thereon. It is not a hard and fast unit of measurement, but is variable according to conditions."[40]

The referee based his determination of the volume of water necessary for irrigation in the Marshall Lake basin on a Washington State University Research Bulletin entitled "Irrigation Requirements for Washington—Estimates and Methodology" (Irrigation Report), and on the expert testimony of Jim Lyerla, the District Supervisor for seven Eastern Washington counties, including Pend Oreille County, in the Water Resources Program of the Department of Ecology. Mr. Lyerla testified that as a part of his work in assigning water quantities to new water permittees, he relied on the Irrigation Report to determine the "water duty" for a proposed use of water. The Irrigation Report provides information for water requirements for specific crops, given in inches per acre per irrigation season, in 40

---

40. *In re Steffens*, 756 P.2d 1002, 1005–06 (Colo.1988) (quoting *Farmers Highline Canal & Reservoir Co. v. Golden*, 129 Colo. 575, 272 P.2d 629 (1954)); *see In re Ahtanum Creek*, 139 Wash. 84, 96, 245 P. 758 (1926).

locations around the state, including Newport, Washington, 5 miles south of Marshall Lake.

Based on the testimony of Mr. Lyerla and the Irrigation Report, the referee determined that an irrigated alfalfa crop grown in the Marshall Lake area requires 21 inches or 1.75 acre feet of water per acre during the irrigation season. The referee then applied an efficiency factor and increased this water duty to 2.5 acre feet per acre per year. The referee found this water duty to be "approximately commensurate with the duty utilized by the Department of Ecology in its quantity allocations in this geographic area under the water right permit system."

Because water rights are characterized in both total yearly allowance and instantaneous flow, the referee also established the maximum rate of diversion at 0.0166 c.f.s. per acre under irrigation. The referee first calculated a standard flow of 1 c.f.s. of water per 60 acres as a reasonable instantaneous flow for alfalfa irrigation in the Marshall Lake basin. In considering the Grimeses' claim, he determined that the Grimeses were entitled to sufficient flow to irrigate 73 acres, or a minimum of 1.21 c.f.s. He then calculated in an efficiency factor to increase this flow by 25 percent and awarded the Grimeses an instantaneous flow of 1.5 c.f.s.

The referee observed that a larger water duty could be awarded to any claimant with specific information proving a right to a larger amount. The 2.5 acre feet/0.0166 c.f.s. water duty was applied when "quantitative evidence of the rate and volume of a right was neither submitted nor made clear during testimony." The referee also observed that "the use of water under all irrigation rights is, however, limited to the amount of water that can be beneficially applied to that number of acres identified in the water right." The referee did not indiscriminately award this water duty to any claim for an irrigation right, but required claimants to prove the number of acres historically irrigated.

* * * The referee's determination of a generic water duty for irrigation of alfalfa in the Marshall Lake basin is supported by a preponderance of the evidence and will not be disturbed by this court.

Waste

From an early date, courts announced the rule that no appropriation of water was valid where the water simply went to waste. Those courts held that the appropriator who diverted more than was needed for the appropriator's actual requirements and allowed the excess to go to waste acquired no right to the excess. A particular use must not only be of benefit to the appropriator, but it must also be a reasonable and economical use of the water in view of other present and future demands upon the source of supply. The difference between absolute waste and economical use has been said to be one of degree only.

Appellant Clarence E. Grimes acknowledged in his testimony that his existing irrigation system required a water flow of up to 3 cubic feet per second in order to deliver 1 cubic foot per second to the field, and that this

system was highly inefficient, causing one-half to two-thirds loss of water.
* * *

While an appropriator's use of water must be reasonably efficient, absolute efficiency is not required. The referee * * * resolved the conflicting testimony by limiting the irrigable acreage to the 73 acres recommended by Ecology. Relying on a standard efficiency factor for irrigation sprinkler systems found in the irrigation report, he confirmed in the Grimeses a water right with one-fourth conveyance loss for a total of 1.5 cubic feet per second. There was at least sufficient evidence for the referee to determine the maximum acreage to which the Grimeses' water right applied, and in limiting the allowable loss for system inefficiency in establishing their instantaneous flow.

The Reasonable Efficiency Test

In limiting the Grimeses' vested water right, the referee balanced several factors, including the water duty for the geographical area and crop under irrigation, the claimants' actual diversion, and sound irrigation practices. In his report, the referee described his method of calculating the Grimeses' water right as a "reasonable efficiency" test.

Amici curiae argue that this test is contrary to judicial decisions which have recognized that the standard of reasonable beneficial use of water for irrigation is limited to consideration of the use of the established means of diversion and application according to the reasonable custom of the locality. Respondent Ecology argues that the 3–part "reasonable efficiency" test cited by the referee provides "the balance sought by the courts between the competing needs of efficiency and maximum utilization of the water, and the existing physical and economic limitations in each situation." Ecology asserts that local custom in irrigation practices is but one of several factors the court must consider in deciding whether a given use of water is reasonable, and, therefore, beneficial.

* * *

Amici curiae urge this court to hold that only "the established means of diversion and application according to the reasonable custom of the locality" may be considered in defining reasonable use. This argument is based on the eminent domain provision of the state Water Code, which prohibits condemnation of a water right when the owner of that right is using the water:

> for the irrigation of his land then under irrigation to the full extent of the soil, by the most economical method of artificial irrigation applicable to such land according to the usual methods of artificial irrigation employed in the vicinity where such land is situated. In any case, the court shall determine what is the most economical method of irrigation.

This court has consistently held that rights of users of water for irrigation purposes are vested rights in real property. Amici curiae assert that the "local custom" test has been employed historically to determine whether given applications of water are wasteful, within the meaning of beneficial use, and that courts should now apply it in the setting of general adjudications. This is the established law in this state.

Decisions of courts throughout the western states provide a basis for defining "reasonable efficiency" with respect to irrigation practices. While customary irrigation practices common to the locality are a factor for consideration, they do not justify waste of water. As this court stated in a case predating the Water Code of 1917:

> [W]hen rights in such an important element as water is in the arid regions are to be measured by the courts, we cannot lay down a rule that would give to the user an arbitrary right to use water at will. [An irrigator's] rights are to be measured by his necessities ... and not by any fanciful notion of his own....
>
>   . . . .
>
> ... [C]ustom can fix the manner of use of water for irrigation only when it is founded on necessity ... [and] an irrigator is entitled to use only so much as he can put to a beneficial use, for the public policy of the people of the United States will not tolerate waste of water in the arid regions.[66]

Local custom and the relative efficiency of irrigation systems in common use are important elements, but must be considered in connection with other statutorily mandated factors, such as the costs and benefits of improvements to irrigation systems, including the use of public and private funds to facilitate improvements.

In limiting the Grimeses' water use by a requirement of reasonable efficiency, the referee properly considered the irrigation report, the Grimeses' actual water use, and their existing irrigation system. The referee alluded to a test incorporating factors that consider impacts to the water source and its flora and fauna. While consideration of these impacts is consonant with the State's obligations under RCW 90.03.005 and 90.54.010(1)(a) and (2), these factors cannot operate to impair existing water rights. * * *

* * * Nowhere in the record does he discuss application of the elements of the so-called "test." If he had in fact applied the "test," it would be necessary for this court to reverse and remand. * * *

Adjudication proceedings cannot be used "to lessen, enlarge, or modify the existing rights of any riparian owner, or any existing right acquired by appropriation, or otherwise." The suggested test would be contrary to the vested rights of water users. "It has long been settled in this state that property owners have a vested interest in their water rights to the extent that the water is beneficially used on the land." Included in the vested rights is the right to diversion, delivery and application "according to the

66. *Shafford v. White Bluffs Land & Irrig. Co.,* 63 Wash. 10, 13–16, 114 P. 883 (1911).

usual methods of artificial irrigation employed in the vicinity where such land is situated." The Legislature sets a standard clearly contradictory to the suggested test in RCW 90.03.040, which relates to eminent domain over water rights. The test is contrary also to long established principles of Western water law.

While we reject use of the specific test suggested by the referee, we affirm because (1) there is no indication in the record that he in fact applied the factors stated in the "test," and (2) he applied the actual beneficial use made by Grimes, taking into account the actual needs and use and the methods of delivery and application in the vicinity. The adjudication and confirmation of a water right in an amount less than claimed by Grimes does not result from application of the so-called test. Rather, as the referee makes clear:

> Quantification of the amount of water to which this right is entitled creates somewhat of a problem in that there has been no direct testimony regarding the amount of water placed to beneficial use other than a reference in the state's investigatory report that 56 sprinklers are utilized in the system.

In the absence of such proof, the referee nevertheless confirmed the right by using a normal duty of water for the type of crops raised and specifically added 25 percent for transportation loss. Making the best of inadequate proof by the claimant, it appears from the record that the referee applied the usual methods of irrigation employed in the vicinity where the Grimeses' land is located.

The Takings Argument

Appellants Grimes argue that diminishment of their prior appropriation in any way is a "taking" of their property right for which they must be compensated or have the decision of the trial court set aside. A vested water right is a type of private property that is subject to the Fifth Amendment prohibition on takings without just compensation. Nevertheless, the concept of "beneficial use," as developed in the common law and as described earlier in this opinion, operates as a permissible limitation on water rights.

NOTES

1. Should the meaning of "reasonable efficiency" change as irrigators' practices in the vicinity change, or as new technologies become available? Would this mean that any use of water is constantly subject to litigation for judicial determination of whether alleged changed conditions have rendered the use unreasonable and therefore nonbeneficial?

In a case concerning one of the nation's first reclamation projects, the Newlands Project in Nevada, the district judge awarded water duties of 3.5 and 4.5 acre-feet per acre per year respectively to bottomland and benchland farmers. The United States objected because landowner contracts with the Bureau of Reclamation limited the water duty to a maximum of 3 acre-feet. The Ninth Circuit Court of Appeals held that § 8 of the Reclamation Act, see *infra* p. 818, required that beneficial use be determined by reference to state law. The court said that "beneficial use expresses a dynamic concept, which is a 'variable according to conditions,' and therefore over time. * * * The district court, in the absence of any earlier administrative or judicial determination of beneficial use, was correct to find beneficial use as of the present time as shown by the best available current information." United States v. Alpine Land & Reservoir Co., 697 F.2d 851, 855 (9th Cir.1983). Thus, the larger decreed rights prevailed over the contracts.

2. Consumptive use of irrigation water, which accounts for about 90% of the West's water use, can be reduced by techniques such as: installation of drip irrigation systems instead of flooding fields; gated pipes instead of open ditches; leveling of fields to reduce runoff; scientific scheduling and moisture sensing devices; and planting drought- and salt-resistant crops. For instance, installation of sprinkler systems instead of surface flooding can reduce waste from 47% to 29%. See generally, Office of Technology Assessment, Water Related Technologies for Sustainable Agriculture in U.S. Arid/Semiarid Lands (1983).

If the waste of water is unwise and conservation measures are truly efficient, why haven't farmers and water distribution institutions already adopted such measures? One study addresses the economic feasibility of requiring greater efficiency:

> Improvements to plug the leaks in [water delivery] systems will not come without significant investment and effort, however. The Soil Conservation Service (SCS) estimates that it will cost about $600 million a year just to repair, and replace as necessary, existing irrigation systems in the country. This would not improve their efficiency, but simply maintain the levels that now exist.

> Another $150 million a year would be needed to maintain irrigation water storage reservoirs. In addition, SCS predicts that it would take another $260 million per year in the 17 western states to get a 4 percent improvement in delivery systems and a 5 percent increase in on-farm efficiency. That total billion-dollar-per-year maintenance bill would amount to about $25 per acre per year, so farmers would no doubt still find it economical if they were faced with loss of their irrigation system.

R. Neil Sampson, Farmland or Wasteland: A Time to Choose 158–59 (1981).

3. Much water "lost" through seepage from ditches and overflows from excess irrigation actually returns to the stream where it can be diverted and used by others. To the extent that return flows can be used by other appropriators, are "waste" figures overstated? Can you conceive of circumstances where excessive application or large quantities of such return flow seepage nonetheless would be "wasteful?"

4. Commentators observe that there are disincentives to conservation in western water law. George W. Pring & Karen A. Tomb, *License to Waste: Legal Barriers to Conservation and Efficient Use of Water in the West,* 25 Rocky Mtn. Min. L. Inst. 25–1 (1979). Reform suggestions include the modification of the beneficial use doctrine, the elimination of community custom as a defense, establishment of water banks, and other institutional changes. Improved irrigations efficiency remains on the list of needed water use improvement throughout the world. However, is there a possible perverse incentive problem? That is, the more water than an irrigator conserves, the more incentive the user has to increase its acreage so that the end result may be a net increase in the amount of water consumed.

5.   Should appropriators get the benefit of improvements in efficiency that enable them to exceed the efficiency of others in the region? In R.T. Nahas Co. v. Hulet, 106 Idaho 37, 674 P.2d 1036 (App.1983), the junior appropriator argued that the senior appropriator's right should be reduced because the senior converted to a more efficient system of irrigation, sprinklers rather than flood irrigation, and because the senior was growing alfalfa, which only required 3.5 acre-feet of water per acre under ideal conditions. Nahas' land is not flat and has porous soil. The senior, however, proved to the court's satisfaction that 5 as opposed to 3.5 acre-feet per acre was reasonable and essential considering the porous soils, sloping land, and dry climate.

6.   Who can raise the question of excessive or wasteful use of water? Under what circumstances? In some states, the occasion arises only when an appropriator invokes administrative or judicial jurisdiction. Because nearly every other appropriator is potentially affected by a wasteful use, should each of them be able to commence an action? Is there a sufficient public interest in preventing waste that even non-appropriators should be able to raise the issue?

In a case seeking to impose mandatory conservation duties on a water district by applying the California Constitution, the California Supreme Court held that the State Water Resources Control Board, not the courts, should decide whether the district has a duty to reclaim wastewater before seeking additional freshwater supplies, citing the doctrine of primary jurisdiction. It also noted that "in administrative proceedings comprehensive adjudication considers the interests of other concerned persons who may not be parties to the court action." Environmental Defense Fund, Inc. v. East Bay Mun. Utility Dist., 20 Cal.3d 327, 142 Cal.Rptr. 904, 572 P.2d 1128 (1977), *vacated by* 439 U.S. 811, 99 S.Ct. 70, 58 L.Ed.2d 103 (1978), *remanded* 26 Cal.3d 183, 161 Cal.Rptr. 466, 605 P.2d 1, 9 (1980). Later proceedings are considered in Stuart L. Somach, *The American River Decision: Balancing Instream Protection with Other Competing Beneficial Uses,* 1 Rivers 251 (1990).

A–B Cattle Company v. United States

Supreme Court of Colorado, 1978.
196 Colo. 539, 589 P.2d 57.

■ Groves, Justice.

* * *

As a part of the Fryingpan–Arkansas Reclamation Project, the United States constructed Pueblo Dam across the Arkansas River a few miles west of Pueblo, creating Pueblo Reservoir. This inundated the headgate and first four miles of the Bessemer Ditch. In exchange for the water formerly transported from the headgate through the ditch, clear water is delivered from the dam into the ditch.

Prior to construction of the reservoir, the United States brought a condemnation proceeding in the United States District Court for the District of Colorado against the Bessemer Co. for the taking of the headgate and the upper portion of the ditch. * * * The Bessemer Co. answered, alleging among other things, that the delivery of clear water instead of silty water would result in substantial damage to the individual stockholders. Subsequently, these shareholders brought the action in the Court of Claims, asking for damages of nearly $100,000,000, plus costs, disbursements and expenses, including reasonable attorney, appraisal and engineering fees. Thereafter, the United States District Court in the condemnation proceeding sustained the Government's motion to dismiss the action as to the silt issue without prejudice to determination of that question by the Court of Claims.

The Court of Claims in its statement of facts has given as the basis for the alleged damages the following:

> "The substitution of clear water from Pueblo Dam for the stream water with silt as diverted from the river has had certain adverse effects on the Bessemer Ditch system and the lands irrigated from the ditch. The silt in the water tended to seal the bed and banks of the ditch. Clear water leaks through the bottom and sides of the ditch in greater volume than silty water. More of the water passing the Bessemer Ditch gauging station about six miles below the original diversion point of the ditch seeps out of the bottom and sides of the ditch so that less of the diverted water reaches the points of delivery to Plaintiffs. There is an increase in the amount of aquatic vegetation growing in the ditch and the laterals. There has been an increase in erosion of the ditch and the laterals in places and sloughing off of material from the sides of the ditches into the bottom. There has been more seepage from the ditch into basements through the Pueblo reach of the ditch. When applied to land for irrigation, clear water does not spread as far as silty water."

[The Court of Claims certified to the Colorado Supreme Court the question of whether the holder of a water right has a right to receive water of the same quality, including the silt content thereof, as has historically been received under the right.]

I

* * *

This leads us to the fundamental question as to whether the original appropriations for the Bessemer Ditch were for silty water. In our view the appropriations were for water, and not for water containing silt. Silt is not a component of water. Rather, it is suspended sediment which comes principally from the banks and bottom of an onrushing stream and which settles to the bottom when there is no longer movement of the water. Thus, there is far more sediment being carried in the waters of the Arkansas River during the flood season of late spring, than in the early spring or fall.

* * *

* * * [W]e regard the storage of water, with consequent settling of silt to the bottom of the reservoir, as not constituting an unreasonable deterioration in quality.

II

There has not been cited any case holding that a senior appropriator has a vested right to the silt content of the water as of the time of his appropriation or at any other time. * * * The trend and philosophy of Colorado law are contrary to the result asked by the plaintiffs. The Arkansas River is overappropriated; water is scarce; and conservation of water and prevention of wastage is the order of the day. The plaintiffs have canals and laterals which leak and seep, thereby, so far as plaintiffs are concerned, wasting the water. They seek to continue their transport of water in leaky ditches by, in effect, calling upon the junior appropriators on the stream to pay for the portion of the leakage which silt will stop.

We said in Fellhauer v. People, 167 Colo. 320, 447 P.2d 986 (1968):

> "For nearly a century the waters of the Arkansas River have been used and reused many times over as they proceed from elevations exceeding 12,000 feet to 3,375 feet at the state line. These uses, and similar uses on other rivers, have developed under article XVI, section 6 of the Colorado constitution which contains *inter alia* two provisions:

>> The right to divert the unappropriated waters of any natural stream to beneficial uses shall never be denied. Priority of appropriation shall give the better right as between those using water for the same purpose;

> Under those provisions and the statutes enacted thereunder a great body of law has been established. In the six briefs, all ably written, sixty Colorado cases have been cited. These decisions are concerned primarily with the respective priorities of *vested rights* which have been established. It is implicit in these constitutional provisions that, along with *vested rights*, there shall be *maximum utilization* of the water of this state. As administration of water approaches its second century the curtain is opening upon the new drama of *maximum utilization* and how constitutionally that doctrine can be integrated into the law of *vested rights*. We have known for a long time that the doctrine was lurking in the backstage shadows as a result of the accepted, though oft violated, principle that the right to water does not give the right to waste it.

"*Colorado Springs v. Bender*, 148 Colo. 458, 366 P.2d 552, might be called the signal that the curtain was about to rise. There it was stated as follows:

> 'At his own point of diversion on a natural water course, each diverter must establish some reasonable means of effectuating his diversion. He is not entitled to command the whole or a substantial flow of the stream merely to facilitate his taking the fraction of the whole flow to which he is entitled. *Schodde v. Twin Falls Land & Water Co.*, 224 U.S. 107.' "

Our answer in the negative to the question propounded by the Court of Claims is a part of the policy of this state that there should be maximum utilization of water and that the maximum utilization doctrine be integrated into the law of vested rights. Without the storage of water, the use thereof cannot be maximized.

It will be noted that in *Colorado Springs v. Bender, supra*, this court cited the United States Supreme Court in *Schodde v. Twin Falls Land & Water Co., supra*. Schodde diverted his water from a shallow canyon and up to his fields by means of water-driven water wheels. Later, others built a dam which slowed the flow until it would not drive the water wheels. Schodde claimed damages against the defendant dam builder. The United States District Court dismissed the complaint on the ground that Schodde's claim to the right to have his water wheels turn was not a reasonable attribute of an appropriation. The Court of Appeals affirmed, as did the United States Supreme Court, stating, "extent of beneficial use was an inherent and necessary limitation upon the right to appropriate." *See Empire Water and Power Co. v. Cascade Town Co.*, 205 F. 123 (8th Cir.1913).

In using its leaky ditches the Bessemer Co. has not attempted to make maximum utilization of the water. As was indicated in 1909 in a case involving the Bessemer Co. and its main canal (*Middelkamp v. Bessemer Irrigating Ditch Co.*, 46 Colo. 102, 103 P. 280), the time may not yet have arrived when all ditches can be required to be lined or placed in pipes. Even assuming that that proposition of 1909 still holds true, this does not change our view that the plaintiffs do not have the right to use silt content to help seal leaky ditches. To view it otherwise would run contra to a basic principle of western irrigation that conservation and maximum usage demand the storage of water in times of plenty for the use in times of drought.

III

* * *

The effect of granting any particular appropriator a constitutionally protected property right in the concentration of silt present in the water at the time of the appropriation would seriously inhibit any subsequent upstream or downstream appropriation. Upstream diversions or impoundments will result in alteration of the silt concentration to downstream users if only due to the slowing impact on stream velocity. Applied in its extreme, an appropriator located on lower reaches of a stream with a very early appropriation date could put a call on the river for the receipt of its natural silt concentration, which would have the practical effect of halting all upstream use and commanding substantially the entire stream flow to satisfy its appropriation.

* * *

■ LEE, ERICKSON and CARRIGAN, JJ., dissent.

■ ERICKSON, JUSTICE, dissenting:

* * * Since a change in water quality can affect the irrigative capacity and utility of a specific quantity of water appropriated, our courts have consistently recognized that appropriators are entitled to protection against detrimental changes in water quality. *Larimer County Reservoir Co. v. People*, [9 P. 794 (1885)]. The question of what constitutes a "diminution" in the quality of water must, therefore, be analyzed in terms of the use to which the water is put. An appropriator's expectations can just as easily be defeated by altering the quality of water as by changing the quantity. Thus, one aspect of an appropriation is the right to continue to receive water of the quality upon which the appropriator relied in making his appropriation. Because the defendants in this case altered the quality of the water which the plaintiffs receive, plaintiffs have been deprived of a quantity of water which they historically received and put to beneficial use.

* * * If a junior appropriator causes a reduction in the quantity of water delivered to a senior appropriator, the injury is obvious. Similarly, a change in the water's natural quality, which denies existing appropriators the full measure of their rights, whether by the addition of a pollutant or by the removal of a naturally-occurring element such as silt, also constitutes injury. The crucial consideration is that water rights which were appropriated for a specific purpose and which were limited in quantity to that amount necessary to achieve that purpose, are no longer sufficient to satisfy that purpose as a result of the change in water quality. The injury inflicted by the change in water quality under such circumstances lessens the value of the water rights and constitutes damage which is cognizable under Colorado Law.

NOTE

The dissenting opinion constituted the decision of the court until a rehearing. If it had remained the court's decision, what would the United States have had to pay in damages? The cost of lining all ditches? Could such a decision become precedent for limiting future appropriations on a stream where any lessening of flow would cause more silt to settle out and jeopardize "natural" ditch lining? Could a senior industrial user accustomed to using stagnant, algae-laden water for cooling demand that its "quality" be maintained because pure water would create more oxidation in the senior's facility?

The dissenting opinion recites "that appropriators are entitled to protection against detrimental changes in water quality." In fact, the right to water quality is enforced narrowly—not only in the strange factual setting of *A–B Cattle*. States tend to limit their control of water quality to regulatory programs implementing federal statutes. See the summary of the Clean Water Act, *infra* p. 673. These regulations target almost exclusively discharges of pollutants into streams.

Lawrence J. MacDonnell, From Reclamation to Sustainability: Water, Agriculture, and the Environment in the American West

239–246 (1999).

Human diversions of water resources from their sources in the American West have been determined as much by cost and the availability of water as by the direct need they are meeting. Thus, for example, senior irrigators are likely to divert more water from a stream than are junior irrigators for an equivalent use. Senior irrigators are likely to have lower-cost, less efficient delivery and use systems. Until people like Elwood Mead started pointing out that these cheap systems often deprive others of the opportunity to develop and use water, states paid no attention to these practices. New appropriators soon found it necessary to begin building storage dams to gain control of water not already claimed. Thus proceeded what might be called the "extensive" development of western water resources—a process by which new demands were satisfied by extending control over more of the resource, rather than by more careful and efficient "intensive" development and use of water.

This was a strategy that worked reasonably well so long as federal subsidies were available to pay most of the cost of this development, and environmental concerns remained in the background. It is a strategy we can no longer afford. Instead, a primary objective of water policy should be to encourage actions that help reduce the considerable gap that presently exists between the diversion or withdrawal of water from its source and the use of water necessary to accomplish the purposes for which it was diverted. According to the U.S. Geological Survey, of the 178.9 million acre-feet of water taken out of surface-water and groundwater sources in 1990 in the nineteen western states for domestic, industrial, thermoelectric power, and irrigation uses, 81.7 million acre-feet were consumed—46 percent.

The place to begin thinking about reducing this gap is with the West's major water diverter: irrigation. Statistics on irrigation-water use over this century suggest that irrigators themselves are using water more efficiently. * * * Irrigators in the Lower Arkansas Valley, for example, have made on-farm changes to utilize their diversions more fully. The Roza Irrigation district in the Yakima Basin made improvements to its water-delivery system. In both cases changes were initiated because of the direct economic gains made possible—measured in terms of increased irrigated acreage, a more reliable water supply for existing irrigated lands, the cultivation of more water-intensive crops, and reduced labor.

The lower Arkansas is a chronically overappropriated river, however, and the Roza is a junior water-right holder in the supply-limited Yakima River. Many irrigators (particularly those with senior water rights) are satisfied with their existing irrigation systems and see little reason to make costly changes for uncertain benefits. Unless they are forced to make changes (as have been irrigators in the Newlands Project) or someone pays the full cost of making the changes (as does the Bureau of Reclamation for the Grand Valley Project), the motivation simply does not now exist.

Moreover, real problems of interdependence have developed over the years that make change both physically and legally difficult. The inefficiencies of traditional surface-water irrigation systems long ago were simply built into other water uses, both upstream and downstream. Upstream users seeking to appropriate water were subject to the full diversion right of senior downstream users. They developed their rights in recognition of this downstream use. Downstream users developed their appropriations on the basis of the water available in the stream, much of which may have included return flows from more senior upstream appropriators. Even within a single irrigation system, the original methods of irrigation are the ones on which water-use patterns were established. Unused water, both surface and subsurface, from higher lands often provides water to users within the system on lower lands. Expectations, sometimes with a legal basis, have developed around these patterns of water use.

It is this reliance on what some would call wasteful or inefficient use of water that causes irrigators to resist calls for water conservation. And they are right to resist conservation that would not account for and protect these reliances. For the most part, however, the debate about irrigation-water conservation has been far too simplistic. Water conservation that works cannot be implemented without a broad, system-wide understanding of how water presently is being used, how existing uses can continue to be met, and whether changes are possible that can produce desired additional benefits while meeting existing uses.

Making more efficient use of water, measured in terms of reducing the gap between the amount of water diverted and the amount usefully consumed, is not an end in itself. It is a means, potentially, of achieving other desired objectives. The most easily achieved of these objectives will be to reduce the amount of direct diversions from surface-water sources, thereby increasing flows that remain in the stream channel between the original point of diversion and the point where unused water returns to the stream. Thus, if a desired objective is to improve stream flows in this particular segment, and the value of that improvement is worth the investment necessary to make a reduction in diversions possible, conservation can be beneficial. This is the primary objective of water-conservation planning in the Yakima Basin. It is also a benefit of reducing diversions in the Grand Valley.

Similarly, if an objective is to reduce the amount of contaminants that return to a water body with irrigation return flows, and the value of that reduction is worth the value of the investment necessary to achieve that reduction, there are ways to make that objective work. This is the sort of effort ongoing in the Newlands Project [in Nevada] to address water-quality concerns in the Lahontan wetlands and, in the Grand Valley [of Colorado], to reduce salinity in the Colorado River.

If, however, the objective is to increase the amount of water available for new consumptive uses, conservation alone is unlikely to help. In a stream system wherein uses of water already are fully committed, new consumptive uses are likely to have to replace existing consumptive uses. Water conservation can reduce consumptive use to some degree, but rarely will these conservation improvements produce substantial *additional* water in the system unless the historical uses have taken water permanently out of a water basin.

Uses of water legally established under the laws of the state in which water is diverted or withdrawn are protected from impairment or harm as a consequence of others changing their use of water. Not all patterns of dependence among water users enjoy legal protection—for example, a user relying on water that leaks from a poorly constructed storage or convey-ance system probably does not have a legal right to require that unintended leakage to continue. Moreover, a downstream use enjoying the benefits of return flows of "imported" water (water from another basin) cannot require the importer to continue to make that water available. In general, however, the laws of the states following prior appropriation require that water legally available to an appropriator remain available in the same amount and timing under which the appropriation was established.

Several states have begun making clarifications of their water laws that should help encourage water conservation. One approach, taken by California, assures appropriators that conservation of water (defined as the use of less water to accomplish the same purpose) is itself a beneficial use. Other states, such as Oregon and Montana, have attempted to define statutorily the legal status of water that is conserved. Oregon authorizes appropriators who have installed conservation measures that reduce exist-ing water uses to make other use, of up to 75 percent, of the conserved water. Montana authorizes appropriators who "salvage" historically divert-ed water to lease or sell the water, or to change its use.

These statutes alter the traditional assumption of prior appropriation that water no longer diverted and used by an appropriator simply becomes available to the next junior appropriator. Instead they offer an important incentive to existing users to consider whether they can make changes reducing historical uses that produce benefits exceeding the cost of the changes, either through additional use of the conserved water or by selling or leasing that water to another. Such an approach recognizes the need to encourage the conservation and reallocation of water and the importance of providing incentives to existing users for this purpose. It provides a means by which existing users may continue their activities, but with more efficient water delivery and use systems.

The broad policy objective of water conservation is to reduce unneeded uses of water where there are more benefits that can be produced by other uses of the water. In some respects this long has been an objective of water law: Appropriations are understood to be limited to the *minimum* amount of water necessary to accomplish the purposes of the appropriation. In practice, however, there has been virtually no effort to apply this so-called "beneficial use" standard to reduce the amount of water diverted under existing water rights. Nor is there much interest today in some kind of across-the-board administrative or regulatory process requiring appropriators to upgrade their practices so that more water is available for other uses.

In some respects it is surprising that there has been so little political support for such an approach. Water is a common resource, shared by many uses and users. The appropriation and private use of a portion of the water are considered necessary and important because of the benefits provided by those uses. Legally, an appropriator holds a "right" to use water to accomplish the beneficial purposes of the appropriation, which is regarded as a property right. The property interest, however, is not to some fixed quantity of water but to a priority date for using an amount of water *necessary* to accomplish a stated purpose or purposes. The amount of water necessary might very well be viewed as changeable over time as new practices and technologies make it economically feasible to reduce total water use to accomplish the same purpose. What is necessary might even be viewed as dependent on other demands on the water resource. As an analogy, consider the widespread use of zoning to direct and limit land uses in urban areas. Just as such laws have greatly altered traditional uses and expectation of uses of private property, so too might water uses in highly competitive or sensitive places become subject to specified use standards.

One explanation for the limited interest to date in such an approach is the costs it would impose, both for government to administer and for users to comply with, relative to the benefits that would be gained. Experience in the lower Truckee and Carson basins emphasizes this point. Many years and many millions of dollars have been spent in an attempt to improve irrigation efficiency of a relatively small irrigated area (roughly sixty thousand acres). It is inconceivable that funding could be found to make possible this kind of effort for the roughly 46 million acres of land irrigated in the western states.

* * *

To survive as a viable activity in the next century, irrigated agriculture must bring its practices more closely in line with the interests and needs of other water users in the West. There is no compelling policy reason why irrigation should somehow be insulated from the changes taking place in this region.

Many in irrigated agriculture do not believe that the problems caused by their water uses are their problems. In their view they were first to establish such practices; others must adjust to them. If others want certain practices to change, they will have to pay the full costs of doing so. Moreover, irrigators should be able to decide whether or not to make the changes—even if others do pay for them.

In my view this is wishful thinking. Sooner or later changes are going to occur—in fact, they are already occurring. Irrigators in the Newlands Project discovered that they controlled far less water than they had originally believed. A similar fate struck irrigators using water from the Central Valley Project of California when Congress unilaterally allocated eight hundred thousand acre-feet of project storage to fish and wildlife uses in 1992. Irrigators in the Grand Valley face the possibility that their water-use practices will be determined to be wasteful, shifting a portion of their historically controlled water to upstream junior appropriators such as cities on the Front Range of Colorado.

At one time I hoped irrigators would themselves take more of the initiative in finding ways to modernize and improve their systems, using funding from others who would benefit from use of the conserved water. The arrangement between the Imperial Irrigation District and the Metropolitan Water District of Southern California seemed to offer a model—urban users providing funding for irrigators to improve their systems in return for the use of conserved water. Now I am less certain. Very likely this deal would not have occurred had IID not been threatened with the loss of a portion of its water right.

* * *

The general understanding under which western water development occurred was that appropriators should take as much water as they could use. Today that should be understood to mean that appropriators should take only as much as they need. Reducing the gap between these two measures for existing appropriators will require a mix of incentives and standards. All new appropriations should already be subject to a heightened standard of need and of efficient use, but state water laws continue only to require the more general "beneficial use" standard. Reducing the gap between diversion and consumption is a slow and difficult process, but one that is essential if western water uses are to be sustainable.

REUSE OF APPROPRIATED WATER

Once water is diverted from a watercourse and used, appropriators may be limited in their ability to reuse it. The extent of reuse may depend on the original source of the water and on whether the appropriator has relinquished control so that the water may be deemed to have returned to the watercourse. Whether to allow reuse may entail technical and policy factors.

Estate of Steed v. New Escalante Irrigation Co.

Supreme Court of Utah, 1992.
846 P.2d 1223.

■ HOWE, ASSOCIATE CHIEF JUSTICE:

* * *

I. Facts

This case involves the use of water in Alvey Wash, which is south of the town of Escalante in Garfield County. The wash is shaped like a horseshoe opening to the south, with one prong of the wash coming from the southwest and the other prong going to the southeast. Escalante is located immediately north of the bend in the horseshoe. The inside of the southwest prong is bordered by tall and impenetrable cliffs. The land inside the horseshoe slopes gently from the base of the east side of those cliffs across the middle of the horseshoe toward the east prong. A substantial part of that land has been irrigated for over one hundred years with water diverted from the Escalante River, which runs north of Escalante in a generally west to east direction, and with water taken from the southeast prong of the wash. The Escalante River is a tributary to the Colorado River. New Escalante's diversions are the last diversions from the Escalante River for irrigation in Utah. The unused water flows to Lake Powell on the Colorado River.

Alvey Wash is a natural watershed, with a drainage area of about 102 square miles. It empties into the Escalante River about 25 miles downstream from the irrigated lands of Steed and New Escalante's shareholders. However, the Escalante River does not naturally contribute any water to Alvey Wash. New Escalante has historically delivered diverted water to the lands of its shareholders through open canals. The shareholders applied the water to their lands by flood-type irrigation. Some of their lands drain toward Alvey Wash, and consequently, runoff and seepage water reached the wash, where it commingled with the natural flow in the wash.

In 1982, New Escalante changed its irrigation system from flood irrigation to a pressurized sprinkler system of enclosed pipes. The open ditches and canals previously used were abandoned. The new system is much more efficient and has substantially diminished the runoff and seepage water which reaches Alvey Wash.

Steed owns a decreed water right in Alvey Wash from which it irrigates its lands. It contends that it had a vested right to receive the same amount of runoff and seepage flow to the wash. It characterizes itself as a downstream water user in the same river system affected by changes made by an upstream user. Steed sought an injunction, a replacement order, and money damages. The trial court held that because there was no natural contribution of water from the Escalante River to the wash, Steed had acquired no vested right, either by appropriation, by adverse use, or otherwise, to compel New Escalante to continue to let the same amount of water run off or seep from the lands of its shareholders into the wash.

II. Vested Right

Utah, along with the majority of western states, follows the appropriation doctrine: First in time, first in right for beneficial use is the basis of the acquisition of water rights. *Gunnison Irrigation Co. v. Gunnison Highland Canal Co.*, 52 Utah 347, 174 P. 852 (1918).

In a long line of cases dating from 1912, this court has dealt with the rights of water users in runoff and seepage water from higher ground. In *Garns v. Rollins*, 41 Utah 260, 125 P. 867 (1912), waste or percolating water from the irrigation of the plaintiff's land ran into a ditch from which the defendant irrigated his adjoining land. The plaintiff brought an action to determine the title and the right to use the runoff irrigation water. The trial court held that the plaintiff was entitled to as much of that water as she could put to beneficial use. On appeal, we reversed and held that the plaintiff had the absolute right to all of the waste water which she could capture before it ran off her land. We stated:

> The law is well settled, in fact the authorities all agree, that one landowner receiving waste water which flows, seeps, or percolates from the land of another cannot acquire a prescriptive right to such water, nor any right (except by grant) to have the owner of the land from which he obtains the water continue the flow.

41 Utah at 272, 125 P. at 872. In *Garns*, we quoted approvingly the following statement from 1 Samuel C. Weil, *Water Rights in the Western States* 54 (3d ed. 1911): "Waste water soaking from the land of another after irrigation need not be continued, and may be intercepted and taken by such original irrigator, and conducted elsewhere, though parties theretofore using the waste are deprived thereof." *Garns*, 41 Utah at 273, 125 P. at 872. Seven years later, in *Stookey v. Green*, 53 Utah 311, 178 P. 586 (1919), we cited *Garns* for the holding that "the run-off, waste, and seepage from irrigation are not subject to appropriation as against the owner of the land irrigated who desires to recapture it and apply it on his own land." 53 Utah at 319, 178 P. at 589.

The question as to what rights one can acquire in water that wastes or seeps from the land of another arose again in *Smithfield West Bench Irrigation Co. v. Union Central Life Insurance Co.*, 105 Utah 468, 142 P.2d 866 (1943). On the second appeal in that case, 113 Utah 356, 195 P.2d 249 (1948), this court gave a clear answer to that question:

> It is well established under the authorities cited in our previous opinion that waters diverted from a natural source, applied to irrigation and recaptured before they escape from the original appropriator's control, still belong to the original appropriator. If the original appropriator has a beneficial use for such waters he may again reuse them and no one can acquire a right superior to that of the original appropriator.

113 Utah at 363, 195 P.2d at 252–53.

* * *

In two later cases, we again recognized and restated the rule that an upstream irrigator had the right to completely consume all the water it diverted by using it over and over again. However, in each case we carved out an exception to the general rule specific to the fact situation before the court. In *East Bench Irrigation Co. v. Deseret Irrigation Co.*, 2 Utah 2d 170, 271 P.2d 449 (1954), we held that the rule did not apply when the runoff or waste water returned to the stream from which it was originally diverted. We quoted from Wells A. Hutchins, *Selected Problems in the Law of Water Rights in the West* 362–68 (1942):

> Appropriations may generally be made of waste water which has been abandoned by the original appropriators, but with important qualifications. Generally, an independent right to the use of abandoned or waste water can be acquired only if the water has not yet returned to the stream from which it was diverted. If such water after abandonment has re-entered a portion of the stream system from which it was originally appropriated, as noted in greater detail below, it becomes a part of that watercourse in legal contemplation as well as physically, and from the standpoint of rights of use, it is just as much a part of the flow as is the water with which it is mingled; hence appropriative rights which before the mingling have attached to the waters of the stream attach with equal effect to the waste waters originally diverted from the stream and then abandoned into it, so that an independent appropriation cannot then be made of the waste waters as such * * *.

2 Utah 2d at 181 n. 6, 271 P.2d at 457 n. 6. In some of the cases relied upon by Steed, the runoff or waste water did return to the stream from which it was diverted.

Another exception was recognized in *Stubbs v. Ercanbrack*, 13 Utah 2d 45, 368 P.2d 461 (1962). Once again, we acknowledged the rule in *Garns* that "water rights could not be acquired in waste water so that the defendant would be obliged to continue to irrigate his higher ground to provide water to be collected in the plaintiffs' drains." 13 Utah 2d at 50, 368 P.2d at 464. However, we held that that rule did not apply because after the irrigation water had been used, it commingled with the water in the natural water table, thereby losing its identity as irrigation water. As such, it could no longer be considered owned by the defendant. Id.

Turning to the present case, we agree with the trial court that the determination of this case is controlled by the rule we adopted in *Garns*, which we have consistently followed for the past eighty years. The trial court properly concluded that the water reaching Alvey Wash by way of seepage and runoff water from irrigation by New Escalante's shareholders was subject to reappropriation in 1909 when Steed's predecessor filed his application to appropriate water in Alvey Wash. However, such reappropriation did not carry with it any vested right to require New Escalante to continue to divert water from the Escalante River or to convey the water through its irrigation system and to restrict its use of the same so that the flow to Alvey Wash would be maintained at its historic level. Neither of the exceptions which we recognized in *East Bench* or in *Stubbs* is applicable in the instant case. In *East Bench*, the water had returned to the stream from which it had been diverted. In *Stubbs*, there was no attempt by the upper water user to capture surplus or waste water before it went into the ground. There, the upper user let the excess water seep into the ground and then attempted to reuse it at the lower end of his land after it had commingled with natural water in the soil. No such fact situation is presented here.

Text writers on water law are in general agreement with our decisions in this area of the law. In the recent treatise *Waters and Water Rights*, it is stated that the only limitations which should compel an appropriator to continue wasting water are "(1) a finding that the amount released has been dedicated to the public and, therefore, the appropriator's water right has been modified to that extent; or (2) a cessation to purposefully harm the intervening user." 2 Robert E. Beck, et al., *Waters and Water Rights* § 13.04, at 150 (1991). That treatise further states that when water is applied to irrigation, there is

> an expectation that it is the water right holder's water and may be used by that owner to the fullest extent possible. Thus, the owner is allowed to "recapture" that water once it has been put to its ultimate use, whether in a sewage facility or on a field to irrigate a crop. The basic exception to allowing recapture is where the portion that would be subject to recapture has become return flow, that is, finds its way back to its source. At that point, if not before, it becomes tributary water and subject to the call of the stream.

Id. at 152–53 (citations omitted).

III.   Balance the Interests of Water Users

Steed contends that regardless of whether it has a vested right, this court needs to balance the interests of upper and lower water users on the same river system. Steed asserts that New Escalante's change to the pressurized system has resulted in a 25 percent increase in efficiency and thus its shareholders now require about 25 percent less water to irrigate the same number of acres. Steed argues that allowing New Escalante to keep the excess water and expand the acreage watered by its shareholders ignores the loss of water to Steed. Steed concedes that increased efficiency in the use of water is desirable, but urges that out of the savings, losses caused to other users should be made up.

Moreover, Steed points out that there has actually been no increased efficiency. To the extent New Escalante now has water for more acreage, Steed has water for less acreage. Thus the basin as a whole has experienced no change. The technology employed by New Escalante has merely shifted water, giving the appearance of increasing efficiency without any real gain.

New Escalante counters that both the evidence and the trial court's findings are contrary to Steed's assertion that the change to the new system has resulted in substantial amounts of excess water. The evidence is to the effect that the pressurized sprinkler system is approximately 25 percent more efficient than flood-type irrigation. However, the new system does not make water. The system distributes an efficient application of the water, allowing the crops to consume more water. With a flood-type irrigation system, crops are somewhat over watered at the upper end and under watered at the lower end.

New Escalante's water right, with an 1875 priority, is for 40 cubic feet per second. The president of New Escalante testified that with the new system, the pipe capacity is 33 cubic feet per second (c.f.s.). The excess water is now stored in reservoirs and consumed in the late summer months when the flow of the Escalante River diminishes and New Escalante is unable to divert its entitlement of 40 c.f.s. He further testified that there is no water left at the end of the season. The trial court's finding on this matter is in accord with New Escalante. Moreover, New Escalante denied Steed's contention that an unauthorized expansion of acreage is being watered by its shareholders. Once again, neither the evidence nor the trial court's findings support Steed's contentions. At the time of trial, New Escalante had the decreed right to irrigate 2,712.28 acres. The evidence indicates that it operated within that limit.

We must therefore reject Steed's suggestions as to how the interests of the two users can be balanced. Unfortunately, both parties cannot "win." The law simply favors the first user by allowing it to capture seepage and runoff before it escapes from the land. When there is not enough water to satisfy the needs of all users, the user who depends upon another's seepage and runoff will suffer.

Underlying Utah's water law is a strong policy to promote conservation. This can be done by encouraging the implementation of improvements in water systems to prevent seepage. In *Big Cottonwood Tanner Ditch Co. v. Moyle*, 109 Utah 213, 174 P.2d 148 (1946), we upheld the right of an irrigation company to cement and waterproof its ditches to prevent seepage even though it might harm trees, shrubs, and other plant life growing along the ditch banks on the servient property. We expressly rejected cases holding to the contrary because they were "decided in states where the need for water conservation does not exist or exists only to a limited degree * * *." 109 Utah at 235, 174 P.2d at 159.

* * * The *Moyle* case is an example of where, in the interest of conservation, an irrigation company was allowed to capture its seepage even though the seepage was serving a beneficial use in supporting the flora along the ditch banks.

In the instant case, New Escalante has expended more than two million dollars to convert its system to a pressurized, enclosed pipe and sprinkler system. The open canals from which water once seeped are no longer used. Sprinklers apply the water to the land so that nearly all the water is absorbed and little runs off. If the water conserved could not be used by New Escalante, there would be no incentive to make improvements. So long as New Escalante diverts only that volume of water to which it is entitled, it should be allowed to make the most efficient use of it.

* * *

V. Conclusion

Because Utah is an arid state, efficient and beneficial use of water should be encouraged. In furtherance of that objective, an appropriator should be encouraged to apply water in the most efficient manner. Any technique which conserves water consumption and reduces waste is commendable. It is unfortunate that Steed lost some water which previously found its way to augment the water in Alvey Wash. However, absent a natural connection between the water in the wash and the water New Escalante diverted from the Escalante River, Steed acquired no vested right to compel New Escalante to allow the water applied to irrigation to run off their shareholders' lands.

Significant amounts of irrigation water can be lost through evaporation, seepage, or other means. We must encourage greater efficiency through water-saving techniques. As former Chief Justice Crockett so appropriately noted in *Wayman v. Murray City Corp.* some 23 years ago: "Because of the vital importance of water * * * both our statutory and decisional law have been fashioned in recognition of the desirability and of the necessity of insuring the highest possible development and of the most continuous beneficial use of all available water with as little waste as possible." 23 Utah 2d 97, 100, 458 P.2d 861, 863 (1969) (citations omitted).

Judgment affirmed.

NOTES

1.   Although many appropriators become dependent on appropriations of waste water that is on its way back to the stream, *Steed* rules that appropriators of waste water do not have a right to demand continuation of deliveries through a drainage system. This is the rule in most states. For instance, in Cleaver v. Judd, 238 Or. 266, 393 P.2d 193 (1964), the court held that waste water could be salvaged and reused by the original appropriator even though a neighboring landowner who had been using the waste water for irrigation purposes would no longer be able to use it.

2.   The general rule is that as soon as the water leaves the appropriator's land and is in or destined for a natural stream, it becomes subject to appropriation by others. See Fuss v. Franks, 610 P.2d 17 (Wyo.1980). The courts in some states consider water to have entered the stream system even before it leaves the land of the appropriator seeking to reuse it. In Ft. Morgan Reservoir & Irrigation Co. v. McCune, 71 Colo. 256, 206 P. 393 (1922), a reservoir owner dug a trench in front of a dam to recapture water that was seeping out and began to put the water to use on the original land. The court held that as soon as water escapes from a ditch or reservoir and becomes percolating water that is destined for a natural stream, it is considered part of the stream and not subject to reuse by the original appropriator. Which rule encourages greater efficiency? Are there other policy considerations that are relevant?

3. Should New Escalante be allowed to apply "saved" water to new fields? Compare this with Salt River Valley Water Users' Ass'n v. Kovacovich, 3 Ariz.App. 28, 411 P.2d 201 (1966), where the court held that a farmer who required less water because of improved irrigation practices could not apply the saved water to new fields and produce new crops. Would a contrary rule make more sense?

4. The California Water Code §§ 1010–11 (West Supp. 2007) provides that reclaimed waste water or water saved through conservation may be sold, leased, exchanged, or otherwise transferred pursuant to the state's general transfer laws. Conservation is defined to include any "use of less water to accomplish the same purpose," and it includes reductions in use from land fallowing and crop rotation. The law also declares that failure to use all or part of one's water rights because of water conservation efforts cannot effect a forfeiture, and actually constitutes a beneficial use of water. Montana allows salvagers to retain the right to the salvaged water for beneficial use. MONT. CODE ANN. § 85–2–402 (2005). A lower court in Montana has allowed additional acreage to be irrigated with water saved by an irrigator by using center-pivot irrigation and other efficient practices. United States v. *In re* Application for Change of Appropriation Water Rights, No. CDV 99–28 (Mont. 1st Jud. Dist. 1999). At the Western Governors' Association 1985 Water Efficiency Workshop, it was noted that there was considerable support for legislation to give the salvager clear title to salvaged water. However, some felt that to allow a "waster" of water to "profit" from his waste was akin to rewarding a "bum." Is it better to penalize or reward efficiency?

5. Just north of the Colorado River Delta is the fertile Imperial Valley of California. The Imperial Irrigation District (IID) is the single largest user of Colorado River water, diverting about 2.9 million acre-feet per year to produce crops that keep large parts of the country in fruits and vegetables all year. In 1984, the California State Water Resources Control Board found that a return flow loss of 38% from the IID to the Salton Sea (over a million acre-feet per year) was unreasonable and violated state constitutional and statutory prohibitions against waste. Imperial Irrigation Dist. v. State Water Resources Control Bd., 225 Cal.App.3d 548, 275 Cal.Rptr. 250 (1990). The Metropolitan Water District of Southern California (MWD) saw these return flows as a potential source of water supply for the Los Angeles area and in 1989, after several years of negotiations spurred on by the court decisions unfavorable to IID, IID and MWD signed a conservation agreement. MWD agreed to pay for structural and nonstructural conservation projects in the Imperial Valley that will conserve 106,100 acre-feet of water annually, which MWD then has the right to use. The actual water right stays with IID. The capital costs to MWD are estimated at $97.8 million, plus $23 million in indirect costs for the conserved water. For a more detailed explanation of the IID–MWD transfer and subsequent transfers, see *infra* p. 1016.

City and County of Denver v. Fulton Irrigating Ditch Co.

Supreme Court of Colorado, 1972.
179 Colo. 47, 506 P.2d 144.

■ GROVES, JUSTICE.

This is an appeal from the decision in a declaratory judgment action by the plaintiffs, City and County of Denver (Denver) and the Adolph Coors Company (Coors). At issue are questions of Denver's rights in water obtained through transmountain diversions. These diversions are of water from the Colorado River basin, which naturally flows westerly from the west side of the Continental Divide to the Pacific Ocean. The waters are diverted to the South Platte River basin on the eastern side of the Continental Divide, the area in which Denver is located. The South Platte flows easterly, to the Missouri River. The defendant ditch companies divert water for irrigation purposes from the South Platte River downstream from the point of discharge of effluent from the plant of Metropolitan Sewage District No. 1 (Metro). Metro receives and processes Denver's sewage.

About half of Denver's water supply is Colorado River basin water. Approximately 100,000 acre feet annually—an average constant flow of about 137 cubic feet per second of time—of this water is placed in the South Platte River in the form of sewage effluent. The water is originally diverted from three Colorado River tributaries, the Fraser River, the Williams Fork River and the Blue River.

* * *

Denver sought a declaratory judgment as to two questions:

1. Whether Denver may make successive uses of the diverted transmountain water while its dominion over the water continues.

2. Whether Denver may make an exchange of water under agreement with Coors dated December 4, 1969.

We hold that Denver, in the absence of an agreement on its part not to do so, (1) may re-use, (2) may make a successive use of, and (3) after use may make disposition of imported water. Further, we affirm the trial court in its determination that, by reason of an agreement dated May 1, 1940 to which Denver is a party, Denver may not exchange water under the Coors agreement.

I.

The terms "re-use" and "successive use" have been used in the arguments with somewhat varying meanings. We add a third term, "right of disposition," and now define the three terms as used in this opinion.

"Re-use" means a subsequent use of imported water for the same purpose as the original use. For example, this could embrace the treatment of sewage resulting in potable water which is re-cycled into the regular water system.

"Successive use" means subsequent use by the water importer for a different purpose. This includes the practice of the City of Aurora and possibly other municipalities which treat sewage containing imported water for further use by the city for irrigation of public parks and facilities and for industrial uses.

"Right of disposition" means the right to sell, lease, exchange or otherwise dispose of effluent containing foreign water after distribution through Denver's water system and collection in its sewer system.

A statute adopted in 1969 apparently authorizes Denver to re-use, make successive uses, and after use to have the right of disposition of imported water, subject, of course, to its contractual obligations otherwise. This statute reads:

> "Whenever an appropriator has heretofore, or shall hereafter lawfully introduce foreign water into a stream system from an unconnected stream system, such appropriator may make a succession of uses of such water by exchange or otherwise to the extent that its volume can be distinguished from the volume of the streams into which it is introduced. Nothing in this section shall be construed to impair or diminish any water right which has become vested."

1969 Perm.Supp., C.R.S.1963, 148–2–6 [now COLO. REV. STAT. § 37–82–106 (2000)].

Even without the statute we think that Denver has the rights of re-use, successive use and disposition of foreign water, subject again to contrary contractual obligations.

Comrie v. Sweet, 75 Colo. 199, 225 P. 214 (1924) and Ripley v. Park Center Land and Water Co., 40 Colo. 129, 90 P. 75 (1907), involved developed water or allegedly developed water produced from mining operations. As the term was used in those opinions, "developed water" is that water which has been added to the supply of a natural stream and which never would have come into the stream had it not been for the efforts of the party producing it. In *Ripley* the water was judicially determined to be "developed water," and the sale of it by the developers to downstream users was validated as against holders of decrees in the stream. If these developers had instead made a completely consumptive use of the water, we believe this court would still have ruled that the holders of stream priorities could not complain. It follows that the developers without hindrance could use, re-use, make successive use of and dispose of the water. As far as the claims of defendants here are concerned, we see no distinction between the rights of owners of developed water from a mine and the rights of Denver as to its imported water.

* * *

In order to minimize the amount of water removed from Western Colorado, eastern slope importers should, to the maximum extent feasible, reuse and make successive uses of the foreign water.

* * *

The trial court determined that, absent negating circumstances, Denver had the right of re-use, successive use and disposition after use of foreign water. This, of course, we affirm. We do not agree, however, and reverse, the following determination of the trial court:

> It is the Court's ruling that pursuant to the evidence in this case [Denver's] dominion [over imported water] is lost at the customer tap delivery, but in any event the loss is final and complete at the point of delivery of Denver's sewage to the Denver Metropolitan Sewer intake line, and no question of loss of dominion at the point Denver's sewage is mixed with that of 15 other municipalities and governmental entities, processed on secondary treatment and delivered to Metro's outfall line to the South Platte River as treated effluent.

* * *

> "[I]dentity of the water is lost, including dominion thereof, that such water has been abandoned with the result that no participant member in the Metro District would have any legal claim or right to any particular percentage of volume of the return sewage effluent, regardless of the source of the water, be it wells, South Platte River water or other transmountain water."

* * * Metro is merely an agent of Denver and other municipalities delivering sewage to it, and rights and responsibilities as between Denver and downstream irrigation users are the same as if Denver itself treated its sewage and returned it to the stream.

We hold that when Denver delivers water to a customer tap, it does not lose dominion over the water later returning to its sewer.

It was stipulated that Denver keeps records designed to disclose the amounts of various classes of water which it diverts, stores and distributes. * * *

There is no issue in this case as to quality of water. With the question of quality not involved, we accept Denver's argument that water is fungible or is to be treated the same as a fungible article. The particles of water do not have to be identified as coming from Western Colorado, but rather water, whether or not contained in effluent, can be divided volumetrically. A percentage of the effluent discharged by the Metro plant can be considered as imported water. Under the stipulated facts, we do not need to go into the processes of division of the water. We note with approval the stipulation that Denver will have the burden of demonstrating the identity of transmountain water.

* * *

NOTES

1. How can Colorado's restrictive rule on recapture and reuse of water stated in *Fort Morgan Reservoir & Irrigation Co. v. McCune, supra* p. 218, be reconciled with the decision in the principal case? At what point do Denver's rights in the imported water cease? Can water be sold downstream in Nebraska? Are there any limits on how the imported water is used? May it be used wastefully in the midst of a drought? Do those in the watershed of origin have a stake in how the water is used? Cf. Public Serv. Co. of Colorado v. Willows Water Dist., 856 P.2d 829 (Colo.1993) (water district did not lose dominion over water used for irrigation so long as there was intent and ability to recapture the water). For a review of Colorado law concerning the right to successive use and reuse, see Allison Maynard, *The Reuse Right in Colorado Water Law: A Theory of Dominion,* 68 Denv. U. L. Rev. 413 (1991).

2.   Suppose Denver concludes that a cheaper means of complying with pollution controls is to evaporate the effluent rather than treat and discharge it. Under *Fulton* could it do so? See Robert G. Berger, Comment, *Water Law—Cessation of Return Flow as a Means of Complying with Pollution Control Laws,* 12 Land & Water L. Rev. 431 (1977).

3.   Can downstream appropriators ever acquire any continuing rights to developed water which the developer returns to the stream? The court in *Fulton* avoided this question by finding that Denver had in mind, "possibly from its first transmountain diversion," reuse, successive use, and disposition of the imported water. In a case factually similar to *Fulton,* appropriators were held not entitled to compensation when the city changed its point of sewage effluent return and bypassed their headgate, in part on the ground that the city could cease importing the water and eliminate the supply in any event. Thayer v. City of Rawlins, 594 P.2d 951 (Wyo.1979). New Mexico reached the same result under a law which classifies waste or drainage water as artificial surface water. N.M. Stat. Ann. § 72–5–27 (2003); Reynolds v. City of Roswell, 99 N.M. 84, 654 P.2d 537 (1982). Suppose the developer never reuses the water. Is the water then available for appropriation? In Dodge v. Ellensburg Water Co., 46 Wash.App. 77, 729 P.2d 631, 633 (1986), the water company diverted water from a creek fed by return flows from the transbasin diversions of upstream irrigation districts. A downstream water user objected to the diversion because the company had never perfected an appropriation, but the court refused to enjoin Ellensburg's use: "Foreign water, once abandoned by its developer, does not become part of the natural flow of the drainage area where it is discharged and may be used by the first person who takes it." However, the company secured only "the *corpus* of the water" and "no water rights, prescriptive or otherwise." Id. at 634.

Southeastern Colorado Water Conservancy Dist. v. Shelton Farms, Inc.

Supreme Court of Colorado, 1974.
187 Colo. 181, 529 P.2d 1321.

■ DAY, JUSTICE.

   This is an appeal from two judgments and decrees awarding appellees Shelton Farms and Colorado–New Mexico Land Company ("the Company") water rights free from the call of any and all senior decreed water rights on the Arkansas River.

This case, so far as we are advised, is of first impression in the United States, dealing with whether the killing of water-using vegetation and the filling of a marshy area to prevent evaporation can produce a superior water right for the amount of water not transpired or evaporated. The Pueblo district court held it could, and granted both Shelton and the Company such a water right.

* * * We hold for the objectors, and reverse each judgment and decree.

I.

To comprehend the importance of this lawsuit, it is necessary to understand the Arkansas River and its tributaries.

In 1863 there were virtually no "water-loving" trees along the banks of the river. Their growth was prevented when the great roaming buffalo herds ate the saplings, and the native Indians used most of the timber. In the next 40 years both the buffalo and the Indians were decimated. Phreatophytes (water consuming plants) and cottonwood began to appear along the Arkansas. After the great Pueblo flood of 1921 the river bottom became thickly infested with tamarisk or salt cedar, a highly phreatophytic growth.

Since 1863 all surface flow of the river has been put to beneficial use, until today the Arkansas is greatly over-appropriated. There is not enough flow to satisfy decreed water rights. The phreatophytes have hindered the situation, for they have consumed large quantities of subsurface water which would otherwise have flowed in the stream and been available for decreed use.

In 1940, appellee Shelton bought 500 acres of land on the Arkansas River. Since then, he has cleared two land areas of phreatophytes, and filled in a third marshy area. Shelton claimed he had saved approximately 442 acre-feet of water per year, previously consumed by phreatophytes or lost to evaporation, which is now available for beneficial use. Shelton had 8 previously decreed wells. He asked for the right to augment his previous water rights with the salvaged water, to use during those times when pumping is curtailed by the State Engineer.

The objectors Southeastern Water Conservancy District, and others, moved to dismiss the augmentation application. The motion was denied and trial was held. The lower court awarded Shelton 181.72 acre-feet of water, free from the call of the river. The lower court analogized to the law of accretion, stating that the capture and use by another of water which ordinarily would be lost is not detrimental to prior holders. The decree contained a comprehensive series of safeguards to protect the prior vested interests. * * *

* * *

II.

* * * The issue can be stated very simply: May one who cuts down water-consuming vegetation obtain a decree for an equivalent amount of water for his own beneficial use free from the call of the river?

Appellees state that the Water Right Determination and Administration Act ("the Act"), 1969 Perm.Supp., C.R.S.1963, 148–21–1 et seq. [COLO. REV. STAT. §§ 37–92–101 to 602 (2000)] permits augmentation or substitution of water captured. Those are flexible terms. Thus, appellees feel that the source of water so provided—whether developed or salvaged—is immaterial, so long as prior vested rights are not injured. They insist that but for their actions the salvaged water would have been available to no one, so now they may receive a water right free from the call of prior appropriators, who are in no way harmed. Appellees conclude that their actions provide maximum utilization of water, protect vested rights, and encourage conservation and waste reduction in the water-scarce Arkansas River Valley.

* * *

The objectors assert that the lower court's resolution of the issue does violence to Colorado's firm appropriation doctrine of "first in time—first in right" on which the priority of previous decrees is bottomed. They point out that the existing case law in Colorado, which was not changed by statute, limits the doctrine of "free from call" to waters which are *truly developed and were never part of the river system.* They argue that appellees' claims were not for developed water, and thus must come under the mandates of the priority system. Furthermore, a priority date free from the call of the river will impinge the entire scheme of adjudication of water decrees as required by the Act.

There is no legal precedent squarely in point for either denying or approving these claims. The answer requires consideration of judicial precedent relating to "developed" and "salvaged" water, as well as consideration of the provisions of the Water Act. Also squarely before us is the equally serious question of whether the granting of such a unique water right will encourage denuding river banks everywhere of trees and shrubs which, like the vegetation destroyed in these cases, also consume the river water.

III.

We first consider existing case law. There is no question that one who merely clears out a channel, lines it with concrete or otherwise hastens the flow of water, without adding to the existing water, is not entitled to a decree therefore.

It is equally true and well established in Colorado that one who *adds* to an existing water supply is entitled to a decree affirming the use of such water. Strong evidence is required to prove the addition of the water. Leadville Mine Development Co., *supra*. There are three important situations, analogous to this case, when these rare decrees have been granted.

The first is when one physically transports water from another source, as when the Water Conservancy District transported water from the Frying Pan River basin to the Arkansas River. The second is when one properly captures and stores flood waters. The third is when one finds water within the system, *which would never have normally reached the river or its tributaries*. An example is trapped water artificially produced by draining a mine. Ripley v. Park Center Land & Water Co., 40 Colo. 129, 90 P. 75 (1907). Another example is trapped water in an independent saucepan-type formation composed of impervious shale which prevents the water from escaping. Pikes Peak v. Kuiper, 169 Colo. 309, 455 P.2d 882 (1969).

* * *

Thus, this case law draws a distinction between "developed" and "salvaged" water. Both terms are words of art. Developed implies *new* waters not previously part of the river system. These waters are free from the river call, and are not junior to prior decrees. Salvaged water implies waters in the river or its tributaries (including the aquifer) which ordinarily would go to waste, but somehow are made available for beneficial use. Salvaged waters are subject to call by prior appropriators. We cannot airily waive aside the traditional language of the river, and draw no distinctions between developed and salvaged water. To do so would be to wreak havoc with our water law. Those terms, and others, evolved specifically to tread softly in this state where water is so precious.

The roots of phreatophytes are like a pump. The trees, which did not have to go to court or seek any right, merely "sucked up" the water from prior appropriators. Appellees now take the water from the trees. Therefore, appellees also are continuing to take from the appropriators, but seek a court decree to approve it. They added nothing new; what was there was merely released and put to a different use. To grant appellees an unconditional water right therefor would be a windfall which cannot be allowed, for thirsty men cannot step into the shoes of a "water thief" (the phreatophytes). Senior appropriators were powerless to move on the land of others and destroy the "thief"—the trees and phreatophytes—before they took firm root. They are helpless now to move in and destroy them to fulfill their own decrees. The property (the water) must return from whence it comes—the river—and thereon down the line to those the river feeds in turn.

IV.

Each appellee decree was assigned an historical priority date. However, each decree was nevertheless to be free from the call of the river. In other words, despite a paper date the decree was to be outside the priority system, in derogation of the "first in time—first in right" water theory normally followed in Colorado.

* * *

Appellees would substitute the priority doctrine with a lack of injury doctrine. In Fellhauer v. People, *supra*, we spoke of the future of water law:

" * * * It is implicit * * * that, along with *vested rights,* there shall be *maximum utilization* of the water of this state. As administration of water approaches its second century the curtain is opening upon the new drama of *maximum utilization* and how constitutionally that doctrine can be integrated into the law of *vested rights.* We have known for a long time that the doctrine was lurking in the backstage shadows as a result of the accepted, though oft violated, principle that the right to water does not give the right to waste it." (Emphasis original.)

The Colorado legislature responded to the *Fellhauer* decision and its twin mandates of protecting vested rights and achieving maximum utilization by enacting various amendments to the 1963 Water Right Determination and Administration Act. 1969 Perm.Supp., C.R.S.1963, 148–21–2(1) [COLO. REV. STAT. § 37–92–102 (2000)] is a declaration of policy that all waters in Colorado have been

" * * * declared to be the property of the public, * * *. As incident thereto, it shall be the policy of this state to integrate the appropriation, use and administration of underground water tributary to a stream with the use of surface water, in such a way as to maximize the beneficial use of all of the waters of this state."

* * *

We do not read into the enactment of the post-*Fellhauer* amendments carte-blanche authority to substitute water consumption and raise it to a preferential right.

Beyond question, the Arkansas River is over-appropriated. Water promised has not been water delivered, for there is simply not enough to go around. Thus, the question is not whether prior appropriators are injured *today* by appellees' actions. The injury occurred *long ago,* when the water-consuming trees robbed consumers of water which would have naturally flowed for their use. The harm was real and enormous. The logical implication of the injury standard is that *until senior consumers have been saturated to fulfillment,* any displacement of water from the time and place of their need is harmful to them.

* * *

We arrive at the instant decision with reluctance, as we are loathe to stifle creativity in finding new water supplies, and do wish not to discourage maximized beneficial use of Colorado's water. But there are questions of policy to consider. If new waters can be had by appellees' method, without legislative supervision, there will be perhaps thousands of such super decrees on all the rivers of the state. S.E. Reynolds, State Engineer of New Mexico for many years, pointed out the dangers inherent in this procedure:

" * * * If one ignores the technical difficulty of determining the amount of water salvaged, this proposal, at first blush, might seem reasonable and in the interest of the best use of water and related land resources.

* * *

"On closer scrutiny, it appears that if the water supply of prior existing rights is lost to encroaching phreatophytes and then taken by individuals eradicating the plants the result would be chaos. The doctrine of prior appropriation as we know it would fall—the phreatophytes and then the individual salvaging water would have the best right. Furthermore, if individuals salvaging public water lost to encroaching phreatophytes were permitted to create new water rights where there is no new water, the price of salt cedar jungles would rise sharply. And we could expect to see a thriving, if clandestine, business in salt cedar seed and phreatophyte cultivation."

If these decrees were affirmed, the use of a power saw or a bulldozer would generate a better water right than the earliest ditch on the river. The planting and harvesting of trees to create water rights superior to the oldest decrees on the Arkansas would result in a harvest of pandemonium. Furthermore, one must be concerned that once all plant life disappears, the soil on the banks of the river will slip away, causing irreparable erosion.

* * *

We believe that in this situation unrestrained self-help to a previously untapped water supply would result in a barren wasteland. While we admire the industry and ingenuity of appellees, we cannot condone the removal of water on an *ad hoc,* farm by farm basis. The withdrawal of water must be orderly, and to be orderly it must come under the priority system.

V.

No one on any river would be adverse to a schematic and integrated system of developing this kind of water supply with control and balancing considerations. But to create such a scheme is the work of the legislature, through creation of appropriate district authorities with right of condemnation on a selective basis, not for the courts. Until such time as the legislature responds, actions such as appellees' should not be given court sanction.

Judgments reversed and cause remanded to the trial court with directions to vacate the decrees.

■ GROVES and KELLEY. JJ. specially concur.

■ GROVES, JUSTICE (specially concurring):

* * *

* * * It is earnestly to be hoped that the General Assembly can provide a solution so that this water, now being lost in such large quantities to the phreatophytes may be brought under reasonable control.

I wish to state, however, that, if the General Assembly does not act within a reasonable time in this area, I hope that the matter will be brought to this Court again. Then, in order to carry out the spirit of Fellhauer v. People, 167 Colo. 320, 447 P.2d 986 (1968), and the legislative intent expressed in the 1971 amendments quoted in the opinion, I intend to urge the Court to reverse the opinion and permit persons in the position of the claimants here to take the water. They will not be taking water from holders of decreed rights, but rather from the robbers of the decreed rights—the phreatophytes.

Water lost is water wasted. The judiciary should not sit by forever and permit this to continue, even though its remedies cannot be as equitable as those that surely the legislature can fashion.

■ KELLEY, J. concurs in this opinion.

NOTES

1.   Does the court destroy all incentive for the eradication of water-wasting vegetation? Under what circumstances will phreatophytes be removed? Who enjoys the benefits of their removal? See COLO. REV. STAT. § 37–92–103(9) (2006) for a codification of the *Shelton* rule.

2.   In the principal case Justice Day asserted that maximum utilization of water could only be accomplished by legislative action because of the necessity for long-range planning and ongoing regulation. Faced with the same problem, the Governor's Commission to Review California Water Rights Law proposed that salvagers be required to obtain a permit from the State Water Resources Control Board in order to appropriate salvaged water. The Commission would grant salvagers a right superior to all users along the stream in order to encourage salvage efforts. Governor's Commission to Review California Water Rights Law, Final Report 61 (1978). Presumably the Water Resources Control Board would balance the environmental effect of removing phreatophytes from streams against the production gains before granting the permit. But other problems remain. A proposal to grant salvagers the water they salvage assumes that the amount of water saved can be accurately measured. See Comment, *Phreatophyte Eradication as a Source of Water Rights in Colorado*, 43 U. Colo. L. Rev. 473 (1972).

3.   Although the court seemed concerned about environmental impacts, it later ruled that a water court could not consider evidence of environmental and social impacts when approving allocations of water rights. See *In re Board of County Comm'rs of County of Arapahoe*, 891 P.2d 952 (Colo. 1995).

4.   Given that developed water is not subject to administration by the state engineer, the court has been skeptical of attempts to characterize water in that way. See City of Aurora ex rel. Utility Enterprise v. Colorado State Engineer, 105 P.3d 595 (Colo. 2005) and Ready Mixed Concrete Co. in

Adams County v. Farmers Reservoir and Irrigation Co., 115 P.3d 638 (Colo. 2005).

3.   TRANSFER

Lawrence J. MacDonnell, Transferring Water Uses in the West
43 Okla.L.Rev. 119 (1990).

An important option for supplying changing western water require-ments is to transfer some existing uses of water to new uses. The economic attractiveness of this option is demonstrated by studies indicating a marked disparity in the value of water in many existing uses compared with water's value in alternative uses. And, in fact, water transfers are occurring in the western states. Economists and others have commented, however, that transfers are not occurring as widely as would be suggested by the apparent economic incentives. Some have suggested that the reasons for this less than economically desirable level of transfer activity can be found in legal barriers or impediments that either absolutely prevent transfers or make the transfers so difficult as to dissipate any economic incentives.

* * *

Water rights may be transferred in a variety of ways. There may be a simple transfer of ownership. For example, the sale of irrigated farmlands typically includes the sale of the associated water rights. Generally, the simple change in ownership of a water right does not require state review or approval. Transfers may also involve a change in the existing manner of use, either with or without a change in ownership. Changes such as the point of diversion, place of use, or type of use, normally do require state review.

Legal mechanisms available in the western states for transferring the use of water also are numerous. The traditional approach has been to go through a change-of-water-right proceeding seeking state approval for a proposed change of use of an existing appropriative water right. Commonly, the person with the new use purchases an existing water right for the purpose of making the change of use.

Instead of a permanent shift in ownership of the right, the transfer may be limited to the water itself. Short-term, seasonal leases of water are common throughout the West and typically occur on an informal basis. Longer leases and leases involving a change of water use may have to go through a change-of-use proceeding.

Water rights also may be exchanged in many western states. Normally, exchanges are voluntary arrangements between holders of water rights who find mutual advantages in trading water rights. In recent years, some states have recognized the potential value of allowing involuntary ex-changes under certain circumstances.

* * *

The Origin of Water Transfer Principles

California courts, which were the first to recognize the right to appropriate water, also were the first to consider an appropriator's right to make changes. * * *

The courts of other western states generally accepted California's water transfer principles. Several states enacted legislative provisions specifically authorizing changes in water rights. These provisions required that there be no injury to other water rights and usually established some kind of state review.

Transfers Reconsidered

This initial acceptance of water transfers began to falter as conditions changed and problems arose. * * *As the miners moved from claim to claim they took their water rights with them. When they decided that they had had enough of mining, often the only valuable asset they had was their water rights and the water conveyance systems they had built. Allowing changes and transfers of water rights under such circumstances made * * * sense.

As irrigated agriculture displaced mining as the dominant water use in the West, circumstances changed. Stability became important since patterns of water use in agriculture generally follow regular cycles. Farmers tended not to move the way miners did. And, in the arid West, farmers generally viewed water less as an asset to be bought and sold and more as an integral and permanent part of their lives. The agricultural community created mutual ditch and storage companies and irrigation districts to cooperatively develop the water supply. With the creation of the Bureau of Reclamation in 1902, major water storage and supply projects were built throughout the West with federal financial and technical support. Settlement and development of the West proceeded through the widespread irrigation of arid and semi-arid but cultivatable lands.

* * *

The major issues that arise in transfer cases are the validity of the original right (e.g., has it been abandoned?), the extent of the right—especially the quantity of water historically used, and whether the transfer will cause injury to other water rights. Each of these issues requires considerable technical and, perhaps, legal analysis. * * * Concerns about injury to other rights have been met by limiting the net depletion of the stream following the transfer to the quantity of water historically consumed in the original use. Additional terms and conditions may be added to the transfer approval if necessary to offset injury. * * *

The second type of concern reflected in these state statutes is the treatment of water as a commodity to be traded or sold. Many in the West, including Elwood Mead, have argued that water is a public resource, that its use is intended to serve the broadest possible public good, and that it should not be the basis for private profit except as results from direct beneficial use.[48] Thus, the Arizona Legislature limited those who could hold rights to irrigation water to those owning the lands on which the water was used.

Linked to this concern is the belief that water is an essential part of the community that it serves. Control and use of the resource should be governed by the collective community, not by individual users whose interests may differ from that of the community generally. This view is reflected most clearly in state statutes giving irrigation districts control over the allocation and use of water resources within their boundaries and limiting transfers of water to locations within the district. Protection provided to areas of origin in several states also recognizes this concern.

The Barriers Come Down But ...

In recent years, water transfers have been viewed more favorably in the West. Shifting economic and demographic forces have increased the power of cities which need the water and reduced the relative value of water used for irrigation. Some environmentalists have seized on water transfers as a means of avoiding the need for construction of environmentally damaging dams. Conservatives are attracted to this market-oriented approach for allocating resources.

In 1962, Arizona eliminated its strict appurtenancy requirement and explicitly allowed the transfer of water rights.[54] Wyoming enacted legislation in 1973 expressly authorizing changes in water rights.[55] In 1980, the California Legislature announced a general policy favoring voluntary water transfers.[56] In 1988, the Utah Legislature removed the restrictions against transfers of water outside conservancy district boundaries,[57] and in 1989, the Colorado Legislature allowed the leasing of water outside conservancy district boundaries.[58] Other western states have eliminated restrictions against transfers in recent years as well.[59]

While many of the absolute barriers to transfers are being removed, limitations beyond the traditional no "injurious consequence" rule are being instituted in their place. For example, the Arizona transfers legislation requires the approval of any irrigation district, agricultural improvement district or water users association affected by a transfer.[60] The

48. Mead, Irrigation Institutions 86–87 (1903). An eminent commentator from the eastern United States, Roscoe Pound, noted a trend in this direction in western water law in 1914. Pound, *The End of Law As Developed in Legal Rules and Doctrines*, 27 Harv. L. Rev. 195, 234 (1914).

54. Ariz. Rev. Stat. § 45–172 (1987).

55. Wyo. Stat. § 41–3–104 (1977). Curiously, the Wyoming legislature did not repeal the 1909 statute restricting water right changes.

56. Cal. Water Code § 109(a) (West Supp. 1989).

57. Utah Code Ann. § 73–9–13(3) (Supp.1989).

58. Colo. Rev. Stat. § 37–83–106 (1989).

59. *See, e.g.,* Neb. Rev. Stat. § 46–289 (1984) (authorizing interbasin transfers of water); SB 178, 1989 S.D. Laws (amending S.D. Codified Laws Ann. § 46–5–34.1) (authorizing transfer of irrigation rights to domestic uses on other lands).

60. Ariz. Rev. Stat. Ann. § 45–172(4), (5) (1987). Approval must be obtained if the water is to be transferred from lands within

Wyoming legislation makes transfers potentially subject to review concerning (1) economic losses to the community and the state related to the transfer, (2) the extent to which these economic losses would be offset by benefits from the new use, and (3) the availability of other sources of water.[61] The new California law requires that transfers not "unreasonably" affect either fish, wildlife, or other instream beneficial uses or the economy of the area from which the water is to be transferred.[62] In 1985, the New Mexico Legislature subjected water transfers to a requirement that the transfers not be detrimental to the public welfare.[63] And in 1989, the Utah Supreme Court ruled that water transfers in that state must pass a public interest review.[64]

In short, while there is more general acceptance of water transfers, there is also a trend towards providing protection for an increasingly broad set of interests. The effect of this trend is difficult to assess. Removing barriers at least makes transfers possible. On the other hand, the imposition of limitations and conditions adds to the cost and complexity of making a transfer. Apparently, the West is now entering a period in which additional obligations of transferors will be identified and defined. Increased definition will be required for presently open-ended public interest standards. The increasingly broad set of water-based values will have to be factored into the decision processes governing transfers of water uses. The decision processes themselves may well have to be changed to accommodate consideration of these matters.

ECONOMICS OF WATER TRANSFERS

Clifford T. Lee, The Transfer of Water Rights in California

Governor's Commission to Review California Water Rights Law, Staff Paper No. 5.
5–10 (1977).

I. *Water as a Marketable Resource*

A. *Theory of Equimarginal Value*

Resources have value because they are scarce, in the sense that the quantity demanded exceeds the supply at zero price. Where scarcity exists, it is necessary to develop some method of resource allocation. Economists have commonly posited the economic efficiency objective as a criterion for optimal resource allocation. The theory of equimarginal value asserts that, as a necessary condition of economic efficiency, all users of a resource must derive equal value from the last unit of the resource each user has consumed.

these entities or from the watersheds supplying water for their use.

61. Wyo. Stat. § 41–3–104(a) (1977).

62. Cal. Water Code § 386 (West Supp. 1989).

63. N.M. Stat. Ann. § 72–5–23 (1978).

64. Bonham v. Morgan, [788 P.2d 497 (Utah 1989)].

The value of any unit of water is essentially measured by the maximum amount which the consumer would be willing to pay for that unit. The marginal value is the value of the last unit consumed. For any consumer, the marginal value will ordinarily decline or rise as the quantity of water consumed in any period increases or decreases. Thus, if the marginal value to consumer "A" of one acre-foot of water is $20, and the marginal value to consumer "B" is $10, then both parties would be better off in terms of their own preferences if B sold A one acre-foot of water at some price between $10 and $20. Since B's consumption of water has decreased due to the sale, his marginal value for water will increase (perhaps to $11 an acre-foot). Similarly, since A's consumption has increased, his marginal value for water will decrease (perhaps to $19 an acre-foot). Economists have therefore concluded that the most efficient allocation of water resources requires the eventual equalization of the marginal values of all water consumers.

Water values will vary substantially depending upon the type of water use. The National Water Commission found a wide variation in values among the same uses and between different uses. The Commission therefore recommended the encouragement of water rights transfers in order to reduce such disparities in value.

B. Problems in Application

1. The Theory of the Second Best

As noted, one condition for the optimal allocation of a resource is the equalization of marginal values among the consumers of the resource. Some economists have argued that where the economy does not conform to *all* conditions for optimal resource allocation then a "second best" conformity may not necessarily increase total system efficiency. For example, where all goods and services are not priced at marginal cost, the introduction of marginal cost pricing in one sector of the economy might worsen the allocation of the resources. The obvious implication of the theory of the second best is that piecemeal efforts to achieve system efficiency may not be desirable.

Commentators on the theory of the second best have noted that the theory assumes an interdependent economic system. However, economic optimization in some broad sector of the economy may be justified where the outputs and relative prices have negligible repercussion in the rest of the economy. The same argument would apply where a geographical area has tenuous economic links with the rest of the economy. Furthermore, where deviations from the conditions of optimal allocation are initially large in the free sectors of the economy and relatively small in the restrained sectors, then movement towards optimalization in the free sectors may still be desirable.

Finally, regardless of its impact on total system efficiency, the theory of the second best does not impair gains achieved by individual parties who seek to improve their position through private transfers. The reallocation of water so as to equalize marginal values will still increase the total value productivity of that water.

2.   *Externalities, Spillover Effects and Third Party Effects*

An economic externality occurs where actions by one individual or a group of individuals affect outside parties because of a failure in markets. The market process fails because it does not cause the individual whose action results in an externality to adjust his behavior in accordance with the consequences. Thus, a private transaction imposes costs or benefits upon a third person who has not been party to the bargaining process.

For example, a paper mill that discharges untreated effluent into a river imposes costs that are not internalized in its transactions with paper purchasers. These wildlife, fishery and recreational losses are examples of negative externalities. On the other hand, the improvement by a private landowner of his property will commonly enhance the value of his neighbor's property. This increase in property value is an example of a positive externality.

It is also important to distinguish between technological externalities and pecuniary externalities. Most commentators agree that one should only consider the impact of technological externalities when evaluating the efficiency of any particular transfer. Technological externalities impose actual losses or gains on the productive capacity of society. The externality affects the actual, physical output or satisfaction that a third party producer or consumer can get from his physical inputs. For example, flooding agricultural land in order to operate a dam imposes actual, physical losses in the productive capacity of agriculture.

Pecuniary externalities, on the other hand, do not change the real productive capacity of society. Instead, the gains or losses suffered by the third parties occur through changes in prices. For example, the reservoir created by the new dam may increase recreational opportunities thereby reducing the existing gains of private recreation facility operators that service any neighboring reservoirs.

A discussion of water rights transfers requires consideration of externality theory because water rights transfers commonly affect third parties. A transfer by an upstream user outside of the watershed may reduce the return flow available to downstream users. Pumping by an overlying landowner for purposes of export to nonoverlying land may affect the availability of groundwater to adjacent landowners. Equalization of private marginal values through transfers would not, in such situations, meet the efficiency objective. The water transfer prices would not properly reflect the costs or the benefits imposed upon third parties. If external costs or benefits are created by these transfers, unadjusted prices would be too low or too high and the number of transfers would be too great or too small.

NOTE: TRANSACTION COSTS

In theory, water transfers can be highly beneficial. Lee discussed the question of externalities. Partly because of those externalities, one must consider the question of transaction costs—the expenses that are incurred reaching and implementing a bargain. One reason that transaction costs can be considerable in water transfers is that the sale of a water right is not as simple as the sale of a car or even a parcel of land. The external impacts can arouse opposition and at least necessitate the involvement of multiple parties in a transaction. The transaction costs may include fees for lawyers, engineers, government permits, and for obtaining needed data and other information. The transaction costs of water transfers were examined in a six-state study of transfers by Dr. MacDonnell. The study found:

> The case studies of transactions costs in Colorado and New Mexico suggest average costs in the range of $200 to $380 per acre-foot of water transferred. There appear to be significant scale economies so that the transfer of larger amounts of water results in lower per-acre-foot costs. The data also show that third party opposition to the transfer increased the acre-foot costs. The average transactions costs found in the Colorado sample of cases were considerably higher than those in New Mexico. This finding corresponds to the findings that the decision time in New Mexico is markedly less than in Colorado and that many fewer cases are protested in New Mexico than in Colorado. However, the average transactions costs in New Mexico appear to have increased dramatically from 1975 to 1987.

> Additional study is necessary to determine the effect of these costs on water rights transfer activity. The New Mexico data show that most applications incur relatively low transaction costs.

Lawrence J. MacDonnell et al., The Water Transfer Process as a Management Option for Meeting Changing Water Demand, vol. I, 68 (1990).

The operation of a free market in water rights has been impeded by several practical difficulties and legal requirements that impose transaction costs. They include:

(1) Junior water rights in return flow must be protected. This rule is applied in all western states; it is likely to continue to be applied for both constitutional and political reasons.

(2) Inadequacy of records and poor administration of water rights. Records of water rights are inadequate in two respects: some rights to use water do not appear of record and some claims that do appear are not legally enforceable because of abandonment or forfeiture. Moreover, administration of rights is sometimes inept; states often provide inadequate funds for professional water rights administration.

(3) Legal and institutional restrictions. Today, absolute legal prohibitions on transfers are few. Costly review procedures and restrictions remain. The Bureau of Reclamation, whose projects distribute about 20% of the water used in the West, mostly for irrigation, has several legal and policy restrictions that inhibit transfers. In addition, states increasingly impose restrictions on, or require review of, transactions to ensure that third parties are protected.

The No–Injury Rule

Since the earliest decisions under the appropriation doctrine, courts have allowed changes of use only if no injury will result to other users. *E.g.*, McDonald v. Bear River and Auburn Water & Min. Co., 13 Cal. 220 (1859). Protection of "rights of others" in cases dealing with transfers or changes of use benefits junior appropriators, since senior appropriators have a prior call on the stream in any event. Ordinarily, the portion of an irrigation right equivalent to the amount of water consumed in the irrigation process is transferable. Juniors often depend on the amount not consumed to satisfy their rights.

A good ball-park figure for irrigation efficiency in the West is 50%. Thus, half of water diverted and turned onto the land is consumed by evapotranspiration, and the other half returns to the hydrologic cycle as return flow to a surface stream, as recharge to a groundwater aquifer, or as evaporation.

Why should junior appropriators be protected? The answer lies in history, economic policy, and common ideas of justice or good policy. Most direct flow rights were created in the nineteenth century. A farmer settled on land and diverted water from a nearby stream to irrigate it. The farmer did not know, and had no way of knowing, whether the water flowing in the river was return flow or original snow melt. The economic policy was to encourage investment. To promote this policy, rules were adopted that maintained the status quo—that gave legal security in the supply upon which the investment was predicated. Lastly, the long persistence of a state of affairs gives rise to expectations that it will continue in the future. While the law certainly does not always fulfill these expectations, it is not unusual for it to do so when investments have been made based on them.

Suppose A Canal Co. obtained an appropriative right on Clear River in 1867 to divert 20 cfs of water during a growing season of 120 days. The annual diversion right would be approximately 4,800 acre-feet. Thereafter, B Canal Co., knowing these facts, obtained a right for its downstream ditch to 10 cfs. Though B does not know it, 10 cfs return to the stream from A's diversion, and this return flow enters the stream above B's headgate. A proposes to sell its water right to Center City, which plans to move the point of diversion to an intake below B's canal. If A can move all 20 cfs, B will have no water supply when the flow of the river at A's old point of diversion is just 20 cfs. Center City could require the 20 cfs to bypass B's headgate, thus depriving B of the return flow from the old diversion. Such a transfer is not permitted; only A's consumptive use of 10 cfs may be transferred, leaving 10 cfs to substitute for the return flow. Our explanation of this rule is that B's expectations would be drastically upset if it lost the 10 cfs represented by return flow and that upsetting such expectations would not only strain the social fabric but would deter investment in partially developed streams. Hence courts and legislatures protect B.

Consider how junior appropriators' rights could be impaired in the following cases: (a) An upstream senior hydroelectric power appropriator proposes to make a transbasin diversion at the power dam site; (b) A downstream senior irrigator is supplied by return flow from a junior and the senior wishes to move its point of diversion upstream, above the junior; (c) A senior irrigator with a diversion right of 20 cfs from May to September wishes to build a reservoir and store 20 cfs continuous flow from May to September.

Green v. Chaffee Ditch Co.

Supreme Court of Colorado, 1962.
150 Colo. 91, 371 P.2d 775.

■ MOORE, JUSTICE.

* * *

Lydia Hoffman Morrison and her brother Milton Coy Hoffman are the owners of seventy-two acres of land along the bank of the river. In the water adjudication of April 11, 1882, under priority No. 13, * * * approximately 16 c.f.s., is owned by Morrison and Hoffman. They entered into a contract to sell to the city of Fort Collins 8 c.f.s. of this water, and the city requests permission to change the point of diversion thirteen miles upstream. Numerous protests were filed to the requested change. These protests contain the assertion that Morrison and Hoffman did not own 16 c.f.s., and that if any such water rights had ever existed they had been abandoned.

The trial court entered findings which, in pertinent part, contain the following:

"That the land owned by said petitioners, Milton Coy Hoffman and Lydia Hoffman Morrison, irrigated by said water is seventy-two acres along the river bottom, the Cache La Poudre River dividing said land. That the top soil is a sandy loam and varies in thickness from about five feet to a few inches and is underlain with coarse gravel, which in some places comes to the surface. That because of the soil conditions and the proximity to the river, all water applied to said land, not consumed by plant life and evaporation, returns to the river within a very short time and again becomes a part of the river and available to other appropriators. That the amount of water necessarily consumed by plant life to produce a maximum crop, in addition to natural rainfall, is * * * one and one-fourth acre feet of water for each acre irrigated, thus requiring 90 acre feet of water each year for the proper irrigation of said land. That the efficiency of water on this particular land is 25%, requiring the application to this land of 360 acre feet of water during each irrigating season to produce maximum crops. That in addition to the 90 acre feet of water consumed on this land, five acre feet are lost by evaporation and seepage while the water is in transit from the headgate of the Coy Ditch to the Hoffman–Morrison farm, making a total consumptive use of 95 acre feet of water each year. That the only domestic use of this water has been a small amount for the watering of livestock. That the irrigating season on this land has been from April 15th to October 15th of each year.

"That the City of Fort Collins, during the period from April 15th and October 15th of each year has an average return flow through its sewage disposal plant, storm sewers and other sources of 50% of the water taken in at its intake pipeline.

"That for many years last past, and ever since the entry of the original adjudication Decree, the petitioners Milton Coy Hoffman and Lydia Hoffman Morrison and their predecessors in title and interest have never beneficially used at any one time more than eight cubic feet of water per second of time for the irrigation of the lands now owned by them. Any diversions by petitioners or others in excess of that amount were a subterfuge and not made in good faith.

"That any diversion of water from said priority from October 16th of any year to April 14th, inclusive, of the following year, except for livestock purposes, would injuriously affect the storage rights of protestants, or some one or more of them, as they have historically depended upon the filling of their storage decrees during said time."

* * *

The court decreed inter alia that:

"No diversion from Priority No. 13 awarded to the Coy Ditch can be transferred without injury to junior appropriators, except under the conditions herein set forth, and any transfer of water, heretofore beneficially used, must be upon condition that the land heretofore irrigated must be forever deprived of irrigation water from this Decree, and cannot be a transfer of water not needed or beneficially used.

"That there can be diverted from the headgate of the Coy Ditch to the headgate of the City of Fort Collins pipeline without injury to the protestants, that amount of water which, when the return flow from the City sewage plant and other sources is considered, permits the City to consumptively use 95 acre feet of water during the irrigating season. Therefore, under the foregoing findings, the City should be permitted to divert 190 acre feet of water during each irrigation season under the conditions that the City at no time shall divert more than eight cubic feet of water per second of time * * *."

* * * There is an abundance of evidence establishing the fact that at no time has an amount of water in excess of 8 c.f.s. been applied to beneficial use on the seventy-two acres of land involved. * * *

* * * Actually they had contracted to sell to the city all the water which they could lawfully have used at any time. Under the specific findings of the trial court that no more than 8 c.f.s. was ever applied to beneficial use, that volume of water was the full measure of the water right acquired.

* * *

[Dismissing the petitioners' contentions, the court said:] * * * Applicable and controlling rules concerning these contentions are to be found in the opinion of this court in Farmers Highline Canal and Reservoir Company, et al., v. City of Golden, et al., 129 Colo. 575, 272 P.(2d) 629. From that opinion we re-state basic concepts which require an affirmance of the judgment in the instant action. The case cited was one involving an application for change in the point of diversion of water. It was there held:

* * *

(2) "It is recognized that water is a property right, subject to sale and conveyance, and that under proper conditions not only may the point of diversion be changed, but likewise the manner of use. It further is recognized that such change may be permitted, by proper court decree, only in such instances as it is specifically shown that the rights of other users from the same source are not injuriously affected by such change, and that the burden of proof thereof rests upon petitioner.

* * *

(4) "Equally well established, as we have repeatedly held, is the principle that junior appropriators have vested rights in the continuation of stream conditions as they existed at the time of their respective appropriations, and that subsequent to such appropriations they may successfully resist all proposed changes in points of diversion and use of water from that source which in any way materially injures or adversely affects their rights. * * *

(5) "All appropriations of water, and all decrees determining the respective rights of users, regardless of whether specific mention be made therein, are subject to all constitutional and statutory provisions and restrictions designed for the protection of junior appropriators from the same stream. * * * "

We think the following language contained in the opinion in the case cited is pertinent to the issues in the instant case:

"Petitioner contends, however, that it is entirely within the right of an appropriator of water to enlarge upon his use, and now that the City of Golden is the owner, it may enlarge upon the use to the extent of the entire decree. Counsel for petitioner here confuse two altogether different principles. This doctrine even on behalf of an original appropriator, may be applied only to the extent of use contemplated at the time of appropriation. It has no application whatever to a situation where a decree is sought for change of point of diversion or use. There the right is strictly limited to the extent of former actual usage. 'The right to change the point of diversion is, of course, nonetheless a qualified right because petitioner acquired it by purchase.' Fort Lyon Co. v. Rocky Ford Co., 79 Colo. 511, 515, 246 Pac. 781.

* * *

" * * * Where the entire amount fixed by the decree was reasonably required in the proper irrigation of the lands to which first applied, then the whole priority properly may be changed for similar usage; but where such irrigation did not require the entire volume of the decree, then only that portion may be changed which previously had been necessary for proper irrigation. It is not a question of whether the amount of water decreed was adequate, but whether it was excessive. The extent of needed use in original location is the criterion in considering change of point of diversion. This, of course, is premised upon the assumption that whatever of the decreed water was not properly used remained in the stream.

* * *

"Where it appears that the change sought to be made will result in depletion to the source of supply and result in injury to junior appropriators therefrom, the decree should contain such conditions as are proper to counteract the loss, and should be denied only in such instances as where it is impossible to impose reasonable conditions to effectuate this purpose."

We conclude that the trial court determined the issues in the instant case in a manner consistent with the foregoing principles, and find no error requiring a reversal of the judgment. There was no abuse of discretion in the assessment of costs.

The judgment accordingly is affirmed.

NOTES

1.   The court in *Green* limits the amount of water that may be transferred to a maximum quantity (acre-feet) and rate of diversion (cubic feet per second). Evidence showed the amount of water needed for crops and the amount transferable accordingly was specified in terms of the quantity that may be consumed (95 acre-feet) and the quantity that may be diverted (190 acre-feet if there will be a 50% return flow as Fort Collins proposed). These amounts were based on evidence concerning the consumption needs of crops from the kind of soils on the Hoffman farm and estimated transit losses for the ditch in question. The maximum rate at which the water could be taken (8 cfs) was based on evidence that this was the maximum historical rate of diversion based on actual records. Water lawyers are generally familiar with these terms and calculations. A table of the equivalents is found in Appendix A at the end of the book.

Sophisticated formulae may be required to determine crop demand. For instance, the Blaney–Criddle formula is frequently used for calculating crop consumptive use requirements. Essentially, the formula considers such factors as mean monthly temperature, length of day, and available moisture to determine monthly consumptive water requirements. The formula is most useful where little or no data, except climatological, may be available. The authors of the formula explain it in Harry F. Blaney &

Wayne D. Criddle, *Determining Water Requirements for Settling Water Disputes,* 4 Nat. Resources J. 29 (1964). More precise methodologies, such as the Penman Monteith formula, are available for estimating crop water demand and evapotranspiration. They tend to be data intensive and thus expensive. Use of such formulae requires engineering and other expertise. For an explanation of the Penman–Monteith formula, see Crop–evapotranspiration–Guidelines for computing crop water requirements, FAO Irrigation and Drainage Paper 56, Chapter 2, Food and Agriculture Organization of the United Nations, Rome (1998).

When a change of use issue reaches the courtroom, the parties typically hire their own experts to help them prove their contentions. In *Green,* for example, the court relied on expert testimony to find that, although Hoffman and Morrison thought they had sold only half of their water right, they had, in fact, sold all the water to which they were entitled.

Where adversarial experts are permitted, they add considerably to the cost of a change of use or transfer. In Colorado, where no binding or presumptively correct determination of how much water may be transferred is made by a state agency or official, cases typically can involve multiple experts. Parties are obliged to hire them or risk loss of their rights. In one change of use case, the Colorado Supreme Court concluded: "The petitioners presented expert witnesses who testified that the junior appropriators would not be injured by the proposed change. The protestants produced no expert testimony. * * * [The protestants] did not meet their burden of going forward with the evidence." CF & I Steel Corp. v. Rooks, 178 Colo. 110, 495 P.2d 1134, 1136 (1972).

2. There are several methods of determining historical beneficial use. In City of Westminster v. Church, 167 Colo. 1, 445 P.2d 52 (1968), a change in point of diversion of a decreed right was limited to the amount historically diverted, despite a finding of nonabandonment of the originally decreed right in connection with an earlier change in point of diversion. The court examined average annual diversions over a twenty-one year period to determine that the amount of water historically used was less than the "paper right." In diversions involving pumping, courts or agencies sometimes examine electricity bills.

3. A wide variety of "changes" in a water right may be subject to the no injury rule. Colorado has the most detailed list. COLO. REV. STAT. § 37–92–103(5) (2006) defines "change of water right" as:

> * * * a change in the type, place, or time of use, a change in the point of diversion, a change from a fixed point of diversion to alternate or supplemental points of diversion, a change from alternate or supplemental points of diversion to a fixed point of diversion, a change in the means of diversion, a change in the place of storage, a change from direct application to storage and subsequent application, a change from storage and subsequent application to direct application, a change from a fixed place of storage to alternate places of storage, a change from alternate places of storage to a fixed place of storage, or any combination of such changes.

The term also includes changes of conditional water rights. The statute further provides that changes in water rights shall not "injuriously affect the owner of or persons entitled to use water under a vested water right or a decreed conditional water right." COLO. REV. STAT. § 37–92–305(3) (2006). Note that a change in point of return (of "waste water" or "return flow") is not listed. Other states apply the no injury limitation to less sharply defined categories of change. See, *e.g.*, NEV. REV. STAT. ANN. § 533.345 (Michie 2006); OR. REV. STAT. § 540.520 (2005); WYO. STAT. ANN. § 41–3–104 (2007).

When the type of use changes, say from agricultural to municipal as in *Green*, the time of use may also change; irrigation is seasonal while municipal use is year-around. As with other changes, the responsible agency or court must either condition the change or deny it in order to avoid injury to other water users who would be deprived of uses they had established during the times of the year when the changed use would occur. The Washington Supreme Court approved changing a water right from seasonal domestic, stockwatering, and irrigation uses to all-year resort uses. It upheld limiting the quantity of water that could be taken to about two-thirds of the historical use because the rights historically had not been used in the winter. R.D. Merrill Co. v. State, Pollution Control Hearings Bd., 137 Wash.2d 118, 969 P.2d 458 (1999). Under what circumstances does it make sense to limit the overall amount of water that can be taken under the right rather than the timing of diversions?

4.   Some change applications may be so ambitious and vague that they run afoul of the bias in western water law against speculation, discussed *supra* at p. 179. In High Plains A & M, LLC v. Southeastern Colo. Water Conservancy Dist., 120 P.3d 710 (Colo. 2005), the application sought a change in water rights from irrigation to more than fifty possible uses in any of twenty-eight counties. The water court balked at what it considered an application for a "new" water right, and denied it as speculative. The supreme court affirmed, holding "as a basic predicate of an application for a decree changing the type and place of use, that the applicant will sufficiently demonstrate an actual beneficial use to be made at an identified location or locations under the change decree, if issued." Id. At 714.

5.   In Basin Electric Power Co-op. v. State Bd. of Control, 578 P.2d 557 (Wyo.1978), the court explained how the historical beneficial use requirement and the concept of abandonment, see *infra* pp. 259–265, both flow from the doctrine of beneficial use:

> We have previously said that the water right of an appropriator is limited to beneficial use, even though a larger amount has been adjudicated. The decreed amount of water may be prima facie evidence of an appropriator's entitlement, but such evidence may be rebutted by showing actual historic beneficial use. Beneficial use is not a concept which is considered only at the time an appropriation is obtained. The concept represents a continuing obligation which must be satisfied in order for the appropriation to remain viable. The state's abandonment statutes are recognition of this requirement. * * *

In other words, the amount of water originally decreed or disclosed in a water permit is not necessarily the amount which may be transferred to a new place of use. In Colorado, at least, the amount which may be transferred is limited to the "Duty of Water," which is defined as the amount reasonably required for proper irrigation under the original appropriation. Contra, *W.S. Ranch Company v. Kaiser Steel Corporation*, 79 N.M. 65, 439 P.2d 714 (1968), where the change-in-use petitioner was allowed to transfer the entire amount of the decreed water right regardless of subsequent actual beneficial use.

The key to understanding the application of beneficial-use concepts to a change-of-use proceeding is a recognition that the issues of nonuse and misuse are inextricably interwoven with the issues of change of use and change in the place of use. This is true even without the formal initiation of abandonment proceedings under the statutes. If an appropriator, either by misuse or failure to use, has effectively abandoned either all or part of his water right through noncompliance with the beneficial-use requirements imposed by law, he could not effect a change of use or place of use for that amount of his appropriation which had been abandoned.

578 P.2d at 563–65.

6. An appropriator has a right to divert 150 acre-feet of water per year to irrigate a particular field. For thirty years the appropriator has grown alfalfa in the field, which has only consumed 50 acre-feet per year. The appropriator decides to plant rice in the field instead. For proper irrigation the rice will consume 100 acre-feet of water per year. Read the excerpt from *Farmers Highline Canal*, quoted *supra* at p. 240. Does the "no injury" rule announced there prevent the original appropriator from "enlarging" on the consumptive use to the full extent of the decree if there is no change in the purpose (agriculture) or the place of use? If the purpose of the no injury rule is to protect expectations of juniors, does allowing this increased consumption make sense? Would you recommend that your alfalfa-growing client, who anticipates future sales of water rights, switch to rice?

Orr v. Arapahoe Water and Sanitation District

Supreme Court of Colorado, 1988.
753 P.2d 1217.

■ QUINN, CHIEF JUSTICE.

This case involves the interpretation of a 1969 decree * * * which changed the points of diversion of certain decreed water rights from surface ditches to wells. In 1981, the applicants * * * sought a change in use from irrigation to municipal purposes. The water court granted the application, but interpreted the 1969 decree to limit the new points of diversion to the amount of water historically used at the original decreed points of diversion. We affirm the judgment of the water court.

I.

A summary of the factual and procedural history of this case is necessary to an understanding of the issues raised in this appeal. In 1950, the Dixon family acquired the Diamond Over D Ranch located approximately two and one-half miles northwest of Parker, Colorado. The deed to the ranch also conveyed to the Dixons [water rights to about 12 c.f.s. from Cherry Creek that had been decreed in 1883 and 1890 to four ditches with appropriation dates of 1862, 1869, 1880 and 1885]. * * * From the time of these decrees until the mid–1930s, the water rights had been used to irrigate portions of the property which would eventually comprise the Diamond Over D Ranch. In the mid–1930s, Cherry Creek flooded and destroyed the headgates of the ditches and portions of the ditches as well. The headgates were never reconstructed, and the property was not again irrigated until after the Dixon family purchased the land in 1950.

* * * By 1963, Diamond Over D Ranch, Inc. had drilled seven irrigation wells on the property through which it diverted water pursuant to the water rights originally decreed to the four ditches. In 1969, Diamond Over D Ranch, Inc. filed a petition in the District Court of Douglas County to change the points of diversion from the four ditches to the seven wells. A hearing was held on the petition on November 10, 1969. Lester Dixon, Jr., vice president of Diamond Over D Ranch, Inc., testified at the hearing that subsequent to the drilling of the wells the Dixon family had used the wells to divert water pursuant to the water rights originally decreed to the ditches, and had done so continuously and without objection from other water users. There was also testimony from a water engineer that a decree changing the points of diversion would have no adverse impact on other appropriators because diverting water through the wells would be the same as diverting water through the ditches. No evidence was presented at the 1969 hearing concerning the amount of land actually irrigated or the amount of water consumptively used in irrigating the land either through the ditches or the wells.

* * *

* * * After finding that a decree changing the points of diversion would not injuriously affect the vested water rights of others, the court granted the decree changing the points of diversion * * *.

Diamond Over D Ranch, Inc. was dissolved in 1972 and undivided interests in the land and the water rights were conveyed to Lester Dixon, Jr., Joann Dixon Morrow, and Bruce Dixon. In 1979, the three Dixons entered into a contract to sell the land and water rights to Castlewood Corporation. The contract required Castlewood to purchase the land and the water rights in increments. As each increment was purchased, Castlewood Corporation sold the land and water rights to James Orr, Cogito N. V., and Erwin Interests, Inc., and they in turn sold it to Cottonwood Water and Sanitation District, which had been formed to provide water and sewer service to the lands formerly comprising the Diamond Over D Ranch.

In 1981, the applicants filed the present proceeding seeking, *inter alia*, a determination with respect to a change of water rights from irrigation to municipal uses for the seven wells which were diverting water pursuant to the 1969 decree. Several parties filed statements of opposition to the application, including the State Engineer and various water and sanitation districts. The water judge referred the application to a water referee, and a hearing was held before the referee in November and December, 1981. It was the applicants' position that the 1969 decree changing the points of diversion from the ditches to the wells confirmed the method and extent of irrigation practiced from 1956 to 1979 by the Dixons and Diamond Over D Ranch, Inc. as being a proper exercise of the water rights originally decreed to the four ditches and then transferred to the seven wells. In keeping with this position, Lester Dixon, Jr., testified that from 1956 to 1979 the Dixons and the family corporation diverted water through the wells to irrigate at least 310 acres of land used as a feedlot operation for raising steers. The parties agreed, pursuant to an oral stipulation, that the actual consumptive use of water from the seven wells was 682 acre feet per year.

It was the position of the objectors, however, that the 1969 decree changing the points of diversion had the effect of transferring to the wells the amount of water consumptively used through the ditches when the ditches were active. The objectors presented evidence that this amount of water was 282.8 acre feet per year. The applicants declined to present any evidence concerning the irrigation practices under the ditches, claiming that the 1969 decree changing the points of diversion was res judicata on their right to divert 682 acre feet of water per year to irrigate the 310 acres of land used in the feedlot operation.

The referee interpreted the 1969 decree as "transferring to the wells the irrigation practice as it existed when the ditches were active," and relied for that interpretation on the following language from the 1969 decree:

> The modifications in the points of diversion, if granted, will result in no change in the place or type of use of water; the rights will continue to be used for the *irrigation of land*s of the Petitioner [Diamond Over D Ranch, Inc.] *which have been historically irrigated by use of said rights.*

* * *

In approving the application for a change in use from irrigation to municipal purposes, the referee ruled that, since the applicants owned a half interest in the water rights decreed to the three ditches from which there had been a consumptive use of 282.8 acre feet per year, the applicants were entitled to withdraw 141 acre feet of water annually through the wells for municipal purposes, based on the priority dates applicable to the ditches * * *

* * *

Since there was no indication in the 1969 proceeding of any "fractional interest" in any of the wells, the water court ruled that paragraph 2B of the 1969 decree was intended to authorize Diamond Over D Ranch, Inc. to divert an amount of water commensurate with its interest "under the surface decrees" as "limited to the historic use under the earlier surface decrees." The court concluded that "diversions will be measured by the historic use of the original decrees rather than what appears to be a somewhat expanded use of it that was taken under the wells," and, accordingly, affirmed the ruling of the referee which limited the applicants to 141 acre feet of water per year from the seven Diamond Over D Wells for municipal purposes.

The applicants then filed this appeal. They initially argue that the water court erred in interpreting the 1969 decree as limiting the amount of water that could be diverted at the new points of diversion to the amount historically used at the original decreed points of diversion. According to the applicants, the water court should have interpreted the 1969 decree as confirming the method and extent of irrigation practiced by the Dixons and the family corporation from 1956 to 1979, which resulted in the diversion through the wells and the consumptive use of 682 acre feet of water per year to irrigate 310 acres of land. The applicants next argue that the 1969 decree is res judicata on their right to withdraw 682 acre feet of water per year from the seven wells.

II.

It has long been the rule in Colorado that if a decree is susceptible of more than one interpretation, one of which is consistent with applicable legal principles and the others of which are inconsistent with those principles, we obviously must choose that interpretation which accords with controlling legal norms. * * *

* * * Before the water court may grant an application for a change in the point of diversion, the applicant must demonstrate that the proposed change will not injuriously affect the vested rights of other water users.[4] Junior appropriators have a vested right to the continuation of stream conditions as they existed at the time of their appropriations, with the result that an application for a change in the point of diversion is always subject to the limitation that such change not injure the rights of junior appropriators. *City of Westminster v. Church*, 167 Colo. 1, 11–12, 445 P.2d 52, 58–59 (1968); *Farmers Highline Canal & Reservoir Co.*, 129 Colo. at

---

4. Section 37–92–305(3), 15 C.R.S. (1973), sets forth the standard by which an application seeking a change in point of diversion must be evaluated:

A change of water right or plan for augmentation, including water exchange project, shall be approved if such change or plan will not injuriously affect the owner of or persons entitled to use water under a vested water right or a decreed conditional water right. If it is determined that the proposed change or plan as presented in the application would cause such injurious effect, the referee or the water judge, as the case may be, shall afford the applicant or any person opposed to the application an opportunity to propose terms or conditions which would prevent such injurious effect. * * *

579–80, 272 P.2d at 631–32; *Enlarged Southside Irrigation Ditch Co. v. John's Flood Ditch Co.*, 116 Colo. 580, 586, 183 P.2d 552, 554–55 (1947).

In order to provide protection to the rights of other appropriators, especially to those junior in priority, several limitations are read into every decree by implication. *E.g., Rominiecki v. McIntyre Livestock Corp.*, 633 P.2d 1064, 1067 (Colo.1981); *Weibert v. Rothe Brothers, Inc.*, 618 P.2d 1367, 1371–72 (1980); *Farmers Highline Canal & Reservoir Co.* One such limitation is that "diversions are limited to an amount sufficient for the purpose for which the appropriation was made, even though such limitation may be less than the decreed rate of diversion." *Rominiecki.* An appropriator, therefore, "has no right as against a junior appropriator to divert more water than can be used beneficially, or to extend the time of diversion to irrigate lands other than those for which the appropriation was made." Id. Nor may a senior appropriator, as against a junior appropriator, lend, rent, or sell any excess water after completing the irrigation of the land for which the water was appropriated. *Enlarged Southside Irrigation Ditch Co.*

Similarly, the right to change a point of diversion is limited in quantity by historical use at the original decreed point of diversion. *Weibert.* " 'Historical use' as a limitation on the right to change a point of diversion has been considered to be an application of the principle that junior appropriators have vested rights in the continuation of stream conditions as they existed at the time of their respective appropriations." Id. at 317, 618 P.2d at 1372. Thus, a senior appropriator is not entitled to enlarge the historical use of a water right by changing the point of diversion and then diverting from the new location the full amount of water decreed to the original point of diversion, even though the historical use at the original point of diversion might have been less than the decreed rate of diversion. As this court succinctly stated in *The New Cache LaPoudre Irrigation Co. v. The Water Supply and Storage Co.*, 49 Colo. 1, 7, 111 P. 610, 612 (1910):

> [A]n order permitting a change in the point of diversion to be made does not, and cannot, in any way enlarge the right of its recipient by conferring upon him power to divert a greater quantity of water from the stream than he theretofore took, or to use it for a greater length of time than he was previously entitled to.

III.

We turn now to the applicants' claim that the water court erred in not interpreting the 1969 decree as confirming the method and extent of irrigation practiced by the Dixons and the family corporation which resulted in a consumptive use of 682 acre feet of water per year. Contrary to the applicants' claim, we are satisfied that long standing principles of Colorado water law relating to a change in the point of diversion fully support the water court's ruling in this case.

The 1969 decree changing the points of diversion limited the amount of water that could be diverted through the seven wells, the new points of diversion, to that same amount historically diverted through the four ditches, the original decreed points of diversion. The fact that the 1969 decree did not expressly limit the well diversions to the amount of water historically diverted through the ditches is not controlling, since such a limitation is read into every water decree by implication.

* * *

IV.

We turn finally to the applicants' claim of res judicata. The applicants argue that the doctrine of res judicata prevents any inquiry into the historical use of the water rights originally decreed to the four ditches. We find this argument devoid of merit.

The applicants' argument is based on the erroneous assumption that the 1969 decree confirmed the Dixons' and the family corporation's consumptive use of 682 acre feet of water pumped through well diversion from 1956 to 1979. As previously discussed, the 1969 decree impliedly limited diversions through the wells to the amount which had been originally decreed to the four ditches, as further limited by the historical use at the original decreed points of diversion, and the water court's ruling in this case was a proper construction of that decree in light of controlling principles of Colorado law.

* * *

The judgment is accordingly affirmed.

NOTES

1. The right to change a point of diversion is also limited in quantity to the duty of water with respect to the original decreed place of use. Weibert v. Rothe Brothers, Inc., 200 Colo. 310, 618 P.2d 1367, 1371 (1980). The duty of water was defined in Farmers Highline Canal & Reservoir Co. v. City of Golden, 129 Colo. 575, 272 P.2d 629, 634 (1954), as follows:

> It is that measure of water, which, by careful management and use, without wastage, is reasonably required to be applied to any given tract of land for such period of time as may be adequate to produce therefrom a maximum amount of such crops as ordinarily are grown thereon. It is not a hard and fast unit of measurement, but is variable according to conditions.

> The historical use of a water right could very well be less than the duty of water if, for example, it was physically impossible in the past to divert water at the optimum rate on a continuing basis. *Weibert*, 618 P.2d at 1372. In such a case, diversions at the new point of diversion would necessarily be limited in quantity to the historical use at the original point of diversion.

2. The limitation that restricts transfers to historical consumptive use exists primarily to protect juniors, though it may also be applied to carry out policies related to overall stream management. In *Basin Electric Power Co-op. v. State Bd. of Control, supra* p. 243, plaintiff had requested a change in type of use and point of diversion of water rights it had acquired from a former agricultural user. The land on which the water had been used straddled a geographical divide. Water used on only 20% of the land returned to the Laramie River (from which it had been withdrawn); the rest of the irrigation was across the divide in a geologically closed basin, and return flows stayed there. Plaintiff, a power company, claimed a right to use all the water diverted by the former user which had not historically returned to the Laramie River. A Wyoming statute stated that a change would be allowed:

> * * * provided that the quantity of water transferred by the granting of the petition shall not exceed the amount of water historically diverted under the existing use, nor exceed the historic rate of diversion under the existing use, nor increase the historic amount consumptively used under the existing use, nor decrease the historic amount of return flow, nor in any manner injure other lawful appropriators.

WYO. REV. STAT. § 41–3–104(a) (2007). The plaintiff claimed that the prohibition of injury to other appropriators was the main purpose of the statute, and that it was therefore entitled to make a change in use so long as other appropriators were not injured. The court rejected that contention, and concluded that "the statute forecloses anyone desiring to effect a change of use from transferring more water than has been historically consumptively used, regardless of the injury or lack thereof to other appropriators." The court found that the closed-basin return flows were not consumptive uses, and thus could not be transferred.

3. The rule established in *Orr* was further clarified in Farmers High Line Canal and Reservoir Co. v. City of Golden, 975 P.2d 189 (Colo.1999). Irrigators and municipalities brought an action claiming the city had expanded its water usage beyond the amount decreed in an earlier change of use proceeding. The plaintiffs argued that the rule in *Orr* should be applied to allow the addition of volumetric limitations based on the fact that the earlier decrees already contained implied limitations. However, the court clarified the ruling in *Orr* and declined to extend the rule to the facts of this case:

> In each individual case, we must review the record of the prior proceeding in order to determine whether historical consumptive use was calculated and relied upon in the formation of the earlier decree. If so, we will not modify the resulting decree by implying volumetric limitations into its terms. The implied volumetric limitation doctrine in *Orr* was developed in order to prevent injury to juniors when a prior change decree did not address or contemplate the question of historical consumptive use. This doctrine was not developed in order to provide juniors with a method to insert volumetric limitations where they were previously absent, even though historical consumptive use formed the basis for the earlier decree.

Id. at 242. The court determined that the earlier decrees were unambiguous, historical consumptive use had been taken into account, and the terms and conditions required to prevent injury to junior appropriators had been determined at the earlier proceedings. On appeal after remand, the court discussed the principles relevant to an evaluation of an impermissible expansion of decreed rights, Farmers Reservoir & Irrigation Co. v. City of Golden, 44 P.3d 241 (Colo. 2002).

4. Suppose a water right held for industrial purposes was leased or transferred to a ditch company to be used for irrigation, but no change of the place or type of use was ever adjudicated and decreed (*i.e.*, approved) by the water court. More than thirty years later the water right was sold to a developer for a subdivision and a change of use proceeding was commenced. Can the usage in agricultural irrigation under the undecreed change of use be considered as historical use? The Colorado Supreme Court applied *Orr*'s "implied limitation restricting usage to that which occurred for the original appropriation" to hold that uses for the undecreed purposes cannot be counted. Santa Fe Trail Ranches Property Owners Assoc. v. Simpson, 990 P.2d 46, 55 (Colo.1999). Whether or not another water right is harmed, "the right to change a water right is limited to that amount of water actually used beneficially pursuant to the decree at the appropriator's place of use." Underlying this rule is a purpose of furthering the public policy of optimum use, that keeps water available for new uses and prevents waste, as well as protecting other users of private water rights. The process for approving a change of use is important in restricting an appropriation to the actual beneficial use because "[p]roperty rights in water are usufructuary; ownership of the resource itself remains in the public." 990 P.2d at 54.

Metropolitan Denver Sewage Disposal Dist. No. 1 v. Farmers Reservoir & Irrigation Co.

Supreme Court of Colorado, 1972.
179 Colo. 36, 499 P.2d 1190.

■ Groves, Justice.

The defendants in error (plaintiffs) have decreed rights for irrigation purposes out of the South Platte River. In about 1937 Denver constructed a sewage treatment facility known as the Denver Northside Plant. Effluent from this plant was discharged into the South Platte River above the common headgate of the plaintiffs. Beginning in about 1966 the effluent from Denver's sewage was placed in the river downstream from this headgate. The plaintiffs brought before the court this declaratory judgment action asking, among other things, that it be adjudged that the plaintiffs are entitled to have the effluent placed in the river above their headgate. The trial court ruled in favor of the plaintiffs. We reverse. * * *

Nearly every decree for South Platte River water diverted downstream from Denver is dependent for its supply upon return flow of waste and seepage waters. See Comstock v. Ramsay, 55 Colo. 244, 133 P. 1107 (1913). The only inference to be drawn from the statement of facts is that, absent either effluent discharge above the headgate or change of the plaintiffs' point of diversion to a place below the plant, the plaintiffs' decrees will be substantially unfilled. * * *

The effluent with which we are concerned here is solely from water arising in the South Platte watershed, which has been acquired by Denver, and, after use within Denver, has been transported through Denver's sewer system to Metro's plant. * * *

We sense an underlying sentiment (or hope) by Denver that the plaintiffs may have the effluent involved to the extent of their decrees. Be that as it may, it is apparent that the parties are concerned primarily with the question of who shall bear the cost of transporting the water from the new place of discharge to the initial (common) section of the plaintiffs' ditch. Before proceeding further, we wish to emphasize that we are not expressing any opinion on the right of plaintiffs to the effluent. Rather, we are concerned with whether Denver, acting through Metro, may change its point of effluent discharge into the stream at the Metro plant with impunity as against the plaintiffs' objection. * * *

In its oral announcement, the trial court stated in effect that the rules governing change of *point of return* (to the stream) are the same as those governing change of *point of diversion*, citing Brighton Ditch Co. v. Englewood, 124 Colo. 366, 237 P.2d 116 (1951), and Fort Collins Milling & Elevator Co. v. Larimer and Weld Irr. Co., 61 Colo. 45, 156 P. 140 (1916). An appropriator may not change his point of diversion except upon conditions which eliminate injury to other appropriators. See Farmers Highline Canal & Reservoir Co. v. Golden, 129 Colo. 575, 272 P.2d 629 (1954) and cases cited therein. The plaintiffs argue similarly that they are entitled to conditions on the stream as they have existed * * *. We cannot agree with the argument of the plaintiffs and the conclusion of the trial court. The cases cited by them and listed above are all change of point of diversion, and not change in point of return, cases. To us, they are not persuasive. Plaintiffs also cite Comstock, State Engineer v. Ramsay, 55 Colo. 244, 133 P. 1107 (1913), which involves the lack of right to intercept waste water which is proceeding toward the stream, and does not involve the right to change the point of return.

Changes of points of return of waste water are not governed by the same rules as changes of points of diversion. Conceivably, there may be instances (perhaps in the case of power water) in which a change of point of return may be enjoined, but this is not one of them. In Green Valley Ditch Co. v. Schneider, 50 Colo. 606, 115 P. 705 (1911) the Tegeler lateral carried waste water which plaintiff used. It was there held as follows:

> "Plaintiff's rights were limited and only attached to the water discharged from the Tegeler lateral, whatever that happened to be, after the defendants and cross-complainants had supplied their own wants and necessities. This does not vest her with any control over the ditches or laterals of appellants, or the water flowing therein, nor does it obligate appellants to continue or maintain conditions so as to supply plaintiff's appropriation of waste water at any time or in any quantity, when acting in good faith."

We believe that it follows from this determination that there is no vested right in downstream appropriators to maintainance [sic] of the same point of return of irrigation waste water.[3]

At least in the absence of bad faith or of arbitrary or unreasonable conduct, the same rule should be applicable to sewage waste or the effluent therefrom of a municipality or sanitation district. Any question of arbitrary or unreasonable conduct here was removed by the agreed statement of facts. It was there stipulated that the Metro plant was placed at a location gravitationally below the Northside Plant and "was selected on the basis of economic feasibility and is a normal engineering selection. * * * "We hold, therefore, that the plaintiffs may not interfere with Denver's change of point of return.

It has not been argued that it may be against public policy for appropriators to prevent change of point of return of sewage effluent, i.e., the vitiation of the public health in a burgeoning urban area. We, of course, make no ruling in this respect, but think it well to suggest that possible public policy questions are worth expression.

We feel we should remark that the General Assembly may well wish to change, prospectively at least, the rule we here announce as to change of point of return.

* * *

* * * Under date of July 29, 1968, Denver, Metro and the plaintiffs entered into an agreement. This recited that Denver had constructed a pumping facility capable of delivering effluent from the Metro plant into the Burlington Ditch. The agreement provides among other things for the ultimate vesting of title to the pumping facility, for the payment of the cost of the facility, and for the payment of operational expenses connected therewith. The identity of the party or parties which obtain title and make payments, and rather complex arrangements relating thereto, are dependent upon the ultimate outcome of the instant case and of City and County of Denver etc. v. Fulton Irrigating Ditch Company * * *.

* * *

■ KELLEY, J., did not participate.

■ ERICKSON, J., dissents.

NOTES

1. The decision in the principal case says that the no injury rule does not apply to changes in the point of return. Why? In fact, most "injuries" triggering application of the rule are the result of an appropriator's being deprived of return flow. Usually, the decrease in return flows is caused by a

---

3. This statement should not be construed as an expression concerning any right or lack of right to enlarge the use of irriga-tion water. See Fort Lyon Canal Co. v. Chew, 33 Colo. 392, 81 P. 37 (1905).

change in point of diversion or place of use. Is there any sound reason that a change in point of return unaccompanied by another such change of use should be exempt from the rule?

2. To apply the no injury rule in *Metro Denver* the court would have had to decide the extent of harm to the farmers deprived of Denver's returns. Presumably, a remedy would extend only to the amount of water Denver was obligated to return (*i.e.*, the diversion right less the amount it had a right to consume). This would have necessitated a determination of the amount of water Denver was entitled to consume. Presumably, that would mean the city's historical consumptive use. Suppose, however, that the city decided to recycle treated sewage indefinitely, giving it a 100% consumptive right without a "change of use" being involved. The result would have been the same as the court's actual decision. Should the court have decided that a municipal right is potentially 100% consumptive and therefore there is no cognizable injury when a municipal point of return is changed?

City of Boulder v. Boulder & Left Hand Ditch Co.

Supreme Court of Colorado, 1976.
192 Colo. 219, 557 P.2d 1182.

■ GROVES, JUSTICE.

* * *

* * * Each of the parties is a decreed appropriator of water out of Boulder Creek. Left Hand and Farmers are mutual ditch companies. Their decrees are for irrigation and are prior to that of Boulder.

The ditch of Farmers (Farmers Ditch) has been used for more than 100 years for the irrigation of lands in the Boulder Creek watershed and the return flow from such irrigation proceeds to Boulder Creek.

The water decreed to the ditch of Left Hand (Left Hand Ditch) for almost 100 years has been used upon lands, the return flow of which returns largely to Dry Creek and South St. Vrain Creek.

The two mutual ditch companies have the same point of diversion out of Boulder Creek, being within the city limits of Boulder, and they utilize a common lateral for the first one and one-half miles from the point of diversion. Then, the ditch of each company proceeds from the lateral to the respective irrigated area served by each.

During the irrigation season, with the consent of Farmers, Left Hand is diverting and transporting in its ditch some of the water decreed to Farmers.[2] If this diversion were not made, the historic return flow therefrom would be used by appropriators out of Boulder Creek, upstream from

---

2. While we have not noted mention of the fact in the complaint nor the decree, it appears from one of the briefs that Left Hand owns stock in Farmers and as a result is entitled to rights in the Farmers Ditch water represented by such stock. This portion of Farmers Ditch water, which Left Hand is taking out of the immediate watershed of Boulder Creek, is the subject of this action.

its confluence with South St. Vrain Creek. Absent this return flow Boulder must permit the same portion of its decreed water to remain in Boulder Creek in order to satisfy the decree of these intervening appropriators.

There has been no decree permitting the change of place of use of the water involved. In the absence of such a decree, the plaintiff contends that it is entitled to injunctive relief whereby Left Hand would be prohibited from diverting the water from the watershed in which it has been historically used.

The fundamental basis for the dismissal of the complaint by the water judge was the rulings of this court in *Metro Denver Sewage v. Farmers Reservoir*, 179 Colo. 36, 499 P.2d 1190 (1972), and *Tongue Creek v. Orchard City*, 131 Colo. 177, 280 P.2d 426 (1955). For reasons which we will later elaborate, these cases are distinguishable.

It has been fundamental law in this state that junior appropriators have rights in return flow to the extent that they may not be injured by a change in the place of use of the irrigation water which provides that return flow. The basic principles were stated in *Farmers Highline Canal v. Golden*, 129 Colo. 575, 272 P.2d 629, 631 (1954) * * *.

* * *

The basic fallacy in the ground of decision used by the water judge is his statement, "there is no distinction * * * between waste water from irrigation and return flow water from irrigation. * * * "A typical example is that of the irrigator who turns water into individual furrows traversing his field. That portion which is not absorbed into the earth or transpires remains in the furrow at the end thereof, and is collected in a waste ditch. The contents of the waste ditch is waste water. When this waste water so collected runs in the waste ditch to the stream, the law is that one who appropriates the waste water from the stream cannot assert a right to have the irrigator continue to discharge the waste water into the stream. * * *

In *Metro Denver Sewage*, the real party in interest, Denver, was discharging at a certain place the effluent from its sewage after treatment into the same river from whence the water was diverted by Denver. Then Denver changed the point of discharge downstream, thereby preventing—or at least hindering—the user of the effluent, who had been diverting it from the stream below the old point of discharge and above the new. Thus, we were asked to determine whether we would follow the rule that one cannot change the point of diversion or place of use to the injury of a junior appropriator or the other rule that the junior appropriator has no right to the continuance—or the continuance of the place of discharge—of waste water. We elected to follow the irrigation waste water rule, saying, "in the absence of bad faith or of arbitrary or unreasonable conduct, the [waste water] rule should be applicable to sewage waste or the effluent therefrom of a municipality or sanitation district."

Return flow is not waste water. Rather, it is irrigation water seeping back to a stream after it has gone underground to perform its nutritional function. As already indicated, the law makes no distinction between change of point of diversion and change of place of use so far as the rights of junior appropriators are concerned. We made it clear in *Metro Denver Sewage* that the change of point of return of waste water or effluent is not governed by the same rules as changes of point of diversion and place of use.

We are here involved with the effect of a change of place of use because *return flow* results from *use* and not from water carried in the surface in ditches and wasted into the stream. Under the allegations of the complaint, therefore, this case should be treated as one of change of place of use and not under the rules of *Tongue Creek* and *Metro Denver Sewage*. We do not speculate as to the extent to which Boulder may prove its case, but do rule that it is entitled under the complaint to its day in court.

* * *

NOTES

1. On remand, how should the water court decide the amount of water that can be taken from Boulder Creek to Left Hand Ditch?

2. The court recited its decision in *Metro Denver*. Is the *Metro Denver* rule necessarily involved? The court goes to considerable lengths to distinguish the case with its sweeping rule that juniors are not protected against a change in a senior's point of return. It contrives a distinction between irrigation waste (water returned to the stream in a ditch) and return flows (water that seeps back to the stream) and says that the former is not subject to the no injury rule while the latter is. *Metro Denver* neither mentioned nor depended on the distinction. In fact, the ancient cases relied upon by the court in *Metro Denver* for exempting return flows from the no injury rule, as well as the additional decisions cited in *Boulder,* make no such distinction. Furthermore, they are not even concerned with whether the no injury rule applies to waste (or return) water. They deal specifically with whether a water right can be perfected, and must be protected, when an alleged appropriator intercepts another's drainage as a source of water. The courts in those cases hold, unremarkably, that the senior is not obliged to continue diverting and using water, thereby producing waste to supply the wastewater user.

Metro Denver dealt with a situation where wastewater had been historically returned to a *stream* at a point above which others had made their appropriations. When the return was moved downstream of the others' diversion, they lost their supply. The old cases said that no one can count on another's continued diversion, use, and return of water to provide water to be appropriated from a drainage *ditch* or gully before it reenters a stream. But *Metro Denver* said appropriators can no longer count on the *stream* as a source of a water right even if stream conditions are changed as the result of a change in point of return. *Boulder* softens the odd *Metro Denver* rule, saying that seepage returns are protected from a change in point of return while returns by ditch are not. In Colorado, water that has seeped into the ground is considered to be in the "natural stream" from which appropriations can be made. See *supra* p. 218. Should junior appropriators be protected from being cut off from seepage water but not from losing a source of supply that historically reaches the stream by a pipe or ditch?

3. Does the decision in *Boulder* prevent an irrigator from lining an irrigation ditch to prevent seepage? Which type of water is subject to reuse by the appropriator? Can the appropriator still decide not to irrigate a field in a particular year, or to abandon a water right altogether if the absence of return flows would deprive downstream appropriators of being able to fulfill their water rights? Can an appropriator consume or sell to others all "waste water"?

4. "Waste water" is a term of art and is different from "water which is being wasted." Baumgartner v. Stremel, 178 Colo. 209, 496 P.2d 705, 706 (1972). What is the distinction?

5. Do the following effects constitute injury under the no injury rule: A diminution in quality? A loss of fishing opportunity? Limitations on future uses in an area of origin? Rendering an old, inefficient means of diversion useless? Cf. City of Roswell v. Reynolds, 86 N.M. 249, 522 P.2d 796 (1974) (change in point of diversion to a well disallowed absent showing by applicant that new wells would not increase salinity levels of others); Leavitt v. Lassen Irrigation Co., 157 Cal. 82, 106 P. 404 (1909) (operator of public water system could not change to private use); Twin Lakes Reservoir & Canal Co. v. City of Aspen, 193 Colo. 478, 568 P.2d 45 (1977) (because transmountain diversions are necessarily 100% consumptive as to basin of origin, court need not inquire into consumption and return flow of the changed use).

6. Under real property law, an owner cannot prevent a change in the use of a neighbor's property that results in costs, inconvenience, or unpleasantness short of a nuisance. Absent regulations, building a bulky, architecturally unpleasing building that increases traffic and noise may be within the neighbor's right. Yet *any* inhibition on another's use of water rights is barred by the no injury rule. Why is this?

National Research Council, National Academy of Science, Water Transfers in the West: Efficiency, Equity, and the Environment

38–39 (1992).

Third Party Impacts and Opportunities

* * *

A water buyer and seller are the two primary parties in a water transfer, each of whom must be satisfied with the results of the negotiations for a transfer to be consummated. These primary parties negotiate in their own best interests and exercise control over whether a transfer will occur. Consequently, their interests are not typically a central concern of public policies governing water transfers. Instead, public policies must be concerned with the interests of so-called third parties, that is, those who stand to be affected by the transfer but are not represented in the negotiations and lack control over or input into the processes by which transfer proposals are evaluated and implemented.

The impacts of transfers and the parties affected are many, diverse, and potentially substantial. Third parties * * * can include

- other water rights holders;
- agriculture (including farmers and agricultural businesses in the area of origin);
- the environment (including instream flows, wetlands and other ecosystems, water quality, and other interests affected by environmental changes);
- urban interests;
- ethnic communities and Indian tribes;
- rural communities; and
- federal taxpayers.

The types of impacts felt by these parties are quite varied but can be broadly thought of as economic, social, and environmental. Economic effects include impacts on incomes, jobs, and business opportunities. Social impacts include changes in community structure, cohesiveness, and control over water resources, and such changes can occur in both rural and urban communities. Environmental effects are broad based, including effects not only on instream flow, wetlands, and fish and wildlife, but also on downstream water quality and on recreational opportunities that are dependent on streamflows, riparian habitats, and aesthetic qualities.

Because local governments in the area of origin are seldom the buyers or sellers in water transfer transactions, their interests and those of community residents frequently are of concern. Damage to the environmental and aesthetic amenities of natural and rural areas may be significant. For example, transfers that involve surface waters may decrease instream flows, leading to degradation of wetlands and water quality and to loss of riparian habitat. Such transfers also can result in increased sewage treatment costs to municipalities that rely on the depleted streams. Where surface water and ground water are closely linked, the export of ground water also can alter surface flows, with potential adverse effects on riparian vegetation and wetlands. Ground water transfers may lower the water levels in the aquifer, affecting other water users pumping from a common aquifer, drying up wetlands, and altering riparian vegetation and wildlife habitat. Negative effects tend to be most serious when transfers involve moving water from one watershed or region to another. In such instances, the benefits associated with that water are lost to the local area. Fiscal impacts include loss of property tax base and bonding capacity, tighter spending limitations, and reduced revenue sharing.

Water transfers from agricultural to other uses may lead to the retirement of irrigated land. Environmental consequences include soil erosion, blowing dust, and tumbleweeds, which arise after crop production ceases. When farmland is retired from production, the loss of agricultural jobs and related businesses may inhibit future economic growth in the area of origin. When the tax base shrinks, causing local services to decline, the area of origin becomes less attractive to new businesses. Also, water and land resources needed for new local development may be unavailable as a result of major water transfers.

––––––––––

Third party effects or "externalities" other than the rights of junior users were not considered under the common law of prior appropriation. They have been addressed to varying degrees by modern statutory systems in some states as discussed *infra*, and under federal environmental laws as discussed *infra* Chapter 7.

4. LOSS

Jenkins v. State, Department of Water Resources

Supreme Court of Idaho, 1982.
103 Idaho 384, 647 P.2d 1256.

■ SHEPARD, JUSTICE.

* * *

Jenkins is the owner of 280 acres of land near the town of Kilgore in Clark County, Idaho. Appurtenant to that property are two separate water rights, one for 2.4 cfs of water from Cottonwood Creek, and the second for 3.2 cfs of water from Ching Creek. Those water rights were adjudicated by decree of federal court in 1930. Both creeks flow southerly in a generally parallel direction from the mountains of Targhee National Forest. Ching Creek is the more easterly and the Jenkins property is located further east of Ching Creek. There are a series of channels approximately 2 miles in length running easterly from Cottonwood Creek to Ching Creek that are the principal subject of this dispute. It is contended by appellant Jenkins that the water representing his Cottonwood right flows from Cottonwood Creek through channels into Ching Creek from whence it is diverted by him together with the water representing his Ching Creek right.

In 1978, Jenkins filed an application with the Department of Water Resources, seeking to transfer the point of diversion for his Ching Creek water right to the location of a recently built headgate. At that time an examination of the records indicated that the decreed point of diversion for Jenkins' Cottonwood right was not located on any stream. Jenkins filed an amended application to transfer the point of diversion of the Cottonwood right and locate that point of diversion on Cottonwood Creek.

Several water users on both Ching and Cottonwood Creeks protested these proposed transfers, and the district water master recommended that the Department deny the transfer of the Cottonwood right. A hearing was held thereon at which all parties were represented by counsel. Thereafter the director of the Department issued an order granting the transfer of the point of diversion of the Ching Creek right but denying the transfer of the point of diversion of the Cottonwood Creek right. The director found that no water had been diverted from Cottonwood Creek for use on Jenkin's land for the previous 18 years. He also found that waters of both Ching and Cottonwood Creeks were overappropriated. He concluded that to allow a resumption of use of the Cottonwood right would represent an enlargement of the use over the prior 18 years, that the water users would be injured thereby, and that I.C. § 42–222 authorized denial of an application in such circumstances. The director relied upon that portion of I.C. § 42–222 which provides for the forfeiture of a water right not used for five years.

From that decision of the director, Jenkins appealed to the district court. * * *

The trial court found that water from Cottonwood Creek only flowed to Ching Creek irregularly during the spring run off and that any such contribution was not the result of a physical diversion. The court also found that Jenkins took only 3.2 cfs of water from Ching Creek which was the amount he was entitled to under his Ching Creek right, and therefore he received no water in excess of his Ching Creek right, which could be construed as Cottonwood right water. * * *

* * * [W]e conclude that the director of the Department of Water Resources has jurisdiction to determine the question of abandonment and forfeiture and such is required as a preliminary step to performance of his statutory duty in determining whether or not the proposed transfer would injure other water rights. While ordinarily abandonment and forfeiture are to be determined in a separate proceeding, it is clear that when a water right is sought to be transferred and protestors allege that it has been abandoned or forfeited, and that to allow resumption of that right would cause some injury, a determination of abandonment or forfeiture is necessary for the performance of his powers of determining injury. The director is statutorily required to examine all evidence of whether the proposed transfer will injure other water rights or constitute an enlargement of the original right, and evidence which demonstrates that the right sought to be transferred has been abandoned or forfeited, is probative as to whether that transfer would injure other water rights. If a water right has indeed been lost through abandonment or forfeiture, the right to use that water reverts to the state and is subject to further appropriation. * * * Hence a person making a subsequent appropriation will be injured by resumption of the abandoned or forfeited water right. If a senior right has been abandoned or forfeited, the priority of the original appropriator is lost, and the junior appropriators move up the ladder of priority. If a senior right which had been forfeited or abandoned were allowed to be reinstated through a transfer proceeding, clearly injury would result to otherwise junior appro-

priators. Priority in time is an essential part of western water law and to diminish one's priority works an undeniable injury to that water right holder.

* * *

* * * We note initially that care must be taken in this type of proceeding to distinguish between abandonment and forfeiture. Each is a related concept but each carries with it distinctive requirements. * * * However, this Court has recently reaffirmed that those terms relate to different legal concepts * * *. *Sears v. Berryman*, 101 Idaho 843, 623 P.2d 455 (1981); *Gilbert v. Smith*, 97 Idaho 735, 552 P.2d 1220 (1976). As stated in *Sears v. Berryman, supra*:

> "Abandonment is a common law doctrine involving the occurrence of (1) an intent to abandon and (2) an actual relinquishment or surrender of the water right. Forfeiture, on the other hand, is predicated upon the statutory declaration that all rights to use water are lost where the appropriator fails to make beneficial use of the water for a continuous five year period. I.C. § 42–222(2)."

101 Idaho at 847, 623 P.2d at 459.

Intent to abandon must be proved by clear and convincing evidence of unequivocal acts, and mere non-use of a water right, standing alone, is not sufficient for a *per se* abandonment. *Sears v. Berryman, supra*; *Gilbert v. Smith, supra*. Intent to abandon is a question of fact to be decided by the trier of fact. *Sears v. Berryman, supra*. As in *Sears*, there was no finding by the trial court, nor by the director of the Department, that Jenkins intended to abandon his Cottonwood water right. The record shows only non-use, disclosing no intent to abandon, and hence Jenkins did not lose his water right by common law abandonment.

We then proceed to a determination of whether the findings are sufficient to support a determination of a statutory forfeiture. * * *

Statutory forfeiture is based upon the legislative declaration in I.C. § 42–222(2) that water rights may be lost if they are not applied to a beneficial use for a period of five continuous years. *Gilbert v. Smith*. Certain defenses to forfeiture have been recognized. Extension of the five year period may be made upon a showing of good cause, providing the application for extension is made within the first five-year period. I.C. § 42–222(2). Also wrongful interference with a water right or failure to use the water because of circumstances over which the water right holder has no control have been recognized as defenses. Further, if use of the water right is resumed after the five year period, but before any third parties make a claim in the water, then the courts will decline to declare a forfeiture. Here Jenkins has raised none of these defenses, and the record is devoid of any evidence to indicate that any of the established defenses would be applicable even if argued. The entire case was tried and appealed on Jenkins' theory that he had used the Cottonwood water the entire time.

Forfeitures are not favored, and clear and convincing proof is required to support a forfeiture. * * *

* * * There is substantial, albeit conflicting, evidence indicating that Jenkins failed to use Cottonwood Creek water for a beneficial use between 1961 and 1979, a period of 18 years. The water master testified that he had delivered water from the two creeks for those 18 years, but has not delivered nor been requested to deliver to Jenkins the 2.4 cfs water out of Cottonwood Creek. The trial court found that the channels from Cottonwood Creek to Ching Creek do not carry a regular flow of water except during the spring runoff. Those facts are supported by clear and convincing evidence, and support the conclusion of statutory forfeiture.

* * *

Accordingly, we affirm the order of the district court, which in turn affirmed the decision of the Director of the Department of Water Resources which denied the application for the transfer of the point of diversion of Jenkins' Cottonwood water right. Costs to respondents.

NOTES

1.   Abandonment is a common law concept that requires proof of intent to relinquish dominion and control over a property interest and the proponent of abandonment bears the burden of proving the requisite state of mind. Given the high value of water rights, instances where the owner of such rights consciously intends to abandon them are rare. Courts say that intent and the act of relinquishment of dominion and control are separate jural acts. In Edgemont Improvement Co. v. N. S. Tubbs Sheep Co., 22 S.D. 142, 115 N.W. 1130, 1131 (1908), the court said "[i]t is well settled that mere non-use of water does not amount to abandonment, nor is mere lapse of time alone sufficient to establish abandonment. In all cases abandonment is a question of intention." See also Gilbert v. Smith, 97 Idaho 735, 552 P.2d 1220 (1976), where it was held that fifty-three years of non-use did not constitute abandonment per se. Nevertheless, mere non-use of water or mere lapse of time may create a presumption of intent to abandon the water right. As a practical matter non-use is the best evidence of intent. In Cundy v. Weber, 68 S.D. 214, 300 N.W. 17 (1941), the court, faced with a forty-seven year period of non-use, held that a prima facie showing of intent to abandon may be made by evidence of failure to apply the water to a beneficial use for an unreasonable period of time. See also City and County of Denver v. Middle Park Water Conservancy Dist., 925 P.2d 283 (Colo.1996) (Denver made no effort for over 40 years to develop its irrigation water rights, demonstrating an intent to abandon).

2.   Statutes in some states create a rebuttable presumption of abandonment after a certain period of time. COLO. REV. STAT. § 37–92–402(11) (2006) (ten years); MONT. CODE ANN. § 85–2–404 (2005) (ten years). What reasons are sufficient to rebut a presumption of intent to abandon? Colorado has held that economic, financial, or legal obstacles may be sufficient, Hallenbeck v. Granby Ditch & Reservoir Co., 160 Colo. 555, 420 P.2d 419 (1966), but economic infeasibility is not an excuse, CF & I Steel Corp. v. Purgatoire River Water Conservancy Dist., 183 Colo. 135, 515 P.2d 456 (1973). Broad assertions, unsupported by evidence are not sufficient to rebut the presumption. *In re* Musselshell River Drainage Area, 255 Mont. 43, 840 P.2d 577 (1992).

The Colorado Supreme Court is moving, albeit uneasily, toward firmer use of abandonment to make more water available for appropriation. It has held that small water rights transfers on paper did not overcome the presumption of abandonment when there was a 29 year period of non-use of hydroelectric rights. City and County of Denver v. Snake River Water Dist., 788 P.2d 772 (Colo.1990). The dissent cited the court's decision in People *ex rel.* Danielson v. City of Thornton, 775 P.2d 11, 19 (Colo.1989) (actual good faith attempts to sell a water right are strongly indicative of an absence of intent to abandon). For a discussion of factors involved in rebutting a presumption of abandonment, see East Twin Lakes Ditches and Water Works, Inc. v. Board of County Commissioners of Lake County, 76 P.3d 918 (Colo. 2003).

Should a more liberal standard apply to users, such as the mining industry that have long periods of nonuse because of low raw commodity prices? See *In re* Clark Fork River Drainage Area, 274 Mont. 340, 908 P.2d 1353 (1995) (rejecting argument that mining water rights should receive special treatment). Does the presumption apply to municipalities? See Okanogan Wilderness League v. Town of Twisp, 133 Wash.2d 769, 947 P.2d 732 (1997) (nonuse for 50 years raises presumption).

3. Abandonment must be voluntary. Although Wyoming law provides that abandonment occurs "[w]here the holder of an appropriation * * * fails, either intentionally or unintentionally, to use the water" (WYO. STAT. ANN. § 41–3–401 (2007)), the Wyoming Supreme Court found that abandonment cannot occur if an appropriator's non-use is not voluntary. Scott v. McTiernan, 974 P.2d 966 (Wyo.1999) (appeal after remand at 31 P.3d 749 (Wyo. 2001)), (where a neighbor intentionally prevented water from flowing to the owners' property, assured them that the matter would be resolved, and then brought an action for abandonment).

4. Forfeiture is the statutory termination of water rights if they are not used for a given period. *E.g.,* NEV. REV. STAT. ANN. § 533.060 (Michie 2006) (failure to put water to beneficial use for five successive years results in forfeiture); N.M. STAT. ANN. § 72–5–28 (2003 & Supp. 2006) (non-use for a period of four years, followed by a one year notice period, results in reversion to the public); WYO. STAT. ANN. § 41–3–401 (2007) (failure to put water to beneficial use for which it was appropriated for five successive years works a forfeiture of the right); and OR. REV. STAT. § 540.610(1) (2005) (five successive years of non-use of all or part of a water right establishes a rebuttable presumption of forfeiture). See Rencken v. Young, 300 Or. 352, 711 P.2d 954 (1985).

5. Periods of non-use may be excused from the operation of a forfeiture statute for a variety of reasons. Exemptions range from not penalizing an appropriator for non-use during a period of drought to allowing non-use while the holder of the right is on active duty with the armed forces. N.M. STAT. ANN. § 72–5–28(E) (2003 & Supp. 2006). Exemptions raise the question whether the running of the statute is merely suspended for the period of the statutorily excused non-use, or whether the end of the period of excused non-use marks the beginning of a new limitations period. The New Mexico statute addresses this problem. N.M. STAT. ANN. § 75–5–28(D) (2003 & Supp. 2006). The statute also allows a one-year grace period during which forfeiture can be avoided by recommencing the use.

Although forfeiture statutes often appear straightforward enough, attempts to apply them have revealed the influence of the common law on defenses to temper the harsh consequences. What happens, for instance, where water is put to a beneficial use during one year in a five-year statutory forfeiture period? See Rocky Ford Irrigation Co. v. Kents Lake Reservoir Co., 104 Utah 216, 140 P.2d 638 (1943). What if water is not used at all for the statutory period, but the appropriator resumes the use before any steps are taken to declare a forfeiture? Compare Bausch v. Myers, 273 Or. 376, 541 P.2d 817 (1975), with Sturgeon v. Brooks, 73 Wyo. 436, 281 P.2d 675 (1955), Application of Boyer, 73 Idaho 152, 248 P.2d 540 (1952), and Sagewillow, Inc. v. Idaho Dept. of Water Resources, 138 Idaho 831, 70 P.3d 669 (2003).

6. Are forfeiture statutes constitutional? The Supreme Court of Nevada has held that they are, even as applied to rights perfected before the state changed applicable law from abandonment to forfeiture. Town of Eureka v. Office of State Engineer, 108 Nev. 163, 826 P.2d 948, 950–51 (1992). Does the allowance of a defense for circumstances similar to those that rebut intent to abandon solve any constitutional problems with terminating a right for a relatively brief period of non-use? See Sheep Mountain Cattle Co. v. State, Dept. of Ecology, 45 Wash.App. 427, 726 P.2d 55 (1986) (water right holder entitled to notice and hearing prior to forfeiture). Would a law holding that the failure to use a surface estate for five years results in an escheat to the state be constitutional?

7. In what kind of proceedings can the issue of forfeiture be raised? Note that in *Jenkins,* the proceeding was for a change in the point of diversion. Jurisdiction over water transfers and related actions may be split between administrative agencies and courts. If the courts have concurrent jurisdiction with administrative agencies, who should make the initial factual determinations? The Wyoming Supreme Court has applied the doctrine of primary jurisdiction. In cases where the issue of abandonment is "intertwined with other issues" the court proposed that the Board of Control adopt rules permitting a trial court to certify the abandonment issue to the board for initial determination. Under the doctrine of primary jurisdiction, when the issue returns to the court with an administrative record, judicial review is circumscribed by the usual limited standards of review provided by state administrative procedure acts. Having said all this, the court concluded by observing that the doctrine of primary jurisdiction is flexible and its application will depend on whether its purpose—allocating the power to make initial determinations of fact and law to the better decider—will be "aided * * * in the particular litigation." Kearney Lake, Land & Reservoir Co. v. Lake DeSmet Reservoir Co., 487 P.2d 324, 328 (Wyo.1971).

An appropriator has rights to 40 cfs and for twenty years raises corn, regularly using 30 cfs. Will the other 10 cfs be held abandoned or forfeited? How could the issue arise?

8. When a claim of forfeiture is being evaluated, the trial court must establish a period over which the level of forfeiture is to be measured. In addition, it may be appropriate to measure water usage on a seasonal basis, or even month by month. The choice of forfeiture "methodology" may have a critical bearing on the amount of water deemed forfeited. The complexities are explored in North Kern Water Storage Dist. v . Kern Delta Water Dist., 147 Cal.App.4th 555, 54 Cal.Rptr.3d 578 (2007).

NOTE: PRESCRIPTION

Many western states have construed the assertion of public ownership in state constitutions or statutes to make compliance with the requirements of the state's prior appropriation law the exclusive method of acquiring a water right. Thus, prescriptive rights both as against the state and among private parties are barred on the same principle of sovereign immunity that precludes gaining rights to government land by adverse possession. See A. Dan Tarlock, Law of Water Rights and Resources § 5:90 (2000).

Several states' statutes specifically prohibit the acquisition of water rights by prescription or adverse possession, including Alaska, Idaho, Nevada, Kansas, and Utah. Utah's law (Utah Code Ann. § 73–3–1 (1989)) was passed after the state supreme court held that water rights could be established by prescription. Hammond v. Johnson, 94 Utah 20, 66 P.2d 894 (1937). In Idaho, although prescriptive claims are barred by statute, the courts continue to entertain adverse possession claims. Boise–Kuna Irrigation Dist. v. Gross, 118 Idaho 940, 801 P.2d 1291 (Idaho App.1990). The issue was extensively debated in California until the state supreme court held that the state's permit system was the exclusive means of acquiring a post–1914 appropriative right as against the state, but left open the question of whether prescriptive rights would be recognized among private users. People v. Shirokow, 26 Cal.3d 301, 162 Cal.Rptr. 30, 605 P.2d 859 (1980).

Independent of theoretical sovereign immunity principles, what practical objections are there to the recognition of prescriptive rights against state-created prior appropriation rights? See Coryell v. Robinson, 118 Colo. 225, 194 P.2d 342 (1948), holding that under a prior appropriation system everyone has a right to assume that persons using water do so pursuant to the priority system. See also Campbell v. Wyoming Dev. Co., 55 Wyo. 347, 100 P.2d 124 (1940).

CHAPTER FOUR

MODERN STATUTORY ADMINISTRATION OF WATER

Water allocation in the West, and increasingly in the East, is governed by statutes that grant water rights to private and public entities that satisfy certain conditions. However, in both regions, prior judge-made law continues to guide the interpretation of these statutes. A water user or a lawyer whose client seeks a water right for a particular use first must complete and file an administrative agency-required application, usually followed by agency review, and a notice to existing water rights holders giving them an opportunity to object. The agency applies statutory or administrative rules and standards in order to decide how much water an applicant will have a right to use. These standards typically require determinations that sufficient water is available, that existing rights will be unharmed, and that the proposed use will benefit the public interest.

In order to ensure that uses are consistent with rights each state has a distinct system for establishing water rights, approving changes in the use of water rights, and administering water uses. The statutory systems of a few illustrative states in different regions are described in this chapter.

The changes wrought by modern statutory systems reflect the difficulty in applying rules developed in an era when society's needs were simpler and competition for water was less keen. In the East, the apparent plentitude of water lulled many states into thinking that it was unnecessary to address the subject with any detailed set of water laws. We have seen in Chapter Three, part A, that courts in riparian states often resorted to the law of torts to mediate disputes post hoc. With global climate change, population growth, increased competing demands and the resulting risk of scarcity in many eastern states, legislatures have developed more sophisticated water law systems. Nevertheless, in conflicts among users, common law tort rules are the default. rules.

In the West, changes in relative need have created scarcity problems: water historically allocated to mining and irrigation is now demanded by growing cities, industries, fishing streams, wetlands, and waterfalls. In the past, a property-rights regime allowed users to acquire firm rights to large amounts of water simply by making a claim and putting the water to use; today, these historical claims make it difficult to apply the already rigid principles of the appropriation doctrine.

In the face of established rights, change comes slowly. Consider the rule of prior appropriation that there is no sharing of shortages in dry years. Holders of the oldest rights are entitled to exercise them fully regardless of the relatively greater social importance or productivity of newer uses. In the 1980s, the dewatering of high quality trout streams became a major issue in Montana and the state adopted an experimental program to lease senior water rights to guarantee minimum streamflows during severe droughts. See Brian Morris, *When Rivers Run Dry Under a Big Sky: Balancing Agricultural and Recreational Claims to Scarce Water Resources in Montana and the American West*, 11 Stan. Envtl. L.J. 259 (1992); MONT. CODE ANN. § 85–2–436. However, the Montana Supreme Court reaffirmed the right of irrigators to dewater a river by taking two-thirds of a drought-stressed flow, over the objections of an environmental group. Baker Ditch Co. v. District Ct. of the 18th Judicial Dist., 251 Mont. 251, 824 P.2d 260 (1992). Thus, old rights can endure as long as uses continue; they are extinguished only if they are not used—or if the weight of public opinion provokes political change. Like many water problems, stresses on Montana's trout streams persist. In 2008, a review of the climate change literature concluded that the West's temperatures had increased 1.7 degrees compared to 1 in the rest of the planet. Stephen Saunders, Charles Montgomery and Tom Easley, *The West's Changed Climate 2* (Rocky Mountain Climate Organization and Natural Resources Defense Council, 2008). Scientists in Montana are concerned that there will be insufficient flows in small streams in hot late summers for grayling wild trout, and farmers argue that taking water from agriculture "will wreck us." Jim Robbins, *A Fight for Water Heats Up, Prized Fish Suffer*. N.Y. TIMES, (April 1, 2008).

With changing conditions and social values, the underlying principles of appropriation are often challenged as obstacles to new demands. Is a diversion always necessary to "use" water? What uses are beneficial, and to what extent are the principles of beneficial use and waste interrelated? Can yesterday's acceptable beneficial use become tomorrow's wasteful practice and no longer legitimate a water right? How can the "public interest" be accommodated within the appropriation system?

The suitability of the doctrine of prior appropriation to the modern West has been vigorously questioned by various commentators. Professor Wilkinson is a leading exponent of the argument that most of the doctrine should be rejected because it promotes the destruction of watersheds. Charles F. Wilkinson, *Aldo Leopold and Western Water Law: Thinking Perpendicular to the Doctrine of Prior Appropriation*, 24 Land & Water L. Rev. 1 (1989). He went so far as to pronounce the doctrine dead. "Prior * * * died this January 19th [1991] when his heart seized up after receiving a fax informing him that * * * the New Director of the Denver Water Board had recommended the water developers not file a law suit challenging EPA's rejection of the dam at Two Forks." Charles F. Wilkinson, *In Memoriam, Prior Appropriation 1848–1991*, 21 Envtl. L. v, xvi (1991). Compare John D. Leshy, *The Prior Appropriation Doctrine of Water Law in the West: An Emperor with Few Clothes*, 29 J. West 5 (July 1990) and A. Dan Tarlock, *New Water Transfer Restrictions: The West Returns to Riparianism*, 27 Water Res. Research 987 (1991), arguing that appropriative water rights are being modified to reflect environmental and other public interest values. But see Gregory J. Hobbs, Jr., *The Reluctant Marriage: The Next Generation (A Response to Charles Wilkinson)*, 21 Envtl. L. 1087 (1991). More recently, two of the casebook authors concluded that as with the announcement of Mark Twain's death, announcements of "Prior's" death were equally premature:

> [I]t appears that "Prior" continues to be alive as he enters his third century. The great Samuel Weil would recognize most of the features that he explicated in his early treatise on water law, despite his prescient warnings that the doctrine would have to adapt to changing conditions (Samuel C. Weil, WATER RIGHTS IN THE WESTERN STATES § 57 [(3d ed. 1911)]. Though alive, Prior is increasingly marginalized as an anachronism, a bit out of touch with the times but with some bite as well as bark. Courts continue to recite the catechism of intent to appropriate, relation back, priority and beneficial use, but on the ground, users are working around the doctrine through transfers, water banks, and other new sharing arrangements, and courts make incremental doctrinal adjustments. Ironically, to the dismay of hard-core riparianists, reverse colonization is occurring. As the East turns to regulated riparianism, eastern state legislatures, regulatory agencies, and courts ... are also finding that the protection of prior users is essential for any allocation regime. It is simply too late in the day to impose substantial disruption on the settled expectations of economic interests. [David H. Getches and A. Dan Tarlock, Water Law and Management: An Urbanizing and Greener West Copes With New Challenges, in The Evolution of Natural Resources Law and Policy (2008).

A. THE STRUCTURE OF PERMIT SYSTEMS

George William Sherk, Meetings of Waters: The Conceptual Confluence of Water Law in the Eastern and Western States

Natural Resources & Environment, Spring 1991, at 3–5, 47–49.

* * * While the eastern states are moving away from the riparian doctrine, the western states have been moving away from a strict doctrine of prior appropriation. The resulting conceptual confluence finds the eastern states adopting some aspects of the prior appropriation doctrine while the western states temper that doctrine by adopting certain historically riparian concepts.

This analysis addresses the conceptual confluence that is occurring in six distinct but interconnected areas: programmatic scope, quantification, priorities/public interest, instream flows, water conservation, and transbasin diversions.

Programmatic Scope

Western states (or territories) adopted the prior appropriation doctrine on a statewide basis. The riparian doctrine applied in eastern states because it was a part of the common law adopted in those states. As eastern states have replaced the riparian doctrine with permit systems, the geographic orientation has shifted from statewide to site-specific.

Regarding surface waters, Recently enacted legislation in Virginia provides for the reestablishment of surface water management areas. Several Great Lakes states have enacted similar laws regarding surface water uses and diversions within the Great Lakes Basin. This approach may also be emerging with regard to the drainage basin of the Chesapeake Bay.

* * *

The site-specific management programs adopted in the eastern states appear to be evolving into comprehensive statewide programs. The statewide programs of the western states are being supplemented by site-specific management programs. The trend is likely to continue, with both statewide and site-specific programs becoming the rule in all of the states. * * *

Quantification

In the western states, beneficial use defines the basis, measure and limit of a water right. This means western water rights are quite specific in terms of quantity, allowable use, point of diversion, and timing of availability, among other things. Under the riparian doctrine, water rights are not quantified. Owners of riparian land in the eastern states were entitled under the common law doctrine to utilize adjacent or subjacent water in any reasonable way, subject only to similar uses by other landowners.

The specificity of western water rights is reflected in the administrative permitting systems that have been adopted recently in many eastern states. Such systems usually require existing riparian uses to be quantified and registered. Following registration, the state program usually provides the riparian water user with a permit which describes the water use with the same specificity ascribed to water rights existing under the prior appropriation doctrine.

At least nineteen eastern states have enacted legislation establishing registration or permitting requirements. Florida, for example, established a two-year period during which permits for existing consumptive uses had to be obtained. Failure to obtain a permit resulted in a conclusive presumption that the use had been abandoned. Several of the eastern states have enacted legislation requiring registration to occur during a shorter period of time following enactment or by a specific date. North Carolina, Virginia, and South Carolina have applied the registration requirement to groundwater uses in limited capacity use areas.

The movement toward quantification and registration of water uses in the eastern states and the issuance of permits to protect those uses has been motivated in part by the growing interest in water marketing. In Virginia, permits within surface water management areas are transferable with the approval of the State Water Control Board. The eastern states are learning what the western states considered obvious: the quantification process is essential to determining the amount of water that a permit holder can transfer.

Quantification of individual rights in eastern water resources is similar, in the words of Professor Tarlock, to "the nineteenth century tradition of dividing the commons among private claimants." Concomitant with this privatization, however, comes increasing regulation to protect the public interest. At least nine eastern and western states (Alaska, California, Idaho, Mississippi, Montana, New Jersey, North Dakota, Texas, and Oregon) have adopted some form of the public trust doctrine as one means of protecting the public interest in state water resources. Definitions of navigability have been expanded to include public uses and recreational values in Arkansas, Montana, and Oklahoma. As more fully discussed below, a majority of the fifty states has enacted minimum water level legislation.

On the issues of quantification and public interest regulation of private water rights, the confluence of eastern and western water law is continuing with every legislative session.

Priorities/Public Interest

The highest priority under the prior appropriation doctrine went to the most senior water use. As a general rule, all unappropriated water was subject to appropriation. In the eastern states, all riparian water users shared the resource. A limited priority was afforded domestic and agricultural water uses. As eastern states move away from riparian water law concepts, western states, through the consideration of factors such as the "public interest," are moving away from a strict rule of prior appropriation.

The prior appropriation concept of temporal priority has been utilized in eastern states, but not as the sole determinant of priority in times of shortage. The emerging eastern approach has been to list a series of factors to be considered in determining whether a permit should be issued or a change in place or type of use should be allowed. As with the western states, one of the factors is the impact of the proposed use on existing water uses. At least twelve eastern states require permit applicants to demonstrate that their proposed uses will not interfere with existing uses. Wisconsin allows for the revocation of a permit if the permitted water use interferes with riparian water users or public water supplies. In addition, several of the eastern states have adopted sections 850A and 858 of the Restatement (Second) of Torts, which favor existing water uses in determining reasonable or unreasonable uses of surface and groundwater.

New legislation in eastern states consistently includes consideration of the public interest in allocation and regulation of water rights. The public interest determines how water will be allocated during a water shortage in

Kentucky. In Florida and Virginia, the public interest includes consideration of environmental values and instream flow requirements.

As eastern states move toward a balance between temporal priority and the public interest, the western states, either by statute or case law, are moving in the same direction. According to Professor George Gould, McGeorge School of Law, all of the western states except Colorado and Montana require consideration of the public interest when an appropriation is initiated. All of the western states require consideration of the public interest following an appropriation when changes in place or type of use are proposed. In Colorado, for example, the regulations of the state engineer [potentially could] provide for the maximum/optimum use of the state's water, not a strict application of the rule of priority. Maximum/optimum use may include economic and environmental considerations.

Eastern and western states are moving toward the concept of "equitable priority," which balances impacts on existing water users (temporal priority) with public interest considerations. This balancing is occurring throughout the regulatory process, from initiation of a water use to a change in the place or purpose of that use.

The critical question emerging in eastern and western states is "Who decides what is in the public interest?" If a proposed change in place or purpose of use is intended to meet the needs of a water market, for example, is the public interest determined by economic benefits *or* by social and environmental costs? Professor Chuck DuMars, University of New Mexico School of Law, has argued that public interest determinations are political in nature and should be resolved in more public and political regional water processes rather than in courts or quasi-judicial administrative agencies. Others question whether the public interest is well served when an issue like water use is politicized. Regardless of who makes the decision, determining the public interest has emerged as a major factor in the management and allocation of water resources in the eastern and western states.

Instream Flows

Historically, the prior appropriation doctrine required diversion of water from a watercourse before a right to the water could be established. There was little recognition or protection in appropriation doctrine states for nonconsumptive instream uses. Even less recognition or protection of such uses was afforded in riparian doctrine states.

In England, the common law prohibited riparian water users from adversely affecting the "natural flow" of a watercourse. In America, the "reasonable use" doctrine replaced the "natural flow" concept in order to encourage economic development in the eastern states. Absent state legislation, however, "reasonable use" does not include instream uses.

The concept of "instream flows" includes the use (or nonuse) of water for a variety of purposes or to protect a variety of interests. Historically, navigation, public water supply, sanitation and fish/wildlife purposes have been recognized as requiring minimum streamflows. Recreational, aesthetic and ecological uses now are being recognized as equally important water uses in a society whose perceptions of the values of the natural world are maturing.

The result is that eastern and western states are taking steps to protect instream flows. In the prior appropriation doctrine states, for example, the diversion requirement has been eliminated in Colorado, Idaho, and Arizona. Legislation authorizing the reservation of water (or the withdrawal of water from the appropriation) to protect instream flows has been enacted in Alaska, Oregon, Montana, and Utah. In addition, instream flows have been protected by case law or statute in Washington, Wyoming, North Dakota, and Nevada.

While the western states integrate protection of instream flows into the prior appropriation doctrine, at least sixteen eastern states have enacted legislation to protect such flows in the context of legislation amending (or superseding) the riparian doctrine. The preferred approach in at least ten eastern states has been to authorize a branch of state government to establish minimum streamflows or water levels.

Recently enacted Virginia legislation illustrates the trend. In Virginia, a surface water management area may be established in order to protect instream and offstream beneficial uses. Offstream beneficial uses may be restricted if the State Water Control Board determines that such uses threaten to reduce streamflows (i.e., affect instream beneficial uses adversely) in a management area. In addition, the legislation mandates the protection of instream beneficial uses and public water supplies.

Massachusetts and South Carolina have protected instream flows by restricting the amount of water available for transbasin diversions. Conversely, Wisconsin allows transbasin diversions for the purpose of maintaining streamflows or lake levels.

Protection of instream flows has been one of the driving forces behind recent legislative activity in the eastern states. Given the growing recognition of the value of instream flows, especially in purely economic terms, it is certain that this trend will continue in the eastern and western states. One recent study of the operation of a reservoir in New Mexico, for example, concluded that recreational use of the water stored in an on-stream reservoir produced a return of between $700 and $1,100 per acre-foot, while use of that water for irrigation produced a return of only $40 per acre-foot.

At the present time, at least twenty-six eastern and western states protect instream flows. The "natural flow" concept of English common law, long ago replaced by the "reasonable use" doctrine, is reflected in the image of state legislation protecting the natural flow of watercourses in eastern and western states.

Water Conservation

"Water conservation" means different things to different people. In the West, it has meant conservation of seasonally available resources through the construction of dams and reservoirs. In the East, more often than not, it has meant those means by which the demand for water might be reduced.

Water conservation has been the subject of recent legislation in both regions. The doctrine of prior appropriation in practical effect discourages water conservation because protectable water rights are limited to that quantity of water that is diverted and put to beneficial use. While waste is prohibited, the owner of a water right has no incentive to reduce consumption through efficient or alternative processes. It is not in the interest of an agricultural water user, for example, to install a more efficient irrigation system because there is no guarantee that the irrigator will be able to claim the amount of water conserved.

States in the West have moved to correct this situation. Oregon and California have given the right to use or convey conserved water to the person implementing the conservation measures. Utah court decisions have reached the same result.

In Texas and at least six eastern states, water conservation must be considered when granting permits for proposed water uses. Massachusetts, South Carolina, Ohio, and Illinois also require that conservation be considered before approving any transbasin diversions. In Virginia, having an approved water conservation program may exempt some water users from the permit requirements that are imposed when a surface water management area is established. Connecticut and Vermont have established water conservation standards for plumbing fixtures. Indiana, Kentucky, Wisconsin, and Florida have authorized a branch of state government to develop water conservation plans.

While water conservation may have meant preserving supply in the western states and reducing demand in the eastern states, the trend is for it to mean both things in all states. Supply limitations are forcing the western states to take additional steps to reduce water demands. The current demand reduction programs of the Metropolitan Water District of Southern California are the kinds of programs that will be required throughout the region. Recent mandates in the eastern states to protect instream flows while increasing demands stretch available supplies have brought a new interest in conservation programs and water storage projects.

Transbasin Diversions

Under the prior appropriation doctrine, water rights are generally transferable provided the rights of downstream water users are not impaired. Because of adverse impacts, however, several western states restrict intrabasin and interbasin diversions. California and Oklahoma protect "areas of origin" by providing that transfers may not unreasonably affect fish and wildlife, instream beneficial uses, or the economy of the area from which the water is diverted. Colorado prohibits the transbasin diversion of Colorado River water by water conservancy districts if such diversions would impair existing rights or future beneficial uses. Arizona and Oregon require State Water Commission approval for such transfers and the consent of adversely affected irrigation districts, agricultural districts, and water user associations. The Texas Water Rights Commission may not approve transbasin diversions if the diversion would prejudice the people or adversely affect property located in the exporting area. In addition, the Texas Water Development Board, in planning for transbasin diversions, must consider the needs of exporting basins for fifty years into the future. Colorado and Arizona have considered legislation that would impose a transfer tax on transbasin diversions to offset adverse impacts on the exporting area.

Under the riparian doctrine of "reasonable use," transbasin diversions were [theoretically] impossible because water uses were restricted both to riparian lands and to the basin of origin. A number of eastern states, however, have enacted legislation authorizing transbasin diversions under certain circumstances. For example, Florida allows such diversions if consistent with the public interest and there is no local government opposition. Kentucky, Massachusetts, Georgia, and South Carolina have established general criteria for approving proposed transbasin diversions. Six of the Great Lakes Basin states have implemented Principle III of the Great Lakes Charter which prohibits diversions from the Great Lakes watershed if significant adverse impacts would result.

Eastern and western states are moving toward allowing certain transbasin diversions while imposing increasing restrictions on those diversions. In general, transbasin diversions will be allowed subject to specific conditions and with the provision of adequate compensation to the exporting basin. As in California, this compensation may be provided in the form of grants or loans to finance water-related activities. It may be provided in the form of crop insurance for low-water years. It may also mean that state authorities, as in Colorado, will require construction of compensatory storage to ensure that the supply of water available to the exporting basin is not reduced by the transbasin diversion.

Professor Larry MacDonnell, University of Colorado School of Law, and Chuck Howe, Professor of Economics at the University of Colorado, have proposed a three-part public interest test for transbasin diversions. First, the proposed diversion should be the least-cost source of reliable supply to the importing basin. Second, the benefits from the diversion should exceed all related costs. Third, no one should be made worse by the diversion. In one form or another, such tests are being utilized in the eastern and western states.

Looking upstream from New Orleans, it is impossible to tell where the waters of the Mississippi River originated. Did they fall as snow in Colorado or as rain in West Virginia? We know only that the circumstances of their passage have consistently, continuously, and irresistibly brought these waters ever closer together.

Like the Mississippi, the conceptual confluence of eastern and western water law, driven by consistent environmental and economic circumstances, is gradually producing a system of water laws in which the harsh rigidity of the prior appropriation doctrine is made more flexible, and the useless vagaries of the riparian doctrine are given new definition. The emerging legal construct is focused on a balance among all natural and man-made uses of a water resource or on what Professor Luna Leopold, University of California at Berkeley, would call the "preservation of the hydrologic continuum." It is hoped that the emerging system of water laws will be both principled and coherent and will work as well in times of shortage as they do in times of abundance.

1. THE RISE OF STATUTORY SYSTEMS

A major effort at providing a standardized framework for comprehensive water legislation was initiated under the leadership of the late Professor Frank E. Maloney. He believed that a model water code which reflected the public's interest in water as a resource, with that interest defined to include wildlife preservation, maintenance of ecological balance, scenic beauty, navigation, recreation, and protection of municipal/public water supplies, was the best allocation regime. See Frank E. Maloney et al., A Model Water Code (1972).

Frank E. Maloney, Sheldon J. Plager & Fletcher N. Baldwin, Water Law and Administration: The Florida Experience
172–73 (1968).

§ 60. Weaknesses of the Common Law Approach to Allocation of Water for Consumptive Use

In theory the standard of relative reasonableness under the reasonable use branch of the riparian system facilitates an adjustment of conflicts between uses in accordance with the demands of each user and the dictates of the general public interest.[1] It allows each riparian a certain amount of flexibility in commencing a new use or in expanding an existing one in the light of changing conditions of water use and supply.

Recently, however, criticism has been leveled at the riparian system and its restrictions on the use of stream water to riparian owners, along with its requirement that the water be used only on riparian land. Many critics feel better use may frequently be made at other places by riparian or nonriparian owners.[2]

The major criticism of the system relates to the element of uncertainty associated with the reasonable use of water for nondomestic purposes. Because the reasonableness of each use is determined by the needs of other riparians, unforeseen conditions arise when others commence or enlarge

---

1. "The advantages of this [reasonable use] theory are that it is entirely utilitarian and tends to promote the fullest beneficial use of water resources." Restatement of Torts at 345–46 (Ch. 41, topic 3, Scope Note) (1939).

2. See Fisher, *Western Experience & Eastern Appropriation Proposals,* in The Law of Water Allocation in the Eastern United States 75 (1958).

uses despite long nonuse of their rights. This uncertainty is increased in many states where a riparian neither making nor intending to make use of water can enjoin an existing use as unreasonable with regard to his right. In practice the court will occasionally regard the fact of priority of use as one element to be considered in assessing reasonableness.

Another criticism of the common law riparian system has concerned the lack of administrative controls in many jurisdictions where the extent of a riparian's right of reasonable use can be determined only by litigation. The critics maintain that this uncertainty results in a needless loss when industries utilizing water resources have their water use patterns upset by competing projects. Probably of greater concern is the waste of water going unused or devoted to less valuable uses because industries fearful of such losses refuse to come into a jurisdiction.

On occasion courts have apportioned streamflow between competing users to give the riparians a clear picture of their rights. The infrequency of such decisions may be accounted for in part by the fact that it would involve the court too closely in the supervision of those uses. Recognizing their lack of expertise and the inefficiency of a case-by-case approach, the courts have been reluctant to become involved. Also the numerous courts are structurally not as capable of uniformity in the application of the law as a single centralized agency.

As population growth and modern technological developments in both agriculture and industry have been making increasingly greater demands on eastern water supplies, the problem of maintaining streamflows and ground water levels has assumed increasingly greater importance. Concern over the adequacy of existing laws to cope with emerging water resource problems has led many executive and legislative study committees to propose new methods to deal with the problems. The legislative creation of administrative authorities in a number of eastern states, with varying powers to grant permits authorizing the withdrawal of water from streams, has raised a number of interrelated legal and physical problems.

These uncertainties occasioned by the flexibility of the riparian system have sparked the recent movement for new water-rights legislation in many eastern states, including provisions for the establishment of permit systems to provide a means of regulation, through administrative agencies, of existing and future water uses.

NOTE

The Model Code deals with water management and regulates uses of groundwater, surface water, and diffused surface water. Under its provisions, a state may reserve rights for minimum stream flows and lake levels, as well as regulate water quality. Use and quality considerations are both under one authority, called the State Water Resources Board. The Board is also given authority over the construction and regulation of wells and surface water works, weather modification operations, and negotiations on behalf of the state in federal and interstate water projects. All uses other than those for individual domestic purposes are subject to permit. Permits are issued for a maximum of twenty years, except where a longer period is required to retire bonds issued by municipalities or other governmental bodies. In the latter event the maximum period is fifty years. In the event of competing permit applications for an inadequate supply of water, the application that "best serves the public interest" prevails. The Code proposes the formulation of a state water use plan, based on water supply and demand information. One objective of the plan is to maximize "reasonable-beneficial use" of water, which is defined by the Code as "[t]he use of water in such a quantity as is necessary for economic and efficient utilization, for a purpose and in a manner which is both reasonable and consistent with the public interest." Frank E. Maloney et al., A Model Water Code (1972), at 4.

2. THE EAST MODIFIES RIPARIANISM

Robert H. Abrams, Replacing Riparianism in the Twenty–First Century

36 Wayne L. Rev. 93 (1989).

Riparianism has been the universal water law of the East for two centuries. The doctrine has served the region well largely because the demand on the water resource has rarely exceeded supply. However, the East is now facing both unprecedented demand and changing climatic conditions that will cause chronic water shortages. Riparianism lacks a reliable method of allocating water uses in times of shortage. Therefore, a search for alternatives to the venerable doctrine must begin. This Article is the final part of a trilogy that outlines the need for a radical departure from riparianism. It proposes to replace riparianism with a hierarchical permit-based water rights system that features transferable permits. The new system will function both in times of ample water supply and in times of water shortage.

I. Rejecting Prior Appropriation and Existing Eastern Administrative Systems

Before presenting the proposed permit system, the inappropriateness of two other water allocation methods as alternatives to riparianism, prior appropriation and administrative permit systems, must be briefly discussed to show that a better alternative is needed. In the arid West, where water shortages are common, prior appropriation replaced riparianism and became the dominant water law. Riparianism's rules of sharing in times of shortage did not offer a sufficiently secure right to water use. To overcome this insecurity, Western water law developed a temporal appropriation system ("first in time, first in right") that erected a quantifiable set of annual usufructuary rights that were far more precise than the rights granted under riparianism. Thus, one might suppose that prior appropriation could successfully replace riparianism in any region facing water shortfalls because its allocative system was designed for water-short areas.

Beyond security of right, two additional aspects of prior appropriation are particularly attractive: (1) its doctrinal promise to avoid waste and promote conservation; and (2) its ability to permit marketing of the water rights that results in the transfer of water from low value uses to high value uses. Both of these features foster efficient use of the water, allowing maximum utilization. Under scrutiny, the expected failure of riparianism on these two counts is not total, nor is the expected exemplary performance of prior appropriation patent. These findings challenge the supposition that prior appropriation is the cure for riparianism and spark the search for still better alternatives.

Waste avoidance and conservation are vital to water-short regions, and the governing water law doctrines must reflect the importance of these practices. Riparianism views a wasteful use as unreasonable, and therefore enjoinable, if it harms another user. More important, in the ad hoc nature of riparian decision making, the presence or absence of conservation efforts can be used to determine whether an otherwise reasonable riparian use is being undertaken in a reasonable fashion during a time of shortage. Prior appropriation guards against waste as a facet of the beneficial use inquiry. Only the amount of water put to a beneficial use is protected; for example, in an irrigation application, water that is applied in excess of the amount needed for the crop can be allocated to another user. In virtually all prior appropriation states, however, the waste doctrine is not strictly applied. One commentator noted that "[prior appropriation] actually encouraged the development of inefficient techniques in areas where greed and speculation were commonplace; the greater the appropriation, the greater the water right claimed.... Only in cases of extreme wastefulness have courts required that irrigation appropriations conform to customary practices of the region."[4]

The second claimed attraction of prior appropriation systems as an improvement on riparianism is the transferability of the water rights. Riparianism's penchant for trying to accommodate competing users through sharing of the shortage offers little promise to a user in a water-short area that water use will continue without diminution. The user cannot increase the certainty of continued water by purchasing additional water rights because none of the coriparians can exclude others from the use of the water. Each riparian will sell the usufructuary right of withdrawal for whatever price it will bring. Low value and high value water users alike have correlative rights, and there is no guarantee that in time of shortage the uses curtailed will be the low, rather than the high, value uses. Riparianism thus impedes the creation of a meaningful water market.

---

4. Shupe, *Waste in Western Water Law: A Blueprint for Change,* 61 Or. L. Rev. 483, 486 (1982). Conformity to local custom is hardly a standard that inspires extensive conservation efforts. *See, e.g.,* Tulare Irr. Dist. v. Lindsay–Strathmore Irr. Dist., 3 Cal.2d 489, 45 P.2d 972 (1935) (condoning transmission loss of almost half of diverted water as consistent with custom).

In contrast, prior appropriation offers the user an opportunity to purchase a senior water right, thereby ensuring more secure water receipt. This buying and selling of water rights leads to the possibility of creating a functioning water market in which the price of water not only measures the cost of its provision, but also reflects its value as a productive scarce resource. Unfortunately, prior appropriation's record of fostering water transfers that move scarce water to more valuable uses merits only faint praise. Appropriative water rights, despite creating a quantified set of usufructuary priorities capable of supporting efficiency-enhancing transfers, are not readily marketable commodities that can be transferred easily to their highest use. The doctrine has always permitted transfers, but the transfers are limited by the "no harm on transfer" rule, which requires deference to the security of the rights of downstream junior water users who depend on making use of water that is withdrawn, but not consumed, by upstream seniors. The no harm rule limits transfers to those in which the disparity in values of the water to the transferee and transferor is sufficiently great to overcome what are almost always very high transaction costs.

Beyond the false promises of efficient water use and marketing of water rights, a final objection to importing prior appropriation to the East is the doctrine's neglect of instream uses, a systemic weakness that is of particular concern in the Eastern United States. The doctrinal insistence that a usufructuary right could only be perfected by a physical diversion of water from the watercourse, and thereafter applying the diverted water to a beneficial use, made it impossible to obtain rights to protect instream flows needed to support recreation or fish and wildlife habitat. Within the last two decades, this shortcoming of appropriation law has been addressed by state governments with statutes that protect instream flows. These statutes mark a departure from appropriation toward a managerial system that accommodates the broader spectrum of interests in ways that are more nearly riparian in flavor. Thus, what is sensibly under consideration as an alternative to riparianism, although flying the banner of prior appropriation, is instead a potpourri of appropriation and regulation. This raises the question of whether it would be preferable to build a replacement for riparianism on a regulatory platform that grows out of riparian, rather than appropriation, traditions.

A more attractive path for improving riparianism is to overlay some government regulation on the traditional pattern of unbridled private decision making and common-law judicial review that has determined water use patterns in the Eastern United States. Two riparian states, Iowa and Florida, have adopted far-reaching permit systems; sixteen other riparian jurisdictions have supplemented their common law with some kind of regulatory system. Although their standards for permit issuance are linguistically similar to the common-law doctrine, these systems typically require some form of administrative issuance of permits for the allocation of surface waters. The systems are thus a significant departure from riparianism because the permit applications are reviewed prospectively before the use is initiated. States can therefore avoid user conflicts before they arise by refusing a permit, conditioning a permit grant, or taking actions that reduce the overall demand for water. These systems are more sensitive than prior appropriation because the permitting agency is empowered to consider the impact of the permit on competing uses, including instream uses of the water, and can control the duration of the permit. Permits, like other methods that quantify uses, allow easy introduction of price-induced conservation methods such as a withdrawal and/or consumption fee on a per unit basis. However, most states have been slow to adopt such fees.

Three evident drawbacks of a standard permit system are its rigidity, its tendency to overregulate, and its lack of articulated policy objectives. Permits in the typical Eastern systems are user specific and are not transferable separate from the land that is benefitted by the use. The system is hyperactive—even users who are not part of the allocation problem are forced to participate in government regulation. Finally, the existing systems offer little guidance to state agencies. Administrative decisions, like their riparian common-law forbearers, continue to be made on an ad hoc basis with little regard for integrated water system management.

The foregoing critique of prior appropriation systems and the bulk of the current permit systems has tried to show that in many ways those systems do not effectively manage the water resource. Neither pose so attractive an alternative to riparianism that adoption is imminent. If a better alternative can be fashioned, the time to act is now, for "damages can be lessened if societies utilize a strategy of proactive risk management rather than one of reactive crisis management." Ideally, integrated intergovernmental long-range water planning might well be the optimal initial proactive step. Comprehensive planning, however, is both a lengthy and expensive process that too often fails to yield the definitive guidance needed to support a coherent resource management system. The need is for a mechanism that is less cumbersome to implement, yet has the capacity to respond to escalating pressure on the water resource. The instrumentalist theory of water law comes to the fore by identifying the principal objective sought—giving legal protection to the most important uses of the water.

* * *

For an early and still timely assessment of the operation of permit systems in riparian states see the trilogy by Professor Robert H. Abrams: *Charting The Course of Riparianism: An Instrumentalist Theory of Change*, 35 Wayne L. Rev. 1381 (1989); *Water Allocation By Comprehensive Permit Systems in the East: Considering A Move Away From Orthodoxy*, 9 Va. Envtl. L.J. 255 (1990); and *Replacing Riparianism in the Twenty–First Century*, 36 Wayne L. Rev. 93 (1989). In 1997, the American Society of Civil Engineers published a model state Regulated Riparian Water Rights and Prior Appropriation Water Rights Codes. The Regulated Riparian Code (Joseph W. Dellapenna ed. 1997), addresses all aspects of Eastern water allocation, state water resources planning, permit standards, transfers, transbasin diversions, area of origin protections, and instream flows. See

Robert Beck, The Regulated Riparian Model Water Code: Blueprint for Twenty First Century Water Management, 25 Wm. & Mary Envtl. L. & Pol'y Rev. 113 (2000).

3. Regulated Ripariansim

a. What Is It?

Eastern permit systems have been characterized by Professor Dellapena as "regulated riparianism," Joseph W. Dellapena, Chapter 9, Regulated Riparianism, in 1 Waters and Water Rights (2007 Replacement vol.), but this term does not capture the variety among them. The core meaning of regulated riparianism is that the common law of riparian rights has been statutorily modified but remains the default rule to resolve conflicts among users. Regulated riparianism's major modification is to overlay a permit system on the common law. A series of droughts in the 1950s initially triggered the first round of reforms. See N. William Hines, A Decade of Experience Under the Iowa Water Permit System 10–12 (University of Iowa College of Law, Agricultural Law Monograph No. 9 1966). One state, Mississippi, actually adopted prior appropriation in 1956, but then replaced it with regulated riparianism in 1988. Today, concerns about shortages triggered by population increases, the heightened competition between consumptive and non-consumptive or instream uses, and global climate change continue to spur interest water law reform. In the eight Great lakes states, the evolving anti-out-basin diversion regime, see pages 1043–1049, *infra*, has produced new water use registration requirements, e.g. McKinney's Consolidated Laws of New York, Environmental Conservation law § 15–1605 (2006), and new withdrawal permit regimes, e.g. Minn. Stat. Ch. 103G (2007); Mich. Comp. Laws §§ 324–32701 et. seq. (2008 Cum. Annual Pocket Part).

Regulated riparianism, following the lead of prior appropriation, asserts the state's power to set the ground rules for water allocation and use, often by asserting that the state "owns" its waters in trust for its citizens. However, state assertion of the trust power and the displacement of the common law can be uneven. E.g., Bausch & Lomb Inc. v. Utica Mutual Insurance Co., 330 Md. 758, 625 A.2d 1021 (1993), which holds that Maryland's regulation of water pollution and surface water fell short of the western states trust ownership, and that any assertion of trust ownership was limited to surface, navigable waters. Thus, the state could not maintain an action against a Superfund site's insurer for natural resources damages to groundwater. See also New Mexico v. General Electric Company, 335 F.Supp.2d 1185 (D.N.M. 2004), discussed at page 666, *infra*. Beyond the assertion of regulatory power, eastern permit systems are seldom comprehensive and leave many questions such as the relationship among permit holders and the transferrability of permit rights unaddressed.

b. The Scope of Regulated Riparian Permit Systems

Many systems are primarily registration systems. Other states have registration for smaller uses and permit requirements for larger ones. For example, Michigan requires annual use reports from industrial and agricultural users who use over 100,000 gallons per day, MICH.COMP.LAWS § 324.32705, and permits for new diversions between 2,000,000–5,000,000 gallons per day, § 324.32713.[1] Several states regulate only withdrawals in stressed areas. In 1989, Virginia required permits for new withdrawals or withdrawals in excess of pre–1989 maximum daily withdrawals in "declared surface management areas." VA.CODE ANN. § 62.1–243 and 247. These areas may be declared to protect "substantial instream values," when low conditions could occur "which would threaten downstream uses," and when current or potential off-steam uses "are likely to exacerbate natural low flow conditions to the detriment of instream flow values." Id at § 62.1–246.

c.   *The Florida Model for Stressed Humid States*

The major exception to the piecemeal and incomplete approach found in most eastern states is Florida's 1972 law, based on Dean Maloney's Model Water Code. Since the Florida statute, many states have adopted elements of the system but no state has adopted a statute as comprehensive as Florida's. Florida, more than other eastern states, shares a crucial characteristic with California and other areas of the world such as Namibia: the relatively less populated and rural north is much better watered than the more populous south.

Richard Hamann, Law and Policy in Managing Florida's Water Resources, *in* Water Resources Atlas of Florida

(Edward A. Fernald and Elizabeth D. Purdum eds., 1998).

Florida's water resources have been shaped by our policy choices and the laws and institutions created to implement them. Until the 1970s, those waters were impounded, drained, filled, diverted, extracted and contaminated on a massive scale, with devastating consequences for the natural environment and the sustainability of our society. Today, they are increasingly being protected, conserved, rationed and restored. * * *

The Legal Framework for Water Management

The Water Resources Act of 1972, codified as Chapter 373 of the Florida Statutes * * * delegates comprehensive authority to manage water to five regional water management districts covering the entire state and [to] the Florida Department of Environmental Protection (DEP). Two of those districts already existed in 1972, the Southwest Florida Water Management district and the South Florida Water Management District (created from the Central and Southern Florida Flood Control District). The three new water management districts, Northwest Florida, Suwannee and St. Johns River Water Management Districts, were created to manage

---

1.   The range is tied to the Great Lakes Compact, *infra* pages 1043–1046, which requires a basin wide review for new diversions over 5,000,000 gallons per day.

water in the northern and central parts of the state. One of the most important features of the districts is that their boundaries are drawn along surface hydrologic basin boundaries, cutting across political subdivisions like counties or cities. Having the responsibility for entire watersheds greatly enhances the ability of a district to address ecosystem-level problems. The watershed of the Everglades, for example, is entirely in the South Florida Water Management District.

Each water management district is headed by a governing board, comprised of unpaid citizens appointed by the Governor and confirmed by the Senate. The governing board hires an executive director and is responsible for approving the district's budget, plans, acquisitions, rules and orders. The districts have the authority to levy ad valorem taxes under an amendment to the Florida constitution approved by the voters in 1976. The Legislature sets a cap on the level of taxes and provides additional funds through appropriations. The activities of the districts are supervised and reviewed by a state level agency, the Florida Department of Environmental Protection (DEP). Much of the regulatory authority of the districts has actually been delegated by DEP. In addition, many district decisions are subject to review by the governor and cabinet.

The authority of the districts is broad and comprehensive. The water management districts can build and operate water management structures such as canals, dikes and pumping stations. They also have the authority to purchase and manage land for water management purposes.

The districts have extensive regulatory authority. The use of district lands and works can be regulated. The development of land for public or private uses is also subject to regulation under the Environmental Regulatory Permitting process. Virtually any construction or other activity that alters the flow of water across the surface of the land may be regulated by the districts to ensure that water quality is not degraded, downstream areas are not flooded, and aquifers and wetlands that wildlife are dependent on are not adversely affected. If any development activity is proposed for a wetland, then it must also meet a public interest test based on review of the impacts to fish and wildlife habitat, recreation and other wetland functions. Such impacts may be offset or compensated for by the preservation, restoration or enhancement of other wetlands. Mitigation banks have been established to facilitate this process and ensure the resulting mitigation areas have high ecological value. The districts also have a role in regulating the use of state-owned submerged lands and in coastal construction regulation.

Another major area for regulation by the districts is in the regulation of activities that affect the quantity of water available for use by humans or the environment. The districts have authority to regulate artificial recharge facilities and consumptive use of water. Consumptive use permitting is one of the most important responsibilities of the districts. Virtually any use of water that involves withdrawing or diverting it from its source can be regulated by a water management district under this authority. Local governments are prohibited from regulating consumptive use.

Consumptive use permits are granted for fixed periods of time. The maximum possible duration for most permits is twenty years. In practice, the districts have been reluctant to grant such lengthy permits because of the need to evaluate the availability of water and of more efficient techniques for using it. Permits can be revoked only under very limited circumstances. Thus, permittees are guaranteed a right to use water for the duration of their permit, subject only to water use restrictions imposed because of drought or emergency conditions. Permits may be freely transferred to the purchasers of the land or other facilities where the water is being used. Upon the expiration of a permit, the user must apply for renewal. New conditions may be imposed at that time to protect the environment or require more efficient use of available supplies. A competing user may be granted the right to use the water where there is some superior public interest to be served, although that has never occurred.

Three criteria must be met for obtaining a consumptive use permit. The applicant must establish that the use: (1) will not interfere with a presently existing legal use of water; (2) is a "reasonable beneficial" use; and (3) is consistent with the public interest. The requirement that a new use cannot interfere with an existing use ensures that the water allocated to one user under that law cannot be taken for use by another. It thus establishes legal certainty that water rights will be protected.

The reasonable beneficial use standard is the most innovative part of the criteria. The statute defines a reasonable beneficial use as "the use of water in such quantity as is necessary for economic and efficient utilization for a purpose and in a manner which is both reasonable and consistent with the public interest." The standard thus mandates water use efficiency and requires the districts to consider the same kinds of factors that were considered under the common law in making determinations of reasonableness. In addition, the public interest must be a factor in determining whether to issue a permit.

Environmental considerations play an important role in the determination of whether to issue a consumptive use permit. A wellfield permit, for example, that would result in dewatering wetlands could be denied for failure to meet the reasonableness or public interest standards. The districts are also required to establish minimum flows and levels as a limit for acceptable environmental impacts. Where those minimum flows and levels have been violated by existing conditions, the districts are required to develop recovery plans. They are also required, however, to consider the effects of hydrologic changes, and the feasibility of attaining minimum flows and levels, in establishing them.

Consumptive use permits allocate the water that is available during "normal" times. Florida, however, is subject to wide variation in climatic conditions, including extended droughts. To prepare for such events, each district is required to adopt a water shortage plan. Under the plan, permits may be classified by source, method of withdrawal, and use. When there is insufficient water available to meet all legal demands, or use must be curtailed to prevent serious harm to the water resources of the area from salt water intrusion or other effects, then the water shortage plan may be put into effect. Restrictions under the plan may be imposed on all users or only on certain classes of users depending on the specific conditions of the water shortage. If implementation of the water shortage plan is not adequate to protect the public and the environment, then an emergency can be declared and orders issued to individual users to limit water use.

One area in which the Water Resources Act differs substantially from the common law is in the treatment of water transport. Under the common law, the right to use water was limited to those who owned riparian land or land overlying a groundwater source. Since 1957, Florida statutes have allowed the transport of water to more distant locations. The current law allows the districts to permit the holders of consumptive use permits to transport water "beyond overlying land, across county boundaries, or outside the watershed from which it is taken" where consistent with the public interest. The 1998 Legislature directed the districts to consider a variety of factors in making that determination, mostly related to the availability and environmental impacts of alternatives. For transfers outside of a water management district, the district is required to consider the needs of both the receiving and producing areas.

The Water Resources Act provides for a variety of water management planning by the districts and the Florida Department of Environmental Protection (DEP). The DEP is directed to adopt a Florida Water Plan, consisting of its existing program and a "water resource implementation rule." Each water management district is required to develop a District Water Management Plan, regional water supply plans, groundwater basin resource availability inventories and Surface Water Improvement Management (SWIM) plans. This planning process should provide the basis for land use planning, restoration activities, water supply development, the establishment of minimum flows and levels and consumptive use permitting.

In considering the legal and institutional framework for water management in Florida, several other governmental entities and programs must be discussed. Local governments have the broadest responsibility for protecting water resources, managing flood hazards and providing water supplies. Local government comprehensive plans are the vehicle for integrating these concerns with community development and other considerations. The Florida Department of Community Affairs and Florida's eleven regional planning councils have important roles in the planning process.

Local governments in several areas of the state have also joined together through interlocal agreements to provide water on a regional basis, most notably in the Tampa Bay area. The West Coast Regional Water Supply Authority controls an extensive network of wellfields, pipelines and pumping stations to supply water to its member local governments, including Pinellas, Pasco, and Hillsborough counties. By working together in such cooperative arrangements, local governments can reduce regional conflict over water supply.

The protection and restoration of water quality is a vital part of water management. Water quality standard are established by the Florida Department of Environmental Protection (DEP), with the guidance and oversight of the U.S. Environmental Protection Agency (EPA). Both DEP and EPA regulate the discharge of pollutants by such major sources as industry, agriculture, mining, construction, and waste treatment. They are both involved with the cleanup of sites that have been contaminated by hazardous wastes, toxic substances, and petroleum. Other agencies with a role in protecting water quality are the Department of Health, which regulates septic tanks and other on-site sewage treatment and disposal systems, and the Florida Department of Agriculture and Consumer Services, which has jurisdiction over the application of pesticides.

Water managers and users increasingly face the need to consider impacts to the endangered and threatened species that inhabit or depend on Florida's waters * * *. Fish and wildlife are an important part of the resource. The Florida Game and Fresh Water Fish Commission, the Marine Fisheries Commission, the U.S. Fish and Wildlife Service and the National Marine Fisheries Service all play important roles in conducting research on fish and wildlife and bringing that information to the attention of water managers.

The federal government is actively involved in water management and has significant investments in such vital resources as the Everglades National Park, the national forests of Florida, and the national wildlife refuges. The federal government also holds several reservations in trust for the Miccosukee and Seminole tribes. The U.S. Army Corps of Engineers is engaged in a massive restudy of the Central and Southern Florida Project that will soon culminate in recommendations for a multibillion dollar reconstruction project to improve water supply, water quality and natural systems protection in South Florida. [The Corps of Engineers and the EPA have] wetlands permitting responsibilities throughout the state * * *. [EPA] has supported a great deal of research on the causes of water quality degradation [throughout Florida].

* * *

Florida's water management system has been the envy of many other states for over 25 years. Because the water management districts encompass entire watersheds, they are able to address environmental problems with less jurisdictional conflict than is usually possible. By having a stable source of ad valorem tax revenue, the districts are able to develop scientific expertise and information over years of data collection and analysis. With an independent source of revenue and appointed boards, the programs of the districts have been less subject to political whim than those of many other agencies. And finally, the scope of authority delegated to the districts has been sufficiently broad and flexible that they have been able to address problems that were only dimly recognized in 1972.

The districts have enjoyed strong political support. That is at least partly because their decisions have been supportive of agricultural, commercial, and residential development. They have provided drainage and flood protection, and they have denied very few consumptive use permits. Water seemed to be abundant.

* * *

One set of issues revolves around the allocation of water for the natural environment through the establishment of minimum flows and levels, reservations of water, or the development of plans for restoring natural ecosystems. * * *

The determination of how to allocate available supplies to meet increasing human demands also raises a host of issues. Increased water efficiency is the most attractive option, but at some point the limits of cost and acceptability will be reached. The reallocation of water from existing users is at least theoretically possible. Upon expiration of a permit, water managers can transfer the supply to competing users who better serve the public interest. The economic and social dislocation that would occur, for example, from depriving agricultural users to serve expanding urban areas, makes this highly unattractive.

Existing users have been pressing in recent years to expand their protection. When permits are renewed, users are often forced to implement more efficient methods for using water or to use alternative sources that are more expensive or less desirable. Longer term permits protect users from having to make such changes. Another option that has been advocated for increasing the level of certainty for existing users is to give them either a guaranteed right to renew their permits or to give them a greater preference against competing users.

One way of obtaining more efficient use of water and providing for the transfer of water rights to new uses would be to provide compensation to displaced users. Some economists argue that water markets should be established, allowing the holder of water rights to sell them for new uses. They believe that a properly designed market would allocate water among competing users better than an administrative agency. Some of the arguments raised against such proposals relate to the practicality of establishing markets for something that cannot be easily transferred to different users without considering place-specific adverse effects. Others focus on the nature of water as a public resource and question whether it is fair to allow private users to gain monetary benefits from selling it. There is also concern whether markets place a value on all of the appropriate factors. The experience of the western states, where water rights are more freely traded, is instructive. In many places aquatic environments cannot be restored without purchasing expensive water rights from the private sector. In other areas, rural communities are being destroyed as the water rights necessary to support agriculture are transferred to more wealthy urban sectors.

* * *

One of the largest unresolved issues in Florida is how to make appropriate linkages between water management and land use decisions. Although any intensive use of land requires a water supply and thus places additional demands on available sources of water, land use planners are currently not required to consider the availability of water and the impacts of water supply development when making land use decisions. Inadequate consideration is given to the potential impacts of land use activity on water resources, through drainage, flood control, contamination, nutrient enrichment, boating traffic, and other effects. * * *

NOTES

1. *Is It Better Than Processed Cheese?* Does Florida's code address the problems cited by Professors Maloney et al., *supra* p. 275–277 How does the Code, as described by Professor Hamann, meet the concerns discussed by Professor Abrams, *supra* p. 278? What changes could make the Florida code even more comprehensive? How does the Code depart from the common law tradition of riparian law? If the code were proposed for adoption in a western state, how would it alter the common law tradition of prior appropriation? One issue noted by Professor Hamann is the limited life of water permits. What potential problems does this feature of the code present? How can these problems be addressed?

2. *What About the Fish and Boaters?* Despite all its positive aspects, there have been persistent calls to amend the Florida code partly as a result of citizen outcries over the failure of water management districts to establish minimum flows and levels for surface waters and aquifers. Conflicts between municipal and agricultural users, rich and poor areas, and coastal versus inland concerns also created pressure for change. In 1997, the Florida legislature amended the code and changed its flavor in many respects. Districts were mandated to undertake water development rather than just their traditional regulatory and allocation functions. FLA. STAT. ANN. § 373.0831(3). Responding to the concerns of water users that their permitted withdrawals could be curtailed for environmental protection, the legislature eased the minimum flow responsibilities of the districts. See FLA. STAT. ANN. §§ 373.042 and 373.0421. It removed the former mandatory language with respect to setting these levels that had led a Florida court of appeals to require one district to take action. Concerned Citizens of Putnam County for Responsive Government, Inc. v. St. Johns River Water Management Dist., 622 So.2d 520 (Fla.App.1993). Now the districts are to produce a "priority list" of the water bodies where they intend to establish flows and levels. Once set, minimum levels can be challenged and subjected to scientific peer review. Moreover, the benchmark for flows and levels is no longer the historic level where there has been substantial alteration of a waterway. The amendments also made several changes in governance of districts by giving the governor and legislature more control of district boards, management, and budgets. See generally Frank E. Matthews & Gabriel E. Nieto, *Florida Water Policy: A Twenty–Five Year Mid–Course Correction*, 25 Fla. St. U. L. Rev. 365 (1998).

3. *Is it Constitutional?* Does the substitution of a permit system for common law riparian or groundwater rights, as Florida has done, constitute a taking a property without due process of law? This concern has been persistently voiced but the issue has seldom arisen in the East. The most authoritative precedent remains in Omernik v. Wisconsin, 64 Wis.2d 6, 218 N.W.2d 734, 743 (1974). The Supreme Court of Wisconsin held that the law applied in Nekoosa–Edwards Paper Co. v. Public Service Comm'n, 8 Wis.2d 582, 99 N.W.2d 821 (1959), discussed in Note 4, *infra*, was not a taking without just compensation but was a "valid exercise of the police power." See also Omernick v. Department of Natural Resources, 71 Wis.2d 370, 238 N.W.2d 114, 116 (1976), in which the court held that the legislature has "abrogated the common law riparian right of irrigation and has substituted the permit procedure...." Thus, the riparian owner must obtain a permit before diverting water for irrigation purposes which requires the consent of all riparians injured by a diversion of non-surplus water. The taking question is discussed generally *infra* p. 486.

One of the reasons that the taking issue does not often arise is that the scope of any claimed riparian rights is likely to be uncertain. City of Waterbury v. Township of Washington, 260 Conn. 506, 800 A.2d 1102 (2002) illustrates the problem of deciding what common law rights, if any, have been diminished. A small downstream town sued Waterbury alleging that its long standing transbasin diversions from a small river, the lower reaches of which were a state wild and scenic river, produced low summer flows diminishing its natural beauty, reducing it as a habitat for river organisms, and limiting the value for fishing and other recreation. The town argued that the diversions were an unreasonable impairment of the public trust value of the river under the Connecticut Environmental Protection Act, CONN.GEN.STAT. § 22a–17, and a violation of the minimum flow provisions statute for stocked rivers, CONN.GEN.STAT. §§ 26–141a–141c. Waterbury asserted prescriptive rights to the water and that there was no evidence of stocking in the reach of its diversion. The court held that the minimum flow statute only requires stocking somewhere along the river and guarantees sufficient water for natural and stocked wildlife and recreation. However, it held that Waterbury could claim prescriptive rights because until 1982 the state followed the natural flow theory, see page 123, *supra*, and "the mere presence of the Shepaug dam was sufficient to satisfy the open and visible requirement necessary to establish a prescriptive easement." 800 A.2d at 1149. The case was remanded with the following observations to determine whether Waterbury had increased its use beyond the scope of the easement and whether or not the city had acquired new prescriptive easements:

> Thus, on the remand, if the trial court determines that Waterbury has exceeded the scope of its easement, without gaining a new easement, the court must determine what remedial action it should take. In this connection, however, several preliminary questions must be addressed. Because the parties have not briefed these issues, we decline to decide them. In order, however, to aid the trial court in its resolution of this issue, should it arise, we offer the following guidance.

The trial court, first, must determine whether the defendants currently possess any riparian rights with respect to the flow down the Shepaug River, or if this common-law right has been superseded by legislative enactment. In 1982, with the enactment of the diversion act, Connecticut made a transition from a common-law riparian rights to a regulated riparian rights state. The major change effectuated by this transition is that, now, a state agency will determine, in advance, what diversions are allowed and to what extent, rather than having trial courts apply common-law riparian rights principles and resolve disputes through litigation. J. Christman, Water Rights in the Eastern United States (K. Wright ed., 1998) pp. 29–30; J. Dellapenna, 1 Waters and Water Rights, *supra*, § 9.03(b)(1), at p. 493 ("[r]egulated riparian statutes delegate to an administrative agency the right to decide who among competing applicants, will receive the right to use water, terms and conditions under which they will hold that right, and when, where, and how that right will end").

The diversion act requires that any party seeking to divert water after July 1, 1982, first obtain a permit from the department. When the legislature enacted the diversion act, it exempted all those current diversions from the permitting system, but ordered the holders of the existing diversions to register with the department "on a form prescribed by [it] the location, capacity, frequency and rate of withdrawals or discharges of said diversion and a description of the water use and water system." General Statutes § 22a–368 (a). The trial court found that Waterbury properly registered its Shepaug River diversion, and thus is exempt from the permitting requirements. Section 22a–377 (c) 1(c)(1) of the Regulations of Connecticut State Agencies provides: "Any person or municipality which registered a diversion pursuant to section 22a–368 of the General Statutes may maintain such diversion *only in accordance with the information provided in the registration form filed with the Commissioner.* Any person or municipality which registered a diversion pursuant to section 22a–368 of the General Statutes may not cause or allow any modification of such diversion, *including but not limited to an increase in withdrawal capacity,* without having first obtained a permit under sections 22a–365 to 22a–378, inclusive, of the General Statutes and 22a–377 (c) 2 of the Regulations of Connecticut State Agencies, unless such modification is exempt under section 22a–377 of the General Statutes or section 22a–377 (b) 1 of the Regulations of Connecticut State Agencies." (Emphasis added.)

The trial court must also determine whether these provisions constitute the sole means by which a party can remedy an excessive diversion, or if the legislature intended to allow riparians additional common-law remedies for grandfathered diversions. For example, the Regulated Riparian Model Water Code, intended "to create a complete, comprehensive, and well integrated statutory scheme for creating or refining a regulated riparian system of water law capable of dealing with the problems of the twenty-first century." J. Dellapenna, A.S.C.E., Regulated Riparian Model Water Code (1997) preface, p. x.

With respect to the effects of grandfathering provisions in a permit system, the code provides: "Most states will choose to exempt some water uses from the permit system. In that case the Code provides that disputes involving such exempted water uses will be governed by the principle of reasonable use. In most cases, that rule is simply the prior law that already applied to them as the common law of riparian rights or the common law of underground water." Id., at § 2R–1–04, commentary, p. 31. The diversion act, passed fifteen years before the publication of this code, contains no such provision. Therefore, the trial court must determine what ramifications, if any, result from this omission.

Additionally, if the trial court determines that the defendants retain riparian rights with respect to the exempted diversion, it must decide what standard will govern its examination of whether Waterbury violated these rights: either some type of reasonableness inquiry, as indicated in the model code and provided for in General Statutes § 22a–373 of the diversion act, or "the prior law that already applied to them as the common law of riparian rights"; J. Dellapenna, Regulated Riparian Model Water Code, *supra*, at § 2R–1–04, commentary, p. 31; which, prior to 1982 in Connecticut, was the natural flow body of law.

4. *Are prior users at greater risk compared to the common law or prior appropriation?* How should prior users be protected? Two interrelated crucial questions are the security of existing permitted uses and the length of permits. Review the debate between proponents of regulated riparianism and prior appropriation on pages 136–137. As in theological disputes, distinctions are crucial. The major criticisms of prior appropriation have been that prior appropriation locks out newer, more efficient or socially important uses and freezes older, often inefficient uses. Thus, the system must, like riparian rights, always be open to new entrants and permit terms should be limited. For example, Delaware issues withdrawal permits "on the basis of equitable apportionment," DEL.CODE.ANN. Title 7, § 6010, and by administrative regulation has limited permits to a maximum of 30 years with annual 5 year reviews. However, regulated riparianism must confront the question that has been at the center of prior appropriation: how much certainty is necessary to trigger the necessary investment in societally beneficial water infrastructure. When the issue has arisen, states have followed the principle of prior appropriation. See pages 610–613, *infra*. Wisconsin once had a statute which required the consent of all riparians along a nonnavigable stream to divert "water other than surplus water." Nekoosa–Edwards Paper Co. v. Public Service Comm'n, 8 Wis.2d 582, 99 N.W.2d 821 (1959) construed the statute to allow the State PublicSP Service Commission to determine if water was being beneficially used by a riparian or whether it was surplus but not to decide whether a diversion would injure other riparian owners. Thus, a downstream hydroelectric facility, which needed the flow from a lake fed by a small creek during the summer, could veto two proposed upstream irrigation diversions. See Jacob

H. Beuscher, Appropriation Law Elements in Riparian Doctrine States, 10 Buffalo L. Rev. 448 (1961).

The recent experience of Georgia in trying to devise a permit system responsive to more prolonged droughts is illustrative of the problems of balancing security and efficiency. The state has both growing urban areas and expanding supplemental irrigation acreage in the Flint River Basin, especially from groundwater. She experienced a series of severe droughts starting in 1998. Atlanta is dependent on a Corps of Engineers reservoir that is the source of an interstate dispute among Alabama, Florida and Georgia. See pages 976–977. In 2002, the state passed the Flint River Drought Protection Act. GA.CODE.ANN. § 12–5–40 et seq. (2003). The Act applies to surface and groundwater in the Flint River Basin. Permits are required for diversions over 100,000 gallons per day. When a drought is declared, the Director of the Environmental Protection Division of the Department of Natural Resources may set the number of acres that must be retired for the irrigation season to meet minimum Flint River flows informally promised to Florida. To meet the target, the Director can hold an auction. If the auction does not produce the target reduction, the Director can begin to revoke the most recent permits and "work chronologically backward with each order issued." Id. at § 12–5–547. Auctions were held in 2001 and 2002. Initially, irrigators bid the amount that they will accept per acre to forego irrigation. Tobacco settlement monies were used fund the auction and 33,101 acres were withdrawn from irrigation. In 2002, the state set an average price which was slightly lower than the 2001 average price, $128.00 per acre versus $135.00, and 40,000 acres were taken out of irrigation at a cost $5.2 million.

The state initially issued farm use permits for groundwater based on use prior to 1998, but has begun to tighten these permits as based on the 1998 data. This made it impossible to determine how much water was actually saved by the auctions because the state did not know the amount of actual—let alone beneficial—use. After 2003, new permits are limited to 25 year terms and existing permits may be renewed at a lower capacity if they "would have unreasonable adverse affects on other water users." GA.CODE.ANN. § 12–5–31(b) (2003). See John L. Fortuna, Water Rights, Public Resources, and Private Commodities: Examining the Current and Future Law Governing the Allocation of Georgia Water, 38 Ga. L. Rev. 1009 (2004) and Wilson G. Barmeyer, The Problem of Reallocation in A Regulated Riparian System: Examining the Law of Georgia, 40 Ga. L. Rev. 207 (2005) for a history of the state's efforts to adjust its water law to more frequent, persistent droughts. Post–2003 wells must be metered and annual withdrawal amounts reported to the state, but the meters will be furnished by the state. Id. at § 12–5–31(b.1)(1) (2003). Permits may not be cancelled for non-use except if use is not commenced within two years after the issuance of the permit. Code Ga.Ann. § 12–5–31(b)(2). Cancellation is subject to financial hardship or circumstances beyond the control of the user defenses. As the drought progressed, Georgia amended its permit statute, subject to a 2008 referendum, to allow the modification of prior permits to accommodate new users on a pro rata or other reasonable use basis, but the Director of the Board of Natural Resources "shall give preference to existing use over an initial application." § 12–5–31(f) (2003). And, permits may now be issued for 10 and 50 years, and requires a supply adequacy determination for permits over 25 years which must be periodically reviewed. § 12–5–31(g) (2003).

Are Georgian farmers are better off than Western water users who are not compensated when priorities are enforced? Which is a fairer, more efficient system?

5. *Water Marketing in Regulated Riparian Jurisdictions: Does it work?* Does regulated riparianism solve the transfer problem? Review pages 277–279. The answer is basically no because proponents of regulated riparianism are extremely skeptical about the merits of water marketing and because statutes seldom directly address the issue. Even in the few states that expressly authorize transfers, problems exist:

> In most states, permits are tied to the original land and/or use for which a permit is issued, much like the case in Georgia. It would appear that three states (Delaware, Maryland, and North Carolina) allow water use permits to be transferred to other users involving changes in point of diversion and/or use . . ., but only after extensive review and approval by the State. Such transfers may be regarded as allowing the sale of a state-issued water use permit. However, we find little evidence of any implementation of such transfers and, generally, little enthusiasm for implementation. . . .
>
> In these regards, an interesting example is seen in rules established for North Carolina's Central Coastal Plain "Capacity Use Area" (CUA). In this CUA a permitted water user may sell or transfer to others any portion of his permitted withdrawal; the original permittee must request a permit modification to reduce his permitted withdrawal and the proposed recipient of the transfer must apply for a new or amended withdrawal permit (which must be approved by the state). However, discussions with personnel in the state's Department of Water Resources (DWR) reveal that, as of December 3, 2003, no transfer under this provision had taken place, although one proposed transfer was, at that time, under consideration. The proposed transfer would be a temporary transfer from Lenoir County to communities in neighboring counties for 5 years; financial arrangements related to this transfer, if indeed such arrangements exist, are unknown. Our information suggests that North Carolina's DWR may have serious concerns about the transfer provisions of the Rule based on the perceived difficulty of managing such transfers in the case of ground water, and the potential for adverse localized effects and the high level of uncertainty that appears to surround any groundwater analysis. Given the DWR's substantial regulatory authority over such transfers, we are told that future trades, if any, will likely be very limited.

[Whitney Rusert and Ronald Cummings, Characteristics of Water–Use Control Policies: A Survey of 28 Eastern States 1, 5 (Water Policy Working Paper No. 2004–001, North Georgia Water Planning and Policy Center, Andrew Young School of Policy studies Georgia State University, 2004).]

Florida allows the transfer of groundwater permits for the use of the Floridian aquifer to those seeking access to fresh water supplies, Grace M. Johns and Jay Yingling, Water Allocation Under Scarcity, Florida Water Resources J. 28 (June, 2000).

4. WESTERN STATES

a. *Overview*

Appropriation, as developed by the courts, was essentially a rule of capture. A right was perfected by diverting water from a stream and putting it to use. At first, these were the only requirements for perfecting a water right. Some states also imposed minor procedural requirements such as posting a notice or filing a paper in a county courthouse.

Now, however, appropriation is controlled by complex state statutes. These statutes regulate every aspect of appropriation, laying out detailed conditions for new appropriations and changes of use and regulating the use and management of water. Today, a practitioner looks first to state statutes and the rules of administrative agencies and only secondarily to doctrines and concepts. A history of practical problems explains why states moved away from the apparent simplicity of the early prior appropriation law.

Early records were notoriously imprecise, and there was no single place one could look to determine rights claimed in a river that might run through several counties. In addition, most appropriators claimed rights to far more water than they actually needed or used. This was partly because of a lack of knowledge by the users and partly because of their desire to ensure that they would have plenty of water to meet any future needs. Poor records and over-appropriation on paper created uncertainty that discouraged investments in expensive diversion and storage facilities.

Judicial decisions in disputes that would arise among appropriators provided some records. The decree in water rights adjudication might be helpful to a prospective appropriator but it was only conclusive as among those who actually were joined in the case. The first step in moving toward more reliable water rights determinations was for states to allow general stream adjudications. All interested parties in a watershed were joined in a lawsuit to decide their relative rights. The court integrated the claims of all parties with any piecemeal adjudications that had been made in the past, and then reviewed and determined the priority dates and quantities of all rights.

General stream adjudications were improvements over the early free-for-all appropriation system but once judgments became final, many states lacked a method for any way of integrating new rights and a system for administering decreed rights. A new wave of general permit stream adjudications has been initiated in states that have adopted permit systems. See *infra* p. 305.

The actual opening and closing of headgates to divert or cut off the flow of water to individual appropriators was often unregulated except by the water users themselves. This lack of supervision sometimes led to gunfire and other forms of self-help. See *Coffin v. Left Hand Ditch Co.*, *supra* p. 71.

Transfers of water rights provided another source of confusion. To the extent that changes in an appropriator's point of diversion were permitted without central coordination, a gap would arise between the record and actual locations of water rights on a given stream.

For general discussions of the conditions which led to the enactment of legislation subjecting appropriation to a state permit process see Elwood Mead, Irrigation Institutions (1903), especially pages 60–87 and 147–59. See generally Michael V. McIntire, *The Disparity Between State Water Rights Records and Actual Water Use Patterns: "I Wonder Where the Water Went?"*, 5 Land & Water L. Rev. 23 (1970).

For compelling, practical reasons, then, most of the western states began to exercise increasing administrative control over the acquisition and administration of water rights. Under the permit statutes adopted in all appropriation states but Colorado, a state administrative agency or official, such as the state engineer, is delegated the authority to administer the acquisition, transfer, and sometimes the loss of surface water rights. The agency has quasi-judicial functions. The same matters in Colorado are left to water courts that have administrative functions. State statutes differ, especially in the roles of administrative agencies and officials, but the perfection and use of water rights nevertheless depend on most of the same factors that are important in the eastern states. The degree of administrative controls varies from state to state.

Wyoming Hereford Ranch v. Hammond Packing Co.

Supreme Court of Wyoming, 1925.
33 Wyo. 14, 236 P. 764.

■ KIMBALL, J. This action involves rights to the use of the waters of Crow creek, a stream rising west of the city of Cheyenne, and flowing in a general easterly direction through that city and through lands owned by the Hammond Packing company and the Wyoming Hereford Ranch. The plaintiff, the Wyoming Hereford Ranch, and the defendant the Hammond Packing company are appropriators of the waters of said creek for the purpose of irrigation. * * *

In addition to its rights under the decree of 1888, the plaintiff claimed an appropriation through the Bolln ditch for the irrigation of about 200 acres. The decree of the district court upheld this claim and established the right as prior and superior to the rights of the defendant under its permits of 1909 and 1911 * * *. It is conceded that whatever right the plaintiff has to divert and use water through the Bolln ditch was acquired since the adoption of the Constitution and the enactment of the state water law of 1890. Article 8 of the Constitution contains the following provisions:

"Section 1. The water of all natural streams, springs, lakes or other collections of still water, within the boundaries of the state, are hereby declared to be the property of the state.

"Sec. 2. There shall be constituted a board of control, to be composed of the state engineer and superintendents of the water divisions; which shall, under such regulations as may be prescribed by law, have the supervision of the waters of the state and of their appropriation, distribution and diversion, and of the various officers connected therewith. Its decisions to be subject to review by the courts of the state.

"Sec. 3. Priority of appropriation for beneficial uses shall give the better right. No appropriation shall be denied except when such denial is demanded by the public interest. * * * "

* * *

At the first session of the state Legislature, there was enacted a law approved December 22, 1890, "providing for the supervision and use of the waters of the state." Chapter 8, Laws of Wyoming 1890–91. Section 34 of that act provided, among other things, that any one thereafter intending to appropriate any of the public waters of the state should, before commencing construction, enlargement, or extension of any distributing works, or performing any work in connection with said appropriation, make an application to the president of the board of control for a permit to make such appropriation. It requires that the application for a permit shall, among other things, state the source from which the appropriation is to be made, the amount of the appropriation, the location and character of the proposed works, and the time at which the application of water to beneficial purposes shall be made, which time is limited to the time required for the completion of the work when prosecuted with due diligence. If it is intended that the water should be used for irrigation, the application should describe the lands to be irrigated. It is further provided that the application shall state additional facts required by the board of control. On receipt of the application, it is filed and recorded in the office of the state engineer, and if on investigation it is found that there is unappropriated water in the source of supply named in the application, and if the appropriation is not otherwise detrimental to the public welfare, the engineer shall approve the application. The application indorsed with such approval is then returned to the applicant, "who shall, on receipt thereof, be authorized to proceed with such work, and to take such measures as may be necessary to perfect such appropriation." It is further provided that—

"If there is no unappropriated water in the source of supply, or if, in the judgment of the state engineer, such appropriation is detrimental to public interests, the state engineer shall refuse such appropriation, and the party making such application shall not prosecute such work, so long as such refusal shall continue in force."

* * *

It is conceded as to the Bolln ditch that the plaintiff has never conformed to the provisions of this law, and we are required to decide whether, under the Constitution and the legislation of 1890, a lawful appropriation of waters can be made without a permit, and without an application therefore. * * *

Directing our attention first to statute law of 1890, there would seem to be little need for construction or interpretation. When it is provided that before commencing the construction or enlargement of any distributing works, there must be an application for a permit, and that, if approval of the permit is refused, the party applying therefore shall not prosecute such work, it would seem quite clear, so far as the statute is concerned, that the permit is a condition precedent to the right to divert and appropriate water. If an applicant for a permit has no right to divert waters until the application is approved, it surely was not intended that a person who has never made such application could legally divert and use the waters of the state. * * *

In determining the meaning of a written law, it is proper to consider the evils sought to be remedied. The laws of the territory had permitted the diversion of water without any state supervision of the works and without any adequate notice and record of the amount, purpose, and date of the appropriation. Defective and badly located diversion works often made the use of water wasteful. No right became definite until it was adjudicated in court, and adjudications were often long delayed and then made on inaccurate testimony and without any disinterested measurements of the ditches or of the lands irrigated. Until such an adjudication, no subsequent appropriation could be made with safety, for no one could tell the amount of unappropriated water in the stream. The evils attendant on such a system, and the importance of providing a different system that would give the state the unquestioned right of control, had become well recognized at the time the Constitution was framed. * * * In interpreting this language, we must give consideration to the contemporaneous recognition not only of the importance of state supervision of the diversion of waters, but also of the fact that such supervision could not be effective, nor intelligently exercised, without accurate and complete information of proposed appropriations. The Legislature has decided that the public interests demand that such information shall be given to the state board by an application for a permit, and that until such an application is approved, no appropriation can be lawfully made. We believe these requirements are reasonable in so far at least as they are questioned in this case.

* * *

It follows that the part of the decree which gives the plaintiff a priority for use of water through the Bolln ditch cannot be upheld.

* * *

NOTE

Before enacting a permit statute, Wyoming had a statutory procedure under territorial law that required all water rights claimants to file statements in the proper district court in order to adjudicate water rights. Irrigation Water Rights Act of 1886, 1886 Wyo. Sess. Laws 61. In 1890, Wyoming passed a comprehensive water rights act immediately upon achieving statehood. Ironically, the "Wyoming" system of water rights administration is based on an approach developed in Northern Colorado that had been rejected by the Colorado legislature twelve years earlier. The Act and Wyoming's constitution incorporated many of the ideas of Elwood Mead, reflecting his belief in centralized control of water. Mead, a young engineer and reformer lawyer while he was at Colorado Agricultural College, later Colorado State University, was the first territorial engineer, then the state engineer of Wyoming, and later the Commissioner of the Bureau of Reclamation. See James R. Kluger, Turning on Water with a Shovel: The Career of Elwood Mead (1992).

As *Wyoming Hereford* shows, an appropriator under this system does not have a choice between judicial and administrative acquisition of a right. The latter is exclusive and use of water without a permit is unlawful. WYO. STAT. ANN. § 41–4–501 (2001). The statute had been attacked on the basis that it unconstitutionally delegated judicial functions to a non-judicial, administrative agency. Farm Investment Co. v. Carpenter, 9 Wyo. 110, 61 P. 258, 264, 267 (1900). The court upheld the statute stating:

> The statute nowhere attempts to divest the courts of any jurisdiction granted to them by the constitution to redress grievances and afford relief at law or in equity under the ordinary and well known rules of procedure. * * * The proceeding is one in which the claimant does not obtain redress for an injury, but secures evidence of title to a valuable right—a right to use a peculiar public commodity. * * * The board, it is true, acts judicially; but the power exercised is quasi-judicial only, and such as, under proper circumstances, may appropriately be conferred upon executive officers or boards.

For and interesting account of the historical context for the development of the Wyoming system and the *Farm Investment v. Carpenter case*, *see* Anne Mackinnon, Historic and Future Challenges in Western Water Law: The Case of Wyoming, 6 Wyo. L. Rev. 291, 295–309 (2006).

To obtain a water right from the State Board of Control, or to enlarge an existing right, one must apply to the state engineer who approves or rejects an application. The Wyoming Constitution provides that "[n]o appropriation shall be denied except when such denial is demanded by the public interests." Wyo. Const. Art. VIII, § 3. Implementing this mandate, the state engineer will approve an application to apply water to a beneficial use so long as the appropriation will not impair the value of existing rights or cause detriment to the public welfare. WYO. STAT. ANN. § 41–4–503 (2001). If the proposed new use will lead to either type of harm the state engineer has a duty to reject the application. Though there is no express authority for the state engineer to impose conditions on the permit, the courts have held that such authority falls within the power to deny permits when it is in the public interest. Big Horn Power Co. v. State, 23 Wyo. 271, 148 P. 1110 (1915).

Once a permit has been issued, and any required work completed within the time set for construction (not to exceed five years), the applicant may submit proof that the appropriation has been perfected to the superintendent of the water division where the right is located. Final proof of appropriation must be made within five years of the time allowed for completion of the application of water to a beneficial use. Notice of permit issuance is given to the public who may contest any of the proposed determinations. All information on the appropriation is transmitted to the Board of Control, which issues a "Certificate of Appropriation" if it is satisfied that the appropriation has been perfected according to the terms of the permit and that no conflicts exist. The priority date of the perfected right dates from the filing of the permit application with the state engineer. Appeals are available to the board from the action of the state engineer or to the district court from the action of the board.

The Wyoming Act also provides a means for adjudicating all existing rights in a stream. WYO. STAT. ANN. §§ 41–4–310 to 316 (2001). All general stream adjudications were complete by 1927 and parties were issued certificates evidencing recognized water rights. The validity of the adjudication procedure was upheld by the Wyoming Supreme Court. Anita Ditch Co. v. Turner, 389 P.2d 1018, 1021 (Wyo.1964). For a thorough review, see Mark Squillace, *One Hundred Years of Wyoming Water Law*, 26 Land & Water L. Rev. 93 (1991); and Mark Squillace, *A Critical Look at Wyoming Water Law*, 24 Land & Water L. Rev. 307 (1989).

b. Other State Variations

A sampling of other systems illustrates the range of differences that developed among the western states.

The Montana System

The Montana permit system has its roots in the Montana Water Use Act of 1973, passed after a new state constitution was adopted in 1972. 1973 Mont. Laws 452, codified in various sections of MONT. CODE ANN. title 85. It developed much later and quite differently from Wyoming's system. Conversion to a permit system necessitated revisiting old rights and created a new system for dealing with new appropriations. Prior to 1973, neither the state engineer, the State Water Conservation Board, nor their 1971 successor, the Department of Natural Resources and Conservation, was involved in the procedures for appropriating or adjudicating water rights. See Albert W. Stone, *The Long Count on Dempsey: No Final Decision On Water Right Adjudication*, 31 Mont. L. Rev. 1 (1969).

Under the Water Use Act, MONT. CODE ANN. §§ 85–2–101 to 907 (2007), the Department of Natural Resources and Conservation was required to establish a centralized record system for existing rights and to initiate adjudications of water rights. The department selected specific areas or sources of water to begin proceedings to determine existing rights. Reviewing and quantifying old rights has proved to be an overwhelming task. The department did an on-site investigation and attempted to ascertain all of the persons who might have rights, as well as the quantity and priority of each. Because many of the rights were not of record, and may not have been in use for long periods, that information was difficult to obtain. This proved to be inefficient and time consuming, and led to amendments to the Act, dividing the state into four large water divisions in an effort to expedite adjudications. The burden of gathering data on existing rights shifted to the users and claimants, who had to file their claims by April 30, 1982 or be conclusively presumed to have abandoned non-filed claims.

Each water division has a district judge designated as the water judge for that division, MONT. CODE ANN. § 3–7–201 (2007). In practice, the water judge issues preliminary decrees within a division. In divisions where there are claims of federal or Indian reserved water rights, the judge will issue a "temporary preliminary decree." The purpose is to adjudicate only state water rights, and later to insert reserved rights as a result of negotiation of "compacts" with the United States and the tribes.

After issuance of a preliminary decree (or temporary preliminary decree), persons may file objections and obtain a hearing which can be complex and time consuming. After objections and hearings, the water judge may revise the preliminary decree, followed by further proceedings. Ultimately the judge issues a final decree that is appealable to the Montana Supreme Court. There may be multiple, legally-unrelated final decrees within a division.

As of 2001, after nineteen years, only 56 percent of the 219,413 claims filed with the water courts had been adjudicated. Final decrees had been issued in 16,354 cases (7.5 percent) and another 106,739 claims (49 percent) had received preliminary or temporary preliminary decrees.

Earlier in the process, an engineering firm on contract with one of the large utilities involved in the adjudication process issued an evaluation critical of the accuracy of the adjudications in two sample sub-basins of the Clark Fork River drainage. The study reported that of the 70,000 claims decreed statewide by early 1986, only 20 had been verified by a field investigation. In one sub-basin, "[t]he Water Court decreed 9.5% more water volume than claimed and 171% more than calculated [by the department] in the verification process." The report concluded that there "is clearly an insufficient number of field investigations to ensure that the adjudication process is factually correct." Hydrometrics, Executive Summary of the Evaluation of the State of Montana Water Rights Adjudication Process for Sub–Basins 76K and 76E of the Clark Fork River Drainage, Montana (May 4, 1987).

The Montana courts have continually upheld the water adjudication process over constitutional challenges. The Montana Supreme Court held that the water court, not the Department of Natural Resources and Conservation, had the authority to promulgate rules for verification of water claims, although the supreme court determined that it would supervise the adoption of verification rules. Swift v. State, Dep't of Natural Resources & Conservation, 226 Mont. 439, 736 P.2d 117 (1987). The supreme court upheld the constitutionality of requiring quantification of both flow rate and volume, McDonald v. State, 220 Mont. 519, 722 P.2d 598 (1986), and most recently the court upheld the constitutionality of barring claims which were filed late. *In re* Yellowstone River, 253 Mont. 167, 832 P.2d 1210 (1992).

Acquiring a new (post–1973) water right, as distinguished from adjudicating existing rights, resembles other states' permit systems. Application is made to the department, which must issue a permit if certain criteria are met as specified by statute. For applications of less than 4,000 acre-feet per year and less than 5.5 cfs, the principal limitations are that there be sufficient unappropriated water, that other appropriators will not be adversely affected, that the diversion will be properly constructed, and that the proposed use is beneficial. For applications in excess of that amount, the department is required by 1985 amendments to consider a broad range of economic and environmental factors, impacts, and benefits to the state. Public interest factors in allocating waters are discussed *infra* p. 319. Private parties may not appropriate water if either: (1) water would be consumed in excess of 4,000 acre-feet per year and 5.5 cfs; or (2) water would be transported out of the basins of the Clark Fork, Kootenai, St. Mary, Little Missouri, Yellowstone, or Missouri rivers. Water in excess of such quantities or for export from these basins must be leased from the state. See John E. Thorson et al., *Forging Public Rights in Montana's Waters*, 6 Pub. Land L. Rev. 1 (1985).

Once the appropriation has been made, the permittee receives a certificate of water right, but the certificate may not be issued for a right to a specific source until there has been a general adjudication of existing rights in that source. Because there have been so few final decrees, there are practically no final certificates of water rights. Objections to applications for water rights may be filed and a hearing will be held if the department either determines that an objection states a valid claim, or the department has imposed terms or conditions on the approval of the permit, and the applicant requests a hearing.

The priority date of a right obtained under the permit system is the filing date of the permit application. The permit system is the exclusive means of obtaining water rights; however, governmental entities may apply to the Board of Natural Resources and Conservation for a reservation of water for present or future use. Mont. Code Ann. § 85–2–316 (2007). These reservations can amount to half the flow of certain named rivers. See *supra* p. 267. Parties opposing decisions of the department may request a hearing before the Board of Natural Resources and Conservation. Both the distribution of water rights and the adjudication of disputes are within the district court's jurisdiction.

The California System

California's prior appropriation permit system is administered by the State Water Resources Control Board. Anyone wishing to appropriate surface water or water in "subterranean streams flowing in known and definite channels" must obtain a permit. California's permit system is not exclusive, so there are users with rights to surface waters who are not required to comply with the permitting process. Riparian owners, appropriators prior to 1914, users of spring waters originating and remaining on their land, and cities with pueblo rights* need not obtain water right permits. In principle, many should file statements of water diversion and use (see CAL. WATER CODE § 5105 (West 2001)), but they often do not. The board's policy is to disregard prescriptive surface rights initiated subsequent to 1914 unless they are supported by a permit, a position sustained by the California Supreme Court. People v. Shirokow, 26 Cal.3d 301, 162 Cal.Rptr. 30, 605 P.2d 859 (1980). Waters already appropriated or waters needed for useful and beneficial purposes on riparian lands are excepted. CAL. WATER CODE § 1201 (West 2001). Although riparian rights are still recognized, a 1928 constitutional amendment limited common law rights by imposing a requirement that all water rights not exceed an amount of water reasonably required for the purposes of the adjacent lands. Cal. Const. art. X, § 2; see *supra* p. 93.

The permit application must provide information on the source, nature, and amount of use, place of use and diversion, and time needed to construct the diversion structure and apply the water to beneficial use. The board must calculate the availability of unappropriated water and, if necessary, the amount that must remain in the source for other beneficial uses, including uses protected by water quality control plans. Notice of the application must be given to the public. Any person, whether or not a water right holder, may protest the approval of an application. The applicant is required to file an answer to every protest.

The board conducts a field investigation to resolve protests. Formal hearings may be held or the parties may agree to a proceeding in lieu of a hearing. Before a permit is issued, each application is reviewed to determine whether an environmental impact report is needed pursuant to the California Environmental Quality Act. Most applications for water rights permits do not require impact reports.

Temporary permits are available to a party who has an urgent need to appropriate water if it is found that unappropriated water is available, the rights of downstream users are not injured, and the environment will not be unreasonably affected. Interim use permits are available to allow use by others of water already appropriated but not yet needed by a municipality. Before a permanent right to appropriate water is granted, the permittee must demonstrate "due diligence" in applying it to a beneficial use. Annual progress reports must be filed with the board or else permits may be revoked. The only exceptions are appropriations by municipalities and applications of the Department of Water Resources. Standard terms and conditions are included in permits, such as continuing authority by the board to prevent waste, unreasonable use, etc. This has become a powerful tool for conserving water. See IID–MWD transfer discussed *infra* pp. 368–

---

* A "pueblo right" is "the paramount right of an American city as successor of a Spanish or Mexican pueblo (municipality) to the use of water naturally occurring within the old pueblo limits for the use of the inhabitants of the city." Wells A. Hutchins, The California Law of Water Rights 256 (1956). See *infra* p. 712. [Eds.]

372. In two situations, the board may reserve jurisdiction to change terms and conditions of a permit: if there was insufficient information to decide which conditions were needed, or if the permit is part of a large project and related applications are pending.

Once a permittee has completed construction of a diversion structure and applied the water to beneficial use, the board investigates to confirm completion and compliance. If all is in order, the board issues a license that may be subject to the terms and conditions included in the permit and others that may be required by statute. See *infra*, p. 426, on the Mono Lake litigation. A license is granted for so long as the water appropriated under it is used for a useful and beneficial purpose. CAL. WATER CODE § 1627 (West 1971). Licenses may be revoked for failure to use the water beneficially or reasonably, or for failure to comply with the terms and conditions imposed on the license.

The hybrid system in which riparian rights coexist with rights by prior appropriation complicates administration of water rights. Superiority among rights depends largely upon the respective times of accrual of the rights, or date of priority. Generally, a riparian's date of priority is the date the lands first passed from public to private ownership.

California has adjudication procedures to determine and integrate all water rights claimed on a stream system, including those established by appropriation, riparian rights, or any other basis. The statutory procedure, created in 1913, underwent a major revision in 1976 in an effort to shorten staff involvement time. CAL. WATER CODE § 2501 (West 1971 & Supp. 2000).

An adjudication is initiated by petition to the board by a claimant on the stream system. Claimants are then notified, and an investigation and report follow. A decree ultimately establishes all rights to the use of water. This procedure does not include underground water supplies other than subterranean streams flowing through known and definite channels, but a specific exception was made by the legislature for the Scott River stream system after it was discovered through investigation that withdrawal of the groundwater caused a reduction in surface flow.

When there is a suit over water rights on an unadjudicated stream, the courts may refer the suit to the board for a determination of physical facts or an investigation of issues. Following this investigation and hearings, the court enters its decree.

The Colorado System

Colorado is the only prior appropriation state that does not have a permit system. Language in the state constitution is similar to many other western states' constitutions. It provides that "[t]he right to divert the unappropriated waters of any natural stream shall never be denied." Colo. Const. art. XVI, § 6. Some commentators and courts have interpreted it to mean that appropriators may not be required to seek agency permission before claiming a water right. See John U. Carlson, *Report to Governor John A. Love on Certain Colorado Water Law Problems*, 50 Denver L.J. 293, 295 (1973). See also People *ex rel.* Park Reservoir Co. v. Hinderlider, 98

Colo. 505, 57 P.2d 894 (1936). Rather, appropriators can claim a water right first and then seek a "decreed" right in court. As a practical matter, however, an appropriation that has not been decreed has little value because it is junior to all decreed rights. Thus, it cannot be enforced until all decreed rights have been satisfied.

Prior to 1969, the adjudication of water rights was the responsibility of the district courts in some seventy water districts, roughly coterminous with county lines. The claimant sought an adjudication, with notice given to all parties. Following a court proceeding where the claims, along with minimal information provided by the state engineer, were considered, a decree was issued listing the rights in priority order. In the early days this system, with little participation by state agencies, resulted in many inflated paper decrees.

The Colorado system was placed within a comprehensive statutory framework with the enactment of the Water Right Determination and Administration Act of 1969, COLO. REV. STAT. §§ 37–92–101 to 602 (2000). Seven water divisions were created in the state, vastly simplifying the earlier administrative arrangements. Each division has a division engineer who reports to the state engineer. "Water matters" are considered in a water court in each division, with a water judge, referee, and a water clerk. Applicants for a conditional water right, absolute water right, or change in an existing water right (including transfer) file an application with the water clerk. Monthly resumes of the applications are published in a local newspaper and sent to potentially affected water rights holders. Objectors then have an opportunity to file statements of opposition to the applications. After consulting with the division or state engineer, the referee makes a ruling, approving, approving in part, or denying each application. Interested parties who are dissatisfied with the ruling may file a protest. A protest results in a hearing at which the water judge determines the issues de novo. Parties typically hire lawyers and engineers to represent them. Multiple party cases therefore can be rather expensive.

The referee's rulings, including those against which no protest has been filed, are reviewed semi-annually by the water judge, who can confirm, modify, or reverse them. Appeals of these rulings go directly to the Colorado Supreme Court. Transfers and other changes in water rights are judged by standards designed to prevent injury to existing water rights, including those with later priorities than the right for which the change is sought. (Protection of "junior" appropriators from injurious changes is a major characteristic of the appropriation system, and is discussed *supra* p. 230.)

Under the Colorado postponement doctrine, no decree may be awarded with a priority date earlier than the most junior decree awarded in the previous calendar year. COLO. REV. STAT. § 37–92–306 (2000). Unadjudicated rights remain valid, however, and retain their early appropriation date. But if they are later adjudicated they receive an adjudication date in the year of adjudication that is prior to all other decrees in that year except other previously unadjudicated rights with earlier appropriation dates that are applied for in the same year.

Water rights can be lost through abandonment in Colorado. There is no statutory forfeiture provision, although non-use for a period of ten years creates a rebuttable presumption of abandonment. COLO. REV. STAT. § 37–92–402 (2000). Every ten years the division engineer prepares a list of absolute water rights which the engineer has determined to have been abandoned in whole or in part. After notification of those whose water rights are on the list, and opportunity for protest, a hearing is held before the water judge, who is empowered to declare water rights conclusively abandoned. COLO. REV. STAT. § 37–92–401 (2000). Division engineers compile and publish a tabulation of all water rights in their division every four years. The tabulation reflects all newly decreed conditional and absolute rights and abandonments. These tabulations may be protested in hearings before the water judge.

c. General Stream Adjudications

Because most states in the West grew up without neat, administrative systems for keeping records of and reconciling all the demands on a river system, some areas of particular scarcity have been plagued by conflicts and uncertainties. As new proposals for development come forward it is sometimes difficult to tell what valid rights exist on a river, how large actual uses under the rights are, and even what the priority dates are. With little or no review of the quantities of many of these rights, some unused or wastefully used rights are surely included. Other rights may have been abandoned. A time-honored solution to these problems has been for a party seeking certainty, or the state itself, to bring a lawsuit that joins as parties everyone claiming a water right in the watershed. The extent of the litigation could range from a single tributary to an entire river system with all its tributaries. Some states have special procedures for general stream adjudications. But completed adjudications have been scattered and few.

In the past three decades a few western states where statutory permit systems are now in force have decided to adjudicate entire river basins in an attempt to put their pre- and post-statute records and administration of water in order. They were motivated in no small part by the Supreme Court's interpretation of a federal law, the McCarran Amendment, to allow the states to join the United States as a party in such litigation and force the government to claim and have quantified reserved water rights pertaining to federal and Indian lands. These rights have a potentially enormous scope because of the presence of large federal and Indian land holdings with typically early priorities, creating considerable uncertainty for other water users. See *Winters v. United States, supra* p. 102, and Chapter 9.

Today, these general stream adjudications are forums for a vast number of the West's water lawyers. Montana's scheme is described *supra* pp. 299–301. Since that massive adjudication began in 1973, Arizona, Washington, Idaho, and Oregon have commenced litigation to adjudicate water rights in entire river basins under special statutes. The Gila River adjudication in Arizona started in 1974 and involves the claims of 24,000 water users. Washington has been litigating the rights of 40,000 water users in the Yakima River basin since 1977. Idaho's Snake River Basin Adjudication has been in active litigation since 1987 and involves 185,000 claims—almost all water rights in the state. In 1990, Oregon started a quasi-administrative process to determine the water rights of 25,000 claimants in the Klamath River basin. See generally John E. Thorson, *State Watershed Adjudications: Approaches and Alternatives*, 42 Rocky Mtn. Min. L. Inst. 22–1 (1996).

In theory, these adjudications eventually will validate and integrate existing rights and provide a basis for future allocation and administration of water rights that is accessible, fair, and efficient. The process, however, can require water users to prove up rights they considered inviolate on paper but which cannot be justified by modern standards of beneficial use. Where old assumptions have come into conflict with modern values in these cases some senior water users have balked and they have gotten the attention of legislators who have sought to change the rules in the middle of the game. For instance, in Idaho, newer, more efficient groundwater uses were in competition with senior, inefficient surface uses that draw on the same sources. When the court in the Snake River Basin Adjudication uniformly applied a standard of reasonable efficiency it disadvantaged senior users whose uses depended on old surface diversion works. See pages 387–395, *infra*. The legislature then tried to change the rules of decision to give the seniors relief. This was held unlawful by the state supreme court. Similarly, judicial invalidation of legislation followed the Arizona legislature's attempt to revise retroactively the standards for finding abandonment and forfeiture, adverse possession, and the filing requirements for water rights applications that had been established in the Gila River adjudication.

Other states have not initiated general stream adjudications on the scale described here. They have proved unwieldy, expensive, and overly contentious and have kept water administration in the affected areas in limbo for many years. Moreover, they have typically neglected some of the biggest issues in modern western rights such as endangered species, water quality, conjunctive use, and the need for more efficient water use. Significantly, they are open only to water rights holders, excluding the public participation that is being demanded in most water matters today. But the pending litigation is bound to continue beyond the retirements of many of the lawyers who have been involved in them for most of their careers.

As the costs of general adjudications mounted, other states began to cast the cold eye of crude benefit-cost analysis to the costs of general stream adjudications and sought faster, less costly ways of quantifying rights, especially Indian reserved water rights. For example, in 2002, the Washington State Department of Ecology and Office of the Attorney General submitted a report on the Yakima general adjudication, now in its third decade. Washington State Department of Ecology and Office of the Attorney General, Streamlining the Water Rights General Adjudication

Procedures, Pub. No. 02–11–019 (December 2002), available at http://www. ecy.wa.gov/biblio/0211019. To speed up the process, it recommended, *inter alia*, a greater role for the Department in making tentative determinations and validating registered water rights. It also suggested allowing limited special adjudications that would allow the Department to initiate an adjudication that would cover a limited number of issues and would not affect all water users in the basin, although it recognized that this would not qualify as a McCarran Amendment general adjudication. Adjudications have morphed into a variety of alternative dispute resolution processes, and increasingly the states have turned to negotiated settlements, backed by federal dollars, to achieve their objectives, and are now only one of several management strategies to cope with continued urbanization, the pressures to maintain and restore degraded watersheds and global climate change. For a mid-decade report on the progress and status of general stream adjudications in the various western states, *see* John K. Thorson, Ramsey L. Kropf, Andrea K. Gerlak and Dar Crammond, Dividing Western Waters: A Century of Adjudicating Rivers and Streams, 8 Denv. Water L. Rev. 355 (2005) and *id.* at 298 (2006).

A. Dan Tarlock, General Stream Adjudications: A Good Public Investment?, 133 Water Resources Research 52, 53–54 (May 2006) concludes that:

> (1) the adjudications, with the help of the United States Supreme Court, have succeeded in cabining the extent of non-Indian federal reserved rights for public lands, (2) the adjudications have allowed Indian Tribes to obtain congressional water rights settlements that give them much more economic and ecological benefits than they would have obtained had they pursued their claims to a final decree, (3) the adjudications will provide some help as the states adjust to the end of the Reclamation Era and the new risks of global climate change, but (4) the adjudications have not been able to deal effectively with federal regulatory water rights arising under the Clean Water and Endangered Species Acts. . . .

to revise retroactively the standards for finding abandonment and forfeiture, adverse possession, and the filing requirements for water rights applications that had been established in the Gila River adjudication.

It appears doubtful that many other states will initiate general stream adjudications on the scale described here. They have proved unwieldy, expensive, and overly contentious and have kept water administration in the affected areas in limbo for many years. Moreover, they have typically neglected some of the biggest issues in modern western rights such as endangered species, water quality, conjunctive use, and the need for more efficient water use. Significantly, they are open only to water rights holders, excluding the public participation that is being demanded in most water matters today. But the pending litigation is bound to continue beyond the retirements of many of the lawyers who have been involved in them for most of their careers.

B. ISSUES UNDER WATER ALLOCATION STATUTES

There are several common issues that arise under the various state statutory systems. Agencies, state officials, or courts regularly must make determinations about availability of water for new uses, protection of existing uses, public interest factors, instream flow protection, changes in use, "reasonable" or "beneficial" use, and water quality. In the following pages we discuss the issues arising from the type of administrative decisions that are most frequently the subject of conflict.

Permit statutes introduce an element of administrative discretion into the decision on whether or not one can get a water right. In the common law of riparian rights all landowners along a stream had water rights. How can an administrative official deny or qualify the inherent water rights of a riparian landowner to make reasonable use of appurtenant waters?

Under the common law of prior appropriation one needed only to divert water to a beneficial use. On what basis should an official be able to deny an application for water rights? Hutchins notes that "[i]n the 16 Western States in which control over appropriation of water is imposed by statute no person has an unqualified right to appropriate water." 1 Wells A. Hutchins, Water Rights Laws in the Nineteen Western States 403 (1971). Typical statutes require at least that an applicant for a new water right must establish that unappropriated water is available and that vested rights will be unimpaired by the new appropriation.

1. THRESHOLD ISSUES

a. Availability of Water

Virtually all water laws prevent new rights from being recognized or permits being granted if it would harm vested rights. This is the most fundamental way of protecting priorities. A related requirement is that there be water available for appropriation before a water right will be granted. This is not a simple or objective matter. A water right is no guarantee that water will be available because rights may exist in flows that occur only occasionally. Administrative agencies must decide as a policy and technical matter how often water must be available in the stream to justify issuing rights in it.

Where the supply of water from a stream regularly exceeds the aggregate of all existing rights, a new water user has no trouble finding available water. But even if a stream in the arid West is described as "over-appropriated" this does not necessarily mean that there is no water available for a new appropriation. "Over-appropriated" means only that there are users who perhaps are not satisfied in some average years, or who are not satisfied during a certain season of the year, usually the drier summer months, which is also the irrigation season.

Besides physical shortages, "over-appropriation" may appear to exist as a result of over-stated rights on paper. Some rights that appear to command water on paper may actually have been lost through abandonments or forfeitures but may not yet be reflected in the records. Conditional rights may survive on paper, though in fact they will not ever be fully utilized and may be cancelled eventually for lack of diligent application to a beneficial use, thus "freeing up" water that had been considered appropriated water for the benefit of the stream and new appropriators. Do these possibilities suggest that appropriations should be liberally allowed, even when water "appears" to be in short supply? In determining what water is "unappropriated," should the water agency look behind the paper rights that exist on a stream and attempt to determine the amount of water that is actually being used, i.e., discount rights exceeding the quantity that can be used beneficially and those that are subject to abandonment or forfeiture?

When administrative agencies are charged with exercising discretion over new appropriations, they are confronted with a dilemma on over-appropriated streams: If a permit is granted, investments may be made on the expectation that water will continue to be available. If a permit is denied, important and valuable uses may be prevented or juniors may be forced to develop more costly alternative supplies. If a junior appropriator is willing to take a chance on making use of water that may in fact be available only every few years or that may be diverted away in the future by seniors with conditional rights, why not allow it? To do so seems consistent with the ideal of maximizing the beneficial use of streams. Are seniors prejudiced by allowing a stream to become over-appropriated? Are there public policy reasons for not doing so?

Oregon, for example, considers a stream over-appropriated if "[t]he quantity of surface water available during a specific period is not sufficient to meet the expected demands from all water rights at least 80 percent of the time during that period." Or. Admin. R. 690–400–010(11)(a). Oregon ordinarily will not issue a permit for a new surface water use unless the state agency expects water to be available throughout the proposed season of use in four years out of five; thus, most of the state is effectively closed to new surface water permits because of the supply/demand picture in the dry months. Nebraska declared a moratorium on new surface water appropriations in several major river basins in 2004, following passage of LB 962 earlier that year. Under this landmark statute, the Department of Natural Resources has designated much of western Nebraska as fully appropriated or over-appropriated. The DNR's 2004 moratorium officially closed the Platte River above the mouth of the Loup River to new appropriations, along with the North Platte, South Platte, Republican River, White River, and Hat Creek Basins; the Upper Niobrara Basin was already covered by an earlier moratorium. The DNR stated that it was in the public interest to close these basins, because continuing to permit new uses where sufficient water is not available "would result in 'paper water rights' that would cause additional costs to the taxpayer because of the costs of processing such applications, the costs of administering such applications, and the costs of canceling such appropriations in the future."

Although the Colorado River in Texas appears fully appropriated on paper, some 1.6 million acre-feet of water flow to the Gulf of Mexico annually. Developers have attempted, unsuccessfully, to convince the state water commission and the state supreme court that they should discount existing paper water rights and find that water is available for appropriation. Lower Colorado River Auth. v. Texas Dept. of Water Resources, 689 S.W.2d 873 (Tex.1984). The court defended a restrictive interpretation of unappropriated water that counted all existing uncancelled permits and filings at their recorded levels, stating that the water agency should be more aggressive in pursuing actions to cancel rights that are subject to forfeiture.

Is the Texas court correct that the best way to protect senior rights is to consider all rights "on the books" as valid and unavailable for appropriation? Are factors other than senior rights protection and physical availability relevant?

The Colorado Supreme Court has said that only historical diversions under absolute decrees are considered in determining water availability; conditional rights are disregarded. Board of County Comm'rs v. Crystal Creek Homeowners Ass'n, 891 P.2d 952, 962 (Colo.1995). The Colorado court also has held that even when a river is over-appropriated, a new appropriation will be allowed if no material injury will occur to senior users. Southeastern Colorado Water Conservancy Dist. v. Rich, 625 P.2d 977 (Colo.1981). What is "material injury"? A later case held that the statutory policy of encouraging maximum (or optimum) utilization of water resources allowed the state engineer to require senior appropriators to drill wells to fulfill their water rights in order to allow for junior appropriations, even though the senior rights were originally for surface diversions. Alamosa–La Jara Water Users Protection Ass'n v. Gould, 674 P.2d 914 (Colo. 1983), *infra* p. 343. The court cautioned, however, that the state engineer must consider a variety of economic and environmental factors in deciding how much water was available for appropriation inasmuch as "the policy of maximum utilization does not require a single-minded endeavor to squeeze every drop of water from the valley's aquifer."

b. *Rights for Future Uses*

Statutes in most western states codify the doctrine of relation back. Permit-granting authorities are normally given the discretion to condition permits on the application of the water to a beneficial use within a certain time period. NEV. REV. STAT. ANN. § 533.380 (Michie 1995) (within ten years); N.M. STAT. ANN. § 72–5–6 (1978) (within nine years); KAN. STAT. ANN. § 82a–713 (1997) (within "reasonable" period of time). The opportunity is provided for an extension in circumstances involving an excusable failure to apply the water to a beneficial use within the required time. UTAH CODE ANN. § 73–3–12 (Michie Supp. 2000); NEB. REV. STAT. § 46–238 (1998). See also Associated Enterprises, Inc. v. Toltec Watershed Improvement Dist., 578 P.2d 1359 (Wyo.1978). Failure to meet the time limits or to procure an extension may result in cancellation of the permit. IDAHO CODE ANN. § 42–311 (Michie 1996) (permit may be cancelled after notice); S.D. CODIFIED LAWS § 46–5–25 (1999) (right under permit forfeited); WYO. STAT. ANN. § 41–4–506 (2001) (state engineer may cancel permit upon default). See also Bailey v. State, 95 Nev. 378, 594 P.2d 734 (1979).

States vary in the rigor that they impose on appropriators who seek to extend the time to complete an appropriation. The Alaska Supreme Court has held that when attempting to show that "diligent effort" has been made toward completing an appropriation, "an applicant must actually do something during the term of the permit to demonstrate diligence; a statement of intent cannot suffice." Tulkisarmute Native Cmty. Council v. Heinze, 898 P.2d 935, 944–945 (Alaska 1995). In *Tulkisarmute*, the water rights permittee failed to demonstrate construction of infrastructure or any actual water use in its extension applications. The applications instead included only a statement that water use would begin at an undetermined future date and that the permittee intended to begin operations during a vague four-year time period. The court determined that the permittee did not show that diligent efforts had been made toward appropriation and therefore reversed the Department of Natural Resources' decision to extend the permits.

Should the standards be the same for *cities* as they are for other water users? Or should they have greater latitude in acquiring present water rights for anticipated future needs?

In *City and County of Denver v. Northern Colorado Water Conservancy District, supra* p. 171, Chief Justice Stone would defer to the needs of a "great city." He opined that "when appropriations are sought by a growing city, regard should be given to its reasonably anticipated requirements." 276 P.2d at 997. In *City and County of Denver v. Sheriff, supra* p. 94, the court upheld large, then unneeded, appropriations by Denver on the western slope of the Rocky Mountains. The court stated that Denver needed flexibility in preparing for future municipal uses opining that: "it is not speculation but the highest prudence on the part of the city to obtain appropriations of water that will satisfy the needs resulting from a normal increase in population within a reasonable period of time." 96 P.2d at 841. *Sheriff* seemed to treat municipalities differently from other appropriators by allowing them to appropriate water beyond their immediate needs. Furthermore, the court held that Denver could lease to farmers water not needed for the city's immediate use. But see Pagosa Area Water and Sanitation Dist. v. Trout Unlimited, *infra*, p. 313.

Four Counties Water Users Ass'n v. Colorado River Water Conservation Dist., 159 Colo. 499, 414 P.2d 469 (1966), held that a court should not substitute its judgment as to future growth projections for that of the Association. Further, the court held that the economic feasibility of completing a project is not a proper test to be used upon the application for a conditional decree: "If they have miscalculated and fail, the loss is theirs—if they succeed, it will be for the eternal benefit of the peoples of the state of Colorado." Id. at 476 (quoting Metropolitan Suburban Water Users Ass'n v. Colorado River Water Conservation Dist., 148 Colo. 173, 365 P.2d 273, 288 (1961)).

Arizona requires a permit application for municipal uses to set forth "the population to be served, and an *estimate of future population requirements*." ARIZ. REV. STAT. ANN. § 45–152(B)(4) (West 1994) (emphasis added). The next section says that "[a]pplications for municipal uses may be approved to the exclusion of all subsequent appropriations if the estimated needs of the municipality so demand after consideration by and upon order of the director." ARIZ. REV. STAT. ANN. § 45–153(B) (West 1994). The California Water Code includes an article entitled "Preferred Priorities of Municipalities." CAL. WATER CODE §§ 1460–1464 (West 1971). The first section states: "The application for a permit by a municipality for the use of water for the municipality or the inhabitants thereof for domestic purposes shall be considered *first in right, irrespective of whether it is first in time*." Id. at § 1460 (emphasis added). The statute also requires an application for municipal water supply to "state the present population to be served, and *as near as may be, the future requirements of the city*." Id. at § 1264 (emphasis added). In Nevada, an application to appropriate water for municipal supply or for domestic use must state the approximate number of persons to be served and the approximate future requirements of that municipality. NEV. REV. STAT. ANN. § 533.340 (Michie 1995). The state of Washington has an identical provision. WASH. REV. CODE ANN. § 90.03.260 (West 1992). Oklahoma extends a municipality's right of eminent domain to include condemnation of land and water within and without its corporate limits to supply its contemplated future needs. 11 OKLA. ST. ANN. § 37–103 and § 37–117 (West 1994). Oregon's water laws put appropriations for hydroelectric power in the most prominent position, but also provide that the Water Resources Commission "may approve an application for a municipal water supply to the exclusion of all subsequent appropriations, if the exigencies of the case demand." OR. REV STAT. § 225.290 and § 537.190(2) (1999).

Colorado has no fixed time limit for use of a water right but uses court-supervised "conditional decrees" to ensure that large water projects will not lose priority to a subsequent appropriator during the typically lengthy development period before water can be put to beneficial use. See Public Service Company of Colorado v. Board of Water Works of Pueblo, 831 P.2d 470 (Colo.1992). The appropriator must make a showing of "reasonable diligence" to the water court every six years in order to perpetuate the conditionally decreed right. COLO. REV. STAT. § 37–92–301(4) (2000). Failure to do so results in a cancellation of the water right. The required showing is not rigorous. Indeed, some conditional rights have survived for more than fifty years, with no actual physical progress toward constructing diversions. See *supra* p. 170. Once the water is actually put to beneficial use, the appropriator can receive an "absolute" decree dating back to the conditional decree date.

Allowing appropriators to speculate on future development by acquiring water rights without clear plans for using the water can lead to monopolization of water resources and impede development by others. An anti-speculation policy was announced in Colorado River Water Conservation Dist. v. Vidler Tunnel Water Co., 197 Colo. 413, 594 P.2d 566 (1979), discussed *supra* p. 179, where the appropriator had neither land nor contracts with others for use of the water. The anti-speculation doctrine was extended to applications for changes of water right in High Plains A & M, LLC v. Southeastern Colo. Water Conservancy Dist., 120 P.3d 710 (Colo. 2005). The broad implications of this extension are discussed in Lawrence J. MacDonnell, Public Water–Private Water: Anti–Speculation, Water Reallocation, and High Plains A & M, LLC v. Southeastern Colorado Water Conservancy District, 10 U. Denver Water L. Rev. 1 (2006).

Interpreting the anti-speculation policy embodied in Colorado statutory law following *Vidler* (COLO. REV. STAT. § 37–92–103(3)(a)), the Colorado Supreme Court noted that there was an exception to the requirement that an appropriator have an interest in the land to be served for "government agencies." This, it said, should embody an exception from the *Vidler* rule for cities as recognized in *Sheriff* and *City and County of Denver*. See City of Thornton v. Bijou Irrigation Co., 926 P.2d 1, 37–42 (Colo.1996). A city must show only that the amount of water is consistent with its "reasonably anticipated requirements based on substantiated projections of future growth." Id. at 39. This somewhat vague standard was sharpened in Pagosa Area Water and Sanitation Dist. v. Trout Unlimited, 170 P.3d 307 (Colo. 2007). There the court held that "a governmental water supply agency has the burden of demonstrating three elements in regard to its intent to make a non-speculative conditional appropriation of unappropriated water: (1) what is a reasonable water supply planning period; (2) what are the substantiated population projections based on a normal rate of growth for that period; and (3) what amount of available unappropriated water is reasonably necessary to serve the reasonably anticipated needs of the governmental agency for the planning period, above its current water supply." Id. at 309–310.

In the wake of the *Vidler* decision the Colorado legislature also added a requirement to be met before a conditional decree can be granted. The statute states:

> No claim for a conditional water right may be recognized or a decree therefor granted except to the extent that it is established that the waters can be and will be diverted, stored or otherwise captured, possessed and controlled and will be beneficially used and that the project can and will be completed with diligence and within a reasonable period of time.

COLO. REV. STAT. § 37–92–305(9)(b) (2000).

The Colorado Supreme Court has applied this latter statute, known as the "can and will" requirement, to defeat an application where the only way there would be sufficient unappropriated water was with an augmentation plan (providing existing water users with another source of supply) that the applicant had not yet implemented. Lionelle v. Southeastern Colorado Water Conservancy Dist., 676 P.2d 1162 (Colo.1984), and Southeastern Colorado Water Conservancy Dist. v. City of Florence, 688 P.2d 715 (Colo.1984). On augmentation plans, see *infra* p. 384. If facilities must be constructed, the applicant must show that there is a substantial probability that they will be constructed within a reasonable time. See Board of County Commissioners v. Crystal Creek Homeowners Ass'n, 891 P.2d 952 (Colo. 1995).

What factors should a court consider when determining whether or not an applicant can and will perfect a water right? How can one be reasonably certain that the claimed waters will be diverted and applied to beneficial use and the project completed diligently within a reasonable period of time? Must financing be secure? How much assurance is necessary that federal permits will be granted? Is it necessary to have firm contracts for all of the water that will be developed? Enough water to make the project financially feasible?

Where access is required across lands owned by others in order to transport water, the Colorado Supreme Court has not required an existing right of access in order to fulfill the "can and will" requirement. City of Black Hawk v. City of Central, 97 P.3d 951 (Colo. 2004). In FWS Land & Cattle Company v. State Division of Wildlife, 795 P.2d 837 (Colo.1990), the court had denied a conditional decree under the "can and will" requirement because it was clear the state lands necessary for the project would not be available without express consent of the Colorado Division of Wildlife. In *In re* Gibbs v. Wolf Land Co., 856 P.2d 798 (Colo.1993), however, the court stated that *FWS* was not dispositive of the issue, and ruled that "an applicant may rely on the potential right of private condemnation in satisfying the can and will requirement" unless the record shows that there are no circumstances under which the needed access may be obtained. Id. at 802.

Availability of water is also an important factor in determining whether the appropriation "can" be completed. Application for Water Rights of

Hines Highlands Ltd. Partnership, 929 P.2d 718 (Colo.1996) and Mt. Emmons Mining Co. v. Town of Crested Butte, 40 P.3d 1255 (Colo. 2002). Although an applicant must show that the water is available based on several factors, it is not necessary to show that the "water will always be available to the full extent applied for in the decree." However, where a Special Use Permit from the U.S. Forest Service was required for the applicant to capture the water,and the Forest Service had denied the permit, the applicant was held not to have met the "can and will" test. West Elk Ranch, L.L.C. v. United States, 65 P.3d 479 (Colo. 2002).

As part of the reasonable diligence showings required every six years to keep a conditional decree alive, the appropriator also must satisfy the can and will requirement. The Colorado Supreme Court determined that the can and will requirement is to be applied by water courts in the hexennial diligence proceedings as well as in issuing initial conditional decrees. Municipal Subdistrict, Northern Colorado Water Conservancy District v. OXY USA, Inc., 990 P.2d 701 (Colo.1999). As a result, the can and will requirement continues to apply until the conditionally decreed right becomes absolute.

In Washington, water rights for future uses were thrown into doubt by *Department of Ecology v. Theodoratus*, 957 P.2d 1241 (Wash. 1998). *Theodoratus* involved a change in the approach for recognizing vested water rights for public water supply. In 1973, the Department of Ecology had issued Theodoratus a permit to pump groundwater for a new residential development; his water supply system was intended to serve a total of 253 lots (including 30 outside his development), but by the early 1990s Theodoratus had built water lines to only 93 lots. Even though he had not actually used all of his permitted water, however, Theodoratus arguably had a vested right to the full amount under the language of his permit and established agency practice:

> The [permit] included language purporting to create a vested water right which would entitle the applicant to a water certificate issued under RCW 90.03.330 once a water supply system was capable of delivering water, even though some or most of the lots were vacant. Quantification of a water right based upon system capacity, rather than the amount of water used, is referred to as a "pumps and pipes method." This method has been used by the Department for at least the past 40 years, and hundreds of permits have been issued with pumps and pipes language.

* * *

The permit originally granted to Appellant called for completion of the development by 1980. Due to various litigation, the project was delayed several times. A recession in the 1980's in the area also slowed the project. The Department granted several extensions to Appellant. From 1985 to 1992 the Department file was inactive. In 1992, Appellant requested an extension to 2001, which the Department at first denied. Appellant appealed the denial. The Department then changed its decision and granted an extension to January 1, 2001. The Department placed four conditions on the extension. * * * The third condition basically provides that a vested water right would be determined based upon actual application of water to beneficial use, not on system capacity. There is no question that this third condition reflected a significant change in the basis for issuance of a final certificate of water right. Appellant appealed the new conditions.

* * *

Read together, the statutes contemplate, in addition to construction of a water system, that an applicant will estimate the time needed to actually apply appropriated water to beneficial use, the Department will establish a time period in which water shall actually be applied to beneficial use, extensions of time will be available depending upon the circumstances, and a final certificate of water right will be issued upon a showing that the appropriation has been perfected. The surface water provisions which require application of water to beneficial use effectuate legislative policy expressly stated in both the surface and groundwater codes. *See* RCW 90.03.010; 90.44.020; 90.44.040.

Case law is in accord with the statutory requirement that a water right must be based on actual application of water to beneficial use and not upon system capacity. "An appropriated water right is established and maintained by the purposeful application of a *given quantity of water* to a beneficial use upon the land." *Grimes,* 121 Wash.2d at 468, 852 P.2d 1044 (emphasis added) (quoting *Neubert,* 117 Wash.2d at 237, 814 P.2d 199). Perfection of an appropriative right requires that appropriation is complete only when the water is *actually applied* to a beneficial use. * * *

In requiring actual application of water to beneficial use in order to perfect an appropriative right before a final certificate of water right may be issued, the statutes codify fundamental western water law.

Appellant argues, however, that RCW 90.44.080 requires only completion of construction in accordance with the pumps and pipes language in his original permit. RCW 90.44.080 states that "[u]pon a showing to the department that construction has been completed in compliance with the terms of any permit issued under the provisions of this chapter, it shall be the duty of the department to issue to the permittee a certificate of groundwater right stating that the appropriation has been perfected under such permit." RCW 90.44.080. The statute requires (1) completion of construction of the water system (2) in compliance with the terms of permit and (3) perfection of the appropriative right. * * * Because both compliance with a permit (containing terms lawful under the statutes) and perfection of the appropriation are required under RCW 90.44.080, we reject Appellant's contention that all the statute requires is completion of construction. * * *

We are also not persuaded by Appellant's claim that a distinction is warranted because his is a public water supply system. Initially, we note that Appellant is a private developer and his development is finite. Appellant is not a municipality, and we decline to address issues concerning municipal water suppliers in the context of this case. We do note that the statutory scheme allows for differences between municipal and other water use. *E.g.,* RCW 90.03.260; 90.14.140(2)(d). We also note that 1997 legislation which would have allowed for a system capacity measure of a water right "[f]or those public water supplies that fulfill municipal water supply purposes," Substitute Senate Bill 5783, 55th Leg., Reg. Sess. § 4(2) (1997), was vetoed by the Governor on the ground that the provision, along with another vetoed section, would have provided an unfair advantage to public water systems by creating great uncertainty in determining water availability for other water rights and new applicants, as well as uncertainty in the protection of instream resources, and would have increased the difficulty of managing the state's waters. * * *

Finally, there is another reason to reject Appellant's contention that system capacity determines the measure and limit of a water right. Water rights may be relinquished. RCW 90.14.130–.180. The failure "to beneficially use all or any part" of the right for five years, without sufficient cause, "shall relinquish" the right in whole or in part. RCW 90.14.160; 90.14.170; 90.14.180. If system capacity defined the quantity of the right, i.e., system capacity equated to beneficial use as a measure and limit of the right, these statutory provisions would be meaningless. * * *

We do note that Appellant has been granted an extension of time in which to perfect his water right. He has at present an inchoate right to water which has not yet been applied to beneficial use. * * *

957 P.2d at 1243–1248. Justice Sanders dissented, concluding that

> the issue before us is whether Ecology could, pursuant to our statute, issue a water certificate based on the pumps and pipes approach. The majority asserts pumps and pipes has never been the law and Ecology's long-standing practice was illegal from the start. In the process the majority compels an absurd result and destabilizes all certificates already issued under the pumps and pipes approach as well as impairs the future of residential development in Washington. Adding insult to error, the majority denies Theodoratus a certificate even though he justifiably relied on Ecology's directive by making a substantial investment of private funds.

Id. at 1250–1251 (Sanders, J., dissenting). In 2003, the Washington Legislature enacted a statute intended re-stabilize all existing "pumps and pipes" certificates as part of a broad revision of state law relating to municipal water rights. The statute prohibited the Department of Ecology from revoking or diminishing a certificate unless the certificate had ministerial errors or was obtained through misrepresentation. The statute specified that this prohibition applied to existing certificates for municipal water supply that were issued "based on an administrative policy for issuing such certificates once works for diverting or withdrawing and distributing water for municipal supply purposes were constructed rather than after the water had been placed to actual beneficial use." After the statute's effective date, however, certificates would be issued "only for the perfected portion of a water right as demonstrated through actual beneficial use." Rev. Code Wash. 90.03.330. Was this statute an unwarranted departure from the bedrock principle of prior appropriation, or a reasonable measure to protect cities' investment-backed expectations? As a policy matter, is "pumps and pipes" a reasonable basis for establishing vested water rights for public supply purposes?

c.   Preferences

The laws of nearly every western state contain preferences for particular types of uses. These are found in state constitutions as well as in statutes. For instance, Colorado's Constitution says:

> [W]hen the waters of any natural stream are not sufficient for the service of all those desiring the use of the same, those using the water for domestic purposes shall have the preference over those claiming for any other purpose, and those using the water for agricultural purposes shall have preference over those using the same for manufacturing purposes.

COLO. CONST. ART. 16, § 6. Although these strongly worded provisions may appear to give an absolute preference to one type of use, such as domestic purposes, over other uses such as agricultural, they are not typically applied to preempt temporal priorities, so that in a shortage an agricultural right would still defeat a domestic right. This is a major difference from riparian jurisdictions.

What then do the preference laws mean? The Colorado provision has been applied only to allow users needing water for a particular purpose to condemn water rights held for a lower preference use. The most common application of the preference laws is to guide administrative officials in issuing water rights permits among competing applicants. Professor Beck explains how these laws have evolved in content and application:

> Prior appropriation statutes started out with hierarchical lists that became longer as uses were subdivided or added and unused water became scarcer. North Dakota exemplifies this evolution with the original 1963 list and its context reading as follows: "*In all cases* where the use of water for different purposes conflict such uses shall conform to the following order of priority: 1. Domestic Use. 2. Livestock Use. 3. Irrigation and Industry," [N.D. CENT. CODE § 61–01–01.01 (repealed 1977)] (emphasis added). The revision that North Dakota made in 1977 affected both the list and the context: "When there are competing applications for water from the same source, and the source is insufficient to supply all applicants, the state engineer shall adhere to the following order of priority: 1. Domestic use. 2. Municipal use. 3.

Livestock use. 4. Irrigation use. 5. Industrial use. 6. Fish, wildlife, and outdoor recreational uses." [N.D. CENT. CODE § 61–04–06.1 (2007)]

Frank Trelease surveyed all seventeen coterminous western states in 1955 and indicated that only five states, Montana, Nevada, North Dakota, and Washington did not have water use preference lists. However, now Montana provides that in "controlled ground water areas," groundwater withdrawals can be limited "for domestic and livestock purposes first and then to withdrawals for other beneficial purposes, including but not limited to agricultural, industrial, municipal (other than domestic), and recreational purposes, in the order that the department considers advisable under the circumstances." [MONT. CODE ANN. § 85–2–506 (1999)]. Nevada also now has a preference provision relating to groundwater. [*See* NEV. REV. STAT. ANN. § 534.120(2) (Michie Supp. 1999)]. North Dakota has the provision [discussed above]. South Dakota provides at least that the "use of water for domestic purposes is the highest use of water" and is preferred over other uses. [S.D. CODIFIED LAWS § 46–1–5 (Michie 1999)]. [And,] Washington gives authority to the Department of Ecology to reserve water for future use and provides that reservations of water by the department "for agriculture, hydroelectric energy, municipal, industrial, and other uses ... or minimum flows or levels ... shall constitute appropriations." [WASH. REV. CODE. ANN. §§ 90.54.050, 90.03.345 (West 1992 & Supp. 2000)]. This statutory language appears to give the Department some authority to establish preferences based on use. * * *

Robert E. Beck, *Use Preferences for Water*, 76 N.D. L. Rev. 753, 767–68 (2000).

2. PROMOTING THE PUBLIC INTEREST

Can a state deny a permit when unappropriated water is available and vested rights will be unimpaired? Qualifications are usually expressed in statutes that allow a state water resources agency to deny applications that are not in the public interest.

Permits for irrigation or agriculture may not be issued in Wisconsin if it appears that public rights will be injured. Wis. Stat. Ann. (West 1998). Conditions are also imposed on the permit that allow it to be amended or rescinded to protect public rights in the stream. See Harold W. Ellis, et al., Water–Use Law and Administration in Wisconsin § 9.06 (1970). The Wisconsin Department of Natural Resources (as successor to the Public Service Commission) grants a permit if "the proposed dam is in the public interest, considering ecological, aesthetic, economic and recreational values * * *. The enjoyment of natural scenic beauty [is a] * * * public [right] to be considered along with other public rights * * *." WIS. STAT. ANN. § 31.06(3) (West 1998). The statute directs the department to weigh the recreational use and natural scenic beauty of the river in its natural state and in its altered state due to the dam, and "if it further appears that the economic need of electric power is less than the value of the recreational and scenic beauty advantage of such river in its natural state," the department shall deny the permit. Thus, the department weighs the public interests against the competing interests. The Supreme Court of Wisconsin has indicated that while the public right in water may have originated in use for navigation, the right will not be "lost by failure of pecuniary profitable navigation," and other uses may be developed, such as "sailing, rowing, canoeing, bathing, fishing, hunting, skating," or other public purposes. Nekoosa Edwards Paper Co. v. Railroad Comm'n, 201 Wis. 40, 228 N.W. 144, 147 (1929).

The Utah Code provides that the state engineer is directed to reject or limit any application to appropriate unappropriated waters where the approval of the application would prove detrimental to the public welfare. UTAH CODE ANN. § 73–3–8 (Michie 1989). In Washington, the statute requires the supervisor to grant the permit only if "the appropriation thereof as proposed will not impair existing rights or be detrimental to the public welfare." WASH. REV. CODE ANN. § 90.03.290 (West 2001). If the proposed appropriation "threatens to prove detrimental to the public interest, having due regard to the highest feasible development of the use of the waters belonging to the public, it shall be the duty of the supervisor to reject such application and to refuse to issue the permit asked for." Id. The Nevada statute requires that "where * * * use or change [of use] threatens or proves detrimental to the public interest, the state engineer shall * * * refuse to issue the requested permit." NEV. REV. STAT. ANN. § 533.370 (Michie Supp. 1999). See also WYO. STAT. ANN. § 41–4–503 (2001). These statutes, however, do not confer unlimited discretion on state agencies to make "optimum" allocation decisions. They have a history.

Early case law provided a very limited application of "public interest." The leading case is Young & Norton v. Hinderlider, 15 N.M. 666, 110 P. 1045 (1910). Hinderlider had applied for a permit to make an appropriation and construct a storage project. Over two months later, a competing applicant filed for a right to the waters of the same stream, and proposed to develop the water at a much lower cost. The territorial engineer found, among other things, "[t]hat it would not be to the best interests of the public to approve the [Hinderlider application], thereby forcing the protestants to pay more than double price for their water rights." Id. at 1047. On appeal, the court refused to limit the meaning of the term "contrary to public interest" to cases in which there was posed a menace to the public health or safety. Instead, it was held broad enough to prevent investors from making worthless investments in the state, thereby allowing the territorial engineer to evaluate the potential success of a proposed project, including economic feasibility. "If there is available unappropriated water of the La Plata river for only 5,000 or 6,000 acres of land, it would be contrary to the public interest that a project for irrigating 14,000 acres with that water should receive an official approval which would, perhaps, enable the promoters of it to market their scheme to sell stock reasonably sure to become worthless, and land which could not be irrigated, at the price of irrigated land." Id. at 1050.

Other courts have followed the *Young & Norton* definition of public interest. *Young & Norton* was applied in Tanner v. Bacon, 103 Utah 494, 136 P.2d 957 (1943). The state engineer denied Tanner's 1925 application to appropriate 100 cfs of the Provo River for power purposes, finding that granting the application would be "detrimental to the public welfare," although unappropriated water was available. In 1922, the State Water Storage Commission had contracted with the Bureau of Reclamation for a study of a reservoir project that would import waters into the Provo River and store them for domestic and supplemental irrigation and industrial supply. In 1936, the Provo River Water Users' Association (a corporation created to act as intermediary between the Bureau of Reclamation and project users) contracted with the United States to construct a storage project. On April 3, 1936 the Association filed for a right to divert and store up to 30,000 acre-feet annually. The trial court found that Tanner's proposed use conflicted with this later-proposed project which was "the more beneficial use of such waters for domestic, and irrigation purposes" and affirmed the state engineer's decision, but ordered the application reinstated subject to the rights of the Provo River Water Users' Association:

> The law which governed the right to make future appropriations when plaintiff filed his application is Sec. 48, Chap. 67, Laws of Utah for 1919 [now amended and codified at UTAH CODE ANN. § 73–3–8], which provides: "Where there is no unappropriated water in the proposed source of supply, or where the proposed use will conflict with prior applications or existing rights, or where the approval of such application would in the opinion of the State Engineer *interfere with the more beneficial use for irrigation, domestic or culinary purposes, stock watering, power or mining development, manufacturing, or would prove detrimental to the public welfare,* it shall be the duty of the State Engineer to reject such application." (Italics added.) * * *

> These statutes may not vest the state with the proprietary ownership of the water but they clearly do enjoin upon the state the duty to control the appropriation of the public waters in a manner that will be for the best interests of the public. * * *

> [T]he legislature intended that upon the filing of an application to appropriate water the State Engineer should determine from the facts and circumstances of each case whether the approval thereof would interfere with the more beneficial use of the water, for one of the purposes mentioned, whether the purpose proposed in the application was for one of the purposes mentioned or for some other purpose. This is the construction placed upon this provision by the District Court. It found that to store the flood waters of the Provo River to be later used for domestic, irrigation and other purposes was the more beneficial use which the approval of plaintiff's application, without making it subject to those rights, would interfere with. This decision not being arbitrary or capricious but based upon experience and well recognized principles must be sustained.

136 P.2d at 962–964.

"Public interest" may also be a factor in a court's determining which "use will be for the greatest public benefit" in a condemnation action. Mack v. Eldorado Water Dist., 56 Wash.2d 584, 354 P.2d 917, 919 (1960).

a. New Uses

Little Blue Natural Resources Dist. v. Lower Platte North Natural Resources Dist.

Supreme Court of Nebraska, 1980.
206 Neb. 535, 294 N.W.2d 598.

■ KRIVOSHA, CHIEF JUSTICE.

* * *

[The Little Blue Natural Resources District is a district formed under Nebraska law to perform multiple functions that historically were performed by several special districts. Neb. Rev. Stat. § 2–3203. The District planned an irrigation project to divert water from a point near the Platte River to District lands in another watershed which could not be irrigated with groundwater because there was no aquifer there.]

The Central Nebraska Public Power and Irrigation District, generally known as Tri–County, operates a supply canal south of the Platte River which transports water from a diversion dam on the Platte River east of North Platte, Nebraska, to a point near Overton, Nebraska, where the supply canal joins the Phelps County canal, a major irrigation canal operated by Tri–County. A wasteway located at this junction is used to return water to the river when it is not to be used for irrigation purposes. A gate located at the junction is used to send water in the supply canal into the Phelps County canal or into the wasteway.

The Little Blue project contemplates taking water at this structure, which would otherwise be returned through the wasteway to the river, and carrying it to the Campbell reservoir for storage for use during the following season. The plan contemplates the use of the Phelps County canal to a point near Axtell, Nebraska, where a new supply canal would be constructed which would connect with the Little Blue River southwest of Minden, Nebraska.

Since the Tri–County district would be using water for irrigation during the months of April through August, the Little Blue project would use the flow in the supply canal from September until January and would take only water which would otherwise be returned to the Platte River through the wasteway.

* * *

The director [of the Department of Water Resources] found there was unappropriated water in the Platte River sufficient to meet the demands of the proposed project, but that approval of the applications would result in water for irrigation purposes being taken from the Platte River and applied to land outside the basin of the Platte River, contrary to the rules announced by this court in *Osterman v. Central Nebraska Public Power and Irrigation District*, 131 Neb. 356, 268 N.W. 334 (1936). The director concluded that the *Osterman* case was controlling and, for that reason, the department was without authority to approve the applications. The applicant has appealed from the order denying the applications.

* * *

The *Osterman* case involved applications by the Central Nebraska Public Power and Irrigation District, generally known as Tri–County, to divert and store water from the Platte River for power purposes and to irrigate land in Gosper, Phelps, Kearney, and Adams Counties. Approximately 60 percent of the water to be used for irrigation purposes would have been transported out of the Platte River basin and applied to lands within the basin of the Blue River.

In the *Osterman* case, this court declared that, at common law, the right to use water was limited to the owners of riparian lands and, of necessity, there was "no right to transport waters beyond or over the divide or watershed that enclosed the source from which obtained."

* * *

The language of the Nebraska Constitution is clear and unambiguous with regard to the use of water. Neb.Const. art. XV, § 4, unequivocally provides: "The necessity of water for domestic use and for irrigation purposes in the State of Nebraska is hereby declared to be a natural want." * * *

Neb.Const. art. XV, § 5, provides: "The use of the water of every natural stream within the State of Nebraska is hereby dedicated to the people of the state for beneficial purposes, subject to the provisions of the following section." It is significant to note that the quoted section refers to the use of the water of *every* natural stream being dedicated to "the people." Nothing in art. XV, § 5, indicates or authorizes limiting the use of the water of every natural stream to *within a particular watershed basin* or dedicating its use to the people living *within a particular watershed basin.* Quite to the contrary, the clear and unambiguous language constitutionally mandates that the use of *every* stream, regardless of its location, be dedicated to *all* of the people of the state, regardless of their location, and not just to those who happen to live within the confines of a particular valley or watershed basin. Nowhere within the Constitution can such limiting words be found.

That fact is further made clear when one looks at Neb.Const. art. XV, § 6, which provides, in part: "The right to divert unappropriated waters of every natural stream for beneficial use shall *never be denied* except when such denial is demanded by the public interest." (Emphasis supplied).

* * *

The *Osterman* decision totally ignored the provisions of the Nebraska Constitution and relied solely upon the provisions of what is now Neb. Rev.

STAT. § 46–265 (Reissue 1978), and what was formerly § 46–620 COMP. STAT. 1929. It reads as follows:

> The owner or owners of any irrigation ditch or canal shall carefully maintain the embankments thereof so as to prevent waste therefrom, and shall return the unused water from such ditch or canal with as little waste thereof as possible to the stream from which such water was taken, *or to the Missouri River.*

(Emphasis supplied). The *Osterman* court concluded that the phrase "or to the Missouri River" had no application, was not a part of the statute, and should be ignored. The court, therefore, concluded that former § 46–620 prohibited transbasin diversion.

There is no basis, however, to conclude that the phrase "or to the Missouri River" has no meaning. All of the water of the State of Nebraska empties into the Missouri River and, therefore, it must be concluded that diversion may occur so long as the unused portion of the water is not in some manner unnecessarily impounded or wasted and is returned to its natural stream of origin or to the Missouri River.

The *Osterman* decision further concluded that former § 46–508, now § 46–206, which provides:

> The water appropriated from a river or stream shall not be turned or permitted to run into the waters or channel of any other river or stream than that from which it is taken or appropriated, *unless such stream exceeds in width one hundred feet, in which event not more than seventy-five per cent of the regular flow shall be taken.*

(emphasis supplied), was superseded by the provisions of § 46–620 and should be disregarded.

* * *

* * * If transbasin diversion is prohibited entirely, as urged by appellees, then the last clause of § 46–206, permitting the diversion of up to 75 percent of the water from a stream more than 100 feet wide is meaningless.

When we then give both sections of the statute their plain meaning, we are left with no other conclusion but that, if a stream is more than 100 feet wide, up to 75 percent of the water not otherwise appropriated may be diverted so long as no waste is permitted, the unused portion is returned to its stream of origin or permitted to find its way back to the Missouri River, and the public interest does not otherwise require that such diversion be denied.

* * *

In *Osterman, supra* at 362, 268 N.W. at 337, we said:

> It would be a sad commentary on our political organization, upon the department of roads and irrigation, and upon this reviewing court, if in rationing this necessity of life this beautiful valley should be left with a dry river bed and ruined farms, because of any mistaken theory that the protection of its natural fertility did not constitute a public interest within the policy of our laws.

We agree with that statement and believe that, under the provisions of our Constitution dealing with water, it is applicable to the entire state so long as the public interest does not otherwise demand. Would it not be a far sadder commentary if, in rationing this necessity of life, large areas of the state outside a particular valley were ruined while unappropriated water flowed into the Missouri River and on to other states.

When there is insufficient water to meet all needs, the Director of Water Resources may, under the law, limit the removal of water in accordance with statutorily established priorities similar to the restrictions imposed by the director and set out in *Cozad Ditch Co. v. Central Nebraska Public Power & Irrigation Dist.* [272 N.W. 560 (Neb.1937)]. Under our present Constitution and statutes, the determination of what constitutes a public interest sufficient to either limit or deny, as the situation may demand, the right to remove unappropriated waters from a stream must, in the first instance, be determined by the director. The Constitution tells us that the desire and need for water for domestic and irrigation purposes is a "natural want" of all our citizens and we should not unnecessarily deny it to any who can obtain it without doing harm to others.

* * *

Reversed and Remanded.

NOTES

1. After the principal case was decided, the Nebraska legislature amended the water transfer statute to enumerate the relevant factors to be considered by the Director of the Department of Natural Resources in determining the public interest:

(1) The economic, environmental, and other benefits of the proposed interbasin transfer and use;

(2) Any adverse impacts of the proposed interbasin transfer and use;

(3) Any current beneficial uses being made of the unappropriated water in the basin of origin;

(4) Any reasonably foreseeable future beneficial uses of the water in the basin of origin;

(5) The economic, environmental, and other benefits of leaving the water in the basin of origin for current or future beneficial uses;

(6) Alternative sources of water supply available to the applicant; and

(7) Alternative sources of water available to the basin of origin for future beneficial uses.

The application shall be deemed in the public interest if the overall benefits to the state and the applicant's basin are greater than or equal to the adverse impacts to the state and the basin of origin.

Neb. Rev. Stat. § 46–289 (1998).

The statute was construed in Little Blue Natural Resources Dist. v. Lower Platte North Natural Resources Dist., 210 Neb. 862, 317 N.W.2d 726 (1982) which held that the director must consult with the Game and Parks Commission to determine whether the proposed appropriations would interfere with endangered species or their habitat. The statute withstood a constitutional challenge in In re Applications A–16027, 242 Neb. 315, 495 N.W.2d 23 (1993). For a description of threats to one endangered species posed by proposed Nebraska water projects, and an analysis of the new transfer statute, see Daniel C. Vaughn, Comment, *The Whooping Crane, the Platte River, and Endangered Species Legislation,* 66 Neb. L. Rev. 175 (1987).

In a later case, irrigation districts challenged the Director of Water Resources' denial of an application to divert water from the South Platte River for storage in Enders Reservoir. In re Application of Hitchcock and Red Willow Irrigation Dist., 226 Neb. 146, 410 N.W.2d 101 (1987). The director's decision was based in part on the transbasin diversion law, which appellants claimed to be unconstitutional. The director also found that the project would harm endangered species habitat on the South Platte River. Most significantly, however, the director found that no water was available for appropriation in the South Platte.

2. In the *Osterman* case construed by the court, a nearly identical scheme for removing water from one basin to another was considered and rejected on the ground that interbasin diversions would be inconsistent with the common law. The court stated:

> "The common-law rules as to the rights and duties of riparian owners are in force in every part of the state, except as altered or modified by statute." Meng v. Coffey, 67 Neb. 500, 93 N.W. 713 * * *
>
> The language of the above rule necessarily implies that the right to use water at common law is limited strictly to riparian lands. * * * This necessitates the further conclusion that at common law there was in general no right to transport waters beyond or over the divide or watershed that enclosed the source from which obtained.

131 Neb. 356, 268 N.W. 334, 339 (1936). In reversing the *Osterman* case based on state constitutional provisions, did the Nebraska court effectively hold the riparian doctrine unconstitutional? What is the effect of the *Little Blue* decision on the rights of riparians? See Regina M. Shields, Note, *Water Law—Transbasin Diversion in Nebraska,* 14 Creighton L. Rev. 887 (1981); and Eric Pearson, *Constitutional Restraints on Water Diversions in Nebraska: The Little Blue Controversy,* 16 Creighton L. Rev. 695 (1983).

Shokal v. Dunn

Supreme Court of Idaho, 1985.
109 Idaho 330, 707 P.2d 441.

■ BISTLINE, JUSTICE.

On December 21, 1978, respondent Trout Co. applied for a permit to appropriate 100 c.f.s. of waters from Billingsley Creek near Hagerman,

Idaho. Numerous protests were filed by local residents, property owners, and Billingsley Creek water users. The Department of Water Resources (Water Resources) [issued a permit].

* * *

* * * [On appeal, the district court] determined that Water Resources had failed to properly evaluate the question of "local public interest," holding that the applicant had the ultimate burden of proving that a proposed water use was in the local public interest under I.C. § 42–203A.

* * * The Director conditionally granted the application upon a subsequent showing by the applicant, Trout Co., that the project would meet certain requirements and restrictions set forth in the order. * * *

Subsequently, Trout Co. submitted a new set of drawings of the facility, and a document entitled "Contemplated Operational Criteria for the Trout Co. Fishraising Facility" (hereinafter "Operational Criteria"). * * *

The protestants filed * * * protests raising many factual issues regarding the "Operational Criteria." After reviewing the "Operational Criteria" and considering the objections raised by the protestants and other parties, Water Resources, without further hearing, issued its final order on July 21, 1982, granting the application for Permit No. 36–7834. Appeal was again taken to the district court, this time before the Honorable W.E. Smith. * * *

III.   THE LOCAL PUBLIC INTEREST

* * * [T]he only matters for the agency to consider on remand are those which relate generally to the local public interest. I.C. § 42–203A(5)(e). We turn first to the interpretation of this provision, a question of first impression before this Court.[2]

A.   *Defining the Local Public Interest.*

Under I.C. § 42–203A(5)(e), if an applicant's appropriation of water "will conflict with the local public interest, where the local public interest

---

2. The requirement that Water Resources protect the public interest is related to the larger doctrine of the public trust, which Justice Huntley comprehensively discussed in Kootenai Environmental Alliance v. Panhandle Yacht Club, Inc., 105 Idaho 622, 671 P.2d 1085 (1983). The state holds all waters in trust for the benefit of the public, and "does not have the power to abdicate its role as trustee in favor of private parties." Id. at 625, 671 P.2d at 1088. Any grant to use the state's waters is "subject to the trust and to action by the State necessary to fulfill its trust responsibilities." Id. at 631, 671 P.2d at 1094. Trust interests include property values, "navigation, fish and wildlife habitat, aquatic life, recreation, aesthetic beauty and water quality." Id. at 632, 671 P.2d at 1095. Reviewing courts must "take a 'close look' at the action [of the legislature or of agencies such as Water Resources] to determine if it complies with the public trust doctrine and will not act merely as a rubber stamp for agency or legislative action." Id. at 629, 671 P.2d at 1092. Justice Huntley concluded, "The public trust at all times forms the outer boundaries of permissible government action with respect to public trust resources." Id. at 632, 671 P.2d at 1095.

is defined as the affairs of the people in the area directly affected by the proposed use," then the Director "may reject such application and refuse issuance of a permit therefor, or may partially approve and grant a permit for a smaller quantity of water than applied for, or may grant a permit upon conditions."

The Utah Supreme Court interpreted a similar provision [UTAH CODE ANN. § 100–8–1] to authorize the State Engineer "to reject or limit the priority of plaintiff's application [for a permit to appropriate water for a power project] in the interest of the public welfare." *Tanner v. Bacon*, 103 Utah 494, 136 P.2d 957, 964 (1943); *see also People v. Shirokow*, 26 Cal.3d 301, 162 Cal.Rptr. 30, 37, 605 P.2d 859, 866 (1980) (In the public interest, the Water Board may impose the condition that the applicant salvage the water required for his or her project.); *East Bay Municipal Utility District v. Department of Public Works*, 1 Cal.2d 476, 35 P.2d 1027, 1029 (1934) ("Where the facts justify the action, the water authority should be allowed to impose [on an application to appropriate water for a power project], in the public interest, the restrictions and conditions provided for in the act," or to reject the application "in its entirety."). Both the Utah and California Supreme Courts have upheld state water agencies which had granted appropriations subject to future appropriations for uses of greater importance—in effect prioritizing among uses according to the public interest. The Director of Water Resources has the same considerable flexibility and authority, which he has already implemented in earlier proceedings in this matter, to protect the public interest.

Indeed, I.C. § 42–203A places upon the Director the affirmative *duty* to assess and protect the public interest. In assessing the duty of the state water board imposed by California's "public interest" provision, the California Supreme Court declared, "If the board determines a particular use is not in furtherance of the greatest public benefit, on balance the public interest must prevail." *Shirokow, supra, accord, Tanner, supra* (The State has "the *duty* to control the appropriation of the public waters in a manner that will be for the best interests of the public.") (emphasis added).

The authority and duty of the Director to protect the public interest spring naturally from the statute; the more difficult task for us is to define "the local public interest." Public interest provisions appear frequently in the statutes of the prior appropriation states of the West, but are explicated rarely. I.C. § 42–203A provides little guidance. Fortunately, however, the legislature did provide guidance in a related statute, I.C. § 42–1501. We also derive assistance from our sister states and from the academic community.

In I.C. § 42–1501 [providing for protection of instream flows,] the legislature declared it "in the public interest" that:

> the streams of this state and their environments be protected against loss of water supply to preserve the minimum stream flows required for the protection of fish and wildlife habitat, aquatic life, recreation, aesthetic beauty, transportation and navigation values, and water quality.

Not only is the term "public interest" common to both §§ 42–1501 and 42–203A, and the two sections common to the same title 42 (Irrigation and Drainage—Water Rights and Reclamation), but also the legislature approved the term "public interest" in both sections on the *same day,* March 29, 1978. Clearly, the legislature in § 42–203A must have intended the public interest on the local scale to include the public interest elements listed in § 42–1501: "fish and wildlife habitat, aquatic life, recreation, aesthetic beauty, transportation and navigation values, and water quality."

In so intending, the legislature was in good company. Unlike other state public interest statutes, the Alaska statute enumerates the elements of the public interest. The public interest elements of I.C. § 42–1501 are almost precisely duplicated within the Alaska statute, which is set out in the margin.[3] * * *

The Alaska statute contains other elements which common sense argues ought to be considered part of the local public interest. These include the proposed appropriation's benefit to the applicant, its economic effect, its effect "of loss of alternative uses of water that might be made within a reasonable time if not precluded or hindered by the proposed appropriation," its harm to others, its "effect upon access to navigable or public waters," and "the intent and ability of the applicant to complete the appropriation." Alaska Stat. § 46.5.080(b).

Several other public interest elements, though obvious, deserve specific mention. These are: assuring minimum stream flows, as specifically provided in I.C. § 42–1501, discouraging waste, and encouraging conservation. *See Shirokow, supra* (The California Supreme Court found water salvage to be sufficiently in the public interest to require it of a permittee.).

The above-mentioned elements of the public interest are not intended to be a comprehensive list. As observed long ago by the New Mexico Supreme Court, the "public interest" should be read broadly in order to "secure the greatest possible benefit from [the public waters] for the public." *Young & Norton v. Hinderlider,* 110 P. 1045, 1050 (N.M. 1910)

---

3. Alaska Stat. § 46.15.080 provides:

(b) In determining the public interest, the commissioner shall consider

(1) the benefit to the applicant resulting from the proposed appropriation;

(2) the effect of the economic activity resulting from the proposed appropriation;

(3) the effect on fish and game resources and on public recreational opportunities;

(4) the effect on public health;

(5) the effect of loss of alternate uses of water that might be made within a reasonable time if not pre-cluded or hindered by the proposed appropriation;

(6) harm to other persons resulting from the proposed appropriation;

(7) the intent and ability of the applicant to complete the appropriation; and

(8) the effect upon access to navigable or public waters.

See also Bank of Am. Nat. Trust & Sav. Assoc. v. State Water Resources Control Bd., 116 Cal.Rptr. 770, 771 (1974) (If supported by the record, the state water board can condition a permit for a reservoir on providing for the public interest element of public access for recreation.).

(Rejects considering only public health and safety; considers relative costs of two projects.). By using the general term "the local public interest," the legislature intended to include any locally important factor impacted by proposed appropriations.

Of course, not every appropriation will impact every one of the above elements. Nor will the elements have equal weight in every situation. The relevant elements and other relative weights will vary with local needs, circumstances, and interests. For example, in an area heavily dependent on recreation and tourism or specifically devoted to preservation in its natural state, Water Resources may give great consideration to the aesthetic and environmental ramifications of granting a permit which calls for substantial modification of the landscape or the stream.

Those applying for permits and those challenging the application bear the burden of demonstrating which elements of the public interest are impacted and to what degree. * * *

However, the burden of proof in all cases as to where the public interest lies * * * rests with the applicant:

> [I]t is not [the] protestant's burden of proof to establish that the project is not in the local public interest. The burden of proof is upon the applicant to show that the project is either in the local public interest or that there are factors that overweigh the local public interest in favor of the project.

The determination of what elements of the public interest are impacted, and what the public interest requires, is committed to Water Resources' sound discretion.

* * *

The above elements of the public interest [including concerns with dewatering of streams and water quality], together with other elements and factors which Water Resources deems relevant, will be considered at the hearing on the amended application. Water Resources should accept relevant testimony and other evidence providing additional information on the public interest.

NOTES

1. The administrator charged with determining the public interest has a difficult balancing task. How comfortable would you be as the Director of Water Resources after *Shokal* in deciding whether to grant a permit? Absent further legislative or judicial direction, the Director of the Department of Water Resources can exercise discretion to decide what is in the public interest. *Shokal* has been applied to deny and to condition permits to preserve environmental and recreational values. For instance, in 1990 the director denied a permit to appropriate water from the Bear River for a small hydroelectric project. He based his denial on the possibility that downstream users would be adversely affected by evaporation losses and his finding that the project was not in the local public interest because the recreational use of a whitewater stretch of the river through a portion of the Bear River Canyon would be hampered, wildlife habitat would be eliminated, and the applicant demonstrated insufficient financial resources. Can the local public interest differ from the statewide public interest?

The state supreme court has held that even objectors who do not own water rights are proper parties to raise objections under the local public interest statute. Hardy v. Higginson, 123 Idaho 485, 849 P.2d 946 (1993). For a history of the development of the public interest requirement in Idaho see Scott W. Reed, *The Public Trust Doctrine in Idaho,* 19 Envtl. L. 655 (1989).

The degree of judicial oversight of officials who determine what is in the "public interest" depends on the extent to which courts defer to the exercise of administrative discretion and the degree to which they are willing to evaluate evidence. Under administrative law principles, courts usually will not second-guess administrative officials. The Nebraska Supreme Court reviewed a decision by the Director of Water Resources finding an appropriation for an instream flow was in the "public interest." *In re* Application A–16642, 236 Neb. 671, 463 N.W.2d 591 (1990). In confirming the director's finding the court stated:

> [T]he several arguments of the complaining objectors are nothing more than attempts to entice this court into reweighing evidence. However, * * * when presented with an appeal from an order of the Director of Water Resources, this court does not reweigh the evidence its review is limited to a search for errors appearing in the record.

Id. at 613.

2. In divining the "public interest," administrative officials and courts have looked to various announcements of legislative intent in other contexts. The court in *Shokal* followed this approach looking even to the laws of other states to give meaning to the term. Nevada has refused to follow this approach. See Pyramid Lake Paiute Tribe of Indians v. Washoe County, 112 Nev. 743, 918 P.2d 697 (1996).

The Washington Supreme Court has interpreted the intent of public welfare considerations in an older statute in light of much more recent environmental legislation. It held that a State Environmental Policy Act, Wash. Rev. Code Ann. § 43.21C.030(2)(a–g) (West 1998) (like the counterpart National Environmental Policy Act, 42 U.S.C. §§ 4321–4370 (West 2008–2009), had made an "ecological ethic" part of the mission and mandate of every agency to which it applied). Therefore, environmental values had to be considered as a part of the public welfare in a request for a permit to divert water from Loon Lake for domestic use when the withdrawn water was used near the lake and then returned to it from septic tanks. Stempel v. Department of Water Resources, 82 Wash.2d 109, 508 P.2d 166 (1973). The Washington Water Resources Act also expressed a concern for public health and preservation of natural resources. Provisions of Wash. Rev. Code Ann. § 90.54.010 referring to protection of water quality, though also passed subsequent to the permit law, were found to require evaluation of pollution reentry problems in applying the public welfare standard.

3. In addition to the criteria applicable to all other applications for water rights, Montana law (see *supra* p. 299) requires public interest review only in the case of large appropriations. The applicant for an appropriation of 4,000 acre-feet per year or more or of 5.5 cfs or more must prove, and the Department of Natural Resources and Conservation must find, that:

(b) The proposed appropriation is a reasonable use. A finding must be based on a consideration of the following:

(i) the existing demands on the state water supply, as well as projected demands, such as reservations of water for future beneficial purposes, including municipal water supplies, irrigation systems, and minimum streamflows for the protection of existing water rights and aquatic life;

(ii) the benefits to the applicant and the state;

(iii) the effects on the quantity and quality of water for existing beneficial uses in the source of supply;

(iv) the availability and feasibility of using low-quality water for the purpose for which application has been made;

(v) the effects on private property rights by any creation of or contribution to saline seep; and

(vi) the probably significant adverse environmental impacts of the proposed use of water as determined by the department. * * *

MONT. CODE ANN. § 85–2–311 (1999).

4. Oregon law provides unusual detail regarding public interest considerations in permitting. OR. REV. STAT. 537.170(8) contains a list of broadly worded factors for the Water Resources Department to consider regarding whether a permit application is in the public interest, including "[c]onserving the highest use of the water for all purposes, including irrigation, domestic use, municipal water supply, power development, public recreation, protection of commercial and game fishing and wildlife, fire protection, mining, industrial purposes, navigation, scenic attraction," or any other beneficial water use which "may have a special value to the public." Another statute, however, requires the agency to presume that a proposed use will not harm the public interest if the use "is allowed in the applicable basin program established pursuant to ORS 536.300 and 536.340 or given a preference under ORS 536.310 (12), if water is available, if the proposed use will not injure other water rights and if the proposed use complies with rules of the Water Resources Commission." The presumption may be rebutted if it is shown, based on a preponderance of the evidence, that one of these prerequisites is not met or that the proposed use would be contrary to a specific public interest under § 537.170(8). OR. REV. STAT. 537.153(2). The statute refers to "rules of the Water Resources Commission," and some of these rules further define the criteria for making public interest determinations. Or. Admin. R. Ch. 690, Div. 33 (restricting new water uses to protect sensitive fish populations in certain areas of the state). The rules contain additional factors for the agency to consider in deciding on the public interest, including whether the proposed use would have broad public benefits, whether there are reasonable alternatives, and whether mitigation measures have been adopted. Or. Admin. R. 690–33–0340. Compared to a "simple" requirement that the permitting agency must consider the (undefined) public interest, do such provisions make Oregon public interest determinations more objective and predictable, or just more complicated?

5.   In absence of specific legislative standards, is there any limit on the factors an agency or a reviewing court should consider to be within the "public interest?" Professor Trelease has poignantly suggested in an aptly titled article that perceptions of the fine line between sound administrative judgment and apparent arbitrariness may depend on one's interest in a particular transaction:

> The Wise Administrator, as every one knows, is the man in a government office who protects "the public interests" (read *my* interests) from actions which would adversely affect those interests, when the public is (I am) otherwise unable to influence the course of those actions. The other fellow is as easy to spot; he is the man in government who makes decisions for me that I would rather, and could better, make for myself.

Frank J. Trelease, *The Model Water Code, the Wise Administrator and the Goddam Bureaucrat,* 14 Nat. Resources J. 207, 207 (1974).

6.   In Colorado, although the constitution says that all unappropriated water is "property of the public, and the same is dedicated to the use of the people of the state," the state supreme court has held that in absence of statute a water court may not consider evidence of environmental or other public interest impacts in deciding whether to grant a decree for conditional water rights. See Board of County Comm'rs v. Crystal Creek Homeowners Ass'n, 891 P.2d 952, 972–75 (Colo.1995).

————

Familiar objections to broad administrative discretion in natural resources allocation include: standards may vary with incumbents in administrative positions; there is unpredictability as to how resources will be allocated; and costs and delays are built into the system. If the goal of water allocation is to maximize the benefits of water for society with a minimum of costs or harms, can it be achieved in a better way? Is planning the answer?

David H. Getches, Water Planning: Untapped Opportunity for the Western States

9 J. Energy L. & Pol'y 1 (1988).

I.   Introduction

The western states face shifting and increasing resource demands that dictate, now more than ever, the implementation of workable, comprehensive state water planning.

* * *

Water planning, like planning for other resources, means articulating policy and applying that policy to specific facts and data. It was characterized by the National Water Commission as "the prelude to informed decisionmaking." To be effective, water planning must be a strategic effort that integrates policy with the best available resource information, providing guidance and assistance for future actions.

* * *

III. The Fundamentals of Water Planning

Water resource planning is widely misunderstood. It is often seen as a centralized, bureaucracy-dominated, inflexible blueprint for specific project development. The use of the terminology "state water plan" contributes to the confusion because it connotes a single, prescriptive document. If planning is to serve public needs, it must be a comprehensive, dynamic process, articulating policies and strategies relative to a state's particular water resources and needs. To be effective, the results of the process should be legally integrated into state decisions, giving "teeth" to the effort.

* * *

B. *Comprehensive Process*

Water resources planning should include a wide range of subjects that affect or are affected by the use of water, including land use, pollution, wildlife, and recreation. A comprehensive planning process must consider all available sources of water, both surface and underground.

It is highly unusual for water planning to be integrated with land use planning, yet the two are inextricably connected. Land use plans and projections depend on the availability of water supplies. Similarly, water resources planning depends heavily upon plans made by state and local governments for future land use. The presence or absence of a water supply has not historically determined how growth will occur but the timing and cost of water supply may influence patterns of growth. If investments in land are to be reliable and a development pattern reasonably predictable, water needs should be anticipated based on land use plans, and the necessary infrastructure should be identified.

Water quality planning is traditionally divorced from water resource planning; most states divide the responsibilities for regulating water quality and allocating water resources between different agencies. Considerable water quality planning has been done in the United States. Congress required and funded water quality plans as a condition of local governments receiving major construction grants under the Clean Water Act, but this was carried out independent of any ongoing state water resources planning. Similarly, detailed plans for construction and operation of specific water projects have ignored water quality concerns. This is especially negligent in the case of irrigation projects, where there is a direct connection between application of water, which seeps and leaches through saline soils, and the pollution of surface and groundwater supplies by increased salinity levels.

* * *

Conjunctive management of groundwater and surface supplies has been urged for years, but the two sources are rarely considered together by water managers. Although some groundwater is hydrologically connected with surface streams, the two are treated as legally separate sources in some states. Even if this anomalous division of ground and surface water allocation is to continue, sound planning could lead to more rational decisions by the agencies or officials who implement the separate schemes.

* * *

States regularly plan for recreation, fish and wildlife management, flood protection, and instream flow needs. These state environmental and other resource plans should be integrated into water planning. Similarly, state economic development goals and plans need to be reflected in a water plan. Industrial expansion, development of new business, and satisfaction of municipal needs all may turn on sound water planning.

Comprehensive water planning requires states to consider how to manage existing supplies better, rather than simply to assume that future needs will be satisfied from newly developed sources. A key planning goal should be to identify optimum uses of a state's water resources and existing facilities, and to consider a variety of sources for those uses. A Western Governors Association report on water efficiency found that a tremendous amount of western water is wasted through inefficient use and management. It found that basin-wide co-operation, water conservation and efficiency, alternative physical solutions, and conjunctive use could satisfy much of the West's foreseeable future demand.

* * *

Legislative authorizations for planning and the actions of an entity carrying out planning responsibilities should be unambiguous about which aspects of the process are to be considered binding. Some parts of planning documents may be merely illustrations or examples of how the policy could be carried out. The identification of water development projects in the planning process is especially susceptible to the interpretation that it is prescriptive, as illustrated by the case of *Johnson Rancho County Water District v. State Water Rights Board,* [235 Cal. App. 2d 863, 45 Cal. Rptr. 589 (3d Dist. 1965)]. In that case, the court considered the propriety of the state Water Rights Board's (predecessor to the state Water Resources Control Board) allowing development of a project at a point on a river that would preclude the future development of another project that was a specific feature of the California Water Plan. The California statutes provide that "it is the policy of the State that The California Water Plan ... is accepted as the guide for the orderly and co-ordinated control, protection, conservation, development, and utilization of the water resources of the State." Interpreting this vague statement, the court pointed out that the statute also said that the declaration "does not constitute approval of specific projects ... nor shall this declaration be construed as a prohibition of the development of the water resources of the State by any entity." Furthermore, the Code said that the Board is required only to "give consideration to ... the California Water Plan...." Thus, the court rejected the contention that the Water Rights Board was legally powerless to grant a permit for a new project that would preclude building a project set out in the plan.

To avoid confusion and uncertainty about the effect and purposes of state water planning, state law should clearly specify the intended uses for the resulting plans and policies. * * *

B.   Public Interest Determinations

Courts and administrative agencies increasingly are being asked to make determinations of "the public interest" in their decisions concerning water rights allocation and transfers. Sixteen states have some form of public interest review.[139] These mandates create difficulties and ambiguities for administrators because they typically lack legislative standards or guidance.

* * *

* * * Even where there is no statutory requirement that administrators' decisions further the public interest, courts increasingly require agencies to consider a variety of environmental and economic factors as they administer water. In Colorado, where administrative agencies exercise virtually no discretion in allocating or administering water, the supreme court has been moving firmly toward demanding that decisions, rules, and regulations ensure optimum utilization of water.[148]

The courts almost certainly will continue in their attempts to inject newly asserted, widely held public values into determinations concerning water, notwithstanding the sparsity of legislative guidance. The absence or

---

139.   Alaska Stat. §§ 46.15.040, –.080(a) (1984 & Supp.1986); Ariz. Rev. Stat. Ann. §§ 45–152, –153 (Supp. 2007); Cal. Water Code §§ 1225, 1255 (West 1971 & Supp. 1987); Idaho Code §§ 42–201, –203A, –203C (Supp. 1986); Kan. Stat. §§ 82a–705, –711 (1984); Mont. Code Ann. §§ 85–2–302, 311(2) (1985) (does not use typical "public interest" or "public welfare" phrasing but a permit can issue for larger appropriations only if the proposed use is "a reasonable use," which is defined in terms of typical public interest criteria); Neb. Rev. Stat. §§ 46–233, –234 (1984); Nev. Rev. Stat. §§ 533.325, .370(5), 533.345 (2005); N.M. Stat. Ann. §§ 72–5–1, –6, –7, 72–12–3, –3E (1985); N.D. Cent. Code §§ 61–04–02, 06 (1985); Or. Rev. Stat. §§ 537.130, –.170(4) (1985); S.D. Comp. Laws Ann. §§ 46–1–15, –2A–9, –5–10, –6–3 (1983); Tex. Water Code Ann. §§ 11.121, –134(3) (Vernon Supp.1987); Utah Code Ann. §§ 73–3–1, –8(1) (1980 & Supp. 1986); Wash. Rev. Code Ann. §§ 90.03.250, –.290, –44.050, –44.060 (1962); Wyo. Stat. §§ 41–4–503, –3–930 to –932 (1977 & Supp. 1986).

148.   See Alamosa–La Jara Water Users Protection Ass'n v. Gould, 674 P.2d 914 (Colo.1983). The Colorado Supreme Court has found a "clear obligation [for the state engineer] to represent the public interest" in water rights determinations. Bar 70 Enterprises, Inc. v. Tosco Corp., 703 P.2d 1297, 1304 (Colo.1985); Wadsworth v. Kuiper, 193 Colo. 95, 562 P.2d 1114 (1977). See also *United Plainsmen,* [247 N.W.2d 457 (N.D.1976)].

vagueness of legislative standards understandably frustrates judicial efforts[149] and, as the New Mexico case quoted above demonstrates, can produce surprising results.

Legislatures prefer to delegate broad discretion to administrative officials and agencies, rather than to catalogue detailed standards. The legislative process is not well suited to developing standards detailed enough to be applied meaningfully in multiple and diverse situations. The legislature can require a state agency to engage in a planning process and thereby to produce comprehensive standards and guidelines, along with a description of how they should be applied and balanced in various circumstances. Although it is unlikely that any comprehensive planning document would be durable enough for all situations, it almost inevitably would be better than the product of a legislative drafting process or, alternatively, ad hoc exercises by an administrative agency. A planning process can consider variables in advance and continue to adjust the approaches taken to reflect changing facts and changing policies. The legislature can oversee the process by making periodic revisions of the agency's articulated plans and policies so far as necessary to keep the agency within the fundamental tenets of state legislative policies.

NOTE: IMPACT ASSESSMENT

Environmental laws have modified water rights administration. Many states have enacted legislation paralleling the National Environmental Policy Act of 1969 (NEPA), see *infra* p. 331, that requires an environmental assessment of major water developments. Thus, water permitting agencies have become increasingly involved with ecological considerations in the evaluation of water use applications. A few states have passed their own versions of NEPA and require consideration of environmental factors not just for major water development but also for water allocation. The Washington statute is discussed *supra* p. 331.

An example with a long history concerns the appropriation of water from the Owens River Valley in California for the City of Los Angeles. In the early 1970s the Los Angeles Department of Water and Power was once again looking to the Owens Valley for the solution to its water supply problems. The city had completed its first aqueduct from the valley to Los Angeles in 1913 and a second was operating by 1970. The system was largely gravity fed, so pumping costs were low. The Owens Valley supplied the city with 80 percent of its water—close to 4.6 million acre-feet of water flow each year through the Owens Valley Aqueduct to Los Angeles. In 1972, Los Angeles moved to increase its pumping of Owens Valley groundwater from 176.2 acre-feet per day (afd) to as much as 623.7 afd. The city told tenants on Los Angeles-owned land that their leases might not be renewed and warned that Lake Diaz, a small recreational lake, might be

---

149. At least one court has expressed uneasiness about the difficulties involved in applying public interest standards without definite criteria. *See* Steamboaters v. Winchester Water Control Dist., 69 Or.App. 596, 688 P.2d 92 (1984).

dried up. Owens Valley residents reacted bitterly to Los Angeles's announcement. "We are a colony of Los Angeles," one rancher said. "Less than two percent of our valley belongs to us. We pay rent to the Department of Water and Power even for our stores and churches. There is more Los Angeles land here than down there in the City." Some Owens Valley dwellers suspected that the city was deliberately trying to drive them from the valley so that it could continue its water exportation without objections.

The valley's residents responded in two ways. The first was violent, reminiscent of the 1920s when farmers dynamited the Los Angeles Aqueduct and closed its gates prompting the City to send trainloads of guards to Owens Valley with sawed off shotguns. In the spring of 1976, Los Angeles locked the gates through which water flows into Lake Diaz. Angry Owens Valley dwellers took welding torches to the gates and forced them open. An explosion destroyed a section of the aqueduct in the fall of 1976, allowing more than 307 acre-feet of water to spill onto a dry riverbed. The day after the aqueduct explosion, a stick of dynamite tied to an arrow was fired into a Los Angeles fountain named for William Mulholland, the engineer who designed the Owens Valley aqueduct and pipeline system.

Inyo County, encompassing much of Owens Valley, reacted in a more restrained manner. It filed an action containing two charges against Los Angeles. First, the county claimed that the city's increased pumping threatened frail plants and wildlife and therefore violated California's Environmental Quality Act (CEQA), CAL. PUB. RES. CODE §§ 21000–21178 (West 1996). See generally Daniel P. Selmi, *The Judicial Development of the California Environmental Quality Act,* 18 U.C. Davis L. Rev. 197 (1984). The second challenge was that Los Angeles' action constituted a wasteful use of water in violation of California's constitution. In reply, the Los Angeles Department of Water and Power contended that its obligation, and the greater need for water, lay with Los Angeles. The state courts determined that because only 50 percent of the estimated cost of construction of the additional wells had actually been spent, the increased groundwater pumping was part of an "ongoing project." This ruling made the pumping subject to CEQA even though the project was begun prior to the effective date of the Act. As a result, the city had to file an environmental impact report (EIR).

In a series of six reported decisions, the California Court of Appeals dealt with challenges to the adequacy of EIRs prepared by the city. Finally, the city and Inyo County settled the case. The city agreed to pay the county about two million dollars a year for environmental impacts caused by continued groundwater pumping and an additional ten million dollars to re-establish a trout fishery in the Lower Owens River and to build recreational facilities. In exchange, Los Angeles was to have the right to take 200,000 acre-feet of water a year, down from 480,000 acre-feet a year which it was taking before the agreement.

When the parties jointly petitioned the court to accept the EIR prepared to support their settlement agreement, others contended that since there was no longer adversity between the city and the county that they should be permitted to challenge the EIR in order to carry out the purposes of CEQA. The court of appeals held, under the "public interest exception" to the mootness doctrine, that the court should scrutinize the EIR with the assistance of adversary amici curiae. County of Inyo v. Los Angeles, C004068 (3d Dist. 1997) (unpublished order discharging preemptory writ of mandate issued August 6, 1993). The litigation reached settlement in 1997 and both Los Angeles and Inyo County formed a standing committee to monitor both vegetation and groundwater around the Los Angeles well fields. City of Los Angeles v. County of Inyo, Case No. 12908 (Super. Ct. Inyo County, Cal. 1997). The goal of the settlement is to make sure that withdrawals do not exceed total recharge over a twenty-year period and avoid possible environmental impacts. See A. Dan Tarlock & Sarah B. Van de Wetering, *Growth Management and Western Water Law From Urban Oases to Archipelagos*, 5 Hastings W.–Nw. J. Envtl. L. & Pol'y 163, 182–83 (1993).

b.   Changes in Existing Rights

Old water rights and uses create the greatest conflicts with public interest factors. They are the ones that were established when the technology of water diversion and use was primitive, water was plentiful (at least by western standards), and society's primary goal was to promote the opening of the West. Water was allocated and developed without regard for efficiency or environmental effects; it often continues to be used in the same manner, protected by legal rights and aided by subsidized facilities.

The prior appropriation doctrine establishing those rights was developed to meet the demands for water in the 1800s; public interest considerations are now being superimposed on it to meet demands. As Professor Joseph Sax put it:

> The problem is really quite simple, it does not require mastery of obtuse legal doctrines to appreciate what is going on. The heart of the matter is that public values have changed, and the use of water has reached some critical limits. One result is that we need to retrieve some water from traditional water users to sustain streams and lakes as natural systems and to protect water quality. Moreover, traditional sources of new supply—such as dams and transbasin transportation of water, on which conventional users depend—are being closed off for a variety of familiar reasons, including both federal reluctance to finance new projects, and environmental objections. Thus, we have a potential head-on conflict between existing water users and their existing and future demands, and future demands of what may broadly be called instream uses.

Joseph Sax, *The Limits of Private Rights in Public Waters*, 19 Envtl. L. 473, 474 (1989).

How "safe" are water rights once they are permitted? What channels are open to review and modify existing water rights through application of the "public interest?"

Bonham v. Morgan

Supreme Court of Utah, 1989.
788 P.2d 497.

■ PER CURIAM:

* * *

Plaintiff Stanley B. Bonham, who is not a water user, protested against a permanent change application filed under Utah Code Ann. § 73–3–3 (1980) in the office of the defendant state engineer (state engineer) in June of 1984 by defendants Salt Lake County Water Conservancy District and Draper Irrigation Company (applicants). Applicants sought to change the point of diversion, place, and nature of use of certain water rights in Bell Canyon, Dry Creek, Rocky Mouth Creek, and Big Willow Creek. At a subsequent hearing, Bonham produced evidence of substantial flooding and damage to plaintiffs' properties and adjacent public lands during 1983 and 1984. Bonham informed the state engineer that the flooding was the result of applicants' construction of a screw gate, pipeline, and diversion works after they obtained preliminary approval of their change application. According to Bonham, the flooding had occurred and would recur on a yearly basis whenever the applicants closed their screw gate, allowing the waters to be diverted down the hillside onto plaintiffs' properties and nearby property contemplated for use as a public park. Bonham objected that the proposed structures and improvements contemplated after final approval would detrimentally impact the public welfare.

The state engineer conducted on-site inspections but eventually issued his memorandum decision in which he concluded that he was without authority to address Bonham's claims in ruling on the permanent change application, as Bonham was not a water user, that the state engineer's authority was limited to investigating impairments of vested water rights, and that there was no evidence before him to indicate that the implementation of the change application would impair those rights. The state engineer then granted the permanent change application.

* * * In count one of their complaint, they claimed that the state engineer failed to review the plans and specifications of the improvements, failed to conduct an investigation as required by Utah Code Ann. § 73–3–8 (1985) to determine what damage the change application would have on private and public property, and failed to comply with section 73–3–3 (1980) by not considering the "duties" of the defendant applicants. Plaintiffs alleged that the state engineer's disclaimer of any authority to consider, in connection with a permanent change application, any damages caused to plaintiffs as a result of his approval of the application, was contrary to the clear mandate of section 73–3–8, which requires an evaluation of the factors there set out, including any and all damage to public and private property and the impact the application will have on the public welfare. Plaintiffs also alleged that they had owned and occupied their approximately ten acres of property for twenty years and that for the approximately one hundred years since Draper Irrigation first constructed open ditches, flumes, pipelines, and other aqueducts to carry water from Bell Canyon Reservoir to its water treatment plant in Draper, Utah, plaintiffs' properties had remained undisturbed. Since the construction of the screw gates, in furtherance of the applied-for change, that was no longer the case. Virtual waterfalls cascaded down the hillside immediately east of plaintiffs' properties whenever applicants closed that gate and caused tremendous damage to plaintiffs' properties and the public area in the vicinity.

* * *

Utah Code Ann. § 73-3-3 (1980), at the time the state engineer rendered his decision, read in pertinent part:

* * *

No permanent change shall be made except on the approval of an application therefor by the state engineer.... *The procedure in the state engineer's office and rights and duties of the applicants with respect to applications for permanent changes of point of diversion, place or purpose of use shall be the same as provided in this title for applications to appropriate water;* but the state engineer may, in connection with applications for permanent change involving only a change in point of diversion of 660 feet or less, waive the necessity for publishing notice of such applications. No temporary change shall be made except upon an application filed in duplicate with the state engineer.... The state engineer shall make an investigation and *if such temporary change does not impair any vested rights of others he shall make an order authorizing the change.*

(Emphasis added.)

Section 73-3-8 (1985), at the time the state engineer rendered his decision, read in pertinent part:

(1) It shall be the duty of the state engineer to approve an application if:

* * *

(e) the application was filed in good faith and not for purposes of speculation or monopoly. *If the state engineer, because of information in his possession obtained either by his own investigation or otherwise, has reason to believe that an application to appropriate water will interfere with its more beneficial use for irrigation, domestic or culinary, stock watering, power or mining development or manufacturing, or will unreasonably affect public recreation or the natural stream environment, or will prove detrimental to the public welfare, it is his duty to withhold his approval or rejection of the application until he has investigated the matter. If an application does not meet the requirements of this section, it shall be rejected.*

(Emphasis added.)

* * *

We agree with the position taken by plaintiffs * * * that both statutory purposes and a reasonable textual interpretation of water allocation statutes support the application of appropriation criteria to permanent change applications. The language critical to our determination was added to section 100–3–3, R.S. Utah 1933, in 1937. *See* L. 1937, ch. 130, § 1. The amendment removed provisions addressing notice requirements and added for the first time language defining permanent and temporary changes. After setting out procedures relating to applications for permanent changes, the 1937 amendment continued:

> The procedure in the state engineer's office *and the rights and duties of the applicant with respect to application for permanent changes* of point of diversion, place, or purpose of use *shall be the same as provided in this title for applications to appropriate water.*

(Emphasis added.)

* * *

* * * The only reasonable meaning to read into section 73–3–3 is that the state engineer must investigate and reject the application for either appropriation or permanent change of use or place of use if approval would interfere with more beneficial use, public recreation, the natural stream environment, or the public welfare. It is unreasonable to assume that the legislature would require the state engineer to investigate matters of public concern in water appropriations and yet restrict him from undertaking those duties in permanent change applications. Carried to its logical conclusion, such an interpretation would eviscerate the duties of the state engineer under section 73–3–8 and allow an applicant to accomplish in a two-step process what the statute proscribes in a one-step process. For all that an applicant would need to do to achieve a disapproved purpose under section 73–3–8 would be to appropriate for an approved purpose and then to file a change application under section 73–3–3.

NOTES

1. The New Mexico Supreme Court applied public interest review to a change in point of diversion but sustained the change where there was a lack of evidence showing that the change in point of diversion was the cause of deteriorating water quality. Stokes v. Morgan, 101 N.M. 195, 680 P.2d 335 (1984).

2. A New Mexico trial court overturned the state engineer's approval of a proposed change of use of water from livestock watering and early season flood irrigating (for soil preparation) to a recreational lake for a new resort. The court found the change improper and disallowed it as contrary to the public interest, citing the importance of preserving the culture and traditions of Hispanic rural communities:

34. The Northern New Mexico region possesses significant history, tradition and culture of recognized value, not measurable in dollars and cents.

35. The relationship between the people and their land and water is central to the maintenance of that culture and tradition.

36. The imposition of a resort-oriented economy in the Ensenada area would erode and likely destroy a distinct local culture which is several hundred years old.

Ensenada Land and Water Association v. Sleeper, No. RA–84–53(C) (District Court, Rio Arriba County, New Mexico, June 2, 1985). Did the decision favor the public interest?

The case was reversed on appeal because the New Mexico transfer statute at the time did not allow such public interest considerations in transfers and the New Mexico Supreme Court refused to hear an appeal. Ensenada Land & Water Association v. Sleeper, 107 N.M. 494, 760 P.2d 787 (App.1988). The transfer never took place, however, because the developer went bankrupt. See Shannon A. Parden, *The Milagro Beanfield War Revisited in Ensenada Land & Water Association v. Sleeper: Public Welfare Defies Transfer of Water Rights,* 29 Nat. Resources J. 861 (1989). *Sleeper* has led to the suggestion that communities be given a veto over major water rights transfers similar to powers that communities exercise through zoning. See Charles T. DuMars & Michele Minnis, *New Mexico Water Law: Determining Public Welfare Values in Water Rights Allocation,* 31 Ariz. L. Rev. 817 (1989).

3. Although Colorado does not allow consideration of public interest factors when conditional rights are sought, the supreme court has upheld the imposition of conditions requiring revegetation of lands that are dried up when there is a change of use. See City of Thornton v. Bijou Irrigation Co., 926 P.2d 1, 86 (Colo.1996) (citing *Shelton Farms, supra* p. 223, for the need to balance maximum beneficial use and natural resource protection). The Colorado Legislature went further in 2007, authorizing water courts to impose conditions for water quality protection on permanent transfers of more than 1,000 acre-feet of water from irrigation to a new use. The courts may impose a term or condition if such a proposed transfer would cause a violation, or contribute to an existing violation, of Colorado water quality standards. COLO. REV. STAT. § 37–92–305(4)(a)(V) (2007). See discussion at page 664, *infra.*

c. Limitations on the Exercise of Rights

Alamosa–La Jara Water Users Protection Ass'n v. Gould

Supreme Court of Colorado, 1983.
674 P.2d 914.

■ DUBOFSKY, JUSTICE.

This is an appeal from a judgment of the district court for Water Division 3 (water court) regarding rules promulgated by the Colorado State

Engineer (proposed rules) limiting the use of surface and underground water in the San Luis Valley. * * * The water court approved rules for administering separate obligations for deliveries from the Conejos River and the Rio Grande mainstem, and disapproved rules which phased out all wells in the San Luis Valley unless each well owner could demonstrate a lack of material injury to senior surface water users or provide a plan of augmentation to replace the water taken by a well. * * *

I.

The San Luis Valley in south-central Colorado extends approximately ninety miles from north to south and fifty miles from east to west at an elevation varying between 7,500 feet and 8,000 feet above sea level. The major mountain boundaries are the San Juan mountains to the west and the Sangre de Cristo mountains to the east. The Rio Grande mainstem rises in the San Juan mountains, flows southeasterly through the valley to Alamosa, and then runs south through a break in the San Luis hills, which border the valley on the south, into the state of New Mexico, then along the border between Texas and Mexico, emptying into the Gulf of Mexico. The Conejos River rises in the Conejos Mountains to the south-west and flows north-easterly along the southern edge of the valley, joining the Rio Grande mainstem at Los Sauces. Despite its high altitude, short growing season, and average annual precipitation of only about 7.5 inches, the valley sustains a productive agricultural economy dependent upon irrigation water.

The upper 6000 feet of fill below the valley surface consists of unconsolidated clay, silt, sand, and gravel, and interbedded lava flows, containing an estimated two billion acre-feet of underground water. Some of the underground water is in an unconfined aquifer system at shallow depths. Beneath the unconfined aquifer are relatively impermeable beds of clay and basalt and beneath these confining layers are substantial quantities of water which comprise the confined aquifer. The confining clay layer generally does not exist around the valley's perimeter, and the confined aquifer system is recharged from surface flow to the underground water system at the edges of the valley. Because the recharge areas are higher in elevation than the floor of the valley, the confined aquifer is under artesian pressure, resulting in the free flow of water from some artesian wells and springs at natural breaks in the confining layer. In some places, where the confining layer is less thick and more transmissive, water from the confined aquifer will leak upward through the confining clay layers into the unconfined aquifer. The unconfined aquifer is directly connected with the surface streams in some places. To varying degrees, the surface streams, the unconfined aquifer, and the confined aquifer are hydraulically connected.[3]

* * *

3. North of the Rio Grande mainstem, a hydraulic divide provides the southern boundary of an area known as the Closed Basin. Four large mutual irrigation systems

In 1975, the state engineer promulgated the proposed rules, publishing them in all counties of Water Division No. 3, which is generally coterminous with the San Luis Valley. * * * Numerous protests to the proposed rules were filed, requiring a hearing before a water judge under section 37–92–501(2)(h), C.R.S.

* * *

A lengthy trial ensued. * * *

II.

A.

The proposed rules are based on the premise that the separate delivery schedules provided for the Conejos and Rio Grande in Article III of the compact mandate separate administration of the rivers. This interpretation of the compact reflects administration of the rivers under the compact since 1968 when, as a result of the stipulation with New Mexico and Texas, the Colorado state engineer began to require curtailment of diversions in order to meet compact obligations.

As a result of separate administration of the rivers, senior water rights on the Conejos River have been curtailed at times when users with more recently acquired rights on the Rio Grande have continued to divert water. Moreover, although the Conejos system contributes only thirty percent of the inflow of water to the San Luis Valley, administration in accordance with the compact schedules requires the Conejos system to provide forty-five percent of Colorado's deliveries at the New Mexico state line. The Conejos District maintains that the Conejos River is a losing stream,[11] and that the state engineer has curtailed a large percentage of inflow at the headgates of the Conejos water users so that the stream will produce the amount required by the compact. In contrast the Rio Grande is a gaining stream, and its delivery obligation is satisfied to a large extent by return flows of water already diverted for irrigation. Since 1968, except for the severe drought years of 1972 and 1977, the state has curtailed diversions to some extent on the Conejos and its tributaries during the irrigation season. The effect of such curtailment in the Conejos area is to reduce the irrigation season by about one week at each end of the season, resulting in numerous hardships on farmers and ranchers in the area. Consequently, intense controversy has developed over whether administration according to the separate delivery schedules of Article III is required by the compact or permissible under state law.

* * *

supply water from the mainstem to irrigate the agricultural land in the basin. Return water from irrigation and small streams within the basin flow toward the sump, the basin's lowest surface area, rather than returning to the mainstem, and consequently, most of the water is lost to evapotranspiration.

11. A losing stream is one in which there are significant river losses other than for diversions below the inflow gauges.

* * * The equitable apportionment of the waters of interstate streams may be accomplished either by the United States Supreme Court, *Kansas v. Colorado*, 206 U.S. 46 (1907), or by interstate compact, *Colorado v. Kansas*, 320 U.S. 383 (1943). Equitable apportionment, a federal doctrine, can determine times of delivery and sources of supply to satisfy that delivery without conflicting with state law, for state law applies only to the water which has not been committed to other states by the equitable apportionment. *Hinderlider v. LaPlata River and Cherry Creek Ditch Co.*, 304 U.S. 92 (1938). In an equitable apportionment, strict adherence to prior appropriations may not always be possible. *Colorado v. New Mexico*, 459 U.S. 176 (1982); *Nebraska v. Wyoming*, 325 U.S. 589 (1945).

* * * The separate delivery rules, therefore, are not inconsistent with constitutional and statutory provisions for priority administration of water rights.

* * *

III.

The proposed underground water rules tie tributary underground water administration in the valley to regulation for compact requirements by integrating tributary underground water diversions into the priority system for surface streams. The rules are intended over a five-year period to curtail well diversions unless individual well owners prove that their wells do not cause injury to senior water rights or remedy such injury through plans for augmentation.

* * *

C.

The water court disapproved the well regulations because they did not contain a requirement that stream appropriators tap the enormous supply of water underlying the surface of the valley. * * *

The state engineer asserts that the proposed rules properly place the burden of remedying the injury caused to senior appropriators on junior water users and that the water court's ruling is a misapplication of law. The state engineer relies upon the principle, codified in section 37–92–102, C.R.S., that the priority system governs water allocation and that junior water rights from whatever source are not entitled to divert water that otherwise would be available for use by senior water rights. *See also* sections 37–92–301(3) and 37–92–501, C.R.S. Under the prior appropriation doctrine, it is argued, the burden of integrating surface and groundwater rights falls upon junior water users, primarily through plans for augmentation under section 37–92–103(9), C.R.S. * * *

* * * [T]he state policy of maximum utilization of water [was] first enunciated in *Fellhauer* [v. People], 447 P.2d [986 (Colo.1969)] at 994,

"It is implicit in these constitutional provisions [the two provisions are in Article XVI, Section 6 of the Colorado Constitution] that, along with *vested rights* there shall be *maximum utilization* of the water of this state. As administration of water approaches its second century the curtain is opening upon the new drama of *maximum utilization* and how constitutionally that doctrine can be integrated into the law of *vested rights*." (Emphasis in original.)

The policy of maximum utilization was codified in the "Water Right Determination and Administration Act of 1969" where the General Assembly declared

"the policy of the state of Colorado that all waters originating in or flowing into this state, whether found on the surface or underground, have always been and are hereby declared to be the property of the public, dedicated to the use of the people of the state, subject to appropriation and use in accordance with law. As incident thereto, it is the policy of this state to integrate the appropriation, use, and administration of underground water tributary to a stream with the use of surface water in such a way as to maximize the beneficial use of all of the waters of this state.

(2) Recognizing that previous and existing laws have given inadequate attention to the development and use of underground waters of the state, that the use of underground waters as an independent source or in conjunction with surface waters is necessary to the present and future welfare of the people of this state, and that the future welfare of the state depends upon a sound and flexible integrated use of all waters of the state, it is hereby declared to be the further policy of the state of Colorado that in the determination of water rights, uses, and administration of water the following principles shall apply:

* * *

(b) The existing use of ground water, either independently or in conjunction with surface rights, shall be recognized to the fullest extent possible, subject to the preservation of other existing vested rights, but, at his own point of diversion on a natural water course, each diverter must establish some reasonable means of effectuating his diversion. He is not entitled to demand the whole flow of the stream merely to facilitate his taking the fraction of the whole flow to which he is entitled.

(c) The use of ground water may be considered as an alternate or supplemental source of supply for surface decrees entered prior to June 7, 1969, taking into consideration both previous usage and the necessity to protect the vested rights of others.

(d) No reduction of any lawful diversion because of the operation of the priority system shall be permitted unless such reduction would increase the amount of water available to and required by water rights having senior priorities."

Section 37–92–102(1) and (2), C.R.S.

The 1969 Act recognized in section 37–92–102(2)(b) that one method of achieving maximum utilization of water is to require that each diverter establish a reasonable means of effectuating his diversion. The section is based upon the holding in *Colorado Springs v. Bender* [366 P.2d 552 (Colo.1961), *infra* p. 560], a case involving senior wells which used tributary water to irrigate farm land and a junior well which supplied water for Colorado Springs. The plaintiffs, senior appropriators, sued to enjoin the defendant's diversion of water in violation of the plaintiffs' rights of prior appropriation, alleging that the defendant's pumping was lowering the water table below the intake of the plaintiffs' pumping facilities. * * * The *Bender* court then directed the trial court to consider whether adequate means for reaching a sufficient supply could be made available to the senior appropriators, and because senior appropriators cannot be required to improve their extraction facilities beyond their economic reach, whether an adequate means should be decreed at the expense of the junior appropriators. The court in *Bender* relied upon *Schodde v. Twin Falls Land and Water Company*, 224 U.S. 107 (1912), which requires a senior's method of diversion to be reasonable in order for it to be protected from injury caused by junior diversions. * * *[34]

Here, several witnesses testified that the water in storage in the valley's aquifers provides the support for the water above it to move to the streams. The well owners and the communities argue that it is not unreasonable to require surface diverters to deepen their headgates if the water from the stream is beneath their feet. The argument continues that the surface owners have lost nothing except a gravity flow source of supply which is cheaper and easier to divert, and that the loss only occurs at times when the surface stream is inadequate to fill the surface diverters' priorities. A reasonable means of diversion in this case, it is argued, is one that eliminates the need for supporting the surface stream, thereby freeing the underground water for maximum beneficial use.

* * *

The water court held that, under certain circumstances, surface stream appropriators may be required to withdraw underground water tributary to the stream in order to satisfy their surface appropriations. We affirm this legal conclusion and return the proposed well rules to the state engineer for consideration of whether the reasonable-means-of-diversion doctrine provides, in this case, a method of achieving maximum utilization of water—a consideration which the state engineer erroneously believed was foreclosed. We note that the policy of maximum utilization does not require a single-minded endeavor to squeeze every drop of water from the valley's aquifers. Section 37–92–501(2)(e) makes clear that the objective of "maximum use"

---

34. The state engineer attempts to distinguish the *Bender* and *Schodde* decisions on the basis that *Bender* concerned conflicts between underground water appropriations and *Schodde,* conflicts between surface appropriations. However, the 1969 Act integrated surface and underground water appropriations, thus allowing a conflict between a surface and underground water appropriation to be subject to the *Bender* doctrine as codified in the same act, section 37–92–102(2), C.R.S.

administration is "optimum use."[36] Optimum use can only be achieved with proper regard for all significant factors, including environmental and economic concerns. *See* section 37–92–102(3), C.R.S. (recognizing the need to correlate the activities of mankind with reasonable preservation of the natural environment); Harrison & Sandstrom, [*The Groundwater–Surface Water Conflict and Recent Colorado Legislation*, 43 U. Colo. L. Rev. 1 (1971)], at 14–15 (An increase of well diversions at the expense of maintenance of a surface flow would increase the efficiency of irrigation at the expense of other environmental and economic values.). *See also* Trelease [*Conjunctive Use of Ground Water and Surface Water*, 27 Rocky Mtn. Min. L. Inst. 1853 (1982)], at 1866–1872 (Determination of what constitutes a reasonable means of diversion may be more a question of the proper allocation of the costs of more efficient diversion than of the quantity of water ultimately diverted.). The water court observed that the state engineer's reconsideration might take the form of requiring senior appropriators to drill new wells before requiring curtailment of junior rights and listed a number of suggestions for increasing utilization.[37] Similarly, the state engineer's reconsideration might result in assessment to junior appropriators of the cost of making those improvements to seniors' diversions which are necessitated by junior withdrawals. Selection among these and other possibilities, including retention of the scheme of the proposed rules, is a policy decision to be made by the state engineer, after consideration of all relevant factors.

We remand the rules to the water court for return to the state engineer.

NOTES

1. Unlike states with permit systems, Colorado initially allocates water without administrative intervention or public interest review. One claims rights to appropriate water for a use beneficial in light of the user's

---

36. Section 37–92–501(2)(e) states: "All rules and regulations shall have as their objective the optimum use of water consistent with preservation of the priority system of water rights."

37. Throughout the latter part of the trial, the parties' expert engineers met off the record in an attempt to agree upon a resolution of the water problems in the valley. At the conclusion of the water judge's opinion, he listed some of the engineers' suggestions as including: (1) Elimination of the wasteful practice of subirrigation; (2) encouragement of improved irrigation efficiency, such as increased use of sprinklers; (3) prohibit the wasteful practice of allowing diverted water to collect in barrow pits, potholes and other areas, only to evaporate; (4) promote the Closed Basin Project; (5) construct new wells and use existing wells to deliver both confined and unconfined water to help satisfy Compact obligations; (6) construct new drains and rehabilitate existing drains to salvage water presently lost to non-beneficial evapotranspiration; (7) initiate channel rectification program to prevent the wasteful overflow losses on critical reaches on the river system in the valley; (8) a systematic augmentation plan for direct flow rights and wells from the confined and unconfined aquifers, pursuant to ongoing research to determine the effect of such augmentation upon senior priority rights; (9) development of reservoirs to store pre-Compact direct flow rights; (10) additional purchase of existing water rights and release of those waters to the streams.

economic needs, and a water court then determines the priority of the new right relative to all others. See *supra* p. 303. Rights can be transferred in private transactions so long as the court finds that other rights will not be injured by a change in the place, manner, or time of the diversion or use of water.

Is the "public interest" ignored? Rights to water for streamflows "to protect the natural environment to a reasonable degree" can be appropriated by a state agency, integrated in the resume of all appropriative rights, and enforced like other rights. See *infra* p. 351. Water quality is controlled by regulatory statutes. Water users are otherwise unconstrained in moving water to the uses having the highest economic values—and which therefore can pay the highest price for water. In light of the decision in *Alamosa–La Jara*, may the state engineer nevertheless administer a water right with regard to environmental and economic (i.e., public interest) factors? If the state engineer fails to do so can the engineer's actions be challenged on the ground that it would not result in optimum utilization of water?

2. The decision in *Alamosa–La Jara* was followed in R.J.A., Inc. v. Water Users Ass'n of Dist. No. 6, 690 P.2d 823, 828 (Colo.1984) ("[T]he general legislative policy of maximizing beneficial and integrated use of surface and subsurface water must be implemented with a sensitivity to the effect on other resources.")

3. In 2004, The Colorado State Engineer filed with the Water Clerk in Water Division Three (the Division involved in *Alamosa–LaJara*), "Rules Governing New Withdrawals of Ground Water in Water Division Three Affecting the Rate or Direction of Movement of Water in the Confined Aquifer System." These Rules were drafted in direct reponse to legislative direction. C.R.S. § 37–92–501(4)(a) through (4)(c) (2007). Among other principles, they strive to maintain a sustainable water supply in the aquifers. The Rules were sustained against constitutional challenge in Simpson v. Cotton Creek Circles, LLC, 181 P.3d 252 (Colo. 2008). The opinion contains a helpful discussion of the complex hydrology of the San Luis Basin, See also the discussion of Idaho's Conjunctive Use Rule at pages 587–595, *infra*.

4. On the subject of accommodating the public interest within the appropriation system, see Charles F. Wilkinson, *Western Water Law in Transition,* 56 U. Colo. L. Rev. 317 (1985).

3.   STATUTORY PROTECTION FOR INSTREAM FLOWS

In the case of Empire Water and Power Co. v. Cascade Town Co., 205 Fed. 123 (8th Cir.1913), *supra* p. 97, the court struggled with the issue of whether water could be appropriated to maintain a waterfall for natural beauty at a resort. The court concluded that: "It may be that if the attention of the lawmakers had been directed to such natural objects of great beauty they would have sought to preserve them, but we think the dominant idea [behind the state laws] was utility * * * and we are constrained to follow it." Id. at 129. But even after the Colorado legislature had passed a law allowing for appropriations of water for fishery purposes, the Colorado Supreme Court refused to interpret the law as allowing for an appropriation without a diversion. Colorado River Water Conservation Dist. v. Rocky Mountain Power Co., 158 Colo. 331, 406 P.2d 798 (1965), *supra* p. 99. In absence of an express statement, it said that "the legislature did not intend to bring about such an extreme departure from well established doctrine * * *." Id. at 800.

One of the major innovations of statutory systems has been the creation of programs for protection of instream flows. Although public interest requirements can address prevention of stream depletions that affect fish and wildlife, recreation, water quality, and other public values that demand instream flows, the most typical way to ensure protection of those values is through programs to protect instream flows. In some cases the statutes are specific to a particular stream or place.

State, Department of Parks v. Idaho Department of Water Administration

Supreme Court of Idaho, 1974.
96 Idaho 440, 530 P.2d 924.

■ Shepard, Chief Justice.

This is an appeal and a cross-appeal from a judgment of the district court in an action wherein the Idaho Department of Parks, pursuant to statute, sought to appropriate in trust for the people of Idaho certain unappropriated waters of the Malad Canyon. * * *

In 1971 the Idaho Legislature enacted I.C. § 67–4307. In essence the statute directs the Department of Parks of the State of Idaho to appropriate in trust for the people of Idaho certain unappropriated natural waters of the Malad Canyon in Gooding County, Idaho. Additionally, it declares (1) that the preservation of the waters for scenic beauty and recreation uses is a beneficial use of water; (2) that the public use of those waters is of greater priority than any other use save domestic consumption, and (3) that the unappropriated state land located between the highwater marks on either bank of these waters is to be used and preserved in its present condition as a recreational site for the people of Idaho.

Pursuant to the statute the Idaho Department of Parks filed an application for a permit to appropriate the waters specified by the statute. * * *

That application was protested by the Idaho Water Users Association, Twin Falls Canal Company, and the North Side Canal Company under the provisions of I.C. § 42–203. Those parties are cross-appellants herein and are hereafter designated "Water Users." * * *

II.

The Water Users * * * assert error in the trial court's determination that the preservation of aesthetic values and recreational opportunities for the citizens of this state is a beneficial use in the sense that they will support an appropriative water right under the Idaho Constitution.

The foundation of the Water Users' argument is that the five uses specified in article 15, section 3 of the Constitution, i.e., domestic, agriculture, mining, manufacturing and power are exclusive and thus are the only uses that are cognizable beneficial uses under our Constitution. We reject that argument.

We find no support for the position of the Water Users in the discussions reported in II Idaho Constitutional Convention, Proceedings and Debate 1889 (1912), as pertaining to article 15, section 3. It appears that insofar as particular uses were mentioned in the debates, discussion was confined to the establishment of preferences for certain uses over others under certain circumstances. Such establishment of preferences appears to be a common feature of water law in the west. While it is well established in western water law that an appropriation of water must be made for a "beneficial use," nevertheless in Idaho at least the generic term "beneficial use" has never been judicially or statutorily defined. Our research does not disclose any case in which any court has attempted to define the term "beneficial use."

Consideration of the statute in question herein indicates clearly that the legislature has declared that "[t]he preservation of water in the area described for its scenic beauty and recreational purposes necessary and desirable for all citizens of the state * * * is hereby declared to be a beneficial use of such water." We note that numerous other western states have recognized through legislation that utilization of water for scenic or recreational purposes is a beneficial use. Such legislation in other states carries no binding effect on this court but, in the absence of persuasive case law to the contrary, it would appear to indicate that the use of water for providing recreational and aesthetic pleasure represents an emerging recognition in this and other states of social values and benefits from the use of water. The statute in question herein recognizes aesthetic and recreational values and benefits which will accrue to the people of the state in respect to the waters of Malad Canyon. We find no basis upon which to disturb that declaration of the legislature that in this instance those values and benefits constitute "beneficial uses." The decision of the district court upon this issue is affirmed.

* * *

We now reach the final issue as to whether there must be an actual physical diversion of the water in order to support an appropriation. * * *

The precise language of article 15, section 3, does not bear on this question but merely declares "[t]he right to divert and appropriate the unappropriated waters of any natural stream to beneficial use, shall never be denied * * *." * * *

We hold that our Constitution does not require actual physical diversion. We deem it clear that until the time of the enactment of the statute in question herein Idaho's statutory scheme regulating the appropriation of water has contemplated an actual physical diversion. * * *

In the statute before us, I.C. § 67–4307, the Idaho legislature has clearly stated a policy at odds with its previous general statutory scheme of water appropriation. I.C. § 67–4307 directs parks "to appropriate [not 'divert and appropriate'] the unappropriated natural spring flow" of the Malad Canyon and declares the "preservation of water in the area described for its scenic beauty and recreational purposes" is a beneficial use. Furthermore, the statute states that "license shall issue at any time upon proof of beneficial use to which said waters are now dedicated." We deem it clear that the legislature intended no physical diversion of water be required in the appropriation of the subject waters.

* * *

■ DONALDSON, J., concurs.

* * *

■ BAKES, JUSTICE (concurring specially):

I concur in the result reached by Chief Justice Shepard in his plurality opinion, although not necessarily everything stated therein. Additionally, I wish to address in a different manner the question of whether or not the preservation of the waters of Malad Canyon in a natural state is a beneficial use that may be appropriated without the means of a diversion. (Parts II and III of that opinion).

The first question to be considered is whether any uses other than the uses referred to in Article 15, § 3, of the Idaho Constitution—domestic, mining, agricultural and manufacturing—can be beneficial uses of water under the Idaho Constitution. * * *

The Idaho Constitution does not explicitly answer this question. * * *

* * * I think we should look to very practical considerations in attempting to construe it. Prior to the time that the Constitution was adopted there were a number of common uses of water which were neither domestic, mining, agricultural nor manufacturing. A community would store water in a tank for use in fighting fires. The operator of a livery stable or a stockyard would water the stock kept there. Logging operations used water both to transport logs and for storage in mill ponds. Communities would use water wagons to settle dust on their dirt streets. The railroad used water for its steam engines and other uses related to the operation of the railroad. All of these uses were undoubtedly considered beneficial, but none of them were domestic, mining, agricultural or manufacturing. I do not believe that by adopting Article 15, § 3, of the Idaho Constitution that it was intended that uses such as these could no longer be considered beneficial uses. * * * I therefore conclude that uses other than those enumerated in Article 15, § 3, can be beneficial uses.

The next question is whether the use at issue in this case is beneficial. * * *

With the exception of those uses elevated to beneficial status by Article 15, § 3, of the Constitution, the concept of what is or is not a beneficial use must necessarily change with changing conditions. For example, if we were now presented with a question of whether or not using water to operate a public swimming pool, a fountain, or to flood a tract to provide ice for a skating rink were beneficial uses, a good argument could be presented that such uses, although not domestic, mining, agricultural or manufacturing uses, were nevertheless beneficial. But we cannot say that such uses will always be beneficial because conditions might so change that these uses would be an unjustifiable use of water needed for other purposes. The notion of beneficiality of use must include a requirement of reasonableness. With the exception of the uses implicitly declared to be beneficial by Article 15, § 3, there is always a possibility that other uses beneficial in one era will not be in another and *vice versa*. As stated in Tulare Irrig. Dist. v. Lindsay–Strathmore Irrig. Dist., 3 Cal.2d 489, 45 P.2d 972, 1007 (1935):

> "What is a beneficial use, of course, depends upon the facts and circumstances of each case. What may be a reasonable beneficial use, where water is present in excess of all needs, would not be a reasonable beneficial use in an area of great scarcity and great need. What is a beneficial use at one time may, because of changed conditions, become a waste of water at a later time."

What we have decided in this case is that the use now before us, although not specifically listed in Article 15, § 3, of the Constitution, is beneficial because, considering today's circumstances, the legislative classification is reasonable based on the record. I would restrict today's holding to the narrow proposition that the use before us is beneficial so long as, and only so long as, the circumstances of water use in the state have not changed to the extent that it is no longer reasonable to continue this use at the expense of more desirable uses for more urgent needs. * * *

Where an appropriative water right does not require a diversion to make it effective and beneficial, in the absence of a statute requiring a diversion there appears to be no practical reason why a diversion should be required. * * * If a beneficial use can be made of the water in its natural channel, Article 15, § 3, should not require the superfluous effort of construction of a diversion as a precondition for obtaining an appropriation. However, in an appropriation without a diversion, the right acquired is not to the stream flow as was the case under the riparian system, but to the use of a specific amount of water which is the subject of the right. That amount must be a reasonable and efficient use of the water.

* * *

■ DONALDSON, J., concurs.

* * *

■ McQuade, Justice, (dissenting).

* * *

* * * It is significant that the conjunctive was used when the Constitution was written, i.e., divert *and* appropriate rather than the disjunctive, i.e., divert *or* appropriate. In the absence of any contrary evidence, we should presume that the framers of the Idaho Constitution chose the conjunctive deliberately and that they intended it be accorded its ordinary meaning.

■ McFadden, Justice (dissenting).

* * *

In my view, the so-called "appropriation" authorized by I.C. § 67–4307 constitutes a denial of the constitutional right to appropriate the unappropriated waters of the Malad Canyon Springs.

I recognize that the state, acting in its proprietary capacity, may appropriate water without offending Article 15, section 3; but as in the case of private appropriators, the state's appropriative right depends upon the application of water to a "beneficial use." In this case, however, the state agency is directed to hold unappropriated waters "in trust for the people of the state" for "scenic beauty and recreational purposes." I.C. § 67–4307. If the state were to hold unappropriated waters in trust for these purposes, it certainly would not be acting in a proprietary capacity; it would be doing nothing more than it already had a duty to do in its sovereign capacity. * * *

* * * Under Article 15, section 3 of the Idaho Constitution, water held by the state in its sovereign capacity—even though being beneficially used by the general public—is subject to being appropriated for specific private (or proprietary) beneficial uses. Thus, in-stream public use of unappropriated water for recreational purposes and for scenic beauty is subject to diminution by the exercise of the constitutional right to appropriate water for private (or proprietary) beneficial uses. * * * [A] reservation by the state of unappropriated waters is completely unauthorized by our Constitution. Unlike the constitutions of some other western states, Idaho's Constitution does not provide that the right to appropriate "shall never be denied *except when such denial is demanded by the public interest.*"[1] Our Constitution provides that the right to appropriate unappropriated waters "*shall never be denied, except* that the state may regulate and limit the use thereof for power purposes." Art. 15, sec. 3, Idaho Const. (emphasis added).

The Idaho provision makes an exception only for power purposes—not for the demands of the public interest (and not for the purposes of recreation and scenic beauty). To allow the state to in effect reserve water from appropriation in furtherance of non-proprietary, non-power purposes—when the framers of the Constitution contemplated that private beneficial users could appropriate water being held by the state in its sovereign capacity—amounts to nothing less than a denial of the constitutional right to appropriate the "unappropriated waters" of any natural

---

1. Neb.Const. art. XV, § 6; *see also* Wyo. Const. art. 8, § 3 ("No appropriation shall be denied except when such denial is demanded by the public interests").

stream. "In other words, the state cannot by legislative act authorize its own agency to *monopolize or withdraw the very rights that section 3 of article 15 of the Constitution says 'shall never be denied' the people of the state.*" State Water Conservation Bd. v. Enking, 56 Idaho 722, 732, 58 P.2d 779, 783 (1936). The proper means to authorize such a withdrawal (or "appropriation") is to amend the Constitution to so provide.

It is beyond dispute that scenic beauty and recreation are both of vital importance to modern day life in Idaho. But this does not ipso facto mean the state has the right to promote these beneficial ends by withdrawing waters from appropriation, given the guarantee contained in the Idaho Constitution. I note, however, that the effect of a proposed appropriation upon scenic beauty and recreation can and should be considered in determining whether the use contemplated is "beneficial" within the meaning of the Constitution. Comment, Water Appropriation for Recreation, 1 Land & Water L. Rev. 209, 221 (1966). In other words, where the benefits of a proposed use are outweighed by the attendant detriment to scenic beauty and recreation, the use is not a "beneficial use," and the application for a permit to appropriate public waters for that use should be denied. As always, the question of beneficial use must be determined on a case by case basis, since the benefits of a particular proposed appropriation may outweigh the detriment to recreation and scenic beauty. Whether a use of water is "beneficial" is a question of fact to be resolved upon a consideration of the circumstances present in a particular case.

* * *

In conclusion, although I believe that recreation and scenic beauty can and should be taken into consideration on a case by case basis, they cannot be used as an excuse to deny all future appropriation of water for other purposes, at least until the Constitution is amended.

NOTES

1. Of what significance is it that the instream appropriation of water in the principal case was at the source of the river? By contrast, an instream appropriation of downstream water would interfere with subsequent private appropriation along the whole course of the river. Would this implicate the Idaho Constitution's provision that the "right to divert and appropriate the unappropriated waters * * * to beneficial uses, shall never be denied"? IDAHO CONST. ART. XV, § 3. Is there any difference analytically between a downstream appropriation by a municipality for domestic consumption, and downstream instream appropriation if there is unappropriated water available and both uses are beneficial?

2. After the Colorado Supreme Court, in *Colorado River Water Conservation Dist. v. Rocky Mountain Power Co., supra* p. 99, held an instream flow appropriation by the district for piscatorial purposes invalid for lack of an actual diversion, the legislature authorized the State Water Conservation

Board to appropriate water for instream flows. The law (as amended) states:

> (3) Further recognizing the need to correlate the activities of mankind with some reasonable preservation of the natural environment, the Colorado water conservation board is hereby vested with the exclusive authority, on behalf of the people of the state of Colorado, to appropriate in a manner consistent with sections 5 and 6 of article XVI of the state constitution, such waters of natural streams and lakes as the board determines may be required * * * to preserve the natural environment to a reasonable degree. * * * Prior to the initiation of any such appropriation or acquisition, the board shall request recommendations from the division of wildlife and the division of parks and outdoor recreation. The board also shall request recommendations from the United States Department of Agriculture and the United States Department of the Interior. * * *

Colo. Rev. Stat. § 37–92–102(3) (2000).

The bill also deleted reference to "diversion" in the definition of "appropriation" (Colo. Rev. Stat. § 37–92–103(4) (2000)) and changed the definition of beneficial use to include instream flows:

> "Beneficial use" is the use of that amount of water that is reasonable and appropriate under reasonably efficient practices to accomplish without waste the purpose for which the appropriation is lawfully made and, without limiting the generality of the foregoing, includes the impoundment of water for recreational purposes, including fishery or wildlife. For the benefit and enjoyment of present and future generations, "beneficial use" shall also include the appropriation by law of such minimum flows between specific points or levels for natural streams and lakes as are required to preserve the natural environment to a reasonable degree.

Given the standard in the statute how much discretion does the Board have in setting the amount of minimum flow? Could it appropriate all of the water flowing in a fishing stream used by a thousand fishermen and thereby preclude a 10,000 employee micro-chip manufacturer? Could it acquire the rights to releases from a dam to maintain a constant flow beneficial to recreational boaters in a stream that seasonally experiences great fluctuations? Although the law allows not only appropriation of new rights but acquisition of the senior rights by purchase or gift, the statute has been amended to prevent the acquisition and conversion of conditional water rights to instream uses. Colo. Rev. Stat. § 37–92–102(3)(c.5) (2000).

3.   Other western states have enacted instream flow statutes and some include instream flows in their water planning. The approaches differ widely. See generally Cynthia F. Covell, *A Survey of State Instream Flow Programs in the Western United States*, 1 Denv. Water L. Rev. 177 (1998); J. Boyd, Hip Deep: A Survey of State Instream Flow Law From the Rocky Mountains to the Pacific Ocean, 43 Nat. Res. J. 1151 (2003); and C. Bonham, Perspectives from the Field: A Review of Western Instream Flow

Issues and Recommendations for a New Western Future, 36 Envtl. L. 1205 (2006).

Two useful studies evaluated the status of state instream flow programs as of the middle of the first decade of the 21st century. The first, produced by the Colorado Water Conservation Board, discussed the legal status of instream flow rights in each of eighteen western states: the legal basis for instream flow rights, the purposes for which such rights could be created, the entities which could acquire and hold such rights, the number of such rights actually created, etc. Sasha Charney, Colo. Water Conservation Bd., Decades Down the Road: An Analysis of Instream Flow Programs in Colorado and the Western United States (July 2005). The second, conducted by Ruth Mathews for The Nature Conservancy, primarily addressed the implementation of state instream flow programs, focusing on the practical challenges facing these programs and suggesting changes that could facilitate flow protection and restoration. Ruth Mathews, Instream Flow Protection and Restoration: Setting a New Compass Point, 36 Envtl. L. 1311 (2006).

Montana has authorized state and federal agencies to apply to the Board of Natural Resources and Conservation to reserve water for instream uses, and the state has reserved substantial amounts in the Yellowstone Basin. MONT. CODE ANN. § 85–2–316 (1999). A 1979 amendment limited minimum flow reservations to 50 percent of the annual flow of gauged streams. The section was again modified in 1985 to restrict reservations to portions of five rivers, including the Yellowstone and Missouri. Oregon very early identified specific waterways for special protection, by withdrawing water from appropriation. OR. REV. STAT. §§ 538.200, 538.270 (1999). Other states allow the designation of "scenic river areas," "wild rivers," or "free-flowing rivers." OKLA. STAT. ANN. 82 §§ 1451–1471 (1990); CAL. PUB. RES. CODE §§ 5093.50–5093.69 (West 1984). In addition to treating some waterways specifically, Oregon now allows the Water Resources Board to withdraw waters in all streams from appropriation. OR. REV. STAT. § 536.410 (1999). Washington also allows administrative withdrawals of waters from appropriation for base flows. WASH. REV. CODE ANN. § 90.22.010 (West Supp. 2001).

Integration of instream flow rights into the ladder of priorities for permitted water rights by treating them as "appropriations" (rather than reserving or withdrawing water from appropriation) has been adopted in a few other states. Wyoming has a law similar to Colorado's, allowing new appropriations and acquisition of existing rights by the State Division of Water Development, but it limits them to quantities of flows that are necessary for fisheries. WYO. STAT. § 41–3–1001 (2001). The statute permits new appropriations to be made for consumptive beneficial uses to the detriment of instream flow appropriations, however, in stream sections within a mile upstream of state boundaries or certain waters. As of 2008, seventy-four instream appropriations covering three hundred stream miles have been issued by the state engineer. Utah has enacted a statute allowing only existing appropriations to be transferred to the State Division of

Wildlife Resources or the Division of Parks for instream flows with the same priorities as the established right. UTAH CODE ANN. § 73–3–3(11) (Supp. 2000). The statute was expanded in 2008 to allow "fishing groups" to file applications for change of use of an existing right for the protection or restoration of stream habitat for native cutthroat trout. However, the change is limited to ten years. UTAH CODE ANN. § 73–3–30. Montana formerly had a system of state appropriation of instream flows from 1947 until the law was amended in 1973 to provide for reservations of flows that would prevent new appropriations that interfere with instream flows. After Trout Unlimited successfully challenged Department of Natural Resources and Conservation rules which allow groundwater pumping in closed basins if there was no immediate impact on surface flows, Montana Trout Unlimited v. Montana Department of Natural Resources and Conservation, 331 Mont. 483, 133 P.3d 224 (2006), the legislature enacted legislation that requires the DNRC to assess the potential impact of new pumping on surface flows. 2007 H.B. 831, enacted as MCA §§ 85–2–361 through 85–2–363 (2007).

4. An interesting dispute arose under Nebraska's instream flow statute, NEB. REV. STAT. §§ 46–2,107 to 46–2,119 (1998). The Central Platte Natural Resources District sought permits for instream flow rights in the Platte River in order to maintain habitat for five species of birds, most of them listed as endangered species. Central Platte Natural Resources Dist. v. Wyoming, 245 Neb. 439, 513 N.W.2d 847 (1994). By assisting in the survival and recovery of these species the district could hope to avoid the impacts of onerous regulatory requirements on present and future water uses. Wyoming, upstream on the Platte (but also a landowner in Nebraska) alleged that the state Director of Water Resources had not complied with the instream flow statute in several respects.

One objection was that the appropriation would interfere with senior water rights. The court held that a proper instream flow right by definition cannot interfere with senior rights since all it does is call water past upstream junior rights. But what if, once the instream flow right is granted, an upstream senior sought to move its diversion point downstream (or a downstream senior sought to move its diversion point upstream) into the stretch of stream protected by the instream flow. Presumably this would be precluded by the no-injury rule. Why is this not an interference with senior rights? Would a new junior appropriation of a consumptive use right be precluded as interfering with a senior right because of the possibility of impeding seniors who may want to change their points of diversion?

5. Riparian common law implied that flows would be maintained because there was no right to deplete waterways unreasonably. But this called for a case-by-case determination. Today, statutes in eastern states generally include provisions for setting minimum streamflows. This is a requirement in fourteen of the eighteen "regulated riparian" jurisdictions. See Water and Water Rights § 9.05(b) (Robert E. Beck ed.).

Typically, minimum flow requirements are implemented by requiring protection of instream flows as part of the process for issuing permits to use water. For instance, Virginia's law requires that anyone seeking to withdraw water from a river must have a Virginia Water Protection Permit. The statute declares that "the preservation of instream flows for purposes of the protection of navigation, maintenance of waste assimilation capacity, the protection of fish and wildlife resources and habitat, recreation, cultural and aesthetic values is a beneficial use of Virginia's waters." VA. CODE § 62.1–44.15:5(B) (Michie Supp. 2000). This is implemented through imposition of conditions or a denial of the permit. When a county was granted a permit for a large lake on Cedar Run, several citizens appealed. Permit conditions required a "floor flow" to maintain a "stream-flow level * * * at all times," control outlet structures to ensure the maintenance of the required flow rates, and monitoring facilities to demonstrate compliance. The court rejected the claims of plaintiffs who challenged the conditions as inadequate and argued that the state was required to "do no harm." It said that to avoid all harm would be "absurd" given the purpose of allowing various uses under the permitting statute that would necessarily disrupt other beneficial uses. Scheer v. Virginia, 2001 WL 803840 (Va.App.2001). See also Mattaponi Indian Tribe v. Virginia, 261 Va. 366, 541 S.E.2d 920 (2001) (upholding standing of tribe and a citizen's group to object to permit conditions as contrary to instream beneficial uses recognized by the statute).

In Florida, citizens have been allowed to challenge the issuance of permits for consumptive use of water where water districts have not yet fulfilled their mandate to set minimum flows. See Concerned Citizens of Putnam County for Responsive Government, Inc. v. St. Johns River Water Management Dist., 622 So.2d 520 (Fla.Dist.Ct.App.1993) and discussion *supra* p. 288.

6. Once a state agency appropriates instream flow rights is it obligated to enforce them? When the Colorado Water Conservation Board agreed to allow a ski area to divert water for snow-making that would deplete the stream below the Board's appropriated instream flow right, a citizen's group sued. The court held that under the statute the agency had a fiduciary duty to the people of the state and therefore its actions were improper. Aspen Wilderness Workshop, Inc. v. Colorado Water Conservation Board, 901 P.2d 1251 (Colo.1995). The legislature then amended the law to allow the Board to relinquish instream water rights if it holds hearings in advance. COLO. REV. STAT. § 37–92–102(3) (2000).

City of Thornton v. City of Fort Collins

Supreme Court of Colorado, 1992.
830 P.2d 915.

■ JUSTICE MULLARKEY delivered the Opinion of the Court.

* * *

* * * This case began when Fort Collins sought approval of conditional surface water rights along a segment of the Cache La Poudre River (Poudre

River) which runs roughly from the northwest boundary diagonally toward the southeast boundary of Fort Collins. Fort Collins refers to that segment of the Poudre River as the Poudre River Recreation Corridor (Corridor). The Corridor is comprised of several parks, open space areas and trail systems. With the development of the Corridor, Fort Collins has enhanced the recreational opportunities and preserved the piscatory and wildlife resources of the Poudre River for the enjoyment of the residents of and visitors to Fort Collins. * * *

* * * The Nature Dam is a relatively new structure designed and built to divert the Poudre River back into its "historic" channel and away from a channel cut after heavy rains and flooding in 1983–84. Along the historic channel, Colorado State University (CSU) owns and maintains property slated for development as the Northern Colorado Nature Center. The Nature Center offers an interpretive trail system and picnic grounds for day use. Future plans include an arboretum and the relocation of the CSU raptor rehabilitation program to the Nature Center. Fort Collins and CSU cooperate with regard to the Nature Center and the continued development of the historic channel. Construction of the Nature Dam began after 1986 but was completed before trial to the water court. The Power Dam is an older structure on the Poudre River owned and maintained by Fort Collins. The Power Dam is so named because of its proximity to a retired municipal power plant which has received local historical designation. The old plant and the Power Dam are in the midst of numerous parks, a visual arts center and a community center, all integral to the Corridor. * * * Recently, Fort Collins renovated the Power Dam by strengthening the structure itself and by adding a boat chute and a fish ladder designed for recreational use and piscatorial preservation respectively. * * *

* * * The water court found that the water appropriation at the Nature Dam was a diversion and not a minimum stream flow and decreed Fort Collins a conditional Poudre River water right of 55 cfs with an appropriation date of February 18, 1986. However, the water court found that the water appropriation at the Power Dam was not a diversion, but a minimum stream flow, and thus did not decree a conditional Poudre River water right for the Power Dam.

Thornton appeals the water court's award of a conditional water right to Fort Collins for the Nature Dam, and Fort Collins cross-appeals the water court's denial of a decree for its claimed conditional water right for the Power Dam. * * *

* * * Thornton argues that because Fort Collins's claimed diversion at the Nature Dam is nothing more than a minimum stream flow right, the conditional decree cannot issue.

* * *

The water court held that the Nature Dam diverts Poudre River water from a more recent channel back into its historic channel. * * *

* * * A diversion in the conventional sense is not required. Under section 37–92–103(7), 15 C.R.S. (1990):

"Diversion" or "divert" means removing water from its natural course or location, or controlling water in its natural course or location, by means of a ditch, canal, flume, reservoir, bypass, pipeline, conduit, well, pump, or other structure or device.

Thus, to effect a diversion under the statute, water either must be removed or it must be controlled. * * *

* * * Controlling water within its natural course or location by some structure or device for a beneficial use thus may result in a valid appropriation. * * *

* * * This statute provides that water appropriated for municipal, recreational, piscatorial, fishery, and wildlife purposes is water put to beneficial uses. * * *

* * * The exclusive authority vested in the CWCB [Colorado Water Conservation Board] to appropriate minimum stream flows does not detract from the right to divert and to put to beneficial use unappropriated waters by removal or control. *See Colo.Const.*, Art. XVI, § 6.

* * *

* * * This is not an appropriation of a minimum stream flow, an appropriation given exclusively to the CWCB. A minimum stream flow does not require removal or control of water by some structure or device. A minimum stream flow between two points on a stream or river usually signifies the complete absence of a structure or device. Furthermore, that an appropriation of a minimum stream flow by the CWCB must put that stream flow to the beneficial use of the preservation of nature does not mean that the beneficial uses to which waters controlled by some structure or device may not also redound to the preservation of piscatorial and other natural resources. Although controlling water within its natural course or location by some structure or device may effect a result which is similar to a minimum flow, that does not mean that the appropriation effected by the structure is invalid under the Act. When the application of water to beneficial use is effected by some structure or device, the resulting appropriation is by a diversion within the meaning of the Act.

The issue then is whether the appropriation of water effected by the Nature Dam is a removal or control of water for beneficial use within the meaning of the foregoing statutes. The water court found that the Nature Dam removes Poudre River water from its natural course or location and puts that water to a beneficial use. We agree. * * * Thornton again argues that Fort Collins's persistent intent to appropriate minimum stream flows means that the appropriation at the Nature Dam is an invalid appropriation. To be sure, re-labeling what is otherwise a minimum stream flow without control by some structure or device as a diversion, that is, removal or control of water by some structure or device, does not transform the former into the latter from a legal point of view. However, it is clear that the Nature Dam is a structure which either removes water from its natural course or location or controls water within its natural course or location given that the Poudre's "historic" channel may be considered the River's natural course or location. The uses of the Poudre River water so controlled are recreational, piscatorial and wildlife uses, all valid under the Act.

The water court also found that Fort Collins does not claim a right to exercise dominion and control of the water after it leaves the point of the Nature Dam. Thornton argues that this means that Fort Collins has not appropriated the waters for the claimed beneficial uses because the water may be appropriated by others after leaving the Nature Dam thereby preventing its beneficial use by Fort Collins. * * * Under the statutes, to control water within its natural course or location means that the appropriator exercises control over the water at least to the extent that the water continues to be put to beneficial use by the appropriator, in this instance by Fort Collins. Thus, Fort Collins may validly exercise dominion over the Poudre River water once it passes the Nature Dam and continues within that segment of the river in which such water is put to beneficial use. If and when the water passes downstream from that controlled segment of the Poudre it may be subject to further appropriation by others.

* * *

On cross-appeal Fort Collins argues that the water court erred in declining to award a conditional water right for the Power Dam.

* * *

The boat chute and the fish ladder were included in the reconstruction and renovation of the Power Dam in 1987. In general, boat chutes and fish ladders, when properly designed and constructed, are structures which concentrate the flow of water to serve their intended purposes. A chute or ladder therefore may qualify as a "structure or device" which controls water in its natural course or location under section 37–92–103(7). * * * That the chute and the ladder control and direct river water *only* at unspecified low flows in the river is not a defect since that is precisely what they are designed to do. We therefore reverse the water court's conclusion that the Power Dam does not effect a diversion within the meaning of the Act.

* * * Whatever the appropriation date, we find that the Nature Dam may effect a valid appropriation. Finally, we hold that the Power Dam qualifies as a structure which controls water and thus also may effect a valid appropriation.

NOTES

1. Following the decision in this case some municipalities acted to protect flows in streams running through their boundaries. The City of Golden sought and was awarded a 1000 c.f.s. water right for a world-class white water boating course. Concerning the Application for Water Rights of the City of Golden, No. 98CW448, Dist. Ct. Water Div., No. 1 (Colo. Jan. 13,

2001). The city constructed seven boat chutes to serve as "control struc-tures," thereby effecting "diversions" to comply with the *Thornton* deci-sion. In reaction, the state legislature enacted special procedures for adjudication of "recreational in-channel diversions." The water court must consider the recommendations of the state Water Conservation Board and findings on several issues including whether the stream is appropriate for the intended use, whether the use would promote maximum use of water, and whether it would impair the state's ability "to fully develop and to place to consumptive beneficial use its interstate compact entitlements," Colo. Rev. Stat. § 37–92–102(6) (2001) A concern of the legislature is that if instream flows were maintained to the state line it could preclude full development of the state's apportionment of interstate waters. In Colorado Water Conservation Board v. Upper Gunnison River Water Conservancy Dist., 109 P.3d 585 (Colo. 2005), the Board reviewed an application under the recreational in-channel diversion law and recommended an amount less than that requested by the applicant. The water court awarded the full amount requested. The supreme court's opinion clarifies the relative roles of the Board and the water court. A 2006 Colorado statute imposed various restrictions on the authority of local governments to obtain, defend, and exercise these recreational in-channel diversions, or "RICDs." Act of May 11, 2006, ch. 197, 2006 Colo. Sess. Laws 906.

2. A Washington statute provides, "Beneficial uses under a municipal water supply purposes water right may include water withdrawn or divert-ed under such a right and used for (1) Uses that benefit fish and wildlife, water quality, or other instream resources or related habitat values...." Rev. Code Wash. 90.03.550. Are these uses consistent with traditional notions of municipal water supply? Do today's western cities have an interest in providing sufficient water to protect these values? For an argument that western water law should allow cities to obtain the water rights necessary to protect public values (including recreation) in their rivers, *see* Reed D. Benson, Rivers to Live By: Can Western Water Law Help Communities Embrace Their Streams? 27 J. Land, Resources & Envtl. L. 1, 18–27 (2007).

3. Most instream flow statutes limit appropriation of instream flows to state agencies. Should states allow the perfection of private instream flow rights? What problems might arise? See James Huffman, Instream Water Use: Public and Private Alternatives, in Water Rights: Scarce Resource Allocation, Bureaucracy, and the Environment 249 (Terry L. Anderson ed., 1983) (arguing that a private market in instream flow rights is desirable). Assuming the state has an interest in ensuring that huge quantities of water are not appropriated for instream flow by speculators, thereby tying up future water development, does the state have a legitimate concern when private interests purchase existing water rights, *e.g.*, irrigation rights, and change them to instream flow rights?

NOTE: WATER TRUSTS

As agricultural, industrial, and residential uses place heavier demands on rivers and streams, fish and wildlife habitat can suffer and recreational uses can be diminished. Minimum streamflow laws have not been completely successful in combating these problems. The fundamental shortcoming of state instream flow laws is that they were created too late. By the time states began adopting legislation allowing state agencies to appropriate water for instream flows, many of the West's rivers and streams were already over-appropriated. In dry years little, if any, water was left over for junior instream flow rights after senior rights were satisfied. See Reed D. Benson, *Symposium: Watershed Issue: The Role of Streamflow Protection in Northwest River Basin Management*, 26 Envtl. L. 175, 206–08 (1996).

A few western states have now enacted legislation designed to allow private interests to acquire water rights by sale, donation, or lease for the purpose of maintaining minimum instream flows. Oregon was the first state to enact such legislation with the passage of the In–Stream Water Rights Act of 1987. Or. Rev. Stat. §§ 537.332–537.360 (2007). The law provides that "[a]ny person may purchase or lease an existing water right or portion thereof or accept a gift of an existing water right or portion thereof for conversion to an in-stream water right." Or. Rev. Stat. § 537.348 (1999). The law further provides that "[a]ny water right converted to an in-stream water right * * * shall retain the priority date of the water right purchased, leased or received as a gift." Id. This statute, and similar statutes in other western states, paved the way for the creation of water trusts.

Modeled after land trusts, water trusts are non-profit organizations created specifically to acquire water rights for instream flows. Private water rights can be purchased, donated, or leased by the trust (depending upon the law of the state) and then converted to instream use.

The Oregon Water Trust (OWT) was created in 1993 and became the nation's first water trust. The non-profit corporation was initially created by four individuals "to test 'market environmentalism'," but it has grown dramatically since its inception. See Janet C. Neuman & Cheyenne Chapman, *Wading Into the Water Market: The First Five Years of the Oregon Water Trust*, 14 J. Envtl. L. & Litig. 135, 136 (1999). Former OWT President Janet Neuman reported that the organization had completed more than 300 deals in its first decade of operations, but explained that OWT continued to face significant challenges and criticism in its effort to restore instream through water right transactions. Janet C. Neuman, The Good, the Bad, and the Ugly: The First Ten Years of the Oregon Water Trust, 83 Neb. L. Rev. 432 (2004).

Other states have followed Oregon's lead. In 1995 Montana amended its water code to allow private interests to make a "temporary" change of consumptive rights to instream flows "for the benefit of the fishery resource." Mont. Code Ann. § 85–2–408 (2001). Appropriators are also able to lease their water rights "to another person for instream flow[s] to benefit the fishery resource." § 85–2–408(2)(a)(ii). Since then, non-governmental organizations such as Trout Unlimited have been able to lease water rights to restore wildlife habitat. Agricultural, industrial, environmental, and other interest groups are now attempting to form a Montana Water Trust.

In 1997 the Texas state legislature created the Texas Water Trust. TEX. WATER CODE ANN. § 15–7031 (Vernon 2000). The Texas Water Trust was established as a part of the larger Texas Water Bank "to hold water rights dedicated to environmental needs, including instream flows, water quality, fish and wildlife habitat, or bay and estuary flows." § 15–7031. After an NGO applied for an appropriation for substantial estuary protection flows, Texas created a complicated, but innovative, adaptive management instream flow reservation protection program for its rivers, lakes, bays, and estuaries. An environmental flows advisory group is charged with developing an environmental flow regime for specific basins, using a consensus, regional, and stakeholder process. TEX. WATER CODE ANN. § 11.0235(d)–11.0237. Appropriation permits may not be issued for bay or estuary flow appropriations, § 11.0235(d)(5), but permits for permitted uses can be conditioned for these purposes. In basins where unappropriated water is available, the Texas Natural Resource Conservation Commission "should establish an environmental set-aside below which water should not be available for appropriation." § 11.0235(d)(3). Set-asides can be supplemented by water markets and donated water rights.

In 1998, the Washington Water Trust (WWT) was created to restore instream flows under the state's Trust Water Rights Program. WASH. REV. CODE ANN. §§ 90.42.005 to 90.42.900 (West 1992 & Supp. 2001). Under this program, "the state may acquire all or portions of existing water rights, by purchase, gift, or other appropriate means * * * from any person or entity * * *." § 90.42.080(1). The WWT began working with landowners in 1999 to acquire water rights for instream flow use.

The Colorado Water Trust (CWT) was incorporated in 2001 to pursue conversions of water rights to instream flow within the bounds of existing state law. The CWT acquires decreed water rights from willing sellers. The rights are changed so that they can be dedicated to instream flow use. To engage in this activity, the CWT works in partnership with the Colorado Conservation Board, the only entity authorized by law to hold such rights. In addition to conducting water rights acquisitions, the CWT uses all tools available to enhance streamflows in critical areas of Colorado, including short term arrangements such as leases, structural solutions such as delivery-system and reservoir outlet upgrades, and alternative use solutions such as changes in points of diversion.

Utah enacted a statute in 2008 which authorized private interests to convert existing water rights to instream use, but imposed numerous limits on this authority. Only nonprofit fishing groups (such as Trout Unlimited) may apply for such a transfer, and only for the purpose of protecting or restoring habitat for one of three named strains of native cutthroat trout. The transfers may only last for a fixed period of one to ten years, and the authority for the transfers themselves will expire at the end of 2018. The fishing group must obtain the approval of the director of the Division of Wildlife Resources, who may approve the transfer only if several specific criteria are met, and may nonetheless deny it if the director finds that the transfer would not be in the public interest. The transfer application must include studies required by the state engineer "demonstrating the necessity for the instream flow in the specified section of the stream and the projected benefits to the public resulting from the change;" the application is otherwise subject to the procedures applicable to new appropriations. Utah Code Ann. 73–3–30(3). Why do you suppose the Utah statute imposes these restrictions on private efforts to convert existing water rights to instream use? Are these restrictions good policy?

4. Transfers and Changed Uses in Statutory Systems

Under riparian common law water rights were tied to the land. Various means were devised to allow uses on non-riparian lands. Now, permit statutes allow for non-riparian uses, but it is rare to allow the permits to be marketable.

Water rights held under the common law prior appropriation doctrine were generally transferable, subject only to the "no injury" rule that protected other water users from the adverse consequences of a transfer on their water rights. See *supra* p. 237. Now most states have statutes that embody the no injury rule developed under the common law of prior appropriation. The Utah statute is exemplary. Utah Code Ann. § 73–3–3 (Michie Supp. 2000) provides:

(2) (a) Any person entitled to the use of water may make permanent or temporary changes in the:

(i) point of diversion;

(ii) place of use; or

(iii) purpose of use for which the water was originally appropriated.

(b) A change may not be made if it impairs any vested right without just compensation.

* * *

(4) (a) A change may not be made unless the change application is approved by the state engineer.

* * *

(5) (a) The state engineer shall follow the same procedures, and the rights and duties of the applicants with respect to applications for permanent changes of point of diversion, place of use, or purpose of use shall be the same, as provided in this title for applications to appropriate water.

* * *

(7) (a) The state engineer may not reject applications for either permanent or temporary changes for the sole reason that the change would impair the vested rights of others.

(b) If otherwise proper, permanent or temporary changes may be approved for part of the water involved or upon the condition that conflicting rights are acquired.

* * *

(9) Any person who changes or who attempts to change a point of diversion, place of use, or purpose of use, either permanently or temporarily, without first applying to the state engineer in the manner provided in this section:

(a) obtains no right; and

(b) is guilty of a crime punishable under Section 73–2–27 if the change or attempted change is made knowingly or intentionally; and

(c) is guilty of a separately punishable offense for each day of the unlawful change.''

* * *

Some state statutes impose standards on transfers beyond the ''no injury'' requirement. A few statutes impose some form of public interest test on transfers; see, e.g. Idaho Code 42–222(1) (local public interest); N.M. Stat. Ann. 72–5–23 (public welfare). The Wyoming statute imposes several standards: no injury, no increase in the historic rate or quantity of diversions, no increase in consumptive use or decrease in return flow. It goes on to require the state agency to

consider all facts it believes pertinent to the transfer which may include the following:

(i) The economic loss to the community and the state if the use from which the right is transferred is discontinued;

(ii) The extent to which such economic loss will be offset by the new use;

(iii) Whether other sources of water are available for the new use.

WYO. STAT. ANN. § 41–3–104(a) (2007).

Are these last three factors relevant to the question of injury? Under the Wyoming statute, can a transfer causing no injury nonetheless be denied based on economic impacts or feasible alternatives? As a policy matter, should such factors (or the public interest) be a basis for denying or conditioning a proposed transfer?

a.   Improving Efficiency Through Transfers and Exchanges

National Research Council, National Academy of Science, Water Transfers in the West: Efficiency, Equity, and the Environment

234–43 (1992).

California's Imperial Valley: A "Win–Win" Transfer?

* * * In early 1989 the Imperial Irrigation District (IID) and the Metropolitan Water District (MWD) of Southern California signed a water conservation agreement. Two other irrigation districts, the Palo Verde Irrigation District and the Coachella Valley Water District, became part of the agreement in late 1989 (IID and MWD, 1989). In brief, MWD will pay for a program of water conservation for IID. In return, IID will reduce its call on the Colorado River by the amount conserved, and MWD will be entitled to divert this amount into its system at Parker Dam. Although MWD prefers not to characterize the agreement as a water transfer, it is otherwise almost universally viewed as the first major rural-to-urban transfer of irrigation water in California and will be a model for future transfers that try to accommodate urban demands and preservation of the state's productive agricultural economy. It is important to realize that the Imperial Irrigation District–Metropolitan Water District transfer was an "easy" case because no existing users were displaced and third party effects were minimal or indirect enough to be ignored. Still, it offers an important illustration of the potential of transfers.

THE SETTING

The Imperial Valley lies on the northern edge of the Sonoran Desert in southern California about 50 mi (80 km) west of the Colorado River (Figure 11.1). The area was originally called the Salton Sink and, for a while in the nineteenth century, the Valley of the Dead. It was renamed the Imperial Valley at the turn of the century by the irrigation pioneer and promoter George Chaffey as part of an effort to attract settlers to the harsh desert.

* * *

* * * It has been said that the Imperial Valley is one of nature's jokes—it contains hundreds of thousands of acres of flat fertile land formed by silt deposited in the ancient delta of the Colorado and the growing season is perpetual, but rainfall averages less than 3 in. (0.7 cm) per year. Ground water resources are minimal, so the valley, actually a geological sink, must rely on the Colorado River for its supply.

* * *

The history of the settlement and cultivation of the Imperial Valley is in large part the history of the regulation of the Colorado River and the growth of agribusiness in the state. As a 1991 appellate court opinion upholding the state's power to curb wasteful use practices in the valley observed, IID "has occupied a position of great strength, discretion and vested right in a geographical part of the country that is 'far western,' embracing a philosophy that is independent in every sense of the word. Recent trends in water-use philosophy and the administration of water law have severely undermined the positions of districts such as IID" (*Imperial Irrigation District v. State Water Resources Control Board,* 1991). That history has enabled the valley to chart its own destiny, but the valley is increasingly vulnerable to criticism that it uses a disproportionate share of southern California's water. Ninety-eight percent of Colorado River water deliveries to the IID go to irrigation, and the average use is more than 5 acre-feet (6 megaliters (ML)) per acre. A wide variety of irrigation techniques are used.

* * *

Figure 11.1 Main waterways and features, California's Imperial Valley

* * *

LEGAL BACKGROUND

* * *

The IID's water rights are subject to the requirement that the water be put to beneficial use. Western water rights are usufructuary—they are limited to the use of the water and cease if the water stops being put to a beneficial use. The prevailing assumption is that water that is not put to beneficial use is either forfeited or abandoned and is open to appropriation by others. Attacks on nonbeneficial or wasteful uses generally are brought by junior water rights holders against seniors. The IID has long been attacked for applying water in excess of crop needs, but its use was not seriously challenged until 1980. The most significant challenge to IID's water use was an ultimately unsuccessful effort by a valley activist to apply the excess land provisions of the Reclamation Act of 1902.

The geography of the valley makes excess use and the resulting drainage a serious problem. The U.S. Supreme Court Special Master, Simon Rifkind, noted in 1960 that much of California's water use was "wasted, as is apparent, for example, in the very large unused runoff each year into the Salton Sea." The IID has been sued by a number of landowners for damages caused by flooding. In 1980 a lawsuit filed by a Salton Sea farmer, who claimed that IID's tailwater drainage was raising the level of the Salton Sea and flooding his land, triggered a series of administrative and judicial orders requiring greater water conservation in the IID, although water salvage investigations had been under way since the mid–1960s. These state orders provided a strong incentive to negotiate a settlement. In 1984, after a lengthy series of hearings in which a variety of interests (e.g., the California Department of Water Resources and the Environmental Defense Fund) presented substantial evidence on IID's water management practices and the potential for a conservation-induced water sale, the State Water Resources Control Board concluded that IID's use of water was unreasonable under California law and constituted waste. The next year the Bureau of Reclamation issued a report identifying measures that could conserve 354,000 acre-feet (436,700 ML) per year.

* * *

THE 1989 WATER CONSERVATION AGREEMENTS

The 1989 Water Conservation Agreement obligates MWD to pay for both structural and nonstructural conservation projects designed to conserve 106,100 acre-feet (130,900 ML) annually, which it can then take for a period of 35 years. Total capital costs are estimated to be $97.8 million, plus $23 million in indirect costs. The program will be implemented over a 5–year period between 1990 and 1994; then the savings will be constant until MWD or another party agrees to an additional conservation program. The legal questions that initially created potential barriers were finessed. Section 6.5 of the agreement is replete with disclaimers that MWD shall not assert a right to the conserved waters, that the rights of the parties "except as specifically set forth in this agreement" to the use of the Colorado are not affected, and that the conserved water will at all times retain its third priority and has not been forfeited by IID. Likewise, the possibility of MWD's banking water in Lake Mead during wet years is acknowledged, but the irrigation districts reserve the right to challenge any future banking agreements.

Canal lining is the major conservation strategy being pursued, but IID will also build new regulating reservoirs and canal spill interceptors and will automate its delivery system. The agreement will be administered and monitored by a program coordinating committee composed of one IID, one MWD, and one neutral representative. The MWD must bear all capital construction costs, the "ongoing direct costs of the nonstructural projects of the program, and operation, maintenance and replacement costs of the structural projects of the program necessary to the keep the projects ... in good operating condition during the terms of this agreement" (IID and MWD, 1989). In addition, MWD must bear $23 million in indirect costs such as lost hydroelectric revenues, "mitigation of adverse impacts on agriculture from increased salinity in the water," and environmental mitigation and litigation costs from any impact on water levels or water quality in the Salton Sea and the New and Alamo rivers (IID and MWD, 1989).

* * *

The IID and MWD Water Conservation Agreement is seen by both parties as a win-win agreement. The MWD, of course, increases its Colorado River supplies by 106,100 acre-feet (130,900 ML), and this additional margin of safety, about 20 percent of its anticipated dry year shortfall, will become important as Arizona takes more of its Colorado River entitlement and supplies become more scarce in both the Colorado basin and northern California. The IID obtains money in return for doing what it may well have become legally obligated to do in any event, while its irrigated acreage is unaffected by the agreement. This is the first such transaction and thus relatively straightforward to negotiate. Future attempts to reach such agreements may be more complicated.

* * *

National Research Council, National Academy of Science, Water Transfers in the West: Efficiency, Equity, and the Environment

30–34 (1992).

Types of Water Transfer Opportunities

Several different types of transactions—including water leases, water banks, dry year option arrangements, and transfers of salvaged water—may be used to transfer water use from one party to another. Water rights may be sold or leased, and the transfer may be permanent or temporary.

Water Leases

A water lease occurs when a water rights owner and a new user negotiate an agreement to use a fixed quantity of water over a specific period of time, instead of purchasing a permanent right. Leases often occur during dry years, when some farmers or cities run low on water supplies in storage and need a temporary way to endure short-term drought. For example, junior rights irrigators with orchards and other high-value perennial crops sometimes lease water on a one-time basis for their late summer irrigations from neighboring seasonal crop growers who hold more senior rights. Orchard crop owners are willing to pay more for this water than it was worth to irrigate field crops because they face the danger of losing their long-term investment if their trees die.

Water lease prices in various areas of the West cover a broad range. For example, in 1988 the Bureau of Reclamation offered to lease water from its Green Mountain Reservoir in western Colorado at $6 per acre-foot ($4.85 per [megaliter] ML) for agricultural use, $10 per acre-foot ($8.10 per ML) for municipal use, and up to $80 per acre-foot ($65 per ML) for industrial use. In the same year, the bureau's central Arizona project office leased surplus water to Phoenix-area customers at prices ranging from $35 to $82 per acre-foot ($28.40 to $66.50 per ML). In another lease arrangement in the late 1980s, the Montana Fish, Wildlife and Parks Department paid $20,000 for a release of 10,000 acre-feet (12,335 ML) from Painted Rocks Reservoir into the Bitterroot River to preserve downstream fisheries.

Water Banks

Water banks are another transfer-related option. A water bank is a formal mechanism for pooling surplus water rights for rental to other users. In Idaho, for example, farmers with surplus entitlements from federal projects sell more than 100,000 acre-feet (123,400 ML) annually through water banks that are sanctioned by the state. Water bank leases generally result in changes in point of diversion of storage water or changes in place or purpose of use. Several tests must be met before reallocation through a water bank is approved, such as whether the lease would cause the use of water to be expanded beyond that authorized under the water right or whether it would conflict with the local public interest. Idaho water bank prices in the late 1980s ranged from $2.75 to $5.50 per acre-foot ($2.23 to $4.45 per ML) for one-time use of the water during the irrigation season. Part of the fees collected goes to the entity supplying the water to the rental pool; part goes to the water district to cover administrative costs. Prices are set by the water banks' governing boards and are actually well below the real market value of the water. * * *

In 1991, California responded to a 5–year drought by establishing a water bank to facilitate market-like transfers of water. The arrangement provides for the state to buy water from voluntary sellers and distribute it at cost to urban and agricultural users with critical needs, urgent fish and wildlife protection needs, and carryover storage to guard against a sixth dry year.

Dry Year Option Arrangements

Many water users have enough water to meet their needs in most years but not in the driest years. As a result, users sometimes attempt to negotiate an option agreement with senior rights holders to use the senior water during dry years only. Dry year option arrangements allow the senior rights holders to continue to use the water (in most cases for farming) in normal years and give the option holder (often a municipal user) a cost-effective way to make its supply more reliable during dry years. For example, a dry year option agreement has been implemented by a Utah city and a nearby irrigator. The city paid the irrigator $25,000 for entering the option arrangement for a 25–year period; during those dry years in which the city takes water, it pays the farmer a set sum plus the quantity of hay the farmer might have grown. The farmer benefited from the cash payments and the guarantee of hay for his livestock; the city was assured more reliable supplies.

On a larger scale, the Metropolitan Water District (MWD) of southern California has proposed a dry year option arrangement to farmers in the Palo Verde Irrigation District. The MWD offered cash payments for each acre placed in the program and additional payments each time it asserts its option to transfer the water during dry years. The irrigators declined that offer, but negotiations continue. It is inevitable that more such agreements will be negotiated in the future. In northern California during the summer of 1988, the East Bay Municipal Utility District (EBMUD) offered irrigators a dry year option based on a payment for the water of $50 per acre-foot ($40.50 per ML). However, the irrigators felt the price was too low, and no agreement was reached.

Transfers of Salvaged Water

Transfers of salvaged water also occur. This is a variation of a water sale, in which a city or business that needs additional supplies finances irrigation improvements in exchange for rights to use the water that is conserved. In Wyoming, the city of Casper paid for upgrading irrigation systems in the Alcova Irrigation District in order to salvage several thousand acre-feet of water from the district for new municipal use. In California in 1989, after years of negotiations, MWD and the Imperial Irrigation District (IID) reached an agreement calling for MWD to pay for irrigation system improvements within IID in exchange for rights to use the water conserved. The IID is at the lower end of the river system, and there are no opportunities to reuse return flows, so the return flow is considered "wasted." In California, MWD has begun a closely watched pilot program with the Coachella Valley Water District to salvage Colorado River water imported to southern California via leaky canals. Through a multi-million dollar canal-lining project, MWD hopes to salvage up to 30,000 acre-feet (37,000 ML) annually for municipal use. Additional transfer arrangements involving water conservation are under serious consideration elsewhere in California.

Other Types of Exchanges

Water transfers also include exchanges in which one user trades some water or combination of water and money for another user's supply because the timing, guarantee of availability, or quality makes that supply more attractive to the first user. This type of exchange is relatively common in Colorado, where cities buy water rights in adjacent basins and exchange them for water that can be piped through existing conveyance systems.

California droughts have spurred exploration of water exchanges. To protect the quality of supplies for urban customers during the anticipated 1989 to 1990 drought, EBMUD, in the San Francisco region, wanted to trade low-quality water to local irrigators in exchange for an equivalent amount of their entitlement to higher-quality mountain runoff from the Mokelumne River, EBMUD's normal source of supply. Again, this proposal was rejected by local irrigators.

Another bank-like type of exchange that has occurred in California and could be used elsewhere involves trading surplus surface waters in wet years for accumulated ground water supplies during droughts. The MWD of Southern California has had a policy of storing imported water in ground water aquifers since 1931. The MWD and other water users in California are recharging and stabilizing ground water aquifers by putting surplus surface water into the ground water in both adjudicated and unadjudicated basins. This activity could be extended to irrigation districts. Surplus surface water would be stored during wet years in exchange for use of local irrigation rights during droughts. During dry years, MWD would use the farmers' surface water rights for municipal use; the farmers would then pump the water that MWD has previously recharged into the ground water beneath their lands.

Several states have enacted legislation to encourage the sale of salvaged or conserved water. Oregon has an innovative water conservation statute that splits the benefits of conservation between the saver and the state. If the state approves a conservation plan as feasible, effective, protective of junior rights, and consistent with the public interest, the salvager is entitled to the saved water, but the state may allocate 25 percent of the water to itself for instream flow maintenance and other environmental uses. Or. Rev. Stat. § 537.470 (1999). The argument that the legislation constitutes a taking is considered but rejected in Joseph L. Sax, *The Constitution, Property Rights and the Future of Water Law,* 61 U. Colo. L. Rev. 257 (1990).

NOTE: BUREAU OF RECLAMATION TRANSFERS

Federal reclamation law has created the expectation of eternally cheap water to be used on project lands. The original vision of the West as an Eden of family farms was never fulfilled and is fading. In many areas of the West—California, Colorado, Nevada, and Texas, for example—federal reclamation projects have been identified as potential pools of water available for reallocation to urban and environmental uses. Water stored and distributed by the Bureau of Reclamation is theoretically available for transfer from agriculture to urban and instream uses, but reclamation law is not structured to encourage or facilitate transfers.

Some transfers of reclamation water have occurred, but there are major political and legal impediments. See Richard W. Wahl, Markets for Federal Waters: Subsidies, Property Rights and the Bureau of Reclamation (1989). The two major legal impediments are the uncertainty over the transferability of reclamation rights and the possibility that the federal government will try to recapture a portion of the value created by the subsidy. Bruce Driver, *The Effect of Federal Reclamation Law on Voluntary Water Transfers*, 33 Rocky Mtn. Min. L. Inst. 26–1, 26–7 (1987). However, there is no absolute prohibition against transfers. The Supreme Court has held that under Section 8 of the Reclamation Act, 43 U.S.C.A. § 372, the Bureau has legal title to the water as a trustee for the project beneficiaries because the Bureau is "simply a carrier and distributor of water * * * with the right to receive the sums stipulated in the contracts as reimbursement for the cost of construction and annual charges for operation and maintenance of the works." Ickes v. Fox, 300 U.S. 82, 95, 57 S.Ct. 412, 81 L.Ed. 525 (1937). The Utah Supreme Court recently applied Section 8 in a case involving a dispute between the Bureau and a water user group over which one had the right to apply for a transfer of project water rights. In re Uintah Basin, 133 P.3d 410 (Utah 2006). The court emphasized the Bureau's duty to follow state water laws, and declared that the government's interest in project water rights gives it nothing more than "a protective role on behalf of the rank-and-file persons who have applied the water to beneficial use." *Id.* at 420–421. Section 8 provides that "[t]he right to the use of water acquired under the provision of this Act shall be appurtenant to the land irrigated, and beneficial use shall be the basis, the measure, and the limit of the right." Id. at 85. A 1955 federal case, however, refused to interpret the appurtenancy requirement to preclude a city's appropriation under state law of storm and flood waters and unused return flows from the Rio Grande Project in Texas. The pervasive deference to state law "makes it very doubtful that the fact water rights in a reclamation project become 'appurtenant to the land irrigated,' renders such rights immune from state law." El Paso County Water Improvement Dist. No. 1 v. City of El Paso, 133 F.Supp. 894, 904 (W.D.Tex.1955), *aff'd in part, rev'd in part* 243 F.2d 927 (5th Cir.1957). More generally, this part of Section 8 may have been repealed by subsequent acts authorizing the use of water for non-irrigation purposes. *E.g.*, Reclamation Projects Act of 1939, 43 U.S.C.A. § 390b (West Supp. 2001). The Miscellaneous Water Supply Act of 1920, 43 U.S.C.A. § 521 (West 1986), allows the Bureau to supply water for non-irrigation purposes under limited conditions and appears to authorize surplus transfers to non-project uses when irrigation is not impaired.

For a useful examination of the problems and benefits of federal water transfers see Brian E. Gray et al., *Transfers of Federal Reclamation Water: A Case Study of California's San Joaquin Valley,* 21 Envtl. L. 911 (1991). See generally, The Law of Waters and Water Rights § 41.06 (Robert E. Beck ed., Supp.).

b. Out of Priority Use

Board of Directors of Wilder Irrigation Dist. v. Jorgensen

Supreme Court of Idaho, 1943.
64 Idaho 538, 136 P.2d 461.

■ HOLDEN, CHIEF JUSTICE.

* * * December 19, 1925, the Wilder Irrigation District was organized. * * *

It was found, in the course of time, the water supply provided under the terms of the contract between the United States and the District, dated April 6, 1926, was not sufficient for the proper irrigation and reclamation of the lands within the district. That led the district to take steps to obtain additional water and to that end, the district entered into another contract with the United States, dated January 13, 1941, also subject to later authorization by the electors of the district, for 33 $^{71}\!/_{100}$ per cent of water to be stored in the Anderson Ranch Reservoir to be constructed by the United States. * * * Thereafter, a petition, in the usual form, was filed in the District Court of Canyon County praying that "each and all of the proceedings had and taken by the Board of Directors of Wilder Irrigation District, for and in connection with the special election * * * 'concerning the construction of Anderson Ranch Reservoir and related matters', between the United States of America and the Wilder Irrigation District * * * be examined, approved and confirmed by this Court, and that the legality and validity of said contract be determined and established by decree of this Court."

At the conclusion of the submission of proof by the District in support of its petition, it was stipulated by counsel for the respective parties that "the following [question] shall be submitted to the Court for its decision:

* * * Has the respondent District power to enter into a contract with the United States whereby the United States may, at some future time, substitute an equal amount of Payette and Salmon River water for District Boise River water?"

The right to substitute waters of one stream for those of another was presented to this Court in Agnes B. Reno et al. v. J. R. Richards et al., 32 Idaho 1, 178 P. 81, 82.

* * *

* * * It thus appears in the Reno case the waters of Birch Creek had been decreed some 24 years before, and, therefore, that the waters of that stream had become appurtenant to the lands for the irrigation of which they had been decreed, just as it is contended by appellants the waters of Boise River have been decreed and become appurtenant to the lands of appellants' and, of course, other landowners in the respondent district. With substantially the same question presented as appellants contend is

presented in the case at bar, this Court, in the Reno case, held that "in the absence of detriment to other users of waters from Birch creek, there is no doubt of [the diverters'] right to make a diversion from Birch creek, at their point of diversion, of the amount of [increased] water which they caused to flow therein for the use of other appropriators farther down the stream."

It follows from this holding the fact water has been decreed for the irrigation of lands and become appurtenant thereto does not, for that reason alone, as contended by appellants, prevent a substitution; and, further, that a decree and the appurtenancy of water to lands do not, in and of themselves, constitute a sufficient reason for denying a substitution or exchange of water.

* * *

It must be kept in mind the contest in the case at bar is between appellant landowners within respondent district and the district itself; that the sole purpose of the contract in question is to provide much-needed additional water for the irrigation of the irrigated lands within the boundaries of the district, including appellants' lands, in the manner and as expressly authorized by statute; that the additional supply of water contracted for from Anderson Ranch Reservoir does not depend upon a possible later substitution of water; that such additional supply is assured in any event; that the proposed contract will not have the effect of reducing the amount of water to which any landowner within the district is entitled; that no landowner is compelled to surrender any right whatsoever; that in the event an exchange of water is later made, such water would be emptied into the Boise River at a point above the diversion works of the respondent district; that in the event an exchange of water takes place as provided in the contract under consideration, then and in that case, a landowner within the district, for instance, instead of receiving as at present, under the 1926 contract, 100 inches of the waters of Boise River, would receive a like amount of the waters of Payette and Salmon Rivers, and that such landowner would also receive his share of the Anderson Ranch Reservoir storage water contracted for, which would not, under the circumstances above stated, operate to the detriment of any landowner.

* * *

We conclude the judgment must be affirmed, and it is so ordered, with costs to respondent.

* * *

■ GIVENS, JUSTICE (dissenting).

* * *

While some courts have stated that a water user is not concerned with and has no right to any specific source of supply or to any particular water, an appropriator does have, after diversion and application to a beneficial use, a constitutional right to the continuation of the source of his supply of water as it physically existed at the time his appropriation was made. It is true no attempt has yet been made to make the change authorized in [the contract]; the clause pertinent to this point, nevertheless, gives the Secretary of the Interior sole power to make such change when and as he may please.

* * *

If Salmon River or Payette River water is substituted for Boise River water to appellants, the water theretofore used by them and obtained from Boise River sources will necessarily have to be transferred to someone else, as without continued application to a beneficial use the appropriation thereof would lapse. If, after a period of time, under such substitution, the water from Payette or Salmon Rivers, due to physical conditions which might arise and over which man would have no control, would fail, even though appellants' rights would be paramount to the interim users, appellants would at least face the probability of a lawsuit to determine such right, and, in the meantime, be subject to the possibility that they would have no water, and hence their lands would be worthless. * * *

* * * The consequences affect vested, substantial rights, and it is not merely a matter of operation or regulation. As stated in the majority opinion, this provision of the contract has absolutely no connection with the supply of water from Anderson Ranch Dam. It is authorizing and accepting uncertainty for certainty. It seems to me, under the expressed theory and general nature of an irrigation district as enunciated by the following, this provision of the contract is in violation of Art. 15, Sec. 4, of the Idaho constitution. * * *

NOTES

1. Colorado allows out-of-priority use or storage of water by juniors without prejudice to senior uses, and seniors are required to accept a substitute water supply:

> (1) In every case in which the state engineer finds that water can be stored out of priority under circumstances such that the water so stored can be promptly made available to downstream senior storage appropriators in case they are unable to completely store their entire appropriative right due to insufficient water supply, the state engineer may permit such upstream storage out of priority * * *.

> (2) Individuals and private or public entities, alone or in concert, may provide a substituted supply of water to one or more appropriators senior to them, * * * and, to the extent that such substituted water is made available to meet the appropriative requirements of such senior, the right of such senior to draw water pursuant to his appropriation shall be deemed to be satisfied. The rights of such senior may be used for effectuating such substitution during the period while it is in operation, and the practice may be confirmed by court order as provided for determining water rights.

(3) Any substituted water shall be of a quality and continuity to meet the requirements of use to which the senior appropriation has normally been put. * * *

COLO. REV. STAT. § 37–80–120 (2000).

2. There are other devices for managing water more efficiently by not adhering religiously to priorities, yet satisfying seniors' needs. Rotation is a practice whereby a schedule is devised, either through an agreement among water users or by court order, giving individual users the right to divert the entire flow of the stream, or that portion owned by the parties to the agreement, for a short period of time. Rotations can be among multiple owners of a single water right (*e.g.*, users within a district), or among owners of independent diversions. Their purpose is to combat the inefficiencies that often result from continuous diversions of small amounts of water. All rotation plans are subject to the rights of other users on the stream. Many states have specific statutory authorizations for rotation plans. Nevada, for example, permits rotation among several users, or among different priorities of one user, to the end that each user will have an irrigation head of at least two cubic feet per second. NEV. REV. STAT. ANN. § 533.075 (Michie 1995). Several states require that proposed rotation plans be submitted in advance to designated state officials. OR. REV. STAT. § 540.150 (1999); WASH. REV. CODE ANN. § 90.03.390 (West 1992); WYO. STAT. ANN. § 41–3–612 (2001). Rotation plans are sometimes imposed by court order, typically where there is not enough water to permit simultaneous use by all parties. What special circumstances would induce a court in an appropriation state to depart from the strict application of priorities and impose rotation among competing users? Compare Hufford v. Dye, 162 Cal. 147, 121 P. 400 (1912), with Cundy v. Weber, 68 S.D. 214, 300 N.W. 17 (1941). Is rotation a potential solution to the problems posed in *Crowley*, *supra* p. 190?

3. Exchange agreements are consensual arrangements for achieving greater flexibility and increased efficiency in the use of water rights. They typically are more complex than substituted supply or rotation arrangements. For instance, exchanges often involve water from two or more sources and do not normally involve the apportionment of water over a fixed time period. Exchange arrangements must avoid injury to other appropriators, both senior and junior to the parties to the exchange. See, *e.g.*, WYO. STAT. ANN. § 41–3–106(d) (2001). Some statutes authorizing exchanges require reductions in the exchanged rights to compensate for losses from seepage and evaporation. See COLO. REV. STAT. §§ 37–83–101 to 105 (2000); N.M. STAT. ANN. § 72–5–26 (1997). Despite the existence of a valid exchange agreement, the parties are limited to the amount they can beneficially use at any given time; in other words, a senior may not be able to transfer all of its "paper" rights, if some of them are deemed "surplus." Johnston v. Little Horse Creek Irrigation Co., 13 Wyo. 208, 79 P. 22 (1904).

4. A thoughtful discussion of the issues surrounding out-of-priority use is Lawrence J. MacDonnell, Out-of-Priority Water Use: Adding Flexibility to the Water Appropriation System, 83 Neb.L.Rev. 485 (2004).

Harrison C. Dunning, The "Physical Solution" in Western Water Law

57 U.Colo.L.Rev. 445, 448, 458–61, 472–74, 477–78 (1986).

* * *

My objective in this article is to examine an approach to promoting optimal utilization while protecting established rights which I shall call the "physical solution." The term comes from twentieth-century California cases, but the practice, under one label or another, is found in several western states. In Utah and New Mexico, a comparable but narrower term is "right of replacement," while Colorado uses "substitute supply" and, more generally, the "plan for augmentation." In these states and others in the West, the idea is the same: in appropriate circumstances, a court or agency may (or, some say, *must*) compel a senior right holder to accept a substituted source of water or a modification of his means of diversion, distribution or use of water at a junior right holder's expense in order to benefit the junior and to achieve better overall utilization of the resource. As the pace of large-scale water development projects in the West slows, and as we are increasingly forced to look to mechanisms other than new water supply projects to balance supply and demand, the physical solution will likely become ever more important in western water law.

* * *

III. The Theory of the Physical Solution

* * * The courts which have approved physical solutions have done so on two different bases. The earliest was to ground the concept on principles of equity appropriate to the granting of injunctive relief. But in this century the courts have more often derived the basis for the physical solution from the practical necessities of the arid West. * * *

A. *Equity as a Basis for Physical Solutions*

An early example of physical-solution doctrine rooted in equity is *Montecito Valley Water Company v. City of Santa Barbara.*[66] There the water company, an appropriator, diverted flow from a creek in order to sell water to the inhabitants of Montecito. Subsequently Santa Barbara and others put tunnels in lands adjacent to the creek in order to collect water for delivery to other service areas. This water was percolating groundwater, a part of which was tributary to the stream.

On the assumption that the tributary water belonged to the water company, the court in *Montecito Valley* noted that an injunction against those operating the tunnels might be appropriate. It then stated, however, the conventional proposition that injunctive relief should be granted only if no other relief was adequate. In light of several factors present, the court observed that if the junior could make good to the senior the amount of

66. 144 Cal. 578, 77 P. 1113 (1904).

water diverted from the stream, then "the judgment, in common equity, should provide accordingly."

* * *

B.   Necessity and the Policy of Optimal Utilization

Another judicial approach to the physical solution doctrine has been to refer to the necessity in the arid West of promoting the optimal utilization of water. An early decision from Utah is illustrative.[73] Salt Lake City and others, senior appropriators from Utah Lake, protested an application to appropriate water from the lake. The protest was overruled by the state engineer, and the seniors brought suit. Their complaint alleged in part that further diversion from the shallow lake would interfere with the pumps which assisted in their diversions.

In affirming the overruling of the protests, the Supreme Court of Utah relied on Utah authority which permits an appropriator by condemnation to acquire a right to the use of the ditches or means of diversion of a prior water user.[74] It reasoned that, given this authority, "the right to apply to a beneficial use water which cannot be so applied without in some way affecting prior rights, where such rights may nevertheless be protected and maintained, cannot well be questioned."[75] The applicant could appropriate, but he would either have to cause water to flow to the seniors' pumping plant "as now constructed" or to pay any additional pumping costs his diversion imposed on them.[76]

In linking physical solutions to statutorily granted authority for a private person to condemn property needed for the impoundment, distribution or drainage of water, the Utah court clearly was grounding itself ultimately on the necessities of the West. * * *

V.   SOME PHYSICAL SOLUTION ISSUES

A.   Hydrological and Legal Uncertainty

Physical solutions are one way a system of water law can respond to the inflexibility which is possible when rules are laid down to protect established property rights in water. Physical solutions are designed to provide an acceptable combination of security for seniors and opportunity for juniors. However, they must themselves be designed to be flexible. It would be ironic and unfortunate if a tool designed to accommodate change became itself a barrier to change.

* * *

73. Salt Lake City v. Gardner, 39 Utah 30, 114 P. 147 (1911).

74. Nash v. Clark, 27 Utah 158, 75 P. 371 (1904), aff'd, 198 U.S. 361 (1905). That decision refers to several statutory provisions in Utah on this type of condemnation.

75. Salt Lake City v. Gardner, 39 Utah 30, 45, 114 P. 147, 152.

76. Id. at 48, 114 P. at 153.

* * * [I]t should be accepted that the essence of the plan is a continuing obligation on the part of the junior to protect the senior if the junior wishes to continue to have favorable access to water. The form of that protection should be able to change over time. It should be permissible to substitute new sources of replacement water for old sources, or it should be possible to give the senior less replacement water, if he can enjoy equivalent benefits because of improvements in the way the water is distributed and used.

To require seniors to rely upon performance of a continuing obligation on the part of juniors obviously exposes the seniors to some degree of risk. The seniors must then look first to the juniors for their water, not to the source. As pointed out long ago by a Utah judge objecting to a physical solution,[155] the situation is one ripe for litigation. And as a practical matter seniors are entitled * * * to wonder how successful they would be, in the event of augmentation plan defaults, in eliminating injurious pumping by thousands of junior wells. To the extent that physical solutions allow new water development to take place, they obviously increase the pressure on a limited resource. They consequently increase the possible difficulties of the earliest resource users, who seek to protect their favored positions.

* * *

B. *Complexity of Administration*

* * *

In practice, tremendous uncertainty often exists as to just how upstream use affects the downstream availability of water. Decisions may turn on computer modeling more than anything else in many situations, and the "physical solution" or "plan for augmentation" may be nothing more than a name lawyers use for an agreed-to state of uncertainty. In such circumstances some of the assumptions made by the computer modelers are bound to prove inaccurate and some seniors are likely to be injured. When this happens, it is unlikely anyone will try to put Humpty–Dumpty together again and restore to the injured seniors their original priority. Prior appropriation in those cases will likely be replaced with a system much more akin to equitable apportionment.

C. *The Need for an Adequate Statutory Foundation*

Physical solution doctrine in the West is rooted in conventional equitable concepts and in notions of necessity drawn from the region's arid condition. Courts have alluded to or developed ideas about physical solutions in a number of cases, and, as explained above, a few states have given some statutory expression to the idea. But no state has provided a fully adequate statutory foundation for physical solutions. Until each western

---

155. "What the plaintiffs need, and they are entitled to, is not a lawsuit, but the use of the waters appropriated by them more than a quarter of a century ago." Salt Lake City v. Gardner, 39 Utah 30, 59, 114 P. 147, 157 (1911) (Straup, J., dissenting). The same point was made in Board of Directors v. Jorgensen, 64 Idaho 538, 136 P.2d 461, 475 (1943) (Givens, J., dissenting).

state does so, it is unlikely that the large potential contribution of physical solutions will be fully realized.

An adequate physical solution statute would apply to all users of water, whether they be appropriators, riparians, holders of contractual rights to water or something else. If the objective is to increase efficiency and reduce waste in the use of the West's limited developed water supply, neither the basis of the senior entitlement nor that of the junior seeking to improve or initiate a use matters. What does matter is that the senior have reasonable security in obtaining needed water and that the junior be allowed to be innovative in taking care of his own needs while protecting the senior against unreasonable injury.

Cache LaPoudre Water Users Ass'n v. Glacier View Meadows

Supreme Court of Colorado, 1976.
191 Colo. 53, 550 P.2d 288.

■ GROVES, JUSTICE.

The applicant Glacier View Meadows, a limited partnership, is a developer of residential lots in the mountains northwest of Fort Collins, Colorado. It filed with the water court two applications for approval of a plan of augmentation. The plans would provide future owners of presently unimproved lots with domestic water from wells to be drilled in the future.
* * *

The objector, North Poudre Irrigation Company, is a ditch and reservoir company. The objector, Cache LaPoudre Water Users Association, is a nonprofit protective association, whose members own substantial reservoir and direct flow decrees on the Cache LaPoudre River.

* * *

The applicant owns 75 "preferred shares" of the Mountain and Plains Irrigation Company, which entitle applicant to both reservoir and direct flow water. Applicant acquired these 75 shares from Ideal Cement Company, Dreher Pickle Company and City of Fort Collins, which historically had made year-around use of their water. Under the plan some of applicant's reservoir rights will be used to replace consumptively used water from proposed wells. The water from the wells will be exclusively devoted to in-house, residential domestic use. Under the two applications which are the subject of the court's decree, there will be a maximum of 1892 single-family residential units. In some cases, one well will furnish water for more than one unit.

The reservoirs containing replacement water and the points of discharge of water therefrom into the stream, as well as all of the residential units and the points of return flow therefrom into the stream, lie above the points of diversion of any water of the objectors.

* * *

Of the 1892 units, at ultimate development 105 units are expected to use an evapotranspiration system of sewage disposal. The consumptive use for these 105 units will be 100% of the water diverted from wells. This 100% will be replaced entirely by reservoir water plus enough to account for evaporative losses during transportation in the stream.

The remaining 1787 units, when ultimately developed, will have septic-soil absorption sewage systems. From these latter diversions there will be a consumptive use of not more than 10% and at least 90% will constitute return flow to the stream. Replacement water for the 10%, plus an amount sufficient to embrace transportation losses, will be replenished by the aforementioned releases from the reservoirs.

The rate of flow permitted and claimed for each well will be four gallons per minute for each dwelling unit to be served by any well. The plan is predicated upon the assumption that each dwelling unit will be occupied by 3.5 persons 365 days a year, and that each person will require 80 gallons of well water per day. The entire consumptive use of well water (including those units having 100% consumptive use) will not exceed 89 acre feet per year. 55 of applicant's 75 shares will be devoted to replacement of this consumptively used water. 55 shares represent an amount of 94.71 acre feet per year. After deducting 5% for transportation losses, 89.97 feet remain for replacement.

* * *

As mentioned earlier, the applicant acquired the 75 shares from Ideal Cement Company, Dreher Pickle Company and the City of Fort Collins. Historically, only 25% of the water used by these three returned to the stream. The plan allocates the water from 20 of the 75 shares of stock for use in the stream in lieu of the 25% return flow which no longer exists.

The return flow from these three sources was obtained for each month of the year, being an annual aggregate of 31.29 acre feet. The decree fixes the discharges of reservoir water into the stream, representing this return flow plus transportation losses and other factors, on a daily basis for each month, thereby assuring more than the historic return flow from the three sources. Using a factor of 30 days per month, we convert the monthly figures into an aggregate annual amount of 34.2 acre feet per year. The decree fixes a maximum for this purpose of 34.44. Within this limitation the Division Engineer may use his discretion in "aggregating" the releases for more efficient administration.

We find no mention of the subject in the record or the briefs, but assume that the replacement of return flow from the three sources just discussed is based upon the ultra-conservative view that the matter is treated as if the water represented by the 75 shares had been transported out of the water shed with no return flow or that such water was entirely consumptively used if devoted for some other purposes in the water shed.

* * *

It is contemplated by the plan that, so long as its provisions are followed, there will be no injury to the holders of prior rights. However, if there is a call by a right superior to the association's priority rights, that call must be met. The water court concluded that the only thing that will upset the plan will be an extended period of drought. If such a drought causes insufficient water to be available for replacement, the well water users will be obliged to acquire additional water by lease or otherwise, or else to reduce their consumptive use, to the end that water consumptively used under the plan will not exceed that available for replacement.

* * *

The principal argument of the objectors is that, except during flood stages, the Cache LaPoudre River is over-appropriated. With this we agree. *Hall v. Kuiper*, 181 Colo. 130, 510 P.2d 329 (1973). The argument continues that, unless there is 100% replacement of the water taken from the wells, senior water rights will be injured and there will be a violation of the Water Right Determination and Administration Act of 1969 (section 37–92–101 *et seq.*, C.R.S.1973, hereinafter called the "Act"), and the rules and regulations of the State Engineer's office.

* * *

Further, it is argued, the reservoir water held in storage in the Cache LaPoudre Basin has been used historically so that, after use (presumably irrigation), 50% returns to the stream. The result is that the reservoir water, used under the plan for replacement of well water consumptively used, is 100% consumptively used with none thereof returning to the stream; and the result is that injury results to senior rights.

* * *

The objectors' assertion that there must be 100% replacement of withdrawn well water brings us to the major subject of the case: Is this plan of augmentation valid?

* * *

Except as specifically noted, we find that the plan of augmentation has been formulated and approved consonant with, and in furtherance of, the purpose and intent of our recent statutes; and that the plan is valid.

We hold here, and in the companion opinion announced contemporaneously with this one, Kelly Ranch v. Southeastern Colorado Water Conservancy District, Colo., 550 P.2d 297 (1976), that under the plans for augmentation involved water is available for appropriation when the diversion thereof does not injure holders of vested rights.

Objectors cite *Southeastern Colorado Water Conservancy District v. Shelton Farms*, 187 Colo. 181, 529 P.2d 1321 (1974), in which this court ruled that one, who cuts down water-consuming vegetation (phreatophytes) along the Arkansas River, does not have a right to a decree for an equivalent amount of water to that consumed by the vegetation, free of the call of the river. * * * *Shelton Farms* involved a factual situation which makes it distinguishable from this and *Kelly Ranch, supra.* * * *

There, the senior rights had adjusted to the loss of the water caused by the growth of phreatophytes; and, once returned to the river, the water would still belong to the senior users in satisfaction of their decrees. In the instant case, the water to be used in replacement never was that of the senior users. Here, there is not displacement *"from the time and place of their need."* Under the findings here, the stream will be the same, irrespective of the well diversions.

Under the circumstances of this case, there is no significant difference between the prior appropriation doctrine, and the lack of injury doctrine. Here, where senior users can show no injury by the diversion of water, they cannot preclude the beneficial use of water by another. *Fellhauer, supra,* was cited as authority in *Shelton Farms.* It is likewise authority here. As was there said, "As administration of water approaches its second century the curtain is opening upon the new drama of *maximum utilization* and how constitutionally that doctrine can be integrated into the law of *vested rights."*

We rule that, in a matter such as this one, water is available for appropriation if the taking thereof does not cause injury. Therefore, the argument of the objectors, to the effect that water withdrawn from the wells must be replaced 100%, falls.

* * *

The next argument of the objectors is that the applicant's reservoir water historically has been used so that 50% thereof has returned to the stream. The argument continues that, since applicant's reservoir water is being used to replace water which has been 100% consumptively used, the usual 50% is not being permitted to return to the stream. If the applicant has answered this, its response is oblique, to say the least. The plain and simple answer is that the reservoir water which the applicant acquired historically had been used in such a way that only 25% of that water returned to the stream after use. As has been already set forth, the applicant is returning all of this 25% flow, plus transportation losses, directly to the stream. The reservoir water used for replacement of well water consumptively used is in addition to the replacement of the 25%. It is clear that there has been no infringement upon the historic return flow to the stream.

NOTES

1. When plans for augmentation involve changes in type and place of use, the timing of water use, as in the principal case, may also change significantly. This makes administration of the plan a matter of critical importance in protecting vested rights. In *Glacier View Meadows,* the trial court on remand approved the plan and granted considerable discretion to the state engineer in managing the release of replacement water into the stream. It noted that well diversions would be limited by restrictive covenants and the terms of the individual well permits, and that the groundwater withdrawals assumed by the plan for augmentation were higher than those projected by the evidence, thus assuring a margin of safety. The water court also commented that:

> Inherent in the hydrological and geological analysis upon which the plan for augmentation herein is founded, is a degree of uncertainty, but the uncertainty is no greater than that inherent in the administration of water rights generally and is not of great significance. The assumptions upon which the plan is based allow more than adequate latitude. If the plan for augmentation is operated in accordance with the detailed conditions herein, it will have the effect of replacing water in the stream at the times and places and in the amounts of the depletions caused by the development's use of water. As a result, the underground water to be diverted by the development wells, which would otherwise be considered as appropriated and unavailable for use, will now be available for appropriation without adversely affecting vested water rights or decreed conditional water rights on the South Platte River or its tributaries.

In re Application of Glacier View Meadows for Water Rights in Larimer County, Nos. W–7438 and W–7629 (Colo. Dist. Ct., Water Div. No. 1, Oct. 6, 1976).

2. The plan for augmentation concept was introduced into Colorado water law by the Water Right Determination and Administration Act of 1969. The Act defines a plan:

> "Plan for augmentation" means a detailed program to increase the supply of water available for beneficial use in a division or portion thereof by the development of new or alternate means or points of diversion, by a pooling of water resources, by water exchange projects, by providing substitute supplies of water, by the development of new sources of water, or by any other appropriate means. "Plan for augmentation" does not include the salvage of tributary waters by the eradication of phreatophytes, nor does it include the use of tributary water collected from land surfaces that have been made impermeable, thereby increasing the runoff but not adding to the existing supply of tributary water.

COLO. REV. STAT. § 37–92–103(9) (2008).

Compare the definition offered by a leading Colorado water lawyer: "Plans for augmentation, a word of art for using a little surface water to divert a larger amount of ground water, became a classic Colorado compromise which both accommodated and restrained the use of wells and surface rights through traditional court proceedings." D. Monte Pascoe, *Plans and Studies: The Recent Quest for a Utopia in the Utilization of Colorado's Water Resources,* 55 U. Colo. L. Rev. 391, 399 (1984).

Plans for augmentation have become an increasingly important means of facilitating development where supplies are fully appropriated. The importance of plans of augmentation is underscored by Empire Lodge Homeowners' Association v. Moyer, 39 P.3d 1139 (Colo.2001), which holds that a water user who made out-of-priority diversions without a plan of augmentation does not have standing to protect its diversions by invoking either the futile call or the enlargement doctrines. Prior to 1977, preliminary plans could be approved by the state engineer but now a plan is submitted to a referee and then reviewed by the water court. COLO. REV. STAT. § 37–92–301 (2000). The state engineer's office is limited to administering the court-approved plans, although it is directed to "exercise the broadest latitude possible in the administration of waters under their jurisdiction to encourage and develop augmentation plans * * * to allow continuance of existing uses and to assure maximum beneficial utilization of the waters of this state." COLO. REV. STAT. § 37–92–501.5 (2000).

3. A plan for augmentation is based on the same principles as a conventional water rights transfer, in that the proponent of a plan has the burden of establishing that vested or conditional rights will not be injured as a result of the plan. Thus, the court will limit augmentation sources to the former duty of water and historical use, and will protect juniors' rights to a continuation of stream conditions. Weibert v. Rothe Bros., Inc., 200 Colo. 310, 618 P.2d 1367 (1980). But the no-injury principle also allows plans that do not provide for replacement of 100 percent of the out-of-priority diversions so long as other water users are not harmed. Water Rights of Park County Sportsmen's Ranch LLP v. Bargas, 986 P.2d 262 (Colo.1999).

As in the principal case, plans for augmentation often involve well drilling, and are further discussed in that context in Chapter Six. Groundwater is not a necessary ingredient of a plan, however. Nor does a valid plan require the introduction of new water into the system. See Kelly Ranch v. Southeastern Colo. Water Conservancy Dist., 191 Colo. 65, 550 P.2d 297 (1976). No new water was to be introduced to the stream in *Glacier View Meadows*, and tributary groundwater was to be used to supply the new homes. Can such a plan truly result in "no injury" to existing users if more water is actually consumed from a fully appropriated stream?

4. What are the risks of drainage basin alteration with which the court was concerned? Unanticipated loss of use of runoff by senior appropriators? General ecosystem disruption?

c. Area of Origin Protection from Transfers

In the prior appropriation system, unlike the riparian system, there is no prohibition against moving water out of the watershed where it originates. Water rights are tied neither to the land nor to the watershed. Some of the earliest cases involved distant transfers, even to another drainage basin. See *Coffin v. Left Hand Ditch Co., supra* p. 71. Yet residents often resist removal of water from their region for use elsewhere. Are there equities or impacts that justify departing from the basic traditions of prior appropriation to inhibit transfers to another area or watershed? Recall our discussion of third-party impacts of transfers *supra* p. 237. Are there additional factors that come into play when water is transferred to another watershed?

National Research Council, National Academy of Sciences, Water Transfers in the West: Efficiency, Equity, and the Environment
257–59 (1992).

Water is not merely a commodity in the normal sense of the word but rather a resource held in common for all citizens, and this should be recognized in the processes used to evaluate water transfers. The interests of communities, local governments, individuals, and the environment in the areas from which water is proposed to be exported are not now adequately represented in the laws and policies of many western states. Communities hold strong values that support maintaining water within its natural watershed. For some, water is the basis of present and future economic vitality and environmental amenities; these values often are augmented by water-related social and cultural concerns and traditions. * * * [T]he threat to cultural values is illustrated dramatically in the case of the acequias of northern New Mexico.

State laws and policies often fail to recognize that when water is removed from its natural watershed a variety of economic, social, and environmental harms can occur. Prior appropriation law has never limited the use of water to the watershed in which it originates, and the committee does not recommend that water be constrained to its watershed of origin. However, states do need to ensure that the special problems caused the public by transbasin export are fully addressed before such transfers are permitted. Although basin-of-origin interests should not have veto power over transfers, their interests should be represented in the evaluation process, to the extent that those interests are important to society.

State tax laws often provide incentives for transfers because local taxing jurisdictions cannot impose taxes or in lieu payments, and these incentives could be revised to address the equities of reallocation. Municipalities and certain quasi-public water utilities that purchase or lease water supplies or build and operate works to use water supplies from outside their service areas ordinarily pay no property taxes to local governments in areas of origin because of intergovernmental immunity from taxation. In addition, western states usually provide by law that private entities may be taxed on the value of water facilities only by the county where the water is used. The inability to tax facilities that dewater areas of origin compounds the disadvantages to the communities in these areas. For instance, states could revise their tax laws to make exporting entities bear a larger portion of the costs of mitigating the third party effects of transfers. Exporters could be subject to local property or other taxes. States might consider developing a transaction tax for water rights transfers. This transaction tax would be analogous to a severance tax and would be used to mitigate adverse environmental effects caused by transfers (interbasin as well as others). Setting the level of such a tax would require careful analysis so that desirable transfers are not discouraged but adequate revenues for mitigation are collected.

RECOMMENDATIONS:

• States and tribal governments should develop specific policies to guide water transfer approval processes regarding the community and environmental consequences of transferring water from one basin to another, because such transfers may have serious long-term consequences.

• Water transfer processes should formally recognize interests within basins of origin that are of statewide and regional importance, and these interests should be weighed when transbasin exports are being considered.

• Although each state or tribe should select the approach that suits its needs best, area-of-origin protection generally would include impact assessment, opportunities for all affected interests to be heard, regulatory mechanisms to help avoid adverse effects, compensation (e.g., financial payments or mitigation), and authority to deny a proposed transfer or water use involving a transbasin export if the effects are judged unacceptable.

• States should revise laws that now exempt water facilities from taxation by the county of origin either because the exporter is a public entity or because of provisions that make such facilities taxable only in the county where the water is used. Mechanisms to compensate communities for transfer-related losses of tax base, such as an annual payment in lieu of taxes, may be needed.

Colorado River Water Conservation Dist. v. Municipal Subdistrict, Northern Colorado Water Conservancy Dist.

Supreme Court of Colorado, 1979.
198 Colo. 352, 610 P.2d 81.

■ ERICKSON, JUSTICE.

The appellant, the Colorado River Water Conservation District (the River District), appeals from a conditional decree entered by the District Court, Water Division No. 5, which granted to the appellee, the Municipal Subdistrict, Northern Colorado Water Conservancy District (the Subdistrict) the conditional rights to the use of water to be exported from the natural basin of the Colorado River. In reaching its decision, the water court determined that the appellee was in compliance with the provisions of section 37–45–118(1)(b)(IV), C.R.S.1973 (hereafter subparagraph IV),[1]

---

1. The subparagraph in issue provides: "(IV) However, any works or facilities planned and designed for the exportation of water from the natural basin of the Colorado river and its tributaries in Colorado, by any district created under this article, shall be subject to the provisions of the Colorado river compact and the 'Boulder Canyon Project Act.' Any such works or facilities shall be designed, constructed and operated in such

which specifies certain requirements for trans-basin exportation of water by water conservancy districts and subdistricts thereof. * * *

A.   Timing of Plan Submission

The trial court determined that a plan in compliance with subparagraph IV need not be demonstrated at the time a claim for conditional water rights is decreed. Under the procedures set forth by the trial court, an applicant's obligation to demonstrate such a plan arises at a later stage in the appropriation process, at which time a "reasonable diligence" hearing is held to determine compliance with subparagraph IV.

We believe that the trial court's interpretation ignores the language and purpose of the statute, and therefore is erroneous. Subparagraph IV is a clear limitation upon the general powers of the water conservancy districts and subdistricts. It begins with the word "however" and conditions the grant of power to "take by appropriation ... water ... water rights ... and sources of water supply...." The intent of the General Assembly was to protect not only present appropriations but "in addition thereto prospective uses of water" within the natural basin of the Colorado River. The mechanism for accomplishing this is the submission of project plans detailing the design, construction and operation of facilities aimed at achieving these stated goals. To allow the required plan to be submitted at a later hearing would subvert the legislative intent of subparagraph IV, which is to obtain a definition and description of the plan in advance of the conditional decree during the early stages of the decree process. In addition, such a procedure would result in substantial expenditures of public funds between the time of the conditional decree and the hearing on reasonable diligence without assurance that the plan would protect the present and future appropriators within the natural basin of the Colorado River.

* * *

We * * * hold that in order to obtain a conditional decree a conservancy district or subdistrict must first comply with the statute "which gave it existence and which imposed conditions upon it before it could obtain such sought-for appropriation."

B.   Adequacy of the Subdistrict's Plan

The following plan was submitted by the Municipal Subdistrict:

1) The Windy Gap Water System will divert water from the upper drainage area of the Colorado River at Windy Gap and transport it back upstream to Granby Reservoir.

manner that the present appropriations of water, and in addition thereto prospective uses of water for irrigation and other beneficial consumptive use purposes, including consumptive uses for domestic, mining, and industrial purposes, within the natural basin of the Colorado river in the state of Colorado, from which water is exported, will not be impaired nor increased in cost at the expense of the water users within the natural basin. The facilities and other means for the accomplishment of said purpose shall be incorporated in and made a part of any project plans for the exportation of water from said natural basin in Colorado."

2) The existing facilities of the Colorado–Big Thompson Project will be used to transport the water from Granby Reservoir to the points of delivery for ultimate use on the Eastern Slope.

3) All diversions will be made strictly under the priority system, thus protecting all conditional and absolute water rights senior in priority to the Windy Gap Water System decrees.

4) Future uses of water in the natural basin of the Colorado River will be protected by:

i) bypassing 75 cubic feet per second of water or the run of the river, whichever is less, at all times at the Windy Gap Diversion Dam, and

ii) complete compliance by the Municipal Subdistrict with all of the terms and provisions of Senate Document 80 (which [describes facilities of the Colorado–Big Thompson federal reclamation project, analyzes prospective water uses, and] contains a finding that operation under its terms will not harm present or prospective uses of waters on the Western Slope) in the design, construction and operation of the Windy Gap Water System.

The water court determined that a plan in compliance with subparagraph IV need only be in "broad conceptual form" at the time of initiation of a conditional decree and accordingly declared the Subdistrict's plan to be adequate.

We hold that the plan did not comply with the statute which required that "[t]he facilities and other means for accomplishment of said purpose shall be incorporated in and made a part of any project plans for the exportation of water from said natural basin in Colorado." Section 37–45–118(1)(b)(IV), C.R.S. 1973.

The plan required by subparagraph IV must be at least as detailed as that necessary to document the elements of an appropriation. * * *

The requirement that a plan need only be in broad conceptual form impermissibly weakens these common law mandates. The purpose of demanding physical acts manifesting intent is to put others on notice as to the demand an appropriation will make upon the available water supply. Consistent with this theme, subparagraph IV was enacted to put in-basin users on notice as to the supply remaining after a proposed appropriation. As noted, the provision appears as a limitation on the otherwise general power to appropriate and must therefore be considered in a determination of whether the intent to appropriate exists in sufficiently specific form. The specificity mandated by subparagraph IV, then, is nothing short of a physical demonstration that any project works or facilities will be "designed, constructed and operated in such a manner that the present appropriations of water, and in addition thereto prospective uses of water ... within the natural basin of the Colorado river ... will not be impaired nor increased in cost at the expense of the water users within the natural basin."

* * *

Accordingly, we reverse and remand for further proceedings consistent with the directions contained in this opinion.

NOTES

1. The court insists not only that adequate compensatory storage facilities ultimately be built, but that they be planned in detail and demonstrated as adequate even before a conditional decree can be issued to divert water over the Continental Divide. Is this an overly technical reading of the statute? Are there practical reasons for the requirement?

2. Following the decision in the principal case, a settlement agreement was reached among the parties and many other interests. The Subdistrict agreed to pay up to $10 million for a western slope compensatory storage reservoir known as the Azure Reservoir. Other concessions were made, including the grant of storage space to a western slope water district in an existing western slope reservoir owned by the Northern Colorado Water Conservancy District. The Subdistrict also agreed to subordinate its rights to the western slope users' rights. Payments were also made to upgrade water treatment facilities and to study salinity problems. Does this type of agreement satisfy the requirement of "a physical demonstration that any project works will not impair or increase the cost of water in the basin?"

It is interesting that five years later the Subdistrict and the Colorado River Water Conservation District agreed that the Azure Project should not be pursued further. Instead, the Subdistrict agreed to pay $10.2 million to the district so that it could build a storage project of its choosing. The water court approved.

3. The compensatory storage requirement read into the conservancy district law in the principal case does not apply to transbasin diversions by Denver or other municipalities. Should it? Why have such protective legislation at all? If future western slope water uses are socially important, why not let the future users buy out senior users on the eastern slope?

4. If it is shown that there are projections for the western slope to grow from its present size (about 100,000 population) to over a million, should any exports be allowed under the statute?

5. The concept of compensatory storage embodied in the Colorado Conservancy District Act is based on an accord reached a few years before the Act was passed. The agreement was necessary to reconcile eastern and western slope interests that were to be affected by the Colorado–Big Thompson (CBT) Project. The Project was planned to take water from the upper reaches of the Colorado River and transport it across the Rocky Mountains to the northern Front Range. Negotiations resulted in a resolution that included several principles for transmountain diversion projects. One was that an "essential part" of such projects should be the "construction of a compensatory reservoir on the western slope of sufficient capacity to hold an amount of water equal to the amount to be annually diverted * * *." This and other principles were included in "Senate Document 80" mentioned in the principal case, which in turn was incorporated by reference in the CBT authorizing legislation. Accordingly, the 152,000 acre-foot Green Mountain Reservoir was built on the western slope as part of the CBT. The Bureau of Reclamation is still searching for purchasers of Green Mountain water; some fifty years after the reservoir's construction, the water remains virtually unused except for electric power generation.

6.   The National Water Commission's 1973 Report was critical of compensatory storage schemes in that they may cause "economic waste because the area of origin may not be prepared to use the compensatory storage for many years." National Water Commission, Water Policies For the Future 324 (1973). Given that future water demand projections will be uncertain (see State and National Water Use Trends To The Year 2000, A Report Prepared For the Congressional Research Service of the Library of Congress for the Committee on Environment and Public Works U.S. Senate, S. 96–12 (1980)), how should determinations about location, capacity, and use of compensatory storage projects be made?

NOTE: AREA OF ORIGIN PROTECTION

Area of origin protection statutes represent political responses to the effects of larger transbasin diversions and are a departure from the original prior appropriation doctrine, which placed no limits on where water could be used. Colorado's "compensatory storage" statute is only one means of protecting the basin of origin.

There are two main approaches. The first is to allocate future local rights so as to preempt exports. This method involves "informed guessing" in order to determine what the future demand will be. These guesses will invariably be wrong. Thus, the area may end up with too little water (at least from its perspective) and no chance of acquiring more because all the existing supplies are under long-term contracts. Or, the area may end up with more water than it needs and be reluctant to release this excess water for use elsewhere.

The second approach is to grant the area of origin a priority right to appropriate whatever water may become necessary for development when it is required. This allows water to be used in another basin until the basin of origin "needs" the water, at which point the basin of origin can recapture its water and invalidate transfer contracts. This method can lead to unsettling results for the holder of water contracts because there would be no guarantee of delivery. In addition, as a practical matter, it may be difficult for an area of origin to interrupt long-standing water deliveries in the importing area.

California's area of origin laws give the exporting area absolute priority to make future use of water over that of the importing area. One statute leaves for the county of origin all the water it may need for future development. Cal. Water Code §§ 10505–10505.5 (West 1992).[1]

1.   § 10505. Restrictions on release or assignment

Who makes the determination of when, and to what extent, water is "necessary for the development of the county"? The California statute provides that it shall be the Water Resources Control Board. This board is a quasi-judicial body set up to regulate water rights, water pollution and water quality control, whose five members are appointed by the Governor. The board is not subject to the California Administrative Procedure Act. Should a genuine dispute develop between, say, the Metropolitan Water District of Southern California (the main recipient of State Water Project water) and Butte County (north of Sacramento on the Feather River) as to the amount of water that has become "necessary for the development of [Butte County]," do you think that both the parties would accept the determination of the Water Resources Control Board as final? In view of the substantial interests involved, it is more likely that the losing party in the board's decision will press for legislative relief. What is the effect of the reapportionment cases on a political solution? Once water from the area of origin has been committed to use in another area, albeit temporarily, what is the effect on investments and plans for growth in the area of origin as opposed to the importing area? If the restrictions were put into the contracts on the calculated assumption that a situation requiring their use would never arise, why put them in at all?

Under the county of origin statute, only those counties in which the water "originates" are protected. This wording is construed to mean that counties are protected only to the extent that water actually originates, in the form of rain or snow, within their boundaries. This interpretation raises difficult problems for the foothill counties. In California, these counties usually receive minimal rainfall but have abundant water in the rivers that are fed by mountain runoff and snow melt. Thus, most of the water "originates" in mountainous counties which are usually too rugged for much development. The foothill counties, whose potential for development is often much greater, receive little protection for the abundant water presently flowing into them. This problem became urgent when the state decided to construct the massive Central Valley Project. To solve it, the legislature enacted the Watershed Protection Act as an integral part of the Central Valley Act of 1933. CAL. WATER CODE §§ 11460–11463 (West 1992).[2]

No priority under this part shall be released nor assignment made of any application that will, in the judgment of the board, deprive the county in which the water covered by the application originates of any such water necessary for the development of the county.

§ 10505.5 Territorial Restrictions on Use

Every application heretofore or hereafter made and filed pursuant to Section 10500, and held by the State Water Resources Control Board, shall be amended to provide, and any permit hereafter issued pursuant to such application, and any license issued pursuant

to such a permit, shall provide, that the application, permit, or license shall not authorize the use of any water outside of the county of origin which is necessary for the development of the county.

2. § 11460. Prior right to watershed water

In the construction and operation by the department of any project under the provisions of this part a watershed or area wherein water originates, or an area immediately adjacent thereto which can conveniently be supplied with water therefrom, shall not be deprived by the department directly or indirectly of the prior right to all of the water

The main idea of the Watershed Protection Act was to extend source area water priorities to the entire watershed area and not limit them to the areas of precipitation. This obviously grants some relief to the foothill areas, as these are almost always included in "the region or area which contributes to the supply of the stream in question." 25 Ops. Cal. Atty. Gen. 8, 19 (1955). The proviso that the "article shall not be so construed as to create any new property rights * * * "precludes the board from assigning water rights to an area based on a determination of its potential need. All that is granted is a priority to water users in the area so that when they require more water, they can "recapture" the water from any other non-watershed user. The statute ran into some unusual difficulties. It was enacted in 1933 and was meant to apply to the state's Central Valley Project (CVP). The Depression was, however, well underway and the state was unable to finance the project. The federal government took over the CVP in 1935 and by 1940 was deeply involved in the water business in California. It was nevertheless assumed that the county of origin and watershed protection acts were still effective because § 8 of the Reclamation law purported on its face to apply state (rather than federal) law. We examine the validity of this assumption and the present status of the protection statutes in connection with California v. United States, *infra* p. 818.

Area of origin protection was always an issue in appropriation applications from the Sierra foothills, but until recently, the statutes were not a constraint on water use. However, California law is changing. El Dorado Irrigation Dist. v. State Water Resources Control Board, 142 Cal.App.4th 937, 48 Cal.Rptr.3d 468, 496–499 (3 Dist. 2006). held that the California Water Resources Control Board could not condition the assignment of a state appropriation with a 1927 priority to a water district by requiring the district to curtail its diversions whenever the Bureau of Reclamation or the State Water Project released stored water to meet the Sacramento–San Joaquin Bay Delta water quality standards, when similar conditions were

reasonably required to adequately supply the beneficial needs of the watershed, area, or any of the inhabitants or property owners therein.

In no other way than by purchase or otherwise as provided in this part shall water rights of a watershed, area, or the inhabitants be impaired or curtailed by the department, but the provisions of this article shall be strictly limited to the acts and proceedings of the department, as such, and shall not apply to any persons or state agencies.

§ 11462. Creation of new property rights

The provisions of this article shall not be so construed as to create any new property rights other than against the department as provided in this part or to require the depart-

ment to furnish to any person without adequate compensation therefor any water made available by the construction of any works by the department.

§ 11463. Exchange of watershed water

In the construction and operation by the department of any project under the provisions of this part, no exchange of the water of any watershed or area for the water of any other watershed or area may be made by the department unless the water requirements of the watershed or area in which the exchange is made are first and at all times met and satisfied to the extent that the requirements would have been met were the exchange not made, and no right to the use of water shall be gained or lost by reason of any such exchange.

not imposed on junior water rights holders. The trial judge also held that the condition violated the area of origin statutes because it protected project exports at the expense of a foothill county. The court held that the area of origin statutes limit the Bureau and the State of California but do not apply to the Board's administration of water rights. It further held that Cal. Water Code § 11462, which provides that the California Department of Water Resources is not required to provide free project water to counties in the watershed of origin, means that "although El Dorado may be entitled to assert a priority under section 11460 over the Bureau and Department to the diversion of water originating in the watershed of the South Fork American River, it does *not* extend to water the projects have properly diverted to storage at an earlier date. If El Dorado wants water properly stored by the projects, it must pay for it." 48 Cal.Rptr.3d at 498. State Water Resources Control Board Cases, 136 Cal.App.4th 674, 39 Cal.Rptr.3d 189, 255–266 (3 Dist. 2006) considered the argument that the Delta Water Plan, which allows water to be withdrawn from New Melones Reservoir on the Stanislaus River for salinity maintenance, violates Section 11460. The court rejected the Board's argument, based on 25 Ops.CalAtty.Gen. 8 (1955), that the statute created only inchoate rights and thus did not apply to a user who has or seeks a contract with the Bureau of Reclamation. "Nothing in the statute itself imposes such a limitation . . ." 39 Cal.Rptr.3d at 256. Thus, an existing contract holder can object to any agency action that reduces the user's allotment for the benefit of uses outside the area of origin. However, the court held that (1) the Delta is in the area of origin for water from the Stanislaus River and (2) the Act "does not establish a preference for any particular use of water within the area of origin, such as irrigation or municipal use, over other uses such as the protection and enhancement of water quality." Id. *El Dorado* was applied in Phelps v. State Water Resources Control Board, 157 Cal.App.4th 89, 68 Cal.Rptr.3d 350 (3 Dist. 2007) (Delta salinity releases are being used "to supply the beneficial needs of the area of origin" and thus § 11140 does not preclude the issuance of water rights conditioned on no diversions of water needed for Delta protection).

Problem: A stream flows through two mountain counties before entering the Central Valley. There are two private diverters, 1 and 2, that use the water within the watershed and a diversion, 3, by the State of California to supply a project that is subject to area of origin restrictions. The three diverters use all the available supply during low flow periods. A fourth diverter petitions the State Water Resources Control Board for a diversion to supply a second home development within the watershed of the stream. What are the respective priorities among the four diverters? See Ronald B. Robie & Russell R. Kletzing, *Area of Origin Statutes—The California Experience*, 15 Idaho L. Rev. 419, 435–36 (1979).

For a discussion of other area of origin protection approaches, see Gary D. Weatherford, *Legal Aspects of Interregional Water Diversion*, 15 UCLA L. Rev. 1299, 1313 (1968); Lawrence J. MacDonnell & Charles W. Howe, *Area-of-Origin Protection in Transbasin Water Diversions: An Evaluation of Alternative Approaches*, 57 U. Colo. L. Rev. 527 (1986).

CHAPTER FIVE

Shared Public and Private Use of Waters

As shown in the preceding chapters, the primary function of water law has been to set the ground rules for the acquisition of private rights to use water and to adjust relationships among users. Although water is often characterized as a public resource, or even "property" of the public, the state or public interest in waters has usually been expressed as a regulatory rather than proprietary function. California's water code declares that the state owns all waters in trust for the people, but it has been held that unless the state follows the same procedures that a private party must follow to obtain a water right, it has no "ownership" of any water in the state. California v. Riverside Superior Court, 78 Cal.App.4th 1019, 93 Cal.Rptr.2d 276, 283–84 (2000) (state not a property owner and thus an "owned property" exclusion cannot be invoked by its insurer to avoid indemnification for state superfund liability).

Private rights to use waters are, however, created by state laws. These are property rights, but water rights are necessarily incomplete because the interests of other users and the public generally are integral elements of the right. The necessity to accommodate other users demonstrates one way in which property rights in water are incomplete. See *In re* Water Use Permit Applications, 94 Haw. 97, 9 P.3d 409 (2000) *infra* p. 434. Water use has always been regulated, and historically the purpose has been to limit individual users to make more water available for other, similarly situated users. This type of regulation has been generally accepted. Because of the physical nature of water, all water rights—riparian or appropriative—are correlative; the use of water must be shared among a wide class of claimants and water rights have a greater dimension of non-exclusivity compared to rights to land or to personal property.

Water rights are also incomplete because some stream and lake waters are considered public, and the use of these waters, and the submerged lands underlying navigable waters, is dedicated to the public. As a result, states may have proprietary—not merely regulatory—rights to the beds for the benefit of the general public, and private water rights owners along these waterways may be subject to greater restrictions on the use of these waters, and on use of the underlying stream and lake beds as compared to "dry" land.

The boundary between private rights and state regulation and between private and public rights is often contested and uncertain. However, the distinction between public and private waters has a long history that can be traced back to Roman law and perhaps earlier. See Eugene F. Ware, Roman Water Law (reprint 1985) (1905). Likewise, there is a long history of state control over water use to promote the public interest. The public interest in water is increasing as more attention is being given to conservation and to restoration of aquatic ecosystems and their watersheds. These restrictions are expressed in new regulations and through the expanded recognition of the proprietary rights of governments.

This chapter explores the sources and scope of public and private rights to use the surface of waterways and submerged lands, the extent to which private rights are burdened with a public trust servitude and other limitations, as well as the constitutional limitations on state regulation of water use.

A.   THE PUBLIC TRUST IN NAVIGABLE WATERS

1.   PUBLIC OWNERSHIP OF BEDS

Everyone who has ever waited for a boat to pass under a drawbridge has seen the oldest public right—navigation—in action. Throughout most of recorded European history, the most important uses of rivers and lakes have been commercial navigation and fishing. This partly explains why public rights have often been bound up with the question of whether a waterbody is navigable. Navigability can be an elusive concept and one can question why state power to limit water or land use should be tied to this standard, especially today as rivers are valued for their public recreational and beneficial ecosystem services regardless of their navigable capacity. Nonetheless, the question of whether or not a river or lake is "navigable" is the legal starting point to decide questions such as bed ownership and whether the overlying waters must be shared between riparians and the general public.

The continuing importance of navigability as well as limitations on the concept are shown by Lehigh Falls Fishing Club v. Andrejewski, 735 A.2d 718 (Pa.Super.1999). A private fishing club sought to bar fishing by non-members on a stretch of the Lehigh River along which it leased land. Dictum in an 1826 case listed the Lehigh as one of the state's navigable rivers along with the Ohio, Monongahela, Allegheny, Susquehanna, Delaware, and others. The Fishing Club proved that an 1874 edition of the 1826 case reports omitted the Lehigh from the list of rivers, that the 1874 edition is the only available edition of the 1826 decision, and that the stretch of the river in question was not in fact navigable. The court rejected these arguments because the precedent had been consistently followed by courts and thus the actual navigability of the river was irrelevant:

> [T]he Lehigh River has been determined to be a navigable river by our Supreme Court. Regardless of the age of the precedent, it is precedent. See *Poor v. McClure*, 77 Pa. 214 (1874) (indicating that once the

question of a waterway's navigability has been determined by the Court, the issue is settled).

* * *

Appellant correctly notes that the test for navigability is whether a river is navigable in fact. It then points to the considerable evidence that it presented regarding the depth and navigability of the portion of the Lehigh River located through its land. It presents compelling argument, based on evidence provided from engineers, that it is not possible, in fact, to navigate the Lehigh River between the Francis E. Walter Dam and a waterfall located upriver from its land.

However, we cannot piecemeal by piecemeal re-examine the navigability of an acknowledged public waterway. The relevant case law necessarily is old since the issue of what rivers are public rivers became important early in the history of our Commonwealth. The Lehigh River unquestionably historically has been considered by our Supreme Court as a navigable, public waterway. Since Appellant's land is on the Lehigh River, the public has the right to fish on the portion of the river located through its land.

Id. at 722.

The navigability of a stream determines two linked questions: (1) the ownership of the bed of the stream or lake, and (2) how private and public uses are allocated. It may also determine whether the river is subject to federal jurisdiction. See *infra* p. 802. We start with the first question.

a. Ancient Origins of Public Ownership

The ownership of the submerged beds of navigable waters has been worked out by a long series of Supreme Court precedents. These precedents drew on a relatively brief but confusing British history. English law evolved from the late sixteenth through the eighteenth century, largely as a result of Henry VIII's break with Rome. Many lands became available to the Crown through forfeiture, and the question of the Crown's right to rivers and seashores became increasingly important. English law initially posited that "[e]very navigable river, so high as the sea flows and ebbs into it, is a royal river, and belongs to the King by his prerogative." The Case of the Royal Fishery of Banne, 80 Eng. Rep. 540 (K.B. 1611). The King's prerogative ownership, which is discussed below, meant that the public had a right to use the land and fisheries and any grants that limited public use had to be express. Dale D. Goble and Eric T. Freyfogle, Wildlife Law 278 (2002). See also Eric T. Freyfogle, *Ethics, Community, and Private Land*, 23 Ecology L.Q. 631 (1996). United States courts used this history first to determine ownership of the beds of navigable waters and then to create the modern public trust doctrine.

Because the Crown of England claimed title to the beds of navigable waters, the first question is whether the federal government or the states are the successors to this prerogative. As between the federal government and the states, title to the beds underlying navigable waters is vested in the states:

> For when the Revolution took place, the people of each state became themselves sovereign; and in that character hold the absolute right to all their navigable waters and soil under them for their own common use, subject only to rights since surrendered by the Constitution to the general government.

Martin v. Waddell, 41 U.S. 367, 410, 10 L.Ed. 997 (1842).

Martin v. Waddell was a conflict between two patentees, both claiming exclusive rights to cultivate oysters in the tidelands of Raritan Bay, New Jersey. One claimed under the patent from the King of England to the Duke of York establishing a colony in New Jersey. His theory was that the Crown owned the tidelands and held them in trust for the public for certain purposes and the Crown could grant title to tidelands subject to the trust, but the patent to the Duke of York conveyed the tidelands in question with an exclusive right of fishery. This theory was adopted by Justice Thompson, dissenting, but the Supreme Court (by Chief Justice Taney) held to the contrary:

> And in deciding a question like this, we must not look merely to the strict technical meaning of the words of the letters patent.
>
> * * * The object in view appears upon the face of them. They were made for the purpose of enabling the Duke of York to establish a colony upon the newly discovered continent, to be governed, as nearly as circumstances would permit, according to the laws and usages of England; and in which the duke, his heirs and assigns, were to stand in the place of the king, and administer the government according to the principles of the British constitution. * * * And the people who were to plant this colony, and to form the political body over which he was to rule, were subjects of Great Britain, accustomed to be governed according to its usages and laws.
>
> It is said by Hale in his Treatise de Jure Maris, Harg. Law Tracts, 11, when speaking of the navigable waters, and the sea on the coasts within the jurisdiction of the British crown, "that although the king is the owner of this great coast, and, as a consequent of his propriety, hath the primary right of fishing in the sea and creeks, and arms thereof, yet the common people of England have regularly a liberty of fishing in the sea, or creeks, or arms thereof, as a public common of piscary, and may not, without injury to their right, be restrained of it, unless in such places, creeks, or navigable rivers, where either the king of some particular subject hath gained a propriety exclusive of that common liberty."
>
> The principle here stated by Hale, as to "the public common of piscary" belonging to the common people of England, is not questioned by any English writer upon that subject. The point upon which different opinions have been expressed, is whether since Magna Charta, "either the king or any particular subject can gain a propriety

exclusive of the common liberty." For, undoubtedly rights of fishery, exclusive of the common liberty, are at this day held and enjoyed by private individuals under ancient grants. But the existence of a doubt as to the right of the king to make such a grant after Magna Charta, would of itself show how fixed has been the policy of that government on this subject for the last six hundred years; and how carefully it has preserved this common right for the benefit of the public.

Id. at 411–12.

b. *Navigability for Title*

A body of case law has developed to define "navigability." The Supreme Court rejected a rule attributed to English common law that limited Crown ownership to navigable waters that were affected by the ebb and flow of the tides. Unlike in the British Isles many segments of major waterways are not affected by the tides. If tidal navigability had prevailed in the United States, the Great Lakes and the great inland river systems would not be subject to federal control. In 1851 the Court held that admiralty jurisdiction extended to non-tidal waters. Propeller Genesee Chief v. Fitzhugh, 53 U.S. 443, 13 L.Ed. 1058 (1851). In Barney v. Keokuk, 94 U.S. 324, 24 L.Ed. 224 (1876), *Genesee Chief* was applied to hold that the states owned the beds to non-tidal navigable waters.

Several old cases related to congressional power under the Commerce Clause, though whether a stream is navigable has little to do with congressional power today. Other cases deal with "the navigation servitude," which allows the federal government to diminish or destroy the value of land in aid of navigation.

The classic federal definition of navigability, which applied in the title cases, is derived from The Daniel Ball, 77 U.S. (10 Wall.) 557, 563, 19 L.Ed. 999 (1870):

Those rivers must be regarded as public navigable rivers in law which are navigable in fact when they are used, or are susceptible of being used, in their ordinary condition, as highways for commerce, over which trade and travel are or may be conducted in the customary modes of trade and travel on water. And they constitute navigable waters of the Unites States * * * when they form in their ordinary conditions by themselves or by uniting with other waters, a continued highway over which commerce is or may be carried on with states or foreign countries.

"Navigability for title" is a backward looking rule that allocates title to the beds of rivers and lakes based on the condition of the waterbody at statehood. There have been frequent title conflicts between states and the United States, and among the grantees of these sovereigns, over which sovereign could grant land ownership in the beds to private parties. The issue may arise where lands along a river were patented by the federal government to a homesteader or other private party. The question is whether the title includes the bed of the abutting river. Some cases have dealt with who (which sovereign or its grantees) can reap income from, say, oil wells drilled in a riverbed.

The navigability for title cases also inform the issue of public use rights because states are subject to limitations on their power to convey lands beneath navigable waters. States take these lands subject to the public trust. The issue of the power of states to sever land from the trust is discussed *infra* p. 416. Navigable waterways are subject to a public trust, and private rights in any such lands that are conveyed may be commensurately limited. In defining rights of public use and access, states have placed limits on owners of private lands underlying or abutting waterways, some of which waterways meet the federal definition of navigable for title and some of which do not. These state laws sometimes refer to "navigability" but this may have a different definition in laws enacted under the state's police power. Only those state laws or regulations that interfere with federally protected public uses or some constitutionally authorized federal activity are prohibited.

Johnson and Austin summarized the teaching of several U.S. Supreme Court cases that deal with navigability for title:

(2) Such navigability is determined by the natural and ordinary condition of the water at that time [statehood], not whether it could be made navigable by artificial improvements. However, the fact that rapids, rocks, or other obstructions make navigation difficult will not destroy title navigability so long as the waters were usable for a significant portion of the time.

(3) Navigability in intrastate commerce is all that is required, not usability in interstate commerce.

(4) The waters must be usable by the "customary modes of trade or travel on water." This may include waters usable for commercial log floating. This includes waters as little as three or four feet deep that are geographically located so they have been, or can be used by canoes and rowboats for commercial trade and travel (fur traders' canoes). This does not include waters which are difficult to access because of surrounding mud flats or the like, *and* which are geographically isolated from habitation and transportation routes, *and* which have never been and are not likely to be used for commercial trade or travel. This probably does not include waters that are geographically isolated from habitation and transportation routes and which have never been and are not likely to be used for commercial trade or travel, even though these waters are deep enough and large enough to float commercial type vessels, and are not physically inaccessible because of mud flats or the like.

Ralph W. Johnson and Russell A. Austin, Jr., *Recreational Rights and Titles to Beds on Western Lakes and Streams*, 7 Nat. Resources J. 1, 24–25 (1967).

In an important case, the Supreme Court held that the Great Salt Lake was navigable at the time Utah entered the Union. It applied the standard "or are susceptible of being used, in their ordinary condition, as highways for commerce" announced in *The Daniel Ball*:

> Although the evidence is not extensive, we think it is sufficient to sustain the findings. There were, for example, nine boats used from time to time to haul cattle and sheep from the mainland to one of the islands or from one of the islands to the mainland. * * *
>
> There was, in addition to the boats used by ranchers, one boat used by an outsider who carried sheep to an island for the owners of the sheep. It is said that one sheep boat for hire does not make an artery for commerce; but one sheep boat for hire is in keeping with the theme of actual navigability of the waters of the lake in earlier years.
>
> There was, in addition, a boat known as the *City of Corinne* which was launched in May 1871 for the purpose of carrying passengers and freight; but its life in that capacity apparently lasted less than a year. In 1872 it was converted into an excursion boat which apparently plied the waters of the lake until 1881. There are other boats that hauled sheep to and from an island in the lake and also hauled ore, and salt, and cedar posts. Still another boat was used to carry salt from various salt works around the lake to a railroad connection.
>
> The United States says the trade conducted by these various vessels was sporadic and their careers were short. It is true that most of the traffic which we have mentioned took place in the 1880's, while Utah became a State in 1896. Moreover, it is said that the level of the lake had so changed by 1896 that navigation was not practical. The Master's Report effectively refutes that contention. It says that on January 4,1896, the lake was 30.2 feet deep. He finds that on that date "the Lake was physically capable of being used in its ordinary condition as a highway for floating and affording passage to water craft in the manner over which trade and travel was or might be conducted in the customary modes of travel on water at that time."

Utah v. United States, 403 U.S. 9, 11–12, 91 S.Ct. 1775, 29 L.Ed.2d 279 (1971).

c. *Federal–State Conflicts Over Ownership*

The Supreme Court has held that states admitted to the Union subsequent to the original thirteen succeeded to the same rights as the original states, *i.e.* on an "equal footing." Pollard v. Hagan, 44 U.S. 212, 11 L.Ed. 565 (1845). *Pollard* was a conflict between federal and state patentees to tidelands under Mobile Bay, Alabama, a state carved out of lands ceded to the federal government by the original states and by Spain. The Supreme Court rejected the argument that the federal government rather than states succeeded to full sovereignty partly on the theory that deeds of cession from the original states imposed the trust in favor of future states. It also assumed that any attempt to assume sovereignty would have been unconstitutional "because the United States has no constitutional capacity to exercise municipal jurisdiction, sovereignty, or eminent domain, within the limits of a state or elsewhere, except in cases in which it is expressly granted." Id. at 223. This limitation on federal legislative power was not accepted in later cases so that state retention of public lands does not violate the equal footing doctrine. But the idea that submerged lands were held in trust by the federal government for future states persisted.

The extent of the trust for future states was thrown into some doubt in Knight v. United Land Ass'n, 142 U.S. 161, 12 S.Ct. 258, 35 L.Ed. 974 (1891). The federal government confirmed a title to tidelands based on the claim of the city of San Francisco as successor to the rights of the former Mexican pueblo as against a state patentee. The Court upheld the pueblo grant because the Treaty of Guadalupe Hildago required the United States to protect property rights which had been created by its predecessor, the Mexican government. *Knight* seems inconsistent with the constitutional theory of *Pollard* for it suggested in dictum that, besides treaty obligations, federal lands might be "subject to trusts which would require their disposition in some other way." Id. at 183. *Knight* gave federal patentees an opening to argue that their grants included tidelands.

In 1894 the Supreme Court reasserted *Pollard* and sought to harmonize it with federal public domain disposition policy in Shively v. Bowlby, 152 U.S. 1, 14 S.Ct. 548, 38 L.Ed. 331 (1894):

> By the Constitution, as is now well settled, the United States, having rightfully acquired the Territories, and being the only government which can impose laws upon them, have the entire dominion and sovereignty, national and municipal, Federal and state, over all the Territories, so long as they remain in a territorial condition. * * *

> We cannot doubt, therefore, that Congress has the power to make grants of lands below high water mark of navigable waters in any Territory of the United States, whenever it becomes necessary to do so in order to perform international obligations, or to effect the improvement of such lands for the promotion and convenience of commerce with foreign nations and among the several States, or to carry out other public purposes appropriate to the objects for which the United States hold the Territory.

* * *

> The Congress of the United States, in disposing of the public lands, has constantly acted upon the theory that those lands, whether in the interior, or on the coast, above high water mark, may be taken up by actual occupants, in order to encourage the settlement of the country; but that the navigable waters and the soils under them, whether within or above the ebb and flow of the tide, shall be and remain public highways; and, being chiefly valuable for the public purposes of commerce, navigation and fishery, and for the improvements necessary to secure and promote those purposes, shall not be granted away during the period of territorial government; but, unless in case of some international duty or public exigency, shall be held by the United States in trust for the future States, and shall vest in the

several States, when organized and admitted into the Union, with all the powers and prerogatives appertaining to the older States in regard to such waters and soils within their respective jurisdictions; in short, shall not be disposed of piecemeal to individuals as private property, but shall be held as a whole for the purpose of being ultimately administered and dealt with for the public benefit by the State, after it shall have become a completely organized community.

Id. at 48–50.

Once title has been allocated to the states, they are free to decide whether the bed shall pass out of state ownership into private hands or shall be retained by the state, although state discretion has been progressively limited in the past century when the public interest was not served by these transfers. Sometimes they have been made advisedly (as when California deeded lands in San Francisco Bay into private ownership). Sometimes private title has been obtained by fraud (as where the surveyor described a lake bed as dry land). And sometimes title has been obtained by legal error (as where the state regarded a water body as non-navigable and hence recognized title as tracing to the federal patentee of land adjoining the bed).

Some states adopted the rule that a lake that has been meandered (shorelines surveyed and mapped) by U.S. Government surveyors is navigable and, correlatively, a lake that has not been meandered is non-navigable. State courts have decided bed titles on the basis of these rules, but the U.S. Supreme Court has indicated that meander lines marking the shores as shown by surveyors do not decide titles to beds of water bodies but were only run to determine the quantity of upland to be sold and the price to be collected. Hardin v. Jordan, 140 U.S. 371, 11 S.Ct. 808, 35 L.Ed. 428 (1891).

Once it is authoritatively decided that the bed of the lake or stream is in private ownership it becomes necessary to determine how the bed is shared among riparian owners and what rights the riparians and members of the public have to use the overlying waters. With respect to rivers, the property line is the center of the stream, sometimes determined as a line midway between the banks of the river at its ordinary level, but sometimes determined as the thread of the main channel of the stream. As to lakes and ponds, various means of apportioning the lake bed have been devised, e.g., on the basis of lake frontage and by extending property lines from the shore to the center of the lake. See Rufford G. Patton & Carrol G. Patton, Patton on Titles §§ 132–133 (2d ed. 1957).

Ownership lines do not necessarily determine the limits of uses that may be made on the surface by riparians themselves. Limits on the extent of any private rights that may exist in water bodies for the benefit of the public are determined, first, by whether the waterway is navigable for title. Second, one must look to state law. State law can extend public rights to use both navigable and non-navigable waterways, but may not defeat certain public rights in navigable waters.

The next case shows the overriding importance of federal law in determining what federal patentees receive from their grants.

Hughes v. Washington

Supreme Court of the United States, 1967.
389 U.S. 290, 88 S.Ct. 438, 19 L.Ed.2d 530.

■ BLACK, J., delivered the opinion of the Court.

The question for decision is whether federal or state law controls the ownership of land, called accretion, gradually deposited by the ocean on adjoining upland property conveyed by the United States prior to statehood. The circumstances that give rise to the question are these. Prior to 1889 all land in what is now the State of Washington was owned by the United States, except land that had been conveyed to private parties. At that time owners of property bordering the ocean, such as the predecessor in title of Mrs. Stella Hughes, the petitioner here, had under the common law a right to include within their lands any accretion gradually built up by the ocean.[1] Washington became a State in 1889, and Article 17 of the State's new constitution, as interpreted by its Supreme Court, denied the owners of ocean-front property in the State any further rights in accretion that might in the future be formed between their property and the ocean. This is a suit brought by Mrs. Hughes, the successor in title to the original federal grantee, against the State of Washington as owner of the tidelands to determine whether the right to future accretions which existed under federal law in 1889 was abolished by that provision of the Washington Constitution. The trial court upheld Mrs. Hughes' contention that the right to accretions remained subject to federal law, and that she was the owner of the accreted lands. The State Supreme Court reversed, holding that state law controlled and that the State owned these lands. 67 Wash. 2d 799, 410 P. 2d 20 (1966). We granted certiorari. 385 U.S. 1000 (1967). We hold that this question is governed by federal, not state, law and that under federal law Mrs. Hughes, who traces her title to a federal grant prior to statehood, is the owner of these accretions.

While the issue appears never to have been squarely presented to this Court before, we think the path to decision is indicated by our holding in *Borax, Ltd. v. Los Angeles*, 296 U.S. 10 (1935). In that case we dealt with the rights of a California property owner who held under a federal patent, and in that instance, unlike the present case, the patent was issued after statehood. We held that

> [t]he question as to the extent of this federal grant, that is, as to the limit of the land conveyed, or the boundary between the upland and the tideland, is necessarily a federal question. It is a question which concerns the validity and effect of an act done by the United States; it

---

1. Jones v. Johnston, 18 How. 150 (1856); County of St. Clair v. Lovingston, 23 Wall. 46 (1874).

involves the ascertainment of the essential basis of a right asserted under federal law. 296 U.S., at 22.

* * *

Recognizing the difficulty of distinguishing *Borax*, respondent urges us to reconsider it. *Borax* itself, as well as *United States v. Oregon, supra,* and many other cases, makes clear that a dispute over title to lands owned by the Federal Government is governed by federal law, although of course the Federal Government may, if it desires, choose to select a state rule as the federal rule. *Borax* holds that there has been no such choice in this area, and we have no difficulty in concluding that *Borax* was correctly decided. The rule deals with waters that lap both the lands of the State and the boundaries of the international sea. This relationship, at this particular point of the marginal sea, is too close to the vital interest of the Nation in its own boundaries to allow it to be governed by any law but the "supreme Law of the Land."

This brings us to the question of what the federal rule is. The State has not attempted to argue that federal law gives it title to these accretions, and it seems clear to us that it could not. A long and unbroken line of decisions of this Court establishes that the grantee of land bounded by a body of navigable water acquires a right to any natural and gradual accretion formed along the shore. In *Jones v. Johnston*, 18 How. 150 (1856), a dispute between two parties owning land along Lake Michigan over the ownership of soil that had gradually been deposited along the shore, this Court held that "land gained from the sea either by alluvion or dereliction, if the same be by little and little, by small and imperceptible degrees, belongs to the owner of the land adjoining." 18 How., at 156. The Court has repeatedly reaffirmed this rule, *County of St. Clair v. Lovingston*, 23 Wall. 46 (1874); *Jefferis v. East Omaha Land Co.*, 134 U.S. 178 (1890), and the soundness of the principle is scarcely open to question. Any other rule would leave riparian owners continually in danger of losing the access to water which is often the most valuable feature of their property, and continually vulnerable to harassing litigation challenging the location of the original water lines. While it is true that these riparian rights are to some extent insecure in any event, since they are subject to considerable control by the neighboring owner of the tideland,[3] this is insufficient reason to leave these valuable rights at the mercy of natural phenomena which may in no way affect the interests of the tideland owner. See *Stevens v. Arnold*, 262 U.S. 266, 269–270 (1923). We therefore hold that petitioner is entitled to the accretion that has been gradually formed along her property by the ocean.

---

3. It has been held that a State may, without paying compensation, deprive a riparian owner of his common-law right to utilize the flowing water, *St. Anthony Falls Water Power Co.* v. *Water Comm'rs*, 168 U.S. 349 (1897), or to build a wharf over the water, *Shively v. Bowlby*, 152 U.S. 1 (1894). It has also been held that the State may fill its tidelands and thus block the riparian owner's natural access to the water. *Port of Seattle v. Oregon & W. R. Co.*, 255 U.S. 56 (1921).

The judgment below is reversed, and the case is remanded to the Supreme Court of Washington for further proceedings not inconsistent with this opinion.

Reversed and remanded.

■ JUSTICE MARSHALL took no part in the consideration or decision of this case.

■ JUSTICE STEWART, concurring.

I fully agree that the extent of the 1866 federal grant to which Mrs. Hughes traces her ownership was originally measurable by federal common law, and that under the applicable federal rule her predecessor in title acquired the right to all accretions gradually built up by the sea. For me, however, that does not end the matter. For the Supreme Court of Washington decided in 1966, in the case now before us, that Washington terminated the right to oceanfront accretions when it became a State in 1889. The State concedes that the federal grant in question conferred such a right prior to 1889. But the State purports to have reserved all post–1889 accretions for the public domain. Mrs. Hughes is entitled to the beach she claims in this case only if the State failed in its effort to abolish all private rights to seashore accretions.

Surely it must be conceded as a general proposition that the law of real property is, under our Constitution, left to the individual States to develop and administer. And surely Washington or any other State is free to make changes, either legislative or judicial, in its general rules of real property law, including the rules governing the property rights of riparian owners. Nor are riparian owners who derive their title from the United States somehow immune from the changing impact of these general state rules. *Joy v. St. Louis,* 201 U.S. 332, 342. For if they were, then the property law of a State like Washington, carved entirely out of federal territory, would be forever frozen into the mold it occupied on the date of the State's admission to the Union. It follows that Mrs. Hughes cannot claim immunity from changes in the property law of Washington simply because her title derives from a federal grant. Like any other property owner, however, Mrs. Hughes may insist, quite apart from the federal origin of her title, that the State not take her land without just compensation. *Chicago, B. & Q. R. Co. v. Chicago,* 166 U.S. 226, 236–241. * * *

We cannot resolve the federal question whether there has been such a taking without first making a determination of our own as to who owned the seashore accretions between 1889 and 1966. To the extent that the decision of the Supreme Court of Washington on that issue arguably conforms to reasonable expectations, we must of course accept it as conclusive. But to the extent that it constitutes a sudden change in state law, unpredictable in terms of the relevant precedents, no such deference would be appropriate. For a State cannot be permitted to defeat the constitutional prohibition against taking property without due process of law by the simple device of asserting retroactively that the property it has taken never existed at all. Whether the decision here worked an unpredictable change in state law thus inevitably presents a federal question for the determination of this Court. * * *

There can be little doubt about the impact of that change upon Mrs. Hughes: The beach she had every reason to regard as hers was declared by the state court to be in the public domain. Of course the court did not conceive of this action as a taking. As is so often the case when a State exercises its power to make law, or to regulate, or to pursue a public project, pre-existing property interests were impaired here without any calculated decision to deprive anyone of what he once owned. But the Constitution measures a taking of property not by what a State says, or by what it intends, but by what it *does*. Although the State in this case made no attempt to take the accreted lands by eminent domain, it achieved the same result by effecting a retroactive transformation of private into public property—without paying for the privilege of doing so. Because the Due Process Clause of the Fourteenth Amendment forbids such confiscation by a State, no less through its courts than through its legislature, and no less when a taking is unintended than when it is deliberate, I join in reversing the judgment.

NOTES

1. *Is There A Presumption of State Ownership?* Since *Hughes*, the Court has become more protective of state ownership and state power to determine title disputes. The State of Utah challenged the federal government's issuance of oil and gas leases in Lake Utah. The 150 square mile lake is navigable and the state's title was asserted based on the equal footing doctrine, in that other states have received title to the beds of navigable waterways. The United States invoked an 1888 statute that had been used to set aside the lake as a future federal reservoir site. Utah became a state in 1896. The United States Supreme Court rejected this theory and said that the test is whether "Congress * * * clearly express[ed] an intention to defeat Utah's claim to the lakebed under the equal footing doctrine." Utah Div. of State Lands v. United States, 482 U.S. 193, 208, 107 S.Ct. 2318, 96 L.Ed.2d 162 (1987). Until 1987 it was generally assumed that pre-statehood withdrawals were effective to preserve federal title to the beds of navigable waters without specific congressional action. For instance, the Supreme Court refused to review the ruling of the Ninth Circuit Court of Appeals that oil deposits under the bed of a navigable lake in the Kenai National Moose Range were federal property because the lands and waters of the 2 million acre range had been withdrawn by executive order prior to Alaska statehood. United States v. Alaska, 423 F.2d 764 (9th Cir.1970), cert. denied 400 U.S. 967, 91 S.Ct. 363, 27 L.Ed.2d 388 (1970).

In a later title decision, the Supreme Court moved away from *Utah Division of State Lands'* extreme presumption in favor of the passage of public lands to the states under the equal footing doctrine. Relying on *Utah Division of State Lands*, Alaska claimed ownership of the submerged lands beneath coastal barrier islands, but the Court rejected the argument and reaffirmed Congress' power as a matter of "congressional policy, not . . . constitutional obligation" to reserve public lands which would otherwise pass to the states under the equal footing doctrine. Justice O'Connor reversed the Special Master's conclusion and held that the submerged lands of the National Petroleum Reserve within the Arctic National Wildlife Refuge did not pass to Alaska when it entered the union in 1959. The critical inquiries are the purpose of the conveyance or reservation and whether Congress intended to defeat future state title claims. The United States met both standards: the claimed state ownership would undermine the strategic purposes of the reservation, naval oil supplies at all times, because oil bearing formations extended beneath both the submerged and upland portions of the reserve. "It is simply not plausible that the United States sought to reserve only the upland portion of the area." The same factors supported the conclusion that Congress intended to defeat state title. United States v. Alaska, 521 U.S. 1, 39–40, 117 S.Ct. 1888, 138 L.Ed.2d 231 (1997).

2. *Federal Law or State Law? Hughes* involved ocean-front property, but the opinion suggested that all post-statehood title disputes to beds underlying navigable waters might be decided by federal rather than state rules. This dictum became the rule in Bonelli Cattle Co. v. Arizona, 414 U.S. 313, 94 S.Ct. 517, 38 L.Ed.2d 526 (1973). The dispute in *Bonelli* was whether the state or a private party whose title was based on a federal patent held title to land that reemerged after completion of a federal rechanneling project. The court said the federal test applied and added:

> The equal-footing doctrine was never intended to provide a State with a windfall of thousands of acres of dry land exposed when the main thread of a navigable stream is changed. It would be at odds with the fundamental purpose of the original grant to the States to afford a State title to land from which a navigable stream had receded unless the land was exposed as part of a navigational or related public project of which it was a necessary and integral part * * *.
>
> The advance of the Colorado's waters divested the title of the upland owners in favor of the State in order to guarantee full public enjoyment of the watercourse. But, when the water receded from the land, there was no longer a public benefit to be protected; consequently, the State, as sovereign, has no need for title. That the cause of the recession was artificial, or that the rate was perceptible, should be of no effect.

Id. at 322–24.

Four years later the court overruled *Bonelli* in Oregon *ex rel.* State Land Bd. v. Corvallis Sand & Gravel Co., 429 U.S. 363, 97 S.Ct. 582, 50 L.Ed.2d 550 (1977). The state of Oregon claimed title to the bed of a navigable channel which became the main channel of Willamette River after a major flood. Mr. Justice Rehnquist explained why state law alone should govern post-statehood title disputes:

Our error, as we now see it, was to view the equal-footing doctrine enunciated in *Pollard's Lessee v. Hagan* as a basis upon which federal common law could supersede state law in the determination of land titles. Precisely the contrary is true; in *Pollard's Lessee* itself the equal-footing doctrine resulted in the State's acquisition of title notwithstanding the efforts of the Federal Government to dispose of the lands in question in another way.

The equal-footing doctrine did not, therefore, provide a basis for federal law to supersede the State's application of its own law in deciding title to the Bonelli land, and state law should have been applied unless there were present some other principle of federal law requiring state law to be displaced.

Id. at 371.

What is the status of *Hughes* and *Borax* (cited and discussed in *Hughes*) after *Corvallis Sand & Gravel*? Justice Rehnquist explained that federal law was applied in *Borax* to determine boundaries between uplands and tidelands at the time of statehood. He continued, saying:

This same principle would require that determination of the initial boundary between a riverbed, which the State acquired under the equal-footing doctrine, and riparian fast lands likewise be decided as a matter of federal law rather than state law. But that determination is solely for the purpose of fixing the boundaries of the riverbed acquired by the State at the time of its admission to the Union; thereafter the role of the equal-footing doctrine is ended, and the land is subject to the laws of the State. The expressions in *Bonelli* suggesting a more expansive role for the equal-footing doctrine are contrary to the line of cases following *Pollard's Lessee*.

Id. at 376–77.

3. *Special Rules for Indian Tribes?* The federal government's power to reserve the beds underlying navigable waters must be exercised under before-statehood circumstances that clearly demonstrate an intention to defeat state ownership. Does this standard apply to reservations of the beds of navigable waters for the benefit of Indian tribes? In Montana v. United States, 450 U.S. 544, 101 S.Ct. 1245, 67 L.Ed.2d 493 (1981), the Crow Tribe asserted the right to regulate fishing by non-Indians in the Big Horn River. The United States claimed that it had conveyed title to the river's bed to the tribe. The state argued that the United States had held the bed in trust, and that upon statehood it passed to Montana. The United States relied on Shively v. Bowlby, 152 U.S. 1, 14 S.Ct. 548, 38 L.Ed. 331 (1894), *supra* p. 406, but the Court held that there is a presumption against any conveyance or retention of title to the bed by the United States, citing United States v. Holt State Bank, 270 U.S. 49, 46 S.Ct. 197, 70 L.Ed. 465 (1926):

The Crow treaties in this case, like the Chippewa treaties in *Holt State Bank*, fail to overcome the established presumption that the beds of navigable waters remain in trust for future States and pass to the new

States when they assume sovereignty. The 1851 treaty did not by its terms formally convey any land to the Indians at all, but instead chiefly represented a covenant among several tribes which recognized specific boundaries for their respective territories. Treaty of Fort Laramie, 1851, [11 Stat. 749] Art. 5. * * * It referred to hunting and fishing only insofar as it said that the Crow Indians "do not surrender the privilege of hunting, fishing, or passing over any of the tracts of country heretofore described," a statement that had no bearing on ownership of the riverbed. * * * The treaty in no way expressly referred to the riverbed, nor was an intention to convey the riverbed expressed in "clear and especial words," Martin v. Waddell, 16 Pet., at 411 [41 U.S., at 349] or "definitely declared or otherwise made very plain," United States v. Holt State Bank, 270 U.S., at 55. Rather, as in *Holt*, "[t]he effect of what was done was to reserve in a general way for the continued occupation of the Indians what remained of their aboriginal territory." *Id*. at 58.

Though Article 2 gave the Crow Indians the sole right to use and occupy the reserved land, and implicitly, the power to exclude others from it, the respondents' reliance on that provision simply begs the question of the precise extent of the conveyed lands to which this exclusivity attaches. The mere fact that the bed of a navigable water lies within the boundaries described in the treaty does not make the riverbed part of the conveyed land, especially when there is no express reference to the riverbed that might overcome the presumption against its conveyance.

Montana, 450 U.S. at 553–54.

Justices Blackmun, Brennan, and Marshall dissented on the ground that the purpose of the reservation indicated an intent to grant the tribe title to that portion of the bed that was totally encompassed by the reservation. See Choctaw Nation v. Oklahoma, 397 U.S. 620, 90 S.Ct. 1328, 25 L.Ed.2d 615 (1970). Title to the beds of navigable waters flowing through reservations continues to be unsettled in part because lower courts do not always apply the *Montana* presumption against tribal ownership. See, *e.g.*, United States v. Washington, 157 F.3d 630 (9th Cir.1998), cert. denied 526 U.S. 1060, 119 S.Ct. 1376, 143 L.Ed.2d 535 (1999), which held that the presumptions applied in *Montana* and *Utah Division of State Lands* do not apply to customary use rights claims as opposed to claims of tidelands ownership. See Thomas H. Pacheco, Indian Bedlands Claims: A Need to Clear the Waters, 15 Harv. Envtl. L. Rev. 1 (1991).

The Supreme Court's formalist Eleventh Amendment jurisprudence,[2] which shields states from legislation seeking to enforce federal rights, creates additional barriers for tribes. The Court has held that the Eleventh Amendment barred a declaratory suit against a state official to affirm that the tribe had the exclusive use of its claimed portion of the bed of Lake

---

2. In Tennessee v. Lane, 541 U.S. 509, 124 S.Ct. 1978, 158 L.Ed.2d 820 (2004), the Court has somewhat retreated from its formalist approach.

Coeur d'Alene in northern Idaho. Idaho v. Coeur d'Alene Tribe of Idaho, 521 U.S. 261, 117 S.Ct. 2028, 138 L.Ed.2d 438 (1997).

Courts continue to apply the two-prong test for federal retention announced in *United States v. Alaska, supra* pp. 411–412 to Indian tribes: there must be both an executive reservation and explicit or implicit congressional ratification. The Coeur d'Alene Tribe ultimately met this test and thus provided its title to a portion of the bed of Lake Coeur d'Alene within its reservation. Idaho v. United States, 533 U.S. 262, 121 S.Ct. 2135, 150 L.Ed.2d 326 (2001). The Court found that the Executive included the submerged lands in the reservation boundaries which were finally fixed in 1889–1890 and Congress, before and after statehood, dealt with the tribe in a way that showed its intent to preserve the tribal interest in land and water absent tribal consent. Formal congressional ratification is not required to overcome the presumption of state title. However, the quantum of congressional action may be difficult for many tribes to meet. It is necessary to show that Congress had notice of the inclusion of submerged lands in reservation boundaries, had the opportunity and power to repudiate the executive reservation, and instead affirmatively dealt with the tribe in a way that preserved the reservation.

2. THE PUBLIC TRUST DOCTRINE AS A LIMIT ON PRIVATE USE

State proprietary claims to navigable waters are different from other government proprietary claims. The state is not simply claiming exclusive, individual ownership of a resource. It is claiming ownership as trustee for the people. State trust ownership is one of the most difficult and contested areas of water law. "The public trust ... expresses three ideas, one grounded in Roman law and the other two resulting from Anglo American common law. The first is that public waters, generally defined as navigable waters, are subject to a public servitude for navigation, commerce, and, later, fisheries. The second idea is that the public owns the beds of submerged waters. The third idea is that the sovereign must use these submerged lands only for trust purposes." A. Dan Tarlock, *Earth and Other Ethics: The Institutional Issues*, 56 Tenn. L. Rev. 43, 56 (1988). The first two meanings reflect longstanding limitations on private water use in the common law and other legal systems. See *The Public Trust Doctrine in Tidal Areas: A Sometime Submerged Traditional Doctrine*, 79 Yale L.J. 762 (1970) and Charles F. Wilkinson, *The Headwaters of the Public Trust: Some Thoughts on the Source and Scope of the Traditional Doctrine*, 19 Envtl. Law 425 (1989). These limitations can be justified on the ground that public retention and use is the most efficient use of navigable waters. Carol Rose, *The Comedy of the Commons: Custom, Commerce, and Inherently Public Property*, 53 U. Chi. L. Rev. 711 (1986). It is the third idea that has excited environmental lawyers because the public trust doctrine is one of the few potential substantive judicial limitations on state and federal resource allocation decisions. For a useful analysis of the historical evolution of the doctrine, see Molly Selvin, *The Public Trust Doctrine in*

American Law and Economic Policy, 1789–1920, 1980 Wis. L. Rev. 1403 (1980).

The source and scope of the public trust doctrine remain the subject of intense debate. Is it a common law doctrine? Is it a federal constitutional doctrine binding on all states? If so, what is the source? The Equal Footing Doctrine? The Commerce Clause? Does the trust extend beyond the protection of public rights to use navigable waters? For example, does it extend to the protection of ecological integrity of aquatic ecosystems? What uses are consistent, inconsistent with trust purposes? What limitations exist on the power of the state to terminate the trust?

Illinois Central Railroad Co. v. Illinois

Supreme Court of the United States, 1892.
146 U.S. 387, 13 S.Ct. 110, 36 L.Ed. 1018.

[The case grew out of the complex history of federal, state and local grants to railroads and the Illinois and Michigan Canal. In 1827 Congress granted Illinois one-half of five sections along the route of the proposed Illinois and Michigan Canal. In 1850, Congress granted land to construct the Illinois Central Railroad from the terminus of the canal on Lake Michigan to Cairo, Illinois, on the Ohio River. In 1852, the City of Chicago authorized the railroad to extend its tracks to the north end of the Lake Michigan harbor. In 1869 the legislature gave the natural fee title to the submerged bed of Lake Michigan east of its tracks to the breakwater for a distance of one mile in return for a yearly rental based on the gross earnings the land conveyed. The court noted in its opinion that the original purpose of the 1869 act was to convey the state lands to the City of Chicago to allow it to enlarge its harbor but "during the passage of the act its purport was changed." In 1873 the legislature had a change of mind and repealed the act of 1869. The state brought a quiet title action and won. In affirming, the Supreme Court addressed the state's power to enact the 1869 and 1873 legislation.]

The question, therefore, to be considered is whether the legislature was competent to thus deprive the State of its ownership of the submerged lands in the harbor of Chicago, and of the consequent control of its waters; or, in other words, whether the railroad corporation can hold the lands and control the waters by the grant, against any future exercise of power over them by the State.

That the State holds the title to the lands under the navigable waters of Lake Michigan, within its limits, in the same manner that the State holds title to soils under tide water, by the common law, we have already shown, and that title necessarily carries with it control over the waters above them whenever the lands are subjected to use. But it is a title different in character from that which the State holds in lands intended for sale. It is different from the title which the United States hold in the public lands which are open to preemption and sale. It is a title held in trust for the people of the State that they may enjoy the navigation of the waters, carry on commerce over them, and have liberty of fishing therein freed from the obstruction or interference of private parties. The interest of the people in the navigation of the waters and in commerce over them may be improved in many instances by the erection of wharves, docks and piers therein, for which purpose the State may grant parcels of the submerged lands; and, so long as their disposition is made for such purpose, no valid objections can be made to the grants. It is grants of parcels of lands under navigable waters, that may afford foundation for wharves, piers, docks and other structures in aid of commerce, and grants of parcels which, being occupied, do not substantially impair the public interest in the lands and waters remaining, that are chiefly considered and sustained in the adjudged cases as a valid exercise of legislative power consistently with the trust to the public upon which such lands are held by the State. But that is a very different doctrine from the one which would sanction the abdication of the general control of the State over lands under the navigable waters of an entire harbor or bay, or of a sea or lake. Such abdication is not consistent with the exercise of that trust which requires the government of the State to preserve such waters for the use of the public. The trust devolving upon the State for the public, and which can only be discharged by the management and control of property in which the public has an interest, cannot be relinquished by a transfer of the property. The control of the State for the purposes of the trust can never be lost, except as to such parcels as are used in promoting the interests of the public therein, or can be disposed of without any substantial impairment of the public interest in the lands and waters remaining. It is only by observing the distinction between a grant of such parcels for the improvement of the public interest, or which when occupied do not substantially impair the public interest in the lands and waters remaining, and a grant of the whole property in which the public is interested, that the language of the adjudged cases can be reconciled. General language sometimes found in opinions of the courts, expressive of absolute ownership and control by the State of lands under navigable waters, irrespective of any trust as to their use and disposition, must be read and construed with reference to the special facts of the particular cases. A grant of all the lands under the navigable waters of a State has never been adjudged to be within the legislative power; and any attempted grant of the kind would be held, if not absolutely void on its face, as subject to revocation. The State can no more abdicate its trust over property in which the whole people are interested, like navigable waters and soils under them, so as to leave them entirely under the use and control of private parties, except in the instance of parcels mentioned for the improvement of the navigation and use of the waters, or when parcels can be disposed of without impairment of the public interest in what remains, than it can abdicate its police powers in the administration of government and the preservation of the peace. In the administration of government the use of such powers may for a limited period be delegated to a municipality or other body, but there always remains with the State the right to revoke those powers and exercise them in a more direct manner, and one more conformable to its wishes. So with trusts connected with public property, or property of a special character, like lands under navigable waters, they cannot be placed entirely beyond the direction and control of the State.

The harbor of Chicago is of immense value to the people of the State of Illinois in the facilities it affords to its vast and constantly increasing commerce; and the idea that its legislature can deprive the State of control over its bed and waters and place the same in the hands of a private corporation created for a different purpose, one limited to transportation of passengers and freight between distant points and the city, is a proposition that cannot be defended.

The area of the submerged lands proposed to be ceded by the act in question to the railroad company embraces something more than a thousand acres, being, as stated by counsel, more than three times the area of the outer harbor, and not only including all of that harbor but embracing adjoining submerged lands which will, in all probability, be hereafter included in the harbor. It is as large as that embraced by all the merchandise docks along the Thames at London; is much larger than that included in the famous docks and basins at Liverpool; is twice that of the port of Marseilles, and nearly if not quite equal to the pier area along the waterfront of the city of New York. And the arrivals and clearings of vessels at the port exceed in number those of New York, and are equal to those of New York and Boston combined. Chicago has nearly twenty-five per cent of the lake carrying trade as compared with the arrivals and clearings of all the leading ports of our great inland seas. In the year ending June 30, 1886, the joint arrivals and clearances of vessels at that port amounted to twenty-two thousand and ninety-six, with a tonnage of over seven millions; and in 1890 the tonnage of the vessels reached nearly nine millions. As stated by counsel, since the passage of the Lake Front Act, in 1869, the population of the city has increased nearly a million souls, and the increase of commerce has kept pace with it. It is hardly conceivable that the legislature can divest the State of the control and management of this harbor and vest it absolutely in a private corporation. Surely an act of the legislature transferring the title to its submerged lands and the power claimed by the railroad company, to a foreign State or nation would be repudiated, without hesitation, as a gross perversion of the trust over the property under which it is held. So would a similar transfer to a corporation of another State. It would not be listened to that the control and management of the harbor of that great city—a subject of concern to the whole people of the State—should thus be placed elsewhere than in the State itself. All the objections which can be urged to such attempted transfer may be urged to a transfer to a private corporation like the railroad company in this case.

Any grant of the kind is necessarily revocable, and the exercise of the trust by which the property was held by the State can be resumed at any time. Undoubtedly there may be expenses incurred in improvements made under such a grant which the State ought to pay; but, be that as it may, the power to resume the trust whenever the State judges best is, we think, incontrovertible. The position advanced by the railroad company in support of its claim to the ownership of the submerged lands and the right to the erection of wharves, piers and docks at its pleasure, or for its business in the harbor of Chicago, would place every harbor in the country at the mercy of a majority of the legislature of the State in which the harbor is situated.

We cannot, it is true, cite any authority where a grant of this kind has been held invalid, for we believe that no instance exists where the harbor of a great city and its commerce have been allowed to pass into the control of any private corporation. But the decisions are numerous which declare that such property is held by the State, by virtue of its sovereignty, in trust for the public. The ownership of the navigable waters of the harbor and of the lands under them is a subject of public concern to the whole people of the State. The trust with which they are held, therefore, is governmental and cannot be alienated, except in those instances mentioned of parcels used in the improvement of the interest thus held, or when parcels can be disposed of without detriment to the public interest in the lands and waters remaining.

This follows necessarily from the public character of the property, being held by the whole people for purposes in which the whole people are interested. As said by Chief Justice Taney, in *Martin v. Waddell*, 16 Pet. 367, 410: "When the Revolution took place the people of each State became themselves sovereign, and in that character hold the absolute right to all their navigable waters, and the soils under them, for their own common use, subject only to the rights since surrendered by the Constitution to the general government." In *Arnold v. Mundy*, 1 Halsted, 1, which is cited by this court in *Martin v. Waddell*, 16 Pet. 418, and spoken of by Chief Justice Taney as entitled to great weight, and in which the decision was made "with great deliberation and research," the Supreme Court of New Jersey comments upon the rights of the State in the bed of navigable waters, and, after observing that the power exercised by the State over the lands and waters is nothing more than what is called the *jus regium*, the right of regulating, improving and securing them for the benefit of every individual citizen, adds: "The sovereign power, itself, therefore, cannot consistently with the principles of the law of nature and the constitution of a well-ordered society, make a direct and absolute grant of the waters of the State, divesting all the citizens of their common right. It would be a grievance which never could be long borne by a free people." Necessarily must the control of the waters of a State over all lands under them pass when the lands are conveyed in fee to private parties, and are by them subjected to use.

* * *

■ Justice Shiras, Dissenting.

* * *

The opinion of the majority, if I rightly apprehend it, likewise concedes that a State does possess the power to grant the rights of property and possession in such lands to private parties, but the power is stated to be, in some way restricted to "small parcels, or where such parcels can be disposed of without detriment to the public interests in the lands and waters remaining." But it is difficult to see how the validity of the exercise of the power, if the power exists, can depend upon the size of the parcel granted, or how, if it be possible to imagine that the power is subject to such a limitation, the present case would be affected, as the grant in question, though doubtless a large and valuable one, is, relatively to the remaining soil and waters, if not insignificant, yet certainly, in view of the purposes to be effected, not unreasonable. It is matter of common knowledge that a great railroad system, like that of the Illinois Central Railroad Company, requires an extensive and constantly increasing territory for its terminal facilities.

NOTES

1. *Illinois Central* remains important in Illinois as the legislature has had a long practice of making substantial grants of Lake Michigan submerged lands. For example, the Illinois Legislature transferred 194.6 acres of land beneath Lake Michigan to United States Steel for $19,460.00 after a legislative finding that the grant would not impair the public interest because a public park was located north of the proposed mill. The Illinois Supreme Court invalidated the grant. The court found that prior cases have never upheld a grant where "the primary purpose was to benefit a private interest." Because the transferred trust lands were "adjacent to waters presently in important public use [which] would be irretrievably removed from the use of the people of Illinois," the court held that "to preserve meaning and vitality in the public trust doctrine, when a grant of submerged land beneath waters of Lake Michigan is proposed under the circumstances here, the public purpose to be served cannot be only incidental and remote. The claimed benefit here to the public through additional employment and economic improvement is too indirect, intangible and elusive to satisfy the requirement of a public purpose." People *ex rel.* Scott v. Chicago Park Dist., 66 Ill.2d 65, 4 Ill.Dec. 660, 360 N.E.2d 773, 780–81 (1976). Accord Lake Michigan Federation v. United States Army Corps of Engineers, 742 F.Supp. 441 (N.D.Ill.1990) (invalidating state legislation conveying 18.5 acres of Lake Michigan bed to private university for a landfill).

2. Most states have allowed the state to sever trust lands from the trust, although most cases have involved small severances. Following *Illinois Central*, most courts have reviewed severances to ensure that they promote the trust purposes. For example the Wisconsin Supreme Court held that a conveyance of trust land to a private party promoted trust because it was "an essential requisite of the entire plan to aid the city in the construction of its proposed outer harbor." City of Milwaukee v. State, 193 Wis. 423, 214 N.W. 820, 826 (1927). Today, many states are becoming more protective of trust lands. Protection can take the form of a presumption that a state grant remains subject to the trust, Gwathmey v. State, 342 N.C. 287, 464 S.E.2d 674 (1995) Query v. Burgess, 371 S.C. 407, 639 S.E.2d 455 (S.C.

App. 2006)., a high standard for alienation, Cinque Bambini Partnership v. State, 491 So.2d 508 (Miss.1986), aff'd sub. nom. Phillips Petroleum Co. v. Mississippi, 484 U.S. 469, 108 S.Ct. 791, 98 L.Ed.2d 877 (1988) ("higher public purpose"), or higher standards for the improvements necessary to perfect title, City of West Palm Beach v. Board of Trustees of the Internal Improvement Trust, 746 So.2d 1085 (Fla.1999) (dredging a marina insufficient to obtain title to submerged lands because the act granting title required the construction of wharves, or the erection of permanent structures or fills in the submerged lands).

States that allow severance generally protect prior fills on a reliance theory. For example, Rhode Island allows prior tideland patentees to obtain fee simple title if they can establish express or implied state approval and that an improvement was made in justifiable reliance on the approval. Greater Providence Chamber of Commerce v. State, 657 A.2d 1038 (R.I. 1995) and Providence & Worcester R.R. Co. v. Pine, 729 A.2d 202 (R.I. 1999). The filled land remains subject to the public trust rights of fishery, commerce, and navigation. The state may not reacquire it based on the public trust doctrine alone but it can impose restrictions any time before the landowner changes position in reliance on the state's inaction. Alabama has reaffirmed that the ownership of submerged lands "is a trust of the most solemn character" and held that a statute allowing a riparian owner to reclaim tidelands and acquire title required a completed fill, not merely a publication of intent to fill. West Dauphin Ltd. v. Callon Offshore Prod., Inc., 725 So.2d 944, 952 (Ala.1998). Ohio has affirmed the public trust doctrine, but held that it does not authorize the state to change the rent standards retroactively for a fifty year lease for a marina issued in 1968 for $2,500.00 per year subject to a vague readjustment standard. Sandusky Marina Ltd. v. Ohio Dep't of Natural Res., 126 Ohio App.3d 256, 710 N.E.2d 302 (1998).

3. Can public trust purposes evolve? California is a case study in the adaptation of the trust to new demands. The courts heard a series of cases requiring them to decide if new uses were logically related to commerce and navigation. *E.g.*, City of Long Beach v. Marshall, 11 Cal.2d 609, 82 P.2d 362 (1938) (oil and gas leasing), and People v. City of Long Beach, 51 Cal.2d 875, 338 P.2d 177 (1959) (YMCA for seamen and naval officers). Trust lands were once deprecated as mud flats, sloughs, and brackish lagoons, but today these lands are valued wetlands or biodiversity reserves. Does the trust extend to the protection of the ecological values of these lands?

The leading case holding that the trust can evolve is Marks v. Whitney, 6 Cal.3d 251, 98 Cal.Rptr. 790, 491 P.2d 374 (1971). The case grew out of California's large-scale conveyance of tide and marshlands in the nineteenth century. Marks was a tidelands patentee whose lands adjoined almost the entire shoreline of Whitney's upland property. Marks sought to fill his tidelands and the trial court held that Whitney had obtained a prescriptive easement to locate a seven-foot wharf across Marks' tidelands. The court reaffirmed the longstanding rule that a tidelands owner owns the title to the soil subject to the trust. It did not determine whether Whitney's easement interfered with Marks' *jus privatum* or the *jus publicum*. The significance of the opinion is the Court's dictum that:

> There is a growing public recognition that one of the most important public uses of the tidelands—a use encompassed within the tidelands trust—is the preservation of those lands in their natural state, so that they may serve as ecological units for scientific study, as open space, and as environments which provide food and habitat for birds and marine life, and which favorably effect the scenery and climate of the area. It is not necessary to here define precisely all public uses which encumber tidelands.

Id. at 380.

The expanded purpose of the public trust in light of modern societal tastes was carried forward in City of Berkeley v. Superior Court of Alameda County, 26 Cal.3d 515, 162 Cal.Rptr. 327, 606 P.2d 362 (1980). The court held that two acts of the California legislature passed in 1868 and 1870 did not convey fee simple title to tidelands and that some of the tidelands remained subject to the public trust. The two statutes allowed some 88 square miles of San Francisco Bay to be conveyed and filled, and in 1915 the California Supreme Court had held that these acts conveyed fee simple interests freed from the trust. Knudson v. Kearney, 171 Cal. 250, 152 P. 541 (1915). Writing for the majority in *Berkeley*, Justice Mosk, the author of *Marks*, reasoned that *Knudson* was wrong. Either the two acts were not intended to promote navigation and thus grants made pursuant to them were not free of the public trust or, in the alternative, even if the purpose was navigation improvement, "*Illinois Central* holds that a state may not grant to private persons tidelands as vast in area as the board was authorized to sell by the 1870 act." 606 P.2d at 371. To balance longstanding reliance on *Knudson* with the court's modern perception of the scope of the trust, the court held that tidal lands in private ownership remained subject to public trust unless they had already been filled, in which case they were held in absolute title free of the trust.

Justice Mosk later wrote in State v. Superior Court of Lake County, 29 Cal.3d 210, 172 Cal.Rptr. 696, 625 P.2d 239 (1981), that the trust extends to non-tidal waters conveyed to private parties. Under California law, riparian and littoral owners own to the low water mark of bodies of water navigable in 1850 (at statehood), but the submerged land between the high and low water marks remains subject to the public trust. Thus, the state could deny a permit to fill the foreshore for ecological reasons or to preserve public recreational opportunities. See also State *ex rel.* Sprynczynatyk v. Mills, 523 N.W.2d 537 (N.D.1994) (state has rights in shore between high and low water marks under public trust doctrine). In State v. Superior Court of Placer County, 29 Cal.3d 240, 172 Cal.Rptr. 713, 625 P.2d 256 (1981), a landowner sued under the Civil Rights Act, § 1983, to prevent the state from asserting its public trust claims to the foreshore, but the California Supreme Court (per Justice Mosk) held that the state cannot be estopped from asserting these claims for public policy reasons.

Justice Mosk continued to apply his theory that public trust severances are limited to situations where no trust purpose could be served without a total restoration in City of Los Angeles v. Venice Peninsula Properties, 31 Cal.3d 288, 182 Cal.Rptr. 599, 644 P.2d 792 (1982). That case held that the trust applied to tidelands ceded by Mexico under the Treaty of Guadalupe Hidalgo. But the U.S. Supreme Court, which is more sensitive to the protection of long-standing expectations, did not agree: "We hold that California cannot at this late date assert its public trust easement over petitioner's property, when petitioner's predecessors-in-interest had their interest confirmed without any mention of such an easement in proceedings taken pursuant to the Act of 1851." Summa Corp. v. California *ex rel.* State Lands Comm'n, 466 U.S. 198, 209, 104 S.Ct. 1751, 80 L.Ed.2d 237 (1984).

4. Is the public trust a legitimate exercise of state judicial or legislative power? The first step in legitimation is to ground the trust in the federal constitution or in common law. In Idaho v. Coeur d'Alene Tribe, 521 U.S. 261, 283–287, 117 S.Ct. 2028, 138 L.Ed.2d 438 (1997), Justice Kennedy offered this analysis of the constitutional basis for the doctrine:

> The Court from an early date has acknowledged that the people of each of the Thirteen Colonies at the time of independence "became themselves sovereign; and in that character hold the absolute right to all their navigable waters and the soils under them for their own common use, subject only to the rights since surrendered by the Constitution to the general government." *Martin v. Lessee of Waddell*, 16 Pet. 367, 410 (1842). Then, in *Lessee of Pollard v. Hagan*, 44 U.S. 212 (1845), the Court concluded that States entering the Union after 1789 did so on an "equal footing" with the original States and so have similar ownership over these "sovereign lands." In consequence of this rule, a State's title to these sovereign lands arises from the equal footing doctrine and is "conferred not by Congress but by the Constitution itself." *Oregon ex rel. State Land Bd. v. Corvallis Sand & Gravel Co.*, 429 U.S. 363, 374 (1977). The importance of these lands to state sovereignty explains our longstanding commitment to the principle that the United States is presumed to have held navigable waters in acquired territory for the ultimate benefit of future States and "that disposals by the United States during the territorial period are not lightly to be inferred, and should not be regarded as intended unless the intention was definitely declared or otherwise made very plain." *United States v. Holt State Bank*, 270 U.S. 49, 46 S.Ct. 197, 70 L.Ed. 465 (1926).

> The principle which underlies the equal footing doctrine and the strong presumption of state ownership is that navigable waters uniquely implicate sovereign interests. The principle arises from ancient doctrines. See, e.g., Institutes of Justinian, Lib. II, Tit. I, § 2 (T. Cooper transl. 2d ed. 1841) ("Rivers and ports are public; hence the right of fishing in a port, or in rivers are in common"). The special treatment of navigable waters in English law was recognized in Brac-

ton's time. He stated that "all rivers and ports are public, so that the right to fish therein is common to all persons. The use of river banks, as of the river itself, is also public." 2 H. Bracton, De Legibus et Consuetudinibus Angliae 40 (S. Thorne trans. 1968). The Magna Carta provided that the Crown would remove "all fish-weirs ... from the Thames and the Medway and throughout all England, except on the sea coast." M. Evans & R. Jack, Sources of English Legal and Constitutional History 53 (1984); see also *Waddell, supra* (tracing tidelands trusteeship back to Magna Carta).

The Court in *Shively v. Bowlby*, 152 U.S. 1, 13 (1894), summarizing English common law, stated:

> "In England, from the time of Lord Hale, it has been treated as settled that the title in the soil of the sea, or of arms of the sea, below ordinary high water mark, is in the King; except so far as an individual or a corporation has acquired rights in it by express grant, or by prescription or usage ... and that this title, *jus privatum,* whether in the King or in a subject, is held subject to the public right, *jus publicum,* of navigation and fishing."

Not surprisingly, American law adopted as its own much of the English law respecting navigable waters, including the principle that submerged lands are held for a public purpose. A prominent example is *Illinois Central R. Co. v. Illinois*, 146 U.S. 387 (1892), where the Court held that the Illinois Legislature did not have the authority to vest the State's right and title to a portion of the navigable waters of Lake Michigan in a private party even though a proviso in the grant declared that it did not authorize obstructions to the harbor, impairment of the public right of navigation, or exemption of the private party from any act regulating rates of wharfage and dockage to be charged in the harbor. An attempted transfer was beyond the authority of the legislature since it amounted to abdication of its obligation to regulate, improve, and secure submerged lands for the benefit of every individual. While *Illinois Central* was "necessarily a statement of Illinois law," *Appleby v. City of New York*, 271 U.S. 364, 395 (1926), it invoked the principle in American law recognizing the weighty public interests in submerged lands.

American law, in some ways, enhanced and extended the public aspects of submerged lands. English law made a distinction between waterways subject to the ebb and flow of the tide and large enough to accommodate boats (royal rivers) and nontidal waterways (public highways). With respect to the royal rivers, the King was presumed to hold title to the river bed and soil while the public retained the right of passage and the right to fish. With public highways, as the name suggests, the public retained the right of passage, but title was typically held by a private party. See J. Angell, A Treatise on The Common Law in Relation to Water–Courses 14–18 (1824).

Do you agree with Professor James Rasband's argument that *Shively v. Bowlby* and *Illinois Central* are irreconcilable because "*Shively* views the question of the validity of sovereign grants of land under navigable waters as one of intent. *Illinois Central* views the question as one of power." James R. Rasband, *The Disregarded Common Parentage of the Equal Footing and Public Trust Doctrines*, 32 Land & Water L. Rev. 1, 67 (1997).

Is the public trust a pre-existing limitation on land and water titles in navigable waters that would limit claims that legislation curbing uses of such property would not be a taking? See discussion *infra* pp. 505–531. Professor Rasband has argued that this step cannot be taken because the trust is not grounded in the common law, let alone Roman law, and thus "[a]pplication of the doctrine can result not only in a dangerous usurpation of legislative authority, but also in a potential violation of the Fifth and Fourteenth Amendments when a prior grant of trust resources is revoked or modified without the payment of just compensation." James R. Rasband, *The Public Trust Doctrine: A Tragedy of the Common Law*, 77 Texas L. Rev. 1335, 1336 (1999); see also James L. Huffman, Trusting the Public Interest 6.

5.   The doctrine of *Illinois Central* has been offered as the basis for a general theory of public rights in natural resources requiring the assertion of state police power to ensure the protection of public rights when administrative or legislative decisions to develop trust resources give insufficient attention to trust values. Joseph L. Sax, *The Public Trust Doctrine in Natural Resource Law: Effective Judicial Intervention*, 68 Mich. L. Rev. 471 (1970). However, courts have not been enthusiastic about extending the trust to other resources such as public lands. *E.g.*, Sierra Club v. Andrus, 487 F.Supp. 443 (D.D.C.1980), aff'd Sierra Club v. Watt, 659 F.2d 203 (D.C.Cir.1981) (national parks). See Steven M. Jawetz, Comment, *The Public Trust Totem in Public Land Law: Ineffective—and Undesirable—Judicial Intervention*, 10 Ecology L.Q. 455 (1982).

6.   Joseph D. Kearney and Thomas W. Merrill, The Origins of the American Public Trust Doctrine: What Really Happened in Illinois Central, 71 U. Chicago L. Rev.799 (2004), is an exhaustive study of the fight to control the development of a harbor south of the Chicago River that led to Illinois Central. The authors conclude that the railroad consistently acted primarily to protect its investment in its lakefront trackage, but that the suspicion that the railroad obtained the 1869 legislation in part through bribery "is more likely than not correct," in part, because "the legislative history of the 1873 repeal suggests that Illinois Central was deeply concerned about the prospect of a formal investigation, and fought to defeat it. This ... suggests that the railroad had something to hide." Id. At 927. Kearney and Merrill's main conclusion is that the decision can not be explained as the simple subordination of the public to private interest because both the city's and railroad's harbor plans provided the same benefits to Chicago and thus "the fact that the railroad was largely motivated to protect its longstanding investment in the lakefront makes its position much more sympathetic than the caricature that comes through in the standard account" on the case. Id. At 926. What implications do these conclusions have for the Sax theory of the trust? Do you agree with the authors' argument that the beds of navigable waters are uniquely subject to more intense use contests because the line between private and public rights is uncertain and thus "caution is in order before extending the [public trust] doctrine to consumption rights in water. . . ."? Id. At 928.

National Audubon Society v. Superior Court of Alpine County

Supreme Court of California, 1983.
33 Cal.3d 419, 189 Cal.Rptr. 346, 658 P.2d 709, cert. denied, 464 U.S. 977, 104 S.Ct. 413, 78 L.Ed.2d 351.

■ BROUSSARD, JUSTICE.

Mono Lake, the second largest lake in California, sits at the base of the Sierra Nevada escarpment near the eastern entrance to Yosemite National Park. The lake is saline; it contains no fish but supports a large population of brine shrimp which feed vast numbers of nesting and migratory birds. Islands in the lake protect a large breeding colony of California gulls, and the lake itself serves as a haven on the migration route for thousands of Northern Phalarope, Wilson's Phalarope, and Eared Grebe. Towers and spires of tufa on the north and south shores are matters of geological interest and a tourist attraction.

Although Mono Lake receives some water from rain and snow on the lake surface, historically most of its supply came from snowmelt in the Sierra Nevada. Five freshwater streams—Mill, Lee Vining, Walker, Parker and Rush Creeks—arise near the crest of the range and carry the annual runoff to the west shore of the lake. In 1940, however, the Division of Water Resources, the predecessor to the present California Water Resources Board, granted the Department of Water and Power of the City of Los Angeles (hereafter DWP) a permit to appropriate virtually the entire flow of four of the five streams flowing into the lake. DWP promptly constructed facilities to divert about half the flow of these streams into DWP's Owens Valley aqueduct. In 1970 DWP completed a second diversion tunnel, and since that time has taken virtually the entire flow of these streams.

As a result of these diversions, the level of the lake has dropped; the surface area has diminished by one-third; one of the two principal islands in the lake has become a peninsula, exposing the gull rookery there to coyotes and other predators and causing the gulls to abandon the former island. The ultimate effect of continued diversions is a matter of intense dispute, but there seems little doubt that both the scenic beauty and the ecological values of Mono Lake are imperiled.

* * *

This case brings together for the first time two systems of legal thought: the appropriative water rights system which since the days of the gold rush has dominated California water law, and the public trust doctrine which, after evolving as a shield for the protection of tidelands, now extends its protective scope to navigable lakes. Ever since we first recognized that the public trust protects environmental and recreational values (*Marks v. Whitney* (1971) 6 Cal.3d 251 [98 Cal. Rptr. 790, 491 P.2d 374]), the two systems of legal thought have been on a collision course. (Johnson, *Public Trust Protection for Stream Flows and Lake Levels* (1980) 14 U.C. Davis L.Rev. 233.) They meet in a unique and dramatic setting which highlights the clash of values. Mono Lake is a scenic and ecological treasure of national significance, imperiled by continued diversions of water; yet, the need of Los Angeles for water is apparent, its reliance on rights granted by the board evident, the cost of curtailing diversions substantial.

Attempting to integrate the teachings and values of both the public trust and the appropriative water rights system, we have arrived at certain conclusions which we briefly summarize here. In our opinion, the core of the public trust doctrine is the state's authority as sovereign to exercise a continuous supervision and control over the navigable waters of the state and the lands underlying those waters. This authority applies to the waters tributary to Mono Lake and bars DWP or any other party from claiming a vested right to divert waters once it becomes clear that such diversions harm the interests protected by the public trust. The corollary rule which evolved in tideland and lakeshore cases barring conveyance of rights free of the trust except to serve trust purposes cannot, however, apply without modification to flowing waters. The prosperity and habitability of much of this state requires the diversion of great quantities of water from its streams for purposes unconnected to any navigation, commerce, fishing, recreation, or ecological use relating to the source stream. The state must have the power to grant nonvested usufructuary rights to appropriate water even if diversions harm public trust uses. Approval of such diversion without considering public trust values, however, may result in needless destruction of those values. Accordingly, we believe that before state courts and agencies approve water diversions they should consider the effect of such diversions upon interests protected by the public trust, and attempt, so far as feasible, to avoid or minimize any harm to those interests. * * *

The board's decision states that "[it] is indeed unfortunate that the City's proposed development will result in decreasing the aesthetic advantages of Mono Basin but *there is apparently nothing that this office can do to prevent it.* The use to which the City proposes to put the water under its Applications ... is defined by the Water Commission Act as the highest to which water may be applied and to make available unappropriated water for this use the City has, by the condemnation proceedings described above, acquired the littoral and riparian rights on Mono Lake and its tributaries south of Mill Creek. This office therefore has *no alternative but to dismiss all protests based upon the possible lowering of the water level in Mono Lake and the effect that the diversion of water from these streams may have upon the aesthetic and recreational value of the Basin.*" (Div. Wat. Resources Dec. 7053, 7055, 8042 & 8043 (Apr. 11, 1940), at p. 26, italics added.) * * *

"By the law of nature these things are common to mankind—the air, running water, the sea and consequently the shores of the sea." (Institutes of Justinian 2.1.1.) From this origin in Roman law, the English common law evolved the concept of the public trust, under which the sovereign owns "all of its navigable waterways and the lands lying beneath them 'as trustee of a public trust for the benefit of the people.' " (*Colberg, Inc. v. State of California ex rel. Dept. Pub. Wks.* (1967) 67 Cal.2d 408, 416, 62 Cal.Rptr. 401, 432 P.2d 3.) The State of California acquired title as trustee to such lands and waterways upon its admission to the union (*City of Berkeley v. Superior Court* (1980) 26 Cal.3d 515, 521, 162 Cal.Rptr. 327, 606 P.2d 362 and cases there cited); from the earliest days its judicial decisions have recognized and enforced the trust obligation.

Three aspects of the public trust doctrine require consideration in this opinion: the purpose of the trust; the scope of the trust, particularly as it applies to the nonnavigable tributaries of a navigable lake; and the powers and duties of the state as trustee of the public trust. We discuss these questions in the order listed.

(a) The purpose of the public trust.

The objective of the public trust has evolved in tandem with the changing public perception of the values and uses of waterways. As we observed in *Marks v. Whitney, supra*, 6 Cal.3d 251, "[p]ublic trust easements [were] traditionally defined in terms of navigation, commerce and fisheries. They have been held to include the right to fish, hunt, bathe, swim, to use for boating and general recreation purposes the navigable waters of the state, and to use the bottom of the navigable waters for anchoring, standing, or other purposes." (P. 259, 98 Cal. Rptr. 790, 491 P. 2d 374.) We went on, however, to hold that the traditional triad of uses—navigation, commerce and fishing—did not limit the public interest in the trust res.

* * *

Mono Lake is a navigable waterway. (*City of Los Angeles v. Aitken, supra*, 10 Cal.App.2d 460, 466.) It supports a small local industry which harvests brine shrimp for sale as fish food, which endeavor probably qualifies the lake as a "fishery" under the traditional public trust cases. The principal values plaintiffs seek to protect, however, are recreational and ecological—the scenic views of the lake and its shore, the purity of the air, and the use of the lake for nesting and feeding by birds. Under *Marks v. Whitney, supra*, it is clear that protection of these values is among the purposes of the public trust.

* * *

We conclude that the public trust doctrine, as recognized and developed in California decisions, protects navigable waters from harm caused by diversion of nonnavigable tributaries.[19]

19. In view of the conclusion stated in the text, we need not consider the question whether the public trust extends for some purposes—such as protection of fishing, environmental values, and recreation interests—to nonnavigable streams. For discussion of

(c) Duties and powers of the state as trustee.

In the following review of the authority and obligations of the state as administrator of the public trust, the dominant theme is the state's sovereign power and duty to exercise continued supervision over the trust. One consequence, of importance to this and many other cases, is that parties acquiring rights in trust property generally hold those rights subject to the trust, and can assert no vested right to use those rights in a manner harmful to the trust.

As we noted recently in *City of Berkeley v. Superior Court, supra*, the decision of the United States Supreme Court in *Illinois Central Railroad Company v. Illinois, supra*, "remains the primary authority even today, almost nine decades after it was decided." The Illinois Legislature in 1886 had granted the railroad in fee simple 1,000 acres of submerged lands, virtually the entire Chicago waterfront. Four years later it sought to revoke that grant. The Supreme Court upheld the revocatory legislation. Its opinion explained that lands under navigable waters conveyed to private parties for wharves, docks, and other structures in furtherance of trust purposes could be granted free of the trust because the conveyance is consistent with the purpose of the trust. But the legislature, it held, did not have the power to convey the entire city waterfront free of trust, thus barring all future legislatures from protecting the public interest.

* * *

* * * [I]n our recent decision in *City of Berkeley v. Superior Court, supra*, 26 Cal.3d 515, we considered whether deeds executed by the Board of Tidelands Commissioners pursuant to an 1870 act conferred title free of the trust. Applying the principles of earlier decisions, we held that the grantees' title was subject to the trust, both because the Legislature had not made clear its intention to authorize a conveyance free of the trust and because the 1870 act and the conveyances under it were not intended to further trust purposes.

Once again we rejected the claim that establishment of the public trust constituted a taking of property for which compensation was required: * * *

In summary, the foregoing cases amply demonstrate the continuing power of the state as administrator of the public trust, a power which extends to the revocation of previously granted rights or to the enforcement of the trust against lands long thought free of the trust (see *City of Berkeley v. Superior Court, supra*). Except for those rare instances in which a grantee may acquire a right to use former trust property free of trust restrictions, the grantee holds subject to the trust, and while he may assert a vested right to the servient estate (the right of use subject to the trust) and to any improvements he erects, he can claim no vested right to bar recognition of the trust or state action to carry out its purposes. * * *

this subject, see Walston, *The Public Trust Doctrine in the Water Rights Context: The* *Wrong Environmental Remedy* (1982) 22 Santa Clara L.Rev. 63, 85.

Our recent decision in *People v. Shirokow* (1980) 26 Cal.3d 301, 162 Cal.Rptr. 30, 605 P.2d 859, described the early history of the appropriative water rights system in California. We explained that "California operates under the so-called dual system of water rights which recognizes both the appropriation and the riparian doctrines. * * * "

In 1926, however, a decision of this court led to a constitutional amendment which radically altered water law in California and led to an expansion of the powers of the board. In *Herminghaus v. South. California Edison Co.* (1926) 200 Cal. 81, 252 P. 607, we held not only that riparian rights took priority over appropriations authorized by the Water Board, a point which had always been clear, but that as between the riparian and the appropriator, the former's use of water was not limited by the doctrine of reasonable use. (Pp. 100–101.) That decision led to a constitutional amendment which abolished the right of a riparian to devote water to unreasonable uses, and established the doctrine of reasonable use as an overriding feature of California water law.

* * *

* * * This amendment does more than merely overturn *Herminghaus*—it establishes state water policy. All uses of water, including public trust uses, must now conform to the standard of reasonable use.

* * *

* * * In our opinion, both the public trust doctrine and the water rights system embody important precepts which make the law more responsive to the diverse needs and interests involved in the planning and allocation of water resources. To embrace one system of thought and reject the other would lead to an unbalanced structure, one which would either decry as a breach of trust appropriations essential to the economic development of this state, or deny any duty to protect or even consider the values promoted by the public trust. Therefore, seeking an accommodation which will make use of the pertinent principles of both the public trust doctrine and the appropriative water rights system, and drawing upon the history of the public trust and the water rights system, the body of judicial precedent, and the views of expert commentators, we reach the following conclusions:

a. The state as sovereign retains continuing supervisory control over its navigable waters and the lands beneath those waters. This principle, fundamental to the concept of the public trust, applies to rights in flowing waters as well as to rights in tidelands and lakeshores; it prevents any party from acquiring a vested right to appropriate water in a manner harmful to the interests protected by the public trust.

b. As a matter of current and historical necessity, the Legislature, acting directly or through an authorized agency such as the Water Board, has the power to grant usufructuary licenses that will permit an appropriator to take water from flowing streams and use that water in a distant part of the state, even though this taking does not promote, and may unavoidably harm, the trust uses at the source stream. The population and economy of this state depend upon the appropriation of vast quantities of water for uses unrelated to in-stream trust values. California's Constitution (see art. X, § 2), its statutes (see Wat. Code, §§ 100, 104), decisions, and commentators all emphasize the need to make efficient use of California's limited water resources: all recognize, at least implicitly, that efficient use requires diverting water from in-stream uses. Now that the economy and population centers of this state have developed in reliance upon appropriated water, it would be disingenuous to hold that such appropriations are and have always been improper to the extent that they harm public trust uses, and can be justified only upon theories of reliance or estoppel.

c. The state has an affirmative duty to take the public trust into account in the planning and allocation of water resources, and to protect public trust uses whenever feasible. Just as the history of this state shows that appropriation may be necessary for efficient use of water despite unavoidable harm to public trust values, it demonstrates that an appropriative water rights system administered without consideration of the public trust may cause unnecessary and unjustified harm to trust interests. As a matter of practical necessity the state may have to approve appropriations despite foreseeable harm to public trust uses. In so doing, however, the state must bear in mind its duty as trustee to consider the effect of the taking on the public trust (see *United Plainsmen v. N.D. State Water Cons. Commission* (N.D. 1976) 247 N.W.2d 457, 462–463), and to preserve, so far as consistent with the public interest, the uses protected by the trust.

Once the state has approved an appropriation, the public trust imposes a duty of continuing supervision over the taking and use of the appropriated water. In exercising its sovereign power to allocate water resources in the public interest, the state is not confined by past allocation decisions which may be incorrect in light of current knowledge or inconsistent with current needs.

The state accordingly has the power to reconsider allocation decisions even though those decisions were made after due consideration of their effect on the public trust. The case for reconsidering a particular decision, however, is even stronger when that decision failed to weigh and consider public trust uses. In the case before us, the salient fact is that no responsible body has ever determined the impact of diverting the entire flow of the Mono Lake tributaries into the Los Angeles Aqueduct. This is not a case in which the Legislature, the Water Board, or any judicial body has determined that the needs of Los Angeles outweigh the needs of the Mono Basin, that the benefit gained is worth the price. Neither has any responsible body determined whether some lesser taking would better balance the diverse interests. Instead, DWP acquired rights to the entire flow in 1940 from a water board which believed it lacked both the power and the duty to protect the Mono Lake environment, and continues to exercise those rights in apparent disregard for the resulting damage to the scenery, ecology, and human uses of Mono Lake.

It is clear that some responsible body ought to reconsider the allocation of the waters of the Mono Basin. No vested rights bar such reconsideration.

We recognize the substantial concerns voiced by Los Angeles—the city's need for water, its reliance upon the 1940 board decision, the cost both in terms of money and environmental impact of obtaining water elsewhere. Such concerns must enter into any allocation decision. We hold only that they do not preclude a reconsideration and reallocation which also takes into account the impact of water diversion on the Mono Lake environment.
* * *

This opinion is but one step in the eventual resolution of the Mono Lake controversy. We do not dictate any particular allocation of water. Our objective is to resolve a legal conundrum in which two competing systems of thought—the public trust doctrine and the appropriative water rights system—existed independently of each other, espousing principles which seemingly suggested opposite results. We hope by integrating these two doctrines to clear away the legal barriers which have so far prevented either the Water Board or the courts from taking a new and objective look at the water resources of the Mono Basin. The human and environmental uses of Mono Lake—uses protected by the public trust doctrine—deserve to be taken into account. Such uses should not be destroyed because the state mistakenly thought itself powerless to protect them.

* * *

■ RICHARDSON, JUSTICE, concurring and dissenting.

I concur with parts 1 through 4 of the majority opinion and with its analysis of the relationship between the public trust doctrine and the water rights system in this state. I respectfully dissent, however, from part 5 of the opinion wherein the majority holds that the courts and the California Water Resources Board (Water Board) have *concurrent* jurisdiction in cases of this kind. In my view, there are several compelling reasons for holding that the Water Board has exclusive original jurisdiction over the present dispute, subject of course to judicial review of its decision.

NOTES

1. The Mono Lake case has a happy ending. In subsequent litigation, an intermediate appellate court held that California Fish and Game Code §§ 5937 and 5946 required the State Water Resources Board to condition Los Angeles Water and Power's tributary diversions that started after the statutes were passed in 1953 in order to protect a pre-existing trout fishery. California Trout, Inc. v. State Water Res. Control Bd., 207 Cal.App.3d 585, 255 Cal.Rptr. 184 (1989). Then, the state legislature appropriated $60 million for the replacement of the lost 50,000 acre-feet, and the parties ultimately agreed to stabilize the lake level at 6,392.6 feet compared to the pre-diversion level of 6,405 feet. John Hart, Storm Over Mono: The Mono Lake Battle and the California Water Future 177 (1996) describes a vision of the post-litigation lake:

> At the tufa groves, the rising tide will spread among the towers. Tufa masses now at the shoreline will become islands; towers now

standing in the bushes. . . . Negrit Island will regain its isolation. . . . Though coyotes are known to swim, the widening waters should eventually discourage them, and the gull colony should return. On the great arc of the lake's eastern rim, the alkali band will shrink until, in most cases, lakewater meets either vegetation or dark-colored sand. From a distance the lake will appear "full." Dust will blow here and there, but the great regional storms should be no more. Along the shore, wetlands will more commonly be found near open water, providing good habitat for ducks.

In 2008, the Los Angeles Times reported that the lake level is rising but that "the water in Mono Lake remains at 34 feet below its pre-diversion level, and it still has 8 vertical feet to rise before it reaches its target of 6,391 feet about sea level that was set by the Water Resources Control Board, and if the mark isn't hit by 2014, the panel will hold a hearing on the matter." Louis Sagahun, There Was a Time When It Was Hard To Find Yellow Warblers At Rush Creek, Los Angeles Times, July 24, 2008. See Gregory Webber, *Articulating the Public Trust, Text, Near–Text and Context*, 27 Ariz St. L.J. 1155 (1996) (assessing the doctrine's application in California water administration).

2. The public trust doctrine has been adopted in other states. *E.g.*, United Plainsmen Ass'n v. North Dakota State Water Conservation Comm'n, 247 N.W.2d 457 (N.D.1976) (holding that state agency must consider potential effect of large appropriation for an energy project on state's future water needs). But some states seem to be moving away from the doctrine. For instance, in Washington, the Supreme Court ruled that the trust does not apply to non-navigable water or groundwater and thus cannot be involved in most disputes. Rettkowski v. Department of Ecology, 122 Wash.2d 219, 858 P.2d 232 (1993). Idaho seemingly adopted the trust in two major decisions, Ritter v. Standal, 98 Idaho 446, 566 P.2d 769 (1977) and Kootenai Environmental Alliance, Inc. v. Panhandle Yacht Club. Inc., 105 Idaho 622, 671 P.2d 1085 (1983). But then the state supreme court held that a conservation organization had no standing to intervene in the Snake River basin-wide adjudication to assert public trust values. The court held that the constitutional right to divert limits the application of trust to the exercise of water rights. The Court did add that the state's trust responsibility is not diminished by the adjudication. Idaho Conservation League v. State, 128 Idaho 155, 911 P.2d 748 (1995). Then, in 1996 the Idaho legislature enacted legislation to make it very difficult, if not impossible, for the state to assert a public trust interest in the state's waters. IDAHO CODE ANN. §§ 58–1201 to –1203 (2008). The legislation allows the alienation of trust lands for agriculture, mining and forestry, or other uses and adopts the federal bed title test of navigability. Is the legislation constitutional under Idaho v. Coeur d'Alene Tribe, *supra* p. 423? See Michael Blumm, Harrison Dunning & Scott Reed, *Renouncing the Public Trust: An Assessment of the Validity of Idaho House Bill 794*, 24 Ecology L. Q. 461 (1997).

In Arizona's Gila River adjudication, a lower court had upheld the state's legislation decision to exclude consideration of the public trust in the adjudication. Then, on appeal, the Arizona Supreme Court reversed, holding that "[t]he public trust doctrine is a constitutional limitation on legislative power" which "[t]he Legislature cannot by legislation destroy." *San Carlos Apache Tribe v. Superior Court,* 193 Ariz. 195, 972 P.2d 179, 198 (1999).

In re Water Use Permit Applications, Petitions for Interim Instream Flow Standard Amendments, and Petitions for Water Reservations for the Waiahole Ditch

Supreme Court of Hawai'i, 2000.
94 Haw. 97, 9 P.3d 409.

[From 1913 to 1995, the Waiahole Ditch collected surface water and dike-impounded groundwater and transported it from the windward (east) to the leeward (west) side of the island of Oahu to irrigate a sugar plantation. After the plantation was discontinued, the Waiahole Irrigation Company (WIC) filed water rights applications with the Hawai'i Water Rights Commission on behalf of other water users. The combined filings exceeded the capacity of the ditch. First, the commission ordered WIC to stop disposing of irrigation wastewater into ditches and instead to release the surplus water to restore depleted windward streams. This experiment in ecosystem management was successful; the flows flushed out exotic species and experts predicted that native species could be reintroduced and thrive in the streams. Then, the commission concluded that it had a public trust duty to establish instream flow standards but those standards could only be established after long-term research and monitoring. Nevertheless, the "precautionary principle" (governments should regulate to prevent environmental harm in the face of scientific uncertainty and the burden of proof is on the regulated party, not the government) required action. The commission allowed irrigation uses on the leeward side of the island but also required substantial releases of water into the stream on the windward side, saying it would revise the instream flow requirements periodically. This was challenged by the water users as exceeding any common law public trust duties. The Court held otherwise.]

Having established the public trust doctrine's independent validity, we must define its basic parameters with respect to the water resources of this state. In so doing, we address: a) the "scope" of the trust, or the resources it encompasses; and b) the "substance" of the trust, including the purposes or uses it upholds and the powers and duties it confers on the state.

a.   Scope of the Trust

The public trust doctrine has varied in scope over time and across jurisdictions. * * * In Hawai'i, this court has recognized, based on founding principles of law in this jurisdiction, a distinct public trust encompassing all the water resources of the state. See *Robinson,* 65 Haw. at 674, 658 P.2d at 310. The Hawai'i Constitution declares that "all public resources are held in trust by the state for the benefit of its people," Haw. Const. art.

XI, § 1, and establishes a public trust obligation "to protect, control, and regulate the use of Hawaii's water resources for the benefit of its people," Haw. Const. art. XI, § 7.

We need not define the full extent of article XI, section 1's reference to "all public resources" at this juncture. For the purposes of this case, however, we reaffirm that, under article XI, sections 1 and 7 and the sovereign reservation, the public trust doctrine applies to all water resources without exception or distinction. KSBE and Castle advocate for the exclusion of ground waters from the public trust. Their arguments, first, contradict the clear import of the constitutional provisions, which do not differentiate between categories of water in mandating the protection and regulation of water resources for the common good.[31] The convention's records confirm that the framers understood "water resources" as "include[ing] ground water, surface water and all other water." Debates, in 2 Proceedings, at 861 (statement by Delegate Fukunaga).

We are also unpersuaded by the contention of KSBE and Castle that the sovereign reservation does not extend to ground waters. Their position rests almost entirely on one decision, *City Mill Co., Ltd. v. Honolulu Sewer & Water Comm'n*, 30 Haw. 912 (1929). Discussing the effect of the Mahele, the *City Mill* court observed that " 'all mineral or metallic mines' were reserved to the Hawaiian government, but there was no reservation whatever of the subterranean waters." *Id.* at 934. Nowhere in the opinion, however, does the court address the reservation of sovereign prerogatives and its surrounding historical and legal context. This fatal oversight, common to other cases subsequently invalidated by this court, discounts the precedential value of City Mill concerning the public trust. * * *

* * *

Even more fundamentally, just as ancient Hawaiian usage reflected the perspectives of that era, the common law distinctions between ground and surface water developed without regard to the manner in which "both categories represent no more than a single integrated source of water with each element dependent upon the other for its existence." *Id.* at 555, 656 P.2d at 73. Modern science and technology have discredited the surface-ground dichotomy. *See id.* (describing the "modern scientific approach" of acknowledging "the unity of the hydrological cycle"); A. Dan Tarlock, *Law of Water Rights and Resources* § 4:5 (2000). * * * In determining the scope of the sovereign reservation, therefore, we see little sense in adhering to artificial distinctions neither recognized by the ancient system nor borne out in the present practical realities of this state.

31. With respect to article XI, section 1, KSBE contends that the provision's reference to "public natural resources" indicates an intent to exclude "privately owned" waters from the public trust. This argument misses the point; at least in the water resources context, we have maintained that, apart from any private rights that may exist in water, "there is, as there always has been, a superior public interest in this natural bounty." Robinson, 65 Haw. at 677, 658 P.2d at 312.

Water is no less an essential "usufruct of lands" when found below, rather than above, the ground. In view of the ultimate value of water to the ancient Hawaiians, it is inescapable that the sovereign reservation was intended to guarantee public rights to all water, regardless of its immediate source. Whatever practices the ancients may have observed in their time, therefore, we must conclude that the reserved trust encompasses any usage developed in ours, including the "ground water" uses proposed by the parties in the instant case. The public trust, by its very nature, does not remain fixed for all time, but must conform to changing needs and circumstances. * * *

In sum, given the vital importance of all waters to the public welfare, we decline to carve out a ground water exception to the water resources trust. Based on the plain language of our constitution and a reasoned modern view of the sovereign reservation, we confirm that the public trust doctrine applies to all water resources, unlimited by any surface-ground distinction.

b. Substance of the Trust

The public trust is a dual concept of sovereign right and responsibility. Previous decisions have thoroughly reviewed the sovereign authority of the state under the trust. The arguments in the present appeal focus on the state's trust duties. In its decision, the Commission stated that, under the public trust doctrine, "the State's first duty is to protect the fresh water resources (surface and ground) which are part of the public trust res," a duty which it further described as "a categorical imperative and the precondition to all subsequent considerations." The public trust, the Commission also ruled, subjects offstream water uses to a "heightened level of scrutiny." *Id.* at 10.

In *Illinois Central*, the United States Supreme Court described the state's interest in its navigable waters as "title," not in a proprietary sense, but "title held *in trust for the people of the State that they may enjoy* the navigation of the *waters*, carry on commerce over them, and have liberty of fishing therein *freed from the obstruction or interference of private parties*." 146 U.S. at 452 (emphases added). The trust, in the Court's simplest terms, "requires the government of the State to *preserve such waters for the use of the public*." *Id.* at 453 (emphasis added).

Based on this formulation, other courts have sought to further define the requirements of the public trust doctrine. The rules developed in order to protect public water bodies and submerged lands for public access and use, however. * * * This court recognized as much in *Robinson*, stating that "[t]he extent of the state's trust obligation over all waters of course would not be identical to that which applies to navigable waters." 65 Haw. at 675, 658 P.2d at 310. Keeping this distinction in mind, we consider the substance of the water resources trust of this state, specifically, the purposes protected by the trust and the powers and duties conferred on the state thereunder.

i. Purposes of the Trust

In other states, the "purposes" or "uses" of the public trust have evolved with changing public values and needs. The trust traditionally preserved public rights of navigation, commerce, and fishing. * * *

As a logical extension from the increasing number of public trust uses of waters in their natural state, courts have recognized the distinct public interest in resource protection. As explained by the California Supreme Court:

> One of the most important public uses of the tidelands—a use encompassed within the tidelands trust—*is the preservation of those lands in their natural state*, so that they may serve as ecological units for scientific study, as open space, and as environments which provide food and habitat for birds and marine life, and which favorably affect the scenery and climate of the area. * * *

This court has likewise acknowledged resource protection, with its numerous derivative public uses, benefits, and values, as an important underlying purpose of the reserved water resources trust. *See Robinson*, 65 Haw. at 674–76, 658 P.2d at 310–11 (upholding the public interest in the "purity and flow," "continued existence," and "preservation" of the waters of the state). The people of our state have validated resource "protection" by express constitutional decree. *See* Haw. Const. art. XI, §§ 1 & 7. We thus hold that the maintenance of waters in their natural state constitutes a distinct "use" under the water resources trust. This disposes of any portrayal of retention of waters in their natural state as "waste." *See Reppun*, 65 Haw. at 560 n.20, 656 P.2d at 76 n.20 (citing article XI, section 1 as an acknowledgment of the public interest in "a free-flowing stream for its own sake").

Whether under riparian or prior appropriation systems, common law or statute, states have uniformly recognized domestic uses, particularly drinking, as among the highest uses of water resources. * * * This jurisdiction presents no exception. In granting individuals fee simple title to land in the Kuleana Act, the kingdom expressly guaranteed: "The people shall . . . have a right to drinking water, and running water. . . ." Enactment of Further Principles of 1850 § 7, Laws of 1850 at 202 (codified at HRS § 7–1 (1993)). *See also McBryde*, 54 Haw. at 191–98, 504 P.2d at 1341–44 (comparing section 7 of the Kuleana act with authority in other jurisdictions recognizing riparian rights to water for domestic uses); *Carter v. Territory*, 24 Haw. 47, 66 (1917) (granting priority to domestic use based on riparian principles and section 7 of the Kuleana Act). And although this provision and others, including the reservation of sovereign prerogatives, evidently originated out of concern for the rights of native tenants in particular, we have no doubt that they apply today, in a broader sense, to the vital domestic uses of the general public. Accordingly, we recognize domestic water use as a purpose of the state water resources trust. * * *

In acknowledging the general public's need for water, however, we do not lose sight of the trust's "original intent." As noted above, review of the early law of the kingdom reveals the specific objective of preserving the rights of native tenants during the transition to a western system of private property. Before the Mahele, the law "Respecting Water for Irrigation" assured native tenants "their equal proportion" of water. Subsequently, the aforementioned Kuleana Act provision ensured tenants' rights to essential incidents of land beyond their own kuleana, including water, in recognition that "a little bit of land even with allodial title, if they be cut off from all other privileges would be of very little value," 3B Privy Council Records 713 (1850). *See also Reppun*, 65 Haw. 549–50, 656 P.2d at 69–70 (analogizing riparian rights under section 7 of the Kuleana Act to water rights of Indian reservations in Winters v. United States, 207 U.S. 564, 28 S.Ct. 207, 52 L. Ed. 340 (1908)); *cf. Peck v. Bailey*, 8 Haw. 658, 661 (1867) (recognizing "appurtenant rights" to water based on "immemorial usage"). In line with this history and our prior precedent, See *Kalipi v. Hawaiian Trust Co.*, 66 Haw. 1, 656 P.2d 745 (1982); *Public Access Shoreline Hawai'i v. Hawaii Planning Comm'n*, 79 Haw. 425, 438–447, 903 P.2d 1246, 1259–68 (1995), *cert. denied*, 517 U.S. 1163, 134 L. Ed. 2d 660, 116 S. Ct. 1559 (1996), and constitutional mandate, See Haw. Const. art. XII, § 7, we continue to uphold the exercise of Native Hawaiian and traditional and customary rights as a public trust purpose.

LURF asserts that the public trust in Hawai'i encompasses private use of resources for "economic development," citing, *inter alia, Territory v. Liliuokalani*, 14 Haw. 88 (1902) (grants of tidal lands to private individuals), *Haalelea v. Montgomery*, 2 Haw. 62 (1858) (konohiki fishing rights), and the Admissions Act, Act of Mar. 18, 1959, Pub. L. 83–3, 73 Stat. 4, § 5(f) (designating "development of farm and home ownership" as one of the purposes of the state ceded lands trust). While these examples generally demonstrate that the public trust may allow grants of private interests in trust resources under certain circumstances, they in no way establish private commercial use as among the public purposes *protected* by the trust.

Although its purpose has evolved over time, the public trust has never been understood to safeguard rights of exclusive use for private commercial gain. Such an interpretation, indeed, eviscerates the trust's basic purpose of reserving the resource for use and access by the general public without preference or restriction. * * *

National Audubon, 658 P.2d at 723–24. * * *

We hold that, while the state water resources trust acknowledges that private use for "economic development" may produce important public benefits and that such benefits must figure into any balancing of competing interests in water, it stops short of embracing private commercial use as a protected "trust purpose." We thus eschew LURF's view of the trust, in which the " 'public interest' advanced by the trust is the sum of competing private interests" and the "rhetorical distinction between 'public trust' and 'private gain' is a false dichotomy." To the contrary, if the public trust is to retain any meaning and effect, it must recognize enduring public rights in trust resources separate from, and superior to, the prevailing private interests in the resources at any given time. See Robinson, 65 Haw. at 677,

658 P.2d at 312 ("[U]nderlying every private diversion and application there is, as there always has been, a superior public interest in this natural bounty.").

ii. Powers and Duties of the State under the Trust

This court has described the public trust relating to water resources as the authority and duty "to maintain the *purity and flow* of our waters for future generations and to assure that the waters of our land are put to *reasonable and beneficial uses.*" *Id.* at 674, 658 P.2d at 310 (emphases added). Similarly, article XI, section 1 of the Hawai'i Constitution requires the state both to "protect" natural resources *and* to promote their "use and development." The state water resources trust thus embodies a dual mandate of 1) protection and 2) maximum reasonable and beneficial use.

NOTES

1. Do the California and Hawai'i Supreme Courts adopt the same theory of the nature of the public trust? California has limited the trust to navigable waters. Golden Feather Community Ass'n v. Thermalito Irrigation Dist., 209 Cal.App.3d 1276, 257 Cal.Rptr. 836 (1989). Does Hawai'i adhere to the navigable non-navigable distinction? In contrast to California, Hawai'i has a statutory scheme that incorporates the protection of instream flows. What is the justification for the imposition of an independent trust duty? What must an applicant in Hawai'i demonstrate to obtain a consumptive use permit?

2. The Court has continued to apply and extend the trust in two cases involving the small, arid and groundwater dependent island of Moloka'i. In In re Wai'ola O Moloka'i, 83 P.3d 664, 103 Hawai'i 401 (2004), the Court remanded a well permit issued to the island's largest land owner, Molokai'i Ranch, because the Commission failed to discharge its trust responsibility to native Hawaiians when it shifted the burden of proof to interveners (1) to establish that there would be no interference with Department of Hawaiian Homelands water reservations and (2) to show that the risk of salt water intrusion from the proposed pumping would impair customary native gathering rights among ahupua's tenants. However, the Court upheld that Commission's decision to allow the use of groundwater on non-overlying land, as allowed by HAW. REV. STAT. § 174C–49(c), in part, because the decision was consistent with state and county land use plans. *In re* Kukui (Molokai), Inc., 116 Hawai'i 481, 174 P.3d 320 (2007), involved a different well permit application by a successor to land originally owned by Molokai'i Ranch. The Court remanded the permit because the Commission failed to discharge its trust responsibilities to the Department of Hawaiian Homelands by failing to consider whether practicable alternative sources of water were available. In addition, the Court held that again the Commission incorrectly placed a burden on other interveners to show that would be no interference with customary native gathering rights. For a critical view of these decisions see David L. Callies and Calvert G. Chipchase, *Water Regulation, Land Use and the Environment*, 30 U. Haw. L. Rev. 49 (2007).

3. ALLOWABLE PRIVATE USE OF SUBMERGED LANDS

At common law a wharf placed in navigable waters was a purpresture (unlawful enclosure of public property). If injury to the public right of navigation was shown, it was also a public nuisance. The difference was that if only a purpresture was proved, the court could decide if it would be more beneficial to the public to abate it or let it remain. But, if a public nuisance existed, the court could not balance and the wharf had to be removed. See Joseph K. Angell, A Treatise On The Right Of Property In Tide Waters And In The Soil And Shores Thereof 196–206 (2d ed. 1847).

Colonial ordinances "early allowed the owners of lands bounding on tide waters greater rights and privileges in the shore below high water mark, then they had in England." Shively v. Bowlby, 152 U.S. 1, 18, 14 S.Ct. 548, 38 L.Ed. 331 (1894). A 1661 Massachusetts ordinance permitted a riparian to wharf out 100 rods from the high water mark. Gradually the eastern and midwestern states came to recognize the right by statute or custom and usage. Modern cases typically are consistent with such rights. *E.g.*, Johnson v. Bryant, 350 So.2d 433 (Ala.1977) (a dock erected pursuant to the common law right to wharf out and authorized by the Corps of Engineers "does not constitute a nuisance per se"). In the Pacific coast states, however, the right has always been entirely statutory as the courts have consistently held that any wharf which is not authorized by the legislature is a purpresture. Other states seem to be moving toward this position.

In California, the state may allow the riparian to wharf out upon the payment of fees or may eject the wharfing-out riparian as a trespasser. If the state elects not to bring suit, another riparian claiming injury from the wharf can only obtain relief upon proof that the wharf is a public nuisance that causes special damage. Woods v. Johnson, 241 Cal.App.2d 278, 50 Cal.Rptr. 515 (1966). A Florida intermediate court of appeals described the right as a "quantified common law right to wharf out in the absence of a statute." Board of Trustees of the Internal Improvement Trust Fund v. Medeira Beach Nominee, Inc., 272 So.2d 209 (Fla.App.1973). The right is subject to regulation by statute, under the common law doctrines of shared surface use to the public right to use navigable waters. See Board of Trustees of the Internal Improvement Trust Fund v. Levy, 656 So.2d 1359 (Fla.Dist.Ct.App.1995), which upheld limitations on the length of docks waterward of the mean high water line. See also Intracoastal North Condominium Ass'n v. Palm Beach County, 698 So.2d 384 (Fla.App.1997), which held that the excavation of a navigable channel which increased the current and diminished the riparian's access to navigable waters was not a taking.

Wharves and piers in navigable waters are also subject to the navigation servitude, which is discussed *infra* p. 479. Thus, the United States may order a pier owner to remove a pier that was lawfully erected but subsequently became an obstruction to navigation. United States v. Alameda Gateway Ltd., 213 F.3d 1161 (9th Cir.2000).

How can the public right to use the surface of the water overlying state-owned beds be reconciled with the riparian's easement to wharf out? Capune v. Robbins, 273 N.C. 581, 160 S.E.2d 881 (1968), offers one answer. Plaintiff was attempting to go from Coney Island, New York, to Florida via surfboard. Defendant owned a fishing pier built into the Atlantic Ocean and it was his policy to keep surfboarders away from it. He failed to realize the epic nature of the plaintiff's trip and when plaintiff passed under the pier, defendant yelled at him not to go under the pier. As plaintiff was trying to turn his board, defendant struck him on the head with a pop bottle. Plaintiff recovered damages in tort and on appeal defendant argued that plaintiff had no legal right to travel under the pier. While it is hard to believe that defendant's force was reasonable even if plaintiff was a trespasser, the court chose in part to rest plaintiff's recovery on his right as a member of the public to use navigable waters for recreational purposes.

On non-navigable lakes surrounded by private lands riparian owners also seek to build docks and fill in privately-owned submerged lands. Though the waterbody is not technically navigable it may support boat traffic and a variety of recreational uses of the surface that are within the correlative rights of other riparian owners, if not the public. The nature of those rights is discussed *infra* pp. 449–461. Conflicts in this setting are essentially disputes among riparians whose competing property rights have equal status, though states may extend public rights in ways that bring them into conflict with private rights.

Wilbour v. Gallagher

Supreme Court of Washington, 1969.
77 Wash.2d 306, 462 P.2d 232.

■ HILL, JUDGE.

We are here concerned with the uses to which privately owned land can be put, which for "thirty-five years" has been submerged each year by waters of a navigable lake. The submergence at its maximum depth (3 to 15 feet) was for approximately 3 months, June 15 to September 15 each year.

* * *

Lake Chelan is a glacial gorge in Chelan County, approximately 55 miles in length, and with a width, generally speaking, of from 1 to 2 miles. Its navigability is conceded. Prior to 1927, it lay in its natural state with the level of its waters at 1,079 feet above sea level. By 1891 the land involved in this action had passed into private ownership being included in the "Plat of the Town of Lake Park." The platter dedicated and quit-claimed all streets and alleys therein to the use of the public forever. All of the platted property subsequently became a part of the town of Lakeside, and is now a part of the town of Chelan. The date of incorporation of Lakeside does not appear from the record, but on May 2, 1927, by ordinance No. 24, the town vacated certain specifically described streets and alleys.

* * *

It should be noted that the public is the beneficiary of the grant in perpetuity of " * * * the right of access * * * over the lands included within the boundaries of those portions of the vacated streets and alleys hereinafter described, to Lake Chelan, at all stages of water * * * "

The Chelan Electric Company constructed a dam, pursuant to a permit by the Federal Power Commission, which permitted the annual raising of the level of the lake to 1,100 feet above sea level, with the requirement that it reach that level by June 15 each year. Thereafter in May of each year the dam was closed and the waters gradually rose to the 1,100 foot level, presumably by June 15th. They were maintained at that level until September when the dam was opened and the waters gradually subsided to the natural 1,079 foot level.

We come now to a consideration of the right claimed by the defendants, Norman G. Gallagher and Ruth I. Gallagher, his wife, to fill their land below the 1,100 foot level to a height 5 feet above that level, and thus prevent its being submerged and making it available for use at all times. (Certain fills have now been completed.)

The claimed right is challenged by the plaintiffs (Charles S. Wilbour and Harriet G. Wilbour, his wife; and Chester L. Green and Ruby Green, his wife) who brought a class action on behalf of themselves and the public asking that the fills be removed, and asking for damages to their own properties caused by the fills.

To assist in an understanding of the situation, we have prepared a drawing, which appears on the following page. It is not drawn to scale, neither is it an exhibit in the case and it has been prepared for illustrative purposes only. It is based primarily on exhibit 5, a large drawing by Mr. Gallagher showing the fills he has made. It shows also the approximate water line of Lake Chelan at both the 1,079 and 1,100–foot levels. The lots, blocks, streets and alleys are as shown in the plat of Lake Park, and State Highway 97 has been superimposed. Unfortunately, the block numbers, other than 2 and 3, were omitted, and they will be supplied in our narrative explanation of the drawing.

The shaded area has been divided into 4 lettered segments. G and W are the properties owned by the plaintiffs (the Greens and the Wilbours), improved with their respective homes, and lying partially above and below the 1,100 foot level (all of block 4, plat of Lake Park). A and B represent the two fills made by the defendants (the Gallaghers), both fills have access to Highway 97, and are now being used as trailer courts. A includes block 3, plat of Lake Park (except lots 1 and 2), including the alley in that block extending from vacated Wharf Street to vacated Main Street; a portion of block 6, plat of Lake Park, between the highway and vacated Main Street;

also portions of vacated Main and Cross[10] Streets. B includes a part of block 4, plat of Lake Park between the highway and vacated Cross Street; lots 18 to 22 inclusive, block 2, plat of Lake Park; and the portion of vacated Cross Street lying between the indicated portions of blocks 4 and 2. A portion of the intersection of vacated Cross and Wharf Streets also has been blockaded by a construction of the defendants, not shown on the drawing.

The trial court found that for 35 years prior to the trial (July and September 1965) and except for the filling by the defendants, commenced in 1961, the waters of Lake Chelan

> covered the lands of Defendants in Blocks 2 and 3, Lake Park, including the streets and alleys in and adjacent to said Blocks 2 and 3, for a period each year from late spring through September, to a depth of three feet to fifteen feet.

And that for the same period

> the general public, including Plaintiffs and their respective predecessors in interest, have used the waters covering the portions of Blocks 2 and 3, Plat of Lake Park, now owned by the Defendants, as well as the water covering portions of the streets and alleys adjacent thereto, for fishing, boating, swimming and for general recreational use and that said use was open adverse, notorious and uninterrupted for said period, during the period of each year when water covers the said portions of Block 2 and 3 and the adjacent streets and alleys.

The trial court ultimately concluded (based upon estoppel) that the defendants should not be compelled to remove their fills, but awarded the plaintiffs damages, finding that the value of the Wilbour property had been lessened $8,500, and the value of the Green property had been lessened $11,000 by reason of the fills established by the defendants.

* * *

This lessening of value was predicated principally on the loss of view, but also on inability to use the water over the filled land for navigation, fishing, swimming, boating and general recreational uses; and because, in consequence of the defendants' fill, "algae has become an increasing problem, which has created an unsightly situation on Plaintiffs' beaches."

From this judgment the defendants appealed, urging that they were simply making their own property usable and that any damages sustained by the plaintiffs were damnum absque injuria.

The plaintiffs have cross-appealed urging that the defendants' fills should have been abated.

The importance of this litigation transcends the consideration it has received from the public authorities. If every owner of property between

---

10. The portion of vacated Cross Street included in A is quite small and is right at the intersection of vacated Main with Cross Streets. The unfilled portion of Cross Street, now a shallow moat at high water, affords the Greens their only access by water to the lake.

the 1,079 foot and the 1,100 foot level around Lake Chelan has the right the defendants claim, the public's right in the navigable waters of that lake above the 1,079 foot level would be practically nil.

The property owners could make any use, not prohibited by law, of their properties—from fills for trailer parks close to the highways to high-rise apartments close to the lake.

Unless the laws applicable to the use of navigable waters apply to this annual artificial extension of the water of Lake Chelan, to preserve the status quo, it would seem that everybody is on his own.

The plaintiffs have made an excellent case on the basis of prescriptive rights. The filling of the vacated streets and alleys by the defendants cannot be sustained on any basis, since they had acquired no title to them and, in any event, the public had the right of access over the lands included within the boundaries of the vacated streets and alleys to Lake Chelan at all stages of water. Further, the obvious purpose of the contemporaneous vacation and the grant to the public of the right of access was to enable the Chelan Electric Company to acquire the right to submerge the streets and alleys and yet to preserve to the public the right of access over them to the lake "at all stages of water."

However, it is unnecessary to rely on prescriptive rights, or on the rights of the public to use the land within the vacated streets and alleys for access to the lake. We prefer to rest our decision on the proposition that the fills made by the defendants constitute an obstruction to navigation.

While this is a matter of first impression and no exactly comparable case has been found, our holding represents the logical extension of established law in somewhat comparable situations.

There was no private ownership of the land under Lake Chelan in its natural state, and no right to obstruct navigation.

It is well settled that if the level of the lake had been raised to the 1,100 foot level and had been maintained constantly at that level for the prescriptive period, the 1,100 foot level would be considered the natural level of the lake with the submerged lands being converted into part of the lake bed and to state ownership. The public would have the right to use all of the water of the lake up to the 1,100 foot level.

We have here, however, not only the raising of the lake level by artificial means, but the distinctive features that the level does not remain constant and that the owners of the land between the 1,079 and the 1,100 foot level can occupy their property during most of the year.

We find a somewhat comparable situation in those navigable lakes which have a natural or seasonal fluctuation in extent, and have a recognized high water line and low water line. However, in those cases the problems involved usually hinge on the rights accorded riparian owners (whose titles go to the low water mark) in the areas between the high and low water marks.

The law is quite clear that where the level of a navigable body of water fluctuates due to natural causes so that a riparian owner's property is submerged part of the year, the public has the right to use all the waters of the navigable lake or stream whether it be at the high water line, the low water line, or in between. In such situations the riparian owners whose lands are periodically submerged are said to have the right to prevent any trespass on their land between the high and the low marks when not submerged. However, title between those lines is qualified by the public right of navigation and the state may prevent any use of it that interferes with that right. When the land is submerged, the owner has only a qualified fee subject to the right of the public to use the water over the lands consistent with navigational rights, primary and corollary.

Thus, in the situation of a naturally varying water level, the respective rights of the public and of the owners of the periodically submerged lands are dependent upon the level of the water. As the level rises, the rights of the public to use the water increase since the area of water increases; correspondingly, the rights of the landowners decrease since they cannot use their property in such a manner as to interfere with the expanded public rights. As the level and the area of the water decreases, the rights of the public decrease and the rights of the landowners increase as the waters drain off their land, again giving them the right to exclusive possession until their lands are again submerged.

When the circumstance of an artificial raising of navigable waters to a temporary higher level is synthesized with the law dealing with navigable waters having a naturally fluctuating level, the logically resulting rule for the protection of the public interest is that, where the waters of a navigable body are periodically raised and lowered by artificial means, the artificial fluctuation should be considered the same as a natural fluctuation with the rights of the public being the same in both situations, *i.e.*, the public has the right to go where the navigable waters go, even though the navigable waters lie over privately owned lands.

* * *

Following the reasoning of these cases we hold that when the level of Lake Chelan is raised to the 1,100 foot mark (or such level as submerges the defendants' land), that land is subjected to the rights of navigation, together with its incidental rights of fishing, boating, swimming, water skiing, and other related recreational purposes generally regarded as corollary to the right of navigation and the use of public waters. When the level of the lake is lowered so that the defendants' land is no longer submerged, then they are entitled to keep trespassers off their land, and may do with the land as they wish consistent with the right of navigation when it is submerged.

It follows that the defendants' fills, insofar as they obstruct the submergence of the land by navigable waters at or below the 1,100–foot level, must be removed.[13] The court cannot authorize or approve an obstruction to navigation.

■ NEILL, JUDGE (dissenting in part).

* * *

The majority opinion reaches the conclusion that the fill on defendants' lots is to be removed on the basis that this fill constitutes an obstruction to navigation. Analogizing from the rule that the public has the right to the use of navigable water at both high levels and low levels, subject to the right of littoral owners to reasonably obstruct them with "aids to navigation" such as docks, wharfs, etc., the majority holds that fluctuations of water levels which are artificially created are no different then fluctuations created by nature.

The difficulty, as I view it, is that under the majority's holding there is a taking of defendants' property right for public use without just compensation. Defendants (through their antecedents in the chain of title) have a full fee title diminished only by the right of the power company to periodically inundate their lands to a specific elevation. I see no reason in law or equity for preventing such an owner from protecting his land against such inundation by raising the grade of the land.

The periodic flooding involved here is entirely different from a natural raising and lowering of the lake level by reason of rains, seasonal runoff, and drought. In the latter instance, the littoral owner's rights to the foreshore lands between high and low water, whatever these rights may be, are subject to the public's navigation rights. Here, the defendants' lots, *all of which lie above natural high water*, are not subject to public navigation rights unless there has been a voluntary conveyance, eminent domain proceedings, estoppel, or loss through prescription. Unless precluded by one of the aforementioned reasons, defendants have the right to use their lots, including the right to change the grade thereof, in order to make any lawful use thereof. Accordingly, I do not agree that the fill on defendants' lots is unlawful. They should not be required to remove it.

NOTES

1. What implications does *Wilbour* hold for patentees of tide and shoreland grants? Are those who have already filled in a better "equity" position

---

13. We are concerned at the absence of any representation in this action by the Town or County of Chelan, or of the State of Washington, all of whom would seem to have some interest and concern in what, if any, and where, if at all, fills and structures are to be permitted (and under what conditions) between the upper and lower levels of Lake Chelan. There undoubtedly are places on the shore of the lake where developments, such as those of the defendants, would be desirable and appropriate. This presents a problem for the interested public authorities and perhaps could be solved by the establishment of harbor lines in certain areas within which fills could be made, together with carefully planned zoning by appropriate authorities to preserve for the people of this state the lake's navigational and recreational possibilities. Otherwise there exists a new type of privately owned shorelands of little value except as a place to pitch a tent when the lands are not submerged.

than those who have not done so? *Wilbour* was distinguished in Harris v. Hylebos Indus., Inc., 81 Wash.2d 770, 505 P.2d 457 (1973), where a state tideland patentee in the Tacoma harbor was allowed to fill his property and cut off an upland owner's access to navigable waters because coastal and bay tidelands as opposed to recreational lake bottoms:

> have never been classified by the state as navigable waters, but rather have been treated as land. * * * In [*Wilbour*], there was no evidence that the legislature or other governing body intended that the lands in question be reclaimed. The legislative intent regarding the use of tidelands in harbors or cities is manifestly that the navigable portions of such harbors, behind the harbor lines, shall consist of commercial waterways, and that the filling and reclaiming of the tidelands which have been sold to private parties shall be encouraged.

Id. at 466. The various state tideland disposition acts were reviewed and the court concluded "[t]hus it is apparent that the legislature has regarded the filling and improving of * * * tidelands, particularly in commercial harbors, as an aid to navigation, rather than an obstruction." Id. at 462. The court also suggested that appropriate governmental bodies could authorize filling in lakes subject to the *Wilbour* rule.

2. Why did the Gallaghers not argue that they had a right to fill as an incident to their common law riparian rights to wharf out? The reason may have been a common assumption in Washington that there are no riparian rights in watercourses navigable for title under the federal test. See Port of Seattle v. Oregon & Wash. R.R., 255 U.S. 56, 64, 41 S.Ct. 237, 65 L.Ed. 500 (1921). Only if the legislature authorizes encroachments into navigable waters are they not considered purprestures.

Professor Johnson has synthesized the Washington judicial decisions, concluding that "the court has effectively restricted private riparian rights on navigable waters where those rights are in conflict with the constitutional power of the State to control such waters. The constitution [Wash. Const. art. XVII, § 1] does not purport to eliminate riparian rights as between individuals, and the court has not so construed it." Ralph W. Johnson, *Riparian and Public Rights To Lakes and Streams*, 35 Wash. L. Rev. 580, 604–05 (1960).

3. Lake Chelan in *Wilbour* had been enlarged by private effort and its navigability was held to extend to increased surface area. Does the public have any right to use a wholly artificial but navigable lake? A plaintiff and defendant each took title to portions of the bottom of an artificial but navigable lake with a deed containing a restrictive covenant limiting surface use of the lake to homeowners' association members. Defendant's apartment tenants then asserted a right to use the surface. The Florida Supreme Court held that the restriction applied. Silver Blue Lake Apartments, Inc. v. Silver Blue Lake Home Owners Ass'n, 245 So.2d 609 (Fla.1971). The dissenting chief justice set forth some conditions under which privately-owned, artificial lakes might be open to public use:

Where, for example, there is acquiescence in the use of the waterbody by persons not members of the designated exclusive group, principles of dedication or abandonment may operate to create public rights therein. Also, for example, where an artificial waterbody was not specifically developed originally pursuant to a given plan or design to exclusively limit the public use thereof and where, as suggested by certain evidence in the instant case, the scheme for limiting the use of the waterbody was advanced by developers subsequent to the actual creation of the man-made lake and subsequent to its use by members of the public for recreation, there may be a weakening of those policy considerations which favor private ownership of the waterbody to the extent that recognition of public rights therein may be warranted by virtue of countervailing considerations, including the anticipated increased pressure in this state for the availability of more water sources for public recreational purposes.

Id. at 618. What difficulties do you see with the chief justice's proposal? See James N. Corbridge, *Surface Rights in Artificial Waters*, 24 Nat. Resources J. 887, 908–09 (1984).

Other states have held that the geographical scope of navigable waters includes the use of artificial lakes created by damming the stream when they cover private property. Bohn v. Albertson, 107 Cal.App.2d 738, 238 P.2d 128 (1951); Diversion Lake Club v. Heath, 126 Tex. 129, 86 S.W.2d 441 (1935); State v. Head, 330 S.C. 79, 498 S.E.2d 389 (App.1997).

4. In Kaiser Aetna v. United States, 444 U.S. 164, 100 S.Ct. 383, 62 L.Ed.2d 332 (1979), discussed *infra* p. 485, a private developer deepened a pond adjacent to the ocean and converted it into a marina with a channel. After the Army Corps of Engineers asserted a right of public access to the pond the Supreme Court held that it was not "navigable" such that access could be obtained without compensation to the owner. The Court said, however, that the Corps had sufficient regulatory power over the pond to prevent activities interfering with navigation. See also Vaughn v. Vermilion Corp., 444 U.S. 206, 100 S.Ct. 399, 62 L.Ed.2d 365 (1979) (no right of public use of manmade canals that connect the Gulf of Mexico with an inland waterway).

5. Once a water body is determined navigable, a state may legislate the extent of public uses to which the water body is subject. The federal navigability for title test classifies the water body, but it may then be opened to the public for uses beyond traditional notions of what constitutes navigation.

Before granting a permit for a hydroelectric project, the Wisconsin Water Power Act requires a finding by the State Public Service Commission that "the proposed dam will not materially obstruct existing navigation or violate other public rights." In applying the statute the Wisconsin Supreme Court held that "other public rights" include boating and other recreational uses. Accordingly, the court held that the Public Service Commission must find whether public rights for recreational enjoyment of the Namekagon River "in its present natural condition outweigh the benefits to the public which would result in the construction of the dam." Muench v. Public Serv. Comm'n, 261 Wis. 492, 53 N.W.2d 514, 525 (1952).

B. Rights to Surface Use Among Riparians

State laws often, but not always, allow owners of land abutting a waterway rights to use the entire surface of the water. If they own the bed of the waterway, they may have rights to fill in the submerged land owned by them or construct improvements on it. Many private riparian owners own the shores and some, as successors to the state, may have title to the beds as well. The determination of ownership of the bed itself may depend on whether a waterbody is navigable for title. In a navigable stream or lake, "property" is effectively burdened with an easement for public use.

Most reported cases dealing with the respective rights of riparians to use water surfaces and submerged lands tend to involve non-navigable waterways because on navigable waters riparian surface rights are generally synonymous with public rights. Thus, plaintiffs, riparian or not, generally assert public rights to use the surface.

Property owners, whether on a navigable or non-navigable waterway, also have rights vis a vis one another—riparian rights—that may allow them to use the surface and submerged lands in ways that others cannot. For instance, the right to wharf out can belong only to a riparian. With these rights go certain reciprocal obligations. A riparian with lakefront property has a right to use the entire surface of the lake, but may own only a portion of the bed. On the other hand, the lakefront owner must allow use by other riparians of the owned portion.

That the principles governing these rights are called "riparian" can be misleading. They are applicable in states that followed prior appropriation laws to allocate water rights as well as in states where water allocation was historically based on the riparian doctrine. The cardinal principle of riparian water law, reasonable use, does control most conflicts among surface users, however. The application of this principle in disputes among users of water for irrigation, water power, and other purposes is covered in Chapter Three.

As with assertions of riparian rights to use the surface of a waterway, riparian owners using the submerged lands must show that the use is truly a "riparian" use and that it is reasonable. In Bach v. Sarich, 74 Wash.2d 575, 445 P.2d 648 (1968), defendants owned the bed of a non-navigable lake and proposed to build an apartment house that would project into the lake approximately 130 feet. The court enjoined the construction of the apartment.

Mere proximity of the apartment to the water does not render it to a riparian use. With respect to a structure, such a use must be so intimately associated with the water that apart from the water its utility would be seriously impaired. This is not the case with defendants' prospective use. The utility of the apartment is in no way dependent upon the waters of Bitter Lake, and its utility as an apartment would be in no way impaired apart from this lake. This is evidenced by the fact that apartments Nos. 2, 3 and 4 are entirely on upland property.

Nor may defendants justify the presence of their apartment by the commercial zoning classification imposed by the city of Seattle or by the issuance of a building permit.

All riparian owners along the shore of a natural, non-navigable lake share in common the right to use the entire surface of the lake for boating, swimming, fishing, and other similar riparian rights so long as there is no unreasonable interference with the exercise of these rights by other respective owners. These rights are vested property rights, and may not be taken or damaged for public or private use without just compensation.

The court's order resulted in the substantial work completed on the project being demolished. Specific relief is sometimes specific.

Restrictions on a riparian owner's property right to use the surface of the lake can give rise to takings claims. The Forest Service's ban on use of sailboats, houseboats, and nonburnable disposable food and beverage containers in the Sylvania Wilderness was found to constitute a taking of rights of riparian landowners who owned about 5% of the lakeshore. Stupak–Thrall v. Glickman, 988 F.Supp. 1055 (W.D.Mich.1997). However, the ability of the Forest Service to regulate the riparian owner's use short of a ban has not been clearly decided. The Sixth Circuit affirmed through an equally divided en banc opinion, wherein the court recognized the difficulties of the takings analysis. "That this case has been controversial is apparent from its effect of splitting our court right down the middle." Stupak–Thrall v. United States, 89 F.3d 1269, 1272 (6th Cir.1996). Takings claims are discussed *infra* in Section F of this chapter.

The common law has not dealt comfortably with these matters. This has led to legislative responses. After *Bach*, Washington enacted a statutory scheme for shoreline management. Shoreline Management Act of 1971, Wash. Rev. Code Ann. §§ 90.58.020–90.58.930 (2004 & Supp. 2007). In brief, developments along the shore now require a permit from the appropriate local government authority consistent with guidelines for local plans promulgated by the state Department of Ecology as well as the state master program.

Beacham v. Lake Zurich Property Owners Ass'n

Supreme Court of Illinois, 1988.
123 Ill.2d 227, 122 Ill.Dec. 14, 526 N.E.2d 154, 156–57.

This appeal grows out of an action brought by Beacham and Sandy Point for declaratory and injunctive relief with respect to her use of Lake Zurich. In count I, the plaintiffs sought a declaration that incident to Beacham's ownership of a part of the lake bed was the right to make reasonable use of the entire lake surface. In count II, the plaintiffs sought to enjoin various attempts by the Property Owners Association to exclude Beacham and her licensees from the lake surface overlying that part of the lake bed controlled by the Association. The Property Owners Association moved for dismissal of the complaint, and the trial judge granted the motion. The trial judge believed that ownership of a part of a private, nonnavigable lake bed entitles the owner to exclude all others from the surface of the lake above his or her property.

The plaintiffs appealed the dismissal of their complaint, and the appellate court reversed. The court held that ownership of a part of a private, nonnavigable lake bed entitles the owner and the owner's licensees to the reasonable use of the surface waters of the entire lake provided they do not interfere with the reasonable use of the waters by other owners and their licensees. Noting that the case presented a question of first impression in Illinois, the appellate court turned to decisions from other States for guidance. A review of the relevant authority disclosed the existence of two conflicting views on the subject: a so-called common law rule supporting the position of the Property Owners Association, and a so-called civil law rule supporting the position of the plaintiffs. The appellate court concluded that the better-reasoned rule was the civil law approach, which provides that ownership of a part of the bed of a private, nonnavigable lake entitles the owner and the owner's licensees to the reasonable use and enjoyment of the entire lake surface provided they do not interfere with the reasonable use of the water by other owners and their licensees.

The Property Owners Association argues here that appellate court's adoption of the civil law rule is inconsistent with this court's decision in *Leonard v. Pearce* (1932), 348 Ill. 518, 181 N.E. 399. *Leonard* involved Lake Zurich, and the Property Owners Association construes the case as holding that the owners of a part of the lake bed could exclude all others from the waters overlying that property.

We agree with the appellate court that *Leonard* does not control the decision here. In *Leonard* the court determined only whether Lake Zurich was navigable and whether members of the general public were entitled to use the lake through either dedication to public use or prescriptive right. The court held that the lake was nonnavigable and therefore private and that the public did not have either a dedicated or prescriptive right to use the lake. The court concluded, "A development of obnoxious conditions caused the owners of the lake to terminate the free and unrestricted use of its waters which the public had formerly enjoyed. This action simply amounted to a cancellation of the permissive right previously extended." (*Leonard*, 348 Ill. at 528, 181 N.E. 399.) Thus, the dispute in *Leonard* was between owners of the lake and those who were unable to claim any ownership interest in the lake. The dispute here flows from different circumstances; it involves the respective rights of the lake bed owners among themselves.

This court has not previously determined the respective rights of lake bed owners in the use and enjoyment of the lake, and, as the appellate court did, we therefore turn to a consideration of the decisions of other States on this issue. Under the common law rule, the owner of a part of a lake bed has the right to the exclusive use and control of the waters above that property. This rule is a corollary of the traditional common law view that the ownership of a parcel of land entitles the owner to the exclusive use and enjoyment of anything above or below the property. (See *Smoulter v. Boyd* (1904), 209 Pa. 146, 58 A. 144.) Courts following the common law principle have held that the owner of a part of a lake bed may exclude from the surface of the overlying water all other persons, including those who own other parts of the lake bed. As the appellate court noted, however, in certain of those decisions the interest of the party challenging the restriction was quite small in comparison with the interest of the majority owner.

In those States in which the civil law rule prevails, the owner of a part of a lake bed has a right to the reasonable use and enjoyment of the entire lake surface. Those courts rejecting the common law rule have noted the difficulties presented by attempts to establish and obey definite property lines and certain other impractical consequences of that rule, such as the erection of booms, fences, or barriers. Moreover, application of the civil law approach promotes rather than hinders the recreational use and enjoyment of lakes. We conclude that the arguments supporting the civil law rule warrant its adoption in Illinois. Restricting the use of a lake to the water overlying the owner's lake bed property can only frustrate the cooperative and mutually beneficial use of that important resource.

We, therefore, affirm the appellate court's holding that where there are multiple owners of the bed of a private, nonnavigable lake, such owners and their licensees have the right to the reasonable use and enjoyment of the surface waters of the entire lake provided they do not unduly interfere with the reasonable use of the waters by other owners and their licensees.

The question remains, however, whether the plaintiffs' use of the lake, including the renting of boats to members of the general public, is a reasonable one that does not unduly interfere with the reasonable use of the lake by other owners and their licensees. Because that question is not before us and remains for consideration by the trial court in the first instance, we express no view on it now.

For the reasons stated, the judgment of the appellate court is affirmed, and the cause is remanded to the circuit court of Lake County for further proceedings not inconsistent with this opinion.

Affirmed and remanded.

NOTES

1. *Stay on Your Pie.* Indiana has reaffirmed its commitment to the common law rule. Carnahan v. Moriah Property Owners Ass'n, Inc., 716 N.E.2d 437 (Ind.1999). The decision recognized that the de facto rule on many small lakes is shared recreational use, but the court allowed littoral owners to assert their right to exclude others from using their wedge

formed by an extension of their property lines to a point in the center of
the lake by foreclosing most prescriptive easement claims. The common law
rule has recently been adopted in Connecticut, Ace Equipment Sales, Inc. v.
Buccino, 273 Conn. 217, 869 A.2d 626 (2005), and in Iowa, Orr v. Mortvedt,
735 N.W.2d 610 (Iowa 2007).

The historical development of the two rules is discussed in Andrea B.
Carroll, Examining a Comparative Law Myth: Two Hundred Years of
Riparian Misconception, 80 Tul. L.Rev. 901 (2006).

2. *Natural versus Artificial Lakes.* Does it make a difference if the lake is
artificially created? Statler v. Catalano, 293 Ill.App.3d 483, 229 Ill.Dec. 274,
691 N.E.2d 384 (1997) (no distinction between natural and artificial lakes);
Mayer v. Grueber, 29 Wis.2d 168, 138 N.W.2d 197, 205 (1965) (right to use
an artificial lake is an incident of ownership vested exclusively "in the
owner of the fee upon which the lake is located"); Publix Super Markets,
Inc. v. Pearson, 315 So.2d 98 (Fla.App.1975) (phosphate pits not surrounded with a subdivision had never been dedicated to recreational use).

If an artificial expansion of a non-navigable waterbody floods a portion
of an existing riparian's land, may the riparian use the entire surface of the
artificially expanded waterbody? Several cases hold that the owners of land
extending beneath artificial or man-made lakes, not navigable as a matter
of law, have surface water rights only in the surface waters above their
land. E.g., Wehby v. Turpin, 710 So.2d 1243 (Ala.1998); Anderson v. Bell,
433 So.2d 1202 (Fla.1983). But there seems to be no valid reason for not
allowing such use in a jurisdiction that follows the common use approach
for natural waterbodies. See Custis Fishing & Hunting Club, Inc. v.
Johnson, 214 Va. 388, 200 S.E.2d 542 (1973).

3. *Can the Public Bootstrap?* Does the public acquire rights when non-
navigable, private waters become navigable by artificial expansion? The
majority rule is that public rights to the surface are not thereby created.
Ten Eyck v. Warwick, 27 N.Y.S. 536 (1894). Where private land is flooded
by navigable waters, the result differs. See People v. Kraemer, 7 Misc.2d
373, 164 N.Y.S.2d 423 (Police Ct., Village of Lloyd Harbor, Suffolk Co.
1957) (private landowner whose lands were flooded is required to accept
the public right of navigation where he allowed the condition to continue).
Some courts have limited the scope of public rights on artificially expanded
waters to those enjoyed on the waterbody in its natural state. Tapoco, Inc.
v. Peterson, 213 Tenn. 335, 373 S.W.2d 605 (1963). Cf. Dycus v. Sillers, 557
So.2d 486 (Miss.1990) (fishing hole connected to public waters by chute or
drain created by Corps of Engineers dredging is a private waterbody, and
the public does not acquire a right to surface use). What if navigable waters
expand over private property through subsidence? In TH Investments, Inc.
v. Kirby Inland Marine, L.P., 218 S.W.3d 173 (Tex.App.–Houston (14th
Dist.) 2007), the state had granted a patent to a parcel of dry land in 1845.
When the land subsequently subsided and was covered by navigable water,
the Texas Court of Appeals held that the dry land conveyance did not
overcome the presumption of state ownership and application of the Public
Trust.

4. *Fixed Water Levels?* If A purchases a littoral tract on a lake formed by construction of a private or state-licensed dam, what rights does A acquire to the maintenance of the water level, absent an express easement? Suppose the dam owner has acquired a flowage easement by prescription that permits the flooding of A's land. Can A subsequently assert a reciprocal negative easement against lowering the lake level based on A's recreational use of the lake for the prescriptive period? In Kiwanis Club Found., Inc. v. Yost, 179 Neb. 598, 139 N.W.2d 359, 361 (1966), the court rejected this argument:

> Construction and maintenance of a dam over a long period of time may well tend to lead persons owning property above the dam to believe that a permanent and valuable right has been acquired, or is naturally present. The very fact that a man-made dam is obviously present, however, is sufficient to charge them with notice that the water level is artificial as distinguished from natural, and that its level may be lowered or returned to the natural state at any time * * *.

> We hold that where a dam has been built for the private convenience and advantage of the owner, he is not required to maintain and operate it for the benefit of an upper riparian owner who obtains advantages from its existence; and that the construction and maintenance of such a dam does not create any reciprocal rights in upstream riparian proprietors based on prescription, dedication and estoppel.

In Green v. City of Williamstown, 848 F.Supp. 102 (E.D.Ky.1994), the court followed *Kiwanis Club* and found that the dam owner has a right to abandon the dam completely. In contrast, a Georgia intermediate appeals court distinguished *Kiwanis Club* and sustained a temporary injunction against further demolition of a dam, where plaintiff homeowners had received their lakeside property from defendant dam owners by warranty deed which referenced a plat; that plat, in turn, referenced the lake which defendants proposed to lower. Dillard v. Bishop Eddie Long Ministries, Inc., 258 Ga.App. 507, 574 S.E.2d 544 (2002).

A riparian might also want to prevent artificial lake levels from rising. In Natural Soda Products Co. v. City of Los Angeles, 23 Cal.2d 193, 143 P.2d 12 (1943), the defendant city, from 1919 to 1937, diverted virtually all the flow of the Owens River, which supplied Owens Lake, a waterbody with no outlet. When the lake dried up, brines containing valuable chemicals collected on the exposed bottom. Plaintiff, a chemical company, built a plant to process the brines. In 1937 the defendant closed its diversion dam and water flooded the lake to a depth of three to four feet, inundating plaintiff's plant. An award of $153,000 in damages was upheld because plaintiff made substantial expenditures in reliance on the city's diversions.

Several midwestern states and the state of Washington have lake level maintenance statutes. They are designed to establish a level through a statutory procedure or an administrative or judicial proceeding that quantifies the littoral owner's common law right and to provide some protection for littoral owners from property damage caused by dams or other structures which cause the alteration of the lake.

5. *Artificial to Natural.* Despite the hostility of the courts to the concept of riparian rights in artificial watercourses, even such wholly artificial structures as manmade canals and ditches may be treated as natural if they have been in place for a substantial period of time. Bollinger v. Henry, 375 S.W.2d 161 (Mo.1964), allowed the owner of lands alongside a century-old millrace to exercise consumptive riparian rights. Ramada Inns, Inc. v. Salt River Valley Water Users' Ass'n, 111 Ariz. 65, 523 P.2d 496 (1974), refused to apply the common law rule of strict liability for flooding caused to another's property with water by an artificial impoundment (Rylands v. Fletcher, L.R. 3 H.L. 330 (1868)). There, the ninety-year old Arizona Canal had been surrounded by expansion of metropolitan Phoenix. The subsequent locators had the same "duty" to avoid losses as would anyone locating next to a natural stream subject to flooding. In Ace Equipment Sales v. Buccino, 273 Conn. 217, 225, 869 A.2d 626, 631 (2005), the court noted by way of dictum that an artificial lake might be treated as natural, where detrimental reliance was shown. For a review of the problems of artificial watercourses, see James N. Corbridge, Jr., *Surface Rights in Artificial Watercourses*, 24 Nat. Resources J. 887 (1984).

Thompson v. Enz

Supreme Court of Michigan, 1967.
379 Mich. 667, 154 N.W.2d 473.

[A land development corporation purchased a riparian parcel of land on a lake that was used primarily for recreational purposes. The corporation subdivided the parcel into lots only 16 of which abutted directly on the lake. The back lots would have access to the lake by a canal dug by the corporation. Other riparians on the lake sued to enjoin the proposed subdivision and the digging of the canal on the grounds that it would constitute an interference with their riparian rights. The riparian owners were unable to prove that the level of the lake would be lowered or that the quality of the water would be impaired.]

■ KAVANAGH, JUSTICE.

* * *

This case concerns certain property rights in and around Gun Lake, which is situated partly in Barry county and partly in Allegan county. The parties agree that this lake has approximately 2,680 acres of surface area and approximately 30 miles of shore line.

The defendant corporation is a contract purchaser of a riparian parcel of land having approximately 1,415 feet of frontage on said lake, and the individual defendants are the sole stockholders of the corporation. * * *

The following questions are raised on appeal:

1. May a right of access to Gun Lake be created by dredging an artificial canal from the lake through lots having frontage on Gun Lake to

back lots having no frontage thereon, and may ownership of such lots carry with it riparian rights?

2.   Does the development by defendants of their property which partially fronts on Gun Lake by the construction of a canal connecting back lots to the lake and granting rights of access to the lake constitute an illegal invasion of the rights of the plaintiffs and an infringement of their riparian rights in and to the surface of Gun lake and in and to the subaqueous land thereunder?

"Riparian land" is defined as a parcel of land which includes therein a part of or is bounded by a natural watercourse. 4 Restatement, Torts, § 843.

* * *

A "riparian proprietor" is a person who is in possession of riparian lands or who owns an estate therein. 4 Restatement, Torts, § 844, p 331.

Land abutting on an artificial watercourse has no riparian rights. * * *

We, therefore, conclude that parcels of land to be subdivided from the main tract of land bordering on Gun lake have no riparian rights as: (1) they neither include therein a part of nor are they bounded by Gun lake, and (2) the canal itself would be an artificial watercourse giving rise to no riparian rights.

The remaining question for decision is whether or not riparian rights may be conveyed to a grantee or reserved by the grantor in a conveyance which divides a tract of land with riparian rights into more than one parcel, of which parcels only one would remain bounded by the watercourse.

In the case of *Harvey Realty Co. v. Borough of Wallingford, supra,* Justice Hinman, writing for the Court, stated:

> "It is clear that the grantees or contractees, from the plaintiff, of lots separated from and not bordering on Pine lake can have, of their own right, no riparian privileges in its waters. *And any attempted transfer of the right made by a riparian to a nonriparian proprietor is invalid.*" (Citing text and cases.) (Emphasis supplied.)

* * *

We hold that what is meant by this "reservation" of riparian rights is merely the reservation of a right-of-way for access to the water course. * * * This, however, cannot and does not give rise to riparian rights.

* * *

We hold that riparian rights are not alienable, severable, divisible, or assignable apart from the land which includes therein, or is bounded, by a natural watercourse.

While riparian rights may not be conveyed or reserved—nor do they exist by virtue of being bounded by an artificial water course—easements, licenses and the like for a right-of-way for access to a water course do exist and ofttimes are granted to nonriparian owners.

We will, therefore, treat the proposal here as though easements for rights-of-way for access are given to the back lot purchasers. We must then consider what right, if any, the owners of the back lots have to use these rights-of-way. In so doing, attention must be given to the use of riparian rights by the defendants and the remaining proprietors on Gun Lake.

Riparian uses are divided generally into two classes. The first of these is for natural purposes. These uses encompass all those absolutely necessary for the existence of the riparian proprietor and his family, such as to quench thirst and for household purposes. Without these uses both man and beast would perish. Users for natural purposes enjoy a preferred nonproratable position with respect to all other users rather than a correlative one.

The second of these is a use for artificial purposes. Artificial uses are those which merely increase one's comfort and prosperity and do not rank as essential to his existence, such as commercial profit and recreation. Users for artificial purposes occupy a correlative status with the other riparians in exercise of their riparian rights for artificial purposes. Use for an artificial purpose must be (a) only for the benefit of the riparian land and (b) reasonable in light of the correlative rights of the other proprietors. It is clear in the case before us that the use made of the property by the defendants is for a strictly artificial purpose and must meet the test of reasonableness.

* * *

The trial court made no finding of fact as to the reasonableness of the use. This record is insufficient for us to make a determination as to reasonableness. Therefore, we remand to the trial court for such determination. The trial court should keep in mind the following factors in determining whether the use would be reasonable:

First, attention should be given to the watercourse and its attributes, including its size, character and natural state. In determining the reasonableness of the use in the case at bar, it should be considered that Gun lake is not a large lake, that it is used primarily for recreational purposes, and that the defendants are changing its natural state by expanding the lake frontage of their property from an actual 1,415 feet to a total, inclusive of the canals, of 12,415 feet, being an increase in frontage of approximately 800 per cent.

Second, the trial court should examine the use itself as to its type, extent, necessity, effect on the quantity, quality, and level of the water, and the purposes of the users. Factors in this particular case that should be considered include: (a) that this use would permanently add approximately one family without riparian rights to each 18 acres of surface area (or 137 families); (b) the possibility that the level of the lake may be reduced by withdrawing trust waters into over 2 miles of the proposed canals, as is alleged by the attorney general in his motion to intervene; (c) the possibility that pollution may result; (d) that there is nothing in the record showing any necessity for this use; and (e) the fact that it appears that the purpose of the defendants herein is merely commercial exploitation.

Third, it is necessary to examine the proposed artificial use in relation to the consequential effects, including the benefits obtained and the detriment suffered, on the correlative rights and interests of other riparian proprietors and also on the interests of the State, including fishing, navigation, and conservation. An additional fact to be considered by the trial court in this litigation is whether the benefit to the defendant subdividers would amount merely to a rich financial harvest, while the remaining proprietors—who now possess a tranquil retreat from everyday living—would be forced to endure the annoyances which would come from an enormous increase in lake users.

Undoubtedly, at the new hearing, the attorney general of the State of Michigan will intervene under his statutory general powers of intervention for the purpose of protecting the rights of the public.

If, after considering all of these factors and any additional testimony the parties may desire to present, the trial court (as chancellor) concludes the use is unreasonable, that court should retain jurisdiction of the matter for the purpose of granting such further necessary or proper relief as may be necessary to protect the rights and interests of plaintiffs, the public, and riparian owners of property abutting this lake. * * * General Court Rules of 1963 No. 521.6.

———

On remand the trial judge held that the defendant's proposed use was unreasonable. Although the Supreme Court approved the trial court's findings, it decided to vacate the judgment because plaintiffs waited until defendant had completed most of the excavation required for construction of the canals before seeking an injunction and therefore the plaintiffs were estopped from obtaining equitable relief. Thompson v. Enz, 188 N.W.2d 579 (1971). Justice Brennan, in a separate opinion, argued that the trial court's decision should be reversed, not just vacated:

> These defendants do not propose to exercise any rights or inaugurate any uses which are in the slightest fashion more detrimental to the lake than the existing uses of other lake owners. In fact all necessary permits were obtained, fees paid and approval granted to proceed with this development. The trial court would brand these defendants' use as the "straw that broke the camel's back," and in the name of preserving to these plaintiffs a quasi-monopoly to use a lake which belongs to the people of Michigan, our Court would approve the arbitrary, unlawful and unconstitutional confiscation of the defendants' property without payment of compensation therefor. That excavation was lawful and, in fact, authorized when undertaken. It is lawful today.

Id. at 587–88.

NOTES

1.   Under the court's test, must each activity (*e.g.*, the canal construction, the decision to subdivide and convey lots, the particular uses of the surface by each new canal lot owner) be judged by the reasonable use standard? Tort law ordinarily awards damages based on actual or imminent harm and existing uses rather than attempting to project future uses and harms.

The trial judge's tipping point analysis modifies the traditional doctrine that equity will not enjoin an activity without proof of imminent irreparable injury. This doctrine requires a plaintiff to show that it is highly probable that injury will occur in the foreseeable future.

2.   Are the owners of the lots connected to the lake by the canal in *Thompson* now riparian to the lake?

3.   Suppose that a riparian owner puts in a parking lot and boat ramp, charges for admission, and allows members of the public to use the lake. Do these licensees have riparian rights? Are there any limitations on the licensor's exercise of littoral rights? Does it matter if the licensor is a government agency and the other riparian owners are private parties? In Botton v. State, 69 Wash.2d 751, 420 P.2d 352 (1966), the state purchased a lot on Phantom Lake near Seattle for a fishing access site. The shoreline of the lake had been privately owned, and the other littoral owners sued the state complaining that thefts, noise, littering, safety hazards, and generally unacceptable social behavior impaired their right to use the lake for recreational purposes. The court held that all littoral owners are subject to the reasonable use standard. Members of the public may be admitted by littoral owners, but the state's failure to control the public's use of the lake was found to be an unreasonable interference with the rights of the other littoral owners. The late Professor Ralph Johnson of the University of Washington School of Law reported that after *Botton* the Department of Game closed the lake to the public for many years because the department was unable to come to an agreement with the littoral owners to limit public access and it lacked the funds to provide a full-time employee to police the area. Some 28 years later following extensive mediation the City of Bellevue proposed and was granted a permit to construct a dock and boat launch at a city park next to the lake, along with parking, trails, and restrooms to support public access. The permit was granted on the conditions that there be no swimming and that only twelve small, non-motorized boats of non-residents be allowed for a maximum of three hours each per day.

4.   Michigan's legislative response to *Thompson* was The Inland Lakes and Streams Act, Mich. Comp. Laws Ann. § 281.951–281.966. (West 1996), recodified as Mich. Comp. Laws Ann. § 324.30101–324.30113 (West 1999 & West Supp. 2007). The statutory requirement of a permit does not eliminate the common law remedy recognized in *Thompson*.

In addition to such direct regulation three other types of statutes can have a significant although indirect impact on riparian development activities. These are (1) state environmental policy acts which superimpose an environmental impact statement requirement on existing permit or regulatory approval procedures, (2) critical areas legislation which requires special local or state approval for activities in a designated area, and (3) legislation which gives the public standing to sue to protect environmental rights.

An example of the third type of legislation is the Michigan Environmental Protection Act (MEPA). Mich. Comp. Laws Ann. §§ 324.1701–324.1706 (West 1999). The Act allowed "the attorney general or any person" to sue to enjoin a public or private entity whose act "has * * * or is likely to pollute, impair or destroy the air, water or other natural resources or the public trust in these resources." §§ 324.1701(1), 324.1702(1). This Act, which has been copied in several other states, offers opportunities to challenge environmentally harmful activities, and for agencies to impose added environmental standards. See, *e.g.*, Attorney General *ex rel.* Natural Resources Commission v. Balkema, 191 Mich.App. 201, 477 N.W.2d 100 (1991) (filling of shallow lake without a permit violated MEPA because the lake was home to black terns and the system acted as a nutrient trap). MEPA was applied in Opal Lake Ass'n v. Michaywe' Ltd., 47 Mich.App. 354, 209 N.W.2d 478 (1973). The court enjoined a proposed lakeshore development, addressing the question of uncertain harm from expanded lake use as follows:

> Here there seems to be little argument that should a significant number of the proposed 2,250 individual lot owners and their guests in Michaywe decide to use the Opal Lake access site at the same time a nuisance to *everyone* will result. Here also plans have been nearly fully developed for the access site. One hundred twenty-five purchasers had already at the time of this suit bought land in the Michaywe project on the apparent representation that they would have access to the Swim'n Sun Club. It seems patently unreasonable to ignore such facts and their probable effects until the clear waters of Opal Lake are muddied, the noise around the Swim'n Sun Club is deafening, and the other private shore owners on Opal Lake have put up "For Sale" signs on their property simply because in some distinguishable past nuisance cases the courts refused to enjoin anticipated harm. We do not believe the unrestricted use of the Michaywe beachfront by hundreds, if not thousands, of non-riparian landowners is so "anticipatory" as to negate the possibility of giving injunctive relief.

209 N.W.2d at 483.

Legislatively conferred standing has been questioned on constitutional grounds by the Michigan courts. See the discussion in Michigan Citizens for Water Conservation v. Nestlé Waters North America Inc., 479 Mich. 280, 737 N.W.2d 447 (2007).

C.   EXPANDING PUBLIC RIGHTS TO SURFACE USE

We have seen that the public has rights to use the surface of bodies of water that fit the federal test of navigability at the time of statehood. But in waters where there is no such public trust interest, and even in such waters where the public wants to assert rights going beyond those protected by the public trust, any right to use the surface is necessarily a result of state law. The growing economic and social importance of recreational uses of water has led to the recognition of public rights to use the surface of waterbodies for boating, fishing, hunting, and other recreational purposes under several legal theories.

One means of deeming the waterbodies open to public access is the adoption of a more liberal state test of navigability. Adoption of a "saw log test" of navigability for title (any river used to float saw logs to the mill is navigable) made it easier for state courts to extend the definition of navigability to those waters capable of supporting noncommercial recreational activities. As an early Minnesota decision observed, "The division of waters into navigable and non-navigable is but a way of dividing them into public and private waters—a classification which, in some form, every civilized nation has recognized; the line of division being largely determined by its conditions and habits." Lamprey v. Metcalf, 52 Minn. 181, 53 N.W. 1139, 1143 (1893). Shortly thereafter, Wisconsin adopted an expanded concept of navigability based in part on the Northwest Ordinance's guarantee of free highways and carrying places for the Mississippi, Saint Lawrence, and rivers in between. Diana Shooting Club v. Husting, 156 Wis. 261, 145 N.W. 816 (1914). Public rights recognized by the ordinance presumably were not superseded by admission to statehood. See Elder v. Delcour, 364 Mo. 835, 269 S.W.2d 17 (1954); Coleman v. Schaeffer, 163 Ohio St. 202, 126 N.E.2d 444 (1955).

More recently, courts have expanded state definitions of navigability in a manner that directly recognizes the public importance of recreational uses. See discussion in White's Mill Colony Inc. v. Williams, 363 S.C. 117, 609 S.E.2d 811 (App. 2005). Others have anchored such rights on state constitutional and statutory declarations that describe the nature of public and private legal interests in water and waterbodies. Still, some courts have resorted to little more than ipsi dixit to expand public rights. *E.g.*, Curry v. Hill, 460 P.2d 933 (Okla.1969).

The expansion of public rights to non-navigable waters carries forward the spirit of both the English and the federal common law. In many instances it requires a change in the common law of the state itself. The effect of the expansion is, of course, to redistribute resources from private ownership and control to public ownership, that is, to make the resource a common good. Does this reallocation diminish the market value of the riparian land? Could the reallocation amount to a taking without just compensation?

State v. McIlroy

Supreme Court of Arkansas, 1980.
268 Ark. 227, 595 S.W.2d 659.

■ HICKMAN, JUSTICE.

W. L. McIlroy and his late brother's estate, owners of 230 acres in Franklin County, sought a chancery court declaration that their rights as riparian landowners on the Mulberry River were, because the stream was not a navigable river, superior to the rights of the public.

McIlroy joined as defendants the Ozark Society, a conservationist group, and two companies that rent canoes for use on the Mulberry and other Ozark Mountain streams. The State of Arkansas, intervening, claimed the Mulberry was a navigable stream and the stream bed the property of the state, not the McIlroys. * * *

The Mulberry River, located in northwest Arkansas, heads up in the Ozark Mountains and flows in a westerly direction for about 70 miles until it joins the Arkansas River. It could best be described as an intermediate stream, smaller than the Arkansas River, the lower White and Little Red Rivers and other deep, wide rivers that have been used commercially since their discovery. But neither is it like the many small creeks and branches in Arkansas that cannot be regularly floated with canoes or flatbottomed boats for any substantial period of time during the year. The Mulberry is somewhere in between. It is a stream that for about 50 or 55 miles of its length can be floated by canoe or flatbottomed boat for at least six months of the year. Parts of it are floatable for longer periods of time. The Mulberry is a typical rock-bottomed Ozark Mountain stream, flowing with relatively clear water and populated by a variety of fish. Smallmouth bass favor such a stream and populate the Mulberry.

For most of its distance it is a series of long flat holes of water interrupted by narrower shoals. These shoals attract the canoeists. McIlroy describes the stream as following a tortuous course; canoeists find it an exciting stream testing the skill of an experienced canoeist. Watergaps, affairs of wire or boards erected across the stream to hold cattle, have at times been erected but, according to W. L. McIlroy, they go down with the first rise of water. It is not a stream easily possessed. In recent years, the Mulberry has claimed the lives of several canoeists.

Annually, since 1967, the Ozark Society has sponsored for its members one or more float trips on the Mulberry River. These trips take them through McIlroy's property, which is located about 23 miles up the river from where the Mulberry enters the Arkansas. McIlroy said he had a confrontation with Ozark Society members in 1975 when about 600 people put in at a low water bridge on his property. The bridge, near Cass, serves a county road, and is undisputably a public bridge. Canoeists and fishermen have regularly used it as an access place to the river.

* * *

The evidence by testimony and exhibits demonstrates conclusively that the Mulberry had been used by the public for recreational purposes for many years. It has long been used for fishing and swimming and is today also popular among canoeists.

Seven witnesses from the locality testified. All testified they had fished or swum in the Mulberry at this locality and had never sought permission nor thought they needed it. * * *

Several state and federal officials testified. Richard Davies, Director of Arkansas State Parks and Tourism, said his agency, along with the Arkansas Game and Fish Commission, published, in 1978, a pamphlet, "The Float Streams of Arkansas," listing 14 of Arkansas' most popular fishing and canoeing streams. The Mulberry was touted as Arkansas' finest white water float stream and as an excellent habitat for smallmouth bass. Davies said he considered the water open to the public. George Purvis of the Arkansas Game and Fish Commission said the Mulberry was included in the pamphlet because it was one of the top five or six streams in the state for both floaters and fishermen. He also considered it open to the public. William E. Keith, an employee of the Game and Fish Commission, said fish were stocked on the Mulberry periodically from 1952 through 1977, sometimes at the low water bridge at Cass.

Nineteen canoeists testified and three others' testimony was offered by stipulation. All had floated the Mulberry, most several times; some numerous times. None had ever sought permission nor thought they needed it. No one's right to canoe was challenged until McIlroy challenged some of them in 1978. Harold Hedges began floating it in 1952, with about 20 other people. Most canoeists had floated the Mulberry in the 60's and 70's. Evidence showed the Ozark Society, a conservationist group, had sponsored floats annually from 1967 to 1978.

* * *

The facts presented prove that the Mulberry River at the point in question is capable of recreational use and has been used extensively for recreational purposes. We must now decide whether such a stream is navigable.

Determining the navigability of a stream is essentially a matter of deciding if it is public or private property. Navigation in fact is the standard modern test of navigability, and, as embroidered by the federal courts, controls when navigation must be defined for federal purposes—maritime jurisdiction, regulation under the Commerce Clause, and title disputes between the state and federal governments. * * *

Arkansas has adopted the standard definition of navigability. * * *

However, in the case of *Barboro v. Boyle*, 119 Ark. 377, 178 S.W. 378 (1915), this Court foresaw, no doubt, that things would change in the future and that recreation would become an important interest of the people of Arkansas. The language in the *Barboro* case is almost prophetic. While adhering to the standard definition of navigability, with its dependence upon a commercial criterion, the Court went on to say:

> It is the policy of this state to encourage the use of its water courses for any useful or beneficial purpose. There may be other public uses than the carrying on of commerce of pecuniary value. * * * Pleasure

resorts might even be built upon the banks of the lake and the water might be needed for municipal purposes. Moreover, the waters of the lake might be used to a much greater extent for boating, for pleasure, for bathing, fishing and hunting than they are now used.

Since that time no case presented to us has involved the public's right to use a stream which has a recreational value, but lacks commercial adaptability in the traditional sense. Our definition of navigability is, therefore, a remnant of the steamboat era.

However, many other states have been presented with this same problem. Back in 1870, the Massachusetts Supreme Court found a stream navigable that could only be used for pleasure. The stream was about two feet deep at low water. The court stated:

> If water is navigable for pleasure boating, it must be regarded as navigable water though no craft has ever been upon it for the purpose of trade or agriculture. *Attorney General v. Woods*, 108 Mass. 436, 440 (1870).

In Ohio, the court recently was faced with this problem and decided to change its definition of navigation. The Ohio court said:

> We hold that the modern utilization of our water by our citizens requires that our courts, in this judicial interpretation of the navigability of such water, consider this recreational use as well as the more traditional criterion of commercial use. *State ex rel. v. Newport Concrete Co.*, 44 Ohio App. 2d 121, 127, 336 N.E. 2d 453, 457 73 Ohio Ops.2d 124 (1975).

Applying a "public trust" to the Little Miami River, the Ohio court found that the State of Ohio "... holds these waters in trust for those Ohioans who wish to use the stream for all legitimate uses, be they commercial, transportational, or recreational." *State, ex rel. v. Newport Concrete Co., supra.*

Michigan reached a similar conclusion in 1974. Navigability in Michigan was significantly affected by whether logs had been, or could be, floated down a stream. That "flotable test" had been used by the Michigan court until it was confronted with the same problem that we have. Michigan readily admitted that its definition needed to be changed:

> We therefore hold that members of the public have the right to navigate and to exercise the incidents of navigation in a lawful manner at any point below high water mark on waters of this state which are capable of being navigated by oar or motor propelled small craft. *Kelley ex. rel. MacMullan v. Hallden, 51 Mich.App. 176, 214 N.W.2d 856, 864 (1974).*

For examples of other states that have adopted similar definitions of navigation, see: *People v. Mack*, 19 Cal.App.3d 1040, 97 Cal. Rptr. 448 (1971); *Lamprey v. State*, 52 Minn. 181, 53 N.W. 1139 (1893); *Luscher v.*

Reynolds, 153 Or. 625, 56 P.2d 1158 (1936).*

Arkansas, as most states in their infancy, was mostly concerned with river traffic by steamboats or barges when cases like *Lutesville, supra,* were decided. We have had no case regarding recreational use of waters such as the Mulberry. It may be that our decisions did or did not anticipate such use of streams which are suitable, as the Mulberry is, for recreational use. Such use would include flatbottomed boats for fishing and canoes for floating—or both. There is no doubt that the segment of the Mulberry River that is involved in this lawsuit can be used for a substantial portion of the year for recreational purposes. Consequently, we hold that it is navigable at that place with all the incidental rights of that determination.

McIlroy and others testified that the reason they brought the lawsuit was because their privacy was being interrupted by the people who trespassed on their property, littered the stream and generally destroyed their property. We are equally disturbed with that small percentage of the public that abuses public privileges and has no respect for the property of others. Their conduct is a shame on us all. It is not disputed that riparian landowners on a navigable stream have a right to prohibit the public from crossing their property to reach such a stream. The McIlroys' rights in this regard are not affected by our decision. While there are laws prohibiting such misconduct, every branch of Arkansas' government should be more aware of its duty to keep Arkansas, which is a beautiful state, a good place to live. No doubt the state cannot alone solve such a problem, it requires some individual effort of the people. Nonetheless, we can no more close a public waterway because some of those who use it annoy nearby property owners, than we could close a public highway for similar reasons.

In any event, the state sought a decision that would protect its right to this stream. With that right, which we now recognize, goes a responsibility to keep it as God made it.

Reversed.

* * *

■ Fogleman, C. J., concurs in part and dissents in part.

I cannot join in the court's new definition of navigability, even though I concur in the reversal of the decree in this case. * * *

* * *

The test of navigability is the means of determining the property rights of riparian owners. As such it is a rule of property. To repudiate this rule of property by judicial decision will have the effect of invalidating titles that were acquired in reliance upon the rule and such a change, if desirable, should be brought about by legislation, which operates only prospectively

---

*Other states that have adopted the pleasure boat test of navigability include: Idaho (Southern Idaho Fish & Game Ass'n v. Picabo Livestock, Inc., 528 P.2d 1295 (Idaho 1974)); and New York (People v. Kraemer, 164 N.Y.S.2d 423 (N.Y.Police Ct.1957)). [Eds.]

and cannot upset titles already vested. We are not free to disregard a rule of property. Where our holdings have become a rule of property, they must not be overruled retroactively or retrospectively.

Even a legislative enactment cannot destroy vested rights which riparian owners have in a nonnavigable stream. * * *

The adoption of a so-called modern test changes a rule of property and apparently divests titles that have been vested under the prior test. In Arkansas, unlike communist states, it is the right of private property, not the rights of the public, that rises above constitutional sanction. Art. 2, § 22, Constitution of Arkansas. This is one of the fundamental distinctions between our system and the communistic form of government and its focus is directed to public rights asserted in streams. The statement that the right of property is before and higher than any constitutional sanction is more than a slogan.

NOTES

1. *Pleasure boat test.* Michigan was included among the states adopting the pleasure boat test. The Michigan Supreme Court later applied a more rigorous version of the test in Bott v. Commission of Natural Resources of the State of Michigan Dept. of Natural Resources, 415 Mich. 45, 327 N.W.2d 838 (1982). In *Bott* landowners owned almost all of the land around two small, spring-fed lakes and the shallow creeks connecting the lakes to somewhat larger lakes. Littoral owners on the larger lakes, joined by the state, sought to establish a right of access through the connecting creeks from the larger to the smaller lakes. The Michigan Supreme Court decided to swim against modern precedent and held that the littoral owners on the two small lakes had exclusive use of them. It found that the small creeks connecting several small lakes were "not of sufficient width and depth to be used for recreation." The court expressed dissatisfaction with the pleasure boat test suggesting that it is not, indeed, the law of Michigan: "Adoption of recreational-boating test would subject many formerly private inland waters to what are in essence recreational easements." Id. at 850.

2. *Recreational Navigability.* Must a river meet a test of navigability to be public? In Montana Coalition For Stream Access, Inc. v. Curran, 210 Mont. 38, 682 P.2d 163 (1984), the Montana Supreme Court held that the Dearborn River, a tributary of the Missouri, was open to public recreational use. It said that navigability for recreational use is a state law question. The recognition of public rights in *Curran* could have been sustained based on the fact that the Dearborn River was determined to be navigable for title by the federal test, and hence "burdened by this public trust," because railroad ties and logs were floated in it prior to Montana statehood. Thus, the state owned the bed under the Equal Footing Doctrine. A month after *Curran*, the Court decided Montana Coalition for Stream Access, Inc. v. Hildreth, 211 Mont. 29, 684 P.2d 1088 (1984):

> We held in *Curran*, *supra*, that the question of title to the underlying streambed is immaterial in determining navigability for

recreational use of State-owned waters. This holding applies equally to the case now before us.

* * *

Since title to the underlying bed is not at issue and is immaterial to the determination of the public's right of use, the District Court did not err in failing to make findings of fact and conclusions of law relative to the ownership of the streambed.

Id. at 1092. The sole issue in determining the availability of waterbodies for public recreational use was said to be "the capability of use of the waters for recreational purposes." Id. at 1091. The court expressly declined to adopt the pleasure boat test of navigability saying that it was "unnecessary and improper to determine a specific test under which to find navigability for recreational use." Id. For a useful analysis of the cases, see John E. Thorson et al., *Forging Public Rights in Montana's Waters*, 6 Pub. Land L. Rev. 1 (1985).

Montana responded to *Curran* and *Hildreth* by passing legislation that created two classes of waters. Class I waters are those owned by the state under the federal navigability for title test or those that are or have been capable of supporting commercial uses such as log floating or fur skin transportation. Class II waters are all other waters. Class II waters capable of no or limited recreational use may be identified and recreational use limited to the actual capacity. All surface waters "capable of recreational use" are subject to public use. The legislation also limited landowner liability to acts of willful or wanton misconduct and barred the acquisition of prescriptive easements by the recreational use of surface streams. Mont. Code Ann. §§ 23–2–301 to –322 (2006). The use of both Class I and II waters is subject to further state regulation. Both Montana cases noted that the public has no right to trespass across private property to get to waters open for recreational use. *Hildreth* did hold that "[t]he public has the right to use the waters and the bed and banks up to the ordinary high water mark," regardless of land ownership. In cases of obstructions, "the public is allowed to portage around such barriers in the least intrusive manner possible, avoiding damage to the adjacent owner's property and his rights." Montana Coalition for Stream Access, Inc. v. Hildreth, 211 Mont. 29, 684 P.2d 1088, 1091 (1984). Provisions of the statute were held unconstitutional in Galt v. State, 225 Mont. 142, 731 P.2d 912 (1987). But see discussion in Madison v. Graham, 126 F.Supp.2d 1320 (D.Mont. 2001). Although the public has an easement to use the land below the high water marks, the statute was overbroad in recognizing a public right to portage, camp, hunt, and erect duck blinds in all cases. The public's right is "only to such use as is necessary to utilization of the water itself." The court also struck down a provision that required landowners to pay the cost of establishing portage routes around artificial barriers, in that the benefit of such routes is to the public, not the landowner, and thus the state should pay the expense.

3. *Prescriptive Rights.* What is the practical effect of a state's adopting the prescription rule urged by Chief Justice Fogleman instead of the pleasure boat test of navigability? Prescriptive rights of recreational boaters had been recognized in Arkansas before *McIlroy*. Buffalo River Conservation & Recreation Council v. National Park Serv., 558 F.2d 1342 (8th Cir.1977). Pursuant to the Buffalo National River Act, 16 U.S.C.A. §§ 460m–8 to 460m–14 (West 2000 & West Supp. 2007), the Park Service acquired several parcels along the Buffalo River in Arkansas. Its congressional appropriation of funds was exhausted, resulting in a checkerboard pattern of acquired and nonacquired land. The Service posted a map showing acquired land at its headquarters and posted "no trespassing" signs on some private lands. Nevertheless, those floating the river "trespassed upon the land of private owners, left gates open, left debris, annoyed owners by requests to use their phones and bathroom facilities." A suit by the nonacquired landowners against the Park Service on a taking theory was dismissed. The Eighth Circuit held that the property owners could fence off their shorelands but could not obstruct the bed of the river because the public had acquired a prescriptive easement of floatation.

Crooked Creek, a major whitewater stream, begins near Dogpatch, Arkansas and eventually flows into the navigable White River. The state claimed title to the bed of Crooked Creek. The evidence consisted of the testimony of 24 canoeists, boaters, and fishermen who used the river for recreation and disputed testimony about the amount of money that river recreation brought to the county. The Chancellor held that the state did not meet the federal test of navigability, discussed *supra* p. 403, because the only evidence of floatable commerce occurred in the past 50 years, but that the public had acquired a prescriptive right to use the river for recreational boating. Arkansas v. Sharp, Chancery Court of Marion County, Ark., June 8, 1999. The opinion contained the following discussion of *McIlroy*:

> This Court is mindful of the Arkansas Supreme Court's colloquy in *State v. McIlroy*, wherein, it said that except for defining maritime jurisdiction, regulations under the Commerce Clause, and Title disputes between State and Federal Governments: ". . . the States may adopt their own definition of navigability."
>
> That is an accurate statement of the law when it is applied to the definition known as "navigability for use." Under the "navigability for use" approach, the plenary ownership of property is not in issue, rather the extent to which a State may regulate the use of water is the sine qua non. Montana Coalition For Stream Access, Inc. v. Hildreth, 684 P.2d 1088 (Mont. 1984); see also A. Dan Tarlock, James N. Corbridge, Jr. and David H. Getches, Water Resource Management (4th ed. 1993). States are free to change their definitions of "navigability for use" as times and needs require because a finding that a river is "navigable for use" does not affect title to the stream's bed. It is a separate concept from the federal question of determining "Navigability for Title," however.

* * *

It has been widely assumed that the *McIlroy* Court affected title to the property of W.L. McIlroy and his brother's estate by redefining "navigability" over 150 years after Statehood and after property rights had vested. In fact, following the decision, the General Assembly of the State of Arkansas voted to relinquish and quitclaim title to the creek bed back to the property owners, Act 872 of 1981, saying:

> "... the Arkansas Supreme Court in holding the Mulberry River to be navigable seriously impaired the oil and gas leases, farming leases, and the sale of property along the Mulberry River; that the boundary lines of property owners have been materially affected in that they now cannot be determined without additional court action ..."

A careful reading of the opinion reveals, however, that the Court avoided the issue of bed ownership and gave no indication that it intended to affect title to the bed of Mulberry Creek. At least the authorities cited in the case suggests that conclusion.

In Reitsma v. Pascoag Reservoir & Dam, LLC, 774 A.2d 826 (R.I. 2001), the Rhode Island Supreme Court upheld a trial court decision that the State had acquired a prescriptive easement for the public to use a boat ramp to access the surface of the lake for recreational purposes. In addition, the State acquired title to a portion of the lake bottom by adverse possession,

4. *Stay in the Canoe.* What protection exists for landowners who are fearful that a flotilla of pleasure boaters will bring large numbers of fishermen, campers, and picnickers wading on the beds and walking along the banks?

It is clear that the landowner in a state following the recreational use test is now prohibited from erecting barriers across the stream to prevent the public from exercising its easement. Equally clear is that absent established custom, discussed *infra* p. 488, most courts would not hold that the state could grant its licensees immunity from trespass if they gained access to the water by walking across private lands. These and other more permanent privileges such as mooring boats must be acquired by prescription. See Shellow v. Hagen, 9 Wis.2d 506, 101 N.W.2d 694 (1960). But does it then follow that the recreationist must remain inside the boat to avoid a trespass suit? Some courts define the public easement as a "right of flotage" and recognize that some right to disembark is a necessary incident of full enjoyment.

To determine the scope of an easement for the purpose of deciding if it is overburdened, courts start by asking if the present use is a substantial increase in the use of the servient estate contemplated by the parties at the time of grant. However, its utility in the case of public recreational rights is limited because: (1) The servitude is imposed by courts and legislatures rather than by a voluntary conveyance. (While this is true for easements by necessity also, the courts insist that the necessity exists at the time that the unified tract is severed, thus limiting the easement to the extent necessary to serve the landlocked tract at that time.) (2) The servitude is explicitly perceived as elastic for it is imposed to accommodate new public demands with the present capacity of the water to support them. The cases dealing with these problems are few and the answers inconsistent. The narrowest servitude is illustrated in Wyoming, which relied on saw log cases and confined the rights of boaters to "disembark and pull, push or carry over shoals, riffles and rapids." Day v. Armstrong, 362 P.2d 137, 146 (Wyo.1961). Michigan, one of the original saw log states, permits fishermen to wade on the bed so long as there is no trespassing on uplands. Rushton *ex rel.* Hoffmaster v. Taggart, 306 Mich. 432, 11 N.W.2d 193 (1943). Missouri permits wading and walking on the bed and use of the channel for recreation. Elder v. Delcour, 364 Mo. 835, 269 S.W.2d 17 (1954). In Conatser v. Johnson, 194 P.3d 897 (Utah 2008), the Utah Supreme Court held that "the scope of the public's easement in state waters provides the public the right to engage in all recreational activities that *utilize* the water and does not limit the public to activities that can be performed *upon* the water."

As mentioned *supra* p. 461, some states apply the Northwest Ordinance as a source of public rights. The ordinance speaks not only of navigable waters, but also provides that "the carrying places between the same, shall be common highways." But see Lundberg v. University of Notre Dame, 231 Wis. 187, 282 N.W. 70, 72 (1938) (rejecting application of the ordinance to a dispute involving a portage to a lake used for recreational purposes).

New York appears to have adopted a similar narrow privilege of dry land use. Adirondack League Club, Inc. v. Sierra Club, 92 N.Y.2d 591, 684 N.Y.S.2d 168, 706 N.E.2d 1192 (1998) (incidental privilege of bank use and portage when "absolutely necessary.") For an interesting account of the problems of obtaining access for kayaking the Greer Spring Branch in Missouri, now part of a wild and scenic river, see John W. Ragsdale, *Greer Spring*, 67 UMKC L. Rev. 3 (1998).

People v. Emmert

Supreme Court of Colorado, 1979.
198 Colo. 137, 597 P.2d 1025.

■ LEE, JUSTICE.

The defendants-appellants were convicted of third-degree criminal trespass in violation of section 18–4–504, C.R.S. 1973.

* * *

* * * The record shows that on July 3, 1976, the defendants entered the Colorado River from public land for a float-trip downstream. The Colorado River flows westerly and bisects the ranch of the Ritschard Cattle Company. As it passes through the Ritschard ranch, it varies in depth from twelve inches to several feet. The rafts on which the defendants floated were designed to draw five to six inches of water, and had leg-holes through which the occupants could extend their legs into the water below the rafts. This enabled the defendants as they floated down the river to touch the bed of the river from time to time to control the rafts, avoid rocks and overhangs, and to stay in the main channel of the river. They touched the riverbed as it crossed the Ritschard ranch. The defendants did not, however, leave their rafts or encroach upon the shoreline or the banks of the river or islands owned by the Ritschard Cattle Company.

* * *

Upon being notified that a party of floaters was approaching, Con Ritschard and his foreman extended a single strand of barbed wire across the river at the location of the Ritschard private bridge. The strand of barbed wire was from eight to ten inches above the surface of the water and was placed in this position specifically to impede the defendants. Ritschard and his foreman remained on the bridge to tell defendants they were trespassing on private property. Defendants Taylor and Wilson were stopped at the bridge and told they were trespassing. They denied this and floated their rafts under the barbed wire and remained under the bridge for a period of time until defendant Emmert, and others in the rafting party, caught up with them. Shortly, a deputy sheriff arrived and placed the defendants under arrest, and they were subsequently charged with third-degree criminal trespass.

The parties stipulated that the river is non-navigable and had not historically been used for commercial or trade purposes of any kind. However, the river had been used in the past by recreational floaters using rafts, tubes, kayaks and flat-bottom boats, despite the express objection of the Ritschards. At the time of this incident, the river had been posted with no-trespassing signs.

Also, it was agreed that substantially all of the Ritschard ranch land was deeded land with no exclusion of the bed of the river, and that the area where the defendants were stopped was such an area, with the land on both sides of the river owned by the Ritschard ranch.

I.

The third-degree criminal trespass statute, section 18–4–504, C.R.S. 1973, provides:

"A person commits the crime of third degree criminal trespass if he unlawfully enters or remains in or upon premises. Third degree criminal trespass is a class 1 petty offense."

Defendants do not argue that they did not intentionally float on the river over the Ritschard ranch property without the owner's consent. Their contention is that they did so lawfully as a matter of right under the authority of section 5, Article XVI of the Colorado Constitution. Thus, if the defendants' interpretation is incorrect, it follows that they committed the offense of third-degree criminal trespass.

II.

It is the general rule of property law recognized in Colorado that the land underlying non-navigable streams is the subject of private ownership and is vested in the proprietors of the adjoining lands. *More v. Johnson*,

193 Colo. 489, 568 P.2d 437 (1977); *Hartman v. Tresise*, 36 Colo. 146, 84 P. 685 (1906); *Hanlon v. Hobson*, 24 Colo. 284, 51 P. 433 (1897). It is clear, therefore, that since the section of the Colorado River here involved is non-navigable the title to the stream bed is owned by the riparian landowner, the Ritschard Cattle Company. Defendants do not dispute the ownership by the Ritschard Cattle Company of the riverbed in question.

The common law rule holds that he who owns the surface of the ground has the exclusive right to everything which is above it (*"cujus est solum, ejus est usque ad coelum"*). This fundamental rule of property law has been recognized not only judicially but also by our General Assembly when in 1937 it enacted what is now codified as section 41–1–107, C.R.S. 1973:

> "The ownership of space above the lands and waters of this state is declared to be vested in the several owners of the surface beneath, subject to the right of flight of aircraft."

Applying this rule, which was implicitly adopted by the court in *Hartman*, *supra*, the ownership of the bed of a non-navigable stream vests in the owner the exclusive right of control of everything above the stream bed, subject only to constitutional and statutory limitations, restrictions and regulations. Thus, in *Hartman*, *supra*, ownership of the streambed was held to include the exclusive right of fishery in the waters flowing over it. It follows that whoever "breaks the close"—intrudes upon the space above the surface of the land—without the permission of the owner, whether it be for fishing or for other recreational purposes, such as floating, as in this case, commits a trespass. *See Restatement (Second) of Torts § 159.*

We have not been cited to any Colorado decisions interpreting constitutional or statutory provisions which may have modified the common law rule of property law upon which we predicate this decision. And we do not feel constrained to follow the trend away from the coupling of bed title with the right of public recreational use of surface waters as urged by defendants. We recognize the various rationales employed by courts to allow public recreational use of water overlying privately owned beds, i.e., (1) practical considerations employed in water rich states such as Florida, Minnesota and Washington; (2) a public easement in recreation as an incident of navigation; (3) the creation of a public trust based on usability, thereby establishing only a limited private usufructuary right; and (4) state constitutional basis for state ownership. We consider the common law rule of more force and effect, especially given its longstanding recognition in this state. As noted in *Smith v. People*, 120 Colo. 39, 206 P.2d 826 (1949): "If a change in long established judicial precedent is desirable, it is a legislative and not a judicial function to make any needed change." We specifically note that it is within the competence of the General Assembly to modify rules of common law within constitutional parameters.

III.

The defendants claim that section 5 of Article XVI of the Colorado Constitution establishes the public right to recreational use of all waters in the state. We do not agree with this interpretation. We note that Article XVI is entitled "Mining and Irrigation." Section 5, under the heading "Irrigation," reads:

> "The water of every natural stream, not heretofore appropriated, within the state of Colorado, is hereby declared to be the property of the public, and the same is dedicated to the use of the people of the state, subject to appropriation as hereinafter provided."

This provision of the Colorado Constitution, upon which the defendants so heavily rely, simply and firmly establishes the right of appropriation in this state. In this regard, we agree with the decision in *Hartman, supra*, where this court rejected an argument similar to defendants' here, that a person had a right under section 5 of Article XVI to fish in a non-navigable stream bounded by private property without the consent of the owner. In rejecting this contention, the court stated:

> " * * * The section of the Constitution relied upon declares the unappropriated waters of our natural streams to be the property of the public, and dedicates the same to the use of the people of the state, subject to appropriation, as in that instrument provided; and the following section provides that the right to divert the same to beneficial uses shall never be denied. It is this right of appropriation which the general government has recognized and confirmed, and subject to which its grants of public lands in the arid states since 1866 have been made. * * * "

The defendants attempt to distinguish *Hartman, supra,* on the grounds that the main thrust of the decision was to hold unconstitutional, as taking of private property without just compensation, that part of Colo.Sess. Laws, 1903, ch. 112, section 7 at 233, which provided: "That the public shall have the right to fish in any stream in this state, stocked at public expense, subject to actions in trespass for any damage done property along the bank of any such stream." The defendants fail to recognize, however, that their misplaced reliance on the constitutional provision was squarely rejected by the language of *Hartman, supra.* We here reaffirm, therefore, that section 5, Article XVI of the Colorado Constitution was primarily intended to preserve the historical appropriation system of water rights upon which the irrigation economy in Colorado was founded, rather than to assure public access to waters for purposes other than appropriation.

Defendants also urge as a better resolution of this controversy that we follow the Wyoming decision in Day v. Armstrong, 362 P.2d 137 (Wyo. 1961). We decline to do so. There, under similar facts to those presented in this case, the Wyoming supreme court declared that the public has the right to the recreational use of the surface waters of non-navigable streams bounded by private property.

This conclusion, the Wyoming court declared, was "based solely upon Wyoming's Constitutional declaration that all waters within its boundaries belong to the State * * *.''[1] Significantly, unlike Colorado's counterpart constitutional provision, the Wyoming provision does not mention appropriation. As such, it has been regarded as a stronger statement of the public's right to recreational use of all surface waters. See Joseph L. Sax, Water Law, 354 (1965).[2]

The interest at issue here, a riparian bed owner's exclusive use of water overlying his land, is distinguished from the right of appropriation. Constitutional provisions historically concerned with appropriation, therefore, should not be applied to subvert a riparian bed owner's common law right to the exclusive surface use of waters bounded by his lands. Without permission, the public cannot use such waters for recreation. If the increasing demand for recreational space on the waters of this state is to be accommodated, the legislative process is the proper method to achieve this end.

* * *

Finally, we note that in 1977, after the incident here in controversy had occurred, the legislature clarified the meaning of the word "premises" by the enactment of section 18–4–504.5, which provides:

"As used in sections 18–4–503 and 18–4–504, 'premises' means real property, buildings, and other improvements thereon, and the stream banks and beds of any non-navigable fresh water streams flowing through such real property."

We hold that the public has no right to the use of waters overlying private lands for recreational purposes without the consent of the owner.

Accordingly, the judgment is affirmed.

■ GROVES and CARRIGAN, JJ., dissent.

■ GROVES, JUSTICE, dissenting:

I respectfully dissent.

The majority opinion narrowly construes *Colo.Const.* Art. XVI, § 5. * * * The provision establishes that the waters of the state are the property of the public and are dedicated to the use of the people of the state. The clause "subject to appropriation as hereinafter provided" functions as a caveat establishing that appropriation for a beneficial use is superior to other uses. The clause in itself does not limit other uses.

---

1. Article 8 of the Wyoming constitution is entitled "Irrigation and Water Rights." Section 1 thereof, entitled "Water is state property," reads: "The water of all natural streams, springs, lakes or other collections of still water, within the boundaries of the state, are hereby declared to be the property of the state."

2. A possible explanation for the Wyoming supreme court's result is that the allocation and use of water in Wyoming is centrally controlled by the state through an administrative permit system whereby a permit may be denied if determined to be detrimental to the public welfare. This approach contrasts Colorado's minimal state control over appropriation of water. See Colo. Const. Art. XVI, Sec. 6, which provides that "[t]he right to divert the unappropriated waters of any natural stream to beneficial uses shall never be denied."

At the beginning of this century, Justice Bailey in a dissenting opinion [Hartman v. Tresise, 84 P. 685 (Colo.1905)], set forth the same interpretation of the constitutional provision:

> "This makes the waters of every natural stream public. They are dedicated to the use of the people, to be used by them in such manner as they see fit, subject only to one condition; that of the right of appropriation for beneficial purposes. Until the waters are appropriated and diverted from the stream, they belong to the public.
>
> "No stronger words could have been used by the people than are used in this declaration. It is idle to say that the waters of the streams are dedicated to the public for the purpose of appropriation, because those are not the words of the Constitution. It is a grant made subject to that right. * * * "

The constitutional language in no way supports any intent to provide for exclusive private use of public waters. * * *

Hartman concerned the constitutionality of a statute which purported to give the public the right to fish in any stream in the state, subject to actions for trespass for damages done to the privately owned banks of a stream. The facts of the case are not explained clearly. Nonetheless, it appears that the defendant entered the plaintiff's land to fish in a natural stream flowing there. Both the statute and the defendant's conduct concerned trespass to land. The majority in *Hartman* held only that the defendant had no right to fish in a stream whose beds and banks were privately owned and that the legislative attempt to create public easements on private land to facilitate access to streams constituted a taking of private property without compensation.

* * *

No determination as to the rights to use of streams in the absence of a trespass to land was necessary. Consequently, the statements to the effect that *Colo.Const.* Art. XVI, § 6 only provides for a right of appropriation are merely *dicta*, not precedent. * * *

In sum, the constitutional language clearly dictates a result opposite to that reached by the majority. Even if the constitutional provision were deemed ambiguous, contemporary concerns with the availability of natural resources for recreation argues for a broad interpretation of the public's rights in the waters of the state, rather than reliance upon inapplicable case law and common law made irrelevant by the express adoption of a scheme of appropriation.

* * *

■ Carrigan, Justice, dissenting:

* * *

* * * Although it is clear that the defendants touched their feet to the stream bed owned by the Ritschards, it is unclear why that contact alone is insufficient to uphold the trespass convictions. If the majority believes that

such "foot-dragging" is an inadequate basis for supporting the trespass convictions, it should say so and say why. But if the touching was a trespass, that violation was ripe for a decision and should have been the only basis for a decision. All of the majority's assertions about landowners' rights to water in adjoining streams, therefore, are assertions that amount to dicta. The majority has decided a major constitutional issue of far-ranging implications but, in so doing, has decided an issue that was not ripe for consideration.

The majority reaches deep into the common law of feudal England for the principle it today imposes on modern Colorado. The principle is of such antiquity that the majority has to express it in Latin: "Cujus est solum, ejus est usque ad coelum."[1]

A long "leap of faith" would be necessary to assume that that ancient rule had been imported into Colorado's early common law. And an even longer leap would be required to conclude that it was intended to govern the controversy at hand. But even if those leaps were made, it would seem obvious that the people of Colorado, in adopting the state constitution, repealed those principles and set forth the rule that unappropriated waters of Colorado's natural streams belong to all the people. *Colo.Const.*, Art. XVI, section 5.

Indeed, if "cujus est solum, ejus est usque ad coelum," is the law in Colorado, the majority opinion creates some serious problems for Colorado. If a landowner, for instance, has the right to all of the air flowing above his or her land, he or she also has the exclusive right to exclude others from trespassing in the airspace. Violators who infringe that airspace may be prosecuted for criminal trespass (as in this case), sued for damages or both. Anyone who floats a balloon, pilots a hang glider, flies a kite or shoots fireworks through another's airspace, therefore, is subject either to criminal prosecution, civil suit or both. Similarly and presumably, so are the owners and operators of industrial, utility and other plants which spew smoke or pollutants into the airstream and over the property of others.

* * *

The majority opinion dramatically alters the law of Colorado as it has been perceived by the many boaters, rafters and tubers who for years have sought rest, recreation and relaxation on our beautiful streams and rivers. As our population grows, so grows the need for surcease from the cares and concerns of city dwelling. Those who in our state constitution dedicated our natural streams "to the use of the people of the state * * * "were not elitists. *Colo.Const.*, Art. XVI, section 5. They did not reserve the enjoyment of these great natural resources to the few. Nor did they exclude from such pleasures all but the few who owned land on stream banks. If the recreational use of streams was not among those uses for which streams were

---

1. He who owns the surface of the ground has exclusive right to everything which is above it.

reserved to the public, it is impossible to conceive what uses were contemplated and reserved by the constitution.

* * *

Ironically the majority opinion, while implying that the General Assembly is competent to change the rule adopted today, has complicated the prospects of having the rule changed in the future. The Court has painted the state into a corner, and its brushwork assures that any effort to alter the rule will be difficult and expensive. The Court, by creating a vested property right in stream water (with the concomitant right to exclude all others from that water), has created a valuable property interest. And the General Assembly, therefore, cannot give the public recreational access to rivers without taking away from landowners their newly recognized property interests and paying them "just compensation." *U.S.Const.*, Amendment V; *Colo.Const.*, Art. II, section 15.

It is difficult to imagine a more stark contrast than the disparity between the result which the majority reaches and the language and spirit of Article XIV, section 5, ("The water of every natural stream, not heretofore appropriated, within the State of Colorado, is hereby declared to be the property of the *public*, and the same is dedicated to the use of the *People* of the State, subject to appropriation as hereinafter provided." (Emphasis added.)).

Eleven states west of the Mississippi River have recognized the right of public or non-owners' use of waters in river beds which are privately owned. Such rights are flourishing in California, Idaho, Iowa, Minnesota, Missouri, New Mexico, Oregon, South Dakota, Texas, Washington, and Wyoming. See Ralph W. Johnson and Russell A. Austin, Jr., *Recreational Rights and Titles to Beds on Western Lakes and Streams*, 7 Nat. Resources J. 38–40 (1967). See also Joseph B. Gaudet, Note, *Water Recreation—Public Use of "Private Waters*," 52 Cal. L. Rev. 171 (1964). But those rights now appear to be floundering in Colorado.

NOTES

1. *Minority Rule.* The decision in *Emmert* placed Colorado in a small minority of states that have rejected the expanded theories of public rights in water that traverses private lands. "Peculiar" Kansas chose to join Colorado in the minority. State *ex rel.* Meek v. Hays, 246 Kan. 99, 785 P.2d 1356 (1990), adopted the narrow federal test for title as the state test of navigability for recreational use, citing the fact that in 1986 the legislature "killed" two bills which would have allowed public use of streams that are non-navigable under the federal test.

2. *Can the Legislature Change the Rule?* The court in *Emmert* did not consider whether the Colorado River was navigable under the federal test because of a stipulation of the parties that it was not navigable. Presumably, in another case sufficient evidence that the river was navigable at statehood would impress the river with a public trust (see *supra* p. 415) and allow public use. But public use of non-navigable streams would depend on the court's consideration of the various theories adopted in other states. Instead of doing that in *Emmert,* the court deferred to the legislature to take any action needed to accommodate the demand for recreational uses. Justice Carrigan in dissent suggests possible constraints (legal and economic) on the legislature after *Emmert.* What can a future legislature do? See Lisa La Belle Scott, Note, *The Public Trust Doctrine—A Tool for Expanding Recreational Rafting Rights in Colorado,* 57 U. Colo. L. Rev. 625 (1986).

3. Prior to the decision in *Emmert,* but after the facts occurred, the state's criminal trespass law was amended to clarify the meaning of "premises". The Attorney General opined that:

> The legislative definition of "premises" in section 18–4–504.5 * * * was restricted to real property and does not include either the waters of streams or the airspace above private property. * * * The statute then would repeal "ad coelum" in the criminal trespass context, and would reverse the *Emmert* result in the situation * * * where persons float over private property but do not touch the river bed or banks.

> * * *

> An examination of the legislative history of section 18–4–504.5 reveals quite clearly that the intent of the legislature was to protect riparian landowners from trespasses to the privately owned banks and beds of streams, while insuring that those who float or boat upon those streams without intruding on real property would not be liable for a criminal trespass. * * *

> * * * Because section 18–4–504.5 speaks to criminal trespass and does not address civil remedies, it cannot be viewed as authorizing the owners of stream banks and beds to prohibit or otherwise control the use for floating of waters passing over their lands.

Op.Colo. Att'y Gen. File No. ONR8303042/KW (1983). Without a remedy in criminal trespass, what recourse does an objecting property owner have to boaters and sportsmen floating through their property? Although, as the Attorney General concludes, the amendment does not "address" civil remedies, are such remedies precluded? Is self-help appropriate? Could the "problem" still be solved with barbed wire?

4. *Consumptive Rights versus Public Rights. Emmert* found that the framers of Colorado's Constitution were primarily concerned with preserving the ability of the citizens to appropriate water and therefore the court could not rely on the provision of the constitution declaring that unappropriated water in streams is "property of the public, and the same is dedicated to the use of the people of the state" as supporting public recreational use. Is the result supported by the difference in Colorado's constitutional provision regarding rights to water from the provision in the Wyoming Constitution quoted in footnote 1 of *Emmert,* which was cited to reach an opposite result in *Day v. Armstrong?* Are the constitutions materially different? See *supra* p. 477. In the *Curran* case discussed *supra* pp. 466–467, the Montana Supreme Court construed a provision in the state constitution referring to prior appropriation as preventing a property owner from excluding the public from using a stream for recreation "except to the extent of his prior appropriation of part of the water for irrigation." 682 P.2d at 170. The Montana Constitution provides: "All surface, underground, flood, and atmospheric waters within the boundaries of the state are the property of the state for the use of its people and are subject to appropriation for beneficial uses as provided by law." Mont. Const. art. IX, § 3.

Is it realistic to expect conflicts between the public's use of water for recreation and the exercise of water rights established by prior appropriation?

A has an 1895 appropriation on Trout Paradise River located in a state like Montana that recognizes a right of public recreational use. In 2000 the river is declared suitable for recreational use and thus open to public use. During the 2002 summer irrigation season A makes a call on the river that is rejected by the water master on the ground that the diversion will interfere with the use of the water for public fishing and flotation rights. Can the state withhold the water from diversion?

In Ritter v. Standal, 98 Idaho 446, 566 P.2d 769 (1977), defendant constructed a fish farm in an estuary of the Snake River that blocked both a private riparian's and the public's access to the river. Idaho Code § 36–907 declared the river navigable for fishing. The court held that the public had use rights to recreation, and that the reach of the river had long been used for these purposes, citing Southern Idaho Fish and Game Ass'n v. Picabo Livestock, Inc., 96 Idaho 360, 528 P.2d 1295 (1974). Defendant was ordered to remove the fish farm and restore the estuary because the farm was a public and private nuisance obstructing free passage of a navigable estuary. Of special interest is the court's rejection of defendant's argument that his state water license allowed him to maintain the farm to the detriment of public rights.

D. THE NAVIGATION SERVITUDE

United States v. Rands

Supreme Court of the United States, 1967.
389 U.S. 121, 88 S.Ct. 265, 19 L.Ed.2d 329.

■ MR. JUSTICE WHITE delivered the opinion of the Court.

In this case the Court is asked to decide whether the compensation which the United States is constitutionally required to pay when it condemns riparian land includes the land's value as a port site. Respondents owned land along the Columbia River in the State of Oregon. They leased the land to the State with an option to purchase, it apparently being contemplated that the State would use the land as an industrial park, part of which would function as a port. The option was never exercised, for the land was taken by the United States in connection with the John Day Lock and Dam Project, authorized by Congress as part of a comprehensive plan for the development of the Columbia River. Pursuant to statute the United States then conveyed the land to the State of Oregon at a price considerably less than the option price at which respondents had hoped to sell. In the condemnation action, the trial judge determined that the compensable value of the land taken was limited to its value for sand, gravel, and agricultural purposes and that its special value as a port site could not be considered. The ultimate award was about one-fifth the claimed value of the land if used as a port. The Court of Appeals for the Ninth Circuit reversed, apparently holding that the Government had taken from respondents a compensable right of access to navigable waters and concluding that "port site value should be compensable under the Fifth Amendment." 367 F.2d 186, 191 (1966). We granted certiorari, 386 U.S. 989, because of a seeming conflict between the decision below and *United States v. Twin City Power Co.*, 350 U.S. 222 (1956). We reverse the judgment of the Court of Appeals because the principles underlying *Twin City* govern this case and the Court of Appeals erred in failing to follow them.

The Commerce Clause confers a unique position upon the Government in connection with navigable waters. "The power to regulate commerce comprehends the control for that purpose, and to the extent necessary, of all the navigable waters of the United States * * *. For this purpose they are the public property of the nation, and subject to all the requisite legislation by Congress." *Gilman v. Philadelphia*, 3 Wall. 713, 724–525 (1866). This power to regulate navigation confers upon the United States a "dominant servitude", *FPC v. Niagara Mohawk Power Corp.*, 347 U.S. 239, 249 (1954), which extends to the entire stream and the stream bed below ordinary high-water mark. The proper exercise of this power is not an invasion of any private property rights in the stream or the lands underlying it, for the damage sustained does not result from taking property from riparian owners within the meaning of the Fifth Amendment but from the lawful exercise of a power to which the interests of riparian owners have always been subject. Thus, without being constitutionally obligated to pay compensation, the United States may change the course of a navigable stream, or otherwise impair or destroy a riparian owner's access to navigable waters, even though the market value of the riparian owner's land is substantially diminished.

The navigational servitude of the United States does not extend beyond the high-water mark. Consequently, when fast lands are taken by the Government, just compensation must be paid. But "just as the navigational privilege permits the Government to reduce the value of riparian lands by denying the riparian owner access to the stream without compensation for his loss, * * * it also permits the Government to disregard the value arising from this same fact of riparian location in compensating the owner when fast lands are appropriated." *United States v. Virginia Elec. & Power Co.*, 365 U.S. 624, 629 (1961). Specifically, the Court has held that the Government is not required to give compensation for "water power" when it takes the riparian lands of a private power company using the stream to generate power. *United States v. Chandler–Dunbar Water Power Co.*, 229 U.S. 53, 73–74 (1913). Nor must it compensate the company for the value of its uplands as a power plant site. *Id.*, at 76. Such value does not "inhere in these parcels as upland," but depends on use of the water to which the company has no right as against the United States: "The Government had dominion over the water power of the rapids and falls and cannot be required to pay any hypothetical additional value to a riparian owner who had no right to appropriate the current to his own commercial use." *Ibid.*

All this was made unmistakably clear in *United States v. Twin City Power Co.*, 350 U.S. 222 (1956). The United States condemned a promising site for a hydroelectric power plant and was held to be under no obligation to pay for any special value which the fast lands had for power generating purposes. The value of the land attributable to its location on the stream was "due to the flow of the stream; and if the United States were required to pay the judgments below, it would be compensating the landowner for the increment of value added to the fast lands if the flow of the stream were taken into account." 350 U.S., at 226.

We are asked to distinguish between the value of land as a power site and its value as a port site. In the power cases, the stream is used as a source of power to generate electricity. In this case, for the property to have value as a port, vessels must be able to arrive and depart by water, meanwhile using the waterside facilities of the port. In both cases, special value arises from access to, and use of navigable waters. With regard to the constitutional duty to compensate a riparian owner, no distinction can be drawn. It is irrelevant that the licensing authority presently being exercised over hydroelectric projects may be different from, or even more stringent than, the licensing of port sites. We are dealing with the constitutional power of Congress completely to regulate navigable streams to the total exclusion of private power companies or port owners. As was true in *Twin City*, if the owner of the fast lands can demand port site value as part of his compensation, "he gets the value of a right that the Government in the exercise of its dominant servitude can grant or withhold as it chooses. * * * To require the United States to pay for this * * * value would be to create private claims in the public domain." 350 U.S., at 228.

Respondents and the Court of Appeals alike have found *Twin City* inconsistent with the holding in *United States v. River Rouge Improvement Co.*, 269 U.S. 411 (1926). In that case, the Government took waterfront property to widen and improve the navigable channel of the Rouge River. By reason of the improvements, other portions of the riparian owner's property became more valuable because they were afforded direct access to the stream for the building of docks and other purposes related to navigation. Pursuant to § 6 of the Rivers and Harbors Act of 1918, the compensation award for the part of the property taken by the Government was reduced by the value of the special and direct benefits to the remainder of the land. The argument here seems to be that if the enhancement in value flowing from a riparian location is real enough to reduce the award for another part of the same owner's property, consistency demands that these same values be recognized in the award when any riparian property is taken by the Government. There is no inconsistency. *Twin City* and its predecessors do not deny that access to navigable waters may enhance the market value of riparian property. And, in *River Rouge*, it was recognized that state law may give the riparian owner valuable rights of access to navigable waters good against other riparian owners or against the State itself. But under *Twin City* and like cases, these rights and values are not assertable against the superior rights of the United States, are not property within the meaning of the Fifth Amendment, and need not be paid for when appropriated by the United States. Thus, when only part of the property is taken and the market value of the remainder is enhanced by reason of the improvement to navigable waters, reducing the award by the amount of the increase in value simply applies in another context the principle that special values arising from access to a navigable stream are allocable to the public, and not to private interest. Otherwise the private owner would receive a windfall to which he is not entitled.

Our attention is also directed to *Monongahela Navigation Co. v. United States*, 148 U.S. 312 (1893), where it was held that the Government had to pay the going-concern value of a toll lock and dam built at the implied invitation of the Government, and to the portion of the opinion in *Chandler–Dunbar* approving an award requiring the Government to pay for the value of fast lands as a site for a canal and lock to bypass the falls and rapids of the river. *Monongahela* is not in point, however, for the Court has since read it as resting "primarily upon the doctrine of estoppel. * * * " *Omnia Commercial Co., Inc. v. United States*, 261 U.S. 502, 513–514 (1923). The portion of *Chandler–Dunbar* relied on by respondents was duly noted and dealt with in *Twin City* itself, 350 U.S. 222, 226 (1956). That aspect of the decision has been confined to its special facts, and, in any event, if it is at all inconsistent with *Twin City*, it is only the latter which survives.

Finally, respondents urge that the Government's position subverts the policy of the Submerged Lands Act, which confirmed and vested in the States title to the lands beneath navigable waters within their boundaries and to natural resources within such lands and waters, together with the right and power to manage, develop, and use such lands and natural resources. However, reliance on that Act is misplaced, for it expressly recognized that the United States retained "all its navigational servitude and rights in and powers of regulation and control of said lands and navigable waters for the constitutional purposes of commerce, navigation, national defense, and international affairs, all of which shall be paramount to, but shall not be deemed to include, proprietary rights of ownership * * * ." Nothing in the Act was to be construed "as the release or relinquishment of any rights of the United States arising under the constitutional authority of Congress to regulate or improve navigation, or to provide for flood control, or the production of power." The Act left congressional power over commerce and the dominant navigational servitude of the United States precisely where it found them.

For the foregoing reasons, the judgment of the Court of Appeals is reversed and the case remanded with direction to reinstate the judgment of the District Court.

Reversed and remanded.

Mr. Justice Marshall took no part in the consideration or decision of this case.

NOTES

1. Suppose the United States had condemned Rands' land for a highway. Would the measure of compensation be the same?

2. Prior to Rands, the two most important cases on the "navigation servitude" were *Chandler–Dunbar* and *Twin City*, both relied on in *Rands*.

In *Chandler–Dunbar*, the owner of the dam site had erected a dam with the revocable permission of the Secretary of War and was producing and selling water power. Congress chose to destroy the water power value in order to promote navigation. In denying recovery of the water power values of the condemned dam site, the Court seemed to state that since Congress could forbid the placing of a dam in a navigable stream, no property interest in water power could be obtained and hence no compensation was due. However, the Court did uphold the landowner's claim for compensation for "lock and canal" values of fast land. It appears that the land was well-suited for development for water transportation as traffic increased on the lake. How can this award be reconciled with the denial of water power values?

Twin City concerned the claim of a dam site owner who planned to develop a hydroelectric power project on a navigable river. Congress authorized a public power project that pre-empted claimant's site. In short, the United States took claimant's hydroelectric power site for its own hydroelectric project. Ruling first that Congress authorized the project at least in part for incidental navigation benefits and that if "the interests of navigation are served, it is constitutionally irrelevant that other purposes may also be advanced," the Court held in a 5–4 decision that *Chandler–Dunbar* controlled the decision: "To require the United States to pay for this water power value would be to create private claims in the public domain."

The dissenting judges relied heavily on the "lock and canal" award in *Chandler–Dunbar*, but the majority dismissed it in a footnote, stating that perhaps the *Chandler–Dunbar* Court had sustained the award because the "lock and canal" values were consistent with the navigation improvement planned by United States. In any event, the "lock and canal" values of *Chandler–Dunbar* seem to afford little ground for argument in the light of the 8–0 decision (and the comment on *Chandler–Dunbar*) in *Rands*.

3.   A certain amount of confusion exists about the effect of the navigation servitude on non-navigable streams. In United States v. Kansas City Life Ins. Co., 339 U.S. 799, 70 S.Ct. 885, 94 L.Ed. 1277 (1950), the Court (5 to 4) granted compensation to a landowner whose farm was ruined by saturation of the subsoil when the United States raised the level of the Mississippi River to the mean high-water mark and thereby backed water up the non-navigable tributary on which the farm lay. Later, in United States v. Grand River Dam Auth., 363 U.S. 229, 80 S.Ct. 1134, 4 L.Ed.2d 1186 (1960), the Court held that the United States owed no compensation for water power values in a dam site condemned on a non-navigable tributary as part of the Arkansas River flood control and navigation project.

Suppose the United States condemns a vacation home on a non-navigable river for a post office. If vacation homes fronting on the river bring higher prices than homes away from the stream must the United States pay the higher value?

4.   The River and Harbors Act of 1970, § 111, 33 U.S.C.A. § 595(a) (West 2001), altered the compensation requirements of *Rands*:

> [C]ompensation to be paid for real property taken by the United States above the normal high water mark of navigable waters of the United States shall be the fair market value of such real property based upon all uses to which such real property may reasonably be put, including its highest and best use, any of which uses may be dependent upon access to or utilization of such navigable waters.

How much of the no-compensation rule of *Rands* survives under the law? How would *Twin City* and *Chandler–Dunbar* be decided today? Does the new law offer any protection to those losing their permits for wharfs or artificial landfills, whose uses and facilities are below the normal high water mark?

Consider the following illustration of how the now-modified rule of *Rands* works: A landowner owns a twenty-acre tract consisting of two adjacent, ten-acre parcels, one on the shore of a navigable stream, one immediately upland of it. The upland parcel is worth $2,000 an acre. The waterfront parcel is worth $4,500 an acre, the difference being attributable to its waterfront location. The United States condemns the waterfront parcel which is to be inundated as part of a federal local and dam project. The upland parcel will become attractive waterfront property (worth $4,500 an acre). The landowner will receive nothing under the *Rands* rule, but is entitled to $20,000 compensation under the rule as modified by the 1970 amendment (because the amendment left intact the rule that the increased value of new waterfront land must be subtracted from the award).

5.   Kuapa Pond is a shallow 523–acre lagoon on Oahu, Hawai'i, separated from a Pacific Ocean bay by a barrier beach. The pond historically had been used as a fishpond, and under Hawaiian land law was the private property of the landowner, the Bishop Estate. Bishop leased 6,000 acres, including the pond, to Kaiser Aetna in 1961 for a marina subdivision. Kaiser Aetna dredged the pond and opened an eight-foot-deep channel to the bay. A dispute arose between Kaiser and the U.S. Army Corps of Engineers. The Corps argued that further filling in the marina required a permit under § 10 of the Rivers and Harbors Act because the channel made the pond navigable and therefore it had become subject to a public navigation easement. The Corps had earlier informed Kaiser that no permit was needed for dredging the pond and subsequently acquiesced to the dredging of the channel. The Supreme Court held that Kuapa Pond was now navigable and subject to the Corps' regulatory jurisdiction, but further held that the imposition of a navigation easement on behalf of members of the public would constitute a taking and could not be characterized as an exercise of the navigation servitude. Kaiser Aetna v. United States, 444 U.S. 164, 100 S.Ct. 383, 62 L.Ed.2d 332 (1979).

Writing for the majority, Justice Rehnquist distinguished the servitude cases:

> There is no denying that the strict logic of the more recent cases limiting the Government's liability to pay damages for riparian access, if carried to its ultimate conclusion, might completely swallow up any private claim for "just compensation" under the Fifth Amendment even in a situation as different from the riparian condemnation cases as this one. But, as Mr. Justice Holmes observed in a very different context, the life of the law has not been logic, it has been experience. The navigation servitude, which exists by virtue of the Commerce Clause in navigable streams, gives rise to an authority in the Government to assure that such streams retain their capacity to serve as continuous highways for the purpose of navigation in interstate commerce. Thus, when the Government acquires fast lands to improve navigation, it is not required under the Eminent Domain Clause to compensate landowners for certain elements of damage attributable to riparian location, such as land's value as a hydroelectric site, *Twin City Power Co.*, or a port site, *United States v. Rands*. But none of these cases ever doubted that when the Government wished to acquire fast lands, it was required by the Eminent Domain Clause of the Fifth Amendment to condemn and pay fair value for that interest. * * *

> Here, the Government's attempt to create a public right of access to the improved pond goes so far beyond ordinary regulation or improvement for navigation as to amount to a taking under the logic of *Pennsylvania Coal Co. v. Mahon*, 260 U.S. 393 (1922). More than one factor contributes to this result. It is clear that prior to its improvement, Kuapa Pond was incapable of being used as a continuous highway for the purpose of navigation in interstate commerce. Its maximum depth at high tide was a mere two feet, it was separated from the adjacent bay and ocean by a natural barrier beach, and its principal commercial value was limited to fishing. It consequently is not the sort of "great navigable stream" that this Court has previously recognized as being "[incapable] of private ownership." See, e.g., *United States v. Chandler–Dunbar Co.*; *United States v. Twin City Power Co.* And, as previously noted, Kuapa Pond has always been

> considered to be private property under Hawaiian law. Thus, the interest of petitioners in the now dredged marina is strikingly similar to that of owners of fast land adjacent to navigable water.

Id. at 177–79.

Justice Blackmun dissented and argued that the navigation servitude was coextensive with navigable waters of the United States and that Kaiser Aetna was not entitled to compensation for the imposition of the servitude: the government had a substantial interest in maintaining free highways of navigability and "[w]hatever expectancy petitioners may have had in control over the pond for use as a fishery was surrendered in exchange for the advantages of access when they cut a channel into the bay." Id. at 190–91. In a companion case, the Court applied the *Kaiser Aetna* reasoning to deny applicability of the navigation servitude to a system of human-made canals in Louisiana that connect the Gulf of Mexico with an inland waterway. Vaughn v. Vermilion Corp., 444 U.S. 206, 100 S.Ct. 399, 62 L.Ed.2d 365 (1979). Courts have continued to recognize that even if a waterway is navigable, this factor alone does not necessarily determine its status as navigable water for all purposes. See, *e.g.*, Dardar v. Lafourche Realty Co., Inc., 55 F.3d 1082 (5th Cir.1995) (despite navigability, navigational servitude was not imposed based on shallow depth, private ownership, and non-navigability in natural state).

The Court later held that the navigation servitude precludes the recovery of damages by an Indian tribe for damages to sand and gravel deposits caused by a navigation improvement project. United States v. Cherokee Nation of Oklahoma, 480 U.S. 700, 107 S.Ct. 1487, 94 L.Ed.2d 704 (1987). The court of appeals had applied a balancing test to award compensation, but the Supreme Court held that no balancing was required "where, as here, the interference with in-stream interests results from the exercise of the Government's power to regulate navigational uses of 'the deep streams which penetrate our country in every direction.' " Id. at 703. The Court also rejected the argument that tribal ownership of title to the bed was an exception to the rule that "all" riparian owners are subject to the servitude. What is the distinction between this case and *Kaiser Aetna*?

6.   Section 10(c) of the Federal Power Act, 16 U.S.C.A. § 803(c) provides in part:

> Each licensee hereunder shall be liable for all damages occasioned to the property of others by the construction, maintenance, or operation of the project works or of the works appurtenant or accessory thereto, constructed under the license, and in no event shall the United States be liable therefor.

Seattle, holding a Federal Power Act license, and proceeding under federal eminent domain power conferred by the Act, claimed that as a federal licensee it enjoyed the same navigation servitude that the federal government would have had if it were constructing the project, and thus that it was not liable for power site values of land it condemned. In Public Util. Dist. No. 1 v. City of Seattle, 382 F.2d 666 (9th Cir.1967), the Court of

Appeals rejected the contention, resting its judgment on two grounds: (1) that the servitude is a privilege held exclusively by the government and is not delegable; (2) in the alternative, if the power is delegable, the United States has not done so, for § 10(c) expressly requires payment for state-created water values taken by licensees. There was one dissent. After certiorari was applied for in the Supreme Court, the petition was dismissed (396 U.S. 803, 90 S.Ct. 22, 24 L.Ed.2d 59 (1969)) under Rule 60 (voluntary settlement by the parties), leaving the legal question unresolved.

7. Is there a state navigation servitude? The California Supreme Court held that the state does not have to compensate shipyard owners whose access to a deep water ship channel was substantially impaired by the construction of two freeway bridges across the channel. Colberg, Inc. v. State *ex rel.* Dept. of Public Works, 432 P.2d 3, 67 Cal.2d 408, 62 Cal.Rptr. 401 (1967). The court said that the state servitude was subject to the same limitation as the federal. *Colberg* recognized that the states are split on the issue of whether private rights impaired as the result of projects in aid of navigation are compensable. See Commonwealth, Dept. of Highways v. Thomas, 427 S.W.2d 213 (Ky.1967) (allowing compensation on similar facts). See also Wernberg v. State, 516 P.2d 1191, 1200–1201 (Alaska 1973).

E.   SHORELINE ACCESS

The right to use water is a function of access to a watercourse. States have passed laws to facilitate access to divert water under a consumptive use right. State laws allowing private condemnation of rights of way for pipes and canals have been upheld as furthering a public use, given the importance of water in the West. *E.g.*, Clark v. Nash, 198 U.S. 361, 25 S.Ct. 676, 49 L.Ed. 1085 (1905). But it is more difficult for the public to obtain access to waters, lakes, rivers, and oceans that are subject to public rights. The problem of access to Atlantic, Pacific, and Great Lakes beaches illustrates the problem. There are 59,157 miles of coastline—including Alaska and the Great Lakes—in the United States. Of these, 21,724 are suitable for public recreation, but only 1209 miles are open to the public. See James F. Lafargue, *Practical Legal Remedies to the Public Beach Shortage*, 5 Envtl. Affairs 447, 448 (1976).

At common law, public rights to use coastal waters are confined to the sea and foreshore (the land covered and uncovered by the regular cycles of the tide), and the foreshore and sea must be reached without trespassing on private property. Federal and state regulatory jurisdiction has been extended over waters that were considered non-navigable at common law and similarly public rights have been extended to smaller and smaller water bodies. It was probably inevitable that the expansion of public rights to use the surface of waters would spill over to the assertion of public rights to use dry shoreland areas.

Because purchase of access rights to beach front property by the state is not always financially feasible, there has been considerable pressure to impress dry sand areas with public rights. Besides purchase or condemnation of beach front land or rights of way, public access rights can be established by judicial decisions recognizing public rights under various common law doctrines or by legislation. These methods all have encountered constitutional objections.

Custom. The most sweeping use of judicial doctrine to open dry sand beaches to the public is the Oregon Supreme Court's expansion of the common law doctrine of custom. As articulated by Blackstone, custom was a local as opposed to general practice that had been continuously exercised from time immemorial, peaceably asserted, reasonable, certain, obligatory on all owners, and not contrary to other laws. See William Blackstone, Blackstone's Commentaries on the Law 57 (Bernard C. Gavit ed. 1941).

Many American courts refused to recognize custom because it was inconsistent with the uniform common law and there were no time immemorial practices in the United States. *E.g.*, State *ex rel.* Haman v. Fox, 100 Idaho 140, 594 P.2d 1093 (1979). The Oregon Supreme Court, however, held that since statehood and before, both Indians and non-Indians assumed that all the state's dry sand beaches were open to public use. State *ex rel.* Thornton v. Hay, 254 Or. 584, 462 P.2d 671 (1969). In recent years, there has been increasingly criticism of the *Thornton* decision as a distortion of the doctrine of custom, see David L. Callies, *Custom and the Public Trust: Background Principles of State Property Law?*, 30 Envtl. L. Rptr. 10003 (2000), and as a judicial taking, see David J. Bederman, *The Curious Resurrection of Custom: Beach Access and Judicial Takings*, 96 Colum. L. Rev. 1375 (1996). In Oregon, there have been post-*Thornton* takings challenges, all unsuccessful. Stevens v. City of Cannon Beach, 317 Or. 131, 854 P.2d 449 (1993), cert. denied 510 U.S. 1207, 114 S.Ct. 1332, 127 L.Ed.2d 679 (1994) held that custom was an inherent limitation in the title of all Oregon littoral owners.

Hawai'i has most dramatically extended the boundary between private and public coastal land. The conventional understanding of the division of land in feudal Hawai'i was that the King granted his chiefs the right to use an ahupua'a, which was basically a watershed that extended from the ocean to the uplands. Tenants lived off the ahupua'a by taro farming, hunting, gathering, and fishing. This system was formally abolished in 1848, when King Kamehameha III acceded to the demands of foreign residents for allodial land titles and formally divided his lands among the chiefs, himself, and the government. See Ralph S. KuyKendall, The Hawaiian Kingdom, Volume 1, Foundation and Transformation 1778–1854, at 269–298 (1938). The break-up of the monarch's land holdings "the Great Mahele," became the basis for the development of Hawai'i's plantation economy controlled by a small group of large landowners. It was thought to be the beginning of the end for the survival of any Native Hawai'ian rights to use the ancient ahupua'as for traditional uses.

Much later, after Hawai'i became a state, its supreme court began to enforce Native Hawai'ian rights. Early decisions relied on ancient use of the seashore to hold that the boundary between private property was the farthest inward vegetation line rather than the traditional "upper reaches of the waves." See Application of Ashford, 50 Haw. 314, 440 P.2d 76 (1968) and County of Hawai'i v. Sotomura, 55 Haw. 176, 517 P.2d 57 (1973). In an eminent domain action, however, a federal district court opined that the Hawai'i Supreme Court's decisions amounted to an unconstitutional taking, at least as applied to land registered under the Torrens system. Sotomura v. County of Hawai'i, 460 F.Supp. 473 (D.Haw.1978). The net result is that large resort developers usually accede to the vegetation line but title to individual shore front property remains uncertain, and property owners often negotiate a boundary line with the state.

Today, custom is thriving in Hawai'i. The Hawai'i Supreme Court has held that Native Hawaiians may exercise traditional gathering, hunting, and religious practices on undeveloped land. Public Access Shoreline Hawaii v. Hawai'i County Planning Comm'n, 79 Haw. 425, 903 P.2d 1246 (1995) (*PASH*). These customary rights were held to have survived the transition to an allodial land tenure regime in the Kingdom and Territory and to be secured by the Hawai'i Constitution. *PASH* concluded: "[o]ur examination of the relevant historical developments in Hawaiian history leads us to the conclusion that the western concept of exclusivity is not universally applicable in Hawai'i." 903 P.2d at 1268. Native customary rights also extend to water use, although these rights are not as developed as is the law of land access. *In re* Water Use Permit Applications, 94 Haw. 97, 9 P.3d 409 (2000) (appeal after remand at 105 Haw. 1, 93 P.3d 643 (2004)) (appeal after remand at 113 Haw. 52, 147 P.3d 836 (2006)), *supra* p. 434.

What are the limits of customary rights? State v. Hanapi, 89 Haw. 177, 970 P.2d 485 (1998), teaches that they must have an evidentiary foundation to link them to a pre-eighteenth century customary or traditional practice. Hanapi, a Native Hawai'ian, owned land next to a non-Native who illegally filled a wetland, and Hanapi complained first to the landowner and then to the U.S. Army Corps of Engineers. The Corps agreed to a voluntary, unsupervised restoration subject to consultation with an anthropologist. Hanapi, acting as a self-appointed "monitor" of the work, was arrested for trespass when he refused to leave the fenced-in restoration area. In affirming the conviction, the court noted that "Hanapi adduced no evidence establishing 'stewardship' or 'restoration and healing of lands' as an ancient tradition or customary native Hawaiian practice." 970 P.2d at 495. See also Ka Pa'akai O Ka'aina v. Land Use Comm'n, 94 Haw. 31, 7 P.3d 1068 (2000). See generally Linda S. Parker, Native American Estate: The Struggle Over Indian and Hawaiian Lands (1989).

Public Trust. The public trust doctrine has also been invoked as a basis for gaining public access across land to reach a waterway that is subject to the public trust. See, *e.g.*, National Ass'n of Home Builders v. New Jersey Dept. of Environmental Protection, 64 F.Supp.2d 354 (D.N.J.1999). The court held that a requirement that a developer maintain a 30–foot walkway along the Hudson River was not a taking because most of it was on land conveyed to private parties but never severed from the trust and the rest was on upland subject to a public right of access under an earlier New Jersey case that held private, dry sand areas adjoining a municipal beach were subject to a public right of access. Matthews v. Bay Head Improvement Ass'n, 95 N.J. 306, 471 A.2d 355 (1984). Public access through privately owned property was further clarified in Raleigh Avenue Beach Ass'n v. Atlantis Beach Club, Inc., 185 N.J. 40, 879 A.2d 112 (2005). An intermediate Connecticut appellate court held that the public trust prevents a town from barring non-residents from its parks and beaches, but reserved judgment on the issue of whether a community could charge non-residents a de minimis differential access charge. Leydon v. Town of Greenwich, 57 Conn.App. 712, 750 A.2d 1122 (2000). On appeal, the Connecticut Supreme Court agreed that the ordinance in question was void, but grounded its opinion on constitutional issues of freedom of expression and association. 257 Conn. 318, 777 A.2d 552 (2001). For a case discussing the public trust doctrine and shoreline access on the Great Lakes, see Glass v. Goeckel, 473 Mich. 667, 703 N.W.2d 58 (2005).

Legislation. Legislation purporting to grant access over private lands to reach trust lands has been held to be an unconstitutional taking by the courts in New Hampshire, Maine, and Massachusetts. Opinion of the Justices (Public Use of Coastal Beaches), 139 N.H. 82, 649 A.2d 604 (1994); Bell v. Town of Wells, 557 A.2d 168 (Me.1989); Opinion of the Justices, 365 Mass. 681, 313 N.E.2d 561 (1974).

The states have also attempted to move public boundary lines landward in order to expand public use. To determine the boundary between public and private land, most coastal states use the mean high tide line or a variant of this standard. Delaware, Massachusetts, Maine, New Hampshire, and Virginia use the low waterline. There are practical reasons for questioning the rule. The mean high tide line is a variable plane that shifts with accretion and erosion and poses considerable risks for property developers who erroneously locate the boundary. Cf. Lechuza Villas West v. California Coastal Comm'n, 60 Cal.App.4th 218, 70 Cal.Rptr.2d 399 (1997). Can a low water mark state shift to the mean high tide line, and therefore expand the amount of submerged land subject to public use? See State v. Ashmore, 236 Ga. 401, 224 S.E.2d 334 (1976), cert. denied 429 U.S. 830, 97 S.Ct. 90, 50 L.Ed.2d 93 (1976). *Ashmore* held that Georgia could change from the mean low tide line, established in 1902, to the mean high tide line (the usual boundary line) because the 1902 statute referring to the low tide line was only intended to grant private rights to take oysters rather than to convey title to littoral owners. However, when the New Hampshire legislature changed the boundary line from the mean high tide to the highest high tide line, the state Supreme Court held that it was an unconstitutional taking. "Property rights created by the common law may not be taken away legislatively without due process of law." Purdie v. Attorney General, 143 N.H. 661, 732 A.2d 442, 447 (1999).

Washington has declared that portion of foreshore lying between the extreme low tide line and the mean high tide line to be a public highway. Seashore Conservation Area, Wash. Rev. Code Ann. §§ 79A.05.600–

79A.05.695 (West 2001 & West Supp. 2007). In Hughes v. State, 67 Wash.2d 799, 410 P.2d 20 (1966), the Washington Supreme Court then construed the vegetation line to be the mean high tide line citing a 1901 precedent, Shelton Logging Co. v. Gosser, 26 Wash. 126, 66 P. 151 (1901) interpreting Shively v. Bowlby, 152 U.S. 1, 14 S.Ct. 548, 38 L.Ed. 331 (1894). The United States Supreme Court did not rule on this issue in *Hughes, supra,* p. 408.

Coastal shoreline access in California is provided for under the California Coastal Act of 1976 that requires new coastal zone developments to dedicate public access to the ocean unless it would interfere with public safety, military security or a fragile coastal area, adequate access exists nearby or agriculture would be threatened. Cal. Pub. Res. Code §§ 30210–30214 (West 2007).

The California Coastal Commission's practice of requiring subdivision exactions for public beach access under the act has been challenged by developers. Several California cases held that the justification for the required dedication is not the need created by the particular project but that the Commission may consider the cumulative impact of many small projects that collectively create a need for access. The U.S. Supreme Court has held that such exactions must be directly or indirectly related to the demand for beach use caused by the subdivision. See Nollan v. California Coastal Comm'n, 483 U.S. 825, 107 S.Ct. 3141, 97 L.Ed.2d 677 (1987), *infra* p. 519.

Gion v. City of Santa Cruz

Supreme Court of California, 1970.
2 Cal.3d 29, 84 Cal.Rptr. 162, 465 P.2d 50.

■ PER CURIAM.

We consider these two cases together because both raise the question of determining when an implied dedication of land has been made.

* * *

In Dietz v. King, plaintiffs, as representatives of the public, asked the court to enjoin defendants from interfering with the public's use of Navarro Beach in Mendocino County and an unimproved dirt road, called the Navarro Beach Road, leading to that beach. The beach is a small sandy peninsula jutting into the Pacific Ocean. It is surrounded by cliffs at the south and east, and is bounded by the Navarro River and the Navarro Beach Road (the only convenient access to the beach by land) on the north. The Navarro Beach Road branches from a county road that parallels State Highway One. The road runs in a southwesterly direction along the Navarro River for 1,500 feet and then turns for the final 1,500 feet due south to the beach. The road first crosses for a short distance land owned by the Carlyles, who maintain a residence adjacent to the road. It then crosses land owned by Mae Crider and Jack W. Sparkman, proprietors of an ancient structure called the Navarro-by-the-Sea Hotel, and, for the final 2,200 feet, land now owned by defendants.

The public has used the beach and the road for at least 100 years. Five cottages were built on the high ground of the ocean beach about 100 years ago. A small cemetery plot containing the remains of shipwrecked sailors and natives of the area existed there. Elderly witnesses testified that persons traveled over the road during the closing years of the last century. They came in substantial numbers to camp, picnic, collect and cut drift-wood for fuel, and fish for abalone, crabs, and finned fish. Others came to the beach to decorate the graves, which had wooden crosses upon them. Indians, in groups of 50 to 75 came from as far away as Ukiah during the summer months. They camped on the beach for weeks at a time, drying kelp and catching and drying abalone and other fish. In decreasing num-bers they continued to use the road and the beach until about 1950.

In more recent years the public use of Navarro Beach has expanded. The trial court found on substantial evidence that "For many years members of the public have used and enjoyed the said beach for various kinds of recreational activities, including picnicking, hiking, swimming, fishing, skin diving, camping, driftwood collecting, firewood collecting, and related activities." At times as many as 100 persons have been on the beach. They have come in automobiles, trucks, campers, and trailers. The beach has been used for commercial fishing, and during good weather a school for retarded children has brought its students to the beach once every week or two.

None of the previous owners of the King property ever objected to public use of Navarro Beach Road. * * *

In 1960, a year after the Kings acquired the land, they placed a large timber across the road at the entrance to their land. Within two hours it was removed by persons wishing to use the beach. Mr. King occasionally put up No Trespassing signs, but they were always removed by the time he returned to the land, and the public continued to use the beach until August 1966. During that month, Mr. King had another large log placed across the road at the entrance to his property. That barrier was, however, also quickly removed. He then sent in a caterpillar crew to permanently block the road. That operation was stopped by the issuance of a temporary restraining order.

The various owners of the Navarro-by-the-Sea property have at times placed an unlocked chain across the Navarro Beach Road on that property. One witness said she saw a chain between 1911 and 1920. Another witness said the chain was put up to discourage cows from straying and eating poisonous weeds. The chain was occasionally hooked to an upright spike, but was never locked in place and could be easily removed. Its purpose apparently was to restrict cows, not people, from the beach. In fact, the chain was almost always unhooked and lying on the ground.

From about 1949 on, a proprietor of the Navarro-by-the-Sea Hotel maintained a sign at the posts saying, "Private Road—Admission 50 please pay at hotel." With moderate success, the proprietor collected tolls for a relatively short period of time. Some years later another proprietor resumed the practice. Most persons ignored the sign, however, and went to the beach without paying. The hotel operators never applied any sanctions to those who declined to pay. In a recorded instrument the present owners of the Navarro-by-the-Sea property acknowledged that "for over one hundred years there has existed a public easement and right of way" in the road as it crosses their property. The Carlyles and the previous owners of the first stretch of the Navarro Beach Road never objected to its use over their property and do not now object.

The Mendocino county superior court ruled in favor of defendants, concluding that there had been no dedication of the beach or the road and in particular that widespread public use does not lead to an implied dedication.

In our most recent discussion of common-law dedication, Union Transp. Co. v. Sacramento County (1954) 42 Cal.2d 235, 240–241, 267 P.2d 10, we noted that a common-law dedication of property to the public can be proved either by showing acquiescence of the owner in use of the land under circumstances that negate the idea that the use is under a license or by establishing open and continuous use by the public for the prescriptive period. When dedication by acquiescence for a period of less than five years is claimed, the owner's actual consent to the dedication must be proved. The owner's intent is the crucial factor. (42 Cal.2d at p. 241, 267 P.2d 10, quoting from Schwerdtle v. County of Placer (1895) 108 Cal. 589, 593, 41 P. 448.) When, on the other hand, a litigant seeks to prove dedication by adverse use, the inquiry shifts from the intent and activities of the owner to those of the public. The question then is whether the public has used the land "for a period of more than five years with full knowledge of the owner, without asking or receiving permission to do so and without objection being made by any one." (42 Cal.2d at p. 240, 267 P.2d at p. 13, quoting from Hare v. Craig (1929) 206 Cal. 753, 757, 276 P. 336.) As other cases have stated, the question is whether the public has engaged in "long-continued adverse use" of the land sufficient to raise the "conclusive and undisputable presumption of knowledge and acquiescence, while at the same time it negatives the idea of a mere license."

In both cases at issue here, the litigants representing the public contend that the second test has been met. Although there is evidence in both cases from which it might be inferred that owners preceding the present fee owners acquiesced in the public use of the land, that argument has not been pressed before this court. We therefore turn to the issue of dedication by adverse use.

Three problems of interpretation have concerned the lower courts with respect to proof of dedication by adverse use: (1) When is a public use deemed to be adverse? (2) Must a litigant representing the public prove that the owner did not grant a license to the public? (3) Is there any difference between dedication of shoreline property and other property?

In determining the adverse use necessary to raise a conclusive presumption of dedication, analogies from the law of adverse possession and easement by prescriptive rights can be misleading. An adverse possessor or a person gaining a personal easement by prescription is acting to gain a property right in himself and the test in those situations is whether the person acted as if he actually claimed a personal legal right in the property. Such a personal claim of right need not be shown to establish a dedication because it is a public right that is being claimed. What must be shown is that persons used the property believing the public had a right to such use. This public use may not be "adverse" to the interests of the owner in the sense that the word is used in adverse possession cases. If a trial court finds that the public has used land without objection or interference for more than five years, it need not make a separate finding of "adversity" to support a decision of implied dedication.

Litigants, therefore, seeking to show that land has been dedicated to the public, need only produce evidence that persons have used the land as they would have used public land. If the land involved is a beach or shoreline area, they should show that the land was used as if it were a public recreation area. If a road is involved, the litigants must show that it was used as if it were a public road. Evidence that the users looked to a governmental agency for maintenance of the land is significant in establishing an implied dedication to the public.

Litigants seeking to establish dedication to the public must also show that various groups of persons have used the land. If only a limited and definable number of persons have used the land, those persons may be able to claim a personal easement but not dedication to the public. An owner may well tolerate use by some persons but object vigorously to use by others. If the fee owner proves that use of the land fluctuated seasonally, on the other hand, such a showing does not negate evidence of adverse user. "[T]he thing of significance is that whoever wanted to use [the land] did so * * * when they wished to do so without asking permission and without protest from the land owners." (Seaway Company v. Attorney General (Tex.Civ.App.), 375 S.W.2d 923, 936.)

The second problem that has concerned lower courts is whether there is a presumption that use by the public is under a license by the fee owner, a presumption that must be overcome by the public with evidence to the contrary. * * *

No reason appears for distinguishing proof of implied dedication by invoking a presumption of permissive use. The question whether public use of privately owned lands is under a license of the owner is ordinarily one of fact. We will not presume that owners of property today knowingly permit the general public to use their lands and grant a license to the public to do so. For a fee owner to negate a finding of intent to dedicate based on uninterrupted public use for more than five years, therefore, he must either affirmatively prove that he has granted the public a license to use his property or demonstrate that he has made a bona fide attempt to prevent public use. Whether an owner's efforts to halt public use are adequate in a particular case will turn on the means the owner uses in relation to the character of the property and the extent of public use. Although "No Trespassing" signs may be sufficient when only an occasional hiker traverses an isolated property, the same action cannot reasonably be expected to halt a continuous influx of beach users to an attractive seashore property. If the fee owner proves that he has made more than minimal and ineffectual efforts to exclude the public, then the trier of fact must decide whether the owner's activities have been adequate. If the owner has not attempted to halt public use in any significant way, however, it will be held as a matter of law that he intended to dedicate the property or an easement therein to the public, and evidence that the public used the property for the prescriptive period is sufficient to establish dedication.

A final question that has concerned lower courts is whether the rules governing shoreline property differ from those governing other types of property, particularly roads. * * *

Even if we were reluctant to apply the rules of common-law dedication to open recreational areas, we must observe the strong policy expressed in the constitution and statutes of this state of encouraging public use of shoreline recreational areas.

Among the statutory provisions favoring public ownership of shoreline areas is Civil Code, section 830. That section states that absent specific language to the contrary, private ownership of uplands ends at the high-water mark. The decisions of this court have interpreted this provision to create a presumption in favor of public ownership of land between high and low tide.

There is also a clearly enunciated public policy in the California Constitution in favor of allowing the public access to shoreline areas:

"No individual, partnership, or corporation, claiming or possessing the frontage or tidal lands of a harbor, bay, inlet, estuary, or other navigable water in this State, shall be permitted to exclude the right of way to such water whenever it is required for any public purpose, nor to destroy or obstruct the free navigation of such water. * * * "(Art. XV, § 2.)

Recreational purposes are among the "public purposes" mentioned by this constitutional provision. Although article XV section 2 may be limited to some extent by the United States Constitution it clearly indicates that we should encourage public use of shoreline areas whenever that can be done consistently with the federal constitution.

* * *

We conclude that there was an implied dedication of property rights in both cases. In both cases the public used the land "for a period of more than five years with full knowledge of the owner, without asking or receiving permission to do so and without objection being made by any one." (Union Transp. Co. v. Sacramento County, *supra*, 42 Cal.2d 235, 240, 267 P.2d 10, 13 quoting from Hare v. Craig, *supra*, 206 Cal. 753, 757, 276

P. 336.) In both cases the public used the land in public ways, as if the land was owned by a government, as if the land were a public park.

NOTES

1.   *Gion* applies the law of dedication to provide access to waters that were open to the public at common law. What if the state stocks a lake with fish at public expense and then argues that the water has been dedicated to the public? This argument has been consistently rejected by the courts on a variety of grounds. At common law, fishing rights were a *profit a prendre* and thus could be transferred only by grant. What if the state enacts a statute granting members of the public the right to fish in stocked streams and grants them a right of access over private lands so long as they compensate the owner for any actual damage that results from their trespass? See Hartman v. Tresise, 36 Colo. 146, 84 P. 685 (1905) (holding the statute unconstitutional).

2.   Statutory enactments in some states may be a basis for expanding the dedication doctrine. Consider, for example, Ind. Code Ann. § 14–26–2–3 (Michie 2003) which defines a public freshwater lake as "a lake that has been used by the public with the acquiescence of a riparian owner." If a riparian permits a non-riparian family to enjoy a swim in the lake, is it now public?

Under the Minnesota lake level statute, a public action may be brought to declare that a flowage easement to maintain the water level in an artificial lake created by a dam has been dedicated to the state if the dam has been maintained for at least 15 years primarily for public purposes like navigation, fishing and hunting, and the lake has been continuously used for those purposes. Minn. Stat. Ann. § 110.31, recodified at § 103G.551 (West 1997). This statute has been interpreted to mean that the common law elements of dedication—intent to dedicate and acceptance by the public—must be shown, but that if the specified conditions are met, a dedication is presumed. See State by Burnquist v. Fischer, 245 Minn. 1, 71 N.W.2d 161, 164–65 (1955).

3.   Issues of public beach use through prescription, dedication and custom are discussed in Trepanier v. County of Volusia, 965 So.2d 276 (Fla.App. 2007). The county argued in that case that easements and rights of way can "migrate" with changes in the tide. The property in question had been severely affected by several hurricanes.

F.   WATER RIGHTS AND CONSTITUTIONAL TAKINGS

1.   CHANGING TO STATUTORY SYSTEMS

Over the years, most riparian and appropriation states have modified their water administration by changing to a permit system. See Chapter 4, *supra*. For riparians, such a change can result in the loss or diminishment of common law rights available to owners of streamside land. Under the common law, riparian land owners typically are entitled to all the water they can reasonably use solely by reason of their location. If a riparian landowner's needs change, or a new use arises, the law allows the riparian to increase the quantity used, subject to being challenged by other users arguing the use is unreasonable. Under the typical permit system, both the quantity of water and the uses to which the water may be put are dictated by the terms of the permit. Changes may not be made without the approval of the permitting authority. If the use is inefficient or unreasonable, it may not be allowed.

In some states, permit holders can lose their rights if the water is not used diligently. Permit holders may forfeit their permits if they fail to put water to use within a specific period of time, usually two or three years. In some states, permits are of a limited duration and may not be automatically renewed, but instead are subjected to the same scrutiny as new applications. This requirement detracts from the value of both appropriative and riparian rights. Holders of expired permits must justify the reasonableness and efficiency of their water use on the same basis as new applicants. This ensures that the permitting process remains responsive to changing needs by aiding the entry of new uses into the system, and encouraging the application of economically efficient technology.

Obviously, riparian landowners suffer significant limitations on their common law rights under such statutory systems. Expectations may be disappointed and the apparent value of a riparian's estate may be diluted. Surprisingly, there have been few suits directly challenging the constitutionality of these statutes.

The three Pacific Coast states and the six states divided by the one-hundredth meridian were first settled in their more humid regions. They applied riparian law on private lands, and only later moved—in varying degrees—toward an appropriation system. They created so-called dual or hybrid systems of water rights. States that have switched to prior appropriation have tried to make the new system the exclusive one, but there may be constitutional objections to a quick transition. When a state shifts from the common law to a property rights system that places substantial limits on the use of a resource, holders of common law rights may argue that the new property rights regime results in an unconstitutional taking of property without due process of law.

In re Waters of Long Valley Creek Stream System

Supreme Court of California, 1979.
25 Cal.3d 339, 158 Cal.Rptr. 350, 599 P.2d 656.

■ MOSK, JUSTICE.

The significant problem in this case is the extent to which the State Water Resources Control Board (Board) has the power to define and otherwise limit prospective riparian rights when, pursuant to the statutory adjudication procedure set forth in Water Code section 2500 et seq., it determines all claimed rights to the use of water in a stream system. * * *

The action arises out of a statutory proceeding to adjudicate the rights of all claimants to the waters of the Long Valley Creek Stream System (stream system) in Lassen, Sierra and Plumas Counties. * * *

Because of the limited water supply, there has been prolific litigation among the various water claimants in the area since at least 1883. In the interest of resolving the conflicts that have fostered such litigation, nine claimants filed a petition in 1966 with the Board for statutory adjudication of all water rights in the stream system. (Wat. Code, § 2525.) The staff of the Board conducted a preliminary investigation and recommended in favor of the petition, which the Board subsequently granted. Thereafter the Board prepared and published a notice of the proceedings (*id.*, §§ 2526, 2527), and all persons claiming a right to the waters of the stream system notified the Board of their intention to file a claim. (*Id.*, § 2528.) As required by Water Code section 2550, the board then conducted an extensive investigation; it published a report containing the results of this investigation for the principal purpose of assisting water users in filing their claims of right.

After filing its report, the Board advised persons who notified it of their intention to file a claim that the claim and proof in support of it must be formally presented. It heard 234 claims and proofs, and 42 contests thereto, concerning the rights of the stream system. After consideration of these claims, proofs and contests, it "entered of record in its office an order determining and establishing the several rights to the water of the stream system." (*Id.*, § 2700.)

Donald Ramelli (Ramelli), as a party aggrieved or dissatisfied with the order of determination, filed a notice of exceptions in the superior court pursuant to Water Code section 2757. Ramelli owns land upon which Balls Creek originates. For the past approximately 60 years he and his predecessors have irrigated 89 acres of this land, but before the Board he claimed prospective riparian rights in the creek for an additional 2,884 acres. The order of determination nevertheless awarded him various amounts of water for only the 89 acres as to which he was currently exercising his riparian rights; it extinguished entirely his claim as a riparian landowner to the future use of water with respect to the remaining 2,884 acres.

The trial court denied Ramelli's exceptions and entered a decree consistent with the Board's order of determination. Ramelli appealed from the decree, and we reverse.

* * *

In this case the Board entirely extinguished Ramelli's riparian claim to the future use of water. Such extinction raises a substantial constitutional issue as a result of our holding in *Tulare Dist. v. Lindsay–Strathmore Dist.* (1935) *supra*, 3 Cal.2d 489, 531, 45 P.2d 972, that section 11 of the Water Commission Act violated article X, section 2 (formerly art. XIV, § 3); the section, as stated above, provided in essence for the complete extinction of riparian rights that remained unused for 10 consecutive years. We consequently decline to construe the statutory adjudication procedure as authorizing the Board to extinguish altogether future riparian rights. * * *

A.

Article X, section 2, acknowledges that in California a riparian landowner has historically possessed a common law right to the future use of water in a stream system. The provision does so by declaring that "The right to water or to the use or flow of water in or from any natural stream or water course in this State is and shall be limited to such water as shall be *reasonably required for the beneficial use to be served* ..." and that "Riparian rights in a stream or water course attach to, but to no more than so much of the flow thereof as may be required or used consistently with this section, for the purposes for which such lands are, *or may be made adaptable,* in view of such reasonable and beneficial uses...." (Cal.Const., art. X, § 2, italics added.)

As the above language also discloses, however, riparian rights are limited by the concept of reasonable and beneficial use. Moreover, they must not be exercised in a manner that is inconsistent with constitutional policy provisions that are to govern interpretations of water rights in California. In light of these policies and of the constitutional intent to limit unduly expansive interpretations of water rights that would contravene them, it becomes clear that article X, section 2, enables the Legislature to exercise broad authority in defining and otherwise limiting future riparian rights, and to delegate this authority to the Board.

* * * This authorization discloses that the framers of article X, section 2, recognized that the promotion of its salutary policies would require granting the Legislature broad flexibility in determining the appropriate means for protecting scarce state water resources.[6]

6. The importance of broad legislative authority for the conservation and regulation of scarce water resources has also been recognized by courts in other states. For example, in *Belle Fourche Irrigation District v. Smiley* (1970) 84 S.D. 701, 176 N.W.2d 239, the South Dakota Supreme Court upheld a statute that recognized riparian rights as vested only "to the extent of the existing beneficial use"; the court reasoned that the statute was an appropriate exercise of the state's power to provide for the "maximum utilization of the water resources of the state." (*Id.,* at p. 245.) In *State v. Knapp* (1949) 167 Kan. 546, 207 P.2d 440, the Kansas Supreme Court sustained a statute that inter alia (1) limited vested riparian rights to those uses actually instituted at the time the legislation was enacted or within three years prior thereto, and (2) required approval from the state for the commencement of any further uses. (See also *Brown v. Chase* (1923) 125 Wash. 542, 217 P. 23, 26 [water of nonnavigable stream subject to appropriation when riparian cannot use it beneficially, "either directly or prospectively, within a reasonable time"]; *In re Hood River,* 114 Or. 112, (1924) 227 P. 1065, 1084 ["state may change its common-law rule as to every stream within its dominion, and permit the appropriation of the flowing water for such purposes as it deems wise"]; c.f. *Baeth v. Hoisveen* (N.Dak.1968) 157 N.W.2d 728, 732 [no absolute ownership of groundwater that has not actually been diverted and applied to a beneficial use]; *Knight v. Grimes* (1964) 80 S.D. 517, 127 N.W.2d 708, 711 [right to take and use percolating groundwater does not constitute actual ownership prior to withdrawal]; *Williams v. City of Wichita* (1962) 190 Kan. 317, 374 P.2d 578, 589, app. dism. (1963) 375 U.S. 7 [legislature may change principles of common law

Our conclusion that article X, section 2, does not preclude legislative or administrative determinations with respect to the nature of future riparian rights becomes even more readily apparent upon examination of the history of the provision. Article X, section 2, was adopted by amendment in 1928. It was a direct response to the decision by this court in *Herminghaus v. Southern California Edison Co.* (1926) 200 Cal. 81, 252 P. 607, which held that a downstream riparian's right against an inferior upstream appropriator permits him to command the entire flow of the stream to flood his pastureland. * * *

We next examine whether such a broad grant of authority to the Board is consistent with the constitutional holding of *Tulare Dist. v. Lindsay–Strathmore Dist., supra.* Ramelli argues that a riparian's prospective right cannot be defined or otherwise limited in a statutory proceeding because of our holding in *Tulare* that section 11 of the Water Commission Act—which declared that 10 years' nonuse, without an intervening use, constituted an abandonment of a riparian right—was "incongruous and in violation of the spirit of the constitutional provision . . ." (*Id.* at p. 531, 45 P.2d at p. 989.) Ramelli's expansive reading of the limits *Tulare* places on legislative authority is unsupportable in light of the amendment's grant of authority to the Legislature to enact laws in the furtherance of the constitutionally expressed state water policy. Moreover, *Tulare* is distinguishable from the issue before us in that the statute therein treated the right as automatically abandoned as a result of 10 years' nonuse, without consideration of other needs and uses of the water in the stream system. The statute therefore was inconsistent with the mandate of the amendment to promote the reasonable beneficial use of state waters.

It is well established that what is a reasonable use of water varies with the facts and circumstances of the particular case. And it appears self-evident that the reasonableness of a riparian use cannot be determined without considering the effect of such use on all the needs of those in the stream system, nor can it be made "*in vacuo* isolated from state-wide considerations of transcendent importance." (*Joslin v. Marin Muni. Water Dist.* (1967) 67 Cal.2d 132, 140, 60 Cal.Rptr. 377, 382, 429 P.2d 889, 894). * * *

* * * The Legislature has enacted a comprehensive administrative scheme for the final determination of *all* rights in a stream system. (Wat. Code, § 2500 et seq.) The statutory adjudication procedure involves a complex balancing of both public and private interests, with the final decree assuring certainty to the existing economy and reasonable predictability to the uses of water in a stream system. In so doing, it falls within the amendment's specific grant of authority to the Legislature. (Cal.Const., art. X, § 2.) That the statutory adjudication procedure promotes the

and abrogate decisions made thereunder when in its opinion it is necessary to the public interest]; *Baumann v. Smrha* (1956) 145 F.Supp. 617, 624, affd. 352 U.S. 863 [state has power "to modify or reject the doctrine of riparian rights because unsuited to the conditions in the state and to put into force the doctrine of prior appropriation and application to beneficial use or reasonable use"].)

policies of the amendment is reflected in a recent report of the Governor's Commission To Review California Water Rights Law. (Final Rep. (Dec. 1978).) This document identifies uncertainty as one of the major problems in contemporary California water rights law, and it discloses that riparian rights are a principal source of this uncertainty.

Uncertainty concerning the rights of water users has pernicious effects. Initially, it inhibits long range planning and investment for the development and use of waters in a stream system. * * *

* * * And, as the Board engineer observed, the inconclusive fragmentary definition of water rights resulting from that litigation was "the prime reason for the proposed adjudication." The principal cause of this untoward effect appears to be that a private suit for determining title to water binds only those who are parties to the suit; such suits are inadequate, however, because shortages in supply or new appropriations or riparian uses have the potential for bringing all water users on the stream in conflict.

Finally, uncertainty impairs the state's administration of water rights. * * *

B.

A more difficult question is whether the Board may constitutionally extinguish a riparian landowner's unexercised claim to the use of water. * * *

* * * In light of *Tulare's* holding that section 11 of the Water Commission Act was unconstitutional, however, we are reluctant to conclude that the Board may altogether extinguish a riparian's future claim when it has not been established that the imposition of other less drastic limitations on the claim would be less effective in promoting the most reasonable and beneficial use of the stream system. Because no such showing has been made in this case, it is clear that the Board's decision to extinguish Ramelli's future riparian claim raises a serious constitutional issue. Thus, since the Legislature has not clearly expressed an intention that the statute should be construed otherwise, we interpret it as not authorizing the Board in these circumstances to extinguish altogether Ramelli's claim to the future use of waters in the Long Valley stream system.

* * *

* * * Thus, the Board is authorized to decide that an unexercised riparian claim loses its priority with respect to all rights currently being exercised. Moreover, to the extent that an unexercised riparian right may also create uncertainty with respect to permits of appropriation that the Board may grant after the statutory adjudication procedure is final, and may thereby continue to conflict with the public interest in reasonable and beneficial use of state waters, the Board may also determine that the future riparian right shall have a lower priority than any uses of water it authorizes before the riparian in fact attempts to exercise his right. In other words, while we interpret the Water Code as not authorizing the Board to extinguish altogether a future riparian right, the Board may make

determinations as to the scope, nature and priority of the right that it deems reasonably necessary to the promotion of the state's interest in fostering the most reasonable and beneficial use of its scarce water resources.

* * *

The judgment is reversed for further proceedings consistent with this opinion.

■ BIRD, C.J., and TOBRINER and NEWMAN, JJ., concur.

■ RICHARDSON, JUSTICE, concurring and dissenting.

* * *

* * * [T]he applicable cases expressly *deny* authority to limit or fix prospective riparian uses "until the need for such use arises," because at all times such uses remain "paramount to any right of the appropriator." (*Tulare, supra.*) Although a *presently exercised* riparian use must be "reasonable and beneficial" under the constitutional provision, no limitation or quantification of a reasonable *future* use is possible in light of the difficulty in predicting future needs. * * *

■ CLARK, J., concurs.

■ MANUEL, JUSTICE, concurring and dissenting.

* * * I agree that although the subject provisions of the Water Code should not be interpreted to permit the Board to altogether extinguish the presently unused portion of a riparian right, they may be interpreted in a manner consistent with the relevant constitutional provision (Cal.Const., art. X, § 2; formerly art. XIV, § 3) to permit the Board to undertake a present quantification of the right in order to bring about certainty and thereby promote the efficient and beneficial use of the water resources of this state. I do not agree, however, that in the course of such a determination the Board has the power to fix such a right at the level of its present use and "determine that the future riparian right shall have a lower priority than any uses of water [the Board] authorizes before the riparian in fact attempts to exercise his right." In my view the exercise of such a power would be plainly inconsistent with the provisions of article X, section 2, of our state Constitution; the considerations which have led the majority to interpret the relevant Water Code provisions to preclude the extinguishment of the unused portion of a riparian right also demand that the same provisions be read to preclude the procedure here approved. I conclude, in short, that in permitting the Board to assign less than riparian status to the unused portion of a riparian right, the majority has essentially approved the extinguishment of that portion of the right—and thereby has reached a result inconsistent with its fundamental holding and the clear command of the Constitution.

* * *

Hearing denied; CLARK, RICHARDSON and MANUEL, JJ., dissenting.

NOTES

1. If there are already more claims to water than there is water in Balls Creek, is it any consolation to Ramelli that the court refused "to extinguish altogether future riparian rights" while making them subject to all existing uses? Does the decision leave Ramelli, as a riparian landowner, with any advantage over nonriparians who may have a future use for water?

2. Was the court's resolution necessary to carry out the purposes of the California constitutional provision and the statutory adjudication procedure? What do you think of Justice Manuel's suggestion that unused riparian rights be quantified? Is the overriding policy to eliminate uncertainty or to eliminate the riparian doctrine?

3. The United States Supreme Court deferred to an interpretation of state law that resulted in denial of a permit to repair and maintain an existing dam in a navigable river. Although this destroyed the value of the plaintiff's investment, it did not violate the constitutional prohibition of taking property because the state defines what is property. "We accept as conclusive the state court's view of the nature of the rights of riparian owners." Fox River Paper Co. v. Railroad Comm'n of Wisconsin, 274 U.S. 651, 47 S.Ct. 669, 71 L.Ed. 1279 (1927).

NOTE: OBJECTIONS TO STATUTES CONVERTING A STATE SYSTEM FROM RIPARIAN TO PRIOR APPROPRIATION

The California adjudication system had important impacts on riparian rights, but laws in other states made more sweeping conversions of their water law systems. Typically, these schemes were "saved" because common law rights were seldom totally eliminated, and holders of unexercised rights could still perfect rights under the new system. Therefore, there was no unconstitutional taking of property rights. Many of the cases raising such a challenge are cited in note 6 of In re *Waters of Long Valley Creek Stream System, supra* p. 497.

A relatively simple change from the riparian system based in common law to an appropriation system like those developed in other states is illustrated in Wasserburger v. Coffee, 180 Neb. 149, 141 N.W.2d 738 (1966). In *Wasserburger* the Nebraska Supreme Court faced several issues: (1) *when* common law riparian rights had been modified by legislative adoption of the prior appropriation doctrine; (2) *what* land patented prior to the legislative modification retained its riparian status; and (3) *how* to resolve the conflicts between riparian and appropriative claims. The court held that the appropriation system was not adopted by the legislature until the Irrigation Act of 1895 expressly dedicated the use of unappropriated water of every stream to the people subject to appropriation for beneficial use. Removing land from the public domain and putting it in private ownership prior to the 1895 Act could, therefore, make a riparian water right superior to an appropriative right. Any land later severed from the riparian tract, however, lost its riparian status. See discussion of the unity of title rule, *supra* p. 114. Finally, the court held that riparian rights would be protected even against appropriations prior in time when an appropriator intentionally caused substantial harm to a riparian proprietor or the harmful appropriation was "unreasonable." The reasonableness of an appropriation turns on the social value of the respective uses, the extent of the harm, the practicality of allowing both the riparian and the appropriative uses, and the time the respective uses were initiated.

The principal problem of moving from riparianism to appropriation is, of course, what to do with unused riparian rights. The Oregon statute mentioned in *California Oregon Power Co., supra* p. 106, simply extinguished them, raising a substantive due process question that the Supreme Court ducked. Lower courts have often had to confront the question. Kansas, for example, was not a Desert Land Act state, but the legislature moved from a riparian system to an exclusive appropriation system in which "vested right" was defined as the right to continue to use water "having actually been applied to any beneficial use" when the statute was enacted. All waters were then declared to be subject to appropriation as provided in the statute, but "vested rights" were excepted from the appropriation regime. Kan. Stat. Ann. § 82a–701, 703 (1997). In Williams v. City of Wichita, 190 Kan. 317, 374 P.2d 578 (1962), appeal dismissed 375 U.S. 7, 84 S.Ct. 46, 11 L.Ed.2d 38 (1963), the constitutionality of the statute was raised. An overlying owner who claimed common law rights to the future use of groundwater sued to enjoin the city from pumping from the aquifer under a statutory appropriation permit. The court sustained the statute and entered judgment for the city. See also F. Arthur Stone & Sons v. Gibson, 230 Kan. 224, 630 P.2d 1164 (1981).

South Dakota has ended up in the same place, although the path was more tortuous. The South Dakota court originally adopted the riparian rule and invalidated a broad appropriation statute enacted in 1907 as an unconstitutional taking of riparian property rights. St. Germain Irrigating Co. v. Hawthorn Ditch Co., 32 S.D. 260, 143 N.W. 124 (1913). Later, however, the court backtracked to some extent by holding that the Desert Land Act severed land and water and that federal patents issued after 1877 carried no water rights with them. Cook v. Evans, 45 S.D. 31, 185 N.W. 262 (1921), and Haaser v. Englebrecht, 45 S.D. 143, 186 N.W. 572 (1922). Although Mr. Justice Sutherland cited these cases in *California Oregon Power Co.*, the South Dakota court refused the compliment, taking advantage of the opportunity provided by that case to declare its previous decisions wrong, and holding that in South Dakota the Desert Land Act did not sever land and water and therefore riparian rights attached to all land grants. Platt v. Rapid City, 67 S.D. 245, 291 N.W. 600 (1940). Then in 1955, the legislature sought to abolish unused riparian rights, invoking the Kansas technique of defining vested rights to include only rights to water in actual use. 1955 S.D. Laws 506 (codified at S.D. Codified Laws §§ 46–1–1 to –11 (West 2004)). The statute was held constitutional in Knight v. Grimes, 80 S.D. 517, 127 N.W.2d 708 (1964). (North Dakota reached a similar result in Baeth v. Hoisveen, 157 N.W.2d 728 (N.D.1968).) A 1970 South Dakota case, Belle Fourche Irrigation Dist. v. Smiley, 84 S.D. 701, 176 N.W.2d 239 (1970), sustained the statute again, but held that when an appeal is taken from a water resources commission finding on the quantity of a riparian's vested right, the commission must present evidence to the trial court to sustain the commission's determination.

The problem of dual rights is especially complex in Texas. Vested riparian rights are recognized for lands granted before July 1, 1895, the date of the enactment of the Irrigation Act of 1895. In brief, riparians were entitled to the ordinary flow of the stream and appropriators to the flood waters. Motl v. Boyd, 116 Tex. 82, 286 S.W. 458 (1926). The 1967 Water Rights Adjudication Act (Tex. Water Code Ann. § 11.303(b) (West 2008)) limited riparian rights to the water actually put to a beneficial use between 1963–1967. An intermediate court of appeals held that the Act was an unconstitutional taking in Schero v. Texas Dep't of Water Res., 630 S.W.2d 516 (Tex.App.1982), but the Texas Supreme Court followed the precedents discussed above and held that the Act was constitutional. *In re* Adjudication of the Water Rights of the Upper Guadalupe Segment of the Guadalupe River Basin, 642 S.W.2d 438 (Tex.1982); *In re* Adjudication of the Water Rights in the Llano River Watershed of the Colorado River Basin, 642 S.W.2d 446 (Tex.1982). In *Upper Guadalupe* the Texas Supreme Court cited Texaco, Inc. v. Short, 454 U.S. 516, 102 S.Ct. 781, 70 L.Ed.2d 738 (1982), which held that the Indiana Dormant Mineral Act, which revests mineral interests unused for twenty years in the surface estate if the interest has not been otherwise maintained, was neither a taking nor a violation of Texaco's right to procedural due process.

Washington switched from the California-type dual system to an exclusive prior appropriation system in 1917. Existing riparian rights were preserved, Wash. Rev. Code Ann. § 90.03.010 (West 2004), and a 1923 decision, Brown v. Chase, 125 Wash. 542, 217 P. 23 (1923), stated that unexercised rights put to a beneficial use within a reasonable period after 1917 were also preserved. The state supreme court has held that all rights must have been put to use by 1932, the year suggested by the state, because fifteen years is a constitutionally sufficient period of notice for riparians to adjust to the new requirements for the perfection of a water right. *In re* Deadman Creek Drainage Basin in Spokane County, 103 Wash.2d 686, 694 P.2d 1071 (1985).

From the precedents it appeared that states were not significantly limited in converting from a riparian to a prior appropriation system. Then the Supreme Court of Oklahoma held unconstitutional a state law similar in most respects to statutes in other states.

Franco–American Charolaise, Ltd. v. Oklahoma Water Resources Board

Supreme Court of Oklahoma, 1990.
855 P.2d 568.

■ OPALA, JUSTICE.

This appeal challenges the constitutionality of the 1963 amendments to Oklahoma's water law insofar as the amendments regulate riparian rights.
* * *

A. Statement of the Facts

Mill Creek is a spring-fed dry weather creek in the Upper Clear Boggy watershed within the Muddy Boggy River Basin. Byrd's Mill Spring flows directly into Mill Creek which in turn flows into Clear Boggy Creek. Clear Boggy Creek is joined by Buck Creek and flows downstream as Clear Boggy Creek where it joins Muddy Boggy Creek to form the Muddy Boggy River. The latter is a tributary of the Red River. In 1980 the area experienced a severe drought and the stream bed in Clear Boggy Creek went dry. In August of 1980 the City of Ada [City] made application, pursuant to 82 O.S.1981 § 105.9, to increase its appropriation of water from Byrd's Mill Spring from 3,360 acre feet per year to 11,202 acre feet per year to meet a projected annual need of 10,523 acre feet per year by the year 2020. * * * Riparian owners and in-basin appropriators objected to the City's application for additional stream water. The OWRB determined that the average yield of Byrd's Mill Spring is 9,820 acre feet per year. Prior appropriations, including that of the City and some appellee riparian owners, total 3,776 acre feet per year. Allowing 584 acre feet to supply domestic needs down to Buck Creek and 120 acre feet for unavoidable loss, the OWRB found the amount available for appropriation was 5,340 acre feet, 2,502 acre feet less than the 7,842 acre feet requested by the City. The City amended its application to conform to the finding. The OWRB then granted all 5,340 acre feet available for appropriation to the City, requiring the City to release at least 1,120 acre feet of water per year downstream. The OWRB order also required the City to meter and record monthly the amount of water taken from Byrd's Mill Spring. In-basin riparian owners and appropriators appealed from the administrative decision to the District Court, Coal County.

B. Common–Law And Statutory Authority Affecting Water Rights

The Organic Act of 1890 extended England's common law over Indian Territory. The same year the Territorial Legislature adopted a * * * codification of the common-law riparian doctrine of water rights [that] remained the law in Oklahoma until legislative adoption of the 1963 amendments.

In 1897 the legislature provided for the appropriation of the ordinary flow or underflow of stream water for the irrigation of arid sections of the State. The statute protected the riparian owner from the appropriation of the ordinary flow of the stream *without* the riparian owner's consent except by condemnation. In 1905 the provision protecting the riparian right was omitted. It was reinstated in 1909, then finally eliminated in 1910. * * *

Since 1897 both the common law and the statutes have operated in Oklahoma to confer riparian and appropriative rights. Though these rights have coexisted in the State for almost 100 years, they are theoretically irreconcilable.[15] The common-law riparian right extends to the reasonable use of the stream *or* to its natural flow, depending on the jurisdiction; the appropriative right attaches to a fixed amount. The last riparian use asserted has as much priority as the first; the appropriator who takes first has the senior right. In 1963 the legislature attempted to reconcile the two doctrines. The amendments, shown in italics, are as follows:

> "The owner of the land owns water standing thereon, or flowing over or under its surface but not forming a definite stream. *The use of groundwater shall be governed by the Oklahoma Ground Water Law.* Water running in a definite stream, formed by nature over or under the surface, may be used by him *for domestic purposes as defined in Section 2(a) of this Act,* as long as it remains there, but he may not prevent the natural flow of the stream, or of the natural spring from which it commences its definite course, nor pursue nor pollute the same, *as such water then becomes public water and is subject to appropriation for the benefit and welfare of the people of the state, as provided by law; Provided however, that nothing contained herein shall prevent the owner of land from damming up or otherwise using the bed of a stream on his land for the collection or storage of waters in an amount not to exceed that which he owns, by virtue of the first sentence of this section so long as he provides for the continued natural flow of the stream in an amount equal to that which entered his land less the uses allowed in this Act; provided further, that nothing contained herein shall be construed to limit the powers of the Oklahoma Water Resources Board to grant permission to build or alter structures on a stream pursuant to Title 82 to provide for the storage of additional water the use of which the land owner has or acquires by virtue of this act.*"[16]

Companion statutes limit riparian domestic use to household purposes, to the watering of domestic animals up to the land's normal grazing capacity, and to the irrigation of land not exceeding a total of three acres. The riparian owner may also store a two-year supply for domestic use. In addition, the 1963 amendments provided a validation mechanism as a method for protecting pre-existing beneficial uses, including those of the riparian owner and pre-existing appropriators. All subsequent rights to the use of stream water, except for riparian domestic uses, are to be acquired by appropriation. The stream's natural flow is considered public water and subject to appropriation. Riparian owners may not assert their common-law right to the use of stream water other than for the domestic uses.

* * *

---

15. This dual system of water rights is known nationally as the "California Doctrine" and at one time was the rule in all West Coast states and the tier of the Great Plains from North Dakota to Texas. Only California and Nebraska retain it. Most dual-system states have since adopted the appro-

priation doctrine as controlling all rights to stream water.

16. Now codified at 60 O.S.1981 § 60. See Rarick, Oklahoma Water Law, Stream and Surface Under the 1963 Amendments, 23 Okla.L.Rev. 19 [1970] (discussing the legislative history and effect of the amendments).

D. The Constitutional Question

The issue here is whether the legislature can validly abrogate the riparian owner's right to initiate non-domestic reasonable uses in stream water without affording compensation. Art. 2, § 24, Okl. Const. provides in part:

> "Private property shall not be taken or damaged for public use without just compensation. Such compensation, irrespective of any benefit from any improvements proposed shall be ascertained by a board of commissioners of not less than three freeholders, in such a matter as may be prescribed by law." * * *

* * * [T]he common-law riparian right to use stream water, as long as that use is reasonable, has been long recognized in Oklahoma law as a private property right.

* * *

We, therefore, hold that the 1963 water law amendments are fraught with a constitutional infirmity in that they abolish the right of riparian owners to assert their vested interest in the prospective reasonable use of the stream. Under the 1963 amendments, riparian owners stand on equal footing with appropriator; ownership of riparian land affords *no right* to the stream water except for limited domestic use.

This case must be remanded for the trial court to determine whether the appellee-riparian owners' claim to the use of the stream flow for the enhancement of the value of the riparian land for recreation, for the preservation of wildlife, for fighting grass fires, and for lowering the body temperature of their cattle on hot summer days is reasonable.

* * *

Although the 1963 water law amendments provided a mechanism for a riparian owner to "perfect" all beneficial uses initiated prior to the legislation, that mechanism falls short of protecting the riparian owner's common-law appurtenant right. The mechanism is constitutionally inadequate first of all because the full sweep of the riparian right is much broader than the validation mechanism could ever shield. The heart of the riparian right is the right to assert a use at *any time* as long as it does not harm another riparian who has a corresponding right. Further, yesterday's reasonable use by one riparian owner may become unreasonable tomorrow when a fellow riparian owner asserts a new or expanded use. After the 1963 amendments, the riparian owner who wants to expand a use or assert a new use may do so *only as an appropriator.* His use is not judged by its reasonableness but only by its priority in time.

Furthermore, the validation mechanism attempted to forever set in stone the maximum amount of stream water the landowner, *as a riparian owner,* can use. Any use asserted by the landowner, *as an appropriator,* is either denied because no water is available or is given a lower priority than all other uses, including those of appropriators who are non-riparian to the stream. It matters not that the riparian owner's use is reasonable when compared with prior uses. This result is antithetical to the very nature of the common-law riparian right, which places no stock in the fact of past use, present use, or even non-use.

* * *

In preserving today the riparian right from its infirm legislative abrogation, we do not disestablish the appropriative right. California and Nebraska, which still maintain the dual regime of water rights, protect appropriative rights, prior reasonable uses of the riparian owner and prospective reasonable uses of the riparian owner. * * *

* * *

Upon remand, should the trial court find that any or all of the riparian owners' asserted uses of the stream for their claimed purposes is unreasonable, such uses do not fall under the mantle of constitutionally protected property rights. On the other hand, should the trial court find that an asserted riparian use of the stream is reasonable, the right to a flow sufficient to supply the riparian owners' reasonable use must be preserved in the owners.

To assure that the state's resources are put to the most reasonable and beneficial use, we adopt the approach of the Supreme Court of Nebraska in *Wasserburger v. Coffee. Wasserburger* holds that the rights of the riparian owner and the appropriator are to be determined by relative reasonableness. * * *

The OWRB shall approve the City's appropriation only if it finds there is surplus water after providing for 1) all prior appropriations; 2) all riparian uses perfected under the 1963 amendments; 3) all *riparian* domestic uses, 4) all riparian uses approved as reasonable on remand and 5) all anticipated in-basin needs. * * *

■ LAVENDER, VICE CHIEF JUSTICE, concurring in part; dissenting in part:

I must respectfully dissent from that part of the majority opinion holding the 1963 legislative amendments to our State's stream water law unconstitutional under the guise the amendments effected a taking of property without just compensation in violation of OKLA. CONST. art. 2, § 24. In reaching this result the majority makes several errors.

Initially, it misperceives that future, unquantified use of stream water by a riparian is a vested property right that can only be limited or modified pursuant to judicially mandated common law factors that were generally used to decide piecemeal litigation between competing riparians in water use disputes. Secondly, it misinterprets the plain and unambiguous legislation at issue and it fails to recognize that even assuming a vested property right is at issue, such rights in natural resources like water, may be subject to reasonable limitations or even forfeiture for failure to put the resource to beneficial use. Thirdly, its analysis of the law as to what constitutes a taking of private property requiring just compensation is flawed. In my view the majority errs in such regard by failing to view the legislation as akin to zoning regulation, which although may limit a riparian's open-ended common law right to make use of the water to benefit his land and thereby effect the value of his land, does not deprive him of all economic use of his land or absolutely deprive him of water. The lack of water to a riparian, if it occurs, is caused by his own neglect or inaction by years of failure either to put the water to beneficial use or failure to gain an appropriation permit from the Oklahoma Water Resources Board (OWRB) for uses being made prior to passage of the 1963 amendments or uses made or sought to be made between passage of the amendments and the City of Ada's appropriation at issue here. This mistake of the majority is particularly egregious because it wholly ignores the virtually admitted fact that neither riparians or appropriators *own* the water they are being allowed to use. All of the people in this State own the water and that ownership interest by the legislation before us is merely being channeled by the Legislature, for the benefit of those owners (i.e. the people), to those uses deemed wise.

The majority has failed to consider persuasive case law from the highest courts of other jurisdictions upholding analogous legislation over similar attacks and pronouncements of the United States Supreme Court which lead me to conclude the legislation *on its face* is constitutional. The majority finally seems to confuse *public* fundamental and preeminent rights in the streams of this State, protected through the public trust doctrine, as being the private property of landowners (riparians) owning land adjacent to the stream waters in Oklahoma.

In place of the statutory scheme drafted by the Legislature after years of study and debate the majority acts as a super-legislature by rewriting the water law of this State in accord with its views of prudent public policy, something neither this Court or any court has the power to do. The foundation of this judicial "legislation", relying as it does on the so-called California Doctrine, is illusory at best because the majority ignores pronouncements from the California Supreme Court which has itself recognized the common law doctrine of unquantified future riparian use of stream water is not a vested right, even in the face of a California constitutional provision specifically interpreted to protect it, *when it may impair the promotion of reasonable and beneficial uses of state waters and, in effect, constitute waste of the resource.*[2]

* * *

In the instant case the majority does not rely for its holding of constitutional infirmity on the loss of any preexisting uses riparians were

---

2. *In Re Waters of Long Valley Creek Stream System,* 25 Cal.3d 339, 158 Cal.Rptr. 350, 355, fn. 3, 599 P.2d 656, 661, f.n. 3 (1979). In said case the California Supreme Court said:

> [A]ppellant also asserts that these common law cases disclose his future right to an unquantified amount of water has become "vested." The assertion is without merit. As discussed *post*, riparian rights are limited by the concept of reasonable and beneficial use, and they may not be exercised in a manner that is inconsistent with the policy declaration of article X, section 2 of the [California] Constitution. *Thus, to the extent that a future riparian right may impair the promotion of reasonable and beneficial uses of state waters, it is inapt to view it as vested.* (emphasis added)

making of the stream prior to passage of the 1963 amendments. It realizes it cannot do so in this facial attack upon the legislation because the amendments provided a mechanism for protection of these uses. Instead it says riparians have a right to insist that things remain as they were under the common law in regard to future use. Other states have concluded differently.

The South Dakota Supreme Court in the case of *Belle Fourche Irrigation District v. Smiley* rejected a similar argument to that raised by Appellees here and approved of by the majority. Said case involved a challenge to that state's comprehensive state water law of 1955 by a riparian owner who asserted he had a vested right to use or divert water from the Belle Fourche River for domestic and irrigation purposes by virtue of his ownership of land contiguous to the river. The riparian claimed that this right became an inseparable incident of his land when it was settled, that use did not create it and disuse could not destroy it, and to deny him said right deprived him of property without just compensation. In rejecting the argument the South Dakota Supreme Court effectively determined that the legislature had the authority to define a vested right in water as that being utilized for beneficial purposes prior to passage of its state water law and that the Legislature of South Dakota could limit the rights of riparians to domestic use or to those uses granted by appropriation under their statutory scheme.

Another court upholding legislation of a similar nature was the Texas Supreme Court in *In re Adjudication of the Water Rights of the Upper Guadalupe Segment of the Guadalupe River Basin*. In pertinent part the legislation at issue in the Texas case provided that water claims would only be recognized to the extent of the maximum actual application of water to beneficial use without waste during any calendar year from 1963 to 1967. The legislation had been passed in 1967 to clear up the confusion and chaotic nature of the water law in Texas, which like Oklahoma had in place a dual system recognizing both the riparian and appropriation doctrines. Even though, as distinguished from the *Belle Fourche* case, the Texas court acknowledged that riparians who acquired their land before a certain date had a vested right to the use of non-flood waters, the court still upheld the legislation at issue in part because it recognized that what the riparians had was only a right to use what the state owned, i.e. the water. The court determined that such a right, like the appropriator's right, was a right to use the resource beneficially, not to waste it.

NOTE

1. As a result of the ruling in *Franco*, Oklahoma's water rights system was converted back into the dual water rights system that the legislature attempted to eliminate in 1963. The litigation had taken more than a decade and the final decision was met with hostility on all sides. The city of Ada then refiled its original appropriation application with the OWRB, which was prepared to act on it until a writ of prohibition was obtained by the original protestants to the application. In the writ, the district judge remanded the proceedings back to the OWRB, directing the Board to evaluate the application using the standards set forth in *Franco*. Gary D. Allison, *Franco–American Charolaise: The Never Ending Story*, 30 Tulsa L.J. 1, 56 (1994).

On remand, the city argued that the reasonableness hearing was moot because of new legislation passed in 1993 in direct response to *Franco*. The legislature expressed its intent to abolish non-domestic riparian rights and create a new unified water rights system:

> It is the intent of the Oklahoma Legislature that the purpose of Section 105.1 through Section 105.32 of this title is to provide for stability and certainty in water rights by replacing the incompatible dual systems of riparian and appropriative water rights which governed the use of water from definite streams in Oklahoma prior to June 10, 1963, with an appropriation system of regulation requiring the beneficial use of water and providing that priority in time shall give the better right. These sections are intended to provide that riparian landowners may use water for domestic uses and store water in definite streams and that appropriations shall not interfere with such domestic uses, to recognize through administrative adjudications all uses, riparian and appropriative, existing prior to June 10, 1963, and to extinguish future claims to use water, except for domestic use, based only on ownership of riparian lands.

Okla. Stat. Ann. Tit. 82, § 105.1A (West Supp. 2007). The OWRB agreed with the City, stating that, as an administrative agency, the OWRB must presume the new statute to be constitutional. On appeal, the district court ruled that § 105.1A is unconstitutional. Rick R. Linker, *Regulatory Structure: The Potential Impact of Franco*, in Oklahoma Water Law Project: The Impact of Franco–American Charolaise, Ltd. v. Oklahoma Water Resources Board 159, 176 (Drew L. Kershen ed., 1995). The Oklahoma Supreme Court has yet to rule on the constitutionality of the statute; presented with an opportunity to do so in 2006, the court declined to reach the question. Heldermon v. Wright, 152 P.3d 855 (Okla. 2006). *Heldermon* involved a dispute between two riparians, in which the Oklahoma Water Resources Board played only a peripheral role. The lower court held § 105.1A unconstitutional, but the supreme court remanded the case without reaching the merits to give the OWRB an opportunity to participate. *Id.* at 860. In sum, *Franco* has resulted in uncertainty for water users in Oklahoma, with the influence reaching agriculture, reservoir management, recreation, tribal and interstate claims, and the basic regulatory structure.

2. Most of the foregoing cases deal with legislative efforts to change a state's system of water rights, typically from riparianism to appropriation. But what if the change in water law systems was dictated not by statute, but by a state supreme court decision? Would the U.S. Constitution protect existing users claiming rights under the "old" system? *See* Barton H. Thompson, Jr., *Judicial Takings,* 76 Va. L. Rev. 1449 (1990). In a case arising from Hawaii, the Ninth Circuit Court of Appeals insisted that a state court cannot divest rights established under prior law:

> The Supreme Court of Hawaii in 1973 *sua sponte* overruled all territorial cases to the contrary and adopted the English common law doctrine of riparian rights. *McBryde Sugar Co. v. Robinson, et al.*, 54 Hawaii 174, 504 P.2d 1330, 1344 (1973) *[McBryde I].* * * *

> The state conceded at oral argument that the Fourteenth Amendment would require it to pay just compensation if it attempted to take vested property rights. The substantive question, therefore, is whether the state can declare, by court decision, that the water rights in this case have not vested. The short answer is no.

* * *

> On April 28, 1930, the Supreme Court of the Territory of Hawaii, in litigation between substantially the same parties that are here today, except for the McBryde Sugar Company, held that the common law doctrine of riparian rights was not in force in Hawaii with reference to surplus waters of the normal flow of a stream. The same court further held that the owner (konohiki) of the land (ili) could use the water collected on his ili as he saw fit, subject to the rights of downstream owners to drinking water and other domestic uses that the parties in all this litigation have agreed have not been in controversy. * * * When that case reached this court, we affirmed in an opinion which stated that the definition of property rights and water rights in light of the feudal history of land tenure in the islands was best left to the local courts. *Territory of Hawaii v. Gay*, 52 F.2d 356, 359 (9th Cir.1931) *(Territory II)*. The water law, at least between the territorial government and the Gay and Robinson interests, thereafter remained settled until statehood. * * *

> The parties concede that the State of Hawaii has the sovereign power to change its laws from time to time as its legislature may see fit, and may, by changing its laws, radically change the definitions of property rights and the manner in which property rights can be controlled or transferred.

> The state may also change its laws by judicial decision as well as by legislative action. Insofar as judicial changes in the law operate prospectively to affect property rights vesting after the law is changed, no specific federal question is presented by the state's choice of implement in changing state law. See *Hughes v. Washington*, 389 U.S. 290 (1967) (Stewart, J. concurring) *[supra*, p. 397]. * * *

> We assume, therefore, for the purposes of this case, that the Supreme Court of Hawaii was acting well within its judicial power under the state constitution when it overruled earlier cases and declared for the first time, after more than a century of a different law, that the common law doctrine of riparian ownership was the law of Hawaii. This declaration of a change in the water law of Hawaii may be effective with respect to real property rights created in Hawaii after

the *McBryde I* decision became final. New law, however, cannot divest rights that vested before the court announced the new law. See *Hughes*, 389 U.S. at 295–98, 88 S.Ct. at 441–43.

Robinson v. Ariyoshi, 753 F.2d 1468 (9th Cir. 1985), remanded for further proceedings, 477 U.S. 902, 106 S.Ct. 3269, 91 L.Ed.2d 560 (1986), opinion vacated, 887 F.2d 215 (9th Cir.1989). Shortly after *Robinson v. Ariyoshi* was decided, Hawai'i adopted a comprehensive water law that modified the born-again riparianism that had resulted in the *McBryde* decision discussed in the case. The 1987 statute established a water rights permitting system under which existing users, as well as new users, must receive a permit if they are in designated water management areas established by a Commission on Water Resource Management. Once an area is designated, holders of common law appurtenant rights are entitled to a permit as a matter of right. Permits are transferable. The legislation grants jurisdiction to the commission to resolve water disputes whether or not they arise in a water management area. Haw. Rev. Stat. § 174C–1 to –95 (Michie 2005). For a review of the Hawai'i water code see Douglas W. MacDougal, *Testing the Current: The Water Code and the Regulation of Hawai'i's Water Resources*, 10 U. Haw. L. Rev. 205 (1988).

2.   CONTROLS AND LIMITS ON USE OF EXISTING RIGHTS

What happens to water rights holders when the state, through its administrative, legislative, or judicial branch, decides to require a more efficient use of water by holders of existing rights?

Enterprise Irrigation District v. Willis

Supreme Court of Nebraska, 1939.
135 Neb. 827, 284 N.W. 326.

■ CARTER, JUSTICE.

* * *

The record discloses that in the year 1889 the Enterprise Ditch Company made an appropriation of water from the North Platte river, in accordance with the law of appropriation then in existence, in an amount in excess of 138.90 second-feet, subject only to the common-law rule that no more water could be diverted and appropriated than could be applied to a beneficial use. * * *

* * * The irrigation law of 1895 limited for the first time the quantity of water that could be appropriated to a specific amount; the statute stating "that no allotment for irrigation shall exceed one cubic foot per second for each 70 acres of land for which said appropriation shall be made." Laws 1895, c. 69, § 20. The same act also provided: "Nothing in this act contained shall be so construed as to interfere with or impair the rights to water appropriated and acquired prior to the passage of this act." Laws 1895, c. 69, § 49. In 1911, the legislature placed a further limitation upon the quantity of water that could be appropriated, the statute providing, "that no allotment for irrigation shall exceed one cubic foot per second of time for each seventy acres of land nor *three acre-feet in the aggregate during one calendar year for each acre of land for which such appropriation shall be made.*" Laws 1911, c. 153, § 19. (Italics ours). These same limitations appear in the irrigation law contained in the civil administrative code law of 1919. Laws 1919, c. 190, p. 837. The 1919 law also provided: "Nothing in this article contained shall be so construed as to interfere with or impair the rights to water appropriated and acquired prior to the fourth day of April, 1895." Laws 1919, p. 832. * * * It is the contention of the defendants that the limitation of three acre-feet in the aggregate during one calendar year for each acre of land for which the appropriation shall have been made * * * applies to plaintiff's appropriation and, that amount having been exceeded at the time this suit was commenced, the plaintiff was not entitled to any more water and defendants should not be enjoined from closing the headgates of plaintiff's canal. Plaintiff contends that its appropriation is a right vested as of March 28, 1889, and that the statute in question has no retroactive force and, if such retroactive construction be placed upon it, it is violative of the due process clauses of the Constitution of Nebraska (article 1, § 3) and the Fourteenth Amendment to the Constitution of the United States, U.S.C.A. Defendants contend that the statute is a proper exercise of the police power of the state and is not inhibited by either the state or federal Constitutions.

* * *

It is a principle of the common law that one may not divert more water, even under a valid appropriation, than he can put to a beneficial use. While many elements must be considered in determining whether water has been put to beneficial use, one is that it shall not exceed the least amount of water that experience indicates is necessary in the exercise of good husbandry for the production of crops. The extent to which landowners need and are entitled to have the benefit of irrigation water under a vested appropriation ordinarily depends upon aridity, rainfall, location, soil porosity, adaptability to particular forms of production and the use to which the irrigable lands are put. In other words, the duty of water may be defined as such a quantity of water necessary, when economically conducted and applied to the land without unnecessary loss, as will result in the successful growing of crops. 2 Kinney, Irrigation and Water Rights (2d Ed.) secs. 902 and 903.

Many persons engaged in farming within the plaintiff district testified that the water used by them had been used in the usual and ordinary way to produce crops, that there had been no waste or misapplication of the irrigation water, and that, at the time the closing of the headgate was threatened, their crops were in need of water. They also testified that a failure to obtain water would have resulted in a material decrease in the crop returns from their lands.

The defendants produced the evidence of two experts who testified that they had made many experiments as to the amount of water required to grow certain kinds of crops on various kinds of lands, including the types of land found in the plaintiff district. The conclusions of these witnesses were that three acre-feet of water was sufficient to grow the kind of crops raised on the lands within the Enterprise Irrigation district. The experiments testified to were made under conditions very dissimilar from those under which the farmers of the plaintiff district were forced to operate. Whether the difference in conditions would account for the difference in the amount of water used would require us to delve into the realms of speculation and conjecture. * * * After a consideration of all the evidence in the record on the subject, we are of the opinion that it will not sustain a finding that irrigation water was wasted or put to other than a beneficial use in the usual, ordinary and recognized method of applying irrigation water in that section of the state.

It must be borne in mind that the quantity of water that can be diverted under a vested water right for irrigation purposes is an element of importance equal to that of its priority in determining its value. While such a right may be regulated and supervised by the state and its administrative officers for the purpose of protecting all adjudicated rights of appropriators having an interest in the waters of the stream, yet a law of this character cannot operate to divest rights already vested at the time it was enacted. While vested water rights may be interfered with within reasonable limits under the police power of the state to secure a proper regulation and supervision of them for the public good, any interference that limits the quantity of water or changes the date of its priority to the material injury of its holder is more than regulation and supervision and extends into the field generally referred to as a deprivation of a vested right.

In a similar situation the legislature of California declared that the term "useful or beneficial purposes" shall not be construed to mean the use in any one year of more than two and one-half acre-feet of water per acre in the irrigation of uncultivated areas of land not devoted to cultivated crops. It was contended that the act of the legislature was justified as a proper exercise of the police power of the state. In holding to the contrary, the supreme court of that state said: " * * * To concede that the state Legislature has the right arbitrarily to fix as to [unadulterated lands] the amount of water which the riparian proprietor may take and use thereon would be to concede an equal power to make a like arbitrary fixation in respect to cultivated areas also, entirely regardless of the foregoing elements which are necessarily the determining factors in such fixation. To concede this would be to concede to the legislative department of the state government the arbitrary power to destroy vested rights in private property of every kind and character." Herminghaus v. Southern California Edison Co., 200 Cal. 81, 252 P. 607, 622. We are of the opinion that the principle of law set forth in the foregoing case is correct and that it has particular application to the facts in the case at bar.

The evidence, as we view it, shows that the plaintiff district has diverted more than three acre-feet of water for every irrigable acre in its district. It further shows that the water used has been applied to a beneficial use without waste. It is not disputed that additional water was required when the injunction was threatened and that plaintiff's appropriation, without the limitations complained of, was sufficient to provide it without infringing upon the rights of prior appropriators. The evidence of the expert witnesses tendered by the defendants was not sufficient to overcome the undisputed evidence offered by the plaintiff. * * *

We fully realize the difficulty of regulating and supervising the holder of an appropriation such as the plaintiff possesses. However, the difficulty must be overcome by regulation and control over the district by virtue of a proper exercise of the police power of the state. The difficulties of the situation cannot be advanced as a justification for violating vested property rights.

NOTE

To what extent does *Willis* curb the ability of legislatures to limit use of water under existing rights by passing "duty of water" statutes like the one at issue in that case? Is the decision inconsistent with the *Alamosa–La Jara* case, *supra* p. 343, in which the court held that the state engineer could require senior users to drill wells to get water they historically had taken from the stream in order to allow for fuller use of water by juniors?

NOTE: U.S. SUPREME COURT CASES REGARDING CONSTITUTIONAL TAKINGS

Since the mid–1970s, the U.S. Supreme Court has decided numerous cases regarding the effect of government actions on private property. Through these cases, the Court has developed a legal framework for analyzing the question of when a government action effects a "taking" of property requiring compensation under the Fifth Amendment. This legal framework is highly complex, and the Court's rules often do not produce clear, predictable results when applied to a particular set of facts. Moreover, takings litigation often involves a clash of values, with one side arguing for private property rights and the other advocating for public interests served by government action. For these and other reasons, disputes over takings are often hotly contested.

In one of the more recent cases involving a claim that government action had taken private property, the Court provided a brief synopsis of the relevant legal framework:

> The paradigmatic taking requiring just compensation is a direct government appropriation or physical invasion of private property. See, *e.g., United States v. Pewee Coal Co.,* 341 U.S. 114 (1951) (Government's seizure and operation of a coal mine to prevent a national strike of coal miners effected a taking); *United States v. General Motors Corp.,* 323 U.S. 373 (1945) (Government's occupation of private warehouse effected a taking). Indeed, until the Court's watershed decision in *Pennsylvania Coal Co. v. Mahon,* 260 U.S. 393 (1922), "it was

generally thought that the Takings Clause reached *only* a 'direct appropriation' of property, or the functional equivalent of a 'practical ouster of [the owner's] possession.' " *Lucas v. South Carolina Coastal Council,* 505 U.S. 1003 (1992) (citations omitted and emphasis added; brackets in original); see also *id.,* at 1028, n. 15 ("[E]arly constitutional theorists did not believe the Takings Clause embraced regulations of property at all").

Beginning with *Mahon,* however, the Court recognized that government regulation of private property may, in some instances, be so onerous that its effect is tantamount to a direct appropriation or ouster—and that such "regulatory takings" may be compensable under the Fifth Amendment. In Justice Holmes' storied but cryptic formulation, "while property may be regulated to a certain extent, if regulation goes too far it will be recognized as a taking." 260 U.S., at 415. The rub, of course, has been—and remains—how to discern how far is "too far." In answering that question, we must remain cognizant that "government regulation—by definition—involves the adjustment of rights for the public good," *Andrus v. Allard,* 444 U.S. 51, 65 (1979), and that "Government hardly could go on if to some extent values incident to property could not be diminished without paying for every such change in the general law," *Mahon, supra,* at 413.

Our precedents stake out two categories of regulatory action that generally will be deemed *per se* takings for Fifth Amendment purposes. First, where government requires an owner to suffer a permanent physical invasion of her property—however minor—it must provide just compensation. See *Loretto v. Teleprompter Manhattan CATV Corp.,* 458 U.S. 419 (1982) (state law requiring landlords to permit cable companies to install cable facilities in apartment buildings effected a taking). A second categorical rule applies to regulations that completely deprive an owner of *"all* economically beneficial us[e]" of her property. *Lucas,* 505 U.S., at 1019 (emphasis in original). We held in *Lucas* that the government must pay just compensation for such "total regulatory takings," except to the extent that "background principles of nuisance and property law" independently restrict the owner's intended use of the property. *Id.,* at 1026–1032.

Outside these two relatively narrow categories (and the special context of land-use exactions discussed below), regulatory takings challenges are governed by the standards set forth in *Penn Central Transp. Co. v. New York City,* 438 U.S. 104 (1978). The Court in *Penn Central* acknowledged that it had hitherto been "unable to develop any 'set formula' " for evaluating regulatory takings claims, but identified "several factors that have particular significance." *Id.,* at 124. Primary among those factors are "[t]he economic impact of the regulation on the claimant and, particularly, the extent to which the regulation has interfered with distinct investment-backed expectations." *Ibid.* In addition, the "character of the governmental action"—for instance whether it amounts to a physical invasion or instead merely affects property interests through "some public program adjusting the benefits and burdens of economic life to promote the common good"—may be relevant in discerning whether a taking has occurred. *Ibid.* The *Penn Central* factors—though each has given rise to vexing subsidiary questions—have served as the principal guidelines for resolving regulatory takings claims that do not fall within the physical takings or *Lucas* rules. See, *e.g., Palazzolo v. Rhode Island,* 533 U.S. 606, 617–618 (2001) *id.,* at 632–634 (O'CONNOR, J., concurring).

Although our regulatory takings jurisprudence cannot be characterized as unified, these three inquiries (reflected in *Loretto, Lucas,* and *Penn Central*) share a common touchstone. Each aims to identify regulatory actions that are functionally equivalent to the classic taking in which government directly appropriates private property or ousts the owner from his domain. Accordingly, each of these tests focuses directly upon the severity of the burden that government imposes upon private property rights. The Court has held that physical takings require compensation because of the unique burden they impose: A permanent physical invasion, however minimal the economic cost it entails, eviscerates the owner's right to exclude others from entering and using her property—perhaps the most fundamental of all property interests. See *Dolan v. City of Tigard,* 512 U.S. 374, 384 (1994); *Nollan v. California Coastal Comm'n,* 483 U.S. 825 (1987); *Loretto, supra,* at 433; *Kaiser Aetna v. United States,* 444 U.S. 164, 176 (1979). In the *Lucas* context, of course, the complete elimination of a property's value is the determinative factor. See *Lucas, supra,* at 1017 (positing that "total deprivation of beneficial use is, from the landowner's point of view, the equivalent of a physical appropriation"). And the *Penn Central* inquiry turns in large part, albeit not exclusively, upon the magnitude of a regulation's economic impact and the degree to which it interferes with legitimate property interests.

Lingle v. Chevron U.S.A. Inc., 544 U.S. 528, 537–40 (2005).

The Court also explained the special rule applicable to land-use "exactions" as developed in *Nollan v. California Coastal Comm'n,* 483 U.S. 825, 107 S.Ct. 3141, 97 L.Ed.2d 677 (1987) and *Dolan v. City of Tigard,* 512 U.S. 374, 114 S.Ct. 2309, 129 L.Ed.2d 304 (1994):

> Both *Nollan* and *Dolan* involved Fifth Amendment takings challenges to adjudicative land-use exactions—specifically, government demands that a landowner dedicate an easement allowing public access to her property as a condition of obtaining a development permit. See *Dolan, supra,* at 379–380 (permit to expand a store and parking lot conditioned on the dedication of a portion of the relevant property for a "greenway," including a bike/pedestrian path); *Nollan, supra,* at 828 (permit to build a larger residence on beachfront property conditioned on dedication of an easement allowing the public to traverse a strip of the property between the owner's seawall and the mean high-tide line).
>
> In each case, the Court began with the premise that, had the government simply appropriated the easement in question, this would

have been a *per se* physical taking. *Dolan, supra,* at 384; *Nollan, supra,* at 831–832. The question was whether the government could, without paying the compensation that would otherwise be required upon effecting such a taking, demand the easement as a condition for granting a development permit the government was entitled to deny. * * * As the Court explained in *Dolan,* these cases involve a special application of the "doctrine of 'unconstitutional conditions,' " which provides that "the government may not require a person to give up a constitutional right—here the right to receive just compensation when property is taken for a public use—in exchange for a discretionary benefit conferred by the government where the benefit has little or no relationship to the property."

Id. at 546–47.

In Lucas v. South Carolina Coastal Council, 505 U.S. 1003, 112 S.Ct. 2886, 120 L.Ed.2d 798 (1992), the Court held that South Carolina had to justify its beach front set-back law, that was intended to prevent erosion of the coastline caused by construction in the zone affected by tidal action, based on background principles of property or nuisance law. The application of the regulation rendered Lucas' property economically valueless and the Court announced a per se rule of compensability when regulations deprive land of all economically beneficial uses unless the limitations are consistent with "existing rules or understandings" concerning use of property. The Court proposed a nuisance-type inquiry looking at the character of the government action, the degree of harm to public resources and neighboring land, the economic impact of the regulation, and the extent to which it interfered with distinct investment-backed expectation. Justice Scalia's plurality opinion explains how state legislation can pass constitutional muster:

Where the State seeks to sustain regulation that deprives land of all economically beneficial use, we think it may resist compensation only if the logically antecedent inquiry into the nature of the owner's estate shows that the proscribed use interests were not part of his title to begin with. This accords, we think, with our "takings" jurisprudence, which has traditionally been guided by the understanding of our citizens regarding the content of, and the State's power over, the "bundle of rights" that they acquire when they obtain title to property. It seems to us that the property owner necessarily expects the uses of his property to be restricted, from time to time, by various measures newly enacted by the State in legitimate exercise of its police powers. * * *

* * * [R]egulations that prohibit all economically beneficial use of land * * * cannot be newly legislated or decreed (without compensation), but must inhere in the title itself, in the restrictions that background principles of the State's law of property and nuisance already place upon land ownership. A law or decree with such an effect must, in other words, do no more than duplicate the result that could have been achieved in the courts—by adjacent landowners (or other uniquely affected persons) under the State's law of private nuisance, or

by the State under its complementary power to abate nuisances that affect the public generally, or otherwise.

> On this analysis, the owner of a lake bed, for example, would not be entitled to compensation when he is denied the requisite permit to engage in a landfilling operation that would have the effect of flooding others' land. Nor the corporate owner of a nuclear generating plant, when it is directed to remove all improvements from its land upon discovery that the plant sits astride an earthquake fault. Such regulatory action may well have the effect of eliminating the land's only economically productive use, but it does not proscribe a productive use that was previously permissible under relevant property and nuisance principles. The use of these properties for what are now expressly prohibited purposes was *always* unlawful, and (subject to other constitutional limitations) it was open to the State at any point to make the implication of those background principles of nuisance and property law explicit.

Id. at 1027–30.

The Court in *Lingle* noted that each of the *Penn Central* factors had given rise to "vexing subsidiary questions." One of these questions was, to what extent is the regulation framework at the time the property owner acquires the property relevant? The Court has held that a person who purchased wetland property after the state regulations restricting filling were in place could claim the full value of the property as filled when the state denied a development request. Palazzolo v. Rhode Island, 533 U.S. 606, 121 S.Ct. 2448, 150 L.Ed.2d 592 (2001). Justice Kennedy wrote that the Rhode Island Supreme Court erred in holding that notice of the regulation absolutely barred a takings claim. Citing *Nollan,* the Court held that prior notice was not a bar: "The State may not put so potent a Hobbesian stick into the Lockian bundle. * * * Were we to accept the State's rule, the postenactment transfer of title would absolve the state of its obligation to defend any action restricting land use, no matter how extreme or unreasonable." Id. at 627. However, the Court affirmed the state supreme court's holding that the petitioner had not proved a total deprivation of all economic value and remanded for further proceedings. Justice O'Connor concurred but emphasized that the timing of the enactment of regulations was relevant to the traditional regulatory takings test announced in *Penn Central,,* that inquired into whether the regulation interfered with investment-backed expectations of the property owner. She defined the term to include both the state of regulation at the time of acquisition and the nature and extent of permitted development under the regulatory regime. *Id.* at 633–636 (O'Connor, J., concurring).

Joseph L. Sax, The Constitution, Property Rights and the Future of Water Law

61 U.Colo.L.Rev. 257 (1990).

* * *

What exactly is the problem? At its crudest the claim would be that whatever uses an appropriator has been making, and that have been recognized as lawful in the past, must as a matter of property right be permitted to continue or be compensated as a taking. If successful, such demands would deny a state effective authority to mandate more efficient use of existing supplies. The notion seems to be that to declare an existing use wasteful, or non-beneficial, is a sort of prohibited *ex post facto* law that impairs a vested right.

* * *

A second property dispute arises from the demand that existing appropriators give up some water in order to restore instream flows. Here the claim is that an appropriator with a recognized right to abstract and use a given quantum of water from a stream cannot be required to divert less, or to make discharges from storage, in order to produce desired stream conditions. The appropriator would say that the right to abstract water from a stream is the very essence of his property right in water and that to diminish that right because the state wants increased instream flows is the most blatant sort of taking without compensation.

* * *

I. Water Rights as Constitutionally Protected Property

* * *

The following is a brief statement of the constitutional situation. The regulatory authority of the state under the aegis of the police power is very broad. Even the Court's most conservative and property-oriented Justices accept the capaciousness of the police power. The reason, no doubt, is reluctance to second-guess legislatures about the need for regulation, and recognition that we live in a regulatory state. Significant changes in takings doctrine would put the court at odds with the modern legislative style of governance. Short of regulation that is forbidden by some other constitutional provision, * * * or is seen as not serving a public function at all, it is difficult to imagine subjects that might garner legislative majorities whose purpose would be viewed today as beyond the police power. Certainly legislation that constrains uses of property to achieve environmental protection goals is firmly within the police power,[12] as is legislation that constrains property use in order to conserve scarce natural resources by requiring more efficient use.[13] The same is true of legislation to promote

---

12. *E.g.* United States v. Riverside Bayview Homes, 474 U.S. 121 (1985) (wetlands); Hodel v. Virginia Surface Mining and Reclamation Ass'n, 452 U.S. 264 (1981) (strip mining); Agins v. City of Tiburon, 447 U.S. 255 (1980) (open space).

13. *E.g.,* State v. Dexter, 32 Wash. 2d 551, 202 P.2d 906 (1949), *aff'd per curiam,* 338 U.S. 863 (1949) (requiring those engaged in commercial logging operations to leave a certain number of trees standing for reseeding and restocking purposes). For a reference to this history of efforts at sustained-yield forestry see Sibley, *An America That Did Not Happen,* High Country News, Dec. 22, 1986, at 8.

efficient administration.[14] Those three categories cover just about all the regulatory proposals that are likely to be made as to western water law.

The question then is under what circumstances compensation is due even for a valid exercise of the police power? There are essentially only two grounds on which it is possible to win a takings case today. The first is where there is a "physical invasion," that is, where government physically appropriates to itself some part of an owner's property, as in the recent *Nollan*,[15] *Loretto*,[16] and *Kaiser Aetna*[17] cases. The second is where the effect of the regulation, though its purpose is valid under the police power, is so greatly to diminish the value of the property that is no longer economically viable. As to this latter test—the so-called diminution of value standard—the Supreme Court has been extremely deferential to regulators. Even diminutions approaching 90% of value have been sustained without compensation. That has been the Court's unvarying position for many decades.

Under these standards, the only new water law regulation that would *prima facie* raise a taking problem is a release requirement: requiring existing appropriators to make releases in order to augment instream flows for public purposes such as ecosystem protection and public recreation. If the appropriator's property right were an unqualified one, such a requirement might well be viewed as a "physical invasion," and would thus be compensable. But, * * * original limitations on the property that can be acquired in water undermines this facially appealing claim for compensation.

Otherwise, the regulations most likely to be challenged are those that require existing uses to be cut back as wasteful. There is no property right to waste water, and that would seem to end the matter. But several claims may nonetheless be anticipated against such regulation. First, that it would be retroactive; conduct previously considered legal would be made illegal. Second, insofar as such regulation is sought to be justified under the preexisting waste doctrine, it may be urged that the doctrine has been

---

14. *E.g.*, Texaco v. Short, 454 U.S. 516 (1982), where the Court upheld (unanimously on the takings issue) a state statute providing that mineral interests unused for many years lapsed unless the owner filed a statement of claim in the county recorder's office.

15. Nollan v. California Coastal Comm'n, 483 U.S. 825 (1987) (state's demand for dedication of right-of-way to allow public to walk across homeowner's oceanfront land as a condition for grant of building permit to enlarge beachfront home held an unconstitutional taking because no causal nexus was found between the public harm created by the home enlargement and the public benefit of walking across beach).

16. Loretto v. Teleprompter Manhattan CATV Corp., 458 U.S. 491 (1982) (governmentally required, virtually uncompensated installation of cable television wiring by landlords to benefit tenants held an unconstitutional taking of landlord's property). For reasons not germane to this discussion, I view *Loretto* as wrongly decided. Be that as it may, it nonetheless demonstrates that physical invasion is the event that primarily triggers a demand for compensation by the Supreme Court. Even physical invasion is not a guarantee of compensation, however. Pruneyard Shopping Center v. Robins, 447 U.S. 74 (1980).

17. Kaiser Aetna v. United States, 444 U.S. 164 (1979) (governmentally required public boating access to privately created marina excavated from non-navigable pond, now (but not formerly) connected to ocean, held an unconstitutional taking of marina developer's property).

unused or loosely construed for a long time and should not be tightened up now. Or it may be urged that definitions of waste should not change over time.

The first of these issues is easily answered. There is no constitutional bar to retroactive regulatory legislation. The U.S. Supreme Court has recently and explicitly sustained retroactive legislation against taking challenges. This issue no longer presents a substantial federal question. Nonetheless, a notion seems to have been advanced in some circles that what might be called the "non-conforming use" rule in land zoning states a constitutional proposition. The claim is that a use that is already being made and that was lawful when initiated cannot be regulated away without compensation, even though similarly situated new uses may be regulated. The short answer is that there has never been a non-conforming use rule in federal constitutional property law. Valid preexisting uses have been subject to rezoning and owners have been required to change their use to conform to the new law.

Although the non-conforming use rule may be a prudent one for certain relatively low priority public purposes (such as removing highway billboards or clearing commercial uses out of residential neighborhoods), it would fundamentally subvert the regulatory process if it were implemented as a constitutional principle. New fire and safety laws could hardly await a whole new generation of buildings, and for that reason required retrofitting of devices like fire sprinklers, or removal of hazards like asbestos, raise no constitutional taking problem.

The notion that a standard once set (such as a waste rule in water law) cannot be subsequently revised is just another version of the "non-conforming use" argument. Indeed, if the argument were correct that standards cannot be upgraded, all of our environmental statutes would be unconstitutional. We could not require industries to retrofit new air and water pollution control equipment to meet new, tighter standards so long as they had been in compliance with the standards that were in effect when their facility was built. Although the Supreme Court has never in so many words sustained the constitutionality of new pollution standards applied to existing facilities, betting on the constitutionality of such laws as against taking claims is as safe a wager as the law has to offer. * * * [T]here are two differences in water doctrine that put holders of water rights in a weaker position than other property owners subject to retrospective regulation. First, there has always been a law saying in effect that water could not be wasted, or could only be used beneficially. While owners of most property have a right to make inefficient uses if they so choose, this is not true of owners of water rights.

Second, new laws defining existing uses as wasteful are more prospective, and less retroactive, than a number of other laws whose constitutionality has been sustained by the Supreme Court. In the leading retroactive regulation cases, property owners were required to make supplemental payments to compensate for conduct wholly in the past which was legal when engaged in. In the water situation, imposition of waste laws would only change the uses that can be made in the future. No reparation would be required for past wasteful uses.

II. The Tradition of Change in Water Law

* * *

Far from being a modern invention of goal-oriented judges, change is the unchanging chronicle of water jurisprudence. When the question was getting timber to market in places which lacked highways or railroads but not rivers, those rivers suitable for floating logs to market magically became navigable. When the needs of commerce required it, navigability was extended from tidal waters (which had been its historical limit) to nontidal waters suitable for waterborne navigation. New needs have always generated new doctrines and, thereby, new property rights.

Water, as a necessary and common medium for community development at every stage of society, has been held subject to the perceived societal necessities of the time and circumstances. In that sense water's capacity for full privatization has always been limited. The very terminology of water law reveals that limitation: terms such as "beneficial," "non-wasteful," "navigation servitude," and "public trust" all import an irreducible public claim on waters as a public resource, and not merely as a private commodity. In the following section I address those doctrines that limit full privatization of water. A discussion of these doctrines will show why, in demanding releases to meet instream flow needs, a state is only asserting a right it has always had and never granted away.

III. A Tradition of Public Servitudes

A. The Public Trust and Its Predecessors

There is a tradition that recognizes a pre-existing right of the State in the flow of its rivers. Private diversions, at least those in tidal or navigable waters and affected tributaries, have always been subject to a servitude and a trust in favor of the public. Only California courts have thus far fully explored the implications of this tradition for the imposition of release requirements on existing appropriators. They have resolved the question strongly in favor of the public, first in the Mono Lake case,[38] then in the intermediate appellate decision in the Delta water case,[39] and most recently in a carefully crafted Superior Court decision, *Environmental Defense Fund v. East Bay Municipal Utility District.*[40]

* * *

---

38. National Audubon Soc'y v. Superior Court, 33 Cal. 3d 419, 658 P.2d 709, 189 Cal. Rptr. 346, cert. denied, 464 U.S. 977 (1983). [*supra* p. 414].

39. United States v. State Water Resources Control Bd., 182 Cal. App. 3d 82, 227 Cal. Rptr. 161 (1986).

40. No. 425955 (Alameda County Sup. Ct., Nov. 27, 1989).

B.   Appropriators as Polluters

Where releases are required to protect downstream water quality, appropriators may be seen as in no better position than conventional polluters. The water rights and uses of industrial and municipal polluters are subject to all controls necessary to restore desired water quality even if such controls prohibit or limit uses that have been lawfully made for many decades. For example, it seems unquestionable that both the intake and discharge of water by industrialists may be extensively regulated where their uses pollute the water body into which they discharge.

The situation of the industrial water user/polluter puts in perspective the appropriator's claim that it has a right to dewater a river and destroy it as a natural system—and that if the state wants now to restore the river, the public should pay. Prior to federal water quality legislation, the shoreline oil refinery or power plant that discharged heated or tainted water back into the source was permitted to destroy the river as a sustaining natural system. Now the public is reclaiming rivers from industrial polluters in order to restore their natural functioning and the public is not paying.

In at least some circumstances the situations of irrigators and industrial polluters seems indistinguishable. The following illustration suggests the similarity. Mineralized return flows from irrigation appropriators contaminated California's Kesterson refuge with selenium, killing birds that roosted there. One way to control the contamination is to reduce the total amount of water flowing through irrigation systems. Reductions in amounts of water diverted and passed over the irrigated lands would decrease the mineral content of the water and reduce the concentration of the contaminated water downstream. Assuming that the reduced-diversion approach is part of the best and most economical strategy for dealing with the contamination issue, and that such a requirement would not deprive the irrigators of all economic viability, would such a release requirement be viewed as a physical invasion (government seizure) of the water, or as a legitimate noncompensable regulation?

No legally or factually significant difference is apparent between the Kesterson-type hypothetical case and a conventional case of industrial pollution. Both involve a physical discharge of water that has been contaminated. Though the issue has not been authoritatively litigated, the operating premise has been that the pollution model applies, so that the government can require releases without incurring an obligation to compensate.

NOTE

Is Professor Sax's analysis consistent with the Supreme Court's regulatory takings analysis ? What is included in the "bundle of rights" which a water right holder acquires? How does the doctrine of beneficial use inform the issue? How far can a water right be reduced before it has "no economically beneficial use?"

3. ENVIRONMENTAL RESTRICTIONS ON WATER USE AS PHYSICAL TAKINGS

When the government restricts water use (or reduces deliveries from a federal water project) in order to preserve endangered species habitat or comply with other environmental requirements, water users may claim that the government has taken their rights and must pay them compensation. A crucial question of law in such cases is whether the court should analyze the restriction as a physical or a regulatory taking. Because the Penn Central test for regulatory takings will almost always be a difficult one for plaintiffs in these cases, they have argued consistently for a physical takings analysis of water use restrictions. The plaintiffs prevailed on this point in a controversial decision by the Court of Federal Claims, Tulare Lake Basin Water Storage Dist. v. United States, 49 Fed. Cl. 313 (2001) (*Tulare*). In that case, endangered species requirements had reduced water deliveries to plaintiffs from the California State Water Project, which operates in concert with the federal Central Valley Project. Regarding the correct takings analysis, Judge Wiese wrote:

> Plaintiffs urge us to consider this action as a case involving a physical taking of property. Under that theory, plaintiffs possessed contract rights entitling them to the use of a specified quantity of water. By preventing them from using that water, plaintiffs argue, the government deprived them of the entire value of their contract right.
>
> Defendant sees the case differently. In defendant's view, the court must examine the government's conduct under the three-part test that *Penn Central* prescribes for the evaluation of regulatory action that interferes with an owner's use of his property. Under that rubric, defendant contends, the claim must fail because plaintiffs' reasonable contract expectations were necessarily limited by regulatory concern over fish and wildlife; and because the economic loss asserted here—a fraction of the master contract's overall value—was de minimis.
>
> Of the two positions, plaintiffs', we believe, is the correct one. Case law reveals that the distinction between a physical invasion and a governmental activity that merely impairs the use of that property turns on whether the intrusion is "so immediate and direct as to subtract from the owner's full enjoyment of the property and to limit his exploitation of it." *United States v. Causby*, 328 U.S. 256, 265 (1946). In *Causby*, for instance, the Court ruled that frequent flights immediately above a landowner's property constituted a taking, comparing such actions to a more traditional physical taking: "If, by reason of the frequency and altitude of the flights, respondents could not use this land for any purpose, their loss would be complete. It would be as complete as if the United States had entered upon the surface of the land and taken exclusive possession of it." *Id.* at 261(footnote omitted).
>
> While water rights present an admittedly unusual situation, we think the *Causby* example is an instructive one. In the context of water

rights, a mere restriction on use—the hallmark of a regulatory action—completely eviscerates the right itself since plaintiffs' sole entitlement is to the use of the water. Unlike other species of property where use restrictions may limit some, but not all of the incidents of ownership, the denial of a right to the use of water accomplishes a complete extinction of all value. Thus, by limiting plaintiffs' ability to use an amount of water to which they would otherwise be entitled, the government has essentially substituted itself as the beneficiary of the contract rights with regard to that water and totally displaced the contract holder. That complete occupation of property—an exclusive possession of plaintiffs' water-use rights for preservation of the fish—mirrors the invasion present in *Causby*. To the extent, then, that the federal government, by preventing plaintiffs from using the water to which they would otherwise have been entitled, have rendered the usufructuary right to that water valueless, they have thus effected a physical taking.

Id. at 318–19.

NOTES

1. The *Tulare* court acknowledged the existence of California's public trust doctrine, but rejected the idea that it is a "background principle" sufficient to save government actions from being compensatory takings. An assistant attorney general who represented the State of California in *National Audubon Society, supra* p. 414, argued that "the public trust doctrine provides the conceptual basis of the water right laws [and] under the water right laws, the state has the right to balance environmental values and economic needs, and also to re-examine and if necessary modify existing rights to reflect changing public needs." Roderick E. Walston, *The Public Trust Doctrine: Implications for State Water Rights Administration*, Speech Delivered Before American Bar Association Natural Resources Section, January 8, 1985. For a more recent discussion regarding the application of the "background principles" aspect of the *Lucas* decision, *see* Michael C. Blumm and Lucus Ritchie, *Lucas's Unlikely Legacy: The Rise of Background Principles as Categorical Takings Defenses*, 29 Harv. Envtl. L. Rev. 321 (2005).

The prior appropriation doctrine was established to protect and define water rights. When states modify existing rights by effectively applying or redefining "beneficial use" under one or more of the methods of "public interest" review discussed *supra* p. 319, how secure are those rights? What remedy, if any, does the holder of a modified right have?

Consider the following answer to the taking argument in the special context of water rights:

Although some commentators have pointed to the fifth amendment's prohibitions against the taking of private property without the payment of just compensation as a potential "limitation on the public trust doctrine," these arguments are dependent on the acceptance of the premise that recipients of water rights from the states had no notice of the retention of sovereign ownership interests by the states and the accompanying public trust obligations. That such a premise is untenable is evident when one recalls that the usufructuary principle of western water law is a universally recognized "expression of the state's trust responsibilities to its citizens in the water rights context." Moreover, given the constitutional and statutory declarations of state or public ownership of water resources upon which western water law was founded, the "no notice" premise of the takings argument is, at best, a strained appeal to equity for it also ignores the numerous judicial affirmations of the public nature of state inland water resources and the common understanding, prevalent throughout the West, that the inland water resources of a state "belong" to all the people of the state. Thus, the acquisition of water rights by a state under the public trust doctrine would, like federal reserved rights acquired by the federal government, not require the payment of just compensation for the infringement of privately-held water rights.

Peter A. Fahmy, *The Public Trust Doctrine as a Source of State Reserved Water Rights*, 63 Denv. U. L. Rev. 585, 600–01 (1986). For a discussion stating that modification of existing water rights through "public interest" is a taking, see John S. Harbison, *Waist Deep in the Big Muddy: Property Rights, Public Values and Instream Waters*, 26 Land & Water L. Rev. 535, 549 (1991).

2. Is the debate represented by these views relevant to the court's physical invasion approach? Would the court's analysis apply if the basis for government regulation were the navigation servitude? Some courts have suggested that the federal government may invoke the servitude when it denies a permit to fill wetlands under the Clean Water Act. *E.g.*, Lambert Gravel Co. v. J.A. Jones Construction Co., 835 F.2d 1105 (5th Cir.1988). But the Court of Federal Claims has held that the government may only invoke the servitude as a defense to a per se taking claim when the purpose of the regulation is related to navigation. Palm Beach Isles Assoc. v. United States, 42 Fed.Cl. 340 (1998).

3. *Tulare* was the first reported case in which a court held that restrictions imposed under the Endangered Species Act had resulted in a taking of property requiring compensation. Melinda Harm Benson, *The* Tulare *Case: Water Rights, The Endangered Species Act, and the Fifth Amendment*, 32 Envtl. L. 551, 552 (2002). Following its 2001 decision on liability, the Court of Federal Claims held a trial to determine plaintiffs' damages. After trial, the court determined that the government had taken roughly 300,000 acre-feet of water from plaintiffs in 1992–1994, and that most of this water should be valued at around $67 per acre-foot. The court calculated total damages at about $13.9 million plus interest. Tulare Lake Basin Water Storage Dist. v. United States, 59 Fed.Cl. 246, 266 (2003). The State of California, the National Marine Fisheries Service and others urged the federal government to appeal the liability decision, but in late 2004 the parties settled the case for $16.7 million. Tulare Lake Basin Water Storage

Dist. v. United States, Verdict, Agreement and Settlement, 2004 WL 3728318 (Dec. 21, 2004). Why do you suppose the government chose not to appeal such a significant decision?

4. Not long after the liability decision in *Tulare*, the Supreme Court decided *Tahoe–Sierra Preservation Council v. Tahoe Regional Planning Agency*, 535 U.S. 302, 122 S.Ct. 1465, 152 L.Ed.2d 517 (2002). The case involved a challenge to a 32–month development moratorium on lands surrounding Lake Tahoe, imposed to allow time to develop a comprehensive land-use plan to protect the Lake's celebrated water quality. *Tahoe–Sierra* clarified the analytical distinction between physical and regulatory takings:

> When the government physically takes possession of an interest in property for some public purpose, it has a categorical duty to compensate the former owner, *United States v. Pewee Coal Co.*, 341 U.S. 114, 115 (1951), regardless of whether the interest that is taken constitutes an entire parcel or merely a part thereof. Thus, compensation is mandated when a leasehold is taken and the government occupies the property for its own purposes, even though that use is temporary. *United States v. General Motors Corp.*, 323 U.S. 373 (1945); *United States v. Petty Motor Co.*, 327 U.S. 372 (1946). Similarly, when the government appropriates part of a rooftop in order to provide cable TV access for apartment tenants, *Loretto v. Teleprompter Manhattan CATV Corp.*, 458 U.S. 419 (1982); or when its planes use private airspace to approach a government airport, *United States v. Causby*, 328 U.S. 256 (1946), it is required to pay for that share no matter how small. But a government regulation that merely prohibits landlords from evicting tenants unwilling to pay a higher rent, *Block v. Hirsh*, 256 U.S. 135 (1921); that bans certain private uses of a portion of an owner's property, *Village of Euclid v. Ambler Realty Co.*, 272 U.S. 365 (1926); *Keystone Bituminous Coal Assn. v. DeBenedictis*, 480 U.S. 470 (1987); or that forbids the private use of certain airspace, *Penn Central Transp. Co. v. New York City*, 438 U.S. 104 (1978), does not constitute a categorical taking. "The first category of cases requires courts to apply a clear rule; the second necessarily entails complex factual assessments of the purposes and economic effects of government actions." *Yee v. Escondido*, 503 U.S. 519, 523 (1992). See also *Loretto*, 458 U.S., at 440; *Keystone*, 480 U.S., at 489, n. 18.

> This longstanding distinction between acquisitions of property for public use, on the one hand, and regulations prohibiting private uses, on the other, makes it inappropriate to treat cases involving physical takings as controlling precedents for the evaluation of a claim that there has been a "regulatory taking," and vice versa. For the same reason that we do not ask whether a physical appropriation advances a substantial government interest or whether it deprives the owner of all economically valuable use, we do not apply our precedent from the physical takings context to regulatory takings claims. Land-use regulations are ubiquitous and most of them impact property values in some tangential way-often in completely unanticipated ways. Treating them

all as *per se* takings would transform government regulation into a luxury few governments could afford. By contrast, physical appropriations are relatively rare, easily identified, and usually represent a greater affront to individual property rights. "This case does not present the 'classi[c] taking' in which the government directly appropriates private property for its own use," *Eastern Enterprises v. Apfel,* 524 U.S. 498, 522 (1998); instead the interference with property rights "arises from some public program adjusting the benefits and burdens of economic life to promote the common good," Penn Central, 438 U.S., at 124.

Id. at 322–325 (footnotes omitted).

In addition, *Tahoe–Sierra* stressed the importance of considering a regulation's effect on the entire property right, not merely a portion of the right. Thus, a regulation that prohibits some uses of property but allows others, or prohibits use of a portion of a parcel of land but allows use of the remainder, does not result in a taking. *Id.* at 327. Similarly, the Court emphasized that a restriction which temporarily imposes severe restrictions on how property may be used does not necessarily take the property while the restriction is in place. *Id.* at 331. Summing up, the Court stated, "An interest in real property is defined by the metes and bounds that describe its geographic dimensions and the term of years that describes the temporal aspect of the owner's interest. See Restatement of Property §§ 7–9 (1936). Both dimensions must be considered if the interest is to be viewed in its entirety. Hence, a permanent deprivation of the owner's use of the entire area is a taking of 'the parcel as a whole,' whereas a temporary restriction that merely causes a diminution in value is not." *Id.* at 331–332.

Does *Tahoe–Sierra* offer clear guidance on whether environmental restrictions on water use should be analyzed as physical takings?

5. The *Tulare* plaintiffs argued that the Endangered Species Act caused a taking of their property by imposing restrictions on the operation of a federal water project, resulting in delivery of less water than they claimed a right to receive. *Tulare* was the first case in which plaintiff water users claimed a taking on these facts, but certainly not the last; several such cases were pending in the federal courts as of 2008. *Tulare* was unusual in one respect: the plaintiffs had contracts with the State of California to receive water from the California State Water Project (which was operated in conjunction with the federal Central Valley Project), rather than contracts with the U.S. Bureau of Reclamation to receive water directly from a federal project built by USBR. (Bureau of Reclamation projects and contracts are discussed in Chapter 8B.) The existence and language of these federal contracts may pose challenges for plaintiffs claiming a taking of their rights. A notable case arose from the Klamath Basin water controversy of 2001, where a drought and the Endangered Species Act resulted in farmers getting little or none of the water they were accustomed to receiving from USBR's Klamath Project. The irrigators sued, alleging that the government took their water rights by cutting deliveries in 2001 to preserve endangered species habitat. The Court of Federal Claims, however, denied compensation in two extensive opinions written by Judge Allegra. In the first, the court held that the plaintiffs could not claim a taking of property rights, but only a breach of contract: "the proper remedy for the alleged infringement lies in a contract claim, not one for a takings." Klamath Irrigation Dist. v. United States, 67 Fed.Cl. 504, 532 (2005). Judge Allegra also rejected arguments based on *Tulare*, and criticized that decision in fairly blunt terms: "With all due respect, *Tulare* appears to be wrong on some counts, incomplete in others, and, distinguishable, at all events." The court faulted *Tulare* for shortcomings relating both to its analysis of federal water contracts and California water law, *id.* at 538, and also noted that *Tulare* had been intensely criticized "by commentators who, *inter alia,* have challenged the court's application of a physical taking theory to what was a temporary reduction in water," citing Michael C. Blumm and Lucus Ritchie, Lucas's Unlikely Legacy: The Rise of Background Principles as Categorical Takings Defenses, 29 Harv. Envtl. L.Rev. 321, 329 (2005); Cori S. Parobek, "Of Farmers' Takes and Fishes' Takings: Fifth Amendment Compensation Claims When the Endangered Species Act and Western Water Rights Collide," 27 Harv. Envtl. L.Rev. 177, 212–23 (2003); and Brittany K.T. Kauffman, "What Remains of the Endangered Species Act and Western Water Rights after Tulare Lake Basin Water Storage District v. United States?," 74 U. Colo. L.Rev. 837 (2003). *Id.* at 538 n. 59,

In its second opinion in *Klamath Irrigation District*, the court held that the federal government had not breached its contracts with the irrigators because the enactment of the ESA was a "sovereign act" that effectively overrode the government's obligation to provide water, and that the government retained authority to take such a sovereign act because the government had not surrendered this power in "unmistakable terms" in the contract. Klamath Irrigation Dist. v. United States, 75 Fed.Cl. 677 (2007). The Court of Federal Claims (Judge Miller) also denied relief to the irrigators in a somewhat similar case. Stockton East Water Dist. v. United States, 75 Fed.Cl. 321 (2007). The court in *Stockton East* held that the plaintiffs had not established that the government had breached its contracts, but did not accept the "sovereign act" argument that had been crucial in the Klamath case. Stockton East Water Dist. v. United States, 76 Fed.Cl. 497 (2007). The plaintiffs appealed both *Klamath* and *Stockton East* to the Federal Circuit.

The 2001 *Tulare* decision had been a major victory for water users, but the next seven years brought them disappointment in the courts. *Tahoe–Sierra* cast doubt on whether water use restrictions should be analyzed as a physical taking. Plaintiffs lost in *Klamath Irrigation District* and *Stockton East*. In a case involving country restrictions on groundwater pumping, the California Court of Appeals criticized *Tulare* and rejected its physical taking analysis. Allegretti & Co. v. County of Imperial, 138 Cal.App.4th 1261, 42 Cal.Rptr.3d 122 (2006). Even Judge Wiese, the jurist who had decided *Tulare*, essentially repudiated his earlier reasoning in Casitas Municipal Water Dist. v. United States, 76 Fed.Cl. 100 (2007). On appeal from that decision, however, the Federal Circuit Court of Appeals resurrected the physical taking analysis.

Casitas Mun. Water Dist. v. United States

Federal Circuit Court of Appeals, 2008.
543 F.3d 1276.

■ MOORE, CIRCUIT JUDGE.

Casitas Municipal Water District (Casitas) appeals the judgment of the United States Court of Federal Claims granting summary judgment in favor of the government holding that there was no governmental breach of contract and no compensable taking under the Fifth Amendment. We affirm-in-part, reverse-in-part, and remand.

Congress authorized the construction of the Ventura River Project (Project) on March 1, 1956. Pub.L. No. 423, 70 Stat. 32 (1956). The Project provides the water supply for farmland irrigation and municipal, domestic, and industrial uses in Ventura County, California. The Project comprises, among other things, the Casitas Dam, Casitas Reservoir, Robles Diversion Dam, and the Robles–Casitas Canal. More specifically, the Project combines water of Coyote Creek and Ventura River in its principal feature, the Casitas Reservoir, generally called Lake Casitas. [Casitas receives water from the Ventura River Project under a 1956 contract with the United States.] * * *

In August, 1997, almost forty years after the construction of the project, the National Marine Fisheries Service (NMFS) listed the West Coast steelhead trout as an endangered species in the Project watershed. Section 9 of the Endangered Species Act (ESA) makes it illegal to "take" any species listed as endangered under the Act. 16 U.S.C. § 1538. To avoid ESA section 9 liability, the Bureau of Reclamation (BOR) sought a biological opinion by the NMFS (BiOp) pursuant to section 7 of the ESA. Id. § 1536(a)(2). For the purposes of this appeal, the government concedes that the BOR's May 2, 2003 directive advising Casitas that it was obligated to comply with the requirement of the BiOp compelled Casitas to: (1) construct a fish ladder facility, which is located at the intersection of the Ventura River, Robles Diversion Dam, and the Robles–Casitas Canal; and (2) divert water from the Project to the fish ladder, resulting in a permanent loss to Casitas of a certain amount of water per year.[4] Under protest Casitas complied, but on January 26, 2005, Casitas filed suit against the government alleging that these actions constituted a breach of contract and a compensable Fifth Amendment taking of its water.

* * *

4. * * * The parties dispute the amount of actual water Casitas has lost due to the diversion to the fish ladder. Casitas argues that the amount of loss is up to 3,200 acre-feet per year. The government argues the amount of loss of water in Lake Casitas due to the operation of the fish ladder was 1,349 acre-feet as of May 2006, but that this amount may decrease in the future.

To begin, we note that the government has conceded that Casitas has a valid property right in the water in question. Specifically, the government has conceded that Casitas has a right both to divert 107,800 acre-feet of water and to use 28,500 acre-feet of such diverted water. ("Plaintiff [characterizes its property interest] in its opposition brief [as follows]: 'In this case, Casitas claims the right to divert through the Ventura River Project 107,800 acre-feet of water from the Ventura River per year and the right to put 28,500 acre-feet of water to beneficial use each year....' [I]n order to streamline this summary judgment process, and to avoid any unnecessary confusion in the resolution of the nature or type of taking at issue in this case (i.e., physical or regulatory) defendant will assume for purposes of this motion that plaintiff's characterization of the scope of its property interests is correct."). However, before considering whether the diversion of Casitas' water to the fish ladder is best analyzed under the rubric of a physical or regulatory taking, it is useful to review the distinctions traditionally made between the two doctrines.

* * *

A trilogy of Supreme Court cases involving water rights provides guidance on the demarcation between regulatory and physical takings analysis with respect to these rights. In International Paper Co. v. United States, 282 U.S. 399 (1931), the United States, during World War I, issued a requisition order for all of the hydroelectric power of the Niagara Falls Power Company (Niagara Power). Id. at 405. At the time that the United States' order was issued, Niagara Power leased a portion of its water to International Paper Company (International Paper), which diverted the water via a canal to its mill. Id. at 404–05. In response to the United States' direction to "cut off the water being taken" by International Paper to increase power production, Niagara Power terminated the diversion of water to International Paper. Id. at 405–06. This termination resulted in International Paper being unable to operate its mill for nearly nine months. Id. The United States did not take over the operations of either Niagara Power or International Paper, nor did it physically direct the flow of the water. Instead, the United States caused Niagara Power to stop International Paper from diverting water to its mill so that the water would instead be available for third party use—"private companies for work deemed more useful [by the government] than the manufacture of paper." Id. at 404. This third party use served a public purpose of supplying power for the war effort. The Supreme Court found that the government directly appropriated water that International Paper had a right to use.

In United States v. Gerlach Live Stock Co., 339 U.S. 725 (1950), the claimants held riparian water rights for irrigation of their grasslands by natural seasonal overflow of the San Joaquin River, id. at 729–30. The BOR built Friant Dam, a part of the Central Valley Project, upstream from the claimants' land. Id. at 730, 734. The Friant Dam was built to store high stage river flows which then were "diverted ... through a system of canals and sold to irrigate more than a million acres of land." Id. at 729. As a result, "a dry river bed" was left downstream of the dam, and the overflow irrigation of the claimants' lands virtually ceased. Id. at 729–30. Thus, the United States caused water to be physically diverted away from the claimants for third party use—delivery under water contracts. The Friant Dam served a public purpose of "mak[ing] water available where it would be of the greatest service." Id. at 728. The Supreme Court analyzed the government's action as a physical taking.

Dugan v. Rank, 372 U.S. 609 (1963), similarly involved claims arising out of the United States' physical diversion of water for third party use, by the Friant Dam. In Dugan, landowners along the San Joaquin River, owning riparian and other water rights in the river, alleged that the BOR's storage of water upstream behind Friant Dam left insufficient water in the river to supply their water rights. Id. at 614, 616. The Supreme Court agreed, and analyzed the government's physical appropriation of water as a physical taking.

We agree with both parties that, in each of these cases, the United States physically diverted the water, or caused water to be diverted away from the plaintiffs' property. We also agree that in each of these cases the diverted water was dedicated to government use or third party use which served a public purpose. Additionally, we agree that the Supreme Court analyzed the government action in each of these cases as a per se taking. Finally, we concur with the government that our focus should primarily be on the character of the government action when determining whether a physical or regulatory taking has occurred.

The government contends that this trio of Supreme Court cases is distinguishable from the instant case because they involve direct appropriations of property as opposed to restrictions on use of natural resources. The government argues that it did not seize, appropriate, divert, or impound any water, but merely required water to be left in the stream.

Here, the government admits for the purposes of summary judgment that it required Casitas to build the fish ladder facility, which is a man-made concrete structure that was not a portion of the existing Ventura River. * * *

The government also admits that the operation of the fish ladder required water, which prior to the fish ladder's construction flowed into the Casitas Reservoir via the Robles–Casitas Canal, to be physically diverted away from the Robles–Casitas Canal and into the fish ladder. Specifically, the government admits that the operation of the fish ladder includes closing the overshot gate, which is located in the Robles–Casitas Canal, and that the closure of this gate causes water that would have gone into the Casitas Reservoir via the Robles–Casitas Canal to be diverted into the fish ladder. These admissions make clear that the government did not merely require some water to remain in stream, but instead actively caused the physical diversion of water away from the Robles–Casitas Canal—after the water had left the Ventura River and was in the Robles–Casitas Canal—and towards the fish ladder, thus reducing Casitas' water supply.

The active hand of the government was also at play in International Paper, where the Court remarked that "[t]he petitioner's right was to the use of the water; and when all the water that it used was withdrawn from the petitioner's mill and turned elsewhere by government requisition for the production of power it is hard to see what more the Government could do to take the use." 282 U.S. at 407. Similar to the petitioner in International Paper, Casitas' right was to the use of the water, and its water was withdrawn from the Robles–Casitas Canal and turned elsewhere (to the fish ladder) by the government. Although Casitas' right was only partially impaired, in the physical taking jurisprudence any impairment is sufficient. See Tahoe–Sierra, 535 U.S. at 322. The Supreme Court in Dugan held that a partial impairment of the petitioner's water rights was a taking,

> Having plenary power to seize the whole of respondents' rights in carrying out the congressional mandate, the federal officers a fortiori had authority to seize less. It follows that if any part of respondents' claimed water rights were invaded it amounted to an interference therewith and a taking thereof. . . .

372 U.S. at 623. Therefore, we conclude that the government physically appropriated water that Casitas held a usufructuary right in.

The government also argues that, in contrast to the trilogy of Supreme Court cases, here, the United States did not appropriate the water for its own use or for use by a third party. We find this argument unpersuasive. The government, by passing the ESA, has recognized the importance of protecting endangered species. In fact, the purpose of the ESA is express in the statute itself. 16 U.S.C. § 1531(a)–(c). Specifically, Congress found that "species of fish . . . have been so depleted in numbers that they are in danger of or threatened with extinction" and that "these species of fish . . . are of esthetic, ecological, educational, historical, recreational, and scientific value to the Nation and its people." Id. § 1531(a)(2)–(3). Congress also found that "encouraging . . . interested parties . . . to develop and maintain conservation programs . . . is a key to meeting the Nation's international commitments and to better safeguarding, for the benefit of all citizens, the Nation's heritage in fish. . . ." Id. § 1531(a)(5). In light of these findings, there is little doubt that the preservation of the habitat of an endangered species is for government and third party use—the public—which serves a public purpose. * * *

Finally, the government attempts to distinguish this trio of Supreme Court cases on the basis that the physical diversion of water by the government in each of these cases was part of an undisputed exercise of the United States' eminent domain powers. The government argues that physical takings are usually obvious and that the government's exercise of eminent domain powers or alternatively the government's offer to purchase the rights in advance is evidence of the obviousness of the physical taking in International Paper, Dugan, and Gerlach. Oral Arg. 34:00–34:23; see, e.g., Tahoe–Sierra, 535 U.S. at 322 n. 17 ("When the government . . . physically appropriates the property, the fact of a taking is typically obvious and undisputed."). However, at the time International Paper, Dugan, and

Gerlach were litigated, the government did not appear to take the position that the takings of water rights in those cases were obvious. * * *

Further, the government argues that the installation and operation of the fish ladder was merely a use restriction on a natural resource, and therefore governed by the regulatory taking jurisprudence. Specifically, the government argues the instant case is similar to United States v. Central Eureka Mining Co., 357 U.S. 155 (1958), where the government issued an order requiring a gold mine to cease operations, and to Penn Central, where the government restricted a building owner's private airspace. In both of these cases, the Supreme Court analyzed the government action as a regulatory taking. The government contrasts the instant case with Pewee Coal, where the government took actual possession and control of a coal mine, and United States v. Causby, 328 U.S. 256 (1946), where government planes utilized private airspace. In each of these cases the Supreme Court analyzed the government's action as a physical taking.

The government is correct that, similar to the regulatory takings cases involving restrictions on use, the owner of the property in this case also had an expectation that was later altered by government action. However, in contrast to the restriction of use cases cited by the government, this case involves physical appropriation by the government. The United States actively caused water to be physically diverted away from Casitas after the water had left the Ventura River and was in the Robles–Casitas Canal. Like Pewee Coal, the government, in this case, took physical possession of the water. By its own admission, the government required construction of the fish ladder and compelled the water to be rerouted to the fish ladder in order for the fish ladder to operate. This is no different than the government piping the water to a different location. It is no less a physical appropriation. This is not like Central Eureka Mining, where the government merely ordered the gold mine to cease operations. 357 U.S. at 165–66. In Central Eureka Mining, the Court expressly distinguished the physical takings cases on the grounds that "[t]he Government had no need for the gold or the gold mines." Id. at 166. The government simply halted mining; it did not commandeer the gold for a public use. At the end of the regulatory restriction, the gold mine still had all of its gold and machinery. In this case, in contrast, the government did commandeer the water for a public use-preservation of an endangered species. When the government diverted the water to the fish ladder, it took Casitas' water. The water, and Casitas' right to use that water, is forever gone. As such, this case is more closely analogous to Pewee Coal and Causby than Penn Central and Central Eureka Mining.

* * *

Moreover, in the instant case, the government admissions make clear that the United States did not just require that water be left in the river, but instead physically caused Casitas to divert water away from the Robles–Casitas Canal and towards the fish ladder. Where the government plays an active role and physically appropriates property, the per se taking analysis applies.

We conclude by noting that the Supreme Court's decision in Tahoe–Sierra did not depart from the substantial body of precedent dictating that the government's physical appropriation of a portion of a water right is compensable. While Tahoe–Sierra emphasized the sharp distinction between physical and regulatory takings, it did not involve a claim of physical taking, nor did it involve water rights. Id. at 322–23. See Steven J. Eagle, Planning Moratoria and Regulatory Takings: The Supreme Court's Fairness Mandate Benefits Landowners, 31 Fla. St. U.L.Rev. 429, 443–55 (2004) (arguing that Tahoe–Sierra decoupled physical and regulatory takings analysis). Tahoe–Sierra did not overrule, modify, or even mention the holdings of International Paper, Dugan, or Gerlach. As such, these cases remain good law. Tahoe–Sierra was a regulatory case—due to a moratorium the landowner was unable to develop his land for thirty-two months. The government in Tahoe–Sierra did not physically appropriate anything, but rather restricted the owner's use of his land. The landowner was prohibited from developing the land during that time. The land itself was in no way changed or diminished due to this restriction, and, as the court held, "the property will recover value as soon as the prohibition is lifted." Tahoe–Sierra, 535 U.S. at 332. The owner's land was the same after the moratorium as it was before. The regulatory restriction merely maintained the status quo.

In this case, in contrast, the water that is diverted away from the Robles–Diversion Canal is permanently gone. Casitas will never, at the end of any period of time, be able to get that water back. The character of the government action was a physical diversion for a public use—the protection of an endangered species. The government-caused diversion to the fish ladder has permanently taken that water away from Casitas. This is not temporary, and it does not leave the right in the same state it was before the government action. The water, and Casitas' right to use that water, is forever gone. Unlike Tahoe–Sierra, the government, in this case, directly appropriated Casitas' water for its own use—for the preservation of an endangered species. The government requirement that Casitas build the fish ladder and divert water to it should be analyzed under the physical takings rubric.

For the foregoing reasons, we affirm the district court's grant of summary judgment in favor of the government with respect to Casitas' breach of contract claim and reverse the district court's grant of partial summary judgment in favor of the government with respect to a taking under the Fifth Amendment. We remand for further proceedings consistent with this opinion.[17]

---

17. In the Court of Federal Claims, Casitas conceded that if the governmental actions at issue in this case were not analyzed under a physical taking rubric, it could not prevail. At the same time, the government made certain conditional concessions in order to put the case in a posture for summary judgment. (For example, the government conceded for the limited purpose of summary judgment that Casitas possessed a cognizable property interest.) The court thereafter granted summary judgment in favor of the government on the takings issue after determining that the governmental actions at is-

■ MAYER, CIRCUIT JUDGE, dissenting-in-part.

In my view, the trial court correctly decided that the water use requirements imposed by the federal government on Casitas do not constitute per se takings of property requiring compensation under the Takings Clause. Because Tahoe–Sierra Preservation Council v. Tahoe Regional Planning Activity, 535 U.S. 302 (2002), controls the question of whether the multi-factor inquiry set out in Penn Central Transportation Co. v. New York City, 438 U.S. 104 (1978), is the proper framework for analyzing whether a taking has occurred in this case, I dissent from the majority's contrary decision.

* * *

No physical taking has occurred. First, because Casitas possesses a usufructuary interest in the water and does not actually own the water molecules at issue, it is difficult to imagine how its property interest in the water could be physically invaded or occupied. Cf. United States v. Causby, 328 U.S. 256, 264–66 (1946) (finding a physical taking when the government literally and physically invaded private airspace with its aircraft). Further, the government has not acquired Casitas' water use license. The United States may not make proprietary use of the water denied to Casitas by the ESA, nor may it divert Casitas' use rights to a third party. Rather, the limitation imposed on the total quantity of water available for Casitas' use is directly correlated to the quantity of water needed to remain in the Ventura River's hydrologic cycle to preserve the endangered Southern California steelhead under a public program to promote the common good.
* * *

Here, the government did not invade, seize, convey or convert Casitas' property to consumptive or proprietary use. Rather, it imposed regulatory operating criteria on Casitas' request to comply with the ESA through use of a fish passage facility that returns a specified amount of water diverted from the Ventura River by the Robles Diversion Dam back to its natural flow for the purpose of endangered species preservation. Mere deprivation of water from the owner of water rights without governmental invasion, appropriation or diversion of the water for consumptive or proprietary use does not amount to a physical taking under Tahoe–Sierra. The government's action restricting Casitas' right to make consumptive use of a portion of the water granted by its license is not possessory. See Loretto, 458 U.S. at 440 (stating that the multifactor Penn Central inquiry is generally applicable to nonpossessory governmental activity). Rather, a classic regulatory restraint on natural resource development has occurred.
* * *

sue did not effect a physical taking. We have reversed the grant of summary judgment in favor of the government based solely upon our determination that the governmental actions at issue in this case are properly analyzed under a physical taking rubric. On re- mand, after receiving the views of the parties and ruling on any matters left open during the summary judgment proceedings, the Court of Federal Claims will be in a position to determine the ultimate question of whether a taking occurred in this case. * * *

For this to be a physical taking requires expanding the definition to the point of erasing the line between physical and regulatory takings. Indeed, any property use restriction—whether on land, air, or water, and whether temporary or permanent—deprives the owner of a pre-existing right to develop at least a portion of his property for certain economic uses. Yet in Tahoe–Sierra, the Supreme Court nevertheless reaffirmed the constitutional distinction between physical acquisitions and regulatory restrictions. 535 U.S. at 321–22. Here, compliance with Section 9 of the ESA ultimately requires Casitas to leave more water in the river, thus augmenting the downstream river flow essential for protection of the endangered steelhead trout. In cooperation with the Bureau of Reclamation, Casitas can presumably accomplish this in any number of ways; for example, by closing the Robles–Casitas Canal entrance gates and allowing fish passage through openings in the Robles Diversion Dam, or by permitting some of the water diverted by the dam to return to the river through a fish passage facility. To differentiate between these two illustrative approaches on a deceptively simple theory of "diversion" creates a perverse system of incentives, whereby form is elevated over substance, because self-selected methods of regulatory compliance can be manipulated and negotiated to arrive at preferred Fifth Amendment results. According to this pretextual logic, in the first example, water never leaves the river's flow, so there is no "diversion." In the second example, Casitas allows some already diverted water to return to the river, creating a "re-diversion." The result is the same, and should not lead to a difference in the characterization of the activity: a private property owner's choice of prophylactic actions cannot dictate whether a future takings claim will be physical or regulatory. This is particularly salient because it was Casitas who initiated Reclamation's Section 7 ESA consultations with the National Marine Fisheries Service and suggested use of the fish passage facility to ensure ESA compliance. Presumably, this approach represented the most economical way to comply with the ESA while still permitting Casitas to divert its maximum allowable allotment of water.

* * * It is logically incongruent to analyze ESA-based land use restrictions as regulatory takings, and ESA-based water use restrictions as physical takings. The government is not appropriating or taking possession of Casitas' property, but rather is prohibiting Casitas from making private use of a certain amount of the river's natural flow under a public program to promote the common good. Labeling such an action a physical taking blurs the line Tahoe–Sierra carefully draws between physical and regulatory takings.

NOTES

1. Is the dissent correct in arguing that the majority opinion could lead to unjustifiably different results depending on whether the facts involve a "diversion" of water for environmental purposes? Is the majority correct in finding that by ensuring water for endangered species, the government appropriated water for its own use, similar to the requisition of water to generate power for the war effort in *International Paper*? Which opinion has the better argument on whether the government's action is a physical occupation of property?

2. The *Casitas* plaintiffs conceded that they could not prove a regulatory taking under *Penn Central*, thus putting all their chips on the physical takings analysis. In an earlier California case, however, a landowner plaintiff argued a taking of water rights under several theories, including *Penn Central*. The facts were very different from those of *Tulare* and subsequent federal cases:

> Allegretti owns property in Imperial County that overlies groundwater basins, which are accessed by Allegretti and its farmer tenant for irrigation purposes via deep-water wells and pumps. In October 1994, Allegretti filed with County an application for a conditional use permit to redrill an inoperable well, one of several existing wells on the property, so that it could add approximately 200 acres of land for crop production. Allegretti's tenant used the remaining operating wells to actively farm portions of the land between 1993 and 2004. In June 1997, County approved the conditional use permit for Allegretti's redrilling project subject to certain conditions, including one limiting Allegretti's draw of groundwater to 12,000 acre-feet per year from all production wells on site. Allegretti did not record the permit and it never took effect. Allegretti acknowledges there are no present restrictions on the use of water from its existing wells.

Allegretti & Co. v. County of Imperial, 138 Cal.App.4th 1261, 1267, 42 Cal.Rptr.3d 122 (2006). After rejecting claims for a physical taking and a *per se* regulatory taking based on a total loss of economic value (as in *Lucas*), the court analyzed plaintiffs' case under *Penn Central*:

> When a regulation does not result in a physical invasion and does not deprive the property owner of all economic use of the property, a reviewing court must evaluate the regulation in light of the Penn Central factors. (Kavanau v. Santa Monica Rent Control Board (1997) 16 Cal.4th 761, 775, 66 Cal.Rptr.2d 672, 941 P.2d 851 (Kavanau).) "Penn Central emphasized three factors in particular: (1) '[t]he economic impact of the regulation on the claimant'; (2) 'the extent to which the regulation has interfered with distinct investment-backed expectations'; and (3) 'the character of the governmental action.'" (Kavanau, 16 Cal.4th at p. 775, 66 Cal.Rptr.2d 672, 941 P.2d 851; accord, Lingle, *supra*, 544 U.S. at pp. 538–539; Palazzolo v. Rhode Island, *supra*, 533 U.S. at p. 633.)
>
> * * *
>
> Applying the three Penn Central factors relied upon by Allegretti does not persuade us to find County's action constitutes a regulatory taking. Importantly, the basis for this factual inquiry "is the owner's entire property holdings at the time of the alleged taking, not just the adversely affected portion." (Buckley v. California Coastal Com. (1998) 68 Cal.App.4th 178, 193, 80 Cal.Rptr.2d 562, citing Keystone Bitumi-

nous Coal Assn. v. DeBenedictis (1987) 480 U.S. 470, 497.) Thus the relevant parcel is Allegretti's 2400 acres, and not merely its right to draw water from it. (E.g., Florida Rock Indus. Inc. v. United States (Fed.Cl.1999) 45 Fed.Cl. 21, 33.)

Beginning with the last mentioned Penn Central factor, the character of the governmental action, County's action did not physically invade or appropriate Allegretti's property or groundwater. Accordingly, that factor does not support a taking. (See Connolly v. Pension Ben. Guar. Corp. (1986) 475 U.S. 211, 225.)

As for the economic impact of County's regulation, Allegretti concedes it did not establish the precise amount of such an impact through expert testimony at trial, but maintains such testimony is unnecessary because it is plain that County's action has restricted Allegretti's ability to draw water to the capacity of its existing wells, thus limiting its farm production to between 400 and 800 acres of a 2,400 parcel. Allegretti criticizes the trial court's reliance on the fact Allegretti was receiving rental income on a portion of the property, claiming the preservation of "some economically beneficial use" is not sufficient to constitute a defense in the County's favor.

In addressing economic impact, we ask whether the regulation "unreasonably impair[s] the value or use of [the] property" in view of the owners' general use of their property. (E.g., PruneYard Shopping Center v. Robins (1980) 447 U.S. 74, 83.) Not only is the use to which the property owner puts his or her property important, but the economic impact needs to be considered in the context of other laws and regulatory schemes. (See Connolly v. Pension Benefit Guar. Corp., *supra*, 475 U.S. 211, 225–226 [evaluating economic impact of imposing withdrawal fees on employers who leave pension funds within context of entire ERISA scheme].) We note the U.S. Supreme Court has repeatedly upheld land use regulations that destroy or adversely affect real property interests. (Keystone Bituminous Coal Assn. v. DeBenedictis, *supra*, 480 U.S. at p. 489, fn. 18.)

Allegretti has not demonstrated any economic impact from County's 12,000 acre-feet per year limitation other than unspecific lay testimony regarding reduced profits via a below-market rental rate or diminution in value as a result of its inability to use the entirety of its 2400–acre property for farming. It is well established that mere diminution in value of property, however serious, does not constitute a taking. (Concrete Pipe and Products of California, Inc. v. Construction Laborers Pension Trust for Southern Cal. (1993) 508 U.S. 602, 645, citing Village of Euclid v. Ambler Realty Co. (1926) 272 U.S. 365 [approximately 75% diminution in value]; Hadacheck v. Sebastian (1915) 239 U.S. 394, 405, [92.5% diminution]; see also Penna. Coal Co. v. Mahon (1922) 260 U.S. 393, 413 ["[g]overnment hardly could go on if to some extent values incident to property could not be diminished without paying for every such change in the general law"].) Under Penn Central, regulations that prohibit the "most beneficial use of the property" or which prohibit "a beneficial use to which individual parcels had previously been devoted and thus cause [ ] substantial individualized harm" are not takings. (Penn Central, *supra*, 438 U.S. at p. 125.) Like most land use regulations, the ordinance may have "the inevitable effect of reducing the value of regulated properties," but even a "significant diminution in value is insufficient to establish a confiscatory taking." (Terminal Plaza Corp. v. City and County of San Francisco (1986) 177 Cal.App.3d 892, 912, 223 Cal.Rptr. 379, quoting Griffin Development Co. v. City of Oxnard (1985) 39 Cal.3d 256, 267, 217 Cal.Rptr. 1, 703 P.2d 339.)

Allegretti has not demonstrated compensable interference with "distinct investment backed expectations" (Penn Central, *supra*, 438 U.S. at p. 124; Kavanau, *supra*, 16 Cal.4th at p. 781, 66 Cal.Rptr.2d 672, 941 P.2d 851) by County's 12,000 acre-feet per year limitation. The sole evidence on which it relies is Joe Allegretti's testimony that he purchased the land for $2.5 million and made improvements with the expectation he could farm all 2,400 acres and make a substantial profit off the investment. It also points to Joe Allegretti's testimony that he could farm more acres if he had more operable wells, and testimony from Allegretti's tenant that he intended to farm all 1,686 acres, but could not because there was not enough water. Citing City of Barstow v. Mojave Water Agency, *supra*, 23 Cal.4th at p. 1224, 99 Cal.Rptr.2d 294, 5 P.3d 853, Allegretti asserts it "has the right to put to use as much of that water as it needs in order to irrigate its cropland."

There are several flaws in this argument. First, the evidence does not reveal distinct, as opposed to abstract, expectations. Joe Allegretti's testimony was only that he had purchased the farm having been given "lots of reassurances that it could be a viable farming operation" (emphasis added) and that his investment had not yet reached expectation. A " 'reasonable investment-backed expectation' " must be more than a " 'unilateral expectation or an abstract need.' " (Ruckelshaus v. Monsanto Co., *supra*, 467 U.S. at pp. 1005–1006.) Further, as our high court in City of Barstow acknowledged, although an overlying user such as Allegretti may have superior rights to others lacking legal priority, Allegretti's water "right" is nonetheless restricted to a reasonable beneficial use consistent with article X, section 2 of the California Constitution. (City of Barstow v. Mojave Water Agency, *supra*, 23 Cal.4th at p. 1240, 99 Cal.Rptr.2d 294, 5 P.3d 853.) Allegretti's claim to an unlimited right to use as much water as it needs to irrigate flies in the face of that standard, and it has not pointed to any evidence in the record that its proposed irrigation of all 2400 acres would be reasonable within the meaning of the constitutional restriction. Second, Allegretti's claim is essentially that it has lost "at least the potential for substantial profits." Allegretti's claim of loss of anticipated profits or gain is not compensable, as it "demonstrate[s] no more than a possible restriction upon more economic uses of its property." (Terminal Plaza Corp. v. City and County of San Francisco

(1986) 177 Cal.App.3d 892, 912, 223 Cal.Rptr. 379.) Because of its very uncertainty, the interest in anticipated gains has traditionally been viewed as less compelling than other property-related interests. (Andrus v. Allard, *supra*, 444 U.S. at p. 66.) For the foregoing reasons, Allegretti's claim of a regulatory taking under Penn Central is not persuasive.

Id. at 1277–1280.

QUESTIONS

1. Which of the following regulatory actions could result in a compensable taking under relevant Supreme Court cases? Under *Casitas*?

a. A senior water rights holder "calls" an upstream junior, demanding that the junior forgo diverting water because the senior needs to satisfy earlier priority uses. The state engineer refuses to enforce the senior right against the junior because the senior could invest in a well to pump groundwater that would draw the same amount of water from the same basic source. The result is to render a costly surface diversion works worthless and to require the senior to make a large expenditure for the well. See Alamosa–La Jara Water Users Protection Ass'n v. Gould, 674 P.2d 914 (Colo.1983), *supra* p. 336.

b. A farmer, who has been using a water right to irrigate the same fields for many years, is ordered to cease using the water. The fields contain highly saline soils and the return flows pollute the stream beyond legislatively adopted water quality standards.

c. A farmer sells a senior water right to a chemical company, but the change of use is refused because the chemical company's return flow will pollute the stream.

d. The legislature passes a law requiring minimum streamflows in all streams valuable as public fisheries. The owner of a hydroelectric dam is required by law to bypass half the water historically used to generate power in order to protect fish populations in the river.

e. The law referred to in d results in an order to remove the dam entirely to avoid total destruction of the fishery.

f. A new water quality law requires limitation of water uses that significantly diminish water quality. A senior irrigator of hay meadows has long diverted much of the flow of a creek just above a natural salt seep. The diminished flow is inadequate to dilute the salty water and the stream is rendered useless for fifty miles below that point. The senior user is ordered to cease the diversion. This incidentally allows dozens of junior agricultural and municipal uses to flourish in the fifty mile stretch and for fish life to be reestablished.

g. Would it make any difference in f if the primary purpose of the law was not to improve water quality but to expand beneficial uses (agriculture, municipal, fish and wildlife, recreation)?

CHAPTER SIX

GROUNDWATER MANAGEMENT

Our need for water—for good, cool mountain water—was very great indeed. Many of the folks had heard of "Water Witches" who could locate underground streams by means of a forked stick, so when one came to town and persuaded the Bishop and several other leading brethren to go with him to run some tests, all were pleased when the forked stick would turn and point downward at the same approximate point in the wash, indicating that there had to be an underground stream along that line * * *. The salesman talked of a gushing stream of clear, cool mountain water from the snows that fell around the Noon Peak. * * * At last they struck mud! Such an excitement as went through the town! When the first buckets of muddy water came out, the workers told themselves that they just hadn't hit the main stream yet. But another day's work convinced them all: the water was brackish like slough water—totally unfit to drink!

Juanita Brooks, Quicksand and Cactus: A Memoir of the Southern Mormon Frontier 8–9 (1982).

This comic but sad tale illustrates an important problem in groundwater law: initial allocation was based on myths rather than geohydrology.[1] Even in the pre-enlightened seventeenth century, scientists did not think that groundwater was derived from rainfall because the supply was assumed to be insufficient and the ground to be too impervious. Ironically, a French lawyer, Pierre Perrault, was the first person to posit a clear understanding of the hydrologic cycle. His studies of the Seine River drainage basin, published in 1674, confirmed that rainfall was the sole source of surface and subsurface flows. David Keith Todd, Groundwater Hydrology 2–3 (1959). Unfortunately for the development of the law, groundwater was early subdivided into three arbitrary and unscientific categories: artesian, percolating, and underground watercourses. Leading water attorney Raphael J. Moses attributes the tripartite division to Clesson S. Kinney as reflected in volume two of his treatise, Law of Irrigation and Water Rights 2095 (2d ed. 1912). Raphael J. Moses, *The Law of Groundwater—Does Modern Buried Treasure Create a New Breed of Pirates?*, 11 Rocky Mtn. Min. L. Inst. 277 (1966).

The laws governing groundwater use are important because groundwater is an important source of supply for municipal, industrial use, and

---

1. Water witches or dowsers are still active, especially in drought-stricken areas. Jesse McKinley, Parched Californians Feel Pull of "Witches" and Forked Sticks, The New York Times, p.1, col. 4, October 9, 2008.

irrigation in many parts of the country. In addition, the "hidden" nature of the resource makes it more difficult to impose conservation regimes in areas where use exceeds recharge rates. The United States Geological Survey estimated that 84,500 million gallons per day of groundwater were withdrawn in 2000,of which 99% was freshwater., Estimated Use of Water in the United States in 2000, U.S. Geological Survey Circular 1268, at 4 (1998). Surface withdrawals accounted for 323,000 million gallons per day, but in areas such as Arizona and Hawai'i, with few surface resources, groundwater is a very important source of supply. In many other areas of the country, contaminated surface waters or other constraints on surface water use make groundwater a critical resource.

The lack of understanding of the nature of groundwater resources has been an impediment to sound policymaking. Different rules have attached to different classes of water, not necessarily based on the hydrologic effects of their withdrawal on surface or other groundwater sources. As a result, it has been difficult for courts and legislatures to develop efficient and fair allocation rules and to coordinate surface and groundwater rights.

Some water users dependent on surface supplies have found them depleted by groundwater pumpers, but have lacked the kind of legal protection they would have if someone interfered with their above-ground diversions. For instance, a water user sunk a shallow well in a small island in the middle of the Platte River that would diminish the water available to users whose surface diversions were downstream. Senior users alleged that the pumper interfered with their rights. But the Nebraska Supreme Court held that the state's prior appropriation law did not extend to "groundwater." Metropolitan Utils. Dist. of Omaha v. Merritt Beach Co., 140 N.W.2d 626 (Neb. 1966). *See also* Spear T Ranch, Inc. v. Knaub, 269 Neb. 177, 691 N.W.2d 116 (2005), where the Nebraska Supreme Court held that surface water appropriation rules do not apply to conflicts between surface and groundwater users. This problem is discussed in more detail at pages 595–598, *infra*.

Some groundwater resources are essentially nonrenewable in time frames that are within the reach of water managers and policymakers. Many important groundwater deposits may be replaced only over extended periods, refilling perhaps only in geologic time. Therefore, pumping from them is essentially mining a finite resource. Most states lack adequate laws to deal wisely with nonrenewable groundwater. If pumpers are allowed to take groundwater out of an aquifer based solely on priority (a rule that may be reasonable for a surface source or with hydrologically connected groundwater), a non-renewable aquifer may be depleted by the first few users or it may be physically destroyed if pumping occurs far faster than recharge. If overlying landowners are considered the "owners" of groundwater, they can develop it at rates that may hurt others, perhaps setting off a race among landowners to deplete the aquifer. Neither the rule of priority nor the rule of ownership considers the needs of society.

Generally, groundwater laws have not required pumpers to compare the present benefits of extraction to the benefits of deferred extraction in order to minimize the overall costs of production and maximize the value of the resource in the future. Many state laws do not even discern whether groundwater sources are essentially renewable or nonrenewable, let alone determine a safe yield that has both scientific validity and economic rationality, based on the length of time it will take to deplete the resource.

Another physical reality that has been ignored in groundwater management has been the connection between contamination of groundwater and how or when groundwater is pumped. At one extreme, there are some states that allocate rights to use groundwater without regard to whether the water is safe to use and without limitations that will protect an aquifer from contamination. Thus, pumpers may pierce more than one aquifer and allow polluted water from one to migrate through the well shaft into a pure source. And pumping rates may be set without regard to rates of natural recharge so that water is withdrawn so fast that salt water from a nearby sea or a contamination plume from a pollution source is drawn into, and destroys, a good source. Thus legal and administrative dichotomies between groundwater allocation and protection of groundwater quality also create obstacles to sound resource management.

Groundwater management involves two basic issues: (1) What protections should be afforded to competing pumpers? and (2) What should be the allowable rate of extraction? The former issue has received more attention, and consequently, has often determined the answer to the latter. Groundwater allocation, then, has been approached largely as a tort issue among holders, or prospective holders, of property rights. In humid regions, like the eastern United States, the common law has dealt principally with the conflicts that have arisen between two neighbors. However, as some groundwater sources have begun to prove unreliable, we are beginning to challenge the assumption that judicial allocation among individuals is adequate to determine access and the scope of use of the resource.

The Report of the National Water Commission, Water Policies for the Future 232 (1973), summarized the major modern management problems:

> (1) integrating management of surface water and groundwater, (2) depletion of groundwater aquifers at rates exceeding recharge (often referred to as the "mining" of groundwater), and (3) impairment of groundwater quality. Lesser, though important, problems are also considered: accelerating collection of groundwater data together with fuller and more meaningful interpretation of it.

How these issues are addressed is tremendously important to the public. Over 24 percent of all freshwater supplies in the United States comes from groundwater. Estimated Use of Water in the United States in 2000, U.S. Geological Survey Circular 1268, 6 (2007). Agricultural irrigation uses 68 percent of all groundwater produced. *Id.* At 9. Remarkably, in recent years about a quarter of all the groundwater withdrawals for western agriculture were overdrafts (*i.e.*, in excess of annual precipitation and natural recharge). James Wilson, Groundwater: A Non–Technical Guide 32 (1982). The rate of growth in the quantities of groundwater used for irrigation began to decline in 1975, reflecting the higher costs of pumping due to rising electric rates and fuel prices and the lowered groundwater levels in some places. Municipal and industrial uses of groundwater, however, have increased 15% since 1975. Conservation Foundation, America's Water: Current Trends and Emerging Issues 5–10 (1984). Increasingly, agricultural uses come into conflict with growing municipal demands for groundwater as deep, high capacity wells draw down aquifers and render wells of farmers and small domestic users inadequate. As southeastern and midwestern farmers invest in supplemental irrigation equipment, heavier pumping occurs and conflicts among them intensify. J.W. Looney, *Modification of Arkansas Water Law: Issues and Alternatives,* 38 Ark. L. Rev. 221 (1984). Resource managers consequently have begun to cope with the question of pumping rates as an issue in which there is a broad public interest.

What kind of institutions should be used to allocate groundwater basins efficiently and fairly? Economists usually answer by suggesting a property rights regime. One argument is that well-defined, enforceable, and transferable property rights will tend to allocate basins efficiently because market prices will emerge and make owners aware of the costs of wasting water:

> Definition and enforcement are necessary to give individuals the incentive to use water efficiently. In order for an exchange to take place, traders must have some idea of what rights are included. Less will be paid for rights that are not well defined and enforced, and in the extreme no trade will occur. * * *

> The transferability of property rights ensures that individuals will take into account the opportunity costs of their actions. As long as individuals are free to buy and sell water rights, market prices will emerge, making owners aware of the cost of wasting water. If rights are not transferable, however, the fact that water has more valuable alternative uses will make little difference; the owner will not be able to sell the rights and capitalize on these higher valued uses.

Terry L. Anderson et al., *Privatizing Groundwater Basins: A Model and Its Application,* in Water Rights: Scarce Resource Allocation, Bureaucracy, and the Environment 223, 227 (Terry L. Anderson ed., 1983).

While the argument for addressing groundwater management by allocation of transferable property rights seems compelling, it may not work as well in practice as in theory. Successful resource management may depend on the initial distribution of property rights, the interrelationship between laws allocating surface and groundwater, and the institutional ability to consolidate or coordinate the management of groundwater throughout all or part of an aquifer. Unless rights are carefully defined, the creation of private rights to use groundwater may lead—as it did at great cost in oil and gas—to a race to develop shallow, high pressure aquifers first.

An alternative approach is to allocate rights in groundwater by assigning rights to overlying landowners. The result of this system may be to allow a few large landowners to monopolize an otherwise public resource.

Unless controls are placed on the manner and rates of pumping by the overlying landowner, rapid depletion of a resource that could be used by the larger community in the future in conjunction with surface water resources may result.

The doctrine of prior appropriation is a third method of allocating groundwater rights. It assigns rights based on existing uses that must be respected by others. But, it is not as well-suited to groundwater allocation as it is to surface water allocation. If the rights of the senior are absolutely protected from any interference, as are surface rights, many aquifers would be limited to a single pumper. Almost every extraction of groundwater potentially affects the level of water in the aquifer and arguably could affect every other pumper. For this reason, most states allow some junior interference with senior pumpers in contrast to the administration of surface priorities. The standard is the familiar "reasonableness" limitation.

Recognition of the special nature of groundwater has led many states to the conclusion that it should be managed as a common resource and administered under rules that respect a variety of public and private concerns. Rights can be defined to optimize the use of available resources over time. Moreover, water managers are recognizing the advantages of integrating plans for surface water development with groundwater management plans.

The problem of groundwater quality is becoming more important with the realization that a contaminated aquifer is tantamount to a depleted aquifer. Federal laws now ban most land disposal of hazardous wastes, regulate deep-well injection of such wastes, and provide for cleaning up existing disposal sites. Control of non-hazardous wastes is largely left to the states. Historically, states did not control groundwater contamination to the extent that they did surface pollution. An exception is New York, which has long required permits to drill wells on Long Island to minimize the effects of salt water intrusion. N.Y. Envtl. Conserv. L. § 15–1527 (McKinney 1997). However, in recent years, federal statutes such as the Safe Drinking Water Act, discussed *infra* p. 689, have resulted in more aggressive state regulatory programs to address groundwater contamination, although problems such as nitrate contamination from agricultural run-off, suburban lawns, golf courses, and vehicle emissions remain regulatory challenges.

The introductory materials in this chapter are designed to provide a basic understanding of groundwater hydrology and the economic and legal barriers to the creation of efficient allocation regimes. We then turn to an examination of various regimes for allocating groundwater rights. Consider whether: (1) the property rights in groundwater that the courts have recognized result in the efficient allocation of the resource, or (2) an administrative allocation regime is superior to a property rights regime.

The public's interest in maintaining a reliable supply of groundwater has influenced modern allocation schemes. Whatever fundamental principles may guide the allocation of property rights and determine the respective rights of competing users, there are broader concerns with the long-term security and quality of groundwater supplies. Section B describes the methods that have been used to allocate rights in groundwater to individuals and to resolve claims among them. Section C explores schemes for regulating production of groundwater to ensure that public concerns with its protection and long-range use are satisfied, consistent with the rights allocated to individuals.

A.   INTRODUCTION TO THE GEOLOGY AND DYNAMICS OF GROUNDWATER

E.C. Pielou, Fresh Water
5–17 (1998).

2.1   Water Young and Old

* * *

All the water below the ground is called, straightforwardly enough, *underground water.*

It occupies a variety of different underground spaces, ranging from tiny pores in the soil and narrow cracks in the bedrock, to enormous limestone caverns. But not all of it is "groundwater." The word *groundwater* has a narrower meaning: it applies only to water that saturates the ground, filling all the available spaces. The ground containing groundwater is known as the *saturated zone,* and the water's upper surface is the *water table.* Unless the water table is at ground level—as it is in swamps and marshes—there is an *unsaturated zone* above the water table in which the pores and cracks are only partially water-filled; they contain some air as well.

* * *

Although all the water below the water table counts as groundwater, it isn't all of one kind: there are three different types. By far the most abundant is *meteoric water;* this is the groundwater that circulates as part of the water cycle. (Its name is related to *meteorology*—nothing to do with meteors.) A small proportion of the water deep underground does not circulate, however, and this non-circulating groundwater is of two kinds.

One kind is *fossil water* (sometimes called *connate* water): it is water that became trapped in ancient sediments when they were laid down, and that remained trapped as the sediment hardened into sedimentary rock.

The other kind is *juvenile water*: it is water given off by subterranean molten rock (*magma*), the material known as lava if it emerges from a volcano, or that forms igneous rocks if it crystallizes deep underground. Water is often an ingredient of magma, and when it cools underground, the water separates from the remaining ingredients to form pockets of liquid inside a mass of hard, cold, crystalline rock.

2.2 Water in "Solid" Ground

Ordinary, meteoric groundwater is water that has soaked into the ground from the surface, from precipitation (rain and melting snow) and from lakes and streams. There it remains, sometimes for long periods, before emerging at the surface again. At first thought it seems incredible that there can be enough space, in the "solid" ground underfoot, to hold all this water.

The necessary space is there, however, in many forms. The commonest spaces are those among the particles—sand grains and tiny pebbles—of loose, unconsolidated sand and gravel. Beds of this material, out of sight beneath the soil, are common. They are found wherever fast rivers carrying loads of coarse sediment once flowed. For example, as the great ice sheets that covered northern North America during the last ice age steadily melted away, huge volumes of water flowed from them. The water was always laden with pebbles, gravel, and sand, known as glacial outwash, that was deposited as the flow slowed down.

* * *

* * * Consolidated (or cemented) sediments, too, contain millions of minute water-holding pores. This is because the gaps among the original grains are often not totally plugged with cementing chemicals; also, parts of the original grains may become dissolved by percolating groundwater (which is never as pure as distilled water), either while consolidation is taking place or at any time afterwards. The result is that sandstone, for example, can be as porous as the loose sand from which it was formed.

Thus a proportion of the total volume of any sediment, loose or cemented, consists of empty space. Most crystalline rocks (igneous and metamorphic) are much more solid; a common exception is basalt, a form of solidified volcanic lava, which is sometimes full of tiny bubbles that make it very porous.

The proportion of empty space in a rock is known as its *porosity*. But note that porosity is not the same as *permeability*, which measures the ease with which water can flow through a material; this depends on the sizes of the individual cavities and the crevices linking them (see section 2.3).

Much of the water in a sample of water-saturated sediment or rock will drain from it if the sample is put in a suitable dry place. But some will remain, clinging to all solid surfaces; it is held there by the force of surface tension but for which water would drain instantly from any wet surface, leaving it dry as a duck's back. * * * The total volume of water in the saturated sample must therefore be thought of as consisting of water that can, and water that cannot, drain away.

The relative amount of these two kinds of water varies greatly from one kind of rock or sediment to another, even though their porosities may be the same. What happens depends on pore size; if the pores are large, the water in them will exist as drops too heavy for surface tension to hold, and it will drain away; but if the pores are small enough, the water in them will exist as thin films, too light to overcome the force of surface tension holding them in place: then the water will be firmly held.

For any rock (consolidated or not), the proportion of water in it that can drain away and the proportion that can't are called, respectively, the *specific yield* and the *specific retention* of the rock. Specific yield and specific retention together add to porosity.

* * *

Some generalizations are possible. For example, clay, with the finest particles, is much more porous than gravel, with the coarsest, which seems surprising until you consider the tremendous weight of wet clay. The material with the greatest yield is sand; although it is less porous than clay, it is much less retentive; gravel is still less retentive, but it yields less water than sand because it holds less—its porosity is less.

* * *

2.3   Moving Groundwater

Groundwater is nearly always moving except, perhaps, at great depths. The rate at which it flows varies enormously but is "glacially" slow by surface standards; 30 meters per year is a typical figure. Ten to 15 meters per day counts as very rapid.

Two factors determine the rate at which groundwater flows. First is the nature of the ground itself. It must be *permeable* as well as porous; its pores and cavities must be linked by channels through which water can flow.

* * *

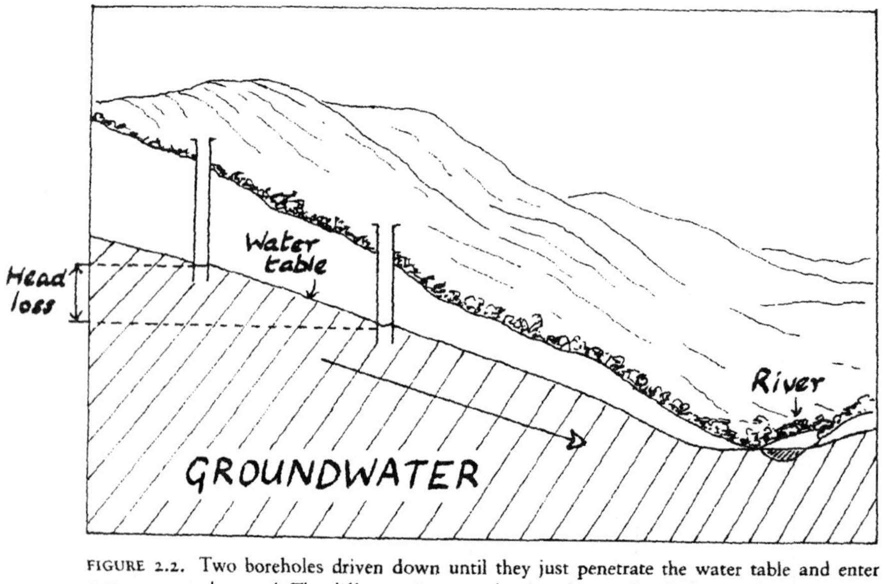

FIGURE 2.2. Two boreholes driven down until they just penetrate the water table and enter water-saturated ground. The difference in water level at the two borehole sites is the head loss between them. The arrow shows the direction of flow of the groundwater.

The second factor determining the rate at which groundwater flows is the strength of the force, or pressure, pushing it. This depends on the *hydraulic head*, or simply the *head*. For example, imagine gently sloping ground with the soil overlying a thick layer of unconsolidated sediments; the sediments hold groundwater (figure 2.2). Imagine that the water table slopes in the same direction as the ground surface above it but much more gently, as would usually be the case. A borehole drilled into the ground anywhere on the slope begins to hold water as soon as it reaches the water table; the height of this water surface above mean sea level is the head.

To judge how the groundwater is moving, you need to compare the heads at two nearby sites. The difference between the heads is the *head loss* between the two sites. Wherever there is a head loss, the groundwater must be flowing toward the site with the lower head. In the example, assume that one borehole is directly downhill of the other; then the head loss divided by the horizontal distance between them is the slope of the water table, known as the *hydraulic gradient*.

The rate at which groundwater flows between the boreholes' sites is found by multiplying the hydraulic gradient by the *hydraulic conductivity* of the material through which the water is flowing. The hydraulic conductivity is the rate (in meters per day) at which water would flow through the material *if* the hydraulic gradient were unity, that is, *if* the water table sloped at an angle of 45. This is a far steeper gradient than would ever be found in nature; hydraulic conductivities are merely numbers allowing the conductivities of different kinds of rocks and sediments to be compared.

* * *

For a great majority of purposes, it is true to say that

Rate of movement = Hydraulic gradient × Hydraulic conductivity

This is the rate of movement of the water as a whole, through the porous ground, and is technically known as the *specific discharge*. It is less than the velocity of the separate tiny "streamlets" flowing through each separate pore.

To consider some numbers, suppose two boreholes are 100 meters apart and the water level in the upper one is two meters above that in the lower one. The head loss is two meters. Therefore, the hydraulic gradient is 0.02, which means that the water table makes an angle of about 1° with the horizontal. If the groundwater is flowing through fine sand with a hydraulic conductivity of 1 meter per day, its rate will be 0.02 × 1 meter/day, that is, 2 centimeters per day.

How fast would the groundwater flow given the same hydraulic gradient but different earth materials? If the material were fine clay, which might have a hydraulic conductivity of 0.1 millimeters per day, the rate would be two micrometers (millionths of a meter) per day. If it were gravel with a hydraulic conductivity of 1,000 meters per day, the rate would be 20 meters per day.

Another way of looking at these flow rates is to consider the time it would take for groundwater to move a distance of 100 meters, again assuming a slope of 1. The times for the clay, the sand, and the gravel are, respectively, 137,000 years, 13.7 years, and 5 days.

* * *

2.4 Aquifers

Many different kinds of sediments and rocks go to make up the ground below the soil, and they are arranged, for the most part, in layers; the layers may be large or small, thick or thin, and can be of varying thickness and tilted at any angle. Intruding into these layers from below are occasional blocks of igneous rock formed of magma that has welled up from a greater depth into the overlying rock and congealed. Each of these different ingredients has its own characteristics so far as water is concerned: in particular, its own specific yield (section 2.2) and its own hydraulic conductivity (section 2.3).

Some layers may be aquifers. An *aquifer* is a body of rock or sediment that holds water in "useful" amounts; that is, the water is abundant enough, and can flow through the ground fast enough, for the aquifer to serve as a natural underground reservoir. Aquifers vary enormously in size and capacity. * * *

* * *

Because of the way sediments and rock strata are layered, it often happens that an aquifer is overlain by a *confining layer*, through which the water in the aquifer cannot escape upward; the confining layer might consist of almost impermeable clay, for example. Or the overlying material may form a so-called *leaky confining layer*, through which water from the aquifer can flow, though much more slowly than through the aquifer itself. Leaky confining layers vary considerably in their leakiness, of course.

An aquifer overlain by a confining layer is a *confined aquifer*, and the water in it behaves differently from that in an *unconfined aquifer* (also called a *water-table aquifer*). An unconfined aquifer is saturated with water up to the level of the water table, and if an open-ended pipe is driven down into it, water will rise in the pipe until the levels coincide inside and out (see section 2.3 and figure 2.2). But if the pipe is driven into an aquifer below a confining layer, water rises in the pipe to a level higher than the top of the aquifer because it is under pressure.

As before, the height of the water in the pipe is described as a head, but now the meaning of the word *head* needs to be pondered. It is less simple than it appears: it has two meanings and implies more than it seems to. It is defined as the *height* of a water surface, which is simply a distance measured in a vertical direction. But it also, implicitly, means *pressure*. In the minds of hydrologists, the notions of pressure and height are interchangeable, and we must consider why this should be.

Suppose you constructed a narrow pipe closed at the bottom by a hinged flap that would open inward when you wanted it to, but not before. Imagine the pipe driven deep into the groundwater. The groundwater exerts pressure on the hinged flap, and now if you open the flap, water will gush up the pipe. When it has come to rest and all is tranquil, visualize the motionless water at the bottom of the pipe, down by the hinged flap; it is *still* under pressure, but now there are equal pressures acting on it both from above and below, which cancel each other out. The upward pressure is the pressure that drove the water up the pipe in the first place: this pressure is still being exerted. The downward pressure is that due to the weight of the water in the pipe. Obviously the two pressures balance each other; if they didn't, the water level in the pipe would rise or fall until they did. The weight of the column of water in the pipe depends on its cross-sectional area as well as its height, of course. The cross-sectional area can be disregarded, however; it makes no difference, because whatever the area, the water in the pipe is pushing against exactly the same area of groundwater. The height alone suffices to measure the pressure.

This, in a nutshell, is why hydrologists use pressure and head (or height) as interchangeable terms. Meteorologists do the same thing, when they use the height of a column of mercury in a barometer as a measure of atmospheric pressure.

A pipe used to find the depth of a water table, or the head at any depth, is called a *piezometer*; the derivation is from the Greek *piezo*, pressure. The amount of water that an unconfined aquifer can hold in storage is found simply by multiplying the saturated volume of the aquifer by the specific yield (see section 2.2) of the aquifer material. The amount that can be held in a confined aquifer is slightly affected by the pressure it is under; the pressure compresses the aquifer material and reduces its porosity; the effect of compression only becomes appreciable in aquifers at considerable depth, however.

Now imagine piezometers driven down through a confining layer into a confined or partly confined aquifer (figure 2.3). The water will rise to different levels in them, levels that correspond with an imaginary surface known as the *piezometric surface*. The piezometeric surface is related to the water in a confined aquifer in the same way that the water is related to the water table in an *un*confined aquifer. In both cases it is the surface to which water rises when a pipe is driven into the aquifer. The only difference is that, whereas a water table is a "real," tangible surface, a piezometric surface is, in a sense, "imaginary." It is where the water level *would* rise to *if* the pressure exerted on it by the confining layer were removed. The piezometric surface is sometimes below and sometimes above ground level; in either case the aquifer, and the water in it, are described as *artesian*, and a well drilled into it is an *artesian well*. Often, however, the term *artesian well* is used only when the piezometric surface lies above-ground at the site of the well, so that water gushes from it spontaneously, without pumping. The word derives from a place-name: Artesium in Roman Gaul, which is now in the province of Artois, in northeast France.

The difference of the water levels in two piezometers is the head loss between them, and the head loss divided by the distance separating them is the hydraulic gradient, as before. Given a gradient, water will flow, but to measure the flow rate through an aquifer, the notions of hydraulic conductivity that we considered above are not particularly useful as they may well be different at different levels in the aquifer. It is better to consider the volume of water passing, per second, through a vertical cross-section of the whole aquifer. This depends on the average hydraulic gradient, the width of the aquifer, and a quantity called the aquifer's *transmissivity*, thus:

Volume of water per second = Transmissivity × Aquifer width × Hydraulic gradient.

Transmissivity is measured in square meters per second. It depends on both the thickness and the permeability of the aquifer.

NOTE

For lawyers practicing in the field of groundwater law, a working knowledge of the principles of hydrology and hydrogeology is an important asset. A detailed treatment can be found in Ralph C. Heath, Basic Ground–Water Hydrology, U.S. Geologic Survey, Water Supply Paper 2220 (1983). Also of interest to the student of current U.S. groundwater problems is Robert J. Glennon, Water Follies: Groundwater Pumping and the Fate of America's Fresh Waters, Island Press (2002).

One of the persistent themes in the law of groundwater is the artificial disconnect between ground and surface rights. Hydrology has advanced considerably as a science, but the law has lagged behind, although courts and legislatures have begun to close the disconnect. See pages 595–598 *infra*. Early cases limited riparian sharing to a small, almost non-existent class of surface waters. Pumpers had to share only groundwater in an underground stream, not percolating underground water. An underground stream has been defined as waters that flow underground within "reasonably ascertainable boundaries" or as "a constant stream in a known and well-defined natural channel." Hayes v. Adams, 109 Or. 51, 218 P. 933 (1923). Underground waters not meeting the narrow definition of an underground stream are said to be percolating waters. Underground streams generally are subject to the law of surface streams; percolating waters are subject to groundwater law. In fact, however, "percolating" waters may be destined for a stream and closely related as a hydrologic matter. Factual determinations of whether waters are percolating are often difficult, making the burden of proof onerous. Furthermore, it may be based on factors other than whether the use of water from the source at issue affects the use of another. In Department of Highways v. Sebastian, 345 S.W.2d 46, 47 (Ky.1961), the following evidence was held sufficient to create a jury issue as to the existence of an underground flowing stream:

> The evidence for the Sebastians was that the course of an underground stream running from a hill on their neighbor's land across the highway right of way and to the springs was identifiable and marked by a line of

green grass which grew on the surface even in dry weather. In Hale v. McLea, 53 Cal. 578 [(1879)], it was held that the presence of a line of bushes usually found nowhere except over watercourses could be sufficient to establish the existence of an underground stream flowing in a known and defined channel. And in Maricopa County Municipal Water Conservation District [No. 1] v. Southwest Cotton Co., 4 P.2d 369 [(Ariz. 1931)], it was said that surface indications such as trees, shrubs, bushes and grasses growing along a defined course are the simplest and surest proofs of the existence of an underground stream as distinguished from percolating water.

Are these sound policy reasons or a scientific basis for distinguishing the legal treatment of percolating waters and so-called underground streams?

Some states have long recognized that where surface water and sub-surface water are connected, they should be administered in an integrated fashion. In Colorado there has been a complete integration of administration of rights to groundwater and surface water that are connected. The state has consistently held that all groundwater is presumed to be tributary to a natural stream. Safranek v. Limon, 123 Colo. 330, 228 P.2d 975 (1951). As such, tributary groundwater is integrated into the administration of surface water priorities. Colo. Rev. Stat. § 37–92–102 (2006). It is defined as "that water in the unconsolidated alluvial aquifer of sand, gravel, and other sedimentary materials and all other waters hydraulically connected thereto which can influence the rate or direction of movement of water in that alluvial aquifer or natural stream" Colo. Rev. Stat. § 37–92–103(11) (2006).

A few state courts have mandated integration without waiting for legislative action. In Postema v. Pollution Control Hearings Bd., 142 Wash.2d 68, 11 P.3d 726 (2000), applicants for groundwater permits appealed after their applications were denied by the Department of Ecology on the basis that a surface stream in hydraulic continuity with the proposed groundwater source was subject to minimum flow rights that were unmet during a substantial portion of the year. The Washington Supreme Court held that:

> [H]ydraulic continuity of an aquifer with a stream having unmet minimum flows is not, in and of itself, a basis for denial of a groundwater application.... However, where there is hydraulic continuity and withdrawal of groundwater would impair existing surface water rights, including minimum flow rights, then denial is required. Ecology may use new information and scientific methodology as it becomes available and scientifically acceptable for determining hydraulic continuity and effect of groundwater withdrawals on surface waters.

Id. at 741.

The lack of integration continues to plague water administration. Small "exempt" wells are a special problem that is just beginning to be addressed. See Robert N. Caldwell, Six–Packs for Subdivisions: The Cumulative Effects of Washington's Domestic Well Exemption, 28 Envtl. L. 1099,

1101–1121 (1998). In 2008, the U.S. Bureau of Reclamation announced that it would issue rules to curb pumping by small domestic wells along the Colorado River, in Arizona, California, and Nevada. These wells tap the river's subsurface flow and withdraw between 9,000 and 15,000 acre feet per year of water. The well owners would have to secure a water right or join a provider with a valid water right. Arizona has 10,000 acre feet of unallocated Colorado River water that it could use to grant state water rights, but the other two states have no surplus water. See pages 1011–1021, *infra*. In New Mexico, the state legislature rebuffed efforts to curb the statutory exemption, but a trial judge held that the exemption was unconstitutional because it interfered with vested appropriative rights. Bounds v. State Engineer (decision issued by Judge J.C. Robinson, Sixth Judicial District Court, Silver City, 2008).

Integrated administration of surface and groundwater supplies requires a sophisticated level of technical information, but has been well within the competence of engineers for many years. Similarly, engineering studies are needed to establish the nature and extent of the effects of pumping from one well to another and the effects of contamination from landfills and other sources or aquifers.

The administration of groundwater rights and resolution of disputes involving aquifers, where causes and effects of water uses must be proved, increasingly depend on the use of advanced computer simulation models. Groundwater models were initially developed to determine the relationship between flow and pressure rates, but the federal and state focus on contamination has stimulated the development of much more sophisticated models. Models are either deterministic or stochastic. The former indicate cause and effect relationships while the latter indicate only probability ranges. Models are further subdivided between hydrogeologic framework and process models. Framework models depict the aquifer, often in three dimensions, and process models describe flow, transport, and chemical characteristics in the aquifer. Conjunctive use models now exist to describe surface and groundwater interaction. Models are relevant evidence in water rights and pollution cases. Typically, experts are employed by parties to a dispute to defend or to challenge the selection and application of a model. After a model has been selected, it must be verified (by proof that the computer code used performs the necessary numerical calculations correctly), validated (by proof that the model successfully "analogues" the real system), and calibrated (adjusted to the known information about the system) before it can be used. Inevitable disagreements among experts are resolved by the usual rules of evidence and judicial review of the record. Courts have generally deferred to an agency's expertise, *e.g.* California *ex rel*. Air Res. Bd. v. U.S. Environmental Protection Agency, 774 F.2d 1437 (9th Cir.1985), but it is possible to challenge successfully the lack of validation studies or a significant discrepancy between the model's assumptions and the hydrogeology of the aquifer. Models used by regulatory agencies are subject to challenge as arbitrary and capricious. Ohio v. U.S. Environmental Protection Agency, 784 F.2d 224 (6th Cir.1986) (affirmed en banc 798 F.2d 880 (6th Cir. 1986)). A useful introduction to groundwater modeling and the law is Michael Sklash et al., *Groundwater Models: Can You Believe What They Are Saying?*, 13 Nat. Resources & Env't 542 (1999).

B. Individual Rights in Groundwater

Jack Hirshleifer, James C. De Haven and Jerome W. Milliman, Water Supply: Economics, Technology, and Policy
59–64 (1960).

1. Common–Pool Problems

The common-pool problem in the exploitation of water resources, in the narrow sense, occurs when a number of overlying property-owners are engaged in competitive pumping of water from a common underlying aquifer. In the wider sense, all cases where users draw competitively on a "fugitive" supply—that is, where the commodity is no one's property until and unless captured for use, wildlife being the classical example—are common-pool problems. Since rights in percolating ground water can normally be obtained only by actual "capture" of the water, pumpers are induced to withdraw at a rate greater than would otherwise be rational for fear that the withdrawals of others will lower water levels in the wells. Or, to look at the matter in another way, each individual considers in his decisions only the effect of his pumping upon the water level in his well—which may be negligible if there are many pumpers, since all are drawing upon a common pool—and does not consider the fact that his pumping will adversely affect all those interested in the pool.

* * *

Three solutions—that is, methods for assuring that the decisions made will meet the criteria of allocative efficiency—have been proposed for common-pool problems. They are (1) centralized decision-making; (2) assignment of pro rata production rights or quotas; and (3) imposition of "use" taxes.

* * *

There are several difficulties in the application of the solution via centralized management to water-resource problems. In the first place, the very concept of a "pool" in the sense of a quantum of a resource effectively localized applies only roughly to water. There will be ground, surface, and atmospheric interconnection between "pools," and only in certain circumstances can the problems of a single area be isolated from others—unless, indeed, the area is made very large, in which case we face both the administrative and political difficulties involved in centralized administration of a resource subject to highly variable local conditions. In California, for example, the natural water supplies of the southern regions largely originate in the snow pack of the Sierras; centralized management of the pool of resources would require a bureaucratic determination of the optimal pattern of consumptive and non-consumptive uses among all the competing ends in widely separated geographical areas which could be served by the use of the resource. Even in limited geographical areas, a highly varied pattern of use may exist which is hardly amenable to centralized government of the resource. Some users may pump water for irrigation, others may impound and divert for municipal supply while still others may want sufficient river flow for navigation or saline-water repulsion. * * *

The advantages of * * * an assignment include its simplicity and directness. A point of great practical importance is that the goal of the assignment is not the difficult and subtle matter of optimal use but an "equitable" apportionment of rights among claimants (some may, indeed, question that the latter is much easier than the former, but in many cases no doubt it is). Under such an apportionment the complicated questions of best use are left up to the successful claimants themselves, though perhaps with some restrictions. Another advantage is that in a certain sense the assignment of quotas does get really to the heart of the problem—the common nature of the resource—by replacing commonality of rights with specificity of shares.

There are, however, difficulties as well. First there is the matter of "equitable" apportionment. Assignment of quotas has not prevented waste in the case of petroleum because apportionment has typically been based on "well potential," so that an incentive to drill unnecessary wells remains. Where historical use is the basis, an incentive is created to initiate use excessively early in order to establish a history of use before final apportionment takes place. Ideally speaking, rights to all water should be assigned once and for all, but this rarely occurs.

A second difficulty turns on the question of efficiency. A single user might, for example, concentrate all his withdrawals on a few wells near the more productive lands, whereas an "equitable" apportionment might give a distribution of quotas whose exploitation through a great many wells leads to some social waste. It might be argued that, in such circumstances, quotas will be bought and sold until they end up in the most efficient distribution. Aside from the fact that certain limitations on transfer of such rights may exist, the process may not work perfectly. Thus there may be a gain in efficiency if both B and C sell their quotas to A, but it may be in the separate interest of each to hold out until the other sells, because, if C ceases pumping, B may be able to capture part of the gain in the form of locally increased water pressure or level, and vice versa. This is analogous to, if not so serious as, the problem of achieving rationality along a river, where intervening users may be in a position to reap a similar unearned benefit. The difficulty rests ultimately on the fact that the quotas really are not perfectly exchangeable between any two uses; the pool, while indeed common, has stream or serial-use aspects.

The third and most serious difficulty turns upon the question of how to achieve rationality in the use of the resource over time. Quotas are normally thought of as being assigned to exhaust the "safe yield" of the common water pool, that is to say, the amount which on the average equals the recharge rate so as to keep water levels constant. But why should water levels be kept constant? To take a ridiculous case, suppose petroleum quotas were similarly based on safe yield—which is, of course, zero. To use more than the safe yield means the water supplied in past years is being "mined," but this is sometimes undoubtedly rational and may even be in the normal case. In the high plains of Texas an extreme instance of this situation exists wherein the accumulation of water over past ages has been immense, but the annual recharge is very small indeed. One other consideration is that steady improvement in the technology of pumping has taken place in the past and may be reasonably projected to the future, so that larger and larger pumping lifts may not always represent increased economic cost of pumping.

* * *

The third or "use-tax" solution to the common-pool problem is in some ways logically the neatest, but it has been applied in practice in only one case to the authors' knowledge—in Orange County, California. The economic theory of the solution is based on the following considerations. Each pumper, in deciding how much to withdraw, compares the marginal cost of pumping with the marginal value in use to him of the water. This will usually be the value of the marginal product, the water being normally used as an intermediate good in the production of goods and services for the market. But his withdrawals will tend to lower the water levels for everyone using the common pool—a consideration which he will ignore or at least not consider fully, because the impact on himself will be partial and may be negligible. (In certain cases, "spillover" costs of pumping may show themselves most conspicuously in the form of salt-water intrusion under someone else's lands.) The use-tax solution would require a payment which would be added to the cost of pumping so that, ideally, the individual would consider the marginal *social* cost in his decision on how much to pump rather than merely the marginal private cost. The payment, of course, would represent the loss of productivity on lands owned by others.

––––––––

Most states once followed rules of reasonable use, correlative rights, prior appropriation, or some combination of these doctrines to determine limits on pumpers. These rules were first applied by courts in tort suits in which one pumper sought damages or an injunction against another. Now the usual mechanism is to issue permits based on certain conditions developed to allocate the available water fairly and to accomplish public purposes such as prolonging aquifer life and preventing contamination. The rules for determining rights remain viable in private lawsuits among pumpers.

1. RIGHTS OF LANDOWNERS

Early systems for allocating rights to use groundwater were based on the ownership of the overlying land. The "absolute ownership" doctrine, sometimes called the English rule, allowed landowners an unlimited right to withdraw water from beneath their property. See Acton v. Blundell, 152 Eng. Rep. 1223 (1843). The doctrine was based on the ancient concept that a landowner's interest extends to the center of the earth. This was adopted as the law in many states in the nineteenth century, but was short-lived in most places. Carried to its logical conclusion, the absolute ownership doctrine allowed even malicious pumping aimed at draining the aquifer under neighboring land. *E.g.*, Huber v. Merkel, 117 Wis. 355, 94 N.W. 354 (1903). Virtually all states now make malicious injury actionable. See Gagnon v. French Lick Springs Hotel Co., 163 Ind. 687, 72 N.E. 849, 852 (1904). The absolute ownership rule still has vitality in some states. Maine recently reaffirmed the rule, see *infra* p. 568, as did Texas, see *infra* p. 623, but Texas has modified the rule by legislation. Vermont was one of the last bastions of the absolute ownership rule. It reaffirmed the rule in 1973, Drinkwine v. State, 131 Vt. 127, 300 A.2d 616 (1973). In 1985, however, the legislature expressly abolished the common law doctrine of absolute ownership of groundwater, and provided a cause of action for unreasonable harm caused by withdrawals, diversions, or pollution, effectively adopting a correlative rights rule. Vt. Stat. Ann. tit. 10, § 1410 (2006).

As groundwater hydrology became a more precise science, and as the effects of groundwater use on others became more apparent, American states rejected the absolute ownership doctrine in favor of rules allowing "reasonable use" or establishing correlative rights that allow all pumpers to share with one another. Today, there are remedies in most of the states for groundwater pumping causing land subsidence or other injury. Even those states that still declare themselves to embrace absolute ownership actually have tempered the doctrine with concepts designed to protect uses of groundwater by other pumpers and to protect the public's interest in conserving the resource.

Tying water rights to land ownership causes obvious problems for municipalities seeking to use groundwater as their source of supply. To address this problem, in many states municipalities are given the power of eminent domain over water and, as a result, injured overlying owners are confined to damage remedies. Examples are Ariz. Rev. Stat. Ann. § 12–1111(12) (West 2003); Cal. Civ. Proc. Code § 1240.110(a) (West 1982); Idaho Code § 50–1801 (Michie 2000); Mont. Code Ann. § 7–7–4404 (2006); Tex. Water Code Ann. § 11.033 (Vernon 2000).

Notions of land ownership remain important in applying modern liability rules and in issuing permits. The extent of overlying land owned by a pumper may determine rights to groundwater. Some systems limit uses of groundwater to uses on or connected with the overlying land. Some allocate rights to pumpers in proportion to the relative amounts of land owned by them.

Higday v. Nickolaus

Kansas City Court of Appeals, Missouri, 1971.
469 S.W.2d 859.

■ SHANGLER, PRESIDING JUDGE.

* * * Appellants are the several owners of some 6000 acres of farm land overlying an alluvial water basin in Boone County known as the

McBaine Bottom. These lands extend from Huntsdale at the north to Easley at the south; they are bordered by a line of limestone bluffs on the east and are enclosed by a sweeping bend of the Missouri River on the west. Underlying this entire plain are strata of porous rock, gravel and soil through which water, without apparent or definite channel, filtrates, oozes and percolates as it falls. This water (much of which has originated far upstream within the Missouri River Valley) has been trapped by an underlying stratum of impervious limestone so that the saturated soil has become a huge aquifer or underground reservoir.

Appellants have devoted the overlying lands to agricultural use with excellent resultant yields. They attribute the fertility of the soil to the continuing presence of a high subterranean water level which has unfailingly and directly supplied the moisture needs of the crops whatever the vagaries of the weather. Appellants also use the underground water for personal consumption, for their livestock, and in the near future will require it for the surface irrigation of their crops.

Respondent City of Columbia is a burgeoning municipality of 50,000 inhabitants which has been, since 1948, in quest of a source of water to replenish a dwindling supply. Following the advice of consulting engineers, it settled on a plan for the withdrawal of water by shallow wells from beneath the McBaine Bottom where appellants' farms are located and thence to transport the water to the City some twelve miles away for sale to customers within and without the City. In December of 1966, the electorate approved a revenue bond issue for the development of a municipal water supply by such a system of shallow wells in the McBaine Bottom. Further scientific analysis and measurement of the basin's water resources followed. With the aid of a test well, it was determined that the underground percolating water table, when undisturbed, rises to an average of ten feet below the soil surface. These waters move laterally through the McBaine alluvium at the rate of two feet per day and in so doing displace 10.5 million gallons of water daily.

Respondent City, by threat of condemnation, has acquired from some of these appellants five well sites totalling 17.25 acres. The City now threatens to extract the groundwater at the rate of 11.5 million gallons daily for purposes wholly unrelated to any beneficial use of the overlying land, but instead, intends to transport the water to its corporate boundaries some miles away for purposes of sale. The mining of the water as contemplated will reduce the water table throughout the basin from the present average of ten feet to a new subsurface average of twenty feet. Appellants complain that this reduction of the water table will divert percolating waters normally available and enjoyed by appellants for their crops, livestock and their personal use and will eventually turn their land into an arid and sterile surface.

On the basis of these pleaded allegations, plaintiffs sought (1) a judicial declaration that defendant City is without right to extract the percolating waters for sale away from the premises or for other use not related with any beneficial ownership or enjoyment of the land from which they are taken when to do so will deprive them, the owners of the adjacent land, of the reasonable use of the underground water for the beneficial use of their own land, and (2) that defendant City be enjoined from undertaking to do so.

* * *

* * * Respondent [City] maintains that since Springfield Waterworks Co. v. Jenkins, 62 Mo.App. 74, was decided by the St. Louis Court of Appeals in 1895, Missouri has recognized the common law rule that a landowner has absolute ownership to the waters under his land and, therefore, may without liability withdraw any quantity of water for any purpose even though the result is to drain all water from beneath his neighbors' lands. Therefore, contends respondent, since the threatened damage plaintiffs plead describes a consequence of the rightful use by respondent of its land, it is *damnum absque injuria* and not actionable. * * *

* * * At an early day, the courts expressed dissatisfaction with the English common law rule and began applying what has come to be known variously, as the rule of "reasonable use", or of "correlative rights", or the "American rule." By the turn of the century, a steady trend of decisions was discernible away from the English rule to a rule of reasonable use. The trend continues.

Generally, the rule of reasonable use is an expression of the maxim that one must so use his own property as not to injure another—that each landowner is restricted to a reasonable exercise of his own rights and a reasonable use of his own property, in view of the similar rights of others.

As it applies to percolating groundwater, the rule of reasonable use recognizes that the overlying owner has a proprietary interest in the water under his lands, but his incidents of ownership are restricted. It recognizes that the nature of the property right is usufructuary rather than absolute as under the English rule. Under the rule of reasonable use, the overlying owner may use the subjacent groundwater freely, and without liability to an adjoining owner, but only if his use is for purposes incident to the beneficial enjoyment of the land from which the water was taken. * * *

The principal difficulty in the application of the reasonable use doctrine is in determining what constitutes a reasonable use. What is a reasonable use must depend to a great extent upon many factors, such as the persons involved, their relative positions, the nature of their uses, the comparative value of their uses, the climatic conditions, and all facts and circumstances pertinent to the issues. However, the modern decisions agree that under the rule of reasonable use *an overlying owner, including a municipality, may not withdraw percolating water and transport it for sale or other use away from the land from which it was taken if the result is to impair the supply of an adjoining landowner to his injury.* Such a use is unreasonable because non-beneficial and "is not for a 'lawful purpose within the general rule concerning percolating waters, but constitutes an actionable wrong for which damages are recoverable'."

The "reasonable use" rule as developed in the law of ground waters must be distinguished from the "correlative rights" rule. In 1902, the California Supreme Court repudiated the English common law rule in favor of the distinctive correlative rights doctrine which is based on the theory of proportionate sharing of withdrawals among landowners overlying a common basin.[9] Under the doctrine, overlying owners have no proprietary interest in the water under their soil. California remains the only important correlative rights state; Utah has abandoned it, and only Nebraska also applies it to some extent. The administration of such a system of rights has proved extremely difficult in times of water shortage and has tendered towards an "equalitarian rigidity" which does not take into account the relative value of the competing uses. However suitable this doctrine may be for California—the prime consumer of ground water in the country—or any other state which may follow it, the reasonable use rule offers a more flexible legal standard for the just determination of beneficial uses of ground water, particularly under the climatic conditions of Missouri.

* * *

* * * The premise that the owner of the soil owns all that lies beneath the surface so that he may use the percolating water in any way he chooses without liability to an adjoining owner fails to recognize that the supply of groundwater is limited, and that the first inherent limitation on water rights is the availability of the supply. Another postulate of the common law doctrine ascribes to percolating waters a movement so "secret, changeable and uncontrollable", that no attempt to subject them to fixed legal rules could be successfully made. Chatfield v. Wilson, 28 Vt. 49, 53 (1855); Frazier v. Brown, 12 Ohio St. 294 (1961). Modern knowledge and techniques have discredited this premise also. The movement, supply, rate of evaporation and many other physical characteristics of groundwater are now readily determinable. In fact, respondent City's decision to turn to the McBaine Bottom as the source of its water supply was made only after careful scientific analysis confirmed that this land was particularly adaptable for water production. * * * The City cannot be permitted to escape liability by appeals to a doctrine which assumes that the very information the City has acted upon was not available to it.

Recently, in Bollinger v. Henry, [375 S.W.2d 166 (1964)] the Supreme Court of Missouri applied the rule of reasonable use to determine the rights of riparian owners. Subterranean streams are governed by the rules applying to natural watercourses on the surface, so the rule of reasonable use is now applicable to them also. We believe the same rule should apply to subterranean percolating waters. It is that legal standard, in absence of a statutory expression of a priority of uses, by which existing water resources may be allocated most equitably and beneficially among competing users, private and public. The application of such a uniform legal standard would

---

9. Katz v. Walkinshaw, 141 Cal. 116, 74 p. 766 (1902).

also give recognition to the established interrelationship between surface and groundwater and would, therefore, bring into one classification all waters over the use of which controversy may arise.

Under the rule of reasonable use as we have stated it, the fundamental measure of the overlying owner's right to use the groundwater is whether it is for purposes incident to the beneficial enjoyment of the land from which it was taken. Thus, a private owner may not withdraw groundwater for purposes of sale if the adjoining landowner is thereby deprived of water necessary for the beneficial enjoyment of his land. Here, the municipality has acquired miniscule plots of earth and by the use of powerful pumps intends to draw into wells on its own land for merchandising groundwater stored in plaintiffs' land, thereby depriving plaintiffs of the beneficial use of the normal water table to their immediate injury and to the eventual impoverishment of their lands. * * *

NOTES

1.   Do you agree with the following analysis of the opinion? "[I]n effect, it appears that the court did not apply the reasonable use doctrine, but rather the doctrine of correlative rights." Rhonda Churchill Thomas, Note, *Water Law—Groundwater Rights in Missouri—A Need for Clarification*, 37 Mo. L. Rev. 357, 362 (1972). Which rule would the city prefer? If on retrial the court decides to award only damages to the plaintiffs, do they have a right to damages for loss of the natural high water table? Does *Higday*'s application of the rule of reasonable use restrict the use of groundwater to overlying land? Does it mean that municipalities can be enjoined from developing a well field unless they purchase the overlying rights of surrounding owners? What is the rationale for restricting the place groundwater is used to overlying land as opposed to basing the right to withdraw groundwater on owning overlying land?

2.   The California rule of correlative rights described in the opinion in *Higday* has been adopted by several other states, at least in dicta. In Woodsum v. Pemberton, 172 N.J.Super. 489, 412 A.2d 1064 (Law Div. 1980), a homeowner whose well pressure declined sued the city for causing the decline, but the court held that the plaintiff's use was not reasonable because the well could have been deepened at a cost of between $750.00–$1,700.00: "[I]f his use is to be described as 'reasonable,' he must dig his well to a depth which anticipates the lowering of the water table by virtue of other 'proper users'." 412 A.2d at 1076. The court balanced the plaintiff's need for the original pressure level against the public's need for the water. Was it correct to do so? The case was affirmed, but on different grounds. All issues were then moot because plaintiff recovered the cost of deepening the well from a settlement with one defendant.

3.   *Higday* was followed in City of Blue Springs v. Central Dev. Ass'n, 831 S.W.2d 655 (Mo.App.1992), which held that a landowner may transfer the right to use underlying water but may not sever title to the water. Under *Higday,* "water is not severable from the land through or under which it

flows." Id. at 659. Thus, the water could not be valued separately when the overlying land was condemned.

4. One semi-arid state, Oklahoma, has enacted legislation allowing overlying owners to receive fixed allocations based on "that percentage of the total annual yield of the basin or subbasin * * * which is equal to the percentage of the land overlying the fresh groundwater basin or subbasin which he owns or leases." Okla. Stat. Ann. tit. 82, § 1020.9 (West Supp. 2007). The determination of the maximum annual yield is an adjudicative decision. Texas County Irrigation and Water Res. Ass'n v. Oklahoma Water Res. Bd., 803 P.2d 1119 (Okla.1990).

In Franco–American Charolaise, Ltd. v. Oklahoma Water Res. Bd., 855 P.2d 568 (Okla.1990), the Oklahoma Supreme Court held unconstitutional a 1963 Act designed to convert the state to the prior appropriation system. This decision has cast a cloud of uncertainty over many aspects of Oklahoma water rights, including groundwater rights. In particular, it perpetuated an unfortunate conflict in Oklahoma law concerning the definition of groundwater as it relates to water in the alluvium of a surface stream. Compare *Franco* with Kline v. Oklahoma Water Resources Board, 759 P.2d 210 (Okla.1988).

In 2003, the state imposed a moratorium on additional pumping from "sensitive sole source" basins. O.S.Supp.2003, §§ 1020.9–1020. B. Jacobs Ranch, L.L.C. v. Smith, 148 P.3d 842 (Okla. 2006) upheld the statute against various state law and federal constitutional challenges. The court followed Tahoe–Sierra Preservation Council, Inc. v. Tahoe, 535 U.S. 302, 122 S.Ct. 1465, 152 L.Ed.2d 517 (2002), to uphold the temporary moratorium as a legitimate conservation measure pending a hydrological study to determine the safe maximum yield of the basin.

5. The Restatement (Second) of Torts, § 858 states:

(1) A proprietor of land or his grantee who withdraws ground water from the land and uses it for a beneficial purpose is not subject to liability for interference with the use of water by another, unless

(a) the withdrawal of ground water unreasonably causes harm to a proprietor of neighboring land through lowering the water table or reducing artesian pressure,

(b) the withdrawal of ground water exceeds the proprietor's reasonable share of the annual supply or total store of ground water, or

(c) the withdrawal of the ground water has a direct and substantial effect upon a watercourse or lake and unreasonably causes harm to a person entitled to the use of its water.

Surprisingly few courts have adopted the Restatement rule, and have generally used it to award dewatered landowners damages against large-scale pumpers. Wisconsin was the first state to apply § 858. State v. Michels Pipeline Construction, Inc., 63 Wis.2d 278, 217 N.W.2d 339 (1974), overruled Huber v. Merkel, 117 Wis. 355, 94 N.W. 354 (1903), which had applied the absolute ownership rule to its logical limit and allowed malicious pumping. Since *Michels Pipeline,* Nebraska (to resolve disputes between users of surface water and hydrologically connected groundwater) and Ohio have adopted § 858. See Spear T Ranch, Inc. v. Knaub, 269 Neb. 177, 691 N.W.2d 116 (2005); Cline v. American Aggregates Corp., 15 Ohio St.3d 384, 474 N.E.2d 324 (1984). In holding that a municipal well field can be both an interference with the common law rights of adjoining land owners and a taking, McNamara v. Rittman, 107 Ohio St.3d 243, 838 N.E.2d 640 (2005), characterized Cline as a rejection of "dark arts" theory of absolue ownership which "greatly expanded water rights protection, reflecting the importance of water rights to every piece of property." 838 N.E.2d at 644. Michigan *appeared to adopt § 858* in Maerz v. United States Steel Corp., 116 Mich.App. 710, 323 N.W.2d 524 (1982), but a subsequent case, Michigan Citizens for Water Conservation v. Nestlé Waters North America, Inc., 269 Mich.App. 25, 709 N.W.2d 174 (2005), rev'd on other grounds, 479 Mich. 280, 737 N.W.2d 447 (2007) noted that "we disagree with defendant's *contention that* Maerz made a wholesale adoption of the Restatement's position...." Id. at 194. Only Indiana and Maine have specifically rejected § 858. See Wiggins v. Brazil Coal & Clay Corp., 452 N.E.2d 958 (Ind.1983). *Maine* reaffirmed the absolute ownership rule because water users had relied on it for over a century, the plaintiffs presented no studies demonstrating that the rule had not functioned well in Maine, and the legislature failed to act on a study commission recommendation that the state adopt the reasonable use rule. Maddocks v. Giles, 728 A.2d 150 (Me.1999).

Who must bear a loss of pressure under an application of the reasonable use rule? The Restatement of Torts (Second) § 858 imposes liability only if the "withdrawal of groundwater unreasonably causes harm * * * through lowering of the water table or reducing artesian pressure." § 858(1)(a). Is the loss of artesian pressure caused by a high capacity agricultural, municipal, or industrial well per se unreasonable?

Several states have permitting statutes that apply rules like the Restatement's "unreasonable harm" rule. For instance, under the Oregon groundwater appropriation act, a permit application may be rejected if the state engineer finds that a well may unduly interfere with existing wells or substantially interfere with surface rights. Or. Rev. Stat. § 537.620(3) (2005).

The Restatement rule in subsection (b) limits the rights of a landowner to a reasonable share of the "annual supply or total store of ground water." This stops short of asserting a public interest in the resource, but nevertheless indicates some limitation besides the immediate effect of pumping on other users. See John S. Lowe et al., *Beyond Section 858: A Proposed Groundwater Liability and Management System for the Eastern United States,* 8 Ecology L.Q. 131 (1979).

NOTE: LAND SUBSIDENCE AND GROUNDWATER PUMPING

As water is pumped from an aquifer, the water occupying the spaces between the rock particles is removed. Without the water, the particles can become more tightly compacted. This reduces the capacity of the geologic structure to store water. In addition, the compression of the aquifer can cause the surface of the overlying land to settle. This is manifested in the lowering of the land surface and in fissures—cracks on the surface. In some places these have turned into gullies up to 50 feet deep and 10 feet wide. Fissures can range in length from a few hundred feet to several miles. The geologic characteristics of an aquifer determine how fast and extensively the land settles.

Some of the most dramatic land subsidence has occurred in the desert Southwest. Near Eloy Arizona hundreds of square miles have subsided, dropping more than 25 feet in some places. This has caused problems for agriculture as irrigation ditches and canals break and as leveled fields have to be re-leveled to allow the proper flow of irrigation water. In urban areas subsidence has made necessary repairs to streets, railroads, sewers, and gas lines and has cracked foundations. In Phoenix, where groundwater pumping has long been the major source of supply, sewers and storm drains that depend on gravity flow have clogged and reversed as the gradient changed due to subsidence.

Besides the obvious implications for the interests of the public, subsidence caused by groundwater pumping has led to litigation against pumpers by damaged neighbors. In Finley v. Teeter Stone, Inc., 251 Md. 428, 248 A.2d 106 (1968), plaintiff farmer alleged that from thirty-five to fifty-seven acres of his land were injured as a result of subsidence, in this case through subterranean and surface collapse caused by removal of water from a limestone formation. Defendant conceded that his pumping to drain a quarry on neighboring land caused the subsidence, but escaped liability on the ground that he was a groundwater user making a reasonable use of his land that was not negligent. See also Adams v. Lang, 553 So.2d 89 (Ala.1989) (extraction of groundwater for catfish pond causing artesian wells on adjoining land to be dewatered was reasonable use).

Plaintiffs in *Finley* relied upon Gamer v. Town of Milton, 346 Mass. 617, 195 N.E.2d 65 (1964). In that case, a town drained a small pond to recover underlying gravel, causing land under some nearby homes to subside. The court imposed liability because of the failure to take reasonable precautions to protect plaintiff's adjacent land. Why is *Gamer* a "negligence" question which imposes the costs on the pumper and *Finley* a "water rights" question? Should liability for withdrawals which cause subsidence depend on the manner in which the court characterizes the problem?

Indiana recently drew a distinction between withdrawals that only reduce water levels and those that cause subsidence. The state follows the absolute ownership rule, but City of Valparaiso v. Defler, 694 N.E.2d 1177 (Ind.App.1998), refused to apply the rule to withdrawals that cause subsidence because "the clear trend * * * [is] toward ameliorating the often harsh consequences which can result from the strict application of the English rule." 694 N.E.2d at 1182.

In a Texas case, an industrial pumper withdrew massive amounts of groundwater with the knowledge that it would damage appellant landowners. It negligently placed its wells, concentrating the land subsidence, and pumped too much water from these wells in too short a time, compounding the damage. Texas had been a leading absolute ownership state, but the court recognized a narrow exception to the general principle of non-liability for damage by negligence in pumping where the negligence was a proximate cause of the subsidence of another's land. Friendswood Dev. Co. v. Smith–Southwest Indus., Inc., 576 S.W.2d 21 (Tex.1978). The court held that the new liability rule applied only prospectively because the common law rule was an established rule of property law. Texas has since enacted legislation to control subsidence. It includes a fee of 1.2 cents per thousand gallons pumped which was upheld in Beckendorff v. Harris–Galveston Coastal Subsidence Dist., 558 S.W.2d 75 (Tex.Civ.App.1977). See *infra* p. 623, for a discussion of Texas groundwater law.

Where pumping by a municipality or other public entity causes subsidence and damage to private property, "takings" issues can arise. Could the municipality avoid liability by asserting police power immunity? In Los Osos Valley Assoc. v. City of San Luis Obispo, 30 Cal.App.4th 1670, 36 Cal.Rptr.2d 758 (1994), the City drilled wells and extracted groundwater to provide municipal supplies during drought conditions. The extraction caused subsidence that damaged buildings in a shopping center owned by Los Osos Valley Associates. Sued in inverse condemnation, the city pleaded as an affirmative defense that it was utilizing its police powers in response to an "emergency" and thus was immune from liability. Affirming a trial court judgment for plaintiffs, the California Court of Appeals noted that

> the City was well aware of the need to conserve water for years. It chose a combination of mild conservation measures and the damaging groundwater pumping. This choice of action over the years does not constitute an emergency. It constituted a choice among many that the City made over a considerable period of time. As such, the City may not rely on its police powers to avoid compensation for the physical destruction of LOVA's buildings due to its groundwater pumping operations.

Id. at 764. What if a municipality adopted a long range plan, adopted strict conservation measures, then declared an emergency and utilized damaging groundwater pumping as a last resort? Would the outcome be different?

2.   PRIOR USERS' RIGHTS

The issue in groundwater appropriation suits is not usually a claim of priority to an absolute amount of water but of a right to a given pressure level. The consequence of losing pressure may be to increase the depth from which water must be pumped (pump lift), requiring the drilling of a deeper well, or installation of a more powerful pump. It may mean conversion of an artesian well whose water once flowed readily above ground to a well requiring expensive drilling and pumps. Groundwater withdrawals may also affect the supply or the accessibility of water available to surface water appropriators because the two sources are hydrologically connected. Only a few states clearly recognize the connection and administer such waters as coming from a single source, despite scientific evidence. A few states apply prior appropriation principles to the use of groundwater that is connected with surface water; priority determines rights among pumpers as well as between pumpers and surface users.

Wayman v. Murray City Corp.

Supreme Court of Utah, 1969.
23 Utah 2d 97, 458 P.2d 861.

■ CROCKETT, CHIEF JUSTICE.

In contest here are rights to water, as to amounts and pressure, in an underground water basin, known as the Murray Artesian Basin. It underlies an area in and adjacent to Murray City, lying between the Wasatch Mountains on the east and the Jordan River on the west. Plaintiffs are five families who own residences along Vine Street in Murray. Each has one or more smart wells (1 ½ to 3 inches in diameter) of varying depths. Each owns established rights to take water by means of their wells approved by the State Engineer. The right of the defendant Murray City derives from its acquisition of seven old wells known as the Baker Wells with rights to use 750 gallons per minute (1.67 c.f.s.) of water from the same underground basin. The rights under some of these wells are prior in time to some of the plaintiffs' wells and later than others. For a period of several years the Baker Wells had not furnished the permitted 750 gallons per minute; and by 1959 the flow had diminished to around 220 gallons per minute. Because of this, Murray City made plans to improve its wells. Pursuant to written permission obtained from the State Engineer on April 10, 1961, it caused a new 16–inch well to be drilled to a depth of 496 feet. It produced an excellent flow, of some variation, up to 1100 gallons per minute. The exact potential of the well is immaterial here because Murray City only contends for its right to draw the 750 gallons of water per minute to which its ownership is not challenged. The Baker Wells were permanently plugged and sealed and the new well was put into continuous operation in May of 1964; and in that month, the change of diversion from the old wells to the new well was approved by the State Engineer, Wayne D. Criddle, by Change Application A–3887.

Plaintiffs brought this suit in the district court against Murray City and the State Engineer to overturn the latter's decision on the ground that the new well had diminished the flow in their own wells and thus deprived them of their entitled water. * * *

Because of the vital importance of water in this arid region both our statutory and decisional law have been fashioned in recognition of the desirability and of the necessity of insuring the highest possible development and of the most continuous beneficial use of all available water with as little waste as possible.[1] * * *

* * * [T]his is not a situation where a party (Murray City) has initiated a *new* withdrawal in a basin which adversely affects the flow of wells prior in time and right.[3] What the City has done is to create a more efficient means of taking the 750 gallons of water per minute from this basin it acquired by its purchase of the Baker Wells. There thus arises the foundational question as to whether a water user, whose well for some reason or another is not producing the water to which he is entitled, may improve his method of taking his entitlement of water from the basin. That in most circumstances this question should be answered in the affirmative is clearly indicated by Sec. 73–3–3, U.C.A. 1953, which provides that:

> Any person entitled to the use of water *may change the place of diversion* or use and may use the water for other purposes than those for which it was originally appropriated, * * *.

* * * Nevertheless, there are other considerations to be reckoned with. The quoted statute, Sec. 73–3–3, further provides: "But no such change shall be made if it impairs any vested right without just compensation." The trial court, upon the trial de novo procedure allowed under Secs. 73–3–14 and 15, found that the new well did adversely affect the flow in the plaintiffs' wells. Inasmuch as there is other substantial evidence in the record to support this finding, under traditional rules of review it cannot be disturbed.

It was in implementation of its finding that the trial court, as authorized under Sec. 73–3–23, provided that Murray City "must at his sole cost *permanently* replace to the plaintiffs water in amount and quality equal to the level of their prior use." This imposes upon Murray City a sweeping and pervasive responsibility. It seems tantamount to requiring it to insure to the plaintiffs a continuous supply of 100% of their allotted flow henceforward, i.e., we assume, forever. * * * From what we have been able to learn about underground water it seems obvious that any decree so "set in concrete" could prove to be highly inequitable and inconsistent with the objectives of our water law as set forth herein. In order to harmonize with those objectives and to have a realistic application to the rights to the use of water any such decree should be understood as relating to the then existing conditions as shown by the evidence in the particular case, and also should be understood as being subject to change if it is shown that there is any substantial change in such conditions.

* * *

1. Title 73, U.C.A.1953, especially Section 73–1–1: "All waters in this state, whether above or under the ground are hereby declared to be the property of the public." And Sec. 73–1–3: "Beneficial use shall be the basis, the measure and the limit of all rights to the use of water in this state," * * *.

3. Thus in that respect different from the case of Current Creek Irrigation Co. v. Andrews, 9 Utah 2d 324, 344 P.2d 528 (1959).

If the water table in such an underground basin must be maintained at a sufficiently high level to sustain pressure in the wells in the higher areas, there may be water above and near the surface in the lower areas, forming ponds, marshes, and swamps. This results in wasteful losses from surface evaporation and from consumption by water-loving plants, tules, reeds and rushes, indigenous to such areas, which are of little or no value. There is often further loss by unproductive drainage from the basin. * * *

From the considerations relating to underground water law hereinabove discussed there has come to be recognized what may be referred to as the "rule of reasonableness" in the allocation of rights in the use of underground water. This involves an analysis of the total situation: the quantity of water available, the average annual recharge in the basin, the existing rights and their priorities. All users are required where necessary to employ reasonable and efficient means in taking their own waters in relation to others to the end that wastage of water is avoided and that the greatest amount of available water is put to beneficial use.

Our neighboring state of Colorado, which has water problems similar to our own, in the case of City of Colorado Springs v. Bender[6] has stated:

> At his own point of diversion on a natural water course, each diverter must establish some reasonable means of effectuating his diversion. He is not entitled to command the whole or a substantial flow of the stream merely to facilitate his taking the fraction of the whole flow to which he is entitled. Schodde v. Twin Falls Land & Water Co., 224 U.S. 107, 119. This principle applied to diversion of underflow or underground water means that *priority of appropriation does not give a right to an inefficient means of diversion*, such as a well which reaches to such a shallow depth into the available water supply that a shortage would occur to such senior even though diversion by others did not deplete the stream below where there would be an adequate supply for the senior's lawful demand.

* * *

That an efficient and practical allocation and regulation of underground waters requires a recognition of this principle is further indicated by the fact that several of our western neighbors have in substance codified such a rule.

We perceive nothing in our statutory law inconsistent with this "rule of reasonableness" just discussed, nor which compels a conclusion that owners of rights to use underground water have any absolute right to pressure. * * *

It is further evident from our statutes on this subject that the legislature, in an awareness of the complexities involved in the regulation and use of underground water, has recognized that it is essential to have the benefit of the expertise of the State Engineer and his staff who are professionally qualified to make such determinations. * * *

---

6. 148 Colo. 458, 366 P.2d 552, 555 (1961).

* * * What is desirable is the best possible adjustment of the rights of these parties in relationship to each other, and without undue or unreasonable burden upon either, and at the same time serve the desideratum of our water law of putting and keeping to the beneficial use the greatest possible amount of available water. Because it is our judgment that the decree of the district court does not achieve that objective, and because of the importance of the rights, not only of the parties here in contention, but of the policy considerations underlying this proceeding, we feel impelled to remand this case for further proceedings and settlement of rights in conformity with the principles we have set forth in this opinion. * * *

NOTES

1. The "right" to static pressure was addressed earlier by the Utah Supreme Court. The court held that "[p]rior appropriators of * * * underground water who have beneficially used it through the natural flow of springs or artesian wells were entitled to have the subsequent appropriators restrained from drawing the water out of and lowering the static head pressure of this underground basin unless they replaced the quality and quantity of the water by pumping or other means to the prior appropriator at the sole cost of the subsequent appropriators." Current Creek Irrigation Co. v. Andrews, 9 Utah 2d 324, 344 P.2d 528, 531 (1959). This has come to be known as the "junior pays" rule. Justice Crockett vigorously dissented:

> I doubt the wisdom of seeking solutions to problems such as the instant ones in such a generality as a rule that a prior user has the absolute right not only to the water, but to have preserved to him the pressure and the means of diversion under all circumstances. Such a rule may seem easy for the court to apply to rid itself of immediate problems, but it is far from easy in practical operation. More important, it does not serve the fundamental purpose of our water law of providing for the fullest conservation and the highest development of water by making it available to all users in the most convenient and economical way. The rule is impractical because in some instances it would produce these bad effects: (1) it would compel wasteful exposures at and near the surface and/or wasteful drainage from the basin; (2) the foregoing would result because in some instances it would be too expensive for later users to pay the cost of lifting their own water and also to bear the expense of maintaining pressure for all prior appropriators; and (3) the problem of administering the allocation of the costs of doing so would be insuperable.

Id. at 534.

Are Justice Crockett's concerns adequately dealt with in *Wayman*?

2. The decision in the principal case relies on Colorado Springs v. Bender, 148 Colo. 458, 366 P.2d 552 (1961). In that case, Bender, who had a small (55 head) cattle operation, sought to prevent the city of Colorado Springs from rendering his shallow, hand-dug well useless. The city had been granted an easement to place its well on the land of Bender's neighbor, a corn farmer. Because the aquifer sloped away from Bender's land, lowering the water table took it out of his reach. The state supreme court instructed the trial court as follows:

> Following such additional evidence as the litigants may desire to present, the following things must be done:
>
> (1) The rate of flow of senior and junior appropriators whose rights are involved, together with the dates of priority of each appropriation, must be determined.
>
> (2) The elevation of water in the aquifer at which each junior appropriator must cease to divert water in order to meet the demands of a senior appropriator must be fixed.
>
> (3) In determining the facts mentioned (under (2)) the conditions surrounding the diversion by the senior appropriator must be examined as to whether he has created a means of diversion from the aquifer which is reasonably adequate for the use to which he has historically put the water of his appropriation. If adequate means for reaching a sufficient supply can be made available to the senior, whose present facilities for diversion fail when water table is lowered by acts of the junior appropriators, provision for such adequate means should be decreed at the expense of the junior appropriators, it being unreasonable to require the senior to supply such means out of his own financial resources. * * *
>
> * * * The court must determine what, if anything, the plaintiffs [seniors] should be required to do to make more efficient the facilities at their point of diversion, due regard being given to the purposes for which the appropriation had been made, and the "economic reach" of plaintiffs. The plaintiffs * * * cannot be required to improve their extraction facilities beyond their economic reach, upon a consideration of all the factors involved.

Id. at 556.

After *Bender,* the state engineer attempted to decide which wells met the "economic reach" rule announced in *Bender* and which did not. In one case, however, he shut down thirty-six wells in the Arkansas Valley without formulating any guidelines. The supreme court held that the action was arbitrary. Fellhauer v. People, 167 Colo. 320, 447 P.2d 986 (1968). Subsequent legislation and administrative regulations established standards. *Fellhauer* has had a broader impact, however, for in dictum the supreme court gave its blessing to new approaches to regulating uses under both ground and surface water rights that extend beyond simple considerations of their relative priorities:

> These uses, and similar uses on other rivers, have developed under article XVI, section 6 of the Colorado constitution which contains *inter alia* two provisions:
>
> > "The right to divert the unappropriated waters of any natural stream to beneficial uses shall never be denied. Priority of appro-

priation shall give the better right as between those using the water for the same purpose;"

* * * It is implicit in these constitutional provisions that, along with *vested rights*, there shall be *maximum utilization* of the water of this state. As administration of water approaches its second century the curtain is opening upon the new drama of *maximum utilization* and how constitutionally that doctrine can be integrated into the law of *vested rights*. We have known for a long time that the doctrine was lurking in the backstage shadows as a result of the accepted, though oft violated, principle that the right to water does not give the right to waste it.

Colorado Springs v. Bender might be called the signal that the curtain was about to rise.

Id. at 994.

3. What rule should a court or administrator formulate to allocate the cost of lower static pressure levels between senior and junior appropriators? Economics provides one set of criteria in the definition of efficiency. Applied to water the resource is efficiently allocated and social welfare maximized when it is consumed to the point that demand equals marginal cost. Marginal cost in the case of groundwater has both an internal (the cost borne by the pumper) and an external (the costs imposed on all other units) component. Demand is a function of the value of the marginal product—the increase in the amount of output by the application of water multiplied by the price of the product.

Consider the outcome in *Wayman* and the economic reach rule of *Bender*. Under what circumstances should the court enjoin a junior pumper or impose damages? Suppose that A has a well from which 10 cfs is pumped to irrigate barley. A usually makes $10,000 a year on the barley. B then drills a well to produce 50 cfs needed for a business that will enjoy a $1 million a year profit. What remedy lies if: (1) B's well makes it impossible for A to produce water, causing A to go out of business? (2) B's well makes it necessary for A to construct a new well at a cost of $10,000? (3) B's well lowers the water table so that A must pay $1000 more a year for electricity to run the pump?

4. One promising conjunctive use of surface water and groundwater is the storage of available surface water in aquifers (through the use of injection wells or natural seepage from the surface) until it is needed for application to a beneficial use. An obvious benefit of such storage would be reduced evaporation as compared with surface reservoirs. Led by California, a few states have authorized aquifer recharge. Legislation is needed to encourage the practice and establish legal protection for rights to the stored water. See, *e.g.*, Ariz. Rev. Stat. Ann. § 45–811.01 (West Supp. 2003); Cal. Water Code § 1242 (West 1971); Idaho Code § 42–4201A (Michie 2003); N.M. Stat. Ann. § 72–5A–1 to –17 (Michie Supp. 2006); 2 Colo. Code Regs. § 402–11 (1995).

Is there any danger that the utilization of aquifers for storage of surface water could lead to injury of other water users? How? What conditions, if any, should be imposed on such storage plans to protect other users? See Board of County Comm'rs of Park County v. Park County Sportsmen's Ranch, L.L.P., 45 P.3d 693 (Colo. 2002). Whatever the conditions, the burden of proving that they have been met is normally on the applicant, often relying on groundwater modeling.

Michigan Citizens for Water Conservation v. Nestlé Waters North America, Inc.

Court of Appeals of Michigan, 2005.
269 Mich.App. 25, 709 N.W.2d 174.

[A water conservation organization and property owners of lands riparian to a spring and a lake brought suit against a company pumping groundwater for bottling. The plaintiffs sought an injunction against the pumping of groundwater that would otherwise reach the surface stream. The trial court granted an injunction and both parties appealed.]

B. Michigan Water Law

In order to provide some much-needed perspective on the applicable law, we shall engage in a discussion of the doctrines historically applied to water disputes and trace the origin and development of water law in Michigan. Traditionally, water law has developed along two distinct lines: (1) the law applicable to water use by riparian owners and (2) the law applicable to groundwater uses.

1. Riparian Water Rights

Under the common law, three main doctrines have developed for dealing with riparian water rights: the English common-law rule, also known as the natural flow doctrine; the reasonable use doctrine; and the appropriation or prior use doctrine. Stoebuck & Whitman, The Law of Property (3d ed.), § 7.4, pp. 422–425. Of these doctrines, the natural flow doctrine and the reasonable use doctrine are relevant to the development of water law in Michigan.

* * *

What constitutes a reasonable use must be determined on a case-by-case basis. *People v. Hulbert,* 131 Mich. 156, 170, 91 N.W. 211 (1902). However, diversions of water from a lake or stream that do not benefit riparian lands were generally considered unreasonable per se. In addition, natural water uses are preferred over artificial uses. *Thompson v. Enz,* 379 Mich. 667, 686, 154 N.W.2d 473 (1967) (plurality opinion of Kavanagh, J.). Hence, under Michigan's riparian authorities, water disputes between riparian proprietors are resolved by a reasonable use test that balances competing water uses to determine whether one riparian proprietor's water use, which interferes with another's use, is unreasonable under the circumstances.

2. Groundwater Water Law

As with riparian water law, there are three main common-law doctrines applicable to groundwater disputes. Stoebuck & Whitman, § 7.5, p 427. The first doctrine is referred to as the English rule or the absolute ownership rule, which was first stated in *Acton v. Blundell,* 12 Mees & W 324; 152 Eng. Rep. 1223 (Exch. 1843). Stoebuck & Whitman, pp. 427–428. Under this rule, "a possessor of land may withdraw as much underground water as he wishes, for whatever purposes he wishes, and let his neighbors look elsewhere than the law for relief." *Id.* at 428, 154 N.W.2d 473.

In America, the most prevalent rule applicable to groundwater disputes is the doctrine of reasonable use, which is also called the American doctrine or the doctrine of correlative rights. *Id.* However, the doctrine of reasonable use is not actually dependent on the reasonableness of the use; rather,

> [a]s the doctrine has developed, it generally has been held that all uses of water upon the land from which it is extracted are "reasonable," even if they more or less deplete the supply to the harm of neighbors, unless the purpose is malicious or the water simply wasted. But ... when the question is whether water may be transported off that land for use elsewhere, this is usually found "unreasonable," though it has sometimes been permitted. Authorities are not all agreed, but a principle that seems to harmonize the decisions is that water may be extracted for use elsewhere only up to the point that it begins to injure owners within the aquifer. [*Id.* at 428–429, 154 N.W.2d 473.]

The last doctrine is a variant of the reasonable use doctrine developed in California, which is often called the correlative rights doctrine. Stoebuck & Whitman, p 429. Under this doctrine,

> [o]wners of land within an aquifer are viewed as having equal rights to put the water to beneficial uses upon those lands. However, an owner's rights do not extend to depleting his neighbor's supply, at least not seriously so, for in the event of a water shortage, a court may apportion the supply that is available among all the owners. It is sometimes said that this is the application of the reasonable use doctrine of flowing streams to underground water.... As to uses outside the land from which the water is drawn, for municipal and other uses, the rule is similar to that under the ordinary reasonable use doctrine: water may be transported only if the overlying owners have been fully supplied. [*Id.*]

a. *Schenk*

The seminal case dealing with groundwater rights in Michigan is *Schenk v. City of Ann Arbor,* 196 Mich. 75, 163 N.W. 109 (1917). In *Schenk,* the city of Ann Arbor purchased land outside the city on which it planned to build a pumping station, and began pumping tests that drew approximately 3.8 million gallons of water daily for several weeks. *Id.* at 77–78, 163

N.W. 109. Numerous persons commenced actions seeking to restrain the city from pumping, including the plaintiff, because of harms allegedly caused by the pumping. *Id.* at 78–80, 163 N.W. 109. However, because the plaintiff in *Schenk* had successfully restored his water supply by lowering his well three feet, the trial court denied the plaintiff's request for an injunction, but granted damages for the actual harm already suffered. *Id.* at 80, 163 N.W. 109.

Before making its decision, the Court noted that the parties were not riparian owners and that the underground waters were percolating waters rather than waters running in a defined underground channel. The Court also noted that the city planned to pipe the water away from the lands from which it was drawn. *Id.* at 81, 163 N.W. 109. The Court then recited the rule of absolute ownership and the authorities for that rule, stating, "While this is the rule applied, and to be applied, in respect to most of the ordinary uses of land, and the ordinary operations carried on upon and in land, there is other doctrine, apparently, but not strictly, a modification of the early common-law doctrine referred to, which is sometimes called the doctrine of reasonable user, and which was introduced by equity to the law." *Id.* at 82, 163 N.W. 109. The Court then adopted the "rule of reasonable user" for the reasons stated by the court in *Meeker v. City of East Orange*, 77 N.J.L. 623, 636–639, 74 A. 379 (N.J.1909). *Schenk, supra* at 82–84, 163 N.W. 109.

> "This [rule] does not prevent the proper user by any landowner of the percolating waters subjacent to his soil in agriculture, manufacturing, irrigation, or otherwise, nor does it prevent any reasonable development of his land by mining or the like, although the underground water of neighboring properties may thus be interfered with or diverted; but it does prevent the withdrawal of underground waters for distribution or sale for uses not connected with any beneficial ownership or enjoyment of the land whence they are taken, if it results therefrom that the owner of adjacent or neighboring land is interfered with in his right to the reasonable user of subsurface water upon his land, or if his wells, springs, or streams are thereby materially diminished in flow, or his land is rendered so arid as to be less valuable for agriculture, pasturage, or other legitimate uses." [*Id.* at 84, 163 N.W. 109, quoting *Meeker, supra* at 638–639, 74 A. 379.]

Although the city was extracting the water for use off the property from which it was extracted, and therefore was subject to the limitations of the reasonable use rule, the Court determined that the plaintiff was not entitled to an injunction because he had lowered his well and regained a supply of water and no other harm was demonstrated entitling him to equitable relief. However, the Court left open the possibility of a future injunction based on a new harm. *Id.* at 92, 163 N.W. 109. Thus, the Court adopted the traditional reasonable use rule, which permits withdrawals of water whose use is not connected with the land from which it is withdrawn, but only to the extent that they do not interfere with an adjacent water user's reasonable use. *Id.* at 84, 163 N.W. 109.

b.   Post–*Schenk* Decisions

After *Schenk,* Michigan courts continued to apply the reasonable use rule stated in *Schenk,* but applied it in a flexible manner to ensure that no one user would be deprived of all beneficial use of its water resources.

* * *

3.   Conclusion

We agree with the *Maerz* Court's conclusion that a reasonable use balancing test is consistent with the Michigan authorities governing water use.[42] Beginning with *Dumont* and *Schenk* and concluding with *Maerz,* Michigan courts have consistently avoided strict rules that permit one water user to utilize water at the expense of an adjacent user. Instead, while employing various tests, the courts have generally sought to ensure the greatest possible access to water resources for all users while protecting certain traditional water uses. See *Dumont, supra* at 423–425. Michigan courts have already recognized the value of the reasonable use balancing test for that purpose. See *Maerz, supra* at 717–720, 323 N.W.2d 524; *Hart, supra* at 322–323, 151 N.W.2d 826; *Dumont, supra* at 423–425. Consequently, in order to recognize the interconnected nature of water sources and fully integrate the law applicable to water disputes, we adopt the reasonable use balancing test first stated in *Dumont* as the law applicable to disputes between riparian and groundwater users.

* * *

2.   Application to the Facts

In the present case, plaintiffs alleged that defendant's groundwater withdrawals interfered with their riparian rights in the Dead Stream, including their right to utilize the stream for recreational boating, wildlife observation, swimming, and fishing, as well as diminishing the aesthetic value of their riparian lands. While some courts have questioned the reasonableness of recreational water uses such as these, see Restatement, § 850A, comment b, p. 223, a plurality of our Supreme Court has determined that recreational uses, including the use of riparian waters as a restful retreat, constitute reasonable uses, *Thompson, supra* at 689, 154 N.W.2d 473. In addition, we recognize that individuals often seek out and invest in riparian property for aesthetic reasons even though they may not partake of recreational activities involving the physical use of the water. Therefore, plaintiffs' use of the stream is a reasonable use worthy of protection.

---

42. However, we do not agree with defendant's contention that the *Maerz* Court intended to make a sweeping adoption of the entire Restatement approach to the resolution of water disputes. Instead, we note that the *Maerz* Court only held that "the *princi-* *ples* expressed in the Restatement . . . should be followed in Michigan." *Maerz, supra* at 720, 323 N.W.2d 524 (emphasis added). Even if the *Maerz* Court had made a sweeping adoption of the Restatement's rule, we would reject it as not binding. See MCR 7.215(J)(1).

It is also uncontested that defendant's use of the disputed water serves a beneficial purpose. Testimony established that defendant's bottling plant employed 140 persons at the time of the trial. This employment directly benefits the workers, their families, and the local community. Likewise, defendant's plant and equipment represent a significant investment in the community and are a source of tax revenue. The provision of water to the general public is also an economically and socially beneficial use of the water. See Restatement, § 850A, comment f, p 226. Therefore, defendant's water use is not inherently unreasonable. Consequently, we must balance the relevant factors to determine whether defendant's use of the water is unreasonable under the circumstances and in light of the harm inflicted on plaintiffs.

Plaintiffs claim that defendant's water withdrawals will harm their recreational and aesthetic use of the Dead Stream, but provide no evidence that defendant's water use has interfered or will interfere with their domestic water supplies. Likewise, defendant's use of the water is for commercial profit. Therefore, both uses are for artificial purposes and neither is entitled to a preference. However, plaintiffs' uses are directly related to the use and enjoyment of their riparian land, whereas defendant's use is not directly related to the land from which the water is withdrawn. Hence, plaintiffs are entitled to some measure of preference as local water users.

All parties agreed that defendant's water withdrawals will capture water that would otherwise have entered the Dead Stream. Hence, defendant's water withdrawals will have a direct effect on the amount of flow in the Dead Stream. In describing the Dead Stream, the trial court noted that it was already a low-flow stream subject to many natural variables. For these reasons, the trial court found that even a modest drop in water level would have dramatic consequences for the stream. Finally, the established uses for the Dead Stream and the lakes to which it connects have traditionally been recreational rather than commercial in character. Considering these factors together, we conclude that the Sanctuary Springs location, with its direct connection to the Dead Stream, is not well suited for high-volume water extractions. Hence, this factor weighs against defendant's use.

In examining the degree of harm to the Dead Stream, the trial court found that it would lose approximately 24 percent of its base flow and 2 inches in stage beyond the stream's natural fluctuations given a withdrawal of 400 gpm. The trial court determined that this reduction in flow would raise the stream's temperature and cause the stream to become choked with plant life. The trial court further found that the loss of flow would cause a narrowing of the channel by at least four feet over a period of time. The trial court determined that these effects would impair the Dead Stream's aesthetic value and its usefulness as a fishery, and would impair recreational navigation of the stream. The loss of recreational use and the physical alteration of the Dead Stream will directly and substantially harm the riparian value of the Dead Stream. Furthermore, while these harms most directly affect those plaintiffs riparian to the Dead Stream, the loss of fishery habitat and recreational value also indirectly affects the quality of fishing and recreation in the entire Tri-lakes area. On the other hand, defendant's bottling enterprise does have significant commercial benefits. The plant directly employs 140 workers and indirectly benefits other workers who provide the plant with necessary goods and services. In addition, the plant provides increased tax revenues to the state and the local community through payroll and property taxes. Overall, under the facts of this case, the harms inflicted on the riparian plaintiffs and the community in general are significantly offset by the economic benefits to society and the local community. Hence, this factor does not favor any party.

In examining the necessity of the manner and amount of defendant's water use, it must be noted that defendant chose the Sanctuary Springs location in order to facilitate its marketing of the extracted water as "spring water." Hence, defendant's options for locating its wells are limited by the nature of the required water source. However, while testimony established that any reduction in the withdrawal rate below 400 gpm will result in the loss of production and jobs, testimony also established that defendant has augmented the supply of water at other plants by shipping it in as needed. In addition, by the time of the trial, defendant had already begun to explore opportunities for obtaining suitable water from other sources. Therefore, defendant does not need to maintain such a high pumping volume at the Sanctuary Spring site in order to continue operations. In contrast, plaintiffs' water uses do not remove water from the system, but do require a minimum level of water, which cannot be mitigated through changes in the manner of use.[59] These factors weigh heavily against defendant's proposed pumping rate of 400 gpm.

3. Conclusion

Although defendant should be permitted to have a "fair participation" in the common water resources of the area, if defendant is permitted to pump at the maximum permitted rate, it will effectively appropriate for its own needs approximately 24 percent of the base flow of the Dead Stream. This is more than a fair participation. While plaintiffs might properly be required to suffer some harm to their use of the Dead Stream, it would be unjust to permit defendant to impose on plaintiffs the entire burden of the harms created by the depletion of the Dead Stream's flow while retaining all the benefits. Furthermore, because defendant is in the best position to spread the costs incurred by a reduction in its use of the water from Sanctuary Springs, it is just that it should bear a greater portion of that burden. See Restatement, § 850A(i), p 220. Therefore, taking all the factors

---

59. The Restatement recognizes that certain water uses, such as boating and recreation, as well as the maintenance of riparian property value, may require the court to protect the integrity of an entire stream or lake. However, such protection is limited to the amount of water needed to preserve the plaintiff's use or the values attributable to the water. Restatement, § 850A, comment i, p 231.

outlined into consideration, we determine that defendant's proposed withdrawal of 400 gpm would be unreasonable under the circumstances.

D. Remedy

Having determined that defendant's proposed withdrawal of water from Sanctuary Springs in the amount of 400 gpm will unreasonably interfere with plaintiffs' riparian water rights in the Dead Stream, we must now determine what the appropriate remedy is under the circumstances. Because of the unique nature of riparian rights, we conclude that an injunction of limited scope is the only adequate remedy.

NOTES

1. The Michigan Supreme Court reversed on standing grounds. See 479 Mich. 280, 737 N.W.2d 447 (2007).

2. In states, like Michigan, that do not follow the prior appropriation doctrine, but where separate judicial doctrines have developed for surface and groundwater, accommodating those doctrines may be particularly challenging. Did the appellate court meet the challenge in Nestlé? Did the court establish principles that will be useful in solving future disputes between other surface and groundwater users?

Musser v. Higginson

Supreme Court of Idaho, 1994.
125 Idaho 392, 871 P.2d 809.

■ JOHNSTON, JUSTICE.

This case is a water distribution case. The primary issue presented is whether the trial court properly issued a writ of mandate ordering the director (the director) of the Idaho department of water resources (the department) immediately to comply with I.C. § 42–602 and distribute water in accordance with the doctrine of prior appropriation.

* * *

Alvin and Tim Musser own real property (the Mussers' property) in Gooding County, Idaho, which has appurtenant to it a decreed right for 4.8 cubic feet per second (cfs) of water from the Martin–Curran Tunnel (the tunnel) with a priority date of April 1, 1892. Howard "Butch" Morris leases the Mussers' property together with the appurtenant water rights. In this opinion, we refer to the Mussers and Morris collectively as "the Mussers."

The Mussers' property is located within water district 36A (the district). The district is served by a watermaster (the watermaster) appointed by the director. The springs which supply the Mussers' water are tributary to the Snake River and are hydrologically interconnected to the Snake plain aquifer (the aquifer).

In the spring of 1993, the Mussers found that the tunnel did not supply them with sufficient water to fulfill their adjudicated water rights. As a result, they contend they planted less acreage than they had previously and that many of their crops were lost and damaged.

On May 25, 1993, other owners of water rights from the tunnel demanded that the watermaster deliver water to them. The watermaster relayed the demand to the director who rejected the demand. On June 16, 1993, the Mussers made a similar demand on the director for the "full and immediate delivery of their decreed water rights from the Curran Tunnel." The director denied the demand on the grounds that "the director is not authorized to direct the watermaster to conjunctively administer ground and surface water within Water District 36A short of a formal hydrologic determination that such conjunctive management is appropriate."

The Mussers sought a writ of mandate to compel the director: (1) to deliver their full decreed water rights, and (2) to control the distribution of water from the aquifer according to the priority date of the decreed water rights.

The director and the department moved to dismiss the Mussers' request for a writ of mandate, arguing that the request was moot because after the Mussers initiated the action, the director issued a notice of intent to promulgate rules and a notice and order for a contested case. The proposed rules would allow the director to respond to the Mussers' demands by providing for the conjunctive management of the aquifer and the Snake River. The contested case would provide a forum for determining how to deliver the Mussers' water pending completion of the proposed rules. Alternatively, the director and the department contended the petition should be dismissed because a writ of mandate is an inappropriate method by which to litigate the relationship between senior and junior ground water rights.

The trial court denied the motion to dismiss and concluded that the director owes the Mussers "a clear legal duty to distribute water under the prior appropriation doctrine." The trial court determined that the director's failure to adopt rules and regulations enabling him to respond to the Mussers' demand for delivery of their water was a breach of his "mandatory, ministerial duty." The trial court also said the director's refusal to honor the Mussers' demand was "arbitrary and capricious" and that the Mussers had no "adequate, plain or speedy remedy at law."

The trial court issued a writ of mandate commanding the director "to immediately comply with I.C. § 42–602 and distribute water in accordance with the Constitution of the State of Idaho and the laws of this state commonly referred to as the Doctrine of Prior Appropriation...." The director and the department appealed and asked the trial court to stay the writ during the appeal. The trial court denied the motion to stay, noting: "I don't see what there is in the writ of mandate that needs to be stayed since the department is proceeding to honor it in its entirety." This Court also denied the request of the director and the department to stay the writ during this appeal.

* * *

The director and the department assert that the trial court should not have issued the writ of mandate. We disagree.

In *Idaho Falls Redev. Agency v. Countryman*, 118 Idaho 43, 794 P.2d 632 (1990), the Court recapitulated the requirements for the issuance of a writ of mandate:

In *Utah Power & Light Co. v. Campbell*, 108 Idaho 950, 953, 703 P.2d 714, 717 (1985), this Court stated that "[m]andamus will lie if the officer against whom the writ is brought has a 'clear legal duty' to perform the desired act, and if the act sought to be compelled is ministerial or executive in nature." Existence of an adequate remedy in the ordinary course of law, either legal or equitable in nature, will prevent issuance of a writ, and the party seeking the writ must prove that no such remedy exists. This Court has repeatedly held that mandamus is not a writ of right and the allowance or refusal to issue a writ of mandate is discretionary. Likewise, Idaho law requires that a writ must be issued in those cases where there is not a plain, speedy, and adequate remedy in the ordinary course of law.

Id. at 44, 794 P.2d at 633 (citations omitted).

I.C. § 42–602 provides:

It shall be the duty of the director of the department of water resources to have *immediate direction and control* of the *distribution of water* from all of the streams, rivers, lakes, ground water and other natural water sources in this state to the canals, ditches, pumps and other facilities diverting therefrom. Distribution of water shall be accomplished either (1) *by watermasters* appointed as provided in this chapter and supervised by the director; or (2) *directly by employees of the department* of water resources under authority of the director in those areas of the state not constituted into water districts as provided in this chapter. *The director must execute the laws relative to the distribution of water in accordance with rights of prior appropriation as provided in section 42–106, Idaho Code.*

The director of the department of water resources shall, in the distribution of water from the streams, rivers, lakes, ground water and other natural water sources, be governed by this title.

I.C. § 42–602 (emphasis added).

We conclude that the director's duty to distribute water pursuant to this statute is a clear legal duty. The director himself testified that he was aware that his duty to deliver water under I.C. § 42–602 is mandatory.

[1]   The director contends, however, that although his duty under I.C. § 42–602 is mandatory, the statute leaves to the director's discretion the means that will be used to respond to calls for water. For more than three-quarters of a century, the Court has adhered to the following principle:

"The fact that certain details are left to the discretion of the authorities does not prevent relief by *mandamus.*" *Beem v. Davis*, 31 Idaho 730, 736, 175 P. 959, 961 (1918) (emphasis in original). *See also Moerder v. City of Moscow*, 74 Idaho 410, 415, 263 P.2d 993, 998 (1953) ("Public officials may, under some circumstances, be compelled by writ of mandate to perform their official duties, although the details of such performance are left to their discretion.")

[2]   This principle applies to this case. The director's duty pursuant to I.C. s 42–602 is clear and executive. Although the details of the performance of the duty are left to the director's discretion, the director has the duty to distribute water.

The director defended his refusal to honor the Mussers' demand by claiming that a "policy" of the department prevented him from taking action. In his testimony at the hearing to consider whether the writ would issue, the director referred to I.C. § 42–226 and stated that "a decision has to be made in the public interest as to whether those who are impacted by groundwater development are unreasonably blocking full use of the resource."

We note that the original version of what is now I.C. § 42–226 was enacted in 1951. 1951 Idaho Sess.Laws, ch. 200, § 1, p. 423. Both the original version and the current statute make it clear that this statute does not affect rights to the use of ground water acquired before the enactment of the statute distribute water to the Mussers, whose priority date is April 1, 1892.

The Mussers presented evidence indicating that suing the director for damages was not a plain, adequate, and speedy remedy in the ordinary course of law because of the ongoing nature of the harm and the difficulty in determining the damages they would incur due to the director's refusal to comply with I.C. § 42–602. The Mussers also contended that suing the director was inadequate because of the director's immunity from damages under I.C. § 6–904, a portion of the Idaho tort claims act.

The director and the department contend that the Mussers could have pursued administrative hearings before the director, administrative appeals, and motions for interim administration of water rights. We note that the only manner in which any of these asserted remedies were presented to the trial court was in the final argument by the attorney for the director and the department at the hearing concerning the request for the writ. There, the attorney argued that the Mussers should seek a hearing and then judicial review pursuant to I.C. §§ 42–237e and 42–1701A. Because these were the only alternative remedies presented to the trial court, these are the only ones we will address.

I.C. § 42–237e states:

> Any person dissatisfied with any decision, determination, order or action of the director of the department of water resources. . . . made pursuant to this act may, if a hearing on the matter already has been held, seek judicial review pursuant to section 42–1701A(4), Idaho Code.

If a hearing has not been held, any person aggrieved by the action of the director. . . . may contest such action pursuant to section 42–1701A(3), Idaho Code.

By its terms, I.C. § 42–1701A(3) applies only to "any applicant for any permit, license, certificate, approval, registration, or similar form of permission required by law to be issued by the director." I.C. § 42–1701A(3) concludes: "Judicial review of any final order of the director issued following the hearing may be had pursuant to subsection (4) of this section." These provisions do not apply to the circumstances presented in this case. The Mussers did not seek a permit, license, certificate, approval, registration, or similar form of permission required by law to be issued by the director. Therefore, these remedies are not available to the Mussers to obtain review of the director's refusal to comply with I.C. § 42–602.

* * *

We affirm the trial court's issuance of the writ of mandate * * *.

■ McDEVITT, C.J., and BISTLINE, TROUT and SILAK, JJ., concur.

NOTES

1. Within a year following the decision in *Musser*, the Idaho Department of Water Resources promulgated Rules for Conjunctive Management of Surface and Ground Water Resources, the "proposed rules" referred to in the case. Idaho Administrative Procedure Act (IDAPA) 37.03.11. (10–7–94).

Selected portions of the Rules follow:

010. DEFINITIONS (RULE 10).

For the purposes of these rules, the following terms will be used as defined below. (10–7–94)

01. Area Having a Common Ground Water Supply. A ground water source within which the diversion and use of ground water or changes in ground water recharge affect the flow of water in a surface water source or within which the diversion and use of water by a holder of a ground water right affects the ground water supply available to the holders of other ground water rights. (Section 42–237a.g., Idaho Code)

02. Artificial Ground Water Recharge. A deliberate and purposeful activity or project that is performed in accordance with Section 42–234(2), Idaho Code, and that diverts, distributes, injects, stores or spreads water to areas from which such water will enter into and recharge a ground water source in an area having a common ground water supply.

03. Conjunctive Management. Legal and hydrologic integration of administration of the diversion and use of water under water rights from surface and ground water sources, including areas having a common ground water supply.

04. Delivery Call. A request from the holder of a water right for administration of water rights under the prior appropriation doctrine.

* * *

07. Full Economic Development of Underground Water Resources. The diversion and use of water from a ground water source for beneficial uses in the public interest at a rate that does not exceed the reasonably anticipated average rate of future natural recharge, in a manner that does not result in material injury to senior-priority surface or ground water rights, and that furthers the principle of reasonable use of surface and ground water as set forth in Rule 42.

08. Futile Call. A delivery call made by the holder of a senior-priority surface or ground water right that, for physical and hydrologic reasons, cannot be satisfied within a reasonable time of the call by immediately curtailing diversions under junior-priority ground water rights or that would result in waste of the water resource.

* * *

14. Material Injury. Hindrance to or impact upon the exercise of a water right caused by the use of water by another person as determined in accordance with Idaho Law, as set forth in Rule 42.

15. Mitigation Plan. A document submitted by the holder(s) of a junior-priority ground water right and approved by the Director as provided in Rule 043 that identifies actions and measures to prevent, or compensate holders of senior-priority water rights for, material injury caused by the diversion and use of water by the holders of junior-priority ground water rights within an area having a common ground water supply.

* * *

18. Reasonable Ground Water Pumping Level. A level established by the Director pursuant to Sections 42–226, and 42–237a.g., Idaho Code, either generally for an area or aquifer or for individual water rights on a case-by-case basis, for the purpose of protecting the holders of senior-priority ground water rights against unreasonable lowering of ground water levels caused by diversion and use of surface or ground water by the holders of junior-priority surface or ground water rights under Idaho law.

* * *

020. GENERAL STATEMENTS OF PURPOSE AND POLICIES FOR CONJUNCTIVE MANAGEMENT OF SURFACE AND GROUND WATER RESOURCES (RULE 20).

01. Distribution of Water Among the Holders of Senior and Junior–Priority Rights. These rules apply to all situations in the state where the diversion and use of water under junior-priority ground water rights either individually or collectively causes material injury to uses of water under senior-priority water rights. The rules govern the distribution of water from ground water sources and areas having a common ground water supply.

02.   Prior Appropriation Doctrine. These rules acknowledge all elements of the prior appropriation doctrine as established by Idaho law.

03.   Reasonable Use of Surface and Ground Water. These rules integrate the administration and use of surface and ground water in a manner consistent with the traditional policy of reasonable use of both surface and ground water. The policy of reasonable use includes the concepts of priority in time and superiority in right being subject to conditions of reasonable use as the legislature may by law prescribe as provided in Article XV, Section 5, Idaho Constitution, optimum development of water resources in the public interest prescribed in Article XV, Section 7, Idaho Constitution, and full economic development as defined by Idaho law. An appropriator is not entitled to command the entirety of large volumes of water in a surface or ground water source to support his appropriation contrary to the public policy of reasonable use of water as described in this rule.

04.   Delivery Calls. These rules provide the basis and procedure for responding to delivery calls made by the holder of a senior-priority surface or ground water right against the holder of a junior-priority ground water right. The principle of the futile call applies to the distribution of water under these rules. Although a call may be denied under the futile call doctrine, these rules may require mitigation or staged or phased curtailment of a junior-priority use if diversion and use of water by the holder of the junior-priority water right causes material injury, even though not immediately measurable, to the holder of a senior-priority surface or ground water right in instances where the hydrologic connection may be remote, the resource is large and no direct immediate relief would be achieved if the junior-priority water use was discontinued.

05.   Exercise of Water Rights. These rules provide the basis for determining the reasonableness of the diversion and use of water by both the holder of a senior-priority water right who requests priority delivery and the holder of a junior-priority water right against whom the call is made.

06.   Areas Having a Common Ground Water Supply. These rules provide the basis for the designation of areas of the state that have a common ground water supply and the procedures that will be followed in incorporating the water rights within such areas into existing water districts or creating new districts as provided in Section 42–237a.g., and Section 42–604, Idaho Code, or designating such areas as ground water management areas as provided in Section 42–233(b), Idaho Code.

07.   Sequence of Actions for Responding to Delivery Calls.
Rule 30 provides procedures for responding to delivery calls within
areas having a common ground water supply that have not been
incorporated into an existing or new water district or designated a
ground water management area. Rule 40 provides procedures for
responding to delivery calls within water districts where areas having a
common ground water supply have been incorporated into the district
or a new district has been created. Rule 41 provides procedures for
responding to delivery calls within areas that have been designated as
ground water management areas. Rule 50 designates specific known
areas having a common ground water supply within the state.

**08.   Reasonably Anticipated Average Rate of Future Natu-
ral Recharge.** These rules provide for administration of the use of
ground water resources to achieve the goal that withdrawals of ground
water not exceed the reasonably anticipated average rate of future
natural recharge. (Section 42–237a.g., Idaho Code)

* * *

**030.   RESPONSES TO CALLS FOR WATER DELIVERY MADE
BY THE HOLDERS OF SENIOR–PRIORITY SURFACE OR
GROUND WATER RIGHTS AGAINST THE HOLDERS OF JUN-
IOR–PRIORITY GROUND WATER RIGHTS WITHIN AREAS
OF THE STATE NOT IN ORGANIZED WATER DISTRICTS OR
WITHIN WATER DISTRICTS WHERE GROUND WATER REG-
ULATION HAS NOT BEEN INCLUDED IN THE FUNCTIONS
OF SUCH DISTRICTS OR WITHIN AREAS THAT HAVE NOT
BEEN DESIGNATED GROUND WATER MANAGEMENT AR-
EAS (RULE 30).**

01.   Delivery Call (Petition). When a delivery call is made by
the holder of a surface or ground water right (petitioner) alleging that
by reason of diversion of water by the holders of one (1) or more
junior-priority ground water rights (respondents) the petitioner is
suffering material injury, the petitioner shall file with the Director a
petition * * *

* * *

07.   Order. Following consideration of the contested case under
the Department's Rules of Procedure, the Director may, by order, take
any or all of the following actions:

   a.   Deny the petition in whole or in part;

   b.   Grant the petition in whole or in part or upon conditions;

   c.   Determine an area having a common ground water supply
which affects the flow of water in a surface water source in an
organized water district;

   d.   Incorporate an area having a common ground water supply into an organized water district following the procedures of
Section 42–604, Idaho Code, provided that the ground water rights

that would be incorporated into the water district have been adjudicated relative to the rights already encompassed within the district;

e. Create a new water district following the procedures of Section 42–604, Idaho Code, provided that the water rights to be included in the new water district have been adjudicated;

f. Determine the need for an adjudication of the priorities and permissible rates and volumes of diversion and consumptive use under the surface and ground water rights of the petitioner and respondents and initiate such adjudication pursuant to Section 42–1406, Idaho Code;

g. By summary order as provided in Section 42–237 a.g., Idaho Code, prohibit or limit the withdrawal of water from any well during any period it is determined that water to fill any water right is not there available without causing ground water levels to be drawn below the reasonable ground water pumping level, or would affect the present or future use of any prior surface or ground water right or result in the withdrawing of the ground water supply at a rate beyond the reasonably anticipated average rate of future natural recharge. The Director will take into consideration the existence of any approved mitigation plan before issuing any order prohibiting or limiting withdrawal of water from any well; or

h. Designate a ground water management area under the provisions of Section 42–233(b), Idaho Code, if it appears that administration of the diversion and use of water from an area having a common ground water supply is required because the ground water supply is insufficient to meet the demands of water rights or the diversion and use of water is at a rate beyond the reasonably anticipated average rate of future natural recharge and modification of an existing water district or creation of a new water district cannot be readily accomplished due to the need to first obtain an adjudication of the water rights.

* * *

040. RESPONSES TO CALLS FOR WATER DELIVERY MADE BY THE HOLDERS OF SENIOR–PRIORITY SURFACE OR GROUND WATER RIGHTS AGAINST THE HOLDERS OF JUNIOR–PRIORITY GROUND WATER RIGHTS FROM AREAS HAVING A COMMON GROUND WATER SUPPLY IN AN ORGANIZED WATER DISTRICT (RULE 40).

01. Responding to a Delivery Call. When a delivery call is made by the holder of a senior-priority water right (petitioner) alleging that by reason of diversion of water by the holders of one (1) or more junior-priority ground water rights (respondents) from an area having a common ground water supply in an organized water district the petitioner is suffering material injury, and upon a finding by the

Director as provided in Rule 42 that material injury is occurring, the Director, through the watermaster, shall:

a. Regulate the diversion and use of water in accordance with the priorities of rights of the various surface or ground water users whose rights are included within the district, provided, that regulation of junior-priority ground water diversion and use where the material injury is delayed or long range may, by order of the Director, be phased-in over not more than a five-year (5) period to lessen the economic impact of immediate and complete curtailment; or

b. Allow out-of-priority diversion of water by junior-priority ground water users pursuant to a mitigation plan that has been approved by the Director.

02.   Regulation of Uses of Water by Watermaster. The Director, through the watermaster, shall regulate use of water within the water district pursuant to Idaho law and the priorities of water rights as provided in Section 42–604, Idaho Code, and under the following procedures:

a. The watermaster shall determine the quantity of surface water of any stream included within the water district which is available for diversion and shall shut the headgates of the holders of junior-priority surface water rights as necessary to assure that water is being diverted and used in accordance with the priorities of the respective water rights from the surface water source.

b. The watermaster shall regulate the diversion and use of ground water in accordance with the rights thereto, approved mitigation plans and orders issued by the Director.

c. Where a call is made by the holder of a senior-priority water right against the holder of a junior-priority ground water right in the water district the watermaster shall first determine whether a mitigation plan has been approved by the Director whereby diversion of ground water may be allowed to continue out of priority order. If the holder of a junior-priority ground water right is a participant in such approved mitigation plan, and is operating in conformance therewith, the watermaster shall allow the ground water use to continue out of priority.

* * *

041.   ADMINISTRATION OF DIVERSION AND USE OF WATER WITHIN A GROUND WATER MANAGEMENT AREA (RULE 41).

01.   Responding to a Delivery Call. When a delivery call is made by the holder of a senior-priority ground water right against holders of junior-priority ground water rights in a designated ground water management area alleging that the ground water supply is insufficient to meet the demands of water rights within all or portions of the ground water management area and requesting the Director to order water right holders, on a time priority basis, to cease or reduce withdrawal of water, the Director shall proceed as follows:

    a.   The petitioner shall be required to submit all information available to petitioner on which the claim is based that the water supply is insufficient.

    b.   The Director shall conduct a fact-finding hearing on the petition at which the petitioner and respondents may present evidence on the water supply, and the diversion and use of water from the ground water management area.

    02.   Order. Following the hearing, the Director may take any or all of the following actions:

    a.   Deny the petition in whole or in part;

    b.   Grant the petition in whole or in part or upon conditions;

    c.   Find that the water supply of the ground water management area is insufficient to meet the demands of water rights within all or portions of the ground water management area and order water right holders on a time priority basis to cease or reduce withdrawal of water, provided that the Director shall consider the expected benefits of an approved mitigation plan in making such finding

    d.   Require the installation of measuring devices and the reporting of water diversions pursuant to Section 42–701, Idaho Code.

* * *

042.   DETERMINING MATERIAL INJURY AND REASONABLENESS OF WATER DIVERSIONS (RULE 42).

    01.   Factors. Factors the Director may consider in determining whether the holders of water rights are suffering material injury and using water efficiently and without waste include, but are not limited to, the following:

    a.   The amount of water available in the source from which the water right is diverted.

    b.   The effort or expense of the holder of the water right to divert water from the source.

    c.   Whether the exercise of junior-priority ground water rights individually or collectively affects the quantity and timing of when water is available to, and the cost of exercising, a senior-priority surface or ground water right. This may include the seasonal as well as the multi-year and cumulative impacts of all ground water withdrawals from the area having a common ground water supply.

    d.   If for irrigation, the rate of diversion compared to the acreage of land served, the annual volume of water diverted, the system diversion and conveyance efficiency, and the method of irrigation water application.

e.   The amount of water being diverted and used compared to the water rights

f.   The existence of water measuring and recording devices.

g.   The extent to which the requirements of the holder of a senior-priority water right could be met with the user's existing facilities and water supplies by employing reasonable diversion and conveyance efficiency and conservation practices; provided, however, the holder of a surface water storage right shall be entitled to maintain a reasonable amount of carry-over storage to assure water supplies for future dry years. In determining a reasonable amount of carry-over storage water, the Director shall consider the average annual rate of fill of storage reservoirs and the average annual carry-over for prior comparable water conditions and the projected water supply for the system.

h.   The extent to which the requirements of the senior-priority surface water right could be met using alternate reasonable means of diversion or alternate points of diversion, including the construction of wells or the use of existing wells to divert and use water from the area having a common ground water supply under the petitioner's surface water right priority.

02.   Delivery Call for Curtailment of Pumping. The holder of a senior-priority surface or ground water right will be prevented from making a delivery call for curtailment of pumping of any well used by the holder of a junior-priority ground water right where use of water under the junior-priority right is covered by an approved and effectively operating mitigation plan.

* * *

2.   The constitutionality of these Rules was challenged in American Falls Reservoir District No. 2 v. Idaho Department of Water Resources, 143 Idaho 862, 154 P.3d 433 (2007). After pointing out the sharp difference between a constitutional challenge as the law is applied in a particular case, and a facial challenge, the court noted that "[f]or a facial constitutional challenge to succeed, the part must demonstrate that the law is unconstitutional in *all* of its applications. In other words, 'the challenger must establish that no set of circumstances exists under which the [law] would be valid.' " [citations omitted]. *Id.* at 441. Holding that the Rules met this standard, the court pointed out that Rule 20.02 specifically "incorporate[s] Idaho law by reference," id. at 444, and commented:

Somewhere between the absolute right to use a decreed water right and an obligation not to waste it and to protect the public's interest in this valuable commodity, lies an area for the exercise of discretion by the Director. This is certainly not unfettered discretion, nor is it discretion to be exercised without any oversight. That oversight is provided by the courts, and upon a properly developed record, this

Court can determine whether that exercise of discretion is being properly carried out. *Id.* at 451.

3. Do the Idaho Conjunctive Management Rules successfully navigate these constitutional waters in situations that are likely to arise? What of the time required to pursue hearings before the Department of Water Resources, determining the presence of "material" injury, or evaluating the "reasonableness" of carry-over storage amounts?

NOTE: INTEGRATION OF SURFACE WATER AND GROUNDWATER ADMINISTRATION

Some courts have found ways to overcome the unscientific treatment of hydrologically connected groundwater and surface water in order to allow for sound practical administration. Under Arizona law, "percolating water" is not appropriable but belongs to the landowner. A spring surfaced in a dry creek bed on land in Arizona owned by the Colliers. They named it "Miracle Spring," dammed the waters flowing from it, and sought a permit to appropriate the water. Because the spring water was percolating water belonging to them, and from which they could have freely pumped before it broke through the surface, the Colliers argued that it was a new appropriable source. Ranchers with vested surface water rights to waters of the creek where it flowed on the surface at lower elevations, contended that they had already appropriated the waters flowing from the creek. Experts testified that Miracle Spring's waters contributed to the flow of the creek. The court held:

> Arizona water law has developed into a bifurcated system in which percolating groundwater is regulated under a set of laws completely distinct from the laws regulating surface water. While this bifurcation provides a workable legal system, it often ignores the scientific reality that groundwater and surface water are often connected. The Colliers also ask us to ignore this reality. Our legislature, however, has tied the approval of new appropriations to their *effect* on existing appropriations. Thus, we are able to look beyond the legal fiction and see that the water the Colliers seek to appropriate is water which has historically fed an appropriated stream. We therefore hold that because the Colliers are seeking to appropriate water which has in the past contributed to Kirkland Creek in an unappropriable form and which now would flow naturally in an appropriable form into the creek above the point where the prior appropriators divert their water, their application to appropriate water was correctly denied on the ground that the appropriation would interfere with prior vested rights.

Collier v. Arizona Dep't of Water Res., 150 Ariz. 195, 722 P.2d 363, 366 (Ariz.App.1986).

Even after *Collier*, Arizona refused to integrate effectively ground and surface rights until 2000. A 1931 opinion had suggested that surface streams included all of the subflow. Maricopa County Municipal Water Conservation Dist. No. 1 v. Southwest Cotton Co., 39 Ariz. 65, 4 P.2d 369

(1931). But a puzzling 1993 opinion expressly refused to adopt a broad definition of subsurface flow and drew a hydrologically unsupportable distinction between streams and percolating groundwater. *In re* General Adjudication of All Rights to Use Water in the Gila River (Gila III), 175 Ariz. 382, 857 P.2d 1236 (1993). However, on remand the trial judge conducted an extensive evidentiary hearing and adopted a more scientifically rational definition that extended the recognition that subflow extended to the "saturated floodplain Holocene alluvium" rather than just the "entrenchment channel." This finding was upheld on appeal. *In re* General Adjudication of All Rights to Use Water in the Gila River (Gila IV), 198 Ariz. 330, 9 P.3d 1069 (2000), cert. denied 533 U.S. 941, 121 S.Ct. 2576, 150 L.Ed.2d 739 (2001). The state supreme court held that the trial judge correctly used the following factors: (1) the subflow was adjacent to and beneath a perennial or intermittent rather than an ephemeral stream, (2) there was a hydrologic connection to the stream from the saturated subflow zone, (3) the floodplain alluvium showed the same flow direction, water level elevations, and chemical composition of the water as the stream, (4) recharge from adjacent tributary aquifers or basin fill had no significant effect on the flood plain alluvium's flow direction, and (5) the location of riparian vegetation demarcated the lateral limits of the aquifer within the saturated floodplain. The net result of the opinion is that all wells on lands above the alluvium, which extends laterally along the stream, fall within the jurisdiction of the Gila River's general stream adjudication of rights on the river.

Surface rights holders may find it more convenient, reliable, and efficient to pump some of their water from the ground. They may face the Catch–22 situation of having their surface rights cancelled for non-use, however. To avoid this, in 1983 Nebraska enacted legislation to authorize the issuance of permits for the use of incidental underground water storage to holders of perfected surface appropriations. Neb. Rev. Stat. § 46–226.01 (2004). The statute was upheld against a takings challenge. Central Neb. Public Power Co. & Irrigation Dist. v. Abrahamson, 226 Neb. 594, 413 N.W.2d 290 (1987) (incidental storage did not harm overlying landowners because no profitable or claimed use of land was foreclosed).

Where surface water and groundwater are hydrologically connected the effects of extracting one on the other may be felt quickly or after a substantial period of time. Where, for instance, water is pumped from an aquifer connected to a surface stream, by means of a well distantly located from that stream, it may be years before the impact on the stream is felt. The existence of such an impact, therefore, creates challenges for water administration. Integrated administration requires sophisticated determinations of when and to what extent junior pumpers must be limited to satisfy the "call" of senior surface users (and vice versa). Computer modeling may be necessary to frame protective decrees, especially where plans for augmentation are proposed to avoid injury to seniors from out-of-priority pumping. Groundwater travels more slowly than surface water so that a cessation in pumping may take a long time to have an effect on stream flows. To implement integrated administration, the Colorado state engineer developed a zone plan along the South Platte River. Wells in Zone A were estimated to affect the river in 10 days, in Zone B in 10–30 days, and in Zone C from 30–75 days. In response to the challenges of junior pumpers arguing that shutting down wells under the zone plan will not cause any water to reach the stream in time of need, the Colorado Supreme Court wrote:

> Three of the findings are related: (1) shutting down of wells will not cause water to reach the stream to satisfy any call in time of need; (2) the regulation promotes and encourages futile calls; and (3) waste results from shutting off of wells. Several witnesses on behalf of the plaintiff testified that by the time water reached the point of diversion of a person making a call the person might no longer need the water by reason of an intervening storm. We are not favorably impressed with this argument because the same thing is true with respect to calls upon inferior surface diversions, albeit to a lesser extent of time. As an illustration, if a ditch near Sterling, Colorado, having senior priority, should make a call under which the ditches with inferior priorities in the upper reaches of the Platte River in the South Park area would have to cease diversion, it is common knowledge that it would take 10 to 14 days for the water to flow from South Park to Sterling. We can see no logical distinction between the result of an intervening storm in the case of a call on surface right and the case of a call on a well.
>
> We found no evidence in the record to support the finding that the regulations promote and encourage futile calls.

Kuiper v. Well Owners Conservation Ass'n, 176 Colo. 119, 490 P.2d 268, 280 (1971).

In *Kuiper*, the court rejected an interpretation of state law requiring senior appropriators, using ground and surface water conjunctively, to satisfy their surface decrees with well water prior to making a call on the river. This view was overruled, however, in Alamosa–La Jara Water Users Protection Ass'n v. Gould, 674 P.2d 914 (Colo.1983), *supra* p. 343. The court reviewed the 1969 Act, *Fellhauer*, and *Bender*:

> We believe that *Well Owners* construed the 1969 Act too narrowly. The prior appropriation doctrine is not a legal barrier to the concurrent consideration by the state engineer of the various methods of implementing the state policy of maximum utilization set out in the 1969 Act. See *Baker v. Ore–Ida Foods, Inc.*, 95 Idaho 575, 513 P.2d 627 (1973). Therefore, to the degree *Well Owners* precludes consideration of a reasonable-means-of-diversion requirement as a method of maximizing utilization of integrated underground and surface waters, we overrule *Well Owners*.

674 P.2d at 934–35. The court further found that the maximum, or optimum, utilization policy of state water law requires the state engineer to make policy judgments in administering groundwater rights that may affect surface rights based on environmental and economic concerns and not simply the respective individual rights of pumpers. See id. at 935.

In Colorado, a junior may be allowed to pump from the tributary aquifer of an overappropriated stream on the condition that senior rights are protected under a plan of augmentation by which some replacement water is added to the stream, discussed *supra* p. 387. Colo. Rev. Stat. § 37–92–301(2) (2006). Colorado Supreme Court decisions have strongly endorsed the use of such plans. See *supra* p. 384.

C.   GROUNDWATER ALLOCATION AND PUBLIC POLICY

As the cases illustrate, absolute principles upon which the rights of competing users may be based—land ownership or priority—resolve disputes only among parties to litigation. The groundwater resource is so broadly important to society that modern courts simply will not settle for a wooden allocation of rights solely to overlying landowners or to the first pumper without regard to the equities of later pumpers or public concerns. Thus, decisionmakers, even within systems that recognize the rights of supplying landowners or prior users, have resorted to rules like "reasonable use" and "correlative rights" in making judgments about how much water a pumper can extract and at what rate. These approaches consider factors other than the interests of the pumpers themselves. Typically, administrators have authority to regulate pumping rates to provide for public and private benefits from the aquifer over the long term.

Most states have enacted extensive statutory schemes to allocate groundwater resources. Although the purpose was originally to provide certainty and predictability among individual users, considerably greater interests are now apparent. In particular, it is important to avoid depleting groundwater too fast. For a survey of western state laws and conservation, see Jeffrey S. Ashley & Zachary C. Smith, Groundwater Management in the West (1999).

There are physical and economic reasons not to pump out all the groundwater that is available from an aquifer. Land subsidence can harm more than private, overlying landowners. The underground formation bearing the water may collapse or compress, reducing the capacity of the aquifer to refill. Furthermore, it may be unwise to take out too much water because the result may be shortages in future years. Thus, water managers have talked of "safe yield"—a term that may refer to the amount of water that can be removed without danger to the aquifer or may refer to the amount that can be removed without jeopardizing the reliability of future supplies for a particular period. The latter usually relates to an average rate of annual recharge. Pumping from an aquifer faster than the recharge rate is considered "mining" the resource.

Essentially nonrenewable groundwater sources, sometimes called nontributary aquifers, demand different considerations. Because any use of them amounts to mining the resource, decisions must be made about how long the aquifer should last. The depletable resource effectively is then amortized over the desired life by setting rate of pumping that will exhaust the stored water in the prescribed time. The objective of nonrenewable resource management is the same as it is for any stock resource: an optimum intertemporal allocation. Harold Hotelling, *The Economics of Exhaustible Resource*, 39 J. Pol. Econ. 137 (1931).

The problem of groundwater "mining" exists world wide. See Yardley, Jim, Beneath Booming Cities, China's Future is Drying Up, The New York Times, September 28, 2007. The article notes that scientists believe the aquifers below the North China Plain may be drained in thirty years, and identifies Yemen, India and Mexico, along with the United States, as countries with groundwater overdraft problems.

In fact, problems of overdraft have rarely been foreseen. More typically, a state will superimpose "critical area legislation" or other regulatory measures on its system of groundwater rights after land begins subsiding, wells begin drying up, or salt water begins to intrude. Many states are beginning to appreciate the desirability of preventing such harm and therefore are taking a more active role in determining pumping rates. They are guided not only by the relative interests of today's pumpers as expressed in a property rights system, but also by concerns for the sustainability of the resource for future users.

In some states it has been necessary to limit sharply the exercise of pre-existing rights to use groundwater in order to place necessary limits on aquifer life. Thus, pumping rates have been curtailed to prevent or regulate mining. Some states, like Arizona, have enacted sweeping laws designed to protect depleting aquifers. This has caused some landowners to challenge groundwater pumping regulation as a deprivation of property without due process of law.

There seems to be little question that states have the regulatory power to limit groundwater pumping among similarly situated users. The rationale of public regulation of groundwater pumping was established by the Supreme Court in a case upholding a New York statute which forbade the drilling of wells over natural mineral springs for the purpose of extracting carbonic gas to be sold as a separate commodity where a large portion of the waters from which the gas was extracted were permitted to run to waste.

> Thus these pumping operations generally result in an unreasonable and wasteful depletion of the common supply and in a corresponding injury to others equally entitled to resort to it. It is to correct this evil that the statute was adopted. * * * It does not take from any surface owner the right to tap from the underlying rock and to draw from a common supply, but, consistently with the continued exercise of that right, so regulates its exercise as reasonable to conserve the interests of all who supply it.

Lindsley v. Natural Carbonic Gas Co., 220 U.S. 61, 77, 31 S.Ct. 337, 55 L.Ed. 369 (1911). Can this rationale extend to a reallocation among different classes of users? How far can a legislature go in making "public welfare" judgments about the allocation of a resource in which individual rights have been established?

Another important interest of the public is in preventing groundwater contamination. In the past, this has rarely been considered in allocating rights to pump groundwater; however, suits have arisen over contamination of a plaintiff's groundwater source allegedly caused by the defendants' activity on the land. The tremendous difficulties of proof and the general public interest in preventing such problems make regulatory schemes more appropriate than litigation for controlling groundwater contamination.

There is an important, but as yet virtually unexplored, relationship between groundwater quality and quantity. For example, to prevent the migration of contaminated plumes, it may be necessary to maintain existing fresh water barriers. Rapid pumping in an area could create "cones of depression" that accelerate the migration of contaminated plumes.

Few states integrate groundwater quality concerns with their systems for allocating rights to pump groundwater. Most of the attention to groundwater contamination has come from the federal government. The resulting laws rarely mesh with state allocation laws, and they almost never are administered as a part of the same system. In addition, legal protection of groundwater quality may demand control of polluting activities on the surface. The relationship between land use planning and the protection of groundwater quality is discussed in Long Island Pine Barrens Soc., Inc. v. Planning Bd. of Brookhaven, 178 A.D.2d 18, 581 N.Y.S.2d 803 (1992). See also Christian Activities Council v. Town Council of Glastonbury, 249 Conn. 566, 735 A.2d 231 (1999) (city properly denied zoning change because proposed residential development might endanger the city's groundwater supply).

U.S. National Water Commission, Water Policies for the Future
238–39 (1973).

Ground Water Mining

Ground water mining occurs when withdrawals are made from an aquifer at rates in excess of net recharge. The problem becomes serious when this practice continues on a sustained basis over time: ground water tables decline, making the pumping of water more and more expensive; compaction may occur in the aquifer, adversely affecting storage capacity and transmissivity; and quality may be threatened by salt water intrusion. Ground water mining may occur in aquifer systems having ample recharge as well as those having negligible recharge. In recharge aquifers, mining results from withdrawals substantially in excess of net recharge. In aquifers with little or no recharge, virtually any withdrawal constitutes mining and sustained withdrawals will, in due course, exhaust the supply or lower water tables below economic pump lifts. A prime example of ground water mining in an aquifer system with negligible recharge is found in the

Ogallala Formation in the High Plains of Texas, an area that also has limited surface water resources.

* * *

Mining ground water is not inherently wrong. It is wrong, however, when the water is mined out without taking account of the future value of the water and the storage capacity of the reservoir. If a ground water aquifer were entirely unrelated to other aquifers and to surface water bodies, and if it were entirely owned by one person or organization, society could leave the decision to mine or not to mine to the owner. Presumably, the owner would seek to balance benefits from present production against anticipated benefits from future production in such a way as to maximize economic return from the resource over time as in the case of any other type of mining. The owner's self-interest would ordinarily coincide with society's interest. But ground water reservoirs are often associated with surface supplies and with other aquifers and are rarely in a single ownership. Accordingly, ground water reservoirs often suffer from the mismanagement associated with other "common pool" resources, namely, excessive use leading to premature exhaustion.

U.S. Geological Survey, National Water Summary, 1983: Hydrologic Events and Issues

36–40 (1984).

A great deal of use has been made of the terms "overdevelopment" and "safe yield" with regard to ground-water development. As it is often used, "safe yield" seems to refer to the pumpage that can be sustained at equilibrium, without continued withdrawal from storage. However, sustained withdrawal from storage or, as it is often termed, "ground-water mining," is no more "unsafe" than the mining of any other mineral resource, provided it is recognized and planned. Neither should pumpage at equilibrium necessarily be considered "safe," unless the attendant impacts, such as reduced streamflow or degradation of water quality, are deemed acceptable. The expression "safe yield" can, in fact, only be defined in terms of specific impacts of pumpage. The consequences of pumpage must be assessed for each level of development, and "safe yield" must be taken as the maximum pumpage for which the consequences are considered acceptable. The term "overdevelopment" then implies pumpage beyond that maximum.

* * *

Pumpage has increased steadily over the last three decades * * *. The total pumpage of ground water in 1980 represented about 20 percent of the total withdrawal of fresh and saline water in the United States. The largest single use of ground water is for irrigation, which accounted for slightly more than 60 bgd in 1980. It is important to note, however, that although irrigation represents the largest withdrawal, roughly half of the population of the country relies on ground water for domestic supply. Some of the factors responsible for the continued increase in ground-water use include significant expansion of irrigation in the humid East as well as in the West, particularly through the increased use of center-pivot systems; water-supply requirements of growing urban areas, particularly in the South and Southwest; water demands associated with energy production; a desire to establish drought-resistant supplies; objections to the construction of surface reservoirs; and objections to export of water from one area to another.

1.   ADMINISTRATIVE REGULATION

Baker v. Ore–Ida Foods, Inc.

Supreme Court of Idaho, 1973.
95 Idaho 575, 513 P.2d 627.

[The Idaho Groundwater Act, Idaho Code § 42–226 (Michie 1996), provides that "while the doctrine of 'first in time is first in right' is recognized, a reasonable exercise of this right shall not block full economic development of underground water resources. Prior appropriators * * * shall be protected in the maintenance of reasonable groundwater pumping levels as may be established by the director of the department of water resources * * *." This case focuses on an aquifer with an average recharge rate of 5,500 acre feet per year where water had been withdrawn "far in excess of safe annual recharge causing a 20 foot per year drop in the aquifer's water level." Pursuant to I.C. § 42–226, the trial court found that the entire average rate of recharge could be pumped by four senior wells and enjoined pumping from all the wells (eight of which were owned by Ore–Ida) and turned the decree over to the Idaho Department of Water Administration (IDWA) for further administration.]

The instant case requires construction of the ground Water Act against the backdrop of the uneven development of our common law concerning ground water. Idaho has vacillated on the question of the appropriability of ground water. * * *

* * *

The Idaho Ground Water Act, I.C. § 42–237a(g) provides in pertinent part:

> "* * * *Water in a well shall not be deemed available to fill a water right therein* if withdrawal therefrom of the amount called for by such right would affect, contrary to the declared policy of this act, the present or future use of any prior surface or ground water right or *result in the withdrawing the ground water supply at a rate beyond the reasonably anticipated average rate of future natural recharge.*" (Emphasis supplied)

We now hold that Idaho's Ground Water Act forbids "mining" of an aquifer. The evidence herein clearly shows that the pumping by all parties was steadily drawing down the water in the aquifer at the rate of 20 ft. per year. Since our statute explicitly forbids such pumping, the district court did not err in enjoining pumping beyond the "reasonably anticipated average rate of future natural recharge."

Perhaps dispositive of this case is the Act's prohibition of ground water "mining." The trial court found that the four senior appropriators would exhaust the aquifer's entire annual recharge. If the junior appropriators were permitted to continue pumping in the amount of their asserted rights they would mine the aquifer. Even so, appellants argue that "under the facts presented, the court of equity should have decreed that each of the parties had a proportional interest in the water resource." Appellants argue that our Act's phrases "reasonable pumping levels" and "full economic development" command a decree granting each of the appropriators, regardless of seniority, a proportionate amount of the aquifer's water.

We reiterate our holding that Idaho's Ground Water Act clearly prohibits the withdrawal of ground water beyond the average rate of future recharge. I.C. § 42–237a(g). In this regard Idaho differs from those of other less fortunate states because we have not yet had to develop legislation regarding withdrawals from non-rechargeable aquifers.

Idaho's Ground Water Act seeks to promote "full economic development" of our ground water resources. I.C. § 42–226. Other western states have enacted analogous ground water legislation enunciating the same policy. We hold that the Ground Water Act is consistent with the constitutionally enunciated policy of promoting optimum development of water resources in the public interest. Idaho Const. art. 15, § 7. Full economic development of Idaho's ground water resources can and will benefit all of our citizens.

* * *

A senior appropriator is only entitled to be protected to the extent of the "reasonable ground water pumping levels" as established by the IDWA. I.C. § 42–226. A senior appropriator is not absolutely protected in either his historic water level or his historic means of diversion. Our Ground Water Act contemplates that in some situations senior appropriators may have to accept some modification of their rights in order to achieve the goal of full economic development.

In the enactment of the Ground Water Act, the Idaho legislature decided, as a matter of public policy, that it may sometimes be necessary to modify private property rights in ground water in order to promote full economic development of the resource. The legislature has said that when private property rights clash with the public interest regarding our limited ground water supplies, in some instances at least, the private interests must recognize that the ultimate goal is the promotion of the welfare of all our citizens. We conclude that our legislature attempted to protect historic water rights while at the same time promoting full development of ground water. Priority rights in ground water are and will be protected insofar as they comply with reasonable pumping levels. Put otherwise, although a senior may have a prior right to ground water, if his means of appropriation demands an unreasonable pumping level his historic means of appropriation will not be protected.

Because of the need for highly technical expertise to accurately measure complex ground water data the legislature has delegated to the IDWA the function of ascertaining reasonable pumping levels. Implicit in this delegation is the recognition that reasonable pumping levels can be modified to conform to changing circumstances. We note that the findings of the IDWA are vested with a presumption of correctness. Idaho's Administrative Procedure Act, I.C. § 67–5215 sets out standards for judicial review of such agency action.

In the case at bar it is apparent under our Ground Water Act that the senior appropriators may enjoin pumping by the junior appropriators to the extent that the additional pumping of the juniors' wells will exceed the "reasonably anticipated average rate of future recharge." The seniors may also enjoin such pumping to the extent that pumping by the juniors may force seniors to go below the "reasonable pumping levels" set by the IDWA.

A necessary concomitant of this statutory matrix is that the senior appropriators are not entitled to relief if the junior appropriators, by pumping from their wells, force seniors to lower their pumps from historic levels to reasonable pumping levels. It should also be noted that those reasonable pumping levels are subject to later modification by the IDWA.

* * *

■ DONALDSON, C.J., and McQUADE, McFADDEN, and BAKES, JJ., concur.

NOTES

1. The director of water resources, pursuant to the statutory mandate, undertook to calculate the amounts of water that the four senior appropriators had historically pumped rather than the maximum allowed under the permits. Using a formula based on power company records, the director found that the four senior appropriators had pumped from 28% to 38% less water than they were entitled to pump under the decrees. Each senior pumper was allowed to pump the amount of water necessary in a dry year so long as the water user did not pump five times his annual historical water use in any consecutive five-year period. The unused water was distributed to the next senior pumper. Procedural problems prevented the supreme court from reaching the issue of whether any excess water allowed under the decree was "water in the bank" for the four seniors to be carried over to future years or was available for redistribution to the juniors. Briggs v. Golden Valley Land & Cattle Co., 97 Idaho 427, 546 P.2d 382 (1976).

2. Historically, entry into a groundwater basin by new pumpers has been relatively easy, but several western states are tightening access. For example, the Nevada Supreme Court has ruled that the state engineer may deny an application because a basin is overappropriated when the amount of outstanding rights, not simply the amount of water being pumped, exceeds the estimated perennial yield. Office of the State Engineer v. Morris, 107 Nev. 699, 819 P.2d 203 (1991). The decision's significance is underscored by pending groundwater applications of the Las Vegas Valley Water District. Las Vegas obtains 85% of its water from Nevada's 300,000 acre-foot share of the Colorado River. This remnant allocation seemed sufficient in 1922, but it is not adequate for a desert urban area approaching a million people. As part of a $2 billion plan to locate and import 250,000 additional acre-feet, the district has filed for 145 groundwater diversions in rural areas north of the city that extend to the town of Ely.

3. *Baker v. Ore–Ida Foods, Inc.* involved an aquifer with sufficient annual recharge to permit some pumping without violating the Ground Water Act's prohibition of "mining." Many aquifers, particularly "deep," non-tributary aquifers, have recharge rates so modest that any significant pumping will mine the aquifer. A celebrated example is the Ogallala Aquifer, which underlies portions of Colorado, Kansas, Nebraska, New Mexico, Oklahoma, South Dakota, Texas, and Wyoming.

> The enormous Ogallala aquifer is groundwater trapped below 174,000 square miles of fertile but dry plains farmland. Unlike most of the world's water supplies, Ogallala groundwater is largely nonrenewable because its sources were cut off thousands of years ago. It is essentially fossil water taken ten thousand to twenty-five thousand years ago from the glacier-laden Rocky Mountains before it was geologically cut off by the Pecos River and the Rio Grande. More than 3 billion acre-feet (an acre-foot is a foot of water on one acre, or 325,851 gallons) are stored under the High Plains. One misconception about the Ogallala aquifer and most groundwater is that it stands in cavernous lakes or flows in thundering underground rivers. In reality, it trickles slowly southeastward through sandy gravel beds, 500 to 1000 feet a year, two to three feet a day. These vast water-saturated gravel beds, 50 to 300 feet below the surface, are 150 to 300 feet thick. More than a half-billion acre-feet of Ogallala water was consumed by irrigation farmers between 1960 and 1990, mostly in southwestern Kansas, the Oklahoma panhandle, and West Texas. This is all the more serious because groundwater replacement occurs only from the surface at the rate of less than an inch a year under irrigated ground and 0.15 inches a year under dry land, while pumping is measured in feet per year. It would take a thousand years to refill the aquifer. Nothing can accelerate the flow, and artificial replacement remains impossible. As to alternatives for water-intensive farming in the region, there are no major rivers like the Mississippi or the Missouri, and rainfall is light.

John Opie, Ogallala: Water for a Dry Land 2–3 (1993).

These hydrological conditions have led overlying states to enact a variety of laws to "conserve" the aquifer. The following case illustrates one approach.

Mathers v. Texaco, Inc.

Supreme Court of New Mexico, 1966.
77 N.M. 239, 421 P.2d 771.

■ LaFel E. Oman, Judge, Court of Appeals.

The applicant-appellant, Texaco, Inc., hereinafter referred to as Texaco, filed applications with the State Engineer for permits to appropriate 700–acre feet of water per year from the Lea County Underground Water Basin. Upon the hearing of the applications and the protests thereto, the respondent-appellant, the State Engineer, hereinafter referred to as the State Engineer, made and entered findings and an order that the applications should be granted for the appropriation by Texaco of 350–acre feet per year for the purpose of water flooding 1,360 acres of oil-bearing formation in a producing oil field. By this water flooding operation, which has been approved by the New Mexico Oil Conservation Commission, it is contemplated that slightly in excess of one million barrels of oil will be recovered.

The protestants-appellees, hereinafter referred to as protestants, who had acquired prior rights to appropriate waters from the Lea County Underground Water Basin, appealed to the district court of Lea County from the findings and order of the State Engineer * * *.

There is no question concerning the following facts:

(1) The use of the water for the proposed flooding of the oil field is a reasonable and beneficial use;

(2) The fresh water in the Lea County Underground Water Basin is found in the Ogalalla formation which varies in thickness from a thin edge to something over 200 feet;

(3) The waters in the basin are replenished only by surface precipitation, which is very limited, and which is just about equalled by a natural discharge from the basin. Thus, for all practical purposes, no recharge takes place, and the pumping of any water from the basin depletes the stock or supply to that extent, and in effect amounts to a mining operation;

(4) In 1952 the State Engineer made a determination of the amount of water in each township in the basin, the amount of water that had been appropriated in each township, and the amount of water that would be drawn from the stock or supply in each township into the surrounding townships, when the waters in the surrounding townships were fully appropriated.

In determining what constitutes full appropriation in each township, and thus in the basin as a whole, he calculated the amount of water that could be withdrawn from each township and still leave one-third of the water in storage at the end of forty years. At that time it was contemplated that some of the remaining water could be economically withdrawn for domestic, and perhaps some other uses, but that it would no longer be economically feasible to withdraw the water for agricultural and most other purposes.

On the basis of this method of administration and operation established in 1952, there remains and is available for appropriation by Texaco the 350–acre feet per year which the State Engineer granted;

(5) The appropriation of the water by Texaco will unquestionably lower the water table in the wells of the protestants, and will result in an increase in pumping costs and in shortening the time during which the protestants can economically pump water from their wells.

* * *

The administration of a non-rechargeable basin, if the waters therein are to be applied to a beneficial use, requires giving to the stock or supply of water a time dimension, or, to state it otherwise, requires the fixing of a rate of withdrawal which will result in a determination of the economic life of the basin at a selected time.

The very nature of the finite stock of water in a non-rechargeable basin compels a modification of the traditional concept of appropriable supply under the appropriation doctrine. Each appropriation from a limited supply of non-replaceable water of necessity reduces the supply in quantity and shortens the time of use to something less than perpetuity. Each appropriator, subsequent to the initial appropriation, reduces in amount, and in time of use, the supply of water available to all prior appropriators, with the consequent decline of the water table, higher pumping costs, and lower yields.

This leads us directly to the main issue on this appeal, and that is whether or not the rights of prior appropriators are impaired, because a subsequent appropriator, by withdrawing waters from a non-rechargeable basin, causes a decline in the water level, higher pumping costs, and lower pumping yields. It was the view of the trial court that the taking of any water from the basin, which could never be replaced, amounted to an impairment of existing rights. He expressed his view in his Finding of Fact No. 11 in the following language:

> "The undisputed evidence in the case supports the premise that the taking of any water from the basin depletes the basin to the extent of the amount of water taken, and this can never be replaced. The undisputed evidence clearly shows impairment to existing rights would result from the granting of the Texaco applications."

Protestants take the position that an application for a permit to withdraw waters from an underground basin must be denied if the evidence establishes that such withdrawal will cause a decline in the water table, because prior appropriators will, of necessity:

> "* * * be damaged and their rights impaired by the lowering of the water table through the shortening of the useful life of the wells, the additional lift costs and the decline in the ability to produce in proportion to a square, making it necessary to drill more wells to produce the same amount of water. * * * "

If the position of protestants be correct, then Texaco, as stated in its brief in chief,

"* * * shot itself out of the saddle with its own undisputed evidence that the Lea County basin is a *non-rechargeable* basin, that the taking of any water from it constitutes a *mining* operation, and that its appropriation for what the court found was a reasonable and beneficial use could 'never be replaced'."

In fact, if the position of protestants be correct, then each and all of the many permits to withdraw waters from this basin issued by the State Engineer, subsequent to the initial permit, have been issued wrongfully and unlawfully, because each withdrawal, to some degree, has caused a lowering of the water level, and thus an impairment of the rights of the initial appropriator.

* * *

The only premise upon which the position of protestants can be logically supported is that "existing rights" embraces the element of perpetuity. As above stated, the beneficial use by the public of the waters in a closed or non-rechargeable basin requires giving to the use of such waters a time limitation. In the case of the Lea County Underground Water Basin, that time limitation was fixed by the State Engineer in 1952 at forty years, after having first made extensive studies and calculations. There is nothing before us to prompt a feeling that this method of administration and operation does not secure to the public the maximum beneficial use of the waters in this basin.

The rights of the protestants to appropriate water from this basin are subject to this time limitation, just as are the rights of all other appropriators. A lowering of the water level in the wells of protestants, together with the resulting increase in pumping costs and the lowering of pumping yields, does not constitute an impairment of the rights of protestants as a matter of law. These are inevitable results of the beneficial use by the public of these waters.

Section 75–11–3, N.M.S.A.1953, provides in part that:

"* * * the state engineer shall, if he finds that there are in such underground stream, channel, artesian basin, reservoir or lake, unappropriated waters, or that the proposed appropriation would not impair existing water rights from such source, grant the said application and issue a permit to the applicant to appropriate all or a part of the waters applied for subject to the rights of all prior appropriators from said source. * * *"

The State Engineer found that there were unappropriated waters, and that the appropriation granted would not impair existing rights. As above stated, on the basis of the method of administration and operation established in 1952, there were available for appropriation by Texaco the 350–acre feet of water per year.

* * *

The judgment of the trial court overruling and reversing the findings and order of the State Engineer is hereby reversed.

It is so ordered.

■ MOISE and COMPTON, JJ., concur.

NOTES

1. Does *Mathers* hold that a senior appropriator is entitled to no protection of the ability to maintain pump lift? The New Mexico Supreme Court held in City of Roswell v. Reynolds, 86 N.M. 249, 522 P.2d 796 (1974), that the state engineer could impose certain conditions on the city as junior pumper to protect seniors. Although *Mathers* denies seniors absolute protection against any lowering of pressure in their wells, the court in *Roswell* said that "it does not follow that the lowering of the water table may never in itself constitute an impairment of existing rights." Id. at 800.

2. What if the holder of a New Mexico surface water right wished to change the point of diversion and purpose of that right to a groundwater right in a different area of the state? If surface water rights in the new area are impacted, is that impairment of these rights as a matter of law? See Montgomery v. Lomos Altos, Inc., 141 N.M. 21, 150 P.3d 971 (2006).

3. The court's decision in *Mathers* prompts two questions: (1) Why should any groundwater mining be allowed (in contrast to *Baker* which disallowed mining)? (2) If mining is allowed, on what legal basis could the state engineer place limits on appropriations so long as there is unappropriated water? What considerations might lead an administrator to choose a forty year aquifer life? Consider the language of the respective statutes and the different physical situations in each case.

4. New Mexico has a long tradition of strong groundwater administration. In 1890 a large artesian aquifer was discovered in the Pecos Valley near Roswell. Farmers immediately drilled wells that flowed day and night. Just as the flaring of natural gas led to pressure for conservation legislation, uncapped artesian wells ultimately led to legislation to prevent waste. After the Wichita Federal Land Bank indicated that it would not lend to farmers in the valley because of waste, civic leaders in Roswell came to the conclusion that an administrative system employing elements of prior appropriation should be applied to limit pumping. Robert G. Dunbar, Forging New Rights in Western Waters 162–72 (1983). Legislation was passed in 1927 allowing the state engineer to designate basins within the state that would be subject to appropriation. The state supreme court declared the legislation unconstitutional because of technical defects in its passage, though it saw no impediment to limiting landowners' rights in favor of appropriators. Yeo v. Tweedy, 34 N.M. 611, 286 P. 970 (1929).

Most states now have regulatory systems to deal with groundwater use. Some have statewide permit systems and some have legislation that focuses on particular areas where pumping has caused problems.

2.   PERMIT SYSTEMS

Minnesota has the most extensive regulation of agricultural groundwater withdrawals in the midwestern United States. All major agricultural withdrawals require a state permit. The state has six priorities or, more accurately, preferences. The first is for domestic use "excluding industrial and commercial uses of municipal water supply." The second is for any use that requires less than 10,000 gallons per day. The third is for agricultural irrigation in excess of 10,000 gallons per day and the use of water for food processing. The fourth is for power production. The fifth is for all other uses in excess of 10,000 gallons per day. And the sixth is for non-essential uses. Minn. Stat. Ann. § 103G.261 (West 1997). The statute specifies two classes of agricultural use permits. Class A permits are required for areas in which adequate groundwater data exist. Class B permits are for all other areas and require the applicant to submit extensive data as a precondition to a permit. Class A or Class B permits may be issued only where the commissioner of natural resources "determines that proposed soil and water conservation measures are adequate based on recommendations of the soil and water conservation districts and that water supply is available for the proposed use without reducing water levels beyond the reach of vicinity wells constructed in accordance with the water well construction code." Minn. Stat. Ann. § 103G.295 (West 1997). What allocation rule has Minnesota adopted? The constitutionality of the statute was upheld in Crookston Cattle Co. v. Minnesota Dep't of Natural Res., 300 N.W.2d 769 (Minn.1980).

Because of Florida's geology, 92 percent of its residents consume groundwater from its extensive aquifers. It is not surprising that Florida has recently experimented with sophisticated conservation legislation. The aquifers have a high rate of recharge, but over-rapid pumping causes salt water intrusion or other contamination. In response to these problems, the Florida Water Resources Act of 1972, Fla. Stat. Ann. § 373.013 to 373.71 (West 2006 & Supp. 2007) (based on a model code drafted by the late Professor Frank E. Maloney), created a permit system for groundwater withdrawals and created districts with the taxing authority to undertake recharge programs. § 373.106. The Florida Supreme Court sustained the permit authority against a challenge that it was an unconstitutional taking of property and held that regulation was necessary to protect the correlative rights of aquifer users. Village of Tequesta v. Jupiter Inlet Corp., 371 So.2d 663 (Fla.1979), cert. denied 444 U.S. 965, 100 S.Ct. 453, 62 L.Ed.2d 377 (1979). The districts must set minimum groundwater levels beyond which further withdrawals would be significantly harmful to the water resources of the area, § 373.042, and may issue twenty-year renewable permits for reasonable beneficial uses. §§ 373.219–223.

The criteria for the issuance of permits are set forth in the following sections:

373.223   Conditions for a permit

(1) To obtain a permit pursuant to the provisions of this chapter, the applicant must establish that the proposed use of water:

(a) Is a reasonable-beneficial use as defined in § 373.019;

(b) Will not interfere with any presently existing legal use of water; and

(c) Is consistent with the public interest.

(2) The governing board or the department may authorize the holder of a use permit to transport and use ground or surface water beyond overlying land across county boundaries, or outside the watershed from which it is taken if the governing board or department determines that such transport and use is consistent with the public interest, and no local government shall adopt or enforce any law, ordinance, rule, regulation, or order to the contrary.

* * *

(4) The governing board or the department by regulation may reserve from use by permit applicants, water in such locations and quantities, and for such seasons of the year, as in its judgment may be required for the protection of fish and wildlife or the public health and safety. Such reservations shall be subject to periodic review and revision in the light of changed conditions. However, all presently existing legal uses of water shall be protected so long as such use is not contrary to the public interest.

373.233 Competing applications

(1) If two or more applications which otherwise comply with the provisions of this part are pending for a quantity of water that is inadequate for both or all, or which for any other reason are in conflict, the governing board or the department shall have the right to approve or modify the application which best serves the public interest.

(2) In the event that two or more competing applications qualify equally under the provisions of subsection (1), the governing board or the department shall give preference to a renewal application over an initial application.

Fla. Admin. Code Ann. r. 17–40.001, adopted in lieu of a state plan, sets out seventeen factors including "other relevant factors" that are to be considered in deciding what is a reasonable beneficial use. Florida's water management law is breaking new ground in the coordination of water supplies and land development. The power of a city to use zoning to preserve an adequate drinking water supply and general aquifer ecosystem stability was upheld in Moviematic Industries Corp. v. Board of County Comm'rs, 349 So.2d 667 (Fla.App.1977).

Proponents of prior appropriation argue that courts will almost inevitably protect prior users regardless of the state's allocation rule. Florida law supports this thesis. The drafters of the Florida code were hostile to the "wasteful" doctrine of prior appropriation and rejected it. However, under the permit system, an applicant must prove that a proposed withdrawal is a reasonable and beneficial use of water and that it will not interfere with existing uses. The intent was that priority would be a non-determinative factor in water allocation. Frank E. Maloney et al., A Model Water Code With Commentary 159–60 (1972). Nevertheless, Harloff v. City of Sarasota, 575 So.2d 1324, 1328 (Fla.App.1991), holds that permittees enjoy "superiority" over subsequent applicants. The court protected municipal well field pressure levels from a 1.7 foot drop in the water table by substantially reducing an 8,500–acre agricultural user's application.

Indiana requires persons who want to begin or increase pumping more than 100,000 gallons per day to obtain a permit. In granting or refusing a permit, the Department of Natural Resources must consider the following:

(1) The effect the withdrawal of additional groundwater from the restricted use area will have on future supplies in the area.

(2) What use is to be made of the water.

(3) How the withdrawal will affect present users of groundwater in the area.

(4) Whether the future natural replenishment is likely to become more or less.

(5) Whether future demands for groundwater are likely to be greater or less.

(6) How the withdrawal of additional groundwater will affect the health and best interests of the public.

Ind. Code Ann. § 14–25–3–8 (Michie 2003). In addition, in granting a permit, the department may:

(1) Impose the conditions or stipulations that are necessary to conserve the ground water of the area and prevent waste, exhaustion, or impairment of ground water.

(2) Require that ground water in a restricted area that is withdrawn and used be returned to the ground through wells, pits, or spreading grounds.

§ 14–25–3–9. Further, the agency director can declare groundwater emergencies whenever there is a substantial lowering of groundwater levels so that wells fail to produce their normal supplies of water. In such emergencies, the director can restrict large pumpers if their withdrawals could exceed natural recharge capabilities. §§ 14–25–4–9 to 14–25–4–12.

What are the limits of a state's legitimate interests in groundwater regulation? It is now clear that the state may not restrict interstate commerce in groundwater (or other water resources). Sporhase v. Nebraska *ex rel.* Douglas, 458 U.S. 941, 102 S.Ct. 3456, 73 L.Ed.2d 1254 (1982), *infra* p. 1030. Constitutionally valid state groundwater regulation that affects interstate commerce must be based on health and welfare considerations, not economic protectionism. The Supreme Court also suggested that Congress has the power to preempt state groundwater regulation should it choose: "Groundwater overdraft is a national problem and Congress has the power to deal with it on that scale." 458 U.S. at 954.

A particular type of permit statute, considered in the following subsection, identifies areas of particular public concern and targets them for special management.

3. SPECIAL GROUNDWATER MANAGEMENT DISTRICTS

Fundingsland v. Colorado Ground Water Commission

Supreme Court of Colorado, 1970.
171 Colo. 487, 468 P.2d 835.

■ PRINGLE, JUSTICE.

On September 2, 1966, Mr. Fundingsland (hereinafter referred to as the plaintiff) filed an application with the Colorado Ground Water Commission (hereinafter referred to as the commission) for a permit to drill a well on certain property located in the Northern High Plains Designated Ground Water Basin in Kit Carson County. No objections to the application were filed. On February 27, 1967, the plaintiff's application was denied by the commission on the basis that there was over appropriation in the area where the well was to be drilled. The plaintiff objected to the ruling of the commission, and a hearing was held before the commission on December 12, 1967. As the result of the hearing the commission sustained its previous denial of the plaintiff's application. * * *

The plaintiff appealed the decision of the commission to the district court, and a trial de novo was held with expert testimony being presented by both the plaintiff and the commission. * * * Under [the Ground Water Management Act, *infra* p. 616] the commission is empowered to deny an application if it finds that the proposed appropriation will unreasonably impair existing water rights from the same source, or will create unreasonable waste. * * *

[T]he trial court determined that a so-called three mile test provided a reasonable basis for assessing the effect of a proposed use on other users in the district. The three mile test was developed for use in the Northern High Plains. It is partly based on policy and partly based on fact and theory. Using that test, a circle with a three mile radius is drawn around the proposed well site. A rate of pumping is determined which would result in a 40% depletion of the available ground water in that area over a period of 25 years. If that rate of pumping is being exceeded by the existing wells within the circle, then the application for a permit to drill a new well may be denied.

The three mile test takes into account all of the considerations specified in the statute. The factors involved in the three mile test were explained to the court by Mr. Erker, senior engineer in the ground water section of the State Engineer's office. He testified that the three mile circle represents the area over which a well, located at the center, would have an effect if permitted to pump intermittently for 25 years. Intermittent pumping, he explained, meant approximately 100 days per year. Other factors which are considered are the saturated thickness of the aquifer within the three mile circle, the number of wells located within the circle, and the yield of those wells. Multiplying the number of wells within the circle times the yield of those wells gives the total, present appropriation within the three mile circle.

Mr. Romero, an assistant water resource engineer for the State of Colorado Division of Water Resources, testified that the modified Theiss equation was used in determining what the draw down effect on the water in the aquifer would be within the three mile circle. He further testified that in determining the balance of water in the aquifer, he considered the fact that there was only intermittent pumping, the amount of recharge to the aquifer due to precipitation and ground water inflow from outlying areas, recharge due to excess irrigation, and possibly recharge from some other source such as leakage from ditches or rivers.

There does not seem to be any contention that the 40% depletion figure is unreasonable or irrational. The assumption in the three mile test is that a 40% depletion of the aquifer within that area would constitute lowering of the water balance beyond reasonable economic limits of with-drawal or use for irrigation.

Likewise, the selection of 25 years as the period during which the 40% depletion is to be allowed is not contested. Mr. Leslie, a farm and ranch loan representative for Northwestern Mutual Life Insurance Company, testified that 25 years was a reasonable, average period in which a loan for the construction of well facilities would have to be repaid.

The testimony and other evidence in the record before the district court support the reasonableness of the three mile test and establish that the three mile test takes into account the factors specified by the statute. If the three mile test was a proper method for the court to use in determining the effect of plaintiff's proposed use on the ground water supply in the district, then the decision of the district court must be upheld.

* * *

The plaintiff calls our attention to Article XVI, Section 6 of the Colorado Constitution which provides: "The right to divert the unappropri-ated waters of any natural stream to beneficial uses shall never be denied." We find, however, that the record clearly supports the finding that there is no unappropriated water within the three mile circle surrounding the plaintiff's proposed well site.

Ground water existing in designated underground water basins is made subject to the doctrine of prior appropriation by 1965 Perm.Supp., C.R.S.1963, 148–18–1 [now codified at Colo. Rev. Stat. § 37–90–102]. The statute further provides:

> " * * * While the doctrine of prior appropriation is recognized, such doctrine should be modified to permit the full economic development of designated ground water resources. Prior appropriations of ground water should be protected and reasonable ground water pumping levels

maintained, but not to include the maintenance of historical water levels. * * * ''

Underground water basins require management that is different from the management of surface streams and underground waters tributary to such streams. In the case of the latter waters, seasonal regulation of diversion by junior appropriators can effectively protect the interests of more senior appropriators and no long range harm can come of over appropriations since the streams are subject to seasonal recharge. The underground water dealt with by 148–18–1 is not subject to the same ready replenishment enjoyed by surface streams and tributary ground water. It is possible for water to be withdrawn from the aquifer in a rate in excess of the annual recharge creating what is called a mining condition. Unless the rate of pumping is regulated, mining must ultimately result in lowering the water balance below a level from which water may be economically withdrawn. Due to the slow rate at which underground waters flow through and into the aquifer, it may be many years before a reasonable water level may be restored to a mined aquifer.

It is clear that the policies of protecting senior appropriators and maintaining reasonable ground water pumping levels set forth by the underground water act require management which takes into account the long range effects of intermittent pumping in the aquifer. In this case all of the experts testifying before the commission and the district court were in agreement that a mining condition exists in the Northern High Plains Designated Ground Water Basin. The commission has determined that proper use of the ground water resource requires that the mining be allowed to continue. However, the maximum allowable rate of depletion, at least when considering applications for permits to drill new wells, has been set at 40% depletion in 25 years. We have pointed out that the depletion rate in the area which would be affected by the plaintiff's proposed well is in excess of the rate allowed by the commission and approved by the district court.

If the plaintiff were permitted to proceed on his theory of "unappropriated water" and pump water from his proposed well until such time as it was no longer economically feasible to withdraw water from the aquifer, then no subsequent regulation of his pumping could protect senior appropriators, and all pumping from the basin within the area of influence of the plaintiff's well would have to cease until a reasonable pumping level was restored through the slow process of recharge. This is not the concept of appropriation contained in the statute, and not the one this Court will follow.

When, as in this case, water is being mined from the ground water basin, and a proposed appropriation would result in unreasonable harm to senior appropriators, then a determination that there is no water available for appropriation is justified.

* * *

NOTE

In drawing the mining circle, Colorado has excluded land in Nebraska, thus altering the volume used to determine if there is a sufficient Colorado water supply for new entrants. Thompson v. Colorado Ground Water Comm'n, 194 Colo. 489, 575 P.2d 372 (1978) upheld the exclusion of 24 percent of the circle on the ground that the rule was a reasonable means of protecting senior appropriators against injury, fostering the full economic development of resources and conserving designated groundwater resources:

> Expert testimony supported the commission's position that overappropriation of the aquifer at the state line, with the intent to stabilize or reverse the aquifer flow to the benefit of Colorado, would seriously injure vested Colorado rights far west of the state line and could ignite a destructive aquifer depletion race with Nebraska, an adjoining state. Evidence that a portion of Colorado's ground water naturally flows into adjoining states, when considered in the context of the commission's overall ground water policy, does not establish a breach of statutory duty by the commission in its determination.

Id. at 377.

Groundwater pumping in Colorado is intense along the Nebraska border. Nebraska has a procedure to designate critical areas, but regulation remains in the hands of local districts and pumping has not yet been curtailed. See generally J. David Aiken & Raymond J. Supalla, *Ground Water Mining and Western Water Rights Law: The Nebraska Experience*, 24 S.D. L. Rev. 607 (1979).

NOTE: STATUTORY CONTROL OF GROUNDWATER IN COLORADO

Some states have long recognized that where surface water and subsurface water are connected, they should be administered in an integrated fashion. In Colorado there has been a complete integration of administration of rights to groundwater and surface water that are connected. The state has consistently held that all groundwater is presumed to be tributary to a natural stream. Safranek v. Limon, 123 Colo. 330, 228 P.2d 975 (1951). As such, tributary groundwater is integrated into the administration of surface water priorities. Colo. Rev. Stat. § 37–92–102 (2006). It is defined as "that water in the unconsolidated alluvial aquifer of sand, gravel, and other sedimentary materials and all other waters hydraulically connected thereto which can influence the rate or direction of movement of water in that alluvial aquifer or natural stream." Colo. Rev. Stat. § 37–92–103(11) (2006). But if the "rate or direction of movement of water" in a natural stream will not be affected, the water is "non-tributary" and outside the appropriation system. Colo. Rev. Stat. § 37–92–103(11) (2006). As such, it may be in a "designated basin" under the Ground Water Management Act as in *Fundingsland*, or it may be administered under a statutory scheme for "non-tributary, non-designated" groundwater.

Tributary or Non–Tributary? A one-hundred year limit on the effects necessary to establish tributariness has been embraced by the state supreme court. Where effects are felt within forty years, groundwater was held to be tributary. Hall v. Kuiper, 181 Colo. 130, 510 P.2d 329 (1973). It is not necessary that groundwater actually reach the stream in 100 years, only that streamflow be affected. District 10 Water Users Ass'n v. Barnett, 198 Colo. 291, 599 P.2d 894 (1979) (groundwater would reach stream in 171 years but pumping would affect stream in forty years). What about effects felt in fifty years? Ninety years?

The Ground Water Management Act. For many years, non-tributary groundwater was not within any regulatory scheme in Colorado. Accordingly, in 1963 the supreme court refused to uphold an adjudication of priorities among non-tributary groundwater pumpers. It found that the deep aquifers there in question were outside the scope of the presumption of tributariness and hence were outside the appropriation system. Whitten v. Coit, 153 Colo. 157, 385 P.2d 131 (1963). The court in *Whitten* alluded to the reasonable use rule as controlling rights among competing users; because the only applicable statute dealt with well drilling there was no administrative or regulatory system to control mining.

In 1965 Colorado enacted the Ground Water Management Act. Colo. Rev. Stat. §§ 37–90–101 to 37–90–143 (2006). The Act subjected designated groundwater basins to principles of prior appropriation "modified to permit the full economic development of designated ground water resources." § 37–90–102(1). Rights to pump groundwater are determined administratively by the Ground Water Commission:

(1) Any person desiring to appropriate ground water for a beneficial use in a designated ground water basin shall make application to the commission in a form to be prescribed by the commission. * * *

(3) After the expiration of the time for filing objections, if no such objections have been filed, the commission shall, if it finds that the proposed appropriation will not unreasonably impair existing water rights from the same source and will not create unreasonable waste, grant the said application, and the state engineer shall issue a conditional permit to the applicant * * * to appropriate all or a part of the waters applied for subject to such reasonable conditions and limitations as the commission may specify.

* * *

(5) In ascertaining whether a proposed use will create unreasonable waste or unreasonably affect the rights of other appropriators, the commission shall take into consideration the area and geologic conditions, the average annual yield and recharge rate of the appropriate water supply, the priority and quantity of existing claims of all persons to use the water, the proposed method of use, and all other matters appropriate to such questions. With regard to whether a proposed use will impair uses under existing water rights, impairment shall include the unreasonable lowering of the water level, or the unreasonable

deterioration of water quality, beyond reasonable economic limits of withdrawal or use.

Colo. Rev. Stat. § 37–90–107 (2006).

The Ground Water Management Act created a two-level system of administrative regulation. The Ground Water Commission is authorized to create "designated groundwater basins." No finding of overdraft need be made. Groundwater management districts may be formed "to regulate the use, control, and conservation" of groundwater in a district that coincides with all or part of a basin. The statutory powers of the commission must be exercised in consultation with districts in areas where they have been formed. Those powers include:

> (a) To supervise and control the exercise and administration of all rights acquired to the use of designated ground water. In the exercise of this power it may, by summary order, prohibit or limit withdrawal of water from any well during any period that it determines that such withdrawal of water from said well would cause unreasonable injury to prior appropriators; except that nothing in this article shall be construed as entitling any prior designated ground water appropriator to the maintenance of the historic water level or any other level below which water still can be economically extracted when the total economic pattern of the particular designated ground water basin is considered; and further except that no such order shall take effect until six months after its entry.

> (b) To establish a reasonable ground water pumping level in an area having a common designated ground water supply. Water in wells shall not be deemed available to fill the water right therefor if withdrawal therefrom of the amount called for by such right would, contrary to the declared policy of this article, unreasonably affect any prior water right, or result in withdrawing the ground water supply at a rate materially in excess of the reasonably anticipated average rate of future recharge.

> * * *

> (e) To order the total or partial discontinuance of any diversion within a ground water basin to the extent the water being diverted is not necessary for application to a beneficial use;

Colo. Rev. Stat. § 37–90–111 (2006).

Where a groundwater management district has been formed, the district board promulgates rules and regulations that set the essential limits on groundwater withdrawals such as allowable depletion rates. Although the Ground Water Commission is required to maintain a priority list for all wells within each designated ground water basin, it is the local groundwater management district that is authorized to administer designated groundwater priorities within its boundaries. Upper Black Squirrel Creek Ground Water Mgmt. Dist. v. Goss, 993 P.2d 1177 (Colo.2000). The power of the Ground Water Commission to coordinate ground and surface rights within a designated basin was reaffirmed in Pioneer Irrigation Dist. v. Danielson, 658 P.2d 842 (Colo.1983).

The Ground Water Management Act has been applied only in the eastern plains of Colorado. Primarily deep, non-tributary agricultural wells in the Ogallala Aquifer are affected. Eight groundwater basins have been designated under the Act and thirteen groundwater management districts have been formed. An amendment to the law prevents designation of groundwater in the Denver Basin, leaving tremendous non-tributary groundwater reserves outside the Act.

Non–Tributary, Non–Designated Groundwater. In 1978, anticipating an energy boom creating new demands for water, four groups filed applications, in all of the state's seven water divisions, for determinations of conditional water rights to over 20 million acre-feet of deep, non-tributary groundwater. The sources were outside designated groundwater basins and at the time statutory law addressed such "non-tributary, non-designated" groundwater only by requiring a well permit. Language in the permit statute allowed such groundwater to be pumped at a rate that would not deplete the water that underlies the land owned by the applicant in less than 100 years. The dearth of statutory treatment left room for applicants to argue that this groundwater was subject to prior appropriation. Others in the case argued that it was the property of the overlying landowners. Some water court judges (who have jurisdiction over surface water appropriation) had assumed jurisdiction to adjudicate rights to non-tributary, non-designated groundwater, but had recognized control by the overlying landowner. Under either theory, vast stores of groundwater would be claimed by a few interests who hoped to market the water to the energy industry. The cases were consolidated in a huge case that the supreme court assigned to a special water judge.

Reviewing the lower court's determination of many issues, the Colorado Supreme Court concluded that only the well permit process applied to rights in non-tributary groundwater:

> * * * [W]e believe that, given the state's plenary control over development of water law, the traditional property concept of fee ownership is of limited usefulness as applied to nontributary ground water and serves to mislead rather than to advance understanding in considering public and private rights to utilization of this unique resource.

* * *

Nontributary ground water is not subject to appropriation under *Colo. Const.* Art. XVI, §§ 5 and 6, or to adjudication or administration under the 1969 Act. The modified doctrine of prior appropriation provided for in the 1965 Act applies to nontributary ground water, and rights to such water in designated ground water basins must be obtained through the procedures established in that Act. Rights to nontributary ground water not located in a designated basin may be obtained only through application for a well permit from the state engineer under section 37–90–137 of the 1965 Act.

Colorado Dept. of Natural Res. v. Southwestern Colo. Water Conservation Dist., 671 P.2d 1294, 1316–19 (Colo.1983) (The *Huston* case). The only statutory restriction on a well permit was to impose a pumping rate that would allow for a 100–year aquifer life.

In 1984, in the wake of the so-called *Huston* case, the General Assembly addressed the issue of how to allocate non-tributary groundwater. First, it clarified the definition of non-tributary groundwater as "that ground water, located outside the boundaries of any designated ground water basins * * * the withdrawal of which will not, within one hundred years, deplete the flow of any natural stream * * * at an annual rate greater than one tenth of one percent of the annual rate of withdrawal." * * * Colo. Rev. Stat. § 37–90–103(10.5) (2006). The most significant legislative pronouncement, contrary to the findings in a report of a blue-ribbon commission appointed by the Governor, was that rights to control access to non-tributary groundwater would depend on overlying land ownership. Colo. Rev. Stat. § 37–90–137(4)(b)(II) (2006). The right to use non-tributary, non-designated groundwater is statutory, and landowners do not have an absolute right to ownership of water under their land, only the right to control access to it. Bayou Land Co. v. Talley, 924 P.2d 136 (Colo.1996).

Well permitting provisions were also expanded in the 1984 Colorado legislation. A clause prohibiting harm to vested rights was retained, but the amendment deemed that injury does not occur as the result of lowering hydrostatic pressure or water levels. Colo. Rev. Stat. § 37–90–137(4)(c) (2006). Water courts were given authority to adjudicate rights in non-tributary groundwater, although the state engineer was authorized to make rules and regulations pertaining to permitting. Colo. Rev. Stat. § 37–90–137(9)(a), (b) (2006).

"Not Non–Tributary" Groundwater. Special rules under detailed statutory specifications in the 1984 law apply to the copious Denver Basin aquifers. Colo. Rev. Stat. § 37–90–137(9)(c) (2006). The four Denver Basin aquifers are essentially non-tributary although in fact, underground water contributes about 50,000 acre-feet of water per year to the South Platte River. Groundwater in these aquifers that is hydraulically connected to a surface stream is characterized as "not nontributary." Colo. Rev. Stat. § 37–90–103(10.7) (2006). "Whether Denver Basin aquifer water underlying a particular parcel of land is nontributary or not nontributary is determined by the state engineer when reviewing a well permit application or by the water court in ruling on a water court decree application." Chatfield East Well Co. v. Chatfield East Prop. Owners Ass'n, 956 P.2d 1260, 1271–72 (Colo.1998).

Any wells that will withdraw groundwater that is not non-tributary require a special plan for augmentation. Normally an augmentation plan replenishes water to avoid all injury to senior rights holders. See *supra* p. 382. But the requirement of protecting seniors from all injurious depletions caused by withdrawals of Denver Basin water applies only within one mile of a stream. Beyond one mile a pumper need only replace a flat percentage of the amount annually pumped from the well back to the affected stream, regardless of actual losses. By regulation, the state engineer draws an outside boundary for a 4 percent "not non-tributary" replenishment zone, beyond which the rules may require up to 2 percent replenishment. This recognizes that nearly all water pumped in the basin is partially tributary. The state engineer's rules consist largely of maps that enable a well permit applicant to determine the applicable replacement duty: 2 percent, 4 percent, or the amount of actual effects on seniors.

Because of the dynamics of the aquifer, stream depletions may continue to occur even after well pumping has ceased. In the context of not non-tributary groundwater, the Colorado Supreme Court has held that plans for augmentation must protect senior appropriators from injury caused by such post-pumping depletions. Danielson v. Castle Meadows, Inc., 791 P.2d 1106 (Colo.1990). In *Danielson*, the state engineer asserted that depletions would continue for two hundred years after well pumping ceased.

NOTE: STATE VARIATIONS IN LOCAL DISTRICT CONTROL OF GROUNDWATER

Some states have opted for special management of specified aquifers but have vested primary authority in local agencies rather than with a state administrative official or boards. For instance, Hawai'i applies the doctrine of correlative rights to non-designated management areas, but the Hawai'ian Water Code applies in designated management areas. *In re* Water Use Permit Applications, 94 Hawai'i 97, 9 P.3d 409, 488–492 (2000). The court justified the dual system because the code reflects "the legislative purpose of substituting in designated management areas, a comprehensive regulatory scheme based on permits in place of the common law regime of water rights administration," citing A. Dan Tarlock, Law of Water Rights and Resources § 3.89 (1988 with annual updates).

Agricultural users in states such as Kansas, Nebraska, and Texas have opposed statewide management. To conserve groundwater, therefore, these states rely on local management initiatives.

Kansas, which applies the law of prior appropriation to groundwater, authorized the creation of local districts with the power to adopt local management programs, subject to state approval. Kan. Stat. Ann. §§ 82a–1020 to –1035 (2006). Several such districts have been created in western and south-central Kansas. Well-spacing requirements to protect existing pumpers have generally been applied, and some districts have adopted safe yield policies resulting in pumping limitations. Professor John Peck of the University of Kansas has described the safe yield program in the Equus Beds Groundwater Management District (GMD), northwest of Wichita:

> The safe yield policy is found in the statement that "a balance will be maintained between recharge to the Equus Beds and total groundwater withdrawals (discharge) from the Equus Beds." To accomplish safe yield, the GMD bases its recommendation for approval or denial of an application permit on a two-mile radius formula as follows: (1) a circle with a radius of two miles is drawn around the proposed well, and

within the circle all of the existing wells as shown on prior applications for permits, certificates of appropriation, or vested rights are totalled as to annual quantity; (2) that annual quantity is added to the quantity of water requested in the application; (3) if the total quantity found by the addition in (2) is less than 4025 acre-feet, approval of the application will be recommended, if it meets other criteria; if the total is greater than 4025 acre-feet, denial of the application will be recommended, unless it is the quantity of the proposed well that puts the total over 4025 acre-feet, in which case the GMD may recommend a quantity that would make the withdrawals equal 4025 acre-feet.

The 4025 acre-feet is the average amount of recharge within an average two mile radius circle in the GMD. This amount is calculated by assuming that out of an average rainfall of thirty inches, twenty percent or six inches returns to the aquifer as recharge.

John C. Peck, *Kansas Groundwater Management Districts*, 29 U. Kan. L. Rev. 51, 75–76 (1980).

A number of other states apply Kansas's circle method for assessing the potential impacts of a well. Professor Peck points out that circle size can have a substantial effect on pumping entitlements: "[A]n applicant might be denied a permit if his requested amount were totalled with existing amounts in a small radius circle because the combined total might exceed the allowable figure. Yet he might be granted a permit if his requested amount were added to existing amounts in a larger circle, even though the density of existing wells were the same in both circles." Id. at 86.

Nebraska applies a combination of correlative rights and appropriative rights to groundwater and has authorized Natural Resources Districts to establish groundwater "control areas." Neb. Rev. Stat. §§ 46–656 to –674, transferred to §§ 46–701 to –702. Control areas may be approved by the State Department of Water Resources after a finding that: (1) the use of groundwater has caused, or is likely to cause, supplies to be inadequate to meet present or reasonably foreseeable future needs; or (2) there is a risk of quality degradation due to groundwater mining. Establishment of a control area is a strong step in Nebraska, and the Director of the Department has refused to designate control areas where the effect on pumping has merely been a seasonal reduction of artesian pressure, not amounting to groundwater mining. J. David Aiken, *Nebraska Ground Water Law and Administration*, 59 Neb. L. Rev. 917, 960–66 (1980). Within designated control areas, well-spacing restrictions, pumping rotations, quantity allocations, transfer restrictions, and well-drilling moratoria may be imposed. Once a control area is established, a state permit is required for new wells, but a permit application can only be denied if approval would violate a condition imposed by a Natural Resources District. In 1996 Nebraska enacted legislation aimed at providing integrated management of surface and groundwater, with primary control at the local district level. L.B. 108, 1996 Neb. Laws 46 (amending various water statutes, specifically Neb. Rev. Stat. § 46–701).

Until recently, management of groundwater in Texas has been neither well-coordinated nor effective. In part this was due to the state's steadfast adherence to the rule of absolute ownership. When Friendswood Dev. Co. v. Smith–Southwest Ind., 576 S.W.2d 21 (Tex.1978), recognized limited liability for negligence in pumping, some Texas water lawyers read the case as the forerunner of the abandonment of the absolute ownership rule, but the courts have continued to adhere to the rule. In a recent case, Sipriano v. Great Spring Waters of America, Inc., 1 S.W.3d 75 (Tex.1999), the Texas Supreme Court declined to reconsider the rule of capture (absolute ownership) doctrine, noting that groundwater regulation was being actively pursued by the legislature.

The rule of capture, which allows well owners virtually unregulated pumping from beneath their land, encourages aggressive investment in groundwater withdrawals, especially in the absence of effective planning and control. See generally, Ronald Kaiser & Frank F. Skillern, *Deep Trouble: Options For Managing the Hidden Threat of Aquifer Depletion in Texas*, 32 Tex. Tech. L. Rev. 249 (2001). Groundwater users in Texas, including agricultural users, have historically opposed statewide control. Legislative responses to anticipated water shortages had been inadequate to address these problems, despite the arguments of planners and commentators that more stringent conservation measures were needed, especially in the High Plains (Ogallala Aquifer) where it was estimated that overpumping could cause irrigated acreage to shrink from 5.9 to 2.9 million acres by 2030.

During the 1990s, two events stimulated political action. First, the State Water Plan was updated in 1996. The new document predicted severe water shortages, and its publication came at a time of severe drought across the state, during which agriculture supplies were strained and many communities suffered failures of municipal water supplies.

During the same period, public attention focused on the Edwards Aquifer, lying between San Antonio and Austin, where the state's adherence to the absolute ownership rule allowed unregulated withdrawals from the aquifer. Withdrawals had long exceeded the 450,000 acre-feet per year safe yield recommended by numerous studies since the 1960s. The Texas Water Commission regulated only withdrawals of water from streams. Efforts to induce the major users, especially farmers and the city of San Antonio, voluntarily to limit their pumping had been unsuccessful. A special district, seeking to protect spring flows, joined with the Sierra Club, seeking to protect the fountain darter and other endangered species, in a suit against the Texas Water Commission. Attempting to take control of the situation in 1992, the commission declared an emergency, and classified the aquifer as an underground river subject to its jurisdiction. See Texas Water Code Ann. § 5.501 (Vernon 2000). The district court then ordered the commission to prepare a plan to maintain water levels in the aquifer. Sierra Club v. Lujan, 1993 WL 151353, 36 ERC 1533 (W.D.Tex.1993). The legislature subsequently enacted the Edwards Aquifer Act, limiting aquifer withdrawals. Act of May 30, 1993, ch. 626, 1993 Tex. Gen. Laws 2350 (amended by Act of May 29, 1995, ch. 261, 1995 Tex. Gen. Laws 2505). The constitutionality of the Act was upheld in Barshop v. Medina County Underground Water Conservation Dist., 925 S.W.2d 618 (Tex.1996).

The events described above led the legislature to enact a sweeping reform of Texas water law in 1997. The new law affected far more than the law of groundwater, as its provisions dealt with: water marketing, transfers, and planning; supplies of surface and groundwater; collection of data regarding the state's water resources; and financial assistance to local governments and small communities. It directed the Texas Water Development Board, the state agency having major responsibility for water planning, to designate and create regional planning areas and groups, and to adopt a state water plan. This set off a flurry of water planning activity in Texas.

The new law failed to modify the absolute ownership rule of capture, however. Instead, it reestablished local groundwater conservation districts as the primary agents of groundwater management in Texas, with the power to regulate well pumping rates within their boundaries. The districts were assigned planning responsibilities and permitting authority over well drilling and the transfer of groundwater, including limiting groundwater exports from a district. See generally John R. Pitts & Janet L. Hamilton, *Texas Water Law for the New Millenium*, 14 Nat. Res. & Environ. 35 (1999).

A Texas court severely limited effective special district control of groundwater. South Plains Lamesa Railroad, Ltd. v. High Plains Underground Water Conservation Dist. No. 1, 52 S.W.3d 770 (Tex.Ct.App.2001). The court held that Texas groundwater rights are absolute and that a district may not revoke a well permit to prohibit the extraction of water because it was disproportionate to the size of the overlying tract. The legislature then specifically authorized districts to prohibit disproportionate extractions. Senate Bill No. 2, R.C. ch. 966, 2001 Tex. Sess. Law Service 1880 (Vernons).

4.   ARIZONA: LEGISLATIVE REDEFINITION OF RIGHTS AND STRONG STATE CONTROL

In 1980, Arizona passed a sweeping new groundwater law. The background of the 1980 Groundwater Management Act is a revealing illustration of the politics of water in the West. The Act purported to limit the rate of extraction, and was clearly intended to shift groundwater from agricultural to municipal and industrial uses. Thus, Arizona became the first state to begin making the hard choices required to shift water systematically from lower-valued agriculture to higher-valued non-agricultural uses.

No arid state is more dependent on declining groundwater supplies than Arizona. Prior to 1980, Arizona was a classic example of non-management. Arizona's agricultural use of groundwater, especially for cotton production, was long considered economically irrational. In the 1970s Arizona used about 4.8 million acre-feet per year of groundwater and

1 million acre-feet per year of surface water. Alternative Futures: Phase II Arizona State Water Plan 3 (Arizona State Water Comm'n 1977). The annual rate of recharge was only 2.6 million acre-feet, leaving a yearly overdraft of 2.2 million acre-feet. The state's "strategy" for controlling groundwater overdraft was premised on a federal bailout, the Central Arizona Project (CAP), first proposed more than a half-century earlier to import new water from the Colorado River. The United States Bureau of Reclamation took the position that the project would not prevent severe water shortages among Arizona water users unless a law was passed that would prevent expansion of groundwater uses from outstripping the supply of new water from the project. When the CAP was authorized by Congress in 1968, it included the stipulation that no CAP water would be delivered to any area that, in the judgment of the Secretary of the Interior, did not have in place adequate measures to control expansion of irrigation from aquifers in the CAP service area. 43 U.S.C.A. § 1524(c) (West 1991 and Supp. 2007).

The delay in securing the CAP created pressures on expanding cities, but it took a series of judicial decisions restricting urban and industrial uses of water to produce an adequate legislative response. Initially, the state supreme court had declared that all groundwater was public and open to appropriation, Bristor v. Cheatham, 73 Ariz. 228, 240 P.2d 185 (1952), then reversed itself and readopted the common law rule, adding a reasonable use limitation. Bristor v. Cheatham, 75 Ariz. 227, 255 P.2d 173 (1953). Sixteen years later, the Arizona Supreme Court confronted the conflict between the reasonable use rule's inherent preference for agriculture (by favoring use on the overlying land) and the municipal needs of Arizona's fast-growing cities. In Jarvis v. State Land Dep't, 104 Ariz. 527, 456 P.2d 385 (1969), the court held for the farmers, enjoining Tucson's pumping and transportation of groundwater from a farming area. Tucson refused to comply, and eighteen months later the court relented in Jarvis v. State Land Dep't, 106 Ariz. 506, 479 P.2d 169 (1970). Citing a provision in the surface water code that put municipal use higher than agricultural use when there were conflicting applications to appropriate, the court allowed Tucson to pump and transport if it purchased and retired the farmland from which it was pumping. In Jarvis v. State Land Dep't, 113 Ariz. 230, 550 P.2d 227 (1976), the court further clarified its earlier decisions by allowing Tucson to pump and transport only as much groundwater as the farmer who had previously owned the land had consumed: "that quantity which, were the lands in cultivation, would not return to the water table." 550 P.2d at 229.

Almost immediately after this decision, however, the court heightened the controversy with another decision, Farmers Invest. Co. v. Bettwy (*FICO*), 113 Ariz. 520, 558 P.2d 14 (1976), which grew out of a fight between a group of pecan farmers, the city of Tucson, and a mining company. The court was forced to resolve an issue that had seldom been addressed by the common law: what constitutes "overlying land" in the context of reasonable use? The court favored the farmers and held unreasonable the use of water for a mine and the city, both outside a designated critical area where the water was pumped. This narrow definition of overlying land "created a storm of protest from the strong Arizona mining lobby," heightened the fears of cities such as Tucson that they would be unable to obtain adequate new supplies, and led directly to the formation of a Groundwater Management Commission in 1977. John L. Kyl, *The 1980 Arizona Groundwater Management Act: From Inception to Current Constitutional Challenge*, 53 U. Colo. L. Rev. 471, 476 (1982).

The final impetus for agricultural, mining, and urban interests to cut a deal came from Secretary of the Interior Cecil Andrus. To carry out a then almost forgotten limitation in the CAP authorizing legislation he announced the federal CAP position: no state groundwater management legislation, no CAP. This spurred the creation of a negotiating group chaired by Governor (subsequently Secretary of the Interior) Bruce Babbitt that included representatives of all major water interests. The cities and the mining industry forged a strong coalition that captured control of the issue from the farmers. They rejected a farmer-backed plan to buy out agricultural lands. The compromises that led to the legislation were not easy. The group rejected specific pro rata pumping cutbacks and the retirement of agricultural lands (though a purchase and retirement program may begin, if necessary, after the year 2006) in favor of granting the Director of Water Resources broad authority to mandate conservation and more efficient use. Desmond D. Connall, Jr., *A History of the Arizona Groundwater Management Act*, 1982 Ariz. St. L.J. 313.

Town of Chino Valley v. City of Prescott

Supreme Court of Arizona, 1981.
131 Ariz. 78, 638 P.2d 1324. Appeal dismissed, 457 U.S. 1101, 102 S.Ct. 2897, 73 L.Ed.2d 1310 (1982).

■ STRUCKMEYER, CHIEF JUSTICE.

* * *

The Town of Chino Valley lies approximately fifteen miles north of the City of Prescott in Yavapai County, Arizona. Prescott owns 164 acres of land in the Chino Valley. In 1948, it drilled wells on some of its Chino Valley property and began transporting groundwater through a seventeen-mile pipeline to its municipal customers. In 1962, pursuant to a petition by Chino Valley residents and A.R.S. § 45–301 et seq., the State Land Department established the Granite Creek Critical Groundwater Area. On September 20, 1970, the Town was incorporated. It was within the Granite Creek Critical Groundwater Area and it owned lands and was withdrawing groundwater from the same underground basin as Prescott. Prescott, itself, was not within the Granite Creek Critical Groundwater Area.

This action was filed on August 21, 1972, seeking to enjoin the pumping of groundwater by Prescott. It did not seek damages for the unlawful pumping or transportation of groundwaters. The lawsuit proceeded at a desultory pace until the order of dismissal on November 3, 1980.

Meanwhile, in 1977 the Legislature amended the Arizona Groundwater Code. The Town in 1978 brought an original action in this Court which challenged the constitutionality of the prohibitions against injunctive relief contained in the 1977 amendments. That challenge was rejected. *Town of Chino Valley v. State Land Department*, 119 Ariz. 243, 580 P.2d 704 (1978).

Thereafter, in June of 1980, the Legislature enacted the Groundwater Management Act, herein called the Act or the 1980 Act.* It repealed the 1977 amendments and abolished critical groundwater areas, substituting geographic units of groundwater management called Active Management Areas and Irrigation Non–Expansion Areas. Certain areas which had been declared critical groundwater areas under former laws were included in the Active Management Areas. By A.R.S. § 45–411(A)(3), the Prescott Active Management Area was established. It includes the Little Chino and Upper Agua Fria Sub-basins. Both the Town of Chino Valley and Prescott are within the Little Chino Sub-basin of the Prescott Active Management Area.

By A.R.S. § 45–541(A) of the 1980 Act, transportation of groundwater is allowed within a sub-basin of an Active Management Area. Prescott, being within the Little Chino Sub-basin from which it was drawing water,

---

* The 1980 Act provided for the establishment of Active Management Areas which are geographical areas where groundwater supplies are imperiled. A.R.S. §§ 45–411 to –637. Active Management Areas encompass a whole groundwater basin or basins. A.R.S. § 45–412(B). Groundwater basins are areas designated as enclosing a relatively hydrologically distinct body or related bodies of groundwater. A.R.S. § 45–402(10). Groundwater sub-basins are areas designated so to enclose a smaller hydrologically distinct body of groundwater found within a groundwater basin. A.R.S. § 45–402(25).

The 1980 Act provides limitations on use of groundwater in Active Management Areas. In general the Act restricts new uses of water drawn from Active Management Areas. The Act sets up a system of determining grandfathered rights to use groundwater in Active Management Areas, A.R.S. §§ 45–461 to –482, defining certain usages of groundwater previously being made and allowing these usages to continue. A.R.S. § 45–462. The Act also establishes the rights of cities, towns, private water companies and irrigation districts in Active Management Areas to withdraw as much groundwater as is needed from within their service areas to serve their customers although restrictions are provided on extensions of service areas and the types of service that may be provided by these entities. A.R.S. § 45–491. The Act also specifies a few other new uses of groundwater that may be made in Active Management Areas. It allows limited new withdrawals for domestic purposes. A.R.S. § 45–454. It also sets up a system for obtaining permits to withdraw new amounts of water for certain specific purposes. A.R.S. §§ 45–511 to –528.

Provided withdrawal is permitted under any of the provisions of the Act, transportation of groundwater within the same sub-basin may be made without payment of damages. A.R.S. § 45–541. Transportation of groundwater between sub-basins or away from Active Management Areas is also authorized if the groundwater is allowed to be withdrawn under the Act's provisions, but damages must be paid for any injury caused. A.R.S. §§ 45l–542, –543. Rules for determining damage are set out in A.R.S. § 45–545. The transportation rules apply whether in or outside of Active Management Areas, A.R.S. § 45–544, although the restrictions on new uses of groundwater do not apply outside of Active Management Areas. A.R.S. § 45–453.

The Act provides for conservation for all uses of groundwater in Active Management Areas. A.R.S. §§ 45–561 to –579. The Act ends with provisions governing the drilling and registering of wells for withdrawing groundwater, A.R.S. §§ 45–591 to –604, and financial and enforcement provisions to carry out the legislation, A.R.S. §§ 45–611 to –615, –631 to –637.

moved for dismissal of the Town's complaint for injunctive relief. The Superior Court granted Prescott's motion, but ordered that the Town have twenty days in which to file an amended complaint specifying any damages. The Town's appeal from that portion of the trial court's order dismissing appellants' claim for injunctive relief is based upon the asserted unconstitutionality of the Act of 1980 since the Act, by permitting the transportation of groundwater, legitimizes the prospective withdrawal of groundwater from the Little Chino Sub-basin by Prescott. Appellants' principal attack is that the Act takes property without due process of law and without just compensation. The Act is also challenged on the grounds that it is a legislative encroachment on judicial powers and that it violates art. 4, part 2, § 13 of the Arizona Constitution in that there are provisions in the Act of 1980 which were not included in the title of the Act.

By the Constitution of Arizona, art. 17, § 1, effective at statehood in 1912, it was provided that the common law doctrine of riparian water rights "shall not obtain or be of any force or effect in the State." Thereafter, in 1919, the Arizona Legislature provided that the water of all sources falling in streams, canyons, ravines, natural channels or definite underground channels belonged to the public and were subject to appropriation for beneficial use. Waters percolating beneath the soil were not included among those subject to appropriation. Appellants rely on the cases of *Howard v. Perrin*, 8 Ariz. 347, 76 P. 460 (1904), and *Maricopa County Water Conservation District No. 1 v. Southwest Cotton Co.*, 39 Ariz. 65, 4 P.2d 369 (1931), for their basic proposition that they own the water percolating beneath their lands under the doctrine of reasonable use.

The Territorial Supreme Court, in *Howard v. Perrin*, commented:

> "Throughout the Pacific Coast, where the doctrine of appropriation obtains, the decisions are uniform to the effect that waters percolating generally through the soil beneath the surface are the property of the owner of the soil * * *." 8 Ariz. at 353, 76 P. at 462.

Howard v. Perrin was a case in which Howard's grantor went upon unsurveyed lands and sank a well, developing a flow of water which he conducted to some water troughs and a reservoir. About six years later, Howard posted a notice that he had appropriated water from a definite underground channel pursuant to the Laws of 1893, Act 86. The issue was whether the waters which Howard claimed to have appropriated were in a definite underground channel or, as the court said: "constituted a running stream flowing in natural channels between well-defined banks * * *." 8 Ariz. at 353, 76 P. at 462. It was held that Howard, having alleged an appropriable subterranean stream, had the burden of proof to establish that fact by competent evidence. The court said it failed "to find sufficient evidence in the testimony of the witnesses * * * to establish the existence of 'a subterranean stream with well-defined channels or banks,' * * *." Id. at 354, 76 P. at 463. Palpably the statement that waters percolating through the soil beneath the surface are the property of the owner of the soil is dictum.

Maricopa County Water Conservation District No. 1 v. Southwest Cotton Co., 39 Ariz. 65, 4 P.2d 369 (1931), was also a case in which it was determined that the proof did not establish an underground stream so as to permit appropriation of water. The court cited to *Howard v. Perrin*, saying:

> "[A]nd therein we held that waters percolating generally through the soil are the property of the owner * * *.
>
> * * * Whether such statement was, strictly speaking, *dicta* or not, it has been accepted as the law of this jurisdiction for so long, and so many rights have been based on it, that only the clearest showing that the rule declared was error would justify us in departing from it." Id. at 82–83, 4 P.2d 369, 4 P.2d at 375–76.

The Town of Chino Valley relies on the two foregoing cited cases, but there are others in which the statement first made in *Howard v. Perrin* was repeated, although there was at no time, according to the way we read the cases, an arguable issue as to the precise nature of the right which the owner of the overlying lands had to the waters beneath.

Dictum thrice repeated is still dictum. It is a court's statement on a question not necessarily involved in the case and, hence, is without force of adjudication. It is not controlling as precedent. We therefore hold that the statement first made in *Howard v. Perrin* and reiterated under circumstances where the exact nature of the overlying owner's rights to the water beneath his property were not in question is not precedent for the decision in this case.

In 1952, in *Bristor v. Cheatham*, 73 Ariz. 228, 240 P.2d 185, a majority of this Court held that waters percolating beneath the surface of the land were subject to appropriation. On rehearing, however, one new judge having been elected and one judge having changed his position, it was held that groundwater was not subject to appropriation. The majority said:

> "[M]any and large investments have been made in the development of ground waters. Under these circumstances the court's announcement of the rule becomes a rule of property * * *." 255 P.2d 173, 175 (1953).

In 1970, in *Jarvis v. State Land Department*, 106 Ariz. 506, 479 P.2d 169, we said:

> "The right to exhaust the common supply by transporting water for use off the lands from which they are pumped is a rule of law controlled by the doctrine of reasonable use and protected by the constitution of the state as a right in property." 106 Ariz. at 509–10, 479 P.2d at 172–73.

The statements in *Bristor* and *Jarvis* do not mean that rights to the use of groundwaters cannot be modified prospectively by the Legislature. They only mean that courts will adhere to an announced rule to protect rights acquired under it and that if any change in the law is necessary, it should be made by the Legislature. The doctrine of rule of property has no operation as against subsequent legislation.

We therefore hold that since the Act of 1980 is prospective in application, it is not a legislative encroachment on judicial powers.

Appellants urge that the 1980 Act denies them due process of law and just compensation. The question therefore is, what are a landowner's rights in the water percolating under his lands?

In our recent case of *Town of Chino Valley v. State Land Dept.*, 119 Ariz. 243, 580 P.2d 704 (1978), we said:

> "Under the doctrine of reasonable use property owners have the right to capture and use the underground water beneath their land for a beneficial purpose on that land * * *." Id. at 248, 580 P.2d at 709.

This statement we think is supported by the better reasoned decisions in this country. In the absolute sense, there can be no ownership in seeping and percolating waters until they are reduced to actual possession and control by the person claiming them because of their migratory character. Like wild animals free to roam as they please, they are the property of no one.

In *Knight v. Grimes*, 80 S.D. 517, 127 N.W.2d 708, 711 (1964), the court noted that South Dakota is largely a semi-arid state and that the legislature was fully justified in finding the public welfare required the maximum protection and utilization of its water supply. It said:

> "The notion that this right to take and use percolating water constitutes an actual ownership of the water prior to withdrawal has been demonstrated to be legally fallacious."

In the recent case of *Village of Tequesta v. Jupiter Inlet Corp.*, 371 So.2d 663, 666–67 (Fla.), cert. denied, 444 U.S. 965 (1979), it was held:

* * *

> "The right of the owner to ground water underlying his land is to the usufruct of the water and not to the water itself."

We therefore hold that there is no right of ownership of groundwater in Arizona prior to its capture and withdrawal from the common supply and that the right of the owner of the overlying land is simply to the usufruct of the water.

This brings us to conclude that appellants' position that the 1980 Act violates the Fifth and Fourteenth Amendments to the Constitution of the United States and art. 2, § 17 of the Constitution of the State of Arizona as a taking of private property without due process of law and just compensation cannot be sustained.

The Legislature, in Ch. 2 of the 1980 Act, A.R.S. § 45–401, declared:

> "A. The legislature finds that the people of Arizona are dependent in whole or in part upon groundwater basins for their water supply and that in many basins and sub-basins withdrawal of groundwater is greatly in excess of the safe annual yield and that this is threatening to destroy the economy of certain areas of this state and is threatening to do substantial injury to the general economy and welfare of this state

and its citizens. The legislature further finds that it is in the best interest of the general economy and welfare of this state and its citizens that the legislature evoke its police power to prescribe which uses of groundwater are most beneficial and economically effective.

B.   It is therefore declared to be the public policy of this state that in the interest of protecting and stabilizing the general economy and welfare of this state and its citizens it is necessary to conserve, protect and allocate the use of groundwater resources of the state and to provide a framework for the comprehensive management and regulation of the withdrawal, transportation, use, conservation and conveyance of rights to use the groundwater in this state."

We do not doubt but that the overdraft of groundwater in this state is a serious problem which has no chance of correcting itself, and that it is necessary for comprehensive legislation to both limit groundwater use and allocate its use among competing interests.

More than twenty-five years ago, this Court decided that the Legislature might choose between competing interests where the supply of groundwater was limited. In *Southwest Engineering Co. v. Ernst*, 79 Ariz. 403, 291 P.2d 764 (1955), we said in holding constitutional the groundwater act of 1948:

* * * that there was a preponderant public interest in the preservation of lands then in cultivation as against lands potentially reclaimable "and that where as here the choice is unavoidable because a supply of water is not available for both, we cannot say that the exercise of such choice, controlled by considerations of social policy which are not unreasonable, involves a denial of due process." *Id.* at 769, 291 P.2d 764. The Legislature in the Act of 1980 again recognized that the supply of groundwater is limited and again exercised a choice for the preservation and use of groundwater.

Legislation which denies or restricts rights to use property necessarily results in a diminution of that property's value. Yet the United States Supreme Court has on numerous occasions upheld under the state's police power regulations of land use which have virtually destroyed private interests. Most recently, in *Agins v. City of Tiburon*, 447 U.S. 255 (1980), it was held that a zoning ordinance restricting the use of a five-acre tract of land to single family residences would not effect a taking of property without compensation. The city ordinance was found to further the legitimate state interest of protecting the residents of the city from the ill effects of urbanization. *Id.* at 262. In the present case, appellants may make such use of their property as they choose, except that their lands may not be irrigated if they were not legally irrigated in the last five years. The 1980 Act furthers legitimate state interests.

Legislatures of various states have from time to time abolished the prevailing uses of groundwater and substituted other plans for its use. State courts have uniformly rejected the idea that groundwater percolating through the soil may not be limited and regulated and must be acquired by eminent domain.

"Like zoning legislation, legislation which limits or regulates the right to use underlying water is permissible. * * * Where regulation operates to arbitrate between competing public and private land uses, however, as does the water priority statute in this case, such legislation is upheld even where the value of the property declines significantly as a result." *Crookston Cattle Co. v. Minnesota Department of Natural Resources*, 300 N.W.2d at 774 (citation omitted).

We hold that the Act of 1980 does not deny appellants due process of law and does not require that they be paid compensation for any possible diminution of their rights which they may have had under the doctrine of reasonable use.

* * *

NOTES

1. The 1980 Act was also upheld in federal court. Cherry v. Steiner, 543 F.Supp. 1270 (D.Ariz.1982), aff'd 716 F.2d 687 (9th Cir.1983). See generally Michael J. Kelly, *Management of Groundwater Through Mandatory Conservation*, 61 Denver L.J. 1 (1983). Does the non-ownership rationale of *Chino* mean that if a landowner's land is condemned for a well field, no recovery for the loss of groundwater use may be had? See Sorensen v. Lower Niobrara Natural Res. Dist., 221 Neb. 180, 376 N.W.2d 539 (1985).

2. Is the *Chino Valley* court saying the reasonable use doctrine has always applied in Arizona? Or does its dismissal, as *dictum*, of statements in *Howard v. Perrin* and its progeny indicate that landowners never had the unqualified right to pump, even for use on their own lands? What rule now applies outside the AMAs or INEAs established by the 1980 Groundwater Management Act?

3. Is the court's statement that "dictum thrice repeated is still dictum" *dictum*? The plaintiffs, including the town of Chino Valley and neighboring farmers, were already pumping groundwater. Therefore, how is the question of what rights a landowner who is not now pumping has in underlying groundwater relevant to the issue before the court in *Chino Valley*? To put the question another way, is the court really being accurate when it says "[w]e therefore hold that there is no right of ownership of groundwater prior to its capture and withdrawal from the common supply."

4. Does the state now have a relatively free hand to devise management plans which stringently regulate existing uses to bring water supply and demand into balance? What constitutional (as opposed to statutory or political) limits on this power remain? See the discussion of takings law *supra* Chapter 5F.

5. A significant provision of the Act requires new developments to have a 100–year guaranteed supply. Because in severely over-drafted basins, it may take many decades to restore the basin to safe yield, one would think that urban growth may be constrained. Alternative supplies have allowed Phoenix and Tucson to continue to grow but the Prescott AMA, on the Mogollon Rim, is still in overdraft and has less surface supply alternatives.

Nonetheless, public and private water providers have continued to issue 100 year assured water supply commitments, as the Act requires, for new subdivisions. A 2000 report by the Arizona Department of Water Resources concluded that the net result is that "committed demand in the AMA ultimately could result in more than doubling the current municipal groundwater use of 11,600 acre feet, significantly exacerbating groundwater overdraft conditions," and thus the "Prescott AMA must join the Phoenix and Tucson region * * * where new subdivisions must rely primarily on water sources other than mined groundwater from within their areas to meet future water needs." Arizona Department of Water Resources, Preliminary Determination Report on the Safe Yield Status of the Prescott Active Management Area. (2000). An update of the hydrology situation in the Prescott AMA is Arizona Department of Water Resources, Prescott Active Management Area, 2003–2004 Hydrologic Monitoring Report (2005).

6. Although Arizona's law required stringent conservation requirements, heavy reliance on groundwater pumping has continued. Demand for CAP water fell far short of the assumptions on which the project was constructed because agricultural users could not afford to pay for their CAP allocations. Under the interstate arrangements for use of the Colorado River, this meant that California could take Arizona's unused portion. See *infra* p. 1021. To create a demand for CAP water the legislature enacted a groundwater storage program, Ariz. Rev. Stat. §§ 45–808 to 45–809 (2000), and created a groundwater replenishment district for the Phoenix and Tucson AMAs. Ariz. Rev. Stat. § 45–611 (2003 and Supp. 2006).

Recent evidence indicates that safe annual yield may not be achieved in the Phoenix and Tucson AMAs because population continues to expand, but there is no consensus about what, if any, new management strategies should be adopted. The State Auditor has suggested that existing reserves will carry the state for 500 years, while other observers argue that agricultural land retirement will be necessary to achieve safe yield. Failing that, the state will be unable to continue promoting unrestricted urban growth. Robert Glennon, *"Because That's Where the Water Is": Retiring Current Water Uses To Achieve the Safe-Yield Objective of the Arizona Groundwater Management Act,* 33 Ariz. L. Rev. 89 (1991). See also William Parsons & Douglas Matthews, *The Californiazation of Arizona Water Politics,* 30 Nat. Resources J. 341 (1990). The relationship between growth control, and urban water supply pricing is further discussed *infra* p. 773. As the title suggests, Paul Hirt, Annie Gustafson and Kelli L. Larson, The Mirage in the Valley of the Sun, 13 Envtl. History 482 (2008), is a pessimistic look at the success of Arizona's efforts to reduce its groundwater mining.

5. CALIFORNIA: BASINWIDE ADJUDICATION

It is appropriate to speak of a water industry in California, because many of the pumpers, especially in Southern California, are large municipal suppliers or industries such as oil companies. California has no statewide groundwater law and has depended largely on adjudication of rights authorized by the legislature to proceed basin by basin. The issue in the several basinwide adjudications has not been simply how to allocate a scarce resource among competing users over time, but the more complex question of how to balance the use of groundwater and use of water imported from the Colorado River and from Northern California rivers. The problem is, of course, cost, as sufficient water to meet existing demands has always been available. For example, in 1945, when an adjudication of rights to groundwater in a portion of the Los Angeles area commenced, the major water supplier, the Metropolitan Water District of Southern California, was potentially able to take 1,212,000 acre-feet of Colorado River water but was selling only 32,000 acre-feet and looking for customers. Because of transportation costs, the price of Colorado River water was higher than that of local supplies, and pumpers desired to maximize their use of the cheaper groundwater. See generally William Blomquist, Dividing the Waters: Governing Groundwater in Southern California (1992).

California followed the rule of absolute ownership until 1903 when the common law was rejected in favor of the correlative rights rule. Katz v. Walkinshaw, 141 Cal. 116, 70 P. 663 (1902), reh'g granted 141 Cal. 116, 74 P. 766 (1903). Correlative rights is a system that allocates a "fair and just portion" of the common pool to each overlying owner. These rights are analogous to riparian rights, for they can be asserted at any time provided the use is reasonable and beneficial under Cal. Const. art. 10, § 2, and subsequent rights are entitled to equal dignity with existing rights. Burr v. Maclay Rancho Water Co., 154 Cal. 428, 98 P. 260 (1908).

Appropriative rights in the basin may also be perfected provided that two conditions are met. First, water must be available in excess of safe annual yield. Second, the water must not be needed by the overlying owners. If the basin is in overdraft and there is insufficient water to satisfy the uses of the overlying owners, the available supply is restricted to overlying owners based on each user's reasonable need. See Tehachapi–Cummings County Water Dist. v. Armstrong, 49 Cal.App.3d 992, 122 Cal.Rptr. 918 (1975). What constitutes overlying use has never been clearly defined. Some cases have equated it with use of land within the groundwater basin rather than the parcel of land beneath which the water is actually pumped. It seems clear, however, that municipalities cannot claim overlying rights to supply customers throughout the basin from which water is pumped. City of San Bernardino v. City of Riverside, 186 Cal. 7, 198 P. 784 (1921). Because most groundwater users in Southern California are cities and industries, the distinction favoring overlying users was less important, at least between 1949 and 1975, when the case of *Los Angeles v. San Fernando, infra* p. 642, was decided.

Pasadena v. Alhambra

Supreme Court of California, 1949.
33 Cal.2d 908, 207 P.2d 17.

■ GIBSON, CHIEF JUDGE.

* * *

The Raymond Basin Area, a field of ground water located at the northwest end of San Gabriel Valley, includes the city of Sierra Madre, almost all of the city of Pasadena, and portions of South Pasadena, San Marino, and Arcadia. The field of ground water contains alluvium consisting of sands, gravels and other porous materials through which water percolates. The northern side is formed by the San Gabriel range of mountains which rise back of the valley to a general elevation of from 5,000 to 6,000 feet. The area comprises 40 square miles and is separated from the rest of the valley along its southern boundary by the Raymond Fault, sometimes known as Raymond Dike, a natural fault in the bedrock constituting a "Barrier in the alluvium * * * which greatly impedes the subsurface movement of water from the area, although it does not entirely stop it, thus creating a vast underground storage reservoir." * * *

Natural underground formations divide the area into two practically separate units. * * *

Our concern is with the Western Unit where the principal ground water movement is from north and west of Monk Hill to the south and east and across Raymond Fault. The water in this unit is replenished by rainfall, by return water arising from the use of water in the unit, and by the runoff and underflow from the San Gabriel Mountains to the north and from the San Rafael hills to the west. Appellant's wells, from which it obtains all its production, are in the southeastern part of this unit, and the underlying water constitutes one ground water body which is a common source of all parties taking water therefrom. The water pumped from the ground in the Western Unit has exceeded the safe yield thereof in every year since 1913–14 (commencing October 1) except during the years 1934–35 and 1936–37. The safe yield of the unit was found to be 18,000 acre feet per year, but the average annual draft was 24,000 acre feet, resulting in an average annual overdraft of 6,000 feet.

With respect to the water rights acquired by the various parties it was stipulated by all of them, including appellant, that "all of the water taken by each of the parties to this stipulation and agreement, at the time it was taken, was taken openly, notoriously and under a claim of right, which claim of right was continuously and uninterruptedly asserted by it to be and was adverse to any and all claims of each and all of the other parties joining herein."

The findings set forth in terms of acre feet per year "the highest continuous production of water for beneficial use in any five (5) year period prior to the filing of the complaint by each of the parties in each of said units, as to which there has been no cessation of use by it during any subsequent continuous five (5) year period." This was designated, for convenience, the "present unadjusted right" of each party, and the court concluded that each party owned "by prescription" the right to take a certain specified amount of water, and that the rights of the parties were of equal priority. The total of the unadjusted rights for the Western Unit was found to be 25,608 acre feet per year, and water pumped by nonparties to the action was 340 acre feet per year. The court also found that a continued draft in these amounts will result in an unreasonable depletion and the eventual destruction of the ground water as a source of supply. * * * The amount of water limited to each party, designated the "decreed right," was set out in the findings, and this allocation gave each party about two-thirds of the amount it had been pumping.

The court enjoined all pumping in excess of the decreed right and appointed a "Water Master" to enforce the provisions of the judgment. It reserved jurisdiction to modify the judgment or make such further orders as might be necessary for adequate enforcement or for protection of the waters in the Raymond Basin Area from contamination.

* * *

The question of who shall bear the burden of curtailing the overdraft, and in what proportion, depends upon the legal nature and status of the particular water right held by each party. Rights in water in an underground basin, so far as pertinent here, are classified as overlying, appropriate, and prescriptive. Generally speaking, an overlying right, analogous to that of a riparian owner in a surface stream, is the right of the owner of the land to take water from the ground underneath for use on his land within the basin or watershed; the right is based on ownership of the land and is appurtenant thereto. The right of an appropriator depends upon an actual taking of water. The term "appropriation" is said by some authorities to be properly used only with reference to the taking of water from a surface stream on public land for nonriparian purposes. The California courts, however, use the term to refer to any taking of water for other than riparian or overlying uses. Where a taking is wrongful, it may ripen into a prescriptive right.

Although the law at one time was otherwise, it is now clear that an overlying owner or any other person having a legal right to surface or ground water may take only such amount as he reasonably needs for beneficial purposes. (Katz v. Walkinshaw, 141 Cal. 116 [70 P. 663, 74 P. 766]; Peabody v. City of Vallejo, 2 Cal.2d 351 [40 P.2d 486]; Cal. Const., art. XIV, § 3.) Public interest requires that there be the greatest number of beneficial uses which the supply can yield, and water may be appropriated for beneficial uses subject to the rights of those who have a lawful priority. Any water not needed for the reasonable beneficial uses of those having prior rights is excess or surplus water. In California surplus water may rightfully be appropriated on privately owned land for nonoverlying uses, such as devotion to a public use or exportation beyond the basin or watershed.

It is the policy of the state to foster the beneficial use of water and discourage waste, and when there is a surplus, whether of surface or ground water, the holder of prior rights may not enjoin its appropriation. Proper overlying use, however, is paramount, and the right of an appropriator, being limited to the amount of the surplus, must yield to that of the overlying owner in the event of a shortage, unless the appropriator has gained prescriptive rights through the taking of nonsurplus waters. As between overlying owners, the rights, like those of riparians, are correlative and are referred to as belonging to all in common; each may use only his reasonable share when water is insufficient to meet the needs of all. As between appropriators, however, the one first in time is the first in right, and a prior appropriator is entitled to all the water he needs, up to the amount that he has taken in the past, before a subsequent appropriator may take any.

Prescriptive rights are not acquired by the taking of surplus or excess water, since no injunction may issue against the taking and the appropriator may take the surplus without giving compensation; however, both overlying owners and appropriators are entitled to the protection of the courts against any substantial infringement of their rights in water which they reasonably and beneficially need. (Peabody v. City of Vallejo, 2 Cal.2d 351, 368–369, 374 [40 P.2d 486].) Accordingly, an appropriative taking of water which is not surplus is wrongful and may ripen into a prescriptive right where the use is actual, open and notorious, hostile and adverse to the original owner, continuous and uninterrupted for the statutory period of five years, and under claim of right. To perfect a claim based upon prescription there must, of course, be conduct which constitutes an actual invasion of the former owner's rights so as to entitle him to bring an action. Appropriative and prescriptive rights to ground water, as well as the rights of an overlying owner, are subject to loss by adverse use. This is in accord with the rule announced in cases dealing with water in a surface stream.

* * *

It follows from the foregoing that, if no prescriptive rights had been acquired, the rights of the overlying owners would be paramount, and the rights of the appropriators would depend on priority of acquisition under the rule that the first appropriator in time is the first in right. The latest in time of the appropriations would then be the first to be curtailed in limiting total production of the area to the safe yield. If such were the case, the overdraft could be eliminated simply by enjoining a part of the latest appropriations, since the record shows that there is ample water to satisfy the needs of all the overlying users and most of the appropriators, and appellant's appropriative rights would depend primarily upon evidence of priority in time of acquisition.

The principal dispute between appellant and respondents, however, concerns whether any water rights in the Western Unit have become prescriptive and, if so, to what extent. Respondents assert that the rights of all the parties, including both overlying users and appropriators, have become mutually prescriptive against all the other parties and, accordingly, that all rights are of equal standing, with none prior or paramount. Appellant, on the other hand, contends that in reality no prescriptive rights have been acquired, and that there has been no actionable invasion or injury of the right of any party using water because each party has been able to take all the water it needed and no party has in any manner prevented a taking of water by any other party. It would follow, under appellant's theory, that not even an overlying owner could have obtained an injunction against a subsequent taking.

* * *

The record shows that there has been an actual adverse user of water in the Western Unit. There was an invasion, to some extent at least, of the rights of both overlying owners and appropriators commencing in the year 1913–1914, when the overdraft first occurred. Each taking of water in excess of the safe yield, whether by subsequent appropriators or by increased use by prior appropriators, was wrongful and was an injury to the then existing owners of water rights, because the overdraft, from its very beginning, operated progressively to reduce the total available supply. Although no owner was immediately prevented from taking the water he needed, the report demonstrates that a continuation of the overdraft would eventually result in such a depletion of the supply stored in the underground basin that it would become inadequate. The injury thus did not involve an immediate disability to obtain water, but, rather, it consisted of the continual lowering of the level and gradual reducing of the total amount of stored water, the accumulated effect of which, after a period of years, would be to render the supply insufficient to meet the needs of the rightful owners.

The proper time to act in preserving the supply is when the overdraft commences, and the aid of the courts would come too late and be entirely inadequate if, as appellant seems to suggest, those who possess water rights could not commence legal proceedings until the supply was so greatly depleted that it actually became difficult or impossible to obtain water. Where the quantity withdrawn exceeds the average annual amount contributed by rainfall, it is manifest that the underground store will be gradually depleted and eventually exhausted, and, accordingly, in order to prevent such a catastrophe, it has been held proper to limit the total use by all consumers to an amount equal, as near as may be, to the average supply and to enjoin takings in such quantities or in such a manner as would destroy or endanger the underground source of water. There is, therefore, no merit to the contention that the owners of water rights were not injured by the additional appropriations made after all surplus waters were taken, and they clearly were entitled to obtain injunctive relief to terminate all takings in excess of the surplus as soon as it became apparent from the lowering of the well levels that the underground basin would be depleted if the excessive pumping were continued.

The lowering of the water table resulting from the overdraft was plainly observable in the wells of the parties * * *.

This evidence is clearly sufficient to justify charging appellant with notice that there was a deficiency rather than a surplus and that the appropriations causing the overdraft were invasions of the rights of overlying owners and prior appropriators. The elements of prescription being present in the record, the statute of limitations ran against the original lawful holders of water rights to whatever extent their rights were invaded.

It must next be determined whether the rights of all of the prior owners were invaded and whether all or only a part of the right of any particular owner was damaged. It has been established that the rights of appropriators as well as of overlying owners will be protected by the courts and that an invasion of either type of right will start the running of the statute. Where, as here, subsequent appropriators reduce the available supply and their acts, if continued, will render it impossible for the holder of a prior right to pump in the future, there is an enjoinable invasion. In this respect there is no difference between an overlying owner and an appropriator. Although neither may prevent a taking of surplus waters, either may institute legal proceedings to safeguard the supply once a surplus ceases to exist and may enjoin any additional user beyond the point of safe yield.

Cases are cited for the proposition that an appropriator's rights are not invaded if he continues to receive the quantity of water to which he is entitled. These cases, however, do not deal with the problem of gradual depletion of water stored in a basin or lake, but, rather, with surface streams or ditches in which water flows but is not retained for future use. The type of injury there considered would immediately deprive the owner of water, and the language in the opinions does not apply to an invasion of rights in a stored supply of water to be used only in future years.

Neither the overlying owners nor the appropriators took steps to obtain the aid of the courts to protect their rights until the present action was instituted, many years after the commencement of the overdraft, and at first glance it would seem to follow that the parties who wrongfully appropriated water for a period of five years would acquire prior prescriptive rights to the full amount so taken. The running of the statute, however, can effectively be interrupted by self help on the part of the lawful owner of the property right involved. Unlike the situation with respect to a surface stream where a wrongful taking by an appropriator has the immediate effect of preventing the riparian owner from receiving water in the amount taken by the wrongdoer, the owners of water rights in the present case were not immediately prevented from taking water, and they in fact continued to pump whatever they needed. As we have seen, the Raymond Basin Area is similar to a large lake or reservoir, and water would be available until exhaustion of the supply. The owners were injured only with respect to their rights to continue to pump at some future date. The invasion was thus only a partial one, since it did not completely oust the original owners of water rights, and for the entire period both the original owners and the wrongdoers continued to pump all the water they needed.

The pumping by each group, however, actually interfered with the other group in that it produced an overdraft which would operate to make it impossible for all to continue at the same rate in the future. If the original owners of water rights had been ousted completely or had failed to pump for a five-year period, then there would have been no interference whatsoever on the part of the owners with the use by the wrongdoers, and the wrongdoers would have perfected prior prescriptive rights to the full amount which they pumped. As we have seen, however, such was not the case, and, although the pumping of each party to this action continued without interruption, it necessarily interfered with the future possibility of pumping by each of the other parties by lowering the water level. The original owners by their own acts, although not by judicial assistance, thus retained or acquired a right to continue to take some water in the future. The wrongdoers also acquired prescriptive rights to continue to take water, but their rights were limited to the extent that the original owners retained or acquired rights by their pumping.

[Affirmed.]

NOTES

1. Determining the relationship between correlative and appropriative rights has plagued California courts. Wright v. Goleta Water Dist., 174 Cal.App.3d 74, 219 Cal.Rptr. 740 (1985) held that California law protects the unexercised correlative rights of overlying landowners, and that they are superior to appropriative rights. The court recognized the unusual correlative rights of overlying landowners in an overdrafted coastal groundwater basin and refused to subordinate them to present beneficial uses of a district. Although the court indicated that it would be logical to extend the principles of *In re* Waters of Long Valley Creek Stream System, 25 Cal.3d 339, 158 Cal.Rptr. 350, 599 P.2d 656 (1979), *supra* p. 497, to groundwater adjudications, it found that the legislature had created a comprehensive adjudication system for surface waters only.

In City of Barstow v. Mojave Water Agency, 23 Cal.4th 1224, 99 Cal.Rptr.3d 294, 5 P.3d 853 (2000), suit was brought to determine priorities in the overdrafted Mojave groundwater basin. In order to resolve a claim that upstream groundwater pumping was adversely impacting downstream users' water supply and contributing to the overdraft, the trial court ordered a physical solution, to which most basin users stipulated, based on equitable principles of apportionment. "The trial court used the phrase 'physical solution' to refer to its equitable distribution of water use in relation to the many parties who stipulated to it." Id. at 858 n.1. On appeal, the California Supreme Court held that "although it is clear that a trial court may impose a physical solution to achieve a practical allocation of water to competing interests, the solution's general purpose cannot simply ignore the priority rights of the parties asserting them. In ordering a physical solution, therefore, a court may neither change priorities among the water rights holders nor eliminate vested rights in applying the solution without first considering them in relation to the reasonable use doctrine." Id. at 869.

2. Salt water intrusion is a serious problem in coastal groundwater basins. Its prevention has been a major motivation in several post-*Pasadena* adjudications in Southern California. Voluntary settlements have been approved by the courts and one unreported, but widely cited, trial court decision has held that the prescriptive period beings to run when salt water intrusion threatens the quality of the basin. San Luis Rey Water Conservation Dist. v. Carlsbad Mun. Water Dist. (San Diego County Superior Court No. 184855, Aug. 3, 1959). Commonly recognized methods of controlling salt water intrusion are:

(1) reduction of pumping or rearrangement of pumping patterns;

(2) recharge of the basin (ordinarily with imported water) to raise the groundwater level above sea level;

(3) creation of a coastal fresh water ridge through injection wells and spreading basins;

(4) construction of an artificial subsurface physical barrier;

(5) creation of a pumping trough along the coast.

The State Water Resources Board may file suit "to restrict pumping, or to impose physical solutions, or both, to the extent necessary to prevent destruction of or irreparable injury to the quality of [ground] water. * * * *" Cal. Water Code § 2100 (West 1971).

Recent jurisprudence makes it much harder for California to follow its generally successful policy in coastal areas of fighting salt water intrusion and remedying groundwater drafts with artificial recharge financed by water user fees. Pajaro Valley Water Management Agency v. Amrhein, 150 Cal.App.4th 1364, 59 Cal.Rptr.3d 484 (2007), held that recharge fees are "property related" fees subject to voter approval under the state's stringent anti-tax constitutional provision, Cal.Const. Art.XIII. It did not follow Richmond v. Shasta Community Services Dist., 32 Cal.4th 409, 9 Cal. Rptr.3d 121, 83 P.3d 518 (2004), which held that a connection charge for new services was not a property related service because the property owner voluntarily applied for the service. But cf. Bighorn–Desert View Water Agency v. Verjil, 39 Cal.4th 205, 46 Cal.Rptr.3d 73, 138 P.3d 220 (2006) (once the property owner pays the connection fee and becomes a resident, the fee is a property-related service). Under *Pajaro* Valley, recharge fees must now be preceded by a written notice of a hearing which specifies the calculation of the proposed charge for every parcel of property in the area; if a majority of affected property owners file a written protest, the agency cannot impose the fee. Unless the fee is for "sewer, water or refuse collection," it must be approved either, at the discretion of the agency, by a vote of a majority of the property owners or two-thirds of the voters residing in the affected area. The court left open he question of whether the exemption applies to recharge fees. See also Note 2, *infra* at p. 653.

3. California has resisted the conjunctive management of groundwater basins by the state or by super-regional agencies. However, through the widespread use of adjudications based on the doctrine of mutual prescription followed by the creation of special districts pursuant to state enabling legislation, a high level of local management has been functionally achieved for the objectives of cutting back pumping to safe annual yield levels and preventing salt water intrusion. The Los Angeles coastal basins were the first to institute litigation after *Pasadena*. First, the West Basin, located on the Pacific Ocean, instituted litigation and then the Central Basin, located adjacent to the West Basin and in effect upstream, followed suit.

The West Basin litigation in Los Angeles has produced the most sophisticated institutional responses to salt water intrusion. After 16 years of litigation, reportedly costing $5 million and resulting in reductions on pumping, salt water intrusion continued to be a problem in the basin. In 1955 the legislature passed the Water Replenishment District Act, Cal. Water Code §§ 60000–65000 (West 1971 & Supp. 2001). Under the enabling legislation a replenishment district may determine the amount of annual overdraft and assess pumpers for the costs of purchasing imported water. If the basin has been adjudicated, assessments may be levied only against those who extract in excess of their declared rights. The district may also levy ad valorem taxes not in excess of $.20 per $100.00 of assessed valuation. As a result of the Act, the Central and West Basin Replenishment District was formed in 1959 after lengthy negotiations with the state and with the major water service organizations in the Los Angeles area. Basically, the district agreed that pumping levies rather than ad valorem taxes would be used to purchase replenishment water from the Metropolitan Water District of Southern California (MWD); the imported water would be spread to recharge the basin and prevent salt water intrusion by the Los Angeles County Flood Control District. The Central Basin benefited from the West Basin's pumping reductions and spreading operations. An adjudication of rights was necessary to assess the pumpers an appropriate amount in order to finance the spreading operations under the Central and West Basin Replenishment District. See Carl Fossette & Ruth Fossette, The Story of Water Development in Los Angeles County (1986); Blomquist, *infra* p. 649.

Los Angeles v. San Fernando

Supreme Court of California, 1975.
14 Cal.3d 199, 123 Cal.Rptr. 1, 537 P.2d 1250.

[In 1955 the City of Los Angeles brought an action against numerous private and public defendants to quiet its title to groundwater in the Upper Los Angeles River Area (ULARA) and enjoin all pumpers from extracting water other than in subordination to the plaintiff's prior rights. Los Angeles pumped from the basin, then spread imported water from the Owens Valley, using the area underlying the river as a reservoir, and subsequently extracted it for delivery to customers within and without the Area. The various pumpers extracted groundwater from four subareas of the ULARA. It was stipulated that 42.5 percent of the basin's supply was derived from imported water and the rest from rain and snow within the watershed. Los Angeles claimed: (1) a right to all the native water on the grounds that the city was the successor of the Pueblo of Los Angeles and this gave it a paramount right to all groundwaters it needed to supply all the original and annexed areas of the Pueblo, and (2) a right to all imported water and return flows therefrom on the grounds that Los Angeles controlled the imported water and thus had not abandoned it by spreading. The defendants denied the existence of a pueblo right, argued that all had pumping rights that had to be determined by the doctrine of mutual prescription, and contended that Los Angeles had abandoned their imported water and thus it went into the mutual prescription pool.

Pueblo rights are primarily important in California, New Mexico, and Texas. The theory is that Spanish law gave the pueblos—early settlements—a paramount claim to supply their needs. The supreme court conceded that prior cases may have misinterpreted Spanish law but held that this was irrelevant because (1) the rights had been consistently recognized by the courts, (2) had been declared a rule of property, and (3) there had been substantial reliance on the part of the City of Los Angeles, because the city had imported Owens Valley water relying on the pueblo right to retain priority to its native supply "once this surplus was exhausted." 527 P.2d at 1283, 1284–85. The right was further limited by the standard that pueblo rights only attach to "waters * * * required for satisfying its municipal needs and those of its inhabitants." See *infra* p. 769.

On the issue of the rights of the various parties to imported water Chief Justice Wright wrote as follows:]

GROUND WATER SUPPLIES ATTRIBUTABLE TO IMPORTED WATER

Return Flow Derived From Delivered Imported Water: San Fernando Basin

* * * Apart from the relatively small quantities of imported water spread by plaintiff for direct recharge of the basin, this ground water consisted of a return flow attributable to *delivered* imported water reaching the ground as waste, seepage, or spillage, or by similar means in the course of use. Most of this delivered water had been imported by plaintiff from Owens Valley and Mono basin; the remainder was Colorado River water purchased by plaintiff and by defendants Glendale and Burbank from the Metropolitan Water District.

Ground water is extracted from San Fernando basin by plaintiff, defendants Glendale and Burbank, and seven private defendants. Plaintiff claims a prior right to the ground water attributable to the return flow from its Owens imports and from the delivered water it purchases from MWD. Plaintiff asserts that defendants Glendale and Burbank are entitled to such return water in the basin derived from their MWD purchases. Those defendants, on the other hand, deny any special rights in return water as such and are joined by the seven private defendant claimants of San Fernando basin ground water in opposing plaintiff's claim to priority in return waters.

In City of Los Angeles v. City of Glendale, 23 Cal.2d 68, 142 P.2d 289, this court affirmed a judgment which declared that plaintiff had prior rights, as against defendants Glendale and Burbank, to "return waters" beneath the San Fernando Valley. These return waters were described as those which were imported by plaintiff and "sold to the farmers of the San Fernando Valley, and which settle after use beneath the surface and join the mass of water below, as anticipated when sold." It was held that plaintiff had a prior right to the water when it was imported and that "[t]he use by others of this water as it flowed to the subterranean basin does not cut off plaintiff's rights."

This holding had a dual basis. One basis for the holding was the trial court's finding that before commencing the importation of Owens water, plaintiff had formed an intention to recapture the return waters used for irrigation in the San Fernando Valley whenever such return waters were needed for its municipal purposes and the use of its inhabitants, and that the Los Angeles Aqueduct had been planned and located to facilitate the availability and recapture of such return waters. Under these circumstances, plaintiff retained its prior right to the return waters wherever they might appear.

The other basis for the *Glendale* holding, found in the reasoning of Stevens v. Oakdale Irr. Dist. (1939) 13 Cal.2d 343, 90 P.2d 58, did not depend on the existence of an intent to recapture return waters *before* importation began. In *Stevens*, water brought from the Stanislaus River into the defendant district's irrigation system reached Lone Tree Creek as seepage, waste and spill from irrigation uses. Lone Tree Creek was in a different watershed from the Stanislaus. After an owner of land traversed by Lone Tree Creek downstream from the district's territory had commenced irrigating with the water, the district for the first time manifested an intention to recapture the water from the creek within its own boundaries for irrigation uses, thereby cutting off the lower user's supply. The district's right to do so was upheld. Even though the district had abandoned the particular quantities of water it had allowed to flow downstream, it retained the right to recapture a subsequent flow as long as it did so within its own irrigation works or on its own land. Applying *Stevens*, the *Glendale* court pointed out that the return waters claimed by plaintiff had "reappeared in the basin of the San Fernando Valley, used by plaintiff for the storage of other imported waters [through spreading] and containing natural waters to which plaintiff had a prior [pueblo] right. Once within the basin en route to plaintiff's diversion works, it was in effect within plaintiff's reservoir." (23 Cal.2d at pp. 77–78, 142 P.2d at p. 295.)

The adjudication in *Glendale* of plaintiff's prior right to return waters derived from delivered Owens water is binding in the present case on defendants Glendale and Burbank. * * *

* * * The recapture right, however, does not necessarily attach to the corpus of water physically traceable to particular deliveries but is a right to take from the commingled supply an amount equivalent to the augmentation contributed by the return. * * *

Defendants Glendale and Burbank each delivers imported MWD water to users within its territory in the San Fernando basin and each has been extracting ground water in the same territory before and during the importation. Accordingly, each has rights to recapture water attributable to the return flow from such deliveries for the same reasons that plaintiff has such a right. These multiple rights necessitate apportionment of the ground water derived from return flow into the amounts attributable to the import deliveries of each defendant and plaintiff. The record in this case, including the referee's report, demonstrates that such apportionment can be made within reasonable limits of accuracy.

Defendants contend that if any party is given rights to a return flow derived from delivered *imported* water, it is "obvious" and "axiomatic" that the same rights should be given to the return flow from delivered water derived from all other sources, including native water extracted from local wells. This argument misconceives the reason for the prior right to return flow from imports. Even though all deliveries produce a return flow, only deliveries derived from imported water add to the ground supply. The purpose of giving the right to recapture returns from delivered imported water priority over overlying rights and rights based on appropriations of the native ground supply is to credit the importer with the fruits of his expenditures and endeavors in bringing into the basin water that would not otherwise be there. Returns from deliveries of extracted native water do not add to the ground supply but only lessen the diminution occasioned by the extractions.

* * *

OVERDRAFT AND PRESCRIPTION

Relationship of Pasadena Decision to Equitable Ground Basin Management

As stated above, the trial court's judgment awarded "mutually prescriptive rights" and "restricted pumping" quotas to the parties purportedly pursuant to the decision in City of Pasadena v. City of Alhambra, *supra*, 33 Cal.2d 908, 207 P.2d 17. * * *

* * *

In the present case, none of the defendants now before us commenced their uses of ground water from the basins of the ULARA after the years in which the trial court found overdraft to have commenced. To the contrary, the amount that each defendant was using at the beginning of overdraft was substantial in relation to such defendant's later use, and there is a notable correlation between the relative levels of usage at the time of overdraft and the restricted pumping quotas allocated in the decree based on awards of prescriptive rights.

Thus, the mutual prescription doctrine was not needed or applied in the present case for the purpose achieved in *Pasadena*—that of avoiding complete elimination of appropriative rights stemming from uses of recent years in favor of those based on earlier uses. Instead, the effect of the trial court's judgment in the present case was to eliminate plaintiff's priorities based not on the timing of its appropriations but on its importation of Owens water and on its pueblo right. * * *

* * *

Effect of Civil Code Section 1007 on Prescriptive Claims Against Cities

The trial court awarded prescriptive water rights against plaintiff to both city and private party defendants in the San Fernando and Sylmar basins. Plaintiff asserts that any prescription of its water rights by defendants was precluded by the 1935 amendment to section 1007 of the Civil Code which provided until 1968 that "no possession by any person, firm or corporation no matter how long continued of any . . . water right . . . or other property . . . dedicated to or owned by any . . . city . . . shall ever ripen into any title, interest or right against such . . . city."

Defendants argue that City of Pasadena v. City of Alhambra, *supra*, 33 Cal.2d 908, 207 P.2d 17, decided that the acquisition of water rights against cities by prescription was not barred by the 1935 amendment to Civil Code section 1007, which had been in effect for two years when the complaint in that action was filed. But this court did not reach the issue in that case.
* * *

We are of the opinion that the 1935 amendment to section 1007 was intended to enlarge the classes of property exempt from prescription by *any* party rather than to immunize such enlarged classes of property from prescription by private parties only. * * *

We construe the word "person," in the 1935 amendment's provision that "no possession by any person, firm or corporation" shall ripen into prescriptive title against certain public entities, to include governmental agencies. This construction does not infringe on their sovereign powers. Such agencies are thereby deprived of nothing except the power to take away the property rights of their fellow public entities through adverse possession. Those other entities are thus protected against prescriptive invasion of their property rights from public as well as private sources. The result is not a diminution of sovereign powers but only the elimination of prescription as a means of transferring property from one arm of the government to another.

Commencement of Overdraft

A ground basin is in a state of surplus when the amount of water being extracted from it is less than the maximum that could be withdrawn without adverse effects on the basin's long term supply. While this state of surplus exists, none of the extractions from the basin for beneficial use constitutes such an invasion of any water right as will entitle the owner of the right to injunctive, as distinct from declaratory, relief. Overdraft commences whenever extractions increase, or the withdrawable maximum decreases, or both, to the point where the surplus ends. Thus on the commencement of overdraft there is no surplus available for the acquisition or enlargement of appropriative rights. Instead, appropriations of water in excess of surplus then invade senior basin rights, creating the element of adversity against those rights prerequisite to their owners' becoming entitled to an injunction and thus to the running of any prescriptive period against them.

* * *

* * * According to plaintiff, overdraft commenced in the ULARA only when (1) total extractions exceeded safe yield and (2) the available water storage capacity of the basin was sufficient to permit cycling of the safe yield throughout the 29–year base period of wet and dry years without causing a waste of water in the wet years. The referee's report as well as other evidence showed that when ground basin levels were relatively high, and storage space correspondingly diminished, waste occurred. Ground basin levels tended to vary in accordance with wide fluctuations in precipitation. Thus if a rising level of extractions were halted at the point of the safe yield based on the 29–year average, ensuing heightening of ground water levels during years of higher-than-average precipitation would cause waste. Since this waste would constitute a loss of basin water in addition to the safe yield extractions, it would eventually create enough additional storage space to stop further similar waste, but the wasted water itself would be lost to any beneficial use. On the other hand, a withdrawal of water from the basin over and above its safe yield in the amount necessary to create the storage space sufficient to prevent the waste would result in a net addition to the beneficially used supply.

We agree with plaintiff that if a ground basin's lack of storage space will cause a limitation of extractions to safe yield to result in a probable waste of water, the amount of water which if withdrawn would create the storage space necessary to avoid the waste and not adversely affect the basin's safe yield is a temporary surplus available for appropriation to beneficial use. Accordingly, overdraft occurs only if extractions from the basin exceed its safe yield plus any such temporary surplus.

* * *

Notice of Adversity as Prerequisite to Commencement of Prescriptive Period

* * *

The fact that one party's taking of water from a basin is open, notorious, and under claim of right does not invade any other party's water rights in the basin so as to entitle the other party to injunctive relief or start the running of any prescriptive period against the other party's rights so long as the taking is only from a surplus of basin water, that is, so long as there is not an overdraft on the basin supply. The commencement of overdraft provides the element of adversity which makes the first party's taking an invasion constituting a basis for injunctive relief to the other party. But if the other party is not on *notice* that the overdraft exists, such adverse taking does not cause the commencement of the prescriptive period.

* * *

Effect of Surplus on Running of Prescriptive Period

* * * Prescriptive rights in the basin were awarded to plaintiff, defendant City of San Fernando and two private defendants based on the "highest continuous annual production of water for beneficial use in any

five (5) year period *subsequent to the commencement of overdraft and prior to the filing of the complaint* by each of the parties from the Sylmar basin as to which there has been no cessation of use by it during any subsequent continuous five (5) year period." (Italics added.) From this formula it appears that the award of prescriptive rights may have been based on extractions of water during a continuous five-year period which included years of surplus.

Years of surplus should not be included in the prescriptive period because the taking of surplus water cannot invade the basin water rights of others. * * *

Appropriate Relief in San Fernando Basin

* * *

The trial court limited the parties' total extractions from the San Fernando basin to an annual 90,680 acre feet, which it found to be the 1964–1965 safe yield, reserving jurisdiction to redetermine the safe yield from time to time in accordance with changed hydrologic conditions. This finding established the basin's available supply for purposes of injunctive relief, the finding being supported by substantial evidence and there being no claim of any temporary surplus over and above the safe yield in 1964–1965.

Undoubtedly injunctive relief is called for in view of the undisputed overdraft prior to rendition of the present judgment. Although by far the largest share of the basin's supply must be allocated to plaintiff, the injunction should restrict plaintiff's as well as defendants' extractions. Plaintiff asserts a need for the entire safe yield of the basin and has demonstrated such need by appropriating substantially more than that amount in 1964–1965. Notwithstanding plaintiff's larger interest the defendant cities have a sufficient interest in maintaining the basin supply to warrant the restriction on plaintiff, stemming from their right to recapture the return flow attributable to their imports, which will probably increase as a result of (1) the defendants' substitution of imported water for the ground supply relinquished in deference to plaintiff's prior rights and (2) the overall expansion of their total water needs. The exercise of the return flow right would become more difficult and eventually impossible if the basin levels were continually lowered by an excess of extractions over safe yield.

On remand, the basin's safe yield should be apportioned between amounts attributable to (1) native waters produced by precipitation within the ULARA and (2) water imported from outside the ULARA. The latter amount should in turn be apportioned among the respective quantities derived from imports by plaintiff, defendant Glendale and defendant Burbank. Plaintiff should be awarded an unadjusted pumping right to the portion of the safe yield derived from native waters and from its own imports, and defendants Glendale and Burbank should each be awarded an unadjusted pumping right to the portion of the safe yield attributable to its own imports.

The new judgment should provide for adjustments in each party's pumping right to be administered by the watermaster under supervision of the court. Plaintiff's pumping right should be adjusted to take into account (1) the separate judgments entered under stipulation between plaintiff and defendants who are not parties to this appeal and (2) the imported water spread by plaintiff. The defendants' pumping rights should be adjusted to reflect return flow from their imports in excess of those for the safe yield year. * * *

Plaintiff seeks injunctive relief against extractions by the private defendants from the San Fernando basin. As already stated, these defendants' rights to the basin ground water are all subordinate to plaintiff's pueblo right and plaintiff's right to the return flow derived from its delivered imported water as well as to such return flow rights of defendants Glendale and Burbank. Accordingly, plaintiff is entitled to have the private defendants' extractions enjoined insofar as they would constitute an overdraft on the basin supply.

Some of the private defendants asserted at the trial, however, that a part or all of their respective uses of the basin water did not diminish the supply available to plaintiff. Certain defendants declared, for example, that their uses were nonconsumptive in that substantially all the extracted water was returned underground after use. Other defendants claimed that geological factors such as underground faults would prevent the water they extracted from ever reaching plaintiff's wells even if it were left in the ground. The trial court did not rule on these contentions in view of its award of prescriptive rights to these defendants based on the historic gross amounts of their extractions. On remand these contentions should be considered in the formulation of any injunctive relief. Plaintiff is not entitled to such relief against extractions which have no immediate or long-range effects on its available supply. If extractions which affect plaintiff's rights nevertheless preserve water for beneficial use that would otherwise go to waste, the trial court should endeavor to arrive at a physical solution which would avoid such waste.

William Blomquist, Dividing the Waters

146–50 (1992).

[The Central and West Basin Water Replenishment District provided a vehicle for pursuing the adjudication of groundwater rights in the Central Basin.]

A settlement committee was appointed by the CBWA to draft an interim agreement for the reduction of pumping. The settlement committee worked with the replenishment district's attorney and engineers to develop a formula for calculating the prescriptive rights acquired in the basin. The committee met every month, and presented a draft of an interim agreement to the Central Basin Water Association on May 3, 1962, just four months after the filing of the complaint. Included as Exhibit A were the engineer's verifications of pumping records to date, which already had accounted for 93 percent of the production from the basin. Meetings with water producers began immediately thereafter to explain the interim agreement and encourage them to sign.

Those who signed the interim agreement would be required after October 31, 1962, to reduce their groundwater production to an "agreed pumping allocation" that was 80 percent of their "assumed relative right." The agreement listed the parties' assumed relative rights, based on their groundwater production and imports of water (which under the Water Code were preserved as rights for producers who had substituted imported water for groundwater). The interim agreement would be presented to the court when parties representing 75 percent of the assumed relative rights had signed.

* * *

Like the West Basin judgment, the Central Basin judgment avoided a statement of the basin's safe yield. A Department of Water Resources estimate of the 1957 safe yield was 137,300 acre-feet. Reducing pumping to that amount would have required a 50 percent cut, rather than the 20 percent decrease the parties negotiated. Central Basin water users chose instead to attempt to restore a balance to the basin by relying on a combination of a 20 percent reduction in groundwater extractions, a guaranteed minimum inflow from the Upper Area, and the artificial replenishment program.

The Central Basin negotiators placed some provisions in their stipulation that differed from those in West Basin. Exchange pool water prices were calculated by a different formula, which made prices significantly higher in Central Basin. As a result, an active market in water right leases emerged in Central Basin, since lease prices negotiated between lessor and lessee were usually lower than exchange pool prices. Watermaster service costs, too, were allocated differently in Central Basin. In the Raymond and West basins, watermaster service costs are apportioned among the parties according to their groundwater rights, which means, for some parties, issuing invoices and collecting payments that are so small the cost of billing them exceeds the amount collected. In Central Basin, a minimum charge of $5.00 is assessed every party; any remaining watermaster service costs are apportioned among parties according to their agreed pumping allocation. If the total cost of watermaster service works out to less than $5.00 per party, each party is assessed that lesser amount equally.

NOTE

Conjunctive use stimulated by basinwide adjudications has not occurred in California's other major area of overdraft, the southern San Joaquin Valley. Large pumpers have resisted direct limitations on groundwater use. However, a study of water use in the area concluded that significant conjunctive use, if not management, has occurred in the area. Surface supplies from federal reservoirs and the state water project have been allocated to influence indirectly, and at a very uneven rate of success, the rate of groundwater use. Andrews and Fairfax's major conclusion was that:

> private and local district groundwater decisionmaking are closely linked with surface water availability and allocation. Surface water quantity, quality, availability, and price are the most important variables in the local groundwater equation. They determine pumping rates and provide the major impetus for undertaking management programs. Groundwater management, therefore, is not direct control over pumping control; rather, it involves the conjunctive use, both planned and unplanned, of surface water and groundwater supplies.

Barbara T. Andrews & Sally K. Fairfax, *Groundwater and Intergovernmental Relations in the Southern San Joaquin Valley of California: What Are All These Cooks Doing To The Broth?*, 55 U. Colo. L. Rev. 145, 200–01 (1984).

California law was complicated by the adoption of Section 1200 of the Water Code in 1914. Section 1200 limits the state's regulatory jurisdiction to streams including "subterranean streams flowing through known and definite channels." Section 1200 was widely read to incorporate an absolute distinction between subterranean streams and percolating groundwater. This interpretation was challenged in Joseph Sax, We Don't Do Groundwater in California: A Morsel of California Legal History, 6 Denver Water L. Rev. 269, 286–306 (2003). To overcome this arbitrary distinction, the State Water Resources Control Board adopted a four-part test to determine whether it has regulatory authority over groundwater. First, a subsurface channel must be present. Second, the channel must have relatively impermeable bed and banks. Third, the course of the channel must be known or be capable of determination by reasonable geologic inference, and fourth, groundwater must be flowing in the channel. The flow need not be parallel to the stream, so long as water is flowing within the channel. In re Garrarapata Water Co., State Water Resources Control Decision No. 1639 (June 17, 1999). This definition was upheld by an intermediate appellate court over alternative constructions of Section 1200 that would limit the Board's jurisdiction to water flowing in narrow bedrock channels bounded by a "significant boundary" to groundwater flow. North Gualala Water Co. v. State Water Resources Control Board, 139 Cal.App.4th 1577, 43 Cal. Rptr.3d 821 (1 Dist. 2006). The decision is a major step toward the integration of ground and surface water rights in California, but nevertheless stops well short of full integration. The court expressly rejected Professor Sax's argument that Section 1200 was intended to eliminate the artificial distinction between ground and surface water. 43 Cal.Rptr.3d at 831, fn. 8.

Deborah A. de Lambert, Comment, District Management for California Groundwater

11 Ecology L.Q. 373, 391–93 (1984).

Orange County Water District—A Case Study

The Orange County Water District (OCWD) is often cited as a model for effective groundwater management in California. Created by a special district act, the OCWD has not needed to resort to adjudication to determine each pumper's rights in the basin. As a result, it has been able to take a more flexible and comprehensive approach to groundwater management.

The OCWD possesses the broad powers necessary for effective groundwater management. The district's express purposes are the protection, conservation, and management of the groundwater supply. Since all pumpers must register with the OCWD, the district is able to monitor the amount of groundwater pumped each year. Further, it is specifically authorized to levy four different types of assessments: *ad valorem* taxes on all property owners, replenishment assessments (pump taxes) on all water pumped when the basin is overdrafted, supplemental replenishment assessments on production of groundwater for all but irrigation purposes, and basin equity assessments. Because of its broad powers, the OCWD is able to carry out all programs and operations it deems necessary to protect the quality and supply of groundwater. Moreover, the OCWD's jurisdiction corresponds roughly to the Orange County groundwater basin.

One of OCWD's most effective management tools has been its extensive replenishment program. Supplemental water supplies are purchased for basin recharge operations and for direct use by consumers. During the 1980–81 water year, over one-half of the total water consumed in the OCWD was imported; most was used directly rather than for replenishment. The efficacy of this program is illustrated by the fact that the accumulated overdraft in the Orange County basin has declined from 700,000 acre-feet in 1956 to 120,634 acre-feet in 1980–81.

The OCWD's replenishment program depends in large part on the district's basin equity assessments and pump taxes, which serve to equalize water costs among users. In 1980–81 the district spent $1,994,445, raised by pump taxes, to purchase supplemental water. Because imported water is more expensive than groundwater for non-irrigation users, incentives are necessary to encourage pumpers to use supplemental water in lieu of pumping. The basin equity assessments provide this incentive by taxing the consumers of groundwater in order to subsidize the users of imported water.

Other factors besides the OCWD's activities have reduced the rate of overdraft in the Orange County basin. Changing trends in land use have allowed population growth without increasing the demand for water because urban uses require much less water than agricultural uses. Changes in agricultural practices may also have contributed to the declining overdraft. Drip and low-flow irrigation, currently used in Orange County, are more efficient than flood irrigation. Additionally, farmers have shifted from irrigated crops, such as deciduous fruits and nuts, to non-irrigated crops, such as pasture. Nonetheless, total groundwater extractions in Orange County actually increased by fifty percent between 1956 and 1981.

Thus, the OCWD's management of Orange County's groundwater has produced significant results. The groundwater level rose from 12 feet below sea level in the 1950's to 17 feet above sea level in 1971. The question remains whether this type of management would work on a statewide basis.

NOTE

There is increasing acceptance of the use of pumping charges to induce conservation. The federal government has the authority under the Reclamation Act of 1902 to impose charges for the use of groundwater which results from spreading surface water distributed to the project. 43 U.S.C.A. § 485(h) (West 1986). Cf. Flint v. United States, 906 F.2d 471 (9th Cir.1990) (maximum charges for operation and maintenance costs are committed to agency discretion by law). In 1987, the Texas legislature authorized the creation of a special district to conserve the Edwards Aquifer, which is the sole source of supply for San Antonio. Act of May 30, 1993 ch. 626, 1993 Tex. Gen. Laws 2350 (amended by Act of May 29, 1995 ch. 261, 1995 Tex. Gen. Laws 2505). The Act allows the imposition of user charges but not taxes. A group of large pumpers challenged the imposition of fees arguing that they were in fact taxes and alleging that they were primarily designed to raise revenue as opposed to regulating the use of water. They contended that the fees would not discourage use as the additional cost would be passed on to the utility's customers. The court of appeals upheld the fee. Creedmoor Maha Water Supply Corp. v. Barton Springs–Edwards Aquifer Conservation Dist., 784 S.W.2d 79 (Tex.App. 1989).

6.   PREVENTION AND CLEAN-UP OF CONTAMINATION

Protection of the public's interest in groundwater is nowhere greater than it is with preserving the quality of underground waters for present and future uses. Yet protecting groundwater from contamination is generally approached as a separate issue. Controlling groundwater quality entirely separately from regulation and allocation of rights to use groundwater seems curious in light of the substantial connection between the two subjects. Although the use of a polluted supply can endanger public health, authorities deciding whether to allow pumping often look only to the quantity of water available, not the quality. The need for integrated management of quality and quantity seems obvious because excessive groundwater pumping may lead to salt water intrusion and contamination of an aquifer. An improperly drilled well can allow a good, clean aquifer to be contaminated by polluted waters migrating from a second aquifer.

Ground water contamination can occur as relatively well defined plumes emanating from specific sources such as spills, landfills, waste lagoons, and/or industrial facilities. Contamination can also occur as a general deterioration of ground water quality over a wide area due to diffuse nonpoint sources such as agricultural fertilizer and pesticide applications, septic systems, urban runoff, leaking sewer networks, application of chemicals, highway deicing materials, animal feedlots, salvage yards, and mining activities. Ground water quality degradation from diffuse nonpoint sources affects large areas, making it difficult to specify the exact source of the contamination.

Ground water contamination is most common in highly developed areas, agricultural areas, and industrial complexes. Frequently ground water contamination is discovered long after it has occurred. One reason for this is the slow movement of ground water through aquifers, sometimes on the order of less than an inch per day. Contaminants in the ground water do not mix or spread quickly, but remain concentrated in slow-moving plumes that may persist for many years.

United States Environmental Protection Agency, National Water Quality Inventory, 1996 Report to Congress ES–31 (1998).

In recent years there have been a number of common law actions to recover damages for groundwater contamination, but there are substantial barriers to recovery. Most of the recovery problems center on the need to prove that the discharged contaminants in fact reached the plaintiff's property and caused injury or property damage. These proof problems have plagued attempts to find tort remedies. Major federal enactments dealing with liability for clean-up eliminate some, but not all of the proof problems by imposing retroactive, strict liability. *E.g.*, Adkins v. Thomas Solvent Co., 440 Mich. 293, 487 N.W.2d 715 (1992) (plaintiffs who had brought suit to recover for the depreciation in value of their properties did not have a cause of action because the polluted groundwater did not, and would not, reach their properties; see Attorney General v. Thomas Solvent Co., *infra* p. 692, for background and outcome of CERCLA suit based on same facts). See also Miller v. Cudahy Co., 567 F.Supp. 892 (D.Kan.1983); Barrett v. Atlantic Richfield Co., 95 F.3d 375 (5th Cir.1996) (landowners living adjacent to superfund site did not prove property for public health damages).

Remedies for groundwater contamination are treated in more detail *infra* pp. 687–701.

CHAPTER SEVEN

ENVIRONMENTAL PROTECTION AND WATER LAW

Historically, rivers, lakes, and aquifers served as sinks for waste disposal and commodities to serve human demands. Waterways were developed—dammed, diverted, and depleted—to serve the needs of the time. Although there is continuing demand for the agricultural, municipal, industrial, and power services produced by water, water resources are also valued for new utilitarian and non-utilitarian reasons. They are now seen, in a larger context, also as part of a natural heritage to be enjoyed for benefits that extend to recreation, aesthetics, and the ecosystem services that they provide. See A. Dan Tarlock, The Great Lakes as an Environmental Heritage of Humankind: An International Law Perspective, 40 Mich. J. L. Reform 995 (2007) and Five Views of the Great Lakes and Why They Might Matter, 15 Minn. J. Int. L. 21 (2006). Others go further, and argue that regardless of the monetary benefits that one can attach to ecosystem services, we should seek to conserve or restore the natural hydrologic functions of rivers. In short, modern water policy seeks to ensure that water resources are used more sustainably, so as not to deprive future generations of the full range of their benefits. As the Western Water Policy Review Advisory Commission concluded, "there is an increasing appreciation of the need to maintain more natural river and aquifer flow patterns to support wildlife and maintain such landscape functions as upstream flood water retention and natural filtration." Water in the West: Challenge for the Next Century 3–6 (1998).

Traditionally, water law's primary function was to allocate water among competing users and to enforce the resulting rights, but these changed attitudes push for a water policy that does more. Water laws across the nation have begun to address environmental issues as evidenced in provisions of permitting statutes that require agencies to consider water quality and other public interest factors that typically implicate environmental issues. The growing concern of state water law with environmental impacts of water use is also illustrated by the enactment of instream flow protection laws by many states.

Environmental protection of aquatic environments goes beyond state water law. Today, no one can develop new sources of water or use existing dams and other facilities as they were used in the past without considering a body of federal and state laws, largely put in place in the environmental decade (1969–1980), designed to advance a variety of public goals that require regulating, limiting, and changing the nature and the extent of water use. These laws pertain primarily to water quality control, wetlands conservation, endangered species protection, and regulation of hydropower development. They are at least as significant as traditional water law for lawyers dealing with water issues. Although they may be administered by states, they are largely federal laws.

The fact that a separate body of largely federal laws may curtail or otherwise clash with the exercise of state-granted water rights creates a special challenge for public policy. Federal environmental laws were enacted with little thought about how they might impact traditional state water allocation. Thus, they remain largely unintegrated with state law as well as with the earlier federal laws enacted to promote and authorize water project development. Like a geological process, they were justed overlain over existing legal regimes. States have found that the principle of federal supremacy over state law that developed during the Reclamation Era, see pages 818–828, has not impeded federal policy as it did in the past; courts have held that much state law is preempted by federal environmental regulation. Students must also be aware of background irony that permeates this area: federal preemption of state water law was first extended to enable massive water development but today is blamed for much of the degradation of the environment.

In the following sections we deal first with the incomplete linkage of water quality control to water allocation law and the possibility of tort remedies. The federal Clean Water Act is considered the primary law in the nation for protecting surface waters. Programs for controlling and cleaning up groundwater contamination are then discussed. Next, we look at several statutory programs that demand environmental protection and that, in the process, often impinge on state water laws. They include the Federal Power Act that licenses private hydroelectric facilities, section 404 of the Clean Water Act that prevents putting "fill" material (including dams) in waters of the United States without a permit, and the Endangered Species Act that targets certain species that are in danger of extinction for special protection.

Case-by-case negotiated problem solving has been advanced as a way to harmonize the values advanced by federal environmental laws with state water law. Given the dearth of laws requiring or even facilitating restoration of aquatic ecosystems collaborative solutions may be the most viable approach presently available. The ultimate solution of restoration of the nation's degraded waters may depend on changing the way water facilities are operated and even removing some dams, an issue raised at the end of the chapter.

A. The Water Quality—Water Law Interface

1. Traditional State Approaches

David H. Getches, Lawrence J. MacDonnell & Teresa A. Rice, Controlling Water Use: The Unfinished Business of Water Quality Protection
89–120 (1991).

States generally do not limit water appropriations or uses to carry out their water quality protection policies

* * *

The need to regulate uses or new appropriations for legitimate water quality purposes becomes more apparent as other means of curbing the production or discharge of pollutants approach the limits of their economic feasibility. Restricting water uses is generally seen as a last resort, however, and the public's interest in water quality is often subordinated to maintaining the integrity of the appropriation system itself. The result has been a categorical resistance to regulating diversions, impoundments, and uses of water to protect water quality; at its extreme, it is manifested in explicit statutory prohibitions against water quality laws being applied in any way that impairs or inhibits the exercise of water rights.

Several states have proclaimed that water quality regulation will not affect water uses or water rights. The New Mexico Water Quality Act specifically denies the Water Quality Control Commission or any other entity power to take away or modify property rights in water.

Similarly, the Arizona Water Quality Control Act declares that the law shall not be interpreted to prevent the exercise of groundwater or surface water rights. Nevada law says that "Nothing in [the Water Pollution Control Law] shall be construed to amend, modify or supersede the [water allocation law] or any rule, regulation or order promulgated or issued thereunder by the state engineer." And Colorado's Water Quality Act states that it "shall not be construed, enforced, or applied so as to cause or result in material injury to water rights." Several other sections of the Colorado Act also limit regulatory authority if it conflicts with the exercise or establishment of water rights.

* * *

A reluctance to administer and enforce water quality laws alongside allocation laws can be explained partly by the usual division of authority between state agencies. Most western states assign responsibilities for water allocation and water quality to separate agencies. These separate agencies usually have different statutory missions and do not coordinate their decisions on specific issues, let alone their policies, with one another. Thus, water rights permits may be granted without regard to the effect of the depletion or manner of use on water quality. On the other hand, the pollution control agency may impose conditions on a pollutant discharge permit that are insensitive to water users' rights.

Nearly every western state has some form of water planning, and water quality concerns are expressed in several state water plans. The plans take many forms: some are processes for ongoing articulation of goals and policies; others primarily address water project development. Many plans contain simply a mention or cursory discussion of water quality issues. Only a few states, such as California and Kansas, actually implement water quality planning goals in the permitting process; permits must be consistent with the plan. Some states are beginning to adopt "planning" processes that are actually dynamic forums for articulating public policies related to all aspects of water use, including quality.

* * *

State efforts to integrate control of water use with water quality protection are in their infancy. * * *

* * * A review of western state water allocation and water quality laws and programs indicates four general ways in which states are seeking to address the relationship between water quality and water quantity:

* * *

> 1. *States have several ways to integrate and coordinate water quality and water allocation responsibilities*

* * *

Cooperative Mechanisms

* * *

The New Mexico State Engineer serves on the Water Quality Control Commission. Similarly, in North Dakota the head of the Water Commission sits on the State Water Pollution Control Board. This approach at least connects the individual with responsibility for water allocation decisions with the entity establishing water quality policy.

Oklahoma has established a Pollution Control Coordinating Board with the heads of a number of state agencies as members, including the Water Resources Board. Oregon has a State Water Management Group and a Governor's Watershed Enhancement Board in which the several water-related agency and commission heads participate. In Utah, the governor established a Water Development Coordinating Committee that includes the directors of the Division of Water Resources, Bureau of Water Pollution Control, Bureau of Public Water Supply, Division of Community Development, and the State Treasurer. The committee coordinates funding requests and actions on water resources, water pollution control, and drinking water projects, and makes recommendations to the legislature when the existing funding is inadequate for needed projects. * * *

Single Agency Coordination

In Washington, the water allocation program and the water quality control program are in a single executive department under the same director. * * * When the water allocation section receives applications for water use permits that appear to have any potential impact on water quality, the water quality section is notified. * * * Fisheries and wildlife officials are notified if an application has a potential impact on these resources.

The Texas Water Commission reviews functions and policies for both water administration and water quality regulation. * * *

Formal Coordination and Planning

Kansas formally coordinates quality and allocation issues in the water planning process but relies on administrative methods to implement policy. The planning process is a dynamic system for exploring policy alternatives and selecting from among options one that becomes a mandate of every agency. The subject matter is wide-ranging to include all aspects of water quality, such as nonpoint sources, wetlands, instream flows, and other issues. Once policy has been set, the agencies coordinate their activities through a number of informal procedures.

* * *

Integrated Responsibility for Allocation and Quality

California is the only state that has merged water resource allocation functions with water pollution and water quality control in a single body. The State Water Resources Control Board issues permits to persons who want to initiate a new water use. * * *

One of the board's mandates in authorizing an appropriation is to coordinate the permitted use with regional water quality control plans. All permits require that a water user adhere to water quality plans even if change becomes necessary after the permit is granted. Thus, the board may limit existing water uses as well as newly permitted uses in order to impose water quality standards when it deems them necessary to fulfill planning objectives and to carry out the public interest. * * *

On balance, it appears that the fullest integration of state water quality and water allocation functions is the most effective and desirable. There are arguments against separating water quality matters and expertise from another agency charged primarily with regulating all other types of pollution (e.g., air, hazardous wastes) and concentrating them in a water agency. Separation arguably will fragment overall, multi-media pollution control efforts. Still, the most integrated and coordinated systems appear to work the best and states should study ways to improve their institutions in ways that will improve water quality and comport with water allocation systems.

* * *

2. *The prior appropriation system offers many opportunities for protecting water quality*

The prior appropriation doctrine recognizes the right to water quality protection to a limited degree. * * *

Protection of Existing Water Rights

* * *

A person whose property rights—including water rights—are harmed by another's pollution may sue in tort for nuisance or trespass.[4] Many early cases involved complaints by one water user of another's pollution. The courts recognized that appropriators have a right to water quality good enough to carry out the uses for which they made their appropriation. Typical cases involved downstream appropriators, often farmers, who successfully pursued remedies against upstream appropriators, often miners.[5] The rule that allows a downstream appropriator to protect beneficial uses from impairment by upstream pollution generally is applied if the downstream plaintiff is a senior appropriator. But it has also been applied to prevent a senior's upstream pollution to the detriment of a downstream user if the senior can prevent the harm to water quality at minimal expense and inconvenience.[6] * * *

* * * Pollution is restricted only if it can be shown to injure the water uses of another appropriator. People who do not hold water rights might want to protect water quality, but only those with appropriative rights can sue.

Appropriators also have difficulties enforcing their private remedies. They must prove causation, deal with multiple parties, and pay the costs of litigation; cost alone may deter them from taking action. When they do assert their rights, they may be inclined to accept a favorable settlement,

4. *E.g.,* Springer v. Joseph Schlitz Brewing Co., 510 F.2d 468 (4th Cir.1975) (polluter liable to property owner for fish kills from pollutant discharges); Atlas Chemical Industries, Inc. v. Anderson, 514 S.W.2d 309 (Tex.Civ.App.1974) (liability to property owners for polluting creek running through property); Cities Service Oil Co. v. Merritt, 332 P.2d 677 (Okla.1958) (nuisance liability for polluting well); Burr v. Adam Eidemiller, Inc., 386 Pa. 416, 126 A.2d 403 (1956) (liability for contaminating water supply with releases of construction debris). These cases involve riparian water rights as well as appropriation rights.

5. *E.g.,* Ravndal v. Northfork Placers, 60 Idaho 305, 91 P.2d 368 (1939); Cushman v. Highland Ditch Co., 33 P. 344 (Colo.App. 1893); Larimer County Reservoir Co. v. People ex rel. Luthe, 8 Colo. 614, 9 P. 794 (1886); State v. California Packing Corp., 105 Utah 182, 141 P.2d 386 (1943); Humphry Tunnel and Mining Co. v. Frank, 105 P. 1093 (Colo. 1909); Helena v. Rogan, 26 Mont. 452, 68 P. 798 (1902).

6. Suffolk Gold Mining & Milling Co. v. San Miguel Consol. Mining & Milling Co., 9 Colo.App. 407, 48 P. 828 (1897); *appeal dismissed,* 24 Colo. 468, 52 P. 1027 (1898). *See also* Wilmore v. Chain O'Mines, 44 P.2d 1024 (Colo.1934).

and that will end the matter although the rights of other water rights holders continue to be affected.

The protection of water quality sufficient to meet the needs of future water appropriators or of recreational or other uses thus should not be left to the private remedies of individual appropriators. The inadequacies of traditional tort litigation to control pollution was one of the factors that led the federal government and the states to enact water pollution control legislation.

Considering Water Quality in the Allocation Process

* * *

In most states, water quality is included directly or indirectly in the considerations of state agencies that issue permits to appropriate water. Thus, state law may require agencies to consider water quality in finding that: the use will not impair existing rights; the use is beneficial; and the administrative decision is in the "public interest." In these cases, decisions to grant or deny a permit, or to impose conditions on uses, may be made on grounds of water quality.

Nonimpairment of existing rights

Existing water users do not have complete protection for their rights unless they are assured that new or changed uses will not interfere with their uses. Kansas law forbids the issuance of a surface or groundwater permit that will impair a use under an existing water right; impairment is defined to include the "unreasonable deterioration of the water quality at the water user's point of diversion beyond a reasonable economic limit." In Colorado, permits to appropriate groundwater within designated groundwater basins may not be issued if the proposed appropriation would "unreasonably impair existing water rights from the same source." Impairment of existing uses is defined to include "the unreasonable deterioration of water quality."

A change in a water right such as for a different purpose or place of use is always subject to a nonimpairment or "no injury" requirement. New Mexico decisions have dealt with water quality impairment to existing groundwater rights caused by a change in well location. These cases have established the authority of the state engineer to deny or condition proposed changes of rights if necessary to protect existing rights from water quality-related injury.

Colorado law promotes exchanges of water and the use of substitute supplies to maximize utilization of its water resources. It requires that exchanged or substituted water be of a quality (as well as quantity) that can "meet the requirements of use" to which the exchanged-for water has been put. * * *

Administrative examination of the water quality effects of new or changed uses can improve protection for existing rights * * *. States seem more inclined to condition or deny water permits or changes if existing water uses will be impaired than if there would be no immediate damage to water rights. Protection against impairment, however, does not fully carry out a policy of protecting water quality for future users or the public unless their interests coincide with those of existing users.

The beneficial use requirement

* * * Since the earliest western water rights decisions, the courts have recognized that there is no right to use water wastefully, *i.e.*, nonbeneficially. The antiwaste principle embodied in the beneficial use requirement has been applied in a limited way, particularly in groundwater allocation. For example, an Oklahoma statute requires the State Water Resources Board to find that waste will not occur before approving an application for a groundwater permit. * * * And, the Montana groundwater code prohibits the waste of groundwater and includes a requirement that all wells be constructed and maintained to prevent waste, contamination, or pollution of groundwater.

The beneficial use requirement is being applied more broadly to prohibit inefficient water use and could be expanded to prohibit undue water degradation. A policy of maximizing beneficial uses of water is inherent in the appropriation doctrine. Courts have interpreted that goal to require reasonably efficient means of diversion. The efficiency principle prevents appropriators from commanding more water than is reasonably necessary to satisfy their own appropriations * * *. Similarly, a polluter should not be able to use the stream to carry away so much waste that it limits other uses. The same principle would prevent depletions so great that pollutants become overly concentrated in the remaining water. Inefficient diversions and uses that result in a polluted stream should not be considered "beneficial uses," since both involve wasteful uses of the resource.

* * * For example, a water allocation agency could deny a right to irrigate a highly saline field, restrict the quantity of water applied to the field or require treatment of saline return flows. It also might deny the right to deplete or impound water that would degrade quality in the remaining stream to the extent of damaging other existing and future beneficial uses. Beneficial uses include recreation and fish and wildlife in most states. Adverse impacts on these uses thus can be considered in the determination that a proposed use will lead to maximum utilization.

The use of water law, specifically the doctrine of beneficial use, as a basis for enacting legislation, exercising police power regulation, and resolving cases in court to control pollution, has great untested potential. Efforts to maintain water quality can be based on the beneficial use doctrine in existing appropriation law, but stronger, more explicit statutes and regulations would bolster this approach.

Public interest review

Nearly all western states now consider the public interest in issuing a permit to use water. In a few states, statutes or case law expressly mention that water quality effects must be examined in determining the public interest. * * * Alaska law requires that "the effect on public health" be among the public interest considerations weighed in water decisions. A Montana statute requires a finding that the public interest, including water quality, be satisfied before a large appropriation is approved. Although some statutes fail to define the factors that are within the "public interest," water quality is probably the most logical and natural choice for inclusion. Accordingly, the Idaho Supreme Court has held that determinations under the Idaho public interest statute must include a consideration of water quality effects.

California water law requires that the State Water Resources Control Board reject an application for a permit to appropriate water found not to be in the public interest. A California Court of Appeal has said that this public interest provision extends to the consideration of water quality standards established under state and federal law.

* * *

Protecting Instream Flows to Safeguard Water Quality
* * *

If a certain quantity of water is required to remain in the stream, at some point existing appropriators may have to forego diverting water and new appropriators will be told that no water is available for appropriation. This may seem inconsistent with the prior appropriation doctrine, which allows diversions by anyone with a beneficial use. In fact, protection of a certain level of instream flows is essential to preserve the capacity of all appropriators to make beneficial uses of the water. If proper streamflows are maintained, appropriators can be assured that diversion and use of water by themselves and others will not adversely affect the quality of the water. * * *

Public Trust Considerations

Courts in a few western states have recognized that the state has a trust responsibility to all citizens in the allocation of state waters. Water is public property under several state constitutions, held and allocated by the state for the benefit of the people. Permits to use state waters must be consistent with the state's fiduciary responsibility for how water is used.

* * *

Professor Ralph Johnson has urged that the public trust doctrine be applied expansively to regulate water uses by prior appropriators in order to protect water quality. He argues that multiple dispersed sources of pollution individually are too insignificant to be controlled as nuisances or invasions of others' rights, although collectively they can profoundly degrade stream quality. Unless these sources are controlled, stream quality could become so degraded that the water would be useless for other appropriators and for the public.

3. Water management areas are sometimes used to protect water quality

Many western states have established special management areas to preserve and equitably allocate water supplies, usually groundwater. Typically, groundwater withdrawals exceed recharge in these areas. Management consists of limiting pumping to control depletions, although water quality protection may be an additional objective. Several states have authorized establishment of these areas specifically to respond to water quality problems.

NOTE

The continuing reluctance to use the law of prior appropriation to address water quality concerns is illustrated by City of Thornton v. Bijou Irrigation Co., 926 P.2d 1, 90–93 (Colo.1996). An appropriator objected to an exchange agreement because it reduced flows available to dilute its discharge to the levels allowed under the water quality statute, but the Colorado Supreme Court found no basis for objection. The state water quality act, C.R.S. Section 28–8–104(1), disclaimed any intent to abrogate water rights, and the court construed this as "a policy decision * * * to focus water quality regulation on uses culminating in unreasonable discharges, as such discharges are not part of any appropriative right under common law." Thornton fared better in In re Concerning Application for Plan for Augmentation of City and County of Denver ex rel. Bd. of Water Com'rs, 44 P.3d 1019 (Colo. 2002). Thornton initially agreed to accept treated sewage rather than Platte River water in a plan for augmentation which allowed Denver to make an out of priority diversion. Seven years after the water court approved the plan, Thornton argued that Denver's treatment plant was now discharging harmful levels of nitrates, phosphorous and other pollutants. It asked for a hearing and for an extension of the court's retained jurisdiction. In reversing the water court's denial of both, the Supreme Court reiterated that a senior appropriator had a right to be free from contamination that interferes with the normal use of water and read *Bijou Irrigation Co.* for the following proposition:

"Because the WQCA [Water Quality Control Act] explicitly provides that it is not to interfere with the water court's role in adjudicating water rights, we conclude that the general assembly did not intend the WQCA to interfere with the water court's ability to protect senior water appropriators [in augmentation plan proceedings].... The WRDAA [Water Right Determination and Administration Act] explicitly requires the water court to to consider water quality issues in the case of an augmentation plan in which water is being actively substituted into a stream for use of other appropriators." [44 P.3d at 1029–1030]

Can the discharge of fresh water ever be pollution? Lee County v. South Florida Water Management Dist., 805 So.2d 893, 897 (Fla.App. 2001), held that the discharge of fresh water from Lake Okeechobee, which was alleged to alter the salinity of an estuary, was not pollution: "nature itself (sic) is not constrained to maintain the optimum contended for by the county is this case." This issue frequently arises under the federal Clean Water Act with inter-watershed transfers. See pages 679–686, *infra*.

2. Tort Remedies

Property owners have used common law actions for trespass and nuisance to deal with discharges of wastes into waterways. Trespass actions are frequently used for ground rather surface water pollution. In riparian jurisdictions the relative rights and obligations of riparian property owners are based on a reasonable use standard. But even in a prior appropriation state, nuisance suits in which liability is based on the reasonableness of one's conduct can be brought against offending polluters.

A trespass is an interference with the *exclusive possession* of property while a nuisance is an interference with the *use and enjoyment* of land. A physical invasion of another's property, such as by causing a pollutant to enter the land, is a trespass. To prevail a plaintiff must show causation, tracing the pollutant to the defendant. Harm is not necessary to sustain a cause of action, but damages (beyond a nominal amount) will be awarded only to the extent they are proved. More recent pollution cases have collapsed the distinction between trespass and nuisance by holding that a trespass based on imperceptible particles or substances requires proof of actual damages. Smith v. Carbide and Chems. Corp., 298 F.Supp.2d 561 (W.D.Ky. 2004). To establish nuisance a plaintiff must prove that the defendant knew or should have known that plaintiff's interests would be injured, that the defendant's conduct was "unreasonable," and that the harm to plaintiff is substantial. The Restatement (Second) of Torts § 826 (1979) calls for a balancing test. The "intentional invasion of another's interest in the use and enjoyment of land is unreasonable if (a) the gravity of the harm outweighs the utility of the actor's conduct, or (b) the harm caused by the conduct is serious and the financial burden of compensating * * * would not make continuation of the conduct not feasible."

Another possible cause of action is for public nuisance. Under Restatement (Second) of Torts § 821B (1979) the court must find the defendant's conduct is unreasonable considering:

(a) Whether the conduct involves a significant interference with the public health, the public safety, the public peace, the public comfort or the public convenience, or

(b) Whether the conduct is proscribed by a statute, ordinance, or administrative regulation, or

(c) Whether the conduct is of a continuing nature or has produced a permanent or long-lasting effect, and, as the actor knows or has reason to know, has a significant effect upon the public right.

Machipongo Land & Coal Co. v. Commonwealth, 569 Pa. 3, 799 A.2d 751 (2002), *cert. denied*, 537 U.S. 1002, 123 S.Ct. 486, 154 L.Ed.2d 397 (2002), held that the public's right, Pa. Const. Art. 1, § 10, to unpolluted water would be a defense to a takings claim by a coal company if the mining would be a public nuisance. The company challenged the designation of a watershed as unsuitable for coal mining under Pennsylvania's Strip Mining Control Act. The trial court refused to allow the Commonwealth to introduce evidence that mining would constitute a public nuisance and thus was a *Lucas* background limitation on the company's claimed common law mining rights.

Typically public nuisance actions must be brought by a public entity; however, a private citizen may bring a public nuisance action if the citizen has suffered injury different in kind, rather than degree. Some state statutes specifically allow private individuals or entities to sue to abate a public nuisance. *E.g.,* Florida Wildlife Fed'n v. State Dep't of Envtl. Regulation, 390 So.2d 64 (Fla.1980). The Restatement (Second) of Torts § 821C (1979) adopts the "harm of a kind different from that suffered by other members of the public exercising the right common to the general public" standard for the recovery damages, but the standard for injunctive relief is more liberal. See Denise E. Antolini, Modernizing Public Nuisance: Solving the Paradox of the Special Injury Rule, 28 Ecology L. Q. 755 (2001).

The distinction between discrete and generalized harm remains a barrier to the use of public nuisance actions to address contaminated waters. New Mexico v. General Electric Company, 335 F.Supp.2d 1185, 1240 (D.N.M. 2004), applied 821C to hold that New Mexico could not recover damages against a factory alleged to contaminate an aquifer south of Albuquerque without a showing "that the State has suffered some discrete physical harm or pecuniary loss apart from the more generalized injury to the public's interest that results from the public nuisance. . . ." New Mexico argued that the state's ownership of the unappropriated groundwater in trust for the public gave them the necessary proprietary interest to recover damages. After a through discussion of the nature of water rights, the court concluded that the state's "proprietary interest" in unappropriated water only becomes a property right when it or a private entity perfects an appropriative rights, and thus "[t]he State's interest. . . . is not 'usufructory' in and of itself, and remains indistinguishable from the public's interest in those waters." 335 F.Supp.2d at 1238. See also Freeman v. Blue Ridge Paper Products, Inc., 229 S.W.3d 694, 706 (Tenn.Ct.App. 2007), which holds that a class action is an appropriate way to adjudicative riparian pollution cases because all riparians suffer common impaired of use of the stream. In what circumstances could the state recover damages for contamination of unappropriated water?

Borough of Westville v. Whitney Home Builders

Superior Court of New Jersey, 1956.
40 N.J.Super. 62, 122 A.2d 233.

[In connection with the development of a residential subdivision, defendant Whitney organized a sewerage company. The plans were approved by the State Board of Health. The treated sewage was discharged into a small natural stream which flowed for a mile into a pond in Westville's principal park. In time of drought, the flow was reduced to a trickle. Two plaintiffs brought suit, the local board of health and the borough as proprietor of the park. The evidence established that it was "highly improbable" that harmful bacteria would survive, and that the principal problem with the discharge was stench. The local health board's suit was dismissed on the ground that exclusive jurisdiction over public nuisance actions for discharge of sewage was in the state board, and no appeal was taken from that ruling. The trial court also dismissed the borough's private nuisance action based on its riparian rights, and the borough has appealed.]

■ CONFORD, J. A. D. * * *

IV.

We thus come to a consideration of the law governing the mutual rights and obligations of riparian owners, *inter sese,* in respect to the use of the water flow. It will be seen that this subject, in New Jersey as elsewhere in this country, is in a state of some doctrinal confusion. * * *

The natural flow theory, long held in England, contemplates that it is the right of every riparian proprietor to have the flow of water across his land maintained in its natural state, not sensibly diminished in quantity or impaired in quality. * * * Maloney, The Balance of Convenience Doctrine, 5 So.Car.L.Q. 159, 169 (1952).

The reasonable use doctrine does not concern itself with the impairment of the natural flow or quality of the water but allows full use of the watercourse in any way that is beneficial to the riparian owner provided only it does not unreasonably interfere with the beneficial uses of others, the court or jury being the arbiter as to what is unreasonable. * * *

An examination of the cases shows that while they sometimes repeat the rule in terms of natural flow and quality, expressions of criteria sounding in reasonable use are also to be found, sometimes in the same case, and that none of the decisions is inconsistent on its facts with the rationale of reasonable use.

* * *

An illuminating variant of the reasonable use doctrine is its expression in terms of "fair participation" between riparian owners. In Sandusky Portland Cement Co. v. Dixon Pure Ice Co., 221 F. 200, L.R.A. 1915E, 1210 (7th Cir.1915), certiorari denied 238 U.S. 630 (1915), a lower owner who manufactured ice from river water was held entitled to an injunction against the heating of the water by an upper proprietor to an extent which materially retarded the formation of ice. The court said (221 F., at page 204):

> "Complainant may not insist on such a use of the water by the defendant as will deprive the latter of any use thereof which may be necessary for its business purposes, provided complainant can by reasonable diligence and effort make the flowing water reasonably answer its own purposes. There must be a fair participation between them. * * * But where, as in the present case, it is shown by the evidence that defendant's use of the river water, while essential for its

own purposes, entirely destroys the right of complainant thereto, there can be no claim by defendant that its use thereof is reasonable. In other words, the emergency of defendant's needs is not the measure of its rights in the water."

On principle, we conclude that the interests of a changing, complex and technologically mushrooming society call for the application of the "reasonable use" doctrine in this field; a rule which enables judicial arbitration, in the absence of controlling legislation, of the fair participation in common waters of those who have a right of property therein on the basis of what all of the attendant circumstances shows to be reasonable. On analysis of the case authorities, we think the courts have actually moved along that course, whatever the occasional ideological conflict in expression. This, moreover, is the approach recently taken by our Supreme Court in the closely cognate area of diversion of surface waters. Armstrong v. Francis Corp., 20 N.J. 320 (1956). The court there alluded to the consideration as to "whether the utility of the possessor's use of his land outweighs the gravity of the harm which results from his alteration of the flow of surface waters" (20 N.J., at page 330). It further said (20 N.J., at page 330):

> "Social progress and the common wellbeing are in actuality better served by a just and right balancing of the competing interests according to the general principles of fairness and common sense which attend the application of the rule of reason."

V.

It remains to apply the foregoing principles to the special problem presented here. We have already taken notice of the plea of plaintiff that the effluent flowing into the ditch and pond is "noisome" and necessarily a pollutant because its origin in association with human *excreta* and *secreta* engenders such revulsion in the average person as assertedly must substantially impair the use of the pond as an important part of the public recreational and park area. The synthesis of the evidence set out in II, *supra*, cannot help but lead to the fair conclusion that the effluent is not reasonably to be regarded as a threat to health, nor offensive, now or in fair prospect, to the senses of sight or smell. No user of the park not knowing of the discharge of the effluent is ever apt to suffer lessened enjoyment ascribable to its flow. Indeed the contrary may be true in times of drought. As recognized by trial court and counsel the question is substantially one of psychological impairment of the recreational function of the park.

We by no means make light of plaintiff's grievance. The problem presented has impressed us as of considerable import. As conceded by the trial court the people of Westville cannot be expected to be happy over the continuous presence of sewage effluent in their park pond, no matter how relatively pure. However, as will be more particularly developed presently, it cannot be said that the discharge of treated sewage effluent into a running stream is *per se* an unreasonable riparian use in today's civilization. Under the reasonable use approach we are called upon to counterweigh social uses and harms. And this we must do in a realistic rather than a theoretical way, and on the basis of the evidence of record, rather than on emotion or runaway imagination.

* * *

These acts of legislation, and others (see, e.g., N.J.S.A. 58:12–2), denote a public policy which recognizes the social importance of sewage disposal plants and the necessity of fair and reasonable accommodation to their functioning of the use of the waters of the State for other purposes, even including that of human consumption, a use not involved in the present case. They tend to refute the idea that treated sewage effluent, as claimed by plaintiff, is necessarily a polluting or contaminating agent.

Clearly inapposite is the body of law that the influx of raw sewage which pollutes a stream is an actionable invasion (in the absence of legislative authorization) of the rights of a lower riparian owner or that a sewage disposal or treatment plant which, because of malfunctioning, inefficiency, or otherwise, is in fact a nuisance or a source of pollution, may be enjoined, Harrisonville v. W.S. Dickey Clay Mfg. Co., 289 U.S. 334 (1933). Research discloses and counsel have cited no case wherein treated sewage effluent has been held *per se* an enjoinable water pollutant. The authorities are uniformly to the contrary.

* * *

On the basis of the entire case we cannot conclude that the denial of injunctive relief by the trial court was erroneous. We do not rest our conclusion on the premise, which plaintiff has properly been at pains to dissipate, that there is required a showing of any particular kind of damages or injury other than psychological where there has, indeed, been the invasion of a property right. Our conception is, rather, that a determination as to the existence of an actionable invasion of the unquestionable property right of a riparian owner in the flow of a water course depends upon a weighing of the reasonableness, under all the circumstances, of the use being made by the defendant and of the materiality of the harm, if any, found to be visited by such use upon the reasonable uses of the water by the complaining owner. For all of the reasons we have set out, we do not consider that the balance of uses and harms reflected by this record points to an injunction. We trust that what we have said will not be read in anywise to impugn the appropriateness of plaintiff's use of the ditch and pond for recreational and park purposes as a riparian owner. If defendants' future operation of the treatment plant is ever shown to be such, in fact, as unreasonably to affect the use and enjoyment by the people of Westville of their park and pond, nothing herein determined upon the basis of the present record will, of course, preclude appropriate relief.

Judgment affirmed.

NOTES

1. The court in *Westville* recognizes that under the riparian doctrine, landowners are entitled to have waters of waterbodies touching their lands unimpaired in quality as well as undiminished in quantity. Recall that riparian law from earliest times allowed for "natural uses" such as drinking and household uses. Does this then mean that a landowner can add pollutants to the water by washing in the stream? Does this entitle a riparian landowner to put household sewage into the stream?

2. The common law did not recognize causes of action in nuisance and trespass against pollution of drinking water by bathers when the bathers were owners of riparian property. Conflicts arose between riparian rights and the exercise of the police power to protect public health. In State v. Heller, 123 Conn. 492, 196 A. 337 (1937), for example, the riparian property owner was convicted of violating a state statute by bathing in a stream which traversed his property. The court found the statute to be a legitimate exercise of the police power, and refused claim for compensation for a taking of property, noting that most of the riparian's rights remained intact, and that private rights must yield to public needs.

In Newton v. City of Groesbeck, 299 S.W. 518 (Tex.Civ.App.1927), the court found that a proposed development of a local swimming hole into a public bathing resort was an unreasonable use in light of a city's claim that the resort would interfere with the quality of its water supply. But see City of Battle Creek v. Goguac Resort Ass'n, 181 Mich. 241, 148 N.W. 441 (1914) (right to operate a bathing resort upheld; court suggested city purchase surrounding lands to prevent bathing in the lake). Cf. Game & Fresh Water Fish Comm'n v. Lake Islands, Ltd., 407 So.2d 189 (Fla.1981) (state regulation prohibiting use of motor boats during duck hunting season was taking of island owners' riparian right of access). Is *Lake Islands, Ltd.* consistent with Central Florida Investments, Inc. v. Orange County Code Enforcement Board, 790 So.2d 593 (Fla.Ct.App.2001)? The case stated that riparian rights are subject to regulation to protect environmentally sensitive lakes from the adverse impacts of jet skis and motor boats.

3. The problem of protecting municipal water supplies from pollution is not new. Until the mid-nineteenth century most cities obtained their water from local free-flowing rivers, small ponds or relatively shallow wells, and wastewater was dispersed in nearby dry well cesspools or privy vaults. Starting in the 1840s, major cities built water supply systems to serve their growing populations, but they did not simultaneously build sanitary sewer systems. The result was an increase in urban pollution as many people installed "water closets." Modern sanitary sewers were built in England in the 1850s and for the next two decades sanitary engineers sought to convince the public that the benefits of lower morbidity and mortality rates outweighed the costs of system construction. By 1880, 103 out of 222 American cities used land disposal to treat wastewater, but many of these had to curtail the practice to protect their own sources of water supply. The battle for sanitary sewers was won, but choices of lower cost, inadequate technology, and decisions to dump untreated or partially treated wastes into available rivers cancelled some of the anticipated benefits. These early decisions and directions continue to shape the law of pollution abatement and municipal sewage treatment policy.

The history of American sewerage development is traced in Joel A. Tarr et al., The Development and Impact of Urban Wastewater Technology:

Changing Concepts of Water Quality Control, 1850–1930, in Pollution and Reform in American Cities, 1870–1930, at 59 (Martin V. Melosi ed., 1980), Joel A. Tarr, The Search for the Ultimate Sink: Urban Pollution in Historical Perspective (1996), and Jamie Benidickson, The Culture of Flushing: A Social and Legal History of Sewage (2007).

Arizona Copper Co. v. Gillespie

Supreme Court of the Territory of Arizona, 1909.
12 Ariz. 190, 100 P. 465.

This action was brought by the appellee against the Shannon Copper Company, the Arizona Copper Company, Limited, and the Arizona Copper Company, to obtain an injunction restraining the defendants from depositing mining debris in streams tributary to the Gila river. * * * The facts found by the trial court are:

"That the Gila river rises in the territory of New Mexico, and flows thence through a generally mountainous country, through the county of Graham, and other counties, in the territory of Arizona, in a westerly direction into the Colorado river at or near the city of Yuma, in the territory of Arizona. That the San Francisco river is an affluent of the said Gila river, emptying its waters into the said Gila river at or near the city of Clifton aforesaid, and above the head of the Montezuma and other canals * * * * * *

* * *

" * * * [N]umerous irrigation ditches, amongst others said Montezuma canal, were taken out of said Gila river at various times in and since the year 1872 by divers persons who were then, and are now, the owners and occupants of irrigable lands lying upon either side of said Gila river, and by means of said ditches the public waters of said river have been ever since appropriated, diverted, and applied to the irrigation and cultivation of a constantly increasing quantity of irrigable lands * * *.

" * * * That the defendant, the Arizona Copper Company, Limited, is engaged in the reduction and treatment of copper ore in said mining district, near the upper branches and affluents of the Gila river. * * * That in the reduction of said copper ores by this defendant said ores are crushed and mixed with water, and that a portion of the slickens, slimes, and tailings therefrom finds its way through the creeks, affluents, and canals upon which the works of said defendant are situated, into the waters of the Gila river, and becomes mingled therewith, and is carried by the waters of said Gila river down to the Upper Gila Valley, in which the farming operations of the plaintiff are carried on, and by and through said river and irrigating ditches, in the ordinary and necessary course of irrigation, to and upon the cultivated lands of plaintiff, and of others like situated.

* * *

" * * * That the plaintiff was injured in the loss of the productivity of his fields of alfalfa upon his said lands in the year preceding the filing of this suit, by reason of the sedimentary deposits upon his fields of alfalfa, in an amount which the court cannot exactly determine, in excess of $1,000. * * *

CAMPBELL, J. (after stating the facts as above). It is insisted by the appellant that, if any wrong is being done by permitting debris from its mining operations to go into the river, the acts constitute a public nuisance, and that the plaintiff may not maintain this action, because it does not appear that the injury sustained by him differs in kind from that sustained by the general public. * * *

* * *

* * * [W]e have no difficulty in concluding that the plaintiff may maintain this action. By reason of the acts of the defendant he, with other owners of land irrigated by water from the Gila river, is suffering a direct individual injury, different from that of the general public. It is true that the general public also suffers an injury from the acts of the defendant, but only in the sense that whatever decreases the general prosperity of the community injures all who are members of the community. * * *

Appellant contends that * * * the right to use the waters of a public stream for mining purposes is recognized by law; that its rights in that respect are equal to those of the agriculturist to use the water for purposes of irrigation; and that in depositing in the river only such of the slimes and tailings as is reasonably necessary in the successful operation of its business it is acting wholly within its rights. Riparian rights do not exist in this territory. The laws of the territory do recognize the right to appropriate the waters of public streams for mining purposes, as well as for agriculture. No superior right, however, is accorded the miner. Under the doctrine of appropriation, he who is first in time is first in right, and so long as he continues to apply the water to a beneficial use, subsequent appropriators may not deprive him of the rights his appropriation gives, either by diminishing the quantity or deteriorating the quality. We do not mean to say that the agriculturist may captiously complain of a reasonable use of water by the miner higher up the stream, although it pollutes and makes the water slightly less desirable, nor that a court of equity should interfere with mining industries because they cause slight inconveniences or occasional annoyances, or even some degree of interference, so long as such do no substantial damage, but to permit a subsequent appropriator to so pollute or burden the stream with debris as substantially to render it less available to the prior appropriator causes him to lose the rights he gained by appropriation as readily as would the diversion of a portion of the water which he appropriated. The plaintiff, by his grantors, appropriated water for the purposes of irrigation in 1872, as did other agriculturists in the community, and, while it does not clearly appear when the defendant first made use of water in connection with its operations, it does appear that it was not prior to 1885.

NOTES

1. What made Gillespie's injury distinct from other members of the public, thereby justifying his bringing an action for public nuisance? See also Ravndal v. Northfork Placers, 60 Idaho 305, 91 P.2d 368 (1939) (plaintiff whose irrigation ditches were filled with sediment and dirty water from defendant's mining operation could sue for public nuisance).

2. Is it necessary that a plaintiff have a water right to sue in trespass or private nuisance for harm from water pollution caused by defendant? In Scheufler v. General Host Corp., 126 F.3d 1261 (10th Cir. 1997), the defendant operated a salt mine near plaintiffs' Kansas land. Salt from the mining operation contaminated an aquifer connected to a surface stream. The aquifer extended underneath plaintiffs' land and made the water unfit for irrigating crops. Plaintiffs claimed that they could not plant irrigated crops on the land because of the contamination. They had applied for water rights under Kansas's prior appropriation law but the state had not acted on the applications, and merely filing an application gives applicants no rights. The court held that the cause of action for nuisance did not depend on the existence of water rights but on interference with the potential use and enjoyment of land.

B. FEDERAL REGULATION OF WATER QUALITY

The popular insistence on clean water for drinking and other domestic uses, and clean waterways for recreation has led to extensive new federal laws. Thanks to them, the United States has succeeded in eliminating many direct discharges of pollutants from factories and publicly owned treatment works. More diffuse sources of pollution—nonpoint sources— such as agricultural and urban runoff, continue to plague waters that are important as sources of supply and for their natural values. Neither state nor federal laws deal comprehensively with nonpoint source pollution. Moreover, the need to restore degraded aquatic ecosystems, which are the legacy of past policy choices, has emerged on the public agenda. Some inroads on aquifer contamination have also been made under federal laws, although the primary impact on groundwater quality has not been prevention but clean-up.

Federal statutes overlay the common law and state water laws. Common law remedies can still be pursued to the extent they would not conflict with federal statutory goals. There are, however, federalism issues. Although the administration of federal pollution laws is often delegated to the states, they are, with a few exceptions, codified and administered separately from state "water law." This can make implementation awkward. Moreover, these federal laws often conflict with state laws causing state-federal clashes.

1. SURFACE WATER—THE CLEAN WATER ACT

a. Basic Structure

In most states, there were few effective laws dealing directly with water pollution before 1972. Since then, the nation's water quality has been primarily controlled by an extensive federal statutory framework implemented through state laws. The most comprehensive federal water pollution statute is the Clean Water Act, 33 U.S.C.A. §§ 1251–1387 (West Supp. 2008). The first Federal Water Pollution Control Act was adopted in 1948. It created a system of federal subsidies for state and local governments, but did not attempt any direct regulation. State regulation proved to be ineffective and uneven. In 1965, Congress enacted the Water Quality Act because state programs were failing to clean up the nation's waters. The Act required classification of all interstate receiving waters, reflecting an underlying belief that water pollution control depended on the capacity of streams to assimilate pollutants. The Act also required the states to act or else the federal government would take over water quality enforcement. But the receiving water quality standards were essentially unenforceable because it was difficult to work backwards from a receiving water standard to the effluent limitation necessary to maintain the desired water quality level over time, especially where multiple discharges were involved. The definitive analysis of the pre-Clean Water Act legislation is N. William Hines, Nor Any Drop To Drink: Public Regulation of Water Quality (pts. 1–3), 52 Iowa L. Rev. 186, 432, 799 (1966–1967).

The continuing ineffectiveness of state programs after the 1965 Act aroused public concern. The 1899 Refuse Act had been revitalized first by the Supreme Court, in United States v. Republic Steel Corp., 362 U.S. 482, 80 S.Ct. 884, 4 L.Ed.2d 903 (1960), then for a short period by enforcement at the hands of the U.S. Army Corps of Engineers. Under that Act any person dumping any kind of refuse in navigable waters violated federal law. The Act was a clumsy mechanism for dealing with ordinary water pollution problems as it lacked specific standards. Furthermore, it did not apply to municipal sewage. Although the states had not done well at controlling pollution, the Refuse Act was not the answer.

Finally, Congress passed the Federal Water Pollution Control Act in 1972 (which has been called the Clean Water Act since 1977) and gave regulatory responsibility to the newly created Environmental Protection Agency (EPA). The goal of the Clean Water Act was to totally eliminate the discharge of pollutants by 1985 and to "restore and maintain the chemical, physical and biological integrity of the Nation's waters." 33 U.S.C.A. § 1251(a) (West Supp. 2008). It set an interim goal of swimmable, fishable waters by 1983. The Act attempted to achieve most of its purposes by the enforcement of two sets of standards: effluent standards limit the concentrations of pollutants that may be discharged from a particular source. Water quality standards limit the concentration of pollutants in the stream.

The basic difference between the 1965 and 1972 Acts is that the later controls water pollution principally by imposing absolute limits on the amounts of pollutants that can be discharged at their source. The receiving water quality standards that were the focus of the earlier act were retained as a backup for the technology-forcing effluent limitations. Upon passage of the 1972 Act, there was finally a comprehensive national water pollution control system. The extent of federal power under the Act is illustrated by

Quivira Mining Co. v. United States Environmental Protection Agency, 765 F.2d 126 (10th Cir.1985), which holds that a uranium mine must obtain a discharge permit under the Clean Water Act for a pond that might overflow into two arroyos that ultimately connect to navigable waters, but that flowed only during period of heavy rainfall and were part of an "underground [where else?] aquifer." Since this case, federal jurisdiction has been potentially limited by the Supreme Court, see *infra*, page 705.

In the Clean Water Act, Congress attempted to promote cooperation between the federal government and the states. Absolute effluent standards were nationally determined, but applied according to state plans. Water quality control was left to the states under the threat of federal intervention if state action was shown to be inadequate. Thus, the Clean Water Act is enforced through an effluent permit system known as the National Pollutant Discharge Elimination System (NPDES). The law simply declares all discharge of pollutants from any "point sources" without a permit to be unlawful. The job of issuing NPDES permits is usually assigned to states adhering to federal standards, otherwise to the EPA. 33 U.S.C.A. § 1251(b) (West Supp. 2008). The rationale for federal floors imposing maximum levels for discharges was to prevent states from competing with each other by offering lower water quality standards.

The federal role has declined in the past two decades as states have devoted more resources to environmental protection and both major political parties have endorsed the need for more devolution of regulatory authority to local entities. Experts claim that there is no logical reason to expect a race to the bottom. *E.g.*, Richard L. Revesz, *Rehabilitating Interstate Competition: Rethinking the "Race-to-the-Bottom" Rationale for Federal Environmental Regulation*, 67 N.Y.U. L. Rev. 1210 (1992) and *Federalism and Environmental Regulation: A Public Choice Analysis*, 115 Harv. L. Rev. 553 (2001). However, evidence is mounting of substantial under-enforcement of the Act by individual states. See David L. Markell, *The Role of Deterrence–Based Enforcement in a "Reinvented" State/Federal Relationship*, 24 Harv. Envtl. L. Rev. 1 (2000), and Rena I. Steinzor, Devolution and Public Health, 24 Harv. Envtl. L. Rev. 351 (2000).

b. NPDES Permit Program: Technology Versus Receiving Water Quality and Quantity

To obtain an NPDES permit, the state or federal agency having jurisdiction over permitting must certify that the discharge will comply with uniform national effluent standards set by the EPA. EPA's power to set binding national effluent limitations that must be incorporated into federal or state individual NPDES permits was upheld in E.I. du Pont de Nemours & Co. v. Train, 430 U.S. 112, 97 S.Ct. 965, 51 L.Ed.2d 204 (1977). The standards are based on the level of pollution control technology that is available for several categories of industries and for publicly owned sewage treatment works. By 1977 all industrial point sources were required to meet effluent limitations requiring "application of the best practicable control technology currently available as defined by the [EPA] Administrator" (BPT). 33 U.S.C.A. § 1311(b)(1)(A) (West Supp. 2008). Use of the best available technology economically achievable (BAT) was required by March 31, 1989 for toxic pollutants and for "nonconventional" pollutants. 33 U.S.C.A. §§ 1311(b)(2)(A), (C), (D) & (F) (West Supp. 2008). "Conventional pollutants" (suspended solids, coliform bacteria, biological oxygen demand, and acidity) were subject to the best conventional control technology (BCT) as of March 31, 1989. 33 U.S.C.A. § 1311(b)(2)(E) (West Supp. 2008). Application of the several statutory standards to particular pollutants is left to the Administrator through rulemaking.

The NPDES permitting process can raise issues that affect the allocation of rights to use quantities of water. In states that administer water resources through a permit system the permitting process can be used to control quality as well as quantity, but rarely is. Florida uses this approach. Water district administrators review permits under a statewide comprehensive plan for water use. No permit may be granted if the anticipated use will affect the quality of the water in any way. All discharges which "alter water quality" (including changes in taste, temperature, and turbidity) must be approved. If a violation occurs, the administrator may rescind the permit, order abatement of the use, and seek civil damages for injury to the resource. Florida's permit system, Fla. Stat. Ann. §§ 373.203–373.250 (West 2000), was adapted from a Model Water Code. See *supra* p. 275.

Courts have made it clear that technology-forcing effluent limitations apply even if the natural waste assimilative capacity of a stream can reduce the pollution. "Congress made the deliberate decision to rule out arguments based on receiving water capacity * * *." Weyerhaeuser Co. v. Costle, 590 F.2d 1011, 1042 (D.C.Cir.1978). However, § 301(8) allows what are in effect waivers based on receiving water characteristics for many pollutants including thermal discharges. 33 U.S.C.A. § 1311(g) (West Supp. 2008).

In addition, a stream's hydrology is a relevant factor in writing NPDES permits and in understanding the fate of pollutants once they enter a stream. As a 2006 United States Geological Survey publication, Surface Water, notes, "[m]any agencies use low-flow characteristics as target conditions or thresholds for making regulatory decisions." Still, reliance on technology rather than natural dilution to limit waste discharges remains a bedrock principle of Clean War Act jurisprudence. However, global climate change challenges many of the assumptions behind existing pollution control strategies including stable stream flows. Climate Change and Water 43 (Intergovernmental Panel on Climate Change Technical Paper VI, June, 2008) [citations omitted] describes the most important potential impacts on water quality:

3.2.1.4 Water quality

Higher water temperatures, increased precipitation intensity, and longer periods of low flows are projected to exacerbate many forms of water pollution, including sediments, nutrients, dissolved organic carbon, pathogens, pesticides, salt and thermal pollution. This will promote algal blooms, and increase the bacterial and fungal content. This will, in turn, impact ecosystems, human health, and the reliability and operating costs of water systems.

Rising temperatures are *likely* to lower water quality in lakes through increased thermal stability and altered mixing patterns, resulting in reduced oxygen concentrations and an increased release of phosphorus from the sediments. For example, already high phosphorus concentrations during summer in a bay of Lake Ontario could double with a 3–4°C increase in water temperature. However, rising temperatures can also improve water quality during winter/spring due to earlier ice break-up and consequent higher oxygen levels and reduced winter fish-kill.

More intense rainfall will lead to an increase in suspended solids (turbidity) in lakes and reservoirs due to soil fluvial erosion (Leemans and Kleidon, 2002), and pollutants will be introduced. The projected increase in precipitation intensity is expected to lead to a deterioration of water quality, as it results in the enhanced transport of pathogens and other dissolved pollutants (e.g., pesticides) to surface waters and groundwater; and in increased erosion, which in turn leads to the mobilisation of adsorbed pollutants such as phosphorus and heavy metals. In addition, more frequent heavy rainfall events will overload the capacity of sewer systems and water and wastewater treatment plants more often. An increased occurrence of low flows will lead to decreased contaminant dilution capacity, and thus higher pollutant concentrations, including pathogens. In areas with overall decreased runoff (e.g., in many semi-arid areas), water quality deterioration will be even worse. In semi-arid and arid areas, climate change is *likely* to increase salinisation of shallow groundwater due to increased evapo-transpiration. As streamflow is projected to decrease in many semi-arid areas, the salinity of rivers and estuaries will increase. For example, salinity levels in the headwaters of the Murray–Darling Basin in Australia are expected to increase by 13–19% by 2050. In general, decreased groundwater recharge, which reduces mobilisation of underground salt, may balance the effect of decreased dilution of salts in rivers and estuaries.

In coastal areas, rising sea levels may have negative effects on stormwater drainage and sewage disposal and increase the potential for the intrusion of saline water into fresh groundwater in coastal aquifers, thus adversely affecting groundwater resources.

c. *Water Quality Standards and TMDLS*

The other water pollution control strategy incorporated in the Clean Water Act is the requirement that water quality standards be set and enforced by the states. 33 U.S.C. § 1313 (West Supp. 2008). These standards deal with the concentrations of pollutants in particular stretches of a stream. State plans and standards for water quality maintenance and control must be submitted to the EPA Administrator. The Administrator determines whether the standards are consistent with the Act's goal for waters of the United States to become "fishable and swimmable." The states must identify "water quality-limited" segments of streams such as areas where discharges that may be consistent with effluent standards nevertheless result in overall water quality that is unacceptable. Section 303(a) further mandates that these areas the state must set "total maximum daily loads" (TMDL) for each pollutant.

The TMDL program lay dormant until a series of citizen law suits forced the states and EPA to administer the section. See Oliver A. Houck, The Clean Water Act TMDL Program: Law, Policy and Implementation (1999) and James R. Rasband, *Who's To Blame? Allocating Watershed Responsibilities Among Multiple Users,* 45 Rocky Mtn. Min. L. Inst. 24–1 (1999). The program has become extremely controversial because of potential cost and because it may require states to allocate waste loads among both point and non-point sources of pollution.

In its administration of the water quality controls under the Clean Water Act, a state may set effluent limitations and water quality standards that are more stringent than those imposed by the United States, Homestake Mining Co. v. United States Environmental Protection Agency, 477 F.Supp. 1279 (D.S.D.1979), and implement antidegradation policy to protect high quality waters that constitute an outstanding national resource, 40 C.F.R. § 131.12 (2000). See generally Jeffrey M. Gaba, *Federal Supervision of State Water Quality Standards Under the Clean Water Act,* 36 Vand. L. Rev. 1167 (1983); N. William Hines, *A Decade of Nondegradation Policy in Congress and the Courts: The Erratic Pursuit of Clean Air and Clean Water,* 62 Iowa L. Rev. 643, 673–81 (1977). If a state does not adopt adequate water quality standards, the Administrator may adopt criteria and standards to override a state's standards and thereby change effluent limitations set in a point source discharge permit. Broad supervisory authority over water quality standards, including discretion in the Administrator to promulgate substitute standards, has been sustained by the courts. E.g., Mississippi Comm'n on Natural Res. v. Costle, 625 F.2d 1269 (5th Cir.1980). Indian tribes have begun to use this power. See *infra* p. 935.

An important case holds that TMDL reduction plans required by the Act should include reduction of non-point source discharges. However, the case also notes that "the CWA leaves to the states the responsibility of developing plans to achieve water quality standards if the statutorily-mandated point source controls will not alone suffice," meaning that the choice of how (or even whether) to reduce nonpoint source pollution of impaired waters is left up to the states. Pronsolino v. Nastri, 291 F.3d 1123 (9th Cir. 2002). Yet a state's reduction of water quality standards and reclassification of waterways to lower quality in order to avoid non-point source regulations (of mining and logging operations) was upheld in American Wildlands v. Browner, 260 F.3d 1192 (10th Cir. 2001).

d.   Point Versus Non–Point Pollution: The Case of Inter–Watershed Transfers

The NPDES is limited to regulation of the "discharge of a pollutant" in point sources. A point source is defined as any discernable, confined and discrete conveyance, including but not limited to any pipe, ditch, channel, tunnel, conduit, well, discrete fissure, container, rolling stock, concentrated animal feeding operation, or vessel or other floating craft, from which pollutants are or may be discharged. This term does not include agriculture stormwater discharges and return flows from irrigated agriculture.33 U.S.C.A. § 1362(14) (West Supp. 2008).

A discharge of a pollutant is "any addition of any pollutant to navigable waters from a point structure." 33 U.S.C. § 1362(14). Therefore, diffused sources of water pollution such as runoff from city streets and seepage from mining operations which are among the greatest threats to streams, but do not fit the definition. Are discharges from a dam that change the quality of a stream discharges from a "point source"? Compare National Wildlife Fed'n v. Gorsuch, 693 F.2d 156 (D.C.Cir.1982), with Committee to Save the Mokelumne River v. East Bay Mun. Utility Dist., 13 F.3d 305 (9th Cir.1993). The water quality impacts of dams are surveyed in M. Collier et al., Dams and Rivers: Primer on the Downstream Effects of Dams (U.S.G.S. Circular 1126 1996).

The exception to the point source definition was added in 1977 after an administrative exemption for agricultural return flows was overturned as inconsistent with the definition. Natural Resources Defense Council, Inc. v. Costle, 568 F.2d 1369 (D.C.Cir.1977). Because point sources are defined to exclude return flows from irrigated agriculture, major pollutant discharges remain unregulated unless states decide to do so. Thus, many agricultural chemicals and salts are put in streams with virtually no regulation.

Catskill Mountains Chapter, Trout Unlimited v. City of New York

United States Court of Appeals, Second Circuit, 2006.
451 F.3d 77.

[New York City's water supply comes from a series of reservoirs in the Catskill Mountains. Part of the system involves a transfer of water from the Schoharie Reservoir through the 18 mile Shandaken Tunnel into Esopus Creek. The reservoir water is more turbid than the natural quality of the creek, a trout stream used for fly fishing. New York refused to apply for an NPDES permit, the Second Circuit held that one was required, a federal district judge imposed a $5,749,000.00 fine against the City, and New York City appealed on the ground that there had been a change in the law since the first Second Circuit opinion.]

II. The Shandaken Tunnel and the Esopus Creek

As part of the water system that supplies New York City with its drinking water, the City maintains the Schoharie Reservoir in the Catskill Mountains. To deliver this water eventually to New York City, water from the Schoharie Reservoir is diverted through the eighteen-mile Shandaken Tunnel and discharged into the Esopus Creek. The Creek's water, in turn, flows into the Ashokan Reservoir, through the Catskill Aqueduct, to a series of reservoirs and tunnels along the east side of the Hudson River, and eventually to New York City. Absent the man-made diversion through the Tunnel, water from the Schoharie Reservoir would never reach the Esopus Creek. *Catskill Mountains Ch. of Trout Unltd. v. City of New York,* 273 F.3d 481, 484 (2d Cir.2001) ("*Catskills I*").

Because water in the Schoharie Reservoir contains suspended solids from both natural and man-made causes, discharges from the Tunnel into the Creek are more turbid than the waters of the Esopus. This turbidity impairs use of the Esopus for fly fishing and other recreational activities. Pursuant to state regulations, the City has been studying ways to reduce the turbidity in the water discharged from the Tunnel but so far has failed to find a way to do so. Until this lawsuit, neither the EPA nor the New York State Department of Environmental Conservation ("NYDEC"), the agency that enforces the CWA in New York State, had ever regulated the turbidity in the Tunnel under the CWA's permitting scheme.

III. Procedural History

In March 2000, Catskills, recreational users of the Esopus Creek, brought this citizen suit under the CWA alleging that the City's discharge of turbid water from the Tunnel violated 33 U.S.C. § 1311(a), which, as we said, prohibits "the discharge of any pollutant" without a discharge permit. The district court dismissed the claim on the pleadings, holding that the discharge from the Tunnel did not constitute an "addition" of a pollutant to the Creek under 33 U.S.C. § 1362(12).

In October 2001, we reversed after concluding that the discharge of water containing pollutants from one distinct water body into another is an "addition of [a] pollutant" under the CWA. *Catskills I,* 273 F.3d at 491–93. As a result, we determined that the discharge from the Tunnel into the Creek requires a permit.

On remand from *Catskills I,* the district court granted summary judgment to the plaintiffs and went on to determine the civil penalties to be assessed against the City. The district court concluded that no penalties should be imposed for the City's actions prior to June 22, 2002, eight months after *Catskills I* put the City on notice that it needed a permit for the Shandaken discharges. Finding a delay of more than eight months unreasonable, however, the district court imposed the maximum penalty for the period from June 22, 2002, to December 31, 2002, when the City filed its permit application; the penalty totaled $5,749,000. This appeal followed.

DISCUSSION

In this appeal, the City asks us to reconsider our holding in *Catskills I* that the discharge of turbid water from the Shandaken Tunnel into the Esopus Creek requires a permit. The City also argues that the penalty of $5,749,000 is too high. In a cross-appeal, Catskills argues that amount is too low.

We are free to reconsider our holding in *Catskills I* if there are cogent, compelling reasons for doing so, such as a change in controlling law or newly discovered facts. *United States v. Tenzer,* 213 F.3d 34, 39 (2d Cir.2000). Determining whether we should reconsider requires briefly revisiting our reasoning in *Catskills I.*

I. *Catskills I*

In concluding that the transfer of turbid water from the Shandaken Tunnel to the Esopus Creek qualified as the "discharge of [a] pollutant," 33 U.S.C. § 1311(a), requiring an NPDES permit, *Catskills I* first noted the CWA's broad definition of the "discharge of a pollutant" as "any addition of any pollutant to navigable waters from any point source." *Id.* § 1362(12). Because the Shandaken Tunnel "plainly qualifies as a point source," *Catskills I,* 273 F.3d at 493, our holding rested, in principal part, on the meaning of "addition," which the CWA leaves undefined. We decided that "addition" means the introduction into navigable water from the "outside world,"[2] with the outside world being defined as "any place outside the particular water body to which pollutants are introduced." *Id.* at 491.

In reaching this result, we distinguished the "dams cases," on which the City relied. In *National Wildlife Federation v. Gorsuch,* 693 F.2d 156 (D.C.Cir.1982), and *National Wildlife Federation v. Consumers Power Co.,* 862 F.2d 580 (6th Cir.1988), two sister circuits held that water taken from a water source and then released back into that same source was not an "addition" to navigable waters under the CWA, despite the fact that the water so released contained "pollutants." 693 F.2d at 183, 862 F.2d at 587. This case differed from the dams cases, we believed, because the Tunnel discharges water into the Creek from a source that is a different, distinct body of water. *Catskills I,* 273 F.3d at 491–92. In *Catskills I,* we analogized the dams cases to a soup ladle scooping soup out of a pot and returning it to that pot, a type of water transfer known as an intrabasin transfer. The Tunnel's discharge, in contrast, was like scooping soup from one pot and depositing it in another pot, thereby adding soup to the second pot, an interbasin transfer. Interbasin transfers, we held in *Catskills I,* constitute "additions," rendering the City's reliance on the dams cases misplaced. *Id.* at 492.

We also rejected the City's "unitary water" theory of navigable waters, which posits that all of the navigable waters of the United States constitute a single water body, such that the transfer of water from any body of water that is part of the navigable waters to any other could never be an "addition." We pointed out that this theory would lead to the absurd result that the transfer of water from a heavily polluted, even toxic, water body to one that was pristine via a point source would not constitute an "addition"

---

2. This phrase comes from the definition of the word "addition" urged by the EPA on the court in *National Wildlife Federation v. Gorsuch,* 693 F.2d 156, 175 (D.C.Cir. 1982). In *Gorsuch,* the EPA argued that an "addition of a pollutant" takes place only if the point source introduces a pollutant into the water from the outside world. *Id.*

of pollutants and would not be subject to the CWA's NPDES permit requirement. *Id.* at 493. *Catskills I* rejected the "unitary water" theory as inconsistent with the ordinary meaning of the word "addition." *Id.*

Finally, we rejected the contention that the provisions of the CWA reserving power to the states could overcome the express permit requirement for water transfers that result in the addition of pollutants. We pointed out that "like many complex statutes ... the CWA balances a welter of consistent and inconsistent goals" but that "none of the statute's broad purposes sways us from what we find to be the plain meaning of its text." *Id.* at 494.

II. Intervening Legal Developments

Following *Catskills I,* there have been two relevant legal developments. The Supreme Court decided *South Florida Water Management District v. Miccosukee Tribe of Indians,* 541 U.S. 95, 124 S.Ct. 1537, 158 L.Ed.2d 264 (2004), and the EPA issued an agency interpretation addressing the applicability of the CWA's NPDES permit requirement to water transfers such as the one at issue in this case.

Miccosukee was a citizen suit contending that an NPDES permit is necessary for the South Florida Water Management District to operate a pump that conveys water from a polluted canal to an undeveloped wetland. The pump serves both to prevent the basin surrounding the canal from flooding and to preserve the wetland area. *Id.* at 100–01, 124 S.Ct. 1537. Consistent with the dams cases, *Miccosukee* held that if the canal and the wetlands are not meaningfully distinct water bodies—an unresolved factual question—no NPDES permit is required. *Id.* at 112, 124 S.Ct. 1537; cf. *S.D. Warren Co. v. Me. Bd. of Envtl. Prot.,* 126 S.Ct. 1843, 1850 (2006) ("[I]f two identified volumes of water are 'simply two parts of the same water body, pumping water from one into the other cannot constitute an "addition" of pollutants.'" (quoting *Miccosukee,* 541 U.S. at 109, 124 S.Ct. 1537)).

On August 5, 2005, the EPA issued an agency interpretation regarding whether the movement of pollutants by a water transfer from one navigable water to a separate one is the "addition" of a pollutant subjecting the activity to the NPDES permitting requirement. According to the EPA, several provisions of the CWA indicate Congress's intent that such transfers be regulated by the states, not by the federal NPDES program. The EPA interpretation argues that, rather than primarily focusing on the meaning of the word "addition," as we did in *Catskills I,* a "holistic" view of the statute that takes this intent into account is appropriate.

The City concedes that this EPA interpretation is not entitled to *Chevron* deference. *See Chevron U.S.A., Inc. v. Natural Res. Def.,* 467 U.S. 837, 104 S.Ct. 2778, 81 L.Ed.2d 694 (1984). Instead, the deference described in *Skidmore v. Swift & Co.,* 323 U.S. 134, 65 S.Ct. 161, 89 L.Ed. 124 (1944), and *United States v. Mead Corp.,* 533 U.S. 218, 121 S.Ct. 2164, 150 L.Ed.2d 292 (2001), is applicable. We thus defer to the agency interpretation according to its " 'power to persuade.' " *Mead,* 533 U.S. at 235, 121 S.Ct. 2164 (quoting *Skidmore,* 323 U.S. at 140, 65 S.Ct. 161).

III. Reconsideration of *Catskills I*

We turn to the City's request that we reconsider our holding in *Catskills I*. Rather than offering "compelling and cogent" reasons for reconsideration, however, the City basically serves us warmed-up arguments that we rejected in *Catskills I*, with the additional contention that either the Supreme Court's *Miccosukee* decision, the EPA interpretation, or both compel a result different from the one we reached earlier. We disagree.

The City first argues that new evidence developed below and the Supreme Court's decision in *Miccosukee* invalidate the distinction between intrabasin and interbasin water transfers. The "new evidence" the City points to simply shows that the release of water from a dam into downstream water is no less likely to add pollutants as would a transfer of water from a distinct water body. Having considered the dams cases in *Catskills I*, we were aware of the presence of pollutants in intrabasin transfers. *Gorsuch* includes an extensive discussion of the nature of water quality changes wrought by dammed water. 693 F.2d at 161–64. And in *Consumers Power*, the water at issue contained fish that were pulverized as they passed through the turbines of a hydroelectric power plant and then were reintroduced into Lake Michigan as biological waste. 862 F.2d at 582. Nonetheless, *Catskills I* concluded that, despite the presence of pollutants in both interbasin and intrabasin transfers, interbasin transfers are properly distinguished because they "add" pollutants to the navigable waters. See *Catskills I*, 273 F.3d at 492. This has not changed.

Nor does the Supreme Court's decision in *Miccosukee* render inter- and intra-basin transfers indistinguishable. *Miccosukee* cited with approval our "soup ladle" analogy and the distinction between inter- and intra-basin transfers. 541 U.S. at 109–10, 124 S.Ct. 1537. The Court remanded the case to the district court to determine whether the water bodies in question were "two pots of soup, not one." Id.; cf. *S.D. Warren Co.*, 126 S.Ct. at 1850 n. 6. This remand would be unnecessary if there were no legally significant distinction between inter- and intra-basin transfers.

The City also reasserts the unitary-water theory of navigable waters. Our rejection of this theory in *Catskills I*, however, is supported by *Miccosukee*, not undermined by it. In that case, the Supreme Court pointed out that several provisions of the CWA seem to distinguish among water bodies that are part of the navigable waters of the United States, implying that, at least in the context of the CWA, the unitary-water theory has no place. 541 U.S. at 105–09, 124 S.Ct. 1537. *Miccosukee* also noted that the EPA has never endorsed the theory in any administrative documents. *Id.* at 107, 124 S.Ct. 1537. Indeed, the Supreme Court pointed out that "the agency once reached the opposite conclusion." *Id.* Thus, *Miccosukee* did no more than note the existence of the theory and raise possible arguments against it. This does not constitute a change of controlling law warranting reconsideration of this court's previous decision on the issue.

Finally, the City points to the "holistic" argument, reflected in the EPA's 2005 agency interpretation, to assert that the proper allocation of rights and responsibilities between the states and the federal government for water regulation necessitates a reconsideration of our holding in *Catskills I*. This proposition is supported by amicus curiae briefs filed by western states who fear that the *Catskills I* rule will upend state regulation of water rights.

This argument, too, was raised by the City in *Catskills I,* albeit less elaborately, and, as with the interbasin/intrabasin distinction and the unitary-waters theory, *Miccosukee* fails to alter the legal landscape to support the "holistic" theory. The power of the states to allocate *quantities* of water within their borders is not inconsistent with federal regulation of water *quality*. Section 510 provides for the preservation of the preexisting rights of states not in conflict with the other requirements of the CWA ("except as expressly proved in this chapter"). Indeed, the Supreme Court has held that "[s]ections 101(g) and 510(2) preserve the authority of each State to allocate water quantity as between users; they do not limit the scope of water pollution controls...." *PUD No. 1 v. Wash. Dep't of Ecology,* 511 U.S. 700, 720, 114 S.Ct. 1900, 128 L.Ed.2d 716 (1994). To be sure, *Miccosukee* acknowledged the possibility that "construing the NPDES program to cover such transfers would ... raise the costs of water distribution prohibitively, and violate" section 101(g). *Miccosukee,* 541 U.S. at 108, 124 S.Ct. 1537. But in the next sentence, the Court recognized that, despite their potential cost, such permits nevertheless might be necessary to protect water quality. *Id.*

Nor does *Miccosukee* support the EPA and the City's argument that the non-point-source provisions of the CWA indicate congressional intent to leave interbasin water transfers outside the NPDES permitting scheme. Section 304(f) of the CWA directs the EPA to study and make recommendations for the regulation of pollutants spread by non-point sources, such as "changes in the movement, flow, or circulation of any navigable waters or ground waters, including changes caused by the construction of ... flow diversion facilities." 33 U.S.C. § 1314(f)(2)(F). From this language, the EPA and the City claim that Congress intended that changes in the circulation of navigable waters caused by the construction of "flow diversion facilities," such as the Tunnel, be exempt from the permit requirements that apply to point sources. As the Supreme Court pointed out in *Miccosukee,* however, "1314(f)(2)(F) does not explicitly exempt nonpoint pollution sources from the NPDES program if they *also* fall within the 'point source' definition." 541 U.S. at 106, 124 S.Ct. 1537.

In the end, while the City contends that nothing in the text of the CWA supports a permit requirement for interbasin transfers of pollutants, these "holistic" arguments about the allocation of state and federal rights, said to be rooted in the structure of the statute, simply overlook its plain language. NPDES permits are required for "the discharge of any pollutant," 33 U.S.C. § 1311(a), which is defined as "any addition of any pollutant to navigable waters from any point source," *id.* § 1362(12). It is the meaning of the word "addition" upon which the outcome of *Catskills I* turned and which has not changed, despite the City's attempts to shift attention away from the text of the CWA to its context. In *Catskills I*, we pointed out that complex statutes often have seemingly inconsistent goals that must be balanced. 273 F.3d at 494. The CWA seeks to achieve water allocation goals as well as to restore and maintain the quality of the nation's waters. The City and the EPA would have us tip the balance toward the allocation goals. But in honoring the text, we adhere to the balance that Congress has struck and remains free to change.

NOTES

1. *EPA Rejects Catskill II.* The EPA turned its 2005 interpretive memorandum into a rule which exempts inter-water body transfers from the NPDES requires of the Clean Water Act and also reaffirmed its acceptance of *Gorsuch.* 73 Fed. Reg. 33,397, June 13, 2008. The agency's primary rationale for the rule is that Congress intended to leave oversight of transfers to the states in cooperation with federal authorities. If a state does not require a new permit for the inter-watercourse transfer of a previously authorized permit, is there a basis for federal-state cooperation? If *Catskill II* refused to accord *Chevron* deference to the agency's 2005 interpretation of the definition of discharge, does restating the statutory interpretation as a rule change the Court's conclusion?

2. *Farms Continue to Pollute.* Although there has been speculation that Congress would act to regulate non-point source pollution from agricultural sources, it has not done so for political reasons. The 1987 Clean Water Act reauthorization provided a major program to assist states in the development of non-point source programs, Water Quality Act of 1987, 33 U.S.C.A. §§ 1251–1387 (West Supp. 2008), but survey after survey finds that non-point sources have not been effectively controlled and often cancel out gains from point source controls. Courts have partially addressed the problem by liberal application of the point source discharge definition. E.g., Concerned Area Residents for the Env't v. Southview Farm, 34 F.3d 114 (2d Cir.1994) (use of lagoons to collect manure so that the liquid can be spread by center pivot irrigation system is a point source discharge).

3. *Pesticide Regulation and the CWA.* A 2001 Ninth Circuit opinion holds that the application of an EPA-approved herbicide along irrigation canals requires an NPDES permit. Headwaters, Inc. v. Talent Irrigation Dist., 243 F.3d 526 (9th Cir.2001). The court held that the application of a herbicide was a discharge into navigable waters because the canals were tributary waters and pesticides were chemical wastes under the CWA. It characterized the district's argument that chemical wastes were pollutants, but toxic chemicals poured directly into the canals were not, as "absurd." EPA initially issued guidance which rejected *Talent*, but League of Wilderness Defenders/Blue Mountains Biodiversity Project v. Forsgren, 309 F.3d 1181 (9th Cir. 2002), held that it was not entitled to *Chevron* deference because it contained no persuasive analysis of the issue. See also No Spray Coalition, Inc. v. City of New York, 351 F.3d 602 (2d Cir. 2003). But cf. Fairhurst v. Hagener, 422 F.3d 1146 (9th Cir. 2005). In 2006, EPA adopted a rule which exempts the applications of pesticides which comply with the Federal Insecticide, Fungicide and Rodenticide Act (FIFRA) of 1947 from Clean Water Act jurisdiction. 71 Fed.Reg. 68,483 (Nov. 27, 2006). The agency has not taken a position of the regulation of drift from terrestrial applications.

NOTE: FEDERAL POLLUTION CONTROL AND THE COMMON LAW

Despite the apparent comprehensiveness of the statutory framework, common law remedies still have an important role to play. Professor Peter Davis concludes that statutory coverage in some areas of water quality control is incomplete. Peter N. Davis, *Theories of Water Pollution Litigation,* 1971 Wis. L. Rev. 738 (1971). He suggests that private use of common law actions such as nuisance and trespass may help fill these legislative gaps. The reasonable use standard applicable among riparian water users presumably includes considerations of water quality. Davis notes that many states have specifically preserved common law rights, either by statute or judicial decision. In the course of an opinion holding that neither the federal nor state Clean Water Acts preempted the riparian's right to be free from unreasonable diminution in quality, the court in Biddix v. Henredon Furniture Indus., Inc., 76 N.C.App. 30, 331 S.E.2d 717, 724 (1985) said:

> We conclude that the Clean Water Act does not abrogate the common law civil actions for private nuisance and trespass to land for pollution of waters resulting from violation of a NPDES permit. First, the Clean Water Act, as amended, does not specifically abrogate these common law civil actions. Assuming for the purposes of this appeal that industrial discharges made under a NPDES permit would constitute a "reasonable use" of water in accordance with the common law, thereby effectively preventing a civil action founded in nuisance or trespass to land, plaintiff's allegations in the case before us allege waste discharges in violation of defendant's NPDES permit.

The Supreme Court has taken a different view of the relationship between the Clean Water Act and non-statutory remedies. It has held that the Act does not authorize an implied right of action for damages suffered as the result of an illegal discharge. Middlesex County Sewerage Auth. v. National Sea Clammers Ass'n, 453 U.S. 1, 101 S.Ct. 2615, 69 L.Ed.2d 435 (1981). Accord Williams Pipe Line Co. v. Bayer Corp., 964 F.Supp. 1300 (S.D.Iowa 1997), and Tiegs v. Watts, 135 Wash.2d 1, 954 P.2d 877 (1998).

Although the Clean Water Act does not necessarily preempt common law actions for polluting activities under a nuisance theory, the result is different when a plaintiff in one state tries to use the common law to remedy polluting activities in another state. Under these circumstances the Supreme Court has held that *federal* common law remedies for interstate pollution are preempted by the Clean Water Act. City of Milwaukee v. Illinois, 451 U.S. 304, 101 S.Ct. 1784, 68 L.Ed.2d 114 (1981). State law causes of action for nuisance can still be pursued but the Supreme Court has held that they too are limited by the Act. In International Paper Co. v. Ouellette, 479 U.S. 481, 107 S.Ct. 805, 93 L.Ed.2d 883 (1987), *infra* p. 975, the Supreme Court held that an individual in one state who is injured by the discharge of pollution in another state may not apply the affected state's nuisance law to the point source in the source state. To do so would "subject the point source to the threat of legal and equitable penalties if the [source state's] permit standards were less stringent than those imposed by the affected state." Id. at 495. Thus, the source would be subjected to another set of standards besides those set in the source state pursuant to the Clean Water Act. However, the Court determined that the injured individual was not without remedy in that a court sitting in the affected (or source) state could apply the source state's nuisance law. The decision effectively holds that the Clean Water Act preempts the affected state's nuisance law, to the extent that it seeks to impose liability on a point source in another state. The dissent responded that no language in the Clean Water Act requires such a result and that the majority failed to consider the conflict of law principles that determine which state's tort law should apply in interstate tort suits.

The Supreme Court also has held that while a downstream state's water quality standards set under the Clean Water Act do not apply to discharges in an upstream polluting state, those standards can be applied to the discharger if they have been incorporated in an NPDES permit issued by the EPA. Arkansas v. Oklahoma, 503 U.S. 91, 112 S.Ct. 1046, 117 L.Ed.2d 239 (1992), *infra* p. 966. This does not apply to the permitting process that is used in most places, where states have been delegated the authority to issue permits.

Violation of an applicable water quality standard or effluent limitation is often asserted as a basis for nuisance or other tort liability. See generally Note, *Water Quality Standards in Private Nuisance Actions,* 79 Yale L.J. 102 (1969). Compliance with applicable standards has not historically been a defense to a nuisance action. Urie v. Franconia Paper Corp., 107 N.H. 131, 218 A.2d 360 (1966); Tiegs v. Watts, 135 Wash.2d 1, 954 P.2d 877 (1998). California's Civil Code mandates that "[n]othing which is done or maintained under the express authority of a statute can be deemed a nuisance." Cal. Civ. Code § 3482 (West 1997). Despite this language, California courts have limited the effect of the statute and continued to follow the historical rule. Varjabedian v. City of Madera, 20 Cal.3d 285, 142 Cal.Rptr. 429, 572 P.2d 43, 47 (1977). In *Varjabedian*, the court stated that a statute must expressly sanction a nuisance for immunity to exist. Why? See Frank I. Michelman, *Pollution as a Tort: A Non–Accidental Perspective on Calabresi's Costs,* 80 Yale L.J. 647 (1971). State standards and effluent limitations were not very strict until the passage of the Clean Water Act. See *supra* p. 673. Now they are, and compliance with nationally applicable NPDES permit requirements of the Act may raise a stronger defense. *E.g.*, Birchwood Lakes Colony Club, Inc. v. Borough of Medford Lakes, 90 N.J. 582, 449 A.2d 472 (1982); Jordan v. City of Santa Barbara, 46 Cal.App.4th 1245, 54 Cal.Rptr.2d 340 (1996) (city not liable for discharges consistent with NPDES permit alleged to increase channel vegetation growth in part because plaintiff's agricultural runoff contributed to the growth).

2.   FEDERAL CONTROL AND CLEAN-UP OF GROUNDWATER CONTAMINATION

The common law of torts provides four primary theories of recovery for groundwater contamination: (1) trespass, (2) nuisance, (3) strict liability, and (4) the intentional discharge of contamination. Plaintiffs with a strong case of cause in fact can generally find a theory on which to try the case, but courts have increasingly modified common law doctrines to make recovery of damages more difficult.

Trespass is an attractive theory of recovery because it does not require proof of damage to plaintiff or his or her property as opposed to proof of interference with the right to exclude. *E.g.*, Scribner v. Summers, 84 F.3d 554 (2d Cir.1996). However, courts have imposed a number of barriers to trespass claims. These include the requirement that plaintiff demonstrate that the contamination interferes with a reasonable and foreseeable use of the subsurface, Chance v. BP Chemicals, Inc., 77 Ohio St.3d 17, 670 N.E.2d 985 (1996), or the invasion must be intentional rather than the result of negligence or an abnormally dangerous condition. Rudd v. Electrolux Corp., 982 F.Supp. 355 (M.D.N.C.1997). See also United Proteins, Inc. v. Farmland Indust., Inc., 259 Kan. 725, 915 P.2d 80 (1996).

Because a nuisance is the substantial interference with the use and enjoyment of another's property, it does not require proof of negligence. Wood v. Picillo, 443 A.2d 1244 (R.I.1982). Some courts allow a plaintiff to prove unreasonable interference by showing a violation of state pollution standards; compare Branch v. Western Petroleum, Inc., 657 P.2d 267 (Utah 1982) and Snyder Ranches, Inc. v. Oil Conservation Comm'n, 110 N.M. 637, 798 P.2d 587 (1990), with *Rudd v. Electrolux Corp, supra.*

Strict liability is the primary basis for the recovery of damages for groundwater contamination. The injection of toxic wastes in an aquifer which contaminates domestic wells has been held to be an abnormally dangerous activity in a number of states. The leading cases include *Branch v. Western Petroleum, supra*, and State v. Ventron Corp., 94 N.J. 254, 463 A.2d 893 (1983). England, however, rejected the theory for past industrial activities. Cambridge Water Co. v. Eastern Counties Leather PLC, 2 A.C. 264 (1993).

Similarly, property owners whose property was near but not over a contaminated plume have argued that they should be awarded stigma damages for the lost property value from the fear of contamination. Courts have divided on the legitimacy of these damages. Compare Adams v. Star Enter., 51 F.3d 417 (4th Cir.1995) (Virginia requires a physical perception of harmful activity), with Lewis v. General Elec. Co., 37 F.Supp.2d 55 (D.Mass.1999) (plaintiffs may recover damages for fear of contracting cancer from contaminated wells if it is more likely than not that the disease will occur). Further complicating recovery, Daubert v. Merrell Dow Pharm., Inc., 509 U.S. 579, 113 S.Ct. 2786, 125 L.Ed.2d 469 (1993), requires federal courts to screen scientific testimony to determine if it is legitimate. The net effect of the decision has been the exclusion of a great deal of evidence needed to prove injury in contamination suits.

Several federal statutory programs deal at least indirectly with groundwater contamination. The effect of regulation, however, is to impose a further dimension of control upon the use of the resource in order to protect the public's interest in it. Federal statutes focus on the protection of public drinking water supplies and on the prevention of groundwater contamination from specific sources. Most pollutants are introduced into groundwater from wastes that have been disposed of in landfills, that percolate from above the ground, or that are injected into the aquifer directly.

The Clean Water Act, controls primarily surface water pollution. Although sections of the Act direct the Environmental Protection Agency (EPA) to cooperate with federal and state agencies to develop programs to control groundwater contamination, the operative provisions of the Act do not directly deal with groundwater. The Act is implemented through a permitting system that is described *supra* p. 675. Permits are required for discharges of pollutants from "point sources" like pipes, but not for pollution from seepage, runoff and other diffused sources. Even deep-well injections are not regulated as "point sources" under the Clean Water Act. Exxon Corp. v. Train, 554 F.2d 1310 (5th Cir.1977). The courts are divided on whether discharges into groundwater connected to surface waters may be point source discharges. Compare Mutual Life Ins. Co. of New York v. Mobil Corp., 1998 WL 160820 (N.D.N.Y.1998) with Umatilla Waterquality Protective Ass'n v. Smith Frozen Foods, Inc., 962 F.Supp. 1312 (D.Or. 1997).

The Safe Drinking Water Act, 42 U.S.C.A. §§ 300f to 300j–26 (West 2009), provides special protection for groundwater quality. The EPA sets end-of-the-pipe standards for public drinking water systems, determines standards for state underground waste injection control (UIC) programs, and designates "sole source aquifers." The heart of the system is the establishment of maximum contaminant goals, maximum contaminant levels, and national primary drinking water regulations. Maximum contaminant goals "shall be set at the level at which no known or anticipated adverse effects on the health of persons occur and which allows an adequate margin of safety." 42 U.S.C.A. § 300g–1(b)(4)(A) (West Supp. 2008). National primary drinking water regulations are based on maximum contaminant levels, which must be as close to the goal "as is feasible." However, these stringent levels may be lowered if the federal Environmental Protection Agency Administrator performs a risk assessment and benefit-cost analysis and publishes a maximum contaminant level that maximizes health benefits "at a cost that is justified by the benefits." § 300g–1(6)(A). This section was added in the 1996 Amendments to the Act and reflects an effort to incorporate risk assessment and limited benefit-cost analysis into the stringent health protection standards that EPA is authorized to adopt. The maximum contaminant goals and levels also can be adopted as clean up standards under section 121 of CERCLA. After designation of an aquifer as a drinking water source, no federal funds or other financial assistance may be used for activities that the EPA determines may contaminate the aquifer "through a recharge zone so as to create a public health hazard." 42 U.S.C.A. § 300h–3(e) (West Supp. 2008). See generally Linda A. Malone, *The Necessary Interrelationship Between Land Use and Preservation of Groundwater Resources,* 9 UCLA J. Envtl. L. & Pol'y 1 (1990).

The Safe Drinking Water Act Amendments of 1986, Pub. L. No. 99–339 100 Stat. 642 (1986) (codified as 42 U.S.C.A. §§ 300f–300j–11), require the states to prepare wellhead protection programs to protect areas surrounding wells used for public water systems from contaminants that may have adverse health effects. EPA, however, cannot impose a program if the state fails to submit one. Wellhead protection programs do not require the states to allocate or regulate the use of ground and surface waters so as to protect drinking water sources. See 42 U.S.C.A. § 300h–7(j) (West 1991). The amendments do provide grants to enable states and local governments to prepare comprehensive management plans for designated sole source aquifers.

Most federal and state efforts under the UIC provisions of the Act have focused on the regulation of Class II wells, those for the production of oil, gas, or geothermal resources. States have expanded the jurisdiction of their oil and gas conservation agencies to identify vulnerable groundwater areas and to regulate the disposal of fluids, usually salt water, produced or used in connection with mineral extraction. To allow uranium mining, EPA exempted 3,000 acres of the Chadron aquifer not currently used for drinking water. This exemption was upheld in Western Nebraska Res. Council v. United States Environmental Protection Agency, 943 F.2d 867 (8th Cir.1991), but the court noted that any migration of contaminants that injured wells outside of the carefully drawn exempt area would be a violation of the permit. Some states have gone beyond the Safe Drinking Water Act and have required permits for the direct or indirect discharge of contaminants into groundwater. *E.g.,* N.M. Stat. Ann. § 74–6–5 (with an exemption for discharges from irrigated agriculture). See generally Roger K. Ferland, *The Protection of Groundwater Quality in the Western States– Regulatory Alternatives and the Mining Industry,* 29 Rocky Mtn. Min. L. Inst. 899 (1983).

Two federal statutes protect groundwater from contamination by releases of hazardous substances. The Resource Conservation and Recovery Act (RCRA) of 1976, 42 U.S.C.A. §§ 6901–6987 (West Supp. 2008), sets up a "cradle-to-grave" system to track wastes from their generation, through transportation, to treatment, storage, or disposal. RCRA originally was not technology-forcing, and allowed the disposal of wastes without treatment or chemical alteration so long as a facility complied with EPA regulations. In 1984, RCRA was amended to prohibit the land disposal of hazardous wastes unless the EPA Administrator determines that prohibition is not necessary for public health protection. 42 U.S.C.A. § 6924(d). Before issuing a permit, EPA must determine that land disposal will be protective of human health for as long as the waste remains hazardous. Deep well injection of hazardous wastes is also extensively regulated under RCRA. Wastes must be pretreated to reduce toxicity. See Chemical Waste Mgmt., Inc. v. United States Environmental Protection Agency, 976 F.2d 2 (D.C.Cir.1992) (dilution may constitute treatment, but only if no hazardous constituents are present following the dilution that would endanger human health or the environment).

The Comprehensive Environmental Response, Compensation, and Liability Act (CERCLA or "Superfund") of 1980, 42 U.S.C.A. §§ 9601–9675 (West Supp. 2008), is not a regulatory statute but an act that allows federal, state, tribal, and local governments to bring suit against parties responsible for the unsafe disposal of hazardous wastes. Most of the damage caused by such disposal is to groundwater. The statute imposes liability on current and past owners or operators, generators who arranged for wastes to be taken to the site, and transporters. 42 U.S.C.A. § 9607(a). Liability has been held to be strict (United States v. Northeastern Pharm. & Chem. Co., 579 F.Supp. 823 (W.D.Mo.1984)), retroactive (United States v. Shell Oil Co., 605 F.Supp. 1064 (D.Colo.1985)), and joint and several. However, more recent cases allow a party to escape joint and several liability if there is a reasonable basis for apportioning liability. See *In re Bell Petroleum Serv.*, 3 F.3d 889 (5th Cir.1993) and U.S. v. Burlington Northern & Santa Fe Ry. Co., 520 F.3d 918 (9th Cir. 2008), cert. granted ___ U.S.___, 129 S.Ct. 30 (2008).

The rights of a party who incurs cleanup costs to seek contribution from other PRPs were limited in Cooper Industries, Inc. v. Aviall, 543 U.S. 157, 125 S.Ct. 577, 160 L.Ed.2d 548 (2004), which holds that Section 113 allows such suits only after a civil cleanup action has been filed by the federal government or a state. Prior to *Cooper Industries*, courts recognized private cost recovery actions under Section 107 for parties who "voluntarily" clean up a site in anticipation of civil cleanup action. Since the case courts have split on the availability of these actions. Compare Consolidated Edison Co. of New York v. UGI Util., Inc., 423 F.3d 90 (2d Cir. 2005) with E.I. DuPont De Nemours and Co. v. United States, 460 F.3d 515 (3d Cir. 2006).

The prima facie case for a Superfund action is a "release" from a "facility." 42 U.S.C.A. § 9607 (West 1995). Proof of a release requires a showing that a substance has begun to contaminate the soil or water in and around a site. See New York v. Shore Realty Corp., 759 F.2d 1032 (2d Cir.1985).

CERCLA allows three basic actions to clean up a hazardous waste site: (1) removal; (2) remedial action; and (3) abatement of an imminent hazard. A removal action may either be a short-term emergency response or a longer term planned removal. Remedial actions are long-term remedies that are designed to produce a permanent clean-up such as the restoration of an aquifer. CERCLA initially contained no statutory standards to determine the appropriate clean-up level. Decisions were made solely on a site-by-site basis. Congress imposed clean-up standards in the 1986 Superfund Amendment and Reauthorization Act.

It is generally conceded that it is too costly to clean up all hazardous waste sites. Enormous sums of money may be spent to achieve solutions that are not permanent and often merely transfer the risks from one community to another. The 1986 Superfund Reauthorization Amendments addressed this problem by requiring that the President (through EPA) select, to the maximum extent practicable, remedies that utilize permanent solutions and alternative treatment or resource recovery technologies that will result in a permanent and significant decrease in the toxicity, mobility, or volume of a hazardous substance or contaminant. Superfund Amendments and Reauthorization Act of 1986, Pub. L. No. 99–499, 1986 U.S.C.C.A.N. (100 Stat.) 1672 (codified as amended in scattered sections of 10, 26, & 42 U.S.C.A.).

Although many reforms have been effected since the passage of the 1986 Amendments, CERCLA remains the target of extensive criticism. The many criticisms of CERCLA generally concern the length of time to remediate sites, the high costs of remediation, and the stringency of the cleanup standards. See generally David B. Spence, *Imposing Individual Liability as a Legislative Policy Choice: Holmesian "Intuitions" and Superfund Reform*, 93 Nw. U. L. Rev. 389 (1999); Alex Geisinger, *Rethinking Risk–Based Environmental Cleanup*, 76 Ind. L.J. 367 (2001); Janet S. Herman, et al., *Groundwater Ecosystems and the Service of Water Purification*, 20 Stan. Envtl. L.J. 479 (2001). In 1995, the Superfund tax on the chemical industry expired, depriving the government of a substantial and stable source of funding for cleanups. Since then the program has been supported by annual appropriations and the recovery of clean up costs. Both sources have declined steeply since 2002.

Attorney General v. Thomas Solvent Co.

Court of Appeals of Michigan, 1985.
146 Mich.App. 55, 380 N.W.2d 53.

■ T. M. BURNS, PRESIDING JUDGE.

Defendant Thomas Solvent Company (hereinafter defendant) appeals by leave granted from an order of the trial court granting a preliminary injunction to abate a public nuisance pursuant to GCR 1963, 782, now MCR 3.601.

In September, 1981, public health officials discovered that the water drawn from 10 to 30 wells which supply water to the City of Battle Creek were contaminated with toxic organic chemicals. Similar contaminants were also found in even higher concentrations in approximately 80 nearby private residential water supply wells. The 30 wells which supply the City of Battle Creek with its water are located in the Verona Well Field which is located just north of the defendant's facility. The private residential wells which are contaminated are located approximately 800 feet northwest of defendant's facilities.

Defendant is engaged in the business of selling industrial solvents and other chemicals and transporting liquid waste to recycling and disposal facilities. Defendant maintains two facilities in the Battle Creek area, the Raymond Road Facility and the Emmett Street Facility. Both of these facilities are located in Emmett Township, Calhoun County, and are a short distance from the Verona Well Field and the contaminated private wells.

At these two facilities, defendant stores a number of industrial solvents in 55–gallon drums. Defendant also has a number of underground tanks on these facilities in which defendant stores such solvents as xylene, toluene, trichloroethylene, perchloroethylene, and 1–1–1 trichloroethane, among others. Defendant uses hoses to transfer these chemicals in the underground tanks to other underground tanks and to trucks.

From 1981 through 1982, a number of soil and water samples were taken from the Verona Well Field area and defendant's facilities sites. Tests were performed with these samples by several federal, state and private agencies, including the United States Environmental Protection Agency (EPA), Michigan Department of Natural Resources (DNR), Michigan Department of Public Health and a Chicago-based technical assistance team known as Ecology and Environment Incorporated. From these tests, officials discovered the existence of a high level of toxic contaminants in the wells and on defendant's property. Accordingly, the EPA designated the Battle Creek Verona Well Field as a "superfund" site on its national priority list under 42 U.S.C. § 9601 *et seq.*

Because of the strong correlation between the types of contaminants found in the soil at both the Raymond Facility and the Emmett Street Facility, and the types of solvents and chemicals discovered in the wells downstream from defendant's site, it was determined by plaintiffs that defendant was at least partially responsible for the groundwater pollution. Therefore, on January 12, 1984, plaintiffs filed the instant complaint against defendant seeking a preliminary injunction, damages, and penalties. Plaintiffs' complaint alleged that defendant had violated § 6(a) and § 7 of the water resources commission act, M.C.L. § 323.1 *et seq.*; M.S.A. § 3.521 *et seq.*, Thomas J. Anderson, Gordon Rockwell Environmental Protection Act, M.C.L. § 691.1201 *et seq.*; M.S.A. § 14.528(201) *et seq.*, and had unlawfully committed a common-law public nuisance.

The trial court held hearings pursuant to GCR 1963, 782, in February, March and April, 1984. On May 2, 1984, the trial court issued a preliminary injunction after finding that an immediate threat of potentially irreparable harm to the public health existed at the defendant's two Battle Creek facilities and that immediate correction was necessary to remove the contaminants from the ground water, stop encroachment of the contaminants onto unpolluted land, and halt the hydrological movement of the contaminated water beneath the two facilities owned by defendant. The order required defendant to install two ground water purge wells and two monitoring wells and to treat all purged ground water with a granular activated carbon filtration system. The order also contained requirements as to the operation of the purge well and treatment system, including the requirements that defendant engage in frequent water sampling and testing procedures. Finally, the order specifically allowed either party to petition the court to modify the purge well and treatment system as necessary.

We note that, while the trial court proceedings were pending, defendant filed a petition under Chapter 11 of the Bankruptcy Code in the United States Bankruptcy Court for the Western District of Michigan. After a hearing, the bankruptcy court determined that the entry of the circuit court's preliminary injunction did not violate the automatic stay provision of the Bankruptcy Code. Subsequently, however, the bankruptcy court issued a preliminary injunction, enjoining all further proceedings to enforce the circuit court's preliminary injunction. While the bankruptcy court's injunction may make this appeal moot, defendant does not provide us with a copy of the bankruptcy court's order. The parties also do not argue that this appeal is moot. Since the validity of the bankruptcy court's injunction is seriously in question, we will consider the merits of this case.

* * *

Contrary to defendant's assertions, the trial court carefully considered the defendant's ability to pay for the clean-up. We specifically note that the trial court did not order the most costly clean-up procedures requested by plaintiff, but instead ordered more conservative measures.

We do not feel that the trial court abused its discretion. Plaintiff's experts testified that the ground water contaminated by defendant's facilities contained extremely high levels of pollutants such as 53,000 parts per billion of TCE, 78,000 parts per billion of PCE, 8,300 parts per billion of dichloroethane, and 1,700 parts per billion of carbon tetrachloride. According to the experts, the presence of these contaminants establish the existence of an emergency situation which had to be stopped immediately to prevent nearby areas from becoming contaminated. These experts also testified that exposure to these chemicals posed substantial risks to individuals including the significant increased risk of developing cancer, detrimental effects on the liver and kidneys, muscular uncoordination, the development of fluid in the lungs, and intoxicating effects such as problems with balance and behavioral changes. Some of these chemicals were also flammable. It is clear that the record supports the trial court's finding that defendant's financial harm was outweighed by the public's health risk.
* * *

* * * There was ample evidence that the toxic substances which contaminated the wells in question flow through the ground water from the defendant's facilities. Defendant's claim that a finding of nuisance was unsupported by the evidence is merely speculation. While there were two other suspected sources contributing to the wells' contamination, there was a well-defined plume of contaminants leaving defendant's property. * * *

Defendant next argues that the circuit court lacked jurisdiction in this matter. First defendant claims that the passage of the Comprehensive Environmental Response, Compensation and Liability Act (CERCLA), 42 U.S.C. § 9601 *et seq.*, directly preempted state law governing the abatement of public nuisances and, therefore, according to defendant, the circuit court in this matter did not have jurisdiction to hear the case. In the alternative, defendant argues that, even if CERCLA did not expressly preempt state law, application of the primary jurisdiction doctrine necessitates a conclusion that the circuit court was required to defer jurisdiction to the EPA.

With regard to its preemption argument, defendant relies primarily upon 42 U.S.C. § 9614(a), which states that nothing in the statute shall be construed as to preempt any state from imposing any "additional liability" or requirement with respect to the release of hazardous substances within that state. We however do not read isolated portions of statutes out of context. A plain reading of § 9614 shows that, instead of preempting state law, that statute provides that states may supplement any liability or requirements that may be imposed under CERCLA. Section 9614 does not state that the individual states are precluded from duplicating liability imposed under CERCLA. Defendant's reliance upon that provision is therefore misplaced. Moreover, § 9606(a) expressly provides that jurisdiction over pollution abatement actions is vested in both the states and local governments and in the President of the United States and his delegates. Both state and federal governments therefore have concurrent jurisdictions over pollution abatement cases. CERCLA was primarily enacted to fill gaps left by earlier federal legislation in dealing with abandoned dump sites and was intended to provide funds for state hazardous waste programs. *Jones v. Inmont Corp.*, 584 F.Supp. 1425, 1428 (S.D.Ohio 1984). It is clear that CERCLA was intended only to supplement hazardous waste programs and not to preempt state programs.

Defendant also claims that, since the EPA is better equipped to handle this case, the trial court should have deferred jurisdiction to the EPA. During the bankruptcy proceeding, an EPA agent testified that, as a result of the circuit court's preliminary injunction, there is no longer an emergency situation regarding the possible contamination of groundwater surrounding defendant's facilities. Since the agency which defendant now claims should control this action admits that the circuit court's actions were proper, we decline to apply the doctrine of primary jurisdiction to this case. In light of the resources of the EPA and the demands on that agency, we do not feel that it would be proper to transfer sole jurisdiction of this matter to the EPA. The circuit court had jurisdiction and properly issued the preliminary injunction.

Affirmed.

NOTES

1. *Measure of Damages.* States and local governments not only have remedies under CERCLA to recover damages for clean-up costs and to obtain equitable relief, but may recover "damages for injury to, destruction of, or loss of natural resources." 42 U.S.C.A. § 9607(a)(4)(C) (West 1995). Natural resources are broadly defined to include "land, fish, wildlife, biota, air, water, ground water, drinking water supplies, and other such resources." 42 U.S.C.A. § 9601(16) (West Supp. 2008). What is the measure of damages? The value of the lost resources or the costs of the restoring the contaminated resource? Initially the Department of Inter, charged with adopting rules, allowed a court to choose the lesser of lost use values or restoration costs. Ohio v. United States Department of Interior, 880 F.2d 432 (D.C.Cir. 1989), invalidated the rule because the statute expressed a preference for restoration. The revised rules were upheld in Kennecott Utah Copper Corp. v. Department of Interior, 88 F.3d 1191 (D.C.Cir. 1996).

2. *Multiple Actors.* Suppose that a plaintiff is injured by several dischargers acting independently. Is each tortfeasor responsible only for the damages caused by that tortfeasor, so that the plaintiff must prove the damage attributable to each discharge? The leading case, Landers v. East Texas Salt Water Disposal Co., 151 Tex. 251, 248 S.W.2d 731 (1952), holds that justice requires that a plaintiff be able to join independent tortfeasors and places the burden of apportioning the wrong on them. The issue of joint and several liability is a major one under CERCLA. See discussion *supra* p. 691. Liability is strict and retroactive. Under the Act, parties with remote connections to a hazardous waste site are potentially responsible for damages. Joint and several liability is the presumptive rule for all contributors to a "superfund" site. United States v. Gurley Refining Co., 788 F.Supp. 1473 (E.D.Ark.1992); B.F. Goodrich Co. v. Murtha, 958 F.2d 1192 (2d Cir.1992); United States v. A & N Cleaners & Launderers, Inc., 788 F.Supp. 1317 (S.D.N.Y.1992). Several decisions allow defendants to apportion their liability based on their individual waste contribution, *In re* Bell Petroleum Services, Inc., 3 F.3d 889 (5th Cir.1993), and a right of contribution among defendants, Colorado v. ASARCO, Inc., 608 F.Supp. 1484 (D.Colo.1985).

3. *How Much is Contaminated Water Worth?* How should societies decide how much an aquifer or a restored stream is worth? If no water right holder or other user is injured, does the resource have any value? It may have no present market value, but does it follow that it has no economic value? There is wide acceptance of the proposition that public resources may have "real" non-market economic values such as non-use, existence, or option values. Economists are attempting to value the demand for these resource uses by techniques such as contingent valuation. See Ronald C. Cummings et al., Valuing Environmental Goods: An Assessment of the Contingent Valuation Method (1986). Contingent valuation generally asks selected people how much they would be willing to pay for an improvement in the quality of a specific resource. Contingent valuation is controversial because any exchange of money is "virtual." For arguments that contingent valuation is too flawed for use in natural resource damage assessments, see Heyde, Comment, is Contingent Valuation Worth the Trouble?, 62 U. Chi. L. Rev. 331 (1995) and Note, "Ask a Silly Question ...": Contingent Valuation of Natural Resource Damages, 105 Harv. L. Rev.

1981 (1992). Most critiques object to CV's bias in favor of resource protection. However, Mark Sagoff, The Economy of the Earth: Philosophy, Law, and the Environment (2nd ed. 2008), argues that the choice to preserve is a legitimate political value choice. Thus, we should not package decisions in the language of economics because it creates the illusion of an objective, value-free choice. Even if contingent valuation is a legitimate indicator of economic value, can it be applied to all natural resources? For example, does a contaminated aquifer have the same non-use values as the Grand Canyon? See National Research Council, Valuing Ground Water: Economic Concepts and Approaches (1997). Contingent valuation can be used in the calculation of natural resource damages after a Blue Ribbon panel of economists endorsed the concept in 1992.

In deciding between diminution in value and restoration as the measure of damages, what assumptions about the future value of the aquifer should be made? Traditionally, economists have assumed a constant value for crops grown with groundwater and thus have put a high discount rate on the future value. The benefits of an immediate clean-up therefore are generally small compared to the costs. However, if the value of crops grown from the aquifer is expected to increase, the equation changes dramatically, easily offsetting the discount rate. A 1992 study showed that the growth in value of specialty crops supported the conclusion that the expense of cleaning up groundwater salinity immediately was justified even if the most unfavorable discount rate set by some economists was used. Richard E. Howitt, *Putting a Price on Ground Water Quality*, in Proceedings, Changing Practices in Ground Water Management—the Pros and Cons of Regulation 31 (University of California Water Resources Center, Report No. 77, 1992). The valuation of a contaminated aquifer with unappropriated water and the value of expert testimony to measure the value were extensively discussed in two pre-trial opinions. New Mexico v. General Electric Co., 335 F.Supp.2d 1185 and 335 F.Supp.2d 1266 (D.N.M. 2004).

Both the assessment of the damages of a degraded ecosystem or the cost of its restoration rest on the same assumption: ecosystems provide valuable services to human kind. In recent years, the cataloging and valuation of these services has emerged as a major justification for the various forms of ecosystem conservation. E.g., Nature's Services: Societal Dependence on Natural Ecosystems (Gretchen Daily ed. 1997) and Millennium Ecosystem Assessment, Living Beyond Our Means: Natural Assets and Human Well–Being (2005). Estimates of the value of these services can yield high numbers to off-set the costs of many environmental regulatory programs. But, is this utilitarian rationale superior to alternative rationales such as the recognition of rights for flora and fauna or the argument that all conservation choices are political choices which cannot be reduced to an economic calculus? For a strong no answer to this question see Mark Sagoff, Price, Principle, and the Environment 135–144 (2007). As Kennecott Copper indicates ecosystem services can be considered as a bi-product of existing regulatory programs. Students of the theory of ecosystem services also recommend that markets be created so that the beneficiaries can pay the providers for the continued production of the service. See J. B.

Ruhl, Steven E. Kraft and Christopher L. Lant, The Law and Policy of Ecosystem Services (2007).

4. *Actually Recovering Natural Resource* Damages. Relatively few natural resource damage awards have been issued. Utah v. Kennecott Corp., 801 F.Supp. 553 (D. Utah 1992), set aside a consent degree for contaminated groundwater from Kennecott's mine west of Salt Lake City. As part of a negotiated settlement of its liability, Kennecott agreed to pay the state $11.7 million in natural resource damages in return for a promise that the state would not sue the company under common law, Utah or federal law for natural resource damages or other remediation costs for the contaminated aquifer. The court found the consent degree deficient because:

> It appears to the court that the area of contamination is not now nor in the future will continue to be neatly contained within water area eight which was identified in the Utah State Engineer's Interim Ground–Water Management Plan and adopted by the State and Kennecott as the Mining Impact Area. There is no physical barrier to prevent the contaminated waters from spreading or moving. Because of the dynamic nature of the plumes in question, it is likely that the area of contamination will shift, spread out and continue to grow larger.

> 2. Determination Regarding the Infeasibility of Restoration

> The State and Kennecott presented evidence that it would be onerous and extremely costly to pump and treat the heavy metals within the low pH plume. Mr. Alkema testified on behalf of the State that pumping the ground water and cleaning it would be unworkable. * * *

> SLCWCD presented expert testimony to the effect that reverse osmosis would be feasible to remediate a portion of the plume. * * *

> The State ultimately may be proven correct in having concluded that it would be infeasible to restore the contaminated waters. However, such finding may well be in error because the State failed to require completion of studies which were begun, and failed to identify and fully discuss possible alternatives for plume remediation and restoration.

> * * *

> It appears to the court that while substantial source remediation has occurred, much more needs to be done. Yet, there is no specific requirement for such set forth in the proposed Consent Decree.

> * * *

> 5. Measure of Damages

> Mr. Alkema testified that the State evaluated the following methods of damage assessment: loss of value, cost of treatment, and replacement. With regard to the loss of value method, Mr. Alkema characterized it as "a market value method" that "looks at the value of the resource strictly as a sale of water rights versus what that overall impact may be to the public." As to the cost of treatment method, Mr. Alkema said that it involved the cost of "pumping water from the mining impact

area and treating it and then using it as a drinking water supply."
* * *

Mr. Alkema testified that the cost of replacement method of damage involves "purchasing water rights for water of comparable quality that would have been there." * * *

It is clear that the loss of value or loss of use method of evaluation was regarded by the State as strictly a market value method of computing damages. In this regard, neither Kennecott nor the State presented evidence of damages suffered by the State for loss of use other than estimated market value of the 13,000 acre feet. No amounts were presented as to existence and option values or damages. Existence value is derived from the satisfaction of simply knowing that a natural resource exists, even if no use occurs. Option value is the value associated with an individual's desire to preserve the option to use the natural resource, even if it is not currently being used. * * *

It appears to the court that the State prematurely utilized the "loss of value" measure of damages since it had not developed sufficient facts to justify its conclusion that the contaminated plumes could not be remediated. In any event, it appears that the loss of value method was not correctly applied. In this regard, the State purported to utilize the loss of value method in determining damages to its ground water resources, but it actually utilized a strictly market value approach, based upon water quantity measured by safe annual yield. Other use and non-use values apart from market value, including option and existence values, were regarded as inapplicable. Failure to take into account damages such as loss of the aquifer apart from market value of the quantity of water the State determined to be contaminated resulted in an inadequate assessment of damages under the loss of use method.

* * *

II. LEGAL ANALYSIS

* * *

The court has determined from a preponderance of the evidence at the hearing that the settlement contained within the proposed Consent decree is deficient in at least three major respects. *First,* lack of sufficient foundation for the State's determination that its ground water natural resource cannot be restored. *Second,* failure to require substantial protection of State natural resources from further contamination. *Third,* failure to apply the proper measure of damages, which resulted in failure adequately to take into account the extent of the damages the State has suffered and will suffer as a result of the contamination. Failure to develop sufficient factual foundation to support the State's determination that contaminated ground waters cannot be restored requires that the proposed Consent Decree be rejected for failure to demonstrate that the remedial purposes CERCLA was intended to achieve cannot be achieved. Failure to mandate containment and management of the contaminated waters, and failure to require further source control does not comport with the CERCLA requirement to "*protect* and restore." * * *

* * * The State simply failed to assess the non-consumptive use values of the aquifer, *i.e.,* option and existence values.*

It appears to the court that significant additional possible damages such as loss of the aquifer are not provided for in the proposed Consent Decree, even assuming that loss of value ultimately is determined to be the proper standard. Moreover, the State failed to calculate into the settlement the costs of preventing the plumes from spreading and contaminating the remaining unspoiled portion of the aquifer, by pumping water or other methods. In addition, the State did not require that the settlement include the cost of further source control which would at least lessen contamination from continuing on a daily basis. Apparently, the State clings to the possibility of future plume remediation to be ordered by EPA. That possibility is not a justifiable reason for the State to fail to adequately study possible alternatives or to fail to require a covenant to "protect and restore" State owned natural resources. In this regard, the settlement as proposed does not "capture fully all aspects of the loss." *Ohio,* 880 F.2d at 463.

This court concludes that inadequate consideration of damages requires that the proposed Consent Decree be rejected for failure to demonstrate to the court the existence of substantive fairness under CERCLA.

5. *Hot Glowing Groundwater.* Other federal statutes directly or indirectly affect groundwater quality. For instance, the Nuclear Waste Policy Act designated Yucca Mountain, Nevada as the sole area to be evaluated as a repository for radioactive waste. 42 U.S.C.A. § 10133(a) (West 1995). As one might except, Nevada has fought federal efforts, and as 2008, no wastes have been desposited in the site. See County of Esmeralda v. United States Dep't of Energy, 925 F.2d 1216 (9th Cir.1991) (Department of Defense acted arbitrarily in refusing to identify Inyo County, California as a potentially affected unit of government in the evaluation even though it shared an aquifer with Yucca Mountain). See also, Nuclear Energy Institute, Inc. v. EPA, 373 F.3d 1251 (D.C.Cir. 2004). EPA adopted a rule which required the Department of Energy to ensure for 10,000 years after disposal individuals living near the site receive no more than a very small dose of radiation. The court set it aside because Congress specifically mandated EPA to set a standard consistent with the findings of the National Academy of Science and the NAS report concluded that there was "no scientific basis for limiting the time period of the individual-risk standard to 10,000 years or any other value." 373 F.3d at 1267. In 2008,

---

*And reflect upon this bit of wisdom from Albert Einstein: "Make everything as   simple as possible, but not more so." [Eds.]

EPA established new rules with up to a million-year horizon for radiation exposure [40 C.F.R. Part 197 (2008)].

C. "Waters of the United States": Wetlands and Small Streams

History shows that border lands are the most likely to experience violent conflict or prolonged disputes over territorial sovereignty. The same holds for federal regulation of wetlands and small streams. The root of the problem is 19th century Supreme Court jurisprudence with the exercise of the Commerce Clause limited to the regulation of "navigable waters." One of the federal government's earliest ventures into the regulation of activities relating to water was in the Rivers and Harbors Act of 1899 mentioned in Appalachian Power, *infra* p. 802. The act restated some earlier laws, the purpose of which was to prevent obstructions to navigation. The Act today states that:

> The creation of any obstruction not affirmatively authorized by Congress, to the navigable capacity of any of the waters of the United States is prohibited; and it shall not be lawful to build [any structure in any port,] navigable river, or other water of the United States * * * except on plans [authorized by the Corps of Engineers]; and it shall not be lawful to excavate or fill, or in any manner to alter or modify the course, location, condition, or capacity of, any port * * * or of the channel of any navigable water of the United States, unless the work has been [authorized by the Corps of Engineers]. * * *

> It shall not be lawful to throw, discharge, or deposit, or cause, suffer, or procure to be thrown, discharged, or deposited material of any kind in any place on the bank of any navigable water, or on the bank of any tributary of any navigable water, where the same shall be liable to be washed into such navigable water, either by ordinary or high tides, or by storms or floods, or otherwise, whereby navigation shall or may be impeded or obstructed * * *.

33 U.S.C.A. §§ 403, 407 (West Supp.2008). Consistent with its mission of promoting commercial navigation, the Corps historically required permits for bridges, dams, dikes, causeways, and obstructions in "large" navigable waters. (In 1966, when the Department of Transportation was created, responsibility for bridges and causeways was turned over to that agency.) The Corps' permitting authority under § 10 of the Act for any activity or structure that would obstruct navigation, and § 9 which requires permission for "any bridge, dam, dike, or causeway over or in" navigable water of the United States was and is a powerful means of regulating water development and water related activities within states. The exercise of the Corps' authority was limited to situations in which a waterway met tests of navigability as set forth in The Daniel Ball, 77 U.S. 557, 19 L.Ed. 999 (1870), quoted *supra* p. 403. Harbor lines were designated and no obstruc-

tions were permitted seaward of the harbor line, but riparians could fill (but not dredge) almost as a matter of right landward of the line.

At the start of the environmental movement in the 1960s, the Act was invigorated as a precursor of the substantial federal role in environmental protection because it was the only legal basis for direct federal regulation of discharges of pollution. In 1968, the Corps expanded its historic jurisdiction and promulgated regulations that allowed it to consider environmental factors in its permit decisions in response to growing criticisms that the former policy was destroying too many wetlands. The regulations were challenged when the Corps denied a permit to dredge and fill in Boca Ciega Bay, Florida after finding that fish and wildlife would be harmed, but that the project would not adversely affect navigation. The Corps' authority to deny dredge and fill permits "for factually substantial ecological reasons even though the project would not interfere with navigation, flood control, or the production of power" was upheld in Zabel v. Tabb, 430 F.2d 199, 203 (5th Cir.1970), cert. denied 401 U.S. 910, 91 S.Ct. 873, 27 L.Ed.2d 808 (1971). It would be hard to read the 1899 Act as a delegation of this broad power, so the court chose to rest its decision primarily on the Fish and Wildlife Coordination Act, 16 U.S.C.A. §§ 661–668ee (West Supp. 2008), which mandated the Secretary "to weigh the effect a dredge and fill permit will have on conservation."

A provision of the Clean Water Act regulating "the discharge of dredged or fill material" opened the door to direct conflicts between state water rights and federal regulatory "uses" of water. Although the Corps' regulatory activities under the Rivers and Harbors Act expanded beyond what was necessary to protect navigability, its authority under the Rivers and Harbors Act nevertheless is narrower than under § 404. The Corps' rules now define the "navigable waters of the United States" covered by the Rivers and Harbors Act as "[a]ll waters which are currently used, or were used in the past, or may be susceptible to use in interstate or foreign commerce, including all waters which are subject to the ebb and flow of the tide." 33 C.F.R. § 328.3 (2000). To protect waters from interference by dredge and fill operations, § 404 of the Act requires anyone who wants to put any fill material in waters of the United States to get a permit from the Army Corps of Engineers.

The Corps has interpreted § 404 expansively, to include within its jurisdiction even wetlands. Lands that are saturated or submerged are vital habitat for birds and other wildlife and essential for flood control and water quality. Most of the nation's wetlands have been filled for farmland or development in eras before the immense ecological value of wetlands was appreciated. Now the primary means of wetlands protection is provided indirectly under § 404. Denial or conditioning of a developer's ability to fill wetlands can limit land uses, draining and filling of lands needed for agriculture, and construction, including construction of facilities needed to store or divert waters to which a water user is entitled under state water law.

The § 404 program is controversial because it affects water resource development projects and land use decisions that have traditionally been subject only to local and state regulation. "Wetland" is not a traditional scientific or geographic classification. It is a regulatory construct informed by scientific criteria. See Mark S. Dennison & James F. Berry, Wetlands: Guide to Science, Law and Technology (1993), and National Research Council, Wetlands: Characteristics and Boundaries (1995) The term emerged within the Corps in the 1950s and now refers to marshes, bogs, swamps and other areas at the border between a water body and dry land. The National Research Council concluded that areas connected to water-courses or those with saturated soils that support hydrophytic vegetation are clearly "wetlands," which it defined as "an ecosystem that depends on constant or recurrent, shallow inundation or saturation at or near the surface of the substrate." Id. at 3. The hard cases are artificial wetlands and isolated wetlands such as prairie potholes. The question of the Corps' jurisdiction has been before the Supreme Court three times, and federal agencies, property owners developers and NGOs must devine the meaning of the Court's 2006 opinion reproduced below.

The first case, United States v. Riverside Bayview Homes, 474 U.S. 121, 106 S.Ct. 455, 88 L.Ed.2d 419 (1985), was challenge to the Corp's assertion of § 404 jurisdiction over a planned housing project on 80 acres of low-lying, marshy land near the shores of Lake St. Clair in Macomb County, Michigan. The Corps classified the area as an adjacent wetland. The agency's then definition of a wetland provided: "The term 'wetlands' means those areas that are inundated or saturated by surface or ground water at a frequency and duration sufficient to support, and that under normal circumstances do support, a prevalence of vegetation typically adapted for life in saturated soil conditions. Wetlands generally include swamps, marshes, bogs and similar areas." 33 CFR § 323.2(c) (1978). The developer argued that Corps jurisdiction was limited to lands which periodi-cally flooded and that the denial of a permit was a taking. Applying Chevron U.S.A., Inc. v. Natural Resources Defense Council, Inc., 467 U.S. 837, 842–845, 104 S.Ct. 2778, 81 L.Ed.2d 694 (1984) and noting that Congress chose not to alter the Corps' definition in the 1977 revisions of the Clean Water Act, the Court concluded:

> Congress chose to define the waters covered by the Act broadly. Although the Act prohibits discharges into "navigable waters," see CWA §§ 301(a), 404(a), 502(12), 33 U.S.C. §§ 1311(a), 1344(a), 1362(12), the Act's definition of "navigable waters" as "the waters of the United States" makes it clear that the term "navigable" as used in the Act is of limited import. In adopting this definition of "navigable waters," Congress evidently intended to repudiate limits that had been placed on federal regulation by earlier water pollution control statutes and to exercise its powers under the Commerce Clause to regulate at least some waters that would not be deemed "navigable" under the classical understanding of that term.

Of course, it is one thing to recognize that Congress intended to allow regulation of waters that might not satisfy traditional tests of navigability; it is another to assert that Congress intended to abandon traditional notions of "waters" and include in that term "wetlands" as well. Nonetheless, the evident breadth of congressional concern for protection of water quality and aquatic ecosystems suggests that it is reasonable for the Corps to interpret the term "waters" to encompass wetlands adjacent to waters as more conventionally defined. Following the lead of the Environmental Protection Agency, see 38 Fed.Reg. 10834 (1973), the Corps has determined that wetlands adjacent to navigable waters do as a general matter play a key role in protecting and enhancing water quality:

"The regulation of activities that cause water pollution cannot rely on * * * artificial lines * * * but must focus on all waters that together form the entire aquatic system. Water moves in hydrologic cycles, and the pollution of this part of the aquatic system, regardless of whether it is above or below an ordinary high water mark, or mean high tide line, will affect the water quality of the other waters within that aquatic system.

"For this reason, the landward limit of Federal jurisdiction under Section 404 must include any adjacent wetlands that form the border of or are in reasonable proximity to other waters of the United States, as these wetlands are part of this aquatic system." 42 Fed.Reg. 37128 (1977).

We cannot say that the Corps' conclusion that adjacent wetlands are inseparably bound up with the "waters" of the United States—based as it is on the Corps' and EPA's technical expertise—is unreasonable. In view of the breadth of federal regulatory authority contemplated by the Act itself and the inherent difficulties of defining precise bounds to regulable waters, the Corps' ecological judgment about the relationship between waters and their adjacent wetlands provides an adequate basis for a legal judgment that adjacent wetlands may be defined as waters under the Act.

* * * In short, the Corps has concluded that wetlands adjacent to lakes, rivers, streams, and other bodies of water may function as integral parts of the aquatic environment even when the moisture creating the wetlands does not find its source in the adjacent bodies of water. Again, we cannot say that the Corps' judgment on these matters is unreasonable, and we therefore conclude that a definition of "waters of the United States" encompassing all wetlands adjacent to other bodies of water over which the Corps has jurisdiction is a permissible interpretation of the Act. Because respondent's property is part of a wetland that actually abuts on a navigable waterway, respondent was required to have a permit in this case.

In United States v. Byrd, 609 F.2d 1204 (7th Cir.1979), a landfill in a small inland lake was held to require a § 404 permit. See also United States v. Robinson, 570 F.Supp. 1157 (M.D.Fla.1983). The criteria for the identification of wetland areas and the areas subject to § 404 jurisdiction are explored in Avoyelles Sportsmen's League, Inc. v. Marsh, 715 F.2d 897 (5th Cir.1983). Until the 1990s, few questioned Congress's power to regulate all wetlands and small water bodies under the Commerce Power. However, in the 1990s, the Court began to adopt a formalist Commerce Clause jurisprudence that stressed limits on federal power that remained only hypothetical after the Court's expansive New Deal reading of the Commerce Clause. E.g. United States v. Lopez, 514 U.S. 549, 115 S.Ct. 1624, 131 L.Ed.2d 626 (1995) and United States v. Morrison, 529 U.S. 598, 120 S.Ct. 1740, 146 L.Ed.2d 658 (2000). Although the Court did not directly invoke its "new" Commerce Clause jurisprudence in Solid Waste Agency of Northern Cook County v. United States Army Corps of Engineers, 531 U.S. 159, 121 S.Ct. 675, 148 L.Ed.2d 576 (2001) (SWANCC), it used federalism principles to ban an extension of Corps jurisdiction over an abandoned sand and gravel pit mining site that had left 200 seasonal ponds that were used as habitat by migratory birds. The Corps denied a § 404 permit for a regional waste disposal facility that would fill the ponds, invoking its jurisdiction under the agency's rule that interpreted navigable waters to include those used by birds protected by international treaties and other migratory birds. In a 5–4 opinion, the Court held that the rule was ultra vires because clear congressional intent is required "[w]here an administrative interpretation invokes the outer limits of Congress' power." Id. at 172. Chief Justice Rehnquist found that allowing federal jurisdiction would impinge on traditional state powers over land and water use. Justice Stevens dissented, arguing that the Corps properly asserted jurisdiction where "[t]he activity being regulated * * * is the discharge of fill material into water" because as "Justice Holmes cogently observed in Missouri v. Holland * * * the protection of migratory birds is a textbook example of a national problem." Id. at 193, 195.

Some experts speculated that *SWANCC* would remove about 20 percent of the nation's water from Corps jurisdiction under § 404. The dividing line now seemed to depend on the existence, or not, of a hydrologic connection or a close proximity between the waters to be regulated and waters used in interstate commerce. For example, a lower court cited *SWANCC* in finding that the Oil Pollution Act did not apply to alleged contamination of the Canadian River via groundwater seepage. The court held that plaintiffs "failed to produce evidence of a close, direct and proximate link between Harken's discharges of oil and any resulting actual, identifiable oil contamination of a particular body of natural surface water that satisfies the jurisdictional requirements of the OPA." Rice v. Harken Exploration Co., 250 F.3d 264, 272 (5th Cir.2001).

Rapanos v. United States

United States Supreme Court, 2006.
547 U.S. 715, 126 S.Ct. 2208, 165 L.Ed.2d 159.

The enforcement proceedings against Mr. Rapanos are a small part of the immense expansion of federal regulation of land use that has occurred under the Clean Water Act—without any change in the governing statute—during the past five Presidential administrations. In the last three decades, the Corps and the Environmental Protection Agency (EPA) have interpreted their jurisdiction over "the waters of the United States" to cover 270– to 300–million acres of swampy lands in the United States—including half of Alaska and an area the size of California in the lower 48 States. And that was just the beginning. The Corps has also asserted jurisdiction over virtually any parcel of land containing a channel or conduit—whether manmade or natural, broad or narrow, permanent or ephemeral—through which rainwater or drainage may occasionally or intermittently flow. On this view, the federally regulated "waters of the United States" include storm drains, roadside ditches, ripples of sand in the desert that may contain water once a year, and lands that are covered by floodwaters once every 100 years. Because they include the land containing storm sewers and desert washes, the statutory "waters of the United States" engulf entire cities and immense arid wastelands. In fact, the entire land area of the United States lies in some drainage basin, and an endless network of visible channels furrows the entire surface, containing water ephemerally wherever the rain falls. Any plot of land containing such a channel may potentially be regulated as a "water of the United States." . . . .

The Corps' current regulations interpret "the waters of the United States" to include, in addition to traditional interstate navigable waters, 33 CFR § 328.3(a)(1) (2004), "[a]ll interstate waters including interstate wetlands," § 328.3(a)(2); "[a]ll other waters such as intrastate lakes, rivers, streams (including intermittent streams), mudflats, sandflats, wetlands, sloughs, prairie potholes, wet meadows, playa lakes, or natural ponds, the use, degradation or destruction of which could affect interstate or foreign commerce," § 328.3(a)(3); "[t]ributaries of [such] waters," § 328.3(a)(5); and "[w]etlands adjacent to [such] waters [and tributaries] (other than waters that are themselves wetlands)," § 328.3(a)(7). The regulation defines "adjacent" wetlands as those—bordering, contiguous [to], or neighboring—waters of the United States. § 328.3(c). It specifically provides that "[w]etlands separated from other waters of the United States by man-made dikes or barriers, natural river berms, beach dunes and the like are 'adjacent wetlands.' " *Ibid.* [The plurality opinion's discussion of Riverside Bayview Homes and SWANCC is omitted]

II

In these consolidated cases, we consider whether four Michigan wetlands, which lie near ditches or man-made drains that eventually empty into traditional navigable waters, constitute "waters of the United States" within the meaning of the Act. Petitioners in No. 04–1034, the Rapanos and their affiliated businesses, deposited fill material without a permit into wetlands on three sites near Midland, Michigan: the "Salzburg site," the "Hines Road site," and the "Pine River site." The wetlands at the Salzburg site are connected to a man-made drain, which drains into Hoppler Creek, which flows into the Kawkawlin River, which empties into Saginaw Bay and Lake Huron. The wetlands at the Hines Road site are connected to something called the "Rose Drain," which has a surface connection to the Tittabawassee River. And the wetlands at the Pine River site have a surface connection to the Pine River, which flows into Lake Huron. It is not clear whether the connections between these wetlands and the nearby drains and ditches are continuous or intermittent, or whether the nearby drains and ditches contain continuous or merely occasional flows of water.

The United States brought civil enforcement proceedings against the Rapanos petitioners. The District Court found that the three described wetlands were "within federal jurisdiction" because they were "adjacent to other waters of the United States," and held petitioners liable for violations of the CWA at those sites. On appeal, the United States Court of Appeals for the Sixth Circuit affirmed, holding that there was federal jurisdiction over the wetlands at all three sites because "there were hydrological connections between all three sites and corresponding adjacent tributaries of navigable waters." 376 F.3d, at 643.

The Carabells were denied a permit to deposit fill material in a wetland located on a triangular parcel of land about one mile from Lake St. Clair. A man-made drainage ditch runs along one side of the wetland, separated from it by a 4–foot–wide man-made berm. The berm is largely or entirely impermeable to water and blocks drainage from the wetland, though it may permit occasional overflow to the ditch. The ditch empties into another ditch or a drain, which connects to Auvase Creek, which empties into Lake St. Clair.

III

The Rapanos petitioners contend that the terms "navigable waters" and "waters of the United States" in the Act must be limited to the traditional definition of *The Daniel Ball,* which required that the "waters" be navigable in fact, or susceptible of being rendered so. See 10 Wall., at 563, 19 L.Ed. 999. But this definition cannot be applied wholesale to the CWA. The Act uses the phrase "navigable waters" as a *defined* term, and the definition is simply "the waters of the United States." 33 U.S.C. § 1362(7). Moreover, the Act provides, in certain circumstances, for the substitution of state for federal jurisdiction over "navigable waters" ... *other than* those waters which are presently used, or are susceptible to use in their natural condition or by reasonable improvement as a means to transport interstate or foreign commerce ... including wetlands adjacent thereto. §§ 1344(g)(1) (emphasis added). This provision shows that the Act's term "navigable waters" includes something more than traditional navigable waters. We have twice stated that the meaning of "navigable waters" in the Act is broader than the traditional understanding of that term, SWANCC, 531 U.S., at 167, 121 S.Ct. 675; Riverside Bayview, 474 U.S., at 133, 106 S.Ct. 455. We have also emphasized, however, that the qualifier is "navigable" is not devoid of significance, SWANCC, supra, at 172, 121 S.Ct. 675.

We need not decide the precise extent to which the qualifiers "navigable" and "of the United States" restrict the coverage of the Act. Whatever the scope of these qualifiers, the CWA authorizes federal jurisdiction only over "waters." 33 U.S.C. § 1362(7). The only natural definition of the term "waters," our prior and subsequent judicial constructions of it, clear evidence from other provisions of the statute, and this Court's canons of construction all confirm that "the waters of the United States" in § 1362(7) cannot bear the expansive meaning that the Corps would give it.

The Corps' expansive approach might be arguable if the CSA defined "navigable waters" as "water of the United States." But "the waters of the United States" is something else. The use of the definite article ("the") and the plural number ("waters") show plainly that § 1362(7) does not refer to water in general. In this form, "the waters" refers more narrowly to water "[a]s found in streams and bodies forming geographical features such as oceans, rivers, [and] lakes," or "the flowing or moving masses, as of waves or floods, making up such streams or bodies." Webster's New International Dictionary 2882 (2d ed.1954) (hereinafter Webster's Second). On this definition, "the waters of the United States" include only relatively permanent, standing or flowing bodies of water. The definition refers to water as found in "streams," "oceans," "rivers," "lakes," and "bodies" of water "forming geographical features." *Ibid.* All of these terms connote continuously present, fixed bodies of water, as opposed to ordinarily dry channels through which water occasionally or intermittently flows. Even the least substantial of the definition's terms, namely "streams," connotes a continuous flow of water in a permanent channel—especially when used in company with other terms such as "rivers," "lakes," and "oceans." None of these terms encompasses transitory puddles or ephemeral flows of water.

> Though scientifically precise distinctions between "perennial" and "intermittent" flows are no doubt available, see, *e.g.,* Dept. of Interior, U.S. Geological Survey, E. Hedman & W. Osterkamp, Streamflow Characteristics Related to Channel Geometry of Streams in Western United States 15 (1982) (Water–Supply Paper 2193), we have no occasion in this litigation to decide exactly when the drying-up of a stream bed is continuous and frequent enough to disqualify the channel as a "wate[r] of the United States." It suffices for present purposes that channels containing permanent flow are plainly within the definition, and that the dissent's "intermittent" and "ephemeral" streams, *post,* at 2260 (opinion of STEVENS, J.)—that is, streams whose flow is "[c]oming and going at intervals ... [b]roken, fitful," Webster's Second 1296, or "existing only, or no longer than, a day; diurnal ... short-lived," *id.,* at 857.

The restriction of "the waters of the United States" to exclude channels containing merely intermittent or ephemeral flow also accords with the commonsense understanding of the term. In applying the definition to "ephemeral streams," "wet meadows," storm sewers and culverts, "directional sheet flow during storm events," drain tiles, man-made drainage ditches, and dry arroyos in the middle of the desert, the Corps has stretched the term "waters of the United States" beyond parody. The plain language of the statute simply does not authorize this "Land Is Waters" approach to federal jurisdiction.

Because of this inherent ambiguity, we deferred to the agency's inclusion of wetlands "actually abut[ting]" traditional navigable waters: "Faced with such a problem of defining the bounds of its regulatory authority," we held, the agency could reasonably conclude that a wetland that "adjoin[ed]" waters of the United States is itself a part of those waters. Id., at 132, 135, and n. 9, 106 S.Ct. 455. The difficulty of delineating the boundary between water and land was central to our reasoning in the case: "In view of the breadth of federal regulatory authority contemplated by the Act itself and *the inherent difficulties of defining precise bounds to regulable waters,* the Corps' ecological judgment about the relationship between waters and their adjacent wetlands provides an adequate basis for a legal judgment that adjacent wetlands may be defined as waters under the Act." Id., at 134, 106 S.Ct. 455 (emphasis added).[7]

When we characterized the holding of *Riverside Bayview* in *SWANCC,* we referred to the close connection between waters and the wetlands that they gradually blend into: "It was the *significant nexus* between the wetlands and 'navigable waters' that informed our reading of the CWA in *Riverside Bayview Homes.*" 531 U.S., at 167, 121 S.Ct. 675 (emphasis added). In particular, *SWANCC* rejected the notion that the ecological considerations upon which the Corps relied in *Riverside Bayview*—and upon which the dissent repeatedly relies today, see *post,* at 2256–2257, 2258, 2258–2259, 2259–2260, 2261–2262, 2263–2264, 2264–2265—provided an *independent* basis for including entities like "wetlands" (or "ephemeral streams") within the phrase "the waters of the United States." *SWANCC* found such ecological considerations irrelevant to the question whether physically isolated waters come within the Corps' jurisdiction. It thus confirmed that *Riverside Bayview* rested upon the inherent ambiguity in defining where water ends and abutting ("adjacent") wetlands begin, permitting the Corps' reliance on ecological considerations *only to resolve*

---

7. Since the wetlands at issue in *Riverside Bayview* actually abutted waters of the United States, the case could not possibly have held that merely "neighboring" wetlands came within the Corps' jurisdiction. *Obiter* approval of that proposition might be inferred, however, from the opinion's quotation without comment of a statement by the Corps describing covered "adjacent" wetlands as those "that form the border of *or are in reasonable proximity to* other waters of the United States." 474 U.S., at 134, 106 S.Ct. 455 (quoting 42 Fed.Reg. 37128 (1977); emphasis added). The opinion immediately reiterated, however, that adjacent wetlands could be regarded as "the waters of the United States" in view of "the inherent difficulties of defining precise bounds to regulable waters," 474 U.S., at 134, 106 S.Ct. 455—a rationale that would have no application to physically separated "neighboring" wetlands. Given that the wetlands at issue in *Riverside Bayview* themselves "actually abut[ted] on a navigable waterway," id., at 135, 106 S.Ct. 455; given that our opinion recognized that unconnected wetlands could not naturally be characterized as "waters" at all, id., at 132, 106 S.Ct. 455; and given the repeated reference to the difficulty of determining where waters end and wetlands begin; the most natural reading of the opinion is that a wetlands' mere "reasonable proximity" to waters of the United States is not enough to confer Corps jurisdiction. In any event, as discussed in our immediately following text, any possible ambiguity has been eliminated by SWANCC, 531 U.S. 159, 121 S.Ct. 675, 148 L.Ed.2d 576 (2001).

that ambiguity in favor of treating all abutting wetlands as waters. Isolated ponds were not "waters of the United States" in their own right, see 531 U.S., at 167, 171, 121 S.Ct. 675, and presented no boundary-drawing problem that would have justified the invocation of ecological factors to treat them as such.

Therefore, *only* those wetlands with a continuous surface connection to bodies that are "waters of the United States" in their own right, so that there is no clear demarcation between "waters" and wetlands, are "adjacent to" such waters and covered by the Act. Wetlands with only an intermittent, physically remote hydrologic connection to "waters of the United States" do not implicate the boundary-drawing problem of *Riverside Bayview,* and thus lack the necessary connection to covered waters that we described as a "significant nexus" in SWANCC. 531 U.S., at 167, 121 S.Ct. 675. Thus, establishing that wetlands such as those at the Rapanos and Carabell sites are covered by the Act requires two findings: First, that the adjacent channel contains a "wate[r] of the United States," (*i.e.,* a relatively permanent body of water connected to traditional interstate navigable waters); and second, that the wetland has a continuous surface connection with that water, making it difficult to determine where the "water" ends and the "wetland" begins.

■ Justice Kennedy, concurring in the judgment:

Contrary to the plurality's description wetlands are not simply moist patches of earth. They are defined as "those areas that are inundated or saturated by surface or ground water at a frequency and duration sufficient to support, and that under normal circumstances do support, a prevalence of vegetation typically adapted for life in saturated soil conditions. Wetlands generally include swamps, marshes, bogs, and similar areas." §§ 328.3(b). The Corps' Wetlands Delineation Manual, including over 100 pages of technical guidance for Corps officers, interprets this definition of wetlands to require: (1) prevalence of plant species typically adapted to saturated soil conditions, determined in accordance with the United States Fish and Wildlife Service's National List of Plant Species that Occur in Wetlands; (2) hydric soil, meaning soil that is saturated, flooded, or ponded for sufficient time during the growing season to become anaerobic, or lacking in oxygen, in the upper part; and (3) wetland hydrology, a term generally requiring continuous inundation or saturation to the surface during at least five percent of the growing season in most years. See Wetlands Research Program Technical Report Y–87–1 (on-line edition), pp. 12–34 (Jan.1987), http://www.saj.usace. army.mil/permit/documents/87ma nual.pdf (all Internet material as visited June 16, 2006, and available in Clerk of Court's case file). Under the Corps' regulations, wetlands are adjacent to tributaries, and thus covered by the Act, even if they are "separated from other waters of the United States by man-made dikes or barriers, natural river berms, beach dunes and the like." §§ 328.3(c) . . . . .

II

The Court in *Riverside Bayview* did note, it is true, the difficulty of defining where "water ends and land begins," id., at 132, 106 S.Ct. 455, and the Court cited that problem as one reason for deferring to the Corps' view that adjacent wetlands could constitute waters. Given, however, the further recognition in *Riverside Bayview* that an overinclusive definition is permissible even when it reaches wetlands holding moisture disconnected from adjacent water-bodies, id., at 135, and n. 9, 106 S.Ct. 455, *Riverside Bayview's* observations about the difficulty of defining the water's edge cannot be taken to establish that when a clear boundary is evident, wetlands beyond the boundary fall outside the Corps' jurisdiction.

For the same reason *Riverside Bayview* also cannot be read as rejecting only the proposition, accepted by the Court of Appeals in that case, that wetlands covered by the Act must contain moisture originating in neighboring waterways. See id., at 125, 134, 106 S.Ct. 455. Since the Court of Appeals had accepted that theory, the Court naturally addressed it. Yet to view the decision's reasoning as limited to that issue—an interpretation the plurality urges here, *ante,* at 2231–2232, n. 13—would again overlook the opinion's broader focus on wetlands' "significant effects on water quality and the aquatic ecosystem," 474 U.S., at 135, n. 9, 106 S.Ct. 455.In any event, even were this reading of *Riverside Bayview* correct, it would offer no support for the plurality's proposed requirement of a "continuous surface connection," *ante,* at 2226. The Court in *Riverside Bayview* rejected the proposition that origination in flooding was necessary for jurisdiction over wetlands. It did not suggest that a flood-based origin would not support jurisdiction; indeed, it presumed the opposite. See 474 U.S., at 134, 106 S.Ct. 455 (noting that the Corps' view was valid "*even* for wetlands that are not the result of flooding or permeation" (emphasis added)). Needless to say, a continuous connection is not necessary for moisture in wetlands to result from flooding—the connection might well exist only during floods.

Consistent with *SWANCC* and *Riverside Bayview* and with the need to give the term "navigable" some meaning, the Corps' jurisdiction over wetlands depends upon the existence of a significant nexus between the wetlands in question and navigable waters in the traditional sense. The required nexus must be assessed in terms of the statute's goals and purposes. Congress enacted the law to "restore and maintain the chemical, physical, and biological integrity of the Nation's waters," 33 U.S.C. § 1251(a), and it pursued that objective by restricting dumping and filling in "navigable waters," §§ 1311(a), 1362(12). With respect to wetlands, the rationale for Clean Water Act regulation is, as the Corps has recognized, that wetlands can perform critical functions related to the integrity of other waters-functions such as pollutant trapping, flood control, and runoff storage. 33 CFR § 320.4(b)(2). Accordingly, wetlands possess the requisite nexus, and thus come within the statutory phrase "navigable waters," if the wetlands, either alone or in combination with similarly situated lands in the region, significantly affect the chemical, physical, and biological integrity of other covered waters more readily understood as "navigable." When, in contrast, wetlands' effects on water quality are speculative or insubstantial, they fall outside the zone fairly encompassed by the statutory term "navigable waters."

In addition, in assessing the hydrology prong of the three-part wetlands test, see *supra,* at 2237–2238, the District Court made extensive findings regarding water tables and drainage on the parcels at issue. In applying the Corps' jurisdictional regulations, the District Court found that each of the wetlands bore surface water connections to tributaries of navigable-in-fact waters.

NOTES

1. *EPA and Corps Cut Back Federal Jurisdiction.* In 2007, an Environmental Protection Agency and U.S. Army Corps of Engineers Guidance, www.apa.gov/owow/wetlands/guidance/CWAwaters.html, interpreting Rapanos was issued which significantly limits federal jurisdiction. Agency guidance is not formally binding and is not automatically entitled to Chevron deference, but courts are free to defer to an agency interpretation of its statutory authority depending on factors such as the quality of the agency's reasoning. United States v. Mead Corp., 533 U.S. 218, 121 S.Ct. 2164, 150 L.Ed.2d 292 (2001). The Guidance adopts the "significant nexus" between a marginal water body or wetland and "traditional" navigable waters test. Federal jurisdiction is a function of the physical, biological and chemical impacts of the volume, frequency and duration of tributary flows of downstream navigable lakes and streams. Non-navigable tributaries are defined as those with a minimum continuous three month flow, and federal jurisdiction does not require a significant nexus determination. Swales, small washes with infrequent flows and ditches are excluded from federal regulation by the guidance. http://www.apa.gov/owow/wetlands/guidance/CWAwaters.html. See generally J. Adler et al., The Supreme Court and the Clean Water Act: Five Essays (Vermont Law School Land use Institute 2007.PAGE 3–42).

Are any of the following water bodies post-*Rapanos* "waters of the United States?" A reach of a river, which eventually flows into a navigable-in fact river, with Class IV rapids used by three rafting companies that advertise in and out of state? A stocked 400 acre lake in State A located 25 miles from a major metropolitan area in State B which attracts fishermen from State B? See William W. Sapp, Rebekah A. Robinson, and Allison Burdette, The Float A Boat Test: How To Use It To Advantage in This Post–Rapanos World, 38 ELR News & Analysis 10439, July, 2008.

2. *What Is the Rule of the Case?* Who wrote the majority opinion? Many courts have concluded that Justice's Kennedy's concurrence is the most persuasive opinion. United States v. Moses, 496 F.3d 984 (9th Cir. 2007) upheld a Conviction for rerouting intermittent Teton Creek upheld because Kennedy concurrence permits a finding that seasonable streams can be waters of the United States.

3. *Rapanos At Work.* The impact of the Guidance can be seen in a 2008 decision of the Corps which concluded that the Los Angeles River ceases to be a federal navigable water body two miles north of the Pacific Ocean, although the CWA applies to flow of the river because it is fed by treated sewage. The river and its watershed, like many urban stream systems, are undergoing restoration, but the Corps decision means that § 404 no longer applies to land development along tributary systems in the upper watershed. Deborah Schoch, Is the L.A. River Up a Creek? If the Waterway Is Not Officially Deemed To Be Navigable, Many of Its Tributaries Could Lose Important Protections, The Los Angeles Times, June 1, 2008. After considerable public outcry, the Assistant Administrator of the EPA announced in August, 2008 that his agency would make the final determination of navigability. Kenneth R. Weiss, Los Angeles River May Get Protection Through Clean Water Act: The EPA Will Define "Traditional Navigable Waters" for the Waterway, The Los Angeles Times, August 19, 2008. However, the Corps may not welcome citizen evidence of the river's navigability. After a civilian Corps biologist joined a three day kayak trip down the river to protest the agency's position and posted two photos of herself paddling on her blog, the Corps proposed suspending her for 30 days. Heather Wylie, Floating to Save the L.A. River, The Los Angeles Times, October 30, 2008.

4. *404 Balancing.* Once the Corps of Engineers has jurisdiction over an activity pursuant to the broad language of § 404, its decision to issue a permit incorporates a variety of considerations. The Corps makes a far-ranging public interest review. Under the Corps' regulations, it engages in a balancing process in which "[t]he benefits which reasonably may be expected to accrue from the proposal must be balanced against its reasonably foreseeable detriments." 33 C.F.R. § 320.4(a) (2000). The Corps is directed to consider

> [a]ll factors which may be relevant to the proposal * * * including the cumulative effects thereof: among those are conservation, economics, aesthetics, general environmental concerns, wetlands, historic properties, fish and wildlife values, flood hazards, floodplain values, land use, navigation, shore erosion and accretion, recreation, water supply and conservation, water quality, energy needs, safety, food and fiber production, mineral needs, considerations of property ownership, and, in general, the needs and welfare of the people. *Id.*

Can the Corps properly consider such concerns, many of which are traditionally state concerns, private concerns, or specifically committed to private decision making by state law and policy? At what point has the Corps by regulation exceeded the purposes of a permit system for dredging and filling in navigable waters? Under the regulations is it not possible for the federal government acting through the Corps of Engineers to take complete control over all, or virtually all, of a state's water development policy and planning? Did Congress intend preemption this broad?

In weighing the public interest factors, the Corps has tempered their effect by deferring to state judgments on many of the public interest factors where there are no "overriding national factors of public interest." 33 C.F.R. § 320.4(j)(4) (2000). Presumably the existence of a state wetlands protection program would be influential in the Corps' decision to defer to the state. Generally speaking, state programs to regulate wetlands are much more limited in their reach than the federal law under § 404. However, some of the programs are more specific and demanding in imposing regulatory requirements on activities in wetlands. States have a veto over a § 404 (or Rivers and Harbors Act § 10) permit. See 33 U.S.C.A. § 1341; 33 C.F.R. §§ 320.3(a), 325.2(b)(i) (West Supp. 2008). The veto is based largely on compliance with state water quality requirements but also extends to other substantive requirements.

5. *Can the EPA Just Say No?* A Corps decision to grant a § 404 permit may be reviewed and the activity prohibited by the Environmental Protection Agency (EPA). This was done in 1990 in the case of the Two Forks Dam in Colorado. In that case, the state had no program to review water development except in the context of determining whether other water rights were adversely affected. Although millions of dollars were spent to review the impacts of the project in the process of preparing the Corps' environmental impact statement (under the National Environmental Policy Act), the EPA found that the project would have "unacceptable and avoidable" environmental effects. The veto was upheld in Alameda Water & Sanitation Dist. v. Reilly, 930 F.Supp. 486 (D.Colo. 1996). See also Bersani v. Robichaud, 850 F.2d 36 (2d Cir. 1988), cert. denied 489 U.S. 1089, 109 S.Ct. 1556, 103 L.Ed.2d 859 (1989) (upholding an EPA permit veto where alternative sites were available for development of a proposed shopping center) and James City County v. Environmental Protection Agency, 12 F.3d 1330 (4th Cir. 1993), cert. denied 513 U.S. 823, 115 S.Ct. 87, 130 L.Ed.2d 39 (1994) (holding that the EPA has no duty to balance the environmental benefits of a veto against the benefits of the foregone project).

D. FEDERAL POWER ACT LICENSING

The 1920 Federal Power Act requires that anyone proposing to develop a hydroelectric facility on a navigable stream must obtain a license from the Federal Energy Regulatory Commission (FERC), formerly the Federal Power Commission (FPC). In Udall v. Federal Power Commission, 387 U.S. 428, 437, 87 S.Ct. 1712, 18 L.Ed.2d 869 (1967), the Supreme Court found a requirement to consider the effects of a project on anadromous fish implicit in the provision of the Act that says that the Commission must find that licensed projects are "best adapted to a comprehensive plan for improving or developing a waterway, * * * and for other beneficial public uses, including recreational purposes." The authority of FERC to impose conditions on licenses to protect fish and wildlife gives it the ability to impose minimum flow requirements contrary to state law as shown in California v. FERC, 495 U.S. 490, 110 S.Ct. 2024, 109 L.Ed.2d 474 (1990), *infra* p. 826. Further, the Fish and Wildlife Coordination Act, 16 U.S.C.A. §§ 661–666c (West Supp. 2008), requires that federal agencies give "equal consideration" to wildlife conservation when undertaking or authorizing water development projects. The latter act is basically toothless, but in the context of FERC licensing it can be used to require mitigation measures such as ladders and hatchery releases as a condition of a project permit. The duty to take environmental considerations into account FERC licensing was strengthened in the Electric Consumers Protection Act of 1986, Pub. L. No. 99–495, § 3, 100 Stat. 1243 (1986) (codified at 16 U.S.C.A. §§ 797(e), 803(a) (West Supp. 2008)), which amended the Federal Power Act to require that:

> in deciding whether to issue any license * * * the Commission, in addition to the power and development purposes for which licenses are issued, shall give equal consideration to the purposes of energy conservation, the protection, mitigation of damage to, and enhancement of, fish and wildlife (including related spawning grounds and habitat), the protection of recreational opportunities, and the preservation of other aspects of environmental quality.

Furthermore, § 10(a) of the Act was amended to specify that comprehensive planning incorporate such environmental considerations and that the state and Indian tribal recommendations for conditions be included in licenses. Conditions requiring mitigation of effects on fish and wildlife also must be included in licenses. Prior to the 1986 Act, it was held in Steamboaters v. FERC, 759 F.2d 1382 (9th Cir.1985), that FERC was not required to impose conditions proposed by the National Marine Fisheries Service of the Department of Commerce. The Commission now must adopt the recommendations of state and federal fish and wildlife agencies unless it publishes findings that to follow those recommendations would be inconsistent with the purposes of the Act. The Act first reached the courts in National Wildlife Federation v. Federal Energy Regulatory Commission, 801 F.2d 1505 (9th Cir. 1986). FERC issued 7 preliminary permits to develop license applications on the Salmon River in Central Idaho. The Nez Peirce Tribe and others objected to the Commission's refusal to either prepare a comprehensive plan for the river, as the Federal Power Act requires, or to require permittees to study the cumulative impacts of the projects. In short, the plaintiffs asked FERC to treat the river as a complex ecosystem. In remanding FERC's decision, the court wrote:

* * *

> In rejecting petitioners' appeal from the Director's action, the Commission gave three reasons for denying petitioners' requests: (1) its usual experience had been that standard permits issued before development of a comprehensive plan were satisfactory; (2) permittees might be put to unnecessary expense and effort if required to conduct cumulative impact studies; and (3) cumulative studies undertaken at the permit stage might be useless if many projects were abandoned before licensing.

> The Commission's decision is not supported by any evidence in the record, let alone "substantial evidence," as required by 16 U.S.C. § 825l(b). We are unable to determine on the present record whether the Commission's decision is "arbitrary, capricious, an abuse of discre-

tion, or otherwise not in accordance with law." 5 U.S.C. § 706(2)(A) (1982).

* * *

The situation is not unlike that before the Supreme Court in Udall v. FPC, 387 U.S. 428 (1967). In Udall, the Federal Power Commission granted a license to build hydroelectric power projects without conducting "an exploration of all issues relevant to the 'public interest,' " id. at 450. Without deciding whether or not the license should have been granted, the Court vacated the Commission's decision, and remanded to the Commission with instructions to provide "an exploration of these neglected phases of the cases, as well as the other points raised by the Secretary." *Id.*

We do not hold the Commission must develop a comprehensive plan before issuing permits, must require permittees to collect data useful for studying cumulative impacts, must develop uniform study guidelines, or must collect baseline environmental data. We do hold the Commission's decision to reject these options is not sustainable on the present record.

* * *

The statute requires the Commission to measure proposed projects against a comprehensive plan. If the Commission had first prepared a comprehensive plan for hydropower development in the Salmon River Basin, establishing the optimal number, type, size and location of hydropower projects in the basin, cumulative impacts could be studied on the assumption that all projects detailed in the comprehensive plan eventually would be brought on line. Alternatively, permittees could have been required to conduct cumulative impact studies and prepare reports based on several development assumptions.

National Wildlife Federation is one small chapter in the decades-long effort to save salmon runs on the Columbia and Snake Rivers. See Michael C. Blumm & Andy Simrin, *The Unraveling of the Parity Promise: Hydropower, Salmon, and Endangered Species in the Columbia Basin*, 21 Envtl. L. 657 (1991); Michael C. Blumm, *NEPA Meets the Northwest Power Act (And Prevails): The Ninth Circuit Orders an EIS on the Bonneville Power Administration's Power Sale Contracts*, 25 Nat. Resources J. 1005 (1985).

NOTES

1. FERC cannot license any facility on or directly affecting a component of the Wild and Scenic Rivers system. Swanson Mining Corp. v. FERC, 790 F.2d 96 (D.C.Cir.1986), holds that § 7 of the Wild and Scenic Rivers Act, 16 U.S.C.A. § 1278 (West 2000), meant what it said when it prohibited development on designated rivers that would interfere with their free-flowing condition. An applicant wanted to develop a project near the bank of the South Fork of the Trinity River in California, a state-administered component of the system, that used water from a tributary of the river. It argued that the project would not impair the values of the river that led to its inclusion in the system, but the court refused to allow FERC to exempt itself from the Wild and Scenic Rivers Act on a case-by-case basis.

2.   Suppose FERC imposes conditions on a license that require the maintenance of certain minimum instream flows below a proposed facility for a certain stretch of the river. If the state does not allow private entities like the licensee to hold instream flow rights (or does not recognize such rights as a beneficial use), how can the flows be assured? Could an appropriator take water just below the facility and thereby defeat the minimum flow condition? Can the state agency issue permits for others to divert water attributable to the flows? Or has FERC, by its minimum flow condition, made an allocation of water rights for some distance below the dam? The more common situation involves FERC refusal to impose minimum flow conditions.

NOTE: DAM REMOVAL

The 20th century was an era of the construction of large, multi-purpose dams, although the impoundment of the country's rivers began in the late 1600s. See generally Christine A. Klein, *On Dams and Democracy*, 78 Or. L. Rev. 641 (1999). A widely noted study argues that most rivers in the mid-Atlantic were originally small anabranching channels with associated wetlands which accumulated little sediment but that today the flood plains of these rivers are the fill terraces formed by breached and abandoned mill dams. Robert C. Walter and Dorothy J. Merritts, Natural Streams and the Legacy of Water–Powered Mills, 319 Science 299, January 18, 2008. There are currently around 75,000 large dams blocking the waterways of the United States. Tens of thousands of smaller dams are also located in rivers and streams. As public concern for the health and vitality of fish and wildlife habitat grows, and environmental concerns rise to the forefront of the political agenda, the benefits of these dams are being questioned and we are reevaluating our infrastructure legacy. Two strategies have emerged to address the environmental costs of dams. First, since large multiple-purpose dams were generally built for the triad of flood control, water supply and hydroelectric generation, there is some potential to reoperate them to promote environmental values. See Lawrence J. MacDonnell, *Managing Reclamation Facilities for Ecosystem Benefits*, 67 U. Colo. L. Rev. 197, 200 (1996). The second strategy is the outright removal of some dams to restore natural flows, which seems to be the most appropriate action in many cases. At least 465 dams have been removed, 100 of these within the past 40 years. Removal of at least another 100 dams around the country is either scheduled or under active consideration.

The idea of removing some dams has gained validity as a reasonable and cost-effective method of river management and restoration. The benefits of removal include restoring flows for fish and wildlife, reinstating natural sediment and nutrient flow, eliminating safety risks, restoring opportunities for whitewater recreations and saving taxpayers' money.

Removal is also driven by the fact that many dams are getting old. The average life expectancy of a dam is 50 years and one-fourth of the dams in the United States are now older than that. FERC-licensed dams are a target for removal advocates as the next case illustrates. The relicensing requirements force privately-owned dams to justify continuing their operations and may refuse or put expensive conditions on licenses for dams where environmental costs outweigh the value of the hydropower. Therefore, during relicensing proceedings several years ago, FERC began considering removal or "decommissioning" of antiquated dams that were doing little good and much harm. The Edwards Dam on the Kennebec River in Maine was ordered to be removed to restore Atlantic salmon runs that had been impeded for almost 200 years.

City of Tacoma v. FERC

United States Court of Appeal, District of Columbia Circuit, 2006.
460 F.3d 53.

These consolidated cases seek our review of a series of orders issued by the Federal Energy Regulatory Commission ("FERC" or "Commission"), granting a conditional license to the City of Tacoma to operate a hydroelectric project on the Skokomish River in the State of Washington. We deny the petitions in part, grant the petitions in part, and remand for further proceedings, without vacating the license.

I

In 1924, Tacoma obtained a license from the Federal Power Commission to flood 8.8 acres of national forest land by damming the North Fork of the Skokomish River at Lake Cushman on the Olympic Peninsula. This license was designated a "minor part license" because it covered only a small part of Tacoma's much larger hydroelectric project (the "Cushman Project"). * * * In the ensuing years, Tacoma built two dams across the North Fork river. The first dam greatly increased the size of Lake Cushman, and the second dam created Lake Kokanee further downstream. Tacoma also constructed two hydroelectric plants, one at the upper dam and a second near Hood Canal, which adjoins Puget Sound. Between Lake Kokanee and Hood Canal, Tacoma diverted virtually all the water from the North Fork riverbed into a pipeline, thereby maximizing the generating power of the river. Nevertheless, some distance downhill from Lake Kokanee, water continued to flow into the North Fork riverbed from McTaggert Creek, and recently Tacoma has released into the riverbed an additional flow of sixty cubic feet per second ("cfs").

The five-thousand-acre reservation of the Skokomish Indian Tribe ("Tribe") is located near the mouth of the Skokomish River, with Hood Canal as its northeastern border and the Skokomish River as its eastern, southeastern, and southern borders. The reservation was established in

1855 by the Treaty of Point No Point, which guarantees certain rights to the Tribe, including the right to take fish from the Skokomish River. The Cushman Project's second hydroelectric plant is situated within the boundary of the reservation, on property Tacoma owns in fee, and an access road and transmission line run across reservation property. The Cushman Project did not remove all water from the section of the Skokomish River that borders the Tribe's reservation; the lower portion of the river continues to be fed by the South Fork and also the small flow that remains in the North Fork. Nevertheless, the Cushman Project sharply reduced water levels, thereby affecting fish populations and increasing silt deposits. The Tribe asserts that the historic mean annual water-flow in the North Fork was eight-hundred cfs. If this figure is accurate, then even accounting for the sixty cfs that Tacoma is now releasing into the North Fork riverbed, Tacoma is still diverting about 92.5 percent of the North Fork's water.

* * *

In 1974, Tacoma's minor part license expired, and Tacoma applied for a new license, expressly seeking a "major project license" that would cover all its project-related facilities. Pursuant to section 15 of the Federal Power Act ("FPA" or the "Act"), 16 U.S.C. § 808(a)(1), which is the section governing relicensing, the Commission is required to issue annual renewals of the existing license during the application review period that precedes issuance of a new long-term license. The Commission therefore issued Tacoma an annual license, and as a consequence of repeated delays, Tacoma of matters addressed during this lengthy review period included: (1) the state certification required under section 401(a) of the Clean Water Act, 33 U.S.C. § 1341(a); (2) the state "concurrence" required under section 307(c)(3)(A) of the Coastal Zone Management Act, 16 U.S.C. § 1456(c)(3)(A); (3) the consultations with state and federal wildlife agencies required under section 10(j) of the FPA, *id.* § 803(j); and (4) the consultations with the Advisory Council on Historic Preservation required under section 106 of the National Historic Preservation Act, *id.* § 470f. In addition, FERC (the successor agency to the Federal Power Commission) prepared an environmental impact statement as required by the National Environmental Policy Act, 42 U.S.C. § 4332(2)(C)l , and the Department of the Interior ("Interior"), as the agency supervising the Tribe's reservation, prepared a list of "conditions" to be included in Tacoma's new license pursuant to section 4(e) of the FPA. *See* 16 U.S.C. § 797(e).

FERC finally completed the application review process in 1998, and on July 30th of that year, FERC issued a forty-year major license for the Cushman Project, imposing a number of conditions designed, among other things, to protect the environment, to remedy past environmental impacts, to restore fish populations, and otherwise to mitigate the effect of the project on the Tribe's reservation. FERC rejected Interior's section 4(e) conditions, but article 407 of the license requires Tacoma to release a minimum flow of 240 cfs (or inflow, whichever is less) into the North Fork riverbed, below Lake Kokanee, and this requirement partially satisfies one of Interior's conditions.

Several parties petitioned for rehearing. Tacoma's petition asserted that, under the terms of the license, the Cushman Project would cost more to operate than the value of the power it generated. The Tribe's petition asserted that the license did not adequately protect the environment or the Tribe's reservation and should have included all of Interior's section 4(e) conditions. The Tribe also contested whether the requirements of the Clean Water Act, the Coastal Zone Management Act, and the National Historic Preservation Act had been satisfied. In a series of orders, FERC (1) denied several petitions for rehearing; (2) clarified that Tacoma could defer its final decision as to whether to accept or reject the new license until after completion of the appeal process; and (3) granted a stay of the new license pending judicial review, thereby permitting Tacoma to continue operations without satisfying any of the license conditions.

Several petitions for review were filed in this court, but we remanded without any decision on the merits because the listing of two salmon species as endangered pursuant to the Endangered Species Act ("ESA") necessitated consultations between FERC and the National Marine Fisheries Service (the "Fisheries Service") regarding the impact of the Cushman Project on these species, and we anticipated that these consultations might result in significant license changes. After remand, FERC also entered into consultations with the Fish and Wildlife Service regarding the impact the project would have on a third species, the bull trout. Pursuant to section 7(b) of the ESA, the Fisheries Service and the Fish and Wildlife Service began preparing biological opinions ("BiOps") detailing their expert findings regarding the impact FERC's proposed action would have on the endangered species and specifying "reasonable and prudent measures" FERC needed to take to minimize any "incidental taking" of the species.

More delays followed, and in September 2003, FERC ordered a "nonadversarial" factfinding hearing before an administrative law judge ("ALJ") in an effort to move the matter forward. In December 2003, the Fisheries Service and the Fish and Wildlife Service issued draft versions of their BiOps, and the ALJ was able to take those draft BiOps into consideration. That same month, the ALJ issued a report emphasizing the critical importance of releasing a minimum flow of 240 cfs into the North Fork riverbed, even on an interim basis, to benefit endangered salmon. A few months later, in March 2004, the Fisheries Service and the Fish and Wildlife Service issued their final BiOps, and in June, FERC amended the license for the Cushman Project, adding specific protections for the endangered species, as recommended in the BiOps. In the same order, FERC partially lifted its stay, thereby requiring the 240 cfs minimum flow the ALJ had recommended in his report. In February 2005, FERC granted in part and denied in part requests for rehearing, making relatively minor additional amendments to the license, and in March 2005, FERC denied rehearing of its February order.

Several petitions challenging FERC's orders are consolidated in this proceeding. On May 3, 2005, we granted a motion for a stay of the 240 cfs minimum-flow requirement. Tacoma thus continues to operate the Cushman Project without any significant license conditions, as it has done for approximately eighty years. It also continues to divert nearly all the water from the North Fork River, as it has done for approximately eighty years. Tacoma has consistently asserted that the 240 cfs minimum flow will necessitate a shut down of the project.

II

B

The Tribe asserts that FERC violated section 4(e) of the FPA by not including Interior's section 4(e) conditions in Tacoma's new license. Section 4(e) of the FPA, 16 U.S.C. § 797(e), provides [t]hat licenses shall be issued within any reservation only after a finding by the Commission that the license will not interfere or be inconsistent with the purpose for which such reservation was created or acquired, and shall be subject to and contain such conditions as the Secretary of the department under whose supervision such reservation falls shall deem necessary for the adequate protection and utilization of such reservation[.]

In this case, Interior is the federal agency under whose supervision the Skokomish Indian Reservation falls, and on August 4, 1997, the Secretary of the Interior submitted section 4(e) conditions to FERC. FERC rejected these conditions because they "were not timely filed."The FPA does not indicate what, if any, time limitation applies in this context, but FERC has imposed a strict time limitation [by rule, requiring all comments and mandatory conditions to be filed within 60 days of FERC's notice that the license application is ready for environmental analysis]. * * *

In accordance with this regulation, Interior's section 4(e) conditions were due on October 31, 1994. Interior, however, did not submit its conditions, or even preliminary conditions, by that date. Instead, Interior submitted a letter stating that, because of the complexity of the project, it would submit *preliminary* conditions within two years. In this letter, Interior also questioned FERC's authority to impose a time restriction on responsibilities the FPA expressly delegated to the Secretary of the Interior. Interior complained that FERC's short time restriction was "unworkable," "as a practical matter . . . not possible," and in conflict with FERC's "trust responsibility to protect the lands and resources of Indian Tribes." Two years later, Interior submitted preliminary section 4(e) conditions, as it said it would do, and about nine months after that, it submitted its final conditions, which FERC rejected as untimely.

We conclude FERC exceeded its statutory authority by placing a strict time restriction on responsibilities Congress delegated to other federal agencies. The FPA provides that licenses "within any reservation" "shall be subject to and contain such conditions as the Secretary of the department under whose supervision such reservation falls shall deem necessary for the adequate protection and utilization of such reservation[.]" 16 U.S.C. § 797(e). The FPA gives FERC no discretion in this regard. Though FERC makes the final decision as to *whether* to issue a license, FERC *shares* its authority to impose license conditions with other federal agencies. To the extent Congress has delegated licensing authority to agencies other than FERC, those agencies, and not FERC, determine how to exercise that authority, subject of course to judicial review. FERC can no more dictate to Interior when Interior should complete its work than Interior can dictate to FERC when FERC should do so. Here, FERC took all the time it needed—a full 24 years—to issue a license to Tacoma. Interior, in contrast, produced its license conditions within about three years of receiving notice on August 1, 1994.

To be sure, Interior and FERC should certainly make every effort to cooperate and to coordinate their efforts, because license conditions imposed by one agency may alter the conditions the other agency deems necessary. Furthermore, when two or more federal agencies have shared authority to impose license conditions, they can certainly agree on an appropriate time frame to govern the process. FERC, however, has no authority to impose a short 60–day limitation unilaterally, thereby effectively stripping Interior of its statutorily delegated authority.

F

The Tribe argues that Tacoma lacks water rights for the water it uses in connection with the Cushman Project. On November 13, 1993, Ecology sent a nine-page letter to FERC, describing in detail the ways in which Tacoma had "mischaracterize[d] the extent of its state water rights." Ecology reiterated its position in two subsequent letters to FERC, one dated January 25, 1994, and the other dated October 27, 1994. The Tribe then raised this issue in its request for reconsideration of the July 30, 1998 order granting the license. FERC rejected the Tribe's argument, noting that Tacoma had applied for additional water rights and that section 27 of the FPA, 16 U.S.C. § 821, deprived FERC of authority to adjudicate issues related to state water rights. The Tribe next brought a motion asking FERC to add two new articles to the license: (1) "an article requiring Tacoma's compliance with its existing state water rights to the in satisfaction of . . . Ecology or a court of competent jurisdiction, including if necessary Tacoma's restricting its water usage to match its authorized amount"; and (2) "an article reserving [FERC's] authority to unilaterally modify the Cushman Project license as may be necessitated by action on Tacoma's water rights taken by . . . Ecology or a court of competent jurisdiction."

We agree with FERC that the articles the Tribe proposed in this motion are unnecessary in light of section 27 of the FPA. Section 27 provides:

> Nothing contained in this chapter shall be construed as affecting or intending to affect or in any way to interfere with the laws of the respective States relating to the control, appropriation, use, or distribution of water used in irrigation or for municipal or other uses, or any vested right acquired therein.

16 U.S.C. § 821. If FERC lacks power to "affect[ ] or . . . interfere with" state water rights, then the license FERC issued for the Cushman Project

does not (and cannot) exempt Tacoma from meeting its water rights obligations under state law. Incorporating those water rights obligations into the license would serve no purpose other than to interpose FERC, in its role as enforcer of the license, into a matter that is not its concern. The Tribe argues that FERC, by issuing the license, has "condone[d] Tacoma's blatant violation" of state water rights law. It cannot under section 27.

III

A

Tacoma argues the license conditions FERC has imposed make the Cushman Project more costly to operate than the value of the power the project generates. On that account, Tacoma asserts the license amounts to a *de facto* decommissioning of the project, in violation of sections 14 and 15 of the FPA.

Under the FPA, any of several things can happen when a license to operate a hydroelectric facility expires: (1) the federal government can take over the project, 16 U.S.C. § 807; (2) FERC can issue a new license to the same licensee "upon reasonable terms," *id.* § 808(a)(1); (3) FERC can issue a license to a different licensee "upon reasonable terms," *id.;* (4) FERC can license all or part of the project for nonpower use, *id.* § 808(f); and (5) FERC can decline to issue a new license. The last option is implicit in section 4(e), which gives to FERC the authority to decide "*whether* to issue any license under this subchapter." If the Commission decides not to issue a new license, however, the Act is silent with respect to the disposition of the project works and any other remedial measures that might be necessary to restore the environment. For example, on the one hand, failure to maintain a dam after a project ceases operations would lead to the gradual deterioration of the dam's structural integrity followed by a possible catastrophe (and huge liability for the landowner) should the dam suddenly give way. On the other hand, the project's former operator may not want to bear the cost of maintaining the dam when it no longer receives revenues from the project, and if the former operator removes the dam, homes and businesses that have come to rely on the presence of the dam may lose much of their value. FERC could, of course, address these issues at the time of licensing by imposing appropriate license conditions, 16 U.S.C. § 799, but it is not clear whether, in the absence of express license conditions, FERC has the authority to impose obligations and costs on a former licensee.

When Congress first enacted the FPA in 1920, its general expectation may have been that FERC would renew hydroelectric project licenses in perpetuity, making post-license disposition of project works unnecessary. At that time, the Act included few provisions protecting the environment, and the general focus was on development of the nation's resources. But with the later addition of various provisions protecting the environment, and also fish and wildlife, the possibility arose that existing projects would be inconsistent with the new values embodied in the law, and FERC might therefore decline to renew a license, or it might issue a renewal on terms the licensee found objectionable. Aware of this possibility, FERC published a "policy statement" in the Federal Register in 1995, claiming authority to decommission existing projects at the time of relicensing and to impose decommissioning costs on the former licensee. *See* Project Decommissioning at Relicensing; Policy Statement, 60 Fed.Reg. 339 (FERC Jan. 4, 1995). The validity of this policy has never been tested in the courts.

Tacoma argues that FERC has no authority to decommission a project unilaterally at the time of relicensing. Rather, sections 14 and 15 of the FPA list several possibilities upon expiration of a license term, and FERC's decommissioning policy is simply not on the list. Tacoma suggests that if FERC does not want to renew Tacoma's 1924 license, and it cannot find another party to take over the Cushman Project, then the federal government must itself take over the project. Of course, FERC did not decommission the Cushman Project; rather, it issued a new license to Tacoma to operate the project. Nevertheless, Tacoma claims FERC loaded up the new license with so many conditions Tacoma has no choice but to shut the project down. In that way, FERC effectively decommissioned the project by the ruse of offering an uneconomic license and saying, in effect, "Take it or leave it." Tacoma argues "FERC may not do indirectly that which it has no authority to do directly—or, in other words, *de facto* decommissioning."

In pressing this argument, Tacoma emphasizes FERC's concession that the new license is uneconomic. Specifically, FERC's own finding is that the "net benefits" of the Cushman Project are "negative $2.06 million" per year. This concession has limited significance, however, in light of FERC's decision in Mead Corp., Publishing Paper Division, 72 FERC 61,027, 1995 WL 414829 (1995). In *Mead Corp.*, FERC concluded it is institutionally unqualified to make business judgments about the long-term economic viability of hydroelectric projects, especially in light of the "new era of competition" in the electric power industry and the unpredictability of market conditions over the course of a thirty- or fifty-year license term. In addition, FERC noted that the potentially high cost associated with decommissioning a project might prompt a licensee to continue operating a project though the project is only marginally viable economically. Accordingly, FERC determined that it would cease the practice of projecting long-term costs when assessing the economic benefits of a project. Instead, it would focus (for the most part) on then-existent conditions, and it would leave to the prospective licensee the decision whether or not to accept the license. FERC expressly noted the possibility that, under this new approach, it might license projects that had "negative economic benefits."

In light of *Mead Corp.*, Tacoma finds far too much significance in FERC's concession that the Cushman Project is uneconomic under the new license. The project may offer advantages to Tacoma that are not readily quantifiable, and market conditions may change significantly over the next forty years, making the project economically viable over the long-term. Tacoma's more persuasive point is that the take-it-or-leave-it attitude FERC expressed in *Mead Corp.* is inconsistent with FERC's statutory obligation under the FPA. Section 15 of the FPA requires FERC to offer a new license on "reasonable terms," or an annual renewal of the old license, and in Tacoma's view, an uneconomic license is *per se* an unreasonable license. FERC responds that its duty is to issue licenses that reflect the congressional mandate irrespective of whether those licenses make good business sense.

In some cases, a change in congressional priorities might cast doubt on a once viable project and lead to closure of the project when its license expires, either because FERC denies a new license outright or because FERC issues a new license that the licensee finds too costly or burdensome. In FERC's decommissioning policy statement, FERC argues persuasively that it cannot guarantee license renewal when Congress has greatly altered the regulatory landscape during the course of the prior license term. 60 Fed.Reg. at 341–43. Moreover, the very fact that a license may not exceed fifty years, *see* 16 U.S.C. § 808(e), indicates Congress's intent that projects be reevaluated from time to time in light of changing circumstances and national priorities, and this reevaluation necessarily implies that in some cases new licenses will not be issued.

One of the major shifts in national priorities since the 1920s has been from a near-exclusive focus on development to an increasing focus on environmental protection, and this shift is reflected in amendments to the FPA. In the 1920s, the FPA contained only two provisions aimed at protecting natural resources: (1) section 4(e) included a provision protecting reservations and authorizing the Secretary of any federal agency overseeing a reservation to impose appropriate license conditions, 16 U.S.C. § 797(e), and (2) section 18 gave the Secretary of Commerce (and later the Secretary of the Interior) the power to impose license conditions governing the construction of fishways, *id.* § 811. Starting in the 1950s, however, environmental protection became an increasingly important concern, and FERC's hydroelectric decisions reflected this shift in national values.

Then, in 1972, Congress enacted the Clean Water Act, under which state water protection agencies must give a water quality "certification" before FERC can license a hydroelectric project. 33 U.S.C. § 1341(a)(1). In addition, section 7 of the ESA, first enacted in 1973, requires FERC to impose license conditions that are necessary to protect any listed species. 16 U.S.C. § 1536(a)(1). Finally, in 1986, Congress amended the FPA to add the following provision to section 4(e):

> In deciding whether to issue any license under this Part for any project, the Commission, in addition to the power and development purposes for which licenses are issued, shall give equal consideration to the purposes of energy conservation, the protection, mitigation of damage to, and enhancement of, fish and wildlife (including related spawning grounds and habitat), the protection of recreational opportunities, and the preservation of other aspects of environmental quality.

Pub.L. No. 99–495, § 3(a), 100 Stat. 1243, 1243 (1986) (codified at 16 U.S.C. § 797(e)). At the same time, Congress also required FERC to consult with state and federal wildlife protection agencies and to include license conditions to protect fish and wildlife. *Id.* § 3(c), 100 Stat. at 1244 (codified at 16 U.S.C. § 803(j)).;F19;F19

In light of these sweeping changes in FERC's statutory mandate, FERC not only has the authority but also the obligation to evaluate existing projects completely anew upon expiration of their license terms. If Congress's enactments are to have any meaning at all, then Congress must have envisioned major changes at some if not all of these existing projects. In cases where these changes render the project impractical, then closure becomes a possibility. As FERC put the point: "[T]he Commission does not read the [Federal Power] Act as requiring it to issue a license."

Nothing in the FPA suggests that Congress intended to "grandfather" existing projects so they could continue to operate indefinitely despite changes in national priorities. Tacoma relies heavily on the provision of the FPA requiring FERC to grant new licenses "upon reasonable terms," 16 U.S.C. § 808(a)(1), but we cannot accept the implication that "reasonable terms" means the same terms that were imposed eighty years ago, or that "reasonable terms" means terms that ignore the present-day statutory mandate. In fact, section 15 of the Act states the opposite: "[T]he commission is authorized [upon expiration of a license] to issue a new license to the existing licensee upon such terms and conditions as may be authorized or required *under the then existing laws and regulations.*" *Id.* (emphasis added).

Therefore, the question we must decide is whether "reasonable terms" can, in some cases, be terms that may have the effect of shutting a project down or occasioning a change of ownership. We think the answer is yes, especially here where, according to FERC's factual finding, Tacoma has recouped its initial investment plus a significant annual return on that investment. The obligation to give "equal consideration" to wildlife protection and the environment, *id.* § 797(e), implies that, at least in some cases, these environmental concerns will prevail. At the very least, the Act is ambiguous, and FERC's interpretation of its statutory authority is reasonable and entitled to deference under Chevron, 467 U.S. at 842–43, 104 S.Ct. 2778.

In conclusion, we find persuasive FERC's argument that Congress implicitly extended to FERC the power to shut down projects either directly, by denying a new license, or indirectly, by imposing reasonable and necessary conditions that cause the licensee to reject the new license. We have no cause to decide in this case whether, and in what circumstances, FERC can impose decommissioning obligations or costs on a former licensee.

* * *

V

In our order of May 3, 2005, we stayed the minimum-flow requirements set forth in article 407 of the license. In light of our conclusion that FERC is obligated to include Interior's section 4(e) conditions in the license, including several conditions imposing minimum flow requirements in excess of those in presently set forth in article 407, we hereby vacate our stay.

[The court ordered FERC to decide whether it would issue the license given the 4(e) conditions.]

NOTES

1. The Energy Policy Act of 2005 established new opportunities for licensees to challenge conditions imposed by agencies in the relicensing process. For a description of the new approach and its application to the relicensing of PacifCorp hydropower dams on the Klamath River *see* Adell Louise Amos, Hydropower Reform and the Impact of the Energy Policy Act of 2005 on the Klamath Basin: Renewed Optimism or Same Old Song? 22 J. Envtl. L. & Litig. 1 (2007). A diverse group of stakeholders has proposed removing the PacifiCorp dams as key to restoring Klamath Basin salmon populations and resolving long and bitter disputes over Klamath River Water. See pages 742–744, *infra.*

2. *Its Money and Salmon.* After a major Supreme Court decision, Washington v. Washington State Commercial Passenger Fishing Vessel Association, 443 U.S. 658, 99 S.Ct. 3055, 61 L.Ed.2d 823 (1979), recognized on and off reservation tribal fishing rights for several reservations in Washington state including one downstream from two dams on the salmon-rich Elwha River, pressure to remove of Glines Canyon and Elwha Dams mounted. Congressional legislation authorized their removal, Elwha River Ecosystem and Fisheries Restoration Act, P.L. 102–495, Oct. 24, 1992, and the two dams were purchased by the federal government in 2000; removal is slated to start in 2012. The removal will be the largest removal to date, and environmentalists are setting their sights on some of the nation's biggest dams. The efforts to restore Salmon runs on the Columbia and its tributaries is an epic tale and illustrates the role that dam removal can play in the future resolution of such conflicts. After a court suggested that the federal government study removing 11 dams on the Columbia and the Snake Rivers, the Clinton Administration (1992–2000) began a study to assess the consequences of breaching four major dams on the Snake River. However, in 2004, the National Oceanographic and Atmospheric Administration concluded that eight large dams are an immutable part of the salmon's environment. Scott K. Miller, *Undamming Glen Canyon: Lunacy, Rationality, or Prophecy?* 19 Stan. Envtl. L.J. 121 (2000), reviews proposals to take down Glen Canyon Dam. See Note 4, page 744, *infra* for further discussion of efforts to save Columbia River salmon.

A Maine conservation organization, the Penobscot River Restoration Trust, raised $25 million to supplement a $15 million federal grant to purchase and remove two hydroelectric dams at the lower end of the river and to build a fish run around a third. The hope is that fish will return to the watershed. The river was a major source of economic development as logs were floated from the headwater forests to downstream paper mills, but much of the resulting pollution has now been cleaned up. Katie Zezima, Maine Conservationists Reach Milestone in Plan to Buy Three Dams, The New York Times, Aug. 22, 2008, p. A13.

3. *What are the Alternatives?* In the case of smaller dams, the loss of the dam's benefits may be off-set by the value of new ecosystem services provided by restoration or replaceable at a reasonable cost. But, the removal of a dam such as O'Shaughnessy Dam in the Hetch Hetchy Valley in Yosemite National Park, which supplies the city of San Francisco, raises series question about replacing the lost benefits. The decision to build the dam was one of the great natural resource fights of the Conservation Era and played a major role in splitting the movement into the utilitarian, multi-use and preservation wings and still resonates in California. See Richard White, "It's Your Misfortune and None of My Own": A History of the American West 413 (1991). California environmentalists have long dreamed on restoring the valley to John Muir's vision of it as the "flow of nature." Michael Cohen, The Pathless Way: John Muir and the American Wilderness 330 (1984). Spreck Rosekrans et al, Paradise Regained: Solutions For Restoring Yosemite Hetch Hetchy Valley (Environmental Defense 2004) is a comprehensive effort to simulate a removal debate. There are many legal issues such as the likely objections if San Francisco were to divert the Tuolumne River downstream from Hetch Hetchy and sent the water directly to its storage facilities south of the city. However, the political overshadow these. In 1987, President Reagan's Secretary of the Interior, Donald Hodel, was the first high ranking official to suggest removal. Environmentalists viewed the suggestion as a ploy to split green northern California. In 2007, the Bush II Administration proposed a $7,000,000.00 removal feasibility study but Senator Diane Feinstein, the former mayor of San Francisco and Hetch Hetchy defender was not amused.

4. *Careful When You Pull the Plug.* The removal of small dams is usually manageable as their impacts on river hydrology are easily defined, although their chemical and biological effects are more uncertain. Large dams present greater challenges. Large reservoirs trap sediments which can also be toxic. One cannot simply blow up the dam. Sediments may have to be treated and downstream dispersal patterns mapped, using the best available science. Dam removal may not be the best option if a dry sediment "lake" takes the place of the former wet reservoir or if the sediment aggrades the downstream river, widening the channel and degrading fish habitat. See Dam Removal Research: Status and Prospects (H.J. William Graf ed. Heinz Center 2002) and symposium, BioScience, Vol. 52, No. 8 (2002).

E.   STATE CERTIFICATION AND FEDERAL ACTIONS

PUD No. 1 of Jefferson County v. Washington Department of Ecology

Supreme Court of the United States, 1994.
511 U.S. 700, 114 S.Ct. 1900, 128 L.Ed.2d 716.

■ JUSTICE O'CONNOR delivered the opinion of the Court.

Petitioners, a city and a local utility district, want to build a hydroelectric project on the Dosewallips River in Washington State. We must decide whether respondent state environmental agency (hereinafter respondent) properly conditioned a permit for the project on the maintenance of specific minimum stream flows to protect salmon and steelhead runs.

I

This case involves the complex statutory and regulatory scheme that governs our Nation's waters, a scheme that implicates both federal and state administrative responsibilities. The Federal Water Pollution Control Act, commonly known as the Clean Water Act, 33 U.S.C. § 1251 *et seq.*, is a comprehensive water quality statute designed to "restore and maintain the chemical, physical, and biological integrity of the Nation's waters." § 1251(a). The Act also seeks to attain "water quality which provides for the protection and propagation of fish, shellfish, and wildlife." § 1251(a)(2).

To achieve these ambitious goals, the Clean Water Act establishes distinct roles for the Federal and State Governments. Under the Act, the Administrator of the Environmental Protection Agency (EPA) is required, among other things, to establish and enforce technology-based limitations on individual discharges into the country's navigable waters from point sources. See §§ 1311, 1314. Section 303 of the Act also requires each State, subject to federal approval, to institute comprehensive water quality standards establishing water quality goals for all intrastate waters. These state water quality standards provide "a supplementary basis . . . so that numerous point sources, despite individual compliance with effluent limitations, may be further regulated to prevent water quality from falling below acceptable levels." *EPA v. California ex rel. State Water Resources Control Bd.,* 426 U.S. 200, 205, n. 12 (1976).

A state water quality standard "shall consist of the designated uses of the navigable waters involved and the water quality criteria for such waters based upon such uses." 33 U.S.C. § 1313(c)(2)(A). In setting standards, the State must comply with the following broad requirements:

> "Such standards shall be such as to protect the public health or welfare, enhance the quality of water and serve the purposes of this chapter. Such standards shall be established taking into consideration their use and value for public water supplies, propagation of fish and wildlife, recreational [and other purposes.]"

A 1987 amendment to the Clean Water Act makes clear that § 303 also contains an "antidegradation policy"—that is, a policy requiring that state standards be sufficient to maintain existing beneficial uses of navigable waters, preventing their further degradation. Specifically, the Act permits the revision of certain effluent limitations or water quality standards "only if such revision is subject to and consistent with the antidegradation policy established under this section." § 1313(d)(4)(B). Accordingly, EPA's regulations implementing the Act require that state water quality standards include "a statewide antidegradation policy" to ensure that "[e]xisting instream water uses and the level of water quality necessary to protect the existing uses shall be maintained and protected." 40 CFR § 131.12 (1993). At a minimum, state water quality standards must satisfy these conditions. The Act also allows States to impose more stringent water quality controls. See 33 U.S.C. §§ 1311(b)(1)(C), 1370. See also 40 CFR § 131.4(a) (1993) ("As recognized by section 510 of the Clean Water Act [33 U.S.C. § 1370], States may develop water quality standards more stringent than required by this regulation").

The State of Washington has adopted comprehensive water quality standards intended to regulate all of the State's navigable waters. See Washington Administrative Code (WAC) 173–201–010 to 173–201–120 (1986). The State created an inventory of all the State's waters, and divided the waters into five classes. Each individual fresh surface water of the State is placed into one of these classes. The Dosewallips River is classified AA, extraordinary. The water quality standard for Class AA waters is set forth at 173–201–045(1). The standard identifies the designated uses of Class AA waters as well as the criteria applicable to such waters.

In addition to these specific standards applicable to Class AA waters, the State has adopted a statewide antidegradation policy. * * *

As required by the Act, EPA reviewed and approved the State's water quality standards. * * *

States are responsible for enforcing water quality standards on intrastate waters. In addition to these primary enforcement responsibilities, § 401 of the Act requires States to provide a water quality certification before a federal license or permit can be issued for activities that may result in any discharge into intrastate navigable waters. Specifically, § 401 requires an applicant for a federal license or permit to conduct any activity "which may result in any discharge into the navigable waters" to obtain from the State a certification "that any such discharge will comply with the applicable provisions of sections [1311, 1312, 1313, 1316, and 1317 of this title]." 33 U.S.C. § 1341(a). Section 401(d) further provides that "[a]ny certification ... shall set forth any effluent limitations and other limitations, and monitoring requirements necessary to assure that any applicant ... will comply with any applicable effluent limitations and other limitations, under section [1311 or 1312 of this title] ... and with any other appropriate requirement of State law set forth in such certification." 33 U.S.C. § 1341(d). The limitations included in the certification become a condition on any federal license.

II

Petitioners propose to build the Elkhorn Hydroelectric Project on the Dosewallips River. If constructed as presently planned, the facility would be located just outside the Olympic National Park on federally owned land within the Olympic National Forest. The project would divert water from a 1.2–mile reach of the river (the bypass reach), run the water through turbines to generate electricity and then return the water to the river below the bypass reach. Under the Federal Power Act (FPA), 41 Stat. 1063, as amended, 16 U.S.C. § 791a *et seq.,* the Federal Energy Regulatory

Commission (FERC) has authority to license new hydroelectric facilities. As a result, petitioners must get a FERC license to build or operate the Elkhorn Project. Because a federal license is required, and because the project may result in discharges into the Dosewallips River, petitioners are also required to obtain state certification of the project pursuant to § 401 of the Clean Water Act, 33 U.S.C. § 1341.

The water flow in the bypass reach, which is currently undiminished by appropriation, ranges seasonally between 149 and 738 cubic feet per second (cfs). The Dosewallips supports two species of salmon, coho and chinook, as well as steelhead trout. As originally proposed, the project was to include a diversion dam which would completely block the river and channel approximately 75% of the river's water into a tunnel alongside the streambed. About 25% of the water would remain in the bypass reach, but would be returned to the original riverbed through sluice gates or a fish ladder. Depending on the season, this would leave a residual minimum flow of between 65 and 155 cfs in the river. Respondent undertook a study to determine the minimum stream flows necessary to protect the salmon and steelhead fishery in the bypass reach. On June 11, 1986, respondent issued a § 401 water quality certification imposing a variety of conditions on the project, including a minimum stream flow requirement of between 100 and 200 cfs depending on the season.

* * *

III

The principal dispute in this case concerns whether the minimum stream flow requirement that the State imposed on the Elkhorn Project is a permissible condition of a § 401 certification under the Clean Water Act. * * *

A

There is no dispute that petitioners were required to obtain a certification from the State pursuant to § 401. Petitioners concede that, at a minimum, the project will result in two possible discharges—the release of dredged and fill material during the construction of the project, and the discharge of water at the end of the tailrace after the water has been used to generate electricity. Petitioners contend, however, that the minimum stream flow requirement imposed by the State was unrelated to these specific discharges, and that as a consequence, the State lacked the authority under § 401 to condition its certification on maintenance of stream flows sufficient to protect the Dosewallips fishery.

If § 401 consisted solely of subsection (a), which refers to a state certification that a "discharge" will comply with certain provisions of the Act, petitioners' assessment of the scope of the State's certification authority would have considerable force. Section 401, however, also contains subsection (d), which expands the State's authority to impose conditions on the certification of a project. Section 401(d) provides that any certification shall set forth "any effluent limitations and other limitations . . . necessary to assure that *any applicant"* will comply with various provisions of the Act and appropriate state law requirements. 33 U.S.C. § 1341(d) (emphasis added). The language of this subsection contradicts petitioners' claim that the State may only impose water quality limitations specifically tied to a "discharge." The text refers to the compliance of the applicant, not the discharge. Section 401(d) thus allows the State to impose "other limitations" on the project in general to assure compliance with various provisions of the Clean Water Act and with "any other appropriate requirement of State law." Although the dissent asserts that this interpretation of § 401(d) renders § 401(a)(1) superfluous, we see no such anomaly. Section 401(a)(1) identifies the category of activities subject to certification—namely, those with discharges. And § 401(d) is most reasonably read as authorizing additional conditions and limitations on the activity as a whole once the threshold condition, the existence of a discharge, is satisfied.

* * *

We agree with the State that ensuring compliance with § 303 is a proper function of the § 401 certification. * * * Although § 303 is not one of the statutory provisions listed in § 401(d), the statute allows States to impose limitations to ensure compliance with § 301 of the Act. Section 301 in turn incorporates § 303 by reference. As a consequence, state water quality standards adopted pursuant to § 303 are among the "other limitations" with which a State may ensure compliance through the § 401 certification process. This interpretation is consistent with EPA's view of the statute. Moreover, limitations to assure compliance with state water quality standards are also permitted by § 401(d)'s reference to "any other appropriate requirement of State law." * * *

B

Having concluded that, pursuant to § 401, States may condition certification upon any limitations necessary to ensure compliance with state water quality standards or any other "appropriate requirement of State law," we consider whether the minimum flow condition is such a limitation. Under § 303, state water quality standards must "consist of the designated uses of the navigable waters involved and the water quality criteria for such waters based upon such uses." In imposing the minimum stream flow requirement, the State determined that construction and operation of the project as planned would be inconsistent with one of the designated uses of Class AA water, namely "[s]almonid [and other fish] migration, rearing, spawning, and harvesting." The designated use of the river as a fish habitat directly reflects the Clean Water Act's goal of maintaining the "chemical, physical, and biological integrity of the Nation's waters." 33 U.S.C. § 1251(a). Indeed, the Act defines pollution as "the man-made or man induced alteration of the chemical, physical, biological, and radiological integrity of water." § 1362(19). Moreover, the Act expressly requires that, in adopting water quality standards, the State must take into consideration the use of waters for "propagation of fish and wildlife." § 1313(c)(2)(A).

Petitioners assert, however, that § 303 requires the State to protect designated uses solely through implementation of specific "criteria." According to petitioners, the State may not require them to operate their dam in a manner consistent with a designated "use"; instead, say petitioners, under § 303 the State may only require that the project comply with specific numerical "criteria."

We disagree with petitioners' interpretation of the language of § 303(c)(2)(A). Under the statute, a water quality standard must "consist of the designated uses of the navigable waters involved *and* the water quality criteria for such waters based upon such uses." (emphasis added). The text makes it plain that water quality standards contain two components. We think the language of § 303 is most naturally read to require that a project be consistent with *both* components, namely, the designated use *and* the water quality criteria. Accordingly, under the literal terms of the statute, a project that does not comply with a designated use of the water does not comply with the applicable water quality standards.

Consequently, pursuant to § 401(d) the State may require that a permit applicant comply with both the designated uses and the water quality criteria of the state standards. In granting certification pursuant to § 401(d), the State "shall set forth any ... limitations ... necessary to assure that [the applicant] will comply with any ... limitations under [§ 303] ... and with any other appropriate requirement of State law." A certification requirement that an applicant operate the project consistently with state water quality standards—*i.e.*, consistently with the designated uses of the water body and the water quality criteria—is both a "limitation" to assure "compl[iance] with ... limitations" imposed under § 303, and an "appropriate" requirement of state law.

* * *

The State also justified its minimum stream flow as necessary to implement the "antidegradation policy" of § 303, 33 U.S.C. § 1313(d)(4)(B). When the Clean Water Act was enacted in 1972, the water quality standards of all 50 States had antidegradation provisions. These provisions were required by federal law. By providing in 1972 that existing state water quality standards would remain in force until revised, the Clean Water Act ensured that the States would continue their antidegradation programs. EPA has consistently required that revised state standards incorporate an antidegradation policy. And, in 1987, Congress explicitly recognized the existence of an "antidegradation policy established under [§ 303]." § 1313(d)(4)(B).

* * *

Petitioners also assert more generally that the Clean Water Act is only concerned with water "quality," and does not allow the regulation of water "quantity." This is an artificial distinction. In many cases, water quantity is closely related to water quality; a sufficient lowering of the water quantity in a body of water could destroy all of its designated uses, be it for drinking water, recreation, navigation or, as here, as a fishery. In any event, there is recognition in the Clean Water Act itself that reduced stream flow, *i.e.,* diminishment of water quantity, can constitute water pollution. First, the Act's definition of pollution as "the man-made or man induced alteration of the chemical, physical, biological, and radiological integrity of water" encompasses the effects of reduced water quantity. 33 U.S.C. § 1362(19). This broad conception of pollution—one which expressly evinces Congress' concern with the physical and biological integrity of water—refutes petitioners' assertion that the Act draws a sharp distinction between the regulation of water "quantity" and water "quality." Moreover, § 304 of the Act expressly recognizes that water "pollution" may result from "changes in the movement, flow, or circulation of any navigable waters ..., including changes caused by the construction of dams." 33 U.S.C. § 1314(f). This concern with the flowage effects of dams and other diversions is also embodied in the EPA regulations, which expressly require existing dams to be operated to attain designated uses.

* * *

IV

Petitioners contend that we should limit the State's authority to impose minimum flow requirements because FERC has comprehensive authority to license hydroelectric projects pursuant to the FPA. In petitioners' view, the minimum flow requirement imposed here interferes with FERC's authority under the FPA. The FPA empowers FERC to issue licenses for projects "necessary or convenient ... for the development, transmission, and utilization of power across, along, from, or in any of the streams ... over which Congress has jurisdiction." § 797(e). The FPA also requires FERC to consider a project's effect on fish and wildlife. In *California v. FERC, supra,* we held that the California Water Resources Control Board, acting pursuant to state law, could not impose a minimum stream flow which conflicted with minimum stream flows contained in a FERC license. We concluded that the FPA did not "save" to the States this authority. No such conflict with any FERC licensing activity is presented here. FERC has not yet acted on petitioners' license application, and it is possible that FERC will eventually deny petitioners' application altogether. Alternatively, it is quite possible, given that FERC is required to give equal consideration to the protection of fish habitat when deciding whether to issue a license, that any FERC license would contain the same conditions as the state § 401 certification. * * *

* * *

■ JUSTICE THOMAS, with whom JUSTICE SCALIA joins, dissenting.

* * *

* * * The terms of § 401(a)(1) make clear that the purpose of the certification process is to ensure that discharges from a project will meet the requirements of the CWA. Indeed, a State's authority under § 401(a)(1) is limited to certifying that "any discharge" that "may result" from "any activity," such as petitioners' proposed hydroelectric project, will "comply" with the enumerated provisions of the CWA; if the discharge will fail to comply, the State may "den[y]" the certification. In addition, under § 401(d), a State may place conditions on a § 401 certification, including "effluent limitations and other limitations, and monitoring requirements," that may be necessary to ensure compliance with various provisions of the CWA and with "any other appropriate requirement of State law." § 1341(d).

The minimum stream flow condition imposed by respondents in this case has no relation to any possible "discharge" that might "result" from petitioners' proposed project. * * * A minimum stream flow requirement, by contrast, is a limitation on the amount of water the project can take in or divert from the river. That is, a minimum stream flow requirement is a limitation on intake—the opposite of discharge. Imposition of such a requirement would thus appear to be beyond a State's authority as it is defined by § 401(a)(1).

* * *

While the Court's interpretation seems plausible at first glance, it ultimately must fail. If, as the Court asserts, § 401(d) permits States to impose conditions unrelated to discharges in § 401 certifications, Congress' careful focus on discharges in § 401(a)(1)—the provision that describes the scope and function of the certification process—was wasted effort. The power to set conditions that are unrelated to discharges is, of course, nothing but a conditional power to deny certification for reasons unrelated to discharges. Permitting States to impose conditions unrelated to discharges, then, effectively eliminates the constraints of § 401(a)(1).

* * *

The Court's reading strikes me as contrary to common sense. It is difficult to see how compliance with a "use" of a body of water could be enforced without reference to the corresponding criteria. * * *

The problematic consequences of decoupling "uses" and "criteria" become clear once the Court's interpretation of § 303 is read in the context of § 401. In the Court's view, a State may condition the § 401 certification "upon *any limitations* necessary to ensure compliance" with the "uses of the water body." (emphasis added). Under the Court's interpretation, then, state environmental agencies may pursue, through § 401, their water goals in any way they choose; the conditions imposed on certifications need not relate to discharges, nor to water quality criteria, nor to any objective or quantifiable standard, so long as they tend to make the water more suitable for the uses the State has chosen. In short, once a State is allowed to impose conditions on § 401 certifications to protect "uses" in the abstract, § 401(d) is limitless.

III

The Court's interpretation of § 401 significantly disrupts the careful balance between state and federal interests that Congress struck in the

Federal Power Act (FPA), 16 U.S.C. § 791a *et seq.* Section 4(e) of the FPA authorizes the Federal Energy Regulatory Commission (FERC) to issue licenses for projects "necessary or convenient ... for the development, transmission, and utilization of power across, along, from, or in any of the streams ... over which Congress has jurisdiction." 16 U.S.C. § 797(e). In the licensing process, FERC must balance a number of considerations: "[I]n addition to the power and development purposes for which licenses are issued, [FERC] shall give equal consideration to the purposes of energy conservation, the protection, mitigation of damage to, and enhancement of, fish and wildlife (including related spawning grounds and habitat), the protection of recreational opportunities, and the preservation of other aspects of environmental quality." *Ibid.* Section 10(a) empowers FERC to impose on a license such conditions, including minimum stream flow requirements, as it deems best suited for power development and other public uses of the waters. See 16 U.S.C. § 803(a); *California v. FERC,* 495 U.S. 490, 494–495, 506 (1990).

* * *

* * * Today, the Court gives the States precisely the veto power over hydroelectric projects that we determined in *California v. FERC* and *First Iowa* they did not possess.

NOTES

1. The Supreme Court applied and extended PUD No. 1 in S.D. Warren v. Maine Board of Environmental Protection, 547 U.S. 370, 126 S.Ct. 1843, 164 L.Ed.2d 625 (2006). The Court held that the state of Maine could intervene in the relicensing of a series of dams on the Presumpscot River which operated on a run-of-the river mode, impounding water to run turbines and then releasing it into the river downstream from the dam. The dam operators argued that the dams did not add anything to the river and thus were not a "discharge" as defined in § 401. Writing for a unanimous court, Justice Souter relied on a technique of statutory construction favored by the current Court. He adopted the dictionary definition of discharge, "flowing or issuing out." Compare the definition of discharge adopted for § 402 in South Florida Water Management District v. Miccosukee Tribe, 541 U.S. 95, 124 S.Ct. 1537, 158 L.Ed.2d 264 (2004), *supra* page 682.

2. Since the principal case was decided, a circuit court has held that FERC must apply state conditions relating to instream flow that are imposed as part of the § 401 certification for the project, leaving it to the license applicant to challenge them. See American Rivers, Inc. v. FERC, 129 F.3d 99 (2d Cir.1997).

3. Can § 401 certification be used to control nonpoint source pollution? For instance, is an application for a federal public lands grazing permit subject to the requirement that the federal activity approving the permit not result in violations of the state's water quality standards? Oregon

Natural Desert Ass'n v. Dombeck, 172 F.3d 1092 (9th Cir.1998), refused to extend the holding of *PUD No. 1* to this situation because, the court said, § 401 only applies to point source discharges. See generally Charles R. Sensiba, *Who's in Charge Here? The Shrinking Role for the Federal Energy Regulatory Commission in Hydropower Relicensing*, 70 U. Colo. L.Rev. 603 (1999).

F.   ENDANGERED SPECIES CONSERVATION

The Endangered Species Act (ESA), 16 U.S.C.A. §§ 1531–1544 (West Supp. 2008), places limits on all actions that may be taken by federal officials. The ESA authorizes the Secretary of the Interior to list endangered or threatened species and to designate critical habitats of these species. Once a species is listed, § 7 of the Act mandates that the agency must insure that its actions are "not likely to jeopardize the continued existence" of an endangered species or adversely modify its habitat. The Act imposes consultation duties between the United States Fish and Wildlife Service and any federal agency planning to take such an action to determine if the action is likely to jeopardize protected species.

Federal duties under the ESA may be triggered by the review of a proposal for federal action or for federal approval of a permit or license for a private action such as a dredge and fill permit pursuant to § 404 of the Clean Water Act. The consultation process may result in a biological opinion showing no jeopardy to threatened or endangered species and thus the project may proceed. If the opinion finds that the action is likely to jeopardize a protected species, the Fish and Wildlife Service must suggest "reasonable and prudent alternatives" to the proposed action. A reasonable and prudent alternative is an approach to meeting the applicant's goals that would not violate the Act. For terrestrial listed species, it is possible to assemble reserves through dedications and purchases of private land along with continuing management. Aquatic species are harder to protect. They usually depend on an historic flow regime that has been compromised by dams and diversions, supported by entrenched water rights or legislation enacted when hatcheries and fish ladders were the answer to all fish conservation problems.

The intersection between the ESA and state water rights is one of the most controversial issues in modern water management. Simply put, the ESA imposes substantive limitations on the operation of state and federal projects as well as the exercise of state-created water rights.

Riverside Irrigation District v. Andrews

United States Court of Appeals, Tenth Circuit, 1985.
758 F.2d 508.

■ McKAY, CIRCUIT JUDGE.

* * *

Plaintiffs seek to build a dam and reservoir on Wildcat Creek, a tributary of the South Platte River. Because construction of the dam involves depositing dredge and fill material in a navigable waterway, the plaintiffs are required to obtain a permit from the Corps of Engineers under Section 404 of the Clean Water Act, 33 U.S.C. § 1344. * * *

A nationwide permit is one covering a category of activities occurring throughout the country that involve discharges of dredge or fill material that will cause only minimal adverse effects on the environment when performed separately and that will have only minimal cumulative effects. Such a permit is automatic in that if one qualifies, no application is needed before beginning the discharge activity. The Corps has the authority and duty, however, to ensure that parties seeking to proceed under a nationwide permit meet the requirements for such action. One condition of a nationwide permit is that the discharge not destroy a threatened or endangered species as identified under the Endangered Species Act, or destroy or adversely modify the critical habitat of such species. 33 C.F.R. § 330.4(b)(2). The regulations thus are consistent with the Corps' obligation, under the Endangered Species Act, to ensure that "any action authorized, funded, or carried out by such agency * * * is not likely to jeopardize the continued existence of any endangered species or threatened species or result in the destruction or adverse modification of habitat of such species which is determined by the Secretary * * * to be critical." 16 U.S.C. § 1536(a)(2).

No one claims that the fill itself will endanger or destroy the habitat of an endangered species or adversely affect the aquatic environment. However, the fill that the Corps is authorizing is required to build the earthen dam. The dam will result in the impoundment of water in a reservoir, facilitating the use of the water in Wildcat Creek. The increased consumptive use will allegedly deplete the stream flow, and it is this depletion that the Corps found would adversely affect the habitat of the whooping crane.

The Endangered Species Act does not, by its terms, enlarge the jurisdiction of the Corps of Engineers under the Clean Water Act. However, it imposes on agencies a mandatory obligation to consider the environmental impacts of the projects that they authorize or fund. As the Supreme Court stated in TVA v. Hill, 437 U.S. 153, 173 (1978):

> One would be hard pressed to find a statutory provision whose terms were any plainer than those of § 7 of the Endangered Species Act. Its very words affirmatively command all federal agencies "to insure that actions authorized, funded or carried out by them do not jeopardize the continued existence" of an endangered species or "result in the destruction or adverse modification of habitat of such species." 16 U.S.C. § 1536. This language admits of no exception.

(emphasis in original). The question in this case is how broadly the Corps is authorized to look under the Clean Water Act in determining the environmental impact of the discharge that it is authorizing.

Plaintiffs claim that the Corps is authorized to consider only the direct, on-site effects of the discharge, particularly the effects on water quality, and that the Corps exceeded its authority by considering downstream effects of changes in water quantity. However, both the statute and the regulations authorize the Corps to consider downstream effects of changes in water quantity as well as on-site changes in water quality in determining whether a proposed discharge qualifies for a nationwide permit. The statute explicitly requires that a permit be obtained for any discharge "incidental to any activity having as its purpose bringing an area of navigable waters into a use to which it was not previously subject, where the flow or circulation of navigable waters may be impaired or the reach of such waters reduced." 33 U.S.C. § 1344(f)(2). The guidelines for determining compliance with section 404(b)(1), developed by the Secretary of the Army and the Environmental Protection Agency, require the permitting authority to consider factors related to water quantity, including the effects of the discharge on water velocity, current patterns, water circulation, and normal water fluctuations. 40 C.F.R. §§ 230.23, 230.24. Thus, the statute focuses not merely on water quality, but rather on all of the effects on the "aquatic environment" caused by replacing water with fill material. 33 U.S.C. § 1344(f)(1)(E). Minnehaha Creek Watershed District v. Hoffman, 597 F.2d 617, 627 (8th Cir.1979).

Plaintiffs argue that, even if the Corps can consider effects of changes in water quantity, it can do so only when the change is a direct effect of the discharge. In the present case, the depletion of water is an indirect effect of the discharge, in that it results from the increased consumptive use of water facilitated by the discharge. However, the Corps is required, under both the Clean Water Act and the Endangered Species Act, to consider the environmental impact of the discharge that it is authorizing. To require it to ignore the indirect effects that result from its actions would be to require it to wear blinders that Congress has not chosen to impose. The fact that the reduction in water does not result "from direct federal action does not lessen the appellee's duty under § 7 [of the Endangered Species Act]." National Wildlife Federation v. Coleman, 529 F.2d 359, 374 (5th Cir.1976). The relevant consideration is the total impact of the discharge on the crane. In National Wildlife Federation, the Fifth Circuit held that the federal agency was required to consider both the direct and the indirect impacts of proposed highway construction, including the residential and commercial development that would develop around the highway interchanges. Similarly, in this case, the Corps was required to consider all effects, direct and indirect, of the discharge for which authorization was sought.

* * *

* * * The reduction of water flows resulting from the increased consumptive use is an effect, albeit indirect, of the discharge to be authorized by the Corps. The discharge thus may "destroy or adversely modify" the critical habitat of an endangered species, and the Corps correctly found that the proposed project did not meet the requirements for a nationwide permit.

Plaintiffs claim that the Corps cannot deny them a nationwide permit because the denial impairs the state's right to allocate water within its jurisdiction, in violation of section 101(g) of the Act (the "Wallop Amendment").[3] Even if denial of a nationwide permit is considered an impairment of the state's authority to allocate water, a question that we do not decide, the Corps acted within its authority. As discussed above, the statute and regulations expressly require the Corps to consider changes in water quantity in granting nationwide permits. Section 101(g), which is only a general policy statement, "cannot nullify a clear and specific grant of jurisdiction, even if the particular grant seems inconsistent with the broadly stated purpose." Connecticut Light and Power Co. v. Federal Power Commission, 324 U.S. 515 (1945). Thus, the Corps did not exceed its authority in denying a nationwide permit based on its determination that the depletion in water flow resulting from increased consumptive use of water would adversely affect the critical habitat of the whooping crane.

The Wallop Amendment does, however, indicate "that Congress did not want to interfere any more than necessary with state water management." National Wildlife Federation v. Gorsuch, 693 F.2d 156, 178 (D.C.Cir.1982). A fair reading of the statute as a whole makes clear that, where both the state's interest in allocating water and the federal government's interest in protecting the environment are implicated, Congress intended an accommodation. Such accommodations are best reached in the individual permit process.

* * *

* * * Plaintiffs are entitled to proceed under a nationwide permit only if they can show that they meet the conditions for such a permit. Thus, plaintiffs must show "that the discharge will not destroy a threatened or endangered species as identified in the Endangered Species Act or destroy or adversely modify the critical habitat of such species." 33 C.F.R. § 330.4(b)(2). The record supports the Corps' finding that the discharge may adversely modify the critical habitat of the whooping crane. Thus, plaintiffs did not meet their burden of showing, as a matter of fact, that the discharge will not have such an adverse impact. The Corps acted within its authority in requiring the plaintiffs to proceed under the individual permit procedure.

Affirmed.

---

3. The Wallop Amendment provides that:

> It is the policy of Congress that the authority of each State to allocate water within its jurisdiction shall not be superseded, abrogated or otherwise impaired by this Act. It is the further policy of Congress that nothing in this Act shall be construed to supersede or abrogate rights to quantities of water which have been established by any State.

33 U.S.C. § 1251(g) (1982).

NOTES

1. *Mitigation Alternatives.* The Fish and Wildlife Service has in some instances allowed water developments that would jeopardize an endangered species if the developer agreed to pay depletion charges that are dedicated to conservation and recovery measures. See Lawrence J. MacDonnell, The Endangered Species Act and Water Development Within the South Platte Basin 32–38 (Colorado Water Resources Research Institute, Research Report No. 137, 1985). Do you think that payment of money can satisfy the requirement that the Secretary take no action that is "likely to jeopardize the continued existence of any endangered or threatened species or result in the destruction or adverse modification of [critical] habitat"? 16 U.S.C.A. § 1536(a)(2) (West Supp. 2008). Is the payment of money a "reasonable and prudent alternative"?

In the early 1980s, water development on the Colorado River in much of Colorado, Utah, and Wyoming appeared to be stalled by the Secretary's proposal that ambitious minimum flows be maintained to avoid jeopardy to endangered fish species (squawfish, humpback chub, bonytail chub). After extensive negotiations, representatives of the Fish and Wildlife Service, the three states, the Bureau of Reclamation, water developers, and environmentalists reached consensus on a multi-faceted recovery plan for the fish. The plan was based on considerable biological data and included measures such as acquisition of instream flows within the state water rights system, releases from federal reservoirs, creation of better habitat, curtailment of planting of exotic (non-native) fish such as bass, construction of passage facilities, artificial propagation, and creation of a fund to support continued recovery efforts from federal and state contributions and one-time payments from new water projects. A committee representing the state and federal agencies oversees the plan's implementation. A similar effort is being made on the Platte River to deal with the whooping crane habitat issue described in the *Riverside* case. See *supra* p. 737. The advantage of such approaches is that they ensure compliance with federal law by means that minimize intrusions on state water law systems.

2. *Diversions as ESA Violations.* Section 3 of the Endangered Species Act (ESA) mandates that the Department of Interior "conserve" endangered species. It has been held that this provision requires the Secretary to operate a federal reservoir so that species preservation is preferred to all other uses until the numbers and condition are restored to a satisfactory level. Carson–Truckee Water Conservancy Dist. v. Clark, 741 F.2d 257 (9th Cir.1984), cert. denied 470 U.S. 1083, 105 S.Ct. 1842, 85 L.Ed.2d 141 (1985). Conflicts between the ESA and state water law are discussed in A. Dan Tarlock, Western Water Rights and the Act, in Balancing on the Brink of Extinction: The Endangered Species Act and Lessons for the Future 167 (Kathryn A. Kohm ed., 1991); see also Melissa K. Estes, The Effect of the Federal Endangered Species Act on State Water Rights, 22 Envtl. L. 1027 (1992).

In the Walla Walla River Basin of eastern Oregon and Washington, irrigators were warned by the Fish and Wildlife Service that their diversions were drying up the river and causing "take" of bull trout, an ESA-listed species. Rather than litigate over their alleged violations, four irrigation districts in the Walla Walla Basin entered into a settlement agreement with the agency, with the support of environmental organizations and the Umatilla Tribes. The settlement essentially absolved the districts of liability for any previous take of bull trout, and provided for a change in irrigation practices—including, most dramatically, a rewatering of the Walla Walla in a stretch that had long been dry during the irrigation season. These settlement agreements have been revised and renewed since the initial 2000 agreement, resulting in dramatically improved habitat conditions for the bull trout and other fish in the Walla Walla River. See David E. Filippi, The Impact of the Endangered Species Act on Water Rights and Water Use, 2002 Proc. Rocky Mtn. Min. L. Inst. 22–1, 22–12–14.

Section 9 of the Act prohibits taking endangered species. "Take" means to "harass, harm, pursue, hunt, shoot, wound, kill, trap, capture, or collect." 16 U.S.C.A. § 1532(19) (West Supp. 2008). Palila v. Hawaii Dep't of Land & Natural Res., 649 F.Supp. 1070 (D.Haw.1986), aff'd 852 F.2d 1106 (9th Cir.1988). At times, the Department of Interior has tried to limit the definition of takings to habitat modification activities that actually kill or injure an individual species, but the courts have defined a taking to include habitat modifications such as irrigation intakes that put a species at risk. United States v. Glenn–Colusa Irrigation Dist., 788 F.Supp. 1126 (E.D.Cal.1992) (district's withdrawals of water from Sacramento River were the proximate cause of death of listed winter run salmon); Department of Fish & Game v. Anderson–Cottonwood Irrigation Dist., 8 Cal. App.4th 1554, 11 Cal.Rptr.2d 222 (1992) (California Endangered Species Act prohibits irrigation withdrawals without proper fish screens because taking not limited to hunting or fishing); and Sierra Club v. Lyng, 694 F.Supp. 1260 (E.D.Tex.1988) (destruction of Red-cockaded woodpecker habitat by clear cutting national forest). The department's definition of habitation modification as a taking was upheld by the Supreme Court in Babbitt v. Sweet Home Chapter of Communities for a Great Oregon, 515 U.S. 687, 115 S.Ct. 2407, 132 L.Ed.2d 597 (1995). Justice O'Connor's concurring opinion reasoned that the modification must be significant and "the regulation's application is limited by ordinary principles of proximate causation, which introduce notions of foreseeability * * * [and thus in] my view, the regulation is limited * * * to actions that actually kill or injure individual animals." Id. at 709. Is impaired breeding a taking? See Marbled Murrelet v. Babbitt, 83 F.3d 1060 (9th Cir.1996).

3. *Water War in the Klamath.* The prospect of water users being impacted by enforcement of the ESA is even greater where they depend on deliveries from federal projects under contracts with the Bureau of Reclamation. The concerns of irrigators with Bureau contracts, and the intensity of their objections, are illustrated by events in the Klamath River Basin. After a challenge by conservation and fishing interests the Bureau was ordered not to release water to contracting farmers until it complied with its ESA obligations. Pacific Coast Federation of Fishermen's Ass'n v. Bureau of Reclamation, 138 F.Supp.2d 1228 (N.D.Cal. 2001). In 2001 the Bureau of

Reclamation announced that it would curtail water deliveries to 90 per cent of the 240,000 acres served by the Klamath Project. One Biop directed that water be kept in the stream for the threatened coho salmon and another required retaining more water upstream in Upper Klamath Lake for two other species of endangered fish. These limitations on the management of the federal project water coincided with a severe drought, resulting in cutting off the irrigation water for over 1000 farmers. This led to civil disobedience including forcing open federal headgates and massive demonstrations by the farmers and their supporters. At one point the sympathetic local sheriff refused to enforce the law against the protesters.

Irrigators had been unsuccessful in seeking legal remedies. They were denied an injunction to prevent implementation of the 2001 Operating Plan because their contractual rights were subservient to the government's ESA requirements as well as trust responsibilities for protecting Indian treaty fishing rights. Kandra v. United States, 145 F.Supp.2d 1192 (D.Or.2001). Earlier, the irrigators were denied status as third-party beneficiaries when they tried to assert rights under a contract between the Bureau and a power company governing releases from Klamath Lake which is also the primary source of irrigation water. Klamath Water Users Protective Ass'n v. Patterson, 204 F.3d 1206 (9th Cir. 1999), cert. denied 531 U.S. 812, 121 S.Ct. 44, 148 L.Ed.2d 14 (2000).

The Secretary of the Interior later decided that conditions allowed her to release more water for the irrigators, but it came too late for most. Several months later, a National Academy of Sciences, National Research Council interim report concluded that the basin was stressed but that there had been "no substantial scientific basis" for the mandated water level, which deprived the irrigators of water. The final report emphasized the need to focus on sucker and salmon recovery and restoration and expressly stated that the Fish and Wildlife's scientific decision was not junk science. However, it reaffirmed its earlier conclusion. Scientific Evaluation of Biological Opinions on Endangered and Threatened Fishes in the Klamath Basin (2002). FWS and NMFS issued a new BiOp in 2002 which called for spring peak flows to help Coho spawning, but postponed full achievement of these until 2010. Pacific Coast Federation of Fishermen's Associations v. United States Bureau of Reclamation, 426 F.3d 1082 (9th Cir. 2005), invalidated the BiOp because it lacked any analysis of the impact of 8 years of low flows on five generations of Coho. On remand, NMFS was told to rethink not better rationalize the opinion and a district court prohibited any Klamath project water deliveriess inconsistent with the long term flow requirements of the 2002 Biop. Holly Doremus and A. Dan Tarlock, Water War in the Klamath Basin: Macho Law, Combat Biology, and Dirty Politics 138 (2008). Since 2001, the headgates have not been shut off due to wet seasons, the use of water banks and the 2002 Biop. However, the net impact of the Department of Interior's decision to favor the farmers over endangered fish has been to move the "problem shed" downstream and to shift the focus to the survival of Coho salmon runs.

The shift of the "problemshed" from the Upper Klamath to the entire basin eventually helped broker a settlement among most of the major interests. In 2004, PacifiCorp's hydroelectric dam licenses were up for renewal, and it announced that it would raise electric rates 1000 percent after a 50 old year sweet heart half-cent per kilowatt hour contract expired. This united the irrigators and the Tribes against the utility. In 2008, a proposed settlement was reached. In brief, it would remove the four PacifiCorps dams that block salmon passage, quantify water rights for the federal wildlife refuges, and offer reduced (but not half-cent per kilowatt hour) power rates to farmers. The farmers versus fish conflict would be solved by cutting irrigation deliveries by 10–25 percent in return for a substantially reduced risk that there will be a repeat of the 2001 total shut-off. The kickers are that the utility and major NGOs such as Oregon Wild and WaterWatch are not parties, the utility has not agreed to remove the dams, and there is no firm funding for the proposed $1 billion budget. See Matt Jenkins, Peace on the Klamath, 40 High Country News No. 12, page 12 (June 23, 2008).

Do the irrigators have a claim for money damages against the United States for losses sustained when the Bureau did not deliver contract water? See pages 527–544.

4. *Salmon at Risk.* Since the 1990s, the Endangered Species Act has been the focus of salmon recovery operations after species began to be listed. Initially, the NMFS relied on smolt transportation around dams, but a 1994 district court opinion invalidated a NMFS biological opinion because trucking and barging would not restore salmon runs. Idaho Dep't of Fish & Game v. National Marine Fisheries Serv., 850 F.Supp. 886 (D.Or.1994). The opinion helped shift the debate away from mitigation solutions, such as transportation and hatcheries, to the merits of increased Snake River flows versus breaching four lower Snake River dams and more generally for the need to restore the river's pre-dam hydrograph. See *Return to the River: An Ecological Vision for the Recovery of the Columbia River Salmon*, 28 Envtl. L. 503 (1998). The case for breaching the dams is reviewed in Michael C. Blumm et al, *Saving Snake River Water and Salmon Simultaneously: The Biological, Economic, and Legal Case for Breaching the Lower Snake River Dams, Lowering John Day Reservoir, and Restoring Natural River Flows*, 28 Envtl. L. 997 (1998). However, the Bush administration took dam removal or breaching off the table in 2006 [right date]. In brief, the federal government kept barging salmon and the courts kept invalidating Biological Opinions. After the 2004 BiOp was found incompatible with the ESA, National Wildlife Federation v. National Marine Fisheries Service, 481 F.3d 1224 (9th Cir. 2007), a new Biop was proposed which outlines a ten year protection program which includes dam modification and tributary and estuary habitat enhancement. See generally Michael C. Blumm, Erica J. Thorson and Joshua D. Smith, Practiced at the Art of Deception: The Failure of Columbia Basin Salmon Recovery Under the Endangered Species Act, 36 Envtl. L. 709 (2006). Proposals to increase flows in the tributaries raise a full range of water rights issues. See Reed D. Benson, *Maintaining the Status Quo: Protecting Established Water Uses in the Pacific Northwest, Despite Rules of Prior Appropriation*, 28 Envtl. L. 881 (1998). One proposal is to eliminate the considerable Bureau of Reclamation water deliveries to ineligible land. The argument that "water spreading" may violate the Endangered Species Act is set out in Peter M. Lacy, *The Irrigated Desert and Imperiled Salmon: "Reclaiming" Illegally Spread Water Via the Endangered Species Act*, 4 Den. Water L. Rev. 351 (2001).

5.   One major point of contention regarding the ESA in the western water context is whether the Bureau of Reclamation, in operating a federal water project, has legal discretion to reduce water deliveries for irrigation (or other uses) in order to provide water for endangered species habitat. In litigation over the operation of Reclamation projects on the Middle Rio Grande in New Mexico, the government and project users argued unsuccessfully that the Bureau lacked discretion to reduce water deliveries for the sake of the Rio Grand Silvery Minnow. Rio Grande Silvery Minnow v. Keys, 333 F.3d 1109 (10th Cir. 2003), vacated as moot, 355 F.3d 1215 (10th Cir. 2004). In 2007, the Supreme Court confirmed that ESA section 7 applies only to discretionary federal actions, and shed some minimal light on what federal actions are non-discretionary for this purpose. National Ass'n of Home Builders v. Defenders of Wildlife, 127 S.Ct. 2518, 168 L.Ed.2d 467 (2007). The effect of this case on Reclamation project operations has yet to be determined, although it is likely to become an issue in the ongoing Silvery Minnow litigation. See Reed D. Benson, Dams, Duties, and Discretion: Bureau of Reclamation Water Project Operations and the Endangered Species Act, 33 Colum. J. Envtl. L. 1 (2008).

A. Dan Tarlock, The Endangered Species Act and Western Water Rights
20 Land & Water L.Rev. 1, 13, 17, 26–30 (1985).

The Endangered Species Act effectively creates de facto regulatory water rights. That is, the federal government now has a new basis to claim that specific but undetermined amounts of water either be released from a reservoir or not be impounded. * * *

The existence of regulatory rights under the Endangered Species Act and section 404 of the Clean Water Act raises the following issue: whether private expectations that the ground-rules under which state water rights are acquired will not be changed are equally as strong when the federal government exercises its constitutional power retroactively to regulate in the public interest. A tentative answer is no. What seems to be emerging out of recent water adjudications is that state-created water rights are not different from any other property rights despite the vast energy dissipated by western water lawyers to will a contrary result. Thus, state water rights are not immune from the retroactive application of state police power or of federal constitutional authority.

* * *

The characterization of permit conditions as "regulatory property rights" is a conceptual analysis: neither Congress nor the courts have adopted it. As permit conditions are imposed, however, the issue of how these "regulatory property rights" should be applied will arise.

The solution which best serves the needs of the federal government and the states is to assign water rights to the project operator. The result is that except in extraordinary cases, the project operator, as a water rights holder, should be subject to state procedural law. The project operator's water rights would also appear in the state record system, notifying subsequent appropriators of the federal government's claims.

State substantive doctrines may operate to frustrate federal water rights claimed under the Endangered Species Act. When conflicts between state law and federal objectives arise, however, state law should be presumptively preempted. * * *

Unlike section 404 of the Clean Water Act, the Endangered Species Act should impose a duty on new and existing federal or private project operators to supply sufficient water to protect the endangered species. Senior water rights holders should not have to suffer uncompensated reallocation, but project beneficiaries and other rights holders may expect to see water allocation patterns that differ from those provided under state law.

* * *

The integration into western water law of the values represented by the Endangered Species Act and section 404 of the Clean Water Act will not be easy. The first step is to recognize that it is legitimate for the federal government to claim water rights under these acts. These Acts represent a federal decision to add to the list of "beneficial" uses served by our water resources. The issue is not whether such rights can be claimed, but under what circumstances and in what manner they can be asserted.

* * *

Courts could start the process of accommodating federal and state interests by adopting a rule requiring the federal government to determine that non-flow release protection strategies are unlikely to preserve the species as compared to flow release strategies. This inquiry will reinforce the federal government's duty to seek mitigation strategies that include active management programs.

* * *

The federal government should be entitled to the minimum amount of water deemed necessary to prevent the species' habitat from a further risk of deterioration. This determination must be based on the best available evidence. Judicial ground rules for species protection should provide sufficient incentives for all interested parties to strike some creative bargains rather than requiring parties to resort to the courts to solve future protection claims.

NOTE: NATIONAL ENVIRONMENTAL POLICY ACT

The National Environmental Policy Act (NEPA), 42 U.S.C.A. §§ 4331–4344 (West 1994), requires federal agencies to prepare an environmental impact statement (EIS) concerning the environmental effects of any proposed projects that constitute "major Federal actions significantly affecting the quality of the human environment." § 4332(c). The federal actions covered can include any approval, license, or permit—such as a Clean Water Act § 404 permit or a Federal Power Act license—as well as decisions to build a federal water project. Whether the project is "major," so as to require an EIS, depends on the magnitude of the impacts. The data developed under the comprehensive planning mandate of § 10(a) of the Federal Power Act and some other programs may be the functional equivalent of an EIS and therefore satisfy NEPA. See National Wildlife Federation v. FERC, 801 F.2d 1505, 17 Envtl. L. Rep. 20,111 (9th Cir.1986).

Initially, courts heard a number of challenges to inadequate environmental impact statements, but these challenges are harder to make today. Agencies have learned how to prepare an adequate EIS. NEPA's duties are procedural not substantive, so that once an adequate EIS is done a project may proceed even if it is environmentally damaging. NEPA does not generally apply to on-going projects where the damage has already been done. Upper Snake River Chapter v. Hodel, 921 F.2d 232 (9th Cir.1990). But, the Act can be applied to the operation of on-going projects when they are modified. For example, in 1989, the Secretary of the Interior agreed to prepare an EIS for the operation of Glen Canyon Dam on the Colorado River. The Department of the Interior had initially refused to do so after it announced plans to rewind existing generators but the Secretary reversed the decision after extensive evidence was shown of potential downstream environmental impacts of the altered flow patterns produced by the dam. The EIS process provides a vehicle for the agency and other interested parties to examine ways to mitigate the tension between historic operating patterns and those that accommodate new values such as environmental protection and recreation enhancement. The 1995 EIS and 1996 Record of Decision ultimately led to an altered flow release schedule and an experimental beach building flow release in 1996, a major precedent in the reoperation of dams for river restoration. See The Controlled Flood in Grand Canyon (Geophysical Monograph 110, Robert C. Webb et al. eds., 1999). See also National Research Council, Downstream: Adaptive Management of Glen Canyon Dam and the Colorado River Ecosystem (1999) and Alejandro E. Camacho, Beyond Conjecture: Learning About Ecosystem Management From the Glen Canyon Dam Experiment, 8 Nev. L. J. 942 (2008).

G.   Accommodating Federal Regulation and State Water Law

1.   Federal Regulation of Water

A tradition of federal deference to states in the allocation and management of water would suggest restraint in the exercise of federal powers that conflict with state water rights. In fact, as this chapter illustrates, Congress has passed several environmental protection laws that often require, or give federal agencies the authority to require, water management practices that may conflict with state-created rights.

Conflicts with state water allocation and control occur when federal law effectively requires that water be used in a particular manner or amount. The effects may be felt when a water user attempts to put the water to use such as when a reservoir or other project is constructed. But there are instances where simply changing the quantity or timing of one's use may conflict with a federal environmental protection law.

Today, this federal-state conflict is one of the most contentious areas of water policy. One reason for the tension is the failure of state laws to keep pace with the public demand for environmental protection. Meanwhile federal legislation has expanded. Where political stand-offs have arisen, often over water development proposals, solutions have been found by convening affected stakeholders. These efforts are typically driven by the stakeholders themselves and include, but are not dominated by, state and federal representatives. One of their major advantages is that the solutions can include restoring the quality and natural flow regimes of waterways. There is little in existing law to require restoration.

David H. Getches, The Metamorphosis of Western Water Policy: Have Federal Laws and Local Decisions Eclipsed the States' Role?

20 Stan.Envtl.L.J. 3, 42–48 (2000).

The most important innovations in water policy in the 1990s have occurred in response to federal pressure and local initiatives, and almost entirely outside the legislatures and courts of the western states. Instead of being produced within the traditional western water institutional framework, changes were generated "outside-the-box." These approaches, more than official state programs, carry forward the kinds of reform-minded ideas that characterized the rhetoric of western governors in the 1980s. Broad segments of the public have gotten involved in solving water problems and have addressed them with attention to their interrelationships with other issues. They have employed solutions that promote more efficient use, market mechanisms, and conjunctive use. Although they are usually ad hoc responses to particular problems, many of these efforts are better examples of a comprehensive approach to planning than state-sponsored water planning.

Although sweeping state institutional reforms are theoretically possible, the experience of the recent past suggests that the most promising advances in the foreseeable future will continue to be ad hoc, outside-the-box, responses to problems arising in specific geographic areas. Unless states can muster the will to embrace reform when the opportunities arise, the federal government along with these local groups will continue to foment constructive change.

1.   Macro-watershed initiatives.

In the watersheds of several major rivers, place-specific problem solving efforts are being conducted by representatives of diverse interests. Although some of these efforts have been supported by state legislation, they generally operate outside traditional water institutions as particularized responses to issues that could not or were not being addressed successfully by existing institutions. Typically, they have tackled a wide range of issues and assembled a diverse group of parties to participate in seeking solutions.

The most notable macro-watershed effort is "CALFED." In this effort, representatives of agricultural, business, environmental, and urban concerns, along with representatives of sixteen state and federal agencies, are cooperatively trying to solve the problems growing out of the so-called Bay–Delta dispute in California. Originally the Bay–Delta matter appeared to be a problem of controlling water quality in the delta of the Sacramento and San Joaquin Rivers at San Francisco Bay. However, it was soon found to implicate water use and protection throughout the state of California. Environmental and supply problems and operations of water diversion facilities were causing serious, ongoing violations of the federal Clean Water Act and Endangered Species Act. State institutions were not equipped to deal comprehensively with the related problems of water quality, watershed protection, ecosystem restoration, water use efficiency, water transfers, instream flow maintenance, flood control, and managing water storage and conveyance facilities. This panoply of issues, formerly addressed in a piecemeal fashion by state legislation, agencies, and courts, became CALFED's portfolio. The participants are now engaged in what amounts to comprehensive statewide water planning to ensure more reliable water supplies, new management practices to improve water quality for the environment, cities, and farms, and ecosystem restoration efforts, including removal of small dams.

Elsewhere, the operations of Glen Canyon Dam, on the Colorado River, are now subject to ongoing review by an "adaptive management work group." A group of states, Indian tribes, power purchasers, recreational users, federal agencies, and environmental organizations is charged with monitoring the effects of policies and plans for operating Glen Canyon Dam. In the past, release of water from the dam, primarily for power generation, has caused serious environmental and social problems. The group now evaluates such issues as the consequences of dam operations for Grand Canyon National Park, and goals such as fulfilling recreational and environmental purposes and recovery of endangered fish species. It then recommends changes in the dam's operating regime to meet various management objectives consistent with the public interest, such as proposing releases necessary to maintain flows required for ecosystem restoration and recreation.

Another macro-watershed effort is underway on the Platte River. After twenty years of conflict over the effects of water development projects on endangered species in the central Platte River, the states of Colorado, Nebraska, and Wyoming have signed a cooperative agreement with the United States Department of the Interior to implement a joint program of restoration and improved management of the river. Environmental groups as well as water users and governments at all levels participate in the program. The agreement addresses endangered species concerns and various collateral issues and is expected to result in delivery of the flows that are needed for habitats of several species.

In the case of the Truckee River–Pyramid Lake issue in Nevada, the results of long and complex negotiations among diverse interests were codified in federal legislation. The legislation resolved many issues, ranging from tribal water rights to interstate allocation of waters between California and Nevada. Important wildlife issues were addressed, including water rights to benefit the Stillwater National Wildlife Refuge and implementation of recovery plans for the Pyramid Lake's imperiled cui-ui and Lahontan cutthroat trout. The act also called for negotiation among all the interested parties of an operating agreement for federal facilities on the Truckee River which, supplies Pyramid Lake. The resulting agreement led to increased efficiencies for the Newlands Reclamation Project that had sapped the river of water needed to maintain the level of the lake and sustain its fishery.

Finally, representatives from Arizona, California, and Nevada have come together with various water and power agencies to form a regional partnership to develop the Lower Colorado River Basin Multi–Species Conservation Program. It is intended to comply with the Endangered Species Act by conserving endangered species and their critical habitat in the 100–year floodplain of the Colorado River within the United States. In addition, it will facilitate further development of Colorado River water. Because species that become endangered in the future may lie in the path of development, the program will attempt to conserve eighty-eight, mostly non-listed, species in the lower Colorado River basin. This will allow present development to proceed as part of an approved habitat conservation plan under provisions of the ESA that allow some incidental harm to endangered species if the plan can provide overall benefits to habitat that otherwise might not be attained.

2. *Local watershed efforts.*

In addition to macro-watershed efforts, there are hundreds of local efforts that involve people in neighborhoods, watersheds, and communities in solving water and other resource problems that affect them. As with the macro-watershed efforts, the approach they follow is far different from the traditional state agency approach to water problems. Instead of looking narrowly at specific projects and limited considerations to address particular issues or problems, these efforts attempt to include as many issues and interests as possible.

In these watershed groups, people and entities representing varied interests may be drawn together by different concerns emanating from use of a common resource. When a river runs through a town or community, for instance, some residents' concerns about pollution caused by an upstream mine may motivate them to seek solutions to the problem, while others may be concerned because an endangered species issue inhibits development. By coming together, disparate interests—from a mine owner to local citizens, business owners to environmentalists, and scientists to school children—become involved in developing multi-faceted solutions, often employing a holistic, or systems approach.

The Animas River Stakeholder Group is typical of collaborative problem solving at the watershed level. Local residents, who shared a common concern for the quality of the Animas River in southern Colorado, convened after water quality studies by the state Department of Health confirmed contamination of the river by cadmium, lead, and other metals leaching from several abandoned mines. Encouraged by a federal Environmental Protection Agency (EPA) policy favoring watershed-based solutions to water quality problems, the state agency hired a facilitator and helped obtain a United States Department of Energy grant to set up the stakeholder group. Participants were attracted to the group for reasons ranging from an altruistic desire to restore the fishery to attempts to avoid Superfund listing and liability. Members included two towns, a county, three state agencies, two federal agencies, a tribe, landowners, mining companies, environmental activists, and other concerned citizens. The group has undertaken monitoring, identification of pollution hot spots, prioritizing sources of contamination, and planning solutions consistent with a comprehensive view of the public interest.

The Natural Resources Law Center at the University of Colorado School of Law has been studying local watershed groups and has published a collection of profiles of many of them. These groups typically are "grassroots" efforts, created and operated from the ground up. Although Oregon and Washington have passed enabling legislation to encourage and provide funding to such groups, most watershed groups in the West operate outside-the-box of traditional state institutions.

NOTES

1. A major legal problem in relying upon outside-the-box efforts to promote aquatic ecosystem management through stakeholder collaboration is that it often has no statutory basis. Ecosystem or watershed management is a scientific rather than legal concept and at present it must be superimposed over existing statutes; these statutes recognize political jurisdictions justified more by history than reason and the specific federal and state agency missions that history has produced. The substitution of voluntary watershed or basin protection efforts for the administration of existing laws is vulnerable to legal challenges, and several recent cases have held that voluntary protection does not comply with the Endangered

Species Act's mandates. As stakeholder groups obtain legal status, either through legislation or the delegation of authority, separation of powers and due process issues arise. See A. Dan Tarlock, *Putting Rivers Back in the Landscape: The Revival of Watershed Management in the United States*, 6 Hastings W–Nw. J. Envtl. L. & Pol'y 167, 192–95 (2000).

2. A successful legal challenge is illustrated in Oregon Natural Res. Council v. Daley, 6 F.Supp.2d 1139 (D.Or.1998). In brief, the populations of evolutionary significant units (ESU) of coastal coho salmon have been declining for a variety of human and natural causes. The decision whether to list the coho as a threatened species under the Endangered Species Act has been a political football throughout the 1990s because the protection and restoration that are triggered by listing require intensive public and private land use controls and water management. The causes include timber harvest practices, livestock grazing, and water diversions. In 1997, the National Marine Fisheries Service (NMFS) withdrew an earlier proposal to list the coho as threatened because the Oregon Coastal Salmon Restoration Initiative, a state-generated effort that involved the affected parties, would reverse the population decline. Scientific opinion within NMFS was divided on the effectiveness of the initiative as well as on the need to list the species. A Magistrate Judge invalidated the decision not to list because a species must be listed if it is likely to become extinct in the foreseeable future. The Service only evaluated the effect of the initiative on population declines over a two-year period. The primary flaw in NMFS's approach was to base its decision not on science but on faith in future actions taken by the legislative and executive branches of Oregon. "NMFS * * * was unwilling to make the hard choice required by the ESA. * * * " Id. At 1152. Thus, reliance on the state's initiative was arbitrary and capricious because it relied on unimplemented, largely voluntary future actions. Oregon's initiative depended in part on local watershed councils where landowner participation was "largely voluntary." NMFS had rejected California's similar action plan, in part, because the state had not funded a proposed watershed initiative and landowner participation was voluntary. The Court found the agency's failure to explain why Oregon's initiative did not pose the same risks as California's "telling." "However laudable Oregon's efforts to employ new management techniques to try to restore the Oregon Coast ESU, such future voluntary conservation effort cannot be a substitute for listing." Id. at 1159. See also National Wildlife Federation v. Babbitt, 128 F.Supp.2d 1274 (E.D. Cal. 2000).

A series of earlier district court opinions, on which the court relied, held that the FWS could not rely on possible future management actions by other agencies. *E.g.*, Biodiversity Legal Foundation v. Babbitt, 943 F.Supp. 23 (D.D.C.1996); Friends of the Wild Swan, Inc. v. United States Fish & Wildlife Ser., 945 F.Supp. 1388 (D.Or.1996). The Ninth Circuit had held that the FWS could not excuse its duty to designate critical habitat for the California Gnatcatcher on a large reserve system created under a voluntary state program. Natural Res. Defense Council v. United States Dep't of Interior, 113 F.3d 1121 (9th Cir.1997).

THE BAY–DELTA: A CASE STUDY IN THE LIMITS OF REASONING TOGETHER

The "Bay–Delta," where the Sacramento and San Joaquin rivers come together at San Francisco Bay, is a 730,000–acre web of islands, sloughs, marshes, wetlands, and open water habitats that has been diked for agriculture. It is economically important as a rich farming district and as the hub for water transfers from the wet north to dry southern California and the San Joaquin Valley. Much of the water that flows into the delta from these systems is extracted using large pumps and put into canals that feed two huge water diversion projects.

Conservation of the Bay–Delta is perhaps the most complex water allocation challenge in the world. Effective conservation requires a comprehensive solution to almost all the state's water conflicts because most of the state's users rely in whole or in part on water passing through or destined for the delta. Solutions require controlling water pollution from point and non-point sources, building storage facilities, instituting urban water conservation, and using water marketing.

From before the first European sighting in 1772 until the Gold Rush, the delta remained a rich storehouse of biodiversity, a vast marsh covered with tules which supported fish, birds, and other wildlife. Beginning with the passage of the federal Swamp and Overflow Act of 1850, seasonally submerged lands of the Bay–Delta were "reclaimed" for farming and farm lands were drained and protected from flooding by levees. In the 19th century, California developed its unique dual system of appropriative and riparian rights which allowed large users to claim large, unquantified quantities of water unsupervised by the state. California's did not adopt a permit system until 1914. In the 20th century, the headwaters of the two rivers were dammed to provide municipal and agricultural supplies.

The first unit of the Central Valley Project (CVP), the Contra Costa Canal, was completed in 1940, and subsequently Shasta Dam was completed at the headwaters of the Sacramento River along with the Delta Cross Channel which helped transfer water from the Sacramento to the Tracy Pumping Plant and into the Delta Mendota Canal for use in the San Joaquin Valley. In 1960, after a bitter sectional political battle, California voters approved the California State Water Project (SWP) to store water in Oroville Dam on the Feather River and then transfer it to southern California. The resulting California Aqueduct came on line in 1973.

Today, the delta is still home to some 750 species of flora and fauna, migrating salmon, and waterfowl. Since 1950, however, the Sacramento River Valley portion of the delta has lost of 98 percent of its riparian habitat, 95 percent of its spawning habitat, and 95 percent of tidal wetlands. Save the Bay, Putting It Back Together: Making Ecosystem Restoration Work 59–60 (2001). Salmon runs are compromised by upstream diversions, dams, and the pumping stations. Winter and Spring Chinook Salmon runs have declined from 30,000 fish in 1971–75 (before the SWP came on line) to 1,000 to 2,000 fish per year.

As upstream diversions began to increase on both rivers, the state became more concerned about salt water intrusion in the Bay–Delta. W. Turrentine Jackson and Alan M. Patterson, The Sacramento–San Joaquin Delta: The Evolution and Implementation of Water Policy (California Water Resources Center Technical Report 163, 1977 is a complete history of the early efforts to protect the Delta). Until the 1980s, the presumed solution was to construct a Peripheral Canal around the Bay–Delta but in 1982, California voters defeated a ballot initiative to finance and construct the canal by a 3–2 margin. Alternative solutions that required limiting diversions for water projects disadvantaged water users who depended on them. When the CVP was planned, San Joaquin Valley riparians had exchanged their water rights for project entitlements. Events came to a head in 1994 after the following legal developments:

> 1986—United States v. State Water Resources Control Board, 182 Cal.App.3d 82, 227 Cal.Rptr. 161 (1986), held that the state had to integrate the maintenance of water quality standards into permits to use existing state and federal water entitlements, limiting water depletions as necessary.

> 1992—Congress passed the Central Valley Project Improvement Act (CVPIA) mandating the creation of an 800,000 acre-feet environmental water account from the uncontracted portion of CVP yield.

> 1993—The Delta Smelt was listed as a threatened species under the Endangered Species Act. Subsequently the Winter Run Chinook from the Sacramento was listed as endangered and the Spring Run Chinook from the San Joaquin was listed as threatened.

> 1994—California Water Plan Update: Bulletin 160–93 (the Bible of California water planning) predicted a state water supply shortfall of 3.7 million acre-feet by 2020 in average years, up to 9 million acre-feet in drought years, as the state's population grows by 53 percent.

> 1994—After the state failed to implement *United States v. State Water Resources Control Board* the EPA acted to set stringent water quality standards. But then the Bay–Delta Accord (discussed *infra* p. 700) was reached, committing the states and the federal government to new water quality standards and to a process for resolving multiple issues with multiple stakeholders at the table.

Sue McClurg, Sacramento–San Joaquin River Basin Study,

Report to the Western Water Policy Review Advisory Commission 5–11 (1997).

Overall, the Sacramento–San Joaquin River Basin is a microcosm of water-related issues throughout the West—water rights, environmental restoration, water marketing and transfers, groundwater use, growth, water pollution. * * *

A. *Environmental Restoration*

The effectiveness and economics of environmental restoration as well as the science behind the decisions are issues facing stakeholders and agency staff within the basin. (The main stakeholders are agricultural, environmental and urban water interests. Other players include commercial and sports fishing groups, major businesses and public interest groups such as the League of Women Voters.) Many of the actions to remediate and improve the environment are required by federal laws such as the Endangered Species Act (ESA), Central Valley Project Improvement Act (CVPIA) and the Clean Water Act (CWA).

While restrictions placed upon traditional water project operations because of these laws have generated complaints from stakeholders and some state agencies (and some efforts to revamp the laws), there is general acknowledgment that these laws have served as a "hammer" to facilitate ultimate cooperation.

The CWA and ESA, for example, were instrumental in the 1994 Bay–Delta Accord and the agreed-upon three-year water quality standards. Environmental groups sued EPA for not enforcing the CWA, creating a deadline for which the federal agency had to promulgate standards, while ESA restrictions on water exports encouraged users of the SWP and CVP to push for a resolution to the problem. Elsewhere within the basin, potential that the spring-run Chinook salmon may be listed under the ESA prompted diverse stakeholders and landowners to join forces on several tributaries to the Sacramento River to boost spring-run population and forestall such a listing.

When it comes to the CVPIA, agricultural stakeholders have expressed frustration that implementation of this law, passed in 1992, has proceeded so slowly. They also say that more money from the environmental restoration fund should be dedicated to projects, not studies. In the meantime, environmentalists also have pushed the U.S. Fish and Wildlife Service (FWS) and USBR to adopt the environmental components of the law and place more restrictions on traditional CVP users.

As work progresses on a comprehensive, collaborative Bay–Delta solution and implementation of the CVPIA, most of the focus on environmental restoration is on:

- **Science**—stakeholders have challenged decisions made by federal and state fishery and water quality agencies through the years on how "good" the science is behind a recommended action. With the shift toward ecosystem management, agency scientists are finding that there are many resource issues that require more research. Urban and agricultural interests increasingly have generated their own scientific evidence on environmental issues through the use of staff or consultant biologists and other scientists.

- **Effectiveness**—agencies and stakeholders both support real-time monitoring to ensure that fish flows, pumping modifications, habitat improvement and other programs that are implemented restore ecosystem functions and lead to increases in fish populations.

- **Economics**—with passage of Proposition 204, the $995 million California water bond, the promise of additional federal funds through

HR 4126, and the environmental restoration fund created by the CVPIA, stakeholders want to make sure projects are prioritized and that money is allocated to measures that will produce the most "bang for the buck." Water users have long complained about the cost of environmental "fixes," such as fish screens, but the availability of state and federal funds to help finance these items has encouraged grassroots efforts to protect fish and habitat.

NOTES

1. *Let Us Reason Together.* What is the most appropriate institutional framework to address the Delta "problem"? The Sacramento–San Joaquin River Basin Study, Report to the Western Water Policy Review Advisory Commission, listed 8 federal agencies, 3 state agencies, and 12 stakeholder organizations representing farmers, environmentalists, urban areas, and others with a primary interest in the outcome, and other agencies and stakeholders with a secondary interest. Should each agency independently decide on issues such as environmental standards, water entitlements, and possible new supply augmentation projects based on its statutory authority and therefore leave many of the final decisions to the courts? The stakeholders instead adopted an "outside-the-box," collaborative solution driven by the fear that the worst-case unilateral action scenario would occur. See Elizabeth A. Rieke, *The Bay–Delta Accord: A Stride Toward Sustainability*, 67 U. Colo. L. Rev. 341 (1996). The Bay–Delta Accord created the framework for a consensus, multi-stakeholder process, called "CALFED," supported by substantial state and federal monies, to develop a long-term solution to the Bay–Delta problem. CALFED is a consortium of federal and state agencies, and its initial mission was to prepare a programmatic environmental impact statement (EIS) on a range of protection alternatives. The accord substituted less stringent ESA and water quality standards than those proposed by the federal agencies in return for a promise to implement the new standards immediately. Water users won a promise that there would be no further reductions on water exports out of the Delta for three years. CALFED was hailed by many as a new model of modular federalism where stakeholders would take ownership of an issue and negotiate a binding new management regime. E.g. Jody Freeman and Daniel A. Farber, Modular Environmental Regulation, 54 Duke L. J. 795 (2005). However, the history of the Bay Delta to 2008 is not encouraging. For a perceptive analysis of the tension between maintaining the water entitlements which depend on water passing through the Delta and conserving its ecosystem see David Owen, Law, Environmental Dynamism, and Reliability: The Rise and Fall of CALFED, 37 Envtl. L. 1145 (2007).

2. *Early Success.* In 1995 the State Water Resources Control Board adopted new Delta water quality standards that required increased outflows from the delta of between 400,000 acre-feet in normal water years and 1.1 million acre-feet in dry years. Subsequent biological opinions for endangered species also contain outflow requirements. Realizing these goals required capital investments in facilities, in 1996 the state's voters approved a $995 million water project bond initiative which included $193 million for immediate physical improvements in the delta.

3. *The CALFED EIA*: Thinking Inside the Box. The initial CALFED agreement formally expired when the provisions of an August 2000 Record of Decision (ROD), which followed the programmatic EIS, are executed. Future actions were to be based on four principles: (1) the provision of good quality water for all beneficial uses, (2) the improvement of aquatic and terrestrial habitats and ecosystem functions in the delta, (3) the reduction of the mismatch between delta supplies and current and projected beneficial uses based on the supply, and (4) the reduction of land use, water supply, infrastructure, and ecosystem risks from a catastrophic breaching of delta levees. The Environmentally Preferred Alternative in the EIS rejected an "isolated conveyance facility" in favor of a through-delta conveyance approach using a variety of measures from modified flows, fish screens, water transfers, and new surface and groundwater storage.

The Bay–Delta Programmatic Environmental Impact Report was challenged on three, principal grounds, the failure to consider reduced exports from the Delta, the failure to assess the environmental impacts of diverting water from existing sources to meet program goals, and the lack of specificity in the sources of water for stabilization flows and for the proposed Environmental Account. In an opinion that was immediately decertified for publication, an intermediate appellate court remanded the Bay–Delta Programmatic Impact Statement. On the first ground, it wrote because "CALFED appears not have considered, as an alternative, smaller water exports from the Bay–Delta region, which might in turn, lead to smaller population growth due to the unavailability of water to support such growth." This alternative had been considered but the use of water markets and land retirement were quickly rejected—because any serious consideration of them exacerbated rather than reduced the conflicts that CALFED was formed to address. The Supreme Court reversed and found the EIR adequate, In re Bay–Delta Programmatic Environmental Impact Report Coordinated Proceedings, 43 Cal.4th 1143, 77 Cal.Rptr.3d 578, 184 P.3d 709 (2008). The final EIS justified the exclusion of export restrictions because it would compromise the objective of water supply reliability, and the Supreme Court concluded that the agency had the discretion to conclude that this was not a reasonable alternative, although it acknowledged that the fact that an alternative would impede the attainment of some project objectives does not per se make it unreasonable. The EIR's lack of specificity of the sources of water to diverted and the adverse impacts of these diversions and the Environmental Account was not fatal. The EIR was a programmatic one which permits a tiered analysis so specificity can be postponed until a specific action or project is proposed.

4. *Water Goes South, Fish Go Away.* Starting in 2000, the vaunted process, which was always long on process and shorter on substance, began to unravel. The basic problem is that the parties could not agree on the necessary Delta flows and thus on limiting exports to south. This would require decisions about which water right holders would suffer cuts to provide the water necessary for flows. Efforts to address the root problems are complicated by the legacy of the 19th and the first half of the 20th century. California did not adopt a permit system until 1914, long after common law riparian and customary appropriative rights vested. The Central Valley Project back-stopped these rights through storage and distribution facilities and reinforced the expectation that the status quo should never be changed. In 2007, the Smelt population declined and the fate of the Delta was placed exactly where the process sought to avoid, state and federal courts. The state's implementation of the various plans to protect the Delta first reached an intermediate appellate court in 2006. State Water Resources Control Board Cases, 136 Cal.App.4th 674, 39 Cal.Rptr.3d 189 (3 Dist. 2006), held that the State Water Resources Control Board's adoption of the 1995 Bay–Delta Plan to increase salinity dilution flows and subsequent refusal to implement it fully violated the Porter–Cologne Water Quality Act. Cal.WaterCode § 13000 et seq. First, the Plan set San Joaquin River flow objectives at Vernalis and included Spring pulse flows. However, the 1998 San Joaquin Agreement did not provide for sufficient flows to meet the Vernalis objectives, and the Board turned to an adaptive management experiment as a substitute for full implementation. The Board acknowledged that the experiment might not fully meet the flow objectives, but approved the San Joaquin River Agreement. The court held that California Water Code § 13050(j) required the Board to implement a previously adopted water quality plan, that adaptive management experiments were not included in the 1995 plan, and thus the subsequent decision to "sequence" implementation was a de facto amendment taken without following the required procedures. Second, the court rejected the argument that a board decision which required the Bureau of Reclamation to meet Delta salinity objectives by releasing water from New Melones Reservoir violated Article X. Section 2 of the California Constitution because the release of water for salinity dilution was an unreasonable use. The court noted that "[t]here certainly may be cases in which the release of water to dilute salinity levels is unreasonable, but that is not always the case." Instead, the use of reservoir releases in conjunction with other salinity control measures was a reasonable beneficial use. Third, the court refused to apply the public trust doctrine to mandate environmental flows; the doctrine does not require that conflicts be resolved in favor of environmental values "whenever possible" because "whenever feasible" is for the State Water Resources Control Board to determine. The court held that the Board adequately balanced competing interests in adopting 1995 Delta Water Quality Plan, although it agreed that the Board erred in failing to achieve minimum flows necessary for salmon protection. 39 Cal.Rptr.3d at 189, 267–272 Another decision held that public trust balancing may permit the state to limit vested rights, but the state "must attempt to preserve priorities to the extent that the priorities do not lead to unreasonable use or a violation of public trust values." The imposition of a curtailment of a senior user but not on junior users to guarantee salinity reduction flows in the Sacramento–San Jaoquin Bay Delta did not demonstrate that Delta flow standards would not be met if the senior's natural flow diversions were curtailed. The Central Valley and State Water Projects would simply have to release more water since the Bureau of Reclamation and the State are responsible for preserving the necessary salinity balance. El Dorado Irrigation District v. State Water Resources Control Board, 142 Cal.App.4th 937 48 Cal.Rptr.3d 468, 491 (3 Dist. 2006). Phelps v. State Water Resources Control Board, 157 Cal.App.4th 89, 68 Cal.Rptr.3d 350 (3 Dist. 2007), holds that Delta water users must anticipate that changing water quality standards will require further diversions reductions, and the state may use valid water quality measures to limit diversions.

In 2007, a federal judge held that the state and federal government had not done enough to protect the listed smelt, and in late 2007 issued a final order which required temporary pumping reductions when certain triggers were met. NDRC v. Interior Dept., 2007 WL 14283, 64 ERC 1718 (E.D.Cal. 2007).

5. *Where should CALFED go?* What is the standard for judging the success of CALFED? One measure is the improved quality of the Bay–Delta ecosystem, but to measure this a baseline must be identified and specific restoration goals set. What is the appropriate baseline? Pre–1848 conditions? Pre–CVP conditions? Pre–SWP conditions? Some synthesis of all three? A new artificial baseline based on the functions that the system could perform on a realistic, improved outflow scenario?

One of the problems with CALFED is that is no baseline nor restoration target has been set. Instead, the "baseline" for flows is a series of government agency prescriptions set forth in the various endangered species biological opinions, the State Water Resources Control Board water quality control plan, and the CVPIA. Models of an undisturbed ecosystem the size of the Bay–Delta do not exist. Is the lack of an ecological target a virtue or defect in the process?

6. *Science to the rescue?* One proposed solution is to save the Delta Smelt population through hatchery releases. Can hatchery fish be added to "wild" populations to prevent listing to to support delisting? In 1991, FWS and NMFS began to classify endangered populations not by species by Evolutionary Significant Units (ESUs). ESU populations are reproductively isolated from other conspecific populations and constitute an important evolutionary component of the species. In 1993, NMFS adopted an interim policy which cautiously allowed some use of hatchery fish to restore and sustain "natural populations." In 1998, the agency listed an ESU of Coho salmon along the Oregon coast and limited the threatened population to naturally spawned populations, conceding that hatchery and natural fish intermingled in the ocean, return to fresh water along with the wild Coho to spawn and interbreed. Alsea Valley Alliance v. Evans, 161 F.Supp.2d 1154 (D. Or. 2001), held that the refusal was arbitrary after evidence showed that up to 87% of naturally spawning salmon were originally hatchery spawned. As was often the case during the Bush II administration, the government did not appeal and the Ninth Circuit dismissed an NGO appeal because the remand order was not final. Alsea Valley Alliance v. Department of Commerce, 358 F.3d 1181 (9th Cir. 2004). In 2004, NMFS issued a Final Hatchery Listing Policy, 70 Fed.Reg. 31, 354 (2004), which allowed NMFs to include hatchery fish "with a level of genetic divergence relative to the local natural population(s) that is no more than occurs within an ESU" in decisions whether to list an ESU. A group of scientists appointed to a NMFS Salmon Recovery Science Review Panel published a peer reviewed article that found significant differences between hatchery and wild salmon. R.A. Myers et al., Hatcheries and Endangered Salmon, 303 Science 1980, March 26, 2004, but claim that they were told to remove this information from the final report that preceded the 2004 NMFS policy. See generally Kristin Carden, Bridging The Divide: The Role of Science in Species Conservation Law, 30 Harv. Envtl. L. Rev. 165 (2006); K. Weiss, Action to Protect Salmon Urged: Scientists Say Their Advice Was Dropped from Report to the U.S. Fisheries Service, Los Angeles Times, March 26, 2004. Trout Unlimited v. Lohn, 2007 WL 1730090, 66 ERC 1020 (W.D. Wash. 2007), invalidated the 2004 policy. See Andrew Long, Defining "Nature" Protected by the Endangered Species Act: Lessons From Hatchery Salmon, 15 NYU Envtl. L. J. 377 (2007).

7. *Wet or "Virtual" Water?* The Clean Water Act has generally rejected the dictum that the solution to pollution is dilution. But dilution—with increased outflows—along with improved river flows, is necessary to conserve the resource. Where will the required water to support these flows be found? In 1992, Congress designated 800,000 acre-feet for environmental purposes in the CVPIA. The CVPIA exempts water contractors with pre-project San Joaquin entitlements so that water users entitled to some 840,000 acre-feet of San Joaquin River and 2.2 million acre-feet of Sacramento River water are not obliged to curtail uses to provide this water. Thus, the major burden to supply the water is borne by only 24 agricultural service contractors in districts south of the Delta. The issue has been addressed in the CALFED process by creating an "environmental water account" (EWA) so as to share the burden of providing environmental water while meeting specific regulatory requirements. The EWA has been established to provide water for the protection and recovery of fish beyond water available through existing regulatory actions related to project operations. The EWA is a cooperative management program whose purpose is to provide protection to the fish of the Bay–Delta estuary through environmentally beneficial changes in SWP and CVP operations. It requires the acquisition of alternative sources of project water supply, called the "EWA assets," which will be used to augment streamflows and delta outflows, to modify exports to provide fishery benefits, and to replace the regular water supply interrupted by the changes to project operations. The replacement water will compensate for reductions in deliveries to existing users. The EWA will be funded jointly by the state and federal governments and managed by the state and federal fishery agencies in coordination with project operators and stakeholders through CALFED.

H.   ENVIRONMENTAL QUALITY AND THE FUTURE OF DAMS

Throughout the world, nations historically avoided many water use conflicts among their citizens and with other countries by constructing large dams and carry-over storage reservoirs. This strategy produced thousands of large dams, but the necessity for continued construction of these facilities is now being re-evaluated. Large dams have produced environmental and social problems and their benefits have often fallen short of projections. Indeed, a report has shown that water development is the single greatest cause of species extinction. Elizabeth Losos et al., *Taxpayer-Subsidized Resource Extraction Harms Species: Double Jeopardy*, 45 BioScience 446, 448 (1995). Many in the United States have concluded that the Reclamation Era is over, largely because of environmental and economic factors. Although history will be the ultimate judge of the validity of the pronouncement, large dam construction has virtually stopped in the United States. Although dam building is alive and well in many developing countries, the case for large dams is becoming more problematic worldwide.

In 2000, the World Commission on Dams, a privately funded organization without official standing or legal status, published its final report, Dams and Development: A New Framework for Decision–Making (2000). The report is the most comprehensive global assessment of the social, economic and environmental impacts of large dams to date and is a balanced but powerful brief against the continued exclusive reliance on large dams to meet the world's water supply demands. The report recognizes that many dams throughout the world provide important benefits, but in large measure it adopts the environmental and social critique of large dams, especially in developing countries, recommends a more rigorous assessment process for proposed new dams, and suggests that much more attention be focused on the reoperation of existing dams and irrigation systems and on the promotion of more sustainable water storage and use technologies.

The Report of the World Commission on Dams, Dams and Development: A New Framework for Decision–Making
xxxi–xxxv (2000).

Performance of large dams

The knowledge base indicates that shortfalls in technical, financial and economic performance have occurred and are compounded by significant social and environmental impacts, the costs of which are often disproportionately borne by poor people, indigenous peoples and other vulnerable groups. Given the large capital investment in large dams, the Commission was disturbed to find that substantive evaluations of completed projects are few in number, narrow in scope, poorly integrated across impact categories and scales, and inadequately linked to decisions on operations.

In assessing the large dams reviewed by the Commission we found that:

- Large dams display a high degree of variability in delivering predicted water and electricity services—and related social benefits—with a considerable portion falling short of physical and economic targets, while others continue generating benefits after 30 to 40 years.

• Large dams have demonstrated a marked tendency towards schedule delays and significant cost overruns.

• Large dams designed to deliver irrigation services have typically fallen short of physical targets, did not recover their costs and have been less profitable in economic terms than expected.

• Large hydropower dams tend to perform closer to, but still below, targets for power generation, generally meet their financial targets but demonstrate variable economic performance relative to targets, with a number of notable under- and over-performers.

• Large dams generally have a range of extensive impacts on rivers, watersheds and aquatic ecosystems—these impacts are more negative than positive and, in many cases, have led to irreversible loss of species and ecosystems.

• Efforts to date to counter the ecosystem impacts of large dams have met with limited success owing to the lack of attention to anticipating and avoiding impacts, the poor quality and uncertainty of predictions, the difficulty of coping with all impacts, and the only partial implementation and success of mitigation measures.

• Pervasive and systematic failure to assess the range of potential negative impacts and implement adequate mitigation, resettlement and development programmes for the displaced, and the failure to account for the consequences of large dams for downstream livelihoods have led to the impoverishment and suffering of millions, giving rise to growing opposition to dams by affected communities worldwide.

• Since the environmental and social costs of large dams have been poorly accounted for in economic terms, the true profitability of these schemes remains elusive.

Perhaps of most significance is the fact that social groups bearing the social and environmental costs and risks of large dams, especially the poor, vulnerable and future generations, are often not the same groups that receive the water and electricity services, nor the social and economic benefits from these. Applying a "balance-sheet" approach to assess the costs and benefits of large dams, where large inequities exist in the distribution of these costs and benefits, is seen as unacceptable given existing commitments to human rights and sustainable development.

Options for water and electricity services

Today, a wide range of options for delivering water and electricity services exists, although in particular situations the cost and feasibility of these options will vary in the face of constraints such as natural resource endowments and site location. The Commission found that:

• Many of the non-dam options available today—including demand-side management, supply efficiency and new supply options—can improve or expand water and energy services and meet evolving development needs in all segments of society.

- There is considerable scope for improving performance of both dam projects and other options.

- Demand management, reducing consumption, recycling and supply and end-use efficiency measures all have significant potential to reduce pressure on water resources in all countries and regions of the world.

- A number of supply-side options at all scales (ranging from small, distributed generation sources or localised water collection and water-recovery systems to regional-interconnection of power grids) have emerged that—on their own or collectively—can improve or expand the delivery of water and energy services in a timely, cost-effective and publicly acceptable manner.

- Decentralised, small-scale options (micro hydro, home-scale solar electric systems, wind and biomass systems) based on local renewable sources offer an important near-term, and possibly long-term, potential particularly in rural areas far away from centralised supply networks.

- Obstacles to the adoption of these options range from market barriers to institutional, intellectual and financial barriers. A range of incentives—some hidden—that favour conventional options limit the adoption rate of alternatives.

Decision-making, planning and institutional arrangements

The decision to build a dam is influenced by many variables beyond immediate technical considerations. As a development choice, the selection of large dams often served as a focal point for the interests and aspirations of politicians, centralised government agencies, international aid donors and the dam-building industry, and did not provide for a comprehensive evaluation of available alternatives. Involvement from civil society varied with the degree of debate and openness to political discourse in a country. However, the WCD Global Review documents a frequent failure to recognise affected people and empower them to participate in the process. In some cases, the opportunity for corruption provided by dams as largescale infrastructure projects further distorted decision-making.

Once a proposed dam project passed preliminary technical and economic feasibility tests and attracted interest from financing agencies and political interests, the momentum behind the project often prevailed over other considerations. Project planning and appraisal for large dams was confined primarily to technical parameters and the narrow application of economic cost-benefit analyses. Historically, social and environmental impacts were left outside the assessment framework and the role of impact assessments in project selection remained marginal, even into the 1990s.

Conflicts over dams have heightened in the last two decades due largely to the social and environmental impacts of dams that were either disregarded in the planning process or unanticipated. However, it also stems from the failure by dam proponents and financing agencies to fulfil commitments made, observe statutory regulations and abide by internal guidelines. Whereas far-reaching improvements in policies, legal requirements and assessment procedures have occurred in particular countries and institutions, in the 1990s it appears that business-as-usual too often prevailed. Further, past shortcomings and inequities remain unresolved, and experience with appeals, dispute resolution and recourse mechanisms has been poor.

Core Values for Decision–Making

As the Global Review of dams makes clear, improving development outcomes in the future requires a substantially expanded basis for deciding on proposed water and energy development projects—a basis that reflects a full knowledge and understanding of the benefits, impacts and risks of large dam projects to all parties. It also requires introducing new voices, perspectives and criteria into decision-making, as well as processes that will build consensus around the decisions reached. This will fundamentally alter the way in which decisions are made and, we are convinced, improve the development effectiveness of future decisions.

The Commission grouped the core values that informed its understanding of these issues under five principal headings:

- equity,
- efficiency,
- participatory decision-making,
- sustainability, and
- accountability.

* * *

The debate about dams is a debate about the very meaning, purpose and pathways for achieving development. This suggests that decision-making on water and energy management will align itself with the emerging global commitment to sustainable human development and on the equitable distribution of costs and benefits. The emergence of a globally accepted framework of norms rests on the adoption of the Universal Declaration of Human Rights in 1948 and related covenants and conventions thereafter. These later resolutions include the Declaration on the Right to Development adopted by the UN General Assembly in 1986, and the Rio Principles agreed to at the UN Conference on Environment and Development in 1992. The core values that inform the Commission's shared understanding are aligned with this consensus and rest on the fundamental human rights accorded to all people by virtue of their humanity.

* * *

Recommendations for a New Policy Framework

* * *[S]even strategic priorities each supported by a set of policy principles, provide a principled and practical way forward for decision-making. Presented here as expressions of an achieved outcome, they summarise key principles and actions that the Commission proposes all actors should adopt and implement.

1. Gaining Public Acceptance

Public acceptance of key decisions is essential for equitable and sustainable water and energy resources development. Acceptance emerges from recognising rights, addressing risks, and safeguarding the entitlements of all groups of affected people, particularly indigenous and tribal peoples, women and other vulnerable groups. Decision making processes and mechanisms are used that enable informed participation by all groups of people, and result in the demonstrable acceptance of key decisions. Where projects affect indigenous and tribal peoples, such processes are guided by their free, prior and informed consent.

2. Comprehensive Options Assessment

Alternatives to dams do often exist. To explore these alternatives, needs for water, food and energy are assessed and objectives clearly defined. The appropriate development response is identified from a range of possible options. The selection is based on a comprehensive and participatory assessment of the full range of policy, institutional and technical options. In the assessment process social and environmental aspects have the same significance as economic and financial factors. The options assessment process continues through all stages of planning, project development and operations.

3. Addressing Existing Dams

Opportunities exist to optimise benefits from many existing dams, address outstanding social issues and strengthen environmental mitigation and restoration measures. Dams and the context in which they operate are not seen as static over time. Benefits and impacts may be transformed by changes in water use priorities, physical and land use changes in the river basin, technological developments, and changes in public policy expressed in environment, safety, economic and technical regulations. Management and operation practices must adapt continuously to changing circumstances over the project's life and must address outstanding social issues.

4. Sustaining Rivers and Livelihoods

Rivers, watersheds and aquatic ecosystems are the biological engines of the planet. They are the basis for life and the livelihoods of local communities. Dams transform landscapes and create risks of irreversible impacts. Understanding, protecting and restoring ecosystems at river basin level is essential to foster equitable human development and the welfare of all species. Options assessment and decision-making around river development prioritises the avoidance of impacts, followed by the minimisation and mitigation of harm to the health and integrity of the river system. Avoiding impacts through good site selection and project design is a priority. Releasing tailormade environmental flows can help maintain downstream ecosystems and the communities that depend on them.

5.   Recognising Entitlements and Sharing Benefits

Joint negotiations with adversely affected people result in mutually agreed and legally enforceable mitigation and development provisions. These recognise entitlements that improve livelihoods and quality of life, and affected people are beneficiaries of the project. Successful mitigation, resettlement and development are fundamental commitments and responsibilities of the State and the developer. They bear the onus to satisfy all affected people that moving from their current context and resources will improve their livelihoods. Accountability of responsible parties to agreed mitigation, resettlement and development provisions is ensured through legal means, such as contracts, and through accessible legal recourse at the national and international level.

6.   Ensuring Compliance

Ensuring public trust and confidence requires that the governments, developers, regulators and operators meet all commitments made for the planning, implementation and operation of dams. Compliance with applicable regulations, criteria and guidelines, and project-specific negotiated agreements is secured at all critical stages in project planning and implementation. A set of mutually reinforcing incentives and mechanisms is required for social, environmental and technical measures. These should involve an appropriate mix of regulatory and non-regulatory measures, incorporating incentives and sanctions. Regulatory and compliance frameworks use incentives and sanctions to ensure effectiveness where flexibility is needed to accommodate changing circumstances.

7.   Sharing Rivers for Peace, Development and Security

Storage and diversion of water on transboundary rivers has been a source of considerable tension between countries and within countries. As specific interventions for diverting water, dams require constructive cooperation. Consequently, the use and management of resources increasingly becomes the subject of agreement between States to promote mutual self-interest for regional co-operation and peaceful collaboration. This leads to a shift in focus from the narrow approach of allocating a finite resource to the sharing of rivers and their associated benefits in which States are innovative in defining the scope of issues for discussion. External financing agencies support the principles of good faith negotiations between riparian States.

If we are to achieve equitable and sustainable outcomes, free of the divisive conflicts of the past, future decision-making about water and energy resource projects will need to reflect and integrate these strategic priorities and their associated policy principles in the planning and project cycles.

Other important examinations of the future role of large dams are Global Perspectives on Large Dams: Evaluating the State of Large Dam Construction and Decommissioning Across the World (Kara D. Francesco and Kathryn Woodruff eds., Yale School of Forestry and Environmental Studies 2008), and Thayer Scudder, The Future of Large Dams: Dealing with Social, Environmental, Institutional and Political Costs (2005).

CHAPTER EIGHT

DEVELOPING AND DISTRIBUTING WATER SUPPLIES

One of the pervasive ironies about water supply, especially in arid regions, is that the supply is in one place and the demand in another. In agriculture, this has meant moving the water from streams to outlying farms and ranches. The expense and inconvenience of building canals and ditches has been mitigated since the mid-nineteenth century by mutual water companies, water districts, and other organizations designed to improve the efficiency and share the costs of water acquisition and delivery. Over time, the special water district, a political subdivision of state government, has gained an important role in water supply projects. With population growth, municipalities, always players in the water business, have become increasingly aggressive in the search for dependable supplies of water. This entire scene is impacted by the water activities of the federal government, exemplified by the many projects constructed by the Bureau of Reclamation under the Newlands Reclamation Act of 1902, as amended on numerous occasions in succeeding years. In addition, the U.S. Army Corps of Engineers has played an important role in controlling rivers, initially for navigation and flood control but later to fulfill multiple purposes including water supply.

This chapter first examines, in note form without "principal" cases, the role of private companies in the distribution of water and various issues raised by municipal water supply and the operation of special water districts. It then turns to the activities of the federal government in developing water, including the reach of congressional power and the preemptive effect of federal legislation.

A. WATER SUPPLY ORGANIZATIONS

For many purposes water service and supply organizations should be, and are, treated like other competitors for available water supplies. The acquisition, exercise, and transfer of water rights by these entities are governed by general rules of water law in the relevant jurisdiction. In addition, there are special laws applicable to them. As the entities charged with allocating water resources among the ultimate users, they are the primary water managers and therefore most lawyers who practice water law are concerned with the affairs of water distribution organizations.

In the settlement of the humid eastern United States, water was primarily needed for domestic purposes, for waterborne transportation, and, with the arrival of industry, for driving mills. These needs could be satisfied through individual enterprise. Rural dwellers dug wells, and industry located alongside streams and rivers. With the development of large towns and cities, however, the urban population soon required organized municipal water distribution facilities.

There are older community supply traditions in the Southwest. The Pueblo Indians of the Southwest had established community ditches five to six hundred years before the first Spanish colonists. Long before the Europeans discovered the New World, irrigation systems of the Anasazi, ancestors of today's New Mexico Pueblo Indians, along the Upper Rio Grande Valley were irrigating substantial areas of desert land. In southern Arizona's Salt River Valley, the Hohokam were using irrigation canals by 700 A.D. They constructed more than 125 miles of canals, allowing them to irrigate over 100,000 acres. The Indians lined the bottoms of many of their ditches, canals, and aqueducts with hardened clay, thereby reducing seepage.

When the Spanish began to settle in the Southwest in the late 1500s, they were impressed with the canal systems of the Tewa Pueblos in New Mexico. The Spaniards promoted systems of community ditches, known as acequias, to support their missions and pueblo lands throughout the region. These irrigation systems were improved in the following two centuries to include sandstone dams, stone aqueducts and clay pipes. One such sandstone structure, Mission Dam at Santa Barbara, California, is still standing. So important was irrigation to the development of Southwest communities that the acequias were usually completed before houses, churches, and town buildings. Institutions were created for the administration of these ditches and canals. A superintendent was appointed to supervise the construction and maintenance of the ditches, to distribute the water among the users, and to arbitrate disputes. The irrigators provided labor according to their land holdings. The historical validity of the pueblo water right has been the subject of lively debate, both academic and judicial. Compare Cartwright v. Public Serv. Co. of New Mexico, 66 N.M. 64, 343 P.2d 654 (1958) (recognizing the pueblo right) with State ex rel. Martinez v. City of Las Vegas, 135 N.M. 375, 89 P.3d 47 (2004) (refusing to recognize the right). The academic discussion can be followed in Pierre Levy, *Which Right is Right: The Pueblo Water Rights Doctrine Meets Prior Appropriation*, 35 Nat. Resources J. 413 (1995), and Peter L. Reich, *Mission Revival Jurisprudence: State Courts and Hispanic Water Law Since 1850*, 69 Wash. L. Rev. 869 (1994). Acequia systems remain important in some communities, especially in northern New Mexico. For interesting discussions of the development of early irrigation practices, see José A. Rivera, Acequia Culture: Water, Land, and Community in the Southwest (1998); Michael C. Meyer, Water in the Hispanic Southwest: A Social and Legal History 1550–

1850 (1984); and Robert G. Dunbar, Forging New Rights in Western Waters (1983).

The Mormons, beginning in the late 1840s, also perfected irrigation techniques in the State of Deseret, later the Utah Territory. Community sites were selected by Brigham Young so that water from the nearby mountains could be used efficiently. Mormon towns were characteristically platted in acre-square blocks; ditches with laterals were dug alongside the streets and can still be seen in small Utah towns. Farming land was adjacent to the town, with separate canals dug to irrigate this land. Within a decade, Mormon settlements were found throughout the entire Utah Territory, southern Idaho, northern Arizona and western Wyoming. Like the Spanish settlers in the Southwest, the Mormons developed community-based institutions governing water use. Brigham Young declared all water the property of the people, allocated land to settlers, and ordered the construction of community dams and ditches. The administration of water was in the hands of local church leaders who distributed the water to those who built projects in proportion to the labor contributed. Leonard J. Arrington, Great Basin Kingdom: Economic History of the Latter Day Saints, 1830–1900, at 52–53 (1958). In the early days of settlement, the church allocated the settlers' land to them and appointed watermasters to distribute the water. The watermaster's duties were similar to those of the superintendent in Southwest communities. Formal prior appropriation came to Utah only after the theocracy gave way to a civil state, but the early church cooperative control over water evolved into the farmer-owned mutual irrigation companies characteristic of Utah today.

Many of the pioneers in the West—early miners and farmers—relied on individual diversion works. Later, it became necessary for them to follow the example of the Indians and the Spanish colonists. When mining and irrigation projects moved away from the few flowing streams, it became obvious that more ambitious cooperative enterprises would be required. Mutual ditch or water companies were formed, with individual users sharing the costs of building and maintaining headgates and ditches. Finally, under the impetus of state statutes and the national reclamation movement, quasi-public conservancy and other special water districts evolved. In some cases, their activities included the generation of electricity and the provision of municipal and industrial (M & I) water, in addition to supplying the needs of irrigators.

The resulting welter of sometimes conflicting water supply institutions is exemplified in California.

At present, general enabling statutes in California provide for the formation of fourteen classes of local public districts which have, or may have, the supplying of water for use as a primary function; in addition, special statutes providing for the formation of specific districts have created in effect two main classes of local districts similarly engaged in water supply. Added to these are numerous municipal water departments, and, outside the public realm, there are a great many private water suppliers in the form of individual proprietorships, mutual water companies, and privately owned public utility companies. This listing omits, moreover, ten more classes of "water" districts, provided for by general statutes, which are not engaged at all, or are only incidentally engaged, in supplying water, and three similar types of district that have been created individually by special statutes none of which are considered in the following discussion.

A. Types of agencies predominantly or entirely engaged in supplying irrigation water

1) Irrigation districts

2) California water districts

B. Types of agencies engaged to significant degree in supplying both irrigation water and urban water

3) Individual proprietorships

4) Mutual water companies

5) Privately owned public utilities

6) Water storage districts

7) Water conservation districts

8) Water storage and conservation districts

9) County water districts

10) Flood control and water conservation districts

11) County flood control and water conservation districts

12) County water authorities

13) County water agencies

C. Types of agencies predominantly or entirely engaged in supplying urban water

14) Municipal water departments

15) County waterworks districts

16) Public utility districts

17) Community service districts

18) Municipal water districts

19) Municipal utility districts

20) Metropolitan water districts.

Joe S. Bain et al., Northern California's Water Industry 77–79 (1966).

There is a pervasive confusion of roles, as water distribution organizations are characterized variously as public and private entities, depending on the issue or occasion. The corporate or public nature of these entities raises a host of legal problems. There is a constant tension between the public purpose in furnishing a reliable water supply and other purposes, such as protecting the public from unfair or excessive economic burdens and managing growth.

The difference between the new and old West is that the old West lived off a narrow colonial economy of raw commodity production, timber and minerals, agriculture, and livestock production. Growth had to be induced to settle what remained a sparsely populated area, except for several urban oases. In the new West, there is no need to induce growth. It is happening. The West is growing for the very reasons people were originally deterred from settlement of the region. The New West's "commodities" now include its climate, mountain and desert wilderness areas, scenery, free-flowing rivers, and open space.

The West is growing faster than the national average and the population is widely dispersed throughout the region with the exception of the Great Plains. Geographically, the "new" West has been characterized as a series of "urban archipelagos" areas of high population density surrounded by a ring of (often quite extensive) suburbs. Some of the archipelago cities include both the older western metropolitan centers and smaller second-tier cities and "towns": Boise, Salt Lake City, Spokane, Denver, Colorado Springs, Las Vegas, Sacramento, Eugene, El Paso, Dallas, Houston, Albuquerque, Tucson, Phoenix, and Missoula. Pamela Case & Gregory Alward, Patterns of Demographic, Economic and Value Change in Western United States, Report to the Western Water Policy Advisory Review Commission 9 (1997). Population dispersal is a function of the West's high amenity levels and its extensive infrastructure, which includes regional air service, educational institutions, interstate highways, and network of communications as well as the plumbing put in place in the last century.

In some areas of the West, the "perfect storm" of decreased federal support for regional water development, continued growth, pressure for protection of endangered species and aquatic ecosystems, and a relatively fixed—perhaps decreasing—water budget due to global climate change, stress existing water allocation systems and highlight the longstanding disconnect between water allocation and land use planning and regulation. See Western Governors Association, Water Needs and Strategies for a Sustainable Future: Next Steps (June 2008). Urban growth impacts four water-related commons: (1) available surface and groundwater supplies, (2) community amenity and survival levels, (3) cultural commons represented by small ranch and farm communities and Indian reservations, and (4) aquatic ecosystems.

Urban areas and the states can no longer count on the federal government to backstop state allocations as they could in the past. As a result, in states such as Arizona, California, Colorado, and Oregon, the responsibility to secure dependable supplies has been de facto assumed by local water providers. And sometimes the responsibility is devolved de jure to local governments, then often indirectly passed to real estate developers by laws that condition new development on an assured water supply. These statutes have created a firmer consumer entitlement to a long-term reliable supply of water than existed in the past. Lincoln L. Davies, *Just a Big, "Hot Fuss"?: Assessing the Value of Connecting Urban Sprawl, Land Use, and Water Rights Through Assured Supply Laws*, 34 Ecology L.Q. 1217 (2007). These statutes have also reopened a long-running debate about the limits that its climate and geography might pose to human settlement. Most students of water policy have concluded that these heightened water supply guarantee duties will not change the bedrock assumption that science and technology can overcome any "natural" barriers to growth, e.g. Peter D. Nichols, Megan K. Murphy, and Douglas S. Kenney, Water and Growth in Colorado: A Review of Legal and Policy Issues (Natural Resources Law Center, University of Colorado School of Law, 2001), and that cities will find the necessary water to keep growing. Still, reports of development denials because of a lack of assured supply are beginning to surface. At a minimum many cities must invest more in aggressive, permanent water conservation including both mandatory and incentive-based strategies, review the historic preference for uniform, constant, average-cost water rates, and reconsider the relationship between special patterns, water use and global climate change. For example, a 2008 San Diego Grand Jury Report, entitled Water Conservation: Sober Up San Diego, the Water Party is Over, found that the City of San Diego has rising block rates for single family residences but uniform rates for multi-family and commercial users. The report recommended that the city adopt a tiered block rate structure for all users "to make charges proportional to use."

NOTE ON ADEQUATE WATER SUPPLY LAWS

Arizona, California, and Colorado have enacted laws which condition the approval of new development on a demonstrated adequate water supply. As part of the Arizona Groundwater Management Act, new development in Active Management Areas, see pages 624–633, *supra*, must have a 100–year guaranteed supply. ARIZ. REV. STAT. ANN. § 45–576.07 (2008). California prohibits the approval of submission maps for developments of over 500 units unless the developer can demonstrate a "sufficient water supply," which is defined as the total supply available during "normal, single-dry, and multiple-dry years within a 20–year projection." CAL. GOV'T CODE § 66473.7(b)(1) (2008). Does this include projected climate change impacts? California's little-NEPA, CAL. PUB. RES. CODE §§ 21000–21006 (Deering 2005), allows courts to probe the assumptions behind assessments of available supply. E.g. Vineyard Area Citizens for Responsible Growth v. Rancho Cordova, 40 Cal.4th 412, 53 Cal.Rptr.3d 821, 150 P.3d 709 (2007). But cf. In re Bay–Delta Programmatic Environmental Impact Report Coordinated Proceedings, page 757, *supra*, and O.W.L. Foundation v. City of Rohnert Park, 86 Cal.Rptr.3d 1 (Cal.App. 2008). Colorado requires an adequate supply for residential developments of over 50 units, COLO REV. STAT. § 29–20–301 et seq. See generally Sarah B. VandeWetering and A. Dan Tarlock, *Western Growth and Sustainable Water Use: If There Are No "Natural Limits," Should We Worry About Water Supplies?*, 27 Pub. Land & Resources L. Rev. 33 (2006).

Litigants are starting to argue that environmental assessments must include the climate change impacts of land use policies on water and energy use. Several trial courts have found that these impacts are still too speculative, but in 2006 the California Legislature enacted AB 32, which seeks a 25% reduction in greenhouse gases by 2020. In November 2006, a non-governmental organization filed a lawsuit against a city to overturn the approval of a 1500–home development. The suit alleged that the project would result in large emissions of carbon dioxide, a greenhouse gas, because the project would increase vehicle trips, and that the environmental impact report prepared for the project under CEQA failed to analyze those emissions or associated global warming impacts. In April 2007, the same organization filed another suit challenging a county's new general plan. The county updated its plan to accommodate a projected 25% increase in the county's population by the year 2030. The state Attorney General joined the suit on the side of the plaintiff, contending that "despite the enactment of AB 32, the FEIR (Final Environmental Impact Report) on the General Plan update ... makes no attempt to analyze the effects of those [greenhouse gas emissions] increases on global warming or the greenhouse gas emissions reductions required by AB 32 ..." In August 2007, Attorney General Jerry Brown and the City of San Bernardino settled the lawsuit. The city agreed to develop a greenhouse gas emissions reduction plan, including the use of its discretionary land use authority to achieve reductions. The settlement is available at http://ag.ca.gov/cms-pdfs/press/2007-08-21_San_Bernardino_settlement_agreement.pdf. Other countries may be ahead of the curve. The Melbourne, Australia Herald Sun, August 8, 2008, reported that the Victoria Civil and Administrative Tribunal reversed a local government development permission for a coastal housing development because of demonstrated foreseeable risks of global climate change-induced storm surges and flooding.

1.   PUBLIC UTILITIES

The law of water service and distribution organizations is fundamentally different in its application to public utilities as compared to private entities. Either by statute or common law, public utilities are legal monopolies authorized to provide a public service. Generally, in return for an exclusive service area, public utilities must serve all those persons within the service area who can afford the service, charging reasonable rates applied in a non-discriminatory manner. A. J. G. Priest, Principles of Public Utility Regulation 227–326 (1969). Most municipal water distribution organizations are now public. In many states, investor-owned water distribution systems have been replaced by public entities, usually municipal water supply systems or special districts. Municipal water supply systems are often exempt from state public utility regulation. See Ann J. Gellis, *Water Supply in the Northeast: A Study in Regulatory Failure,* 12 Ecology L.Q. 429 (1985). Still, municipal water distribution may be subject to judicial controls based on traditional public utility principles. A case illustrating the difference that public utility status might make to a water service organization is Thayer v. California Development Co., 164 Cal. 117, 128 P. 21 (1912)

2.   MUNICIPAL SERVICE

"Until very recently, the universal objective of land use and related water use has been to protect public health and support economic growth and its resultant opportunities for landowners, job seekers, and people from throughout the world who seek a better life." Jerome B. Gilbert, *Water Supply and Land Use Planning: Respecting the Boundaries,* 1 Land Use Forum 338, 340 (1992). The historic policy that water should not be a barrier to urban growth was driven by three economic and legal factors. See Robert A. Gottlieb & Margaret Fitzsimmons, A Thirst For Growth: Water Agencies as Hidden Government in California (1991). First, the distributive politics of water made supply augmentation the cheapest policy for urban water suppliers as well as for irrigators. Second, the politics of local governments forced communities to compete with one another for property tax revenues. Third, the endless extension of water service was supported by public utility law. The basic premise of utility service law is that service must be made available to all who can afford it. Water rates were based on average rather than marginal cost. Over the last thirty years, municipalities in rapidly growing areas have changed their water distribution financing, but this has not altered the notion that a city should obtain supplies adequate to accommodate the maximum future growth.

The transition from the Reclamation Era when large project construction was the preferred solution to growth to an era of reallocation and environmental restoration has forced urban water suppliers to focus on water transfers and demand management (conservation) to meet new service demands. Municipal authorities hope to secure dependable rights, which, in those states following the appropriation system, means senior rights. Many of the older appropriations are agricultural, and therefore there has been pressure on farmers to sell and transfer their water rights to municipalities. For an example of the sort of pressure that can arise, see City of Thornton v. Farmers Reservoir and Irrigation Co., 194 Colo. 526, 575 P.2d 382 (1978).

Usually, a municipality must look to sources outside its boundaries for the acquisition of water supplies. This raises the question of municipal authority to act beyond the city limits. In the absence of statutory authorization, many early cases held there was implied authority. See, e.g., Hall v. Mayor & Council of Calhoun, 140 Ga. 611, 79 S.E. 533 (1913). The problem is now addressed by statute in most states. A useful discussion of the issues is John C. Feirich, Note, *Municipal Power Arising from the Ownership of Extraterritorial Property,* 1957 Ill. L. Forum 99. A Colorado statute limiting municipal condemnation of land to property located within five miles of the city limits was held to be inapplicable to Denver under the constitutional grant of condemnation powers in the provision discussed in *Thornton.* City & County of Denver v. Board of Comm'rs of Arapahoe County, 113 Colo. 150, 156 P.2d 101 (1945).

Is condemnation of water by a municipality always for a "public use"? Courts have generally held that if the primary purpose of the condemnation is to supply water, incidental benefits are permissible, or that incidental private benefits will be disregarded where it is difficult to segregate the private from the public uses. See Richard S. Harnsberger, *Eminent Domain and Water Law,* 48 Neb. L. Rev. 325, 366–69 (1969). Condemnation of water rights to serve users located outside a city's boundaries was upheld in *Thornton*. But the Nebraska Supreme Court has held that condemnation of water rights by a municipality for use by a single industry outside the municipal boundaries is not a public use, although the city would, of course, benefit from the revenues. Burger v. City of Beatrice, 181 Neb. 213, 147 N.W.2d 784 (1967). See also City of Aurora v. Commerce Group Corp., 694 P.2d 382 (Colo.App. 1984) (city cannot condemn stream outside its boundaries for fishing purposes).

The primary duty which drives growth accommodation is the duty to serve. A leading case analyzing this duty is Dateline Builders, Inc. v. City of Santa Rosa, 146 Cal.App.3d 520, 194 Cal.Rptr. 258 (1983), where the court held that the city was not required to connect its sewer trunk line to proposed housing development outside the city's boundaries, where the proposed development was not consistent with the city's land use and development policy.

Public utilities have a duty to serve all customers within a service area provided the customer can be served at a reasonable cost and the customer can pay the tariff. Cities have long assumed that because they had a public duty to service all customers who could pay for service, that they had a duty to acquire the necessary water to fulfill this duty. Courts have generally agreed. A leading California case extended the duty to serve to include a duty on water providers to anticipate future growth and acquire the necessary supplies to meet projected demand. Lukrawka v. Spring Valley Water Co., 169 Cal. 318, 146 P. 640 (1915).

The case for the subordination of utility service to land use planning is that public utility law undermines the traditional power of cities to control their growth rates and their discretion to distribute the growth. This rationale is not inconsistent with the duty to serve, which is ultimately based on basic ideas of fairness and estoppel, and is intended primarily to protect those who had entered into a service relationship with a common carrier or were within the service area of a public utility but were denied service when the carrier or the utility was able or should have been able to provide it. See A. Dan Tarlock, *Western Water Law, Global Warming, and Growth Limitations*, 24 Loy. L.A. L. Rev. 979 (1991).

Courts have suggested that cities may use phased growth regulation to protect new residents from developments with inadequate public services. This allows rapidly growing cities the discretion to time the rate of growth through water and sewer-connection permits. San Mateo County Coastal Landowners' Ass'n v. County of San Mateo, 38 Cal.App.4th 523, 45 Cal. Rptr.2d 117 (1995); First Peoples Bank of New Jersey v. Township of Medford, 126 N.J. 413, 599 A.2d 1248 (1991).

Cities generally are not required to sell their water outside the city boundaries, but often have excess water that they wish to sell to outsiders. May they? The usual answer is yes, subject to the dangers of acquiring public utility status as illustrated in Robinson v. City of Boulder, 190 Colo. 357, 547 P.2d 228 (1976). But see County of Del Norte v. City of Crescent City, 71 Cal.App.4th 965, 84 Cal.Rptr.2d 179 (1999) (the city was allowed to establish policy that it would not provide new water service to unincorporated areas, and despite the fact the permit extended beyond city limits, there was no duty to serve the entire designated territory). Many states have authorized outside sales by statute. See, for instance, Utah Code Ann. § 10–8–14 (1999).

A longstanding source of controversy has been the rates charged by municipalities when they choose to supply water beyond their boundaries. Can the rates for outsiders be higher than those charged residents? The historical answer was that because cities had no duty to supply water to outsiders, they could condition the services on their own terms, including use of discriminatory rate setting. E.g., Zepp v. Mayor & Council of Athens, 180 Ga.App. 72, 348 S.E.2d 673 (1986) (sale of water to non-residents subject to U.C.C. but rate not unconscionable because city has unrestricted authority to set price). The majority rule now is that cities that choose to serve outsiders must do so on reasonable and nondiscriminatory terms. E.g., City of Texarkana v. Wiggins, 151 Tex. 100, 246 S.W.2d 622 (1952). The reasonableness rule rejects differential rates that are based solely on the "outsider" status of the customer, but there may be other, valid reasons, for a higher charge to outsiders, including a higher cost of service in a given case.

May a municipality expand its sphere of influence by conditioning its willingness to supply water to neighboring areas outside their boundaries on an agreement to comply with other municipal requirements, such as annexation, building codes, or land use regulations? See Brookens v. City of Yakima, 15 Wash.App. 464, 550 P.2d 30 (1976), where the city, having provided water to a portion of plaintiff's land, refused to increase deliveries to plaintiffs' remaining acreage when a proposed mobile home park failed to comply with the city's general plan. A related issue involves a municipality's refusal to provide a building permit unless an adequate water supply is available for the proposed development. See Associated Home Builders of Greater Eastbay, Inc. v. City of Livermore, 18 Cal.3d 582, 135 Cal.Rptr. 41, 557 P.2d 473 (1976).

Regulation of rates and requirements that services be provided on an equitable basis are generally imposed under state utility regulation schemes. Typically municipal water service agencies are exempt from such laws. In Board of County Comm'rs of Arapahoe County v. Denver Board of Water Comm'rs, 718 P.2d 235 (Colo. 1986), the municipal water service agency for the City and County of Denver was sued by neighboring counties seeking to have water supplied by Denver to their citizens and to have reasonable rates charged for the service. Denver had supplied water to users outside its boundaries for many years under distributors' contracts for prices higher than the cost of service, and greater than rates charged within the city and county. The state supreme court had previously held in City of Englewood v. City & County of Denver, 123 Colo. 290, 229 P.2d 667 (1951) that the Denver Water Department was not a public utility. The counties argued that the proliferation of extraterritorial service arrangements since Englewood was decided amounted to a change of circumstances. The supreme court held that the test for determining public utility status was no longer the *Englewood* test, and instead referred to the definitions in the "comprehensive scheme for regulation of public utilities by the [Public Utilities Commission]." The regulatory scheme, based on language in a 1954 constitutional amendment (three years after *Englewood*), broadly defined "public utility" to include "every * * * water corporation, person, municipality operating for the purpose of supplying the public." The court held that Denver "clearly fits this definition of a 'public utility.'" While the court found no constitutional barrier to the regulation of municipalities as public utilities by the Public Utility Commission (PUC), it found that the public policy of the state expressed in the statutes is "that municipal utilities have total authority over the provision of water service to users inside and outside municipal boundaries." 718 P.2d at 245. See also Thompson v. Salt Lake City Corp., 724 P.2d 958 (Utah 1986).

Communities faced with growth problems and perceived water shortages sometimes respond by imposing a moratorium on new water hookups or by raising the fees charged for water hookups to prohibitive levels. Such practices have been challenged on constitutional grounds, including claims that they amount to regulatory takings. See Lockary v. Kayfetz, 917 F.2d 1150 (9th Cir. 1990). Although moratoria long have been used to freeze development while a city formulates or revises a land use plan, a moratorium cannot become a de facto permanent freeze without encountering constitutional problems.

3.   MUTUAL IRRIGATION COMPANIES

A peculiar type of private entity for distributing water is the mutual irrigation company. "The mutual irrigation companies grew out of neighborhood or community construction of ditches. After ditches were constructed it was necessary to determine the quantity of water to which each farmer was entitled and to create an institutional structure for the upkeep of the project and the division of water among the users." Robert G. Dunbar, Forging New Rights in Western Waters 28 (1983). Mormon community control of ditches in Utah is sometimes cited as the origin of the mutual irrigation company, but similar early cooperative efforts among farmers were reported in Arizona and Colorado.

Mutual ditch or water companies, sometimes called water users associations, are nonprofit entities and are under the control of local water users. Consequently, they have been exempted from regulation as public utilities in some states. They should be distinguished from commercial irrigation enterprises, sometimes called "carrier ditch" companies. The latter are organized to distribute irrigation water for the profit of investors, who provide the capital and retain ownership of the works, and who are normally not local users. Beset by regulation as public utilities, and plagued by financial reverses, the commercial irrigation companies have virtually passed from the water scene. Mutual ditch companies and water companies, in contrast, have continuing importance.

Mutual water companies were often formed by land speculators as part of their schemes to develop and market lands. Many mutual ditch companies were created to sponsor and operate projects begun around the turn of the century under the Carey Act of 1894, 43 U.S.C.A. §§ 641–647 (West 1986), though most such projects were operated by irrigation districts, discussed *infra* p. 828. In many cases mutuals were reorganized into irrigation districts. The Act, named after its proponent, Senator Joseph M. Carey of Wyoming, authorized grants of millions of acres of land to each of the eleven westernmost states and territories for reclamation, with the expectation that private enterprises would finance irrigation projects on these lands. Only a few original Carey Act projects, such as the Twin Falls South Side Project in Idaho, still operate today. Many of the projects suffered from miscalculated project costs, overestimated water supplies, and a shortage of settlers to buy into the operating companies. The Act was amended several times in an effort to ensure greater project stability and success, but economic and legal problems continued and only one-eighth of the land applied for under the Act actually was patented to settlers. Mutual ditch companies were also sometimes used to contract with the Secretary of the Interior for repayment of project costs and operations of projects constructed under the Reclamation Act of 1902. See *infra* p. 829.

The rights represented by stock certificates in a mutual ditch company and the company's relationship to shareholders may vary from state-to-state. The Utah Supreme Court described the relationship as follows:

> The board of directors of a mutual water company, as a matter of law, owes the duty to distribute to each stockholder his proper proportion of the water available for distribution among the stockholders. A mutual irrigation company has a duty to use reasonable care and diligence in maintaining its canal and keeping it supplied with water, and of regulating and dividing its use among the shareholders in accordance with their interests. The company is liable and must respond in damages to a shareholder injured by its neglect or failure to discharge such duty.
>
> * * * However, [the company] does not have the duty to extend its canal and thereafter maintain it to [the shareholders'] property as they contend. There is neither a provision in the articles of incorporation nor has there been established by custom, a duty to deliver the water to the property of a shareholder.

Swasey v. Rocky Point Ditch Co., 617 P.2d 375, 379 (Utah 1980).

The local water users who control mutual ditch companies are predictably sensitive about changes in the water rights held by the company's shareholders, particularly changes from agriculture to some other use, and those that involve moving the water outside the company's service area. Board of Directors approval is often required for such changes. Given current pressures on agricultural water for use in a variety of non-agricultural schemes, these local sensitivities have assumed high visibility. Some of the issues are discussed in Fort Lyon Canal Co. v. Catlin Canal Co., 642 P.2d 501 (Colo. 1982), an ongoing saga where the State of Colorado owned shares in a mutual water company, and desired to change the point of diversion of water represented by those shares.

Despite a setback in the *Fort Lyon* case, the state continued to press forward in its attempts to provide a permanent pool of water in John Martin Reservoir on the Arkansas River by exchanging the water rights represented by its share of Catlin stock with the Fort Lyon Canal Company. In a further proceeding, In re Water Rights of the Fort Lyon Canal Co., 762 P.2d 1375 (Colo. 1988), the Colorado Supreme Court reiterated the position it adopted in the earlier case, and sustained a water court decision that the Catlin board of directors had not acted arbitrarily or capriciously or abused its discretion in turning down the state's application for a change of water right.

In City of Thornton v. Bijou Irrigation Co., 926 P.2d 1 (Colo. 1996), the city (located outside a conservancy district) acquired land within the district and sought to use the water to exchange for other water in order to provide benefits to the city. The district objected. The court noted that mutual ditch companies may impose reasonable restrictions beyond applicable statutory restrictions on the rights of a water user, and that this rule applied to conservancy districts. It then held that rules of the Northern Colorado Water Conservancy District, precluding extra-district use and benefit, were reasonable limitations on the City of Thornton's exercise of its contractual right to use water supplied by the district.

The consequences of transferring water rights in the Arkansas Valley from irrigation to urban uses outside the valley are ably described in Lawrence J. MacDonnell, From Reclamation to Sustainability: Water, Agriculture, and the Environment in the American West (1999). For a perceptive discussion of the issues raised by transfer of water outside of a district's boundaries, see also Barton H. Thompson, Jr., *Institutional Perspectives on Water Policies and Markets*, 81 Cal. L. Rev. 673 (1993).

Shareholders rights are limited, even as to matters within the service area. In East Jordan Irrigation Co. v. Morgan, 860 P.2d 310 (Utah 1993), the Utah Supreme Court reversed a district court ruling and held that a shareholder in a mutual irrigation company does not have standing to change the point of diversion or use of water without the consent of the corporation. This rule was extended in Badger v. Brooklyn Canal Co., 922 P.2d 745 (Utah 1996), where shareholders in an irrigation company voted to apply for a change in point of diversion as part of a move from flood to sprinkler irrigation. Minority shareholders subsequently challenged the state engineer's approval of the application. The court held the challenge invalid.

The shareholders are not always at the mercy of the corporation. In Left Hand Ditch Co. v. Hill, 933 P.2d 1 (Colo. 1997), a shareholder was refused access to the ditch corporation's shareholder list. The shareholder brought suit to inspect the corporate records and the court held that while the ditch company was under no statutory obligation to disclose the list, there was a common law duty of disclosure. What was the ditch company trying to achieve by denying access to one of its own shareholders?

What protection exists for shareholders of a ditch company to receive water in times of shortage? A mutual ditch company's rights to establish classes of shares based on the priority of different shareholders' appropriations for the purpose of water distribution schedules and to assess those with earlier priorities higher maintenance expenses have been upheld, Robinson v. Booth–Orchard Grove Ditch Co., 94 Colo. 515, 31 P.2d 487 (1934), but such pro rata allocations have been held not to be a conclusive adjudication of priorities among shareholders. Brose v. Board of Dirs. of Nampa and Meridian Irrigation Dist., 24 Idaho 116, 132 P. 799 (1913). Otherwise, the rule is that among shareholders of the same class there is no priority. Sanderson v. Salmon River Canal Co., 34 Idaho 303, 200 P. 341 (1921). Suppose a shareholder-landowner argues that its water rights are being jeopardized by sales of stock to new irrigators or other users. See Laramie Rivers Co. v. Watson, 69 Wyo. 333, 241 P.2d 1080 (1952).

Who owns the water rights held by a mutual ditch company? The company itself? The shareholders? Does the answer depend on the purposes for which ownership is being determined?

A shareholder may wish to transfer the use of water to other lands held by the shareholder, to the lands of other shareholders, or to non-shareholders outside of the company service area. Each shareholder is considered to be the beneficial owner of a water right. Great Western Sugar Co. v. Jackson Lake Reservoir and Irrigation Co., 681 P.2d 484 (Colo. 1984). Thus, shareholders have a duty not to injure the rights of other shareholders. For example, in In re Application for Water Rights of Certain Shareholders in the Las Animas Consol. Canal Co., 688 P.2d 1102 (Colo. 1984), the court approved the sale of the water rights of two mutual ditch companies to a power plant on the condition that no junior rights would be injured, and the water court reserved jurisdiction to consider the question of injury for five years. The court assumed that water under junior priorities was distributed to the shareholders on the basis of their pro rata ownership interests because there was insufficient evidence of actual consumption by each shareholder. The presumption that water is used on the basis of legal entitlements

> permits applicants who can demonstrate gross patterns of historic use of water rights to seek beneficial changes in such patterns of use which otherwise would be prohibited not because of demonstrable injury to the legal rights of others but because of the practical problem of the unavailability of reliable records. A shareholder asserting that historic use differed from use based on legal ownership may, of course, attempt to rebut the presumption.

688 P.2d at 1107–08. Stock may be made appurtenant to the land in order to protect the company from having to make uneconomical water deliveries. Thus shares may pass only with the transfer of the land, or the shares may be made severable. See John H. Davidson, Distribution and Storage Organizations, in Waters and Water Rights §§ 26.02(e)–(e)(2) (Robert E. Beck ed., 1991).

In Jacobucci v. County of Jefferson District Court, 189 Colo. 380, 541 P.2d 667 (1975), a municipality sought to condemn water rights held by the Farmers Reservoir and Irrigation Company. The rights in question were used to irrigate 15,000 acres of land farmed by 271 shareholders of the ditch company. Emphasizing that "the shares of stock owned by Farmers' shareholders represent a definite and specific water right, as well as a corresponding interest in the ditch, canal, reservoir, and other works by which the water is utilized," the court held that the shareholders were indispensable parties to the condemnation proceedings, and must be joined. The court cited Wadsworth Ditch Co. v. Brown, 39 Colo. 57, 88 P. 1060 (1907), in which it was held that the right of a mutual ditch company shareholder to change the point of diversion of use from within to without the area served by the ditch was a property right. Exercise of the right is subject, however, to the company's bylaws providing for assessments of shareholders and the company's right to withdraw the individual share-holder's appropriation through the ditch headgate for others to use when the shareholder has no immediate use for the water.

4.   SPECIAL DISTRICTS

Surprisingly little has been written about the role and governance of special water districts, despite the important functions they perform in the distribution of water, especially in the western states. Three helpful treat-ments are: Timothy De Young, Special Water Districts: Their Role in Western Water Use, in Western Water: Expanding Use/Finite Supplies, Seventh Annual Summer Program, Natural Resources Law Center, Univer-sity of Colorado School of Law (1986); Timothy De Young, Discretion Versus Accountability: The Case for Special Water Districts, in Special Water District: Challenge for the Future 31 (James N. Corbridge, Jr., ed., 1983); and the following article by Professor Leshy.

John D. Leshy, Special Water Districts—The Historical Background, in Special Water Districts: Challenge for the Future 11–27 (James N. Corbridge, Jr., ed., 1983)

I. Introduction

* * *

Special governmental districts today fulfill a dizzying array of pur-poses, including transportation, housing, education, soil conservation, re-creation and, more recently, such specialized functions as mosquito and weather control and industrial development.

* * *

Special water districts remain among the most important of these districts, particularly in the west. Of the nearly 1000 special districts nationwide engaged in 1977 in supplying water for various uses, more than

95% are in the seventeen western states (not including Alaska and Hawaii), and about 40% are in California, Arizona, New Mexico, Utah and Colorado.

* * *

By definition, special water districts have been legislatively classified as governmental entities; more precisely, as political subdivisions of state governments. Historically, the primary reason to give these entities governmental status was to overcome difficulties private enterprise had in raising money to build more ambitious water supply projects.

Table II.

Population and Acres Irrigated (by Irrigation Districts and the Bureau of Reclamation) 17 Western States, 1890–1970

Year	Popula-tion	Total Acres Irrigated	By Special (No.)	District (Acres)	By Bureau of Reclamation
1890	8,322,503	3,631,559	NA	NA	—
1900	11,187,961	7,542,782	NA	NA	—
1920	19,943,531	NA	NA	1,822,887	1,254,569
1930	24,749,633	14,085,967	363	3,452,275	1,485,028
1940	27,036,281	17,243,396	441	3,807,967	3,284,474
1950	34,009,255	24,270,566	483	4,962,413	683,413
1960	43,995,031	30,738,117	558	6,920,527	710,904
1970	52,504,548	34,785,717	687	9,689,181	363,320

* * *

Another modification state legislatures often made in second-generation irrigation districts was to enlarge their functions to embrace purposes other than agricultural irrigation. Some of these were so closely related to the core irrigation purpose or so insignificant as not to change markedly the district or its financial position; e.g., flood control, drainage, and supplying water for fire protection. Two others in particular, however, had a lasting impact on many irrigation districts: authority to deliver water for general purposes other than agricultural irrigation, and authority to generate and sell electric power.

The broadening of districts' authority over water delivery has become increasingly important as the west has grown in population, especially in metropolitan areas, and farmlands have been converted into residential and industrial areas. Moreover, such urbanization has created substantial stress on the management of these districts, and in some areas created substantial tensions between rural and urban interests a tension exacerbated by the typical voting schemes which invest rural interests with political control of district policies.

Giving some districts the authority to generate and sell electricity (and concomitantly, to use the revenues to meet district financial obligations such as bond payments) has had similar far-reaching effects. Some have aggressively exercised this authority, to such an extent that power now far outstrips water as a source of revenue. (Districts' authority is typically not limited to generating electricity with falling water; i.e., hydropower, but instead covers power generated from any source whatsoever.) Coupled again with the voting mechanisms by which rural landowners are vested with political control, this has allowed power producing districts to subsidize agricultural irrigation with power revenues. Moreover, as groundwater has become more important as a source of water supply for districts in many areas, district power production can be used to drive the pumps necessary to retrieve the water.

IV.   The Federal Government Steps In

Though the Reclamation Act of 1902 marked the entry of the federal government into the business of directly financing western agricultural development, it did not have any immediate influence on the formation or functioning of special water districts. The initial act, which actually contemplated a modest federal role (the federal government financing and constructing the projects and the beneficiaries repaying the outlay in full, though without interest, within 10 years), was bottomed on the premise that the federal government would deal directly with individual landowners. Despite the fact that the Wright Act had been in existence for a decade and a half and had already been adopted in seven other states, in other words, Congress expected the federal government to make the necessary repayment arrangements directly with individual water users or their (private) associations. In part this organizational approach reflected the program's original design to further settlement of the federal lands in the west with small yeoman farmers in Jefferson's vision of an agrarian ideal. Because Congress thought federal lands would be homesteaded, cultivated, and obtained mostly by reclamation beneficiaries, and it limited the amount of land on which any beneficiary could receive reclamation water to 160 acres, it seemed to make sense to Congress for the federal government to deal directly with individual beneficiaries.

* * *

* * * Congress between 1911 and 1926 largely substituted special governmental districts for individuals and water users associations as the contact point (and contracting entity) between farmers and the federal government.

In 1926, in fact, Congress recognized special water districts as the exclusive form of local participation in new federal reclamation projects. Though it retreated a bit from that rigid view in 1939, it is still common for Congress, in authorizing construction of a particular reclamation project, to require the formation of a special water district under state law to contract with the federal government for project water delivery and payment of the designated charges.

* * *

Given the substantial financial advantage governmental status affords to water supply entities, it is not surprising that, according to Wells Hutchins, whose surveys of special water districts across the west are the most extensive available, "the chief object in forming many irrigation districts has been to issue (tax exempt) bonds." * * *

* * *

* * * These districts typically have authority to levy taxes on real and personal property within the district as well as the more traditional "assessments." The procedures for formation and selection of governing officers vary widely, as do their management authorities, and may or may not be analogous to the more traditional irrigation districts.

Even more recently, special water districts have been created to oversee withdrawal of groundwater where the rate of extraction exceeds recharge or aquifer contamination is a problem. * * *

* * *

While the proliferating complexity of modern special water districts defies easy description or categorization, a few issues of policy and law are present in most of them, and bear brief mention here.

The first is the relationship between the special water district and the actual water users within it (as well as any other special water districts which may exist covering the same area) in the matter of legal rights to allocate and use water. Generally, state laws governing appropriation and use of water apply to districts of all kinds like they do to private entities, but this has scarcely answered the numerous difficult questions which have arisen from the earliest days of special water districts. The district statutes are often quite opaque on water rights matters, and in this legislative vacuum state courts have fashioned a number of approaches: Some regard the district as holding formal title to the water right while the actual users have a beneficial or equitable ownership interest in it. Others have deemed the actual users to hold legal and equitable title, with the district holding title only to the project's physical works and acting as trustee in delivering the water. One state views the district and actual users to hold the water right in common. Numerous variations on these approaches are found from district type to district type, or where a district was formed after a water supply had already been developed, or where a federal reclamation project is involved.

The matter can be crucial. First and most obviously, it affects the apportionment of water supplies among numerous potential recipients in a district, a question of utmost importance when water is in short supply, as in a drought. It also has a great deal of influence over the district's financial arrangements with its water users and, ultimately, over its ability to act as a water manager, promoting efficient and discouraging inefficient uses of project water. Functionally, the various approaches adopted by the states range from regarding districts as mere deliverers of water to satisfy already established water rights, to giving districts substantial power to allocate and distribute water to actual users according to the district's own determination of equity and efficiency.

When a federal reclamation project is involved, some additional wrinkles are present. Though the applicable statutes are far from clear, and judicial interpretations not wholly reconcilable with each other, recently the Supreme Court has characterized the federal government's ownership interest in reclamation water rights as "mere title" and "at most nominal," with the beneficial interest found in the owners of land within the project to which the water is applied. Thus it appears, as a lower court has held, that the federal government has little management control over the water it makes available (at mostly federal expense), and may not reduce the amount of water supplied to project beneficiaries in order to promote more efficient use or help satisfy other needs, even where the applicable contract with the local beneficiaries reserves this right to the federal government.

The matter of promoting more efficient use is one of growing importance in the West as more demands are placed on existing water supplies and large new supplies seem out of reach. Another aspect of this problem concerns the role of these districts in transferring water from one place or type of use to another, because such transfers are often the best or even the only way of improving efficiency in water use. Here, too, the power of districts to effect, prevent or otherwise influence transfers of water uses is both murky and variegated. It appears that some kinds of districts possess considerable power in this regard (even, as in Arizona, to the extent of possessing an absolute veto over applications to transfer any water rights within all watersheds whether or not within the district itself in which the district possesses water rights). Others, however, may have little or no authority over transfers, approval of which seems to remain in the hands of the state water rights agency.

Another generic issue concerns district governance, more specifically, the procedures for selecting district governing boards. As districts assume new functions and cover wider geographic areas, and as the areas in which they are found undergo substantial demographic, economic and cultural change, the matter of control becomes increasingly important and, concomitantly, controversial. Here too district laws reflect substantial variation: one resident or one landowner—one vote, one acre—one vote, or even voting based on assessed valuation of the property owned. Furthermore, corporations and other entities are sometimes excluded from the franchise even if they own property within or are served by the district.

* * *

A third generic issue is closely related to the previous ones; namely, the appropriate degree of control which should be exercised by the states over district activities. All western states have traditionally administered their water laws on a statewide basis; moreover, many of these states have moved in the direction of adopting state-wide plans to govern the allocation and use of water. Further, as has been described, the trend has been to provide more state oversight of special water district activities. In the abstract, the issue is whether special water districts should be regulated much as other non-governmental water users in the state are regulated, or whether instead their existing governmental stature should be built upon to allow them to play a more directly managerial and regulatory role in implementing state water policy.

Existing state laws generally manifest a schizophrenic approach to this issue. To some extent districts are treated much as private entities would be, but in other areas they are given special treatment because of their cloak of government authority. Perhaps the most prominent example of the latter is their exemption from statewide regulation in carrying out such "natural monopoly" functions as delivering water or generating and selling electric power—regulation to which ordinary business entities exercising similar monopoly power have traditionally been subject. The Advisory Commission on Intergovernmental Relations has recommended, in this connection, that pricing policies of all special districts be made subject to review and approval by state regulatory agencies if they are not otherwise reviewed by the governing body of a unit of general government.

Irrigation Districts and the Wright Act. The Wright Act, ch. 34, 1887 Cal. Stat. 29, was an early attempt by California to enable local farmers to organize irrigation districts. Its constitutionality was upheld in Fallbrook Irrigation District v. Bradley, 164 U.S. 112 (1896). Ten years after its passage, it was superseded by the Wright–Bridgeford Act, ch. 189, 1897 Cal. Stat. 254, CAL. WATER CODE §§ 20500 et seq. (West 1984), which continued the theme of the original Act, and became the model for irrigation district statutes in all of the seventeen western states. The Wright Act was an attempt to undo the results of Lux v. Haggin, 69 Cal. 255, 10 P. 674 (1886), *supra* p. 90. For a discussion of the Act, see Donald Worster, Rivers of Empire 108–09 (1985).

When an irrigation district was formed under the Wright Act, its board of directors was empowered to manage the general affairs of the district, including the acquisition of property, water rights, and irrigation system. The board could also call elections regarding the issuance of bonds and, most importantly, levy assessments to repay bond obligations and to support general expenditures. Although hearings were provided to consider excluding land within district boundaries that was not irrigable from the common source, the Act enabled districts to include, and assess, recalcitrant landowners whose lands could be benefited. This feature of irrigation districts is in sharp contrast to the mutual irrigation company, in which membership was completely voluntary.

By allowing the district to incur indebtedness for which all of the potentially benefited landowners in the district were liable, the Act was intended to add financial stability to local irrigation enterprises. Nevertheless, many districts suffered financial failure. Wells Hutchins has suggested that among the reasons for this were inadequate water supplies, inclusion within districts of non-productive lands, engineering difficulties, and exploitation by speculators who were more concerned with profits than with sound economics. See Wells A. Hutchins, *Irrigation Districts: Their Organization, Operation and Financing, in U.S. Dep't of Agriculture*, Tech. Bull.

No. 254 (1931). Amendments to the Wright Bridgeford Act, and to the irrigation district statutes of other states, have attempted to remedy some of the perceived deficiencies. Representation in district elections has continued to be a particular bone of contention, however. See Ball v. James, 451 U.S. 355, 101 S.Ct. 1811, 68 L.Ed.2d 150 (1981).

Irrigation districts are creatures of state law. As populations have increased in formerly agricultural areas, posing new problems for districts, many state statutes have been modified to expand district powers beyond irrigation, to include drainage, flood control, and the generation of electric power. Some irrigation districts have evolved into more complex water distribution entities. A useful discussion of the history and future of irrigation districts is Lenni Beth Benson, *Desert Survival: The Evolving Western Irrigation District,* 1982 Ariz. St. L.J. 377. In their efforts to address the new problems, irrigation districts may exceed their statutory powers. In Cowden v. Kennewick Irrigation Dist., 76 Wash.App. 844, 888 P.2d 1225 (1995) the district was reined in by the court when it tried to develop real property for residential purposes.

When water distribution organizations organized primarily to supply irrigation water are faced with the transition from farmland to residential development, they can become embroiled in multi-faceted conflicts. In Nueces County Water Control and Improvement Dist. No. 3 v. Texas Water Rights Comm'n, 481 S.W.2d 930 (Tex.Civ.App. 1972), a conservation and reclamation district had been converting water from irrigation to municipal use over a period of several decades. The court rejected an attempt of the Texas Water Rights Commission to cancel a converted right on the ground that such a conversion could not be made without commission approval. At the very same time the City of Corpus Christi had sued the improvement district over the right to scarce water in the Nueces River. See Nueces County Water Control & Improvement Dist. No. 3 v. Texas Water Rights Comm'n, 481 S.W.2d 924 (Tex.Civ.App. 1972).

More than 83% of the residents of the western United States live in cities. This urbanization has exacerbated the conflict between cities and rural irrigation water suppliers. In recognition of the need for representation of urban water interests, a Western Urban Water Coalition (WUWC) was formed in 1992. Members of the WUWC include Denver, Las Vegas, Reno, Phoenix, Portland, Salt Lake City, and Seattle water suppliers, the California Urban Water Agencies, and others. The WUWC is expected to play a pivotal role in water politics and assist western metropolitan areas in finding new approaches to obtaining water supplies. The new alliance shatters the historic coalition between urban and agricultural users that was powerful in moving Congress to appropriate funds for major water projects.

The development of irrigation districts was encouraged by federal reclamation law. See *infra* p. 829. The original Reclamation Act of 1902, Pub. L. No. 161, 32 Stat. 388 (1902), contemplated that the Bureau of Reclamation, in seeking repayment of reclamation project costs to the federal government, would deal directly with private users or irrigation companies. The 1911 Warren Act, 43 U.S.C.A. §§ 523–525 (West 1986), permitted an irrigation district to contract for project water. General authority for the Secretary of the Interior to contract directly with irrigation districts for repayment was forthcoming in 1922. 43 U.S.C.A. § 511 (West 1986). Thereafter, the Bureau encouraged both the formation of such districts and the passage of state laws enabling them to contract with the United States in regard to reclamation projects.

Federal reclamation projects, designed in the main to provide irrigation water, are a significant potential source for transfers to municipal and other uses. Who owns project water, and what are the impediments to transfers? The Supreme Court, in Ickes v. Fox, 300 U.S. 82, 57 S.Ct. 412, 81 L.Ed. 525 (1937), held that the irrigator was the owner of the water right, and characterized the government as "simply a carrier and distributor of the water, with the right to receive the sums stipulated in the contracts as reimbursement for the cost of construction and annual charges for operation of the works." Id. at 95. That case, however, involved a situation where the repayments had been completed. What of the case, likely to exist under today's lengthy repayment periods, where reimbursement is continuing? Professor Tarlock identifies the Bureau of Reclamation as the presumptive holder of legal title "as a trustee for the project beneficiaries." A. Dan Tarlock, Law of Water Rights and Resources § 5.81 (1998 with annual updates). See In re Uintah Basin, 133 P.3d 410 (Utah 2006) (dispute between the Bureau and water user organization over which entity controls return flows from use of project water). Whatever the state of title, proposed transfers must run the gamut of state law deferred to by Section 8 of the Reclamation Act, 43 U.S.C.A. § 372 (West 1986) including state no-injury rules, Bureau of Reclamation contract provisions, approval of the Secretary of the Interior, and whatever anti-transfer protections are imposed by the special districts that customarily hold project water rights.

In many cases, landowners actively seek benefit from the district's power of taxation. In other cases, special districts have been opposed because they could pose too great a threat to existing social and political institutions. A special irrigation district can superimpose new influences upon existing formal and informal allocations of political power that are based on control of water. An economist and a political scientist have described the defeat of a proposed federal irrigation project in Taos County, New Mexico, after Hispanic farmers became concerned about how the local repayment obligation might affect existing water use patterns. See F. Lee Brown and Helen M. Ingram, Water and Poverty in the Southwest (1987).

Special District and the Election of Directors. An historically important issue is the manner of electing directors of special water districts. The landmark Supreme Court case dealing with this issue is Ball v. James, 451 U.S. 355 (1981). The Arizona Legislature had allowed the Salt River Project Agricultural Improvement and Power District to limit voting for its board of directors to voters who owned land in the district, and to apportion voting power based on the amount of land held by each qualified voter. The Supreme Court held, 5–4, that "the peculiarly narrow function of this local governmental body and the special relationship of one class of citizens to that body releases it from the strict demands of the one-person, one-vote principle of the Equal Protection Clause of the Fourteenth Amendment.'' Id. at 357.

Ball has been followed in other cases involving water districts. E.g., Stelzel v. South Indian River Water Control Dist., 486 So.2d 65 (Fla.Dist. Ct.App. 1986) (one vote per acre in district that exercised road construction and maintenance functions and aquatic weed abatement authority).

Representational issues arise even in the grassroots context of traditional acequia organizations. In Wilson v. Denver, 125 N.M. 308, 961 P.2d 153 (1998), interest holders in a community ditch challenged the election of acequia association officers. The court held that voting in ditch elections can be conducted based proportionately on water rights, proportionately on ditch ownership, or based on a majority of those using the ditch for distribution of water, and that ditch officer elections are not subject to the Equal Protection Clause requirement of one person, one vote, citing *Ball*.

State constitutional provisions may impose stricter requirements for voting than the United States Constitution. The Washington Supreme Court has struck down a law limiting the right to vote for irrigation district board members to owners of agricultural land. Foster v. Sunnyside Valley Irrigation Dist., 102 Wash.2d 395, 687 P.2d 841 (1984). The limitation was found to be inconsistent with the state constitution's guarantee of ''free and equal'' elections. The court specifically found that a *Ball* analysis, focusing on the primary purpose of special districts in allowing only landowners to vote, was inconsistent with the state constitution. The court did hold that a district exercising largely non-governmental powers, as determined by the *Ball* test, could apportion votes among the affected class based on the different relative impacts of the district's activities on some members rather than being bound to a one-person, one-vote requirement. The scheme in question in *Foster* gave owners of one to ten acres of agricultural land one vote, and owners of additional agricultural land an additional vote. Because owners of non-agricultural land were completely denied suffrage, the scheme was inadequate. The court said it will subject any apportionment scheme to strict scrutiny to ensure that votes are apportioned according to the level of the district's impact on definable classes of voters.

A related issue is whether directors of irrigation and other water districts should be elected or appointed, and if appointed, by whom. In Choudhry v. Free, 17 Cal.3d 660, 131 Cal.Rptr. 654, 552 P.2d 438 (1976), the California Supreme Court struck down a statute requiring candidates for the board of directors of the Imperial Irrigation District to be landowners within the district. The court held that the requirement violated the constitutional rights of the candidates and the voters.

Under Colorado law, members of conservancy district boards are appointed by the local district court judge. The board must reflect a balance among beneficial water users in the district. This approach (along with a variety of broad powers given to districts) was upheld in People ex rel.

Rogers v. Letford, 102 Colo. 284, 79 P.2d 274 (1938). In districts organized after 1945, an election may be triggered by a petition of 10% of the "registered electors" of the district. COLO. REV. STAT. § 3–45–114 (2000).

Appointment of board members is often criticized on the ground that it tends to perpetuate control of district affairs in the hands of agricultural interests, when the district's problems may be increasingly urban in nature. What are the advantages and disadvantages of appointed, as opposed to elected, boards?

Special Districts and Water Efficiency. Water districts are in a position to play a major role in promoting the efficient allocation of water resources. But there are legal and political impediments to the promotion of efficiency. Districts have been criticized as providing undue subsidies to agriculture. Their ability to spread costs among all taxpayers insulates the districts from the cost of developing or using water. Many charge very little or nothing for water usage. If anything is charged for the water used, it is generally a flat rate or a rate based on the average cost of developing water.

The "energy crisis" of the late 1970s stimulated intense interest in resource use conservation, especially in electric utility rates. Environmentalists and welfare economists argued that average cost rates often created incentives to use more electricity because rates declined with increased usage. The suggested remedy was to base rates on the marginal costs of power generation. The theory was that costs would rise with use and thus there would be incentives to conserve. The same criticism is made of water prices: "The use of taxpayer revenues, fee assessments, and historical average cost pricing procedures sends water price signals to users which are far below the marginal costs of new supply projects. In some cases, particularly in agriculture, no water price signal is sent at all." Zach Willey, Least Cost Approaches For Satisfying Water Demand: An Alternative Analysis, in Western Water: Expanding Uses/Finite Supplies, Seventh Annual Summer Program, Natural Resources Law Center, University of Colorado School of Law (1986). As in the case of electric power, marginal, variable cost pricing is suggested as the proper standard for water rates. The assumption is that this will result in higher prices and more efficient use of water. See generally Zamora et al., *Pricing Urban Water: Theory and Practice in Three Southwestern Cities,* 1 Sw. Rev. Mgmt. Econ. 89 (1981).

There are some important examples of districts where water has been marketed among users in the service area. By allowing agricultural, municipal, and industrial water users to buy and sell rights to use water annually, greater economic efficiency is achieved. The use of water markets in the Northern Colorado Water Conservancy District is illustrative.

The federal Colorado Big Thompson Project (C–BT) was started in 1937 and completed in 1957 to bring supplemental irrigation water from the western side of the Rocky Mountains to Northeastern Colorado. The Northern Colorado Water Conservancy District (NCWCD) was established to contract with the federal government for purchase of the water, repayment of project costs, and distribution of the water to final users. C–BT has provided an historical average of 2.83 x 10^8 m^3 (230,000 acre-feet) or about 17% of the total water supply of the region. While this supply is primarily for supplemental irrigation, towns and a growing number of industries use C–BT as a raw water supply. This supply represents the easily tradable margin needed to provide flexibility in allocation.

The area encompassed by NCWCD included areas of quite different natural water supplies in relation to the amount of arable land. As a result, potential users did not want a mandatory, uniform assignment of water to the land. These sentiments led, in 1957, to a system in which water was to be delivered to the owners of NCWCD shares, a share representing a freely transferable contract between the District and the holder entitling the holder to 1/310,000th of the water available to NCWCD (this has averaged approximately 863.8 m^3 (0.7 acre-feet) of water per year). The transferable nature of the allotments stimulated the creation of a market in which they could be traded.

Much of the water needed for urban and nonagricultural industrial growth has been provided by the sale of NCWCD allotments from agriculture. These nonagricultural users often "rent" excess water back to irrigation on a short-term (annual) basis. In the early years many irrigators gave away their allotments because they did not want to pay the $1.50 annual charge. Allotment prices increased from $30 in 1960 to $291 in 1973. This trend accelerated sharply in 1974 with average prices reaching a peak of $2161 in 1980. Since 1980, prices have fallen back to about $900, partly because of the completion of a premature water supply project that will bring 5.92 x 10^7 m^3 (48,000 acre-feet) of water to towns in the region.

Rentals are transfers of water among users for one season only without transferring the allotment titles. The NCWCD office facilitates communications among prospective buyers and sellers, so that rentals are easily effected in response to relatively small discrepancies in water values among users. About 30% of the C–BT water is involved in rental transactions each year, with towns being big renters of water to agriculture.

Charles W. Howe et al., Innovative Approaches to Water Allocation: The Potential for Water Markets, 22 Water Resources Res. 439, 443–44 (1986).

This market in CBT shares has been described as "the most structured water market in the West.... Irrigators, developers, and municipal water suppliers buy and sell CBT units through a well-defined process," averaging about 8 transactions per month. *Water Market Indicators*, Water Strategist, January 2007, at 12. Growth on the northern Front Range has driven CBT share prices dramatically higher since 1980. In the extreme drought year of 2002, prices exceeded $13,000 per share, although they had fallen below $11,000 by 2006. Id. at 13.

It is difficult to provide incentives for public entities to function efficiently when the economic returns seem attenuated and the idea of "selling out" an important resource is politically unpopular. See Dwight R. Lee, Political Provision of Water: An Economic/Public Choice Perspective, in Special Water Districts: Challenge For the Future 51 (James N. Corbridge, Jr., ed., 1983). If transfers within districts can promote more efficient water use, the opportunities for efficiency are multiplied when transfers outside the district are considered. So are the difficulties multiplied. Typically, district bylaws, state laws, and provisions in federal reclamation contracts provide for water to be supplied to a specific service area defined by district boundaries. For them to be changed usually requires political action. This may be difficult because out-of-district transfers are often politically unpalatable, though they may be economically rewarding. Political opposition also rises to proposals to transfer agricultural water to municipal uses.

There have been some advantageous transactions in which water conserved in a district was transferred to a municipality. When the city of Casper, Wyoming needed an additional water supply it negotiated an agreement with the Alcova Irrigation District under which the city promised to rehabilitate and line portions of the district's 59 miles of canals and 160 miles of laterals in order to reduce seepage. This enabled the district to reduce the amount of water it diverted from the North Platte River, but still deliver the same quantity of water for crop irrigation. Casper gained the benefit of some 7000 acre-feet a year of saved water.

The role of districts in facilitating agricultural to municipal transfers is significant. The most notable example is the Metropolitan Water District–Imperial Irrigation District agreement, discussed *supra* pp. 368–375, and *infra* pp. 1016–1020.

The Western Governors Association (WGA) accepted a report in 1986 calling for greater efficiency in water use and finding that "local special water districts are central to the implementation of policies to enhance western water use; however, they usually operate outside the effective scope of state water policy." The report went on to recommend that:

> States could authorize special water districts to transfer water to users outside of their boundaries, by sale, sale and leaseback, lease with an option to use in wet years, and a wide array of other arrangements. (In many instances state authorization of transfers outside of district boundaries would not be sufficient to enable such transfers due to restrictions contained in Reclamation law and district contracts with the Bureau of Reclamation. This is another area where states and the Bureau will need to work together to effect change.) California has also taken this step by authorizing special districts to transfer water that is "surplus" to their needs. "Surplus" has been defined broadly to include conserved water.

* * *

Special districts could be encouraged to permit the development of markets for water rights, shares or contracts within their boundaries perhaps using some of the auction and other procedures implemented by the Northern Colorado Water Conservancy District. Means of encouragement include conditioning state financial assistance for new projects on the allowance of markets or inclusion in the charters of new districts of requirements to encourage intra-district markets.

* * *

Provisions of western state law that constrain the mobility of water by requiring transferees to purchase land with water or that give special districts veto power over the transfer of water that is not used within their boundaries could be eliminated.

Bruce Driver, Western Water: Tuning the System, Report to the Western Governors Association 52–55 (1986).

In 1988, the Department of the Interior, as part of its self-declared transition from a construction to a management agency, adopted a policy that encourages federal water transfers.

Special Districts for Urban Growth. Although most legal issues pertaining to special districts have arisen in the context of irrigation districts formed long ago, some types of special districts have continued to proliferate, especially to provide water for suburban expansion. Water and sanitation districts, for instance, are widely used by developers in Colorado to organize taxing entities that can finance water supply and distribution facilities for large housing developments in areas not served by existing water suppliers. The process for their formation is typical of the steps in forming any special district. They are formed pursuant to state law, with applicants in a particular area following a set of rather straightforward, prescribed procedures.

These districts sometimes carry their own set of problems. They are easily formed when a developer owns all or virtually all of the land in the proposed district. As houses are sold, the homeowners become the taxpayers in the districts; when all the houses are sold the developer's connection with the district ends. This has led to concerns where the homeowners inherit a substantial debt and, in some cases, limited water supplies, such as a depleting aquifer.

The following excerpt summarizes the steps under a Colorado statute for forming water and sanitation districts.

§ 5.9 Water and Sanitation Districts.

* * * Water and sanitation districts can be located entirely or partly within a municipality or county

All provisions concerning water and sanitation districts are included within the Special Districts Act which provides the same procedures and provisions for water and sanitation as for other districts such as fire protection districts, hospital districts, metropolitan districts, or park and recreation districts. * * *

The organization of a water and sanitation district is initiated by submitting a service plan and processing fee to the county clerk for the applicable board of county commissioners in each county which has territory included in the proposed district. * * * The board of county commissioners must hold a public hearing on the record and may either approve the plan with any conditions it deems necessary or disapprove it. * * *

After approval of a service plan, a petition must be filed with the district court. The petition must be signed by either 30 percent or 200 of the taxpaying electors with the district, whichever number is smaller. * * * Upon a finding that the petition is sufficient, the court directs that an election be held on the question of the organization of the special district. After approval by the electors and a determination that the election was conducted in conformity with applicable election rules and procedures, the court enters an order declaring the district organized, at which point it becomes a quasi-municipal corporation and a political subdivision of the state. * * *

Once a special district is formed, its boundaries can be altered through inclusion or exclusion of property as well as by consolidation with another district. There are also procedures for total dissolution. * * *

* * *

Districts providing water and/or sanitation services are given additional powers. Such a district can compel property owners to connect the property with district water and sewer lines. The district's board can divide the district into areas according to the services furnished and fix charges and taxes accordingly. It can construct, operate, or maintain facilities along public ways, vacant public lands and streams, or watercourses, subject to reasonable regulation by counties and municipalities and payment of fees for restoration. It can assess reasonable penalties for failure to pay fees, and can assess charges for the availability, as opposed to actual use of facilities. It can also condemn property in and outside the district, except to acquire water rights.

* * *

* * * The Act also established exclusion procedures to prevent overlap between special districts and municipalities. Municipalities are automatically excluded, upon request, during district formation, municipalities may also have lands excluded after formation upon a showing that the municipality can provide comparable service within a reasonable time.

* * *

George Vranesh, Vranesh's Colorado Water Law 336–350 (James N. Corbridge, Jr. & Teresa A. Rice eds. rev. ed. 1999).

B.   FEDERAL PLANNING AND DEVELOPMENT OF WATER RESOURCES

After the passage of the Reclamation Act of 1902, huge federal water resources programs were devoted to promoting the settlement of the arid West. The goal of the Bureau of Reclamation, created under the Act, was to conserve and distribute water in the West, primarily for agricultural irrigation of otherwise dry and unproductive lands. However, other regions of the country also have demanded federal intervention in water resource development. Throughout the nineteenth century, federal water resources policy was concentrated on the protection and the promotion of navigation by the building of canals and locks and the dredging and improving of harbors and inland waterways, principally in the East and Southeast. See Beatrice H. Holmes, A History of Federal Water Resources Programs, 1800–1960 (Dept. of Agriculture Misc. Pub. 1233, 1972). The leading history of the triumph of multiple purpose development is Samuel P. Hays, Conservation and the Gospel of Efficiency: The Progressive Conservation Movement, 1890–1920 (1959).

In the twentieth century the authority of the chief navigation protection agency, the United States Army Corps of Engineers, was expanded to include controlling floods, enhancing recreation, supplying municipal water, and, finally, to protecting the environmental quality of water. This opened the arid West to greater water development possibilities under the auspices of the Corps.

John R. Mather, Water Resources: Distribution, Use, and Management
294–305 (1984).

A History of Federal Water Resources Legislation

* * *

Promoting commerce and transportation has long been one of the major concerns of the Federal government (witness the present emphasis on our interstate highway system). In the early 1800s, this interest was expressed in the government's desire to promote river improvements and canal developments to aid in inland transportation. It was clearly stated that navigable waters would be treated as public highways and would be maintained free for the use of all. The westward movement of the nation after the Louisiana Purchase resulted in the Senate asking Secretary of the Treasury Albert Gallatin to prepare a national plan for the development of roads and canals. The Gallatin Report of 1808 called for a nationwide system of canals and other river improvements that could be justified on the basis of the economic development of the West, national defense, and political unity.

While the Gallatin Report, and its later revision by Secretary of War Calhoun in 1819, suggested that Congress had the power to spend money on river improvements because of its concern for national defense and the general welfare, the famous Gibbons v. Ogden decision by the Supreme Court in 1824 acknowledged that the power of Congress to regulate interstate commerce also included the power to regulate navigation within each of the states insofar as that navigation was connected with commerce.

* * *

As farmers moved into drier and drier areas, the need for irrigation became obvious. The Desert Land Act of 1877 authorized sale of 640 acre parcels of land in certain arid states and territories provided the purchasers would irrigate them within 3 years. Various land speculation scandals severely limited the implementation of this Act.

The period from 1900 to 1920, under the administrations of Roosevelt, Taft, and Wilson, marked a most significant and what might be called progressive period in Federal water resources programs and developments. The principles directing the water resources development during this period were (a) conservation of national resources for the use of present and future generations; (b) elimination of control and/or exploitation of the resources by monopolies; (c) elimination of "giveaways" of resources to special interests; (d) encouragement of individual, independent groups such as the family farm.

* * *

A number of agencies were established to coordinate planning and development of water resources. For example, the Reclamation Act of 1902 established, among other things, the Reclamation Fund with money made available from the sale of public lands * * *. The Secretary of the Interior was authorized to use the fund to plan and construct irrigation works in those states. * * *

* * *

During the 1920s (until 1933) under Republican administrations, the general trend was to deemphasize the antimonopolistic policies of the previous two decades and to eliminate, as much as possible, government competition with private enterprise. For a while, work was stopped on the nearly completed Wilson Dam near Muscle Shoals while a private purchaser was sought. Hoover, as Secretary of Commerce, recommended national planning of public works as well as multi-purpose planning by the various governmental drainage basin commissions. But the matter of public vs. private control of power continued to be one of the most sensitive political issues in the nation for years.

* * *

The depression of the 1930s and the new administration under Franklin Roosevelt resulted in the formulation of many construction plans in the form of public works projects in order to stimulate the economy. Multipurpose water resource development with public power programs was promoted to provide regional economic growth and to benefit the largest numbers of people. Planning the development of "national" resources, which included both human and natural resources, became a key to the programs proposed. Roosevelt enlarged the role of the Executive in the proposing of legislation and Congress accepted its role to consider and modify the programs initiated in the Executive Branch.

A number of new water planning agencies were established to push new concepts of regional resources development. One cornerstone of this concept was the creation of the Tennessee Valley Authority in 1933, an agency authorized to exercise all Federal functions of development and management of water and land resources within a large geographic region. As such, it had the power to plan, build, and operate dam and reservoir projects for navigation, flood control, and power. Even more uniquely, it had to obtain only the approval of the House and Senate Appropriations Committees before undertaking any proposed work. The TVA could also make and sell electric power from thermally-driven generators, build transmission lines, direct soil conservation, recreation development, and fish and wildlife improvements.

* * *

Current Federal water laws and programs are quite involved and complex. More than 40 Federal agencies have some water programs or statutory responsibilities and the programs keep changing. * * *

––––––––

A wide repertoire of federal water development possibilities has allowed regional political combinations to capture major federal programs for all parts of the country. The demand for cheap public power led to the establishment of federal authorities, such as the Tennessee Valley Authority and the Bonneville Power Authority, to construct reservoirs for hydroelectric power generation. Flood control structures are, of course, useful in all regions of the country. Promotion of water resources development for a variety of purposes created powerful development constituencies and united political parties and factions around particular development projects. During most of this century water resources development has been equated with progress. The widespread national distribution of federal monies also minimized interregional political checks.

Even those who appreciate the value of the many existing water projects now ask whether it makes sense for the federal government to build more large projects. There is little doubt that such projects as Hoover Dam enriched not only the Southwest but the nation by providing flood protection, a supply of water for growing cities and productive farms, and copious cheap power for homes and industries. But the damming and diversion of western rivers permanently changed the landscape of the West. See, e.g., W. Eugene Hollon, The Great American Desert: Then and Now

(1966). We are just now beginning to ask whether the effort was worth the price. For a clear "no" answer, see Donald Worster, Rivers of Empire: Water, Aridity, and the Growth of the American West (1985). Soaring federal deficits during the 1980s necessitated rethinking all large federal expenditures. But even in the brighter economic times of the sixties and seventies the climate had begun to change for water development projects.

A concern about the need for more comprehensive planning, rather than simple political logrolling, led to passage of the Water Resources Planning Act of 1965, Pub. L. 89–80, 79 Stat. 244 (1965). The Act encouraged state, local, and regional water resources planning. However, many projects had already been authorized because they were feasible from an engineering standpoint and the proponent states had enough political clout to move them through Congress. The belated concern for water resources planning also prompted Congress to establish the National Water Commission in 1968. The Commission was directed to study future water requirements and alternative means of meeting them,

> giving consideration * * * to conservation and more efficient use of existing supplies, increased usability by reduction of pollution, innovations to encourage the highest economic use of water, interbasin transfers, and technological advances * * * [and to] consider economic and social consequences of water resource development on regional economic growth, on institutional arrangements, and on esthetic values affecting the quality of life of the American People. * * *

Pub. L. No. 90 515, § 3(a), 82 Stat. 868 (1968).

The resulting report of the National Water Commission has become a cornerstone for national decision-making about water resources. See U.S. National Water Commission, Water Policies For the Future: Final Report to the President and to the Congress of the United States (1973). As the authorizing language suggested, the federal focus was to change from responding to requests for funds to build water projects to considering a variety of broad public concerns about the use of water resources.

In 1977 a newly-elected President Carter targeted thirty-three water projects for elimination from the federal budget. Henceforth, he announced, all projects would be reviewed in light of environmental factors and benefit-cost ratios. The trend of federal policy away from narrow, structural responses to water issues was supported by strong public sentiment for wise resources protection and use. Still, the tradition of federal water development runs deep, and the Carter "hit list" rocked the West and water development interests throughout the nation. To have the government change the rules of federal financial assistance dashed expectations for construction projects that could assist local economies. Many westerners had resented federal controls on water use and development as being intrusive and unnecessary. As federal assistance receded, westerners viewed such controls as intolerable.

Although the "hit list" was modified after it created a political maelstrom, and a few of the targeted projects were built, the Carter policy eventually became conventional wisdom. Most of the economic and environmental tests for water projects have remained. Later administrations also have insisted that states and other non-federal entities bear a portion of the initial costs of constructing water projects funded by the Bureau of Reclamation or the Corps of Engineers. New Corps projects are subject to specific non-federal cost-sharing requirements under 1986 and later legislation. See Water Resources Development Act of 1986, Pub. L. No. 99–662, 100 Stat. 4082 (1986), as amended at Pub. L. No. 101–640, 104 Stat. 4604 (1990).

Federal water project construction has all but ceased, but the government continues to have a role in operating existing projects. The largest project to be built under the Reclamation program, the Central Arizona Project was one of the last to be completed A drastically redesigned and downsized Animas–La Plata project in Colorado is nearing completion. The Central Utah Project, authorized in 1956, is under construction, but appropriations to fund its completion have been made subject to new conditions that enable the fulfillment of broad environmental purposes. In the future it is likely that only a few, mostly small, projects will be built, as the Bureau of Reclamation focuses its limited resources on maintaining and rehabilitating existing projects. The mission of federal water development agencies is evolving. The Bureau of Reclamation announced in 1988 that it has a new mission that includes improving water use efficiency. Title XXXIV of the Reclamation Projects Authorization and Adjustment Act of 1992 (Pub. L. 102–575, 106 Stat. 4600 (1992)) changes the purposes and operations of California's Central Valley Project to shift water from agriculture to urban uses, to facilitate marketing of water, to promote greater water use efficiency, and to fulfill major environmental goals. The Act may provide a model for reforming much of the present Reclamation system.

There are several themes that run through this section:

Federal power. Federal involvement in water resources, the scope of federal constitutional authority, and much of the law of federal water resources development is a history of the expansion of federal power. Assertions of federal control over water resources are inevitably resisted as intrusions on state sovereignty. The issue that arose early in the history of federal water development was whether state law, and hence policy, is preempted by the assertion of federal regulatory or spending authority. Because the federal government first deferred to the states to set water policy and then began to assert a federal interest in water allocation, federalism issues are especially intense in water law. See generally Reed D. Benson, Deflating the Deference Myth: National Interests vs. State Authority under Federal Laws Affecting Water Use, 2006 Utah L. Rev. 241, 242–267 (2006).

Regional politics. Federal water resources investment has always raised questions about regional equity in the distribution of national wealth. Federal funding of water resources projects has long been criticized by economists as an inefficient allocation of national resources. E.g., John V. Krutilla & Otto Eckstein, Multiple Purpose River Development: Studies in

Applied Economic Analysis (1958). Furthermore, development has rarely followed principles of river basinwide planning, although the wisdom of that approach has been perceived since at least the New Deal era. For a concise history of this idea and its limitations see James L. Wescoat, Jr., Integrated Water Development: Water Use and Conservation Practice in Western Colorado 7 21 (1984). Regional political alliances have historically resisted efforts to apply rational criteria to water resources development proposals, although Congress has attempted to legislate the river basin idea over the years. The longstanding partnership among large water users, the states and the Bureau of Reclamation is the subject of a fast-paced history of the post-World War II Bureau. Marc Reisner, Cadillac Desert: The American West and Its Disappearing Water (1986). Rational allocation takes on more urgency as the era of large-scale federal water resources development draws to an end.

Trend toward improved management. There is a growing appreciation of new uses of water, of non-structural management options, and of marketing project water. Historically, "water conservation" meant storing water for consumptive use, power generation, and flood control; it meant constructing dams and other facilities. See generally A. Dan Tarlock, *The Changing Meaning of Water Conservation in the West*, 66 Neb. L. Rev. 145 (1987). A national environmental consciousness has produced a greater recognition of the value of instream uses and more efficient use practices. The repercussions of this apparent fundamental shift in national thinking about natural resources is reflected, for example, in pollution control and species diversity protection programs discussed *supra* Chapter 7.

Increasingly, the market provides solutions to the demand for reallocation to achieve efficiency and environmental protection. The rejection of large-scale structural responses to water demands is related to the growing appreciation of instream uses and a greater willingness to employ decentralized solutions to produce or free up supplies. For instance, water can be reallocated from existing federal water projects by market transfers of water as an alternative to building more projects to create new supplies. Marginal cost pricing has taken root in other areas such as public utility rate structure and air pollution emission trading w and is now having a profound influence on water resources policy. However, fulfillment of a policy of managing existing federal projects more efficiently in keeping with public values and sound market principles remains incomplete.

1.   The Reach of Congressional Power

The federal government was the greatest force in planning, construction, and operation of flood control, hydroelectric, and irrigation projects for one hundred years. Under the United States Constitution, the federal government's authority is limited to the exercise of powers expressly delegated it, and powers necessary and proper in carrying out those enumerated powers. Federal involvement in water planning and development can find its justification in many of the powers enumerated in the Constitution. Dams and power plants have been justified under the war power as necessary for national defense. The Newlands Act of 1902, creating the Bureau of Reclamation, was premised on the Property Clause, art. IV, § 3, cl. 2, granting Congress the power to control the use of federal public lands.

The power most often relied on in the exercise of federal jurisdiction over water planning and development is the commerce power. In the exercise of its power to promote and regulate interstate commerce under art. I, § 8, cl. 3, the federal government is involved in navigation, flood control, watershed development, power production, and environmental protection. A wide array of subject matter can be included under the rubric of "interstate commerce" based on the Supreme Court's acceptance of even the most attenuated theoretical connection with commercial intercourse that concerns more than one state. See generally Laurence H. Tribe, American Constitutional Law §§ 5–4 to 5–5 (3d ed. 2000). Rather, the question has been whether, in the case of a particular law or project, the geographic impact is so limited that it lies outside Congress's commerce power. In recent years, however, the Court has struggled with whether the Constitution authorizes federal efforts to regulate certain waters and wetlands, and has interpreted the Clean Water Act narrowly so as to avoid those questions. See Solid Waste Agency of Northern Cook County v. U.S. Army Corps of Engineers, 531 U.S. 159, 174, 121 S.Ct. 675, 148 L.Ed.2d 576 (2001); Rapanos v. United States, 547 U.S. 715, 738, 126 S.Ct. 2208, 165 L.Ed.2d 159 (2006) (see chapter 7.C, *supra*). In the early cases, the Court focused on whether a waterway was navigable as an indicator that it was surely within the realm of interstate commerce.

United States v. Appalachian Elec. Power Co.

Supreme Court of the United States, 1940.
311 U.S. 377, 61 S.Ct. 291, 85 L.Ed. 243.

■ MR. JUSTICE REED delivered the opinion of the Court.

This case involves the scope of the federal commerce power in relation to conditions in licenses, required by the Federal Power Commission, for the construction of hydroelectric dams in navigable rivers of the United States. To reach this issue requires, preliminarily, a decision as to the navigability of the New River, a water-course flowing through Virginia and West Virginia. The district court and the circuit court of appeals have both held that the New River is not navigable, and that the United States cannot enjoin the respondent from constructing and putting into operation a hydroelectric dam situated in the river just above Radford, Virginia.

Sections 9 and 10 of the Rivers and Harbors Act of 1899 make it unlawful to construct a dam in any navigable water of the United States without the consent of Congress. By the Federal Water Power Act of 1920, however, Congress created a Federal Power Commission with authority to license the construction of such dams upon specified conditions. Section 23 of that Act provided that persons intending to construct a dam in a nonnavigable stream may file a declaration of intention with the Commission. If after investigation the Commission finds that the interests of interstate or foreign commerce will not be affected, permission shall be granted for the construction. Otherwise construction cannot go forward without a license.

* * *

[The power company argued before the commission that no license was necessary because the stream was not navigable and therefore the 1920 Act did not apply. In the alternative, the company argued that if the stream were navigable, the conditions imposed on licenses by the Act were invalid because they related to regulation of electric power companies, not to navigation. Respondent offered to take a "minor-part" license one without regulatory condition but the commission denied such a license and forbade construction of the dam without a "full-condition" license, which respondent declined to take. Thereafter, the company started building its project, precipitating the litigation.]

* * *

Navigability. The power of the United States over its waters which are capable of use as interstate highways arises from the commerce clause of the Constitution. "The Congress shall have Power * * * To regulate Commerce * * * among the several States." It was held early in our history that the power to regulate commerce necessarily included power over navigation. To make its control effective the Congress may keep the "navigable waters of the United States" open and free and provide by sanctions against any interference with the country's water assets. It may legislate to forbid or license dams in the waters; its power over improvements for navigation in rivers is "absolute."

The states possess control of the waters within their borders, "subject to the acknowledged jurisdiction of the United States under the Constitution in regard to commerce and the navigation of the waters of rivers." It is this subordinate local control that, even as to navigable rivers, creates between the respective governments a contrariety of interests relating to the regulation and protection of waters through licenses, the operation of structures and the acquisition of projects at the end of the license term. But there is no doubt that the United States possesses the power to control the erection of structures in navigable waters.

The navigability of the New River is, of course, a factual question but to call it a fact cannot obscure the diverse elements that enter into the application of the legal tests as to navigability. We are dealing here with the sovereign powers of the Union, the Nation's right that its waterways be utilized for the interests of the commerce of the whole country. It is obvious that the uses to which the streams may be put vary from the carriage of ocean liners to the floating out of logs; that the density of traffic varies equally widely from the busy harbors of the seacoast to the sparsely settled regions of the Western mountains. The tests as to navigability must take these variations into consideration.

Both lower courts based their investigation primarily upon the generally accepted definition of The Daniel Ball.[21] In so doing they were in accord with the rulings of this Court on the basic concept of navigability. Each application of this test, however, is apt to uncover variations and refinements which require further elaboration.

In the lower courts and here, the Government urges that the phrase "susceptible of being used, in their ordinary condition," in the Daniel Ball definition, should not be construed as eliminating the possibility of determining navigability in the light of the effect of reasonable improvements. * * *

To appraise the evidence of navigability on the natural condition only of the waterway is erroneous. Its availability for navigation must also be considered. "Natural and ordinary condition" refers to volume of water, the gradients and the regularity of the flow. A waterway, otherwise suitable for navigation, is not barred from that classification merely because artificial aids must make the highway suitable for use before commercial navigation may be undertaken. Congress has recognized this in § 3 of the Water Power Act by defining "navigable waters" as those "which either in their natural or improved condition" are used or suitable for use. The district court is quite right in saying there are obvious limits to such improvements as affecting navigability. These limits are necessarily a matter of degree. There must be a balance between cost and need at a time when the improvement would be useful. When once found to be navigable, a waterway remains so. This is no more indefinite than a rule of navigability in fact as adopted below based upon "useful interstate commerce" or "general and common usefulness for purposes of trade and commerce" if these are interpreted as barring improvements. Nor is it necessary that the improvements should be actually completed or even authorized. The power of Congress over commerce is not to be hampered because of the necessity for reasonable improvements to make an interstate waterway available for traffic.

Of course there are difficulties in applying these views. Improvements that may be entirely reasonable in a thickly populated, highly developed, industrial region may have been entirely too costly for the same region in the days of the pioneers. The changes in engineering practices or the coming of new industries with varying classes of freight may affect the type of the improvement. Although navigability to fix ownership of the river

---

21.   10 Wall. 557, 563:

" * * * Those rivers must be regarded as public navigable rivers in law which are navigable in fact. And they are navigable in fact when they are used, or are susceptible of being used, in their ordinary condition, as highways for commerce, over which trade and travel are or may be conducted in the customary modes of trade and travel on water. And they constitute navigable waters of the United States within the meaning of the acts of Congress, in contradistinction from the navigable waters of the States, when they form in their ordinary condition by themselves, or by uniting with other waters, a continued highway over which commerce is or may be carried on with other States or foreign countries in the customary modes in which such commerce is conducted by water."

bed[29] or riparian[30] rights is determined as the cases just cited in the notes show, as of the formation of the Union in the original states or the admission to statehood of those formed later, navigability, for the purpose of the regulation of commerce, may later arise. An analogy is found in admiralty jurisdiction, which may be extended over places formerly nonnavigable. There has never been doubt that the navigability referred to in the cases was navigability despite the obstruction of falls, rapids, sand bars, carries or shifting currents. The plenary federal power over commerce must be able to develop with the needs of that commerce which is the reason for its existence. It cannot properly be said that the federal power over navigation is enlarged by the improvements to the waterways. It is merely that improvements make applicable to certain waterways the existing power over commerce.[35] In determining the navigable character of the New River it is proper to consider the feasibility of interstate use after reasonable improvements which might be made.

Nor is it necessary for navigability that the use should be continuous. The character of the region, its products and the difficulties or dangers of the navigation influence the regularity and extent of the use. Small traffic compared to the available commerce of the region is sufficient * * *. With these legal tests in mind we proceed to examine the facts to see whether the 111 mile reach of this river from Allisonia to Hinton, across the Virginia West Virginia state line, has "capability of use by the public for the purposes of transportation and commerce."

Physical Characteristics. * * *

We come then to a consideration of the crucial stretch from Radford to below Wiley's Falls where junction is made with the interstate reach from Wiley's Falls to Hinton. * * *

Use of the River from Radford to Wiley's Falls. Navigation on the Radford Wiley's Falls stretch was not large. Undoubtedly the difficulties restricted it and with the coming of the Norfolk & Western and the Chesapeake & Ohio railroads in the 80s, such use as there had been practically ceased, except for small public ferries going from one bank to the other. Well authenticated instances of boating along this stretch, however, exist. * * *

In 1861 the Virginia General Assembly appropriated $30,000 to improve the New River to accommodate transportation of military stores by bateaux from Central depot [Radford] to the mouth of the Greenbrier. While there is no direct proof that this particular appropriation was spent,

29. Shively v. Bowlby, 152 U.S. 1, 18 and 26; United States v. Utah, 283 U.S. 64, 75.

30. Oklahoma v. Texas, 258 U.S. 574; United States v. Oregon, 295 U.S. 1, 14.

35. Illustrative of this natural growth is United States v. Cress, 243 U.S. 316, involving riparian proprietors' rights where improvements raise the river level so that uplands are newly and permanently subjected to the servitude of public use for navigation. Compensation was decreed for the taking with a declaration that the waterways in question, as artificially improved, remained navigable waters of the United States (243 U.S. pages 325 and 326). Cf. Arizona v. California, 283 U.S. 423.

reports of the War Department engineers make it clear that the Confederate government effected some improvements on the river. * * *

From the end of the Civil War to the coming of the railroads, the evidence of elderly residents familiar with events along the banks of the river between Radford and Wiley's Falls leaves no doubt that at least sporadic transportation took place in and throughout this stretch. * * *

In addition to the testimony of use in the days before railways and good roads, there was a demonstration of the possibility of navigation by a government survey boat with an outboard motor, 16 feet long, five feet wide, drawing 2½ to 3 feet, loaded with a crew of five and its survey equipment. * * * Going upstream it was not necessary to pull or push the boat more than a mile and a quarter and not more than a few hundred feet on the return trip.

Use of a stream long abandoned by water commerce is difficult to prove by abundant evidence. Fourteen authenticated instances of use in a century and a half by explorers and trappers, coupled with general historical references to the river as a water route for the early fur traders and their supplies in pirogues and Durham or flat-bottomed craft similar to the keelboats of the New, sufficed upon that phase in the case of the Des-Plaines. Nor is lack of commercial traffic a bar to a conclusion of navigability where personal or private use by boats demonstrates the availability of the streams for the simpler types of commercial navigation.

The evidence of actual use of the Radford Wiley's Falls section for commerce and for private convenience, when taken in connection with its physical condition, makes it quite plain that by reasonable improvement the reach would be navigable for the type of boats employed on the less obstructed sections. * * *

Effect of Improvability. Respondent denied the practicability of artificial means to bring about the navigability of the New River and the effectiveness of any improvement to make the river a navigable water of the United States. The Government supported its allegation of improvability by pointing out that the use of the section for through navigation and local boating on favorable stretches of the Radford Wiley's Falls reach showed the feasibility of such use and that little was needed in the way of improvements to make the section a thoroughfare for the typical, light commercial traffic of the area. Keelboats, eight feet wide, drawing two feet, were the usual equipment. In the 1872 report of the Chief of Engineers, Major Craighill in charge of New River reports that to get "good sluice navigation of 2 feet at all times" for 54 miles up from the mouth of the Greenbrier River, near Hinton, would cost $30,000 and for 128 miles, Greenbrier to the lead mines (above Allisonia), would cost $100,000. * * *

* * * By 1912 the region's need for use of the river had so diminished that the army engineers advised against undertaking improvements again, and even referred to the cost as "prohibitive". From the use of the Radford Wiley's Falls stretch and the evidence as to its ready improvability at a low cost for easier keelboat use, we conclude that this section of the New River

is navigable. It follows from this, together with the undisputed commercial use of the two stretches above Radford and Hinton, that the New River from Allisonia, Virginia, to Hinton, West Virginia, is a navigable water of the United States.

License Provisions. The determination that the New River is navigable eliminates from this case issues which may arise only where the river involved is nonnavigable. But even accepting the navigability of the New River, the respondent urges that certain provisions of the license, which seek to control affairs of the licensee, are unconnected with navigation and are beyond the power of the Commission, indeed beyond the constitutional power of Congress to authorize. * * *

* * * There is no contention that the provisions of the license are not authorized by the statute. In the note below[65] the chief statutory conditions for a license are epitomized. The license offered the respondent on May 5, 1931, embodied these statutory requirements and we assume it to be in conformity with the existing administration of the Power Act. We shall pass upon the validity of only those provisions of the license called to our attention by the respondent as being unrelated to the purposes of navigation. These are the conditions derived from §§ 10a, 10c, 10d, 10e and 14. * * *

The respondent's objections to the statutory and license provisions, as applied to navigable streams, are based on the contentions (1) that the United States' control of the waters is limited to control for purposes of navigation, (2) that certain license provisions take its property without due

---

65. Section 4(a) of the Act allows the Commission to regulate the licensee's accounts.

Section 6 limits licenses to 50 years.

Section 8 requires Commission approval for voluntary transfers of licenses or rights granted thereunder.

Section 10(a), as amended in 1935, requires that the project be best adapted to a comprehensive plan for improving or developing the waterway for the use or benefit of interstate or foreign commerce, for the improvement and utilization of water-power development, and for other beneficial public uses, including recreational purposes. Under § 10(c) the licensee must maintain the project adequately for navigation and for efficient power operation, must maintain depreciation reserves adequate for renewals and replacements, and must conform to the Commission's regulations for the protection of life, health and property; (d) out of surplus earned after the first 20 years above a specified reasonable rate of return, the licensee must maintain amortization reserves to be applied in reduction of net investment; (e) the licensee must pay the United States rea-

sonable annual charges for administering the Act, and during the first 20 years the United States is to expropriate excessive profits until the state prevents such profits; (f) the licensee may be ordered to reimburse those by whose construction work it is benefited.

By § 11, for projects in navigable waters of the United States the Commission may require the licensee to construct locks, etc., and to furnish the United States free of cost (a) lands and rights-of-way to improve navigation facilities, and (b) power for operating such facilities.

Section 14 gives the United States the right, upon expiration of a license, to take over and operate the project by paying the licensee's "net investment" as defined, not to exceed fair value of the property taken. However, the right of the United States or any state or municipality to condemn the project at any time is expressly reserved.

Section 19 allows state regulation of service and rates; if none exists, the Commission may exercise such jurisdiction.

process, and (3) that the claimed right to acquire this project and to regulate its financing, records and affairs, is an invasion of the rights of the states, contrary to the Tenth Amendment.

Forty-one states join as amici in support of the respondent's arguments. * * *

The respondent is a riparian owner with a valid state license to use the natural resources of the state for its enterprise. Consequently it has as complete a right to the use of the riparian lands, the water, and the river bed as can be obtained under state law. The state and respondent, alike, however, hold the waters and the lands under them subject to the power of Congress to control the waters for the purpose of commerce. The power flows from the grant to regulate, i.e., to "prescribe the rule by which commerce is to be governed." This includes the protection of navigable waters in capacity as well as use. This power of Congress to regulate commerce is so unfettered that its judgment as to whether a structure is or is not a hindrance is conclusive. Its determination is legislative in character. The Federal Government has domination over the water power inherent in the flowing stream. It is liable to no one for its use or non-use. The flow of a navigable stream is in no sense private property; "that the running water in a great navigable stream is capable of private ownership is inconceivable." Exclusion of riparian owners from its benefits without compensation is entirely within the Government's discretion.

Possessing this plenary power to exclude structures from navigable waters and dominion over flowage and its product, energy, the United States may make the erection or maintenance of a structure in a navigable water dependent upon a license. This power is exercised through § 9 of the Rivers and Harbors Act of 1899 prohibiting construction without Congressional consent and through § 4(e) of the present Power Act.

It is quite true that the criticized provisions summarized above are not essential to or even concerned with navigation as such. Respondent asserts that the right of the United States to the use of the waters is limited to navigation. * * *

In our view, it cannot properly be said that the constitutional power of the United States over its waters is limited to control for navigation. By navigation respondent means no more than operation of boats and improvement of the waterway itself. In truth the authority of the United States is the regulation of commerce on its waters. Navigability in the sense just stated, is but a part of this whole. Flood protection, watershed development, recovery of the cost of improvements through utilization of power are likewise parts of commerce control. As respondent soundly argues, the United States cannot by calling a project of its own "a multiple purpose dam" give to itself additional powers, but equally truly the respondent cannot, by seeking to use a navigable waterway for power generation alone, avoid the authority of the Government over the stream. That authority is as broad as the needs of commerce. Water power development from dams in navigable streams is from the public's standpoint a by-product of the general use of the rivers for commerce. To this general power, the respondent must submit its single purpose of electrical production. The fact that the Commission is willing to give a license for a power dam only is of no significance in appraising the type of conditions allowable. It may well be that this portion of the river is not needed for navigation at this time. Or that the dam proposed may function satisfactorily with others, contemplated or intended. It may fit in as a part of the river development. The point is that navigable waters are subject to national planning and control in the broad regulation of commerce granted the Federal Government. The license conditions to which objection is made have an obvious relationship to the exercise of the commerce power. Even if there were no such relationship the plenary power of Congress over navigable waters would empower it to deny the privilege of constructing an obstruction in those waters. It may likewise grant the privilege on terms. It is no objection to the terms and to the exertion of the power that "its exercise is attended by the same incidents which attend the exercise of the police power of the states." The Congressional authority under the commerce clause is complete unless limited by the Fifth Amendment. * * *

Reversed.

NOTES

1. Many years after the decision in the principal case, the Court, per Justice Rehnquist, wrote in Kaiser Aetna v. United States, 444 U.S. 164, 173–174, 100 S.Ct. 383, 62 L.Ed.2d 332 (1979), discussed *supra* pp. 484–486.

> Reference to the navigability of a waterway adds little if anything to the breadth of Congress' regulatory power over interstate commerce. It has long been settled that Congress has extensive authority over this Nation's waters under the Commerce Clause. Early in our history this Court held that the power to regulate commerce necessarily includes power over navigation. Gibbons v. Ogden, 9 Wheat. 1, 189 (1824). * * * The pervasive nature of Congress' regulatory authority over national waters was more fully described in United States v. Appalachian Power Co.: [quoting from the last paragraph of the opinion as edited]. * * *

> Appalachian Power Co. indicates that congressional authority over the waters of this Nation does not depend on a stream's "navigability." And, as demonstrated by this Court's decisions in NLRB v. Jones & Laughlin Steel Corp., 301 U.S. 1 (1937), United States v. Darby, 312 U.S. 100 (1941), and Wickard v. Filburn, 317 U.S. 111 (1942), a wide spectrum of economic activities "affect" interstate commerce and thus are susceptible of congressional regulation under the Commerce Clause irrespective of whether navigation, or, indeed, water, is involved. The cases that discuss Congress' paramount authority to regulate waters used in interstate commerce are consequently best understood when viewed in terms of more traditional Commerce Clause analysis than by reference to whether the stream in fact is capable of supporting

navigation or may be characterized as "navigable water of the United States."

If congressional power did not depend on navigability, why did the Court in *Appalachian Power* spend so much time discussing whether the New River was navigable?

2. Where the United States conceded the non-navigability of a stream, could it legislate a water development program?

Nearly ten years before *Appalachian Power*, Justice Brandeis used the navigation power to sustain congressional authorization of Hoover Dam, a multipurpose project designed principally to provide municipal and irrigation water and electric energy. Recitals in the Colorado River Compact had declared the river no longer to be navigable and Arizona, opposing the dam, said that the facilities and the diversion of water would destroy navigable capacity even if it were navigable. Brandeis seemed reluctant to venture into any other manifestations of Congress's commerce power, choosing instead to defer to Congress's declaration of "navigation purposes" in the first Arizona v. California, 283 U.S. 423, 51 S.Ct. 522, 75 L.Ed. 1154 (1931).

3. By the time of *Appalachian Power* the Court had already decided that irrigation projects in the West could be undertaken by Congress exercising powers outside the Commerce Clause. In Kansas v. Colorado, 206 U.S. 46, 27 S.Ct. 655, 51 L.Ed. 956 (1907), *infra* p. 943, Kansas brought suit in the original jurisdiction of the Supreme Court to enjoin Colorado from making diversions from the Arkansas River. The United States petitioned to intervene, asserting its interest in reclamation under the 1902 Act. The Court addressed the issue as follows:

> We must look beyond [the Commerce Clause] for Congressional authority over arid lands, and it is said to be found in the second paragraph of section 3 of Article IV, reading: "The Congress shall have power to dispose of and make all needful rules and regulations respecting the territory or other property belonging to the United States; and nothing in this Constitution shall be so construed as to prejudice any claims of the United States, or of any particular State."
>
> * * *
>
> This very matter of the reclamation of arid lands illustrates this: At the time of the adoption of the Constitution, within the known and conceded limits of the United States there were no large tracts of arid land, and nothing which called for any further action than that which might be taken by the legislature of the state in which any particular tract of land was to be found; and the Constitution, therefore, makes no provision for a national control of the arid regions or their reclamation. * * *
>
> * * * These arid lands are largely within the territories, and over them, by virtue of the second paragraph of § 3 of article 4, heretofore quoted, or by virtue of the power vested in the national government to acquire territory by treaties, Congress has full power of legislation, subject to no restrictions other than those expressly named in the

Constitution, and therefore, it may legislate in respect to all arid lands within their limits. As to those lands within the limits of the states, at least of the Western states, the national government is the most considerable owner and has power to dispose of and make all needful rules and regulations respecting its property. * * *

206 U.S. at 88–92.

In a later case, the U.S. Supreme Court rejected the navigation power as enabling a federal reclamation project. Absent the presence of public lands, it cited the spending power as the basis of Congress's action. United States v. Gerlach Live Stock Co., 339 U.S. 725, 70 S.Ct. 955, 94 L.Ed. 1231 (1950). The Supreme Court held that congressional authorization of a hydroelectric dam in the National Defense Act of 1916 was a proper exercise of constitutional authority under the defense power. Ashwander v. Tennessee Valley Auth., 297 U.S. 288, 56 S.Ct. 466, 80 L.Ed. 688 (1936). Because uses of waterways implicate national and international commerce, the United States has far-reaching interests in how waterways are used. *See* Oklahoma *ex rel.* Phillips v. Guy F. Atkinson Co., 313 U.S. 508, 61 S.Ct. 1050, 85 L.Ed. 1487 (1941) (upholding a multipurpose federal dam on a nonnavigable portion of a Mississippi River tributary, despite Oklahoma's vigorous objections that the project's hydropower and flood control elements were beyond Congress' power). The difference between a flood control and reclamation project is still important. The federal government is immune from liability for flood damage from the operation of a federal flood control project, 33 U.S.C. § 702c, but it is liable when water released from a multiple purpose project for irrigation use damages a farmer. Central Green Co. v. United States, 531 U.S. 425, 121 S.Ct. 1005, 148 L.Ed.2d 919 (2001) (damage resulted from leaking irrigation canal).

Strictly speaking, there can be no federal-state conflicts over water management; either the federal government has the constitutional power to act or it does not. If it does, the Supremacy Clause of the Constitution (art. VI, cl. 2) overrides all state opposition. Disputes between the federal government and the states over water management related to federal reclamation projects are nonetheless grave. The issues are: To what extent did Congress exercise federal power? To what extent did Congress intend to preempt the field and oust state power? To what extent did Congress explicitly provide for continuing, coordinate, or subordinate power in the states? The issues require a close look at the particular statutes authorizing the project.

First Iowa Hydro–Electric Cooperative v. Federal Power Commission

United States Supreme Court, 1946.
328 U.S. 152, 66 S.Ct. 906, 90 L.Ed. 1143.

■ Mr. Justice Burton delivered the opinion of the Court.

This case illustrates the integration of federal and state jurisdictions in licensing water power projects under the Federal Power Act. The petitioner is the First Iowa Hydro Electric Cooperative, a cooperative association organized under the laws of Iowa with power to generate, distribute and sell electric energy. On January 29, 1940, pursuant to § 23(b) of the Federal Power Act, it filed with the Federal Power Commission a declaration of intention to construct and operate a dam, reservoir and hydroelectric power plant on the Cedar River, near Moscow, Iowa.

On April 2, 1941, it also filed with the Commission an application for a license, under the Federal Power Act, to construct an enlarged project essentially like the one it now wishes to build. * * *

On January 29, 1944, after extended hearings, the Commission rendered an opinion including the following statements:

"As first presented, the plans of the applicant for developing the water resources of the Cedar River were neither desirable nor adequate, but many important changes in design have been made. [The opinion here quoted, in a footnote, § 10(a) of the Federal Power Act.] The applicant has also agreed to certain modifications proposed by the Chief of Engineers of the War Department. The present plans call for a practical and reasonably adequate development to utilize the head and water available, create a large storage reservoir, and make available for recreational purposes a considerable area now unsuitable for such use, all at a cost which does not appear to be unreasonable.

"Further changes in design may be desirable, but they are minor in character and can be effected if the applicant is able to meet the other requirements of the act." Re First Iowa Hydro Electric Cooperative, 52 PUR(NS) 82, 84.

We believe that the Commission would have been justified in proceeding further at that time with its consideration of the petitioner's application upon all the material facts. Such consideration would have included evidence submitted by the petitioner pursuant to § 9(b) of the Federal Power Act[6] as to the petitioner's compliance with the requirements of the laws of Iowa with respect to the petitioner's property rights to make its proposed use of the affected river beds and banks and to divert and use river water for the proposed power purposes, as well as the petitioner's right, within the State of Iowa, to engage in the business of developing, transmitting, and distributing power, and in any other business necessary to effect the purposes of the license. * * *

---

6. "Sec. 9. That each applicant for a license hereunder shall submit to the commission * * *

"(b) Satisfactory evidence that the applicant has complied with the requirements of the laws of the State or States within which the proposed project is to be located with respect to bed and banks and to the appropriation, diversion, and use of water for power purposes and with respect to the right to engage in the business of developing, transmitting, and distributing power, and in any other business necessary to effect the purposes of a license under this Act." 41 Stat. 1068, 16 U.S.C. § 802(b).

The findings made by the Commission on June 3, 1941, in response to the petitioner's declaration of intention are not in question. For the purposes of this application it is settled that the project will affect the navigability of the Cedar, Iowa and Mississippi Rivers, each of which has been determined to be a part of the navigable waters of the United States; will affect the interests of interstate commerce; will flood certain public lands of the United States; and will require for its construction a license from the Commission. The project is clearly within the jurisdiction of the Commission under the Federal Power Act. The question at issue is the need, if any, for the presentation of satisfactory evidence of the petitioner's compliance with the terms of Chapter 363 of the Code of Iowa. This question is put in issue by the petition for review of the order of the Commission which dismissed the application solely on the ground of the failure of the petitioner to present such evidence. The laws of Iowa which that State contends are applicable and require a permit from its Executive Council to effect the purposes of the federal license are all in §§ 7767–7796.1 of the Code of Iowa, 1939, constituting Chapter 363, entitled "Mill Dams and Races." Section 7767 of that chapter is alleged to require the issuance of a permit by the Executive Council of the State and is the one on which the Commission's order must depend. It provides:

"7767 Prohibition permit. No dam shall be constructed, maintained, or operated in this state in any navigable or meandered stream for any purpose, or in any other stream for manufacturing or power purposes, nor shall any water be taken from such streams for industrial purposes, unless a permit has been granted by the executive council to the person, firm, corporation, or municipality constructing, maintaining, or operating the same."

To require the petitioner to secure the actual grant to it of a state permit under § 7767 as a condition precedent to securing a federal license for the same project under the Federal Power Act would vest in the Executive Council of Iowa a veto power over the federal project. Such a veto power easily could destroy the effectiveness of the Federal Act. It would subordinate to the control of the State the "comprehensive" planning which the Act provides shall depend upon the judgment of the Federal Power Commission or other representatives of the Federal Government.
* * *

* * * For example, § 7776 of the State Code requires that "the method of construction, operation, maintenance, and equipment of any and all dams in such waters shall be subject to the approval of the Executive Council." This would subject to state control the very requirements of the project that Congress has placed in the discretion of the Federal Power Commission. A still greater difficulty is illustrated by § 7771. This states the requirements for a state permit as follows:

"7771 When permit granted. If it shall appear to the council that the construction, operation, or maintenance of the dam will not materially obstruct existing navigation, or materially affect other public rights, will not endanger life or public health, and *any water taken from the stream in connection with the project is returned thereto at the nearest practicable place* without being materially diminished in quantity or polluted or rendered deleterious to fish life, it shall grant the permit, upon such terms and conditions as it may prescribe." (Italics supplied.)

This strikes at the heart of the present project. The feature of the project which especially commended it to the Federal Power Commission was its diversion of substantially all of the waters of the Cedar River near Moscow, to the Mississippi River near Muscatine. Such a diversion long has been recognized as an engineering possibility and as constituting the largest power development foreseeable on either the Cedar or Iowa Rivers. It is this diversion that makes possible the increase in the head of water for power development from a maximum of 35 feet to an average of 101 feet, the increase in the capacity of the plant from 15,000 kw. to 50,000 kw. and its output from 47,000,000 kwh. to 200,000,000 kwh. per year. It is this diversion that led the Federal Power Commission, on January 29, 1944, to make its favorable appraisal of the enlarged project in contrast to its unfavorable appraisal, and to the State's rejection, of the smaller project. It is this feature that brings this project squarely under the Federal Power Act and at the same time gives the project its greatest economic justification.

If a state permit is not required, there is no justification for requiring the petitioner, as a condition of securing its federal permit, to present evidence of the petitioner's compliance with the requirements of the State Code for a state permit. Compliance with state requirements that are in conflict with federal requirements may well block the federal license. * * *

In the Federal Power Act there is a separation of those subjects which remain under the jurisdiction of the States from those subjects which the Constitution delegates to the United States and over which Congress vests the Federal Power Commission with authority to act. To the extent of this separation, the Act establishes a dual system of control. The duality of control consists merely of the division of the common enterprise between two cooperating agencies of government, each with final authority in its own jurisdiction. The duality does not require two agencies to share in the final decision of the same issue. Where the Federal Government supersedes the state government there is no suggestion that the two agencies both shall have final authority. In fact a contrary policy is indicated in §§ 4(e), 10(a), (b) and (c), and 23(b). * * *

The Act leaves to the States their traditional jurisdiction subject to the admittedly superior right of the Federal Government, through Congress, to regulate interstate and foreign commerce, administer the public lands and reservations of the United States and, in certain cases, exercise authority under the treaties of the United States. These sources of constitutional authority are all applied in the Federal Power Act to the development of the navigable waters of the United States.

* * *

Sections 27 and 9 are especially significant in this regard. Section 27 expressly "saves" certain state laws relating to property rights as to the use of water, so that these are not superseded by the terms of the Federal Power Act. It provides:

"Sec. 27. That nothing herein contained shall be construed as affecting or intending to affect or in any way to interfere with the laws of the respective States relating to the control, appropriation, use, or distribution of water used in irrigation or for municipal or other uses, or any vested right acquired therein." 41 Stat. 1077, 16 U.S.C. § 821.

Section 27 thus evidences the recognition by Congress of the need for an express "saving" clause in the Federal Power Act if the usual rules of supersedure are to be overcome. Sections 27 and 9(b) were both included in the original Federal Water Power Act of 1920 in their present form. The directness and clarity of § 27 as a "saving" clause and its location near the end of the Act emphasizes the distinction between its purpose and that of § 9(b) which is included in § 9, in the early part of the Act, which deals with the marshalling of information for the consideration of a new federal license. In view of the use by Congress of such an adequate "saving" clause in § 27, its failure to use similar language in § 9(b) is persuasive that § 9(b) should not be given the same effect as is given to § 27.

The effect of § 27, in protecting state laws from supersedure, is limited to laws as to the control, appropriation, use or distribution of water in irrigation or for municipal or other uses of the same nature. It therefore has primary, if not exclusive, reference to such proprietary rights. The phrase "any vested right acquired therein" further emphasizes the application of the section to property rights. * * *

Section 9(b) does not resemble § 27. It must be read with § 9(a) and (c). The entire section is devoted to securing adequate information for the Commission as to pending applications for licenses. Where § 9(a) calls for engineering and financial information, § 9(b) calls for legal information. This makes § 9(b) a natural place in which to describe the evidence which the Commission shall require in order to pass upon applications for federal licenses. This makes it a correspondingly unnatural place to establish by implication such a substantive policy as that contained in § 27 and which, in accordance with the contentions of the State of Iowa, would enable Chapter 363 of the Code of Iowa, 1939, to remain in effect although in conflict with the requirements of the Federal Power Act. There is nothing in the express language of § 9(b) that requires such a conclusion.

It does not itself require compliance with any state laws. Its reference to state laws is by way of suggestion to the Federal Power Commission of subjects as to which the Commission may wish some proof submitted to it of the applicant's progress. The evidence required is described merely as that which shall be "satisfactory" to the Commission. The need for compliance with applicable state laws, if any, arises not from this federal statute but from the effectiveness of the state statutes themselves.

When this application has been remanded to the Commission, that Commission will not act as a substitute for the local authorities having jurisdiction over such questions as the sufficiency of the legal title of the applicant to its riparian rights, or as to the validity of its local franchises, if any, relating to proposed intrastate public utility service. Section 9(b) says that the Commission may wish to have "satisfactory evidence" of the progress made by the applicant toward meeting local requirements but it does not say that the Commission is to assume responsibility for the legal sufficiency of the steps taken. The references made in § 9(b) to beds and banks of streams, to proprietary rights to divert or use water, or to legal rights to engage locally in the business of developing, transmitting and distributing power neither add anything to nor detract anything from the force of the local laws, if any, on those subjects. In so far as those laws have not been superseded by the Federal Power Act, they remain as applicable and effective as they were before its passage. The State of Iowa, however, has sought to sustain the applicability and validity of Chapter 363 of the Code of Iowa in this connection, on the ground that the Federal Power Act, by the implications of § 9(b), has recognized this chapter of Iowa law as part of a system of dual control of power project permits, cumbersome and complicated though it be. If it had been the wish of Congress to make the applicant obtain consent of state as well as federal authorities to each project, the simple thing would have been to so provide. * * *

[T]he Federal Power Act * * * was the outgrowth of a widely supported effort of the conservationists to secure enactment of a complete scheme of national regulation which would promote the comprehensive development of the water resources of the Nation, in so far as it was within the reach of the federal power to do so, instead of the piecemeal, restrictive, negative approach of the River and Harbor Acts and other federal laws previously enacted.

* * *

The detailed provisions of the Act providing for the federal plan of regulation leave no room or need for conflicting state controls. The contention of the State of Iowa is comparable to that which was presented on behalf of 41 States and rejected by this Court in United States v. Appalachian Power Co., 311 U.S. 377. * * *

Reversed.

■ Mr. Justice Jackson took no part in the consideration or decision of this case.

■ Mr. Justice Frankfurter, dissenting.

* * *

With due respect, I have not been able to discover an adequate answer to the position of the Federal Power Commission, thus summarized in the Solicitor General's brief:

"Unless Section 9(b) is to be given no effect whatever, some evidence of compliance with at least some state laws is a prerequisite to the issuance of a federal license, and the view of the court below, that there is no occasion, in this case, to anticipate conflicts between state and federal authority and the consequent invalidity of the state law, is not an unreasonable one. 'To predetermine, even in the limited field of water power, the rights of different sovereignties, pregnant with future controversies, is beyond the judicial function.' United States v. Appalachian Electric Power Co. Here petitioner, since the modification of its plans, has given the State Executive Council and the Iowa courts no opportunity to express their views on its proposed project with reference to matters which may be peculiarly of local concern; without such an expression, it is difficult to assess the propriety of what is only an anticipated exercise of the State's power.''

Accordingly, I think that the judgment should be affirmed.

NOTES

1. With a Federal Power Act license goes some of the United States' preemptive power. Should courts presume that Congress did not intend to bestow its ability to override state law upon non-federal entities in absence of a clear legislative statement to that effect? In City of Tacoma v. Taxpayers of Tacoma, 357 U.S. 320, 78 S.Ct. 1209, 2 L.Ed.2d 1345 (1958), the Supreme Court held that a license effectively delegated condemnation authority to a licensee city so that the city could condemn state property contrary to state law. The state property, a fish hatchery, was located where it would be flooded by waters impounded behind the city's proposed dam.

2. The tension between state water rights and the Federal Energy Regulatory Commission's (FERC's) regulatory authority became more acute when Congress decided to promote small-scale hydroelectric development. In an early effort to legislate a national energy policy, Congress enacted the Public Utility Regulatory Policies Act of 1978 (PURPA), Pub. L. 95–617, 92 Stat. 3117 (1978). PURPA, along with the Energy Security Act of 1980, attempted to stimulate the increased development of alternative renewable energy sources. PURPA's main stimulus for low-head hydroelectric facilities was to create a market for their power. Public utilities were not historically enthusiastic about purchasing small amounts of alternative energy, but Congress mandated enthusiasm. Utilities must purchase the output from qualifying facilities at "a rate that exceeds the incremental cost to the electric utility of alternative electric energy." To carry out PURPA's goal of promoting secure, renewable alternative energy sources, FERC defined incremental cost as full avoided cost.

Activity related to licensing small hydroelectric projects surged as a result of PURPA, accounting for much of the increase in FERC business, which grew from 76 preliminary applications in 1979 to 1856 in 1981, then declined to 636 in 1985 and 60 in 2000. The growth in FERC activity increased the opportunity for FERC to argue that it can preempt state and federal environmental laws and state water laws. The original boom in hydro activity was a result of rising fuel costs and environmental concerns about fossil- and nuclear-fueled plants in the 1970s. The boom began to abate in 1985 as fuel costs declined; in addition, the Tax Act of 1986 removed many tax advantages that previously benefited the hydropower industry. In 2001 FERC's hydrolicensing workload consisted primarily of post-licensing work, as the number of licensing and relicensing applications declined. Today, FERC is heavily involved in relicensing hundreds of existing projects with licenses that have expired or soon will expire. See *supra* pages 714–728.

3.   Short of prohibiting a project, how far may a state go in imposing conditions on FERC applicants? At what point are conditions effectively prohibitions?

California v. United States

Supreme Court of the United States, 1978.
438 U.S. 645, 98 S.Ct. 2985, 57 L.Ed.2d 1018.

■ MR. JUSTICE REHNQUIST delivered the opinion of the Court.

* * *

I

Principles of comity and federalism, which the District Court and the Court of Appeals referred to and which have received considerable attention in our decisions, are as a legal matter based on the Constitution of the United States, statutes enacted by Congress, and judge-made law. But the situations invoking the application of these principles have contributed importantly to their formation. Just as it has been truly said that the life of the law is not logic but experience, see O. Holmes, The Common Law 1 (1881), so may it be said that the life of the law is not political philosophy but experience.

* * *

In order to correctly ascertain the meaning of the Reclamation Act of 1902, we must recognize the obvious truth that the history of irrigation and reclamation before that date was much fresher in the minds of those then in Congress than it is to us today. "[T]he afternoon of July 23, 1847, was the true date of the beginning of modern irrigation. It was on that afternoon that the first band of Mormon pioneers built a small dam across City Creek near the present site of the Mormon Temple and diverted sufficient water to saturate some five acres of exceedingly dry land. Before the day was over they had planted potatoes to preserve the seed."[1] During the subsequent half century, irrigation expanded throughout the arid States of the West, supported usually by private enterprise or the local community. By the turn of the century, however, most of the land which

---

1.   A. Golzé, Reclamation in the United States 6 (1961). The author was at the time of publication the Chief Engineer of the California Department of Water Resources and had been formerly Assistant Commissioner of the United States Bureau of Reclamation.

could be profitably irrigated by such small scale projects had been put to use. Pressure mounted on the Federal Government to provide the funding for the massive projects that would be needed to complete the reclamation culminating in the Reclamation Act of 1902.

* * *

If the term "cooperative federalism" had been in vogue in 1902, the Reclamation Act of that year would surely have qualified as a leading example of it. In that Act, Congress set forth on a massive program to construct and operate dams, reservoirs, and canals for the reclamation of the arid lands in 17 western States. Reflective of the "cooperative federalism" which the Act embodied is § 8, whose exact meaning and scope are the critical inquiries in this case:

"*[N]othing in this Act shall be construed as affecting or intended to affect or to in any way interfere with the laws of any States or Territory relating to the control, appropriation, use or distribution of water used in irrigation*, or any vested rights acquired thereunder, *and the Secretary of the Interior, in carrying out the provisions of this Act, shall proceed in conformity with such laws*, and nothing herein shall in any way affect any right of any State or of the Federal Government or of any landowner, appropriator, or user of water in, to or from any interstate stream or the waters thereof: *Provided*, that the right to the use of water acquired under the provisions of this Act shall be appurtenant to the land irrigated, and beneficial use shall be the basis, the measure, and the limit of the right." [43 U.S.C.A. § 383] (emphasis added).

* * *

The New Melones Dam, which this litigation concerns, is part of the California Central Valley Project, the largest reclamation project yet authorized under the 1902 Act. The Dam, which will impound 2.4 million acre-feet of water of California's Stanislaus River, has the multiple purposes of flood control, irrigation, municipal use, industrial use, power, recreation, water quality control and the protection of fish and wildlife. The waters of the Stanislaus River that will be impounded behind the New Melones Dam arise and flow solely in California.

The United States Bureau of Reclamation, as it has with every other federal reclamation project, applied for a permit from the appropriate state agency, here the California State Water Resources Control Board, to appropriate the water that would be impounded by the Dam and later used for reclamation. After lengthy hearings, the State Board found that unappropriated water was available for the New Melones Project during certain times of the year. Although it therefore approved the Bureau's applications, the State Board attached 25 conditions to the permits. California State Water Resources Control Board, Decision 1422 (April 14, 1973). The most important conditions prohibit full impoundment until the Bureau is able to show firm commitments, or at least a specific plan, for the use of the water.[8] The State Board concluded that without such a specific plan of beneficial use the Bureau had failed to meet the California statutory requirements for appropriation.

* * *

II

The history of the relationship between the Federal Government and the States in the reclamation of the arid lands of the western States is both long and involved, but through it runs the consistent thread of purposeful and continued deference to state water law by Congress.

* * *

[The Court discusses several Supreme Court decisions, the Acts of 1866, 1870 and 1877, the decision in California Oregon Power Co., *supra* p. 107, and proceeds with an analysis of the several legislative acts that led to the enactment of the comprehensive Reclamation Act.]

III

* * *

From the legislative history of the Reclamation Act of 1902, it is clear that state law was expected to control in two important respects. First, and of controlling importance to this case, the Secretary would have to appropriate, purchase, or condemn necessary water rights in strict conformity with state law. * * *

Second, once the waters were released from the dam, their distribution to individual landowners would again be controlled by state law. * * *

A principal motivating factor behind Congress' decision to defer to state law was thus the legal confusion that would arise if federal water law and state water law reigned side by side in the same locality. Congress also intended to "follow the well-established precedent in national legislation of recognizing local and state law relative to the appropriation and distribution of water." [35 Cong. Rec. 6678 6679] (Cong. Mondell). * * *

Both sponsors of and opponents to the Reclamation Act also expressed constitutional doubts as to Congress' power to override the States' regulation of waters within their borders. * * *

---

8. Other conditions prohibit collection of water during periods of the year when unappropriated water is unavailable; require that a preference be given to water users in the water basin in which the New Melones Project is located; require storage releases to be made so as to maintain maximum and minimum chemical concentrations in the San Joaquin River and protect fish and wildlife; require the United States to provide means for the release of excess waters and to clear vegetation and structures from the reservoir sites; require the filing of additional reports and studies; and provide for access to the project site by the State Board and the public. Still other conditions reserve jurisdiction to the Board to impose further conditions on the appropriations if necessary to protect the "beneficial use" of the water involved. The United States did not challenge any of the conditions under state law, but instead filed the federal declaratory action that is now before us.

IV

For almost half a century, this congressionally mandated division between federal and state authority worked smoothly. No project was constructed without the approval of the Secretary of the Interior, and the United States through this official preserved its authority to determine how federal funds should be expended. But state laws relating to water rights were observed in accordance with the congressional directive contained in § 8 of the Act of 1902. In 1958, however, the first of two cases was decided by this Court in which private land owners or municipal corporations contended that state water law had the effect of overriding specific congressional directives to the Secretary of the Interior as to the operation of federal reclamation projects. In Ivanhoe Irrigation District v. McCracken, 357 U.S. 275 (1958), the Supreme Court of California decided that California law forbade the 160 acre limitation on irrigation water deliveries expressly written into § 5 of the Reclamation Act of 1902, and that therefore, under § 8 of the Reclamation Act, the Secretary was required to deliver reclamation water without regard to the acreage limitation. Both the State of California and the United States appealed from this judgment, and this Court reversed it, saying:

> "Section 5 is a specific and mandatory prerequisite laid down by the Congress as binding in the operation of reclamation projects, providing that '[n]o right to the use of water * * * shall be sold for a tract exceeding one hundred and sixty acres to any one landowner. * * *' Without passing generally on the coverage of § 8 in the delicate area of federal-state relations in the irrigation field, we do not believe that the Congress intended § 8 to override the repeatedly reaffirmed national policy of § 5." 357 U.S., at 291 292.

Five years later, in City of Fresno v. California, 372 U.S. 627 (1963), this Court affirmed a decision of the United States Court of Appeals for the Ninth Circuit holding that § 8 did not require the Secretary of the Interior to ignore explicit congressional provisions preferring irrigation use over domestic and municipal use.[24]

---

24. "Section 9(c) of the Reclamation Project Act of 1939 * * * provides: 'No contract relating to municipal water supply or miscellaneous purposes * * * shall be made unless, in the judgment of the Secretary [of the Interior], it will not impair the efficiency of the project for irrigation purposes.' * * * It therefore appears clear that Fresno has no preferential rights to contract for project water, but may receive it only if, in the Secretary's judgment, irrigation will not be adversely affected." 372 U.S., at 630 631.

The Court also concluded in a separate portion of its opinion "§ 8 does not mean that state law may operate to prevent the United States from exercising the power of eminent domain to acquire the water rights of others. * * * Rather, the effect of § 8 in such a case is to leave to state law the definition of the property interests, if any, for which compensation must be made." [372 U.S.,] at 630. Because no provision of California law was actually inconsistent with the exercise by the United States of its power of eminent domain, this statement was dictum. It also might have been apparent from examination of the congressional authorization of the Central Valley Project that congress intended the Secretary to have the power to condemn any necessary water rights. We disavow this dictum, however, to the extent that it implies that state law does not control even where not inconsistent with such expressions of congressional intent.

Petitioners do not ask us to overrule these holdings, nor are we presently inclined to do so. Petitioners instead ask us to hold that a State may impose any condition on the "control, appropriation, use or distribution of water" through a federal reclamation project that is not inconsistent with clear congressional directives respecting the project. Petitioners concede, and the government relies upon, dicta, in our cases that may point to a contrary conclusion. Thus, in Ivanhoe, the Court went beyond the actual facts of that case and stated:

> "As we read § 8, it merely requires the United States to comply with state law when, in the construction and operation of a reclamation project, it becomes necessary for it to acquire water rights or vested interests therein. * * * We read nothing in § 8 that compels the United States to deliver water on conditions imposed by the State." 357 U.S. 275, at 291 292.

Like dictum was repeated in City of Fresno, [372 U.S.] at 630, and in this Court's opinion in Arizona v. California, 373 U.S. 546 (1963), where the Court also said:

> "The argument that § 8 of the Reclamation Act requires the United States in the delivery of water to follow priorities laid down by state law has already been disposed of by this Court in Ivanhoe Irr. Dist. v. McCracken, * * * and reaffirmed in City of Fresno v. California * * *. Since § 8 of the Reclamation Act did not subject the Secretary to state law in disposing of water in [Ivanhoe], we cannot, consistently with Ivanhoe, hold that the Secretary must be bound by state law in disposing of water under the Project Act." Id., at 586 587.

While we are not convinced that the above language is diametrically inconsistent with the position of petitioner, or that it squarely supports the United States, it undoubtedly goes further than was necessary to decide the cases presented to the Court. Ivanhoe and City of Fresno involved conflicts between § 8, requiring the Secretary to follow state law as to water rights, and other provisions of Reclamation Acts that placed specific limitations on how the water was to be distributed. Here the United States contends that it may ignore state law even if no explicit congressional directive conflicts with the conditions imposed by the California State Water Control Board.

In Arizona v. California, the States had asked the Court to rule that state law would control in the distribution of water from the Boulder Canyon Project, a massive multistate reclamation project on the Colorado River. After reviewing the legislative history of the Boulder Canyon Project Act, 43 U.S.C.A. § 617 et seq., the Court concluded that because of the unique size and multistate scope of the Project, Congress did not intend the States to interfere with the Secretary's power to determine with whom and on what terms water contracts would be made. While the Court in rejecting the States' claim repeated the language from Ivanhoe and City of Fresno as to the scope of § 8, there was no need for it to reaffirm such language except as it related to the singular legislative history of the Boulder Canyon Project Act.

But because there is at least tension between the above quoted dictum and what we conceive to be the correct reading of § 8 of the Reclamation Act of 1902, we disavow the dictum to the extent that it would prevent petitioner from imposing conditions on the permits granted to the United States which are not inconsistent with congressional provisions authorizing the project in question. Section 8 cannot be read to require the Secretary to comply with state law only when it becomes necessary to purchase or condemn vested water rights. That section does, of course, provide for the protection of vested water rights, but it also requires the Secretary to comply with state law in the "control, appropriation, use, or distribution of water." Nor, as the United States contends, does § 8 merely require the Secretary of the Interior to file a notice with the State of its intent to appropriate but to thereafter ignore the substantive provision of state law. The legislative history of the Reclamation Act of 1902 makes it abundantly clear that Congress intended to defer to the substance, as well as the form, of state water law. The Government's interpretation would trivialize the broad language and purpose of § 8.

* * *

* * * Assuming, arguendo, that the United States is still free to challenge the consistency of the conditions, resolution of their consistency may well require additional factfinding. We therefore reverse the judgment of the Court of Appeals and remand for further proceedings consistent with this opinion.

Reversed and remanded.

■ Mr. Justice White, with whom Mr. Justice Brennan and Mr. Justice Marshall join, dissenting.

* * *

The majority reads Ivanhoe as holding that § 5 and similar explicit statutory directives are exceptions to § 8's otherwise controlling mandate that state law must govern both the acquisition and distribution of reclamation water. This misinterprets that opinion. It is plain enough that in response to the argument that § 8 subjected the § 5 contract provisions to the strictures of state law, the Court squarely rejected the submission on the ground that § 8 dealt only with the acquisition of water rights and required the United States to respect the water rights that were vested under state law. That the Court might have saved the § 5 provision on a different and narrower ground more acceptable to the present Court majority does not render the ground actually employed any less of a holding of the Court or transform it into the discardable dictum the majority considers it to be.

It is also beyond doubt that both Fresno and Arizona considered Ivanhoe to contain a holding that § 8 was limited to water-right acquisition and did not reach the distribution of reclamation water. But whatever the proper characterization of the Court's pronouncement in Ivanhoe might be, Fresno itself held that in distributing project water the United States, despite state law and § 8, not only was not bound by the municipal preference laws of California, which were contrary to a specific federal statute, but also could export water from the watershed without regard to the county- and watershed-of-origin statutes. The Court held the latter even though no provision of federal law forbade the federal officers from complying with the preferences assertedly established by those state laws.

Much the same is true of Arizona, where the Court heard two arguments totaling over 22 hours and considered voluminous briefs that dealt with a variety of subjects, including the important issue of the impact of § 8 on the Secretary's freedom to contract for the distribution of water. In its opinion, the Court not only dealt with both Ivanhoe and Fresno as considered holdings that § 8 did not bear on distribution rights, but also expressly disagreed with its Special Master and squarely rejected claims that the Secretary could not contract for the sale of water except in compliance with the priorities established by state law. Nor, as suggested by the majority, is there anything in the Arizona case to suggest that the Court arrived at its conclusion by factors peculiar to the statutes authorizing the project. The particular terms of the Secretary's contracts were not authorized or directed by any federal statute. The Court's holding that he was free to proceed as he did was squarely premised on the proposition that § 8 did not control the distribution of the project water.

The short of the matter is that no case in this Court, until this one, has construed § 8 as the present majority insists that it be construed. All of the relevant cases are to the contrary.

* * *

Only the revisionary zeal of the present majority can explain its misreading of our cases and its evident willingness to disregard them. Congress has not disturbed these cases, and until it does, I would respect them. * * * All of the relevant cases are contrary to today's holding, and in none of them was the Court on a frolic of its own. * * *

Even less explicable is the majority's insistence on reaching out to overturn the holding of this Court in Fresno, which reflected the decision in Dugan [v. Rank, 372 U.S. 609 (1963),] and was in turn grounded on a similar approach in Ivanhoe, that state law may not restrict the power of the United States to condemn water rights. The issue was squarely presented and decided in both Dugan and Fresno. In both cases it was claimed and state attorney's general's opinions supported the claim that some of the rights at issue were not condemnable under state law and that § 8 therefore forbade their taking by the Federal Government. In both cases, the claim was rejected by this Court, just as it was in the Court of Appeals. Without briefing and argument, the majority now discards these holdings in a footnote. See n. 24.

Section 7 of the Reclamation Act, now 43 U.S.C.A. § 421, authorizes the Secretary to acquire any rights or property by purchase or condemnation under judicial process, and the Attorney General is directed to institute suit at the request of the Secretary. Also, as Mr. Justice Jackson explained for the Court in Gerlach, 339 U.S., at 735 n. 8, when the Central Valley Project was authorized in 1937, the Secretary of Interior was "authorized to acquire 'by proceedings in eminent domain, or otherwise, all lands, rights-of-way, water rights, and other property necessary for said purposes * * *.' 50 Stat. 844, 850." Furthermore, § 10 of the Reclamation Act, now 43 U.S.C.A. § 373, authorizes the Secretary to perform any and all acts necessary to carry out the Act. * * * Never has there been a suggestion in our cases that Congress, by adopting § 8, intended to permit a State to disentitle the Government to acquire the property necessary or appropriate to carry out an otherwise constitutionally permissible and statutorily authorized undertaking. Gerlach, Ivanhoe, Dugan and Fresno are to the contrary.

The Court's "disavowal" of our prior cases and of the Government's power to condemn state water rights, all without briefing and argument, is a gratuitous effort that I do not care to join and from which I dissent.

NOTES

1. On remand, the district court upheld state conditions that prohibited the impoundment of surplus waters until the Bureau of Reclamation had potential contract buyers and limited the use of water for consumptive purposes to four counties. The state's restrictions on the impoundment of water for hydroelectric generation to save a portion of the Stanislaus for white water rafting were, however, found inconsistent with the purposes of the project. United States v. State, 509 F.Supp. 867 (E.D.Cal.1981). The state fared better in the Ninth Circuit Court of Appeals, which held that, before impounding water behind the dam, the United States must demonstrate a clear need for that water to fulfill project purposes where the storage would flood out fish, wildlife, and recreation uses above the dam. United States v. California, 694 F.2d 1171 (9th Cir.1982). Because of extreme winter flooding, the New Melones Reservoir quickly filled and the white waters of the Stanislaus River were virtually destroyed in spite of the Ninth Circuit's opinion. With many environmental concerns mooted by intervening events, the California State Water Resources Control Board issued Order WR 83–3 the next year, amending the federal government's permit, and allowing it to fill the reservoir and generate its full capacity of hydroelectric power. The litigation is the subject of a case study that places the decisions in the broader context of state and federal water resources development. Barbara T. Andrews & Marie Sansone, Who Runs the Rivers? Dams and Decisions in the New West (1983). See also Amy K. Kelley, *Staging a Comeback: Section 8 of the Reclamation Act*, 18 U.C. Davis L. Rev. 97 (1984).

2. In City of Fresno v. California, 372 U.S. 627, 83 S.Ct. 996, 10 L.Ed.2d 28 (1963), the Supreme Court held that California's statutory preferences for domestic uses and for uses in the area of origin could not be applied to limit the operation of Friant Dam, which is part of the federally supported Central Valley Project. The Court found that the command of § 8 of the Reclamation Act was overridden where observing state law would conflict with § 9(c) which gives specific preference to irrigation uses.

Years later, however, a court held that the operation of Friant Dam was subject to another California state statute. Section 5937 of the California Fish and Game Code mandates that a dam owner "shall allow sufficient water at all times to pass through a fishway, or in the absence of a fishway, allow sufficient water to pass over, around or through the dam, to keep in good condition any fish that may be planted or exist below the dam." Relying on California v. United States, a federal district court held that § 8 requires the Bureau of Reclamation to comply with this statute in operating Friant Dam. Natural Resources Defense Council v. Patterson, 333 F.Supp.2d 906, 913–14 (E.D. Cal. 2004). The court rejected arguments that § 5937 was not the type of state law covered by § 8, and that § 5937 was contrary to Congressional directives regarding Friant Dam operations. *Id.* at 917 (restating its earlier decision in the same litigation, 791 F.Supp. 1425, 1433–35 (E.D. Cal. 1992)). Having found § 5937 applicable to Friant Dam, the court had no trouble finding that the Bureau had violated the statute, because operation of the dam had almost entirely dried up the San Joaquin River to the severe detriment of fish populations. Id. at 924–925. Does this result seem consistent with § 8 as interpreted by the Supreme Court?

3. With its strong language regarding congressional deference to state water laws, California v. United States raised hopes that the Supreme Court might reinterpret the Federal Power Act to expand state authority to impose conditions on non-federal hydropower projects licensed by FERC. Those hopes were dashed by the Court's unanimous decision in California v. Federal Energy Regulatory Comm'n, 495 U.S. 490, 110 S.Ct. 2024, 109 L.Ed.2d 474 (1990). The case involved a FERC license for a new hydropower project on Rock Creek, a tributary of the American River in California. After FERC issued the license with instream flow requirements that state officials considered too low, the Water Resources Control Board imposed significantly higher instream flow requirements as a condition of the licensee's water rights under state law. California claimed the power to impose the condition under Federal Power Act § 27, which says that the Act does not affect or "interfere with the laws of the respective States relating to the control, appropriation, use, or distribution of water used in irrigation or for municipal or other uses...." The Court held that its decision in *First Iowa* was controlling, and that California had not made a sufficient case for overturning established precedent. The Court continued:

> Petitioner also argues that our decision in California v. United States, 438 U.S. 645 (1978), construing § 8 of the Reclamation Act of 1902, requires that we abandon First Iowa's interpretation of § 27 and the FPA. Petitioner reasons that § 8 is similar to and served as a model for FPA § 27, that this Court in California v. United States interpreted § 8 in a manner inconsistent with First Iowa's reading of

§ 27, and that that reading of § 8, subsequent to First Iowa, in some manner overrules or repudiates First Iowa's understanding of § 27. California v. United States is cast in broad terms and embodies a conception of the States' regulatory powers in some tension with that set forth in First Iowa, but that decision bears quite indirectly, at best, upon interpretation of the FPA. The Court in California v. United States interpreted the Reclamation Act of 1902; it did not advert to or purport to interpret the FPA, and held simply that § 8 requires the Secretary of the Interior to comply with state laws, not inconsistent with congressional directives, governing use of water employed in federal reclamation projects. California v. United States, *supra*. Also, as in First Iowa, the Court in California v. United States examined the purpose, structure, and legislative history of the entire statute before it and employed those sources to construe the statute's savings clause. Those sources indicate, of course, that the FPA envisioned a considerably broader and more active federal oversight role in hydropower development than did the Reclamation Act.

* * * Although California v. United States and First Iowa accord different effect to laws relating to water uses, this difference stems in part from the different roles assumed by the federal actor in each case, as reflected in § 8's explicit directive to the Secretary. The Secretary in executing a particular reclamation project is in a position analogous to a licensee under the FPA, and need not comply with state laws conflicting with congressional directives respecting particular reclamation projects; similarly, a federal licensee under the FPA need not comply with state requirements that conflict with the federal license provisions established pursuant to the FPA's directives. An additional textual difference is that § 8 refers only to "water used in irrigation" and contains no counterpart to § 27's reference to "other uses," the provision essential to petitioner's argument. Laws controlling water used in irrigation relate to proprietary rights, as the First Iowa Court indicated, 328 U.S., at 176, and n. 20, and § 8 does not indicate the appropriate treatment of laws relating to other water uses that do not implicate proprietary rights.

Id. at 503–505. The Court stated that a state measure is preempted if it is impossibly to comply with both state and federal law, or if the state law presents "an obstacle to the accomplishment of the full purposes and objectives of Congress." Id. at 506, citing Silkwood v. Kerr–McGee Corp., 464 U.S. 238, 248, 104 S.Ct. 615, 78 L.Ed.2d 443 (1984). It concluded that the California instream flow requirements were preempted, because FERC had issued the license "after considering which requirements would best protect wildlife and ensure that the project would be economically feasible, and thus further power development. Allowing California to impose significantly higher minimum stream flow requirements would disturb and conflict with the balance embodied in that considered federal agency determination." Id.

4. For the view that Congress should overrule the preemptive power of FERC see Michael C. Blumm, *Federalism, Hydroelectric Licensing and the Future of Minimum Streamflows After California v. Federal Energy Regulatory Commission*, 21 Envtl. L. 113 (1991).

5. What are the standards for determining if federal law preempts state law? Should a "clear" statement of congressional intent be required? Why would Reclamation cases call for a different standard of preemption?

2. THE RECLAMATION ACT AND RECLAMATION POLICY

John Wesley Powell, after an historic voyage down the Colorado River, recommended in his 1879 Report on the Lands of the Arid Region of the United States that there be a coordinated, communal effort to develop irrigation throughout the West as a means of settling the region. He also criticized the homestead laws because the maximum authorized entries were too small for the successful settlement of the arid West. The Preemption Act and Homestead Law allowed a farmer to acquire title to only 320 acres. The Desert Land Act of 1877 had expanded the maximum amount to 640 acres if the land was irrigated but, as Wallace Stegner observed, "the Desert Land Act of 1877, linked as it was to the rectangular surveys, and making no allowance for the problems of bringing water to claims, served only to delude the hopeful and to encourage fraud by large land owners, principally cattlemen." Wallace Stegner, Introduction, in John Wesley Powell, Report on the Lands of the Arid Region of the United States, With a More Detailed Account of the Lands of Utah (Belknap Press of Harvard University Press 1962). Powell spent the rest of his life after his 1879 report fighting for land and water laws adapted to aridity.

Powell's irrigation survey work laid the groundwork for the Newlands Act of 1902, creating the Reclamation Service (later renamed the Bureau of Reclamation) in the year of his death. A series of national irrigation congresses had been held beginning in 1891, which helped promote government participation in the development of irrigation. A concerted political effort growing out of these congresses led to the 1902 Act. *See* Donald Pisani, To Reclaim a Divided West 273–325 (1992).

It was the federal government's second attempt to promote an irrigation program. The first was the 1894 Carey Act. Under that Act, the western states received millions of acres of federal lands that were to be sold for the benefit of reclamation programs conducted by the states. The states, however, did not in most instances establish any viable irrigation programs. This convinced many that only a national program could suffice.

Under the leadership of then Congressman Newlands of Nevada, a national water development program was pushed and ultimately succeeded in Congress. The Act created a reclamation fund from the sale of public lands to finance federal irrigation projects. Farmers were required to repay project costs in ten interest-free installments. The funds repaid in this way were then available for other projects. Sixteen western states were to be the beneficiaries. Texas was added in 1906. Although it was a national program, as opposed to the state programs envisioned under the Carey Act, congressional intent to defer to state prior appropriation laws was clear. Thus, federal funding was not to mean an invasion of the state's control over the allocation and distribution of water. As President Theodore Roosevelt stated: "Irrigation works should be built by the National Government * * * the distribution of the water, the diversion of the streams among irrigators, should be left to the settlers themselves, in conformity with State laws and without interference with those laws or with vested rights." Attempts to reflect this intention in the Act resulted in language, chiefly in § 8, that has been a frequent subject of litigation as most of the cases in this subsection demonstrate.

Although several important projects were built in the first three decades following the passage of the 1902 Reclamation Act, the New Deal marked a new era for the Reclamation program. See Donald Pisani, Water and American Government: The Reclamation Bureau, National Water Policy, and the West, 1902–1935 (2002). In the Great Depression of the 1930s, reclamation projects became part of the Roosevelt Administration's effort to restore the economy through government investment in public works projects. The Boulder Canyon Project Act to benefit the Imperial Valley was the federal government's entry into giant-scale reclamation projects. In the 1930s the government started the Columbia Basin Project the largest federally-financed irrigation enterprise ever that led to other projects in Washington, Idaho, Oregon, Montana, and in Canada, and bailed out California's state-sponsored Central Valley Project. The federal investment in completed project facilities since the inception of the Reclamation program totaled $14.9 billion as of 1995. The Bureau today is the nation's largest water wholesaler, providing water to irrigate about 10 million acres throughout the West. It is also a major producer of hydropower, generating enough electricity to serve about six million homes. Reclamation projects also serve additional purposes such as supplying water for municipal purposes and providing reservoir recreation.

NOTE: RESTRICTIONS ON THE DELIVERY OF RECLAMATION PROJECT WATER

The Reclamation Act was designed to promote settlement of the public lands by independent farmers. Thus, the Act included provisions that were designed to deter speculation. Reclamation water was not to be used on more than 160 acres in a single ownership and water users were required to be bona fide residents on or near the land. These provisions were intended to prevent project benefits from being diverted by large, wealthy interests and absentee landlords. Thus, § 5 of the Act (43 U.S.C.A. § 381) prohibited the sale of reclamation water for more than 160 acres in single ownership (320 acres for a husband and wife).

Congress was determined to curb speculation and to prevent monopolization of public land. This effort to avoid the mistakes of the homestead laws failed, however. Generally speaking, the acreage limitations did not work. Speculators tried a variety of devices to subvert the limitations. In some cases lands were put in the names of individuals in a speculator's family or company to evade the 160 acre limitation. Leasing allowed a single operator to control a large area. In other cases, excess lands were held out of production, then later sold to settlers who were eligible to hold them as nonexcess lands, with substantial profits being reaped by the speculators because land that they had bought unirrigated would be eligible for irrigation in the buyer's hands.

In 1926 Congress passed the Omnibus Adjustment Act and attempted to clamp down on speculation. 43 U.S.C.A. § 423e (West 1986). Section 46 of the Act provided that owners must enter into a "recordable contract" with the Secretary of Interior agreeing to sell the excess land. The terms of the contracts, which are specified by the Secretary, usually gave the Secretary a power of attorney to sell the lands if the owner failed to do so within ten years. Several individual projects were also specifically exempted from the acreage requirements (e.g., San Luis Valley Project, Colorado Big Thompson Project). After an epic litigation, the Supreme Court found there were implied exemptions under the Boulder Canyon Project Act. See Bryant v. Yellen, 447 U.S. 352, 100 S.Ct. 2232, 65 L.Ed.2d 184 (1980).

The excess land law was controversial in many parts of the West, but nowhere more so than in the Central and Imperial Valleys of California where large land holdings had been assembled prior to the construction of the projects. The fight over the enforcement of the "excess land" law in California is a rich history involving almost every major political figure in the state from the 1930s on. It is either a history of the triumph of "special interests" or a case study in the futility of economically irrational limitations on resource use. The first view was vigorously advocated by an economist from the University of California, Berkeley, Paul Taylor. Professor Taylor's studies and polemics against state and federal attitudes toward the excess land law are essential reading for anyone who wishes to understand the history of the issue. The writings are collected in Paul S. Taylor, Essays on Land, Water and the Law in California (1979).

The residency requirement, also in § 5, was rarely enforced. The Department of the Interior took the position for about fifty years that this requirement was superseded by the recordable contract provisions of the 1926 Act.

The Reclamation Reform Act of 1982, Pub. L. No. 97–293, 96 Stat. 1261 (1982), repealed the residency requirement and raised the acreage limitation in § 4 from 160 (320 for husband and wife) to 960 acres. Because acreage limitations had regularly been avoided by leasing lands and other technical legal devices, an overall, combined ownership and acreage leasing limit of 2,080 acres was imposed. The Act provided that when lands are leased in excess of the overall ownership and leasing limitations, recipients of irrigation water must pay the "full cost" of irrigation water, a factor that includes many costs such as full amortization of construction costs and unpaid operation and maintenance obligations for which other irrigation users are not liable. Districts were required to amend their contracts with the Bureau of Reclamation to conform with the law in order to enjoy the larger acreage limitations. Individuals in districts that did not do so would be subject to the old law and, under a "hammer clause" in the Reclamation Reform Act, they were required to pay the full cost rate for water delivered to more than 160 acres beginning in April, 1987. The Secretary's implementing regulations, however, allowed a number of management arrangements (other than leasing, which is directly prohibited by the Act) for treating large acreages as separately held, enabling some operations to skirt the acreage limitation. 43 C.F.R. § 426 (2000).

Even after the passage of the Reclamation Reform Act, Central Valley Project (CVP) water users continued to resist efforts to eliminate project water deliveries to large landholdings. Various California water districts challenged the constitutionality of the statute's "hammer clause," arguing that it interfered with their contractual rights, but the Ninth Circuit Court of Appeals held that those contract rights were more limited than the district thought:

> In sum, the fact that the reclamation laws had as their end the dismantling of large landholdings in the West and the redistribution of that land to families, effectively undercuts the Water Districts' argument that they were given an implied right to deliver the water to farms regardless of size, as long as the land was not actually owned by the operator of the farm. To find a vested contract right with these facts, we believe, would seriously impair Congress's sovereign power to pass laws for the public welfare. Were we to accept the Water Districts' argument, parties that enter into contracts with the government pursuant to such legislation could claim vested rights to engage in all conduct not expressly forbidden in the contracts. We do not believe that Congress must exhaustively proscribe conduct in a regulated field to prevent parties from claiming an "implied vested right" to engage in conduct found by later Congresses to be harmful to the public welfare.

Peterson v. United States Dept. of Interior, 899 F.2d 799, 811 (9th Cir. 1990).

Statutes such as the 1902 Reclamation Act, the 1926 Omnibus Adjustment Act, and the 1982 Reclamation Reform Act have established generally applicable rules for the Reclamation program, but they are certainly not the only source of law governing the construction and operation of Bureau water projects. Most reclamation projects have one or more specific federal statutes which address subjects such as acceptable uses of project water, repayment of project costs, and limits on project operations. Under § 8 and *California v. United States, supra* p. 818, state water laws and water rights also govern reclamation projects (unless state measures are inconsistent with congressional directives). And, importantly, contracts between the Bureau of Reclamation and water providers (typically irrigation districts) establish various rights and obligations regarding project water use; each contract is unique, but a contract typically gives a district a qualified right to receive a specific amount of water while imposing a duty to make certain annual payments to the federal government. In short, the legal arrangements governing Reclamation project water are complex and project-specific. See generally Reed D. Benson, *Whose Water Is It? Private Rights and Public Authority over Reclamation Project Water*, 16 Va. Envtl. L.J. 363 (1997).

Many of the key cases involving the interpretation of reclamation contracts have arisen from the CVP in California, the largest and perhaps the most contentious project in the Reclamation program. CVP water users have challenged federal contract restrictions and requirements for more than 50 years. Ivanhoe Irrigation Dist. v. McCracken, 357 U.S. 275, 78 S.Ct. 1174, 2 L.Ed.2d 1313 (1958) (upholding federal contracts for CVP water despite arguments that they violated California law). In *Peterson v. United States Dept. of Interior*, 899 F.2d 799 (9th Cir. 1990). the water users failed to establish that their contracts for CVP water gave them a vested right to deliver water to certain kinds of large landholdings.

Many CVP users have "water service" contracts which last for a certain number of years and then must be renewed. In *Madera Irrigation Dist. v. Hancock*, 985 F.2d 1397 (9th Cir. 1993), the district established that it had a permanent right to water (even though its contract was time-limited), but the court upheld certain provisions of the renewal contract over the district's objections. First, the district challenged an increase in the price rate designed to compensate for costs not charged in the first contract. The court determined that even though the district had a vested property right to permanent water under the contracts, the price change did not violate the existing contract rights. The increase was not a retroactive charge, but instead a "retroactive means of calculating the price of new water" under the new contract. Id. at 1403. The district also challenged a provision that made the new contract subject to modification dependent upon an Environmental Impact Statement under the National Environmental Protection Act (NEPA) and a consultation under section 7 of the Endangered Species Act (ESA). The court once again determined that the contract provisions did not deprive the district of a contract right because the provisions were part of a new contract and not an amendment to an existing contract.

NEPA and the ESA, however, are not the only federal statutes that impose "new" environmental requirements on CVP operations. In 1992, Congress enacted the Central Valley Project Improvement Act (CVPIA) as Title XXXIV of the Reclamation Projects Authorization and Adjustment Act of 1992. Pub. L. No. 102–575, 106 Stat. 4600 (1992). The CVPIA mandated the first major reallocation of CVP water since the federal government assumed control of the project from the state in the 1930s. The Central Valley is stressed by two major demands. Along with the Imperial Valley southeast of Los Angeles, CVP water is the most likely source of new water for an urbanizing Southern California. As population growth concentrates political power in urban areas where residents strongly support environmental protection and the legal mandates of federal and state water quality laws and the Endangered Species Act, there is pressure for addressing the environmental costs of irrigation. The CVPIA added fishery and wildlife protection to the stated project goals and dedicated 800,000 acre-feet of water for the benefit of fish, wildlife, and habitat restoration. In the case below, the Ninth Circuit Court of Appeals decided the crucial question of whether the Bureau of Reclamation must deliver the full amount of project water provided in the contract, despite environmental water demands imposed under the ESA and CVPIA.

O'Neill v. United States

United States Court of Appeals, Ninth Circuit (1995).
50 F.3d 677.

■ CHOY, CIRCUIT JUDGE:

Landowners and water users within "Area I" of the Westlands Water District appeal the district court's denial of their motion to enforce a stipulated judgment which required the United States to perform a 1963 long-term water service contract with the Westlands Water District. The district court held that the contract does not obligate the government to furnish to Westlands the full contractual amount of water when that water cannot be delivered consistently with the requirements of the Endangered Species Act ("ESA"), 16 U.S.C. § 1531 et seq., and the Central Valley Project Improvement Act ("CVPIA"), Pub.L. No. 102–575, 106 Stat. 4706 et seq. The district court further held that Area I could seek judicial review of the agency actions which culminated in the contested water allocation, but that it must do so in a separate suit. We affirm these rulings.

I.

In 1963, the United States entered into a long-term water service contract with Westlands Water District pursuant to federal reclamation statutes. Under this contract, the United States agreed to construct the San Luis Unit of the Federal Central Valley Project ("CVP") in part to furnish water to the Westlands Water District. The CVP is the country's largest federal water reclamation project. The United States agreed to furnish, and the District agreed to pay for, 900,000 acre-feet of water annually subject to Article 11(a) which limits the government's liability for water shortages caused by "errors in operation, drought, or any other causes." Prior to executing the contract, the government conducted feasibility studies and the landowners and other interested parties testified before Congress in support of the project.

Until 1978, both parties performed the contract. Except for one year of drought, a minimum of 900,000 acre-feet of water was delivered annually to Area I landowners and water users. Bolstered by the water supply from the San Luis Unit, the landowners were able to expand their farming operations. However, in 1978, the government refused to perform the contract, maintaining that it was invalid. From that year until 1986, the government required the Westlands District to enter into interim contracts which permitted the government to divert water from Area I "for reasons other than dry or critically dry year," for reasons of "water quality control" in the Delta, or "for any environmental ... reasons." Then, in 1986 the parties stipulated to, and the court entered, a judgment ordering the United States to perform the 1963 contract.

In November of 1990, the Sacramento River winter-run chinook salmon was listed as a threatened species under the Endangered Species Act. ESA was enacted in 1973 to "halt and reverse the trend toward species extinction, whatever the cost." Tennessee Valley Auth. v. Hill, 437 U.S. 153, 184 (1978). ESA Section 7(a)(2) requires all federal agencies "in consultation with and with the assistance of the Secretary [of the Interior or Commerce, to] insure that any action authorized, funded, or carried out by such agency ... is not likely to jeopardize the continued existence of any endangered species or threatened species...." 16 U.S.C. § 1536(a)(2). Accordingly, when the winter-run chinook salmon was listed as a threatened species, the Bureau of Reclamation ("Bureau") entered into ESA consultation with the National Marine Fisheries Service ("NMFS"). As a result of this consultation, NMFS issued a biological opinion which concluded that the Bureau's continued operation of the CVP in the water year 1992–1993 was likely to jeopardize the continued existence of the salmon population. The opinion noted that jeopardy to the salmon could be avoided if the Bureau operated the CVP in accordance with certain prescribed alternatives.

While the Bureau was developing its initial 1993 CVP water allocation, the United States Fish and Wildlife Service issued a notice of intent to list another species of fish indigenous to the Sacramento–San Joaquin Delta, the delta smelt, as a threatened species. The delta smelt was listed on March 5, 1993. Consultation and a biological opinion followed with a result analogous to that in the salmon case.

In October 1992, Congress enacted CVPIA, amending the 1937 CVP reauthorization statute. CVPIA seeks to achieve "a reasonable balance among competing demands for use of Central Valley Project water, including the requirements of fish and wildlife, agricultural, municipal and industrial and power contractors." Section 3402(f). Section 3406(b)(2) of the CVPIA directs the Secretary to

> dedicate and manage annually eight hundred thousand acre-feet of Central Valley Project yield for the primary purpose of implementing the fish, wildlife and habitat restoration purposes and measures authorized by this title; to assist the State of California in its efforts to protect the waters of the San Francisco Bay/Sacramento–San Joaquin Delta Estuary; and to help meet such obligations as may be legally imposed upon the Central Valley Project under State or Federal law following the date of enactment of this title, including but not limited to additional obligations under the Federal Endangered Species Act.

On February 15, 1993, the Bureau announced its initial allocation of CVP water for 1993. Under the final allocation, agricultural contractors south of the Sacramento–San Joaquin Delta, such as the Westlands District, were to receive only 50 percent of their contractual supply of water.

Contractors north of the Delta were to receive 100 percent of their supply, as were "exchange contractors" south of the Delta.

On March 26, 1993, Area I filed a motion to enforce the 1986 stipulated judgment. The government argued that compliance with ESA and CVPIA required it to reduce the amount of water supplied to Area I and that such a reduction was covered by the liability limitation in Article 11 of the contract. The district court agreed with the government that Article 11 limited Area I's contractual rights to delivery of the 900,000 acre-feet of CVP water. The court also held that Area I could seek judicial review of the agency actions which culminated in the 1993 water allocation, but that it must do so in a separate suit. At the time of the district court's decision, the Westlands Water District had already filed such a suit in the same court; Area I has subsequently intervened. Westlands Water Dist. et al. v. United States et. al., 850 F.Supp. 1388 ("Westlands case").

In this appeal, Area I raises the following issues: (1) whether Article 11(a) of the water service contract, which absolves the government of liability for water shortages due to drought or "any other causes," excuses the government from supplying the full contractual amount of water; (2) whether the district court should have considered extrinsic evidence in interpreting the water service contract; (3) whether the government expressly warranted that the contractual amount of water would be available; (4) whether Article 11 is valid and enforceable; and (5) whether the district court should have decided if environmental statutes did, in fact, mandate the reduction in water delivery to Area I.

II.

* * *

A.

Article 11(a) of the water service contract provides that the government shall not be held liable for "any damage, direct or indirect, arising from a shortage on account of errors in operation, drought, or any other causes."[1] The government contends this language is broad and unambigu-

---

1. Article 11 provides:

UNITED STATES NOT LIABLE FOR WATER SHORTAGE(a) There may occur at times during any year a shortage in the quantity of water available for furnishing to the District through and by means of the Project, but in no event shall any liability accrue against the United States or any of its officers, agents, or employees for any damage, direct or indirect, arising from a shortage on account of errors in operation, drought, or any other causes. In any year in which there may occur a shortage from any cause, the United States re-

serves the right to apportion the available water supply among the District and others entitled under the then existing contracts to receive water from the San Luis Unit in accordance with conclusive determinations of the Contracting Officer * * *.

(b) In the event that in any year there is delivered to the District by reason of any shortage or apportionment as provided in subdivision (a) of this article or any discontinuance or reduction of service as set forth in subdivision (d) of Article 9 hereof, less than the quantity of water which the District otherwise would be entitled

ous and that shortages stemming from mandatory compliance with ESA and CVPIA are shortages resulting from "any other cause." Therefore, the government concludes, it is not liable for its failure to deliver the full contractual amount of water to Area I. Area I maintains that the contract language is ambiguous, and limits the government's liability for water delivery only in the event of a "temporary emergency" such as a "rare time[ ] of severe drought."

"A contract is ambiguous if reasonable people could find its terms susceptible to more than one interpretation." Kennewick, 880 F.2d at 1032. Area I finds ambiguity where none exists; the terms of Article 11(a) admit of one meaning and are internally consistent. On its face, Article 11(a) unambiguously disclaims any liability for damages in the event the United States is unable to supply water in times of shortage. Clearly captioned "United States Not Liable for Water Shortage," Article 11 explicitly recognizes that "[t]here may occur at times during any year a shortage in the quantity of water available for furnishing to the District" and provides that "in no event shall any liability accrue against the United States ... for any damages ... arising from a shortage on account of errors in operation, drought, or any other causes." (emphasis added). As the district court duly noted, there are no enumerated exceptions to this provision: "Westlands, as the contracting party, did not include any language of limitation in the contract." Barcellos and Wolfsen, Inc. v. Westlands Water Dist., 849 F.Supp. 717, 723 (E.D.Cal.1993).

* * *

We conclude that the contract's liability limitation is unambiguous and that an unavailability of water resulting from the mandates of valid legislation constitutes a shortage by reason of "any other causes."

B.

The inquiry, however, does not necessarily stop at the four corners of the contract. The district court's opinion asserted, "[t]he terms at issue are not defined in the contract but they are clear on their face.... There is no need to examine extrinsic evidence as to the parties' intended meaning." 849 F.Supp. at 723. To the extent the district court's opinion could be read to hold extrinsic evidence is inadmissible to interpret the terms of a facially unambiguous written instrument, the opinion misstates the law. To the contrary, under the Uniform Commercial Code extrinsic evidence of usage

to receive, there shall be made an adjustment on account of the amounts paid to the United States by the District for water for said year in a manner similar to that provided for in Article 7. To the extent of such deficiency, such adjustment shall constitute the sole remedy of the District or anyone having or claiming to have by, through, or under the District the right to the use of any of the water supply provided for herein.

(c) The United States assumes no responsibility with respect to and does not warrant the quality of the water to be furnished pursuant to this contract....

of trade, course of dealing and course of performance may be considered in determining whether a contract is ambiguous. U.C.C. § 2–202.

* * *

Nevertheless, we affirm the district court's refusal to consider the extrinsic evidence proffered by Area I as it is not the kind of evidence that U.C.C. Section 2–202 renders admissible. Area I points to government statements in news releases and feasibility reports as evidencing intent contrary to the language of the contract, and seeks to establish that subsequent to signing the contract certain Westlands landowners subjectively believed that Article 11's liability limitation could only be triggered by drought. This evidence is not relevant to usage of trade, which is defined in U.C.C. Section 1–205(2) as "any practice or method of dealing having such regularity of observance in a place, vocation or trade as to justify an expectation that it will be observed with respect to the transaction in question." Nor does this evidence purport to establish a course of dealing, defined as "a sequence of previous conduct between the parties to a particular transaction which is fairly to be regarded as establishing a common basis of understanding for interpreting their expressions and other conduct." U.C.C. § 1–205(1). Nor is this evidence relevant to establishing a "course of performance accepted or acquiesced in without objection." U.C.C. § 2–208.

C.

Area I argues that Article 11(a)'s liability limitation is inoperative because the government expressly warranted that water would be available to fulfill the contract. Area I contends that statements of "high government officials," including former President John F. Kennedy, created such an express warranty. We decline, however, to consider these statements. Although the U.C.C. permits extrinsic evidence to be considered in determining whether a contract is ambiguous, once a contract is found to be unambiguous the parol evidence rule excludes statements offered to contradict a clear contract term in a final expression of agreement. U.C.C. § 2–202; Pierce County Hotel Employees & Restaurant Employees Health Trust v. Elks Lodge, B.P.O.E., No. 1450, 827 F.2d 1324, 1327 (9th Cir. 1987). An express warranty of availability would contradict Article 11's unambiguous disclaimer of liability for shortages in water available for supply to Westlands. * * *

D.

Even if the water service contract did obligate the government to supply, without exception, 900,000 acre-feet of water, the district court correctly held that Area I would still not be entitled to prevail as the contract is not immune from subsequently enacted statutes. 849 F.Supp. at 730. The Supreme Court has held that Congress's power to exercise sovereign authority " 'will remain intact unless surrendered in unmistakable terms.' " Bowen v. Public Agencies Opposed to Social Sec. Entrapment, 477 U.S. 41, 52 (1986) (quoting Merrion v. Jicarilla Apache Tribe,

455 U.S. 130, 148 (1982)). "[C]ontractual arrangements, including those to which a sovereign itself is party, 'remain subject to subsequent legislation' by the sovereign." Id. (quoting Merrion, 455 U.S. at 147). Nothing in the 1963 contract surrenders in "unmistakable terms" Congress's sovereign power to enact legislation. Rather, the contract was executed pursuant to the 1902 Reclamation Act and all acts amendatory or supplementary thereto. 1963 Contract Preamble. See Madera Irr. Dist. v. Hancock, 985 F.2d 1397, 1407 (9th Cir.) (Hall, J., concurring), cert. denied, 510 U.S. 813 (1993). The contract contemplates future changes in reclamation laws in Article 26, and Article 11 limits the government's liability for shortages due to any causes. As Area I recognized in its oral argument, CVPIA marks a shift in reclamation law modifying the priority of water uses. There is nothing in the contract that precludes such a shift.

E.

Area I argues that Article 11 as interpreted by the district court is unenforceable on five grounds. None of these grounds is tenable.

Area I first asserts that Article 11 as interpreted is inoperative, as it would unreasonably negate the government's express warranty of availability. Our finding that no express warranty of availability exists disposes of this argument.

Area I then argues that the district court's interpretation of Article 11 would deny Westlands landowners any damages for their losses and would therefore constitute an unenforceable liquidated damages clause. As the district court concluded, however, Article 11 does not contain a liquidated damages clause. Article 11 operates such that, where, as here, a water shortage prevents the government from delivering the entire contractual amount of water, the government is excused from full performance and no breach therefore occurs.

Relying on U.C.C. Section 2–719(2), as adopted by California, Area I next maintains that the essential purpose of Article 11's remedy provision has failed and that the provision is therefore unenforceable. That section provides, "Where circumstances cause an exclusive or limited remedy to fail of its essential purpose, remedy may be had as provided in this Act." As the district court held, "[t]here is no evidence that the essential purpose of the remedy provision has failed." 849 F.Supp. at 723 n. 10. * * * Here, the contractual remedy provided for in the contract is a reduction in the price paid for water deliveries. There is no evidence that Area I has been deprived of this remedy.

Nor is Article 11 unconscionable. The district court correctly found that the water service contract was the product of bargaining by sophisticated parties who foresaw that circumstances might limit the government's ability to deliver the contracted quantity of water in the future. "Where two equal bargainers ... agree as to the appropriate remedy ... they should be held to the terms of their bargain." Id. Area I has not established that there has been a cost or allocation of risk "which is overly harsh and was not justified by the circumstances under which the contract was made." Carboni v. Arrospide, 2 Cal.App.4th 76, 83, 2 Cal.Rptr.2d 845, 849 (1991). Area I points out that Article 11 is a "standard" provision which appeared in other water service contracts. It does not, however, assert that the government refused to bargain over this term. See id. at 85–86, 2 Cal.Rptr.2d at 850–51. The mere fact that a provision is standard does not render it unconscionable.

Finally, Area I claims that Article 11 is void as against the policy of the law because it would exempt the government from responsibility for willful injury to Area I landowners' property. Following the statutory mandates of ESA and CVPIA can hardly be said to be an effort to willfully injure the landowners' property.

Consequently, the unambiguous language of Article 11(a) is enforceable.

* * *

IV.

In conclusion, the district court correctly interpreted the water service agreement between the United States and the Westlands Water District. Article 11(a) unambiguously absolves the government from liability for its failure to deliver the full contractual amount of water where there is a shortage caused by statutory mandate. Area I's challenge to the Bureau's compliance with ESA and CVPIA will be resolved in the separate proceeding in the Westlands case.

NOTES

1. In Madera Irrigation Dist. v. Hancock, *supra* p. 838, the court declared:

> Congress can change federal policy, but it cannot write on a blank slate. The old policies deposit a moraine of contracts, conveyances, expectations and investments. Lives, families, businesses, and towns are built on the basis of the old policies. When Congress changes course, its flexibility is limited by those interests created under the old policies which enjoy legal protection. Fairness toward those who relied on continuation of past policies cuts toward protection. Flexibility, so that government can adapt to changing conditions and changing majority preferences, cuts against. Expectations reasonably based upon constitutionally protected property rights are protected against policy changes by the Fifth Amendment. Those based only on economic and political predictions, not property rights, are not protected.

985 F.2d 1397, 1400 (9th Cir.1993). Do you think the *O'Neill* court fairly applied these principles?

2. Since *O'Neill*, some reclamation project water users have brought litigation in the Court of Federal Claims alleging that their contract water deliveries have been reduced because of restrictions imposed under the ESA, and that the federal government thus owes them compensation for a "taking" of property. In the first such case to reach the Federal Circuit

Court of Appeals, the Casitas Municipal Water District won a key ruling when the appeals court determined that the government's action should be analyzed as a physical (not a regulatory) taking. Casitas Mun. Water Dist. v. United States, 543 F.3d 1276 (Fed. Cir. 2008), *supra* p. 533.

NOTE: RECLAMATION PROJECT SUBSIDIES AND WATER TRANSFERS

Reclamation has been a costly and controversial experiment for the federal government.

> The federal projects were elaborate ones, projects that private enterprise would not undertake. The earlier simpler works that cost not more than $15 or $20 per acre of land [served] had already been built by private enterprise. The federal projects have been built at a rate of from $43 to $162 an acre, with an average of $85 an acre. Land so costly did not produce return enough to repay the investment.

Frederick Merk, History of the Westward Movement 511 (1978).

Reclamation projects have been lyrically defended as the realization of the Jeffersonian dream in the West, but others have questioned the wisdom of reliance on these "soft" benefits. A debate over the efficiency of large-scale reclamation projects arose in the late 1930s when economists began to probe the relationship between irrigation subsidies and federal crop surplus policy. A renewed debate today fuels efforts to reform the Reclamation program.

In 1987, the Bureau of Reclamation issued a short report concluding that its mission should change. The Assessment '87 report stated that: "[t]he Bureau's primary role as the developer of large federally financed agricultural projects is drawing to a close * * *. The Bureau of Reclamation must change from an agency based on federally supported construction to one based on resource management." United States Department of the Interior, Assessment '87, A New Direction for the Bureau of Reclamation, in The Law of Water and Water Rights app. 41B (Robert E. Beck ed., Supp. 2000). To that end, the Department of the Interior in 1988 issued a set of principles to guide the Bureau in review and approval of voluntary water transfers involving Bureau facilities. See *infra* p. 844.

The precursor for this change had been President Carter's executive order calling for consideration of conservation in all proposals for new projects. The Reagan Administration then introduced policies requiring states to share an unspecified portion of the initial costs of any project to be funded by the federal government. The recognition that states could no longer rely on the federal government to finance water projects led to calls for state financing programs and policies well before the Bureau released its 1987 report. See Rodney T. Smith, Troubled Waters: Financing Water in the West (1984).

Richard W. Wahl, Markets for Federal Water: Subsidies, Property Rights, and the Bureau of Reclamation
27–46 (1989).

Bureau of Reclamation publications frequently claim that the costs of the reimbursable functions of reclamation projects will be repaid to the United States:

> It has long been the philosophy of the Nation that all reclamation project costs for the purpose of irrigation, power, and municipal and industrial water supply should be repaid in full. (U.S. Department of the Interior, Bureau of Reclamation, 1972, p. ix)

In reality, the situation is far different. * * *

Irrigation subsidies in Reclamation law take two forms: interest-free repayment and the basing of irrigators' repayment on the bureau's estimate of their "ability to pay." Revenues from federal hydropower are used to "repay" costs beyond the irrigators' "ability to pay." However, repayment by hydropower embodies a substantial subsidy as well, both because it is interest-free and because it occurs after forty or fifty years of irrigation repayment. If federal borrowing costs 4 percent annually, then repayment forty years later interest-free returns to the United States only 20.8 percent of the true cost of the loan. At a borrowing cost of 7 percent, only 6.7 percent is returned * * *. * * *

The Gradual Enlargement of Irrigation Subsidies

* * *

The Reclamation Act of 1902 did not specifically exclude interest from the charges to be recovered for irrigation, but this has become standard bureau practice. The act stated that "charges shall be determined with a view of returning to the reclamation fund the estimated cost of construction of the project." The bureau's administrative interpretation not to charge interest was based on the fact that the act did not specifically mention interest charges and on the implicit approval of Congress, which did not object to bureau practice over the years. * * *

* * * [I]nterest-free repayment over ten years at the federal long-term borrowing rates of 1902 would have provided a subsidy of 14 percent of project construction costs. However, settlers had difficulty meeting repayment even under these terms. As a result, in 1914 Congress passed the Reclamation Extension Act (38 Stat. 686), which stretched the repayment period to twenty years. * * * [T]his provision increased the interest subsidy to 42 percent of construction costs. The 1914 act also provided for a graduated repayment schedule. For new projects, a settler was to pay 5 percent of the construction charges for each of the first five years and 7 percent annually starting in the sixth year until all costs were repaid. Relief was also provided for settlers on existing projects. Repayment was extended to twenty years from the date of the act on a graduated scale based on the remaining construction charges: 2 percent for the first four years, 4 percent

for the next two years, and 6 percent for the next fourteen years. However, the act levied a 1 percent penalty on all payments more than three months late and provided that no water should be delivered to lands for which payments were more than one year in arrears. * * *

Still, repayment continued to be a problem. In 1921, "in view of the financial stringency and the low price of agricultural products," the Secretary of the Interior was authorized to continue water deliveries to settlers for that year even if the settlers were more than one year behind in repayment (42 Stat. 4). Similar legislative deferrals were granted in 1922 (42 Stat. 489) and 1923 (42 Stat. 1324): upon a showing of hardship, both capital and operation and maintenance charges could be deferred for the two-year period. * * * Then, in 1926 the secretary was given the authority to defer repayment of operation and maintenance charges for another five years and to defer the repayment of construction charges on whatever schedule he found necessary (44 Stat. 479). In either case, the amount deferred carried an interest charge of 6 percent. * * * [A]ll told this legislation would have allowed qualifying settlers to defer operation and maintenance charges from 1922 through 1931 and to defer capital charges for at least as long, provided interest charges were added to the amount deferred.

* * *

The Omnibus Adjustment Act of 1926 (44 Stat. 636) allowed the Secretary of the Interior to double the interest-free repayment period for irrigation construction costs to forty years, which * * * increased the subsidy to more than 50 percent of costs given the 4 percent rate of government borrowing prevailing at the time. * * *

Since 1939, inflation has raised the level of the interest subsidy for newly constructed projects (or new construction in established projects). * * *

In summary, various pieces of general reclamation legislation have lengthened the interest-free repayment period for irrigation, thereby increasing the value of the interest subsidy. The effect of the interest subsidy in the Reclamation Act of 1902 was to forgive about 14 percent of construction costs, but by 1939 this level had reached 50 percent. In addition, the gradual rise in nominal interest rates has greatly increased the value of the subsidy since 1960, reaching levels as high as 95 percent. The various deferrals granted by additional reclamation legislation also resulted in extensions of the repayment period, thereby further increasing the effective subsidy * * *.

Conclusions: Effects of the Irrigation Subsidy

* * * The provision of federal subsidies increases the amount of land that will yield sufficient private returns in comparison with private costs. The provision of subsidies merely changes the quantity of arid land on

which farming can be economical, but farming on the most marginal lands may be just as difficult.

Therefore, the principal effects of the irrigation subsidy have been locational. In general, it can be said that federal water subsidies have resulted in more irrigation development in the western states at the expense of bringing additional land into production in the Midwest and South. For example, cotton grown on reclamation projects in California with subsidized water competes with privately developed cotton grown in the South. Of course, this locational effect was one of the principal goals of establishing the original Reclamation Act that is, to encourage the settlement of the arid West through the provision of water to lands that could be homesteaded.

From the standpoint of national economic development, these extensive water subsidies have led to inefficient use of land and water resources as well as capital, labor, and materials. Since the 1950s, reclamation projects have been subject to benefit-cost analyses. In principle, if projects were designed and constructed so that incremental benefits were greater than costs, then there would be no distortions of resource use. As has been shown, however, many projects have been located where benefits fail to exceed costs * * *. Consequently, dams have been placed where the rivers, in the absence of the irrigation subsidy, would have been left in their natural state. Furthermore, low-cost water has provided little incentive for careful use of the resource. This means that water has been diverted to uses other than those that would produce the greatest economic benefits and has, for the most part, continued to be used for the original purposes.

Significant amounts of hydropower on reclamation projects are dedicated to the pumping of irrigation project water supply. Hydropower is provided at a very low charge because of the interest-free subsidy for irrigation pumping. This means that reliable and relatively inexpensive hydropower has been diverted from other productive uses to provide for irrigation. In some cases, the Bureau of Reclamation has found it necessary to participate in the construction of thermal power plants to provide necessary power for project pumping. In general, in the absence of the irrigation subsidy, many of the natural and human resources dedicated to these water diversions and power plants would have been devoted to other, more productive uses.

———

About the same time as Dr. Wahl's criticisms were published, the Bureau of Reclamation announced a policy of facilitating transfers of project water. This was meant to introduce elements of the free market into a system that had been built on a foundation of massive federal subsidies. By allowing for transfers of project water the policy would also respond to the demand for reallocation to higher-valued uses often urban and to improve the operational efficacy of projects.

Department of the Interior, Principles Governing Voluntary Water Transactions That Involve or Affect Facilities Owned or Operated by the Department of the Interior

(1988).

Transactions that involve water rights and supplies are occurring pursuant to State law with increasing frequency in the Nation, particularly in the Western United States. Such transactions include direct sale of water rights; lease of water rights; dry-year options on water rights; sale of land with associated water rights; and conservation investments with subsequent assignment of conserved water.

The Federal Government, as owner of a significant portion of the Nation's water storage and conveyance facilities, can assist State, Tribal, and local authorities in meeting local or regional water needs by improving or facilitating the improvement of management practices with respect to existing water supplies. Exchanges in type, location or priority of use that are accomplished according to State law can allow water to be used more efficiently to meet changing water demands, and also can protect and enhance the Federal investment in existing facilities. In addition, water exchanges can serve to improve many local and Indian reservation economies.

DOI's interest in voluntary water transactions proposed by others derives from an expectation that, to an increasing degree, DOI will be asked to approve, facilitate, or otherwise accommodate such transactions that involve or affect facilities owned or operated by its agencies. The DOI also wishes to be responsive to the July 7, 1987, resolution of the Western Governors' Association, which was reaffirmed at the Association's July 12, 1988, meeting, that the DOI "develop and issue a policy to facilitate water transfers which involve water and/or facilities provided by the Bureau of Reclamation."

The following principles are intended to afford maximum flexibility to State, Tribal, and local entities to arrive at mutually agreeable solutions to their water resource problems and demands. At the same time, these principles are intended to be clear as to the legal, contractual, and regulatory concerns that DOI must consider in its evaluation of proposed transactions.

For the purpose of this statement of principles, all proposed transactions must be between willing parties to the transaction and must be in accordance with applicable State and Federal law. Presentation of a proposal by one party, seeking Federal support or action against other parties, will not be considered in the absence of substantial support for the proposal among affected non-Federal parties.

Voluntary Water Transaction Principles

1. Primacy in water allocation and management decisions rests principally with the States. Voluntary water transactions under this

policy must be in accordance with applicable State and Federal laws.

2. The Department of the Interior (DOI) will become involved in facilitating a proposed voluntary water transaction only when it can be accomplished without diminution of service to those parties otherwise being served by such Federal resources, and when:

   (a) there is an existing Federal contractual or other legal obligation associated with the water supply; or

   (b) there is an existing water right held by the Federal government that may be affected by the transaction; or

   (c) it is proposed to use Federally-owned storage or conveyance capacity to facilitate the transaction; or

   (d) the proposed transaction will affect Federal project operations; and

   (e) the appropriate State, Tribal, or other non-Federal political authorities or subdivisions request DOI's active involvement.

3. DOI will participate in or approve transactions when there are no adverse third-party consequences, or when such third-party consequences will be heard and adjudicated in appropriate State forums, or when such consequences will be mitigated to the satisfaction of the affected parties.

4. As a general rule, DOI's role will be to facilitate transactions that are in accordance with applicable State and Federal law and proposed by others. In doing so, DOI will consider the positions of the affected State, Tribal, and local authorities. DOI will not suggest a specific transaction except when it is part of an Indian water rights settlement, a solution to a water rights controversy, or when it may provide a dependable water supply the provision of which otherwise would involve the expenditure of Federal funds. Such a suggestion would not be carried out without the concurrence of all affected non-Federal parties.

5. The fact that the transaction may involve the use of water supplies developed by Federal water resource projects shall not be considered during evaluation of a proposed transaction.

6. One of DOI's objectives will be to ensure that the Federal government is in an acceptable financial, operational, and contractual position following accomplishment of a transaction under this policy. Unless required explicitly by existing law, contracts, or regulations, DOI will refrain from burdening the transaction with additional costs, fees or charges, except for those costs actually incurred by DOI in performance of its functions in a particular transaction.

7. DOI will consider, in cooperation with appropriate State, Tribal and local authorities, necessary measures that may be required to

mitigate any adverse environmental effects that may arise as a result of the proposed transaction.

NOTE

A study by the National Research Council observed of the policy: "[m]ore transactions probably will be facilitated than would have been without the principles, criteria, and guidance, but the DOI policy by no means provides clear sailing for western water transfers involving federal facilities or federal water rights." Water Transfers in the West: Efficiency, Equity, and the Environment (National Research Council, National Academy of Sciences 1992). For a general discussion of the transfer of project water rights, see Bruce C. Driver, *The Effect of Reclamation Law on Voluntary Transfers of Water*, 33 Rocky Mtn. Min. L. Inst. 26–1 (1988), and Brian E. Gray et al., *Transfers of Federal Reclamation Water: A Case Study of California's San Joaquin Valley*, 21 Envtl. L. 911 (1991).

In 1992, Congress officially encouraged water transfers from the Central Valley Project (CVP), operated by the Bureau of Reclamation. See *supra* p. 830. The Central Valley Project Improvement Act specifies that one of its goals is to assist California urban areas by authorizing all individuals or districts who receive CVP water to transfer all or a portion of the water to a number of designated users, agencies or, organizations, for any beneficial use. All transfers are subject to approval by the Secretary of the Interior, and the water subject to any transfer is limited to water that would have otherwise been consumptively used or irretrievably lost to beneficial use during the transfer period.

In recent years, the West's most active water "market" has been in northern Colorado, where water users exchange (permanently or temporarily) shares of water from a federal reclamation project, the Colorado–Big Thompson (CBT). According to a publication that tracks water transactions, the market in CBT shares is "the most structured water market in the West. The Northern Colorado Water Conservancy District manages the project, with its board of directors approving transfers of CBT units and setting quotas to determine the yield of each unit. . . . Irrigators, developers, and municipal water suppliers buy and sell CBT units through a well-defined process." *Water Market Indicators*, WATER STRATEGIST, January 2007, at 12. At the end of 2006, there were about eight CBT share transactions per month, at an average price of just over $10,000 per share for a permanent sale.

NOTE: CORPS OF ENGINEERS WATER PROJECT OPERATIONS

Like the Bureau of Reclamation, the U.S. Army Corps of Engineers operates hundreds of federal water projects. But the Corps' portfolio of water projects differs from the Bureau's in some significant respects. For one thing, while Reclamation projects are located in the seventeen western states from the Great Plains to the West Coast, Corps of Engineers water projects are found throughout the United States (including the arid West). And whereas Reclamation projects were built and are operated primarily for water supply purposes, Corps project purposes are primarily flood control, hydropower, and recreation. As of 2008, the Corps of Engineers operated 368 reservoirs for flood control, generated about a quarter of the nation's hydropower, and managed recreation areas at 463 lakes drawing over 400 million visitor days annually. The U.S. Supreme Court upheld Congress' power to authorize water projects for such purposes, *Oklahoma ex rel*. Phillips v. Guy F. Atkinson Co., 313 U.S. 508, 61 S.Ct. 1050, 85 L.Ed. 1487 (1941), thus confirming that the Corps' water management role extends far beyond its traditional authority over navigation.

The most important statute establishing the general legal regime for Corps project operations is the Flood Control Act of 1944, Pub. L. No. 78–534, 58 Stat. 887 (1944). The history and purposes of this statute—including its authorization of the Pick–Sloan program for construction of several major reservoirs in the Missouri River basin—is outlined in ETSI Pipeline Project v. Missouri, 484 U.S. 495, 499–505, 108 S.Ct. 805, 98 L.Ed.2d 898 (1988). Although the Flood Control Act does not address project operations in detail, it does authorize the Corps to contract for delivery of "surplus" project water for domestic and industrial uses, but only if such contracts do not impair existing lawful uses of the water. 33 U.S.C. § 708 (2000). The Flood Control Act is not the only statute that limits the Corps' authority, as illustrated by the next case.

Southeastern Federal Power Customers v. Geren

United States Court of Appeals, District of Columbia Circuit (2008).
514 F.3d 1316.

■ Rogers, Circuit Judge.

This case arises out of the requirements of three States for water stored in a federal reservoir. The States of Alabama and Florida appeal the order of the district court approving a Settlement Agreement between Southeastern Federal Power Customers, Inc. ("Southeastern"), a group of Georgia water supply providers ("Water Supply Providers"), the U.S. Army Corps of Engineers (the "Corps"), and the State of Georgia. The Agreement provides for a ten or twenty year "temporary" reallocation of over twenty percent (20%) of the water storage in the Lake Lanier reservoir, which is located in the State of Georgia and operated by the Corps. Alabama and Florida contend that the Agreement violates the Water Supply Act ("WSA"), 43 U.S.C. § 390b(d), the Flood Control Act ("FCA"), 33 U.S.C. § 708, and the National Environmental Protection Act ("NEPA"), 42 U.S.C. § 4321 et. seq. We need address only one of the statutory challenges. Under the WSA, the Corps must obtain prior Congressional approval before undertaking "major ... operational changes." § 301(d), 43 U.S.C. § 390b(d). Because the Agreement's reallocation of Lake Lanier's storage space constitutes a major operational change on its face and has not been authorized by Congress, we reverse the district court's approval of the Agreement.

I.

The setting for this case is Lake Sidney Lanier, a federally owned reservoir operated by the Corps and located in Georgia. It was created by the construction of the Buford Dam on the Chattahoochee River, approximately fifty miles northeast of the city of Atlanta. To the south of the Buford Dam, the Chattahoochee joins the Flint River and the two become the Apalachicola River, which flows through northern Florida and eventually into the Gulf of Mexico. The three river systems make up the Apalachicola–Chattahoochee–Flint river basin ("ACF Basin"), which includes counties in Alabama.

Congress authorized the Corps to design and build Buford Dam in 1946, and the project was completed in the mid–1950s. Beginning in the 1970s, the Corps entered into a series of five-year renewable contracts that allowed some of Lake Lanier to be used for storage of local water supply. See Se. Fed. Power Customers, Inc. v. Harvey, 400 F.3d 1, 2 (D.C.Cir.2005). The last of the local water storage contracts expired in 1990, but the Corps has permitted the withdrawal of water, in increasing amounts, under the terms of the expired contracts. Id.

In 1989, before the expiration of the last temporary local water storage contract, the Corps transmitted a report to Congress recommending that 207,000 acre-feet of storage in Lake Lanier be reallocated from hydropower to local consumption, noting that this might require Congressional approval. USACE, Post Authorization Change Notification Report for the Reallocation of Storage from Hydropower to Water Supply at Lake Lanier, Georgia ("Pac Report") 1, 12, 26 (1989). In response, Alabama sued the Corps in the federal district court in the Northern District of Alabama, seeking to enjoin reallocation of Lake Lanier's storage space to water supply. This litigation resulted in a stay order, Alabama v. USACE, No. CV90–H–1331–B (N.D.Ala. Sept. 19, 1990), and no permanent water storage reallocation was undertaken despite the recommendations of the Pac Report. In 1992, Alabama, Florida, Georgia and the Corps entered into a Memorandum of Agreement allowing existing withdrawals to continue or increase in response to reasonable demand; in 1997, the same three States and Congress approved the Apalachicola–Chattahoochee–Flint River Basin Compact ("Compact") to facilitate water storage allocation, planning and dispute resolution in the ACF Basin. Pub.L. No. 105–104, 111 Stat. 2219. The Compact, which did not assign rights to any quantity of water, id. at 8, terminated on August 31, 2003, without resulting in an agreement on the allocation of water storage resources.

In 2000, Southeastern sued the Corps in the federal district court in the District of Columbia, challenging the Corps' statutory authority to divert water from Lake Lanier to the detriment of hydropower users and alleging economic injury stemming from increased withdrawals of water from Lake Lanier, which allegedly compromised use of Lake Lanier's water for power generation. Georgia thereafter petitioned the Assistant Secretary of the Army for Civil Works to formally reallocate reservoir storage space for local consumption—effectively requesting a threefold increase in the amount of space devoted to local water supply. In 2001, not having received a response to its request, Georgia sued the Corps in the federal district court in the Northern District of Georgia. In 2002, Georgia's request was denied. By letter of April 15, 2002, the Acting Assistant Secretary of the Army for Civil Works explained that because "[t]his request involves substantial withdrawals from Lake Lanier and accommodating it would affect authorized project purposes . . . [the matter had been referred to] the Office of the Army General Counsel, [and t]hat office has . . . concluded that it cannot be accommodated without additional Congressional authorization." * * *

Meanwhile, in March 2001, the D.C. district court referred the parties to mediation, where they were eventually joined by Georgia and the Water Supply Providers. The parties negotiated the Agreement at issue and signed it in January 2003. The Agreement specifies that Lake Lanier's storage space is 1,049,400 acre-feet. It requires the Corps to allocate between 210,858 and 240,858 acre-feet of Lake Lanier's water storage to local municipal and industrial uses for a once-renewable period of ten years; the exact amount of space allocated depends on whether Gwinnett County chooses to purchase all of the storage space to which it is entitled. If, under the Agreement, all of the storage space that may be officially dedicated to local consumption is, then the reallocation constitutes more than twenty-two percent (22%) of the total storage space in Lake Lanier and approximately nine percent (9%) more of the total storage space than was being allocated for local use in 2002. The interim ten-year leases will become permanent if Congress approves the change in use or a final court judgment holds that such approval is not necessary, and the Corps commits to recommending that Congress formally "make the storage covered by the Interim Contracts available on a permanent basis." The Agreement also provides hydropower generators with payments in the form of "credit to be reflected in hydropower rates," based on "revenues paid into the United States Treasury [under contracts based on the Agreement]," to compensate for lost opportunities related to its reallocation of water storage rights.

In October 2003, after the Agreement was signed, the D.C. district court allowed Alabama and Florida to intervene and denied the motions to transfer the case to the Georgia district court; Alabama and Florida also resuscitated the Alabama lawsuit that was filed in 1990. On October 15, 2003, the Alabama district court entered a preliminary injunction, preventing the Agreement from being implemented. The D.C. district court approved the Agreement on February 10, 2004, contingent upon the "dissolution of the [Alabama district court's] injunction." Se. Fed. Power Customers v. Caldera, 301 F.Supp.2d 26, 35 (D.D.C.2004). * * *

II.

Alabama and Florida contend that the Agreement should be set aside because it violates the WSA, the FCA, and NEPA. They maintain that the reallocation in the Agreement requires Congressional approval under the WSA because it both constitutes a major operational change and seriously affects project purposes. They also contend that the Agreement violates the FCA because it allows only the short-term sale of surplus water, whereas the Agreement is a long-term transaction involving water that is not surplus; because the FCA prohibits negatively affecting existing uses of affected water; and because the Agreement is contrary to the Corps' internal FCA contracting guidelines. Finally, they contend that the Agreement violates NEPA by "irrevocably committ[ing] [the Corps] to executing the [Agreement] at the completion of its NEPA analysis," effectively bypassing the statute.

The court reviews the fairness of a settlement agreement for abuse of discretion. Moore v. Nat'l Ass'n of Sec. Dealers, Inc., 762 F.2d 1093, 1106 (D.C.Cir.1985). Although there are few precedents on review of a settlement agreement for compliance with statutory requirements, the district court could hardly approve a settlement agreement that violates a statute, see, e.g., Sierra Club, Inc. v. Elec. Controls Design, Inc., 909 F.2d 1350, 1355 (9th Cir.1990), and this court owes the district court no deference in its legal interpretations. Our statutory review then is de novo, although this is largely a matter of semantics: "A district court by definition abuses its discretion when it makes an error of law," Koon v. United States, 518 U.S. 81, 100 (1996); see also Donovan v. Robbins, 752 F.2d 1170, 1178 (7th Cir.1984). * * *

Section 301 of the WSA, 43 U.S.C. § 390b, addresses the development of "water supplies for domestic, municipal, industrial, and other purposes," specifically acknowledging that primary responsibility for their development is lodged in States and localities. Id. § 301(a), § 390b(a). It authorizes storage "in any reservoir project surveyed, planned, constructed or to be planned ... by the Corps of Engineers or the Bureau of Reclamation" so long as the costs of construction or modification are adequately shared by the beneficiaries. Id. § 301(b), § 390b(b). The WSA provides, however, that:

> Modifications of a reservoir project heretofore authorized, surveyed, planned, or constructed to include storage as provided in subsection (b) of this section which would seriously affect the purposes for which the project was authorized, surveyed, planned, or constructed, or which would involve *major* structural or *operational changes* shall be made only upon the approval of Congress as now provided by law.

Id., § 301(d), § 390b(d) (emphasis added).

Alabama and Florida contend that the Agreement's reallocation of up to 240,858 acre-feet of storage space to the Water Supply Providers constitutes a "major ... operational change[ ]" and thus requires Congressional approval. They point to previous analyses prepared by the Corps and the Office of the Army General Counsel indicating that operational changes on a similar scale would require Congressional approval. See, e.g., Pac Report at 12; Army Legal Memorandum at 12. Appellees offer that the Agreement "merely leaves in place ... [t]he status quo [of] incremental increases in withdrawal amounts by the Water Supply Providers as those increases are permitted by Georgia," and thus does not constitute an operational change. They would distinguish the 2002 Army Legal Memorandum on the basis that Georgia's request involved a larger percentage of Lake Lanier than the storage allocated by the Agreement and included projections that were thirty as opposed to ten years in the future. Appellees further offer that the Agreement provides for compensation payments to hydropower producers, thus "retaining the hydropower benefit and adding the water benefit." Finally, Appellees offer that the reallocation is temporary rather than permanent, and thus does not require Congressional approval.

1.

As a threshold matter, we hold that Alabama and Florida have standing to challenge the Agreement insofar at it constitutes a major operational change to the Lake Lanier reservoir. They credibly claim to fear that the proposed reallocation of water storage will result in "diminish[ed][ ] flow of water reaching the downstream states." The Agreement does potentially reduce the amount of water flowing downstream, and the ACF basin would thereby be affected by changes to the quantity of water in the Chattahoochee River for as long as twenty years. As the ACF basin includes parts of both Alabama and Florida, they would be directly impacted by the Agreement's proposed changes to water storage uses; in its complaint, Florida alleged various negative environmental impacts from reduced water flow.
* * *

2.

Section 301 of the WSA plainly states that a major operational change to a project falling within its scope requires prior Congressional approval. Consistent with this plain text, the Corps has long recognized that its discretion to alter a project's operations without Congressional approval is limited to non-major matters. It acknowledged in the 1989 Pac Report, at 12, that Congressional approval might be required for reallocation of 207,000 acre-feet, or approximately twenty percent (20%) of Lake Lanier's total current storage as specified in the Agreement. In 2002, on the basis of a legal opinion from the Office of the Army General Counsel, the Corps rejected Georgia's request that 370,930 acre-feet, approximately thirty-five percent (35%) of Lake Lanier's total storage, be reallocated to local use. That legal opinion concluded that Georgia's request was of a magnitude that would "involve substantial effects on project purposes and major operational changes" and therefore required prior Congressional approval. This conclusion was based on a comprehensive analysis: The Army Legal Memorandum identified the "specifically authorized purposes [of Lake Lanier].... [as] navigation, hydropower generation, and flood control—with water supply as an incidental benefit; reviewed relevant congressional authorizations, beginning with the Rivers and Harbor Acts of 1945, noting that, according to engineers' reports, water supply was an 'incidental benefit' " of the Dam; and cited statutory limitations on the Corps' authority to modify any existing project under the WSA, referencing a House subcommittee report contrasting the Corps' authority to make "minor modifications" as distinct from "major changes in a project" and observing that "[t]he Corps' view of its discretionary authority in this area comports with that of Congress," (quoting U.S. House Comm. On Public Works, Subcomm. To Study Civil Works, Report on the Civil Functions Program of the Corps of Engineers, 82nd Congress at 22 (1952)). The Corps' legal defense of then-existing water withdrawals was limited to a footnote, without citation to authority, which stated that "the agency does have the discretionary authority to meet the current water supply needs of the municipalities surrounding the reservoir."

On its face, then, reallocating more than twenty-two percent (22%, approximately 241,000 acre feet) of Lake Lanier's storage capacity to local consumption uses, constitutes the type of major operational change referenced by the WSA; the reallocation's limitation to a "temporary" period of twenty years does not change this fact. Even a nine percent (9%, approximately 95,000 acre feet) increase over 2002 levels for twenty years is significant. Appellees' contrary arguments are unpersuasive.

First, Appellees maintain that the Agreement simply reflects the status quo of gradual water storage reallocation, and consequently does not constitute a major operational change. But the appropriate baseline for measuring the impact of the Agreement's reallocation of water storage is zero, which was the amount allocated to storage space for water supply when the lake began operation. Otherwise, under Appellees' logic, even if the Agreement had simply kept in place a series of interim agreements that allocated all of Lake Lanier to storage for local consumption, no major operational change would have occurred—a chain of logic that would effectively bypass section 301(d) of the WSA, 43 U.S.C. § 390b(d). Even taking the status quo as the consumption level in 2002, the reallocation of approximately nine percent (9%, approximately 95,000 acre feet) of storage space for a twenty-year period is still significant. As the Corps acknowledged during oral argument, the change from current local usage storage to the storage levels envisioned by the Agreement would be the largest acre-foot reallocation ever undertaken by the Corps without prior Congressional approval.

Second, Appellees maintain both that the amount of storage space reallocated by the Agreement is too limited to qualify as a major operational change, and that the Agreement's compensation of hydropower users prevents the reallocation from constituting a major operational change. But in defending the Agreement, Appellees provide no rational reason to explain why a reallocation of approximately thirty-five percent (35%) of total storage, taking into account thirty years of future local needs, constitutes a major operational change; whereas a reallocation of more than twenty-two (22%) of total storage, taking into account twenty years of future local needs, does not. In suggesting that the Agreement's compensation for the loss of hydropower uses is meaningfully different from Georgia's reallocation request in 2000, Appellees ignore the fact that even if compensation provides hydropower producers the full financial benefit they would have received from use of Lake Lanier in the absence of the water storage reallocation, a major operational change still occurs because there is less flow through as a result of increased water storage for local use.

Third, Appellees maintain that the absence of a permanent reallocation under the Agreement removes the need for prior congressional approval. But it is unreasonable to believe that Congress intended to deny the Corps authority to make major operational changes without its assent, yet meant for the Corps to be able to use a loophole to allow these changes as long as they are limited to specific time frames, which could theoretically span an infinite period. Appellees' attempt to respond by suggesting a time period of ninety-nine years " 'might cause a serious impact,' " fails to explain why a twenty year term would not cause the same "serious impact."

In other circumstances it is conceivable that the difference between a minor and a major operational change might be an ambiguous matter of degree, where the Court would consider whether an agency's authoritative interpretation should be accorded deference under Chevron step two in defining the term "major operational change." But the Agreement's reallocation of over twenty-two percent (22%) of Lake Lanier's storage space does not present that situation. It is large enough to unambiguously constitute the type of major operational change for which section 301(d) of the WSA, 43 U.S.C. 390b(d), requires prior Congressional approval. This conclusion is reinforced by the Corps' prior consideration of reallocation proposals. The same conclusion applies to a reallocation of approximately nine percent (9%) of Lake Lanier's storage space, for it too presents no ambiguity. This is illustrated by the Corps' acknowledgment of the reallocation's unprecedented scale. Vaguely committing to request Congressional approval of the reallocation at some future date does not accord with the plain text of the WSA.

The Corps may understandably be of the view that it faces a "difficult situation," and is attempting to balance multiple interests and achieve a "creative solution." However, Congress envisioned that changed circumstances or "difficult situations" might arise and specified that any solution involving "major operational . . . changes" required its prior authorization. WSA § 301(d), 43 U.S.C. § 390b(d). We therefore need not reach the other contentions of Alabama and Florida. The Agreement's reallocation of Lake Lanier's storage capacity to local consumption is a major operational change that under section 301(d) of the WSA, 43 U.S.C. § 390b(d), may not occur without Congress' prior authorization. Accordingly, because no authorization has been obtained, we hold that the district court erred in approving the Agreement and reverse.

■ Silberman, Senior Circuit Judge, concurring in the judgment:

I agree with the majority's conclusion that, notwithstanding our limited scope of review of a district court's approval of a settlement agreement, we are obliged to reject this one. I write separately to discuss issues appellants raise which I think should be disposed of—and should be rejected so as not to complicate any further possible litigation—and to disagree with my colleagues on one important point.

Appellants argued that the Agreement violated the Flood Control Act ("FCA"), as well as the Water Supply Act ("WSA"). I think that alternative claim is quite weak. The relevant provision of the FCA states:

> Sale of surplus waters for domestic and industrial uses; disposition of moneys—The Secretary of the Army is authorized to make contracts with States, municipalities, private concerns, or individuals, at such prices and on such terms as he may deem reasonable, for domestic and industrial uses for surplus water that may be available at any reservoir under the control of the Department of the Army: Provided, that no contracts for such water shall adversely affect then existing lawful uses of such water....

33 U.S.C. § 708. By its plain terms, this provision sets the conditions under which the Secretary may sell "surplus water." However, the Corps does not contend that the Settlement Agreement disposes of "surplus" water. The Agreement does reallocate a certain amount of reservoir capacity to water storage, but reallocations are governed by the Water Supply Act, not the Flood Control Act. Section 301(d) of the WSA requires Congressional approval of "[m]odifications of a reservoir project ... which would involve major structural or operational changes...." 43 U.S.C. § 390b(d). It is abundantly clear, then, that the Water Supply Act, not the Flood Control Act, is the statute that governs the Corps' actions in this case, and I would accordingly explicitly reject the appellants' FCA claims.

* * *

My fundamental disagreement with my colleagues' determination that the Agreement works a "major operational change" is with their conclusion that the appropriate baseline for measuring the impact of the Agreement's reallocation of water storage is zero. That seems to imply that the project was never intended to provide water to the city of Atlanta, which is in tension with the 11th Circuit's observation mentioned *infra*, and is an issue which the settling parties agreed was not determined by the Agreement; it is an open question that has not really been briefed.

Beginning in the 1970s, the Corps allocated a steadily increasing volume of storage space to the water supply providers. [Alabama v. U.S. Army Corps of Engineers, 424 F.3d 1117, 1122 (11th Cir. 2005).] It does not appear that Alabama and Florida challenged this policy until 1990, when the Corps was seeking Congressional approval to enter into permanent water supply contracts. Id. at 1122–23. Thus, for over a decade, the appellants acquiesced to a policy of increasingly large withdrawals. Even after Florida and Alabama initiated litigation in 1990, the states entered into two agreements that allowed the Corps to increase water withdrawals "to satisfy reasonable increases in [ ] demand" while settlement negotiations were pending.

By asserting that the baseline is zero, the majority implicitly suggests that for many years some amount of water stored for (and supplied to) the city of Atlanta was illegal. That is a draconian conclusion I do not think warranted by the record.

I nevertheless agree with the majority's determination that the Settlement Agreement is unlawful. To be sure, the definition of major operational change is by no means clear. Typically we would defer to an agency's interpretation of that ambiguous term, but we cannot do so here because we are not reviewing an agency rulemaking or adjudication, but only a settlement agreement (which does not even purport to interpret the crucial language). See United States v. Mead Corp., 533 U.S. 218, 230 (2001). * * *

The Agreement appears to me to constitute a "major operational change" because it substantially increases the amount of reservoir space allocated to water supply compared to the allocation in 2002, which is all we have to conclude. The total storage capacity of Lake Lanier is 1,049,400 acre-feet. In a 2002 memorandum regarding Georgia's request for more water storage, the General Counsel of the Department of the Army stated that, "[c]urrently, municipal and industrial interests, through direct withdrawals and releases from the reservoir, utilize the equivalent of 145,460 acre-feet of storage in Lake Lanier for water supply." Thus, in 2002, approximately 13.9% of the reservoir's capacity was being used for water supply. Under the Settlement Agreement, up to 240,858 acre-feet of the reservoir would be set aside for water storage (175,000 acre-feet for Gwinnett County, 20,675 acre-feet for the City of Gainesville, and 45,183 acre-feet for the Atlanta Regional Commission). This represents an increase of 95,398 acre-feet, which is a 65.6% increase over the 2002 level. Put another way, under the Agreement, approximately 9% more of Lake Lanier's total capacity will be set aside for water storage—in 2002, 13.9% of the total capacity was allocated to water supply, but under the Agreement that figure increased to 22.9%. Like the majority, I also find it noteworthy that the storage levels permitted by the Agreement "would be the largest acre-foot reallocation ever undertaken by the Corps without prior Congressional approval."

* * *

NOTES

1. In its majority opinion, the court noted that it had "no occasion to opine whether the Corps' previous storage reallocations were unlawful." 514 F.3d 1316, 1324 n. 4. Judge Silberman, however, thought that by analyzing the "major operational change" question using a baseline of zero (as opposed to established practice), the court was casting doubt on the Corps' existing allocation of 145,460 acre-feet of Lake Lanier water for public supply. Do you agree that the majority rationale calls into question the legality of the pre-existing allocations?

2. The Flood Control Act also provides for the use of Corps project water for irrigation. It authorizes the Interior Department "to construct, operate, and maintain ... such additional works in connection [with a Corps project] as he may deem necessary for irrigation purposes," in accordance with federal reclamation laws. 43 U.S.C. § 390 (2000). But the statute also provides that the Corps must first determine that its project "may be utilized for irrigation purposes," and specifies that Corps projects "may be utilized hereafter for irrigation purposes only in conformity with the provisions of this section." Id. Based on this language, the Supreme Court held that the Interior Department had no authority to enter into a contract for industrial water supply from Lake Oahe, a Corps project on the Missouri River, without the Corps' approval. "The language of the Act is plain in every respect, and the conclusion is unavoidable that if the Interior Secretary wishes to remove water from an Army reservoir for *any* purpose, the approval of the Army Secretary must be secured." ETSI Pipeline Project v. Missouri, 484 U.S. 495, 505–06, 108 S.Ct. 805, 98 L.Ed.2d 898 (emphasis in original).

3. Even in the absence of new demands for consumptive uses, the Corps often faces difficult challenges in operating its projects to satisfy both upstream and downstream demands. The multi-state flurry of litigation over operation of a string of Corps reservoirs on the Missouri River dramatically illustrates these challenges. The Eighth Circuit Court of Appeals summarized the dispute as follows:

> The Missouri River originates in Montana and runs through North Dakota, South Dakota, Nebraska, Iowa, Kansas and Missouri before emptying into the Mississippi River. In its natural state, the river subjected the surrounding basin to extensive flooding every spring. With the Flood Control Act of 1944 ("FCA"), Congress authorized the construction of a dam and reservoir system on the upper river to control the flooding. In addition to flood control, the FCA envisioned that the reservoirs would provide water for local irrigation projects, steady release into the river during the summer months to support downstream navigation, hydroelectric power generation and lake recreation. The FCA delegated construction and management of the main stem reservoir system to the Corps.

> The current challenges to the Corps' operation of the system arise from two directions. First, a persistent drought in the Missouri River basin has led to a recurring conflict between upstream and downstream water-use interests. In 2002, the Corps planned to release water from Lake Oahe into the river to maintain downstream navigation throughout the summer. South Dakota, fearing a negative impact on the seasonal fish spawn in Lake Oahe and concordantly on the reservoir's sport fishing industry, obtained an injunction in federal district court preventing the Corps from lowering any reservoir in South Dakota until after spawning season. When the Corps decided to lower Lake Sakakawea instead, North Dakota obtained a similar injunction. Not to be outdone, Montana obtained an injunction to prevent releases from Fort Peck Lake. In response, Nebraska obtained an injunction ordering the Corps to make the required releases to support navigation as called for by the Corps' Missouri River Main Stem Reservoir System Master Water Control Manual ("1979 Master Manual").

> In a consolidated appeal of these injunctions, we ruled that the FCA vested the Corps with discretion to balance the competing water-

use interests. *South Dakota v. Ubbelohde,* 330 F.3d 1014, 1027 (8th Cir.2003). Because the FCA's legislative history and its interpretation by the Supreme Court "indicate [ ] that the Corps's primary concerns should be flood control and navigation," we upheld the Corps' decision to follow the 1979 Master Manual and draw down the reservoirs to support downstream navigation. *Id.* at 1032.

The second point of conflict has been that flood prevention and steady summer flows for downstream navigation disrupt the natural habitat of protected bird and fish species in the Missouri River ecosystem. In litigation initially separate from the *Ubbelohde* cases, environmental groups have attempted to force the Corps to operate the system to produce more "natural" river flows to benefit the protected species. To understand the current stances of the parties in this litigation, it is necessary to review in some detail the Corps' previous attempts to accommodate competing interests while developing its operating procedures.

The Corps sets forth its general operational guidelines for the Missouri River reservoir system in a Master Manual and the operational details for each year in an Annual Operating Plan. The first Master Manual was published in 1960 and revised in 1973, 1975 and 1979. The year 1987 brought the onset of the first persistent drought in the region since the reservoir system had become fully operational. Because it found that the operational procedures in the 1979 Master Manual were not well-tailored to handle a persistent drought, the Corps began the revision process for what would become the 2004 Master Manual.

* * *

The Corps followed the [Endangered Species Act § 7 consultation] process with three protected species in the Missouri River basin: the pallid sturgeon, a fish listed as endangered since 1990; the least tern, a migratory bird listed as endangered since 1985; and the piping plover, a migratory bird listed as threatened since 1985. The pallid sturgeon spends its entire life cycle in the Missouri and Mississippi Rivers and their tributaries, while the tern and plover both nest in the summer on sparsely vegetated sandbars along the rivers. In 2000, the FWS issued a Biological Opinion ("2000 BiOp") finding that the Corps' proposed operation of the reservoir system was likely to jeopardize the continued existence of the three species.

* * *

In an attempt to support downstream water-use interests despite the continuing drought in the basin, the Corps released a draft Annual Operating Plan for 2003 that did not incorporate the flow changes from the 2000 BiOp [reasonable and prudent alternative, or] RPA. Environmental interest groups filed suit under the ESA in the United States District Court for the District of Columbia to enjoin operations under that plan. * * * *Am. Rivers v. United States Army Corps of*

Eng'rs, 271 F.Supp.2d 230 (D.D.C.2003). * * * [T]he district court granted the injunction and ordered the Corps to comply with the summer low flow provisions of the 2000 BiOp. *Id.* at 263. Citing a conflict with this Court's *Ubbelohde* holding that required operation consistent with the 1979 Master Manual, the Corps initially failed to comply with the injunction and was held in conditional contempt. *See Am. Rivers v. United States Army Corps of Eng'rs,* 274 F.Supp.2d 62 (D.D.C.2003). Two days later, the Federal Judicial Panel on Multi–District Litigation consolidated all litigation regarding the operation of the Missouri River main stem reservoir system, including new suits by the parties involved in *Ubbelohde,* in the District of Minnesota ("MDL court"). On the order of that court, the Corps complied with the summer low flow provisions of the 2000 BiOp RPA for the brief remainder of the 2003 summer period.

* * *

After the issuance of the 2004 Master Manual and 2004 Annual Operating Plan, various parties filed motions for summary judgment. The district court granted summary judgment to the Federal Defendants on all claims on the bases that (1) the FCA does not create a non-discretionary duty in the Corps to maintain minimum navigation flows or a minimum length for the navigation season, and (2) the discretionary decisions made by the Federal Defendants in balancing water-use interests under the FCA and in avoiding jeopardy to the protected species were not arbitrary and capricious.

In re Operation of the Missouri River System Litigation, 421 F.3d 618, 624–28 (8th Cir. 2005). The Eighth Circuit upheld the federal agency actions. Regarding navigation flows, the court held that while "the dominant functions of the Flood Control Act were to avoid flooding and to maintain downstream navigation, the Act does not dictate how the Corps should strike the balance between these purposes and "secondary" interests such as recreation or wildlife." Id. at 629. For background on the litigation see National Research Council, The Missouri River Ecosystem: Exploring the Prospects for Recovery (2002); John Davidson & Thomas Earl Geu, *The Missouri River and Adaptive Management: Protecting Ecological Function and Legal Process,* 80 Neb. L. Rev. 816 (2001); and Sandra B. Zellmer, *A New Corps of Discovery for Missouri River Management,* 83 Neb. L. Rev. 305 (2004). The Missouri River ESA litigation is typical of the pressures that the Corps faces to augment its historic mission. Corps projects are controlled by specific congressional authorizations; it has no organic act. Thus, as the previous case illustrates, it can either claim that it has no discretion to modify the operation of a dam and reservoir or face a legal challenge when it does so. The National Research Council has conducted several reviews of Corps operations and made suggestions for agency reform. These studies are summarized in National Research Council, U.S. Army Corps of Engineers Water Resources Planning: A New Opportunity for Service (2004) and A. Dan Tarlock, *A First Look at a Modern Legal Regime for A "Post–Modern" United States Army Corps of Engineers,* 52 Kan. L. Rev. 1285 (2004).

CHAPTER NINE

RESERVED RIGHTS FOR INDIAN AND FEDERAL LANDS

In the nineteenth century, the national policy was to use and distribute the public lands that constituted nearly all the lands west of the Mississippi River in order to encourage settlement and development of the nation. Virtually all of these lands came under the governing authority of the United States as the result of treaties or purchases from foreign nations that had claimed them by "discovery." The U.S. gained property rights in the lands by subsequent treaty or agreement with the Indian tribes who had the aboriginal right to use and occupy the territory regardless of whether the United States or a European power claimed sovereignty over them. Lands so acquired by the government were made available to citizens under the mining and homesteading laws. Other laws provided for the distribution of public lands to states for the benefit of education and for other purposes. See Paul Gates, History of Public Land Law Development (1968); George C. Coggins, et al. Federal Public Land and Resources Law (2007).

Individuals taking up mining claims or homesteads on the public lands could establish water rights under the emerging common law doctrine of prior appropriation. The doctrine accommodated certain realities of the West. There was no prohibition on moving water to lands separated from the streams and this allowed development of an arid region with waterways that were few and far between. Security for otherwise precarious investments was provided by recognizing the best right to water in the person who was first to appropriate it and put it to a beneficial use. The simplicity of the essentially customary law of "first in time, first in right" fit a society where, at first, there were few institutions to administer or enforce a complicated legal system.

In Chapter Two, *supra* p. 70, we traced the triumph of the idea that the pioneers should not be treated as trespassers on the public domain but rather as invitees and potential beneficiaries of federal grants that would ripen into fee simple title. While he was a member of the California Supreme Court, Stephen Field adopted the trespass theory; but later, "when a member of the supreme court of the United States, [he gave] up his former stand, and, [because] the war [was] over, [became] a strong supporter of the theory of the pioneers regarding the obligations of the Federal Government." 1 Samuel A. Wiel, Water Rights in the Western States 109 (3d ed. 1911). Field construed the Mining Act of 1866 and subsequent acts to validate existing uses based on local custom. Wiel described the leading opinion, Jennison v. Kirk, 98 U.S. (8 Otto) 453, 25 L.Ed. 240 (1878) as "merely a condensation of the Congressional Globe report of Senator Stewart's [the Nevada sponsor of the Act of 1866] speech in the Senate * * *." Another westerner, Justice Sutherland, went farther and held that the Desert Land Act, 43 U.S.C.A. §§ 321–339 (as amended), resulted in a severance of water from the public lands, leaving unappropriated waters of non-navigable sources open to appropriation for use by the citizens of the territories or states. California Oregon Power Co. v. Beaver Portland Cement Co., 295 U.S. 142, 55 S.Ct. 725, 79 L.Ed. 1356 (1935), *supra* p. 107.

First customs, then judicial decisions, and finally statutes of the western states recognized the prior appropriation doctrine. The series of federal enactments in 1866, 1870, and 1877 dealing with mining and settlement on public lands recognized the validity of state and local laws and customs in allocating water on and transporting it across the public lands. For many years, the trend of judicial decisions, as well as political philosophy, had been to defer to state law in the use of waters on the public domain. This was consistent with the then-reigning public land policy of disposal. Little attention was given to the question of what water rights attached to the federal lands and to the Indian lands that ultimately were not transferred to settlers. If all the public lands were to be distributed eventually, this was not a great concern. Further, the dominant Indian policy in the period was one of assimilation. The Indian land base was being diminished as former Indian lands were opened up for settlement and Indians were confined to increasingly smaller reservations. Until at least the 1830s, it was widely assumed that Indians would become extinct as a separate people through the forces of civilization. Part of the civilizing plan for Indians was the development of skills in agriculture so they could become independent farmers. For the plan to succeed, irrigation water would be needed. Further, by the late nineteenth century, it became apparent that some federal lands would be needed for federal purposes and would have to be retained from disposal. In some cases these federal purposes would demand water.

It was necessary to reconcile an early deference to state water law with the need for water to fulfill the nation's goals on Indian reservations and on the federal public lands that were kept or set aside for particular purposes. In United States v. Rio Grande Dam & Irrigation Co., 174 U.S. 690, 19 S.Ct. 770, 43 L.Ed. 1136 (1899), the Supreme Court said that the states' power to create water rights in streams within their borders was subject to two limitations:

> First, that in the absence of specific authority from Congress a State cannot by its legislation destroy the right of the United States, as the owner of the lands bordering on a stream, to the continued flow of its waters; so far at least as may be necessary for the beneficial uses of the government property.

Id. at 703. The second limitation was that state water law could not impede the federal power to protect the navigable capacity of streams. Few people then perceived the great potential for conflict between the use of water pursuant to the prior appropriation doctrine and the future needs for water on Indian lands or on the public lands that were reserved for a particular government purpose.

In the late nineteenth century, the government was vigorously pursuing a policy of allotting parcels of Indian tribal land holdings among individual Indians. Indians were supposed to become like homesteaders and learn to farm and become self-sufficient. However, many of the lands distributed to Indians under the allotment policy were unsuitable for agriculture without irrigation. This was also true of many of the western homestead lands taken up by non-Indians who then organized themselves to press for federal assistance with irrigation projects. This led to the heavy involvement of the United States government in western water development beginning in the 1880s.

Funding and political support for Indian irrigation projects lagged far behind non-Indian projects. The proponents and the beneficiaries of projects developed under the Reclamation Act, *supra* p. 797, were mostly non-Indians. Although the Reclamation Service itself recognized in its early reports the potential for neglect and loss of Indian lands for lack of water, little attention was given to the subject. The collision course of the reclamation program with American Indian policy should have been evident. The National Water Commission found:

> With the encouragement, or at least the cooperation, of the Secretary of Interior—the very office entrusted with protection of all Indian rights—many large irrigation projects were constructed on streams that flowed through or bordered Indian Reservations, sometimes above and more often below the Reservations. With few exceptions the projects were planned and built by the Federal Government without any attempt to define, let alone protect, prior rights that Indian tribes might have had in the waters used for the projects * * *. In the history of the United States Government's treatment of Indian tribes, its failure to protect Indian water rights for use on the Reservations it set aside for them is one of the sorrier chapters.

U.S. National Water Commission, Water Policies for the Future—Final Report to the President and to the Congress of the United States 474–75 (1973).

The possibility of conflict between Indian and non-Indian uses crystallized in Winters v. United States, 207 U.S. 564, 28 S.Ct. 207, 52 L.Ed. 340 (1908), *supra* p. 102, in which the Supreme Court held that when the United States sets aside an Indian reservation, it impliedly reserves sufficient water to fulfill the purposes of the reservation. The Court further held that the priority date of Indian reserved rights does not depend on when the rights are put to a beneficial use, but on when the reservation was established. Since most Indian reservations were created at an early date by federal treaties, agreements, statutes, or executive orders, the *Winters* doctrine placed rights of indeterminate quantities higher on the ladder of priorities than most of the established appropriations of non-Indian settlers in the vicinity who depended on the same water sources.

The federal government's commitment to retaining and using federal lands for specific purposes such as parks, wildlife refuges, and forests increased the possibilities for conflict with state-created water rights. Although the earliest conflict to reach the Supreme Court, and the one leading to the creation of the doctrine of reserved rights, was in the context of an Indian reservation, the same principles ultimately were applied to reserved public lands. See Arizona v. California, 373 U.S. 546, 83 S.Ct. 1468, 10 L.Ed.2d 542 (1963), *infra* p. 1001. In practice, however, there have been only a few actual conflicts between the use of water rights on federal public lands and the use of state-created water rights.

The most difficult and persistent questions concerning rights recognized by the courts for Indian lands and federal reservations have been how to quantify those rights and how to integrate them with state water rights. Because of the McCarran Amendment, a federal statute consenting to state jurisdiction and waiving sovereign immunity, adjudication of federal rights is ordinarily in state courts. General stream adjudications are proceeding in many of the western states to determine the rights of all water users in entire river basins. See *supra* p. 305. A major motivation for bringing these huge lawsuits was to provide greater certainty for non-Indian water users about the quantities of water that would be legally available to them.

1.   NATURE AND EXTENT OF RESERVED RIGHTS

In 1874, a vast area had been set aside in Northern Montana for the Great Blackfeet Indian Reservation. In 1888, the reservation was reduced to the much smaller Fort Belknap Reservation to allow a vast area to be opened for settlement by non-Indians. In 1898, non-Indians began diverting water out of the Milk River. The federal government, through the Bureau of Indian Affairs, had established a Fort Belknap Indian Irrigation project by which Indians on the Fort Belknap Reservation also began using the waters of the Milk River for irrigation. Then a drought made it impossible for Indian and non-Indian irrigators to divert sufficient water for their lands.

When the settlers upstream of the Fort Belknap Reservation took virtually all of the river's flow, the Bureau of Indian Affairs requested the Department of Justice to assist in protecting the Indians' rights. The United States Attorney in Montana sought an injunction against the non-Indian water users. He could not use the prior appropriation doctrine as the basis for the injunction because the non-Indians produced evidence that they had begun appropriating the water under Montana law four days before the Indian irrigation project. Thus, the U.S. Attorney argued that the reservation had riparian rights. But he also asserted that to deprive the reservation of water would violate treaties between the Indians and the government and destroy the federal government's ability to carry out federal purposes. At the same time, the United States Department of Justice was arguing in Kansas v. Colorado, 206 U.S. 46, 27 S.Ct. 655, 51

L.Ed. 956 (1907), *infra* p. 943, that the doctrine of riparian rights was not the law in western states, and instead, that the United States government had sanctioned and approved the prior appropriation doctrine there. See John Shurts, Indian Reserved Water Rights: The Winters Doctrine and its Social and Legal Context (2000). The injunction sought by the United States Attorney was granted, not based on riparian rights but on the treaty claim. The case was affirmed in the Ninth Circuit Court of Appeals and by the Supreme Court. Interestingly, the opinion was written by Justice Field's successor, Justice McKenna, a self-educated California lawyer.

Winters v. United States

Supreme Court of the United States, 1908.
207 U.S. 564, 28 S.Ct. 207, 52 L.Ed. 340.

[The opinion is found in Chapter Two, p. 102.]

NOTES

1.   Cases and commentators generally agree that the effective date of the reservation—whether it is created by treaty, act of Congress, or executive order—should be regarded as the priority date of the water rights necessary to fulfill the purposes of that reservation. However, under a theory of "aboriginal rights," when the land reserved is part of a tribe's traditional homeland, it can be argued that Indian water rights date back to "time immemorial" and are thus superior to any right held by a non-Indian. See, e.g., U.S. National Water Commission, Water Policies for the Future 473 (1973) ("Where the Reservation is located on lands aboriginally owned by the Indian tribe, their water rights may even be said to have existed from time immemorial"); United States v. Adair, 723 F.2d 1394, 1414 (9th Cir.1983), *infra* p. 899.

2.   Who reserved the water? In *Winters,* the Court said that "the power *of the Government* to reserve the waters and exempt them from appropriation under state laws is not denied and could not be." 207 U.S. at 577 (emphasis added.) From the perspective of federal Indian law, it is axiomatic that—in the context of treaties—it is the tribe that reserves rights not explicitly granted away. See David H. Getches, Charles F. Wilkinson & Robert F. Williams, Federal Indian Law, Cases and Materials, chap. 11 (5th ed. 2005). Indeed, Justice McKenna wrote in *United States v. Winans,* a precursor of *Winters* dealing with fishing rights, "the treaty was not a grant of rights to the Indians, but a grant of rights from them—a reservation of those not granted." 198 U.S. 371, 381, 25 S.Ct. 662, 49 L.Ed. 1089 (1905). Language in *Winters* tends to support this theory. The Court held that the absence of an explicit reservation of water rights by the Indians on lands they ceded so the government could open them for non-Indian homesteading—land that likewise would be valueless without irrigation—created a "conflict of impli-cations." However, the Court concluded that the implication of a "retention of waters is of greater force than that which makes for their cession," because the Indians would not have voluntarily given up their "command of the lands and the waters" which made them "valuable or adequate." 207 U.S. at 576.

3. Is the case wrong? One Indian historian thinks that *Winters* was contrary to the expectations of the assimilation movement. That movement wanted to give the Indians a chance to adopt non-Indian values but expected that the resources of the Indians who failed this test would be quickly shifted to non-Indian settlers. Frederick B. Hoxie, A Final Promise: The Campaign to Assimilate the Indians, 1880–1920, 171 (1984).

4. After *Winters,* a 10,425 acre irrigation project was constructed on the Fort Belknap Reservation to allow the tribes to enjoy their water right, which amounts to the approximate annual natural flow of the Milk. The Milk is an international river that originates in Glacier National Park. As part of the Boundary Waters Treaty of 1909, the United States was awarded 75 percent of the Milk's flow and Canada received similar rights to the Saint Mary's River that also originates in the park and flows almost due north into Alberta. In 1946 the Bureau of Reclamation built a dam and reservoir on the Milk some fifty miles upstream from the reservation. The tribe's natural flow right was recognized in a Bureau of Reclamation–Bureau of Indian Affairs operating agreement; the agreement gave the tribes an additional 1/7 interest in the waters of the Milk stored behind Fresno Dam near Havre, Montana. (The right does not include waters of the Saint Mary's River diverted into the Milk.) Between 1983 and 1985 there was a severe drought in Montana, and by July of 1985 the entire natural flow of the Milk had dried up and the tribes used up their full 1/7 interest in the Fresno Reservoir. The Bureau of Reclamation requested that the Bureau of Indian Affairs close the Fort Belknap Irrigation Project diversion. In August of that same year, "[d]ue to insufficient water and fear of 'water pirates' who might divert the water before the Tribes could receive it, BOR and BIA decided not to release any water and the Fort Belknap Irrigation Project remained closed." Gros Ventre and Assiniboine Tribes of Fort Belknap Indian Community of the Fort Belknap Indian Reservation v. Hodel, No. CV–85–213–GF (D. Mont. August 22, 1985) (Defendant's Motion to Dismiss, p. 10). The tribes immediately filed suit to protect their senior *Winters* rights, but August rains made it possible for BOR and BIA to agree to a temporary schedule of reservoir releases. The suit was dismissed without prejudice. In 2001, Congress passed the Fort Belknap Indian Water Rights Settlement Act confirming that the tribe had its original right to 125 cfs and provided some 70,000 plus additional acre-feet for use on or off the reservation.

Arizona v. California

Supreme Court of the United States, 1963.
373 U.S. 546, 83 S.Ct. 1468, 10 L.Ed.2d 542, decree entered. 376 U.S. 340, 84 S.Ct. 755, 11 L.Ed.2d 757, 376 U.S. 340 (1964).

■ Mr. Justice Black delivered the opinion of the Court.

Claims of the United States

In these proceedings, the United States has asserted claims to waters in the main river and in some of the tributaries for use on Indian

Reservations, National Forests, Recreational and Wildlife Areas, and other government lands and works. While the Master passed upon some of these claims, he declined to reach others, particularly those relating to tributaries. We approve his decision as to which claims required adjudication, and likewise we approve the decree he recommended for the government claims he did decide. We shall discuss only the claims of the United States on behalf of the Indian Reservations.

The Government, on behalf of five Indian Reservations in Arizona, California, and Nevada, asserted rights to water in the mainstream of the Colorado River. The Colorado River Reservation, located partly in Arizona and partly in California, is the largest. It was originally created by an Act of Congress in 1865, but its area was later increased by Executive Order. Other reservations were created by Executive Orders and amendments to them, ranging in dates from 1870 to 1907. The Master found both as a matter of fact and law that when the United States created these reservations or added to them, it reserved not only land but also the use of enough water from the Colorado to irrigate the irrigable portions of the reserved lands. The aggregate quantity of water which the Master held was reserved for all the reservations is about 1,000,000 acre-feet, to be used on around 135,000 irrigable acres of land. Here, as before the Master, Arizona argues that the United States had no power to make a reservation of navigable waters after Arizona became a State; that navigable waters could not be reserved by Executive Orders; that the United States did not intend to reserve water for the Indian Reservations; that the amount of water reserved should be measured by the reasonably foreseeable needs of the Indians living on the reservation rather than by the number of irrigable acres; and, finally, that the judicial doctrine of equitable apportionment should be used to divide the water between the Indians and the other people in the State of Arizona.

The last argument is easily answered. The doctrine of equitable apportionment is a method of resolving water disputes between States. It was created by this Court in the exercise of its original jurisdiction over controversies in which States are parties. An Indian Reservation is not a State. And while Congress has sometimes left Indian Reservations considerable power to manage their own affairs, we are not convinced by Arizona's argument that each reservation is so much like a State that its rights to water should be determined by the doctrine of equitable apportionment. Moreover, even were we to treat an Indian Reservation like a State, equitable apportionment would still not control since, under our view, the Indian claims here are governed by the statutes and Executive Orders creating the reservations.

Arizona's contention that the Federal government had no power, after Arizona became a State, to reserve waters for the use and benefit of federally reserved lands rests largely upon statements in *Pollard's Lessee v.*

Hagan, 3 How. 212 (1845), and *Shively v. Bowlby*, 152 U.S. 1 (1894). Those cases and others that followed them gave rise to the doctrine that lands underlying navigable rivers within territory acquired by the Government are held in trust for future States and that title to such lands is automatically vested in the States upon admission to the Union. But those cases involved only the shores of and lands beneath navigable waters. They do not determine the problem before us and cannot be accepted as limiting the broad powers of the United States to regulate navigable waters under the Commerce Clause and to regulate government lands under Art. IV., § 3, of the Constitution. We have no doubt about the power of the United States under these clauses to reserve water rights for its reservations and its property.

Arizona also argues that, in any event, water rights cannot be reserved by Executive Order. Some of the reservations of Indian lands here involved were made almost 100 years ago, and all of them were made over 45 years ago. In our view, these reservations, like those created directly by Congress, were not limited to land, but included waters as well. Congress and the Executive have ever since recognized these as Indian Reservations. Numerous appropriations, including appropriations for irrigation projects, have been made by Congress. They have been uniformly and universally treated as reservations by map makers, surveyors, and the public. We can give but short shrift at this late date to the argument that the reservations either of land or water are invalid because they were originally set apart by the Executive.

Arizona also challenges the Master's holding as to the Indian Reservations on two other grounds: first, that there is a lack of evidence showing that the United States in establishing the reservations intended to reserve water for them; second, that even if water was meant to be reserved the Master has awarded too much water. We reject both of these contentions. Most of the land in these reservations is and always has been arid. If the water necessary to sustain life is to be had, it must come from the Colorado River or its tributaries. It can be said without overstatement that when the Indians were put on these reservations they were not considered to be located in the most desirable area of the Nation. It is impossible to believe that when Congress created the great Colorado River Indian Reservation and when the Executive Department of this Nation created the other reservations they were unaware that most of the lands were of the desert kind—hot, scorching sands—and that water from the river would be essential to the life of the Indian people and to the animals they hunted and the crops they raised. In the debate leading to approval of the first congressional appropriation for irrigation of the Colorado River Indian Reservation, the delegate from the Territory of Arizona made this statement:

> "Irrigating canals are essential to the prosperity of these Indians. Without water there can be no production, no life; and all they ask of you is to give them a few agricultural implements to enable them to dig an irrigating canal by which their lands may be watered and their

fields irrigated, so that they may enjoy the means of existence. You must provide these Indians with the means of subsistence or they will take by robbery from those who have. During the last year I have seen a number of these Indians starved to death for want of food." Cong. Globe, 38th Cong., 2d Sess. 1321 (1865).

The question of the Government's implied reservation of water rights upon the creation of an Indian Reservation was before this Court in *Winters v. United States*, 207 U.S. 564, decided in 1908. Much the same argument made to us was made in *Winters* to persuade the Court to hold that Congress had created an Indian Reservation without intending to reserve waters necessary to make those reservations livable. The Court rejected all of the arguments. * * * The Court in *Winters* concluded that the Government, when it created that Indian Reservation, intended to deal fairly with the Indians by reserving for them the waters without which their lands would have been useless. *Winters* has been followed by this Court as recently as 1939 in *United States v. Powers*, 305 U.S. 527. We follow it now and agree that the United States did reserve the water rights for the Indians effective as of the time the Indian Reservations were created. This means, as the Master held, that these water rights, having vested before the Act became effective on June 25, 1929, are "present perfected rights" and as such are entitled to priority under the Act.

We also agree with the Master's conclusion as to the quantity of water intended to be reserved. He found that the water was intended to satisfy the future as well as the present needs of the Indian Reservations and ruled that enough water was reserved to irrigate all the practicably irrigable acreage on the reservations. Arizona, on the other hand, contends that the quantity of water reserved should be measured by the Indians' "reasonably foreseeable needs," which, in fact, means by the number of Indians. How many Indians there will be and what their future uses will be can only be guessed. We have concluded, as did the Master, that the only feasible and fair way by which reserved water for the reservations can be measured is irrigable acreage. The various acreages of irrigable land which the Master found to be on the different reservations we find to be reasonable.

* * *

The Master ruled that the principle underlying the reservation of water rights for Indian Reservations was equally applicable to other federal establishments such as National Recreation Areas and Forests. We agree with the conclusions of the Master that the United States intended to reserve water sufficient for the future requirements of the Lake Mead National Recreation Area, the Havasu Lake National Wildlife Refuge, the Imperial National Wildlife Refuge and the Gila National Forest.

* * *

NOTES

1. *Federal lands.* Eight years before deciding *Arizona v. California*, the Court had held that a reservation of federal land for particular purposes (not public land available for disposition or general purposes) removes sources of water on the land from appropriation. Federal Power Comm'n v. Oregon, 349 U.S. 435, 75 S.Ct. 832, 99 L.Ed. 1215 (1955).

2. *Quantities set.* The Supreme Court's decree in Arizona v. California, 376 U.S. 340, 84 S.Ct. 755, 11 L.Ed.2d 757 (1964), specified quantities of water reserved for various Indian reservations and federal lands along the Colorado River. The tribes were awarded over 900,000 acre-feet of water a year. More than 79,000 acre-feet a year was reserved for federal lands including the Havasu Lake National Wildlife Refuge, the Imperial National Wildlife Refuge, and the Lake Mead National Recreation Area. The quantities, of course, were not based on former use of water. For the Fort Mojave Reservation the Court awarded 130,000 acre-feet, although the largest amount of land ever irrigated before the decision had been twenty-three acres, and only one family lived there in 1957.

3. *Quantities revised.* In 1979 the tribes whose reservations are located along the Colorado River moved to intervene on their own behalf in *Arizona v. California* and to reopen the case, in which the Supreme Court maintained continuing jurisdiction. They had been represented by the United States Department of Justice in the earlier litigation, but alleged that the government claimed too little irrigable acreage. They claimed rights to an expanded allocation of water based on arguments that irrigable acreage had been calculated erroneously and that circumstances had changed. 439 U.S. 419, 99 S.Ct. 995, 58 L.Ed.2d 627 (1979). A Court-appointed special master recommended that the tribes' annual entitlement to water be increased by about thirty-five percent—317,000 acre-feet—because of the United States' failure to claim all the irrigable acreage that the tribes owned. The Supreme Court allowed only a slight expansion of the tribes' entitlement—about 10,000 acre-feet. 460 U.S. 605, 103 S.Ct. 1382, 75 L.Ed.2d 318 (1983). This represented additional water attributable only to the final resolution of boundary disputes that were left open by the Court in its 1964 decree.

In striking down the tribes' claims that they had been inadequately represented, and limiting any expansion of rights to lands omitted from the original claims because of boundary disputes, the Supreme Court noted a "strong interest in finality" where "[c]ertainty * * * with respect to water rights in the Western United States" is at stake. The Court concluded that "[t]he doctrine of prior appropriation, the prevailing law in the western states, is largely a product of the compelling need for certainty in the holding and use of water rights." 460 U.S. at 620. Do the Indian tribes have any legal remedies for the loss of water rights not claimed by the United States in *Arizona v. California*? See Fort Mojave Indian Tribe v. United States, 32 Fed.Cl. 29 (Fed.Cl.1994) (denying tribal claim for additional water rights).

In a later chapter of the *Arizona v.* California litigation, the Supreme Court allowed the Fort Yuma Reservation to reopen a nineteenth-century land surrender and claim 75,000 additional acre-feet. 530 U.S. 392, 120

S.Ct. 2304, 147 L.Ed.2d 374 (2000); 531 U.S. 1, 121 S.Ct. 292, 148 L.Ed.2d 1 (2000) (decree).

The five lower Colorado River tribes have committed some 700,000 acre-feet, about 83 percent of their entitlement, to irrigate about 100,000 acres. Reliable irrigation figures for Indian lands are difficult to ascertain, since much irrigated reservation land is owned or leased by non-Indians. See Reid P. Chambers & John E. Echohawk, *Implementing the Winters Doctrine of Indian Reserved Water Rights: Producing Indian Water and Economic Development Without Injuring Non–Indian Water Users?*, 27 Gonz. L. Rev. 447, 457 (1991/92).

4. *Quantification and equity.* The magnitude of potential Indian reserved water rights claims is tremendous. The possibilities of disruption of established non-Indian uses created great uncertainty for appropriative rights perfected after reservations were established. Furthermore, many tribes have not yet asserted all their rights. One estimate of Navajo reserved rights claims based on an irrigable acreage formula is two million acre-feet (maf) a year. William A. Back & Jeffrey S. Taylor, *Navajo Water Rights: Pulling the Plug on the Colorado River,* 20 Nat. Resources J. 71, 74 & n. 12 (1980). Other estimates range as high as 15 million acre-feet—the entire flow of the Colorado River in most years. See Indian Water Rights in the West 26 (Western States Water Council 1983). The Navajo Nation reached a settlement agreement with the State of New Mexico in 2005, agreeing to receive roughly 610,000 acre-feet of water from the San Juan River Basin where a portion of the reservation lives. Congress had not approved the settlement as of its October 2008 adjournment.

What equities do non-Indians have when claims to inchoate rights are raised that may conflict with their water uses? Is it fair to assert the *Winters* doctrine against non-Indian water users long after they and their predecessors established their uses and their investments based on state water rights? Homesteaders were induced by the government to take up lands in the West and allowed to get water rights under state law. Later, as the quotation from the National Water Commission, *supra* p. 861, observed, the government encouraged and abetted the development of water by non-Indians. How could non-Indian water users know that their water rights would be subordinated to long unused Indian water rights as much as a century later?

In 1911 water lawyers could read in Samuel A. Wiel, Water Rights in the Western States, that: "The Supreme Court of the United States says in Winters v. United States that the right of the reservation to water flowing through it, even in the absence of actual use thereon (if necessary for use in the future), cannot be destroyed by private appropriators who first put it to use under local law so permitting, even in States following the Colorado doctrine which ignore the proprietary rights of the United States as riparian proprietor in other aspects." 1 Wiel at 239.

Historian John Shurts, whose work traces the aftermath of *Winters,* concludes that "from 1905 on, whenever a water use or allocation [involving water for Indians and for public lands] arose, the *Winters* doctrine was there, as people tried to make sense of it, apply it, extend or contain it, or contest its use." Indian Reserved Water Rights 252 (2000). Whatever the outcome of these efforts, it seems fair to conclude that the doctrine was not so unknown that its later assertion later in the century should come as a surprise.

5. *Tribal Water Marketing.* The National Water Commission made several recommendations to deal fairly with Indian reserved rights without causing dislocations to non-Indian uses. Consider this one:

> *Recommendation No. 14–5:* Congress should make available financial assistance to Indian tribes which lack the funds to make economic use of their water to permit them to make economic use of it. In addition, Congress should enact legislation providing that on fully appropriated streams the United States shall make a standing offer of indefinite duration to Indian tribes to lease for periods not to exceed 50 years any water or water rights tendered by the Indian owners at the fair market value of the interest tendered.

National Water Commission, Water Policies for the Future—Final Report to the President and to the Congress of the United States 481 (1973). Tribal water marketing as a solution was also strongly endorsed by the Report of the Western Water Policy Review Advisory Commission, Water in the West: Challenge for the Next Century 3–46 to 3–47 (1998). What are the pros and cons of these approaches?

6. *Practicably Irrigable Acreage.* The special master in the 1963 litigation of *Arizona v. California* recommended and the Court accepted the argument that reserved rights of the tribes in question should be determined based on the amount of practicably irrigable acreage (PIA) on the reservations. The PIA approach is based on the master's determination from historical information showing that the purpose of the Colorado River Indian reservations was to enable the tribal members "to develop a viable agricultural economy."

Adjudications to quantify Indian reserved rights are being pursued in multiple cases throughout the western states. Litigation is typically expensive and time-consuming because the parties must hire not only lawyers but experts in soils, hydrology, and engineering to determine how much PIA the reservations contain. Economics also plays a role in determining whether certain irrigable land should be counted as practicably irrigable.

After *Arizona v. California* was reopened, the special master found that economic feasibility was part of the determination of whether land is practicably irrigable. The master's 1982 report noted that many of the lands the 1962 master's report found to be practicably irrigable could not be cultivated profitably under the best of circumstances. But the master rejected state contentions that a benefit-cost analysis must show a margin of profit. Instead, the master found it to be sufficient that benefits are equal to costs. The master also rejected the argument that practicability should be determined based on nineteenth century farming technology. The master's determinations on these points were not challenged. See Arizona v. California, 460 U.S. 605, 103 S.Ct. 1382, 75 L.Ed.2d 318 (1983).

Many "benefits" to Indian tribes from future use of water rights would have a discounted present value of zero. Should such benefits be considered? Is it appropriate to use the economies of heavily subsidized non-Indian reclamation projects (*i.e*, cost per acre irrigated or per acre-foot of water) as a benchmark for defining the economic feasibility of developing Indian water? A new consciousness of water conservation is moving some states to change their laws to require more efficient water use. Should the standard of efficiency be the same as that which applies in the state in question at the time of the adjudication?

7. *Other standards for quantifying rights.* Most Indian water rights claims are based on the PIA formula, but what purposes other than agriculture might the United States and the tribes have had in setting aside an Indian reservation? See United States v. New Mexico, 438 U.S. 696, 98 S.Ct. 3012, 57 L.Ed.2d 1052 (1978), *infra* p. 878, suggesting that water could also have been reserved for a non-agricultural purpose. Cf. Nevada v. United States, 463 U.S. 110, 103 S.Ct. 2906, 77 L.Ed.2d 509 (1983) (noting the Pyramid Lake Paiute Tribe's claim for water for a fishery but rejecting it on grounds of res judicata). See also U.S. National Water Commission, Water Policies for the Future 476 (1973) ("Indian Reservations created for other types of occupations may have water rights measured by different formulas."). Would those purposes command greater quantities of water than would be needed for agriculture?

The purposes of many Indian reservations are stated generally in treaties, statutes, or executive orders. Presumably every reservation was meant to provide a permanent homeland where a tribe could become economically self-sufficient and govern itself. The Supreme Court in *Winters* referred to the general purposes of encouraging "habits of industry" and "advancing the civilization and improvement of the Indians." But see In re General Adjudication of All Rights to Use Water in the Big Horn River System, 835 P.2d 273 (Wyo.1992), *infra* p. 911 (rejecting a master's recommendation to quantify rights based on "homeland" purpose).

The Arizona Supreme Court rejected the exclusive use of the PIA standard because it does not effectively redress Indians for past injustices involved in forcing them onto reservations, frustrates the right of tribes to determine future reservation development, and treats tribes lacking arable lands inequitably. In re the General Adjudication of All Rights to Use Water in the Gila River System and Source, 201 Ariz. 307, 35 P.3d 68 (2001). The court said that in determining the minimal amount of water necessary to accomplish the present and future homeland purpose of an Indian reservation, a trial court may consider the tribe's: (1) history, (2) culture, (3) geography, topography and natural resources, including groundwater availability, (4) economic base, (5) past water use, and (6) present and projected population because "water will always be used, most importantly, for human needs. Therefore, the number of humans is a necessary element in quantifying water rights." Could some tribes be disadvantaged by this broader test? Under what circumstances?

8. *Use of quantified rights for other purposes.* Can reserved rights quantified based on the original purpose of the reservation be put to other uses (e.g., mining, power generation, recreation, municipal uses)? The special master in *Arizona v. California* stated that the fact that the PIA formula had been used "does not necessarily mean, however, that water reserved for Indian Reservations may not be used for purposes other than agriculture and related uses." The Supreme Court later acknowledged this. 439 U.S. 419, 422, 99 S.Ct. 995, 58 L.Ed.2d 627 (1979). Several of the Colorado River tribes have put their water to more productive uses than agriculture. Interestingly, most of the agricultural development on the reservations—and use of water—is actually by non-Indians. Nationally, non-Indians produce 69 percent of Indian farm land income and use 78 percent of all irrigated reservation lands.

9. *Pueblo rights.* When the State of New Mexico instituted suit to adjudicate rights in tributaries of the Rio Grande, Indian pueblos asserted reserved rights to all the water they needed for irrigation. Indians living on pueblo lands trace their tenure centuries back to before the Spanish and Mexican governments ruled the area. Titles recognized by these predecessor sovereigns had been confirmed by the United States, consistent with the government's promise to respect pre-existing titles in the Treaty of Guadalupe Hidalgo, 9 Stat. 922 (1848). The court held that because, unlike other tribes, pueblos held fee title to their land, the reserved rights doctrine was not applicable. New Mexico v. Aamodt, 537 F.2d 1102 (10th Cir.1976), cert. denied 429 U.S. 1121, 97 S.Ct. 1157, 51 L.Ed.2d 572 (1977). Accord State *ex rel.* Martinez v. Kerr–McGee Corp., 120 N.M. 118, 898 P.2d 1256 (App.1995). *Aamodt* held, however, that the water rights of the pueblos were prior to the water rights of all non-Indians whose land ownership was recognized under 1924 and 1933 Acts of Congress that confirmed the pueblos' land titles. It reasoned that a "recognition of any priority date for the Indians later than, or equal to, a priority date for a non-Indian" would violate the mandate of Congress. 537 F.2d at 1113. The result, then, appeared to be essentially what it would have been if *Winters* had applied. The court remanded the case to the district court, suggesting that it consider the applicability of Spanish or Mexican law. In a subsequent decision, New Mexico *ex rel.* Reynolds v. Aamodt, 618 F.Supp. 993 (D.N.M. 1985), the court confirmed that Pueblo Indians held aboriginal title to their traditional lands and retained prior rights to use water thereon, absent specific legislation by Congress to the contrary. Moreover, the pueblos' rights to use water extended to all water of a stream system necessary for domestic and irrigation uses, except where explicitly terminated by the Pueblo Lands Act of 1924. As a result, the pueblos had priority to irrigate all irrigable acreage within the boundaries of lands reserved by Executive Order or congressional statute, subject to prior uses established before the creation of the reservation. Applying this rule, the court said that rights would attach only to lands that had been irrigated between 1846–1924.

This it found to be about 10 percent of the amount of water recommended by the master. Findings and Conclusions, dated April 29, 1987.

The "pueblo water rights doctrine" relates not to the Indian pueblos of New Mexico, but rather to cities in the Southwest that existed before they became part of the United States. A modern city may claim a pueblo water right based on, and dating back to, an action of the Spanish or Mexican government establishing a settlement in a certain location. See *supra* p. 769. The Treaty of Guadalupe Hidalgo by which Mexico ceded its holdings to the United States assures continued respect for property rights vested prior to the 1848 treaty. Thus, under the pueblo water rights doctrine, those cities whose existence traces to Spanish or Mexican land grants that predated U.S. rule have a *Winters*-type water right. The California grants were for pueblos that were to produce agricultural supplies for the presidios. In City of Los Angeles v. City of San Fernando, 14 Cal.3d 199, 123 Cal.Rptr. 1, 537 P.2d 1250 (1975), *supra* p. 642, the California Supreme Court looked to the purpose of the pueblo (now Los Angeles) to find that Spanish law provided rights to sufficient water for its present and future needs:

> The pueblo was deliberately located to take maximum advantage of the Los Angeles River as a source of water for irrigation and the orders for the pueblo's founding included detailed provisions for an irrigation dam and canals. These circumstances strongly suggest a governmental policy of assuring the pueblo a supply of water sufficient for its maintenance and growth, at least in the absence of any other town or settlement of comparable importance competing for the same water supply.

537 P.2d at 1275. The New Mexico Supreme Court originally followed California's lead in recognizing pueblo water rights, but later rejected them as fundamentally inconsistent with the prevailing doctrine of prior appropriation. State of New Mexico v. City of Las Vegas, 135 N.M. 375, 89 P.3d 47 (2004).

2.   JURISDICTION TO DETERMINE RESERVED RIGHTS

United States v. District Court in and for Eagle County

Supreme Court of the United States, 1971.
401 U.S. 520, 91 S.Ct. 998, 28 L.Ed.2d 278.

■ MR. JUSTICE DOUGLAS delivered the opinion of the Court.

Eagle River is a tributary of the Colorado River; and Water District 37 is a Colorado entity encompassing all Colorado lands irrigated by water of the Eagle and its tributaries. The present case started in the Colorado courts and is called a supplemental water adjudication under Colo. Rev. Stat. Ann. 148–9–7 (1963). The Colorado court issued a notice which, *inter alia,* asked all owners and claimants of water rights in those streams "to file a statement of claim and to appear * * * in regard to all water rights owned or claimed by them." The United States was served with this notice pursuant to 43 U.S.C.A. § 666.[1] The United States moved to be dismissed as a party, asserting that 43 U.S.C.A. § 666 does not constitute consent to have adjudicated in a state court the reserved water rights of the United States.

The objections of the United States were overruled by the state District Court and on a motion for a writ of prohibition the Colorado Supreme Court took the same view. 169 Colo. 555, 458 P.2d 760. The case is here on a petition for certiorari, which we granted. 397 U.S. 1005.

We affirm the Colorado decree.

It is clear from our cases that the United States often has reserved water rights based on withdrawals from the public domain. As we said in *Arizona v. California*, 373 U.S. 546, the Federal Government had the authority both before and after a State is admitted into the Union "to reserve waters for the use and benefit of federally reserved lands." *Id.* at 597. The federally reserved lands include any federal enclave. In *Arizona v. California* we were primarily concerned with Indian reservations. *Id.* at 598–601. The reservation of waters may be only implied and the amount will reflect the nature of the federal enclave. *Id.* at 600–601. Here the United States is primarily concerned with reserved waters for the White River National Forest, withdrawn in 1905, Colorado having been admitted into the Union in 1876.

The United States points out that Colorado water rights are based on the appropriation system which requires the permanent fixing of rights to the use of water at the time of the adjudication, with no provision for the future needs, as is often required in case of reserved water rights. Since those rights may potentially be at war with appropriative rights, it is earnestly urged that 43 U.S.C.A. § 666 gave consent to join the United States only for the adjudication of water rights which the United States acquired pursuant to state law.

* * * [T]he first clause of § 666(a)(1), read literally, would seem to cover this case for "rights to the use of water of a river system" is broad enough to embrace "reserved" waters.

---

1. 66 Stat. 560, 43 U.S.C.A. § 666(a), provides:

"Consent is given to join the United States as a defendant in any suit (1) for the adjudication of rights to the use of water of a river system or other source, or (2) for the administration of such rights, where it appears that the United States is the owner of or is in the process of acquiring water rights by appropriation under State law, by purchase, by exchange, or otherwise, and the United States is a necessary party to such suit. The United States, when a party to any such suit, shall (1) be deemed to have waived any right to plead that the State laws are inapplicable or that the United States is not amenable thereto by reason of its sovereignty, and (2) shall be subject to the judgments, orders, and decrees of the court having jurisdiction, and may obtain review thereof, in the same manner and to the same extent as a private individual under like circumstances: *Provided,* That no judgment for costs shall be entered against the United States in any such suit."

The main reliance of the United States appears to be on Clause 2 of § 666(a) which reads:

" * * * for the administration of such rights, where it appears that the United States is the owner of or is in the process of acquiring water rights by appropriation under State law, by purchase, by exchange, or otherwise."

This provision does not qualify § 666(a)(1), for (1) and (2) are separated by an "or." Yet even if "or" be read as "and", we see no difficulty with Colorado's position. Section 666(a)(2) obviously includes water rights previously acquired by the United States through appropriation or presently in the process of being so acquired. But we do not read § 666(a)(2) as being restricted to appropriative rights acquired under state law. In the first place, "the administration of such rights" in § 666(a)(2) must refer to the rights described in (1) for they are the only ones which in this context "such" could mean; and as we have seen they are all-inclusive, in terms at least. Moreover, (2) covers rights acquired by appropriation under state law and rights acquired "by purchase" or "by exchange," which we assume would normally be appropriative rights. But it also includes water rights which the United States has "otherwise" acquired. The doctrine of *ejusdem generis* is invoked to maintain that "or otherwise" does not encompass the adjudication of reserved water rights, which are in no way dependent for their creation or existence on state law. We reject that conclusion for we deal with an all-inclusive statute concerning "the adjudication of rights to the use of water of a river system" which in § 666(a)(1) has no exceptions and which, as we read it, includes appropriative rights, riparian rights, and reserved rights.

It is said that this adjudication is not a "general" one as required by *Dugan v. Rank*, 372 U.S. 609, 618. This proceeding, unlike the one in *Dugan,* is not a private one to determine whether named claimants have priority over the United States. The whole community of claims is involved and as Senator McCarran, Chairman of the Committee reporting on the bill, said in reply to Senator Magnuson: "S. 18 is not intended * * * to be used for any other purpose than to allow the United States to be joined in a suit wherein it is necessary to adjudicate all of the rights of various owners on a given stream. This is so because unless all of the parties owning or in the process of acquiring water rights on a particular stream can be joined as parties defendant, any subsequent decree would be of little value."

* * *

Affirmed.

NOTES

1. Dugan v. Rank, 372 U.S. 609, 83 S.Ct. 999, 10 L.Ed.2d 15 (1963) is cited in the principal case. As a result of the Central Valley Project (described *supra* p. 831), water flow in the San Joaquin River near plaintiff's property was severely diminished. Plaintiff sought to enjoin local officials of the United States Bureau of Reclamation from diverting the water. The United States was joined as a party defendant. The Supreme

Court in *Dugan* held that the McCarran Amendment was not applicable in that case:

> * * * Rather than a case involving a *general* adjudication of "all of the rights of various owners on a given stream," S.Rep. No. 755, 82d Cong., 1st Sess. 9 (1951), it is a private suit to determine water rights solely between the respondents and the United States and the local Reclamation Bureau officials. In addition to the fact that all of the claimants of water rights along the river are not made parties, no relief is either asked or granted as between claimants, nor are priorities sought to be established as to the appropriative and prescriptive rights asserted.

372 U.S. at 618. Is a state adjudication with mixed administrative and judicial functions a general adjudication? See United States v. Oregon, 44 F.3d 758 (9th Cir.1994), cert. denied, sub nom. Klamath Tribe v. Oregon, 516 U.S. 943, 116 S.Ct. 378, 133 L.Ed.2d 302 (1995) (holding that the Oregon proceedings were subject to the McCarran Amendment).

2. Once it proceeds with its claims in state court under the McCarran Amendment, is the United States subject to procedural requirements that may prevent the assertion of certain federal claims? The United States filed reserved water rights claims in state court after losing the principal case. One such federal claim was for 200,000 acre-feet per year for Naval Oil Shale Reserves with priority dates of 1916 and 1924. The claim described the source of waters as "the Colorado and White rivers and water tributary thereto, which are located in or on the [oil shale reserves]." In fact, no part of the reserves was actually located on the rivers, the nearest point to the Colorado River being about one-half mile away. In 1983, the claims had not yet been ruled upon and the federal government sought to amend its application to specify that it asserted the right to divert its water at a particular point on the Colorado River mainstem. The motion to amend was granted, but the water court held that the claims were new ones, not amendments to the original claims which asserted 1916 and 1924 priorities. The Colorado Supreme Court affirmed. United States v. Bell, 724 P.2d 631 (Colo.1986). In order to preserve the original priority date of a reserved right claim, the United States must file that claim in the same year that the federal government was first joined in an adjudication of the relevant area. Park Center Water District v. United States, 781 P.2d 90 (Colo. 1989) (upholding 1936 priority date for a reserved water right claim which was timely filed in 1979 and amended in 1981). Later claims are untimely and can only have priority as of the year in which the application is filed. This way of handling reserved rights claims is similar to the Colorado court's handling of private appropriative claims with old priority dates that are not filed in the first available adjudication after the adjudication law was passed.

The United States Supreme Court has not ruled on the extent to which such state procedural rules may preclude or limit assertions of reserved rights. It has ruled that the McCarran Amendment's waiver of sovereign immunity, which specifically exempts the U.S. from a "judgment for costs," did not require the government to pay filing fees (totaling over $10 million) in an Idaho adjudication. United States v. Idaho, 508 U.S. 1, 113 S.Ct. 1893, 123 L.Ed.2d 563 (1993).

3. Neither the McCarran Amendment nor *Eagle County* specifically addressed the issue of Indian reserved rights. The amendment consents to suits only where "the United States is the owner of * * * water rights." Tribal water rights and other property are held in trust by the government for the benefit of tribes, and tribes are themselves sovereign. The U.S. therefore objected that it should not be forced to claim rights for Indian lands in the Colorado adjudication.

In Colorado River Water Conservation District v. United States, 424 U.S. 800, 96 S.Ct. 1236, 47 L.Ed.2d 483 (1976), the Court decided that the McCarran Amendment created state court jurisdiction to adjudicate Indian reserved rights as well as federal rights. The Court found that "not only the Amendment's language, but also its underlying policy, dictates a construction including Indian rights in its provisions." Id. at 810. Likewise, its "legislative history demonstrates that the McCarran Amendment is to be construed as reaching federal water rights reserved on behalf of Indians. It was unmistakably the understanding of proponents and opponents of the legislation that it contemplated water rights reserved for Indians." Id. at 818. See also Arizona v. San Carlos Apache Tribe, 463 U.S. 545, 556, 103 S.Ct. 3201, 77 L.Ed.2d 837 (1983) (holding that the McCarran Amendment extended state jurisdiction even to states whose constitutions "disclaim all right and title to ... [Indian] lands" and promised that those lands "shall remain under the absolute jurisdiction and control of the United States").

Not only did *Colorado River* extend the McCarran Amendment's reach to include Indian reserved rights, but it also fashioned a doctrine of federal court abstention for cases involving concurrent adjudication of water rights in a state forum in apparent deference to the policies underlying the McCarran Amendment. In *Colorado River,* a federal case was pending before the state case commenced. The Court cited the litigants' ready access to the state's comprehensive regulatory scheme and convenient forum, as well as the McCarran Amendment's policy against piecemeal adjudication as reasons for its deference to the state adjudicative process. See Martin H. Redish & Gene R. Nichol, Federal Courts: Cases, Comments, and Questions 706–720 (3d ed. 1994). *Colorado River* has been read as expressing a strong preference for state over federal adjudication of Indian reserved rights. *E.g.*, United States v. Oregon, 44 F.3d 758 (9th Cir.1994), cert. denied sub. nom. Klamath Tribe v. Oregon, 516 U.S. 943, 116 S.Ct. 378, 133 L.Ed.2d 302 (1995); State Engineer of Nevada v. South Fork Board of Te–Moak Tribe, 114 F.Supp.2d 1046 (D.Nev.2000). *See* Scott B. McElroy & Jeff J. Davis, *Revisiting Colorado River Water Conservation District v. United States—There Must Be A Better Way*, 27 Ariz. St. L.J. 597 (1995).

Major McCarran Amendment adjudications are underway as a part of general stream adjudications in Arizona, Idaho, and Washington. Other states have on-going adjudications, but many tribal rights have yet to be quantified. The process and progress of adjudications in each of the western states is summarized in John E. Thorson, Ramsey L. Kropf, Andrea K. Gerlak & Dar Crammond, *Dividing Western Waters: A Century of Adjudicating Rivers and Streams, Part II,* 9 U. Denv. Water L. Rev. 299, 337–356 (2006).

A Montana decision underscores the importance, at least under some state laws, of determining reserved rights. In the Matter of Application for Beneficial Water Use Permits, 278 Mont. 50, 923 P.2d 1073 (1996) (*Ciotti*) held that the state cannot process new appropriation applications from non-Indians living on the Flathead Reservation prior to the settlement or adjudication of the tribe's water rights:

> Clearly the only way to determine if an applicant's use will unreasonably interfere with the Tribe's reserved water rights is to decide how much water is reserved and how much is available * * *. Instead of resolving doubts in favor of appropriation, the Montana Water Use Act requires an applicant to make explicit statutory showings that there are unappropriated waters in the source of supply, that the water rights of a prior appropriator will not be adversely affected, and that the proposed use not unreasonably interfere with a planned use for which water has been reserved.

Id. at 1079–80.

After the *Ciotti* decision, Montana amended the Water Use Act to require proof of the availability of water only by a preponderance of the evidence. The state supreme court questioned the constitutionality of the statute in Confederated Salish & Kootenai Tribes v. Clinch, 297 Mont. 448, 992 P.2d 244 (1999), and reaffirmed *Ciotti*. However, a divided Montana Supreme Court later held that unquantified tribal reserved rights do not prevent the state from processing claims for changes to existing state-law water rights. Confederated Salish & Kootenai Tribes v. Clinch, 336 Mont. 302, 158 P.3d 377 (2007). In any such proceeding, the change applicant would have to establish by a preponderance of the evidence that the proposed change would not harm the use of existing water rights, including tribal reserved rights. Id. at 388. The extensive dissent in the 2007 case examined the tension in Montana between protecting the tribes' unadjudicated water rights and allowing non-tribal development and use of water resources. Id. at 389 (Nelson, J., dissenting). Questioning the Montana water resources agency's "long-standing position that unquantified tribal rights are being 'adequately protected'" by the agency, Judge Nelson concluded: "Indeed, given the political and economic pressure put on the DNRC, to which it routinely succumbs as demonstrated by its track record over the last twenty years, it is pure fantasy to expect that the agency . . . will satisfactorily protect Indian water rights in the course of its proceedings." Id. at 418.

3.   INTENT TO RESERVE

United States v. New Mexico

Supreme Court of the United States, 1978.
438 U.S. 696, 98 S.Ct. 3012, 57 L.Ed.2d 1052.

■ MR. JUSTICE REHNQUIST delivered the opinion of the Court.

The Rio Mimbres rises in the southwestern highlands of New Mexico and flows generally southward, finally disappearing in a desert sink just north of the Mexican border. The river originates in the upper reaches of the Gila National Forest, but during its course it winds more than 50 miles past privately owned lands and provides substantial water for both irrigation and mining. In 1970, a stream adjudication was begun by the State of New Mexico to determine the exact rights of each user to water from the Mimbres. In this adjudication the United States claimed reserved water rights for use in the Gila National Forest. The State District Court held that the United States, in setting the Gila National Forest aside from other public lands, reserved the use of such water "as may be necessary for the purposes for which [the land was] withdrawn," but that these purposes did not include recreation, aesthetics, wildlife preservation, or cattle grazing. The United States appealed unsuccessfully to the Supreme Court of New Mexico. *Mimbres Valley Irrigation Co. v. Salopek*, 564 P.2d 615 (1977). We granted certiorari to consider whether the Supreme Court of New Mexico had applied the correct principles of federal law in determining petitioner's reserved rights in the Mimbres. We now affirm.

I

The question posed in this case—what quantity of water, if any, the United States reserved out of the Mimbres River when it set aside the Gila National Forest in 1899—is a question of implied intent and not power. In *California v. United States*, [438 U.S. 645, 653–63 (1978), *supra* p. 804,] we had occasion to discuss the respective authority of Federal and State governments over waters in the Western States. The Court has previously concluded that whatever powers the States acquired over their waters as a result of congressional acts and admission into the Union, however, Congress did not intend thereby to relinquish its authority to reserve unappropriated water in the future for use on appurtenant lands withdrawn from the public domain for specific federal purposes. *Winters v. United States*, 207 U.S. 564, 577 (1908); *Arizona v. California*, 373 U.S. 546, 597–598 (1963); *Cappaert v. United States*, 426 U.S. 128, 143–146 (1976).

Recognition of Congress' power to reserve water for land which is itself set apart from the public domain, however, does not answer the question of the amount of water which has been reserved or the purposes for which the water may be used. Substantial portions of the public domain *have* been withdrawn and reserved by the United States for use as Indian reservations, forest reserves, national parks, and national monuments. And water is frequently necessary to achieve the purposes for which these reservations are made. But Congress has seldom expressly reserved water for use on these withdrawn lands. If water were abundant, Congress' silence would pose no problem. In the arid parts of the West, however, claims to water for use on federal reservations inescapably vie with other public and private claims for the limited quantities to be found in the rivers and streams. This competition is compounded by the sheer quantity of reserved lands in the

Western States, which lands form brightly colored swaths across the maps of these States.[3]

The Court has previously concluded that Congress, in giving the President the power to reserve portions of the federal domain for specific federal purposes, *impliedly* authorized him to reserve "appurtenant water then unappropriated *to the extent needed to accomplish the purpose of the reservation.*" *Cappaert,* [426 U.S.,] at 138 (emphasis added). While many of the contours of what has come to be called the "implied-reservation-of-water doctrine" remain unspecified, the Court has repeatedly emphasized that Congress reserved "only that amount of water necessary to fulfill the purpose of the reservation, no more." *Cappaert,* [426 U.S.,] at 141. Each time this Court has applied the "implied-reservation-of-water doctrine," it has carefully examined both the asserted water right and the specific purposes for which the land was reserved, and concluded that without the water the purposes of the reservation would be entirely defeated.[4]

This careful examination is required both because the reservation is implied, rather than expressed, and because of the history of congressional

---

3. The percentage of federally owned land (*excluding* Indian reservations and other trust properties) in the Western States ranges from 29.5% of the land in the State of Washington to 86.5% of the land in the State of Nevada, an average of about 46%. Of the land in the State of New Mexico, 33.6% is federally owned. General Services Administration, Inventory Report on Real Property Owned by the United States Throughout the World as of June 30, 1974, at 17, 34, and App. I, table 4. Because federal reservations are normally found in the uplands of the Western States rather than the flatlands, the percentage of water flow originating in or flowing through the reservations is even more impressive. More than 60% of the average annual water yield in the 11 western States is from federal reservations. The percentages of average annual water yield range from a low of 56% in the Columbia–North Pacific water resource region to a high of 96% in the Upper Colorado region. In the Rio Grande water resource region, where the Rio Mimbres lies, 77% of the average runoff originates on federal reservations. C. Wheatley, C. Corker, T. Stetson, & D. Reed, Study of the Development, Management and Use of Water Resources on the Public Lands 402–406, and table 4 (1969).

4. * * * In *Cappaert,* Congress had given the President the power to reserve "objects of historic and scientific interest that are situated upon the lands owned or con-

trolled by the Government." American Antiquities Preservation Act, 34 Stat. 225, 16 U.S.C.A. § 431 et seq. Pursuant to this power, the President had reserved Devil's Hole as a national monument. Devil's Hole, according to the Presidential Proclamation, is " 'a unique subsurface remnant of the prehistoric chain of lakes which in Pleistocene times formed the Death Valley Lake System' "; it also contains " 'a peculiar race of desert fish, and zoologists have demonstrated that this race of fish, which is found nowhere else in the world, evolved only after the gradual drying up of the Death Valley Lake System isolated this fish population from the original ancestral stock that in Pleistocene times was common to the entire region.' " 426 U.S. at 132. As the Court concluded, the pool was reserved specifically to preserve its scientific interest, principal of which was the Devil's Hole pupfish. Without a certain quantity of water, these fish would not be able to spawn and would die. This quantity of water was therefore impliedly reserved when the monument was proclaimed. Id., at 141. The Court, however, went on to note that the pool "need only be preserved, consistent with the intention expressed in the Proclamation, to the extent necessary to preserve its scientific interest.... The District Court thus tailored its injunction, very appropriately, to *minimal need,* curtailing pumping only to the extent necessary to preserve an adequate water level at Devil's Hole, thus implementing the stated objectives of the Proclamation."

intent in the field of federal-state jurisdiction with respect to allocation of water. Where Congress has expressly addressed the question of whether federal entities must abide by state water law, it has almost invariably deferred to the state law. See *California v. United States* [438 U.S.] at 653–670, 678–679. Where water is necessary to fulfill the very purposes for which a federal reservation was created, it is reasonable to conclude, even in the face of Congress' express deference to state water law in other areas, that the United States intended to reserve the necessary water. Where water is only valuable for a secondary use of the reservation, however, there arises the contrary inference that Congress intended, consistent with its other views, that the United States would acquire water in the same manner as any other public or private appropriator.

* * *

II

A

* * *

The United States contends that Congress intended to reserve minimum instream flows for aesthetic, recreational, and fish-preservation purposes. An examination of the limited purposes for which Congress authorized the creation of national forests, however, provides no support for this claim. In the mid– and late–1800's many of the forests on the public domain were ravaged and the fear arose that the forest lands might soon disappear, leaving the United States with a shortage both of timber and of watersheds with which to encourage stream flows while preventing floods. It was in answer to these fears that in 1891 Congress authorized the President to "set apart and reserve, in any State or Territory having public land bearing forests, in any part of the public lands wholly or in part covered with timber or undergrowth, whether of commercial value or not, as public reservations." Creative Act of March 3, 1891, 26 Stat. 1095, 1103, 16 U.S.C.A. § 471 (repealed 1976).

The Creative Act of 1891 unfortunately did not solve the forest problems of the expanding Nation. To the dismay of the conservationists, the new national forests were not adequately attended and regulated; fires and indiscriminate timber cutting continued their toll. To the anguish of Western settlers, reservations were frequently made indiscriminately. President Cleveland, in particular, responded to pleas of conservationists for greater protective measures by reserving some 21 million acres of "generally settled" forest land on February 22, 1897. President Cleveland's action drew immediate and strong protest from Western Congressmen who felt that the "hasty and ill considered" reservation might prove disastrous to the settlers living on or near these lands.

Congress' answer to these continuing problems was three fold. It suspended the President's Executive Order of February 22, 1897; it carefully defined the purposes for which national forests could in the future be reserved; and it provided a charter for forest management and economic uses within the forests. Organic Administration Act of June 4, 1897, 30 Stat. 31, 16 U.S.C.A. § 473 et seq. In particular, Congress provided

"No national forest shall be established, except to improve and protect the forest within the boundaries, or for the purpose of securing favorable conditions of water flows, and to furnish a continuous supply of timber for the use and necessities of citizens of the United States; but it is not the purpose or intent of these provisions, or of [the Creative Act of 1891], to authorize the inclusion therein of lands more valuable for the mineral therein, or for agricultural purposes, than for forest purposes." 30 Stat. 35, as amended, 16 U.S.C.A. § 475 (1976 ed.) (emphasis added).

The legislative debates surrounding the Organic Administration Act of 1897 and its predecessor bills demonstrate that Congress intended national forests to be reserved for only two purposes—"[t]o conserve the water flows and to furnish a continuous supply of timber for the people." 30 Cong. Rec. 967 (1897) (Cong. McRae). See *United States v. Grimaud*, 220 U.S. 506, 515 (1911). National forests were not to be reserved for aesthetic, environmental, recreational, or wildlife-preservation purposes.

"The objects for which the forest reservation should be made are the protection of the forest growth against destruction by fire and ax, and preservation of forest conditions upon which water conditions and water flow are dependent. The purpose, therefore, of this bill is to maintain favorable forest conditions, without excluding the use of these reservations for other purposes. They are not parks set aside for nonuse, but have been established for economic reasons." 30 Cong. Rec. 966 (1897) (Cong. McRae).

Administrative regulations at the turn of the century confirmed that national forests were to be reserved for only these two limited purposes.

Any doubt as to the relatively narrow purposes for which national forests were to be reserved is removed by comparing the broader language Congress used to authorize the establishment of national parks. In 1916, Congress created the National Park Service and provided that the

"fundamental purpose of said parks, monuments, and reservations ... is to conserve the scenery and the natural and historic objects and the wild life therein and to provide for the enjoyment of the same ... unimpaired for the enjoyment of future generations." National Park Service Act of 1916, 39 Stat. 535, 16 U.S.C. § 1 et seq.

* * *

B

[Petitioner's] claim that Congress intended to reserve water for recreation and wildlife-preservation is not only inconsistent with Congress' failure to recognize these goals as purposes of the national forests, but would also defeat the very purposes for which Congress did create the national forest system.

* * *

C

In 1960, Congress passed the Multiple–Use Sustained–Yield Act of 1960, 74 Stat. 215, 16 U.S.C.[A.] § 528 et seq., which provides

"It is the policy of Congress that the national forests are established and shall be administered for outdoor recreation, range, timber, watershed, and wildlife and fish purposes. The purposes of Sections 528 to 531 of this title are declared to be supplemental to, but not in derogation of, the purposes for which the national forests were established as set forth in the [Organic Administration Act of 1897.]"

* * * While we conclude that the Multiple–Use Sustained–Yield Act of 1960 was intended to broaden the purposes for which national forests had previously been administered, we agree that Congress did not intend to thereby expand the reserved rights of the United States.

* * * Without legislative history to the contrary, we are led to conclude that Congress did not intend in enacting the Multiple–Use Sustained–Yield Act of 1960 to reserve water for the *secondary* purposes there established.[22] A reservation of additional water could mean a substantial loss in the amount of water available for irrigation and domestic use, thereby defeating Congress' principal purpose of securing favorable conditions of water flow. Congress intended the national forests to be administered for broader purposes after 1960 but there is no indication that it believed the new purposes to be so crucial as to require a reservation of additional water. By reaffirming the primacy of a favorable water flow, it indicated the opposite intent.

III

What we have said also answers the Government's contention that Congress intended to reserve water from the Rio Mimbres for stockwatering purposes. The United States issues permits to private cattle owners to graze their stock on the Gila National Forest and provides for stockwatering at various locations along the Rio Mimbres. The United States contends that, since Congress clearly foresaw stockwatering on national forests, reserved rights must be recognized for this purpose. * * *

While Congress intended the national forests to be put to a variety of uses, including stockwatering, not inconsistent with the two principal purposes of the forests, stockwatering was not itself a direct purpose of reserving the land. If stockwatering could not take place on the Gila

---

22. We intimate no view as to whether Congress, in the 1960 Act, authorized the subsequent reservation of national forests out of public lands to which a broader doctrine of reserved water rights might apply.

National Forest, Congress' purposes in reserving the land would not be defeated. * * *

IV

Congress intended that water would be reserved only where necessary to preserve the timber or to secure favorable water flows for private and public uses under state law. This intent is revealed in the purposes for which the national forest system was created and Congress' principled deference to state water law in the Organic Administration Act of 1897 and other legislation. * * *

■ MR. JUSTICE POWELL, with whom MR. JUSTICE BRENNAN, MR. JUSTICE WHITE, and MR. JUSTICE MARSHALL join, dissenting in part.

I agree with the Court that the implied-reservation doctrine should be applied with sensitivity to its impact upon those who have obtained water rights under state law and to Congress' general policy of deference to state water law. I also agree that the Organic Administration Act of 1897, 30 Stat. 11, cannot fairly be read as evidencing an intent to reserve water for recreational or stockwatering purposes in the national forests.

I do not agree, however, that the forests which Congress intended to "improve and protect" are the still, silent, lifeless places envisioned by the Court. In my view, the forests consist of the birds, animals, and fish—the wildlife—that inhabit them, as well as the trees, flowers, shrubs, and grasses. I therefore would hold that the United States is entitled to so much water as is necessary to sustain the wildlife of the forests, as well as the plants. I also add a word concerning the impact of the Court's holding today on future claims by the United States that the reservation of particular national forests impliedly reserved instream flows.

I

My analysis begins with the language of the statute. The Organic Administration Act of 1897, as amended, 16 U.S.C.[A.] § 475, provides in pertinent part:

> "No national forest shall be established, except to improve and protect the forest within the boundaries, or for the purpose of securing favorable conditions of water flows, and to furnish a continuous supply of timber for the use and necessities of citizens of the United States . . ."

Although the language of the statute is not artful, a natural reading would attribute to Congress an intent to authorize the establishment of national forests for three purposes, not the two discerned by the Court. The New Mexico Supreme Court gave the statute its natural reading in this case when it wrote:

> "The Act limits the purposes for which the national forests are authorized to: 1) improving and protecting the forest, 2) securing favorable conditions of water flows, and 3) furnishing a continuous

supply of timber." *Mimbres Valley Irrigation Co. v. Salopek*, 412, 564 P.2d 615, 617 (1977).

Congress has given the statute the same reading, stating that under the Organic Administration Act of 1897 national forests may be established for "the purposes of improving and protecting the forest, securing favorable conditions of water flows, or to furnish a continuous supply of timber ..." H.R.Rep. No. 1551, 86th Cong., 2d Sess., 4 (1960).

* * * It is inconceivable that Congress envisioned the forests it sought to preserve as including only inanimate components such as the timber and flora. Insofar as the Court holds otherwise, the 55th Congress is maligned and the Nation is the poorer, and I dissent.

II

Contrary to the Court's intimations, I see no inconsistency between holding that the United States impliedly reserved the right to instream flows, and what the Court views as the underlying purposes of the 1897 Act. The national forests can regulate the flow of water—which the Court views as "the very purpose for which Congress did create the national forest system"—only for the benefit of appropriators who are downstream from the reservation. The reservation of an instream flow is not a consumptive use; it does not subtract from the amount of water that is available to downstream appropriators. Reservation of an instream flow therefore would be perfectly consistent with the purposes of the 1897 Act as construed by the Court.

I do not dwell on this point, however, for the Court's opinion cannot be read as holding that the United States never reserved instream flows when it set aside national forests under the 1897 Act. The State concedes, quite correctly on the Court's own theory, that even in this case "the United States is not barred from asserting that rights to minimum instream flows might be necessary for erosion control or fire protection on the basis of the recognized purposes of watershed management and the maintenance of timber." Brief for Respondent. Thus, if the United States proves, in this case or others, that the reservation of instream flows is necessary to fulfill the purposes discerned by the Court, I find nothing in the Court's opinion that bars it from asserting this right.

NOTES

1. In *New Mexico,* the Supreme Court relied heavily upon one of the few cases in which the government has asserted non-Indian reserved rights that were in direct conflict with established uses under state water law, Cappaert v. United States, 426 U.S. 128, 96 S.Ct. 2062, 48 L.Ed.2d 523 (1976), discussed in footnote 4 of the principal case. Devil's Hole, a deep cavern in Nevada containing an underground pool inhabited by a unique species of desert fish, was reserved as a national monument by a presidential proclamation in 1952. In 1968, the Cappaerts, who own a ranch nearby, began pumping groundwater coming from the same source as the water in

Devil's Hole, thereby reducing the water level in the underground pool to levels that endangered the fish. The United States sought an injunction to limit the pumping, which the district court granted and the court of appeals approved. The Supreme Court, in addition to affirming the lower courts by holding that sufficient water had been reserved to maintain the level of the underground pool, discussed the reserved rights doctrine:

> This Court has long held that when the Federal Government withdraws its land from the public domain and reserves it for a federal purpose, the Government, by implication, reserves appurtenant water then unappropriated to the extent needed to accomplish the purpose of the reservation. In so doing the United States acquires a reserved right in unappropriated water which vests on the date of the reservation and is superior to the rights of future appropriators. Reservation of water rights is empowered by the Commerce Clause, Art. I, § 8, which permits federal regulation of navigable streams, and the Property Clause, Art. IV, § 3, which permits federal regulation of federal lands. The doctrine applies to Indian reservations and other federal enclaves, encompassing water rights in navigable and nonnavigable streams.

* * *

> In determining whether there is a federally reserved water right implicit in a federal reservation of public land, the issue is whether the Government intended to reserve unappropriated and thus available water. Intent is inferred if the previously unappropriated waters are necessary to accomplish the purposes for which the reservation was created. See, e.g., *Arizona v. California,* [373 U.S.,] at 599–601; *Winters v. United States,* [207 U.S.,] at 576. Both the District Court and the Court of Appeals held that the 1952 Proclamation expressed an intention to reserve unappropriated water, and we agree. The Proclamation discussed the pool in Devil's Hole in four of the five preambles and recited that the "pool ... should be given special protection." Since a pool is a body of water, the protection contemplated is meaningful only if the water remains; the water right reserved by the 1952 Proclamation was thus explicit, not implied.

* * *

> The implied-reservation-of-water-rights doctrine, however, reserves only that amount of water necessary to fulfill the purpose of the reservation, no more. *Arizona v. California,* [373 U.S.,] at 600–601. Here the purpose of reserving Devil's Hole Monument is preservation of the pool. Devil's Hole was reserved "for the preservation of the unusual features of scenic, scientific, and educational interest." The Proclamation notes that the pool contains "a peculiar race of desert fish * * * which is found nowhere else in the world" and that the "pool is of ... outstanding scientific importance ..." The pool need only be preserved, consistent with the intention expressed in the Proclamation, to the extent necessary to preserve its scientific interest. The fish are one of the features of scientific interest. The preamble noting the scientific interest of the pool follows the preamble describ-

ing the fish as unique; the Proclamation must be read in its entirety. Thus, as the District Court has correctly determined, the level of the pool may be permitted to drop to the extent that the drop does not impair the scientific value of the pool as the natural habitat of the species sought to be preserved. * * *

Id. at 138–41.

The events preceding and following the *Cappaert* decision have been summarized:

> The 1960s witnessed the beginning of major physical changes in Ash Meadows [near the southern Nevada desert wetland area occupied by the pupfish], as a large farming operation came to the area. With cultivation of the land and installation of an extensive irrigation system, the water level in the springs decreased. This activity was well on its way toward causing the extinction of the endangered Devil's Hole pupfish and several other endemic species until a Supreme Court decision in 1976 limited the withdrawal of groundwater in Ash Meadows. This court decision forced the farming operation to close.
>
> In 1980, a land development company bought the farming operation's approximately 13,000 acres of land and promptly announced plans for the construction of its first 4000–lot subdivision, one of several it intended to develop in Ash Meadows. With the construction of roads and the clearing of land adjacent to springs, several of the endangered plants and animals were pushed to the brink of extinction Fortunately for the wildlife, these activities allowed conservationists to invoke the protective measures of the Endangered Species Act of 1973. And once the destructive actions of the developers had been halted the Nature Conservancy, a national conservation organization, began discussions with the owning company to purchase its land in Ash Meadows. In 1984, The Nature Conservancy purchased the 12,614 acres of Ash Meadows held by the developer and subsequently sold it to the US Fish and Wildlife Service This land plus additional public domain lands in the area are now part of the recently established Ash Meadows National Wildlife Refuge.

James D. Williams & Ronald M. Nowak, *Vanishing Species in Our Own Backyard: Extinct Fish and Wildlife of the United States and Canada,* in The Last Extinction 107, 127–28 (Les Kaufman & Kenneth Mallory eds., 1986). Even after pumping was restricted, the pupfish population continued to decline due to various causes. In 2006, only 36 were counted compared to 500 in the mid–1990s. However, chances of the pupfish's survival may be improving. After federal scientists began feeding the fish to compensate for a shortage of nutrients, the population increased to 126 in the Fall of 2008. See *A tiny fish's upward move; Imperiled Devil's Hole Pupfish, found only in a deep desert pool, sees numbers increase,* The Los Angeles Times, Oct. 4, 2008, at B1. The relationship between the federal Endangered Species Act and water law is explored *supra* p. 737.

2. Does *New Mexico* rule out reserved rights for instream flows on the public lands? In United States v. Denver, 656 P.2d 1 (Colo.1982), the Colorado Supreme Court held that recreational boating was clearly not within the purposes of the Dinosaur National Monument, pursuant to the federal Antiquities Act of 1906, 16 U.S.C.A. § 431 (which protects "objects of historic and scientific interest"), but remanded the question of "whether the reservation purpose of the Monument includes preservation of fish habitats." Id. at 36. On remand, the water court reviewed the documents leading up to the monument's creation and found that "neither the Presidential Proclamation nor the relevant underlying documents contemporaneous with its issuance suggests that fishes or other wildlife were thought by the President to be of scientific, biological, or historic importance at the time the reservation was made." In the Matter of the Application for Water Rights of the United States of America in Dinosaur National Monument, District Court, Water Division No. 6, Colorado, Case No. W–85 (March 21, 1985).

The *Denver* case also ruled that the U.S. Forest Service could present evidence on the amount of water needed for "channel maintenance" for the purpose of "preserving favorable conditions of water flows." In one trial court, the United States then attempted to show (with evidence from the field of fluvial geomorphology) that certain flushing flows were necessary to maintain the stream channel and thereby to "conserve the water flows" consistent with the Forest Service Organic Act. The water court rejected the claim finding that there was "little evidence of observed ill effects" on the channel from years of irrigation diversions and water storage. Further, the court was unimpressed with the expert testimony and theories saying they "gave a scientific tone to what was essentially speculation." According to the court, if a claim of reserved rights for instream flows for channel maintenance is to succeed it will be "only to a reasonable degree consistent with both the requirements of stream flows and the necessities of efficient irrigation and domestic use." In the Matter of the Amended Application of the United States of America for Reserved Water Rights in the Platte River, District Court, Water Division No. 1, Colorado, Case No. W–8439–76 (February 12, 1993).

3. Can the federal government be compelled to assert reserved rights? In Sierra Club v. Andrus, 487 F.Supp. 443 (D.D.C.1980), the Sierra Club argued that the United States had a public trust duty to participate in a state water rights adjudication in southern Utah because proposed energy development projects threatened to jeopardize the future assertion of reserved rights. The district court held that although the issue was not ripe, "in the event of a real and immediate water supply threat to the scenic, natural, historic or biotic resource values of the Glen Canyon National Recreation Area or the Grand Canyon National Park, the Secretary [of Interior] must take appropriate action." Id. at 448. The Sierra Club appealed only the district court's refusal to decide if the Federal Land Policy and Management Act, 43 U.S.C.A. §§ 1701–1784, "confers by implication federal reserved water rights." In the meantime, the United States did join the state proceeding. The court of appeals expressed grave doubts about instructing the United States to take a particular position in litigation and rejected the Sierra Club's argument that reserved rights attach in the absence of a withdrawal of land from the public domain and reservation of the land for a specific use. Sierra Club v. Watt, 659 F.2d 203, 206 (D.C.Cir.1981).

The Sierra Club later sued to force the federal government to file reserved water right claims for twenty-four designated wilderness areas on national forest lands in Colorado. The district court held that the establishment of these wilderness areas did create reserved water rights, but that the government had no statutory duty to assert these rights in state water right adjudications; the court thus refused to order the government to file wilderness reserved right claims in the Colorado courts. Sierra Club v. Block, 622 F.Supp. 842 (D.Colo. 1985). The Tenth Circuit declined to reach the merits on appeal because it held that the case was not ripe. Sierra Club v. Yeutter, 911 F.2d 1405 (10th Cir. 1990). The court found the issues unfit for judicial review, largely because the government had taken no final action regarding the possible reserved right claims. It also found that the plaintiffs would not be harmed by delaying review until some water development activity caused a more immediate threat to wilderness values. The court reached its decision on ripeness after stating that the government's failure to assert claims would be reviewable "only if its inaction is irreconcilable with the [Wilderness] Act's mandate to preserve the wilderness character of the wilderness areas." Id. at 1415. A more recent Supreme Court decision suggests, however, that the government's failure to claim reserved water rights would ordinarily be unreviewable in the absence of a specific statutory command. Norton v. Southern Utah Wilderness Alliance, 542 U.S. 55, 124 S.Ct. 2373, 159 L.Ed.2d 137 (2004). The Court in that case denied review of a claim that an agency failed to exclude off-road vehicles from wilderness study areas and therefore failed to prevent the impairment of these areas' wilderness characteristics, declaring that agency inaction is reviewable under the APA "only where a plaintiff asserts that an agency failed to take a *discrete* agency action that it is *required to take.*" Id. at 64 (emphasis original).

4. Given its acknowledged status as a trustee for Indian tribes, does the United States have less discretion over whether and to what extent it will assert Indian reserved water rights? After a district judge admonished federal officials that the Secretary had a trust responsibility to protect Indian water rights (Pyramid Lake Paiute Tribe of Indians v. Morton, 354 F.Supp. 252 (D.D.C.1972)) the Supreme Court declined to correct the underlying inequity caused by the government's early disregard for the water rights of the same tribe and refused to allow the tribe itself to reopen the adjudication. It cited the value of not disturbing non-Indian expectations implicit in notions of finality and res judicata in water rights decisions. Nevada v. United States, 463 U.S. 110, 103 S.Ct. 2906, 77 L.Ed.2d 509 (1983).

In the Truckee–Carson–Pyramid Lake Water Rights Settlement Act of 1990, Title II of Pub. L. No. 101–618, 104 Stat. 3294, Congress intervened to accomplish what the Interior Department and courts refused to do—assure more water for Pyramid Lake. The dedication of more water to maintaining the Pyramid Lake fishery has forced making the Truckee–Carson Irrigation District more efficient. Not only is less water available to the district, but return flows to the wildlife refuge have been decreased. See *infra* p. 1026.

High Country Citizens' Alliance v. Norton

United States District Court for the District of Colorado, 2006.
448 F.Supp.2d 1235.

■ CLARENCE A. BRIMMER, DISTRICT JUDGE, sitting by designation.

The Black Canyon of the Gunnison National Park (the Black Canyon or the canyon) is located in west-central Colorado in the center of the Gunnison River Basin. This action involves the right to water from the Gunnison River for the preservation of the canyon.

* * *

In 1933, acting pursuant to the Antiquities Act of 1906, 16 U.S.C. § 431, President Herbert Hoover designated the Black Canyon of the Gunnison as a national monument "for the preservation of the spectacular gorges and additional features of scenic, scientific, and educational interest." * * *

The final major development within the Gunnison River Basin was the construction of the Aspinall Reservoirs by the United States Bureau of Reclamation. The reservoirs were authorized by Congress in the Colorado River Storage Project Act of 1956. The act authorized the Secretary of the Interior to construct four storage projects, including the Aspinall Unit on the Gunnison River above the Black Canyon * * *.

The Aspinall Unit is comprised of a series of three dams which begin about a half-mile upstream from the Black Canyon, the Blue Mesa Dam and Reservoir, the Morrow Point Dam and Reservoir, and Crystal Dam and Reservoir. The Aspinall Reservoirs have significantly altered the natural flow regime of the Gunnison River upstream from the Black Canyon by diverting and regulating flows.

* * *

In 1999, taking into account the Black Canyon's ecological, geological, scenic, historical and wildlife features, Congress passed the Black Canyon Act which upgraded the Black Canyon national monument to a national park. 16 U.S.C. §§ 410fff, 410fff–2. In upgrading the monument to a national park, Congress provided that nothing in the Black Canyon Act affected any water right in existence and that any new water right that the Secretary of the Interior determined necessary for the purposes of the act would be established in accordance with the procedural and substantive requirements of the laws of Colorado. 16 U.S.C. § 410fff–8(b)

* * *

In 1952, Congress enacted the McCarran Amendment which permitted the determination of federal water rights by state courts. The McCarran Amendment eventually led to claims by the United States in the Colorado District Courts in and for Water Divisions 4, 5, and 6 (Colorado water court) for reserved water rights covering national forests and monuments, including the Black Canyon of the Gunnison National Monument. On March 6, 1978, after several years of proceedings, the water court issued an interlocutory decree awarding the United States an absolute and conditional water right for the Black Canyon (the "water court decree"). The water court decree granted the United States a "conditional and absolute" right to a quantity of water necessary to conserve and maintain in an unimpaired condition the scenic, aesthetic, natural, and historic objects of the monument, as well as the wildlife in the monument, in order that the monument might provide a source of recreation and enjoyment for all generations. This purpose includes the utilization of water in the form of direct flow, storage rights, transportation rights, and well rights for the development, conservation, and management of resident and migratory wildlife; forest improvement and protections; wilderness preservation uses; uses for fish culture, conservation, habitat protection and management, including but not limited to, minimum stream flows as are necessary to insure the continued nutrition, growth, conservation, and reproduction of those species of fish which inhabited such waters on the applicable reservation dates, or those species of fish which are later introduced. The decree recognized the United States' priority dates of 1933, 1938 and 1939.

The water court decree directed the United States to file with the court a final and specific quantification of the amount of water necessary to fulfill the purposes for which the land was reserved. The decree provided that, "Such quantification shall take the form of an application to make a conditional water right absolute and shall be subject to the notice and hearing requirements of Colorado law." Twenty-three years later, in January, 2001, the United States filed an application to quantify the water right of the Black Canyon (2001 quantification application). In the 2001 quantification application, the United States claimed a year-round base instream flow of 300 cubic feet per second (cfs) and higher peak and shoulder flows tied to the expected natural spring run-off each year. The priority date of the right claimed was March 2, 1933.

The federal Defendants note that one of the difficulties faced by the government in developing the 2001 quantification application was reconciling the congressional purpose of the Black Canyon with other federal agencies' mandates requiring the use of the water of the Gunnison River. According to the federal Defendants, those agencies include the Bureau of Reclamation which operates the Aspinall Unit, the Department of Energy's Western Area Power Administration which markets the hydroelectric power produced at the Aspinall Unit, the Bureau of Land Management which manages the Gunnison Gorge National Recreation Area immediately below the Black Canyon, and the Fish and Wildlife Service which has responsibility over endangered fish downstream from the Black Canyon in the Colorado River. To address the concerns of these agencies, a remark was added to the 2001 quantification application that the Secretary of the Interior would confer with the agencies and other affected interests in implementing the claim. * * *

More than 380 parties filed statements in opposition to the 2001 quantification application. The Colorado water court granted two stays so that the United States could enter into settlement discussions with some of the parties opposing the application. It is not clear who participated in the negotiations concerning settlement.

On April 2, 2003, the United States Department of the Interior and the Colorado Water Conservation Board (CWCB), a division of the Colorado Department of Natural Resources, entered into an agreement as to the amount of water the National Park Service would be entitled to receive for the Black Canyon (the April agreement). The parties agreed that the National Park Service would relinquish its reserved right to peak and shoulder flows and claim a year-round base flow of the lesser of 300 cfs or natural flow. This base flow would have a 1933 priority date. The parties also agreed that the CWCB would seek to appropriate additional instream flow water under Colorado law with a 2003 priority date. * * *

On July 31, 2003, the United States and the State of Colorado entered into a Memorandum of Agreement (July agreement) as contemplated by the April agreement. The July agreement recited that:

> H. ... [the April agreement] addresses two water rights benefiting the Black Canyon.... The [April agreement] provides that the Park Service will hold a reserved water right for 300 cfs or natural flow, whichever is less, with a 1933 priority date, and the Board will hold an instream flow water right under Colorado law with a 2003 priority date, which will be for water beyond that which satisfies present and future obligations of the authorized purposes of Aspinall, as specified in the Colorado River Storage Project Act, 43 U.S.C. § 620 et seq. as in effect on April 2, 2003, and under the Aspinall Unit's existing water rights decrees obtained under Colorado law.

* * *

Plaintiffs commenced this action in September, 2003 in response to the April and July agreements.

Plaintiffs' motion to set aside agency action challenges the relinquishment of federal water rights on four bases:

1. The April and July agreements are major federal actions that may significantly affect the environment but were undertaken without the environmental impact analysis mandated by the National Environmental Policy Act (NEPA).

2. The federal Defendants' entry into the April and July agreements unlawfully delegated to the State of Colorado responsibility for the performance of duties that Congress consigned to the federal Defendants.

3. The federal Defendants unlawfully disposed of federal property without Congressional authorization.

4. The federal Defendants' entry into the April and July agreements violated their nondiscretionary duties to protect the Black Canyon's resources.

* * *

The Court has carefully analyzed and considered the federal Defendants' and the intervenor Defendants' thorough history of the Gunnison River and the needs and demands for the river water. The Gunnison River unquestionably provides a critical water supply for numerous users. The Defendants clearly describe the competing interests of the state of Colorado and the upper and lower basin states for this invaluable resource. Defendants contend the competing needs for the river water justified entering into the April and July agreements, and that the agreements were a creative solution to meeting multiple needs. In fact, the federal Defendants present their case from a position of urgency on the part of the Bureau of Reclamation and the present and future users of the Aspinall unit.

The Court recognizes that the agreements entered into by the federal Defendants and the state of Colorado bring a sense of relief to a number of users of the river because the agreements eliminate uncertainty created by competition for a crucial water supply. The critical and competing nature of the interests involved in this case, however, illustrate the magnitude of the action which the Defendants have undertaken in entering into the April and July agreements. * * *

The federal Defendants perceive the April and July agreements as a clever compromise which will benefit the significant interests involved. In fact, the federal Defendants suggest that even after public consideration of the 2001 quantification application by the water court, the Black Canyon would have most likely received only the base amount of 300 cfs of water anyway. In their zeal to reach a resolution to the competing interests, however, the Defendants ignore the right of the public to be involved in such a major and significant decision. Unlike a decision to place a call on a water right in a given year, relinquishing a water right with a 1933 priority date is permanent. Although an annual decision as to how much water to release and whether or not to place a call on senior water rights may be a discretionary matter best left to the National Park Service and the Secretary of the Interior, the same cannot be said for permanently passing up a priority date. A permanent relinquishment of a water right with a 1933 priority date for such a scientifically, ecologically and historically important national park must be viewed as a major action requiring compliance with NEPA. * * *

* * *

The National Park Service Organic Act of 1916 created the National Park Service to promote and regulate the use of national parks so as to "conserve the scenery and the natural and historic objects and the wild life therein and to provide for the enjoyment of the same in such manner and by such means as will leave them unimpaired for the enjoyment of future generations." 16 U.S.C. § 1. The National Park Service was consequently charged with the administration of the Black Canyon of the Gunnison National Park. 16 U.S.C. § 410fff–2(b). The Black Canyon of the Gunnison National Park and Gunnison Gorge National Conservation Area Act of 1999 affirmed that the Black Canyon Monument "was established for the preservation of its spectacular gorges and additional features of scenic, scientific, and educational interests." 16 U.S.C. § 410fff(1).

* * *

Plaintiffs complain that although the July agreement recognizes that the "National Park Service is the federal agency responsible for protecting the natural resources, including the water resources, of the Black Canyon of the Gunnison National Park," the April agreement delegates a significant portion of this responsibility to the state of Colorado. The responsibility is delegated through reliance on the Colorado Water Conservation Board to produce instream flows above 300 cfs when the Park Service concedes that flows above 300 cfs are necessary to preserve the canyon.

Plaintiffs contend that the delegation of authority and responsibility to the Colorado Water Conservation Board is prohibited. This Court agrees. While federal agency officials may subdelegate their decision-making authority to subordinates absent evidence of contrary congressional intent, they may not subdelegate to outside entities—private or sovereign—absent affirmative evidence of authority to do so. * * *

Despite the water court's decree of a quantity sufficient to meet the needs of the Black Canyon, the federal Defendants insist that because the water court has not decreed an exact amount of water it deems necessary to fulfill the needs of the canyon, the United States has somehow not given up a water right which the canyon needs. The reality of the matter, however, is that the federal Defendants reached a compromise which satisfied a number of interests. The Court does not judge the value of the compromise, but does judge the manner in which the compromise was reached. The compromise was reached through delegating the determination and acquisition of the proper peak and shoulder flows to the state of Colorado. The federal Defendants urge that the compromise was innovative considering all of the demands on the Gunnison River. Such a delegation, however, was neither necessary nor permissible. The Colorado water court will be able to determine the exact amount of water necessary for the Black Canyon, and that water, with its 1933 priority, will preserve the canyon long after this administration and its successors have left office.

Plaintiffs also challenge the April and July agreements as a partial relinquishment of a federal reserved water right for the Black Canyon without specific authorization from Congress. Plaintiffs reason that the federal reserved water right for the Black Canyon is a property interest that cannot be given up without Congressional authorization. The federal and intervenor Defendants respond that the government has retained the entire property right awarded by the Colorado water court, and for this Court to decide otherwise would intrude upon the water court's jurisdiction.

[A] federal reserved water right constitutes property, not just from the time the right is quantified, but from the time the reservation is created. The right arises on the date of the reservation and continues to exist even if it has not been asserted:

> [W]hen the Federal Government withdraws its land from the public domain and reserves it for a federal purpose, the Government, by implication, reserves appurtenant water then unappropriated to the extent needed to accomplish the purpose of the reservation. In so doing the United States acquires a reserved right in unappropriated water which vests on the date of the reservation and is superior to the rights of future appropriators.

Cappaert v. United States, 426 U.S. at 138, 96 S.Ct. 2062.

The right to a volume of water necessary to serve the canyon's purpose arose when the United States established the Black Canyon of the Gunnison National Monument in 1933. There is consensus that the Black Canyon requires a greater quantity than the federal Defendants proposed in the 2003 amended quantification application. Accordingly, the decision to seek adjudication of a smaller amount than needed represents a disposition of federal property. Only Congress, and not an executive branch agency, can authorize the disposition of federal property. * * *

Plaintiffs allege that the April and July agreements and the relinquishment of a reserved water right in return for a an instream flow right held by the Colorado Water Conservation Board violate the duty to protect park resources imposed on the Park Service by the National Park Service Organic Act, the Black Canyon Act, and the Wilderness Act. Plaintiffs assert that the federal Defendants' actions were consequently arbitrary, capricious, and an abuse of discretion or otherwise not in accordance with law in violation of the Administrative Procedure Act (APA), 5 U.S.C. § 706(2)(A).

* * *

The evidence relied on by the federal Defendants and the Plaintiffs, and the April and July agreements themselves, show that the canyon needs periodic peak and shoulder flows. * * *

* * *

The federal Defendants acknowledge that the 2001 quantification application was filed three days before a change in administrations. * * *

This Court finds that the effect of the April and July agreements was actually to remove the administration of the Black Canyon resources from the National Park Service in direct contravention of the National Park Service Organic Act, the Black Canyon Act and the Wilderness Act. Unlike forgoing a call on the river in dry years, as contemplated by the 2001 quantification application, the April and July agreements were a means to deprive the National Park Service of ever exercising a right to peak and shoulder flows of the Gunnison River. The agreements protected the Black Canyon's competitors, and once the Colorado water court approved the 2003 amended quantification application, those opposing the amended application would have no recourse as res judicata would prevent the reopening of the quantification decree.

The April and July agreements also run counter to the evidence before the National Park Service. The parties to this action agree that the Black Canyon needs peak and shoulder flows. There is no indication that the canyon would be denied these flows by the Colorado water court. To the contrary, the Colorado water court specifically found that the Black Canyon would receive the water necessary to conserve and maintain the canyon for all generations. Accordingly, the National Park Service cannot rationally base the agreements on speculation that the water court might deny the canyon needed water.

Finally, this Court further finds that the federal Defendants' justification that the Secretary of the Interior entered into the agreements in an effort to compromise the needs of the Aspinall unit and the Black Canyon is no more than an after-the-fact rationalization by counsel. The 2001 quantification application included a remark that provided protection for the Aspinall unit and others. The April and July agreements were executed, however, to secure permanent priority for the Aspinall unit and other water interests. The agreements were not to ensure the protection of the canyon because the Black Canyon was already protected. The Court accordingly finds that it was arbitrary, capricious and an abuse of discretion to enter into the agreements and relinquish a 1933 priority to the full quantity of water necessary for the preservation of the Black Canyon. Such a relinquishment is nonsensical. * * *

NOW, THEREFORE, IT IS HEREBY ORDERED that the federal Defendants' entry into the April and July agreements is SET ASIDE. This matter is remanded to the National Park Service for further proceedings consistent with this decision. * * *

NOTES

1. Was it contrary to the McCarran Amendment's policy against piece-meal litigation to allow a federal court challenge to the proposed state court settlement of the Black Canyon reserved right? A divided Colorado Supreme Court said no, and upheld the water court's stay of the Black Canyon quantification proceeding pending resolution of the federal lawsuit:

> The scope of the waiver of sovereign immunity under the McCarran Amendment is not so broad that it allows state courts to evaluate or adjudicate the federal agency decision making processes leading the

United States to make a particular water application in a given case. The Environmental Opposers have brought claims in federal court that can only be decided by that court. Thus, there is no question that there will be both state and federal proceedings before the United States' reserved water right for the Black Canyon can be fully resolved. The federal case will decide whether the United States' amended application complied with the applicable federal law, and the state case will quantify the reserved water right.

In re Application for Water Rights of the United States of America, 101 P.3d 1072, 1080 (Colo. 2004). Justice Hobbs dissented, arguing that: "In my view, the plaintiffs' federal court litigation results in a piecemeal approach to the quantification and administration issues properly before the water court, the very result Congress sought to avoid" with the McCarran Amendment. Id. at 1085 (Hobbs, J., dissenting).

2. The Wild and Scenic Rivers Act of 1968 includes a rare, express statutory acknowledgment that reserved rights exist for instream flows. 16 U.S.C.A. §§ 1271–1287. The Act is designed to protect free flowing rivers from incompatible development projects and to provide for the management of land along the river corridor. Rivers may be designated for inclusion within the system either by an Act of Congress or by the Secretary of the Interior's approval of state legislation nominating a river for inclusion. The Act provides:

> (c) Reservation of waters for other purposes or in unnecessary quantities prohibited.

> Designation of any stream or portion thereof as a national wild, scenic or recreational river area shall not be construed as a reservation of the waters of such streams for purposes other than those specified in this Act, or in quantities greater than necessary to accomplish these purposes.

> (d) State jurisdiction over included streams.

> The jurisdiction of the States over waters of any stream included in a national wild, scenic or recreational river area shall be unaffected by this Act to the extent that such jurisdiction may be exercised without impairing the purposes of this Act or its administration.

16 U.S.C.A. § 1284(c)–(d). If the United States fails to claim reserved rights for a wild and scenic river in a McCarran Amendment adjudication, should a court order it to do so? The Idaho Supreme Court has unanimously held that the Wild and Scenic Rivers Act was an express, if imprecise, assertion of federal reserved water waters. Potlatch Corp. v. United States, 134 Idaho 912, 12 P.3d 1256 (2000). See also Potlatch Corp. v. United States, 134 Idaho 916, 12 P.3d 1260 (2000) (Hells Canyon National Recreation Area Act expressly reserved water).

3. Section 4(d)(6) of the federal Wilderness Act provides only that "[n]othing in this [Act] shall constitute an express or implied claim or denial on the part of the Federal Government to an exemption from state water law." 16 U.S.C.A. § 1133(d)(6). Thus, the issue is whether reserved rights could be implied from the purpose of the Wilderness Act. In 1999, the Idaho Supreme Court held in a 3–2 decision that the Wilderness Act of 1964 created implied reserved water rights and the amount of water needed to fulfill the Act's purpose of preserving wilderness values was all the unappropriated water. The majority reasoned that an implied reservation was compelled by Winters v. United States, 207 U.S. 564, 28 S.Ct. 207, 52 L.Ed. 340 (1908), because the text of the Wilderness Act contemplates that wilderness areas will be maintained in their natural state, which includes stream flows at the time of designation. In re SRBA Case No. 39576, 1999 WL 778325 (Idaho 1999). But then, in 2000 the court reversed itself in another 3–2 decision. In the meantime, Justice Silak, the author of the first opinion, had been defeated for retention in a vicious campaign that included attacks on the earlier decision. The 2000 majority reasoned that *United States v. New Mexico* taught that if the purpose of the reservation would not be entirely defeated for lack of water, the inference is that the United States would acquire any necessary water under state law. Potlatch Corp. v. United States, 134 Idaho 916, 12 P.3d 1260 (2000). Under this narrow standard, it concluded that the Wilderness Act was intended only to withdraw land from development rather than protect watersheds, in part, because "[a] review of the Frank Church papers brings home the reality that Senator Church would not have voted for the Wilderness Act but for his understanding that the Act would not cripple the economic growth of portions of Idaho outside the wilderness." See Karin P. Sheldon, *Water for Wilderness*, 76 Denv. U. L. Rev. 555 (1999). To simplify a very complex subject, statutory construction involves analyzing the text of the statute, the statute's general remedial purpose, and specific legislative intent as revealed by legislative history. Which factor influenced the Idaho Supreme Court? For a discussion of the litigation and a critical view of the Idaho decision, *see* Michael C. Blumm, *Reversing the Winters Doctrine?: Denying Reserved Water Rights for Idaho Wilderness and its Implications*, 73 U. Colo. L. Rev. 173 (2002).

The Idaho Supreme Court also has rejected any implied rights for the non-wilderness portions of the Sawtooth National Recreation Area in an extremely narrow interpretation of the Supreme Court's implied intent standard. State v. United States, 134 Idaho 940, 12 P.3d 1284 (2000). The 3–2 opinion conceded that the purpose of the Act was to protect the wilderness and non-wilderness portions from mining and to protect fish and wildlife values, but concluded that the purpose was "not simply to protect fish habitat, but rather to protect that habitat * * * from the dangers of unregulated mining operations." Id. at 1290. Government land use regulations fulfilled this objective and thus "it is clear that the purpose of the reservation will not be entirely defeated without water." Id. Fish & Wildlife Service v. State, 135 Idaho 655, 23 P.3d 117 (2001) continued the Idaho Supreme Court's implied intention jurisprudence and held that the United States could not claim reserved rights for a wildlife refuge consisting of 94 islands in the Snake River. Although the purpose of the refuge was to create sanctuaries for migratory birds to protect them from hunters and predators, and the existence of islands depends on the land being surrounded by water, the court found any inference of implied reserved rights would be inconsistent with the then prevailing policy of arid land reclamation.

United States v. Adair

United States Court of Appeals, Ninth Circuit, 1983.
723 F.2d 1394, cert. denied 467 U.S. 1252, 104 S.Ct. 3536, 82 L.Ed.2d 841.

■ Before KILKENNY, GOODWIN and FLETCHER, CIRCUIT JUDGES.

■ FLETCHER, CIRCUIT JUDGE:

* * *

I

BACKGROUND

* * *

A. *History of the Litigation Area*

The Klamath Indians have hunted, fished, and foraged in the area of the Klamath Marsh and upper Williamson River for over a thousand years. In 1864 the Klamath Tribe entered into a treaty with the United States whereby it relinquished its aboriginal claim to some 12 million acres of land in return for a reservation of approximately 800,000 acres in south-central Oregon. This reservation included all of the Klamath Marsh as well as large forested tracts of the Williamson River watershed. Treaty between the United States of America and the Klamath and Modoc Tribes and Yahooskin Band of Snake Indians, Oct. 14, 1864, 16 Stat. 707. Article I of the treaty gave the Klamath the exclusive right to hunt, fish, and gather on their reservation. Article II provided funds to help the Klamath adopt an agricultural way of life. 16 Stat. 708.

For 20 years, until 1887, the Klamath lived on their reservation under the terms of the 1864 treaty. In 1887 Congress passed the General Allotment Act, ch. 119, 24 Stat. 388 (1887) which fundamentally changed the nature of land ownership on the Klamath Reservation. Prior to the Act, the tribe held the reservation land in communal ownership. Pursuant to the terms of the Allotment Act, however, parcels of tribal land were granted to individual Indians in fee. Under the allotment system, approximately 25% of the original Klamath Reservation passed from tribal to individual Indian ownership. Over time, many of these individual allotments passed into non-Indian ownership.

The next major change in the pattern of land ownership on the Klamath Reservation occurred in 1954 when Congress approved the Klamath Termination Act. Under this Act, tribe members could give up their interest in tribal property for cash. A large majority of the tribe chose to do this. In order to meet the cash obligation, in 1961, the United States purchased much of the former Klamath Reservation. The balance of the reservation was placed in a private trust for the remaining tribe members. * * * In 1973, to complete implementation of the Klamath Termination Act, the United States condemned most of the tribal land held in trust. Payments from the condemnation proceeding and sale of the remaining trust land went to Indians still enrolled in the tribe. This final distribution of assets essentially extinguished the original Klamath Reservation as a source of tribal property.

* * *

B.   Proceedings in the District Court

In September of 1975, the United States filed suit in federal district court seeking a declaration of water rights within the Williamson River drainage [within the former Klamath Reservation]. In January of 1976, the State of Oregon initiated formal proceedings under state law to determine water rights in the Klamath Basin including that portion of the Williamson River drainage covered by the Government's suit. Later in 1976, the State of Oregon moved to intervene as a defendant in the United States suit. The Klamath Tribe also moved to intervene in the federal suit as a plaintiff. Both motions were granted. Subsequently, the State, joined by the individual defendants, moved for dismissal of the federal court water rights adjudication in favor of the state proceeding under the rule announced by the Supreme Court in *Colorado River Water Conservation District v. United States,* [*supra*, p. 854]. The district court in effect denied the defendants' motion to dismiss when on November 14, 1977, it entered a Pretrial Order to govern the conduct of the federal suit.

This order, in listing the issues to be decided, significantly limited the nature of the federal proceeding. The district court did not agree to decide any question concerning the actual quantification of water rights. * * *

III

WATER RIGHTS

The district court declared reserved water rights within the litigation area to the Klamath Tribe, the Government, individual Indians, and non-Indian successors to Indian land owners. * * *

A.   A Reservation of Water to Accompany the Tribe's Treaty Right to Hunt, Fish, and Gather

Article I of the 1864 treaty with the Klamath Tribe reserved to the Tribe the exclusive right to hunt, fish, and gather on its reservation. This right survived the Klamath Termination Act. The issue presented for decision in this case is whether, as the district court held, these hunting and fishing rights carry with them an implied reservation of water rights.

1.   Reservation of Water in the 1864 Treaty

* * * *New Mexico* and *Cappaert*, while not directly applicable to *Winters* doctrine rights on Indian reservations, *see* F. Cohen, *Handbook of*

Federal Indian Law 581–85 (1982 ed.), establish several useful guidelines. First, water rights may be implied only "[w]here water is necessary to fulfill the very purposes for which a federal reservation was created," and not where it is merely "valuable for a secondary use of the reservation." Second, the scope of the implied right is circumscribed by the necessity that calls for its creation. The doctrine "reserves only that amount of water necessary to fulfill the purpose of the reservation, no more." * * *

Article I of the Klamath Treaty expressly provides that the Tribe will have exclusive on-reservation fishing and gathering rights. * * * In view of the historical importance of hunting and fishing, and the language of Article I of the 1864 Treaty, we find that one of the "very purposes" of establishing the Klamath Reservation was to secure to the Tribe a continuation of its traditional hunting and fishing lifestyle. This was at the forefront of the Tribe's concerns in negotiating the treaty and was recognized as important by the United States as well.

At the same time, as the State and individual defendants argue, Articles II through V of the 1864 Treaty evince a purpose to convert the Klamath Tribe to an agricultural way of life. Article II provides that monies paid to the Tribe in consideration for the land ceded by the treaty "shall be expended * * * to promote the well-being of the Indians, advance them in civilization, *and especially agriculture,* and to secure their moral improvement and education." A similar focus on agriculture is reflected in the language of Articles III, IV and V. It is apparent that a second essential purpose in setting aside the Klamath Reservation, recognized by both the Tribe and the Government, was to encourage the Indians to take up farming.

Neither *Cappaert* nor *New Mexico* requires us to choose between these activities or to identify a single essential purpose which the parties to the 1864 Treaty intended the Klamath Reservation to serve. In fact, in *Colville Confederated Tribes v. Walton,* 647 F.2d 42 (9th Cir.), *cert. denied,* 454 U.S. 1092 (1981), this court found that provision of a "homeland for the Indians to maintain their agrarian society," as well as "preservation of the tribe's access to fishing grounds" were dual purposes behind establishment of the Colville Reservation. Consequently the court found an implied reservation of water to support both of these activities. President Grant established the Colville Reservation in a one-paragraph Executive Order that stated only that the land would be "set apart as a reservation for said Indians." Thus the court in *Colville* discovered the purposes of the reservation and implied water rights from a much less explicit text than that provided by the 1864 Klamath Treaty, Articles I through V. We therefore have no difficulty in upholding the district court's finding that at the time the Klamath Reservation was established, the Government and the Tribe intended to reserve a quantity of the water flowing through the reservation not only for the purpose of supporting Klamath agriculture, but also for the purpose of maintaining the Tribe's treaty right to hunt and fish on reservation lands.

A water right to support game and fish adequate to the needs of Indian hunters and fishers is not a right recognized as a part of the common law doctrine of prior appropriation followed in Oregon. Indeed, one of the standard requirements of the prior appropriation doctrine is that some diversion of the natural flow of a stream is necessary to effect a valid appropriation. But diversion of water is not required to support the fish and game that the Klamath Tribe take in exercise of their treaty rights. Thus the right to water reserved to further the Tribe's hunting and fishing purposes is unusual in that it is basically non-consumptive. * * * The holder of such a right is not entitled to withdraw water from the stream for agricultural, industrial, or other consumptive uses (absent independent consumptive rights). Rather, the entitlement consists of the right to prevent other appropriators from depleting the stream's waters below a protected level in any area where the non-consumptive right applies. * * *

2. Effect of the Klamath Termination Act on the Tribe's Hunting and Fishing Water Rights

In 1954, Congress terminated federal supervision of the Klamath Tribe. The state and individual appellants now argue that the Termination Act also abrogated any water rights reserved by the 1864 Treaty to accompany the Tribe's right to hunt and fish. Appellants contend that when federal supervision was terminated, former reservation lands were sold at full market value without limitations on use. They conclude that recognition of a reserved water right to sustain the Tribe's hunting and fishing rights would impose a servitude or limitation on the use of former reservation lands in contravention of the Termination Act policy of unencumbered sale.

Appellants' argument, however, overlooks the substantive language of the Termination Act,[20] the canons of construction for legislation affecting Indian Tribes, and the implications of our [previous] decision. * * * Section 564m(a) of the Termination Act provides, "[n]othing in sections 564–564w of this title shall abrogate any water rights of the tribe and its members." This provision admits no exception, nor can it be read to exclude reserved water rights. Congress presumably was aware of the importance of such rights to Indian tribes at the time it drafted section 564m of the Klamath Termination Act * * *.

* * * In sum, we agree with the district court that the water rights reserved to the Klamath Tribe by Treaty in 1864 were not abrogated by enactment of the Klamath Termination Act in 1954.

3. Priority of the Water Right Reserved to Accompany the Tribe's Treaty Right to Hunt and Fish

The district court found that the Tribe's water right accompanying its right to hunt and fish carried a priority date for appropriation of time

---

20. Appellants cite language from subsection 28(c) of the 1958 amendments to the Termination Act, 72 Stat. 817. Subsection (c) details the method for appraising the fair market value of Klamath Reservation lands: "each appraiser shall estimate the fair market value of such forest units and marshlands *as if they had been offered for sale on a competitive market without limitation on use* * * *." Id. (emphasis added.) These appraisal instructions cannot be read to dictate the substantive conditions of termination.

immemorial. *United States v. Adair*, 478 F. Supp. at 350. The State and individual appellants argue that an implied reservation of water cannot have a priority date earlier than establishment of the reservation. The Government and the Tribe argue that a pre-reservation priority date is appropriate for tribal water uses that pre-date establishment of the reservation. We have been unable to find any decisions that squarely address this issue. We therefore begin our analysis by turning to well-established principles of Indian treaty interpretation and Indian property rights for guidance.

Foremost among these is the principle that "the treaty is not a grant of rights to the Indians, but a grant of rights from them—a reservation of those not granted." Further, Indian treaties should be construed as the tribes would have understood them. And any ambiguity in a treaty must be resolved in favor of the Indians. A corollary of these principles, also recognized by the Supreme Court, is that when a tribe and the Government negotiate a treaty, the tribe retains all rights not expressly ceded to the Government in the treaty so long as the rights retained are consistent with the tribe's sovereign dependent status.

In 1864, at the time the Klamath entered into a treaty with the United States, the Tribe had lived in Central Oregon and Northern California for more than a thousand years. This ancestral homeland encompassed some 12 million acres. Within its domain, the Tribe used the waters that flowed over its land for domestic purposes and to support its hunting, fishing, and gathering lifestyle. This uninterrupted use and occupation of land and water created in the Tribe aboriginal or "Indian title" to all of its vast holdings. * * * The Supreme Court has specifically held that the Tribe had aboriginal title to timber on the Klamath Reservation. The Tribe's title also included aboriginal hunting and fishing rights, and by the same reasoning, an aboriginal right to the water used by the Tribe as it flowed through its homeland. * * *

With this background in mind, we examine the priority date attaching to the Klamath Tribe's reservation of water to support its hunting and fishing rights. In Article I of the 1864 Treaty the Tribe expressly ceded "all [its] right, title and claim" to most of its ancestral domain. In the same article, however, the Tribe reserved for its exclusive use and occupancy the lands that became the Klamath Reservation, the same lands that are the subject of the instant suit There is no indication in the treaty, express or implied, that the Tribe intended to cede any of its interest in those lands it reserved for itself. Nor is it possible that the Tribe would have understood such a reservation of land to include a relinquishment of its right to use the water as it had always used it on the land it had reserved as a permanent home. Further, we find no language in the treaty to indicate that the United States intended or understood the agreement to diminish the Tribe's rights in that part of its aboriginal holding reserved for its permanent occupancy and use. Accordingly, we agree with the district court that within the 1864 Treaty is a recognition of the Tribe's aboriginal water rights and a confirmation to the Tribe of a continued water right to support its hunting and fishing lifestyle on the Klamath Reservation.

Such water rights necessarily carry a priority date of time immemorial. The rights were not created by the 1864 Treaty, rather, the treaty confirmed the continued existence of these rights. * * * To assign the Tribe's hunting and fishing water rights the later, 1864, priority date argued for by the State and individual appellants would ignore one of the fundamental principles of prior appropriations law—that priority for a particular water right dates from the time of first use. Furthermore, an 1864 priority date might limit the scope of the Tribe's hunting and fishing water rights by reduction for any pre–1864 appropriations of water. This could extinguish rights the Tribe held before 1864 and intended to reserve to itself thereafter. Thus, we are compelled to conclude that where, as here, a tribe shows its aboriginal use of water to support a hunting and fishing lifestyle, and then enters into a treaty with the United States that reserves this aboriginal water use, the water right thereby established retains a priority date of first or immemorial use.[22] * * *

B. *Water Rights of Successors-in-Interest to Klamath Indian Allottees*

* * *

1. Indian Successors to Allotted Reservation Lands

* * * The scope of Indian irrigation rights is well settled. It is a right to sufficient water to "irrigate all the practicably irrigable acreage on the reservation." Individual Indian allottees have a right to use a portion of this reserved water. Moreover, the full measure of this right need not be exercised immediately. As with rights reserved to the Tribe, water may be used by Indian allottees for present and future irrigation needs.[25]

This right is limited here only by section 14 of the Klamath Termination Act, 25 U.S.C. § 564m (1976). This section provides, first, that "[n]othing in [The Termination Act] shall abrogate any water rights of the tribe and its members," and second, that "the laws of the State of Oregon

---

22. In the present case, the Klamath Tribe, as we have noted, has depended upon the waters in question to support its hunting and fishing activities for over 1,000 years. It would be inconsistent with the principles we follow in today's decision to hold that the priority of the Tribe's water rights is any less ancient than the "immemorial" use that has been made of them. See United States v. Shoshone Tribe, 304 U.S. 111, 117, 58 S.Ct. 794, 798, 82 L.Ed. 1213 (1938); F. Cohen, *Handbook of Federal Indian Law* 591 & n. 100 (1982).

25. The water rights of Indian irrigators, as the district court noted, are subordinate to the Tribe's right to water for support of its hunting and fishing lifestyle. 478 F. Supp. at 346. This hierarchy among Indian water rights arises, not from any implication in the 1864 treaty that the purpose of hunting and fishing should predominate over any of the other purposes for which the Klamath Reservation was established, but rather from the analytically separate question of what priority date for appropriation the various water rights reserved in the treaty carry. Analysis of this latter question, under the unique circumstances of this case, leads to the conclusion that the Tribe's hunting and fishing water rights carry an earlier priority date for appropriation, because of historical use, than do water rights for irrigation.

with respect to abandonment of water rights by non-use shall not apply to the tribe and its members until fifteen years after the date of the proclamation [of termination]." *Id*. The State and individual appellants argue that the second part of section 564m was meant to apply all Oregon water law, except that respecting abandonment of water rights by non-use, to the Tribe immediately upon the proclamation of termination.

* * *

In order to effectuate the Termination Act's explicit command that Klamath water rights survive unimpaired, we must interpret the second part of section 564m to mean that starting in 1976, fifteen years after the proclamation of termination in 1961, reserved water actually appropriated for use by members of the Tribe on allotments, could be lost under Oregon laws "with respect to abandonment of water rights by non-use." However, no other provision of Oregon water law that might preclude appropriation of the full measure of Klamath reserved water rights may be applied to the Tribe or its members consistently with the unequivocal language of protection in the first sentence of section 564m. To hold otherwise would sanction destruction of treaty rights in the absence of the required express Congressional approval.

2.   Non–Indian Successors to Allotted Reservation Lands

The district court held that:

> a non-Indian successor to an Indian allottee acquires an appurtenant right to water for the actual acreage under irrigation when he gets title from his Indian predecessor. The priority date of that right is 1864.

> The non-Indian also acquires a right, with an 1864 priority date, to water for additional acreage which he, with reasonable diligence, may place under irrigation.

478 F. Supp. at 349. The sole claim raised by the Tribe in its cross-appeal is to this aspect of the district court's decision.

The claim, however, is foreclosed by our recent decision in *Colville Confederated Tribes v. Walton*, 647 F.2d at 42. There we held the "[t]he full quantity of water available to the Indian allottee thus may be conveyed to the non-Indian purchaser." The limitations on this transfer, recognized in *Colville* are, first, that the non-Indian successor's right to water is "limited by the number of irrigable acres [of former reservation lands that] he owns," *id*, and second, that the non-Indian purchaser may lose the right to that quantity of water through non-use. Thus, citing the district court's opinion in the instant case, in *Colville,* we limited a non-Indian successor to lands allotted to a member of the Colville Tribe to the amount of water used by the Indian predecessor plus additional water that "he or she appropriates with reasonable diligence after the passage of title."

NOTES

1. *Adair* established the existence and certain aspects of the Klamath Tribes' water rights, but left the quantification of those rights to an Oregon state adjudication of Klamath Basin water rights. In 1999, the Oregon Water Resources Department's Adjudicator issued a "Summary and Preliminary Evaluation" of claims filed in that adjudication, in which the Adjudicator took the position that the tribes' instream flow claims "are proper if the record shows that the claimed amount is the minimum quantity of water necessary to protect treaty fish and wildlife resources as they existed in 1979," the year of the original *Adair* decision. The tribes and the United States believed that this standard was contrary to *Adair*, and that the instream flow reserved rights would be unduly reduced if the Oregon adjudication applied this standard. The United States returned to federal court, but the Ninth Circuit Court of Appeals held that the case was not ripe for federal judicial review. United States v. Braren, 338 F.3d 971 (9th Cir. 2003). "[T]he United States and the Tribes seek a clarification of the *Adair* standard to determine if the Preliminary Evaluation announced the right standard. That question can only be answered when the Adjudication is complete." Id. at 976. As of September 2008, 56 of the 64 Klamath tribal claims in the Klamath Basin Adjudication were still contested; by contrast, all of the 666 non-Indian claims had been settled, withdrawn, or otherwise resolved.

2. If reserved rights based on hunting and fishing have not yet been adjudicated, may federal water project operators nonetheless take account of these unquantified tribal claims to provide minimum lake levels and instream flows? *See* Joint Board of Control of the Flathead, Mission and Jocko Irrigation Districts v. U.S., 832 F.2d 1127 (9th Cir. 1987). A Bureau of Indian Affairs water project provided water for irrigation and for tribal fisheries on the Flathead Reservation, and in the midst of a drought the BIA established certain minimum flows and lake levels to protect fish habitat based on the tribes' not-yet-quantified reserved rights. Irrigators sued to overturn this decision and the district court issued an injunction, stating that the agency had a duty to make a "just and equal distribution" of all waters of the reservation. The Ninth Circuit overturned the injunction:

> The action of the BIA in establishing stream flow and pool levels necessary to protect tribal fisheries is not unreviewable. In making its determination, however, the BIA is acting as trustee for the Tribes. Because any aboriginal fishing rights secured by treaty are prior to all irrigation rights, neither the BIA nor the Tribes are subject to a duty of fair and equal distribution of reserved fishery waters. Only after fishery waters are protected does the BIA, acting as Officer-in-Charge of the irrigation project, have a duty to distribute fairly and equitably the *remaining* waters among irrigators of equal priority.

Id. at 1132 (emphasis original). The Bureau of Reclamation has had to consider the unquantified water rights of Klamath Basin tribes, and the federal trust responsibility to these tribes, in managing the waters of the Klamath Project. *See* Reed D. Benson, *Giving Suckers (and Salmon) an Even Break: Klamath Basin Water and the Endangered Species Act,* 15 Tulane Envtl. L.J. 197, 210–221 (2002).

3. Several other courts have held that Indian tribes possess reserved water rights to minimum flows. The Ninth Circuit Court of Appeals recognized that the specific purposes of Indian reservations "were often unarticulated," and that because "the general purpose, to provide a home for the Indians, is a broad one [it] must be liberally construed." Colville Confederated Tribes v. Walton, 647 F.2d 42, 47 (9th Cir.1981), cert. denied 454 U.S. 1092, 102 S.Ct. 657, 70 L.Ed.2d 630 (1981), *supra* p. 905. Citing the Colville Tribes' traditional dependence on fishing for salmon and trout, the court found that preservation of the tribes' fishing grounds was a purpose for creating the reservation in addition to the agricultural purposes. Consequently, the court held that the tribes had a reserved right to sufficient water to maintain a fishery in Omak Lake (as a replacement for the fishery it lost when the Columbia River was dammed). See also Colville Confederated Tribes v. Walton, 752 F.2d 397 (9th Cir.1985), cert. denied 475 U.S. 1010, 106 S.Ct. 1183, 89 L.Ed.2d 300 (1986); United States v. Anderson, 736 F.2d 1358 (9th Cir.1984); Muckleshoot Indian Tribe v. Trans–Canada Enterprises, Ltd., 713 F.2d 455 (9th Cir.1983), cert. denied 465 U.S. 1049, 104 S.Ct. 1324, 79 L.Ed.2d 720 (1984).

Is it "necessary to fulfill the purposes of the reservation" to allow reserved water rights with early priority dates to pass to non-Indian purchasers of allotments? For differing views see Richard B. Collins, *Indian Allotment Water Rights,* 20 Land & Water L. Rev. 421 (1985) and David H. Getches, *Water Rights on Indian Allotments,* 26 S.D. L. Rev. 405 (1981).

4. Should private persons who use federal lands be able to use the reserved water right of the federal government? For instance, suppose a timber contractor with a federal timber cutting permit in a national forest wishes to use water in connection with the timber operation or a concessionaire in a national park needs water to operate a campground or hotel. See United States v. Denver, 656 P.2d 1, 34 (Colo.1982). What limitations might there be on private use of federal reserved water rights? If the United States lawfully transfers a portion of a federal reservation to a private individual, does a portion of the federal reserved rights that attached to that land pass with it?

5. Should Indian tribes be able to sell or lease water held by them under reserved rights to non-Indians for use off the reservations? See *infra* p. 923.

NOTE: FEDERAL POWERS, RESERVED AND NONRESERVED FEDERAL WATER RIGHTS

Basis of Reserved Rights

The Supreme Court in *Arizona v. California* said that there was "no doubt about the power of the United States * * * to reserve water rights for its reservations and its property." 373 U.S. 546, 598, 83 S.Ct. 1468, 10 L.Ed.2d 542 (1963). The constitutional basis relied upon by the Court in *Arizona* was primarily the Property Clause, which provides that "The Congress shall have Power to dispose of and make all needful Rules and

Regulations respecting the Territory or other property belonging to the United States * * *.'' U.S. Const. art. IV, § 3, cl. 2. Until the late nineteenth century, the United States owned almost all of the land, and all of the water appurtenant to that land, in sixteen of the seventeen western states. The federal government thus possessed the constitutional power to dispose of this land and water.

The *Arizona* Court also cited the Commerce Clause of the Constitution, which gives Congress powers over navigable waters. The same clause gives Congress extensive power over Indian affairs, including Indian reservations, speaking of authority ''to regulate Commerce * * * with the Indian Tribes.'' U.S. Const. art. I § 8 cl. 3. In addition, reserved rights for Indian reservations may be based on the treaty power found in article II, § 2, cl. 2, which furnishes power to establish reservations by treaty.

Initially, the federal government took no action regarding water on the western public lands. Early western settlers, when faced with a need for water, simply took what they needed. The Mining Act of 1866, 43 U.S.C.A. § 661, validated these uses, as it confirmed water rights recognized by custom and local law, and provided that pre–1866 appropriative rights would not be defeated by riparian claims of federal patentees. In 1877, Congress passed the Desert Land Act, providing that the right to the use of water should depend upon prior appropriation and that all water not appropriated should ''remain and be held free for the appropriation and use of the public * * *.'' 43 U.S.C.A. § 321. The Act severed appropriated water from the public domain, and the states and territories were permitted to establish water rights systems allocating rights to use water according to their laws. See California Oregon Power Co. v. Beaver Portland Cement Co., 295 U.S. 142, 158, 164, 55 S.Ct. 725, 79 L.Ed. 1356 (1935), *supra* p. 187. Until rights to those waters are actually appropriated by individuals under state law, however, there is nothing preventing the United States from putting the water to use itself, thereby precluding future appropriations by others.

To the extent the U.S. decides to use the unappropriated water, then, it becomes unavailable for appropriation under state law. The question is more difficult when the U.S. decides to commit its land to water-demanding purposes but does not actually start using the water.

The reserved rights doctrine holds that when the United States withdraws land from the public domain, that is, sets it aside for particular federal purposes like a park, forest, or military base, it impliedly reserves unappropriated water sufficient for the purposes of the reservation. At that point, the federal government effectively revokes its permission for the state to allocate rights in the water as granted under the Desert Land Act. Any water appropriated as of the date of the reservation is, however, unavailable to the United States unless it compensates the prior appropriators. The water ''reserved'' by the United States can be used by private parties until the United States decides to put it to use, but they are junior in priority to the federal government. Their uses can be disputed, and if the water is later put to use by the federal government, the junior appropriators are owed no compensation, because they had no rights superior to the United States in the waters they were using.

Suppose the United States has not reserved land for purposes that require water but it needs to use water to carry out some federal program. The government does not have reserved water rights for the program. In *United States v. New Mexico, supra* p. 878, the Court insisted that rights are reserved by the United States only to the extent they are needed to fulfill the primary purposes for which the reservation was established. Thus, the government may not rely on reserved rights for any water needed to fulfill "secondary" purposes, or for water needed to carry out statutory programs and management mandates on and off federal lands. The federal agencies may proceed to acquire water rights under state law, however, and they have done so extensively throughout the country, especially in connection with federal public lands.

Federal Appropriations of Water and Preemption

Must the government adhere to all the requirements of state law as it proceeds to appropriate water within the state system? It seems clear that any water rights appropriated by the United States will have a priority as of the date they are actually perfected. The early date of reserved rights is not available. But suppose the state system involves an administrative determination that could deny or limit the quantity of rights sought by the land manager. Or suppose the land manager seeks water for a purpose not recognized as a beneficial use by the state system (for example, for instream flows in a state where such rights are not allowed). A traditional preemption analysis applies to these situations. The question in each instance is whether Congress, in exercising a constitutionally enumerated power, intended to preempt state water law. Courts will find such an intent if conformity to state water law would frustrate "the accomplishment and execution of the full purposes and objectives of Congress." Laurence H. Tribe, American Constitutional Law 1176 (3rd ed. 2000), citing Hines v. Davidowitz, 312 U.S. 52, 61 S.Ct. 399, 85 L.Ed. 581 (1941).

There has been considerable debate within the Executive Branch as to the extent to which the government can and should assert that its appropriative water rights claims preempt state water law. For a time the federal government asserted a theory of federal "non-reserved" water rights. 86 Interior Dec. 553 (1979). A later administration rejected the position but allowed avoidance of state water law in cases where Congress intended to exercise its constitutional powers to preempt state water law. See Office of Legal Counsel, United States Department of Justice, Memorandum, "Federal Non–Reserved Water Rights," June 17, 1982. The memorandum said that the agencies should read a "presumption" into the language and legislative history of federal statutes that authorize the management of federal lands that Congress intended to follow a general practice of deferring to state water law. Otherwise, public land management statutes like the Federal Land Policy and Management Act (FLPMA), 43 U.S.C.A. §§ 1701–1782, will not be read as preempting state water law. In practice, the United States ordinarily follows state water law in appropriating water rights, but when its attempts to carry out federal purposes are impeded by substantive provisions of state law, the latter may be preempted. See Charles F. Wilkinson & H. Michael Anderson, *Land and Resources Planning in the National Forest,* 64 Or. L. Rev. 1, 232 (1985). In addition, federal regulatory authority can preempt the operation of state law, a matter discussed in Chapter 7B. See generally County of Okanogan v. National Marine Fisheries Service, 347 F.3d 1081 (9th Cir. 2003) (upholding limits on water withdrawals to benefit fish protected by the Endangered Species Act, despite adverse effects on irrigators with established state water rights).

In one case, Congress expressly created a "non-reserved" water right. The law establishing Great Sand Dunes National Park authorized the Secretary of the Interior to appropriate water using state procedures but made it clear that the purpose of the right was "maintaining ground water levels, surface water levels, and stream flows" in the park so that any substantive provisions of inconsistent state law are necessarily preempted. Pub. L. No. 106–530, § 9(b)(2)(B), 114 Stat. 2527, 2533–34. See John D. Leshy, Water Rights for New Federal Land Conservation Programs: A Turn-of-the-Century Evaluation, 4 U. Denver Water L.Rev. 271, 286–87 (2001).

Consider several possible federal needs for water. In which cases do reserved rights exist? In which must the government proceed to acquire water rights entirely according to state law? In which may aspects of state law be preempted when the government seeks to acquire water rights?

1. The Department of Defense needs water to serve barracks built on a military reservation.

2. The Forest Service seeks instream flow rights for fish and wildlife purposes in a national forest, but state law does not recognize instream flows as a beneficial use.

3. The Park Service seeks to convert state-permitted agricultural rights it purchased from a farmer to instream flow rights for a national park, but state law allows instream flow rights to be held only by a state agency.

4. The Bureau of Land Management (BLM) seeks water rights to maintain a fishery in a stream on unreserved lands in a state that does not recognize instream flows as a beneficial use.

5. The Forest Service desires to use water to irrigate a "community garden" operated by employees and their families who live within a national forest.

4. QUANTIFICATION

As the jurisdiction of state courts to adjudicate reserved rights was clarified, states and non-Indian water users pressed for determinations that would provide them with certainty. State court adjudications of federal and

Indian reserved rights are proceeding throughout the West and many have resulted in settlements. Only one such case has resulted in a "final" judicial decision on the existence, priority, and quantity of Indian reserved rights. It also provided an opportunity for the United States Supreme Court to revisit its practicably irrigable acreage (PIA) standard announced in Arizona v. California. Although the decision quantified rights for the Wind River Reservation, it left several issues unresolved.

In re General Adjudication of All Rights to Use Water in the Big Horn River System

Supreme Court of Wyoming, 1988.
753 P.2d 76, affirmed sub nom. Wyoming v. United States, 492 U.S. 406, 109 S.Ct. 2994, 106 L.Ed.2d 342 (1989).

■ Before BROWN, C.J., and THOMAS, CARDINE, and MACY, JJ., and HANSCUM, DISTRICT JUDGE.

I.   INTRODUCTION

This appeal is from the district court's order adjudicating rights to use water in the Big Horn River System and all other sources within the State's Water Division No. 3. * * *

The primary drainage system in the division is the Wind River–Big Horn River which originates in northern Fremont County and leaves the Division at the Wyoming–Montana border in northern Big Horn County. * * *

The history of the Big Horn Basin for purposes of this case begins in the early 1800's when explorers, trappers and traders began traveling into northwestern Wyoming, part of the vast hunting grounds of the peripatetic Shoshone Indians. Neither group encroached on the other and relations were friendly. Nonetheless, in 1865, the United States, hoping to preserve the peace and stability, reached an agreement delineating the area within which the Eastern Shoshone roamed, a 44,672,000 acre region comprising parts of Wyoming, Colorado and Utah. Following the Civil War, as the westward movement gained momentum, the United States government realized the size of the region set aside for Indians only was unrealistic, and on July 3, 1868, executed the Second Treaty of Fort Bridger with the Shoshone and Bannock Indians, establishing the Wind River Indian Reservation.

* * *

B.   *Procedural History of the Instant Litigation*

On January 22, 1977, Wyoming enacted § 1–1054.1, W.S.1957 (now § 1–37–106, W.S.1977), authorizing the State to commence system-wide adjudications of water rights. The State of Wyoming filed the complaint commencing this litigation and naming the United States as a defendant on

January 24, 1977, in the District Court of the Fifth Judicial District of Wyoming.

* * *

The special master signed his 451–page Report Concerning Reserved Water Right Claims by and on Behalf of the Tribes in the Wind River Reservation on December 15, 1982, covering four years of conferences and hearings, involving more than 100 attorneys, transcripts of more than 15,000 pages and over 2,300 exhibits.

The report recognized a reserved water right for the Wind River Indian Reservation and determined that the purpose for which the reservation had been established was a permanent homeland for the Indians. A reserved water right for irrigation, stock watering, fisheries, wildlife and aesthetics, mineral and industrial, and domestic, commercial, and municipal uses was quantified and awarded.

* * *

The State of Wyoming, the United States, the Shoshone and Arapahoe Tribes, and numerous private parties presented objections to the master's report, and on May 10, 1983, Judge Joffe entered his Findings of Fact, Conclusions of Law and Judgment approving that portion of the master's report awarding reserved water rights for practicably irrigable acreage within the Wind River Indian Reservation and refusing to accept that portion of the master's report recommending an award of reserved water rights for other than agricultural purposes.

* * *

The treaty establishing the Wind River Indian Reservation, Treaty of Ft. Bridger, 15 Stat. 673 (1869), is silent on the subject of water for the reservation. Yet both the district court and the special master found an intent to reserve water. We affirm.

* * *

IV. PURPOSES OF THE WIND RIVER INDIAN RESERVATION

The government may reserve water from appropriation under state law for use on the lands set aside for an Indian reservation. *Winters v. United States, supra* 207 U.S. 564. A reserved water right is implied for an Indian reservation where water is necessary to fulfill the purposes of reservation. *United States v. Adair, supra* p. 874, cert. denied sub nom. *Oregon v. United States,* 467 U.S. 1252 (1984). The quantity of water reserved is the amount of water sufficient to fulfill the purpose of the lands set aside for the reservation. * * * We have already decided that Congress intended to reserve water for the Wind River Indian Reservation when it was created in 1868, and we accept the proposition that the amount of water impliedly reserved is determined by the purposes for which the reservation was created.

The special master's finding that the principal purpose for the creation of the reservation was to provide a permanent homeland for the Indians is not a factual determination. The master determined the purpose of the Indian reservation from the face of the treaty as a matter of law. Where the contract is unambiguous, the meaning or intent is derived from the instrument itself as a matter of law. * * * The district court ascertained the purpose of the reservation from the treaty itself, stating: "On the very face of the Treaty, it is clear that its purpose was purely agricultural." This legal determination is fully reviewable by this court.

A. The Treaty

The Treaty with the Shoshones and Bannacks, July 3, 1868, provides in pertinent part:

* * *

"ARTICLE IV. The Indians herein named agree * * * they will make said reservations their permanent home, and they will make no permanent settlement elsewhere; but they shall have the right to hunt on the unoccupied lands of the United States so long as game may be found thereon, and so long as peace subsist * * *.

* * *

"ARTICLE VI. If any individual belonging to said tribes * * * shall desire to commence farming, he shall have the privilege to select * * * a tract of land within the reservation of his tribe * * * which tract * * * shall cease to be held in common * * *.

* * *

"ARTICLE VII. In order to insure the civilization of the tribes entering into this treaty, the necessity of education is admitted, especially of such of them as are or may be settled on said *agricultural reservations* * * *.

"ARTICLE VIII. When the head of a family or lodge shall have selected lands and received his certificate as above directed, and the agent shall be satisfied that he intends in good faith to commence cultivating the soil for a living, he shall be entitled to receive seeds and agricultural implements for the first year * * * and for each succeeding year he shall continue to farm, for a period of three years more * * *.

"And it is further stipulated that such persons as commence farming shall receive instructions from the farmers * * * and whenever more than one hundred persons on either reservation shall enter upon the cultivation of the soil, a second blacksmith shall be provided * * *.

"ARTICLE IX. * * * the United States agrees to deliver at the agency house on the reservation [items of clothing].

" * * * and in addition to the clothing herein named, the sum of ten dollars shall be annually appropriated for each Indian roaming and twenty dollars for each Indian engaged in agriculture, for a period of ten years, to be used by the Secretary of the Interior in the purchase of such articles as from time to time the condition and necessities of the Indians may indicate to be proper.

* * *

"ARTICLE XII. It is agreed that the sum of five hundred dollars annually for three years from the date when they commence to cultivate a farm, shall be expended in presents to the ten persons of said tribe, who in the judgment of the agent, may grow the most valuable crops for the respective year." (Emphasis added.)

The court in *Colville Confederated Tribes v. Walton, supra* 647 F.2d 42, did not mandate that a single purpose for the reservation be found. Rather, the court applied the specific purpose test outlined in *United States v. New Mexico*, [*supra* p. 856], in an Indian reserved water case and found two primary purposes: "to provide a homeland for the Indians to maintain their agrarian society," 647 F.2d at 47, for which practicably irrigable acreage was the measure, and to preserve the "tribes' access to fishing grounds." 647 F.2d at 48. * * * In *United States v. Adair*, the ninth circuit agreed that non-Indian federal reservation reserved water rights cases only provide useful guidelines to Indian reserved water rights.

* * *

* * * Considering the well-established principles of treaty interpretation, the treaty itself, the ample evidence and testimony addressed, and the findings of the district court, we have no difficulty affirming the finding that it was the intent at the time to create a reservation with a sole agricultural purpose. Indian treaties should be interpreted generously, * * * and should not be given a crabbed or restrictive meaning. *McClanahan v. State Tax Commission of Arizona, supra* 411 U.S. at 176. Nor should treaties be improperly construed in favor of Indians, for " '[W]e cannot remake history,' " *Rosebud Sioux Tribe v. Kneip, supra* 430 U.S. at 615 and courts should not distort the words of a treaty to find rights inconsistent with its language.

Article 7 of the treaty refers to "said agricultural reservations." Article 6 authorizes allotments for farming purposes; Article 8 provides seeds and implements for farmers; in Article 9 "the United States agreed to pay each Indian farming a $20 annual stipend, but only $10 to 'roaming' Indians"; and Article 12 establishes a $50 prize to the ten best Indian farmers. The treaty does not encourage any other occupation or pursuit. The district court correctly found that the reference in Article 4 to "permanent homeland" does nothing more than permanently set aside lands for the Indians; it does not define the purpose of the reservation. Rather, the purpose of the permanent-home reservation is found in Articles 6, 8, 9, and 12 of the treaty.

* * *

* * * The fact that the Indians fully intended to continue to hunt and fish does not alter that conclusion.

Agreements subsequent to the treaty acknowledge the continuance of non-agricultural activities on the reservation. The reports of the Indian agents are replete with descriptions of and plans for other activities. Yet not one of the cited reports neglects to report also on the progress of the farming and ranching operations. The primary activity was clearly agricultural.

B. Fisheries

Reserved water rights for fisheries have been recognized where a treaty provision explicitly recognized an exclusive right to take fish on the reservation or the right to take fish at traditional off-reservation fishing grounds, in common with others.

Instream fishery flows have also been recognized where the Indians were heavily, if not totally, dependent on fish for their livelihood. *United States v. Adair*, 723 F.2d at 1409; *Colville Confederated Tribes v. Walton*, 647 F.2d at 48. In the case at bar, the Tribes introduced evidence showing that fish had always been part of the Indians' diet. The master, erroneously concluding that a reserved right for fisheries should be implied when the tribe is "at least partially dependent upon fishing," awarded an instream flow right for fisheries. The district court, however, finding neither a dependency upon fishing for a livelihood nor a traditional lifestyle involving fishing, deleted the award. The district court did not err. The evidence is not sufficient to imply a fishery flow right absent a treaty provision.

C. Mineral and Industrial

The Tribes were denied a reserved water right for mineral and industrial development. All parties to the treaty were well aware before it was signed of the valuable mineral estate underlying the Wind River Indian Reservation. The question of whether, because the Indians own the minerals, the intent was that they should have the water necessary to develop them must be determined, of course, by the intent in 1868. Neither the Tribes nor the United States has cited this court to any provision of the treaty or other evidence indicating that the parties contemplated in 1868 that a purpose of the reservation would be for the Indians to develop the minerals. The fact that the Tribes have since used water for mineral and industrial purposes does not establish that water was impliedly reserved in 1868 for such uses. The district court did not err in denying a reserved water right for mineral and industrial uses.

D. Municipal, Domestic and Commercial

A reserved water right for municipal, domestic and commercial uses was included within the agricultural reserved water award. Domestic and related use has traditionally been subsumed in agricultural reserved rights. See, e.g., *United States ex rel. Ray v. Hibner*, 27 F.2d at 911 (the treaties fixed the rights of the Indians—"to a continuous use of a sufficient amount of water for the irrigation of their lands, and domestic purposes"); *United States v. Powers*, 305 U.S. at 533 ("waters essential to farming and home making"). Practicably irrigable acreage (PIA) was established as the measure of an agricultural reserved water right in *Arizona v. California*, 373 U.S. at 601. The special master there indicated that PIA was the measure of water necessary for agriculture and related purposes. The court properly allowed a reserved water right for municipal, domestic, and commercial use.

E. Livestock

For the reasons stated above, the district court did not err in finding a sole agricultural purpose for the reservation or in subsuming livestock use within that purpose.

F. Wildlife and Aesthetics

The special master awarded 60% of historic flows for wildlife and aesthetic uses, consistent with his determination that the purpose of the reservation was to be a permanent homeland. The district court deleted this award, reciting not only that the purpose was solely agricultural, but that insufficient evidence had been presented to justify an award for these uses. The district court did not err in holding that the Tribes and the United States did not introduce sufficient evidence of a tradition of wildlife and aesthetic preservation which would justify finding this to be a purpose for which the reservation was created and for which water was impliedly reserved.

The district court did not err in finding a sole agricultural purpose in the creation of the Wind River Indian Reservation. The Treaty itself evidences no other purpose, and none of the extraneous evidence cited is sufficient to attribute a broader purpose.

V. SCOPE OF THE RESERVED WATER RIGHT

A. Groundwater

The logic which supports a reservation of surface water to fulfill the purpose of the reservation also supports reservation of groundwater. See *Tweedy v. Texas Company*, 286 F. Supp. 383, 385 (D.Mont.1968) ("whether the [necessary] waters were found on the surface of the land or under it should make no difference"). Certainly the two sources are often interconnected. See § 41–3–916, W.S.1977 (where underground and surface waters are "so interconnected as to constitute in fact one source of supply," a single schedule of priorities shall be made).

Acknowledging the above, we note that, nonetheless, not a single case applying the reserved water doctrine to groundwater is cited to us. The ninth circuit indicated that groundwater was reserved in *United States v. Cappaert*, 508 F.2d 313, 317 (9th Cir.1974). The United States Supreme Court, however, found the water in the pool reserved for preservation of the pupfish was not groundwater but surface water, protected from subsequent diversions from either surface or groundwater supplies *Cappaert v. United States.* * * *

The district court did not err in deciding there was no reserved groundwater right. Because we hold that the reserved water doctrine does not extend to groundwater, we need not address the separate claim that the district court erred in determining that the State owns the groundwater. The State has not appealed the decision that the Tribes may continue to satisfy their domestic and livestock needs (part of the agricultural award) from existing wells at current withdrawal rates; therefore, we do not address that question.

B. Exportation

The district court held that "[t]he Tribes can sell or lease any part of the water covered by their reserved water rights but the said sale or lease cannot be for exportation off of the Reservation." The Tribes did not seek permission to export reserved water, and the United States concedes that no federal law permits the sale of reserved water to non-Indians off the reservation. Because of our holding on the groundwater issue, we need not address the separate constitutional attack on the prohibition of exportation of groundwater.

* * *

VI.   QUANTIFICATION

A. The Measure

The measure of the Tribes' reserved water right is the water necessary to irrigate the practicably irrigable acreage on the reservation. In *Arizona v. California*, a needs test was rejected as too uncertain, the Court opting instead for practicably irrigable acreage as the measure of a tribal agricultural reserved water right. Two subsequent non-Indian reserved water right cases, *Cappaert v. United States*, and *United States v. New Mexico*, indicate that necessity is the measure of a reserved water right. And in Washington v. *Washington State Commercial Passenger Fishing Vessel Association*, the Court recognized the propriety of reducing the Indians' proportion of the fish harvest as their needs diminished. Nonetheless, the Court declined the invitation to re-examine the PIA standard in *Arizona v. California*, and reaffirmed the value of the certainty inherent in the practicably irrigable acreage standard. The district court was correct in quantifying the Tribes' reserved water right by the amount of water necessary to irrigate all of the reservation's practicably irrigable acreage.

B. Future Lands

The Tribes and the United States claimed a reserved water right for lands on the reservation not yet developed for irrigation, but which were in their view, practicably irrigable acreage. Counsel for the State, the Tribes and the United States agreed upon a definition of practicably irrigable acreage: "those acres susceptible to sustained irrigation at reasonable costs." The determination of practicably irrigable acreage involves a two-part analysis, i.e., the PIA must be susceptible of sustained irrigation (not only proof of the arability but also of the engineering feasibility of irrigating the land) and irrigable "at reasonable cost."

The United States presented evidence on all these factors to support its ultimate claim for 53,760 practicably irrigable acres (210,000 acre-feet/year), and Wyoming presented evidence in opposition. * * *

The Amended Judgment and Decree * * * resulted in the total final award being 48,097 acres.

1. Arability

* * *

The master determined that the arable land base was 76,027 acres. Wyoming claims on appeal that the arability investigation did not meet Bureau of Reclamation Standards for 60% of the land as to the depth to barrier, maximum slope, hydraulic conductivity, barrier definition and maximum drain spacing standards. The special master accepted the approach of the United States as meeting its burden of establishing the land base for the determination of arability. There was substantial evidence to support this determination, and looking, as we must, only to the evidence of the United States, we affirm the master's finding of 76,027 acres of arable land base.

2. Engineering Feasibility

* * *

The master did not abuse his discretion in accepting the engineering feasibility work which incorporated 35% project efficiencies rather than a 50% project efficiency. * * *

The master determined that practicably irrigable acreage should be based on present standards.

* * *

The sensitivity doctrine takes its name from this passage: "I agree with the court that the implied-reservation doctrine should be applied with sensitivity to its impact upon those who have obtained water rights under state law and to Congress' general policy of deference to state water law." United States v. New Mexico, 438 U.S. at 718 (Powell, J., dissenting in part). * * *

It is thus not clear whether the sensitivity doctrine, requiring the quantification of reserved water rights with sensitivity to the impact on state and private appropriators, applies here.

Assuming, arguendo, that it does apply, we cannot accept the City of Riverton's argument that it was ignored by the district court. * * *

VIII. MONITORING OF THE DECREE BY THE STATE ENGINEER

The issue of whether the state engineer may monitor the decree is a controversy conferring jurisdiction upon this court. * * *

* * * The decree entered in the instant case does not require application of state water law to the Indian reservation. The decree recognizes reserved water rights based on federal law. The role of the state engineer is thus not to apply state law, but to enforce the reserved rights as decreed under principles of federal law. This court is also cognizant of the fact that exercise of the reserved water rights are intimately bound up with the state water rights of off-reservation users. The state water appropriators are not in a position to jeopardize the decreed rights of the Tribes. The decree only requires the United States and the Tribes first to turn to the state engineer to exercise his authority over the state users to protect their reserved water rights before they seek court assistance to enforce their rights; it does not preclude access to the courts. Incidental monitoring of Indian use to this end has carelessly been termed "administration" of Indian water by the state engineer. Should the state engineer find that it is the Tribes who are violating the decree, it is clear that he must then turn to the courts for enforcement of the decree against the United States and the Tribes and that he cannot simply close the headgates. Any fear that the state engineer may be unfair must be dispelled by Article 1, § 31 of the Wyoming Constitution which provides that the State "shall equally guard all of the various [water] interests involved." The state engineer has sworn to uphold this constitution. Thus it is readily apparent that the provisions authorizing the state engineer to monitor reserved water rights contemplate neither the application of state law nor the authority to deprive the Tribes of water without the assistance of the courts in a suit for the administration of the decree.

* * *

The district court did not err in including provisions giving the state engineer authority to enforce the decree against state appropriators.

* * *

■ THOMAS, JUSTICE, dissenting with whom HANSCUM, DISTRICT JUDGE, joins.

I differ from the majority with respect to three propositions and must dissent from the disposition made in the majority opinion. Except for my three points of difference, I am in accord with the resolution of this case as set forth in that opinion. My three points of difference are: first, I do not agree that reserved water rights, to the extent that they properly are recognized under the reserved rights doctrine, should be limited in the manner suggested by the majority opinion; second, I believe that there should be a pragmatic limitation on the standard for quantification, the practicably irrigable acreage, which would eliminate those lands from the quantification formula which only could be irrigated by the construction of some future water project; and third, but most important, I do not believe that the reserved rights doctrine is applicable to that portion of the lands lying north of the "Big Wind River," i.e., the ceded portion of the Wind River Indian Reservation.

The purpose of establishing an Indian reservation, such as the Wind River Indian Reservation, is to provide a homeland for Indian peoples. If one is to assume that, pursuant to the reserved rights doctrine relating to water, there is an implied reservation of those waters essential to accomplish the purpose of the reservation of land, then I cannot agree that the implied reservation of water with respect to the Wind River Indian Reservation should be limited, as the majority has held in approving the judgment of the district court. The fault that I find with such a limitation is that it assumes that the Indian peoples will not enjoy the same style of evolution as other people, nor are they to have the benefits of modern civilization. I would understand that the homeland concept assumes that the homeland will not be a static place frozen in an instant of time but that the homeland will evolve and will be used in different ways as the Indian society develops. For that reason, I would hold that the implied reservation of water rights attaching to an Indian reservation assumes any use that is appropriate to the Indian homeland as it progresses and develops. The one thing that I would not assume is that using the reserved water as a salable commodity was contemplated in connection with the implied reservation of the water. I would limit its use to the territorial boundaries of the reservation.

Deeming it unnecessary to detail further the formula for allocation of water which involves the concept of practicably irrigable acreage (*Arizona v. California*, 460 U.S. 605, 103 S. Ct. 1382, 75 L. Ed. 2d 318 (1983)), I am convinced that there has to be some degree of pragmatism in determining practicably irrigable acreage. It is clear from the majority opinion that there was included in quantifying the water reserved to the Indian peoples lands not now irrigable but deemed to be practicably irrigable acreage upon the assumption of the development of future irrigation projects. I would be appalled, as most other concerned citizens should be, if the Congress of the United States, or any other governmental body, began expending money to develop water projects for irrigating these Wyoming lands when far more fertile lands in the midwestern states now are being removed from production due to poor market conditions. I am convinced that, because of this pragmatic concern, those lands which were included as practicably irrigable acreage, based upon the assumption of the construction of a future irrigation project, should not be included for the purpose of quantification of the Indian peoples' water rights. They may be irrigable academically, but not as a matter of practicality, and I would require their exclusion from any quantification. * * *

NOTES

1. *Supreme Court Deadlock.* The decision in the principal case, *"Big Horn I,"* resulted in a quantification of the tribes' reserved rights amounting to over 500,000 acre-feet. After the state petitioned for U.S. Supreme Court review, the tribes cross-petitioned on several grounds. What grounds would you raise as tribal attorney? Certiorari was granted solely on a ground urged by the state: that the PIA standard should not have applied to the case. The case was briefed and argued on that point, but the court divided equally, with Justice O'Connor not participating. Research into the late

Justice Thurgood Marshall's papers revealed a complete draft majority opinion by Justice O'Connor for a 5–4 majority. Her opinion would have modified the PIA standard applying a "sensitivity doctrine" whenever junior water rights of non-Indians would be put at risk by the recognition of reserved rights. This would respond to Wyoming Supreme Court Justice Thomas's dissent from the state court decision. However, four days before the opinion was to be issued, Justice O'Connor recused herself because her family owned a ranch in Arizona that was a party to the Gila River Adjudication which included several tribes. See David H. Getches, *Conquering the Cultural Frontier: The New Subjectivism of the Supreme Court in Indian Law*, 84 Cal. L. Rev. 1573, 1640–41 (1996). See also Andrew Mergen & Sylvia Liu, *A Misplaced Sensitivity: The Draft Opinions in Wyoming v. United States*, 68 U. Colo. L. Rev. 683 (1997).

2.   *Instream flows vs. Agriculture.* Shortly after the Wyoming Supreme Court's decision, the tribes closed the headgates to the Crowheart Irrigation Unit of the Wind River Indian Reservation severely restricting the water for the non-Indian irrigators. The tribes contended that the non-Indian irrigators had used more water than had been allotted to them. In February of 1989, Wyoming's Governor and the tribes resolved the dispute in a one-year agreement in which the state paid approximately $5 million and the tribes agreed to limit their exercise of *Winters* rights. In times of shortage, the tribes would share equally with other water users in restricting their use of water, regardless of priority. The state also agreed to improve the water works projects serving the reservation and to look into water storage sites.

Then, in April of 1990, when the agreement with the state expired, the tribes issued an "Instream Flow Permit" to the Shoshone and Northern Arapahoe Tribes for a term of six months authorizing the dedication of 252 cfs of water from the Wind River that had been quantified for future agricultural project uses to maintain instream flows for purposes including fisheries, groundwater recharge, and habitat restoration and enhancement. This again restricted the available water for non-Indian irrigators, who claimed that the court decision did not authorize use of the tribes' water for instream flows. The state argued that the tribes' attempt to convert their reserved water rights to instream flows would severely damage many non-Indian junior appropriators in the area and the Wyoming State Engineer declined to enforce the tribes' "Instream Flow Permits." The tribes then asked the state district court to appoint a special master to resolve the conflict over the tribes' right to apply their water rights to instream flows and, ultimately, to hold the State Engineer in contempt of court. Based on the report of the special master, the district court declared that the tribes were entitled to use their reserved water rights on the reservation as they deemed advisable, including instream flow use, without regard to Wyoming water law. Furthermore, the district court appointed the tribal water agency to administer water rights of Indians and non-Indians on the reservation, instead of the State Engineer.

On appeal, the Wyoming Supreme Court, in a deeply divided plurality decision, held that its 1989 decision (*Big Horn I*) had already determined that instream flow was not an allowable use of water on the Wind River Indian Reservation, which had been created exclusively for agricultural purposes and not for fisheries. The decision allowed the tribes to change the use of their own quantified rights from the established use in agriculture to instream flow uses. However, *Big Horn II* precluded them from changing the purpose of rights quantified for future agricultural projects to instream flows when doing so would deprive non-Indian appropriators of their use rights. The decision also found it improper for the lower court to assign the State Engineer's statutory duty of administering state water rights to the tribal agency. In re General Adjudication of All Rights to Use Water in the Big Horn River System, 835 P.2d 273 (Wyo.1992). The tribes decided for strategic and practical reasons not to seek review of the decision in the U.S. Supreme Court.

Later, major non-Indian irrigators who had purchased Indian lands in the irrigation district successfully argued that they were entitled to the same water rights and priority dates as the Indian sellers. The decision followed *Colville Confederated Tribes v. Walton, supra*, p. 905. The court limited their water rights to an amount of water that had been used by a predecessor or was used within a reasonable time after the purchase. In re General Adjudication of All Rights to Use Water in Big Horn River System, 803 P.2d 61 (Wyo.1990). In further proceedings the court held that in determining the reasonable time for putting water to use in order to establish these rights, the fact that the United States Bureau of Reclamation was constructing an irrigation project for the district was evidence of due diligence. In re General Adjudication of All Rights to Use Water in Big Horn River System, 48 P.3d 1040 (Wyo.2002).

3. *Groundwater.* The *Big Horn I* decision that the tribes do not have reserved rights to groundwater is a minority view. The Arizona Supreme Court applied the reasoning of *Cappaert, supra*, p. 885, to hold that under *Winters*, the government intended to reserve sufficient water from the sources available to the reservation. It also refused to apply state law limitations on Indian groundwater use. *In re* General Adjudication of All Rights to Use Water in the Gila River System and Source, 195 Ariz. 411, 989 P.2d 739, 749–750 (1999), cert. denied 530 U.S. 1250, 120 S.Ct. 2705, 147 L.Ed.2d 974 (2000). A federal court in Washington State and the Montana Supreme Court reached the same conclusion. United States v. Washington Dep't of Ecology, 375 F.Supp.2d 1050, 1058 (W.D. Wash. 2005); Confederated Salish and Kootenai Tribes of the Flathead Reservation v. Stults, 312 Mont. 420, 59 P.3d 1093, 1099 (2002).

4. *"Secondary" Purposes.* The Court in *United States v. New Mexico, supra* p. 878, held that the quantity of water reserved for a national forest was the quantity needed for the primary purposes of producing timber and favorable supplies of water. Thus, no water was reserved for secondary purposes of forests such as stockwatering and fisheries. The Court stressed that water is reserved only if without it the primary "purpose of the reservation would be entirely defeated.'' Does this restrictive language apply to reserved rights for Indian reservations as well as to federal public lands? The Arizona Supreme Court has held that the primary-secondary distinction was not applicable to Indian reserved rights because the federal government's trust responsibilities require that treaties be interpreted expansively so as to further the goal of Indian self-determination and the creation of a permanent, economically self-sufficient homeland for Indian peoples. In re General Adjudication of All Rights to Use Water in the Gila River System and Source, 201 Ariz. 307, 35 P.3d 68 (2001).

5. *Marketing Reserved Rights.* Can the Wind River tribes sell or lease the right to use quantified reserved rights outside the reservation? Indian property ordinarily cannot be sold or leased without congressional consent. See 25 U.S.C.A. § 177. Several settlements of *Winters* doctrine water rights approved by Congress have included provisions for the tribes to market their water off the reservation. See *infra* p. 921.

Should there be any conditions placed on Indian off-reservation water marketing? What protection should there be for junior appropriators injured by the transfer? Should protections be imposed for the tribe's benefit? Off-reservation water marketing could limit future generations of Indians in their possibilities for maintaining economic security and cultural integrity. Can a transfer of water to non-Indians who may become dependent upon it be truly temporary? If a transfer is not temporary, what are the effects on Indian society? See generally David H. Getches, *Management and Marketing of Indian Water: From Conflict to Pragmatism*, 58 U. Colo. L. Rev. 515 (1988) and Chris Seldin, *Interstate Marketing of Indian Water Rights: The Impact of the Commerce Clause*, 87 Cal. L. Rev. 1545 (1999).

NOTE: QUANTIFICATION OF INDIAN RESERVED WATER RIGHTS WITHOUT LITIGATION

One possible alternative to litigation of Indian reserved rights is congressional quantification. Several bills have been introduced in Congress that would provide a general framework for quantification of reserved rights, but they all have died before coming to a vote. Can you suggest the ingredients of a generic solution to Indian reserved water rights claims given the wide variations in geographic, economic, and cultural situations of tribes? Lacking such legislation, tribes and non-Indian water users are left to litigate or negotiate.

In some cases litigation may be useful in determining quantification, but many complex practical problems are best left for negotiated solutions. This led to a series of tribal water rights settlements that addressed unresolved *Winters* rights questions, such as off-reservation and non-agricultural use, on an ad hoc basis. Often the negotiations commence in the course of litigation. Negotiated settlements can be attractive as a way of avoiding the enormous transaction costs of water rights litigation. The *Big Horn* adjudication, *supra* p. 911, cost the state of Wyoming more than $7 million in legal fees alone. In addition, a negotiated solution can provide for delivery of "wet water" to Indians—not just the paper water rights that result from a courtroom victory. In many cases, the non-Indian parties can persuade the federal government to provide them with facilities and other benefits as well.

Many tribal claims were settled in the 1980s, and when the President signed the Puyallup Tribe of Indians Water Settlement of 1990 he issued a statement that such claims would be resolved by negotiation rather than by litigation. The Department of the Interior then issued guidelines for settlements. The thrust of official policy is to provide a framework for negotiating settlements of Indian water rights within which: 1) the United States can participate in a manner consistent with its trust responsibilities to the tribes; 2) Indians receive benefits commensurate with the claims they may release as part of a settlement; 3) Indians obtain the ability to realize value from the confirmed water rights resulting from a settlement; and 4) the costs of the settlement are appropriately shared by its beneficiaries.

Despite the announced policy, the pace of settlements slowed in the 1990s, becoming largely opportunistic since then. The ability of a state's congressional delegation to achieve passage of legislation, the will of the state, and the current policy of the federal government are all factors in whether it is realistic to settle tribal reserved rights claims. Since 1993, Congress has approved only a handful of settlements, most involving relatively small amounts of water.

The settlements have been tailored to the individual reservations and surrounding non-Indian water uses, but they reveal a pattern of common features. Nearly all guaranteed a specific quantity of water to the tribes. Several provided for water to be supplied from a federal project. Virtually all created trust funds of mostly federal money for tribes to invest in water development or economic development activities. The funds ranged from $6 million to over $150 million. Nearly all allowed for some tribal water marketing, though provisions are usually drafted to specify limits on the amount, the lessee (or purchaser), or the place of use.

To judge the "success of negotiations" one must know the motives of the participants. Indian tribes usually seek to retain intact their water rights and the sovereignty they need to exercise, to protect, and to use those rights. Non–Indian water users and state water administrators generally seek certainty of rights and maximum protection of existing uses, particularly by appropriators junior to the tribe whose interests are exposed in litigation. The federal government seeks to mollify political constituencies allied with non-Indians and state authorities, but within the constraints of its trust responsibility to the tribes. Some officials have been reluctant to commit the government to expenditures beyond the cost of defending litigation.

Where—as in the West—water is a scarce and already over-appropriated resource, one might expect negotiated settlements to be a zero-sum game. In fact, and not surprisingly, the lubricant that allows seemingly intractable conflicts to come "unstuck" is federal money, used either to fund water projects that produce more water by adding storage capacity, or to provide tribal development funds that enable tribes to take advantage of their rights by putting some of their water to use on the reservation. Settlements have produced about $693 million for tribes. Furthermore, off–reservation use and marketing of Indian water under them could allow tribes to reap economic benefits when water is not needed for on-reservation uses, though it is subject to limiting conditions and state water transfer laws. Non–Indian interests have also benefited from the settlements, gaining greater certainty, water from federal projects and expenditures for their use, and, in most cases, the availability of additional water supplies.

Indian water settlements, nevertheless, have received mixed reviews. See, for example, Lloyd Burton, American Indian Water Rights and the Limits of the Law (1991). Describing the early Navajo and Uintah–Ouray deferral agreements, Burton concluded that: "It appears in retrospect that the tribes either deferred or surrendered [the use of] potent, senior, and superior rights to a great deal of water in return for promises made but not yet fulfilled * * * or for economic development that has proved largely illusory." Id. at 69. Another concern is that the costs associated with settlements can "cannibalize" resources for other Indian programs. "The money to implement the federal share has * * * come from the Bureau of Indian Affairs (BIA) budget, competing within a limited budget with other priority programs...." Western Water Policy Review Advisory Commission, Water in the West: Challenge for the Next Century, 3–46 (1998).

Tribal Water Settlements

Date	Reservation	Funding*	Water Uses	Marketing
1982, 1992	Tohono O'odham (Papago), AZ	$15 trust, $5.2 O & M, $5.5 stat; U.S. constructs irrig. works	Tribe guaranteed 66,000 af of CAP and reclaimed water; 10,000 af of groundwater	Yes (in Tucson area only)
1985	Fort Peck, MT	none	Tribal–State compact gave tribe 525,236 af of water to irrigate 291,798 acres and allowed use of tribal water for instream flows	Yes (limited to 50,000 af per year unless state authorizes)
1978, 1984, 1992	Ak–Chin, AZ	$18.4 $10.5 to irrigation districts; U.S. constructs irrig. works	Tribe guaranteed 75,000 af from CAP to irrigate 16,000 acres	Yes (leasing in defined areas)
1987	Seminole Tribe, FL	$7.25 state and local	15% of water from South Florida Water Management District	No
1988	Mission Bands of California	$30 trust	Five bands form joint authority to administer 16,000 af rights	No

Date	Reservation	Funding*	Water Uses	Marketing
1988	Salt River, AZ	$47.47 $96 local	Tribe guaranteed 122,400 af to irrigate 27,200 acres	Yes (leasing 13,000 af to cities in Phoenix area)
1988, 2000	Ute Mountain Ute and Southern Ute, CO	$49.5 trust + $40 water fund; $16 state and local; $250 construction	Rights quantified in conjunction with the Animas–La Plata Project; 20,000 af/tribe for M & I	Yes (subject to state law)
1990	Fallon Paiute–Shoshone & Pyramid Lake Paiute, NV	$43 trust for Paiute–Shoshone; $40 trust + $25 fisheries for PL Paiute		Yes (subject to state law)
1990	Fort Hall, ID	$10 trust + $7 water mgmt + $5 land $0.5 state	Guaranteed 581,031 af diversion, 354,239 af consumption	Yes, certain stored water (on and off reservation)
1990, 2006	Fort McDowell, AZ	$23 trust + $13 loan $44 state, local, tribal	35,950 from Verde River & CAP; permitted irrigation of 22,350 acres	Yes (leasing in defined areas)
1992	Northern Cheyenne, MT	$21.5 trust; $43 to rehab dam $21.80 state	91,000 af, including 50,000 af from reservations	Yes (after ten years)
1992	Jicarilla Apache, NM	$6 trust	Authorized new diversions of 40,000 af, depletions of 32,000 af + historic uses	Yes (not inconsistent with state law)
1992	Uintah–Ouray Ute, UT	$125 trust + $73.5 development	Corrected inequities of 1965 deferral agreement; granted tribe proprietary interest in 35,500 af; other rights to be quantified	Yes (subject to state law)
1992	San Carlos Apache, AZ	$38.4 $3 state	76,435 af	Yes (100–year contracts for CAP water)
1994	Yavapai–Prescott Tribe, AZ	Up to $1.02 trust; $.2 state	1,000 af surface and 550 af CAP	Yes (only surface water from reservation)
1997	Warm Springs, OR		324,000 af consumptive use; 250 cfs—on-reservation use 200 cfs—off-reservation use plus minimum flows for fish in rivers	Yes (subject to federal and state law)
1999	Rocky Boys, MT	$48 trust and project design	20,000 af, including 10,000 af stored in federal reservoir	Yes (with federal and state approval)

Date	Reservation	Funding*	Water Uses	Marketing
2000	Shivwits Paiute, UT	$21 trust; $15.75 and $1.5 state and local for construction	4,000 af	Yes (off-reservation use subject to state and federal law)
2001	Fort Belknap	Bill has not yet passed Congress; still in negotiation	645 cfs from Milk River plus other amounts for specific lands, and tribes can divert hydrologically connected groundwater	
2003	Zuni Pueblo	$26.5 million to acquire water and settle claim. ($19.25 million from federal gov't)	1,500 af from groundwater Up to 3,500 af surface water may be purchased	Yes, but only to Zuni fee land, after which it becomes subject to state law.
2004	Gila River Indian Community	$24 million	655,000 af from the CAP, & the Gila, Salt, Verde Rivers	Yes, off-reservation sale or leasing, but not out of state
2004	Nez Perce	$23 million for water and sewer projects; acquisition of BLM land worth $7 million	50,000 af	Allows leasing
2008	Crow Tribe, MT	$44 (pending congressional approval)	300,000 af stored in Bighorn Lake	Yes (limited to contracts for 50,000 af or less)
2008	Soboba Band of Luiseno Indians, CA	$29 ($18 from water districts) + 128 acres of land	9000 af	Yes (100 year contracts)
2009	Navajo Nation, NM	Construction of $870 pipeline (pending congressional approval)	600,000 af	Yes (only within NM)
2009	Duck Valley–Shoshone and Paiute, NV	$12 (pending congressional approval)	111,476 af from East Fork Owyhee River + full flow of springs and creeks on reservation	Yes (only 265 af to upstream users)
2009	White Mountain Apache, AZ (under framework of Gila River Settlement)	Pending congressional approval	27,000 af from Salt and Little Colorado; 25,000 af from CAP	Yes (leases of 22,500 af CAP water to cities for 100 year terms)

* All figures in millions and are federal funds except as specified.

Settlement negotiations over tribal water claims are always long and difficult, and the compromises needed to reach agreement can be painful—especially for tribes, whose senior claims under *Winters* are commonly subordinated to existing (and sometimes future) non-Indian uses. Yet both tribes and states have consistently chosen settlement over litigation as the preferred approach to resolve these claims. Why? For a comprehensive review of the history and the issues surrounding tribal water settlements, see Bonnie G. Colby, John E. Thorson, and Sarah Britton, *Negotiating Tribal Water Rights: Fulfilling Promises in the Arid West* (2005).

One of the largest and most innovative tribal water settlements was the 2004 Nez Perce agreement that was concluded under Idaho's Snake

River Basin Adjudication, Pub. L. 108–447, 108 Stat. 3431 (2004). The tribe's water rights claims were unusually complex in that it sought three distinct kinds of rights: traditional on-reservation *Winters* rights for consumptive uses, unique off-reservation rights to springs on lands formerly occupied by the tribe, and instream flow rights for fish habitat. Moreover, the settlement addressed numerous matters beyond water rights, such as transfer of certain lands to the tribe, management of two fish hatcheries, and compliance with the Endangered Species Act for water projects and non-Indian users in Idaho.

A special issue of the *Idaho Law Review* includes seven articles addressing various aspects and perspectives on the settlement. 42 Idaho L. Rev. No. 3 (2006). The tribe's perspective was summarized as follows:

> The Tribe's goals in negotiation and mediation had been to obtain decreed rights for the three categories of water right claims filed in 1993. Nearly as important was to obtain an improved role for the Tribe in natural resource management issues affecting its reservation and members. Many beneficial provisions of the settlement were simply not available through litigation. The SRBA Court's limited jurisdiction could have produced at best nothing other than water rights. The funding to make those rights benefit the Tribe and its members, the transfer of land within the reservation, and the creation of many beneficial inter-governmental relationships through subsidiary settlement agreements, were all beyond the power of the water court.

K. Heidi Gudgell, Steven C. Moore, and Geoffrey Whiting, *The Nez Perce Tribe's Perspective on the Settlement of Its Water Right Claims in the Snake River Basin Adjudication,* 42 Idaho L. Rev. 563, 593 (2006). The settlement offered different benefits from the State of Idaho's point of view:

> The settlement agreement * * * resolved not only the instream flow claims but all of the Tribe's other water right claims as well. Such claims, including the claims for "on-reservation" instream flows, claims for consumptive water rights, and claims for springs and fountains, had a stronger foundational basis than the off-reservation instream flow claims and were more likely to be decreed. By resolving such claims through negotiation, the State was able to gain concessions that protected existing water rights. Such protections could not have been gained through litigation.

> Perhaps more importantly, resolving the Tribe's claims by means of the settlement agreement allowed the State to address other threats to water rights, primarily threats posed by the Endangered Species Act.
> * * *

Steven W. Strack, *Pandora's Box or Golden Opportunity? Using the Settlement of Indian Reserved Water Right Claims to Affirm State Sovereignty Over Idaho Water and Promote Intergovernmental Cooperation,* 42 Idaho L. Rev. 633, 671 (2006).

5. TRIBAL WATER MANAGEMENT

While most litigation involving Indian water rights concerns the quantity of water reserved under *Winters,* a separate issue concerns governmental authority to regulate water use. Under what circumstances do state or tribal governments have authority to regulate and manage water rights of Indians and non-Indians within reservation boundaries?

Generally, tribes have jurisdiction to regulate Indians and Indian property within reservation boundaries. Many non-Indians live within Indian reservations and, indeed, own or lease land there. As tribes have begun to clarify their reserved rights entitlements and to develop economically, they have also become more sophisticated in their ability to manage resources. Many have enacted tribal water codes and hired administrative, technical, and enforcement staffs to deal with water resources.

The exclusive right of Indian tribes to regulate Indians within Indian country is well-established. More difficult questions arise, however, when tribes regulate water use by non-Indians on non-Indian land located within reservation boundaries. But that does not mean that the state can regulate water use of the non-Indians either. See *infra*, pp. 935–937.

Few Indian water rights settlement agreements have dealt comprehensively with water rights administration and jurisdiction. This phenomenon is explained by some commentators as follows:

> Many of the water quantity settlements have adopted an approach that delays or avoids altogether the difficult issues of water administration * * *. This "jurisdictional finesse" is particularly appropriate for settlements on reservations with substantial nonmember populations, where issues of water management have roots in history and complex, checkerboard landholdings. In the Colorado Ute * * * and 1986 Fort Peck settlements, for example, the parties deferred issues of water administration until the final stages of discussion, when water allocations had been established. In the 1990 Pyramid Lake settlement, the parties left water administration issues (including selection of an agency or court to oversee operation of the Truckee River and its reservoirs) for negotiation by the states and Interior in a later operating agreement.
>
> * * * Indian water administration issues are only arising now. For example, in [*Big Horn I, supra* p. 911], the state court effort to quantify tribal reserved water rights took more than fifteen years, but did not resolve administration questions * * *. Now the state engineer asserts primary jurisdiction over the tribes' effort to change use of the reserved water right from agricultural to instream use. In a similar vein, in the Carson, Walker, and Truckee River decrees, the federal courts turned to the state engineer to make preliminary rulings on transfer applications, including those of tribes.

Peter W. Sly & Cheryl A. Maier, *Indian Water Settlements and EPA,* 5 Nat. Resources & Env't, Spring 1991, at 23, 24–25.

Steven J. Shupe, Water in Indian Country: From Paper Rights to a Managed Resource

57 U. Colo. L. Rev. 561, 577 (1986).

* * *

C. Impediments to Tribal Water Regulation

* * *

* * * Two unresolved issues continue to create uncertainty for tribes wanting to regulate the use of water on the reservation. * * *

1. Non–Indian Water Use

The land ownership pattern within many Indian reservations is a patchwork of tribal lands and parcels owned by various individuals. This checkerboarding was spawned by the General Allotment Act of 1887 wherein many tracts of reservation lands were distributed to individual tribal members. Subsequently, many of the allotments passed into non-Indian ownership, as did other tribal lands that had been deemed "surplus" by the government and opened to homesteading.

This patchwork of land ownership has created a complex pattern of Indian and non-Indian water use within many reservations. This, in turn, led to controversy over which government, tribal or state, has jurisdiction to regulate water use of non-Indians on the reservation. One specific issue that has reached the courts is whether water rights permits issued by the state to non-Indians on the reservations are valid. Tribes have argued that such permits are of no effect and that appropriators, both Indian and non-Indian, must follow tribal law in order to establish a valid right to use water on the reservation. Tribal authority to allocate and regulate limited supplies, they argue, extends not only to tribal water rights reserved under the *Winters* doctrine, but also includes any waters within the reservation.

* * *

2. The Secretarial Moratorium

In [*Walton* and *Anderson*], both the Spokane and Colville tribal governments had enacted water codes in order to assert their regulatory control over reservation water. On many reservations, such codes can be an important tool for implementing tribal policies and effectuating comprehensive water management. Numerous tribes, however, are currently inhibited from utilizing this tool due to the longstanding requirement that their codes receive the approval of the Secretary of the Interior.

In 1934, Congress passed the Indian Reorganization Act (IRA) to stem the erosion of tribal strength that had resulted from the previous allotment policy. Many tribal governments reorganized under the IRA provisions and adopted model constitutions. These IRA constitutions typically contained the provision that all codes enacted by the tribal government needed approval of the Secretary of the Interior in order for them to be valid.

In 1975, Interior Secretary Morton sent a two-paragraph memorandum to the Commissioner of Indian Affairs stating that "any tribal ordinance, resolution, code or other enactment which purports to regulate the use of water on Indian reservations" and which requires approval for its validity shall be automatically disapproved.[105] The moratorium on code approval was to remain in effect until the Department of the Interior promulgated rules providing guidelines for the adoption of tribal water codes. The Secretary expressed his concern that, without such rules, independent tribal water codes "could lead to confusion and a series of separate legal challenges which might lead to undesirable results."

On March 7, 1977, Interior Secretary Andrus published proposed rules regarding the adoption of tribal water codes. Under the proposed rules, the Secretary of the Interior must approve a tribal water code if it comports with certain conditions. First, the code must afford procedural due process to all water users on the reservations. This includes establishing a method for a just distribution of water that ensures that all those similarly situated will be given an equal opportunity to make beneficial use of supplies. Second, it must provide aggrieved persons with the opportunity to seek judicial review of administrative decisions made under the code. Third, the tribe must demonstrate its capacity to administer the code. Fourth, the code must comport with pertinent federal laws and not regulate water use within federal irrigation projects in Indian Country. Finally, and importantly, the code is limited to administering only tribal water rights under the *Winters* doctrine, and cannot regulate other waters of the reservation.

This final condition was particularly offensive to tribes, as was a provision that empowered the Secretary to enact and enforce a water code on the reservation if the tribe failed to act. Many state interests were also dissatisfied by the proposed rules. As a consequence, the Secretary did not attempt to finalize them.

The next set of proposed rules was published in early 1981. They were very similar to the 1977 provisions, including limitation of tribal code jurisdiction exclusively to the regulation of reserved *Winters* rights. Also, they spelled out the rights of non-Indians who had obtained former allotments. The rules further provided that the tribe could not prevent existing water users, Indian or non-Indian, from using the tribe's reserved

---

105. Memorandum from the Sec'y of the Interior, Rogers C.B. Morton, to the Comm'r of Indian Affairs (Jan. 15, 1975):

As you know, the Department is currently considering regulations providing for the adoption of tribal codes to allocate the use of reserved waters on Indian reservations. Our authority to regulate the use of water on Indian reservations is presently in litigation. I am informed, however, that some tribes may be considering the enactment of water use codes of their own. This could lead to confusion and a series of separate legal chal-

lenges which might lead to undesirable results.

I ask, therefore, that you instruct all agency superintendents and area directors to disapprove any tribal ordinance, resolution, code, or other enactment which purports to regulate the use of water on Indian reservations and which by the terms of the tribal governing document is subject to such approval or review in order to become or to remain effective, pending ultimate determination of this matter.

rights "until such time as an authorized tribal permittee or the tribe is prepared to make beneficial use of such reserved water." These 1981 proposed rules were more palatable to state interests, but they were never issued in final form either. Consequently, the moratorium on tribal water code approval remains in effect, bringing uncertainty to tribes that desire to implement water management systems.

Tribes have responded to the moratorium in a variety of ways. Some have chosen to ignore it and enforce water codes without Secretarial approval. Others are attempting to manage waters without enacting an ordinance or code that requires Secretarial approval. In one instance, a tribe has argued successfully for an exemption from the moratorium and is currently drafting a water code for Secretarial review.[112] The next section of this article discusses the various strategies and administration techniques which tribes are currently pursuing in order to manage and control important water resources.

III.   Tribal Water Management Strategies

* * *

* * * As the focus shifts from paper rights to a managed resource, numerous tribes are addressing the many questions involved in comprehensive water management. Among the decisions to be made are: what kind of water administration office to establish, whether to create a permit system, and how best to regulate groundwater use. There is a century of state experience in this field for tribes to assess in evaluating water management strategies. Also, tribal decisionmakers are ensuring that any water administration system on their reservation is designed to accommodate the customs and culture of the tribal members.

As discussed in the following sections, different tribes are currently at various stages of the process. Some, such as those at the Umatilla, Navajo, and Colville reservations, are already implementing their water policies through comprehensive water codes and sophisticated offices. Others are still in the formative stages and are only beginning to assess alternatives for managing tribal water resources.

A.   The Umatilla Experience

The Confederated Tribes of the Umatilla Indian Reservation began their water management process in the 1970's by assessing the reservation's water resources and how they were being used. The process involved a number of scientific investigations, including both field work and document review. Specifically, the tribes compiled streamflow data, inventoried wells on the reservation, compiled diversion and other water use records, and monitored groundwater fluctuations in critical areas.

In addition to the physical inventory, the tribes analyzed how water rights in the area were being administered by the State of Oregon. Specific

---

112. The United States acquiesced to a provision in the Fort Peck/Montana Compact that the tribes be allowed to enforce a water code applicable to the use of reservation waters by tribal members.

areas of dissatisfaction arose from the tribes' findings that state permits were being issued for large irrigation wells despite evidence that the aquifer was in an overdraft condition. It also appeared to the tribes that diversion permits for surface waters were still being approved by the state in the overappropriated Umatilla River basin. These findings helped motivate the tribe to assert regulatory authority over water resources within the reservation boundaries.

* * *

A key component of the management strategy on the Umatilla reservation is the interim water code. * * *

The code established a regulatory system under which water users, both Indian and non-Indian, are required to apply for permits. A focus of the code is the amelioration of groundwater problems associated with overuse of aquifers in portions of the reservation. Any proposed well drilling or modification to an existing well receives close scrutiny under the tribal program before it is permitted or denied. Since Oregon asserts authority over non-Indian well permitting, potential jurisdictional conflicts exist that have yet to be litigated or otherwise resolved.

B. The Navajo Regulatory System

* * * In July[, 1983], the council consolidated authority for water management under a new Division of Water Resources created to achieve numerous water policy objectives.

Five departments, employing more than two hundred people, were created within the Division to achieve these objectives. First, the Water Management Department has primary authority to regulate and manage water on the reservation and the responsibility to inventory water resources and use. It employs a groundwater geologist, soil scientist, hydrologist, water quality specialist, and other personnel to perform its duties.

Second, the Department of Water Development is the construction arm of the Division. It constructs all wells on the reservation as well as structures relating to flood control, irrigation water distribution, and impoundments.

The third department, Operations and Maintenance, is responsible for repair of water distribution facilities and the installation and repair of the many windmills needed by the Navajo people for pumping groundwater.

The Department of Planning and Design applies its economic and engineering expertise to create, assess, and implement various water development strategies. It also pursues water conservation practices in conjunction with the Navajo Young Adult Conservation Program.

Finally, the Department of Agriculture, within the Division of Water Resources, provides technical assistance on irrigation and other matters to ranchers and farmers throughout Navajo lands.

In 1984, the tribal council enacted the Navajo Nation Water Code which asserts authority "over all actions taken within the territorial jurisdiction of the Navajo Nation which affect the use of water within the Navajo Nation." * * *

The code became effective on August 2, 1984. Within one year from that date, all persons desiring to divert water from any source on the reservation were required to file an application for a water use permit. Water users, both Navajo and non-Navajo, generally have responded favorably to this requirement, and the tribe is in the process of issuing numerous water permits. Initially, some energy companies operating on Navajo lands did not respond, but following the *Kerr–McGee* decision, they too filed for water use permits. Also, to date, none of the three states affected by this assertion of jurisdiction has initiated a legal challenge to the code.

C.   The Colville Program

* * * As seen above in the *Walton* case, the Colville tribes have enacted a water code with judicially recognized authority over reservation water use. In addition, the tribes have been very active in pursuing comprehensive water quality control.

Through the efforts of their leaders, the Colville tribes were selected by the EPA for a pilot program involving the control of water pollution in Indian Country. Under this program, the tribes received financial and technical support to assess water quality problems caused by timber harvesting, mining, irrigation return flows, and other potential sources of nonpoint pollution. Following extensive scientific investigation, the tribes enacted measures designed to minimize pollution of reservation waters. These measures included a Mining Practices Water Quality Act, an Onsite Wastewater Treatment and Disposal Code, a Forest Practices Water Quality Act, and Water Quality Standards for streams running through the reservation.

* * * [T]he State of Washington recognized the desirability of coordinating its water quality programs with those of the tribes. As a consequence, the tribes and the state entered a cooperative agreement for water quality control.

* * *

* * * The state will undertake primary enforcement efforts of its regulations on fee lands within the reservation, while the tribes maintained jurisdiction over the remainder of the reservation.

Phase Two of the agreement provides for enforcement of both state and tribal regulations by a person or persons designated by the state and employed by the tribes. * * *

NOTES

1. The question of whether a tribal water code applies to non-Indians must be resolved on a case-by-case basis. In Holly v. Confederated Tribes &

Bands of the Yakima Indian Nation, 655 F.Supp. 557, 558–559 (E.D.Wash. 1985), a federal district court dealt with the Yakima Tribal Code:

> The Code in question is comprehensive, purporting to regulate all waters underlying, arising upon or flowing through or along the border of the Reservation. To determine whether the Yakima Nation's sovereign power is sufficient to apply its Code to nonmembers of the Tribe using excess waters on fee lands requires analysis under *Montana v. United States*, 450 U.S. 544 (1981). * * * Indians have lost the right to govern nonmembers residing within Reservations except in certain instances. One exception exists where nonmembers enter into consensual relationships with a tribe or its members. More importantly in this case, a tribe also retains inherent power to civilly regulate the conduct on non-Indians on fee lands "when that conduct threatens or has some direct effect on the political integrity, the economic security, or the health or welfare of the tribe." 450 U.S. at 566.
>
> Significantly, in a case arising in this district, the reviewing court held that conduct threatening the health or welfare of an Indian tribe may include conduct involving the tribe's water rights. *Walton II*, 647 F.2d at 52. In *Walton*, a non-Indian's water appropriation imperiled the Colville Confederated Tribes' downstream use of agricultural and fisheries water. On the other hand, a contrary conclusion was reached, under different circumstances, in a later action also initiated in this district. See, generally, United States v. Anderson, 736 F.2d 1358, 1365 (9th Cir.1984) (political and economic welfare of the Spokane Tribe unaffected by the conduct of nonmembers using excess water [from source located substantially off the reservation] on fee land).
>
> Here, for purposes of this motion, it is undisputed that surplus waters exist and are used by non-Indians on Reservation fee land and off the Reservation. As the facts demonstrate, the state has met its burden of demonstrating a peaceful co-existence of the non-Indian water users with the Tribes. The [defendants have] not come forward with facts to show existence of a material factual question with respect to whether non-Indian conduct related to non-Indian use of excess waters threatens the political integrity, economic security, or health and welfare of the Tribes. Nor have the non-Indians entered into agreements or dealings with the Tribes with a result of subjecting themselves to tribal civil jurisdiction. Consequently, the inescapable conclusion is the Yakima Nation has not retained the power to regulate excess water use by nonmembers on their fee land within or without the Reservation. It follows, then, that the Code is invalid to the extent it purports to bestow upon the Yakima Nation civil regulatory jurisdiction over non-Indian use of surplus waters. * * *

The Ninth Circuit Court of Appeals affirmed in Holly v. Totus, 812 F.2d 714 (9th Cir.1987) with no published opinion.

2. Most of the federal environmental laws give tribes the ability to assume the same type of primacy over the administration and enforcement of those laws that is available to states. See Clean Water Act, 33 U.S.C.A. § 1377;

Safe Drinking Water Act, 42 U.S.C.A. § 300j–11; Federal Insecticide, Fungicide and Rodenticide Act, 7 U.S.C.A. § 136u; Comprehensive Environmental Response, Compensation and Liability Act, 42 U.S.C.A. § 9626. Indian tribes thus have the power to set environmental standards stricter than state standards and therefore have power to influence up- and downstream water uses. Checkerboard patterns of Indian and non-Indian land ownership on reservations means that in most cases non-Indians must comply with tribal water quality standards if they are to be effective. Therefore, tribal management of reservation resources often requires the regulation of non-Indian land uses. See Judith V. Royster, *Oil and Water in Indian Country*, 37 Nat. Resources J. 457,460–461 (1997).

EPA regulations, 56 Fed. Reg. 64, 876 (1991), require that a tribe demonstrate the basis under the *Montana* test for its assertion of jurisdiction over non-Indians on the reservation in order to take primacy under the Clean Water Act. Tribal power to set water quality standards under the Act can also apply to off-reservation dischargers. In Albuquerque v. EPA, 97 F.3d 415 (10th Cir.1996), cert. denied 522 U.S. 965, 118 S.Ct. 410, 139 L.Ed.2d 314 (1997), the Isleta Pueblo, located on the Rio Grande downstream from Albuquerque, designated the portion of the river flowing through its boundaries as "Primary Contact Ceremonial" for member immersion and ingestion. EPA approved the designation and the tribe set arsenic levels at 17 parts per trillion versus the 50 parts per billion federal drinking water standard. The tribe was concerned that arsenic from the city's wells would endanger fish and the pueblo's centuries-old squash and corn fields. To avoid an upgrade of its treatment plant, Albuquerque argued that the Clean Water Act did not authorize EPA to approve tribal standards more stringent than New Mexico's. The Tenth Circuit upheld EPA's powers under Chevron v. Natural Resources Defense Council, 467 U.S. 837, 104 S.Ct. 2778, 81 L.Ed.2d 694 (1984). The Ninth Circuit later sustained tribal regulation of non-Indians on the Flathead Reservation in Montana. Montana v. EPA, 137 F.3d 1135 (9th Cir.1998). See Denise Fort, *State and Tribal Water Quality Standards Under the Clean Water Act: A Case Study*, 35 Nat. Resources J. 77 (1995); Robin Kundis Craig, *Borders and Discharges: Regulation of Tribal Activities Under the Clean Water Act in States with NPDES Authority*, 16 UCLA J. Envtl. L. & Pol'y 1 (1998); and Jessica Owley, *Tribal Sovereignty Over Water Quality*, 20 J. Land Use & Envtl. L. 61 (2004–2005).

3. The federal Endangered Species Act (ESA) has been a double-edged sword for tribes. Some tribes, like the Pyramid Lake Paiutes, have used the Act to obtain more water for reservation fisheries management. See Carson–Truckee Water Conservancy Dist. v. Clark, 741 F.2d 257 (9th Cir. 1984), cert. denied 470 U.S. 1083, 105 S.Ct. 1842, 85 L.Ed.2d 141 (1985), and discussion *supra* p. 741. But other tribes have found it an impediment to increased irrigation and other planned water uses. Development of water and other natural resources on reservations has lagged behind off-reservation development. Several tribes have begun to find that by the time they have the capital to pursue economic development, including making use of *Winters* rights, the streams in question are already in such distress that some species of fish and wildlife may be faced with extinction. Thus, new tribal activity may face limitations under the ESA. After considerable negotiation with tribal leaders, the Secretaries of the U.S. Departments of Interior and Commerce issued a secretarial order directing their agencies to comply with the ESA "in a manner that harmonizes the federal trust responsibility to tribes, tribal sovereignty, and statutory missions of the departments, and that strives to ensure that Indian tribes do not bear a disproportionate burden for the conservation of listed species, so as to avoid or minimize the potential for conflict and confrontation." Secretarial Order No. 3206, "American Indian Tribal Rights, Federal–Tribal Trust Responsibilities, and the Endangered species Act," June 5, 1997. See Charles F. Wilkinson, Symposium, *Indian Law Into the Twenty–First Century: The Role of Bilateralism in Fulfilling the Federal–Tribal Relationship: The Tribal Rights–Endangered Species Secretarial Order*, 72 Wash. L. Rev. 1063 (1997). For competing views on the interplay of tribal water rights and the ESA in the San Juan River Basin, *see* Hannah Gosnell, *Section 7 of the Endangered Species Act and the Art of Compromise: The Evolution of a Reasonable and Prudent Alternative for the Animas–La Plata Project*, 41 Nat. Resources J. 561 (2001) and David J. Hayes, *Integrating ESA Goals into a Larger Context: The Lesson of Animas–La Plata*, 41 Nat. Resources J. 627 (2001).

CHAPTER TEN

TRANSBOUNDARY WATERS: INTERSTATE AND INTERNATIONAL ALLOCATION

A. INTERSTATE ALLOCATION

After his pioneering exploration of the Colorado River, John Wesley Powell urged that political boundaries follow the divides among river drainages. Report on the Lands of the Arid Region of the United States, With a More Detailed Account of the Lands of Utah (1879). He foresaw that the West's success, perhaps its survival, would depend on the ability of people to cooperate in the allocation and development of water. Powell's vision was largely ignored as counties were laid out and as state boundaries were drawn. Few western state lines coincide with the divides between watersheds; most are straight lines drawn on a map. Idaho's Panhandle is an exception—the Continental Divide forms the eastern boundary between Idaho and Montana so that most of Montana is in the Missouri Basin and most of Idaho in the Columbia. Water boundaries, but not watershed lines, are much more common east of the Mississippi. In several cases they are the centerlines or edges of a river, providing rich fodder for conflicts over the respective interests of neighboring states in the waterway. From the Progressive Conservation Era through the 1970s, there were many federal proposals and legislative experiments to manage large-drainage basins on an integrated hydrologic basis but, with few exceptions, the states and local water users successfully opposed these efforts.

As a result, disputes abound among states that share common waterways along their borders or within their territories. Many relate to allocation of rights to use the resource. Others concern pollution in one state that affects another. These battles have often been fought in courts, leaving to federal judges the task of dividing the waters or controlling their use. In a number of cases the disputant states have taken another approach, bargaining with one another to reach agreement in the form of an interstate compact, which must be ratified by the United States Congress. A third means of interstate water allocation, congressional action, has been used only once, in the apportionment of the waters of the Colorado River. Congress also ratified a settlement which allocated the Truckee River between California and Nevada users.

The chore of allocating rights of states, or individuals in more than one state, to use shared waterways raises a variety of questions. What court has jurisdiction over a waterway that is in more than a single state? Should it matter what legal systems for water allocation are applied within the individual states? Of what importance is it that water use commenced earlier in one state than in another? Is it significant that water is used to produce more economic benefit in one state than the other? How can a slower developing state plan for its future needs and expansion? How are non-consumptive uses valued compared to consumptive ones?

Thus, resolution of interstate conflicts over rights in streams is a *sine qua non* of major development, whether conducted by private enterprise or by the state or federal government. Until state claims have been reduced to definite rights in specified quantities of water, private capital cannot afford the investment risk, states will have difficulty selling bonds, and even the federal government will not authorize projects.

1. ADJUDICATION

Disputes over rights to use interstate waters have regularly been resolved by courts. Competing claimants continue to turn to the courts; in recent years, however, there have been efforts to use a variety of alternative dispute processes to resolve these disputes. Problems with adjudication arise when the dispute is between individuals on different sides of a state line. In the usual case of an upstream user (in State A) interfering with a downstream user (in State B), the latter can enter the courts of State A and obtain personal service on the defendant, or can go into federal district court in either state on diversity of citizenship jurisdiction (assuming the requisite jurisdictional amount is in controversy), similarly obtaining personal service on the defendant within State A.

Jurisdiction over the subject matter raises a conceptual problem, since the court's decree affects a water right not only in State A but also in State B, where the court's writ does not run, whether it be a federal or a state court. Bean v. Morris, 221 U.S. 485, 31 S.Ct. 703, 55 L.Ed. 821 (1911), *infra*, p. 940, offers guidance on this question.

States also find themselves parties in conflicts over water uses. Such disputes are adjudicated in the United States Supreme Court, which under art. III, § 2, cl. 2 has original jurisdiction in "all cases * * * in which a state shall be a party." The Supreme Court's original jurisdiction has been invoked in disputes on the Arkansas, Colorado, Connecticut, Delaware, Laramie, Mississippi, North Platte, Potomac, Pecos, Republican, Rio Grande, Vermejo, Walla Walla, and the Yellowstone Rivers.

In its original jurisdiction, the Supreme Court acts in the capacity of a trial court, although it does not directly take evidence. The proceeding commences with the filing of a complaint, which is then subject to various motions including a motion to dismiss. If the complaint survives the motion stage, the respondent state is required to answer and then, typically, a special master (usually a retired federal judge or a distinguished water lawyer) is appointed to take evidence, prepare findings of fact and conclusions of law, and recommend a decree. The Court then considers the matter on exceptions to the master's report. Usually the Court writes an opinion and enters a decree. The Court may or may not agree with the master. New Jersey v. New York, 283 U.S. 336, 51 S.Ct. 478, 75 L.Ed. 1104 (1931), *infra* p. 948, illustrates interstate stream adjudications by the Court.

The Supreme Court has developed its own common law in exercising its jurisdiction over interstate water disputes. The Court has announced the doctrine of "equitable apportionment" for allocating rights to use waters among states. A line of cases spanning over a century has set forth the several considerations the Court will weigh in making its apportionments. The cases culminate in Colorado v. New Mexico, 467 U.S. 310, 104 S.Ct. 2433, 81 L.Ed.2d 247 (1984), *infra* p. 961.

The evolution of federal common law in interstate disputes over water pollution has been affected by extensive federal water quality legislation. Milwaukee v. Illinois and Michigan, 451 U.S. 304, 101 S.Ct. 1784, 68 L.Ed.2d 114 (1981), held that the federal common law of nuisance in the area of water quality was preempted by the 1972 Amendments to the Federal Water Pollution Control Act (Clean Water Act). International Paper Co. v. Ouellette, 479 U.S. 481, 107 S.Ct. 805, 93 L.Ed.2d 883 (1987), confirmed that analysis and held that, since the Clean Water Act had preempted interstate nuisance law, the only state law applicable to a pollution point source was that of the state in which the point source was located. Later, Arkansas v. Oklahoma, 503 U.S. 91, 112 S.Ct. 1046, 117 L.Ed.2d 239 (1992), *infra* p. 966, held that the water quality standards of a downstream state could be incorporated into an EPA permit under the Clean Water Act and applied against a polluter in an upstream state, in the exercise of EPA discretion.

a. Litigation Between Water Users

Bean v. Morris

Supreme Court of the United States, 1911.
221 U.S. 485, 31 S.Ct. 703, 55 L.Ed. 821.

■ MR. JUSTICE HOLMES delivered the opinion of the court.

This suit was brought by the respondent, Morris, to prevent the petitioners from so diverting the waters of Sage Creek in Montana as to interfere with an alleged prior right of Morris, by appropriation, to two hundred and fifty inches of such waters in Wyoming. Afterwards the other respondent, Howell, was allowed to intervene and make a similar claim. Sage Creek is a small creek, not navigable, that joins the Stinking Water in Wyoming, the latter stream flowing into the Big Horn, which then flows back northerly into Montana again, and unites with the Yellowstone. The Circuit Court made a decree that Morris was entitled to 100 inches miner's measurement, of date April, 1887, and that, subject to Morris, Howell was entitled to one hundred and ten inches, of date August 1, 1890, both parties being prior in time and right to the petitioners. 146 Fed.Rep. 423. On appeal the findings of fact below were adopted and the decree of the Circuit

Court affirmed by the Circuit Court of Appeals. 159 Fed. 651; 86 C.C.A. 519.

It was admitted at the argument that but for the fact that the prior appropriation was in one State, Wyoming, and the interference in another, Montana, the decree would be right, so far as the main and important question is concerned. It is true that some minor points were suggested, such as laches, abandonment, the statute of limitations, etc., but the findings of two courts have been against the petitioners upon all of these, and we see no reason for giving them further consideration. So we pass at once to the question of private water rights as between users in different States.

We know no reason to doubt, and we assume, that, subject to such rights as the lower State might be decided by this court to have, and to vested private rights, if any, protected by the Constitution, the State of Montana has full legislative power over Sage Creek while it flows within that State. Kansas v. Colorado, 206 U.S. 46. Therefore, subject to the same qualifications, we assume that the concurrence of the laws of Montana with those of Wyoming is necessary to create easements, or such private rights and obligations as are in dispute, across their common boundary line. Missouri v. Illinois, 200 U.S. 496, 521. Rickey Land & Cattle Co. v. Miller & Lux, 218 U.S. 258, 260. But with regard to such rights as came into question in the older States, we believe that it always was assumed, in the absence of legislation to the contrary, that the States were willing to ignore boundaries, and allowed the same rights to be acquired from outside the State that could be acquired from within. * * *

There is even stronger reason for the same assumption here. Montana cannot be presumed to be intent on suicide, and there are as many if not more cases in which it would lose as there are in which it would gain, if it invoked a trial of strength with its neighbors. In this very instance, as has been said, the Big Horn, after it has received the waters of Sage Creek, flows back into that State. But this is the least consideration. The doctrine of appropriation has prevailed in these regions probably from the first moment that they knew of any law, and has continued since they became territory of the United States. It was recognized by the statutes of the United States, while Montana and Wyoming were such territory, Rev.Stat., §§ 2339, 2340, p. 429, Act of March 3, 1877, c. 107, 19 Stat. 377, and is recognized by both States now. Before the state lines were drawn of course the principle prevailed between the lands that were destined to be thus artificially divided. Indeed, Morris had made his appropriation before either State was admitted to the Union. The only reasonable presumption is that the States upon their incorporation continued the system that had prevailed theretofore, and made no changes other than those necessarily implied or expressed.

It follows from what we have said that it is unnecessary to consider what limits there may be to the powers of an upper State, if it should seek to do all that it could. The grounds upon which such limits would stand are referred to in Rickey Land & Cattle Co. v. Miller & Lux, 218 U.S. 258, 261.

So it is unnecessary to consider whether Morris is not protected by the Constitution; for it seems superfluous to fall back upon the citadel until some attack drives him to that retreat. Other matters adverted to in argument, so far as not disposed of by what we have said, have been dealt with sufficiently in two courts. It is enough here to say that we are satisfied with their discussion and confine our own to the only matter that warranted a certiorari or suggested questions that might be grave.

Decree affirmed.

NOTE

1.   Applications to transfer water across state lines and the administration of Supreme Court decrees raise similar issues. See Hagan v. Upper Republican Natural Resources Dist., 261 Neb. 312, 622 N.W.2d 627 (2001) (irrigators potentially injured by depletion of aquifer have standing to challenge permit allowing a cross border transfer); Kansas v. Colorado, 514 U.S. 673, 115 S.Ct. 1733, 131 L.Ed.2d 759 (2004), discussed *infra* at page 947, rejected Kansas's objection to the final decree in an interstate compact interpretation that allowed Colorado Water Courts to determine the amount of replacement credits Colorado could earn by putting non-Arkansas River water into the system and by retiring lands in the basin. Kansas had a remedy; she can seek original jurisdiction review of any Colorado decision.

2.   Bean applies to small scale disputes which do not rise to the dignity of an equitable apportionment, but it is always possible to characterize the dispute as one between states which must be litigated as an original jurisdiction action. Badgley v. New York, 606 F.2d 358 (2d Cir. 1979), cert. denied, 447 U.S. 906, 100 S.Ct. 2989, 64 L.Ed.2d 855 (1980), was a challenge to proposed New York diversions by Pennsylvania residents, and the court held that any challenges to one state's use of the Delaware must be brought by another state as an original action in the Supreme Court. However, a subsequent case by the same judge, repeated the rule only as dictum. Hudson River Fishermen's Ass'n v. City of New York, 751 F.Supp. 1088, 1093 (S.D.N.Y. 1990), aff'd mem., 940 F.2d 649 (2d Cir. 1991). Compare Alabama v. U.S. Army Corps of Engineers, 424 F.3d 1117 (11th Cir. 2005). The U.S. Corps of Engineers approved a settlement between power suppliers and Georgia water suppliers over the management of Lake Lanier in northern Georgia. Alabama and Florida sued the Corps because the settlement would permit increased withdrawals of water from Lake Lanier to the benefit of Georgia and to possible detriment of the downstream states. The Eleventh Circuit held that a state has standing to sue the federal government to force it to comply with federal law (NEPA) in the operation of a federal reservoir. The fact that the action will impact the allocation of interstate stream does not per se transform the action into a request for an equitable apportionment. The broader controversy is discussed at page 976, *infra*; the opinion on the merits is at page 847, *supra*.

b.   Litigation Between States

Kansas v. Colorado

Supreme Court of the United States, 1907.
206 U.S. 46, 27 S.Ct. 655, 51 L.Ed. 956.

■ MR. JUSTICE BREWER, * * * delivered the opinion of the court. * * *

Turning now to the controversy as here presented, it is whether Kansas has a right to the continuous flow of the waters of the Arkansas River, as that flow existed before any human interference therewith, or Colorado the right to appropriate the waters of that stream so as to prevent that continuous flow, or that the amount of the flow is subject to the superior authority and supervisory control of the United States. * * * [W]hen the States of Kansas and Colorado were admitted into the Union they were admitted with the full powers of local sovereignty which belonged to other States, * * * and Colorado by its legislation has recognized the right of appropriating the flowing waters to the purposes of irrigation. Now the question arises between two States, one recognizing generally the common law rule of riparian rights and the other prescribing the doctrine of the public ownership of flowing water. Neither State can legislate for or impose its own policy upon the other. A stream flows through the two and a controversy is presented as to the flow of that stream.

[W]henever, * * * the action of one State reaches through the agency of natural laws into the territory of another State, the question of the extent and the limitations of the rights of the two States becomes a matter of justiciable dispute between them, and this court is called upon to settle that dispute in such a way as will recognize the equal rights of both and at the same time establish justice between them. In other words, through these successive disputes and decisions this court is practically building up what may not improperly be called interstate common law. This very case presents a significant illustration. Before either Kansas or Colorado was settled the Arkansas River was a stream running through the territory which now composes these two States. Arid lands abound in Colorado. Reclamation is possible only by the application of water, and the extreme contention of Colorado is that it has a right to appropriate all the waters of this stream for the purposes of irrigating its soil and making more valuable its own territory. But the appropriation of the entire flow of the river would naturally tend to make the lands along the stream in Kansas less arable. It would be taking from the adjacent territory that which had been the customary natural means of preserving its arable character. On the other hand, the possible contention of Kansas, that the flowing water in the Arkansas must, in accordance with the extreme doctrine of the common law of England, be left to flow as it was wont to flow, no portion of it being appropriated in Colorado for the purposes of irrigation, would have the effect to perpetuate a desert condition in portions of Colorado beyond the power of reclamation. Surely here is a dispute of a justiciable nature which must and ought to be tried and determined. If the two States were absolutely independent nations it would be settled by treaty or by force. Neither of these ways being practicable, it must be settled by decision of this court.

* * *

This changes in some respect the scope of our inquiry. It is not limited to the simple matter of whether any portion of the waters of the Arkansas is withheld by Colorado. We must consider the effect of what has been done upon the conditions in the respective States and so adjust the dispute upon the basis of equality of rights as to secure as far as possible to Colorado the benefits of irrigation without depriving Kansas of the like beneficial effects of a flowing stream.

* * * [W]e are justified in looking at the question not narrowly and solely as to the amount of the flow in the channel of the Arkansas River, inquiring merely whether any portion thereof is appropriated by Colorado, but we may properly consider what, in case a portion of that flow is appropriated by Colorado, are the effects of such appropriation upon Kansas territory. For instance, if there be many thousands of acres in Colorado destitute of vegetation, which by the taking of water from the Arkansas River and in no other way can be made valuable as arable lands producing an abundance of vegetable growth, and this transformation of desert land has the effect, through percolation of water in the soil, or in any other way, of giving to Kansas territory, although not in the Arkansas Valley, a benefit from water as great as that which would inure by keeping the flow of the Arkansas in its channel undiminished, then we may rightfully regard the usefulness to Colorado as justifying its action, although the locality of the benefit which the flow of the Arkansas through Kansas has territorially changed. * * * May we not consider some appropriation by Colorado of the waters of the Arkansas to the irrigation and reclamation of its arid lands as a reasonable exercise of its sovereignty and as not unreasonably trespassing upon any rights of Kansas? And here we must notice the local law of Kansas. * * *

"The use of water by a riparian proprietor for irrigation purposes must be reasonable under all the circumstances, and the right must be exercised with due regard to the equal right of every other riparian owner along the course of the stream.

"A diminution of the flow of water over riparian land caused by its use for irrigation purposes by upper riparian proprietors occasions no injury for which damages may be allowed unless it results in subtracting from the value of the land by interfering with the reasonable uses of the water which the landowner is able to enjoy."

* * *

As Kansas thus recognizes the right of appropriating the waters of a stream for the purposes of irrigation, subject to the condition of an equitable division between the riparian proprietors, she cannot complain if the same rule is administered between herself and a sister State. * * *

Comparing the tables of population it will be perceived that both the counties in Colorado and Kansas made a considerable increase in the years from 1880 to 1890; that while the Colorado counties continued their increase from 1890 to 1900, the Kansas counties lost. As the withdrawal of water in Colorado for irrigating purposes became substantially effective about the year 1890, it might, if nothing else appeared, not unreasonably be concluded that the diminished flow of the river in Kansas, caused by the action of Colorado, had resulted in making the land more unproductive, and hence induced settlers to leave the State. As against this it should be noted, as a matter of history, that in the years preceding 1890, Kansas passed through a period of depression, with crops largely a failure in different parts of the State. But, more than that, in 1889 Oklahoma, lying directly south of Kansas, was opened for settlement and immediately there was a large immigration into that territory, coming from all parts of the West, and especially from the State of Kansas, induced by glowing reports of its great possibilities. The population of Oklahoma, as shown by the United States census, was, in 1890, 61,834, and in 1900, 348,331.

Turning to the tables of the corn and wheat products, they do not disclose any marked injury which can be attributed to a diminution of the flow of the river. While there is a variance in the amount produced in the different counties from year to year, it is a variance no more than that which will be found in other parts of the Union, and although the population from 1890 to 1900 in fact diminished, the amount of both the corn and wheat product largely increased. Not only was the total product increased, but the productiveness per acre seems to have been materially improved. Take the corn crop, and per acre, it was, in 1890, 12 bushels and a fraction; in 1895, 21 and a fraction, in 1900, 15, and in 1904, 28 bushels. Of wheat, the product per acre in 1890 was nearly 15 bushels; in 1895 it was only about 3 bushels. (For some reason, while that was a good year for corn, it seems to have been a bad year for wheat.) But in 1900 the product per acre rose to 19 bushels, and in 1904 it was 12 bushels.

These are official figures taken from the United States census reports, and they tend strongly to show that the withdrawal of the water in Colorado for purposes of irrigation has not proved a source of serious detriment to the Kansas counties along the Arkansas River. It is not strange that the western counties show the least development, for being nearest the irrigation in Colorado, they would be most affected thereby. At one time there were some irrigating ditches in these western counties, which promised to be valuable in supplying water and thus increasing the productiveness of the lands in the vicinity of the stream, and it is true that those ditches have ceased to be of much value, the flow in them having largely diminished.

It cannot be denied in view of all the testimony (for that which we have quoted is but a sample of much more bearing upon the question), that the diminution of the flow of water in the river by the irrigation of Colorado has worked some detriment to the southwestern part of Kansas, and yet when we compare the amount of this detriment with the great benefit which has obviously resulted to the counties in Colorado, it would seem that equality of right and equity between the two States forbids any interference with the present withdrawal of water in Colorado for purposes of irrigation.

* * *

Summing up our conclusions, we are of the opinion * * * that the appropriation of the waters of the Arkansas by Colorado, for purposes of irrigation, has diminished the flow of water into the State of Kansas, that the result of that appropriation has been the reclamation of large areas in Colorado, transforming thousands of acres into fertile fields and rendering possible their occupation and cultivation when otherwise they would have continued barren and unoccupied, that while the influence of such diminution has been of perceptible injury to portions of the Arkansas Valley in Kansas, particularly those portions closest to the Colorado line, yet to the great body of the valley it has worked little, if any, detriment, and regarding the interests of both States and the right of each to receive benefit through irrigation and in any other manner from the waters of this stream, we are not satisfied that Kansas has made out a case entitling it to a decree. At the same time it is obvious that if the depletion of the waters of the river by Colorado continues to increase there will come a time when Kansas may justly say that there is no longer an equitable division of benefits and may rightfully call for relief against the action of Colorado, its corporations and citizens in appropriating the waters of the Arkansas for irrigation purposes.

The decree which, therefore, will be entered will dismiss the bill of the State of Kansas as against all the defendants, without prejudice to the right of the plaintiff to institute new proceedings when ever it shall appear that through a material increase in the depletion of the waters of the Arkansas by Colorado, its corporations or citizens, the substantial interests of Kansas are being injured to the extent of destroying the equitable apportionment of benefits between the two States resulting from the flow of the river. * * *

NOTES

1. In an earlier case, Kansas v. Colorado, 185 U.S. 125, 22 S.Ct. 552, 46 L.Ed. 838 (1902), the first water rights case over which the United States Supreme Court exercised original jurisdiction, Kansas alleged that Colorado diversions had caused irreparable damage to crops and livestock but the Court declined to address the claim absent proof of an actual threat by Colorado's use to exhaust the supply of water in Kansas. After further evidence was presented in 1907, the Court decided the principal case. After the 1907 decision, several Kansas ditch companies sued Colorado ditch companies to adjudicate priorities. When attempts at settlement failed, Colorado sued to enjoin Kansas and the ditch companies from bringing suit against Colorado ditch companies. Colorado v. Kansas, 320 U.S. 383, 64 S.Ct. 176, 88 L.Ed. 116 (1943). The Court again held that the benefit to Colorado outweighed the injury to Kansas, and ruled for Colorado. After the first three lawsuits, Kansas and Colorado, with congressional permission, entered into the Arkansas River Compact in 1948, the same year the John Martin Reservoir (located on the Arkansas River in Colorado) was completed. See Mark J. Wagner, Note, *The Parting of the Waters—The Dispute Between Colorado and Kansas Over the Arkansas River,* 24 Washburn L.J. 99 (1984) and David W. Robbins and Dennis M. Montgomery, *The Arkansas River Compacts* 5 U. Denv. Water L. Rev. 58 (2001).

2. In March 1986, Kansas presented a fourth suit in its 100 plus years dispute over Colorado's alleged illegal diversion of water. The suit alleged that Colorado had "materially depleted" the river's flow contrary to the commitments made in the 1948 Compact. The trial was bifurcated into a liability and a remedy phase. The Special Master found that post-Compact groundwater use in Colorado "materially depleted" the Arkansas and thus violated Article IV–D of the Arkansas River Compact. Kansas v. Colorado, 543 U.S. 86, 125 S.Ct. 526, 160 L.Ed.2d 418 (2004). Colorado's argument that Kansas was barred by laches was rejected because Kansas never had clear evidence of Compact violations. For an argument that the Court should entertain laches arguments see Douglas Grant, Limiting Liability for Long–Continued Breach of Interstate Water Allocation Compacts, 43 Nat. Res. J. 373 (2003).

In the damages phase, the Special Master ruled that damages should be measured by Kansas's losses not Colorado's profits, that the damages could be paid in money not water, and that Kansas was entitled to prejudgment interest. Kansas v. Colorado, 533 U.S. 1, 121 S.Ct. 2023, 150 L.Ed.2d 72 (2001). Colorado argued that the Eleventh Amendment barred state damage actions, but the Court held that the Amendment only bars suits by citizens of another state and does not bar suits where a state has a "direct interest" in the outcome. "[I]n Texas v. New Mexico we held that enforcement of an interstate water compact by means of recovery of money damages can be within a State's proper pursuit of the 'general public interest' in an original action." 121 S.Ct. at 2028. The Court also affirmed the Special Master's conclusion that the law allows prejudgment interest for unliquidated damages and dismissed Colorado's objections to the methods used to calculate interest. Kansas's losses were measured by calculating the amount of farmland affected by Colorado's violations, the crops planted on the land, the price of the crops, and the difference in yield likely to be produced by the availability of more water. Both parties "were in agreement concerning most of the facts bearing on the Special Master's calculations" of damages. Id. at 2033. They only "parted ways on the question of exactly how much additional yield would have been produced with the missing water." Id. Although both states developed models to demonstrate the quantitative lost yield, the Colorado expert was forced to "abandon his position when confronted with flaws in his data." Id. With "[i]ts own expert having recanted his alternative proposal" Colorado argued that Kansas's crop loss estimates could not be correct because "if they were it would have been economically profitable for the affected farmers to drill wells" and because they did not do so, the diverted water [could not have been] "as valuable as Kansas's experts claim[ed]." Id. The Court agreed with the Special Master's conclusion that Kansas farmers had many reasons, including lack of money, for not drilling wells and observed that Colorado was trying "to poke holes in Kansas' methodology through a speculative application of abstract economic theory." Id. The case was remanded to the Special Master for a calculation of damages and preparation of a final judgment. Kansas v. Colorado, 543 U.S. 86, 125 S.Ct. 526, 160 L.Ed.2d 418 (2004) considered several damage and compliance issues. It rejected Kansas's motion to appoint a River Master to resolve technical disputes relating to the enforcement of the decree and accepted the Special Master's recommendation that he be allowed to resolve them if the parties could not do so themselves. Administration of the decree involved a complex hydrologic model, and "modeling disputes ... involve not just measurement inputs, but basic assumptions underlying the model." The Court also rejected Kansas's argument that the computer model could be run with one year's data and agreed with the Special Master that 10 years of data are required to match simulations with historic data. Justice Breyer also accepted the Special Master's "equitable" conclusion that in light of its 2001 decision, pre-judgment interest should only be calculated on post–1985 or "late" damages. Kansas thus recovered $38 million rather than $53 million.

New Jersey v. New York

Supreme Court of the United States, 1931.
283 U.S. 336, 51 S.Ct. 478, 75 L.Ed. 1104.

■ Mr. Justice Holmes delivered the opinion of the Court.

This is a bill in equity by which the State of New Jersey seeks to enjoin the State of New York and the City of New York from diverting any waters from the Delaware River or its tributaries, and particularly from the Neversink River, Willowemoc River, Beaver Kill, East Branch of the Delaware River and Little Delaware River, or from any part of any one of them. The other rivers named are among the headwaters of the Delaware and flow into it where it forms a boundary between New York and Pennsylvania. The Delaware continues its course as such boundary to Tristate Rock, near Port Jervis in New York, at which point Pennsylvania and New York are met by New Jersey. From there the River marks the boundary between Pennsylvania and New Jersey until Pennsylvania stops at the Delaware state line, and from then on the River divides Delaware from New Jersey until it reaches the Atlantic between Cape Henlopen and Cape May.

New York proposes to divert a large amount of water from the above-named tributaries of the Delaware and from the watershed of that river to the watershed of the Hudson River in order to increase the water supply of the City of New York. New Jersey insists on a strict application of the rules of the common law governing private riparian proprietors subject to the same sovereign power. Pennsylvania intervenes to protect its interests as against anything that might be done to prejudice its future needs.

We are met at the outset by the question what rule is to be applied. It is established that a more liberal answer may be given than in a controversy between neighbors members of a single State. Connecticut v. Massachusetts, 282 U.S. 660. Different considerations come in when we are dealing with independent sovereigns having to regard the welfare of the whole population and when the alternative to settlement is war. In a less degree, perhaps, the same is true of the quasi-sovereignties bound together in the Union. A river is more than an amenity, it is a treasure. It offers a necessity of life that must be rationed among those who have power over it. New York has the physical power to cut off all the water within its jurisdiction. But clearly the exercise of such a power to the destruction of the interest of lower States could not be tolerated. And on the other hand equally little could New Jersey be permitted to require New York to give up its power altogether in order that the River might come down to it undiminished. Both States have real and substantial interests in the River that must be reconciled as best they may be. The different traditions and practices in different parts of the country may lead to varying results, but the effort always is to secure an equitable apportionment without quibbling over formulas.

This case was referred to a Master and a great mass of evidence was taken. In a most competent and excellent report the Master adopted the principle of equitable division which clearly results from the decisions of the last quarter of a century. Where that principle is established there is not much left to discuss. The removal of water to a different watershed obviously must be allowed at times unless States are to be deprived of the most beneficial use on formal grounds. In fact it has been allowed repeatedly and has been practiced by the States concerned.

New Jersey alleges that the proposed diversion will transgress its rights in many respects. That it will interfere with the navigability of the Delaware without the authority of Congress or the Secretary of War. That it will deprive the State and its citizens who are riparian owners of the undiminished flow of the stream to which they are entitled by the common law as adopted by both States. That it will injuriously affect water power and the ability to develop it. That it will injuriously affect the sanitary conditions of the River. That it will do the same to the industrial use of it. That it will increase the salinity of the lower part of the River and of Delaware Bay to the injury of the oyster industry there. That it will injure the shad fisheries. That it will do the same to the municipal water supply of the New Jersey towns and cities on the River. That by lowering the level of the water it will injure the cultivation of adjoining lands; and finally, that it will injuriously affect the River for recreational purposes. The bill also complains of the change of watershed, already disposed of; denies the necessity of the diversion; charges extravagant use of present supplies, and alleges that the plan will violate the Federal Water Power Act, 16 U.S.C.A.

§§ 791–823 (but see U.S.Code, Tit. 16, § 821 [16 U.S.C.A. § 821]),* interfere with interstate commerce, prefer the ports of New York to those of New Jersey and will take the property of New Jersey and its citizens without due process of law.

The Master finds that the above-named tributaries of the Delaware are not navigable waters of the United States at and above the places where the City of New York proposes to erect dams. Assuming that relief by injunction still might be proper if a substantial diminution within the limits of navigability was threatened, United States v. Rio Grande Dam & Irrigation Co., 174 U.S. 690, 709, he called as a witness General George B. Pillsbury, Assistant Chief of Engineers of the United States Army, who was well acquainted with the River and the plan, and who, although not speaking officially for the War Department, satisfied the Master's mind that the navigable capacity of the River would not be impaired. * * *

With regard to water power the Master concludes that any future plan of New Jersey for constructing dams would need the consent of Congress and of the States of New York and Pennsylvania and, though possible as a matter of engineering, probably would not pay. He adds that there is no such showing of a present interest as to entitle New Jersey to relief. We have spoken at the outset of the more general qualifications of New Jersey's rights as against another State. The Master finds that the taking of 600 millions of gallons daily from the tributaries will not materially affect the River or its sanitary condition, or as a source of municipal water supply, or for industrial uses, or for agriculture, or for the fisheries for shad. The effect upon the use for recreation and upon its reputation in that regard will be somewhat more serious, as will be the effect of increased salinity of the River upon the oyster fisheries. The total is found to be greater than New Jersey ought to bear, but the damage can be removed by reducing the draft of New York to 440 million gallons daily; constructing an efficient plant for the treatment of sewage entering the Delaware or Neversink (the main source of present pollution) thereby reducing the organic impurities 85% and treating the effluent with a germicide so as to reduce the Bacillus Coli originally present in the sewage by 90%; and finally, subject to the qualifications in the decree, when the stage of the Delaware falls below .50 c.s.m. at Port Jervis, New York, or Trenton, New Jersey, by releasing water from the impounding reservoirs of New York, sufficient to restore the flow at those points to .50 c.s.m. We are of opinion that the Master's report should be confirmed and that a decree should be entered to the following effect, subject to such modifications as may be ordered by the Court hereafter.

1.   The injunction prayed for by New Jersey so far as it would restrain the State of New York or City of New York from diverting from the Delaware River or its tributaries to the New York City water supply the equivalent of 440 million gallons of water daily is denied, but is granted to

---

* 16 U.S.C.A. § 821 reads:

Nothing contained in this chapter shall be construed as affecting or intending to affect or in any way to interfere with the laws of the respective States relating to the control, appropriation, use, or distribution of water used in irrigation or for municipal or other uses, or any vested right acquired therein. [Eds.]

restrain the said State and City from diverting water in excess of that amount. The denial of the injunction as above is subject to the [conditions concerning effluent treatment and reservoir releases in the preceding paragraph].

2.   The diversion herein allowed shall not constitute a prior appropriation and shall not give the State of New York and City of New York any superiority of right over the State of New Jersey and Commonwealth of Pennsylvania in the enjoyment and use of the Delaware River and its tributaries.

* * *

6.   Any of the parties hereto, complainant, defendants or intervenor, may apply at the foot of this decree for other or further action or relief and this Court retains jurisdiction of the suit for the purpose of any order or direction or modification of this decree, or any supplemental decree that it may deem at any time to be proper in relation to the subject matter in controversy.

* * *

NOTES

1.   The decree was amended in 1954 to allow increased diversions after completion of the Cannonsville Reservoir, but the decree required at such time a minimum flow at Montague (which became the measuring point in place of Point Jervis). New Jersey v. New York, 347 U.S. 995, 74 S.Ct. 842, 98 L.Ed. 1127 (1954). Who bears the risk of a drought under the initial and amended decrees?

2.   After two hurricanes caused extensive flooding, a congressionally-mandated study recommended a new location for the mainstem reservoir anticipated in the decree. Eventually the four states entered into a compact responding to the new conditions and varying the terms of the decree, and they added the federal government as a party. The compact is discussed in Joseph W. Dellapenna, *Delaware and Susquehanna River Basins* in 6 Water and Water Rights 137. See page 983, *infra* for further discussion of the Compact.

A. Dan Tarlock, The Law of Equitable Apportionment Revisited, Updated, and Restated

56 U. Colo. L. Rev. 381, 385–400 (1985).

The Court first announced its power to apportion equitably interstate streams in *Kansas v. Colorado*.[15] This seminal case arose when Kansas sued Colorado to enjoin Colorado diversions on the Arkansas River. The Court rejected both Kansas's argument that Colorado could not use the river and Colorado's argument that territorial sovereignty gave it the right

15.   206 U.S. 46 (1907).

to deplete the entire flow of the stream, in favor of a sharing rule. Kansas, then a dual system state, argued both that priority of settlement and the riparian rule that "the owners of land on the banks are entitled to the continual flow of the stream ..." gave it the right to relief. In addition to its assertion of territorial sovereignty, Colorado, the originator of pure prior appropriation, asserted the right to the full flow as a riparian making a reasonable use, but further confused the issue by invoking a classic prior appropriation defense. Kansas, it said, was not entitled to any water because its call would be futile; the Arkansas was a dry stream through western Kansas. Colorado prevailed and Kansas's complaint was dismissed without prejudice.[18] Each state, the Court held, had an equal right to use the flow, and Colorado's irrigation withdrawals were reasonable under the common law of riparian rights and did not exceed her rights, whatever they were, under the doctrine of equitable apportionment because Colorado had developed faster than Kansas.

* * *

III.   1907–1945: Barriers to Relief and the Integration of Local and Federal Common Law

A.   *Barriers to Relief: Political Question, the Eleventh Amendment and Lack of Ripeness*

To make equitable apportionments, Supreme Court jurisdiction had to be sustained against two challenges. First, states argued that despite the express recognition of original jurisdiction in the Constitution, the issues were non-justiciable because they were political. Second, they argued that the eleventh amendment, which bars suits by citizens of one state against another state, precluded original actions for equitable apportionment simply to protect holders of state-created rights. At the same time that the Court eliminated these two per se barriers to jurisdiction, it imposed a major limitation on original jurisdiction suits. An action may be dismissed for lack of ripeness if there is insufficient proof of injury.

* * *

Missouri v. Illinois[42] was the first case to set a high standard of injury as a prerequisite to Supreme Court relief. In an epic environmentally

---

18. Kansas was subsequently unsuccessful in reopening the decree in light of increased Colorado withdrawals. Colorado v. Kansas, 320 U.S. 383 (1943). In 1948, the two states negotiated a compact, Kan. Stat. Ann. § 82a–520 (1977), but the dispute between the two states is on-going and it is not clear whether the compact provisions or the doctrine of equitable apportionment will control future litigation. See Note, The Parting of the Waters—The Dispute Between Colorado and Kansas Over the Arkansas River, 24 Washburn L.J. 99 (1984).

42. 200 U.S. 496 (1906). [In Nebraska v. Wyoming, 507 U.S. 584 (1993), the Court drew a distinction between the enforcement of a prior degree and the modification of a prior decree. The former requires no showing of injury, but the latter requires a showing of substantial injury. Two years later, the Court suggested that the standards for the enforcement of prior degrees and compacts are the same, Kansas v. Colorado, 115 S.Ct. 1733 unsound public works project, Illinois reversed the flow of the Chicago River to flush Chicago's sewage into the Illinois River, a tributary of the Mississippi, instead of treating and discharging it into its frontyard—Lake Michigan. Alarmed, Missouri sued to protect the health of residents of St. Louis and other riparian cities. Missouri invoked the common law rule that a riparian had a right to the flow of a stream unimpaired in quality and quantity. To dismiss Missouri's suit, a higher standard of proof than would be applied to a suit for equitable relief between private parties was articulated: "Before this Court ought to intervene the case should be of serious magnitude, clearly and fully proved, and the principle applied should be one which the Court is prepared deliberately to maintain against all considerations on the other side."[43] Relief was not warranted on the facts.

* * *

In 1931 the Court similarly dismissed Connecticut's attempt to prevent a Massachusetts transbasin diversion to benefit Boston.[46] Connecticut relied on the strict common law rule that all uses outside of the watershed were per se unreasonable,[47] but the Court found at least three reasons to dismiss the action. Connecticut, the lower riparian state, failed to prove any injury and thus the case arguably fell within the more "modern" common law rule that only transwatershed diversions that actually caused injury to downstream riparians were actionable.

Four years later, the Court applied its high standards of injury to a familiar western water law doctrine, and dismissed a suit by Washington against Oregon because the former's call would be futile.[50]

B. Standards for Equitable Apportionment

Once the Court accepts original jurisdiction and appoints a master to take the evidence, the issue becomes what law to apply. The Court initially rejected local law as the basis for an apportionment, then accepted it as the basis among states that followed the same law, and finally downgraded local law to a "guiding principle." Fair allocation rather than consistency with locally generated expectations became the touchstone of equitable apportionment. Local law remains, however, central to an equitable apportionment inquiry. Although the Court has never been very precise about the source of the law of equitable apportionment, its early decision makes it clear that the grant of original jurisdiction requires a federal law and a federal law that will not allow one state to use its law to gain an unfair advantage over another. The use of local law as a basis for allocation is thus

(1995), and held that the substantial injury standard applies to amended original action complaints. Nebraska v. Wyoming, 115 S.Ct. 1933 (1995).]

43. Id. at 521.

46. Connecticut v. Massachusetts, 282 U.S. 660 (1931).

47. Stratton v. Mt. Hermon Boys' School, 216 Mass. 83, 103 N.E. 87 (1913).

50. Washington v. Oregon, 297 U.S. 517 (1936).

not compelled by the constitution. But local law may serve as a source of principles to apply since a federal common law must of necessity examine the most relevant sources of substantive law.

In 1911, in Bean v. Morris, [221 U.S. 485 (1911), *supra* p. 915], Justice Holmes enforced priorities on an interstate stream on the theory that when all states through which it flowed had adopted the same system of water law, they estopped themselves from asserting the power to ignore out-of-state priorities. * * *

Eleven years later, Wyoming's action against Colorado to protect prior Wyoming irrigators from the upstream state's proposed diversions of the Laramie River produced the Court's first substantive decision and required the Court to begin integrating state water laws into the federal doctrine of equitable apportionment. In the Laramie litigation, Wyoming successfully urged the application of *Bean* to counter Colorado's argument—prophetic in light of subsequent developments in the state—that priority is a rule of the past, not of the future.[59] The Court upheld Wyoming's priority and awarded it, with minor qualifications, 272,000 out of the river's 288,000 acre feet of dependable supply. Colorado's argument that it could put the water to more beneficial use because the site of the proposed trans-watershed diversion, the Cache La Poudre Valley, was more developed was not seriously considered, although it had carried the day for the state in *Kansas v. Colorado*.

While *Wyoming v. Colorado* has been criticized because it freezes existing, and presumably inefficient, uses in place to the detriment of future, presumably more efficient, uses, the Court's reasoning may actually lead to better conservation practices. Undoubtedly, the rigid adherence to prior appropriation throughout a large river basin might produce inefficiencies. However, there is a strong case for reliance on a modified doctrine of prior appropriation, as the Court has done, on smaller streams. First users build up legitimate expectations of security, and subsequent users can not claim surprise when prior uses are protected. Recognition of prior uses need not freeze all existing uses. It operates more to place the burden of water conservation on new users. This is a difficult but not impossible burden to discharge as the Court's most recent equitable apportionment case, *Colorado v. New Mexico*, [*infra* p. 956] illustrates. * * *

New York City's plans to divert water from the Delaware River watershed produced the Court's major equitable apportionment case among riparian states, and although the Court stressed that its primary objective was an equitable apportionment, again the decision was based primarily on local law. * * * Justice Holmes began by saying, in an oft-quoted phrase, that "[t]he different traditions and practices in different parts of the country may lead to varying results, but the effort is always to secure an equitable apportionment without quibbling over formulas." But he in fact made a riparian apportionment. * * *

New Jersey v. New York is a creative adaption of the law of riparian rights to interstate conflicts. Historically, instream uses have been of

---

59. Wyoming v. Colorado, 259 U.S. 419 (1922). * * *

greater importance compared to consumptive uses in riparian states, and the Court gave full weight to this aspect of riparianism by apportioning the most valuable attribute of the river, its base flow, and it gave full weight to another core riparian concept, preservation of the status quo among similar users. The decree required that the essential benefits of the flow, pollution dilution and salt water intrusion prevention, be preserved as a condition to New York City's withdrawals from the watershed for consumptive uses.

The importance of riparian principles and marginal reductions in base water levels is also illustrated by the litigation over Illinois's reversal of the Chicago River and construction of a channel to link Lake Michigan with the Mississippi. Illinois was able to fend off challenges by downstream states, but was not as successful in defending the necessary diversions from Lake Michigan to flush Chicago's sewage against challenges by the Great Lakes states that the diversions impaired navigation of the lakes.* * * *

Dust bowl conditions in the Great Plains produced the Court's most complex equitable apportionment and statement of current doctrine. To protect the flow of the North Platte River for irrigation purposes, Nebraska sued the upstream state of Wyoming, which impleaded Colorado.[71] Relying on *Wyoming v. Colorado*, Nebraska alleged that the dependable natural flow of the river during irrigation season on a critical reach of the river had long been over-appropriated. The case also involved federal and state claims to water stored in Wyoming reservoirs for the benefit of Wyoming and Nebraska users. Nebraska did benefit substantially from the litigation, but the Court departed from the application of the rule of priority followed in *Wyoming v. Colorado*. Writing for the majority, Justice Douglas concluded that strict adherence to the doctrine of prior appropriation may not be possible if justice and equity are to be done among states, and substituted the following and oft quoted multifactor standard of equitable apportionment:

> So far as possible those established uses should be protected though strict application of the priority rule might jeopardize them. Apportionment calls for the exercise for an informed judgment on a consideration of many factors. Priority of appropriation is the guiding principle. But physical and climatic conditions, the consumptive use of water in the several sections of the river, the character and rate of return flows, the extent of established uses, the availability of storage water, the practical effect of wasteful uses on downstream areas, the damage to upstream areas as compared to the benefits to downstream areas if a limitation is imposed on the former—these are all relevant factors.

NOTE

If the United States has interests in water, such as reserved rights to water for public lands, it must be joined in an equitable apportionment suit

---

* [Wisconsin v. Illinois, 281 U.S. 179 (1929), affirmed *per curiam* 281 U.S. 696 (1930).]

71. Nebraska v. Wyoming, 325 U.S. 589 (1945). * * *

as an indispensable party. This can be a formidable barrier to adjudication of interstate claims. Arizona sued California for an equitable apportionment of the lower Colorado River. As discussed in the next section of this chapter, the waters of the river had been apportioned between states of the upper basin and states of the lower basin by the 1922 Colorado River Compact, but an allocation was not made among the states in each basin. Arizona's suit to effect such a division among the lower basin states was dismissed because the United States, which had extensive land holdings, was an indispensable party and had not consented to be sued. Arizona v. California, 298 U.S. 558, 56 S.Ct. 848, 80 L.Ed. 1331 (1936). A later adjudication, in which the United States consented to be sued, resulted not in an equitable apportionment, but in a finding that Congress had already apportioned the river among the lower basin states by the Boulder Canyon Project Act of 1928. Arizona v. California, 373 U.S. 546, 83 S.Ct. 1468, 10 L.Ed.2d 542 (1963), *infra* p. 1001.

Colorado v. New Mexico

Supreme Court of the United States, 1982.
459 U.S. 176, 103 S.Ct. 539, 74 L.Ed.2d 348.

■ JUSTICE MARSHALL delivered the opinion of the Court.

* * *

I

The Vermejo River is a small, nonnavigable river that originates in the snow belt of the Rocky Mountains in southern Colorado and flows southeasterly into New Mexico for a distance of roughly 55 miles before it joins the Canadian River. The major portion of the river is located in New Mexico. The Colorado portion consists of three main tributaries that combine to form the Vermejo River proper approximately one mile below the Colorado–New Mexico border. At present there are no uses of the water of the Vermejo River in Colorado, and no use or diversion has ever been made in Colorado. In New Mexico, by contrast, farmers and industrial users have diverted water from the Vermejo for many years. * * *

In 1975, a Colorado corporation, Colorado Fuel and Iron Steel Corp. ("C.F. & I."), obtained in Colorado state court a conditional right to divert 75 cubic feet per second from the headwaters of the Vermejo River. C.F. & I. proposed a transmountain diversion of the water to a tributary of the Purgatoire River in Colorado to be used for industrial development and other purposes. Upon learning of this decree, the four principal New Mexico users—Phelps Dodge Corp. ("Phelps Dodge"), Kaiser Steel Corp. ("Kaiser Steel"), Vermejo Park Corp. ("Vermejo Park"), and the Vermejo Conservancy District ("Conservancy District")—filed suit in the United States District Court for the District of New Mexico, seeking to enjoin any diversion by C. F. & I. that would violate their senior rights. On January 16, 1978, the District Court enjoined C. F. & I. from diverting any water from the Vermajo River in derogation of the senior water rights of New

Mexico users. The court found that under the doctrine of prior appropriation, which both New Mexico and Colorado recognize, the New Mexico users were entitled to have their needs fully satisfied because their appropriation was prior in time. * * *

In June 1978 Colorado moved for leave to file an original complaint in this Court. New Mexico opposed the motion. On April 16, 1979, we granted Colorado's motion and appointed the Honorable Ewing T. Kerr, Senior Judge of the United States District Court for the District of Wyoming, as Special Master in this case. After a lengthy trial involving an extensive presentation of evidence, the Special Master submitted a report to the Court on January 9, 1982. * * *

The Special Master found that most of the water of the Vermejo River is consumed by the New Mexico users * * *. He thus recognized that strict application of the rule of priority would not permit Colorado any diversion since the entire available supply is needed to satisfy the demands of appropriators in New Mexico with senior rights. Nevertheless, applying the principle of equitable apportionment established in our prior cases, he recommended permitting Colorado a transmountain diversion of 4,000 acre-feet of water per year from the headwaters of the Vermejo River. * * *

Explaining his conclusion, the Special Master noted that any injury to New Mexico would be restricted to the Conservancy District, the user in New Mexico furthest downstream, since there was sufficient water in the Vermejo River for the three other principal New Mexico water users, Vermejo Park, Kaiser Steel, and Phelps Dodge. He further found that the "Vermejo Conservancy District has never been an economically feasible operation."

* * *

We conclude that the criteria relied upon by the Special Master comport with the doctrine of equitable apportionment as it has evolved in our prior cases. We thus reject New Mexico's contention that the Special Master was required to focus exclusively on the rule of priority. * * *

II

Equitable apportionment is the doctrine of federal common law that governs disputes between States concerning their rights to use the water of an interstate stream. Kansas v. Colorado, 206 U.S. 46, 98 (1907); Connecticut v. Massachusetts, 282 U.S. 660, 670–671 (1931). It is a flexible doctrine which calls for "the exercise of an informed judgment on a consideration of many factors" to secure a "just and equitable" allocation. Nebraska v. Wyoming, 325 U.S. 589, 618 (1945). We have stressed that in arriving at "the delicate adjustment of interests which must be made," ibid., we must consider all relevant factors * * *.

The laws of the contending States concerning intrastate water disputes are an important consideration governing equitable apportionment. When, as in this case, both States recognize the doctrine of prior appropriation, priority becomes the "guiding principle" in an allocation between competing States. But state law is not controlling. Rather, the just apportionment of interstate waters is a question of federal law that depends "upon a consideration of the pertinent laws of the contending States and *all other relevant facts*." Connecticut v. Massachusetts, 282 U.S., at 670–71, 51 S.Ct., at 289 (emphasis added).

In reaching his recommendation the Special Master did not focus exclusively on the rule of priority, but considered other factors such as the efficiency of current uses in New Mexico and the balance of benefits to Colorado and harm to New Mexico. New Mexico contends that it is improper to consider these other factors. It maintains that this Court has strictly applied the rule of priority when apportioning water between States adhering to the prior appropriation doctrine, and has departed from that rule only to protect an existing economy built upon junior appropriations. Since there is no existing economy in Colorado dependent upon the use of water from the Vermejo River, New Mexico contends that the rule of priority is controlling. We disagree with this inflexible interpretation of the doctrine of equitable apportionment.

Our prior cases clearly establish that equitable apportionment will protect only those rights to water that are "reasonably required and applied." Wyoming v. Colorado, 259 U.S. 419, 484 (1922). Especially in those Western States where water is scarce, "[t]here must be no waste . . . of the 'treasure' of a river. . . . Only diligence and good faith will keep the privilege alive." Washington v. Oregon, 297 U.S. 517, 527 (1936). Thus, wasteful or inefficient uses will not be protected. Similarly, concededly senior water rights will be deemed forfeited or substantially diminished where the rights have not been exercised or asserted with reasonable diligence.

We have invoked equitable apportionment not only to require the reasonably efficient use of water, but also to impose on States an affirmative duty to take reasonable steps to conserve and augment the water supply of an interstate stream. In *Wyoming* v. *Colorado*, Wyoming brought suit to prevent a *proposed* diversion by Colorado from the Laramie River. This Court calculated the dependable supply available to both States, subtracted the senior Wyoming uses, and permitted Colorado to divert an amount not exceeding the balance. In calculating the dependable supply we placed on each State the duty to employ "financially and physically feasible" measures "adapted to *conserving and equalizing* the natural flow." 259 U.S., at 484 (emphasis added). Adopting a position similar to New Mexico's in this case, Wyoming objected to a requirement that it employ conservation measures to facilitate Colorado's proposed uses. The answer we gave is especially relevant to this case:

> "The question here is not what one State should do for the other, but how each should exercise her relative rights in the waters of this interstate stream. * * * Both States recognize that conservation within practicable limits is essential in order that needless waste may be prevented and the largest feasible use may be secured. This comports with the all-pervading spirit of the doctrine of appropriation and takes

appropriate heed of the natural necessities out of which it arose. We think that doctrine lays on each of these States a duty to exercise her right reasonably and in a manner calculated to conserve the common supply."

We conclude that it is entirely appropriate to consider the extent to which reasonable conservation measures by New Mexico might offset the proposed Colorado diversion and thereby minimize any injury to New Mexico users. Similarly, it is appropriate to consider whether Colorado has undertaken reasonable steps to minimize the amount of diversion that will be required.

In addition, we have held that in an equitable apportionment of interstate waters it is proper to weigh the harms and benefits to competing States. In *Kansas* v. *Colorado*, where we first announced the doctrine of equitable apportionment, we found that users in Kansas were injured by Colorado's upstream diversions from the Arkansas River. Yet we declined to grant any relief to Kansas on the ground that the great benefit to Colorado outweighed the detriment to Kansas. Similarly, in *Nebraska* v. *Wyoming*, we held that water rights in Wyoming and Nebraska, which under state law were senior, had to yield to the "countervailing equities" of an established economy in Colorado even though it was based on junior appropriations. We noted that the rule of priority should not be strictly applied where it "would work more hardship" on the junior user "than it would bestow benefits" on the senior user. The same principle is applicable in balancing the benefits of a diversion for *proposed* uses against the possible harms to existing uses.

We recognize that the equities supporting the protection of existing economies will usually be compelling. The harm that may result from disrupting established uses is typically certain and immediate, whereas the potential benefits from a proposed diversion may be speculative and re-mote. Under some circumstances, however, the countervailing equities supporting a diversion for future use in one State may justify the detriment to existing users in another State. This may be the case, for example, where the State seeking a diversion demonstrates by clear and convincing evidence that the benefits of the diversion substantially outweigh the harm that might result. In the determination of whether the State proposing the diversion has carried this burden, an important consideration is whether the existing users could offset the diversion by reasonable conservation measures to prevent waste. This approach comports with our emphasis on flexibility in equitable apportionment and also accords sufficient protection to existing uses.

* * *

IV

The flexible doctrine of equitable apportionment clearly extends to a State's claim to divert water for future uses. Whether such a diversion should be permitted will turn on an examination of all factors relevant to a just apportionment. It is proper, therefore, to consider factors such as the extent to which reasonable conservation measures by existing users can offset the reduction in supply due to diversion, and whether the benefits to the State seeking the diversion substantially outweigh the harm to existing uses in another State. We remand for specific factual findings relevant to determining a just and equitable apportionment of the water of the Vermejo River between Colorado and New Mexico.

It is so ordered.

■ JUSTICE O'CONNOR, with whom JUSTICE POWELL joins, concurring in the judgment.

* * *

Colorado would have the Court assess the Conservancy District's "waste" and "inefficiency" by a new yardstick—i.e., not by comparing the economic gains to the District with the costs of achieving greater efficiency, but by comparing the "inefficiency" of New Mexico's uses with the relative benefits to Colorado of a new use. * * *

Today the Court has also gone dangerously far toward accepting that suggestion. The Court holds, *ante*, at 186, that it is appropriate in equitable apportionment litigation to weigh the harms and benefits to the competing States. It does so notwithstanding its recognition that the potential benefits from a *proposed* diversion are likely to be speculative and remote, and therefore difficult to balance against any threatened harms, and its concession that the equities supporting protection of an existing economy will usually be compelling.

* * * Where, as here, however, no existing economy in Colorado depends on the waters of the Vermejo and the actual uses in New Mexico rank in equal importance with the proposed uses in Colorado,[6] the difficulty of arriving at the proper balance is especially great.

* * * Protection of existing economies does not require that users be permitted to continue in unreasonably wasteful or inefficient practices. But the Court should be moved to exercise its original jurisdiction to alter the status quo between States only where there is *clear and convincing evidence*, that one State's use is unreasonably wasteful. * * *

NOTE

Justice Marshall held that the equitable apportionment doctrine required not only efficient water use, but also imposed "on states an affirmative duty to take reasonable steps to conserve and augment the water supply of an interstate stream." Justice O'Connor took issue with this point in her concurring opinion. Was such a duty apparent prior to the decision in *Colorado I*?

6. According to Colorado, the diverted water would be used "in industrial operations at coal mines, agriculture, timbering, power generation, domestic needs and other industrial operations." * * * Reply Brief for Colorado 8.

Colorado v. New Mexico

Supreme Court of the United States, 1984.
467 U.S. 310, 104 S.Ct. 2433, 81 L.Ed.2d 247.

■ Justice O'Connor delivered the opinion of the Court.

[The Court reviewed the decision in Colorado v. New Mexico, 459 U.S. 176 (1982) ("*Colorado I*").]

* * *

[W]e found the Master's report unclear and determined that a remand would be appropriate.

* * *

Requiring Colorado to present clear and convincing evidence in support of its proposed diversion is necessary to appropriately balance the unique interests involved in water rights disputes between sovereigns. The standard reflects this Court's long-held view that a proposed diverter should bear most, though not all, of the risks of erroneous decision * * *. * * * In addition, the clear-and-convincing-evidence standard accommodates society's competing interests in increasing the stability of property rights and in putting resources to their most efficient uses * * *. In short, Colorado's diversion should and will be allowed only if actual inefficiencies in present uses or future benefits from other uses are highly probable.

With these principles in mind, we turn to review the evidence the parties have submitted concerning the proposed diversion. As our opinion noted last Term, New Mexico has met its initial burden of showing "real or substantial injury" because "*any* diversion by Colorado, unless offset by New Mexico at its own expense, [would] necessarily reduce the amount of water available to New Mexico users." Accordingly, the burden shifted on remand to Colorado to show, by clear and convincing evidence, that reasonable conservation measures could compensate for some or all of the proposed diversion and that the injury, if any, to New Mexico would be outweighed by the benefits to Colorado from the diversion. * * *

A.

To establish whether Colorado's proposed diversion could be offset by eliminating New Mexico's nonuse or inefficiency, we asked the Master to make specific findings concerning existing uses, supplies of water, and reasonable conservation measures available to the two States. After assessing the evidence both States offered about existing uses and available supplies, the Master concluded that "current levels of use primarily reflect failure on the part of existing users to fully develop and put to work available water." Moreover, with respect to reasonable conservation measures available, the Master indicated his belief that more careful water administration in New Mexico would alleviate shortages from unregulated stockponds, fishponds, and water detention structures, prevent waste from blockage and clogging in canals, and ensure that users fully devote themselves to development of available resources. He further concluded that "the heart of New Mexico's water problem is the Vermejo Conservancy District," which he considered a failed "reclamation project [that had] never lived up to its expectations or even proved to be a successful project, ... and [that] quite possibly should never have been built." Though the District was quite arguably in the "middle range in reclamation project efficiencies," the Master was of the opinion "that [the District's] inefficient water use should not be charged to Colorado." Furthermore, though Colorado had not submitted evidence or testimony of any conservation measures that C.F. & I. would take, the Master concluded that "it is not for the Master or for New Mexico to say that reasonable attempts to conserve water will not be implemented by Colorado."

We share the Master's concern that New Mexico may be overstating the amount of harm its users would suffer from a diversion. Water use by appropriators along the Vermejo River has remained relatively stable for the past 30 years, and this historic use falls substantially below the decreed rights of those users. Unreliable supplies satisfactorily explain some of this difference, but New Mexico's attempt to excuse three decades of nonuse in this way is, at the very least, suspect. Nevertheless, whatever the merit of New Mexico's explanation, we cannot agree that Colorado has met its burden of identifying, by clear and convincing evidence, conservation efforts that would preserve any of the Vermejo River water supply.

For example, though Colorado alleged that New Mexico could improve its administration of stockponds, fishponds, and water detention structures, it did not actually point to specific measures New Mexico could take to conserve water. * * * Similarly, though Colorado asserted that more rigorous water administration could eliminate blocked diversion works and ensure more careful development of water supplies, it did not show how this would actually preserve existing supplies. Even if Colorado's generalizations were true, they would prove only that some junior users are diverting water that senior appropriators ultimately could call; they would not prove that water is being wasted or used inefficiently by those actually diverting it. * * *

Colorado's attack on current water use in the Vermejo Conservancy District is inadequate for much the same reason. Our cases require only conservation measures that are "financially and physically feasible" and "within practicable limits." * * * A State can carry its burden of proof in an equitable apportionment action only with specific evidence about how existing uses might be improved, or with clear evidence that a project is far less efficient than most other projects. Mere assertions about the relative efficiencies of competing projects will not do.

Finally, there is no evidence in the record that "Colorado has undertaken reasonable steps to minimize the amount of the diversion that will be required." Nine years have past since C.F. & I. first proposed diverting water from the Vermejo River. Yet Colorado has presented no evidence concerning C.F. & I.'s inability to relieve its needs through substitute sources. Furthermore, there is no evidence that C.F. & I. has settled on a definite or even tentative construction design or plan, or that it has prepared an economic analysis of its proposed diversion. Indeed, C.F. & I. has not even conducted an operational study of the reservoir that Colorado contends will be built in conjunction with the proposed diversion. It may be impracticable to ask the State proposing a diversion to provide unerring proof of future uses and concomitant conservation measures that would be taken. But it would be irresponsible of us to apportion water to uses that have not been, at a minimum, carefully studied and objectively evaluated, not to mention decided upon. Financially and physically feasible conservation efforts include careful study of future, as well as prudent implementation of current, water uses. Colorado has been unwilling to take any concrete steps in this direction. * * *

B.

We also asked the Master to help us balance the benefits and harms that might result from the proposed diversion. The Master found that Colorado's proposed interim use is agricultural in nature and that more permanent applications might include use in coal mines, timbering, power generation, domestic needs, and other industrial operations. The Master admitted that "[t]his area of fact finding [was] one of the most difficult [both] because of the necessarily speculative nature of [the] benefits ..." and because of Colorado's "natural reluctance to spend large amounts of time and money developing plans, operations, and cost schemes...." Nevertheless, because the diverted water would, at a minimum, alleviate existing water shortages in Colorado, the Master concluded that the evidence showed considerable benefits would accrue from the diversion. Furthermore, the Master concluded that the injury, if any, to New Mexico would be insubstantial, if only because reasonable conservation measures could, in his opinion, offset the entire impact of the diversion.

Again, we find ourselves without adequate evidence to approve Colorado's proposed diversion. Colorado has not committed itself to any long-term use for which future benefits can be studied and predicted. Nor has Colorado specified how long the interim agricultural use might or might not last. All Colorado has established is that a steel corporation wants to take water for some unidentified use in the future.

By contrast, New Mexico has attempted to identify the harms that would result from the proposed diversion. New Mexico commissioned some independent economists to study the economic effects, direct and indirect, that the diversion would have on persons in New Mexico.

* * * New Mexico, at the very least, has taken concrete steps toward addressing the query this Court posed last Term. Colorado has made no similar effort.

* * * We have only required that a State proposing a diversion conceive and implement some type of long-range planning and analysis of the diversion it proposes. Long-range planning and analysis will, we believe, reduce the uncertainties with which equitable apportionment judgments are made. If New Mexico can develop evidence to prove that its

existing economy is efficiently using water, we see no reason why Colorado cannot take similar steps to prove that its future economy could do better.

* * *

■ JUSTICE STEVENS, dissenting.

[Justice Stevens reviewed the record and found ample evidence to support the conclusion that New Mexico was using its share of the river wastefully and that additional conservation measures were available to New Mexico.]

* * *

Colorado is correct when it states that "New Mexico should not be permitted to use its own lack of administration and record keeping to establish its claim that no water can be conserved. That position, if accepted by the Court, would encourage states to obscure their water use practices and needs in order to avoid their duty to help conserve the common supply." Last Term we explicitly rejected New Mexico's inflexible interpretation of the doctrine of equitable apportionment under which priority would not merely be a guiding principle but the controlling one. * * *

NOTE

1. After the two *Colorado v. New Mexico* decisions, what would your advice be for future uses to a state concerned about protecting its share of an interstate stream, in regard to planning? In regard to water management and conservation? Does Virginia v. Maryland, 540 U.S. 1101, 124 S.Ct. 1127, 157 L.Ed.2d 884 (Mem) (2004), shed any light on these questions? Under a 1795 Compact and subsequent arbitration, Maryland owns the bed of the Potomac River to the low water mark on the Virginia side. Fairfax County, Virginia applied for a Maryland permit to withdraw water from the River. Several Maryland officials objected because the water would divert growth from Maryland to northern Virginia, and Maryland initially denied the permit because the county had not demonstrated a sufficient need for the water. In 2001, she reversed course and approved the permit. However, the legislature placed a limit on the amount of water which could be withdrawn. Maryland conceded Virginia's right to withdraw water, but argued that its sovereignty over the bed gave it the right to regulate Virginia's withdrawals. In an opinion written by the late Chief Justice Rehnquist, the Court held that the 1795 Compact gave Virginia immunity from Maryland's sovereignty over a portion of the bed of the Potomac awarded to Maryland in an arbitration over a century after the Compact became law. Chief Justice Rehnquist reasoned that the language in Article VII of the compact giving the citizens of each state "full property in the shore of the Potowmack river adjoining their land, with all emoluments and advantages thereunto belong, and the privilege of making and carrying out wharves and other improvements . . ." settled the issue at a time when the location of the boundary between the two states and thus

control over the River was contested. Article 4 of the subsequent boundary award gave Virginia "a right to such use of the river as may be necessary to the full enjoyment of her riparian ownership, without impeding navigation or otherwise interfering with the proper use of it by Maryland ...," and the Court held that Virginia therefore gained the right "to use the River beyond the low-water mark ... qua sovereign." Maryland conceded that her objections to Virginia's use of the River to hoard water for herself and her unilateral determination of Virginia's share of the River violated the Dormant Commerce Clause and the doctrine of equitable apportionment. However, the Court's subordination of Compact interpretation to equitable apportionment troubled Justice Stevens who dissented. Virginia v. Maryland was significantly qualified in New Jersey v. Delaware, ___ U.S. ___, 128 S.Ct. 1929, 170 L.Ed.2d 743 (2008). The issue was whether Delaware could use its authority under the Coastal Zone Management Act to veto a proposed liquid natural gas facility, approved by New Jersey, on the New Jersey shore that would extend into the bed of the Delaware River owned by Delaware. New Jersey v. Delaware, 291 U.S. 361, 54 S.Ct. 407, 78 L.Ed. 847 (1934), confirmed that a 1682 grant from the Duke of York to William Penn gave Delaware title to the bed of the River to the low-water mark on the New Jersey side. But, New Jersey argued that a 1905 Compact, 34 Stat. 860 (1907), which allowed each state "to exercise riparian jurisdiction of every kind and nature...." and which was negotiated before the boundary was settled, precluded Delaware from regulating her own territory. In a 6–3 opinion, the Court agreed with the Expert Report of Professor Joseph L. Sax that "riparian jurisdiction" was not a term of art in 1905 and that Delaware did not surrender its right to regulate activities in its soil that extend beyond "ordinary and usual" exercises of the right to wharf out. The proposed facility "goes well beyond the ordinary or usual." Virginia v. Maryland was limited to its facts because the 1877 arbitration award gave Virginia the right to use the River beyond its territory without being subject to regulation by Maryland. Justice Stevens concurred and argued that Delaware's sovereignty gives it the right to object to all extensions into its territory. He also reiterated his dissent in Virginia v. Maryland that Maryland had the power, without defining fully its scope, to prevent the construction of the intake.

2. Does the doctrine of equitable apportionment apply to groundwater? Interstate groundwater conflicts are becoming more common, and the widespread assumption among water lawyers is that the Supreme Court will apply equitable apportionment to groundwater. The settlement of litigation among Colorado, Kansas and Nebraska over the construction of the Republican River Compact, Kansas v. Nebraska and Colorado, No. 126 Original (December 15, 2002), provides an important precedent. The Compact, 57 Stat. 86 (1943), allocates the flow of the river by a percentage allocation to each state. In 1998, Kansas sued Nebraska and Colorado claiming that groundwater pumping in Nebraska violated the Compact by depleting downstream surface flows. Nebraska responded that the Compact only restricted the consumption of water directly diverted from a stream. However, the Special Master recommended that the Supreme Court hold that "[t]he Republican River Compact restricts a compacting State's consumption of groundwater to the extent the consumption depletes stream flow in the Republican River Basin and, therefore, Nebraska's Motion to Dismiss should be denied." *First Report of Special Master 45* (2000). In 2003, the Supreme Court approved a settlement which confirms the compact allocations, requires that ground and surface depletions be used to calculate stream flow depletions for purposes of whether a state has exceeded its allocation, imposes a moratorium on most new wells in Nebraska (where most basins along the Republican are fully appropriated) confirms Colorado's and Kansas's restrictive well regulations, and calculates excess depletions on a five year average. See Aaron M. Popelka, *The Republican River Dispute: An Analysis of the Parties' Compact Interpretation and Final Settlement Stipulation*, 83 Neb. L. Rev. 596 (2004).

3. As New York v. New Jersey illustrates, the Supreme Court's original jurisdiction can be invoked to allocate flows for water quality control as well as for consumptive uses. However, modern litigation among states to protect interstate waterways from pollution by dischargers in another state tends to be dominated by tort principles and federal pollution statutes rather than the notions of equitable apportionment discussed in New Jersey v. New York, *supra* p. 948, and does not always invoke the Supreme Court's original jurisdiction.

Arkansas v. Oklahoma

Supreme Court of the United States, 1992.
503 U.S. 91, 112 S.Ct. 1046, 117 L.Ed.2d 239.

■ JUSTICE STEVENS delivered the opinion of the Court.

* * *

I

In 1985, the City of Fayetteville, Arkansas, applied to the EPA, seeking a permit for the City's new sewage treatment plant under the National Pollution Discharge Elimination System (NPDES). After the appropriate procedures, the EPA, pursuant to § 402(a)(1) of the Act, 33 U.S.C. § 1342(a)(1), issued a permit authorizing the plant to discharge up to half of its effluent (to a limit of 6.1 million gallons per day) into an unnamed stream in northwestern Arkansas. That flow passes through a series of three creeks for about 17 miles, and then enters the Illinois River at a point 22 miles upstream from the Arkansas–Oklahoma border.

The permit imposed specific limitations on the quantity, content, and character of the discharge and also included a number of special conditions, including a provision that if a study then underway indicated that more stringent limitations were necessary to ensure compliance with Oklahoma's water quality standards, the permit would be modified to incorporate those limits. App. 84.

Respondents challenged this permit before the EPA, alleging, *inter alia,* that the discharge violated the Oklahoma water quality standards. Those standards provide that "no degradation [of water quality] shall be allowed" in the upper Illinois River, including the portion of the River immediately downstream from the state line.

Following a hearing, the Administrative Law Judge (ALJ) concluded that the Oklahoma standards would not be implicated unless the contested discharge had "something more than a mere *de minimis* impact" on the State's waters. He found that the discharge would not have an "undue impact" on Oklahoma's waters and, accordingly, affirmed the issuance of the permit.

On a petition for review, the EPA's Chief Judicial Officer first ruled that § 301(b)(1)(C) of the Clean Water Act "requires an NPDES permit to impose any effluent limitations necessary to comply with applicable state water quality standards."[3] He then held that the Act and EPA regulations offered greater protection for the downstream State than the ALJ's "undue impact" standard suggested. He explained the proper standard as follows:

"[A] mere theoretical impairment of Oklahoma's water quality standards—*i.e.,* an infinitesimal impairment predicted through modeling but not expected to be actually detectable or measurable should not by itself block the issuance of the permit. In this case, the permit should be upheld if the record shows by a preponderance of the evidence that the authorized discharges would not cause an actual *detectable* violation of Oklahoma's water quality standards." Id., at 117a (emphasis in original).

On remand, the ALJ made detailed findings of fact and concluded that the City had satisfied the standard set forth by the Chief Judicial Officer. Specifically, the ALJ found that there would be no detectable violation of any of the components of Oklahoma's water quality standards. The Chief Judicial Officer sustained the issuance of the permit.

Both the petitioners in No. 90–1262 (collectively Arkansas) and the respondents in this litigation sought judicial review. Arkansas argued that the Clean Water Act did not require an Arkansas point source to comply with Oklahoma's water quality standards. Oklahoma challenged the EPA's determination that the Fayetteville discharge would not produce a detectable violation of the Oklahoma standards.

* * *

3. Section 301(b)(1)(C) provides, in relevant part, that

"there shall be achieved—

. . .

"(c) not later than July 1, 1977 . . . any more stringent limitation, including those necessary to meet *water quality standards . . . established pursuant to any State law or regulations* * * * or required to implement any applicable water quality standard established pursuant to this chapter." 33 U.S.C. § 1311(b)(1)(C) (emphasis supplied).

II

Interstate waters have been a font of controversy since the founding of the Nation. *E.g.*, Gibbons v. Ogden, 9 Wheat. 1, 6 L.Ed. 23 (1824). This Court has frequently resolved disputes between States that are separated by a common river, see, *e.g.*, Ohio v. Kentucky, 444 U.S. 335 (1980), that border the same body of water, see, *e.g.*, New York v. New Jersey, 256 U.S. 296 (1921), or that are fed by the same river basin, see, *e.g.*, New Jersey v. New York, 283 U.S. 336 (1931).

* * * Among these cases are controversies between a State that introduces pollutants to a waterway and a downstream State that objects. See, *e.g.*, Missouri v. Illinois, 200 U.S. 496 (1906). In such cases, this Court has applied principles of common law tempered by a respect for the sovereignty of the States. In forging what "may not improperly be called interstate common law," Illinois v. Milwaukee, 406 U.S. 91, 105–106 (1972) (*Milwaukee I*), however, we remained aware "that new federal laws and new federal regulations may in time pre-empt the field of federal common law of nuisance." Id., at 107.

In Milwaukee v. Illinois, 451 U.S. 304 (1981) (*Milwaukee II*), we held that the 1972 Amendments to the Federal Water Pollution Control Act did just that. In addressing Illinois' claim that Milwaukee's discharges into Lake Michigan constituted a nuisance, we held that the comprehensive regulatory regime created by the 1972 Amendments pre-empted Illinois' federal common law remedy. We observed that Congress had addressed many of the problems we had identified in *Milwaukee I* by providing a downstream State with an opportunity for a hearing before the source State's permitting agency, by requiring the latter to explain its failure to accept any recommendations offered by the downstream State, and by authorizing the EPA, in its discretion, to veto a source State's issuance of any permit if the waters of another State may be affected. *Milwaukee II*, 451 U.S., at 325–326.

In *Milwaukee II*, the Court did not address whether the 1972 Amendments had supplanted *state* common law remedies as well as the federal common law remedy. See id., at 310, n. 4. On remand, Illinois argued that § 510 of the Clean Water Act, 33 U.S.C. § 1370, expressly preserved the State's right to adopt and enforce rules that are more stringent than federal standards. The Court of Appeals accepted Illinois' reading of § 510, but held that that section did "no more than to save the right and jurisdiction of a state to regulate activity occurring within the confines of its boundary waters." Illinois v. Milwaukee, 731 F.2d 403, 413 (C.A.7 1984), cert. denied, 469 U.S. 1196 (1985).

* * * This Court subsequently endorsed that analysis in International Paper Co. v. Ouellette, 479 U.S. 481 (1987), in which Vermont property owners claimed that the pollution discharged into Lake Champlain by a paper company located in New York constituted a nuisance under Vermont law. The Court held the Clean Water Act taken "as a whole, its purposes and its history" preempted an action based on the law of the affected State and that the only state law applicable to an interstate discharge is "the law of the State in which the point source is located." Id., at 487, 493. Moreover, in reviewing § 402(b) of the Act, the Court pointed out that when a new permit is being issued by the source State's permit-granting agency, the downstream State

"does not have the authority to block the issuance of the permit if it is dissatisfied with the proposed standards. An affected State's only recourse is to apply to the EPA Administrator, who then has the discretion to disapprove the permit if he concludes that the discharges will have an undue impact on interstate waters. § 1342(d)(2). . . . Thus the Act makes it clear that affected States occupy a subordinate position to source States in the federal regulatory program." Id., at 490–491.

Unlike the foregoing cases, this litigation involves not a State-issued permit, but a federally issued permit. To explain the significance of this distinction, we comment further on the statutory scheme before addressing the specific issues raised by the parties.

III

The Clean Water Act anticipates a partnership between the States and the Federal Government, animated by a shared objective: "to restore and maintain the chemical, physical, and biological integrity of the Nation's waters." 33 U.S.C. § 1251(a). Toward this end, the Act provides for two sets of water quality measures. "Effluent limitations" are promulgated by the EPA and restrict the quantities, rates, and concentrations of specified substances which are discharged from point sources. See 33 U.S.C. §§ 1311, 1314. "[W]ater quality standards" are, in general, promulgated by the States and establish the desired condition of a waterway. See 33 U.S.C. § 1313. These standards supplement effluent limitations "so that numerous point sources, despite individual compliance with effluent limitations, may be further regulated to prevent water quality from falling below acceptable levels." EPA v. California ex rel. State Water Resources Control Board, 426 U.S. 200, 205, n. 12 (1976).

The EPA provides States with substantial guidance in the drafting of water quality standards. See generally 40 CFR pt. 131 (1991) (setting forth model water quality standards). Moreover, § 303 of the Act requires, *inter alia,* that state authorities periodically review water quality standards and secure the EPA's approval of any revisions in the standards. If the EPA recommends changes to the standards and the State fails to comply with that recommendation, the Act authorizes the EPA to promulgate water quality standards for the State. 33 U.S.C. § 1313(c).

The primary means for enforcing these limitations and standards is the National Pollution Discharge Elimination System (NPDES), enacted in 1972 as a critical part of Congress' "complete rewriting" of federal water pollution law. *Milwaukee II,* 451 U.S., at 317. Section 301(a) of the Act, 33 U.S.C. § 1311(a), generally prohibits the discharge of any effluent into a navigable body of water unless the point source has obtained an NPDES permit. Section 402 establishes the NPDES permitting regime, and describes two types of permitting systems: state permit programs that must satisfy federal requirements and be approved by the EPA, and a federal program administered by the EPA.

Section 402(b) authorizes each State to establish "its own permit program for discharges into navigable waters within its jurisdiction." 33 U.S.C. § 1342(b). Among the requirements the state program must satisfy are the procedural protections for downstream States discussed in *Ouellette* and *Milwaukee II*. See 33 U.S.C. §§ 1342(b)(3), (5). Although these provisions do not authorize the downstream State to veto the issuance of a permit for a new point source in another State, the Administrator retains authority to block the issuance of any state-issued permit that "is outside the guidelines and requirements" of the Act. 33 U.S.C. § 1342(d)(2).

In the absence of an approved state program, the EPA may issue an NPDES permit under § 402(a) of the Act. (In this case, for example, because Arkansas had not been authorized to issue NPDES permits when the Fayetteville plant was completed, the permit was issued by the EPA itself.) The EPA's permit program is subject to the "same terms, conditions, and requirements" as a state permit program. 33 U.S.C. § 1342(a)(3). Notwithstanding this general symmetry, the EPA has construed the Act as requiring that EPA-issued NPDES permits also comply with § 401(a). That section, which predates § 402 and the NPDES, applies to a broad category of federal licenses, and sets forth requirements for "[a]ny applicant for a Federal license or permit to conduct any activity including, but not limited to, the construction or operation of facilities, which may result in any discharge into the navigable waters." 33 U.S.C. § 1341(a). Section 401(a)(2) appears to prohibit the issuance of any federal license or permit over the objection of an affected State unless compliance with the affected State's water quality requirements can be insured.

IV

* * * The parties have argued three analytically distinct questions concerning the interpretation of the Clean Water Act. First, does the Act require the EPA, in crafting and issuing a permit to a point source in one State, to apply the water quality standards of downstream States? Second, even if the Act does not *require* as much, does the Agency have the statutory authority to mandate such compliance? Third, does the Act provide, as the Court of Appeals held, that once a body of water fails to meet water quality standards no discharge that yields effluent that reach the degraded waters will be permitted?

In this case, it is neither necessary nor prudent for us to resolve the first of these questions. In issuing the Fayetteville permit, the EPA assumed it was obligated by both the Act and its own regulations to ensure that the Fayetteville discharge would not violate Oklahoma's standards.

* * * As we discuss below, this assumption was permissible and reasonable and therefore there is no need for us to address whether the Act requires as much. Moreover, much of the analysis and argument in the briefs of the parties relies on statutory provisions that govern not only federal permits issued pursuant to §§ 401(a) and 402(a), but also state permits issued under § 402(b). It seems unwise to evaluate those arguments in a case such as this one, which only involves a federal permit.

* * * Our decision not to determine at this time the scope of the Agency's statutory *obligations* does not affect our resolution of the second question, which concerns the Agency's statutory *authority*. Even if the Clean Water Act itself does not require the Fayetteville discharge to comply with Oklahoma's water quality standards, the statute clearly does not limit the EPA's authority to mandate such compliance.

* * * Since 1973, EPA regulations have provided that an NPDES permit shall not be issued "[w]hen the imposition of conditions cannot ensure compliance with the applicable water quality requirements of all affected States."[10] 40 CFR § 122.4(d) (1991); see also 38 Fed.Reg. 13533 (1973); 40 CFR § 122.44(d) (1991). Those regulations—relied upon by the EPA in the issuance of the Fayetteville permit—constitute a reasonable exercise of the Agency's statutory authority.

Congress has vested in the Administrator broad discretion to establish conditions for NPDES permits. Section 402(a)(2) provides that for EPA-issued permits "[t]he Administrator shall prescribe conditions for such permits to assure compliance with the requirements of [§ 402(a)(1)] and *such other requirements as he deems appropriate.*" 33 U.S.C. § 1342(a)(2) (emphasis supplied). Similarly, Congress preserved for the Administrator broad authority to oversee state permit programs:

> "No permit shall issue ... if the Administrator ... objects in writing to the issuance of such permit as being outside the guidelines and requirements of this chapter." 33 U.S.C. § 1342(d)(2).

The regulations relied on by the EPA were a perfectly reasonable exercise of the Agency's statutory discretion. The application of state water quality standards in the interstate context is wholly consistent with the Act's broad purpose, "to restore and maintain the chemical, physical, and biological integrity of the Nation's waters." 33 U.S.C. § 1251(a). Moreover, as noted above, § 301(b)(1)(C) expressly identifies the achievement of state water quality standards as one of the Act's central objectives. The Agency's regulations conditioning NPDES permits are a well-tailored means of achieving this goal.

* * * Notwithstanding this apparent reasonableness, Arkansas argues that our description in *Ouellette* of the role of affected States in the permit process and our characterization of the affected States' position as "subordinate," indicates that the EPA's application of the Oklahoma standards was error. We disagree. Our statement in *Ouellette* concerned only an affected State's input into the permit process; that input is clearly limited by the plain language of § 402(b). Limits on an affected State's direct participation in permitting decisions, however, do not in any way constrain

---

10. This restriction applies whether the permit is issued by the EPA or by an ap- proved state program. See 40 CFR § 123.25 (1991).

the *EPA's* authority to require a point source to comply with downstream water quality standards.

Arkansas also argues that regulations requiring compliance with downstream standards are at odds with the legislative history of the Act and with the statutory scheme established by the Act. Although we agree with Arkansas that the Act's legislative history indicates that Congress intended to grant the Administrator discretion in his oversight of the issuance of NPDES permits, we find nothing in that history to indicate that Congress intended to preclude the EPA from establishing a general requirement that such permits be conditioned to ensure compliance with downstream water quality standards.

Similarly, we agree with Arkansas that in the Clean Water Act Congress struck a careful balance among competing policies and interests, but do not find the EPA regulations concerning the application of downstream water quality standards at all incompatible with that balance. Congress, in crafting the Act, protected certain sovereign interest of the States; for example, § 510 allows States to adopt more demanding pollution-control standards than those established under the Act. Arkansas emphasizes that § 510 preserves such state authority only as it is applied to the waters of the regulating State. Even assuming Arkansas's construction of § 510 is correct, cf. id., at 493, that section only concerns *state* authority and does not constrain the *EPA's* authority to promulgate reasonable regulations requiring point sources in one State to comply with water quality standards in downstream States.

* * * For these reasons, we find the EPA's requirement that the Fayetteville discharge comply with Oklahoma's water quality standards to be a reasonable exercise of the Agency's substantial statutory discretion.

V

* * * The Court of Appeals construed the Clean Water Act to prohibit any discharge of effluent that would reach waters already in violation of existing water quality standards. We find nothing in the Act to support this reading.

* * *

VI

* * * The Court of Appeals also concluded that the EPA's issuance of the Fayetteville permit was arbitrary and capricious because the Agency misinterpreted Oklahoma's water quality standards.

* * *

In sum, the Court of Appeals made a policy choice that it was not authorized to make. Arguably, as that court suggested, it might be wise to prohibit any discharge into the Illinois River, even if that discharge would have no adverse impact on water quality. But it was surely not arbitrary for the EPA to conclude—given the benefits to the River from the increased flow of relatively clean water and the benefits achieved in Arkansas by allowing the new plant to operate as designed—that allowing the discharge would be even wiser. * * *

Accordingly, the judgment of the Court of Appeals is

Reversed.

NOTE

After this decision, if a downstream state tried to set protective water quality standards that could limit development in an upstream state, would you expect the upstream state to object? Wyoming strongly opposed Montana standards to protect water quality in the Powder and Tongue River basins; Wyoming argued that Montana's standards were unreasonably tough, and could inhibit production of coal bed methane gas in the Wyoming portion of these energy-rich interstate river basins. EPA set up a process to encourage the states to settle, but when that effort failed after a year of negotiations, EPA approved Montana's standards. Cf. Friends of Pinto Creek v. U.S. E.P.A., 504 F.3d 1007 (9th Cir. 2007). EPA issued an NPDES permit for a copper mine on Pinto Creek, "a desert river located near Miami, Arizona," although the amount of dissolved copper in the stream already exceeded Arizona water quality standards. EPA regulations, 40 C.F.R. § 122.4(i), prohibits discharges that "will cause or contribute to the violation of water quality standards". The mine and EPA argued that *Oklahoma* stood for the proposition that new discharges into water quality-impaired waters should not be prohibited. However, the Court found no conflict with the decision because Friends of Pinto Creek did not simply argue for an absolute ban but established that EPA violated § 122.4(i) by failing to set a compliance schedule to bring the stream segment into compliance with applicable water quality standards.

NOTE: INTERSTATE POLLUTION REMEDIES

Preemption of Federal Tort Law. In Section II of the Court's unanimous decision in *Arkansas*, Justice Stevens traced the evolutionary interaction between the common law—both state and federal—and congressional enactments pertaining to water pollution. For all practical purposes, the Court in Milwaukee v. Illinois and Michigan, 451 U.S. 304, 101 S.Ct. 1784, 68 L.Ed.2d 114 (1981) (*Milwaukee II*), arrested the development of a federal common law of torts to fill in gaps left by antipollution regulatory programs. The decision states that "federal courts, unlike state courts, are not general common law courts and do not possess a general power to develop and apply their own rules of decision," citing Erie v. Tompkins, 304 U.S. 64, 78, 58 S.Ct. 817, 82 L.Ed. 1188 (1938). This rationale for the decision is troubling, since it was traditionally assumed that the power to develop a federal common law of interstate water allocation and pollution came from either the constitutional grant of original jurisdiction or an act of Congress. See Martin H. Redish, Federal Jurisdiction: Tensions in the Allocation of Judicial Power 79–107 (1980).

In fact, Judge Friendly argued that *Erie* did not impeach the constitutionality of the development of a federal common law. He pointed out that Hinderlider v. La Plata River and Cherry Creek Ditch Co., 304 U.S. 92, 58 S.Ct. 803, 82 L.Ed. 1202 (1938), *infra* p. 954, decided the same day as *Erie*, stands for the proposition that "the Constitution can well be deemed to *require* that the federal courts should fashion a law when the interstate nature of the controversy makes it inappropriate that the law of either state should govern" (emphasis added). Henry J. Friendly, *In Praise of Erie and of the New Federal Common Law*, 39 N.Y.U. L. Rev. 383, 408 n. 119 (1964). But cf. Note, *Federal Common Law and Interstate Pollution*, 85 Harv. L. Rev. 1439 (1972).

In an earlier phase of the litigation, Illinois v. Milwaukee, 406 U.S. 91, 92 S.Ct. 1385, 31 L.Ed.2d 712 (1972) (*Milwaukee I*), the Supreme Court based the availability of a common law remedy on both its original jurisdiction to hear interstate equitable apportionment actions and on congressional pollution control statutes. The Clean Water Act (CWA) was passed after *Milwaukee I* but before *Milwaukee II*, however. *Milwaukee II* found nothing in the Act to indicate that Congress intended to preserve federal common law remedies. Indeed, it found that a system of federal statutory standards would be fundamentally at odds with allowing separate federal common law remedies that might result in different standards being applied. See generally A. Dan Tarlock, *Upstream, Downstream: Rationalizing Different State Water Quality Standards on Interstate Streams*, 37 Rocky Mtn. Min. L. Inst. 23–1 (1991).

State Law Remedies. If the federal common law of nuisance is preempted by a statutory scheme, can similar actions be pursued under state law? Section 510 of the CWA allows states to impose stricter limits on pollutant discharges than apply under federal standards. Suppose that a polluter discharges a pollutant in State A that injures citizens of State B. Can the victims sue in the state courts of State B and apply the state law of State B? In Ohio v. Wyandotte Chemicals Corp., 401 U.S. 493, 91 S.Ct. 1005, 28 L.Ed.2d 256 (1971), the state of Ohio brought an original action against a corporation for dumping mercury into Lake Erie in Michigan. The Court declined to take original jurisdiction, suggesting that Ohio could exercise long-arm jurisdiction to obtain adequate relief in its own courts. In such an action, what law would apply?

After the decision in *Milwaukee II*, Illinois sought the same type of relief in U.S. District Court that it had pursued in the Supreme Court, but this time under Illinois statute and common law. The case was consolidated with a class action commenced in the Northern District of Illinois by the state Attorney General against the City of Hammond, Indiana, which was dumping raw sewage into Lake Michigan and was thereby allegedly causing a public and private nuisance under Illinois law. In *Milwaukee III*, the Seventh Circuit said that "in the ordinary interstate tort, the Constitution does not preclude the application of one state's law to afford a remedy for

acts done in another state and producing injury within the forum state."
Illinois v. Milwaukee, 731 F.2d 403, 411 n. 3 (7th Cir.1984), cert. denied
469 U.S. 1196, 105 S.Ct. 979, 83 L.Ed.2d 981 (1985). However, it also held
that the issue here was "the equitable reconciliation of competing uses of
an interstate body of water, Lake Michigan." Id. at 410. As a result, "[t]he
very reasons the Court gave for resorting to federal common law in
Milwaukee I, the need for equitable apportionment, are the same reasons
that the state claiming injury cannot apply its own law to out-of-state
dischargers now." Id. at 403.

The Court resolved this issue in International Paper Co. v. Ouellette,
479 U.S. 481, 107 S.Ct. 805, 93 L.Ed.2d 883 (1987), but not by resorting to
federal common law. Instead, the Court held that the CWA preempted an
action based on Vermont tort law alleging a cause of action for nuisance
caused by a polluter discharging effluent on the New York side of Lake
Champlain. The Court found that the CWA preempts suits based on the
laws of an affected state to curb pollution originating in another state.
Thus, it limited the effect of Section 510 to allowing state laws stricter than
federal laws to be applied only by the polluting state. It is interesting that
the CWA has little provision for dealing with interstate pollution. Therefore, the Court in *Ouellette* noted that the Vermont plaintiff could still
bring a nuisance claim based on New York statutory or common law
inasmuch as stricter standards could be imposed by the source state,
according to the Court's interpretation of the CWA.

Equitable Apportionment. Apparently lost in the volley of *Milwaukee*
litigation was any serious consideration of equitable apportionment. After
federal tort remedies were ruled out, the parties went scurrying for courts
in which to bring a state law tort suit.

The law of equitable apportionment is a kind of federal common law
that is well-accepted in interstate water litigation. Are interstate water
pollution cases effectively cases that seek to "apportion" the right to use
waters shared by two or more states? One "use" is to carry away discharged pollutants and it competes with uses in a neighbor state—drinking
water, recreation, other pollutant discharge. Indeed, a remedy for pollution
is to leave more water in the stream. Recall that the Supreme Court in New
Jersey v. New York, *supra* p. 948, required reductions in diversions and
additional releases from reservoirs to prevent harm to water quality. The
theory and basis for the decision was equitable apportionment, not tort.

An allocation of waters was not specifically sought in *Milwaukee II* or
in *Arkansas v. Oklahoma*. Are remedies like those in *New Jersey* still viable
where present or future actions in one state cause or exacerbate a pollution
problem? Is the federal common law of equitable apportionment preempted
by the Clean Water Act (that targets the discharge of effluent, not the
availability of water to dilute concentrations of effluents)? In other words,
did Congress intend to apportion the use of interstate waters when it set up
the scheme in the Clean Water Act?

NOTE: ON THE FUTURE OF EQUITABLE APPORTIONMENT

Interstate water conflicts increasingly involve a mix of traditional consumptive use allocation issues, water quality issues, and issues related to the conservation of endangered species and ecosystem services. The long-running dispute over the waters of the Apalachicola–Chattahoochee–Flint rivers in Georgia, Alabama, and Florida and the Alabama–Coosa–Tallapoosa rivers in Alabama and Georgia was once thought to be a potential prototype modern interstate dispute. Georgia, which occupies 3/4 of the basin, is a fast growing upper basin state that wants to use more water from the existing federal reservoirs, primarily Lake Lanier north of Atlanta, on the Chattachoochee for municipal and industrial use in the Atlanta metropolitan area and to construct new reservoirs in the head waters of both systems. The Flint River runs through the agricultural regions of southeastern Georgia and is impacted by groundwater pumping. Water quality is decreasing in downstream reaches due to urban run-off, agricultural run-off and new industrial sites. Florida is concerned with low flows and the quality of the estuary at the end of the Apalachicola, formed by the Chattahoochee and Flint, because of the valuable oyster fisheries that the estuary supports. Alabama also fears that upstream diversions will foreclose economic growth along its eastern border with Georgia. See Carl Erhardt, The Battle Over the "Hootch": The Federal–Interstate Water Compact and the Resolution of Rights in the Chattahoochee River, 11 Stan. Envtl. L. J. 200 (1992).

In 1989, the U.S. Army Corps of Engineers triggered the conflict by asking Congress to reallocate 207,000 acre feet from Lake Lanier hydropower production to water supply. Alabama, concerned about downstream navigation, sued the Corps to enjoin the reallocation. In 1992, the three states agreed to continue existing withdrawals, and in 1997 Congress approved an interstate compact for each basin which required that the states negotiate an allocation of basins. Pub. L. No. 105–104, 111 Stat. 2219 (1997). In 2000, Alabama and Georgia reached an agreement on the Alabama–Coosa–Tallapoosa with the help of a mediator, but Georgia made it contingent on a further agreement on the larger Apalachicola–Chattahoochee–Flint, and Florida refused to agree to extend the negotiating deadline. In early 2002, the three states informally agreed to a proposal not to set downstream minimum flow requirements on Alabama and Georgia but instead to require that the Atlanta region begin conserving water or seek alternative supplies after 2030, the date the area is expected to use all existing available supplies. However, in the ensuing years, marked by a severe drought in 2006–2007, the states negotiated and used mediators but were unable to agree on an allocation. Balancing the demands of the Atlanta and Georgia supplemental irrigation needs with downstream nonconsumptive interests, especially Florida's demand for natural rather than minimum flows, proved impossible to resolve, and the Compact expired in 2003. A settlement among the Corps of Engineers, the state of Georgia, water suppliers and several utilities unilaterally shifted 248,858 acre feet of Lake Lanier to water supply for the Atlanta metro area. Southeastern

Federal Power Customers v. Geren, 514 F.3d 1316 (D.C. Cir. 2008), page 847, *supra*, held that the settlement violated the Water Supply Act, 43 U.S.C. § 390b(d), because major reservoir operational changes require Congressional approval; the reallocation constituted over 22 percent of the reservoir's storage capacity, would be the second largest Corps reallocation taken without Congressional approval, and might increase to 35 percent in light of future growth of the region.

In light of the A–C–F experience, what response would you give if asked the merits of continued negotiation and compromise versus an original action adjudication? If the case went to the Supreme Court, how would be it be resolved? Florida argues that the ecosystem services that the natural flow of the Apalachicola are entitled to equal dignity with Georgia's consumptive demands. Is the risk of the destabilization of an aquatic ecosystem, which is estimated to have a $5 billion annual value, a sufficient injury to trigger original jurisdiction? Should the Court apportion the flow of the River or the average annual supply constrained by a minimum base flow? See J.B. Ruhl, Water Wars, Eastern Style: Divvying Up the Apalachicola–Chattahoochee–Flint River Basin, 131 J. Contemp. Water Res. & Educ. 47 (2005).

Georgia has come up with a new solution to Atlanta's water supply. After trying to purchase Tennessee River water from Tennessee, Georgia now claims that she is a riparian state. The basis of the claim is that Congress set the boundary of Georgia's northern border at the first point where the River touched the 35th parallel, but the 1818 survey fixing the boundary erroneously located it a mile south of the River. Georgia's position is set out in *Tapping the Tennessee River at Georgia's Northwest Corner: A Solution to North Georgia's Water Supply Crisis.*

2. ALLOCATION BY INTERSTATE COMPACT

Interstate compacts are contractual arrangements, like treaties, that are used to carry out the objectives of two or more states. The Supreme Court has indicated several times its reluctance to adjudicate interstate stream disputes and has urged the parties to resolve their differences by compact. Compacts are authorized by art. I, § 10, cl. 3 of the Constitution subject to congressional consent.

There are dozens of interstate compacts dealing with water allocation, pollution control, flood control, project development, and basin planning in interstate waters. Interstate stream compacts that allocate water among the signatory parties vary in their terms from an apportionment of a percentage of streamflow to a requirement that a certain quantity of water be delivered at a specified point on the stream.

Apportioning the rights of states to use interstate waters by compact offers flexibility that may not be available in judicial apportionment. Furthermore, adjudication may not be available because the Supreme Court generally refuses jurisdiction unless there is imminent injury, a condition that does not usually arise until a stream is overappropriated.

Thus, compacting states can anticipate their respective future needs and provide for them. This is essential to long range planning by the respective states. The United States may also be a party to an interstate compact to represent the government's needs for federal lands or other national interests.

Compact formation generally begins with congressional authorization of negotiation, often providing for a federal representative to participate. States then commence negotiations, usually after passing enabling legislation designating their negotiators. Negotiations may take many years. The final step is for Congress to consent, a requirement of the compact clause, which states: "No state shall, without the consent of Congress * * * enter into any agreement or compact with another state, or with a foreign power* * *." U.S. Const. art. I, § 10, cl. 3.

Many compacts require the establishment of commissions or similar agencies to deal with matters of compact administration. Often the commissioners are appointed by the governors of the participating states and a federal member who may not have a vote. Commissions allocating waters between states have much administrative power, relegating enforcement to the courts. Some compacts, like the Delaware River Compact, delegate considerable power to a compact agency. However, the Colorado River Compact, *infra* p. 989, created no compact agency at all. The enforcement problems of ordinary compacts are multiplied when the federal government is a signatory, for the question remains unresolved whether congressional consent to such a compact binds future Congresses in matters such as the exercise of Commerce Clause powers that may be contrary to the compact provisions.

Notwithstanding their promise, compacts can leave many problems unresolved. Compact negotiations may succeed only because difficult points are plastered over with ambiguity. Some compacts are based on errors of fact, but once the compact is accepted it is nearly impossible to get the parties to agree to changes. Compacts may be difficult to enforce because the United States is sometimes regarded as an indispensable party, and cannot be sued without its consent. Furthermore, enforcement suits can be expensive and lengthy because they are usually within the original jurisdiction of the Supreme Court of the United States. Compacts often lack the flexibility to deal with changing conditions and they cannot be easily amended.

The classic study of the compact is Felix Frankfurter & James M. Landis, *The Compact Clause of the Constitution—A Study in Interstate Adjustments*, 34 Yale L.J. 685 (1925). A useful supplement is Frederick Lloyd Zimmerman & Mitchell Wendell, The Interstate Compact Since 1925 (Council of State Governments, 1951). The United States Department of the Interior published a reference book: T. Richard Witmer, Documents on the Use and Control of the Waters of Interstate and International Streams: Compacts, Treaties and Adjudications (1956). See also Jerome C. Muys, Interstate Water Compacts: The Interstate Compact and Federal–Interstate Compact, National Water Commission Legal Study No. 14 (1971).

State ex rel. Dyer v. Sims

Supreme Court of the United States, 1951.
341 U.S. 22, 71 S.Ct. 557, 95 L.Ed. 713.

■ MR. JUSTICE FRANKFURTER delivered the opinion of the Court.

After extended negotiations eight States entered into a Compact to control pollution in the Ohio River system. See Ohio River Valley Water Sanitation Compact, 54 Stat. 752. Illinois, Indiana, Kentucky, New York, Ohio, Pennsylvania, Virginia and West Virginia recognized that they were faced with one of the problems of government that are defined by natural rather than political boundaries. Accordingly, they pledged themselves to cooperate in maintaining waters in the Ohio River basin in a sanitary condition through the administrative mechanism of the Ohio River Valley Water Sanitation Commission, consisting of three members from each State and three representing the United States.

The heart of the Compact is Article VI. This provides that sewage discharged into boundary streams or streams flowing from one State into another "shall be so treated, within a time reasonable for the construction of the necessary works, as to provide for substantially complete removal of settleable solids, and the removal of not less than forty-five per cent (45%) of the total suspended solids; provided that, in order to protect the public health or to preserve the waters for other legitimate purposes, ... in specific instances such higher degree of treatment shall be used as may be determined to be necessary by the Commission after investigation, due notice and hearing." Industrial wastes are to be treated "to such degree as may be determined to be necessary by the Commission after investigation, due notice and hearing." Sewage and industrial wastes discharged into streams located wholly within one State are to be treated "to that extent, if any, which may be necessary to maintain such waters in a sanitary and satisfactory condition at least equal to the condition of the waters of the interstate stream immediately above the confluence."

Article IX provides that the Commission may, after notice and hearing, issue orders for compliance enforceable in the State and federal courts. It further provides: "No such order shall go into effect unless and until it receives the assent of at least a majority of the commissioners from each of not less than a majority of the signatory States; and no such order upon a municipality, corporation, person or entity in any State shall go into effect unless and until it receives the assent of not less than a majority of the commissioners from such state."

By Article X the States also agree "to appropriate for the salaries, office and other administrative expenses, their proper proportion of the annual budget as determined by the Commission and approved by the Governors of the signatory States...."

The present controversy arose because of conflicting views between officials of West Virginia regarding the responsibility of West Virginia under the Compact.

The Legislature of that State ratified and approved the Compact on March 11, 1939. W. Va. Acts 1939, c. 38. Congress gave its consent on July 11, 1940, 54 Stat. 752, and upon adoption by all the signatory States the Compact was formally executed by the Governor of West Virginia on June 30, 1948. At its 1949 session the West Virginia Legislature appropriated $12,250 as the State's contribution to the expenses of the Commission for the fiscal year beginning July 1, 1949. W. Va. Acts 1949, c. 9, Item 93. Respondent Sims, the auditor of the State, refused to issue a warrant upon its treasury for payment of this appropriation. To compel him to issue it, the West Virginia Commissioners to the Compact Commission and the members of the West Virginia State Water Commission instituted this original mandamus proceeding in the Supreme Court of Appeals of West Virginia. The court denied relief on the merits, 134 W. Va. [278], 58 S.E.2d 766, and we brought the case here, 340 U.S. 807, because questions of obviously important public interest are raised.

The West Virginia court found that the "sole question" before it was the validity of the Act of 1939 approving West Virginia's adherence to the Compact. It found that Act invalid in that (1) the Compact was deemed to delegate West Virginia's police power to other States and to the Federal Government, and (2) it was deemed to bind future legislatures to make appropriations for the continued activities of the Sanitation Commission and thus to violate Art. X, § 4 of the West Virginia Constitution.

Briefs filed on behalf of the United States and other States, as *amici*, invite the Court to consider far-reaching issues relating to the Compact Clause of the United States Constitution. Art. I, § 10, cl. 3. The United States urges that the Compact be so read as to allow any signatory State to withdraw from its obligations at any time. Pennsylvania, Ohio, Indiana, Illinois, Kentucky and New York contend that the Compact Clause precludes any State from limiting its power to enter into a compact to which Congress has consented. We must not be tempted by these inviting vistas. We need not go beyond the issues on which the West Virginia court found the Compact not binding on that State. That these are issues which give this Court jurisdiction to review the State court proceeding, 28 U.S.C. § 1257, needs no discussion after Delaware River Comm'n v. Colburn, 310 U.S. 419, 427.

Control of pollution in interstate streams might, on occasion, be an appropriate subject for national legislation. * * * But, with prescience, the Framers left the States free to settle regional controversies in diverse ways. Solution of the problem underlying this case may be attempted directly by the affected States through contentious litigation before this Court. * * *

Indeed, so awkward and unsatisfactory is the available litigious solution for these problems that this Court deemed it appropriate to emphasize the practical constitutional alternative provided by the Compact Clause.

* * *

The growing interdependence of regional interests, calling for regional adjustments, has brought extensive use of compacts. A compact is more than a supple device for dealing with interests confined within a region. That it is also a means of safeguarding the national interest is well illustrated in the Compact now under review. Not only was congressional consent required, as for all compacts; direct participation by the Federal Government was provided in the President's appointment of three members of the Compact Commission. Art. IV; Art. XI, § 3.

But a compact is after all a legal document. Though the circumstances of its drafting are likely to assure great care and deliberation, all avoidance of disputes as to scope and meaning is not within human gift. Just as this Court has power to settle disputes between States where there is no compact, it must have final power to pass upon the meaning and validity of compacts. It requires no elaborate argument to reject the suggestion that an agreement solemnly entered into between States by those who alone have political authority to speak for a State can be unilaterally nullified, or given final meaning by an organ of one of the contracting States. A State cannot be its own ultimate judge in a controversy with a sister State. To determine the nature and scope of obligations as between States, whether they arise through the legislative means of compact or the "federal common law" governing interstate controversies (Hinderlider v. La Plata Co., 304 U.S. 92, 110) is the function and duty of the Supreme Court of the Nation. Of course every deference will be shown to what the highest court of a State deems to be the law and policy of its State, particularly when recondite or unique features of local law are urged. Deference is one thing; submission to a State's own determination of whether it has undertaken an obligation, what that obligation is, and whether it conflicts with a disability of the State to undertake it is quite another.

The Supreme Court of Appeals of the State of West Virginia is, for exclusively State purposes, the ultimate tribunal in construing the meaning of her Constitution. Two prior decisions of this Court make clear, however, that we are free to examine determinations of law by State courts in the limited field where a compact brings in issue the rights of other States and the United States.

* * * The issue before us is whether the West Virginia Legislature had authority, under her Constitution, to enter into a compact which involves delegation of power to an interstate agency and an agreement to appropriate funds for the administrative expenses of the agency.

That a legislature may delegate to an administrative body the power to make rules and decide particular cases is one of the axioms of modern government. * * * The Compact involves a reasonable and carefully limited delegation of power to an interstate agency. Nothing in its Constitution suggests that, in dealing with the problem dealt with by the Compact, West Virginia must wait for the answer to be dictated by this Court after harassing and unsatisfactory litigation.

* * *

The State court also held that the Compact is in conflict with Art. X, § 4, of the State Constitution and for that reason is not binding on West Virginia. This section provides:

> "No debt shall be contracted by this State, except to meet casual deficits in the revenue, to redeem a previous liability of the State, to suppress insurrection, repel invasion, or defend the State in time of war; but the payment of any liability, other than that for the ordinary expenses of the State, shall be equally distributed over a period of at least twenty years."

The Compact was evidently drawn with great care to meet the problem of debt limitation in light of this section and similar restrictive provisions in the constitutions of other States. Although, under Art. X of the Compact, the States agree to appropriate funds for administrative expenses, the annual budget must be approved by the Governors of the signatory States. In addition, Article V provides: "The Commission shall not incur any obligations of any kind prior to the making of appropriations adequate to meet the same; nor shall the Commission pledge the credit of any of the signatory States, except by and with the authority of the legislature thereof." In view of these provisions, we conclude that the obligation of the State under the Compact is not in conflict with Art. X, § 4 of the State Constitution.

Reversed and remanded.

* * *

NOTES

1. The Court said that it was not answering the "inviting" question of whether a state which is signatory to a compact can withdraw from its obligations at any time. However, in ruling that it has supervening authority to interpret state law alleged to be in conflict with an interstate compact, the Court does "reject the suggestion that an agreement solemnly entered into between States * * * can be unilaterally nullified, or given final meaning by an organ of one of the contracting States." Has the Court decided the issue that it said it was avoiding?

2. The principal case arose on review of a state court decision. Do federal courts have jurisdiction to interpret compacts in the first instance? Is such interpretation a federal question within the meaning of 28 U.S.C.A. § 1331(a) (i.e., arising "under the Constitution, laws, or treaties of the United States")? League to Save Lake Tahoe v. Tahoe Regional Planning Agency, 507 F.2d 517 (9th Cir.1974), cert. denied 420 U.S. 974, 95 S.Ct. 1398, 43 L.Ed.2d 654 (1975), says yes, but several cases reach contrary results. E.g., Port Auth. Bondholders Protective Committee v. Port of New York Auth., 270 F.Supp. 947 (S.D.N.Y.1967); Delaware River Joint Toll Bridge Comm'n v. Miller, 147 F.Supp. 270 (E.D.Pa.1956); Rivoli Trucking Corp. v. American Export Lines, 167 F.Supp. 937 (S.D.N.Y.1958). In 1994, in a 5–4 decision, the Supreme Court held that interstate compact agencies do not enjoy Eleventh Amendment immunity because they are not states.

Hess v. Port Authority Trans–Hudson Corp., 513 U.S. 30, 115 S.Ct. 394, 130 L.Ed.2d 245 (1994).

3. Is every interstate agreement a "compact" requiring congressional consent? Does the Court in *Dyer* shed light on the question? An earlier case suggested that consent is required only for agreements that exercise the political power of states. Virginia v. Tennessee, 148 U.S. 503, 518–19, 13 S.Ct. 728, 37 L.Ed. 537 (1893).

4. Interstate compacts are often entered into to avoid the risks of an equitable apportionment, but a compact may also follow a Supreme Court decree. In 1930 the Supreme Court apportioned the flow of the Delaware River among New York, Pennsylvania, New Jersey, and Delaware. New Jersey v. New York, 283 U.S. 336, 51 S.Ct. 478, 75 L.Ed. 1104 (1931), *supra* p. 948. The decree allowed New York state to supply New York City by transwatershed diversions from tributaries of the Delaware in the Catskills, subject to several conditions. The Delaware River Basin Compact, Pub. L. 87–328, 75 Stat. 688 (1961), provided that the decree of 1954 may not be changed without the unanimous consent of the parties to the lawsuit, except that the basin commission (made up of one representative from each signatory state and the United States) could declare an emergency and thereafter, upon unanimous vote, vary the terms of the decree during the emergency. The emergency powers of the compact have been employed to reduce the delivery obligations and diversions and to require releases to the river from storage. The Delaware River Basin Compact is a rare example of an interstate compact which creates a regulatory authority. Art. 10, allows the Commission to require the issuance of permits of designated "protected areas." But, this authority is delegated to states with adequate regulatory programs. The Compact delegates authority to issue permits for withdrawals or diversions to the states that have enacted a regulated riparian system of water law. The state permits are to be superseded when the Commission declares a water emergency, yet every water emergency declared under the Compact, the Commission has deferred to the state authorities so long as the states were acting consistently with the drought management plans adopted by the Commission. Three of the states—Delaware, New Jersey and New York—regulate withdrawals. For these states, the Commission operates as a planning agency rather than as a water-permitting agency. Since Pennsylvania does not have comparable regulation, the Commission operates as the permitting authority for users within protected areas of the basin in Pennsylvania. Not surprisingly, all challenges to the Commission's regulatory authority have arisen in Pennsylvania—thus far without success. See Badgley v. New York, 606 F.2d 358 (2d Cir. 1979), cert. denied, 447 U.S. 906, 100 S.Ct. 2989, 64 L.Ed.2d 855 (1980); Delaware River Basin Comm'n v. Bucks Cty. Water Auth'y, 545 F.Supp. 138 (E.D. Pa. 1982); and Dublin Water Co. v. Delaware River Basin Comm'n, 443 F.Supp. 310 (E.D. Pa. 1977).

5. The legal force of an interstate compact as federal law, the supreme law of the land, "trumps" any conflicting law of signatory states. Hinderlider v. La Plata River and Cherry Creek Ditch Co., 304 U.S. 92, 58 S.Ct.

803, 82 L.Ed. 1202 (1938). In *Hinderlider,* the state engineer administered water rights perfected under Colorado law by withholding water from in-state appropriators in order to satisfy delivery requirements mandated by the La Plata River Compact between Colorado and New Mexico. Pursuant to the compact, the state engineer curtailed diversions entirely from time to time, rotating deliveries between users in the two states. The Colorado Supreme Court held the compact to be unconstitutional, as enabling an infringement on vested private property interests.

The U.S. Supreme Court reversed. Since the La Plata was an interstate watercourse being beneficially used in both states, its waters must be equitably apportioned between the two. A compact is a constitutional means of effecting an equitable apportionment and therefore it is binding on the citizens of both states. Further, giving discretion to state officials to rotate uses rather than making a continuous equal division was a "detail" within Congress's constitutional power. Finally, the Court in *Hinderlider* concluded that Colorado users had not been divested of a compensable property interest because the state could allocate only its equitable share of the interstate watercourse and therefore any allocations in excess of that equitable share could not have created a vested property right subject to "taking."

6. Assume that River A and River B both rise in Colorado and flow into New Mexico. Invoking the doctrine of equitable apportionment, a compact allocates all the water of River A to Colorado and all the water of River B to New Mexico. Plaintiff has an adjudicated appropriative right on River B in Colorado senior to some users on River A, but the state engineer shuts down the plaintiff's headgate pursuant to the compact. Is plaintiff entitled to relief?

7. Who is responsible for the satisfaction of Indian water rights in an equitable apportionment or compact adjudication? Arizona has estimated that the claims of the Navajo Reservation could be as high as 15 million acre-feet per year. In *Arizona v. California,* in a portion of the decision reprinted *infra* p. 1001, the special master held that Indian rights were present perfected rights (having priority over virtually all others) and must be satisfied by the state in which the reservation lies. Arizona's total apportionment under compacts and the Supreme Court's interpretation of federal statutes is 2.8 million acre-feet. If tribal claims approach or exceed a state's apportionment, should all states sharing the waterway share respon-sibility for satisfying those rights? Is the satisfaction of Indian claims a federal responsibility since the federal government has a trust responsibili-ty to the tribes to protect their water rights? See generally A. Dan Tarlock, *One River, Three Sovereigns: Indian and Interstate Water Rights,* 22 Land & Water L. Rev. 631 (1987).

8. Interstate compacts are primarily focused on permanently allocating a river's presumed supplies among existing competing users. With limited exceptions such as the Delaware River Basin Compact and the 2008 Great Lakes Compact, *infra* p. 1045, discussed in Note 4, *supra,* the states have been reluctant to include long term management institutions which can deal with changed conditions and new uses. The Utton Transboundary Resources Center at the University of New Mexico School of Law has prepared a model compact. The model compact includes effective management institutions, dispute settlement procedures and the incorporation of environmental interests into allocation regimes. For the text and commentary see Jerome Muys, George William Sherk and Marilyn O'Leary, Utton Transboundary Resources Center Model Interstate Water Compact, 47 Nat. Res. J. 17 (2007).

Intake Water Company v. Yellowstone River Compact Commission

United States Court of Appeals, Ninth Circuit, 1985.
769 F.2d 568, cert. denied 476 U.S. 1163, 106 S.Ct. 2288, 90 L.Ed.2d 729 (1986).

■ J. BLAINE ANDERSON, CIRCUIT JUDGE:

* * *

The Yellowstone River Compact fixes the water usage of all waters of the Yellowstone River Basin. It was enacted by Congress on October 10, 1951. Act of Consent to the Yellowstone River Compact, 65 Stat. 663, Ch. 629, Pub.L. 231 (1951). The signatory states, Montana, Wyoming and North Dakota, approved the Compact and codified it in their laws prior to congressional ratification. The Yellowstone River Compact Commission is charged by Congress with implementation of the Compact.

In June, 1973, appellant Intake appropriated 80,650 acre feet per year of Yellowstone River water. Intake planned construction of a diversion works, including a reservoir near Dawson, Montana. Some of the water was to be diverted outside the Yellowstone Basin for use elsewhere in Montana and North Dakota and thus outside the jurisdiction of the Compact.

Intake challenged the validity of Article X of the Compact, contending that it discriminated against, unreasonably impeded and exerted an undue burden on the flow of interstate commerce in violation of the Commerce Clause of the Constitution. Art. I, § 8, cl. 3. Article X of the Compact restricts interbasin or interstate transfer of Yellowstone River waters, providing that:

> No waters shall be diverted from the Yellowstone River Basin without unanimous consent of all the signatory states:

* * *

Intake alleges that Article X of the Compact, as state law, places a constitutionally impermissible burden on inter-state commerce by requiring unanimous consent of the signatory states for out-of-basin transfers of Yellowstone River water. Appellees, while not challenging the sufficiency of this argument, contend that: the Yellowstone River Compact was approved by Congress; because it was approved by Congress, it is federal, not state, law for purposes of Commerce Clause objections; therefore, the Compact cannot, by definition, be a state law impermissibly interfering with commerce but is instead a federal law, immune from attack.

The three-judge district court, in a well-reasoned decision, concluded that appellees' argument was the compelling one. Intake Water Co. v. Yellowstone River Compact Commission, 590 F.Supp. 293, 296–97 (1983). On the basis of that reasoning, we agree.

When Congress approved this compact, Congress was acting within its authority to immunize state law from some constitutional objections by converting it into federal law. Cuyler v. Adams, 449 U.S. 433, 438, 101 S.Ct. 703, 706, 66 L.Ed.2d 641 (1981). Accord, NYSA–ILA Vacation & Holiday Fund v. Waterfront Comm'n of New York Harbor, 732 F.2d 292 (2d Cir.), cert. denied, 469 U.S. 852 (1984). Nor can there be any question as to whether Congress in fact approved the state law from which immunity from Commerce Clause attack is claimed: The Compact was before Congress and Congress expressly approved it.

We find additional support for this holding in the Supreme Court's recent decision of Northeast Bancorp Inc. v. Board of Governors of the Federal Reserve System, 472 U.S. 159 (1985). There, the Court rejected the argument that regional limitations contained in Massachusetts and Connecticut statutes burdened interstate commerce. The Court held: "When Congress so chooses, state actions which it plainly authorizes are invulnerable to constitutional attack under the Commerce Clause." 472 U.S. at 174. Thus, as a federal law, the Compact authorizes those actions included within its provisions.

* * *

■ TASHIMA, DISTRICT JUDGE, concurring:

* * *

The real issue raised by appellant is what inference should be drawn from an essentially silent congressional record, which is the case here. Neither the Act of Consent to the Yellowstone River Compact, nor its legislative history, discloses that Commerce Clause immunity was expressly considered. Appellant contends that such a silent record compels the conclusion that Congress, in approving a compact, intended not to immunize it from Commerce Clause attack.

By rejecting appellant's contention, we merely ascribe to Congress the intent plainly to be inferred from its action, *i.e.*, that it intended to do what it did—approve the Yellowstone River Compact without reservation.

NOTES

1. It is well established that Congress may expressly consent to state legislation affecting interstate commerce that would otherwise be unconstitutional. E.g., Prudential Insurance Co. v. Benjamin, 328 U.S. 408, 66 S.Ct. 1142, 90 L.Ed. 1342 (1946). Likewise, congressional consent to an interstate compact may immunize the compact's restrictions from Commerce

Clause attack. Is a state law that is intended to implement an interstate compact also immunized from attack under the Commerce Clause because of congressional approval of that compact? In 1984, an entrepreneur unveiled an ambitious plan to export water from the Yampa River in Colorado to water-short San Diego by simply "appropriating" it in Colorado under state law and leaving it in the river to be used in San Diego. Colorado law allows a water export upon a showing that it will not deprive Coloradans of the beneficial use of water and that it will not impair the state's ability to comply with interstate apportionments pursuant to compacts. COLO.REV.STAT. § 37–81–101(3)(a). Unlike the Yellowstone River Compact, the Colorado River Compact is silent on taking water out of the basin. However, the San Diego scheme would have resulted in 10% of Colorado's total apportionment being used in California. If a Colorado water court denied approval to the proposal on the grounds that it would interfere with the interstate allocation scheme, would the Colorado law as applied offend the Commerce Clause as interpreted under *Sporhase, infra* p. 1030?

2. The Yellowstone River Compact Commission was unable to resolve a dispute between Montana and Wyoming, resulting in Montana suing Wyoming in the U.S. Supreme Court. Montana argues that Wyoming failed to meet her compact obligations, resulting in less water flowing into Montana from the key Yellowstone River tributaries. Wyoming argues that she is in full compliance with the compact, and that the water shortages in both states are primarily due to drought. The Supreme Court decided in 2008 to allow the case to proceed. Montana v. Wyoming, ___ U.S. ___, 128 S.Ct. 1332, 170 L.Ed.2d 56 (2008).

David H. Getches, Competing Demands for the Colorado River

56 U. Colo. L. Rev. 413, 415–20 (1985).

In the early years of the twentieth century, Southern California's growing need for federal assistance in building delivery facilities for Colorado River water came into conflict with the desire of states in the Upper Basin to secure the right to develop River water for future needs. Rich farms in California's Imperial Valley were irrigated with water brought from the River by a canal through Mexico. The Imperial Irrigation District sought the security of an "all-American" canal that would not leave the Valley's farmers at the mercy of Mexico. The federal government began investigating the possibilities. At the same time, rapidly expanding Los Angeles was feeling the need for new sources of electric power and anticipating new water needs. Leaders in the Upper Basin states, especially Colorado, objected. They knew that they would eventually need to develop Colorado River water to meet the needs of growing areas like Denver. They feared that if California were allowed to develop the River's water first, it would perfect a better legal claim. Their fears were justified by contemporary jurisprudence.

In 1922 it was reasonable to assume that the United States Supreme Court would recognize greater legal rights in a state that developed water first than in a state developing later. The Court allocates waters of interstate streams by the principle of "equitable apportionment." The Court applied the doctrine of prior appropriation in a 1922 equitable apportionment between Colorado and Wyoming, both of which use prior appropriation to allocate water within the states. Interstate apportionment of the Colorado River under that approach could have resulted in the Upper Basin states getting very little water.

The 1922 Colorado River Compact was intended to strike an accommodation between the expanding demands of the Lower Basin and the desire to preserve adequate water for future use in the less developed Upper Basin, the source of virtually all the River's water. Compacts had been used to settle or avoid conflicts between states on other issues since the signing of the Constitution, but the Colorado River Compact was the first compact negotiated to resolve claims to an interstate stream. The Compact enabled construction of storage facilities to protect the Lower Basin from floods and allowed the Lower Basin to use water needed for a growing population. The Upper Basin states relied on the Compact to prevent River water from being monopolized by California and Arizona through the establishment of legal priorities.

Under the Compact* the waters of the Colorado River were apportioned on an essentially equal basis between the Upper Basin states—Colorado, Utah, Wyoming, and New Mexico—and the Lower Basin states—Arizona, California and Nevada. The Compact guaranteed the Lower Basin states a flow of 75,000,000 acre-feet over a progressive series of ten-year periods. The drafters intended that Article III(a) would give each Basin, Upper and Lower, an average of 7,500,000 acre-feet a year. In addition, under Article III(b) the Lower Basin may consume another 1,000,000 acre-feet in years when flows permit. Article III(e) allows the faster developing Lower Basin to use any water the Upper Basin cannot use. Further, under Article III(c), the two basins are to share equally any burden that might be imposed to deliver water to Mexico, an obligation later set at 1,500,000 acre-feet annually.[8]

The water apportioned to the two basins was later allocated to individual states. In 1949, the Upper Colorado River Basin Compact gave each Upper Basin state a percentage share of that Basin's apportionment.[9] California, Arizona, and Nevada, however, were unable to agree on how to divide the Lower Basin share. After years of intense dispute and litigation, Congress enacted legislation making federal financing of Hoover Dam

---

* Excerpts of the Compact are reprinted *infra* pp. 959–961. [Eds.]

8. The obligation to Mexico was quantified in the Treaty with Mexico, T.S. No. 994, 59 Stat. 1219 (1944).

9. Upper Colorado River Basin Compact, ch. 48, 63 Stat. 31, 33 (1949). The states received the following shares: Colorado, 51.75%; Utah, 23%; Wyoming, 14%; New Mexico, 11.25%; Arizona, 50,000 acre-feet.

contingent on a prescribed Lower Basin allocation formula. Later the Supreme Court found that the Act had effectively apportioned the water.[10]

* * *

The allocation scheme in the 1922 Compact was to give the two basins equitable shares of available water. It is now apparent that the apportionment was made on the incorrect assumption that there would be an average annual flow of at least 16,000,000 acre-feet. Data spanning three centuries, however, reveal an average annual flow of only about 13,500,000 acre-feet. Furthermore, annual flows have been erratic, ranging from 4,400,000 acre-feet to over 22,000,000 acre-feet. The erroneous assumption about average flows resulted in the Lower Basin's being guaranteed substantial minimum deliveries by the Upper Basin, leaving far less water available for Upper Basin use than the negotiators apparently expected.

The Compact contemplates storage facilities to smooth out fluctuating flows and to allow for the average annual usage described in Articles III(a) and III(b). Adequate storage exists on the River to protect Lower Basin Compact entitlements except in the most severe and prolonged drought. Lake Mead, behind Hoover Dam, can hold 27,400,000 acre-feet. Lake Powell has a capacity of 25,000,000 acre-feet. Together, all reservoirs in the Colorado River system have a storage capacity of 62,489,200 acre-feet. With sixty percent of this storage effectively inaccessible to Upper Basin users, however, the burdens of cyclical water shortages fall largely on the Upper Basin. These inherent burdens, as well as practical limits on Upper Basin storage, should inform Compact interpretation. For instance, Article III(e) says that the Upper Basin may not withhold water from Lower Basin uses unless it can "reasonably be applied to domestic and agricultural uses." But the provision should not be read to preclude storage of water to meet future compact delivery requirements under Article III(d) or for reasonably foreseeable Upper Basin needs.

* * *

The Colorado River Compact
Colo. Rev. Stat. § 37–61–101.

* * *

The States of Arizona, California, Colorado, Nevada, New Mexico, Utah, and Wyoming, having resolved to enter into a compact under the Act of the Congress of the United States of America approved August 19, 1921 (42 Stat. 141) and the Acts of the Legislatures of the said States, have

---

10. Arizona v. California, 373 U.S. 546 (1963). The Court held that allocation of the Lower Basin share is governed by the Boulder Canyon Project Act, 43 U.S.C. §§ 617–617f (1982). The Act gives Arizona 2.8 million acre-feet, California 4.4 million acre-feet, and Nevada 300,000 acre-feet of the first 7.5 million acre-feet. Deliveries in excess of such amounts are apportioned 46 percent to Arizona, 50 percent to California and 4 percent to Nevada.

through their Governors appointed as their Commissioners * * * who, after negotiations participated in by Herbert Hoover appointed by The President as the representative of the United States of America, have agreed upon the following articles:

Article I

The major purposes of this compact are to provide for the equitable division and apportionment of the use of the waters of the Colorado River System; to establish the relative importance of different beneficial uses of water; to promote interstate comity; to remove causes of present and future controversies; and to secure the expeditious agricultural and industrial development of the Colorado River Basin, the storage of its waters, and the protection of life and property from floods. To these ends the Colorado River Basin is divided into two Basins, and an apportionment of the use of part of the water of the Colorado River System is made to each of them with the provision that further equitable apportionments may be made.

Article II

As used in this compact—

(a) The term "Colorado River System" means that portion of the Colorado River and its tributaries within the United States of America.

(b) The term "Colorado River Basin" means all of the drainage area of the Colorado River System and all other territory within the United States of America to which the waters of the Colorado River System shall be beneficially applied.

* * *

(e) The term "Lee Ferry" means a point in the main stream of the Colorado River one mile below the mouth of the Paria River.

(f) The term "Upper Basin" means those parts of the States of Arizona, Colorado, New Mexico, Utah, and Wyoming within and from which waters naturally drain into the Colorado River System above Lee Ferry, and also all parts of said States located without the drainage area of the Colorado River System which are now or shall hereafter be beneficially served by waters diverted from the System above Lee Ferry.

(g) The term "Lower Basin" means those parts of the States of Arizona, California, Nevada, New Mexico, and Utah within and from which waters naturally drain into the Colorado River System below Lee Ferry, and also all parts of said States located without the drainage area of the Colorado River System which are now or shall hereafter be beneficially served by waters diverted from the System below Lee Ferry.

(h) The term "domestic use" shall include the use of water for household, stock, municipal, mining, milling, industrial, and other like purposes, but shall exclude the generation of electrical power.

Article III

(a) There is hereby apportioned from the Colorado River System in perpetuity to the Upper Basin and to the Lower Basin, respectively, the exclusive beneficial consumptive use of 7,500,000 acre-feet of water per annum, which shall include all water necessary for the supply of any rights which may now exist.

(b) In addition to the apportionment in paragraph (a), the Lower Basin is hereby given the right to increase its beneficial consumptive use of such waters by one million acre-feet per annum.

(c) If, as a matter of international comity, the United States of America shall hereafter recognize in the United States of Mexico any right to the use of any waters of the Colorado River System, such waters shall be supplied first from the waters which are surplus over and above the aggregate of the quantities specified in paragraphs (a) and (b); and if such surplus shall prove insufficient for this purpose, then the burden of such deficiency shall be equally borne by the Upper Basin and the Lower Basin, and whenever necessary the States of the Upper Division shall deliver at Lee Ferry water to supply one-half of the deficiency so recognized in addition to that provided in paragraph (d).

(d) The States of the Upper Division will not cause the flow of the river at Lee Ferry to be depleted below an aggregate of 75,000,000 acre-feet for any period of ten consecutive years reckoned in continuing progressive series beginning with the first day of October next succeeding the ratification of this compact.

(e) The States of the Upper Division shall not withhold water, and the States of the Lower Division shall not require the delivery of water, which cannot reasonably be applied to domestic and agricultural uses.

* * *

[Paragraph (f) provides for further apportionment "of the waters of the Colorado River System unapportioned by paragraphs (a), (b) and (c)" after 1963 if either Basin reaches its total beneficial consumptive use under (a) and (b). Paragraph (g) allows any two signatory states to call for such an equitable apportionment.]

Article IV

(a) Inasmuch as the Colorado River has ceased to be navigable for commerce and the reservation of its waters for navigation would seriously limit the development of its Basin, the use of its waters for purposes of navigation shall be subservient to the uses of such waters for domestic, agricultural, and power purposes. If the Congress shall not consent to this paragraph, the other provisions of this compact shall nevertheless remain binding.

(b) Subject to the provisions of this compact, water of the Colorado River System may be impounded and used for the generation of electrical power, but such impounding and use shall be subservient to the use and consumption of such water for agricultural and domestic purposes and shall not interfere with or prevent use for such dominant purposes.

(c) The provisions of this article shall not apply to or interfere with the regulation and control by any State within its boundaries of the appropriation, use, and distribution of water.

* * *

Article VII

Nothing in this compact shall be construed as affecting the obligations of the United States of America to Indian tribes.

Article VIII

Present perfected rights to the beneficial use of waters of the Colorado River System are unimpaired by this compact. Whenever storage capacity of 5,000,000 acre-feet shall have been provided on the main Colorado River within or for the benefit of the Lower Basin, then claims of such rights, if any, by appropriators or users of water in the Lower Basin against appropriators or users of water in the Upper Basin shall attach to and be satisfied from water that may be stored not in conflict with Article III.

All other rights to beneficial use of waters of the Colorado River System shall be satisfied solely from the water apportioned to that Basin in which they are situate.

NOTES

1. Consider the following questions in light of the Colorado River Compact:

a.   Suppose that beneficial consumptive uses in the upper basin average 3.5 million acre-feet (maf) annually, while beneficial uses in the lower basin average 7.5 maf annually. Can the states in the lower basin increase their beneficial consumptive uses? By how much?

b.   When flows are sufficient to satisfy a total of 15 maf of consumptive uses in both basins and the lower basin has beneficial consumptive uses of 8.5 maf and the upper basin 3.0, there would be a surplus of 3.5 maf of the upper basin's allocation in the mainstream at Lee Ferry. The Mexican Treaty obligation is 1.5 maf. Can the upper basin withhold in reservoir storage all but 750,000 acre-feet (half of the Mexican obligation) of the remaining 3.0 maf? Consider both Articles III(c) and III(e).

c.   If it takes the release of 2.0 maf at Lee Ferry to supply 1.5 maf at the Mexican border, what responsibility is borne by the two sub-basins regarding the loss?

d.   Assume the upper basin has delivered only 65 maf to the lower basin over the preceding 9 year period. While the lower basin's agricultural and domestic uses have been satisfied, the lower basin demands delivery this year of 10 maf from the upper basin, to bring the 10 year delivery to 75 maf. The water is to be used to generate electric power at Hoover Dam (the revenue from which repays the lower basin's financial obligations to the U.S.). Does the compact require the delivery even if the reservoirs are low and the upper basin would have to reduce its agricultural uses to supply the water?

e. Suppose the upper basin has delivered 75 maf over the preceding 10 year period but had, in addition, stored 15 maf in Lake Powell (the reservoir behind Glen Canyon Dam). All domestic and agricultural uses in both basins have been satisfied. The lower basin demands delivery to Lake Mead of one-half of the supply stored in Lake Powell for use in generating electric power. What result under the compact?

f. The Gila River joins the mainstream of the Colorado near the Mexican border. It produces more than 2 maf of water a year, much of which flows beneath its bed and is extracted by wells. Nearly all of the annual flow is consumed in Arizona so that no water actually flows into the mainstream. Should the water produced by the Gila be considered in satisfaction of the lower basin's apportionment? Should it diminish the upper basin's obligation to deliver 75 maf each ten years? Should it be counted against the lower basin's allowable annual consumptive use? Should the Gila's waters be considered available to meet obligations to deliver water to Mexico?

2. Many questions of interpretation of the Colorado River Compact have been avoided by adoption of "operating criteria" for the two major reservoirs on the Colorado River–Lake Mead, behind Hoover Dam, and Lake Powell, behind Glen Canyon Dam. Congress, in section 602(a) of the Colorado River Basin Project Act of 1968, imposed a hierarchy of priorities on the release of water stored in Lake Powell, required that storage in Lake Powell be equalized with that in Lake Mead, and authorized the Secretary of the Interior to promulgate implementing regulations. The Secretary subsequently adopted long-range operating criteria for Glen Canyon Dam which require minimum annual releases from Lake Powell of 8.23 maf (consisting of the lower basin's 7.5 maf plus Mexico's .75 maf, less the 20,000 acre-feet annual flow of the Paria River, which enters the mainstream below Glen Canyon Dam but above Lee Ferry). Does this depart from the compact delivery requirements?

3. Could the upper basin successfully assert that the compact should be voided or reformed because of a mutual mistake of fact (because average flows are far lower than were supposed in 1922)? The prolonged history of Texas v. New Mexico, 446 U.S. 540, 100 S.Ct. 2911, 64 L.Ed.2d 485 (1980), is instructive. Texas and New Mexico entered into the Pecos River Compact in 1948, and based New Mexico's required deliveries to Texas on "the 1947 condition" of the river. That condition was defined in terms of inflows into the basin and projected outflows therefrom, based on New Mexico's water uses in 1947. This "inflow-outflow method" was recommended by the Compact Engineering Advisory Committee and incorporated in a manual that was in turn made part of the compact itself.

Since the manual was incorrect, calculations made in accordance with it operated to understate New Mexico's annual delivery obligation. The Compact Commission (composed of one voting representative from each state and one nonvoting federal representative) became aware of the mistake, but became hopelessly deadlocked over how to resolve the matter.

Texas then sued, alleging that New Mexico owed it 1.2 million acre-feet of water for the years 1950 through 1972. The Court subsequently ruled at 462 U.S. 554, 103 S.Ct. 2558, 77 L.Ed.2d 1 (1983) that it could not restructure the Compact Commission to break the tie, but remanded the case to a master with directions to develop and retroactively apply an accurate rendition of the "inflow-outflow method." Over the objections of both parties, the Court accepted the resulting master's report in its entirety. 467 U.S. 1238, 104 S.Ct. 3505, 82 L.Ed.2d 816 (1984).

By applying the corrected methodology, the master, Charles J. Meyers, determined that New Mexico's cumulative "water debt" to Texas was 340,100 acre-feet for the years 1950 through 1983, to which "water interest" was to be applied. 482 U.S. 124, 107 S.Ct. 2279, 96 L.Ed.2d 105 (1987). While the master presumed that the debt would be paid by means of increased water deliveries over the following ten years, New Mexico sought the option of a cash settlement. The Court enjoined New Mexico to comply with the compact, remanding to the master the issue of whether New Mexico should be allowed to retire its obligation using money rather than water. New Mexico estimated damages to Texas at $5.3 million, but Texas estimated them at $49.7 million, with the cumulative benefit to New Mexico at nearly $1 billion. The two states ultimately agreed to a stipulated judgment under which New Mexico paid Texas $14 million. For a fascinating history of the litigation see Em Hall, High and Dry: The Texas–New Mexico Struggle for the Pecos River (2002). New Mexico has taken various steps in recent years for the purpose of ensuring future compliance with its delivery obligations to Texas.

4.   One danger of seeking reformation of an interstate compact based on mutual mistake of fact is uncertainty as to the outcome. Once a compact is subjected to the scrutiny of the Supreme Court, the parties in effect lose control of its contents—even as to the definition of terms. For example, in Oklahoma v. New Mexico, 501 U.S. 221, 111 S.Ct. 2281, 115 L.Ed.2d 207 (1991), Oklahoma and Texas brought an original action alleging that New Mexico had been violating the Canadian River Compact by storing and diverting more than its share of water.

The compact gave New Mexico exclusive rights to water "originating" above the Conchas Dam, but limited New Mexico to 200,000 acre-feet of water originating below the dam. To avoid the need to measure below-dam waters, the compact limited New Mexico's storage capacity below Conchas to 200,000 acre-feet. However, New Mexico had increased its storage capacity beyond that limit and was using it to capture water that originated above Conchas Dam, but had seeped under or spilled over the dam.

In a 5–4 decision, the Court first concluded that the language of the compact was sufficiently ambiguous to justify an examination of the negotiating history to determine the true intentions of the parties. The Court then held that, based on the practicalities at the time, "storage capacity" actually meant "stored water," and that water seeping around or spilling over Conchas Dam should be treated as having originated (entered the stream) *below* the dam.

Given the many ambiguities and the massive but conflicting record associated with the Colorado River Compact, it is not surprising that the states of the upper basin have been extremely cautious about opening the potential Pandora's box of a court reformulation of the compact. How might the results of the known mistake be more favorable to the upper basin than would the implications of its correction? What are the risks to the upper basin if the Court applies equitable apportionment standards to the adjudication?

3. CONGRESSIONAL APPORTIONMENT: THE SPECIAL CASE OF THE COLORADO RIVER

Apportionment of the Colorado River between the upper and lower basins in the Colorado River Compact was to provide the upper basin states (Colorado, Utah, Wyoming, and New Mexico) with sufficient water for their later development. But it did not resolve differences over allocation of the lower basin states' (Arizona, California, and Nevada) share among themselves. Likewise, it did not specify how the upper basin states were to share their apportionment of the river. The sparsely populated, slower developing upper basin states were able to work out an agreement allocating percentages of the upper basin share to each state in the 1949 Upper Basin Colorado River Compact. See *supra* p. 988.

Agreement among the lower basin states on an allocation of their water was frustrated by intense conflicts that raged on for years. California wanted extensive development of the river to provide a stable supply of water for the Imperial Valley (which had been irrigated since the early 1900s) and to provide a new supply for the rapidly growing city of Los Angeles. Arizona also wanted development and envisioned a project to bring Colorado River water to central Arizona. But Arizona was extremely fearful of California's taking a disproportionate share of the lower basin supply. Consequently, Arizona withheld its agreement to the compact pending resolution of its concerns. For several years, Arizona was able to thwart California's attempts to develop Colorado River water. Year after year, beginning in 1922, members of the California congressional delegation introduced bills to authorize the construction of a Boulder (later Hoover) Dam. Arizona prevented their enactment, principally through the efforts of Senator Carl Hayden who resorted to a variety of tactics, including filibuster.

Finally, a compromise was arranged in the Senate resulting in the Boulder Canyon Project Act which became law June 25, 1929. The Act overrode the resistance of Arizona to signing the compact, allowing it to become effective upon approval of any six states, so long as California was one of them. With that approval, work on Hoover Dam could begin. Whether intended or not, the Boulder Canyon Project Act became the first, and only, legislative allocation of interstate waters. Arizona v. California, 373 U.S. 546, 83 S.Ct. 1468, 10 L.Ed.2d 542 (1963), *infra* p. 1001, held that Congress had the power to apportion the water of a navigable interstate stream among the states that touch the stream. However, the decision did not face the question of whether Congress can create legal interests in favor of one state in navigable (or non-navigable) streams within another state and not crossing into the favored state—as is the case with the Gila River.

As you read the following excerpts from the Boulder Canyon Project Act, consider whether Congress intended to apportion waters between California and Arizona when it passed the Act in 1928.

The Boulder Canyon Project Act

Pub. L. No. 642, 45 Stat. 1057 (1928).

Be it enacted by the Senate and House of Representatives of the United States of America in Congress assembled, That for the purpose of controlling the floods, improving navigation and regulating the flow of the Colorado River, providing for storage and for the delivery of the stored waters thereof for reclamation of public lands and other beneficial uses exclusively within the United States, and for the generation of electrical energy as a means of making the project herein authorized a self-supporting and financially solvent undertaking the Secretary of the Interior, subject to the terms of the Colorado River compact hereinafter mentioned, is hereby authorized to construct, operate, and maintain a dam and incidental works in the main stream of the Colorado River at Black Canyon or Boulder Canyon adequate to create a storage reservoir of a capacity of not less than twenty million acre-feet of water and a main canal and appurtenant structures located entirely within the United States connecting the Laguna Dam, or other suitable diversion dam, which the Secretary of the Interior is hereby authorized to construct if deemed necessary or advisable by him upon engineering or economic considerations, with the Imperial and Coachella Valleys in California, the expenditures for said main canal and appurtenant structures to be reimbursable, as provided in the reclamation law, and shall not be paid out of revenues derived from the sale or disposal of water power or electric energy at the dam authorized to be constructed at said Black Canyon or Boulder Canyon, or for water for potable purposes outside of the Imperial and Coachella Valleys: *Provided, however*, That no charge shall be made for water or for the use, storage, or delivery of water for irrigation or water for potable purposes in the Imperial or Coachella Valleys; also to construct and equip, operate, and maintain at or near said dam, or cause to be constructed a complete plant and incidental structures suitable for the fullest economic development of electrical energy from the water discharged from said reservoir; and to acquire by proceedings in eminent domain, or otherwise, all lands, rights-of-way, and other property necessary for said purposes.

* * *

Section 4(a)

This Act shall not take effect and no authority shall be exercised hereunder and no work shall be begun and no moneys expended on or in connection with the works or structures provided for in this Act, and no water rights shall be claimed or initiated hereunder, and no steps shall be taken by the United States or by others to initiate or perfect any claims to the use of water pertinent to such works or structures unless and until (1) the States of Arizona, California, Colorado, Nevada, New Mexico, Utah, and Wyoming shall have ratified the Colorado River compact, mentioned in section 13 hereof, and the President by public proclamation shall have so declared, or (2) if said States fail to ratify the said compact within six months from the date of the passage of this Act then, until six of said States, including the State of California, shall ratify said compact and shall consent to waive the provisions of the first paragraph of Article XI of said compact, which makes the same binding and obligatory only when approved by each of the seven States signatory thereto, and shall have approved said compact without conditions, save that of such six-State approval, and the President by public proclamation shall have so declared, and, further, until the State of California, by act of its legislature, shall agree irrevocably and unconditionally with the United States and for the benefit of the States of Arizona, Colorado, Nevada, New Mexico, Utah, and Wyoming, as an express covenant and in consideration of the passage of this Act, that the aggregate annual consumptive use (diversions less returns to the river) of water of and from the Colorado River for use in the State of California, including all uses under contracts made under the provisions of this Act and all water necessary for the supply of any rights which may now exist, shall not exceed four million four hundred thousand acre-feet of the waters apportioned to the lower basin States by paragraph (a) of Article III of the Colorado River compact, plus not more than one-half of any excess or surplus waters unapportioned by said compact, such uses always to be subject to the terms of said compact.

The States of Arizona, California, and Nevada are authorized to enter into an agreement which shall provide (1) that of the 7,500,000 acre-feet annually apportioned to the lower basin by paragraph (a) of Article III of the Colorado River compact, there shall be apportioned to the State of Nevada 300,000 acre-feet and to the State of Arizona 2,800,000 acre-feet for exclusive beneficial consumptive use in perpetuity, and (2) that the State of Arizona may annually use one-half of the excess or surplus waters unapportioned by the Colorado River compact, and (3) that the State of Arizona shall have the exclusive beneficial consumptive use of the Gila River and its tributaries within the boundaries of said State, and (4) that the waters of the Gila River and its tributaries, except return flow after the same enters the Colorado River, shall never be subject to any diminution whatever by any allowance of water which may be made by treaty or otherwise to the United States of Mexico but if, as provided in paragraph (c) of Article III of the Colorado River compact, it shall become necessary to supply water to the United States of Mexico from waters over and above the quantities which are surplus as defined by said compact, then the State of California shall and will mutually agree with the State of Arizona to supply, out of the main stream of the Colorado River, one-half of any deficiency which must be supplied to Mexico by the lower basin, and (5) that the State of California shall and will further mutually agree with the States of Arizona and Nevada that none of said three States shall withhold water and none shall require the delivery of water, which cannot reasonably be applied to domestic and agricultural uses, and (6) that all of the provisions of said tri-State agreement shall be subject in all particulars to the provisions of the Colorado River compact, and (7) said agreement to take effect upon the ratification of the Colorado River compact by Arizona, California, and Nevada.

* * *

Section 5

That the Secretary of the Interior is hereby authorized, under such general regulations as he may prescribe, to contract for the storage of water in said reservoir and for delivery thereof at such points on the river and on said canal as may be agreed upon, for irrigation and domestic uses, and generation of electrical energy and delivery at the switchboard to States, municipal corporations, political subdivisions, and private corporations of electrical energy generated at said dam, upon charges that will provide revenue which, in addition to other revenue accruing under the reclamation law and under this Act, will in his judgment cover all expenses of operation and maintenance incurred by the United States on account of works constructed under this Act and the payments to the United States under subdivision (b) of section 4. Contracts respecting water for irrigation and domestic uses shall be for permanent service and shall conform to paragraph (a) of section 4 of this Act. No person shall have or be entitled to have the use for any purpose of the water stored as aforesaid except by contract made as herein stated.

* * *

Section 6

That the dam and reservoir provided for by section 1 hereof shall be used: First, for river regulation, improvement of navigation, and flood control; second, for irrigation and domestic uses and satisfaction of present perfected rights in pursuance of Article VIII of said Colorado River compact; and third, for power. The title to said dam, reservoir, plant, and incidental works shall forever remain in the United States, and the United States shall, until otherwise provided by Congress, control, manage, and operate the same, except as herein otherwise provided: * * *

NOTES

1.   The tri-state compact authorized in Paragraph 2 of § 4(a) was never agreed upon. Can the terms of the proposed compact aid in the interpretation of paragraph 1 of § 4(a)?

2.   In what ways does the Act modify or determine the meaning of the Colorado River Compact?

3.   Is an apportionment of water between Arizona and California made in the Act? If not, in what tribunal and on what basis would such apportionment be made traditionally?

4.   Does the Act delegate power to the Secretary to apportion water to Arizona and California? What standards control the exercise of that power?

The following article summarizes the events between the passage of the Boulder Canyon Project Act and its definitive interpretation in Arizona v. California, *infra* p. 1001.

Charles J. Meyers, The Colorado River
19 Stan. L. Rev. 1, 39–43, 51–53 (1966).

* * * In its first suit[169] Arizona sued the Secretary of the Interior and all six of the other Colorado River Basin states to enjoin the building of Hoover Dam and the All–American Canal, to stop the formation and performance of contracts for delivery of water from the projected reservoir, and to declare the Colorado River Compact and the Project Act unconstitutional. The case was heard by the Supreme Court on the plaintiff's bill of complaint and defendants' motions to dismiss. Holding that the Boulder Canyon Project Act was a valid exercise of congressional power under the commerce clause, the Court dismissed the bill without prejudice to a later suit for relief if the dam should be operated so as to interfere with Arizona's rights. Apart from its significance to the parties, the case has a general importance since the Supreme Court, for the first time, upheld congressional power under the commerce clause to authorize construction of multipurpose dams on navigable streams.[170] While the Court preserved the fiction that a navigation purpose would be served, it recognized that other purposes not authorized by the navigation power would also be served, primarily the generation and sale of electric power. On this foundation rest many mighty dams that dry up the stream below, thus destroying navigability entirely, if indeed any ever existed.

In its second suit[171] Arizona changed tactics. Conceding that there was as yet no interference with her water rights (Hoover Dam was under construction but had yet to be closed in), Arizona alleged that such interference was threatened in the future. In order to prepare for the

169. Arizona v. California, 283 U.S. 423 (1931).

170. See Morreale, Federal Power in Western Waters: The Navigation Power and the Rule of No Compensation, 3 Natural Resources J. 1, 10–11 (1963).

171. Arizona v. California, 292 U.S. 341 (1934).

lawsuit to come, she sought to commence an action to perpetuate testimony relating to her interpretation of the Project Act and the compact. In essence, Arizona relied upon the act and compact and desired to obtain and record testimony favorable to her construction of each—namely, that the article III(b) water was intended to belong exclusively to Arizona. This bill was dismissed, one ground being that the testimony sought to be preserved would be inadmissible as evidence of the meaning of the compact and the act.

After this rebuff events moved rapidly. In 1934 work began on Parker Dam, the diversion point for the Colorado River Aqueduct. (The aqueduct was designed to carry about 1.3 million acre-feet of water per year to the southern California coastal plain.) Claiming that construction of the dam, which had one foot on Arizona soil, was unauthorized, Arizona's governor sent troops to halt the work.[172] The United States sued for an injunction in the Supreme Court, but lost when the Court determined that Congress had not authorized the dam.[173] Within months after the decision Congress specifically authorized the dam,[174] and Arizona withdrew her troops.

In November of 1935 Arizona filed suit for a general equitable apportionment of the unappropriated water in the river.[175] The United States had not consented to be sued and was not a party. The Court dismissed the complaint without reaching the merits, holding that joinder of the United States was indispensable.

Upon the rendition of this judgment, Arizona found herself stymied. She could secure no judicial relief until the United States consented to be sued. She had not ratified the Colorado River Compact and had no contract for delivery of water from Lake Mead. Her rival, California, on the other hand, had contracts calling for the delivery of water from the main stream to satisfy 5.362 million acre-feet of consumptive use per year, and work was going forward in California on projects which would enable her to make full use of this water.

For nearly ten years Arizona was beset by drought and racked with dissension over the proper course of action. The agricultural interests of central Arizona suffered greatly from lack of water but also feared the effect that compact ratification might have on the Gila supply. Finally, Arizona did what she had to do—she ratified the compact and obtained a contract for the delivery of water from the main stream to supply 2.8 million acre-feet of consumptive use per year.

Unfortunately for Arizona, a contract for water and the actual receipt of water are two very different things. For another ten years she struggled in vain to obtain federal authorization and financing of the works necessary to bring water to her central farming region. Every step of the way she was fought by California, who had a telling argument in the enormous cost of

172. D. Mann, The Politics of Waters in Arizona 85–86 (1963).

173. United States v. Arizona, 295 U.S. 174 (1935).

174. Act of Aug. 30, 1935, 49 Stat. 1039.

175. Arizona v. California, 298 U.S. 558 (1936).

the Central Arizona Project—roughly one billion dollars. Bills to authorize the project were introduced in the 79th, 80th, 81st, and 82d Congresses, and, while some passed in the Senate, all failed in the House, where California was immensely more powerful than Arizona.

* * * On June 14, 1956, twenty-six years after Arizona made her first attempt to obtain an adjudication of her water rights in the Colorado, the trial on the merits began before a Special Master.

* * * [Four and one half years later, on December 5, 1960, the Special Master] filed his final report with the Supreme Court, having heard some 106 witnesses (who filled 22,500 pages of transcript) and having received volumes of exhibits numbering in the hundreds. In addition, depositions were taken from 234 witnesses, filling a transcript of 3,742 pages, on a minor dispute between Arizona and New Mexico. The final report (with a proposed decree) ran 433 pages.

Coming then before the Supreme Court, the case was first argued for sixteen hours in the 1961 term and then, with the retirement of Mr. Justice Whittaker, was set for reargument in the 1962 term. By the time the second argument was held, Mr. Justice Frankfurter had also retired; so the bench contained two new Justices, Goldberg and White. Both voted with the majority, providing the necessary difference in the five-to-three division (Mr. Chief Justice Warren not participating). The Supreme Court gave its judgment on June 3, 1963,[182] and entered the decree on March 9, 1964.[183]

Arizona v. California

Supreme Court of the United States, 1963.
373 U.S. 546, 83 S.Ct. 1468, 10 L.Ed.2d 542, decree entered. 376 U.S. 340, 84 S.Ct. 755, 11 L.Ed.2d 757.

■ MR. JUSTICE BLACK* delivered the opinion of the Court.

* * *

The Special Master appointed by this Court found that the Colorado River Compact, the law of prior appropriation, and the doctrine of equitable apportionment—by which doctrine this Court in the absence of statute resolves interstate claims according to the equities—do not control the issues in this case. The Master concluded that, since the Lower Basin States had failed to make a compact to allocate the waters among themselves as authorized by §§ 4(a) and 8(b), the Secretary's contracts with the States had within the statutory scheme of §§ 4(a), 5, and 8(b) effected an apportionment of the waters of the mainstream which, according to the Master, were the only waters to be apportioned under the Act. The Master further held that, in the event of a shortage of water making it impossible for the Secretary to supply all the water due California, Arizona, and

---

182. 373 U.S. 546 (1963).

183. 376 U.S. 340 (1964).

* Justice Black was a Senator when the Boulder Canyon Project Act was passed in 1928. [Eds.]

Nevada under their contracts, the burden of the shortage must be borne by each State in proportion to her share of the first 7,500,000 acre-feet allocated to the Lower Basin, that is, 44/75 by California, 28/75 by Arizona, and 3/75 by Nevada, without regard to the law of prior appropriation.

Arizona, Nevada, and the United States support with few exceptions the analysis, conclusions, and recommendations of the Special Master's report. These parties agree that Congress did not leave division of the waters to an equitable apportionment by this Court but instead created a comprehensive statutory scheme for the allocation of mainstream waters. Arizona, however, believes that the allocation formula established by the Secretary's contracts was in fact the formula required by the Act. * * *

California is in basic disagreement with almost all of the Master's Report. She argues that the Project Act, like the Colorado River Compact, deals with the entire Colorado River System, not just the mainstream. This would mean that diversions within Arizona and Nevada of tributary waters flowing in those States would be charged against their apportionments and that, because tributary water would be added to the mainstream water in computing the first 7,500,000 acre-feet available to the States, there would be a greater likelihood of a surplus, of which California gets one-half. The result of California's argument would be much more water for California and much less for Arizona. California also argues that the Act neither allocates the Colorado River waters nor gives the Secretary authority to make an allocation. Rather she takes the position that the judicial doctrine of equitable apportionment giving full interstate effect to the traditional western water law of prior appropriation should determine the rights of the parties to the water. Finally, California claims that in any event the Act does not control in time of shortage. Under such circumstances, she says, this Court should divide the waters according to the doctrine of equitable apportionment or the law of prior appropriation, either of which, she argues, should result in protecting her prior uses.

* * *

I.

Allocation of Water Among the States and Distribution to Users.

We have concluded, for reasons to be stated, that Congress in passing the Project Act intended to and did create its own comprehensive scheme for the apportionment among California, Arizona, and Nevada of the Lower Basin's share of the mainstream waters of the Colorado River, leaving each State its tributaries. Congress decided that a fair division of the first 7,500,000 acre-feet of such mainstream waters would give 4,400,000 acre-feet to California, 2,800,000 to Arizona, and 300,000 to Nevada; Arizona and California would each get one-half of any surplus. Prior approval was therefore given in the Act for a tri-state compact to incorporate these terms. The States, subject to subsequent congressional approval, were also permitted to agree on a compact with different terms. Division of the water did not, however, depend on the States' agreeing to a compact, for Congress gave the Secretary of the Interior adequate authority to accomplish the division. Congress did this by giving the Secretary power to make contracts for the delivery of water and by providing that no person could have water without a contract.

A. *Relevancy of Judicial Apportionment and Colorado River Compact.*—We agree with the Master that apportionment of the Lower Basin waters of the Colorado River is not controlled by the doctrine of equitable apportionment or by the Colorado River Compact. It is true that the Court has used the doctrine of equitable apportionment to decide river controversies between States. But in those cases Congress had not made any statutory apportionment. In this case, we have decided that Congress has provided its own method for allocating among the Lower Basin States the mainstream water to which they are entitled under the Compact. Where Congress has so exercised its constitutional power over waters, courts have no power to substitute their own notions of an "equitable apportionment" for the apportionment chosen by Congress.* Nor does the Colorado River Compact control this case. Nothing in that Compact purports to divide water among the Lower Basin States nor in any way to affect or control any future apportionment among those States or any distribution of water within a State. That the Commissioners were able to accomplish even a division of water between the basins is due to what is generally known as the "Hoover Compromise."

> "Participants [in the Compact negotiations] have stated that the negotiations would have broken up but for Mr. Hoover's proposal: that the Commission limit its efforts to a division of water between the upper basin and the lower basin, leaving to each basin the future internal allocation of its share."

And in fact this is all the Compact did. However, the Project Act, by referring to the Compact in several places, does make the Compact relevant to a limited extent. To begin with, the Act explicitly approves the Compact and thereby fixes a division of the waters between the basins which must be respected. Further, in several places the Act refers to terms contained in the Compact. For example, § 12 of the Act adopts the Compact definition of "domestic," and § 6 requires satisfaction of "present perfected rights" as used in the Compact. Obviously, therefore, those particular terms, though originally formulated only for the Compact's allocation of water between basins, are incorporated into the Act and are made applicable to the Project Act's allocation among Lower Basin States. The Act also declares that the Secretary of the Interior and the United States in the construction, operation, and maintenance of the dam and other works and in the making

---

* The Court does not give the constitutional basis for congressional apportionment at this point in the opinion; the justification appears 20 pages later in one off-hand sentence (373 U.S. at 587): "[The Project] * * * Act was passed in the exercise of congressional power to control navigable water for purposes of flood control, navigation, power generation, and other objects, and is equally sustained by the power of Congress to promote the general welfare through projects for reclamation, irrigation, or other internal improvements." (Citing the 1931 decision in *Arizona v. California* and United States v. Gerlach Live Stock Co., 339 U.S. 725 (1950)). [Eds.]

of contracts shall be subject to and controlled by the Colorado River Compact. These latter references to the Compact are quite different from the Act's adoption of Compact terms. Such references, unlike the explicit adoption of terms, were used only to show that the Act and its provisions were in no way to upset, alter, or affect the Compact's congressionally approved division of water between the basins. They were not intended to make the Compact and its provisions control or affect the Act's allocation among and distribution of water within the States of the Lower Basin. Therefore, we look to the Compact for terms specifically incorporated in the Act, and we would also look to it to resolve disputes between the Upper and Lower Basins, were any involved in this case. But no such questions are here. We must determine what apportionment and delivery scheme in the Lower Basin has been effected through the Secretary's contracts. For that determination, we look to the Project Act alone.

B. *Mainstream Apportionment.*—The congressional scheme of apportionment cannot be understood without knowing what water Congress wanted apportioned. Under California's view, which we reject, the first 7,500,000 acre-feet of Lower Basin water, of which California has agreed to use only 4,400,000, is made up of both mainstream and tributary water, not just mainstream water. Under the view of Arizona, Nevada, and the United States, with which we agree, the tributaries are not included in the waters to be divided but remain for the exclusive use of each State. Assuming 7,500,000 acre-feet or more in the mainstream and 2,000,000 in the tributaries, California would get 1,000,000 acre-feet more if the tributaries are included and Arizona 1,000,000 less.

California's argument that the Project Act, like the Colorado River Compact, deals with the main river and all its tributaries rests on § 4(a) of the Act, which limits California to 4,400,000 acre-feet "of the waters apportioned to the lower basin States by paragraph (a) of Article III of the Colorado River compact, plus not more than one-half of any excess or surplus waters unapportioned by said compact. * * * "And Article III(a), referred to by § 4(a), apportioned in perpetuity to the Lower Basin the use of 7,500,000 acre-feet of water per annum "from the Colorado River System," which was defined in the Compact as "that portion of the Colorado River and its tributaries within the United States of America."

Arizona argues that the Compact apportions between basins only the waters of the mainstream, not the mainstream and the tributaries. We need not reach that question, however, for we have concluded that whatever waters the Compact apportioned the Project Act itself dealt only with water of the mainstream. In the first place, the Act, in § 4(a), states that the California limitation, which is in reality her share of the first 7,500,000 acre-feet of Lower Basin water, is on "water of and from the Colorado River," not of and from the "Colorado River System." But more importantly, the negotiations among the States and the congressional debates leading to the passage of the Project Act clearly show that the language used by Congress in the Act was meant to refer to mainstream waters only. Inclusion of the tributaries in the Compact was natural in view of the upper States' strong feeling that the Lower Basin tributaries should be made to share the burden of any obligation to deliver water to Mexico which a future treaty might impose. But when it came to an apportionment among the Lower Basin States, the Gila, by far the most important Lower Basin tributary, would not logically be included, since Arizona alone of the States could effectively use that river. Therefore, with minor exceptions, the proposals and counterproposals over the years, culminating in the Project Act, consistently provided for division of the mainstream only, reserving the tributaries to each State's exclusive use.

* * *

C.   *The Project Act's Apportionment and Distribution Scheme.*—The legislative history, the language of the Act, and the scheme established by the Act for the storage and delivery of water convince us also that Congress intended to provide its own method for a complete apportionment of the mainstream water among Arizona, California, and Nevada.

* * *

In the first section of the Act, the Secretary was authorized to "construct, operate, and maintain a dam and incidental works . . . adequate to create a storage reservoir of a capacity of not less than twenty million acre-feet of water . . ." for the stated purpose of "controlling the floods, improving navigation and regulating the flow of the Colorado River, providing for storage and for the delivery of the stored waters thereof for reclamation of public lands and other beneficial uses * * *," and generating electrical power. The whole point of the Act was to replace the erratic, undependable, often destructive natural flow of the Colorado with the regular, dependable release of waters conserved and stored by the project. Having undertaken this beneficial project, Congress, in several provisions of the Act, made it clear that no one should use mainstream waters save in strict compliance with the scheme set up by the Act. Section 5 authorized the Secretary "under such general regulations as he may prescribe, to contract for the storage of water in said reservoir and for the delivery thereof at such points on the river * * * as may be agreed upon, for irrigation and domestic uses. . . ." To emphasize that water could be obtained from the Secretary alone, § 5 further declared, "No person shall have or be entitled to have the use for any purpose of the water stored as aforesaid except by contract made as herein stated." The supremacy given the Secretary's contracts was made clear in § 8(b) of the Act, which provided that, while the Lower Basin States were free to negotiate a compact dividing the waters, such a compact if made and approved after January 1, 1929, was to be "subject to all contracts, if any, made by the Secretary of the Interior under section 5" before Congress approved the compact.

These several provisions, even without legislative history, are persuasive that Congress intended the Secretary of the Interior, through his § 5 contracts, both to carry out the allocation of the waters of the main Colorado River among the Lower Basin States and to decide which users within each State would get water. The general authority to make contracts normally includes the power to choose with whom and upon what terms the contracts will be made. When Congress in an Act grants authority to contract, that authority is no less than the general authority, unless Congress has placed some limit on it. In this respect it is of interest that in an earlier version the bill did limit the Secretary's contract power by making the contracts "subject to rights of prior appropriators." But that restriction, which preserved the law of prior appropriation, did not survive. It was stricken from the bill when the requirement that every water user have a contract was added to § 5. Significantly, no phrase or provision indicating that the Secretary's contract power was to be controlled by the law of prior appropriation was substituted either then or at any other time before passage of the Act, and we are persuaded that had Congress intended so to fetter the Secretary's discretion, it would have done so in clear and unequivocal terms, as it did in recognizing "present perfected rights" in § 6.

* * *

The argument that Congress would not have delegated to the Secretary so much power to apportion and distribute the water overlooks the ways in which his power is limited and channeled by standards in the Project Act. In particular, the Secretary is bound to observe the Act's limitation of 4,400,000 acre-feet on California's consumptive uses out of the first 7,500,-000 acre-feet of mainstream water. This necessarily leaves the remaining 3,100,000 acre-feet for the use of Arizona and Nevada, since they are the only other States with access to the main Colorado River. Nevada consistently took the position, accepted by the other States throughout the debates, that her conceivable needs would not exceed 300,000 acre-feet, which, of course, left 2,800,000 acre-feet for Arizona's use. Moreover, Congress indicated that it thought this a proper division of the waters when in the second paragraph of § 4(a) it gave advance consent to a tri-state compact adopting such division. While no such compact was ever entered into, the Secretary by his contracts has apportioned the water in the approved amounts and thereby followed the guidelines set down by Congress. And, as the Master pointed out, Congress set up other standards and placed other significant limitations upon the Secretary's power to distribute the stored waters. It specifically set out in order the purposes for which the Secretary must use the dam and the reservoir:

> "First, for river regulation, improvement of navigation, and flood control; second, for irrigation and domestic uses and satisfaction of present perfected rights in pursuance of Article VIII of said Colorado River compact; and third, for power." § 6.

The Act further requires the Secretary to make revenue provisions in his contracts adequate to ensure the recovery of the expenses of construction, operation, and maintenance of the dam and other works within 50 years after their construction. § 4(b). The Secretary is directed to make water contracts for irrigation and domestic uses only for "permanent service." § 5. He and his permittees, licensees, and contractees are subject to the Colorado River Compact, § 8(a), and therefore can do nothing to upset or encroach upon the Compact's allocation of Colorado River water between the Upper and Lower Basins. In the construction, operation, and management of the works, the Secretary is subject to the provisions of the reclamation law, except as the Act otherwise provides. § 14. One of the most significant limitations in the Act is that the Secretary is required to satisfy present perfected rights, a matter of intense importance to those who had reduced their water rights to actual beneficial use at the time the Act became effective. § 6. And, of course, all of the powers granted by the Act are exercised by the Secretary and his well-established executive department, responsible to Congress and the President and subject to judicial review.

* * *

III.

Apportionment and Contracts in Time of Shortage.

We have agreed with the Master that the Secretary's contracts with Arizona for 2,800,000 acre-feet of water and with Nevada for 300,000, together with the limitation of California to 4,400,000 acre-feet, effect a valid apportionment of the first 7,500,000 acre-feet of mainstream water in the Lower Basin. There remains the question of what shall be done in time of shortage. The Master, while declining to make any findings as to what future supply might be expected, nevertheless decided that the Project Act and the Secretary's contract require the Secretary in case of shortage to divide the burden among the three States in this proportion: California 44/75; Arizona 28/75; Nevada 3/75. While pro rata sharing of water shortages seems equitable on its face, more considered judgment may demonstrate quite the contrary. Certainly we should not bind the Secretary to this formula. We have held that the Secretary is vested with considerable control over the apportionment of Colorado River waters. And neither the Project Act nor the water contracts require the use of any particular formula for apportioning shortages. While the Secretary must follow the standards set out in the Act, he nevertheless is free to choose among the recognized methods of apportionment or to devise reasonable methods of his own. This choice, as we see it, is primarily his, not the Master's or even ours. And the Secretary may or may not conclude that a pro rata division is the best solution.

It must be remembered that the Secretary's decision may have an effect not only on irrigation uses but also on other important functions for which Congress brought this great project into being—flood control, improvement of navigation, regulation of flow, and generation and distribution of electric power. Requiring the Secretary to prorate shortages would strip him of the very power of choice which we think Congress, for reasons satisfactory to it, vested in him and which we should not impair or take away from him. For the same reasons we cannot accept California's contention that in case of shortage each State's share of water should be determined by the judicial doctrine of equitable apportionment or by the law of prior appropriation. These principles, while they may provide some guidance, are not binding upon the Secretary where, as here, Congress, with full power to do so, has provided that the waters of a navigable stream shall be harnessed, conserved, stored, and distributed through a government agency under a statutory scheme.

None of this is to say that in case of shortage, the Secretary cannot adopt a method of proration or that he may not lay stress upon priority of use, local laws and customs, or any other factors that might be helpful in reaching an informed judgment in harmony with the Act, the best interests of the Basin States, and the welfare of the Nation. It will be time enough for the courts to intervene when and if the Secretary, in making apportionments or contracts, deviates from the standards Congress has set for him to follow, including his obligation to respect "present perfected rights" as of the date the Act was passed. At this time the Secretary has made no decision at all based on an actual or anticipated shortage of water, and so there is no action of his in this respect for us to review. Finally, as the Master pointed out, Congress still has broad powers over this navigable international stream. Congress can undoubtedly reduce or enlarge the Secretary's power if it wishes. Unless and until it does, we leave in the hands of the Secretary, where Congress placed it, full power to control, manage, and operate the Government's Colorado River works and to make contracts for the sale and delivery of water on such terms as are not prohibited by the Project Act.

* * *

■ MR. JUSTICE HARLAN, whom MR. JUSTICE DOUGLAS and MR. JUSTICE STEWART join, dissenting in part.

I dissent from so much of the Court's opinion as holds that the Secretary of the Interior has been given authority by Congress to apportion, among and within the States of California, Arizona, and Nevada, the waters of the mainstream of the Colorado River below Lee Ferry. I also dissent from the holding that in times of shortage the Secretary has discretion to select or devise any "reasonable method" he wishes for determining which users within these States are to bear the burden of that shortage. (In all other respects Mr. Justice Stewart and I—but not Mr. Justice Douglas—agree with and join in the Court's opinion, though not without some misgivings regarding the amounts of water allocated to the Indian Reservations.)

In my view, it is the equitable principles established by the Court in interstate water-rights cases, as modified by the Colorado River Compact and the California limitation, that were intended by Congress to govern the apportionment of mainstream waters among the Lower Basin States, whether in surplus or in shortage. *A fortiori*, state law was intended to control apportionment among users within a single State.

The Court's conclusions respecting the Secretary's apportionment powers, particularly those in times of shortage, result in a single appointed federal official being vested with absolute control, unrestrained by adequate standards, over the fate of a substantial segment of the life and economy of three States. Such restraint upon his actions as may follow from judicial review are, as will be shown, at best illusory. Today's result, I venture to say, would have dumbfounded those responsible for the legislation the Court construes, for nothing could have been farther from their minds or more inconsistent with their deeply felt convictions.

The Court professes to find this extraordinary delegation of power principally in § 5 of the Project Act, the provision authorizing the Secretary to enter into contracts for the storage and delivery of water. But § 5, * * * had no design resembling that which the Court now extracts from it. Rather, it was intended principally as a revenue measure, and the clause *requiring* a contract as a condition of delivery was inserted at the insistence not of the Lower but of the Upper Basin States in an effort to insure that nothing would disturb that basin's rights under the Colorado River Compact. There was no thought that § 5 would give authority to apportion water among the Lower Basin States. * * *

It is manifest that § 4(a), on which the Court so heavily relies, neither apportions the waters of the river nor vests power in any official to make such an apportionment. The first paragraph does not *grant* any water to anyone; it merely conditions the Act's effectiveness on seven-state ratification of the Compact or on six-state ratification, plus California's agreement to a limitation, i.e., a *ceiling*, on her appropriations. The source of authority to make such appropriations must be found elsewhere. And the second paragraph of § 4(a), suggesting a particular interstate agreement, similarly makes no apportionment of water among the States and delegates no power to any official to make such an apportionment. * * *

This history bears recapitulation. *First*, the law of appropriation, basic to western water law, was greatly respected, and the solution of interstate water disputes by judicial apportionment in this Court was well established and accepted. *Second*, the problems created by these doctrines as applied in *Wyoming* v. *Colorado* were narrow ones, not requiring for their solution complete abrogation of well-tried principles; existing law was quite adequate to deal with all questions save those Congress expressly solved by imposing a ceiling on California. *Third*, Congress throughout the dispute exhibited great reluctance to interfere with the division of water by legislation, because of a deep and fundamental mistrust of federal intervention and a profound regard for state sovereignty, shared by many influential members. *Finally*, when Congress was forced to legislate with respect to this problem or face defeat of the entire Project Act, it chose narrow terms appropriate to the narrow problem before it, and even then acted only indirectly to require California's consent to limiting her consumption.

It is inconceivable that such a Congress intended that the sweeping federal power which it declined to exercise—a power even the most avid partisans of national authority might hesitate to grant to a single administrator—be exercised at the unbridled discretion of an administrative officer, especially in the light of complaints registered about "bureaucratic" and "oppressive" interference of the Department which that very officer headed. It is utterly incredible that a Congress unwilling because of concern for States' rights even to limit California's maximum consumption to 4,400,000 acre-feet without the consent of her legislature intended to give the Secretary of the Interior authority without California's consent to reduce her share even below that quantity in a shortage.

* * *

The Lack of Standards Defining the Limits of the Secretary's Power.

* * * How is the burden of any shortage to be borne by the Lower Basin States? This question is not decided; the Court simply states that the initial determination is for the Secretary to make.

What yardsticks has Congress laid down for him to follow? There is, it is true, a duty imposed on the Secretary under § 6 to satisfy "present perfected rights," and if these rights are defined as those perfected on or before the effective date of the Act, it has been estimated that California's share amounts to approximately 3,000,000 acre-feet annually. This, then, would be the floor provided by the Act for California, assuming enough water is available to satisfy such present perfected rights. And the Act also has provided a ceiling for California: the 4,400,000 acre-feet of water (plus one-half of surplus) described in § 4(a).

But what of that wide area between these two outer limits? Here, when we look for the standards defining the Secretary's authority, we find nothing. Under the Court's construction of the Act, in other words, Congress has made a gift to the Secretary of almost 1,500,000 acre-feet of water a year, to allocate virtually as he pleases in the event of any shortage preventing the fulfillment of all of his delivery commitments.

The delegation of such unrestrained authority to an executive official raises, to say the least, the gravest constitutional doubts. See Schechter Poultry Corp. v. United States, 295 U.S. 495; Panama Refining Co. v. Ryan, 293 U.S. 388; cf. Youngstown Sheet & Tube Co. v. Sawyer, 343 U.S. 579, 587–589. * * *

NOTE

The Meyers article argues that the Court was correct in finding an intent to apportion 7.5 million acre-feet (maf) of mainstream water but expresses doubt about the Court's conclusion that Congress intended to delegate power to the Secretary to deal with lesser amounts as his discretion should prescribe. Although the Congress had never before apportioned an interstate stream, its authority was not questioned. Is the facile treatment of the issue, noted by the editors in the footnote *supra* p. 1003, satisfactory? The leading historian of the Colorado River, Norris Hundley, Jr., Water and the West: The Colorado River Compact and the Politics of Water in the American West 270 (1975), concluded that the Court misread the legislative history:

While some congressmen thought that Congress was infringing upon states' rights by even suggesting a lower-basin pact, Pittman strenuously disagreed. "If California and Nevada and Arizona do not like this agreement," he explained, "they do not have to approve it." "All I have in mind," he protested, is "trying to save six or seven months' time." If the lower-basin states were to enter into an agreement that already had congressional approval, he observed, then they would not have to return later to Congress for approval. "I may not be accomplishing anything; but Arizona seems to be wedded to a certain plan. If the California Legislature does not like it, it does not put us in any worse fix than we are in if we do not adopt it."

Congress agreed, and Pittman's proposal was incorporated into section 4(a) of the bill. Thirty-five years later the U.S. Supreme Court would misconstrue this action and decide that the Boulder Canyon Act provided a statutory apportionment of the waters of the lower Colorado. In 1928, however, Congress appeared confident that it was merely suggesting a way in which the lower states *might* settle their problem themselves.

4. INTERSTATE PROBLEM SOLVING IN THE COLORADO RIVER BASIN

With all three of the legal mechanisms for interstate allocation of water attempted or employed within the Colorado River basin, one would think that there would be a framework for dealing with practical issues. In fact, the basin has struggled with monumental issues of water shortage in the face of growth, drought, and climate change. At least the first two phenomena were anticipated by those who earnestly pursued compacts and legislation after litigation was not fruitful. It was always anticipated that significant dam construction would facilitate solutions to increased water demand. From the start, the architects of the system knew that structural solutions would fall short, but they did not realize the extent of difficulties the future would bring. Neither the severity of natural limits nor the institutional barriers to problem solving were anticipated.

David H. Getches, Water Allocation During Drought in Arizona and Southern California: Legal and Institutional Responses

(NRLC Research Report Series, Nat. Resources L. Center, Univ. of Colo. Sch. of L., January 1991, at 1–3).

A Heavy Dependence on Water

Despite the scarcity of its indigenous natural water supplies, the study area is populated by over 19 million people, about five-sixths of them in Southern California; the area includes the fastest growing cities in the nation. The expansion of human population in the area has accompanied intense economic activity. Much of the activity is water-dependent, including massive production of agricultural goods requiring heavy irrigation. In half a century of almost uninterrupted prosperity and growth there have been few concessions to the area's aridity.

* * *

The government agencies and special districts charged with providing the area with adequate water historically succeeded in keeping supply ahead of demand. Until the last decade they insulated consumers from pressure to restrict usage. And there has always been sufficient water available to accommodate population growth in the region. Engineering ingenuity supported by public investment has created facilities to move water long distances and to store enough to smooth out annual fluctuations in precipitation. Political action and interstate accords have secured rights to use definite quantities of water in Southern California and Arizona vis a vis other states and Northern California.

The region has not yet confirmed the limits of its ability to grow. It is, however, struggling to cope with the economic, social and environmental symptoms of rapidly expanding population. The area managed to keep water supplies ahead of growing demand by importing new water and exceeding safe groundwater pumping levels locally. Recently, however, governments and water suppliers in Arizona and Southern California have recognized that encouraging consumers to reduce water demand can relieve some of the pressure to develop new supplies which are increasingly difficult and costly to find.

Cyclical droughts have occasionally broken the illusion of security, reminding water consumers that some uses are more important than others. Legal principles for allocation of water are frequently invoked to determine which combination of streams, aquifers and reservoirs will provide water in a particular year. But ordinarily there is no apparent difference felt by consumers from one year to the next. Only in extraordinary episodes, such as the Southern California dry spell of [1988–1992], have supplies been so low that a few local curtailments in use have been necessary. Yet these droughts have been less severe, shorter and less widespread than the droughts revealed in tree ring studies that reveal historical precipitation patterns.

The moderately severe, multi-year dry spells the area has experienced in the post-war years, since demand has so dramatically increased, have caused localized minor intrusions on lifestyle—brown lawns, reduction in car washing, attention to leaky plumbing. These episodes have aroused considerable citizen concern in recent years. In Southern California the effects have been confined to a few communities but, because of the publicity, for the first time in seventy years water is being perceived as a potential restraint on the quality of life and on ability to expand. In Arizona, precautionary legal reductions in per capita use in urban areas and controversy over retirement of agricultural uses to provide more water for urban growth have raised Arizonans' consciousness of the finite nature of water in the desert and its linkages to population growth and lifestyle.

* * *

NOTES

1. The Colorado River basin states have always known that they faced serious risks of inadequate water supplies. The concern has been exacerbated as the reality of climate change becomes more apparent. In 2007, the National Research Council confirmed how perilous the future might be. Colorado River Basin Water Management: Evaluation and Adjusting to Hydroclimatic Variability 153–154 (2007) concluded:

> A future of increasing population growth and urban water demand in a hydroclimatic setting of limited—and likely decreasing—supplies presents a sobering prospect for elected officials and water managers. If the region's water resources are to be managed sustainably and continue to provide a broad range of benefits to an increasing number of users, the realities of Colorado River water demand and supply will have to be addressed openly and candidly.... There is no technical cure-all or panacea capable of resolving the region's increasing water supply-and-demand tensions. As the report indicates, future events may necessitate a new level of federal and interstate collaboration on Colorado River water management.

2. What should legal experts do to address water problems like those in the Colorado River basin? To what extent are they made more difficult by the existence of state lines crossing the watershed? Consider the challenges confronted in the Colorado River basin notwithstanding pursuit of available mechanisms for interstate allocation.

NOTE: A FRUSTRATING QUEST FOR SOLUTIONS

The end of the Reclamation Era

Beginning with Hoover Dam, the government financed and built an impressive system of large water projects on the Colorado River. The Court's finding in Arizona v. California that Congress had allocated the waters of the Colorado River in 1928 by means of the Boulder Canyon Project Act finally helped clear the way for further development of the river for the benefit of Arizona, which had withheld its approval of the Compact, after most of the other basin states had benefited from dam building.

As early as the 1940s, the importation of Colorado River water into central Arizona was advanced as a solution for the state's groundwater overdraft problem. In 1947, the Bureau of Reclamation completed a feasibility study of the Central Arizona Project (CAP), which called for annually pumping 1.5 maf of water some 2,100 feet uphill from the Colorado River into an aqueduct that would carry it over 330 miles to Phoenix and Tucson.

Arizona vigorously supported the CAP and for years sought its approval in Congress. California—realizing that its demand for water exceeded its allocation and fearing that CAP would further impinge its future growth—strenuously opposed it. However, once the Court in *Arizona v. California* affirmed Arizona's entitlement to 2.8 maf annually, California's concern shifted from maximizing the amount of its own allocation (which the Court set at 4.4 maf) toward assuring the certainty of its delivery. In exchange for California's support of the project, the priority of CAP's upstream diversion was specified as being junior to California's downstream entitlement to 4.4 maf. The CAP therefore must suffer all cutbacks necessary in a shortage.

The support of the upper basin was secured through the inclusion of several other water projects in the authorization package—including the Animas–La Plata, Dolores, Dallas Creek, West Divide, and San Miguel projects in Colorado, which were to be built concurrently with CAP—and increased funding for the Dixie Project in Utah. It took almost 18 years from the time of the authorization to complete the basic works for CAP. The estimated final cost for CAP of more than $4 billion makes it the most expensive Bureau of Reclamation project in the nation. The later appropriations were difficult to obtain. Further, the Carter administration invoked a provision of the 1968 Act which banned use of CAP water in areas that did not effectively control the expansion of groundwater use for agricultural irrigation. This led to the passage of the Arizona Groundwater Management Act in 1980, *supra* pp. 624–633. However, ever since the CAP began delivering water, its price has caused Arizonans to avoid it. In 1991, less than one third of the 1.5 maf capacity was utilized. Faced with the problem of how to pay for the expensive, oversized project and what to do with the water it delivers, Arizona renegotiated its repayment obligation with the federal government and created a "water bank" to store CAP water underground. See *infra*, p. 1020. Meanwhile, of the five Colorado projects, two have been built (Dolores and Dallas Creek), two have apparently died (San Miguel and West Divide), and construction is now virtually completed on the Animas–La Plata Project, which Congress drastically pared down in size after the original version drew strong objections for its cost and environmental impacts. Some commentators cite Animas–La Plata as the last of the nation's major Reclamation projects.

Salinity as a Curb on Development

Apart from the political disenchantment with water project development, construction and operation of dams—and even storage in existing reservoirs—had become problematical as a solution in the Colorado River basin. Salt concentrations can render the river's waters practically useless by the time water reaches the lower basin states and Mexico. Repeated irrigation diversions and return flows result in the addition of salts leached from the land. The effects of salt loading were vivid when Lake Powell behind Glen Canyon Dam reduced river flows. Mexico experienced crop losses in the Mexicali Valley and claimed the 1944 U.S.–Mexico treaty guaranteeing water delivery to Mexico had been violated. The 1944 treaty said nothing about water quality guarantee. Still the U.S. was forced to agree to limit concentrations of salt in the water reaching Mexico.

To accomplish this, Congress passed the Colorado River Basin Salinity Control Act in 1974 (PL 93–320) [43 U.S.C.A. § 1592 et seq.] creating a vast structural program to control salinity in the Colorado River. It involved canal lining, a groundwater pumping program in the border area, construction of numerous projects to prevent salty water from getting to the river, and even a huge, reverse osmosis desalination plant. Faced with potential violations of the Clean Water Act as saline water in the river crossed state lines the basin states organized the Colorado River Basin Salinity Control Forum, and convinced EPA to allow for implementation of a plan for achieving reductions with federal assistance.

Inefficacy of Dams in Adapting to Climate Change

Adaptation to climate change poses new challenges for the United States Corps of Engineers and the Bureau of Reclamation. Some dams may be in the wrong places and sized incorrectly to deal with changed precipitation patterns. For example, many dams in the Colorado River system are designed to capture snowmelt. With climate change, there may be less snow in the mountains, and what snow does fall may melt and run off during the winters rather than during the springs and summers. Changed runoff patterns will also create pressure to operate reservoirs differently. There may be increased demand for the dedication of more storage space in Bureau of Reclamation reservoirs to flood control at the expense of hydropower and consumptive use releases if runoffs occur earlier in the year. In severe sustained droughts, it may not be possible to generate power while satisfying calls for irrigation and municipal supplies. On other interstate rivers, such as the Missouri where navigation is important, the release of water for navigation presents another competing demand and cause of conflict.

For Southern California, resorting to the State Water Project becomes less tenable as well. Annual deliveries could decline by 7 percent to 15 percent. At the same time, global warming may cause the demand for electricity to increase by 4 percent to 6 percent over the expected increase without global warming. In addition, warmer temperatures could increase spring runoffs, recreating the pattern of flooding followed by inadequate summer supplies. See generally, Peter H. Gleick, Water: The Potential Consequences of Climate Variability and Change for Water Resources of the United States (2000).

Importation Schemes and Dreams

Although some people envisioned continued dam-building on the Colorado, it was clear that the river had natural limits. To accommodate anticipated growth in the basin, there were ambitious—and bizarre— proposals to import water to the basin. The more notable proposals included:

- The Southwest Water Plan: Proposed by Secretary of the Interior Udall shortly after the decision in Arizona v. California was announced, the plan called for building two additional dams (Bridge Canyon and Marble Canyon) at either end of the Grand Canyon

National Monument, the Central Arizona Project (CAP), an experimental desalinization plant in California, and a proposal to divert the waters of wild rivers of Northern California as far south as Arizona. Only the CAP survived the subsequent debate.

- Snake–Colorado Project: Five million acre-feet of water would be brought south through eastern Oregon to the lower Colorado at a cost of $3.2 billion.

- Western Water Plan: Fifteen million acre-feet would be brought through an elaborate system of pumping stations and reservoirs from the Columbia River to Lake Mead on the Colorado at an estimated cost of $11 billion.

- NESCO Plan: A $20 billion fiberglass pipeline would follow the continental shelf of California, carrying four million acre-feet of north coast river water to serve population centers along the coast.

- North American Water and Power Alliance: Water supplies would move from as far north as the Yukon River through Canada, connecting with major rivers there and then linking waterways from coast to coast to augment supplies at a cost of some $200 billion.

A variety of ideas to augment Colorado River water supplies from sources other than imports were also discussed by the states. One possibility was massive cloudseeding. Another scheme was to tow icebergs from Alaska. The Missouri River Basin was studied as a water source by private industry considering oil shale development in the upper basin states. Though the importation schemes eventually died, drought in California in the 1990s sparked new suggestions for importation of Alaskan water using an offshore pipeline or single-hulled oil tankers retired from service after the Exxon Valdez oil spill.

Conservation and Reallocation.

There is still sufficient water in the basin to satisfy most present beneficial uses, considering the availability of groundwater in Arizona and California, and the inefficient uses of water in agriculture. In the long run, however, continued growth of population and consequent water demand cannot be sustained at present levels, forcing consideration of demand management. For the immediate future, the essential problem may be the present allocation of the existing supply of water. California is the fastest growing and hardest hit by scarcity. Most efforts at reallocation are accordingly focused there.

The most promising approaches have been water marketing, salvage, and exchange agreements under which the Metropolitan Water District of Southern California (MWD) obtains the right to use Colorado River water to serve the Los Angeles–San Diego basins. The water is allocated to the irrigation districts along the Colorado River, especially the Imperial Irrigation District (IID). MWD is the major water wholesaler for all of Southern California and the major municipal contractor for California's apportionment of Colorado River water. MWD has been forced to examine and consider a gamut of potentially available alternative sources of water and to enter into a number of innovative agreements with irrigation districts. The first agreement was the MWD–IID water salvage agreement.

IID serves rich agricultural lands in the southernmost portion of California and is the largest single contractor for Colorado River water in the state. One court observed that IID "has occupied a position of great strength, discretion and vested right in a geographical part of the country that is 'far western,' embracing a philosophy that is independent in every sense of the word. Recent trends in water-use philosophy and the administration of water law have severely undermined the positions of districts such as IID." Imperial Irrigation District v. State Water Resources Control Board, 225 Cal.App.3d 548, 275 Cal.Rptr. 250, 266 (1990). IID for many years had every incentive to divert and apply as much water as it could in the district and no incentive to market its water to urban suppliers because no entity was willing to apply the beneficial use doctrine to the district. This began to change in the 1980s and by the end of the decade IID was under orders from the State Water Resources Control Board to stop its wasteful use of irrigation water.

After lengthy negotiations, IID concluded an agreement with MWD that solved IID's immediate problems and provided more municipal water for MWD. The agreement finessed all the asserted obstacles to marketing Colorado River water that were posed by the "Law of the River" and California water law. Under the "Water Conservation Agreement Between the MWD of Southern California and IID" of December 1989, the IID agreed to conserve 100,000 acre-feet per year, which MWD then could divert through its facilities upstream. In return, MWD agreed to pay IID $233 million in direct and indirect costs of the water conservation program, including lining ditches and canals, constructing new regulating reservoirs, and installing automatic control structures to regulate water flow throughout the system.

Is the agreement a transfer? Is it a sale or lease of a water right? Part G provides:

> IID and MWD recognize that they have differences of opinion over various legal questions relating to the transfer of certain water and entitlement of junior priorities to certain water, but each wishes to go forward with the Agreement embodied herein without regard to current or future legal differences, and both agree that nothing herein is intended to or should have the effect of adding to or subtracting from the legal position heretofore or hereafter taken by either, as is more specifically set forth in Article VI hereof.

Under the Seven Party Agreement of 1931, by which seven large water users in California carved up and defined their relative priorities to California's share of Colorado River water that was made available upon completion of the Hoover Dam, any water not used by a higher priority user goes to the next party in line. Since IID holds the second and third priorities, while MWD holds the fourth and fifth, MWD could argue that it is entitled to water conserved by IID at no cost. Thus, Article VI, Section 6.2(d) of the 1989 agreement explicitly waives any potential claim by MWD that saved water reverts to the stream and is thus available for use by those with lower priorities, and estops MWD from claiming that IID forfeited any right by its participation in the agreement. Interestingly, IID did not actually reduce its consumption or diversions after implementing the conservation agreement. Instead, it put more lands under irrigation.

The MWD–IID salvage agreement led to proposals for additional transactions. One was an ill-fated 1997 transfer of 200,000 acre feet to San Diego, which is served by MWD. A corporation bought 45,000 acres and then planned to sell the associated water to San Diego. The sale never took place. Later, IID entered into direct negotiations for selling water to San Diego. Any such sale is fraught with problems. One is, how to transport the water from IID to the San Diego because the only pipeline is MWD's Colorado aqueduct. The State Water Resources Board Control approved a 1998 transfer to San Diego but required IID to propose a Salton Sea restoration plan. In re Imperial Irrigation Dist., Rev.Order No. WRO 2002–0013 (Cal.Water Resources Control B. Oct. 28, 2002). To ensure that MWD treats transferors and transferees fairly, California enacted mandatory "wheeling" legislation. California Water Code Sections 1810–1814 require public entities to wheel (allow their facilities to be used to transport) water from bona fide transfers if unused facility capacity is available. Metropolitan Water District v. Imperial Irrigation District, 80 Cal.App.4th 1403, 96 Cal.Rptr.2d 314 (2000), upheld MWD's fee structure, which was based on the volume of water rather than the distance transported and on the recovery of system-wide costs, but the court indicated a willingness to police discriminatory refusals to wheel. See Craig Bell, *Promoting Conservation By Law: Water Conservation and Western State Initiatives,* 10 U. Denv. Water L. Rev. 313 (2007).

Conservation agreements and transfers can result in serious third party effects. One major impact is on the Salton Sea, originally created when the Colorado River flooded early in the 20th century. The Sea is highly saline and toxic and has depended on run-off from IID to maintain safe salinity levels. See William DeBuys, Salt Dreams (1996). Proposed transfers threaten to decrease these flows. Current multi-million dollar proposals to save the sea include the construction of solar evaporation ponds. As of 2008, studies and small restoration efforts are underway, but no concrete restoration plan has been approved and funded. Other conservation efforts such as the lining of the All–American Canal that serves IID also raise third party effects issues.

A major complication resulting from the project is the adverse effect on Mexican irrigators, who have been relying on seepage from the All–American Canal for over 100,000 acre-feet of water annually that they pump from wells just south of the border. Do these users have potential legal or political claims? See Douglas Hayes, *The All–American Canal Lining Project: A Catalyst for Rational and Comprehensive Groundwater Management on the United States–Mexico Border,* 31 Nat. Resources J. 803 (1991); Alfonso Cortez–Lara & Maria Rosa Garcia–Acevedo, *The Lining of the All–American Canal: The Forgotten Voices,* 40 Nat. Resources J. 261

(2000). The state of California financed the lining of the canal and this resulted in a lawsuit. Litigation opposing the lining came to an end when Congress attached a rider to the Tax Relief and Health Care Act of 2006 which directed the Secretary of Interior to proceed with the project without delay "[n]ot withstanding any other provision of law...." PUB. LAW NO. 109–432, 120 Stat. 2922, § 397. Consejo de Desarrollo Economico de Mexicali v. United States, 482 F.3d 1157 (9th Cir. 2007), dismissed all claims. The court found the language of the statute clear and followed Robertson v. Seattle Audubon Society, 503 U.S. 429, 112 S.Ct. 1407, 118 L.Ed.2d 73 (1992), which holds that Congress may change the substantive law applicable to a pending case consistent with separation of powers principles. Plaintiff's Tenth Amendment challenge was rejected because the United States was not compelling state participation since California had agreed to fund the project after the federal government did not. Plaintiff's equal protection argument, based on the selective denial of the right to healthy environment only to Latinos, was dismissed because the organization failed to identify any member who would have individual standing.

Exchanges and Groundwater Storage.

MWD is pursuing a variety of arrangements to transfer, exchange, and store water to extend its reliable supplies. The Coachella Valley groundwater storage program allows MWD to "bank" Colorado River water underground in the depleted aquifers of two desert districts. Under the agreement negotiated with the Coachella Valley Water District, MWD delivers water from the Colorado River aqueduct for recharge into the Coachella Valley groundwater basin. During dry years, MWD will cease deliveries to Coachella and receive water from the California State Water Project (SWP) to which Coachella Valley users would otherwise have been entitled. Meanwhile, Coachella Valley users will pump groundwater, previously replenished by MWD's Colorado River water. A similar project is being studied in the IID. Another arrangement with the Arvin–Edison Water Storage District, hundreds of miles north in the Central Valley, provides for MWD to store its SWP water in the district during wet years and to receive Arvin–Edison's dry year entitlements from the SWP while farmers pump the stored water.

MWD's other projects include several short-term purchases from San Joaquin Valley water agencies and land fallowing agreements. MWD has also entered into a two-year test agreement with the Palo Verde Valley Irrigation District, holder of the most senior water rights in California to the Colorado River, to fallow about 25 percent of the district's 100,000 acres freeing up 93,000 acre-feet of water for MWD to use in dry years.

Interstate Water Banking and Markets.

There is a significant convergence in the thinking of academics, economists, and water rights experts that water marketing is both long overdue and essential to achieving a more efficient beneficial use of the total water resource. See David H. Getches, *Colorado River Governance; Sharing Federal Authority As an Incentive to Create a New Institution*, 68 U. Colo. L. Rev. 573 (1997). It is also an important adaptation strategy for dealing with climate change. Water apportioned to the upper basin states is under-utilized—providing an obvious source of supply for downstream markets. In the depths of the 1988 to 1992 drought, California suggested the establishment of an escrow account, into which it would pay cash for the privilege of using water in excess of its allotted maximum under the compact. In turn, the cash would be distributed among the states of the upper basin to promote conservation and purchase water rights in order to make water available. Second, California suggested that the upper basin states establish a water bank, through which existing laws permitting the intrastate sale and transfer of water rights could be harnessed to make additional water available for interstate transfer. These proposals were roundly rejected by the other basin states who were unwilling to discuss the concept of interstate water marketing.

For an argument that interstate transfers are consistent with the doctrine of equitable apportionment and that compacts should be construed to allow them unless there is an express prohibition see Olen Paul Matthews and Michael Pease, *The Commerce Clause, Interstate Compacts, and Interstate Boundaries*, 46 Nat. Res. J. 601 (2006).

Arizona's difficulty in putting its share of Colorado River water to use because of the charges that users must pay for CAP project water led to the creation of a "water bank." Arizona has begun to take (and pay for at state expense) CAP water, which it then stores in aquifers. In dry years, Arizona will pump and use the stored groundwater while MWD and Las Vegas may take an equivalent amount of the CAP entitlement directly from the river. Utah has indicated its willingness to consider selling some of its apportionment, but the other states are not yet prepared to consider marketing arrangements between the upper and lower basin states. In 1999, the Department of Interior issued rules to permit transfers among the three Lower Basin States. 43 C.F.R. § 414 (2000). Arizona may store unused Colorado River entitlements in off-stream reservoirs and aquifers. If entitlement holders in the state do not need the water, the Secretary of the Interior may release the water pursuant to a voluntary agreement for use in another Lower Basin state (read California or Nevada).

California's Inability to Stay Within its Allocation.

California grew to depend on the use of other states' unused water from the Colorado River. Southern California was able to use about a million acre-feet of water a year in excess of its apportionment before the Central Arizona Project was completed. But the explosive growth of Las Vegas, Nevada and Arizona's physical ability to deliver its full CAP allotment raised the possibility that California would actually have to live within its 4.4 million acre-feet allotment rather than the 5.2 million acre-feet that it actually withdrew and consumed.

Anticipating the problem, Southern California hoped to complete the vast California State Water Project (SWP) by construction of a peripheral canal to divert water from the Sacramento–San Joaquin Delta that would otherwise flow into San Francisco Bay. But when the state's voters soundly defeated a proposal to build the canal in 1982, the growing Los Angeles area had to look elsewhere. In recent years even the security of existing supplies from the north through the SWP was thrown into doubt by serious environmental issues in the San Francisco Bay Delta. Those problems triggered the CALFED process, *supra* pp. 753–760 and renewed interest in dam construction.

The search for a way to make California comply with the letter of the Compact occupied the Clinton Administration between 1992–2000. As his final act in office, Secretary of the Interior Bruce Babbitt issued new regulations that make it easier for the Secretary to allow California to take more than its apportionment in the guise of a "surplus." The Surplus Criteria are designed to allow the three lower basin states to have more water as California gradually implements its promise to reduce its Colorado River withdrawals toward its 4.4 million acre-feet Compact allocation over fifteen years. The criteria allow Lake Mead to be lowered as much as nineteen feet during California's "soft landing" and it changes the previous surplus allocation formula from Arizona's 46%, California's 50%, and Nevada's 4% to one which shares the surplus equally among the three lower basin states. Nevada will be allowed to store its portion of the surplus in a groundwater bank in Arizona. California's good faith is subject to sanctions; if the state does not meet its surplus reduction targets, California's share of the surplus and access to Lake Mead may be further reduced. Colorado River Interim Surplus Criteria, 65 Fed. Reg. 48,531 (2000). In 2003, all Lower basin parties signed a quantification agreement to implement the rules that itself took years to develop.

Even as the Colorado River basin states agonized over the sharing of "surplus" water in the river, a drought that began in 1999 was ongoing. The impacts on the Colorado River were the worst in 500 years and the drought was continuing in 2008. Like typical multi-year droughts, some years have been worse than others, but during some portions of the most recent drought the huge reservoirs in the Colorado River basin have been depleted to levels that portend an inability to fulfill the allocations in the Law of the River.

James H. Davenport, Softening The Divides: The Seven Colorado River Basin States' Recommendation to the Secretary of the Interior Regarding Lower Basin Shortage Guidelines and the Operation of Lakes Mead and Powell in Low Reservoir Conditions
10 U. Denv. Water L. Rev. 287, 289–290, 296–306, 311 (2007).

* * *

Federal law and practice, including Section 602(b) of the 1968 Colorado River Basin Project Act and the Secretary's Criteria for Coordinated Long-Range Operation of Colorado River Reservoirs Pursuant to the Colorado River Basin Project Act, call upon the Secretary of the Interior to consult with the states through "Governors' Representatives," who represent the governors and their respective states, regarding the operation of Lakes Powell and Mead. * * *

In 2001, the Secretary of the Interior adopted interim surplus guidelines ("ISG") for utilization in the Lower Basin of the Colorado, based in large part on a proposal from the states' representatives. In the years following the adoption of the ISG, drought conditions in the Colorado River Basin caused a significant reduction in water stored in Lakes Powell and Mead, and precipitated discussions by and among the states' representatives, and with the United States through the Department of the Interior and the Bureau of Reclamation.

Upper Basin states—Colorado, Wyoming, Utah, and New Mexico— began to express concern about actual shortages and insufficient water availability in headwaters and tributaries to meet all permitted rights, conditions which had been occurring in those states. Dendrochronological (tree ring) studies raised questions in the academic and environmental communities about the factual reliability of Colorado River hydrological data as a basis for water allocation. The Honorable J. Steven Griles, Deputy Secretary of the Interior, on behalf of Secretary of the Interior Gale Norton, announced at the Colorado River Water Users' Conference in Las Vegas in December 2004, that the Colorado River drought of 2001–2004 compelled the Secretary to consider the adoption of rules through which to govern the distribution of Colorado River water in the Lower Basin during shortage conditions. He requested, on behalf of Norton and the Department, that the Lower Basin states, Arizona, California, and Nevada, negotiate to propose rules for operation in a shortage regime. The states' representatives began to discuss whether the United States has a right to deliver less than 1.5 million acre feet to Mexico under the U.S.–Mexico 1944 Water Treaty's "extraordinary drought" provision when only Upper Basin water users had suffered actual shortages.

* * *

A.   Seven Basin States' Proposal Regarding Colorado River Interim Operations

[Negotiations proceeded for over two years, culminating in several documents.] The seven Colorado River Basin states recommended interim operations that would minimize shortages in the Lower Basin and avoid the risk of curtailment in the Upper Basin through conservation, more efficient reservoir operations, and long-term alternatives to bring additional water into the Colorado River community. The states' recommendation has three key elements: management of Lake Powell and Lake Mead to minimize shortages and avoid curtailments; actions that fully utilize and conserve water in the Lower Basin; and apportionment of shortages in the Lower Basin.

1.   Coordinated Operation of Lakes Powell and Mead

* * *

2. Actions That Fully Utilize and Conserve Water in the Lower Basin

Modification and Extension of the Interim Surplus Guidelines

The Proposed Interim Guidelines * * * are intended as a replacement for those Guidelines. The Proposed Interim Guidelines extend the interim period to 2025 (through operating year 2026) [changing the time limit for California to reduce it use of Colorado River water to the amount required by the Compact and specifying other variations in allocations and limitations on water use] * * *.

Storage of Water in Lake Mead

The states' representatives proposed that the Secretary develop a policy and accounting procedure that would create opportunities for Lower Basin Colorado River contractors to store water in Lake Mead on a multi-year basis. * * * Storage under the shortage program would permit augmentation of water supplies through "projects that create water system efficiency, extraordinary conservation, and the importation of non-Colorado River System water into the Colorado River Mainstream."

The seven states' Proposed Interim Guidelines recommend an accounting approach referred to as "intentionally created surplus" or "ICS." That approach develops the notion that water intentionally not used in a given year creates a "surplus" available for use in another year. * * *

Extraordinary Conservation ICS

Lake Mead storage opportunities depend, in a number of instances upon "extraordinary conservation" by Colorado River contractors. "Extraordinary conservation" activities include: fallowing of land that is, was, or would in the next year be irrigated; canal lining; desalination; * * * and other "extraordinary conservation" measures as agreed upon by the states. The Metropolitan Water District of Southern California ("MWD") and the Imperial Irrigation District ("IID") were the first contractors to arrange for Lake Mead storage, even in advance of the Secretary's adoption of guidelines establishing any process for recovery of the stored water. In 2006, utilizing a "pilot program" approach, established through correspondence with the Bureau of Reclamation, MWD and IID left water in Lake Mead of which they were entitled to take delivery. * * *

System Efficiency ICS

Another means by which contractors can create ICS under the states' representatives' proposal is through the creation of system efficiencies. The states' representatives recommended that a contractor be able to make contributions of capital to the Secretary for use in Secretarial projects designed to realize efficiencies that save water that would otherwise be lost from the Colorado River system in the United States. The Secretary, in consultation with the states, would identify system efficiency projects, terms for capital participation in such projects, and types and amounts of benefits the Secretary would provide in consideration of non-federal capital contributions to system efficiency projects, including a portion of the water saved by the project. * * *

Tributary Conservation ICS

Under the states' representatives' proposal, a contractor could create "Tributary Conservation ICS" by purchasing documented water rights on Colorado River System tributaries upstream of Hoover Dam within the contractor's state. The water rights must have been used for a significant period of years and have been created prior to the effective date of the Boulder Canyon Project Act (June 25, 1929). * * * The recovered water would be available for domestic use only. This water would be in addition to the state's basic apportionment and would be available during declared shortages as "Developed Shortage Supply." * * *

Imported ICS

The states' representatives' proposal would allow creation of an ICS by introduction of non-Colorado River system water in a contractor's state into the Colorado River Mainstream. This water is in addition to a state's basic apportionment and may be used whenever the Secretary declared the existence of an "ICS Surplus" or a shortage condition.

* * *

Normal Operations

In years when Lake Mead elevation as of January 1 is projected to be above elevation 1075 ft. and below 1145 ft., the Secretary would determine a normal operating condition. ICS water would be available during the normal operating condition, provided the Secretary had also determined that an "ICS Surplus" exists.

Shortage Operations

On February 3, 2006, the states representatives proposed to the Secretary that, in years when the projected content of Lake Mead on January 1 is at or below an elevation of 1075 ft. but at or above 1050 ft., a quantity of 400,000 acre-feet would not be delivered to the Lower Basin states and Mexico. In years when Lake Mead projected content is below elevation 1050 ft. but at or above 1025 ft., a quantity of 500,000 acre-feet would not be delivered to the Lower Basin states and Mexico. In years when Lake Mead projected content is below 1025 ft., a quantity of 600,000 acre-feet would not be delivered to the Lower Basin states and Mexico. Under the states' representatives' February 3, 2006, proposal, whenever Lake Mead reaches elevation 1025 ft., the Secretary would consult with the states to determine whether Colorado River hydrologic conditions, together with the delivery of 8.4 million acre-feet of Colorado River water to Lower Basin users and Mexico, would cause the elevation of Lake Mead to fall below 1000 ft. Discussion would then ensue regarding further measures that may then need to be undertaken to avoid or reduce further increases in shortage determinations.

The states' representatives also proposed that United States should reduce deliveries to Mexico pursuant to Article 10 of the 1944 Treaty in any year in which the Secretary had declared that a shortage condition existed pursuant to Article II(B)(3) of the Decree in Arizona v. California. The Secretary would base the total quantity of water that would not be delivered to Mexico on Lower Basin water deliveries during normal water supply conditions. The states' recommendation proposed that Mexico bear 17% of any declared shortage.

Although the hydrologic modeling incorporated in the Bureau of Reclamation's Draft Environmental Impact Statement published on February 28, 2007, incorporated the states' representatives' recommendation that Mexico share 17% of any reduced deliveries of Colorado River water in a declared shortage, the text of the DEIS itself was somewhat more equivocal on the willingness or commitment of the United States to do so:

> In order to assess the potential effects of the alternatives, it was assumed that Mexico would share proportionately in Lower Basin shortages. Allocation of Colorado River water to Mexico is governed by the 1944 Treaty. The proposed federal action is for the purpose of adopting additional operational strategies to improve the Department's annual management and operation of key Colorado River reservoirs for an interim period through 2026. However, in order to assess the potential effects of the proposed federal action in this Draft EIS, certain modeling assumptions are used that display projected water*306 deliveries to Mexico. Reclamation's modeling assumptions are not intended to constitute an interpretation or application of the 1944 Treaty or to represent current or future United States policy regarding deliveries to Mexico. The United States will conduct all necessary and appropriate discussions regarding the proposed federal action and implementation of the 1944 Treaty with Mexico through the IBWC in consultation with the Department of State.

Understanding the uncertainty of the shortage allotment relationship of the United States and Mexico, Arizona, and Nevada negotiated a Shortage Sharing Agreement between themselves in February 2007, which divided 83% of the reduced deliveries that had been recommended to the Secretary on February 3, 2006 between those two states [in specified amounts of water at each tier of reduced deliveries]. * * * The Proposed Interim Guidelines transmitted to the Secretary on April 30, 2007, thus proposed a three-step reduction program in which the reductions of deliveries that would be made in the Lower Division states were stated as 333,000, 417,000, and 500,000 acre-feet per year, respectively.

* * *

In November 2007 the Department of the Interior completed an environmental impact statement on proposed rules that were based on the states' proposal. Then, in December 2007 the Secretary of the Interior signed a Record of Decision, adopting the rules and implementing the essential aspects of the state proposal described in the Davenport article.

NOTES

1. As global climate change and continued urban growth especially in Las Vegas, and the prospect of increased Upper Basin use become more likely, the Bureau and the basin states continue to seek ways to produce more water from the system. For a hard look at this strategy see National Research Council, Colorado River Water Management: Evaluating and Adjusting to Hydroclimatic Variability (2007).

2. The Secretary of the Interior has enormous powers in operating the dams on the Colorado and effectively controlling when and how water is allocated. Should the Secretary defer to the states as she did for the many years it took to propose the rulemaking described in the Davenport article and historically in governing the river? What are the advantages and disadvantages of this approach?

3. What objections might Mexico have to the states' approach described in the article? The treaty with Mexico requires that the United States deliver 1.5 million acre-feet annually. Article X allows the United States' delivery duty to be relaxed in the case of extraordinary drought or a serious accident to the irrigation system of the United States in "proportion as consumptive uses in the United States are reduced." Would a continued decrease in available supply allow the United States to modify its delivery obligation on a long-term basis? See Holly Doremus and Michael Hanemann, *The Challenges of Dynamic Water Management in the American West,* 26 UCLA J. Envtl. L. & Pol'y 55 (2008). Cf. A. Dan Tarlock, *How Well Can International Water Allocation Regimes Adapt to Global Climate Change?*, 15 J. Land Use & Envtl. L. 423 (2000).

4. How could the Colorado River basin states and the nation be better served in attempting to solve the huge practical problems, the solutions to which are so often encumbered with state, local, and private self-interest and purported legal barriers attributed to the Compact and other laws? Should the Compact be revised or scrapped? Should the federal government exert the full extent of its power through use of existing Secretarial authority and new legislation? Should a new commission or multi-interest entity be created with the task of addressing and resolving issues like those discussed in the Davenport article and the preceding note? See David H. Getches, *Colorado River Governance: Sharing Federal Authority as an Incentive to Create a New Institution,* 68 U. Colo. L. Rev. 573 (1997).

NOTE: CONGRESSIONAL APPROVAL OF MULTI–PARTY, MULTI–ISSUE INTERSTATE DISPUTE RESOLUTION

Just as the future of judicial equitable apportionment is changing so is the role of Congress in facilitating resolution of complicated issues tangential to interstate allocation. As parties negotiate comprehensive solutions, federal participation and funding is often necessary. In 1990, Congress basically ratified a de facto apportionment when it adopted the Truckee–Carson–Pyramid Lake Water Rights Settlement Act, Pub.L. No. 101–618, 104 Stat. 3294 (1990). The waters of the Carson and Truckee rivers originate on the eastern slope of the Sierra Nevada Mountains in California and flow into Nevada where they eventually drain into Great Basin sinks. These rivers were effectively apportioned by a series of lawsuits, adjudications, and agreements. The Act is the most precise and comprehensive congressional settlement of a longstanding interstate water dispute. See John Kramer, *Lake Tahoe, the Truckee River, and Pyramid Lake: The Past, Present and Future of Interstate Water Issues*, 19 Pac. L.J. 1339 (1988).

The focus of the Act is on a four-way, intra-Nevada, dispute among the Pyramid Lake Paiute Tribe, who wants increased Truckee River flows to preserve and restore native fisheries, the Truckee–Carson Irrigation District, that holds most water rights on the lower Truckee, the Sierra Pacific Power Company, that supplies water to the growing cities of Reno and Sparks, and environmental interests who seek to maintain flows into the Lahontan Valley wetlands. A byproduct of this settlement is the apportionment of interstate waters.

A series of agreements, lawsuits, and adjudications spanned almost a century, but the two states had never formally apportioned the waters. California and Nevada began compact negotiations in 1956, negotiated one in 1965, and approved it in 1969–70. Congress refused to ratify it because of federal government, tribal, and California state senatorial opposition. However, eventually the tribe, the federal government, and the cities of Reno and Sparks reached an agreement that Congress ratified. The legislation made the same allocation of the Truckee as provided in the compact but agreement was possible because other issues were being addressed. Lake Tahoe basin diversions are limited to 34,000 acre-feet per year; California gets 23,000 acre-feet, and Nevada 11,000 acre-feet. Notably both surface and groundwater are included in this allocation.

Most of the Truckee is used in Nevada and allocated by the 1944 Orr Ditch decree. United States of America v. Orr Ditch Co., Equity Docket No. A3 (D. Nev. 1944). The settlement preserves these prior uses by limiting California to 32,000 acre-feet of gross diversions from surface and groundwater in the Truckee River basin. Maximum annual surface diversions are limited to 10,000 acre-feet. All future California commercial and irrigation withdrawals are junior to all Nevada beneficial uses for the maintenance and preservation of the Pyramid Lake fishery. The apportionment contains novel features such as the protection of return flows from sewage treatment plant discharges and the allocation of water used for winter snowmaking. The legislation required an operating agreement for the Truckee River. Eventually all the major users with the exception of the Truckee–Carson Irrigation District, entered into an agreement, Truckee River Operating Agreement (TROA), that will make more water available for the Pyramid Tribe fishery and give Reno–Sparks drought reserves through a complex reservoir use and storage accounting system. Federal and state parties signed the Record of Decision in September 2008. See generally A. Dan Tarlock, *The Creation of New Risk Sharing Water Entitlement Regimes: The Case of the Truckee–Carson Settlement*, 25 Ecology L. Q. 674 (1999) and Barbara Cosens, *Farmers, Fish, Tribal Power and Poker:*

Reallocating Water in the Truckee River Basin, Nevada and California, 10 Hastings W. Nw. J. Envtl. L. & Pol'y 89 (2003).

Beginning in the 1980s, there have been a number of other "outside-the-box" experiments to solve interstate disputes by collaborative, stakeholder processes that seek consensus. Not all involve apportionment of quantities of water. However, these solutions take place in the shadow of the three traditional allocation methods—original actions, compacts, and congressional apportionment. The threat of litigation or congressional intervention remains an important stimulus to cooperation. The Platte River is a case in point. In 1986, Nebraska reopened *Nebraska v. Wyoming,* discussed *supra* p. 955, after Wyoming planned additional diversion and storage facilities on the North Platte and its tributaries. Since the original action, the maintenance of flows through central Nebraska to sustain the habitat of three endangered species—whooping cranes, piping plovers, and least terns—had become a major interstate issue. See Leo Eisel & David J. Aiken, Platte River Basin Study (Report to the Western Water Policy Review Advisory Commission 1997). Nebraska tried to amend the decree to include instream flows for habitat maintenance in the Central Platte, and the Supreme Court indicated that the state could raise future fish and wildlife injuries in an original jurisdiction action. Nebraska v. Wyoming, 515 U.S. 1, 115 S.Ct. 1933, 132 L.Ed.2d 1 (1995).

In addition to this Supreme Court opinion, the expiration of the Federal Energy Regulatory Commission license for Kingsley Dam on Lake McConaughy in 1987 raised fears that substantial releases for whooping crane habitat below the dam would be mandated in the relicensing. Recall that Congress amended the Federal Power Act in 1986 to require that wildlife conservation be given parity with power generation in all relicensing proceedings. 16 U.S.C. Section 797(e). See David Aiken, *Balancing Endangered Species Protection and Irrigation Water Rights: The Platte Cooperative Agreement,* 3 Great Plains Nat. Resources J. 119 (1999). The fears of Supreme Court—or Department of Interior—ordered instream flows on the river triggered a federal-state-stakeholder process similar to the CALFED process described *supra* pp. 697–702, but unlike CALFED, which has exalted process over substance, the Platte River Agreement got down to brass tacks. Professor Joseph L. Sax has called the Platte River process "the most encouraging model we have for the new biodiversity era." Joseph L. Sax, *Environmental Law at the Turn of the Century: A Reportorial Fragment of Contemporary History,* 88 Cal. L. Rev. 2377, 2394 (2000). Others are less sanguine. See John D. Echeverria, *No Success Like Failure: The Platte River Collaborative Water Planning Process,* 75 Wm. & Mary Envtl. L. & Pol'y Rev. 559 (2001).

Nebraska, Colorado, Wyoming, and the United States Department of the Interior have entered into a "Cooperative Agreement" to develop a basin-wide recovery program for threatened and endangered species in the Central Platte River Basin. The program's primary purpose is to provide recovery-oriented habitat and water for the three endangered species previously mentioned, as well as the pallid sturgeon. The proposed "program" takes a phased, adaptive management approach, and the first phase is expected to be 10 to 13 years in length.

The proposed recovery program has three primary components, including a Water Action Plan, a Depletion Plan, and a Habitat Plan. The Water Action Plan (WAP) addresses maintenance of the flow levels needed to provide adequate habitat for the targeted species. The USFWS believes actual daily flows currently fall short of the targeted flows by an average of 417,000 acre-feet per year. Some parties, however, dispute whether the target flows are the best way to address habitat and recovery of the species. Several different projects are proposed to reach the target flows based on storing water during times of excess flows and releasing water when needed.

While the WAP is designed to put "new water" into the river (water that would not normally be there), the Depletion Plan is designed to prevent increased shortages to target flows caused by new or expanded uses of water. New uses that contribute to target flow shortages would be subject to mitigation, either with water or with dollars that could be used to produce water. Additionally, water right leasing and water banking are other potential ways to secure water for offset purposes. A water bank would allow for purchasing of water to offset new depletions and for deposits resulting from retiring existing uses.

Finally, terrestrial habitat is also necessary to meet the needs of the species. The proposed program would result in the development and protection of 29,000 acres of terrestrial riverine habitat over time. In addition to property already dedicated to the program, habitat would be acquired from willing participants via leasing, conservation easements, and (as a last option) through purchase. Focus would be placed on riverine and wet meadow type habitat. The controversial target flows and the program for terrestrial habitat would be continually re-evaluated and adjusted under a regime of "adaptive management." Thus, initial actions will be modified based on the results of the program. Adaptive management is increasingly being used to allow solutions to complex natural resources management issues to proceed where scientific information is necessarily incomplete.

However, the cooperative agreement process has been very slow to deliver actual benefits to the Platte River ecosystem. The parties signed the Cooperative Agreement in 1997, but it took another nine years of negotiations, planning, and scientific study before the Interior Department and the States approved a Platte River Recovery Implementation Program. Interior Secretary Dirk Kempthorne in 2006 praised the program as "an outstanding collaborative effort among interest groups to cooperatively address the needs of endangered species and ensure that current uses of basin water can continue," but its success in restoring habitat for the protected species remains to be seen.

B.   Federal Limits on State Export Restrictions

Interstate disputes can arise when parties in one state attempt to export water to another state. Large interstate diversions expose sharp regional differences. In the 1960s, a number of ambitious interstate diversion schemes were proposed as described *supra* p. 1015, but they were either prohibited by Congress or collapsed as the Reclamation Era ended. The energy boom of the late 1970s triggered another round of interstate and interbasin transfer proposals, although no large-scale projects were built. With greater attention to economics and to environmental impacts, the prospect of large-scale transbasin diversions becomes more remote. Nevertheless, potential exporting states continue to be concerned about protecting their interests against interstate transfers.

Many states have tried various means to prevent exports. In a case involving a small, cross-border transfer, the United States Supreme Court ruled that states may not prevent exports of water from within their boundaries for abstract economic or political reasons. Unless the restriction on export is found to be for the health or welfare of state citizens, it will be deemed an unconstitutional interference with interstate commerce. At what point are state interests in controlling exports ever sufficiently substantial for export restrictions to be constitutional? In recent years, some commentators have suggested that international trade law, which is based on non-discrimination principles similar to those of the dormant Commerce Clause, may also trump national legislation seeking to limit exports. See Daniel A. Farber & Robert E. Hudec, *Free Trade and the Regulatory State: A GATT's–Eye View of the Dormant Commerce Clause*, 47 Vand. L. Rev. 1401 (1994).

Sporhase v. Nebraska ex rel. Douglas

United States Supreme Court, 1982.
458 U.S. 941, 102 S.Ct. 3456, 73 L.Ed.2d 1254.

■ JUSTICE STEVENS delivered the opinion of the Court.

Appellants challenge the constitutionality of a Nebraska statutory restriction on the withdrawal of ground water from any well within Nebraska intended for use in an adjoining State. The challenge presents three questions under the Commerce Clause: (1) whether ground water is an article of commerce and therefore subject to Congressional regulation; (2) whether the Nebraska restriction on the interstate transfer of ground water imposes an impermissible burden on commerce; and (3) whether Congress has granted the States permission to engage in ground water regulation that otherwise would be impermissible.

Appellants jointly own contiguous tracts of land in Chase County, Nebraska, and Phillips County, Colorado. A well physically located on the Nebraska tract pumps ground water for irrigation of both the Nebraska tract and the Colorado tract. Previous owners of the land registered the well with the State of Nebraska in 1971, but neither they nor the present owners applied for the permit required by § 46–613.01 of the Nebraska Revised Statutes. That section provides:

"Any person, firm, city, village, municipal corporation or any other entity intending to withdraw ground water from any well or pit located in the State of Nebraska and transport it for use in an adjoining state shall apply to the Department of Water Resources for a permit to do so. If the Director of Water Resources finds that the withdrawal of the ground water requested is reasonable, is not contrary to the conservation and use of ground water, and is not otherwise detrimental to the public welfare, he shall grant the permit if the state in which the water is to be used grants reciprocal rights to withdraw and transport ground water from that state for use in the State of Nebraska."

Appellee brought this action to enjoin appellants from transferring the water across the border without a permit. * * *

I

In holding that ground water is not an article of commerce, the Nebraska Supreme Court and appellee cite as controlling precedent Hudson County Water Co. v. McCarter, 209 U.S. 349 (1908). In that case a New Jersey statute prohibited the interstate transfer of any surface water located within the State. The Hudson County Water Company nevertheless contracted with New York City to supply one of its boroughs with water from the Passaic River in New Jersey. The state attorney general sought from the New Jersey courts an injunction against fulfillment of the contract. Over the water company's objections that the statute impaired the obligation of contract, took property without just compensation, interfered with interstate commerce, denied New York citizens the privileges afforded New Jersey citizens, and denied New York citizens the equal protection of the laws, the injunction was granted. This Court, in an opinion by Justice Holmes, affirmed.

Most of the Court's opinion addresses the just compensation claim. Justice Holmes refused to ground the Court's holding, as did the New Jersey state courts, on "the more or less attenuated residuum of title that the State may be said to possess." Id., at 355. For the statute was justified as a regulatory measure that, on balance, did not amount to a taking of property that required just compensation. Putting aside the "problems of irrigation," the State's interest in preserving its waters was well within its police power. That interest was not dependent on any demonstration that the State's water resources were inadequate for present or future use. The State "finds itself in possession of what all admit to be a great public good, and what it has it may keep and give no one a reason for its will." Id., at 357.

Having disposed of the just compensation claim, Justice Holmes turned very briefly to the other constitutional challenges. In one paragraph, he rejected the Contract Clause claim. In the remaining paragraph of the opinion, he rejected all the other defenses. His treatment of the Commerce Clause challenge consists of three sentences: "A man cannot acquire a right to property by his desire to use it in commerce among the States. Neither can he enlarge his otherwise limited and qualified right to the same end.

The case is covered in this respect by *Geer v. Connecticut,* 161 U.S. 519 [(1896)]."

While appellee relies upon *Hudson County,* appellants rest on our summary affirmance of a three-judge District Court judgment in City of Altus v. Carr, 255 F.Supp. 828 (W.D.Tex.), summarily aff'd, 385 U.S. 35 (1966). The city of Altus is located near the southern border of Oklahoma. Large population increases rendered inadequate its source of municipal water. It consequently obtained from the owners of land in an adjoining Texas county the contractual right to pump the ground water underlying that land and to transport it across the border. The Texas Legislature thereafter enacted a statute that forbade the interstate exportation of ground water without the approval of that body.[7] The city filed suit in Federal District Court, claiming that the statute violated the Commerce Clause.

The city relied upon West v. Kansas Natural Gas Co., 221 U.S. 229 (1911), which invalidated an Oklahoma statute that prevented the interstate transfer of natural gas produced within the State,[8] and Pennsylvania v. West Virginia, 262 U.S. 553 (1923), which invalidated a West Virginia statute that accorded a preference to the citizens of that State in the purchase of natural gas produced therein. The Texas Attorney General defended the statute on two grounds. First, he asserted that its purpose was to conserve and protect the State's water resources by regulating the withdrawal of ground water. The District Court rejected that defense because similar conservation claims had met defeat in *West v. Kansas Natural Gas Co., supra,* and *Pennsylvania v. West Virginia, supra.* Second, the State argued that the statute regulated ground water and that ground water is not an article of commerce, citing *Geer v. Connecticut,* 161 U.S. 519 (1896), and *Hudson County Water Co. v. McCarter,* 209 U.S. 349 (1908). The court rejected this argument since the statute directly regulated the interstate transportation of water that had been pumped from the ground, and under Texas law such water was an article of commerce. The court then had little difficulty in concluding that the statute imposed an impermissible burden on interstate commerce.[11]

---

7. The District Court quoted the statute: " 'No one shall withdraw water from any underground source in this State for use in any other state by drilling a well in Texas and transporting the water outside the boundaries of the State unless the same be specifically authorized by an Act of the Texas Legislature and thereafter as approved by it.' " 255 F.Supp., at 830.

8. Justice Holmes, the author of the Court's opinion in *Hudson County,* noted his dissent.

11. "Considering the statute in question only with regard to whether it regulates the transportation and use of water after it has been withdrawn from a well and becomes personal property, such statute constitutes an unreasonable burden upon and interference with interstate commerce. Moreover, on the facts of this case it appear[s] to us that [the Texas statute] does not have for its purpose, nor does it operate to conserve water resources of the State of Texas except in the sense that it does so for her own benefit to the detriment of her sister States as in the case of West v. Kansas Natural Gas Co. In the name of conservation, the statute seeks to prohibit interstate shipments of water while indulging in the substantial discrimination of permitting the unrestricted intrastate production and transportation of water be-

In summarily affirming the district court in *City of Altus*, we did not necessarily adopt the court's reasoning. Our affirmance indicates only our agreement with the result reached by the district court. That result is not necessarily inconsistent with the Nebraska Supreme Court's holding in this case. For Texas law differs significantly from Nebraska law regarding the rights of a surface owner to ground water that he has withdrawn. According to the district court in *City of Altus*, the "rule in Texas was that an owner of land could use all of the percolating water he could capture from the wells on his land for whatever beneficial purposes he needed it, on or off the land, and could likewise sell it to others for use on or off the land and outside the basin where produced, just as he could sell any other species of property." Since ground water, once withdrawn, may be freely bought and sold in States that follow this rule, in those States ground water is appropriately regarded as an article of commerce. In Nebraska the surface owner has no comparable interest in ground water. As explained by the Nebraska Supreme Court, " 'the owner of land is entitled to appropriate subterranean waters found under his land, but he cannot extract and appropriate them in excess of a reasonable and beneficial use upon the land which he owns, especially if such use is injurious to others who have substantial rights to the waters, and if the natural underground supply is insufficient for all owners, each is entitled to a reasonable proportion of the whole.' " 305 N.W.2d at 617 (quoting *Olson v. City of Wahoo*, 248 N.W. 304, 308 (1933)).

City of Altus, however, is inconsistent with *Hudson County*. For in the latter case the Court found *Geer v. Connecticut, supra*, to be controlling on the Commerce Clause issue. *Geer*, which sustained a Connecticut ban on the interstate transportation of game birds captured in that State, was premised on the theory that the State owned its wild animals and therefore was free to qualify any ownership interest it might recognize in the persons who capture them. One such restriction is a prohibition against interstate transfer of the captured animals. This theory of public ownership was advanced as a defense in *City of Altus*. The State argued that it owned all subterranean water and therefore could recognize ownership in the surface owner who withdraws the water, but restrict that ownership to use of the water within the State. That theory, upon which the Commerce Clause issue in *Hudson County* was decided, was rejected by the district court in *City of Altus*. In expressly overruling *Geer* three years ago, this Court traced the demise of the public ownership theory and definitively recast it as " 'but a fiction expressive in legal shorthand of the importance to its people that a State have power to preserve and regulate the exploitation of an important resource.' " *Hughes v. Oklahoma*, 441 U.S. 322, 334 (1979) (quoting *Toomer v. Witsell*, 334 U.S. 385, 402 (1948)). In *Hughes* the Court found the State's interests insufficient to sustain a ban on the interstate transfer of natural minnows seined from waters within the State.

tween points within the State, no matter how distant; for example, from Wilbarger County to El Paso County, Texas. Obviously, the statute had little relation to the cause of conservation." 255 F. Supp., at 839–840.

* * * Appellee, and the *amici curiae* that are vitally interested in conserving and preserving scarce water resources in the arid Western States, have convincingly demonstrated the desirability of state and local management of ground water. But the States' interests clearly have an interstate dimension. Although water is indeed essential for human survival, studies indicate that over 80% of our water supplies is used for agricultural purposes. The agricultural markets supplied by irrigated farms are worldwide. They provide the archetypical example of commerce among the several States for which the Framers of our Constitution intended to authorize federal regulation. The multistate character of the Ogallala aquifer—underlying appellants' tracts of land in Colorado and Nebraska, as well as parts of Texas, New Mexico, Oklahoma, and Kansas—confirms the view that there is a significant federal interest in conservation as well as in fair allocation of this diminishing resource. Cf. *Arizona v. California*, 373 U.S. 546 (1963).

The Western States' interests, and their asserted superior competence, in conserving and preserving scarce water resources are not irrelevant in the Commerce Clause inquiry. Nor is appellee's claim to public ownership without significance. Like Congress' deference to state water law, these factors inform the determination whether the burdens on commerce imposed by state ground water regulation are reasonable or unreasonable. But appellee's claim that Nebraska ground water is not an article of commerce goes too far: it would not only exempt Nebraska ground water regulation from burden-on-commerce analysis, it also would curtail the affirmative power of Congress to implement its own policies concerning such regulation. If Congress chooses to legislate in this area under its commerce power, its regulation need not be more limited in Nebraska than in Texas and States with similar property laws. Ground water overdraft is a national problem and Congress has the power to deal with it on that scale.

II

Our conclusion that water is an article of commerce raises, but does not answer, the question whether the Nebraska statute is unconstitutional. For the existence of unexercised federal regulatory power does not foreclose state regulation of its water resources, of the uses of water within the State, or indeed, of interstate commerce in water. Determining the validity of state statutes affecting interstate commerce requires a more careful inquiry:

> "Where the statute regulates evenhandedly to effectuate a legitimate local public interest, and its effects on interstate commerce are only incidental, it will be upheld unless the burden imposed on such commerce is clearly excessive in relation to the putative local benefits. If a legitimate local purpose is found, then the question becomes one of degree. And the extent of the burden that will be tolerated will of course depend on the nature of the local interest involved, and on whether it could be promoted as well with a lesser impact on interstate activities." *Pike v. Bruce Church, Inc.*, 397 U.S. 137, 142 (1970).

The only purpose that appellee advances for § 46–613.01 is to conserve and preserve diminishing sources of ground water. The purpose is unquestionably legitimate and highly important, and the other aspects of Nebraska's ground water regulation demonstrate that it is genuine. Appellants' land in Nebraska is located within the boundaries of the Upper Republican Ground Water Control Area, which was designated as such by the Director of the Nebraska Department of Water Resources based upon a determination "that there is an inadequate ground water supply to meet present or reasonably foreseeable needs for beneficial use of such water supply." Neb. Rev. Stat. § 46–658(1). Pursuant to § 46–666(1), the Upper Republican Natural Resources District has promulgated special rules and regulations governing ground water withdrawal and use. * * *

The State's interest in conservation and preservation of ground water is advanced by the first three conditions in § 461613.01 for the withdrawal of water for an interstate transfer. Those requirements are "that the withdrawal of the ground water requested is reasonable, is not contrary to the conservation and use of ground water, and is not otherwise detrimental to the public welfare." Although Commerce Clause concerns are implicated by the fact that § 46–613.01 applies to interstate transfers but not to intrastate transfers, there are legitimate reasons for the special treatment accorded requests to transport ground water across state lines. Obviously, a State that imposes severe withdrawal and use restrictions on its own citizens is not discriminating against interstate commerce when it seeks to prevent the uncontrolled transfer of water out of the State. An exemption for interstate transfers would be inconsistent with the ideal of evenhandedness in regulation. At least in the area in which appellants' Nebraska tract is located, the first three standards of 46–613.01 may well be no more strict in application than the limitations upon intrastate transfers imposed by the Upper Republican Natural Resources District.

Moreover, in the absence of a contrary view expressed by Congress, we are reluctant to condemn as unreasonable measures taken by a State to conserve and preserve for its own citizens this vital resource in times of severe shortage. Our reluctance stems from the "confluence of [several] realities." *Hicklin v. Orbeck*, 437 U.S. 518, 534 (1978). First, a State's power to regulate the use of water in times and places of shortage for the purpose of protecting the health of its citizens—and not simply the health of its economy—is at the core of its police power. For Commerce Clause purposes, we have long recognized a difference between economic protectionism, on the one hand, and health and safety regulation, on the other. Second, the legal expectation that under certain circumstances each State may restrict water within its borders has been fostered over the years not only by our equitable apportionment decrees, 353 U.S. 953 (1957), but also by the negotiation and enforcement of interstate compacts. Our law therefore has recognized the relevance of state boundaries in the allocation of scarce water resources. Third, although appellee's claim to public ownership of Nebraska ground water cannot justify a total denial of federal regulatory power, it may support a limited preference for its own citizens in the utilization of the resource. In this regard, it is relevant that appellee's claim is logically more substantial than claims to public ownership of other natural resources. Finally, given appellee's conservation efforts, the continuing availability of ground water in Nebraska is not simply happenstance; the natural resource has some indicia of a good publicly produced and owned in which a State may favor its own citizens in times of shortage. See *Reeves, Inc. v. Stake*, 447 U.S. 429 (1980). A facial examination of the first three conditions set forth in § 46–613.01 does not, therefore, indicate that they impermissibly burden interstate commerce. Appellants, indeed, seem to concede their reasonableness.

Appellants, however, do challenge the requirement that "the state in which the water is to be used grants reciprocal rights to withdraw and transport ground water from that state for use in the State of Nebraska"— the reciprocity provision that troubled the Chief Justice of the Nebraska Supreme Court. Because Colorado forbids the exportation of its ground water,[17] the reciprocity provision operates as an explicit barrier to commerce between the two States. The State therefore bears the initial burden of demonstrating a close fit between the reciprocity requirement and its asserted local purpose.

The reciprocity requirement fails to clear this initial hurdle. For there is no evidence that this restriction is narrowly tailored to the conservation and preservation rationale. Even though the supply of water in a particular well may be abundant, or perhaps even excessive, and even though the most beneficial use of that water might be in another State, such water may not be shipped into a neighboring State that does not permit its water to be used in Nebraska. If it could be shown that the State as a whole suffers a water shortage, that the intrastate transportation of water from areas of abundance to areas of shortage is feasible regardless of distance, and that the importation of water from adjoining States would roughly compensate for any exportation to those States, then the conservation and preservation purpose might be credibly advanced for the reciprocity provision. A demonstrably arid state conceivably might be able to marshall evidence to establish a close means-end relationship between even a total ban on the exportation of water and a purpose to conserve and preserve water. Appellee, however, does not claim that such evidence exists. We therefore are not persuaded that the reciprocity requirement—when superimposed on the first three restrictions in the statute—significantly advances the State's legitimate conservation and preservation interest; it surely is not narrowly tailored to serve that purpose. The reciprocity

---

17. Colo.Rev.Stat. § 37–90–136 provides as follows:

"For the purpose of aiding and preserving unto the state of Colorado and all its citizens the use of all ground waters of this state, whether tributary or nontributary to a natural stream, which waters are necessary for the health and prosperity of all the citizens of the state of Colorado, and for the growth, maintenance, and general welfare of the state, it is unlawful for any person to divert, carry, or transport by ditches, canals, pipelines, conduits, or any other manner any of the ground waters of this state, as said waters are in this section defined, into any other state for use therein."

requirement does not survive the "strictest scrutiny" reserved for facially discriminatory legislation.

III

Appellee's suggestion that Congress has authorized the States to impose otherwise impermissible burdens on interstate commerce in ground water is not well-founded. The suggestion is based on 37 statutes in which Congress has deferred to state water law, and on a number of interstate compacts dealing with water that have been approved by Congress.

* * * Neither the fact that Congress has chosen not to create a federal water law to govern water rights involved in federal projects, nor the fact that Congress has been willing to let the States settle their differences over water rights through mutual agreement, constitutes persuasive evidence that Congress consented to the unilateral imposition of unreasonable burdens on commerce. In the instances in which we have found such consent, Congress' " 'intent and policy' to sustain state legislation from attack under the Commerce Clause" was " 'expressly stated.' "

* * *

■ Justice Rehnquist, with whom Justice O'Connor joins, dissenting.

* * *

In my view, [the] cases appropriately recognize the traditional authority of a State over resources within its boundaries which are essential not only to the well-being, but often to the very lives of its citizens. In the exercise of this authority, a State may so regulate a natural resource so as to preclude that resource from attaining the status of an "article of commerce" for the purposes of the negative impact of the Commerce Clause. It is difficult, if not impossible, to conclude that "commerce" exists in an item that cannot be reduced to possession under state law and in which the State recognizes only a usufructuary right. "Commerce" cannot exist in a natural resource that cannot be sold, rented, traded, or transferred, but only *used*.

* * *

NOTES

1.   How would you advise a state that was intent on prohibiting exports to go about drafting legislation that will pass constitutional muster? What changes in state law may be necessary?

2.   Nebraska has a long history of confining rights to groundwater to overlying land in the state. See Chadd v. Lower Platte South Natural Resources Dist., 261 Neb. 90, 621 N.W.2d 299 (2001). But the state subsequently amended its law to allow interstate transfers. In evaluating an application for an interstate transfer permit, the Director of the Department of Water Resources considers: (1) whether the proposed use is beneficial; (2) the availability to the applicant of alternative surface and groundwater resources; (3) any negative effects of the withdrawal on the ability of surface and groundwater supplies in the area to meet reasonable future demands; and (4) other relevant factors. NEB. REV. STAT. § 46–613.01 (1999). A cross-border permit denial was challenged in Ponderosa Ridge LLC v. Banner County, 250 Neb. 944, 554 N.W.2d 151 (1996). The court admitted that the statute applied only to interstate uses but concluded that "when compared with the regulation of intrastate uses of groundwater, the overall regulation relevant to this litigation is evenhanded." 554 N.W.2d at 165. See generally Richard S. Harnsberger et al., *Interstate Transfers of Water: State Options After Sporhase*, 70 Neb. L. Rev. 754 (1991).

3.   The Supreme Court continues to subject state statutes that prohibit the export or import of resources to a high level of scrutiny. However, narrow seams of opportunity still exist. The Court has distinguished water export prohibitions from statutes prohibiting the import of hazardous wastes because water is essential to survival. Oregon Waste Systems v. Department of Environmental Quality, 511 U.S. 93, 114 S.Ct. 1345, 128 L.Ed.2d 13 (1994). And in Maine v. Taylor, 477 U.S. 131, 106 S.Ct. 2440, 91 L.Ed.2d 110 (1986) the Court upheld Maine's ban on imported baitfish. The Court accepted Maine's ecological argument that imported baitfish would expose native fish to the risk of parasites. Only Justice Stevens concluded that the state had not met of its burden of proving that non-discriminatory alternatives existed to meet its environmental concerns. See generally Donald Regan, *The Supreme Court and State Protectionism: Making Sense of the Dormant Commerce Clause*, 84 Mich. L. Rev. 1091 (1986).

Recall Georgia's claim that she has riparian rights in the Tennessee River, page 977, *supra*. Suppose that the Supreme Court ultimately decides to leave the 1818 boundary in place, given all the boundary adjustments that would follow from a contrary ruling. Georgia claims that the river has sufficient excess capacity to supply the Atlanta metro area. When the Atlanta Regional Commission approached Chattanooga's water supplier about purchasing water from the Chickamauga, the Tennessee legislature passed the Interbasin Transfer Act to block the sale. TENN.CODE.ANN. §§ 69–7–201 et seq. (2001). What are Atlanta and Georgia's options? Is Georgia still entitled to a share of the Tennessee River if several of its Tributaries arise in Georgia? If she is, to how much is she entitled? The negotiations over the Upper Colorado River Basin Compact are instructive. See Charles J. Meyers, The Colorado River, 19 Stan. L. Rev. 1, 27–34 (1966). If Georgia is not entitled to an equitable share of the river, does *Sporhase* compel Tennessee to sell water to Atlanta? If so, must Tennessee sell Atlanta all the "surplus" water in the system? Are any of the factors that would be used in an equitable apportionment relevant to decide Tennessee's Dormant Commerce Clause obligations?

4.   *New Mexico's Attempts to Prevent Exports to Texas.* Justice Stevens' opinion in *Sporhase* offers states some hope that interstate transfer restrictions and perhaps even prohibitions will be found constitutional in arid states. New Mexico immediately tried to exploit this "window of opportunity" in its efforts to stave off a "water raid" by El Paso, Texas, and the ensuing litigation remains the most important post-*Sporhase* case law. El Paso has historically obtained most of its water supplies from an interstate aquifer, the Hueco Bolson, underlying New Mexico and Texas. El Paso estimated that by 2010 the aquifer would become too salty for a primary water supply. After considering various alternatives, the city decided to augment its supplies from two aquifers that support agricultural uses in adjacent New Mexico. The city filed under New Mexico law to appropriate water in two designated underground basins in the southwestern part of the state. That law, since repealed, prohibited the transfer of water out of the state, and the state engineer denied the applications. N.M. STAT. ANN. § 72–12–19 (repealed 1983). The statute was challenged by El Paso as unconstitutional. New Mexico attempted to defend by showing that it was a "demonstrably arid state" where water was needed for human survival and the restriction was needed to prevent a long-term, statewide shortage for all users. Evidence was produced to show that the state as a whole would have a 626,000 acre-foot shortage by 2020, but the district court would not buy this reading of *Sporhase:* "Outside of fulfilling human survival needs, water is an economic resource." El Paso v. Reynolds, 563 F.Supp. 379 (D.N.M.1983).

New Mexico then repealed its flat export prohibition and enacted a statute that required permits for water exports. It provided that:

> In order to approve an application under this act, the state engineer must find that the applicant's withdrawal and transportation of water for use outside the state would not impair existing water rights, is not contrary to the conservation of water within the state and is not otherwise detrimental to the public welfare of the citizens of New Mexico.
>
> D. In acting upon an application under this act, the state engineer shall consider, but not be limited to, the following factors:
>
> (1) the supply of water available to the state of New Mexico;
>
> (2) water demands of the state of New Mexico;
>
> (3) whether there are water shortages within the state of New Mexico;
>
> (4) whether the water that is the subject of the application could feasibly be transported to alleviate water shortages in the state of New Mexico;
>
> (5) the supply and sources of water available to the applicant in the state where the applicant intends to use the water; and
>
> (6) the demands placed on the applicant's supply in the state where the applicant intends to use the water.

N.M. STAT. ANN. § 72–12–1.

The statute was challenged by El Paso. A federal court rejected two of the city's arguments that the statute discriminated against interstate commerce but accepted the third. El Paso v. Reynolds, 597 F.Supp. 694 (D.N.M.1984) (*El Paso II*). El Paso first argued that the "conservation within the state" standard prohibited all transfers because, by definition, exported water cannot be conserved or kept within the state. The court reasoned that "water within the state" did not mean that all water must be retained in-state. It further found that because the state had a tradition of public interest review for in-state uses, "it cannot be concluded that the conservation and public welfare criteria are on their face meaningless as applied to in-state uses." Id. at 699. El Paso next argued that the "public welfare of the citizens of New Mexico" standard was intrinsically discriminatory and precluded even-handed regulation of water use. The court's rejection of this argument was quite different from its conclusion in *El Paso I:*

> New Mexico need not wait until the appropriate time and place of shortage arises to enact a statute limiting exports. The State may enact a law to provide for future contingencies. If facially valid, any constitutional attack on such a statute for violation of the Commerce Clause must await its application.

Id. at 701.

In 1986, a statewide study recommended that New Mexico take a new approach to controlling exports. It concluded that the state should enter the intrastate and interstate water markets directly as a market participant by engaging in large-scale state appropriations of unappropriated groundwater. Water Resources Research Institute and University of New Mexico Law School, State Appropriation of Unappropriated Groundwater: A Strategy for Insuring New Mexico a Water Future (1986).

Recall Justice Stevens' citation of Reeves, Inc. v. Stake, 447 U.S. 429, 100 S.Ct. 2271, 65 L.Ed.2d 244 (1980), in *Sporhase.* In that case, the state of South Dakota, which had owned a cement plant since 1919, responded to the excess demand for cement created by a regional construction boom by giving in-state purchasers preference over out-of-state purchasers. A Wyoming ready-mix distributor, who had purchased cement from South Dakota for twenty years before being denied service in 1978, challenged the preference as unconstitutional. The Court held that the decision to prefer in-state residents in the sale of state-produced goods did not violate the Commerce Clause because the state was acting in a proprietary capacity and "[t]here is no indication of a constitutional plan to limit the abilities of the states themselves to operate freely in a free market." The Supreme Court continues to adhere to the market participation doctrine. White v. Massachusetts Council of Constr. Employers, Inc., 460 U.S. 204, 103 S.Ct. 1042, 75 L.Ed.2d 1 (1983); College Savings Bank v. Florida Prepaid Postsecondary Education Expense Board, 527 U.S. 666, 119 S.Ct. 2219, 144 L.Ed.2d 605 (1999).

After ten years of litigation, El Paso settled the case by withdrawing its claims to New Mexico groundwater. In exchange, El Paso received the cooperation of New Mexico to conduct regional water studies to be coordinated through a joint commission with members from El Paso and New Mexico. More generally, the litigation changed El Paso's water strategy from the traditional sole reliance on new supplies to a regional, more economically rational approach. El Paso has developed a regional strategy to augment its water use by utilizing Texas-based water resources. The strategy: (1) increased the capacity of its well field along the Rio Grande; (2) implemented water conservation programs; (3) increased access to additional Bureau of Reclamation Rio Grande Project surface water; and (4) clarified water rights through adjudication of the Rio Grande from the New Mexico line to the Fort Quitman gauging station. See A. Dan Tarlock & Darcy Alan Frownfelter, *State Groundwater Sovereignty After Sporhase: The Case of the Hueco Bolson*, 43 Okla. L. Rev. 27 (1990). Texas now estimates the recoverable groundwater in its share of the Hueco Bolson, which it fought so hard to expand into New Mexico, will be depleted by 2025. To cope with growth in a chronically water short area, El Paso has implemented a more aggressive conservation strategy, including a seasonal excess use rate structure. This inverted rate structure charges users a charge based on the customers' percentage use above their average winter consumption. See Octavio E. Chavez, *Mining of Internationally Shared Aquifers: The El Paso–Juarez Case*, 40 Nat. Resources J. 1299 (2000). Cross-border cooperation is essential for an effective conservation strategy. Mexico has a centralized water allocation law that includes groundwater. Ley de Aguas Nacionales, D.O. 1 de Diciembre de 1992 translated in Mexico: Environmental Laws and Norms (2001).

5. *Slurry Pipelines.* The power of a state to prevent interstate transfers of water arose in connection with proposals during the 1970s to transport Rocky Mountain coal to other areas of the country through coal slurry pipelines. Slurry is composed of roughly equal parts of pulverized coal and water. A slurry pipeline is an efficient means of transporting coal, but western states feared that the water requirements for several projected pipelines could hamper agricultural production. Environmentalists suggested that the pumping necessary to supply the pipelines' demands could damage groundwater reserves in the Northern Great Plains. See Nancy T. Reed, Comment, *An Analysis of Technical and Legal Issues Raised By the Development of Coal Slurry Pipelines,* 13 Houston L. Rev. 528 (1976). Some states have responded to these concerns by restricting the use of appropriated water outside the state. Wyoming prohibits the use of water in amounts greater than 1000 acre-feet per year for coal slurry pipelines outside the state "without the specific prior approval of the legislature." WYO. STAT. ANN. § 41–3–115(B). Oklahoma bars use of Oklahoma water for slurry pipelines "within or through" the state. OKLA. STAT. ANN. § 7.6. Louisiana prohibits slurry use unless it is administratively determined not to be detrimental to water supply in the exporting area. LA. REV. STAT. ANN. § 723F. The tension between state and federal interests in waters available for slurry pipelines is discussed in Clyde O. Martz & Stanley L. Grazis, *Interstate Transfers of Water and Water Rights—The Slurry Issue,* 23 Rocky Mtn. Min. L. Inst. 33 (1977).

In 1982, the state of South Dakota granted a permit to the ETSI Pipeline Company for consumptive use of 50,000 acre-feet of water per year from the 23 million acre-foot Oahe Reservoir located on the mainstream of the Missouri River in South Dakota. ETSI intended to use the water to transport coal by slurry pipeline from Wyoming to the Gulf Coast. ETSI also obtained a water service contract from the Bureau of Reclamation and a pumping permit from the Army Corps of Engineers, federal agencies charged with managing Oahe, and other projects on the Missouri. The proposal first met a state court challenge. Then the downstream states of Iowa, Missouri, and Nebraska brought a lawsuit in federal district court in Nebraska to block the diversion from Lake Oahe. The issue, then, was whether Congress intended Oahe Reservoir to be a reclamation facility subject to the water marketing authority of the Secretary. The Supreme Court found that the Secretary of Interior lacked authority under the 1944 Flood Control Act to make a contract allowing the state to use (and sell) water for industrial purposes, and thus held the contract void. ETSI v. Missouri, 484 U.S. 495, 108 S.Ct. 805, 98 L.Ed.2d 898 (1988). The Missouri Basin is operated under the Flood Control Act of 1944, 33 U.S.C.A. §§ 701–709 (Pick–Sloan Act), under which the development of the upper basin of the Missouri River was undertaken. Large reservoirs were authorized by the legislation for multiple purposes. See generally, John Thorson, River of Promise, River of Peril: The Politics of Managing the Missouri (1994). Most benefits flowed to the lower basin in the form of flood control and navigation enhancement, while the upper basin states and tribes got a string of recreation reservoirs and hydroelectric power, but little increased acreage under irrigation. See generally, John P. Guhin, *The Law of the Missouri*, 30 S.D. L. Rev. 347 (1985). Today, the focus of interstate disputes on the Missouri is shifting from efforts to increase upper basin consumptive use to the partial restoration of the river's pre-dam hydrograph. See National Research Council, The Missouri River Ecosystem: Exploring the Prospects for Recovery (2002) and pages 855–858, *supra*.

6.   Can a state decide to sell its compact allocation to another state? Upper Colorado River Basin states, which still have unused entitlements, have resisted this notion. See Simms & Davis, Water Transfers Across State Systems, Rocky Mountain Mineral Law Inst. 22–1 (1985). How would you respond to the argument put forth in anti-trust litigation in South Dakota growing out of the failure of a coal slurry pipeline project in the 1980s. After the pipeline project was abandoned, South Dakota, which wanted to sell Oahe Reservoir water to the pipeline, sued the Kansas City Southern Railroad for conspiring to block the pipeline through the railroad's extensive intervention in numerous environmental and water proceedings, thus interfering with the contract South Dakota had with the pipeline. One of Kansas City Southern's arguments was that South Dakota had no water to transfer for out of state use. As the railroad put it in its brief appealing from a $600,000,000.00 judgment that South Dakota won in 1988:

> Two key principles governing [equitable apportionment] are (1) that only citizens of states with natural access to an interstate water source may make the claim to that source and (2) that existing uses at the time of apportionment are accorded a high level of protection.... These principles of equitable apportionment require the prohibition of interstate, interbasin transfers. Water transfers outside a basin—prior to apportionment and absent the consent of all basin states—deprive

citizens of their natural right to an interstate stream. Recipients of out of basin water will build up equities ... [that] will undermine the principle of natural access.

Brief of Kansas City Southern Railroad in Janklow et al. v. Kansas City Southern Industries, Inc. (Civil No. 83–5046, United States Circuit Court of Appeals for the Eighth Circuit, 1988). Compare Olen Paul Matthews and Michael Pease, *The Commerce Clause, Interstate Compacts, and Interstate Boundaries*, 46 Nat. Resources J. 601 (2006), who argue that interstate transfers are consistent with the doctrine of equitable apportionment and that compacts should be construed to allow them unless there is an express prohibition.

NOTE: THE GREAT LAKES—A CASE STUDY IN DIVERSION POLICY MAKING

The five Great Lakes contain approximately one-fifth of the world's freshwater resources, but despite the amount of water available for consumptive use—most of which is currently dedicated to in situ uses—proposals to divert water out of the lakes and out of the Great Lakes Basin have generated a great deal of controversy and some creative legal responses. Some water is taken from the lakes, but the amounts are small by western standards. In fact, transbasin diversions into the lake exceed out of basin diversions. Existing consumptive uses have lowered the lakes by at most 2.4 inches. See International Joint Commission, Protection of the Waters of the Great Lakes (Final report to the Governments of Canada and the United States 2000). Relatively small diversions, however, can have potentially serious system-wide impacts, in part because the lake levels naturally fluctuate between one and two feet; global climate change may result in even lower average levels. Navigation and recreation suffer substantially when water levels drop.

Proposals to divert water from the lakes either by pipeline or by tanker have triggered strong anti-export responses among the eight basin states, the provinces of Ontario and Quebec, and the governments of the United States and Canada. Current diversion "fears" take place against the long history of legal opposition to Chicago's diversion from Lake Michigan, which remains the major transbasin diversion in the entire Great Lakes system. To prevent infectious disease outbreaks, Chicago reversed the flow scheme of the Chicago River and sent its sewage into the Mississippi Basin instead of into Lake Michigan. It also modified the Des Plaines River, the Calumet River, and dug other major drainage canals. These manipulations of nature set off the litigation between Illinois and the United States, and later between Illinois and her sister states (and Canada). Ultimately, the federal government refused to issue a permit for an additional canal after the Corps of Engineers expressed concern about the effects of Chicago's planned diversions on lake levels. The basic conclusion of government studies was that small changes in lake levels could cause several different types of injury to navigation including exposure of wooden docks and wharves to rot, the need for additional dredging, as well as decreased cargo loadings. Recreational shoreline property also suffered potential damage from exposed and often rocky lake beds.

The federal government's basic position was that the diversions were within the exclusive power of Congress to control under a predecessor to the Rivers and Harbors Act of 1899 which made "any obstruction to the navigable capacity" of water subject to federal jurisdiction. *United States v. Rio Grande Dam & Irrigation Co.*, 174 U.S. 690, 708, 19 S.Ct. 770, 43 L.Ed. 1136 (1899). The littoral states asserted that ownership of the Great Lakes entitled them to "have the waters of the Great Lakes and their connecting waters maintained at their normal and natural level." Herbert H. Nanjoks, *The Chicago Diversion Controversy*, 30 Marg. L. Rev. 228, 259 (1947).

The other Great Lakes states began a parallel original equitable apportionment action to stabilize lake levels after Illinois increased lake diversions, even after the Secretary of the Army refused to issue the necessary permits. The gist of the littoral states' argument was that the Chicago diversion violated their right to the natural lake level. In Wisconsin v. Illinois, 278 U.S. 367, 49 S.Ct. 163, 73 L.Ed. 426 (1929), the Court entered a decree ordering the restoration of the navigable capacity of the lakes. The decision rests primarily on federal supremacy, but principles of equitable apportionment are also involved. The Great Lakes states argued that any transbasin diversion is unconstitutional, but the Court based its decision primarily on Illinois' persistent refusal to abide by the federal government's decision to limit diversions that would impede the navigable capacity of the lake. The decree was reopened following a drought in 1955–56. *Wisconsin v. Illinois*, 388 U.S. 426, 87 S.Ct. 1774, 18 L.Ed.2d 1290 (1967). Ironically, in light of the current efforts to prevent all discharges of pollution into the lakes, Wisconsin wanted to ensure that Chicago's reclaimed sewage was put back into the lake. See Illinois v. Milwaukee, 406 U.S. 91, 92 S.Ct. 1385, 31 L.Ed.2d 712 (1972); Milwaukee v. Illinois, 451 U.S. 304, 101 S.Ct. 1784, 68 L.Ed.2d 114 (1981). The net result was that the total diversions were capped. Chicago continued to exceed its allocation and in 1996, the state of Illinois agreed to make up the excess diversions by 2019.

In the 1980s, fears that there may be plans to divert water from Lake Superior to reduce overdraft from the Ogallala aquifer in the central plains states, and a Canadian scheme to take water from James Bay into Lake Huron for export to western provinces and states triggered another chapter in the law of the Great Lakes. Instead of litigation, the basin states and the provinces of Ontario and Quebec signed the Great Lakes Charter. The Charter is neither an interstate compact nor international treaty. It commits the governors and premiers of the basin to monitor existing and future diversions, pass state or provincial legislation to regulate diversions in excess of two million gallons per day, and to notify all other states and provinces of any new or increased diversion over five million gallons per day. In 1986, Congress authorized any governor to veto a proposed out-of-basin diversion. Water Resources Development Act of 1986, 42 U.S.C.A. § 1926d–20. Congress has the power to authorize state legislation that would otherwise violate the dormant Commerce Clause. The Court has not suggested any limitations on this power that would restrain congressional approval of Great Lakes protective efforts, except that the power must be express. New England Power Co. v. New Hampshire, 455 U.S. 331, 102 S.Ct. 1096, 71 L.Ed.2d 188 (1982). Great Lakes diversions which harm either Canada or the United States are also controlled by the 1909 Boundary Waters Treaty between Great Britain (now Canada) and the United States.

Under the Charter, two small communities in Ohio and Wisconsin obtained approval for small diversions. The Charter also played a role in stopping a proposal by the Governor of Illinois to increase the Chicago diversion during a 1988 drought in order to lift grain barges on the Illinois and Mississippi rivers. See Maureen Irish, *Canadian Practice in International Law*, 27 Can. Y. B. Int'l L. 407–409 (1989). In 1999, there was another round of diversion fears. A Canadian company expressed interest in transporting Great Lakes waters by tanker to the Middle East or another water-short area. In addition, a memorandum prepared for the Council of Great Lakes Governors suggested that the Water Resources Development of Act of 1986 violated the non-delegation doctrine and was not a sufficiently clear waiver of the dormant Commerce Clause. The basin states responded with proposed federal legislation and Charter Annex 2001. The report is a strong statement of the environmental and social values of the lakes at the their current levels and provides the basis for a legal regime premised on natural lake level maintenance.

The new federal legislation, Water Resources Development Act of 2000 Section 504, directed the states, in cooperation with the two Canadian provinces, "to develop and implement a mechanism that provides a common conservation standard embodying the principles of water conservation and resource improvement for making decisions concerning the withdrawal and use of water from the Great Lakes Basin." In 2001, the Great Lakes Governors and the Premiers of Ontario and Quebec adopted Annex 2001 which committed them to pursuing a binding agreement "to protect, conserve, restore, improve, and manage use of the Waters and Water–Dependent Natural Resources of the Great Lakes Basin." In 2005, the eight Great Lakes Governors signed the Great Lakes–St. Lawrence Basin Sustainable Water Resources Agreement.

The compact was approved by Congress in 2008. Public Law 110–342, 122 Stat. 3739 (2008). Canadian nationalist greens pushed for a strong anti-diversion regime by stoking the traditional fear that the United States is always poised to grab and export all of Canada's natural resources, including its abundant clean water, to support strong federal and provincial anti-diversion legislation. In the United States, the continued erosion of political power of the Great Lakes region, as the nation's population drifts south and west, provided the necessary urgency for the eight states to maintain the Lakes as a functioning ecosystem in a way that they hope will be difficult to change as the Basin's federal political power erodes. See Noah D. Hall, *Toward a New Horizontal Federalism: Interstate Water Management in the Great Lakes Region*, 77 U. Colo. L. Rev. 405 (2006); Peter Annin, Great Lakes Water Wars (2006); Joseph Dellapenna, *International law's Lessons for the Law of the Lakes*, 40 U. Mich. J. L. Reform 747 (2007); A. Dan Tarlock, *The Great Lakes as an Environmental Heritage of Humankind: An International law Perspective*, 40 U. Mich. J. L. Reform 995 (2007); and Christine Klein, *The Law of the Lakes From Protectionism to Sustainability*, 2006 Mich. St. L. Rev. 1259 (2007).

The two agreements virtually prohibit all diversions from a Great Lakes sub-watershed to a watershed outside of the Great Lakes watershed. A limited exception potentially allows inter-basin transfers for communities located just outside the watershed, which is a narrow band in some states, but it will be difficult to invoke. Parallel legislation exists in Canada. In 2002, Canada enacted a law which prohibits virtually all diversions from her portion of the Great lakes either by traditional conveyances or bulk tanker transport, and Ontario and Quebec promised to adopt parallel legislation. International Boundary Waters Treaty A 20. ct, R.S. c 1. The Compact divides withdrawals into four major categories. New and increased diversions, which are defined as transfers of water outside the Great Lakes basin or between the watersheds of one lake to another, are prohibited subject to limited exceptions. Great Lakes–St. Lawrence River Basin Water Resources Compact § 4.8 (approved 2008). New or increased intra-basin withdrawals under 100,000 gallons per day over a 90 day period are regulated only by the jurisdiction where they originate. Id. at § 4.9(2)(a). Proposed intra-basin uses between 100,000 and 5,000,000 gallons over a 90 day period must meet stringent basin-wide standards such as return flow requirements and a showing that there is no reasonable available alternative water supply. Id. at § 4.9(2)(b). Withdrawals over 5,000,000 gallons over a 90 day period must meet the same standards and are subject to regional review. Id. at § 4.9(1)(c). The only inter-basin transfers allowed are those for cities or counties that straddle the Basin.

Recall that the 2000 Water Resources Development Act included resource improvement standards. The requirement to improve the waters and water dependent natural resources appears to have come from the Clean Water Act's section 404 wetlands mitigation program, which allows developers to drain natural wetlands if they build new, artificial ones. It also comes from the two Ohio and Wisconsin diversions which were conditioned on the promise that they cause no net loss to the lakes. The final version of the Compact dropped an earlier resource improvement standard. There was great concern, especially in Canada, that the resource improvement standard "commodified" the Lakes and would pave the way for diversions and bulk water transport.

NOTE: EXPORT RESTRICTIONS AND INTERNATIONAL TRADE LAW

Are national water export prohibitions illegal under international trade law? In considering proposals to allow bulk sales of water from the Great

Lakes, some international trade experts, especially in Canada, have opined that Article XI of the General Agreement on Tariffs and Trade (GATT) and the North American Free Trade Agreement (NAFTA) invalidate all flat export bans. Article XI outlaws "prohibitions other than duties, taxes or other charges" on exports and imports, but Article XX(g) allows a state to defend an export ban that is necessary to conserve exhaustible natural resources. The conclusion that nations lack the power to prevent the export of water is based on several World Trade Organization (WTO) decisions which have rejected the conservation defense when a nation has attempted to conserve marine resources outside of its territory. GATT Dispute Settlement Panel Report on U.S. Restrictions on Imports of Tuna, Sept. 1, 1991, GATT, B.S.I.D. (39th Supp.) 155 and GATT Dispute Settlement Panel Report on U.S. Restrictions on Imports of Tuna, July, 1994, 33 I.L.M. 839 (1994).

Subsequent WTO appellate decisions have qualified Article XX further by holding that export restrictions must not only fall within the enumerated list in Article XX but they must also be consistent with the "chapeau" which provides that "such measures are not to be applied in a manner which would constitute a means of arbitrary or unjustifiable discrimination between countries where the same conditions appear, or a disguised restriction on international trade." World Trade Organization Appellate Body Report, United States Standards for Reformulated and Conventional Gasoline, 35 I.L.M. 603 (1996); World Trade Organization Appellate Body Report, United States Import Prohibitions of Certain Shrimp and Shrimp Products, WT/DS58/AB/R (1998). See David Driesen, *What is Free Trade: The Real Issue Lurking Behind the Trade and Environment Debate*, 41 Va. J. Int'l L. 279 (2001). However, the Shrimp–Turtle decision limited its holding to the United States' failure to justify the application of different standards to different exporting countries and acknowledged the right of WTO members to preserve their environmental resources. A 2000 decision upheld an import ban for the first time on environmental grounds. WTO Dispute Settlement Panel Report on E.C. Measures Affecting Asbestos and Asbestos Containing Products, 2000 WL 1449942 (Sept. 18, 2000).

Does traditional water conservation management violate the fundamental premise of trade law that all trade partners be treated in a non-discriminatory manner? Do either GATT or NAFTA change the basic principle that state sovereignty allows a state to decide whether or not to allow trade in raw natural resources? The threshold questions are whether water is a product or good for purposes of trade law and whether water is an "exhaustible resource" under Article XX(g). See generally Isabel Dendauw, The Great Lakes Region and Bulk Water Export: Issues of International Trade in Water, 25 Water International 565 (2000). GATT does not define "product," although the term is generally defined as a creation, commodity, produce, or end-result. Consistent with this understanding, in 1993, the three NAFTA countries agreed that:

> [t]he NAFTA creates no rights to natural water resources of any party * * * unless water, in any form, has entered into commerce and

become a good or product. And nothing in NAFTA would oblige a NAFTA party to either exploit its water for commercial use, or to begin exporting water in any form. Water in its natural state in lakes, rivers, reservoirs, aquifers, water basins, and [the] like is not a good or product, is not trade, and therefore is not and never has been subject to the terms of any trade agreement.

A. Dan Tarlock, Law of Water Rights and Resources § 11.14 1, n20 (1988, with Annual Updates). See generally Scott Philip Little, *Canada's Capacity to Control the Flow: Water Export and the North American Free Trade Agreement*, 8 Pace Int'l L. Rev. 127 (1996).

A leading international environmental lawyer, Edith Brown–Weiss, argues that raw or bulk water should not be a GATT or NAFTA good:

it is essential to consider that water is different from other resources. It is a unique resource.... Thus, it would be prudent to adopt an approach of 'anticipatory caution', to strike the appropriate balance between the need to conserve water resources and the need to ensure a level playing field in trade relationships. Anticipatory caution means that in the face of uncertainty about the future, a country should be able to exercise its full sovereignty to maintain its fresh water resources without having to convince the trade community of the legitimacy of its actions.

Edith B. Weiss, *Water Transfers and International Trade Law*, in Fresh Water and International Economic Law 61, 83 (Edith B. Weiss et al. eds., 2005).

Efforts to block exports may also be attacked as illegal expropriations. Customary international law and Chapter 11 of NAFTA allow investors to sue for damages caused by state regulatory decisions. Chapter 11 is especially powerful because it applies to both direct and indirect expropriations and measures "tantamount to nationalization or expropriation," Article 1110(1), and this article has been applied to environmental regulation. *Metalclad Corporation v. United Mexican States,* Award, Case No. ARB (AF)/97/1 (August 30, 2000). In 2005, a group of Texas irrigators brought a Chapter 11 claim against Mexico for its admitted failure, starting in 1992, to honor its Rio Grande Treaty delivery obligations during periods of drought. The basis of the claim was that flowing surface water was a "good" under NAFTA and that favoring Mexican over Texan users violated the equal national treatments provisions of Chapter 11. Mexico moved to dismiss the action because Chapter 11 applies only to investments made in the country which takes the allegedly NAFTA illegal action. The United States State Department filed a brief agreeing with this position, and in 2007 the tribunal dismissed the claim and ruled that Chapter 11 does not apply to investments "wholly confined to their own national states" and that the treaty does not give Texas water right holders a property right in water in Mexican streams because the water belongs to Mexico even though she is under a treaty obligation to deliver it to Texas users. The irrigators are pursuing the Chapter 11 appeal process which allows review in the courts of the neutral NAFTA party, in this case Canada. In 2005, the

United States and Mexico agreed to the terms for the repayment of the deficits. See Gregory F. Szydlowski, *The Commodification of Water: A Look at Canadian Bulk Water Exports, the Texas Water Dispute, and the Ongoing Battle Under NAFTA for Control of Water Resources*, 18 Colo. J. Int'l Envtl. L. & Pol'y 665 (2007).

C. INTERNATIONAL WATER ALLOCATION LAW

Rivers often form or cross national boundaries, and aquifers often straddle two or more countries. For example, the United States shares important aquifers, lakes, and rivers with Canada and Mexico and consequently has had considerable experience with the shared use and management of surface international waters. Thus, international issues are an inseparable part of domestic issues involving international rivers. The Colorado, Columbia, and the Rio Grande rivers are allocated by treaty and there is a complex management regime for the Great Lakes. The tradition of shared groundwater use is much less developed. Even though transboundary water issues involving Canada, Mexico, and the United States are primarily addressed in the context of specific treaties, underlying these is the evolving customary international law of the non-navigational uses of international watercourses. The state practice of the three countries has played an important role in the development of modern international water law. See Albert E. Utton, Part IX, International Waters, in 5 Waters and Water Rights 31–42 (1998).

International water law's importance for the United States is increasing as new water management issues that are not adequately addressed in the existing treaty regimes arise and as the provision of irrigation and domestic water supplies becomes more privatized throughout the world. This section is designed to introduce the student to the basic principles and procedures of international water law. Consistent with our primary focus on the Colorado River to illustrate many of the issues of interstate water allocation we do so in the context of a Mexico–United States water-related environmental issue that is not addressed in the existing treaty regime. Below is a 1999 Report on the environmental degradation of the Colorado River Delta in Mexico caused by upstream dams and diversions in Mexico and the United States. What role, if any, can international water law play in the allocation of international rivers as well as the role, if any, that it might play in promoting environmentally sustainable water use?

Daniel F. Luecke et al., A Delta Once More: Restoring Riparian and Wetland Habitat in the Colorado River Delta

Environmental Defense Fund Report 4–6, 13–20 (1999).

The Delta Today—A Contemporary Geography

* * *

Although the Colorado basin drains 244,000 square miles, including 2000 square miles in northern Mexico, most of its water does not reach the delta. During the twentieth century, river flows into the delta have been reduced nearly 75 percent, from an annual average between 1896 to 1921 of 16.7 million acre-feet (maf), to an annual average between 1984 and 1999 of 4.2 maf. This reduction in water has resulted in major changes to the delta: less silt, fewer nutrients, higher salinity, and higher concentrations of pollutants. Erosion—rather than accretion—is now the dominant physical process in the delta, a highly unusual condition for a river delta. Like other river deltas at risk, such as the Nile's, the Colorado's delta has actually begun to decrease in size.

The loss of freshwater flows to the delta over the past century has reduced delta wetlands to about 5 percent of their original extent, and nonnative species have compromised the ecological health of much of what remains. Stress on ecosystems also has allowed invasive plants to choke out native species along Colorado River riparian areas. Native forests of cottonwood and willow have yielded to sand and mudflats dominated by the nonnative tamarisk (also known as salt cedar), arrowweed, and iodinebush, a transformation that has decreased the habitat value of the riparian forest.

* * *

Nevertheless, despite its diminished state, the delta plays a significant ecological role that goes far beyond its bounds. For migratory birds, the delta is a key stop-over along the Pacific Flyway, and it supports large numbers of wintering waterfowl. Although resident and migratory bird densities have not been studied extensively, the delta is considered a key element of the flyway, and the only significant fresh-water wetland among the Mexican Pacific Coast marshes. Species under threat elsewhere in the Colorado basin still find refuge in the delta, which is also home to the largest known populations of two endangered species, the desert pupfish and the Yuma clapper rail. Delta marshes still have the capacity to provide nursery habitat for marine life that, in turn, supports other marine life across the entire upper Gulf.

Significant riparian areas and wetlands include:

- riparian areas along the Colorado River from the border to the delta (82,000 acres, which have recovery potential, in part because gallery forests of cottonwood and willow have shown a capacity for self-restoration during recent floods);

- the Rio Hardy/Rio Colorado wetlands, an area that fluctuates with floods and was recently measured at 23,719 acres, in the western delta near the confluence of the Rio Hardy and the Colorado, supported by flows from the Rio Hardy and Colorado River flood flows;

- about 20,000 acres of intertidal wetlands, which can be found up to 34 miles upstream from the Gulf supported by high tides; and

- la Ciénega de Santa Clara, a wetland in the eastern delta that was unintentionally created by agricultural return flows from the U.S. and Mexico that arrive via drainage canals, and the adjacent El Doctor and El Indio wetlands, both of which are supported by artesian springs—these wetlands encompass some 44,000 acres.

* * *

Tides and Floods

Two sources of water—tides and floods—continue to sustain parts of the delta much as they have for centuries. Tides are a daily given in the delta, and the topography of the long and narrow Gulf creates an exceptionally high tidal swing of 10 feet or greater at its northern end. This allows high tides to flow more than 34 miles inland in some places and spread over a total of 81,500 acres. Tides have sustained vast areas of the delta through the last several decades, although without freshwater flows to dilute the seawater, tides can have a deleterious effect as well.

Since 1980, floods have once again reached the delta, though they are no longer a guaranteed springtime occurrence as they once were. The Colorado's system of dams can regulate much of the variation between wet and dry years, but extraordinarily wet years will probably continue to bring flooding to the delta when releases exceed the capacity of users in the United States and Mexico to divert the water. Since the filling of the Colorado River's reservoirs, these releases have reestablished an active floodplain from Morelos Dam [Mexico's diversion point at the border] to the tidal zone in the Gulf of California.

Near-record flood releases in the winter of 1983 were at first considered an aberrant event, but occasional flooding has continued, coinciding with El Niño events. From 1980 to 1993, average annual flood flows across the border (cross-border flows minus Mexico's treaty allotment) were 3.9 maf. This is nearly three times Mexico's 1.5 maf treaty allotment, and 25 percent of the historic flow into the delta before dam construction. The largest releases occurred in the early 1980's, with flows after 1986 more sporadic and smaller in volume. In 1997–1998, flows exceeding 1.5maf were released to the delta.

These floods are significant, sustaining the delta's ecosystems through the periodic inundation of its riparian areas and wetlands. * * *

Given the apparent importance of floods, one possible way to support delta ecosystems would be to deliberately manage flood releases for maximum benefit. Water management agreements on the Colorado River include provisions for allocating water under shortage and surplus flow conditions. These agreements could be revised to ensure that a portion of surplus flood flows are stored for, or delivered to, water-dependent ecosystems in amounts and rates, and at times, that would be most beneficial.

Agricultural Wastewater

Delta wetlands with significant conservation interest also survive on agricultural wastewater. Seventeen agricultural drains from the Mexicali

Valley flow into the Rio Hardy/Colorado River system, carrying an average annual volume of 51,000 acre-feet. Another 125,000 acre-feet of mildly saline agricultural wastewater pumped from Arizona's Wellton–Mohawk Irrigation District is delivered to Mexico at the Southern International Boundary. This water is disposed in the eastern delta after traveling 48 miles in a concrete canal called the Main Outlet Drain Extension (MODE). MODE water joins about 25,000 acre-feet of agricultural wastewater * * * to support la Ciénega de Santa Clara.

* * *

Agricultural wastewater can change ecosystem health since it tends to affect the concentration of pollutants, salts, and minerals. High levels of selenium, for example, are found in many delta areas that receive wastewater, and selenium is known to affect birds and other wild-life. Although agricultural wastewater has been a fairly constant source for la Ciénega de Santa Clara, over the years the MODE canal has carried less water and its salinity has declined. This is due to lower pumping rates and lower groundwater salinity. Wastewater flows from the Mexicali Valley annually carry 70,000 tons of fertilizer and 110,000 gallons of insecticide. While agricultural wastewater may not be an ideal source of water, its benefits may, for the present, outweigh its liabilities, particularly since there are few other potential sources for restoring delta ecosystems.

* * *

The Delta's Ecological Significance

Productivity and diversity in the delta have declined over the last century, but the delta ecosystem remains an important biological resource nevertheless. It remains an oasis of life in the midst of the arid Sonoran Desert. Although reduced flows and the construction of levees have transformed the delta, floodwaters, agricultural drainage, municipal wastewater, and seawater in the tidal zone continue to support large riparian areas and marshes. The size of these areas tends to vary dramatically from one season to the next * * * In 1997, flood releases reestablished native vegetation along the delta's Colorado River floodplain and riparian zones as well as in southeastern delta wetlands.

The delta supports a variety of wildlife, including several threatened and endangered species. Mexico's Environmental Regulations on Endangered Species lists the following endangered species found in the terrestrial and aquatic regions of the delta:

- the desert pupfish, also listed as an endangered species in the U.S.— the largest remaining population anywhere is in La Ciénega de Santa Clara;

- the Yuma clapper rail, also listed as an endangered species in the U.S.;

- the bobcat;

- the vaquita porpoise, the world's smallest marine mammal, listed as a species of special concern by the U.S. Marine Mammal Commission; and

- the totoaba, now virtually extinct, a steel-blue fish that grows up to seven feet and 300 pounds, and once supported a commercial fishery that closed in 1975.

In addition, Mexico lists five threatened species: the yellow-footed gull, Heermann's gull, elegant tern, red-dish egret, and peregrine falcon; three species for special protection: the brant, house finch, and mockingbird; and one rare species: the great blue heron.

Although not extensively studied, the delta's significance for migratory birds is indisputable, as it is the principle freshwater marsh in the region. From 1980 to 1985, some 45,000 ducks and 200 geese wintered in the delta. A 1992 winter survey found more than 160,000 birds in the delta * * *.

* * *

Delta wetlands provide habitat for a number of mammals, including raccoons, skunks, bats, coyotes, bobcats, muskrats, rabbits, jackrabbits, desert rats, gophers, and squirrels.

The tidal zone and near shore marine habitats of the Gulf of California also support endangered species and important fisheries. Fish species include catfish, carp, tilapia, mullet, and largemouth bass, and the last remaining populations of desert pupfish, which still survive in backwaters and lagoons. The delta is a negative estuary (where the salinity is greater than the ocean's due to evaporation that exceeds precipitation and river flow) that is a rich breeding ground for marine species and has a significant influence on fish populations, possibly throughout the entire Gulf. Reduction of freshwater flows into the Gulf has reduced the transport of nutrients and changed the characteristics of this critical nursery habitat. * * * The shrimp fishery has dropped off steeply and other fisheries are in decline. The totoaba is now virtually extinct, and the vaquita porpoise is thought to number only a few hundred.

The loss of upper Gulf fisheries may be the most costly effect of reduced flows to the delta. Over fishing certainly contributes to the problem, but scientists have noted a correlation between shrimp catches and flood flows to the delta. This corroborates anecdotal evidence and reports from local fishermen that indicate trends such as a temporary increase in the number of fish species observed in the mid–1980's after high flood flows reached the delta.

* * *

Flood Flows and Water Requirements of Delta Vegetation

Water deliveries below Morelos Dam since 1980 have been extremely variable in frequency and volume. * * *

Since 1980, there have been two prolonged periods with-out flow: a four-year period from 1988 to 1993, and a three-year period from 1994 to 1997. However, the 1997 inspection showed cottonwood and willow trees dating back to both the 1980's and 1993 flow events. It appears that germination correlates with flood flows. * * * Apparently, delta riparian vegetation can survive a period of several years without water deliveries from the United States, once flood flows have allowed the seeds to germinate.

* * * [A]nnual volume releases totaling 260,000 acre-feet in winter and spring are sufficient to produce a vegetation response in summer. * * *

Based on these observations, it is apparent that irregular flows since 1980 have contributed to revegetation of the floodplain despite three-to-four-year intervals of no cross-border flows. * * *

NOTES

1. Does the United States as an upstream state owe any duty to Mexico to provide a share of the necessary restoration flows? Conversely, can an upstream state use all the water originating within its borders to the complete detriment of downstream states? There is no clear answer to the first question, but the widespread assumption in the international water community is that the answer to the second is no.

In 1895, Justin Harmon, the United States Attorney General, asserted that the United States did not have to share the Colorado River with Mexico, but the so-called "Harmon Doctrine" has been repudiated in practice. See Stephen C. McCaffrey, *The Harmon Doctrine: One Hundred Years Later: Buried Not Praised*, 36 Nat. Res. J. 549 (1996). The United States Supreme Court's rejection of the principle of absolute territorial sovereignty between states and the adoption of a rule of limited territorial sovereignty is the foundation of the doctrine of equitable apportionment, and similarly international water law rests on the principle that absolute territorial sovereignty is unfair and inequitable. Equitable apportionment equally rejects the absolute territorial sovereignty principle, which largely benefits upstream states, and the natural flow principle, which would benefit downstream states.

2. The United States abandoned the principle of absolute territorial sovereignty when it agreed to the 1944 United States–Mexico Treaty guaranteeing Mexico 1,500,000 acre-feet per year. See *supra*, p. 962. In addition, the Trail Smelter Arbitration (United States v. Canada 1941), 3 U.N.R.I.A.A. 1938 (1949), which is the foundation of modern international environmental law, applied the Supreme Court's common law pollution cases to hold that "no State has a right to use or permit the use of its territory in such a manner as to cause injury * * * in or to the territory of another or the properties or persons therein, when the case is of serious consequence and the injury is established by clear and convincing proof."

Modern international water law thus starts from the premise that all riparian states have a duty to share the use of international waters. One of the central projects of international water law is to promote the fair and equitable distribution of scarce resources and to curb excessive, unilateral use projects that threaten to foreclose opportunities in other states.

Dante Caponera, The Role of Customary International Water Law, in Water Resources Policy for Asia 365, 385 (Mohammed Ali ed. 1985) asserts that international water law rests on three key principles:

1. All riparians have a right to an equitable and reasonable share of international rivers.

2. Each riparian has a duty not to cause substantial injury—both as to quantity and quality—to other riparian states.

3. Each state has a duty to inform other affected states of water development plans and projects that violate the first two rules and to engage in good faith negotiations to mitigate the injuries.

Nevertheless, absolute rather than limited territorial sovereignty is often the real practice among states, without regard to the interests of co-riparians,. The following are among the best works on international water law: F.J. Berber, Rivers in International Law (1959); The Law of International Drainage Basins (Albert H. Garretson et al. eds. 1968); Johan G. Lammers, Pollution of International Watercourses (1984); Codification and Progressive Development of International Water Law: The Work of the International Law Commission of the United Nations (Patricia Wouters ed. 2008); and Slavako Bogdanovic, International Law of Water Resources: Contribution of the International Law Association (2001). Ludwik A. Teclaff, *The Checkered Development of International Water Law: Fiat or Custom*, 31 Nat. Resources J. 45 (1991) is a useful introduction to the subject.

3. At the time of the 1944 Treaty there was little national, let alone international, consciousness or concern about the environmental harms that result from depleting rivers. Owen McIntyre, Environmental Protection of International Watercourses Under International Law (2007). As discussed *supra* pp. ___–___, much of the work of modern water law is restoration of natural environments damaged or lost because of the damming and diverting of rivers. This has forced modifications of water use rights that were once considered vested and immutable. But cf. Alam, An Examination of the International Environmental law Governing the Proposed Indian river-Linking Project and an Appraisal of its Ecological and Socio–Economic Implications for Lower Riparian Countries, 19 Geo. Int'l Envtl. L. Rev. 209 (2007) who argues that optimum development does not require the maintenance of environmental flows because water flowing to the sea is waste. Can the United States rely entirely on the 1944 quantification of its obligations to Mexico from the Colorado River?

Compare the United States' response to Mexico's outcry when the salinity of the water delivered under the treaty became so severe that it was essentially useless for irrigation. Ultimately, the treaty obligation was modified by a "minute" added to the treaty that caps the salinity levels of water delivered to Mexico. See *supra* p. 1014. The United States may be moving toward a similar response to the newly realized environmental consequences of its diversions of Colorado River water. In 2001, the two countries agreed to Minute 306 to the Treaty. Although it merely creates a framework for bilateral studies of technical issues and options for ensuring water for ecological purposes in the Delta, the minute may be the first step in efforts to ensure protection of the Delta's ecosystems. Kevin C. Wheeler et al., Alternatives to Restoring the Colorado River Delta, 47 Nat. Resources J. 917 (2007), examines the impacts of proposed changes in the operation of the American reach of the River on Delta flows and analyzes the impacts of Lake Mead releases and water transfers on the "Law of the River" and existing water users.

The most recent and authoritative formulation of allocation rules for international rivers is the United Nations Convention on the Law of the Non–Navigational Uses of International Watercourses. See generally Shlomi Dinar, International Water Treaties: Negotiation and Cooperation Among Transboundary Rivers (2008); Stephen McCaffrey, The Law of International Watercourses (2007); Attila Tanzi & Maurizio Arcari, The United Nations Convention on the Law of International Water Courses (2001), and Stephen C. McCaffrey & Mpazi Sinjela, *The 1997 United Nations Convention on International Watercourses*, 92 Am. J. Int'l L. 98 (1998).

Convention on the Law of the Non–Navigational Uses of International Watercourses

U.N. Doc. A/51/869, 36 I.L.M. 700, 700–711 (1997).

On May 21, 1997, by Resolution 51/229, the UN General Assembly adopted the Convention on the Law of Non-navigational Uses of International Watercourses, by a vote of 103 in favor to 3 against, with 27 abstentions.

* * *

Article 1

Scope of the present Convention

1. The present Convention applies to uses of international watercourses and of their waters for purposes other than navigation and to measures of protection, preservation and management related to the uses of those watercourses and their waters.

* * *

Article 2

Use of terms

For the purposes of the present Convention:

(a) "Watercourse" means a system of surface waters and groundwaters constituting by virtue of their physical relationship a unitary whole and normally flowing into a common terminus;

* * *

Article 3

Watercourse agreements

1. In the absence of an agreement to the contrary, nothing in the present Convention shall affect the rights or obligations of a watercourse State arising from agreements in force for it on the date on which it became a party to the present Convention.

2. Notwithstanding the provisions of paragraph 1, parties to agreements referred to in paragraph 1 may, where necessary, consider harmonizing such agreements with the basic principles of the present Convention.

3. Watercourse States may enter into one or more agreements, hereinafter referred to as "watercourse agreements", which apply and adjust the provisions of the present Convention to the characteristics and uses of a particular international watercourse or part thereof.

* * *

Article 5

Equitable and reasonable utilization and participation

1. Watercourse States shall in their respective territories utilize an international watercourse in an equitable and reasonable manner. In particular, an international watercourse shall be used and developed by watercourse States with a view to attaining optimal and sustainable utilization thereof and benefits therefrom, taking into account the interests of the watercourse States concerned, consistent with adequate protection of the watercourse.

* * *

Article 6

Factors relevant to equitable and reasonable utilization

1. Utilization of an international watercourse in an equitable and reasonable manner within the meaning of article 5 requires taking into account all relevant factors and circumstances, including:

(a) Geographic, hydrographic, hydrological, climatic, ecological and other factors of a natural character;

(b) The social and economic needs of the watercourse States concerned;

(c) The population dependent on the watercourse in each watercourse State;

(d) The effects of the use or uses of the watercourse in one watercourse State on other watercourse States;

(e) Existing and potential uses of the watercourse;

(f) Conservation, protection, development and economy of use of the water resources of the watercourse and the costs of measures taken to that effect;

(g) The availability of alternatives, of comparable value, to a particular planned or existing use.

2. In the application of article 5 or paragraph 1 of this article, watercourse States concerned shall, when the need arises, enter into consultations in a spirit of cooperation.

3. The weight to be given to each factor is to be determined by its importance in comparison with that of other relevant factors. In determining what is a reasonable and equitable use, all relevant factors are to be considered together and a conclusion reached on the basis of the whole.

Article 7

Obligation not to cause significant harm

1. Watercourse States shall, in utilizing an international watercourse in their territories, take all appropriate measures to prevent the causing of significant harm to other watercourse States.

2. Where significant harm nevertheless is caused to another watercourse State, the States whose use causes such harm shall, in the absence of agreement to such use, take all appropriate measures, having due regard for the provisions of articles 5 and 6, in consultation with the affected State, to eliminate or mitigate such harm and, where appropriate, to discuss the question of compensation.

Article 8

General obligation to cooperate

1. Watercourse States shall cooperate on the basis of sovereign equality, territorial integrity, mutual benefit and good faith in order to attain optimal utilization and adequate protection of an international watercourse.

* * *

Article 9

Regular exchange of data and information

1. Pursuant to article 8, watercourse States shall on a regular basis exchange readily available data and information on the condition of the watercourse, in particular that of a hydrological, meteorological, hydrogeo-

logical and ecological nature and related to the water quality as well as related forecasts.

* * *

Article 10

Relationship between different kinds of uses

1. In the absence of agreement or custom to the contrary, no use of an international watercourse enjoys inherent priority over other uses.

2. In the event of a conflict between uses of an international watercourse, it shall be resolved with reference to articles 5 to 7, with special regard being given to the requirements of vital human needs.

* * *

Article 12

Notification concerning planned measures with possible adverse effects

Before a watercourse State implements or permits the implementation of planned measures which may have a significant adverse effect upon other watercourse States, it shall provide those States with timely notification thereof.

* * *

Article 20

Protection and preservation of ecosystems

Watercourse States shall, individually and, where appropriate, jointly, protect and preserve the ecosystems of international watercourses.

Article 21

1. For the purpose of this article, "pollution of an international watercourse" means any detrimental alteration in the composition or quality of the waters of an international watercourse which results directly or indirectly from human contact.

2. Watercourse States shall, individually and, where appropriate, jointly, prevent, reduce and control the pollution of an international watercourse that may cause significant harm to other disputes.

3. Watercourse States shall, at the request of any of them, consult with a view to arriving at mutually agreeable measures and methods to prevent, reduce and control pollution of an international watercourse, such as:

    (a) Setting joint water quality objectives and criteria;

    (b) Establishing techniques and practices to address pollution from point and non-point sources:

(c) Establishing lists of substances the introduction of which into the waters of an international watercourse is to be prohibited, limited, investigated or monitored.

Article 22

Introduction of alien or new species

Watercourse States shall take all measures necessary to prevent the introduction of species, alien or new, into an international watercourse which may have effects detrimental to the ecosystem of the watercourse resulting in significant harm to other watercourse States.

NOTES

1. Is environmental degradation "pollution" under Article 7? Article 7 initially enjoined states to use water "in such a way as not to cause appreciable harm to other watercourse states," but two objections surfaced that led to a major revision. The final version of Article 7 was changed in the United Nations General Assembly prior to adoption to accord equitable utilization a strong preference over the no-harm doctrine. See Charles B. Bourne, *The Primacy of the Principle of Equitable Utilization in the 1997 Watercourses Convention,* 1997 Can. Y.B. of Int'l Law. 215, 221–24 (1997); Charles B. Bourne, *The International Law Commission's Draft Articles on the Law of International Water Courses: Principles and Planned Measures,* 3 Colo. J. Int. L. & Pol'y 65 (1992). Proponents of multiple use development criticized the Article 7 standard, which was an application of the *Trail Smelter Arbitration* (U.S. v. Canada), U.N. 3 R.I.A.A. 1905 (1941), as a departure from the common understanding of equitable apportionment because it subordinated development to environmental quality. The ILC defended the standard on the ground that the use of a watercourse that caused appreciable harm to another state was not an equitable use of an international watercourse. For a history of the evolution of Article 7, see Edith Brown Weiss et al., International Environmental Law and Pol'y 875–80 (1998). As adopted, Article 7 is a victory for slower developing states. Do you understand why? See Stephen C. McCaffrey, *A Human Right to Water: Domestic and International Implications,* 5 Geo. Int'l. Envtl. L. Rev. 1, 12 (1993) and Aaron Schwabach, *The United Nations Convention on the Law of International Watercourses, Customary International Law, and the Interests of Developing Upper Riparians,* 33 Tex. Int'l. L.J. 257 (1998).

2. What claims might Mexico assert under the Convention concerning the Delta?

3. Assume that it can be credibly established that flows in the Colorado River average approximately 1,000,000 acre-feet less per year due to global climate change. Does international water law provide a basis to distribute this burden. Article X of the United States–Mexico Treaty of 1944, provides that the United States does not have to fulfill its 1,500,000 delivery obligation in case of "an extraordinary drought." Would a global climate change-induced shortage be an extraordinary drought? See generally Joseph W. Dellapenna, *Adapting the Law of Water Management to Global Climate Change and Other Hydrological Stresses*, 55 J. Am. Water Res. Ass'n 1301 (1999); A. Dan Tarlock, *How Well Can International Water Allocation Regimes Adapt to Global Climate Change*, 15 Fla. St. Land Use & Envtl. L. 423 (2000); Greta Goldenman, *Adapting to Climate Change: A Study of International Rivers and Their Legal Arrangements*, 17 Ecology L.Q. 741 (1990).

4. The Lac Lanoux Arbitration, (Spain v. France), 12 U.N.R.I.A.A. 281 (1957) held that Spain could not object to France's decision to construct a hydroelectric plant which would raise the level of a transboundary lake because Spain, although concerned about the possibility that future irrigation projects would be foreclosed, had not established any damage and had no customary right to veto the project. If a state does not have a right to pre-dam flow, does international water law provide any basis for a downstream state to claim a minimum flow? See Albert Utton, *The International Law of Minimum Stream Flows*, 10 Colo. J. Int'l Envtl. L. & Pol'y 7 (1999). See generally Andre Nollkaemper, *The Contribution of the International Law Commission to International Water Law: Does It Reverse the Flight From Substance*, 28 Neth. Y.B. of Int'l Law 39 (1996); Jutta Brunnee & Stephen J. Toope, *Environmental Security and Freshwater Resources: A Case for International Ecosystem Law*, 5 Y.B. of Int'l Envtl. L. 41 (1995).

5. The success of any revised flow regime intended to restore a degraded aquatic ecosystem will be uncertain. In the case of the Mexican Delta preliminary evidence suggests that large continuous flows of water are not necessary to support the Delta's remaining riparian habitats. Conservation and restoration might only require the delivery of small amounts of annual flows plus occasional pulses from existing Colorado River surpluses, and the maintenance of existing agricultural waste flows. On other rivers, more regular yearly flow regimes may be necessary. Existing users will often invoke scientific uncertainty as an excuse for not providing additional water. Proponents of restoration will invoke the precautionary principle to argue that the success of a restoration experiment need not be guaranteed before it is undertaken. This much contested principle is one of the foundations of international environmental law. The precautionary principle posits that nations have a right (if not a duty) to take measures to prevent harm in advance of conclusive scientific evidence of the cause of the harm or that the harm is occurring. This broad formulation needs to be refined for specific applications. Questions such as the allocation of the burden of proof and the degree of scientific information about the potential future harm necessary to trigger the principle remain unanswered. See Harold Hohmann, Precautionary Legal Duties and Principles of Modern International Environmental Law (1994) and James Hickey & Vern Walker, *Refining the Precautionary Principle in International Environmental Law*, 14 Va. Envtl. L.J. 423 (1995). The application of the precautionary principle was raised in a case concerning the Gabicikovo–Nagymoros Project, *infra*, but it was not applied.

6. In addition to the United Nations Convention, the rules adopted by the International Law Association, an organization somewhat analogous to the American Law Institute, are an important source of non-binding allocation standards. In 2006, the ILA adopted the Berlin Rules on Water Resources. International Law Association, Revision of the Helsinki Rules on the Use of the Water of International Rivers, report of the Fifty–Second ILA Conference, Berlin (2006). The Rules reaffirm the principle that riparian states have "a multi-factor right to the equitable utilization of shared rivers, but they impose greater ecosystem protection duties compared the Helsinki Rules and the 1997 United Nations Convention on the Non–Navigable Uses of International Watercourses." See Owen McIntyre, The Role of Customary Rules and Principles of International Environmental Law in the Protection of Shared International Freshwater Resources, 46 Nat. Resources J. 157 (2006). The Rules recognize the right of international drainage basin states to participate in the management of the resource "in an equitable, reasonable and sustainable manner" and impose a duty of good faith cooperation on all states. Indigenous peoples and other vulnerable communities are singled out for a specific protection. In addition to the establishment of water pollution protection regimes, states must take "all appropriate steps" to protect the interests of these groups when a river is developed. All appropriate measures must also be taken "to protect the ecological integrity necessary to sustain ecosystems dependent on particular waters." Art. 22. A rigorous environmental impact process must be undertaken before undertaking activities with adverse environmental or sustainable development impacts, Art. 28, as recommended by the Report of the World Commission on Dams, Dams and Development (2000).

7. Recall the definition of "groundwater" in Article 2 of the United Nations Convention, *supra* p. 1057. The Convention is limited to shared groundwater systems hydrologically linked to surface waters. The United Nations International Law Commission has prepared draft rules for aquifers not covered by the Convention. See Gabriel E. Eckstein, *Commentary on the U.N. International Law Commission's Draft Articles on the Law of Transboundary Aquifers*, 18 Colo. J. Int'l Envtl. L. & Pol'y 537 (2007) and Gabriel Eckstein and Y. Eckstein, *A Hydrological Approach to Transboundary Ground Water Resources and International Law,* 19 Am. U. Int'l L. Rev. 201 (2003).

Case Concerning The Gabcikovo–Nagymaros Project (Hung. v. Slovakia)

1997 I.C.J. 7, at 39–45 (Sept. 25).

[In 1977 at the height of the Cold War, Hungary and what was then Czechoslovakia signed a joint river basin investment treaty for the construction of the multiple-purpose Gabcikovo–Nagymaros hydroelectric, navigation improvement, and flood control lock and dam project on the Danube River between Bratislava and Budapest. See generally Paul R. Williams, *International Environmental Dispute Resolution: The Dispute Between Slo-*

vakia and Hungary Concerning Construction of the Gabcikovo and Nagymaros Dams, 19 Colum. J. Envtl. L. 1 (1994). Article 14 of the 1977 Treaty provided that the two countries would ensure that the contemplated Gabcikovo bypass canal and hydroelectric plant to be built in Czechoslovakian territory did not impair the flow of the Danube for navigation. During the 1980s, the project became controversial in Hungary for economic and environmental reasons. By the Spring of 1989, the Gabcikovo dam was 85 percent complete and the bypass canal was between 60 and 95 percent complete; Hungary, however, had only constructed the coffer dam for its promised downstream Nagymaros Dam. Hungary unilaterally suspended work on the project in 1989 and one year later suspended the treaty as a "mistake" after she broke away from the then Soviet Union. The possible ecological risks raised by Hungary included the replacement of Danube groundwater flow with stagnant upstream reservoir water, the silting of the Danube, eutrophication, and the threat to aquatic habitats from peaking power releases. After the 1993 division of the two countries, Slovakia continued to implement an alternative solution formulated by Czechoslovakia which involved a dam and diversion solely on her territory. Hungary unilaterally terminated the Treaty in 1992 and justified its 1989 suspension as an "ecological state of necessity."

The International Court of Justice decided the respective states' rights under the 1977 treaty but did not directly apportion the Danube's flow or seek to apply new emerging principles of international environmental law. To justify termination, Hungary invoked a number of familiar contract defenses, including impossibility and changed circumstances, and asserted that the emerging precautionary principle imposed an obligation to prevent damage and thus precluded her continued performance of the treaty. To defend its suspension, she argued that a "state of necessity" existed.]

50.   In the present case, the Parties are in agreement in considering that the existence of a state of necessity must be evaluated in the light of the criteria laid down by the International Law Commission in Article 33 of the Draft Articles on the International Responsibility of States ["State Responsibility"] that it adopted on first reading. That provision is worded as follows:

"Article 33. State of Necessity

1.   A state of necessity may not be invoked by a State as a ground for precluding the wrongfulness of an act of that State not in conformity with an international obligation of the State unless:

   (a) the act was the only means of safeguarding an essential interest of the State against a grave and imminent peril; and

   (b) the act did not seriously impair an essential interest of the State towards which the obligation existed.

2.   In any case, a state of necessity may not be invoked by a State as a ground for precluding wrongfulness: * * *

(c) if the State in question has contributed to the occurrence of the state of necessity." (*Yearbook of the International Law Commission*, 1980, Vol. II, Part 2, p. 34.)

In its Commentary, the Commission defined the "state of necessity" as being the situation of a State whose sole means of safeguarding an essential interest threatened by a grave and imminent peril is to adopt conduct not in conformity with what is required of it by an international obligation to another State (ibid., para. 1) * * *

51. The Court * * * observes * * * that [the state of necessity] can only be accepted on an exceptional basis. * * *

[According to the Commission, the state of necessity can only be invoked under certain strictly defined conditions which must be cumulatively satisfied; and the state concerned is not the sole judge of whether those conditions have been met.]

52. In the present case, the following basic conditions set forth in Draft Article 33 are relevant; it must have been occasioned by an "essential interest" of the State which is the author of the act conflicting with one of its international obligations; that interest must have been threatened by a "grave and imminent peril"; the act being challenged must have been the "only means" of safeguarding that interest; that act must not have "seriously impaired an essential interest" of the State towards which the obligation existed; and the State which is the author of that act must not have "contributed to the occurrence of the state of necessity." Those conditions reflect customary international law.

The Court will now endeavor to ascertain whether those conditions had been met at the time of the suspension and abandonment, by Hungary, of the works that it was to carry out in accordance with the 1977 Treaty.

53. The Court has no difficulty in acknowledging that the concerns expressed by Hungary for its natural environment in the region affected by the Gabcikovo–Nagymaros Project related to an "essential interest" of that State, within the meaning given to that expression in Article 33 of the Draft of the International Law Commission.

The Commission, in its Commentary, indicated that one should not in that context, reduce an "essential interest" to a matter only of the "existence" of the State, and that the whole question was, ultimately, to be judged in the light of the particular case; at the same time, it included among the situations that could occasion a state of necessity, "a grave danger to . . . the ecological preservation of all or some of [the] territory [of a State]" (ibid., p. 35, para. 3); and specified, with reference to State practice, that "It is primarily in the last two decades that safeguarding the ecological balance has come to be considered an 'essential interest' of all States." (Ibid., p. 39, para. 14).

The Court recalls that it has recently had occasion to stress, in the following terms, the great significance that it attaches to respect for the environment, not only for States but also for the whole of mankind:

the environment is not an abstraction but represents the living space, the quality of life and the very health of human beings, including generations unborn. The existence of the general obligation of States to ensure that activities within their jurisdiction and control respect the environment of other States or of areas beyond national control is now part of the corpus of international law relating to the environment.

Legality of the Threat or Use of Nuclear Weapons, Advisory Opinion, I.C.J. Reports 1996, pp. 241–242, para. 29.

54. The verification of the existence, in 1989, of the "peril" invoked by Hungary, of its "grave and imminent" nature, as well as of the absence of any "means" to respond to it, other than the measures taken by Hungary to suspend and abandon the works, are all complex processes.

As the Court has already indicated * * *, Hungary on several occasions expressed, in 1989, its "uncertainties" as to the ecological impact of putting in place the Gabcikovo–Nagymaros barge system, which is why it asked insistently for new scientific studies to be carried out.

The Court considers, however, that serious though these uncertainties might have been they could not, alone, establish the objective existence of a "peril" in the sense of a component element of a state of necessity. The "peril" certainly evokes the idea of "risk"; that is precisely what distinguishes "peril" from material damage. But a state of necessity could not exist without a "peril" duly established at the relevant point in time; the mere apprehension of a possible "peril" could not suffice in that respect. It could moreover hardly be otherwise, when the "peril" constituting the state of necessity has at the same time to be "grave" and "imminent." "Imminence" is synonymous with "immediacy" or "proximity" and goes far beyond the concept of "possibility." As the International Law Commission emphasized in its commentary, the "extremely grave and imminent" peril must "have been a threat to the interest at the actual time" (Yearbook of the International Law Commission, 1980, Vol. II, Part 2, p. 49, para. 33). That does not exclude, in the view of the Court, that a "peril" appearing in the long term might be held to be "imminent" as soon as it is established, at the relevant point in time, that the realization of the peril, however far off it might be, is not thereby any less certain and inevitable.

The Hungarian argument on the state of necessity could not convince the Court unless it was at least proven that a real, "grave" and "imminent peril" existed in 1989 and that the measures taken by Hungary were the only possible response to it. * * *

57. The Court concludes * * * that, with respect to both the Nagymaros and Gabcikovo, the perils invoked by Hungary, without prejudging their possible gravity, were not sufficiently established in 1989, nor were they "imminent"; and that Hungary had available to it at that time means of responding to these perceived perils other than the suspension and abandonment of works with which it had been entrusted. What is more, negotiations were under way which might have led to a review of the Project and the extension of some of its time-limits, without there being

need to abandon it. The Court infers from this that the respect by Hungary, in 1989, of its obligations under the terms of the 1977 Treaty would not have resulted in a situation "characterized so aptly by the maxim *summun jus summa injuria*" * * *.

Post–Judgment Developments

Slovakia was unable to convince the Court to order Hungary to complete the project because she also breached the treaty. The court held that Slovakia's alternative, which temporarily diverted 90 percent of the River's flow, violated the Treaty regime that contemplated joint not unilateral actions. Slovakia's territorial alternative was an illegal diversion under customary international water law because she deprived "Hungary of its right to an equitable and reasonable share of the natural resources of the Danube * * *." In the end, the Court voted thirteen to two that the two states must undertake good faith negotiations consistent with both international environmental norms such as sustainable development and the law of international water courses to come up with a new management scheme in the context of the already constructed projects in Slovakia.

Since 1997, the two countries have carried on extensive technical negotiations, but the project continues to generate great controversy. Hungary proposed a reconfigured Nagymaros dam or the construction of a substitute dam in the newly created Danube–Ipoly National Park. After massive 1998 demonstrations in Budapest, the Hungarian government postponed signing an agreement until a full environmental assessment of proposed projects was done. In December of 1999, Hungary proposed that Slovakia divert the Danube back to its original course in the region that borders Slovakia. In return, Hungary would waive its right to its allocation of power from the Gabcikovo/Bos power station. Between 2004 and 2005, the parties attempted to negotiate a settlement, but the case remains on the IJC docket. In March 2008, Hungary filed a submission which, inter alia, accused Slovakia of violating the treaty by its attempts to sell the Gabcikovo Dam in 2000 and prayed for a reversal of the 1997 judgment.

The Danube Bend is not the only threatened stretch of this historic river. At the mouth, the biologically rich Delta is threatened by the Ukraine's construction of a canal to the Black Sea. The Delta is both a Ramsar Convention designated wetland and UNESCO World Heritage, but protests by Romania and international environmental NGOs have been unsuccessful. See A. Dan Tarlock, Possible Lessons from a Comparison of the Restoration of the Danube and Colorado Deltas, 19 Pacific McGeorge Global Business & Develop. J. 61 (2006) for a discussion of the possible legal objections to the canal.

NOTE: WATER ALLOCATION IN THE MIDDLE EAST

One of the most bitter water disputes in the world centers on the use of the limited resources of the Jordan River among Israel, Jordan, and the Palestinian Authority. The river is initially formed by tributaries that arise in Israel, Lebanon, and the Israeli-occupied Golan Heights. South of Lake Tiberias, the Jordan is joined by the Yarmuk which arises in Syria. States extract water directly from the river and from associated aquifers. A joint study by the Israel Academy for Sciences and Humanities, the Palestine Academy for Science and Technology, the Royal Scientific Society of Jordan, and the United States National Academy of Sciences estimated that the renewable resources of the basin were 2,600–2,788 million cubic meters per year versus a total ground and surface use of 3,183 cubic meters per year. Water for the Future: The West Bank and Gaza Strip, Israel, and Jordan 46, 48 (1999).

The Jordan River was allocated by the 1994 Treaty of Peace Between the State of Israel and the Hashemite Kingdom of Jordan. Article 6 of the treaty deals with water. The Yarmuk River and the Jordan River are dealt with separately. Jordan is entitled to the majority of the flow of the Yarmuk. The treaty gives Israel the major entitlement to the Jordan.

* * * The most significant point about the agreement between the states is the mutual obligation to cooperate in finding and developing new resources, in eliminating waste, in improving efficiency, in participating in joint engineering and research projects, and in the joint pursuit of water quality protection and the optimal utilization of the shared waters. This too is the core requirement of the principle of equitable utilization.

The agreement also recognizes the bias in favor of the status quo found within the attitude of the law. * * * [M]ost of the provisions relating to the quantity of allocation simply reflect the manner and extent of existing use. Nevertheless, where the balancing of the equities revealed some gross unremedied disparity, such as the severe lack of Jordanian water supplies of drinkable quality, the agreement has provided for reallocation to contend with the disparity. This tiered approach is reflected in the structure of the agreement, which first clarifies general use and then provides for the supply of drinkable water in a separate sub-section entitled "Additional Water."

In terms of the role and direction of international water law, there is a striking lesson to be learned from the peace treaty between Israel and Jordan. In the international community of sovereign states, where international law is engaged in an ongoing struggle for supremacy and legitimacy, success comes from the adoption of a broad perspective and approach which facilitates agreement and promotes universal benefit. An overly narrow focus on the delineation of rights will relegate international law to a background role or even to failure.

Here at least, international law is in touch with the reality of politics. It has moved the parties toward agreement and has consolidated their water arrangements. It confirms the importance of cooperation, but points out the limitations of a watercourse agreement that does not include all the states of the watercourse. In international law, and in the conclusions of the political agreement, there are references both to the duty to cooperate, and to the obligation not to cause harm.

In recognizing that the "water resources are not sufficient to meet their needs," the parties are accepting a conservative application of the principle of no appreciable harm.

Finally, the establishment of the Joint Water Committee to oversee future developments reflects an interpretation of the principle of equitable utilization not as an allocatory formula, but as an ongoing source of obligations.

Jonathan M. Wenig, *Water and Peace: The Past, the Present, and the Future of the Jordan River Watercourse: An International Law Analysis*, 27 N.Y.U. J. Int'l L. & Pol., 331, 363–64 (1995). See also Fadia Daibes, *A Progressive Multidisciplinary Approach for Resolving the Palestinian–Israel Conflict Over Shared Groundwater: What Lessons Learned from International Law?* 8 U. DENV. WATER L. REV. 93 (2004).

TABLE OF WATER EQUIVALENTS

1 gallon	=	8.34 pounds
	=	231 cubic inches
	=	0.134 cubic foot
1 million gallons	=	3.07 acre-feet
1 million gallons per day (mgd)	=	1,120 acre-feet per year
	=	1.55 cubic feet per second
	=	694.4 gallons per minute (gpm)
1 cubic foot	=	7.48 gallons
	=	62.4 pounds
1 cubic foot per second (cfs)	=	646,317 gallons per day
	=	448.8 gallons per minute
	=	1.98 acre-feet per day
	=	38.4 miner's inches (CO)
	=	40 miner's inches (AZ, CA, MT, NV, OR)
	=	50 miner's inches (ID, NE, NM, ND, SD, UT)
1 miner's inch	=	.02–.028 c.f.s. (depending on state)
1 acre-foot (af)	=	325,851 gallons
	=	43,560 cubic feet
1 inch of rain	=	27,200 gallons per acre
	=	113 tons per acre

METRIC CONVERSION FACTORS

Multiply:	By:	To Obtain:
foot (ft)	0.3048	meter (m)
cubic foot per second (cfs)	0.02832	cubic meter per second (m³/s)
mile (mi)	1.609	kilometer (km)
acre	0.405	hectare (ha)
acre-foot (af)	1,233.	cubic meter (m³)
gallon	3.785	liter (l)
million gallons per day	3,785.	cubic meter per day

SOURCES OF WATER LAW AND RESOURCES LITERATURE

1. Introduction

Water allocation, especially in the West, has inspired lawyers, historians, economists, political scientists and others to study and write about water resources issues. The literature runs from classic late nineteenth and early twentieth century legal treatises to rich, technical studies and impassioned polemics. The role of water in the development of the West has attracted a number of younger Western historians.

To enrich the work of students and teachers, we suggest some sources for further reading and research the sources that have been most useful to us, along with some general comments about their significance and quality. This bibliography includes sources that address issues raised in this book, as well as sources that provide the full context to understand the drama of water resources allocation.

2. The Law

For students who seek reference sources in water law the current sources are: David H. Getches, Water Law Rights in a Nutshell (4th ed. 2009); A. Dan Tarlock, Law of Water Rights and Resources (1988 with annual updates) (one volume survey with annual updates); and Water and Water Rights (Robert Beck ed., 1996) (multi-author, multiple volume treatise with frequent supplements). Older and regional treatises abound. Henry Philip Farnham, The Law of Waters and Water Rights (1904), is the oldest and the first major treatise that was national in scope. It is still cited by courts, especially in riparian jurisdictions.

The other major treatises are regional. Samuel Charles Wiel, Water Rights in the Western States (3d ed. 1911), and Clesson Selwy Kinney, A Treatise on the Law of Irrigation and Water Rights and the Arid Region Doctrine of Appropriation of Water (2d ed. 1912) are two, still cited treatises on western water law. Wiel is the superior analytical work and courts continue to refer to it for basic and arcane points of law. Kinney is a useful source on the law of prior appropriation in its formative period and is essential reading to catch the spirit of those who converted the West to irrigation farming. A water law scholar in the U.S. Department of Agriculture, Wells A. Hutchins, capped his 62–year career of the study of western water institutions with the posthumous publication of a three-volume treatise, Water Rights Laws in the Nineteen Western States (completed by Harold H. Ellis & J. Peter DeBraal, 1971). The work is somewhat repetitive, but contains a wealth of information and insights into western water law and the development of law in each state. A concise treatment of the law of each state is National Water Commission, A Summary–Digest of State Water Laws (Richard L. Dewsnup & Dallin W. Jensen eds., 1973), remains useful. Water Rights in the Eastern United States (Kenneth R. Wright ed., 1998) is the most recent treatment of eastern water rights.

Some treatises have specialized subject matter. Joseph K. Angell, A Treatise on the Right of Property in Tidewaters and in the Soil and Shores Thereof (1847), was the first major American work on the law of navigable waters. Moses M. Frankel, Law of Seashore Waters and Water Courses: Maine and Massachusetts (1969), is a modern book on the same subject. As the title suggests, George William Sherk, Dividing The Waters: The Resolution of Interstate Conflicts in the United States (2000), is a specialized treatment of interstate conflicts.

In addition to the national, regional, or specialized treatises, there are some very useful treatises specific to individual states. Frank B. Maloney, Sheldon J. Plager & Fletcher N. Baldwin, Jr., Water Law and Administration: The Florida Experience (1968), is an essential source of information about Florida's water and riparian rights in general. Thanks to the efforts of the pioneering water resources law scholar at the University of Wisconsin, Jacob Beuscher, there is a good treatise on Wisconsin law, Harold H. Ellis et al., Water–Use Law and Administration in Wisconsin (1970). Wells Hutchins published a series of Department of Agriculture monographs on the law of water rights of various western states, and these useful volumes are in many law libraries. Other books that are helpful in understanding the water laws of specific states include: Robert I. Reis, Connecticut Water Law: Judicial Allocation of Water Resources (1967); and Charles W. Wixom & Karl F. Zeisler, Industrial Uses of Water in Michigan (1966). California law is described for the practitioner in Harold E. Rogers & Alan H. Nichols, Water For California: Planning, Law & Practice, Finance (2 vols. 1967) and Arthur Littleworth & Eric Gardner, California Water Law (1995). Vranesh's Colorado Water Law, Revised Edition (James N. Corbridge & Teresa A. Rice, eds., 1999), is an updated single volume synthesis of Colorado's well-developed and elaborate water law. Statutes, treatises, forms, and cases relating to Colorado water law are collected in Colorado Water Laws (George Radosevich ed., 1979). Traditions, Innovation and Conflict: Perspectives on Colorado Water Law (Lawrence J. MacDonnell ed., 1986), focuses on modern Colorado water problems.

Water law casebooks also can be important sources for reference and research. Indeed, the very first American casebook on any subject was Angell on Water Courses (1824). Jacob H. Beuscher, Water Rights (now James B. McDonald & Jacob H. Beuscher, Water Rights (2d ed. 1973)), was the first effort to focus a casebook around Midwestern and eastern issues. There are two current, national water law casebooks besides this book: a recent revision of the pioneering effort of the late Dean Frank J. Trelease, the most prominent water law scholar of the post-World War II generation, Frank J. Trelease & George A. Gould, Water Law (4th ed. 1986), now George A. Gould, Douglas L. Grant and Gregory S. Weber, Water Law (7th ed. 2005). The second builds on Joseph Sax's innovative Water Law, Planning & Policy (1968). The most recent edition is Joseph L. Sax, Robert J. Abrams, Barton H. Thompson, Jr., John D. Leshy & Robert H. Abrams, Legal Control of Water Resources (4th ed. 2006).

3.   History

Classical scholars may find a 1905 publication by a Topeka, Kansas lawyer to be interesting reading. Eugene F. Ware, Roman Water Law: Translated from the Pandects of Justinian. The book has been reprinted by Fred B. Rothman & Co.

The development of western water law is tied to the history of the settlement and development of the West. Bernard DeVoto's trilogy, Course of Empire (1952), Across the Wide Missouri (1947), Year of Decision: 1846 (1943), is a fine introduction to the politics of the opening of the West. The relationship between land, climate, and human institutions was first comprehensively explored in Walter Prescott Webb's The Great Plains (1931). Frederick Jackson Turner's successor at Harvard, Frederick Merk, summed up a life of teaching about the West in History of the Western Movement (1978), in which the role of water development is covered extensively. William L. Graf, Wilderness Preservation and the Sagebrush Rebellions (1990), surveys the history of public land and water resources management from the failed efforts to establish a scientific national irrigation policy in the 1870s and 1880s to the failure of the Sagebrush Rebellion in the 1980s to cause the divestment of federal lands.

Books about the history of water law and water development have begun to appear with increasing frequency. For example, Robert G. Dunbar, Forging New Rights in Western Waters (1983), is a very readable introduction to the history of the development of water law. Michael C. Meyer, Water in the Hispanic Southwest: A Social and Legal History, 1550–1850 (1984), is an inquiry into the Spanish origins of irrigation. Water in the American West: Essays in Honor of Raphael J. Moses (David H. Getches ed., 1988), is a balanced evaluation of many aspects of western water development.

Much of western water law and practice is a product of the irrigation movement. Donald J. Pisani, From the Family Farm to Agribusiness: The Irrigation Crusade in California and the West 1850–1931 (1984) is now the standard history. Until recently federal water policy was based on multiple-purpose river basin development. The standard (and excellent) history of the origins of this idea is Samuel P. Hays, Conservation and the Gospel of Efficiency: The Progressive Conservation Movement, 1890–1920 (1959). The role of the counter-preservation tradition in natural resource thinking is traced in Roderick Nash, Wilderness and the American Mind (3d ed. 1982). Beatrice H. Holmes, A History of Federal Water Resources Programs, 1800–1960 (U.S. Dep't of Ag. Misc. Pub. No. 1233, 1972), and History of Federal Water Resources Programs and Policies, 1961–1970 (U.S. Dep't Ag. Misc. Pub. No. 1379, 1979), are useful sources of information about the growth of federal involvement in water management. Karen M. O'Neill, Rivers by Design: State Power and the Origins of the U.S. Flood Control (2006) is the most recent history of the evolution of this important aspect of United States water policy.

Donald Worster has written a provocative, critical history of western water development, Rivers of Empire: Water, Aridity, and the Growth of the American West (1985). A balanced assessment that traces the competition of local and national interests can be found in Donald Pisani's three books, To Reclaim A Divided West: Water, Law, and Public Policy, 1848–1902 (1992); Water, Land, Law in the West: The Limits of Public Policy, 1850–1920 (1996), and Water and American Government: The Reclamation Bureau, National Water Policy, and the West, 1902–1935 (2002). Mark Ferge, Irrigated Eden: The Making of an Agricultural Landscape in the American West (1999) examines the impact of Snake River dams on the region's agriculture. John Opie, Ogallala, Water for a Dry Land, 2d ed. (2000) is a useful description of the development and overdevelopment of the Ogallala Aquifer. William D. Rowley, Reclaiming the Arid West: The Career of Francis G. Newlands (1996) is a biography of the chief sponsor of the Reclamation Act of 1902. The judicial development of special doctrine for determination of Indian water rights is an important slice of the history of the West. The most comprehensive work is based on revealing original research. John Shurts, Indian Reserved Water Rights (2000). A thorough analysis of the politics of water development and the resulting inequities to tribes is Daniel McCool's Command of the Waters: Iron Triangles, Federal Water Development, and Indian Water (1987). Lloyd Burton, American Indian Water Rights and the Limits of Law (1991) is a critical assessment of the law's treatment of tribal water rights in practice. Tribal Water Rights: Essays in Contemporary Law, Policy, and Economics (John E. Thorson, Sarah Britton and Bonnie G. Colby, 2006), is useful examination of the use of legislative settlements to address to Indian water claims. The same authors produced a comprehensive study analyzing and compiling these settlements, Negotiating Tribal Water Rights: Fulfilling Promises in the Arid West (Bonnie G. Colby, John E. Thorson, and Sarah Britton, 2005).

Environmental histories of the West and the nation now being written stress the adverse consequences of human effort to mold nature rather than to adapt to natural conditions. The model articulation of the idea that "[m]an might limit the demands he makes on a basin's water processes" is Henry C. Hart's study of the taming of the Missouri, The Dark Missouri (1957). Joseph M. Petulla, American Environmental History: The Exploitation and Conservation of Natural Resources (1977), is an adequate introduction for the nonspecialist. William N.L. Andrews, Managing the Environment, Managing Ourselves: A History of American Environmental

Policy (1999), is the most comprehensive history of the rise of environmentalism in the United States. An important environmental history, not directly related to water, is William Cronon's Changes in the Land: Indians, Colonists, and the Ecology of New England (1983), which traces the early roots of the creation of private property in resources held in common by the public. Richard White, It's Your Misfortune and None of My Own: A History of the American West (1991), is another important reinterpretation of the West with a strong emphasis on natural resources management issues, as is William G. Robbins, Colony and Empire: The Capitalist Transformation of the American West (1994). The classic of revisionist western history is Patricia Nelson Limerick, The Legacy of Conquest (1987). A. Dan Tarlock and Holly D. Doremus, Water War in the Klamath: Macho Law, Combat Biology, and Dirty Politics (2008) is a case study of the first shut down of an irrigation project to protected endangered species. Other useful books are Dan Flores, The Natural West–Environmental history in the Great Plains and Rocky Mountains (2001); Nancy Langston, Where Water & Land Meet: A Western Landscape Transformed (2003). And finally, essential reading for anyone trying to understand water in the context of the "new" West is William E. Riebsame & James J. Robb, Atlas of the New West: Portrait of a Changing Region (1997). Lawrence J. MacDonnell's From Reclamation to Sustainability: Water, Agriculture, and the Environment in the American West (1999), is a somewhat sympathetic look at western irrigators' efforts to adapt to a rapidly changing world.

Wallace Stegner's Beyond the Hundredth Meridian: John Wesley Powell and the Second Opening of the West (1954), is the standard biography of Powell and a classic book on the West. However, Donald Worster's recent, A River Running West: The Life of John Wesley Powell (2000), may become the primary source to understand Powell's contribution to western understanding and settlement. James R. Kluger, Turning on the Water With a Shovel: The Career of Elwood Mead (1992), is a good biography of this pivotal figure.

Edward Goldsmith & Nicholas Hildyard, The Environmental and Social Effects of Large Dams (1984), is a critical Sierra Club book survey of the consequences of a technology that we have perfected in the United States and exported world-wide. Richard L. Berkman & W. Kip Viscusi, Damming the West (1973), is an earlier Nader exposé of the Bureau of Reclamation. Many of the long-standing criticisms of large dams are validated in the Report of World Commission on Large Dams, Dams and Development: A New Framework for Decision–Making (2000). A commissioner has written his own analysis. Thayer Scudder, The Future of Large Dams: Dealing With Social, Environmental, Institutional and Political Costs (2005).

Individual rivers, specific projects, and water issues of individual states have attracted scholarly attention. The Colorado River has inspired its own literature. Norris Hundley's Water and the West: The Colorado River Compact and the Politics of Water in the American West (1975), and Dividing the Waters: A Century of Controversy Between the United States and Mexico (1966), provide a rich history of the 1922 Compact, the Boulder Canyon Project Act, and our relations with Mexico. A River No More: The Colorado River and the West (1981 updated 1996), by Philip L. Fradkin is an artful blend of history, law, ecology, and social commentary. R. Martin, A Story That Stands Like a Dam: Glen Canyon and the Struggle for the Soul of the West (1989) focuses on one of the two major dams on the river. Evan Ward Tucker, Border Oasis: Water and the Political Ecology of the Colorado River Delta, 1940–1975 (2003) looks at what upstream dam development did to the end of the system. In 1983 a group of scholars and water specialists gathered at the Bishop's Lodge in Santa Fe, New Mexico to assess the Colorado River Compact, and the conference produced New Courses for the Colorado River: Major Issues for the Next Century (Gary D. Weatherford & F. Lee Brown eds., 1986). Dean Mann, The Politics of Water in Arizona (1963), tells how that state developed its dependence on Colorado River water for future growth. Francis J. Welsh, How to Create a Water Crisis (1985); Douglas E. Kupel, Fuel for Growth: Water and Arizona's Urban Environment (2003); and Arizona Water Policy: Management Innovations in an Urbanizing, Arid Region (Bonnie G. Colby and Katherine L. Jacobs, 2006), carry the story forward with a well-documented dissection of the federal bailout of Arizona, the Central Arizona Project.

Conflicts over the use of the water supply of the Owens Valley have been central to California water law. William L. Kahrl, Water and Power: The Conflict over Los Angeles' Water Supply in the Owens Valley (1982), is a fine chronology of the on-going conflict. Abraham Hoffman, Vision or Villainy: Origins of the Owens Valley–Los Angeles Water Controversy (1981), is also good. John Walton, Western Times and Water Wars: State, Culture and Rebellion in California (1992), carries the history of the controversy through the 1980s. Norris Hundley, Jr.'s The Great Thirst: Californians and Water, 1770s–1990s (1992, rev'd ed. 2001), is the most comprehensive history of California's efforts to solve water problems by massive public works. The same landscape is also covered in David Carle, Drowning the Dream: California's Water Choices at the Millenium (2000). Gary D. Libecap, Owens Valley Revisited: A Reassessment of the West's First Great Water Transfer (2007) is very much a revisionist history of this seminal water conflict.

Ira Clark, Water in New Mexico: A History of Its Management and Use (1987), traces the influence of environmental values in that state. Another fine addition to New Mexico and western water history is G. Emlin Hall, High and Dry: The Texas–New Mexico Struggle for the Pecos River (2002). A new compilation of essays focusing on the Southwest is Fluid Arguments: Five Centuries of Western Water Conflicts (Char Miller ed., 2001).

In the 1950s and 1960s, Rivers of America, a series of histories of individual river basins was published. Among the best are Paul Horgan, The Great River: The Rio Grande in North American History (1954), and Stewart H. Holbrook, The Columbia River (1965). Tim Palmer, The Snake River: Window to the West (1991), continues this tradition. Eastern water allocation problems are the subject of Roscoe C. Martin, Water for New

York: A Study in State Administration of Water Resources (1960). Preston J. Hubbard, Origins of the TVA: The Muscle Shoals Controversy, 1920–1932 (1961), examines the origins of our most famous experiment with a river basin authority. Peter Annin, The Great lakes Water Wars (2006), chronicles the successful state and Canadian provincial and federal efforts to limit diversions in the Great Lakes watershed.

Controversies over whether to destroy whitewater for a dam often produce case studies. Among the best are Elmo R. Richardson, Dams, Parks and Politics: Resource Development and Preservation in the Truman–Eisenhower Era (1973); B. Andrews & M. Sansone, Who Runs the Rivers: Dams and Decisions in the New West (1983); and Thomas J. Schoenbaum, The New River Controversy (1979), a good case study of the use of the Wild and Scenic Rivers Act to block a FERC license. More recent books focus on the need to remove dams, e.g., Elizabeth Grossman, watershed: The Undamming of America (2002), or the problem of free-flowing river conservation and restoration. E.g., Ellen Wohl, Virtual Rivers: Lessons from the Mountain Rivers of the Colorado Front Range (2001); William R. Lowry, Dam Politics: Restoring America's Rivers (2003); and Jim W. Johnson, Rivers Under Siege: The Troubled Saga of West Tennessee's Wetlands (2007).

The endless and unsuccessful efforts of the upper and lower basin Missouri River states to allocate and manage the river is the subject of three recent important books. John R. Ferrell, Big Dam Era (1993); John E. Thorson, River of Promise, River of Peril: The Politics of Managing the Missouri River; and Robert Kelly Schneiders, Unruly River: Two Centuries of Change Along the Missouri (1999). Peter Carrels, Uphill Against Water (1999), chronicles a struggle against federal development in the basin.

There is a substantial body of "crisis" literature that predicts a water shortage, surveys wasteful uses and pollution practices, and calls for reform. Books include James C. Wright, The Coming Water Famine (1966); William A. Ashworth, Nor Any Drop to Drink (1982); Fred Powledge, Water: The Nature, Uses, and Future of Our Most Precious and Abused Resource (1982); Frank B. Moss, The Water Crisis (1967); David A. Francko & Robert G. Wetzel, To Quench Our Thirst: The Present and Future Status of Fresh Water Resources of the United States (1983); Robin Clark, Water: The International Crisis (1993); and Sandra Postel, Last Oasis: Facing Water Scarcity (1997) and Pillar of Sand: Can the Irrigation Miracle Last? (1999). In Tapped Out (1998), former Senator Paul Simon argues that the world's water problems have potential for inciting war or becoming a nexus for international cooperation, and he goes on to suggest a range of solutions from conservation to desalination. The literature continues to flow as issues such as water security, privatization and bottled water come to the fore. Among the newer books are Marq de Villiers, Water: The Fate of Our Precious Resource (2001); Vananda Shiva, Water Wars: Privatization, Pollution, and Profit (2002): Maude Barlow, Blue Gold: The Fight to Stop Corporate Theft of the World's Water (2005); Fred Pearce, When Rivers Run Dry: The Defining Crisis of the Twenty-first Century (2007);

Maude Barlow, Blue Covenant: The Global Water crisis and the Coming Battle for the Right to Water (2008); and Elizabeth Royte, Bottlemania: How Water Went on Sale and We Bought It (2008).

4.   Official Documents

Water policy is always being studied at the federal and state levels. Two classic reports are John Wesley Powell's Report on the Lands of the Arid Region of the United States, With a More Detailed Account of the Lands of Utah (1879), and Elwood Mead's U.S. Dep't of Agriculture, Office of Experiment Stations, Report of Irrigation Investigations in California, Bulletin S. Doc. 108 (1901). The 1962 Belknap Press of Harvard University's edition of Powell's report, edited by Wallace Stegner, is the edition of Powell most used by scholars today.

Among the most important modern government studies are the three volumes, A Water Policy for the American People, Ten Rivers in America's Future, and Water Resources Law, The Report of the President's Water Resources Policy Commission (1950); and Water Policies For the Future, Final Report to the President and to the Congress of the United States by the National Water Commission (1973). Water Policies For the Future is the most searching analysis of state and federal water policy to date and frames the policy debate in a still-poignant manner. A commission was formed in the 1990s to examine western water issues and the report reflects the changed values of water in the "new" West but does not recommend the range of comprehensive solutions that its 1973 predecessor was able to do. Report of the Western Water Policy Advisory Review Commission, Water in the West: Challenge for the Next Century (1998).

A 1968 National Academy of Sciences Study, Water and Choice in the Colorado Basin: An Example of Alternatives in Water Management, is a high-powered model of water policy analysis. Forecasts of future water demands are summarized in State and National Water Use Trends to the Year 2000, A Report Prepared By the Congressional Research Service of the Library of Congress for the Committee on Environment and Public Works, U.S. Senate, S. No. 96–12, 96th Cong., 2d Sess. 227–297 (1980).

The Water Science and Technology Board of the National Academy of Sciences and National Research Council, formed in 1982, has published many reports of interest, including Water for the Future: The West Bank and Gaza Strip, Israel, and Jordan (1999); A New Era for Irrigation (1996); Water Transfers in the West: Efficiency, Equity, and the Environment (1992); and Irrigation–Induced Water Quality: What Can Be Learned from the San Joaquin Valley Experience (1989); Managing the Columbia River: Instream Flows, Water Withdrawals, and Salmon Survival (2004); Colorado River Basin Water Management: Evaluating and Adjusting to Hydroclimatic Variability (2007). In 2004, the National Research Council completed a comprehensive evaluation of the U.S. Army Corps of Engineers planning procedures and policies. National Research Council, U.S. Army Corps of Engineers Water Resources Planning: A New Opportunity for Service (2004), offers a blueprint for a post-"Big Dam Era" Corps.

5. Economics

As in other areas, economists have had a major influence on the debate about water allocation policy. Among the modern classics are Otto Eckstein, Water–Resource Development: The Economics of Project Evaluation (1958); John V. Krutilla & Otto Eckstein, Multiple Purpose River Development: Studies in Applied Economic Analysis (1958); Jack Hirshleifer, James C. DeHaven & Jerome W. Milliman, Water Supply: Economics, Technology and Policy (1960). Economics and Public Policy in Water Resource Development (Stephen C. Smith & Emery N. Castle eds., 1964), remains an important collection of papers on the use of economic analysis to guide water development decisions. W. Douglas Shaw, Water Resource Economics and Policy: An Introduction (2005), is a more modern treatment of the problems of water management with equal emphasis on quantity and quality issues. Arthur Maass & Raymond L. Anderson, And the Desert Shall Rejoice: Conflict, Growth, and Justice in Arid Environments (1978), is a worthwhile recent evaluation of reclamation. Charles W. Howe, Benefit–Cost Analysis for Water System Planning (1971), is a fine introduction to formal cost-benefit analysis. Professor Howe's important work on water transfers includes Charles W. Howe & K. William Easter, Interbasin Transfers of Water: Economic Issues and Impacts (1971). The early California experience in water marketing is evaluated in Sharing Scarcity: Gains & Losers in Water Marketing (Harold Carter, Henry J. Vaux, Jr. & Ann F. Scheuring eds., 1994); and Brent H. Haddad, Rivers of Gold: Designing Markets to Allocate Water in California (2000). Carl Bauer, Siren Song: Chilean Water Law as a Model of International Water Reform (2004) is the definitive study of the problems that arose when Chile adopted the United States market model for water allocation. Franklin M. Fisher, Liquid Assets: An Economic Analysis for Water Management and Conflict Resolution in the Middle East and Beyond (2005), is a careful, technical effort to show how water markets might function to help alleviate bitter water conflicts.

Terry L. Anderson, Water Crisis: Ending the Policy Drought (1983), is a popular introduction to current market-based reform proposals. Recent developments are covered in Water Marketing—The Next Generation (Terry L. Anderson & Peter J. Hill eds., 1997). A. Willey, Economic Development and Environmental Quality in California's Water System (1985), applies economic analysis to propose an environmental and marketing reform agenda for that state. Richard W. Wahl, Markets for Federal Water: Subsidies, Property Rights, and the Bureau of Reclamation (1989), is a blueprint for a reformed, market-oriented Bureau.

In the late 1980s mainstream resource economists began to incorporate the concept of "sustainable development into water allocation analysis." Noteworthy texts include David W. Pearce & R. Kerry Turner, Economics of Natural Resources and the Environment (1990), and David W. Pearce et al., Sustainable Development: Economics and Environment in the Third World (1990). Much of the recent work in economics has been devoted to valuing the ecosystem services that biodiversity, including aquatic environments, produce. National Research Council, Valuing Ground Water: Economic Concepts and Approaches (1997), is a good introduction to this literature.

6. Political Science

Political scientists have devoted considerable effort to explaining the "logic" of federal subsidies. The effect of state water attitudes on western state legislatures is examined in Helen M. Ingram, Nancy K. Laney & John R. McCain, A Policy Approach to Political Representation: Lessons from the Four Corners States (1980). Professor Ingram's earlier book, Patterns of Politics in Water Resource Development (1969), is a revealing study of the formation of a coalition to secure congressional funding for a basin-wide development project—in this case the Colorado River Basin Project Act. Merrill R. Goodall, John D. Sullivan & Timothy DeYoung, California Water: A New Political Economy (1978), is the major study of the role of the special districts in water allocation and distribution. David Lewis Feldman, Water Resources Management: In Search of an Environmental Ethic (1991) and Water Policy for Sustainable development (2007), survey the tension between the development mission of the water agencies and environmental protection, as is William Blomquist, Dividing the Water (1992). Ken Conca, Governing Water: Contentious Transnational Politics and Global Institution Building (2006) brings together the lessons—positive and negative—from efforts to improve the management of shared rivers.

Two important books on the water allocation and social equity are F. Lee Brown and Helen Ingram, Water and Poverty in the Southwest (1987) and John Whitley, Helen Ingram and Richard Perry, Water, Place and Equity (2008).

7. Law Reviews

Water law articles and student comments and notes can be found in all law reviews. The greatest concentration of academic writing is in specialized journals, the University of Wyoming Law Review, formerly the Land and Water Law Review, and the University of New Mexico's Natural Resources Journal; an additional source that includes frequent attention to water issues is the University of Colorado Law Review. The numerous specialized environmental law reviews also frequently publish water law articles. The University of Denver College of Law began publishing the Water Law Review in 1997. The journal of the American Water Resources Association, Water Resources Research, publishes technical, policy and legal papers.

8. Popular Literature

Marc Reisner, Cadillac Desert: The American West And Its Disappearing Water (1986), is a lively, well-researched, and critical account of the ability of the Bureau of Reclamation to develop and hold power in the West. This book was followed by Marc Reisner & Sarah Bates, Overtapped Oasis: Reform or Revolution for Western Water (1990). The late Wallace Stegner's

The American West As Living Space (1987), sums up this great author's thoughts on how the West should be used. Charles Wilkinson has carried forward Stegner's thinking in two books, The Eagle Bird: Mapping a New West (1990), and Crossing the Next Meridian (1992).

Another popular book, The Milagro Beanfield War (1976), part of a trilogy by John T. Nichols, chronicles the fictional conflicts between wealthy developers and local farmers in the Southwest. The role of water scarcity in shaping the fiction of the West is studied in David W. Cassuto, Dripping Dry: Literature, Politics, and Water in the Desert Southwest (2001).

9. Miscellaneous

Thomas V. Cech, Principles of Water Resources: History, Development, Management, and Policy (2003), is a general overview of the major water issues. Law students and lawyers will find the discussions of hydrologic principles the most useful aspect of the book. Peter Gleick's bi-annual publications, The World's Water, are rich source of global water use and quality trends.

INDEX

References are to pages.

ABANDONMENT
Foreign waters, 223
Prior appropriation rights, 259–65

ACCRETION AND AVULSION
Common law rule for ocean, 408–11
Loss of riparian rights, 147–50
Reliction, 147

ARIZONA
Colorado River, 995–1011
Central Arizona Project, 624–26, 633, 983–84, 990–91
Groundwater management, 624–33

ARTIFICIAL WATERCOURSES
Defined, 445–59
Expansion artificial to natural, 453
Riparian rights, 455–56
Right to maintain, 454–55

BENEFICIAL USE
See Prior Appropriation

CALIFORNIA
4.4 Plan, 1004, 1020–21
Area of origin protection, 395–98
Bay Delta, 753–761
CALFED, 748, 756–61
California Doctrine, 89–94
Central Valley Project, 386–87, 396–97, 754–756, 800–801, 819, 830–4, 846
Conservation, 219
Constitutional provisions, 93–94, 137, 146, 154, 203, 302, 430, 758
Groundwater management, 565, 633–53
    Salt water intrusion, 640–41
History, 79–82, 89–94
Imperial Irrigation District (IID), 219, 368–72, 790, 1016–19
Metropolitan Water District of Southern California (MWD), 1016–1019, 1023
Public trust rights, 426–33
Quality, 659, 754–760
Owens Valley, 337–38, 644
Shoreline access, 491–96
Statutory system, 301–03

CLEAN WATER ACT
See also Pollution
    Generally, 673–79
Climate change impacts, 676–77
Dredge and fill permits (Section 404), 701–13
Effluent limitations, 676
Enforcement by states, 676
Groundwater, 689
Indian tribes, 935–37
Interbasin transfers, 679–85
Interstate pollution, 686–87, 966–76
National Pollutant Discharge Elimination System, 675–77, 966–73
Non-point sources, 678–79, 685–86
Planning requirements, 659
Point sources defined, 678–79
Relation to common law, 686–87, 973–75
Sources, 676–77
State certification water quality standards, 728–737
Water Quality Standards and TMDLs, 677–678
Wallop Amendment, 740
Wetlands covered, 701–12

COLORADO
Augmentation plans, 384–89
Groundwater administration, 596–98, 613–21
    Groundwater Management Act, 586–88, 616–21
    Management Districts, 613–16
Instream flow, 99–102, 356–57, 360–64
Public rights, 470–77
Prior appropriation adoption, 71–76
Statutory system, 303–05
Water marketing, 232, 777–78, 791–92
Water and sanitation districts, 794–95

COLORADO DOCTRINE
See Prior Appropriation

COLORADO RIVER
Boulder Canyon Project Act, 995–99
Central Arizona Project, 624–26, 633, 1013–14, 1020
Colorado River Delta, 1019–25, 1029–30
Compact of 1922, pp. 987–95, 999–1005, 1020–21
Global warming, 1013, 1015
Instream flows, 741
Legislative apportionment, 995–1011

COLORADO RIVER—Cont'd
Lower Colorado River Basin Multi Species Conservation Program, 741, 750
Mexican Treaty of 1944, 998, 1051, 1054–56
Navigability, 810
Reserved rights,
    Federal, 878–99
    Indian, 102–05, 877, 920, 926–27
Reservoir operation, 1021–25
Salinity, 1014–15

COMMERCE CLAUSE
See Federal Activities; Interstate Allocation; Navigability, Federal navigation power

DAMS
    Generally, 760–67
Colorado River reservoir reoperation, 1021–25
See Federal Power Act; Reclamation Act; Storage
    Removal, 717–18
World Commission on Dams, 760–67

DESERT LAND ACT OF 1877
Prior appropriation recognized, 109, 156, 908

DITCH RIGHTS
See Rights of Way; Service and Supply Organizations

ECONOMICS
    Generally, 33–47
Common-pool, 559–60
Community values, 37–38
Ecosystem values, 696–98
Equalmarginal value, 233–34
External costs, 39–40
Existence values, 696–98
Literature, 1078
Marginal cost pricing, 773
Markets, need for 34–36
Market transfers, 36–40, 233–36, 368–75, 1016–18
    Opportunity Costs, 39–40,
Pricing, 33–36, 41–42
    Second best, 234–35
    Secondary transfer impacts, 40–41, 257–59
Pollution, 652–53
Public goods, 38–39
Scarcity, causes of, 41–47
Water allocation systems evaluated, 48–56

EMINENT DOMAIN
See Navigability; Flowage Rights

ENDANGERED SPECIES ACT
    Generally, 737–47, 936–37
Columbia River, 744–45
Klamath Basin, 742–44
Missouri River, 856–858
Regulatory water rights, 745–745
State water rights, 737–44
Takings, 527–44

EQUITABLE APPORTIONMENT
See Interstate Allocation, Adjudication

FEDERAL ACTIVITIES
    Generally, 796–801
Acquisition of water rights, 69–70, 105–11, 818–25
Basin planning, 798–99
Clean Water Act,
    See Clean Water Act
Commerce clause, 479–483, 667, 802–11, 795–97, 882
Federal preemption of state laws, 105–11, 886–87, 966–75
History, 796–798
Hydroelectric power licensing, 714–28, 802–09
International treaties, 1054–55
Interstate allocation,
    Generally, 796–858
    Compact formation, 977–89
    Corps of Engineers reservoir operation, 847–56
Legislation, 996–98
McCarran Amendment, 873–78
Non-reserved rights, 907–911
Pollution control, 673–686, 686–87, 688–701, 966–75
Powers, 801–11, 794–97, 881–85
Reclamation projects, 784–89, 800–801, 818–41
Rivers and Harbors Act, 674
Takings,
    See Property Rights; Public Trust Doctrine
Wetlands protection, 701–714
    See also Clean Water Act, Dredge and fill permits
Wild and Scenic Rivers Act, 716–17, 897
Wilderness Act, 897–99
Wildlife protection, 737–47, 751–61, 870–99

FEDERAL AND INDIAN LANDS
See Reserved Rights

FEDERAL POWER ACT
    Generally, 714–17, 797–804, 811–18
Congressional power to enact, 788–97
Dam removal, 717–18
Fish and wildlife protection, 714–15
Licenses for hydroelectric dams, 714, 812–16
Relicensing for licensed dams, 718–728
State law conflicts, 811–818
Trial license conditions, 721–723

FISH AND WILDLIFE
    See also Instream Flow
Appropriations for, 99–102
Endangered Species Act, 737–47
Fish and Wildlife Coordination Act, 714–15
Hydroelectric power development, 714–28
Indian treaty rights, 899–904, 906–07, 915
Wild and Scenic Rivers Act, 716–17, 897

FLOWAGE RIGHTS
Condemnation, 479–83
Navigation servitude, 479–86
Prescription, 153–54, 289–91

FLORIDA
A–C–F, A–C–T conflict, 976–77
Groundwater, 610–12
Permit System, 282–89
Water Resources Act of 1972, 282–88

FOREIGN WATERS
Ownership and reuse, 220–23, 643–44
Transbasin diversions, 322–26

FORFEITURE
Prior appropriation, 259–65
Riparian rights, 150–54

GENERAL STREAM ADJUDICATIONS
Effectiveness, 305–08
McCarran Amendment, 873–878

GEORGIA
A–C–F, A–C–T conflict, 976–77
Drought management, 292–93
Groundwater permits, 292

GLOBAL WARMING
Generally, 26–32, 1013, 1015
Groundwater impacts, 30
Water use impacts, 29–32

GREAT LAKES
Generally, 1043–49
Anti-diversion treaty, 1045–48
Trade law, 1046–49

GROUNDWATER
Generally, 545–50
Absolute ownership, 561–62,623
Administrative regulation, 446–50, 598–609
Aquifers, 554–56
Artesian water, 555
Central Arizona Project, 624–26, 633, 1019–20
Common-pool resource, 559–61
Conjunctive use,
    Augmentation, 384–89, 576–78
    Hydrologically connected sources, 556–59, 577–83, 587–595
    Surface-aquifer delineation, 595–98
    Imported water, 643–44
    Management for, 559–61, 649–53
Contamination, 562, 653–54, 562–67 533–34, 536, 568–69, 610, 621–22, 646–61, 992
Correlative rights, 565, 556, 634
Federal interests, 653–54, 688–701
Hydrology, 550–56
Interstate allocation, 965–66, 1030–41
Legislative redefinition of rights, 609–12
Mining and overdraft, 598–601, 605–10, 624–33, 633–53
Mutual prescription, 634–40
Natural resources damages, 698–701

GROUNDWATER—Cont'd
Nature of rights,
    See also Absolute ownership; Correlative rights; Liability rules; Permit systems, Reasonable use this topic
    Prior appropriation, 571–77, 583–87, 595–98, 602–09
    Public resource subject to police power, 595–601
    Reasonable use, 562–66, 549, 577–83
Non-tributary, 586–90
Optimum yield, 558–63
Organizations and districts, 613–16, 621–24, 649–53
Percolating waters, 556–67,564–65, 595–98
Permit systems,
    Generally, 610–613
    Critical areas, 590–94
    Pre-existing uses, 583–601
    Pumping charges, 640–42
    Pumping limits, 582–90, 595–601
Pollution,
    See Contamination, this topic
Prescription, 634–40, 642–49
Pueblo rights, 642–43, 769
Pumping costs, 571–76
    See also Liability rules, this topic
Reasonable use, 562, 564–66, 577–83
Reserved rights, federal and Indian, 916–17, 922–23
Restatement (Second) of Torts (Section 858), 567–68, 577–83
Safe yield, 567, 601–02
    See also Mining and overdraft, Optimum yield, this topic
Springs, 564
Storage, 564, 989–90
Static pressure, right to, 571–77
Subsidence of land, 568–70
Tributary, 613–17
Underground watercourses, 556–57
Water quality, 653–54, 688–701

HAWAII
Navigational servitude, 484–86
Public rights, 488–89
Public trust, 434–39
Shoreline access, 488–89
Water rights, 123–24, 434–39, 512–514

HYBRID SYSTEMS
Generally, 301–03
Adjudication of unused riparian rights, 497–514
Administration, 301–03
California, 84–94, 301–03, 497–503
Division of land,
    See also Riparian Rights, Riparian lands
    Source of title rule, 113–115
History, 89–94
Loss of rights, 265
Prescription, 154–55
Riparian rights modified, 503–14
States applying, 89, 301–03, 503–05

HYDROELECTRIC GENERATION
See also Federal Power Act
Federal licensing, 714–17, 802–818
Storage rights, 180–81

HYDROLOGY
Groundwater hydrology, 550–56, 601–02
Hydrologic cycle, 4–6, 550
Impact of Global Warming, 26–30

IDAHO
Snake River Plain conjunctive use, 587–595

INSTREAM FLOW
Generally, 11–15, 350–64
Minimum lake levels, 454
Prior appropriation,
    Beneficial use, 97–99, 164–67, 351–56
    Diversion requirement, 99–102, 161–68
    Reservations from appropriation, 356, 663
Reserved rights, federal and Indian, 878–99,
    915–16
Wild and Scenic Rivers Act, 897
Wilderness, 898
Wildlife protection, 714–17, 885–87

**INTERNATIONAL WATER ALLOCA-
TION**
Generally, 1049–68
Colorado River Delta, 1049–55
Customary law, 1055, 1062–66
Danube River, 1062–66
Environmental damage, 1060, 1062, 1064–66
Export restrictions, 1045–46
Harmon Doctrine, 1054–55
International trade law, 1046–49
International watercourses, non-navigational
    uses of 1056–62
Middle East, water allocation in 1066–68
Precautionary principle, 1062–66
Treaties, 1055–56, 1056–60, 1067–68

INTERBASIN TRANSFERS
See Transbasin Diversions

INTERSTATE ALLOCATION
Generally, 938–1049
A–C–F, A–C–T conflict, 976–77
Adjudication,
    Generally, 939–66
    Equitable apportionment, 943–66
    Jurisdiction, 939–48
    Private parties, 939–42
    States as parties, 942, 942–53
Commerce clause limits on states, 1030–46
Compacts,
    Generally, 977–87
    Colorado River, 987–1027
    Constitutional authority, 943–44
Conflicts with state law, 940–42, 938–48,
    979–83
Congressional apportionment, 995–1011

INTERSTATE ALLOCATION—Cont'd
Federal legislation, 996–98, 1044–45
Global warming, 1013, 1015
Groundwater, 965–66, 1030–41
Pollution,
    Generally, 966–75
    Discharge state duties, 966–73
Remedies, 973–76
State export restrictions, 1030–46
WTO, 1046–49

LAKES AND PONDS
See also Watercourses
Great Lakes, 1043–49
Minimum lake levels, 132, 454
Navigability, 403–05, 407, 423–25
Surface use, 449–59

LITTORAL RIGHTS
See Lakes and Ponds, Riparian Rights

LOSS OF RIGHTS
See Abandonment; Forfeiture

MINING ACTS OF 1866 AND 1870
Recognition of prior appropriation, 106–111,
    859–60

MODEL WATER CODE
See also Statutory Administration; Ripari-
    an Rights; Permit Systems
Provisions, 275–77

MONTANA
Instream flow, 161–67, 358
Fish and Wildlife, beneficial use, 161–167
Public access to streams, 466–67
Public interest factors, 301
Statutory system, 299–301
Water trusts, 365

MUNICIPAL USE
See also Service and Supply Organizations
Distribution of water, 774–78
Prior appropriation, 94–97, 311–318
Riparian rights, 118
Wastewater treatment, 666–71

**NATIONAL ENVIRONMENTAL POLICY
ACT**
Generally, 337–39
Hydroelectric power projects, 746–47

NAVIGABILITY
Definitions, 401–07, 461–69, 454–55,
    705–712, 802–810
Federal navigation power, 461–69, 802–12,
    1005
Indian reservations, 413–15
Lakes, 404–05
Navigability for title, 403–05
Navigation servitude,
    Generally, 479–487
    Access to formerly non-navigable waters,
        484–86
    Obstructions to navigation, 440–46

NAVIGABILITY—Cont'd
Navigation servitude—Cont'd
    Property in navigable waterway damaged, 473–77
    Property on non-navigable tributary damaged, 474
    Site value, 479–84
    Water power value, 481–83
Public trust doctrine,
    See Public Trust Doctrine
State law, 408–13
Title to beds of navigable waterways, 401–07

OREGON
Columbia River salmon, 744–45
Klamath conflict, 742–44

PERMIT SYSTEMS
    See also Prior Appropriation; Riparian Rights; Statutory Administration
Generally, 268–305

POLLUTION
    Generally, 655–56
Comprehensive Environmental Response, Compensation, and Liability Act (CERCLA), 691–701
Clean Water Act,
    See Clean Water Act
Common law remedies, 660–61, 665–73, 686–87
Groundwater, 653–54, 536, 688–701
Interstate, 986–87, 966–75
Prior appropriation, 660–61, 671–73
Reasonable use, 666–70
Riparian rights, 666–70
Salinity, 1014–15
Sewage treatment, 666–71
State protection, 657–64
Superfund, 649–61
Tort Remedies, 665–73, 646–47
Tribal regulation, 935–37

PRESCRIPTION
See Prior Appropriation; Riparian Rights

PRIOR APPROPRIATION
    Generally, 154–58
Abandonment, 259–65
Administration and enforcement, 292–305
    See also Procedures, this topic
Adverse possession, 265
Anti-speculation doctrine, 313–15
Augmentation, 384–89, 986–91
Availability of water, 308–311, 358
Beneficial use, 182–203
California doctrine, 89–94
Conservation, 202–203, 208–219
Change of use,
    Diversion point, 238–244
    Exchanges, 370
    Historical use limitation, 242–251
    Manner of use, 190–95
    No-injury rule, 236–257, 378–79
    Place of use, 251–54

PRIOR APPROPRIATION—Cont'd
Change of use—Cont'd
    Procedures,
        See Procedures, this topic
    Purpose of use, 233–46
    Return point, 251–57
    Salvaged water, 213–19, 388–72
    Storage, 180–82
    Time of use, 377–80
    Third-party impacts, 257–59
Condemnation of rights, 318
Conditional rights, 171–180, 381–87
Conjunctive use, 189, 343–50, 564–65, 576
    See also Groundwater, this topic
Diversion requirement, 158–168, 360–64
    Conditional rights, 171–180
    Exceptions, 377–80
    Means of, 97–99, 190–95
    Physical diversions, 159–168
Duty of water, 198, 198–200
Efficiency,
    See Beneficial use, this topic
Elements,
    Beneficial use, 182, 182–203, 629–30
    Diversion, 162–64, 360–64
    Intent, 168–179
Extent of right,
    Beneficial use, 161–68, 174–208, 662–33
    Continuation of stream conditions, 203–08
    Duty of water limitations, 197–202, 514–17
    Efficient means of diversion, 190–95
Federal control,
    See also Federal Activities
        See also Reserved rights, this topic;
    Commerce power, 801–02, 908
    History, 76–84, 859–60
    Hydroelectric power development, 811–28
    Interstate allocation, 943–66, 1001–1010
    Navigation, 469–77, 788–97
    Pollution, 203–08, 627–32
    Reclamation projects, 818–284
    Wildlife protection, 359–60, 751–52, 878–90
Foreign waters, 220–23
Forfeiture, 259–265
Futile call, 184–89, 596–97
Groundwater, 571–76, 602–09, 617–19
History,
    Early systems, 67–84
    California doctrine, 89–94
    Federal severance water from land, 107–11
    Hybrid systems, 84–94
    Literature, 1070
    Miners custom, 77–84
    Public lands, 67–71, 88–92
    Riparian doctrine repudiated, 71–75
Inefficiencies, 184–195, 202–03
Initiation of rights,
    See Procedures, this topic
Indian reservations, tension with, 102–105
Instream flows, 99–102, 267–68, 350–64
Intent to appropriate, 162, 164–76

PRIOR APPROPRIATION—Cont'd
Interstate allocation, 948–52, 927–38, 1002–18
  Limitations on right,
    See Change of use; Federal control, this topic
  Duty of water, 197–202, 514–17
  Efficient means of diversion, 190–95
  Interstate allocations, 1043–66, 1001–08, 598–605
  Public interest, 319–33
  Statutory criteria, 294–303, 330–34
Loss of rights, 259–265
Municipal use, 94–97, 171–77, 311–18
No-injury rule, 237–257, 378–79
Silt entitlement, 203–208
  See also Change of use, this topic
Nonuse, 259–65
Perfection of rights,
  See Procedures, this topic
Permits, 294–95
Phreatophyte reduction, 223–230
  Procedures, 294–305
  Storage, 176–77
Place of use,
  See Change of use, this topic
Preferences, 318–19
Prescription, 265
  See also Loss of rights, this topic
Priority, deviation from, 377–80
  See also Relation back doctrine, this topic
Procedures,
  Change of use, 238–257
  Colorado system, 303–05
  Constitutional issues, 295–99
  General stream adjudications, 305–308
  Permitting, 295–99
  Statutory systems described, 293–305
Public interest, 319–33, 319–24, 328–29, 331–42, 629–30
Public "ownership" and state police power, 399–449
Public trust doctrine, 336–42, 389–440, 528
Physical solution, 381–84
  See also Public Trust Doctrine
Purpose of use,
  See Beneficial use; Change of use, this topic
Recreation use, 97–99
Relation back doctrine, 168–180, 311–18
Reserved rights, 102–106, 878–90
  See also Reserved Rights
Reuse,
    Generally, 212–23
  Foreign waters, 220–23
  Limitations, 213–14
  Salvaged water, 213–219
Riparian landowners' rights, 84–89
Storage, 176–77
Time of use, 377–80
  See also Change of use, this topic

PRIOR APPROPRIATION—Cont'd
Transfers,
    Generally, 230–59, 367–76
    See also Change of use, this topic
  Area of origin protection, 395–98
  Economics of, 233–38
  Foreign waters, 220–223
  Junior appropriators, protection of, 230–59
  Opportunities, 362–65
  Salvaged water, 223–230, 358–66
  Third-party effects, 257–59, 340–342, 989
  Transbasin diversions, 273–75, 389–98
Waters subject to,
  Foreign waters, 220–23
  Groundwater, 219–25
  Instream flows, 161–68, 350–67
    See also Public "ownership" and state police power, this topic
  Reserved rights, 878–90, 909–11
    See also Reserved Rights
  Salvaged waters, 213–19, 223–30, 389
  Springs, 564
  Watercourses, 158
  Waters withdrawn from appropriation, 358

PROPERTY RIGHTS
Takings, 450, 517–26

PUBLIC LANDS
  See also Reserved Rights
Acquisition of water rights, 67–61, 859–60
Prior appropriation doctrine, 89–94, 106–11
Rights of way, 485–86

PUBLIC RIGHTS
  See also Prior Appropriation, Public "ownership" and state police power
Access to beaches and shores, 467–70, 487–96
Custom as source of, 488–89
Dedication, 491–96
Navigable waters, 399–407, 451
Non-navigable waters, 470–79
Pleasure boat test, 461–67
Prescriptive rights, 467–69
Recreation capability, 461–67
Shore access, 467–70

PUBLIC TRUST DOCTRINE
    Generally, 415–49, 528
Beach access, 489–91
Hawaiian water rights, 434–39,
History, 401–03
Limiting appropriations, 426–34, 631
Navigable waters, 415–16, 479–80
Severance of trust lands, 416–23
Submerged lands,
    Limit on private use, 416–26
    Private use, 440–49
Takings, 441, 525–26, 529
Wharfing out, conflicts with, 440–41

PUEBLO RIGHTS
Generally, 642–43, 769

RECLAMATION ACT
Acreage limitation, 829–32
Congressional power to enact, 811
Congressional power amend service contracts, 833–40
Costs, 840
Districts, 784–89
Hammer clause, 831–32
History, 828–29
Projects, 818–26, 829–33
Residency requirement, 830
State law deferred to, 818–26
Subsidies, 841–43
Transfer of water rights, 375–76, 844–46

RESERVED RIGHTS
Generally, 104–06, 859–864
Aboriginal Indian rights, 863, 904
Groundwater, 916–17, 922–23
Indian allotments, 104–06, 861, 904–05
Indian reservations, 104–106, 402–03, 864–72, 899–904, 911–23
Instream flow, 878–85, 888–90, 890–99, 915–16, 921
"Non-reserved" rights, 909–10
Origins, 104–106, 859–64
Power to create,
    Generally, 865–67, 907–909
    Commerce clause, 866, 908
    Property clause, 907–909
Prior appropriation system, 104–06, 859–864
Priority, 104–06, 861–62, 902–03
Public lands, 907–09
Pueblo rights, 872–73
Quantification,
    Generally, 868–69, 891–72, 906–07, 917–19, 923–28
    Adjudication, 873–78
    McCarran Amendment, 873–78
    National forests, 878–85, 888
    National monuments, 885–88, 890–97
    National parks, 888–89, 890–97
    National recreation areas, 898
    Practicably irrigable acreage, Indian lands, 868–71, 917–18
    Purpose of reserving land, 871–72, 878–85, 894–99, 912–916
Settlement, Indian reserved rights, 923–29
Sovereign immunity, 873–75
Regulation of,
    State law, 873–78, 929, 934–35
    Tribal law, 889–907, 929–37
State water law inferior, 861–63
Transfer,
    Indian allotments, 861, 899–900
    Leases, public and tribal lands, 879–80, 898
Treaty basis, 863–64
Tribal water management, 929–35
Waters reserved,
    Groundwater, 916–17, 922–23
    Outside reservations, 923–28
    Streams on or bordering reservation, 862–67
Wildlife refuges, 865
Wilderness areas, 869, 897–98

RESTATEMENT (SECOND) OF TORTS
Section 821B, pp. 632
Section 826, p. 632
Section 850, p. 132–33
Section 850A, pp. 133–36
Section 855, pp. 140–41
Section 856, pp. 141–42
Section 858, pp. 867–68

RIGHTS OF WAY
Appurtenant to water rights, 143–44
Condemnation, 487
Water access easements, 143–44

RIPARIAN RIGHTS
Generally, 25–26, 112–54
Abrogation by state law, 277–82, 275–80, 287–92
Accretion and avulsion, 147–150
Apportionment of uses, 124–125
Appropriation elements, 135–136, 291–93
Appropriation, transition to, 486–502
Appurtenance, 114, 145–47
Artificial uses,
Access via canal, 455–60
    Natural uses distinguished, 115–17
Artificial watercourses, 453, 455
Constitutionality modification common law, 289–291, 503–514
Consumptive use, 129–30
Conveyance of land,
    Appurtenance, 114, 145–47
Domestic use, 117
    See also Natural uses, this topic
Extent,
    Appurtenance to land, 114, 145–47
    Watershed limitation, 145–47, 315–19
Foreign waters, 315–19
Hawaiian water rights, 125–126, 434–39, 512–514
History,
    American precedents, 60–63, 122
    English precedents, 63–66
    French precedents, 63
    Literature, 1070
Hybrid systems,
    See Hybrid Systems
Littoral rights, 131
Loss, 150–54
Minimum flows, 351
Minimum lake levels, 454
Model Water Code, 275–77
Modifications,
        See also Reasonable use theory, Statutes limiting, this topic
    Hybrid systems, 406–502
Natural flow theory,
    Generally, 123–24, 128
    Preference for natural uses, 115–118
    Prescription, 150–54
Nonconsumptive rights, 130
Nonriparian uses, 137–142

RIPARIAN RIGHTS—Cont'd
Nonuse, effect of, 496–97
Permit systems,
> See also Hybrid Systems; Statutory Administration
> Generally, 268–94
> Criteria, 284–85, 293–94
> Modification of existing rights, 503–14
> Nonriparian uses, 137–142
> Preferences, 117–18
Pollution, 632–39
Prescription, 150–54
Reasonable use theory,
> Generally, 60–67, 118–123, 128–27, 137, 149, 276, 633–34
> History, 63–67
> Municipal uses, 633–36
> Natural versus artificial use, 117
> Nonconsumptive use, 131–132
> Nonriparian uses, 137–42
> Permit systems, applicability to, 275–77, 351
> Pollution, 666–71, 686
> Preference for natural uses, 116–17
> Prescription, 150–54
Reasonable beneficial use (Model Water Code), 277
Regulated riparianism, 281–94
Restatement (Second) of s rules, 132–137, 140–42 , 632
Restatement (Second)'s impact, 136–137
Reserved rights,
> See Reserved Rights
Riparian lands,
> See also Title To Beds of Streams and Lakes
> Avulsion and accretion, 147–150
> Defined, 147–150
> Division,
>> Grants and reservations, 152–53
>> Partition, 142–44
>> Source of title rule, 113–15
>> Unity of title rule, 113–15
>> Watershed limitation, 145–47
Source of title rule, 113–15
Surface use, 449–60
Surplus water defined, 291–92
Transfer, 142–44, 293–94
> Appurtenance, 145–46
> Grants and reservations, 152–53
Unity of title rule, 113–15
Use restricted to riparian land, 145–47
Watershed limitation, 145–47, 322–26

SAFE DRINKING WATER ACT
Groundwater protection, 689–90

SALVAGED WATER
Recapture and reuse by appropriator, 208–25, 770

SCARCITY
> Generally, 1–4, 41–47
Western water policy, 47–56

SERVICE AND SUPPLY ORGANIZATIONS
> Generally, 768–73
Adequate water supply laws, 773–774
Allocation of waters, 739–46, 776–81, 825–27
Assessments, 785
Carey Act, 738–39, 779
Carrier ditch companies, 778–82
Condemnation, 775–76
Conservancy districts, 780
> See also Irrigation districts, this topic
District formation, 790–91, 794–95
Groundwater, 652–53
Growth accommodation, 773–74, 776, 794
Irrigation districts, 784–89
Municipal water districts, 777–78
Municipalities, 774–78
Mutual ditch companies
> Generally, 78–782
> Shareholder rights, 781–82
Mutual water companies, 780
Political accountability, 789–91
Public and private companies, 770–71
Reclamation projects, 789
Special water districts, 782–787
Utilities, 774, 774–76
> Sewer services, 794–95
Water markets, 791–794
Water rates, 777, 791–91
Wright Act, 787–88

SETTLEMENT PATTERNS
American West, 15–19, 772–73
Water use impacts, 19–25, 772–73

SPRINGS
> See also Groundwater
Ownership, 595
Subject to appropriation, 595

STATUTORY ADMINISTRATION
> Generally, 266–308
Conservation, 268–70
Eastern States, 266–94
Environmental Impact Assessment, 337–339
Instream flows, 271–72, 342–57
Model Water Code, 275–77
Planning, 333–37
Public interest, 319–33, 342–343
Quantification, 268–70
Transbasin diversions, 273–75
Transfers, 367–375
Water banks, 373
Water trusts, 364–367
Western States, 294–308, 326–29
Wyoming System, 295–99

STORAGE
Groundwater, 576–77, 633, 649–53
Prior appropriation, 180–82, 391–95
Water banking, 373, 1020

STREAMS
See Watercourses

SUBMERGED LANDS
See Navigability

SURFACE USE
See Riparian Rights

TAKINGS
See Property Rights

TITLE TO BEDS OF STREAMS AND LAKES
See also Navigability
Equal footing doctrine, 412–13
Federal versus state ownership, 403–08
Public rights, 400–03

TRANSBASIN DIVERSIONS
Generally, 273–74, 389–98
Interstate, 916
Restrictions on, 388–98

TRANSFER OF WATER RIGHTS
See also Prior Appropriation, Transfers
Generally, 225–54, 367–75
Area of origin protection, 379–87
Bureau Reclamation, 375–76
Economics of, 229–32
Junior appropriators, protection of, 232–53
Return flow, protection of rights in, 232–53
Riparian rights, 142–145
Third-party impacts, 390–91

TREATIES
Indian, 836–42, 875–77
International, 1055–56, 1056–60, 1067–68

UNDERGROUND WATERCOURSES
See Groundwater

WASHINGTON
Instream flow, 358
Lake level maintenance, 444–45
Shoreline access, 449–50

WATER DISTRIBUTION ORGANIZATIONS
See Service and Supply Organizations

WATER LAW
Function, 58–59
See generally this index

WATER MEASUREMENT TERMS
Description and conversions, 6–7, 1069

WATER QUALITY
See Pollution

WATER SUPPLY AND DEMAND
Demand, 7–11
Supply, 4–6

WATER TRUSTS
Generally, 364–67

WATERCOURSES
Artificial, 445
Land abutting, defined, 112–13, 145–47
Subject to appropriation, 220–23
Title to beds, 400–407
Underground watercourses, 556–57

WELLS
See also Groundwater
Optimum yield, 571–77
Permits, 610–13

WESTERN WATER
Generally, 19–25
Changing demographics, 14–17, 715–17
Prior appropriation, 154–59
Reform, 49–56, 326–29
Statutory administration, 294–308

WETLANDS
Federal protection, 701–14

WORLD COMMISSION ON DAMS
Existing dams performance, 761–62
New Dam evaluation, 764–766

WYOMING
Public rights, 470
Statutory system, 295–99

†